D1234590

THE ENCYCLOPEDIA OF JAZZ

There is no truer truth obtainable by man than comes of music.

ROBERT BROWNING

Medicine, to produce health, has to examine disease,

and music, to create harmony, must investigate discord.

PLUTARCH

by Leonard Feather

Appreciations by

DUKE ELLINGTON, BENNY GOODMAN and JOHN HAMMOND

THE ENCYCLOPEDIA OF JAZZ

Horizon Press, New York

ISBN: 0-8180-1203-X

Library of Congress Catalog Number: 55-10774

Manufactured in the United States of America

Design: N. Sylvester

Author's prefaces

PREFACE TO FIRST EDITION

Ira Gitler was my assistant through the whole project. His tireless research work in amplifying the biographies, particularly in the addition of data on LP records, was fortified by his extensive knowledge of the subject and by an enthusiasm for the job that made him an invaluable and congenial associate. He also made many helpful suggestions concerning the other sections of the Encyclopedia.

I am deeply indebted to Professor Marshall Stearns for placing the files of his Institute of Jazz Studies at my disposal, and to Bill Grauer and Orrin Keepnews for providing similar research facilities.

In Los Angeles Howard Lucraft of Jazz International, Charles Emge of *Down Beat* and David Stuart of Good Time Jazz and Contemporary Records were especially helpful, as were Dr. Edmond Souchon in New Orleans, publisher Norman Weiser and editor Jack Tracy of *Down Beat* in Chicago and Ralph Gleason in San Francisco. Acklowledgments are also due to Jan Rugolo for her indefatigable stenographic assistance, as well as to Charles Delaunay in Paris, Dede Emerson in New York, Jack Crystal of the Commodore Music Shop and many others who went out of their way to be helpful.

In thanking my wife for her help, as typist, proofreader and general *aide-de-camp*, I can only add that it would be flattering to Job to say that he had the patience of Jane.

My debt to John Hammond transcends any formal expression of gratitude. His bringing together of author and publisher, a move directly responsible for this entire venture, was typical of the way he has spent much of his life, arranging meetings in the hope of bringing about results beneficial to the people concerned and to the music he loves.

Sincere thanks to Jack Tracy, editor of *Down Beat,* for placing that publication's picture files in Chicago at my disposal; to Orrin Keepnews and Bill Grauer of *The Record Changer* for supplying a number of historical pictures, and to George Simon and Bill Coss of *Metronome* for filling in numerous gaps in the photograph collation.

Herman Leonard, one of the foremost artists ever to train his lens on a jazzman, and Francis Wolff, the fine cameraman of Blue Note Records, were especially cooperative in providing some of their greatest pictures.

PREFACE TO NEW EDITION

In the five years since the above acknowledgments were written other correspondents have helped to broaden the scope of The Encyclopedia of Jazz by providing material for the intermediary yearbooks or for the present volume, which combines the original *Encyclopedia*, the two yearbooks and a considerable quantity of new material.

Certain passages in the chapters *Sixty Years of Jazz, Jazz in American Society* and *The Anatomy of Jazz* were excerpted or adapted from the author's *The Book of Jazz* (Horizon Press, 1957; paperback edition Meridian Books, 1959); however, most of these excerpts have been expanded or revised to bring them up to date.

Ira Gitler has continued to work on the series, as has Howard Lucraft in Los Angeles. I am indebted to the following for their generous expenditure of time and effort: Ralph J. Gleason in San Francisco; Jean Barnett Stearns in New York; Don Gold in Chicago; Donald R. Stone in Detroit; the editors of *Jazz News,* and Vic Lewis in London; Frank Tenot in Paris; Joachim-Ernst Berendt in Baden-Baden; Carl-Erik Lindgren in Stockholm; Arrigo Polillo in Milan; Hans de Wild in Amsterdam; Tay Muraoka in Tokyo; also Samuel B. Charters, Willis Conover, Barbara Dane, Franklin S. Driggs and Lucille Butterman.

Special thanks are due to Chuck Suber, Eugene Lees and the entire *Down Beat* staff for making available so much material, including the *Blindfold Test* excerpts; to Martin Williams, a major contributor during the second yearbook phase; and to the many photographers whose work illustrates the book, among them Hanns E. Haehl of *Jazz im Bild,* Carole Reiff Galletly, Victor Tanaka, Richard Schaefer and Tony Scott.

Contents

PREFACES 5

APPRECIATIONS:

THE ENCYCLOPEDIA OF JAZZ, by Duke Ellington 13

THE JAZZ TREND, by Benny Goodman 16

ABOUT THE AUTHOR, by John Hammond 17

SIXTY YEARS OF JAZZ: AN HISTORICAL SURVEY 21

CHRONOLOGY 52

THE ANATOMY OF JAZZ 60

JAZZ IN AMERICAN SOCIETY 79

GIANTS OF JAZZ 89

INTRODUCTION TO BIOGRAPHIES 91

ABBREVIATIONS 94

BIOGRAPHIES 96

THE JAZZMAN AS CRITIC: THE BLINDFOLD TEST 474

INTERNATIONAL POLLS 481

JAZZ OVERSEAS 486

JAZZ AND CLASSICAL MUSIC, by Gunther Schuller 497

HISTORIES OF JAZZ ON RECORDS; RECOMMENDED JAZZ RECORDS 500

MUSICIANS' BIRTHDAYS 505

MUSICIANS' BIRTHPLACES 513

JAZZ ORGANIZATIONS, SCHOOLS AND BOOKING AGENCIES 521

JAZZ RECORD COMPANIES 522

BIBLIOGRAPHY: BOOKS AND PERIODICALS 524

Illustrations

Adderley, Julian "Cannonball" 366
Adderley, Nat 366
Akiyoshi, Toshiko 357
Allen, Red 44
Allen, Steve 125
Allison, Mose 363
Ammons, Albert 42
Armstrong, Louis 33, 35, 36, 38
Auld, Georgie 124

Bailey, Benny 368
Bailey, Buster 38, 123, 193
Bailey, Mildred 123
Baker, Chet 286
Baker, Harold 114
Ballard, Red 124
Barbarin, Paul 34
Barber, Bill 283
Barker, Danny 198
Barnet, Charlie 197
Basie, Count 46, 120, 121
Bauer, Billy 282, 283
Bechet, Sidney 41
Beiderbecke, Bix 37
Bellson, Louis 114
Berigan, Bunny 48
Berman, Sonny 276
Berry, Leroy 46
Best, Denzil 203, 280
Bigard, Barney 34, 116
Blake, Jerry 198
Blakey, Art 273
Blanton, Jimmy 197
Bown, Patti 368
Braff, Rudy 278
Brockman, Gail 203
Brookmeyer, Bob 287
Broonzy, Big Bill 128
Brown, Andrew 198
Brown, Clifford 361
Brown, Les 199
Brown, Marshall 364
Brown, Pete 123
Brown, Ray 353
Brubeck, Dave 286
Bryant, Ray 366
Burns, Ralph 277
Byas, Don 203

Caceres, Ernie 282
Calloway, Cab 198
Candoli, Conte 278
Candoli, Pete 276
Carey, Mutt 34
Carney Harry 114, 285
Carroll, Barbara 359
Carry, Scoops 203
Carter Benny 116
Casey, Al 202
Catlett, Buddy 368
Catlett, Sidney 198, 202
Chaloff, Serge 277, 283
Chambers, Elmer 38
Chambers, Paul 364
Charles, Teddy 288
Christian, Charlie 124, 125
Christian, Emil 33
Christy, June 205
Clarke, Kenny 275
Clayton, Buck 120, 122

Cleveland, Jimmy 367, 368
Cobbs, Bert 34
Cohn, Al 277
Cole, Cozy 200
Cole, Nat King 196
Coleman, Ornette 367
Collette, Buddy 354
Collins, Junior 283
Coltrane, John 367
Condon, Eddie 128
Cooper, Bob 205
Crosby, Bing 199
Crump, A. 203

Dameron, Tadd 273
Dankworth, Johnny 356
Davis, Miles 206, 207, 208, 282, 283, 284
De Franco, Buddy 282, 283, 284
Desmond, Paul 286
Dickenson, Vic 120, 278
Dixon, Charlie 38
Dodds, Baby 33, 37, 196
Dodds, Johnny 33
Domnerus, Arne 355
Dorham, Kenny 362
Dorsey, Jimmy 118
Dorsey, Tommy 37, 118, 199
Durham, Ed 46
Dutrey, Honore 33

Eager, Allen 207
Eckstine, Billy 206
Edison, Harry 120, 122
Eldridge, Roy 196, 197
Ellington, Duke 113, 114, 115, 204
Elliott, Don 288
Elman, Ziggy 124
Escudero, Bob 38
Evans, Bill 365
Evans, Gil 284

Farlow, Tal 287
Farmer, Art 365
Fazola, Irving 47
Feather, Leonard 202
Field, George 34
Finegan, Bill 358
Fitzgerald, Ella 36, 127, 194, 353
Folus, Mickey 276
Freeman, Bud 128
Fuller, Curtis 367

Gardner, Andrew 203
Gardner, Julie 203
Gargano, Tommy 37
Garner, Erroll 279
Geller, Herb 357
Getz, Stan 277, 281, 283
Gezzo, Conrad 276
Gibbs, Terry 288
Gillespie, Dizzy 198, 203, 274, 282, 283
Giuffre, Jimmy 355
Glenn, Tyree 198
Golson, Benny 365
Gonsalves, Paul 114
Goodman, Benny 124, 126, 127
Goodman, Harry 124
Granz, Norman 353
Grappelly, Stephane 117
Green, Benny 203
Green, Charlie 38
Greene, Freddie 120
Griffin, Chris 124
Gullin, Lars 355

Hackett, Bobby 122
Haggart, Bobby 47
Haig, Al 283
Hall, Edmond 45, 128, 202
Hall, Jim 354, 355
Hamilton, Chico 354
Hamilton, Jimmy 114
Hammond, John 127
Hampton, Lionel 47, 127, 197
Hardin, Lil 33
Harris, Benny 203
Harris, Bill 276
Harris, Joe 355, 368
Hawkins, Coleman 38, 197, 202, 203, 361
Hayes, Thamon 46
Heard, J. C. 353
Heath, Percy 363
Henderson, Fletcher 38
Hendricks, Jon 365
Herman, Woody 125, 276, 277
Hilaire, Andrew 39
Hines, Earl 120, 203
Hinton, Milt 200
Hite, Les 47

Hodges, Johnny 113
Holiday, Billie 123
Horne, Lena 276
Howard, Darnell 34
Hyams, Margie 280

Jackson, Chubby 279
Jackson, Mahalia 279
Jackson, Milt 362, 363
Jackson, Quentin 114, 198, 368
Jacquet, Illinois 275
Jamal, Ahmad 359
James, Harry 124, 197
Jefferson, Hilton 198
Johnson, Bill 33
Johnson, Bud 368
Johnson, Bunk 40
Johnson, James P. 39
Johnson, Jay Jay 282, 287
Johnson, Keg 198
Johnson, Lennie 368
Jones, Hank 360
Jones, Jo 120, 198
Jones, Jonah 117, 198
Jones, Philly Joe 364
Jones, Quincy 368
Jones, Thad 360
Jordan, Louis 193

Katz, Fred 354
Kay, Connie 363
Kenton, Stan 204
Kessel, Barney 288, 353
Kiefer, Ed 276
Kilbert, Porter 368
Killion, Al 120
Kirby, John 193
Koenig, George 124
Konitz, Lee 283, 284, 285
Krupa, Gene 124, 125, 353
Kyle, Billy 193

Lambert, Dave 365
Lamond, Don 276
Lang, Eddie 42
LaPorta, John 276
La Rocca, Nick 33
Leadbelly 195
Lee, Peggy 127
Leonard, Harland 46
Levy, John 280
Lewis, Cappy 276
Lewis, Ed 46, 120
Lewis, George 40, 41
Lewis, John 362, 363
Lewis, Meade Lux 43
Lindsay, John 39
Liston, Melba 368
Lunceford, Jimmie 113

Manne, Shelly 280, 282
Margolis, Sam 278
Marowitz, Sam 276
Marsh, Warne 285
May, Billy 358
McConnell, Shorts 203
McEachern, Murray 124
McPartland, Marian 354
McShann, Jay 206
Merrill, Helen 357
Mertz, Paul 37
Metronome All Stars 282, 283
Mezzrow, Mezz 120
Middleton, Velma 116
Miller, Glenn 119
Mills Brothers, The 47
Mingus, Charlie 287
Minor, Dan 120
Mitchell, Billy 360
Mitchell, George 39
Mondragon, Joe 276
Monk, Thelonious 203, 208
Montgomery, Wes 364
Moore, Oscar 196
Morello, Joe 286
Morton, Jelly Roll 39
Moten, Bennie 46
Moten, Bus 46
Mulligan, Gerry 283, 285
Murphy, Turk 357
Murray, Don 37
Musso, Vido 124

Navarro, Fats 275, 282
Nicholas, Albert 34
Nichols, Red 42
Noone, Jimmie 196
Norvo, Red 123, 126, 276, 287

O'Connor, Father 286
O'Day, Anita 356
Oliver, Joe King 33, 34

Oliver, Sy 204
Original Dixieland Jazz Band 33
Ory, Kid 34, 39

Page, Oran (Hot Lips) 46, 128
Page, Vernon 46
Page, Walter 120
Parker, Charlie 203, 206, 207, 282
Pavageau, Alcide 40
Payne, Cecil 275
Pena, Ralph 355
Persson, Aake 355, 368
Peterson, Oscar 353
Pettiford, Oscar 202, 273
Pfiffner, Ralph 276
Phillips, Flip 276, 353
Potter, Tommy 206
Powell, Bud 208
Previn, André 359
Prince, Wesley 196
Procope, Russell 114, 193

Quicksell, Howdy 37

Raney, Jimmy 276
Redman, Don 38, 48
Reid, Neal 276
Reinhardt, Django 114
Reuss, Alan 124
Rich, Buddy 273
Richardson, Jerome 368
Roach, Max 273, 283, 361
Robinson, Russell 33
Rogers, Shorty 276, 281
Rollini, Adrian 46
Rollini, Arthur 124
Rollins, Sonny 361
Ross, Annie 365
Rowles, Jimmy 276
Rubinwitch, Sam 276
Rugolo, Pete 282, 283
Rushing, Jimmy 46, 356
Russell, George 205
Russell, Luis 34
Russell, Pee Wee 43

Safranski, Eddie 282, 283, 284
St. Cyr, Johnny 39
Sauter, Eddie 358
Schertzer, Hymie 124
Schuller, Gunther 363
Scott, Bud 34
Scott, Howard 38
Scott, Tony 360
Shank, Bud 280
Shavers, Charlie 193, 353
Shaw, Artie 119
Shaw, Arvell 126
Shearing, George 280, 281
Shields, Larry 33
Shihab, Sahib 368
Shoffner, Bobby 34
Shulman, Joe 283
Silver, Horace 365
Simeon, Omer 39
Simkins, Jesse 203
Sims, Zoot 277
Sinatra, Frank 199
Smith, Bessie 45
Smith, Carson 354
Smith, Stuff 117
Smith, Tab 120
Smith, Willie 114, 353
Spanier, Muggsy 48
Spann, Les 368
Spargo, Tony 33
Spencer, O'Neil 193
Stacy, Jess 124
Standifer, Floyd 368
Steward, Herbie 277
Stewart, Slam 193
Stitt, Sonny 362
Strayhorn, Billy 276
Sullivan, Maxine 123

Tate, Buddy 120
Tatum, Art 195, 202
Taylor, Billy 354
Teagarden, Jack 118, 125, 356
Terry, Clark 368
Tharpe, Sister Rosetta 199
Thomas, Walter "Foots" 198
Thompson, Lucky 274
Timmons, Bobby 366
Tizol, Juan 114
Tjader, Cal 288
Tough, Dave 124, 125
Tristano, Lennie 282, 283, 284
Trumbauer, Frankie 37
Turner, Joe 127

Vaughan, Sarah 203, 205
Ventura, Charlie 282

Walder, Woodie 46
Waller, Fats 38
Washington, Booker 46
Washington, Dinah 279
Washington, Jack 46, 120
Washington, Willie Mac 46
Watkins, Julius 368
Wayne, Chuck 276, 280
Webb, Chick 194
Webster, Ben 113
Wein, George 361
Wells, Dickie 120
Williams, Cootie 124, 197, 202
Williams, Joe 360
Williams, John 203
Williams, Mary Lou 194
Wilson, Shadow 203
Wilson, Teddy 125, 126
Winding, Kai 207, 282, 283, 287
Wolverine Orchestra 37
Woodman, Britt 114
Woods, Phil 368
Wright, Lammar 198

Young, Lester 120, 201, 353
Young, Trummy 116

Appreciations by Duke Ellington, Benny Goodman and John Hammond

THE ENCYCLOPEDIA OF JAZZ*

BY DUKE ELLINGTON

It is strange that I should be contributing the foreword to Leonard Feather's book, because at one time I was involved in a similar project myself; I almost did a history of jazz.

This happened in 1941, when we were appearing, with the band, in our musical show *Jump for Joy* in Hollywood. One evening Orson Welles came to see the show; the next day he called me and asked me to come over to RKO studios to talk about an idea he had for a history of jazz.

I went to see Welles and was very much impressed. He told me he knew all about me, and spoke very knowingly of my music and of jazz in general. He even showed me how much he knew about *Jump for Joy* by spouting whole lines from it, even whole sequences, though he had only seen the show once, the night before.

Then he went on to tell me that he was planning to make a motion picture entitled *It's All True,* which would be a history of jazz. Since he felt I was best qualified to participate as an authority on the subject and would be aware of all the different types of music to be used in it, he wanted to engage me to write the score, write the book, conduct the orchestra, use my own band and anybody else I wanted to, and they would pay for everything. My salary was to start immediately: a thousand dollars a week for twelve weeks, and the last week would be fifteen hundred. (This was 1941 money, too.)

That would last until we were through with our preparations. In other words, this was just my salary as technical director. In addition, there would be the various other credits and the corresponding salaries—ten thousand for the arrangements, ten thousand for conducting, so much for playing in the picture, so much for the band, and so forth.

"That's the deal," said Welles, "and you're a fool if you don't take it."

"All right," I said, "let's get the first check signed right now."

With that, I went up and started my research. I had all the books on jazz that had been written up to 1941, and I went through them pretty thoroughly. Every now and then I would run into one of those big fat snags—errors made by people who obviously did not know what they were writing about. I began to think to myself, "Oh, this is awful!" and after reading them all I sat down again and started to write one of my own.

The way I visualized my story, the way the picture was supposed to start, the first scene was to take place in New Orleans, with a boat coming down the canal and the King of the Zulus getting off as the boat docked at Basin Street. The King of the Zulus was the big Negro man of the town; they elected a different one every year, in fact they still do. Our opening scene would show this big coronation celebration over on Congo Square, where they re-enact scenes and rituals from slavery days, with the sexual and the religious symbolism and dancing. And this particular year, Buddy Bolden was to be the King of the Zulus.

Buddy Bolden was a guy who had a barber shop,

* Transcribed from a tape recording made by Duke Ellington especially for this book.

ran a newspaper, played the trumpet and was quite a ladies' man on the side. He was a pretty progressive type kid. So one day when he closed his barber shop, we would see one chick putting a newspaper under her arm, and another putting a trumpet under her arm; one of them would have his hat and the other would have his coat, and down the street they would go, the three of them.

They would get as far as the hall where Buddy was going to play that evening. It was all dark. While the chicks were going in to run upstairs and open the windows, you would hear Buddy Bolden tuning up. And when he tuned up on his trumpet it was not just like a musician hitting an A. It was melodic. And while he was using these little melodic ideas to tune up with, by the time he really called himself in tune, why, you could hear that powerful horn of his clear across the Mississippi River.

In the next scene, we would show the people flocking from across the river, coming from all over town, from everywhere around, to this little place where Buddy was about to play. And when he played the crowd would holler "Yeah, Buddy!" and he'd play some more and they'd holler "Yeah, Buddy, yeah, Buddy!"

I wrote a piece of music for this scene—just twenty-eight bars, for a trumpet solo. It was a gasser; real great, I confess it. And I lost it. I always said, and I say to this day, that it was the greatest thing I ever wrote. Nothing but a trumpet solo. And that's the only thing I ever did for this $12,500. I got the money, but they never got the twenty-eight bars. Mr. Welles is a great man; I am sorry that his project never materialized. If he were being subsidized today as he was then, perhaps I would be in Rome now, writing my history of jazz.

The true story has not been told, because most of the histories have been written from too great a distance. I often felt, when I read them, that they were written because their authors had the necessary schooling, the writing ability for the job; but they didn't really know anything about the subject.

The history of jazz, of course, begins with the rhythm coming to America from Africa. It stops in the West Indies, then takes two courses: one across the Gulf of Mexico to New Orleans, and the other up the East Coast. The East Coast was inclined to favor strings—violins, banjos and guitars—while the other development, the one that went to New Orleans and then up the Mississippi to Chicago, came out in the form of clarinets, trombones and trumpets. And then they all converged in New York and blended together, and the offspring was jazz.

Many of the real forerunners of jazz were people who are completely forgotten. Aside from the carnivals and people like W. C. Handy and Will Marion Cook, there were the piano players—a lot of them in New York, many in Washington and Boston and Philadelphia, all up and down the East Coast, and many of them playing in houses of ill repute.

The piano was a great instrument in those days; they used to do everything on the piano that you do with an orchestra nowadays. There were people like Sticky Mack, and Louie Brown: men who would play with a full left hand, and conceived beautiful melodic ideas without ever breaking the rhythm. Yes, they used to play pretty; jazz used to be real pretty.

One of the prettiest things from those days was a tune they played in all the houses, one that was sometimes known as *The Dream*. It was a tango-type thing; tangos were very popular, and West Indian rhythms were an early influence too. The piano players were very important in the early days, and the great piano players were always on the East Coast; there never was anybody in the West who could play two notes. (By "West" I mean New Orleans; in those days there was no other West to speak of, west of that.) Jelly Roll Morton, who was mainly a writer and had more music published than anyone else, played piano like one of those high school teachers in Washington; as a matter of fact, high school teachers played better jazz. Among other things, his rhythm was unsteady; but that's the kind of piano the West was geared up to. On the other hand the piano players on the East Coast did the most impossible things. If you dig up the early piano rolls or records by James P. Johnson you will hear the most beautiful and perfect performances.

Willie "The Lion" Smith was a giant of those days, too. It is one of my great regrets that when the Lion used to come up to my house I didn't have a recording machine so that I could preserve some of those early performances of his.

Yes, in my story you would see men like this developing jazz in the East—the pianists, and the fiddle players, and the men who played banjo and guitars—men like Elmer Snowden and Banjo Bernie—and some real crazy drummers who were beginning to develop in the early days along the East Coast. At the same time I would show some of the great horn men who came out of the West—men like Barney Bigard, who is the greatest clarinet player I know, and Sidney Bechet, the greatest soprano sax.

A lot of the early musicians, especially men like James Reese Europe and Lucky Roberts, had pretty good schooling. Of course the story of jazz has to show all the changes that have taken place along those lines. Today the musician who comes into jazz is better prepared than the musician of yesterday. He is aware not only of what has been happening in present-day music with the jazz people, but also of what happened so far as the old masters are concerned. So he should have much broader musical scope.

Whether he has the imagination is something else again. There are a lot of youngsters coming into jazz today who feel that everything has been done before, up to a certain point, so they try to find something new and they wind up trying for parallels to Picasso and other moderns.

I approve of any development, mind you, as long as the artist is honest about it. I believe that freedom of expression is one of the things we are supposed to enjoy, and everybody should take advantage of it; but I also feel that jazz at this point has been taken over by certain intellectuals. Some have become critics, and some have become patrons of the music. Some have subsidized both the performer and the critic, and jazz has developed into one of those intellectual art forms that scare people away.

A lot of people nowadays are afraid of jazz. Strangely enough this situation is an exact parallel of what has been happening in other musical forms, in opera, in Bach and Mozart, in string quartets. A couple of years ago I was discussing this problem with the director of a string quartet, and he told me that he feels people are afraid to be exposed to what he is doing because they do not know enough about it and want to avoid the embarrassment.

Similarly, people will not come into places where jazz enthusiasts congregate if they are going to be made to feel ignorant. They may be afraid to buy a ticket and sit in the audience because the man next to them might look down his nose at them, so to speak, with a flatted fifth. And nothing can be worse than to have somebody look down his nose with a flatted fifth, believe me.

If you say "What is a square?" they may say they don't know quite what it is, but nobody wants to *be* one. And they automatically become squares if the man who's sitting next to them knows four more names in jazz than they do.

With this book, which gives everybody the chance to read about the names that have made jazz history through the years as well as those that are making it today, nobody need be a square. That's why I think this book is a wonderful idea, and I was very happy to learn that Leonard Feather was the man who had decided to undertake this project.

I don't think there is anyone who is better equipped, musically, for this assignment. He has listened with a musical ear, has accepted, or respected, the artists' original intent, and has always been fair in weighing these factors. Of course Feather was a musician first, and became a listener second, and a writer third, and was thrown into the category of critic.

We have found that one of the respects in which some appraisers of the aural arts have fallen short is that they deem it necessary to categorize a performance—as either good or bad, hot or cold, high or low, always one extreme or the other. I don't think there are enough words in the English language to do all of this right, and unless a man has a grasp of other languages it may be impossible for him to find all the shadings, the nuances and subtleties, the varying degrees of quality, in music. Leonard Feather's knowledge of the romance languages has contributed a lot to his musical vocabulary and also to his department of weights and measures, insofar as dividing these things up and giving them their proper pigeonhole is concerned.

Everybody who listens to jazz should have *The Encyclopedia of Jazz.* It will do a great deal to increase the knowledge and understanding of this music everywhere. I wish it every success.

THE JAZZ TREND

BY BENNY GOODMAN

Since the readers of this book are already familiar with the subject, I suppose it will come as no revelation when I point out that many changes, many advances, have taken place in jazz during the past few years. Once ignored or looked on with condescension by laymen who were willing to accept all the other contemporary art forms on an esthetic level, jazz has at last undergone a number of important changes, both in the channels of creation and in the way it is being appreciated.

For one thing, jazz is no longer looked on merely as dance music. I am sure there will always be people who will dance to it, but there is no longer any need for the best jazz musicians to perform primarily in dance halls or cater only to the demands of dancers. Carnegie Hall in New York, Symphony Hall in Boston, and scores of other concert halls both in America and overseas, have opened up to jazz during the past decade. Today there are a dozen concert "packages" making cross-country and Transatlantic tours, playing all the halls that once were completely closed to jazz.

Similarly, many of the night clubs, those that cater to big bands as well as the spots that use only small combos, are tending more and more to eliminate dancing and to use the extra floor space for spectators who simply want to listen to the music, and listen with an intelligent, critical ear. This is another of the many signs that jazz and its audiences have come of age. Some of those audiences may be the fans who once danced the Lindy Hop, the Shag and the Big Apple to jazz, and now prefer to sit and listen. Others are youngsters just developing an appreciation for the music and learning from the start that this is music for the ears, not merely for the feet.

At one time, back in the years when my band was first becoming known, our audiences consisted chiefly of youngsters in their teens and early twenties who reacted directly and very emotionally to our music; they thought it was stimulating and exciting, and great for dancing. They never analyzed this emotional response, the happiness and enjoyment they experienced. The kids didn't read or write books about the music; they just liked it.

Today, as I say, those kids may still be around, listening to the same music with a feeling of nostalgia. But although these same people constituted a segment of our audiences in the spring of 1956, when I reorganized the band for the Waldorf-Astoria in New York and a series of out-of-town dates, there was an even larger part of the audiences that consisted of a new generation who found the music as fresh and exciting as their parents had in the 1930s. Their reaction, again, was direct and emotional, but today it takes place against a different background. Swing music, in fact all forms of jazz, may be said to have been adopted by the intellectuals.

Since jazz is, in my opinion, one of our most original contributions to Twentieth Century culture and seems likely to go down in history as the real folk music of our country, it is a commendable thing that it has enjoyed this degree of intellectual acceptance. But although we have many competent critics in the newspapers, magazines and the book world writing capably about the subject, among them my brother-in-law John Hammond, the fact remains that there are a number of others who tend to go overboard, approaching the subject as if it were some kind of occult science. One of them, as a matter of fact, seems to be incapable of writing anything in words of less than four syllables, and he doesn't always get the syllables right either. Once he used the word "contrapointal." What does he mean by that? Contrapuntal? I wonder what his readers get out of reading that kind of stuff; my own reaction is simply bewilderment and a touch of dismay, because there seems to be no really deep emotional feeling in this sort of writing; there is nothing but pompousness behind this over-intellectual approach. The same situation exists in Europe, where a number of critics have gone about the business of analyzing and criticizing jazz from the most complicated and didactic standpoint, even though they themselves cannot create any of the music they discuss, and in the vast majority of cases the truly important jazz talents continue to come out of this country. The general public in those overseas countries continues to react to the music with a happy and healthy enthusiasm, as I found out firsthand when we toured Europe in 1950.

The jazz fans in those countries are quite amazing. I remember once meeting a Greek youth, from

Athens, who was about 21 years old when he first came to America. He knew so much about me and my records that I had to ask *him* questions! He told me he corresponded regularly with record collectors in other countries.

Similarly, a year or so ago, I met Count Bernadotte's son, Bertil, who was not more than seventeen, and he turned out to be a jazz fan. He asked me so many questions about records I had made and forgotten about many years ago that I was actually embarrassed. Yet it is heartening to know that in Sweden, France, England and so many other countries, youngsters like this are growing up with a real and avid interest in the music and a desire to help foster its growth. The record collector represents an amazing and unique breed, sometimes as fanatic as any stamp collector or other hobbyist, but it certainly is a healthy trend.

This trend, in these past years, led to the publication of Leonard Feather's *Encyclopedia of Jazz,* which gave the fans, the musicians, and the whole music world a long-needed permanent reference work.

I have known Leonard for many years and I know he has always been aware that facts, as well as opinions, are vitally important in the study of any art. I believe the new, enlarged *Encyclopedia of Jazz* will add a wealth of important facts to the fast growing library of information about the most internationally popular branch of American music.

ABOUT THE AUTHOR

BY JOHN HAMMOND

It has been almost a quarter of a century since I first came across Leonard Feather, that indefatigable chronicler of the jazz scene. Then, as now, our opinions about music were often in violent conflict; but his resourcefulness and industry could always be envied.

Leonard has had a quite unbelievable career in jazz. He once operated simultaneously as composer, arranger, instrumentalist, publicist and critic—a feat never duplicated, before or since. What's more, he has been effective in all these fields, except possibly as pianist. His energy is legendary, and his knowledge awesome. Both in his private and public life he has been a consistent and effective foe of Jim Crow.

All of us in jazz can be deeply grateful to him for *The Encyclopedia of Jazz,* without which only a few could pose as authorities on the subject. It is the *Who's Who, Webster's* and *Grove's* of the field, and it has been a motivating force in the appreciation of jazz as a serious art form.

How ironic it is that our leading writer on what is supposed to be America's most significant contribution to the arts is an ex-Britisher who arrived here in the middle thirties. The fact is that the English jazz fan of the early thirties was far better informed about America's improvising musicians than we were. At that time, there were a great number of Englishmen with even more knowledge than Leonard—but none with his energy or drive. Incidentally, I shall never forget that it was English Columbia that gave me my first job, in 1933, recording jazz for which there was a demand in Great Britain that the American companies were unwilling to satisfy.

Leonard Feather's first visit to America was in 1935, and I recall being on the pier waiting for the *Normandie* to dock. Within a few days, he had combed Harlem, placed some songs with Clarence Williams, and arranged to become (gratis) the London correspondent of the *New York Amsterdam News.* For the next four years he shuttled between the two countries; it was then that he acquired the experience that made him the unique figure he has become in American jazz. He wrote tunes for Irving Mills' publishing firm; later he became confidant and press agent to his idol, Duke Ellington; supervised recording sessions, wrote for every conceivable musical publication here and abroad, and in 1943 joined *Esquire* as a staff writer. During the war there was great interest in jazz, both among servicemen and civilians; Leonard was directly responsible, with Robert Goffin, for the yearly polls run by *Esquire,* the first non-specialized publication to take jazz seriously. Many writers and musicians voted for their favorite instrumentalists, singers, bands and arrangers; *Esquire* sponsored annual jazz concerts, the first of which was held at the Metropolitan Opera House, featuring the winners.

Up to 1949 Leonard was about the busiest man

on the jazz scene, writing, promoting, recording, broadcasting, and becoming involved with various artists. Then his life suddenly changed. While crossing a street on a wintry day, he and his wife were run over by a driverless car whose parking brakes had slipped. For weeks he was on the brink of death.

Those months in the hospital transformed Leonard in many ways. In recent years his musical horizons have widened; today he is a great, constructive force on the musical scene, a selfless, considerate human being, eager to help others, and always working toward the elevation of jazz as an art form.

In the first volume of *The Encyclopedia of Jazz,* the author imposed the sensible limitation of biographies to those musicians whose work was available on long playing records. In 1955 many of the great performances of the earlier jazz stars had not been reissued on LPs, whereas now there is a really representative grouping of all types of jazz available at all speeds.

In 1960 it remains just as difficult as ever to agree on a definition of jazz. Certainly much of the tortured, cerebral gropings of the Tristano and Ornette Coleman schools have more to do with the League of Composers' concerts of the twenties and thirties than with the uninhibited improvisation of earlier days.

Even though it was said in reviews of the original *Encyclopedia of Jazz* that virtually nobody of importance had been omitted, Leonard has continued to expand the horizons of the book not only by adding many new artists but by incorporating country blues singers, early recording artists and many more who, for one reason or another, could not be included in the first book.

As a result, the new, revised *Encyclopedia of Jazz* contains many valuable added features. Besides the biographies, which now number more than two thousand, there are the fascinating blindfold tests of famous musicians, the results of polls, reports from overseas, and greatly expanded chapters on the history and nature of jazz.

I believe the *New Encyclopedia of Jazz* is the most complete and valuable reference work on the subject to date. Though Leonard and I still do not altogether agree about what constitutes jazz, I will always be in his debt for his cataloguing of its achievements in this indispensable new volume.

THE ENCYCLOPEDIA OF JAZZ

Sixty years of jazz: an historical survey

From the perspective of the 1960s, at a time when jazz is enjoying world-wide acceptance, the respect of intellectuals and the official endorsement of the United States government as an instrument of international goodwill, it is difficult for the observer, especially if born after 1930, to form a true and detached perspective. Jazz today needs no apologies, no camouflage or euphemistic disguise, although for the first five decades of its existence it was relegated to the cultural backdoors of our society, an esthetic Cinderella, passively neglected or actively despised.

In order to understand more fully the difficulties under which jazz labored, it must be remembered that during that inaugural half-century it was restricted, in one form or another, to the role of a utilitarian music. The first pre-jazz groups were essentially brass bands playing marching music in the streets. Out of them grew the early units to which the new word "jass" was attached. From the World War I years that saw the rise of the Original Dixieland Band, through the Prohibition decade that was known, for reasons not necessarily bearing directly on the music, as the Jazz Age, these bands were essentially providers of entertainment in cafes and night clubs.

The advent of the swing era brought a slight shift of accent as jazz in its big band manifestations became the dominantly publicized form and was used most often in dance halls and hotels. Not until the mid-1950s was it firmly established that jazz, in addition to its value as music to which one could march, drink or dance, merited the attention of the serious listener, whether in a concert hall or on a long-play record.

Admittedly the onset of the 1960s still found jazz in widespread utilitarian use, but by now the dance halls, dives and smoke-filled rooms that had been its almost exclusive association had receded to secondary importance in the scheme. How this was accomplished, and how the music made more headway in 1955-60 than in the entire preceding 55 years, will be recounted later in this chapter. First it is necessary to examine the sources, nature and development of the music.

There are many common misconceptions about jazz, most of them the result of special pleading on the part of experts in whom romanticism has displaced realism. The most widespread is the concept that New Orleans was the exclusive American nursery of jazz. A second is that jazz originally was African music. Another is the racial theory of jazz nurtured since the 1930s by critics in France.

Largely because several of the important pioneers (notably Louis Armstrong and King Oliver) came from New Orleans, attention was focussed on this city from the earliest days of the documentation of jazz. As a result, a tremendous volume of material has been brought to light concerning virtually any musician whose background could be tied to the colorful story of the New Orleans brass bands: this is reflected in the preponderance of New Orleans musicians to be found among the birthplace listings later in these pages.

Since there was hardly any recording of jazz until the 1920s, and since many of those who were a part of its earliest years have died or are unable to offer anything more than confused and contradictory stories, it is highly unlikely that the real story of the crystallization of jazz will ever be pieced together.

There are, though, a number of older musicians whose recollections tend to bear out the belief that jazz was born in New Orleans but also in many other areas of the United States, spontaneously and more or less simultaneously.

Wilbur De Paris, the trombonist and bandleader whose memories go back to the years not long after the turn of the century when, as a child, he toured with his musician father, has confirmed that there were many groups playing in the brass band style throughout the Southwest and Midwest; that their instrumentation included one or two cornets, clarinet, trombone, guitar, bass and drums; and that these bands, playing at picnics and riding in advertising wagons and often marching in the streets, played a polyphonic music that had many qualities in common with what was later called jazz.

Many of the urban centers made an early contribution, and helped to set styles, says De Paris: "For instance, the type of trumpet playing that came to be identified later with Bix Beiderbecke was quite common in the Midwest among Negro musicians . . . brass band and orchestra men played dances; and they played jazz. There was a whole other school that should complement the New Orleans school, and that was the school I came up in. Basically these men were better, musically and technically, than most of the New Orleans musicians . . . Jazz was growing up in different parts of the country without one part necessarily knowing what the other part was doing."

According to Eubie Blake, the composer and pianist born in 1883, ragtime was played at funerals in his native Baltimore at least as early as similar events in New Orleans that have since been far more widely publicized. "Joe Blow would die, and maybe he belonged to some society, so they would get the money together and have a band for his funeral . . . they sure played ragtime on their horns on the way back from the graveyard. There were dozens of fine musicians who played ragtime in the parades and at the funerals. Trumpet players like Pike Davis and Preston Duncan; a musician named Emil Daverage, who played the euphonium. We called the music ragtime, whether it was a piano or a band playing. We never heard the word jazz until many years later."

The late W. C. Handy, in an interview with the author in 1957, stated that he drew the musicians for his early bands "from all over the country"—many from Mississippi and Louisiana, others from Florida and Tennessee, even a few from Philadelphia and New York. The music that grew into jazz, some of it born in "shout songs" in churches, he added, could be heard "wherever slavery was practiced."

Texas and Oklahoma had parade bands around the turn of the century: one such group in Oklahoma City, with Jim Bronson on clarinet, Andrew Rushing (father of the singer Jimmy Rushing) on trumpet, Millidge Winslett on trombone and George Sparks on peckhorn, may have been the equal or superior of any of the highly publicized bands in which Bunk Johnson and his New Orleans contemporaries marched.

The late Walter Gould, a ragtime pianist from Philadelphia (born 1875), had similar misgivings about the New Orleans myth. "It all started because Louis Armstrong and King Oliver happened to come from there," he said shortly before his death in 1957, adding that when there were dozens of great musicians in the East, "you couldn't find but two or three good piano players in the whole of New Orleans." Willie "The Lion" Smith, the ragtime pianist born in Goshen, New York in 1897, states emphatically that as far back as he can remember the East had its equivalents of the Louis Armstrongs and Bunk Johnsons. Leonard De Paur, the choir director and Negro musicologist, ascribes the lopsided evaluation of jazz origins to the fact that "the boys who chronicled the development around New Orleans did a much more effective job than the people who were East, and it also seems that the whites were more aware of its value around New Orleans and they really did a job of promoting." De Paur recalls that his mother, born around 1887, was completely conversant with jazz as it was practiced by wandering groups from Charleston, South Carolina.

A synthesis of the evidence offered by these and other authorities bears out the belief that jazz, whether in the form of written ragtime for piano or of church shouts, spirituals or brass band music, was born in the United States of America, and that any further pinpointing must remain a subject for considerable speculation.

The second misconception—that jazz grew wholly out of "African music"—is based on what is at best a half-truth. The music we recognize today as jazz is a synthesis of six main sources: rhythms from West Africa; harmonic structure from European classical music; melodic and harmonic qualities from nineteenth-century American folk music; religious music; work songs, and minstrel show music; with, of course, a substantial overlapping of many of these areas.

Negro spirituals and blues bear a slight and debatable relationship, in scale concept and rhythmic values, to African origins; there is a stronger resemblance, in melody and spirit, among the American Negro work songs. Barry Ulanov, in his *History of Jazz in America,* wrote (referring to André Gide's *Travels in The Congo*): "The music that Gide describes is vaguely related to jazz, but is by no means the same thing; it has only a general resemblance to many different kinds of primitive music, European as well as American . . . a comparative analysis of African and American music does not yield clear parallels. . . . There is far more of the sound of jazz in mid-European gypsy fiddling than there is in a whole corps of African drummers."

It is true that while the slave ships brought with their human cargo some of the cultural patterns of the African Negro, there were developing in the United States many folk themes that had melodic and harmonic qualities discernibly related to what was later known as ragtime, jazz and/or the blues. *Frankie and Johnny,* a song of obscure origin, was known in St. Louis in the 1880s, according to one source; originated in 1850 and was sung at the siege of Vicksburg, according to another; dates back as far as 1840, in the opinion of a third. What is important about this song is that it has the classic twelve-measure blues structure, with the first four measures based on the chord of the tonic, the next on the subdominant, and so on through the regular 1-4-5-1 blues pattern. Doubt exists whether *Frankie and Johnny* is of Negro or white origin; the harmonic formula it represents was commonly heard among folk artists of both races a century ago and the twelve-measure form can even be found in English and French balladry of the thirteenth century. Thus the blues, often called the lifeblood of jazz, certainly is not of African descent; structurally it is of white origin, melodically and harmonically it has been nurtured in an American Negro environment. (This is one of many indications that jazz is a social, not a racial music: it was the segregated American Negro, not simply "the Negro", who contributed most of its essential characteristics.) Such tunes of the 1850s as *Arkansas Traveler* and *Turkey in the Straw* bear a closer resemblance to the early jazz than does any known African music, in melodic and harmonic construction.

The third misconception, referred to parenthetically above, is easily explained. More than half the greatest jazz artists have been Negroes; the music stemmed from a specific social environment, originally conditioned by slavery, in which a group of people largely shut off from the white world developed highly personal cultural traits. As soon as the rigid segregation under which they had lived began to relax, it became clear that given a freer interchange of ideas anyone could play jazz, according to his environment, his ability and his value as an individual, not as white or Negro. Place an infant from Australia or China in the care of a jazz-oriented New York family and his chances of growing up to be a great jazzman are as good as those of any other child.

There is considerable evidence that parallel with the development of the Negro brass bands there were similar groups of white musicians, some of whom played an important part in bringing this new music to a wide public through minstrel shows. One was the band of Jack "Papa" Laine, who led a minstrel band in New Orleans during the 1890s. Whether the white groups drew their material exclusively from Negro sources or created themes of their own has been the subject of many claims and counter-accusations. What seems certain is that during the Civil War and postwar years the Negro was fashioning his own music on plantations and in chain gangs, in levee camps and on railroads, poverty confining his expression to the human voice or to crude homemade fiddles, guitars and banjos; that at the same time he was developing spirituals that owed more to white sources than his secular melodies (as an inspection of "white spirituals" reveals), and that it was not until the white and Negro, secular and religious influences spread through the country during the 1890s that a form of music directly linked with jazz developed. This was the era of the cakewalk, and it was probably because of the national popularity of that dance that ragtime began to evolve as a distinct musical style.

Though it tended, after public acceptance, to

become formalized as written music for the piano, ragtime undoubtedly originated as spontaneous music created on guitars and banjos as well as pianos, and just as surely it merged into the "ragtime bands"—Bunk Johnson's and other brass bands are known to have made a specialty of some of the early ragtime tunes. These performances could not be preserved, since there was in effect no phonograph recording; ragtime in its primary, pianistic form, can be heard in a collection of authentic rags, transcribed from the original piano rolls and released on Riverside Records. The best-remembered exponent of ragtime piano was Scott Joplin, a Texan who settled in Sedalia, Missouri during the 1890s. Tom Turpin, another ragtime pioneer, was a saloon keeper and pianist in St. Louis. Among the brass bands that flourished during the same period were Buddy Bolden's band, Freddie Keppard's Olympia band, the Original Creole band, the Eagle band and the Tuxedo band. And "Papa" Laine's Reliance Brass band, playing for picnics, marches and carnivals, was prominent during the same era, playing tunes of undetermined origin that were later to become globally known when the Original Dixieland Band recorded them.

A later Laine group, his Ragtime Band, formed the nucleus of a unit that opened in 1915 at the Lambs' Cafe in Chicago under the leadership of the trombonist Tom Brown. First known as Brown's Dixieland Band, the combo reached Chicago from New Orleans and, despite the objection of local musicians' union officials who were uncomfortably aware of the then sordid meaning of the word "jazz" as a verb, expanded its name to "Brown's Dixieland Jass Band." In 1916 Alcide "Yellow" Nunez, a clarinetist who had worked in Laine's Reliance band, came to Chicago along with cornetist Nick La Rocca, pianist Henry Ragas and trombonist Eddie "Daddy" Edwards. The last three, with Larry Shields, who had been playing clarinet in Brown's band, and a young drummer, Tony Sbarbaro, moved to New York to open early in 1917 at Reisenweber's Cafe just off Columbus Circle.

The band was a phenomenal success. "Jass" was the new popular fad, and before long the word had replaced "ragtime" in the public vocabulary, though the musical distinction was an extremely vague one. The Original Dixieland Jass Band, as the quintet at Reisenweber's was called, recorded for Victor in February 1917. These were the first jazz discs ever made; no Negro jazz orchestra was recorded on a major label until King Oliver's first session six years later.

1917 was a significant year for jazz in several respects. The federal order closing the Storyville area of legalized prostitution in New Orleans left many sporting-house musicians jobless and, in effect, marked the end of an era. During 1917, Louis Armstrong, with a drummer named Joe Lindsey, formed a little band and began to make a local name as a musician of more than ordinary merit. Fate Marable, long a pianist on the Missisippi riverboats, embarked in 1917 on the bandleading career that was to take many great Negro jazzmen on their first trip North.

One musician who did not need the riverboat trip to transport him from New Orleans was Joe "King" Oliver, Louis Armstrong's friend and trumpet idol. Oliver, having worked for several years with trombonist Kid Ory, received an offer to open at the Lincoln Gardens in Chicago. When he left New Orleans in the summer of 1917, taking with him Jimmie Noone to play clarinet, Louis Armstrong took his place in the Ory band.

Jazz was on the move, on both the domestic and international levels, in the years during and after World War I. Jelly Roll Morton had shifted his barrelhouse piano style from the shuttered halls of Storyville to the happier climate of California. Kid Ory followed him there in 1919. Around that time jazz came to Europe as the Original Dixieland Band became the sensation of London society, and Sidney Bechet, former clarinetist with the Eagle Band in New Orleans, appeared on the Continent with Will Marion Cook's concert orchestra.

During these early years the music played by Negro and white musicians drew its material from the music of the old brass bands and from the folk blues that had filtered into urban ragtime and jazz. Harmonically and melodically there was little demonstrable difference between Negro and white jazz, yet there was a distinction, unmistakable to any discerning listener, as subtle and as hard to describe as the difference in taste between wines.

Many of the early musicians were musically illiterate, or were at best indifferent readers. It was not until the early 1920s that the increasing use of written arrangements by both Negro and white bands produced an ever larger proportion of men who had studied music and were capable readers. Improvisation on set harmonic patterns and free interpretations of familiar themes provided the substance of every jazz performance, so written music was rarely needed.

The New Orleans Rhythm Kings, who opened at the Friars' Inn in Chicago in 1921, played much the same kind of jazz as the Original Dixieland group, but gained special distinction from the presence of two soloists who outshone the leader, trumpeter Paul Mares, in inspired solo flights. They were Leon Rappolo, a gifted and ill-fated clarinetist who was to end his days in a mental hospital, and George Brunies, the big-toned trombonist who was among the first to emphasize humor in jazz. Brunies (who later changed his name to Brunis on the advice of a numerologist) entertained his audiences by controlling the trombone slide with his foot.

The comedy aspect was necessary in those days to put jazz across with the public. In order to consolidate its position as a novelty, jazz had to be identified with cacophony; it had to be profane, never sacred. The results could be found in such titles as *Barnyard Blues, Livery Stable Blues, Ostrich Walk, Bow Wow Blues, Skeleton Jangle.* The use of such effects as the "laughing clarinet" and "crying trombone," prominent in the tongue-in-cheek performances of Ted Lewis and other satirists, was prevalent, even among the more dedicated jazzmen, until the music had a secure enough footing to dispense with these tricks.

While the New Orleans Rhythm Kings (or Friars' Society Orchestra, as they were called then) were gaining a firm foothold in Chicago, Kid Ory took an important step in Los Angeles. His band had its first record session, accompanying two singers and playing two tunes on its own, for a small independent label. During the same year, 1921, James P. Johnson made the first jazz piano solo record, *Carolina Shout,* for Okeh.

In 1922 and '23, the newly found market for "race" records, aimed at the Negro market, gave added impetus to jazz. King Oliver, whose Chicago band now included Louis Armstrong and clarinetist Johnny Dodds, traveled to Richmond, Indiana, to record there for the Gennett company; Jelly Roll Morton was among the others who visited the Richmond studio for sessions with the crude acoustical equipment then available. In New York, Fletcher Henderson made records with his own band, the first Negro outfit to specialize in orchestrations; at other sessions he accompanied such leading blues singers as Bessie Smith and Ma Rainey.

Most of these events passed unobserved by the white public. Paul Whiteman, busy trying to "make a lady out of jazz," introduced George Gershwin's *Rhapsody in Blue* in a widely publicized concert at the Aeolian Hall in February 1924. Much of the harmonic and melodic quality but little of the rhythmic content of jazz could be detected in the ambitious Gershwin work. Like so many pseudo-jazz concert works that were later introduced in European concert halls and Hollywood movie studios and on New York radio shows, the *Rhapsody* lacked the blend of orchestration and individual improvisation that has long been a part of every real jazz performance. It has the surface characteristics but few of the basic elements that had already established jazz as an internationally successful, if unladylike, musical innovation.

There were many other events in 1924 that seem, in retrospect, more important than the night at Aeolian Hall. 1924 was the year Louis Armstrong came to New York to join Fletcher Henderson's band; the year Thomas "Fats" Waller recorded *Birmingham Blues* in his initial session; the year a twenty-one-year-old cornetist named Bix Biederbecke came to New York to play at a Times Square dance hall with a band known as the Wolverines. It was the year Ethel Waters showed that vocal jazz was limited neither to the blues nor to the "race" trade when she introduced *Dinah* in a smart night club revue.

The mid-1920s saw a steady rise in the quantity and quality of recorded jazz. With Fletcher Henderson, with various recording groups assembled by Clarence Williams, and with his own special units, Louis Armstrong began to build the stockpile of performances that were to bring him greater fame abroad than he had yet found at home. Duke Ellington, a successful pianist and bandleader in Washington since the war years, had moved to New York in 1923; three years later he was rapidly gaining recognition at the Kentucky Club on Broadway and had composed and recorded the *East St. Louis Toodle-O,* later famous as his radio theme. Starting in 1925 Red Nichols became the central figure in a clique of white jazz musicians, many of whom, well-versed in music, made their living playing in "commercial" bands, though they were best known for the records they made with such groups as the Red Heads, and later Red Nichols and his Five Pennies. Among them were Jimmy Dorsey on clarinet, Miff Mole on trombone, Joe Venuti on violin and Eddie Lang on guitar.

These were the principal New York figures. In Chicago there were King Oliver's Dixie Syncopators at the Plantation, Jimmie Noone's band with Earl Hines at the Apex, and several bands in which trumpeter Freddie Keppard was a key figure. Detroit had produced two orchestras that were to prove historically important: McKinney's Cotton Pickers, whose direction was taken over in 1927 by Don Redman, a gifted saxophonist-arranger; and the Jean Goldkette band, which in 1926-7 included such men as Bix, Frank Trumbauer with his C-Melody saxophone, and Pee Wee Russell on clarinet and saxes. Soon after Goldkette broke up his band in 1927, Bix and several other jazz stars who had worked with him were absorbed into the Paul Whiteman colossus. Limited to occasional solos with Whiteman, they found their esthetic outlet in numerous record sessions.

To many students and collectors the years from 1926 to 1929 mark the golden era of jazz recording. Many of the small units were in their prime: Armstrong's Hot Five and Hot Seven, Jelly Roll Morton and his Red Hot Peppers, Nichols and the Pennies, Bix and Trumbauer, Venuti and Lang. The "Austin High gang" from Chicago was at its peak. Composed originally of five high school students, Jimmy and Dick McPartland on cornet and banjo, Bud Freeman on C-Melody and tenor sax, Frank Teschemacher on clarinet and Jim Lannigan on bass, the group had a fluctuating personnel. Members of its inner circle, on records and for many dates in person in Chicago and later in New York, were Floyd O'Brien and Jack Teagarden on trombone, Mezz Mezzrow and Fud Livingston on saxophones, Dave Tough and Gene Krupa on drums.

The same years saw the birth of Duke Ellington's enlarged band at the Cotton Club in Harlem, of Andy Kirk's "Twelve Clouds of Joy" in Kansas City, of Earl Hines' first big band in Chicago, and of Jimmie Lunceford's group in Memphis.

Among the bigger Negro bands in those years the line between utilitarian orchestrated music for dancing and sincere artistic jazz for listening was thinly drawn; the success of Fletcher Henderson at the Roseland Ballroom on Broadway, of King Oliver and Louis Armstrong at the Savoy Ballroom in Harlem, proved this conclusively. But the line was more distinctly drawn among the big white bands ("big" in those days meant anything with two cornets, a trombone and three saxophones). Perhaps the sole exception was Ben Pollack, the only white bandleader who granted a certain amount of freedom to his soloists and featured a fair proportion of arrangements built on jazz themes. A former New Orleans Rhythm Kings drummer, Pollack had organized his band on the West Coast in 1926 with personnel that included the sixteen-year-old Benny Goodman. During the next three years he produced a series of Victor records in Chicago and New York that showed how the worlds of commercial dance music and authentic jazz could find common ground.

Although the white jazzmen rarely found opportunities for expressing themselves freely on "in-person" jobs, the work they were doing on jazz recording sesions compensated for this restriction by helping them earn international reputations. In many foreign countries records by the Dorsey Brothers, Bix Beiderbecke, Venuti and Lang were the subject of serious discussion and lengthy printed analysis. The London *Melody Maker*, founded in 1926 as a monthly magazine and converted seven years later into a weekly newspaper, devoted many columns to intensely analytical reviews of American records.

Many American musicians who were virtually unknown to the public in their own country found that they had prophets with honor abroad. One bandleader in London sent for Adrian Rollini and others to lend his band the authentic American touch. Jimmy Dorsey and Muggsy Spanier, visiting Great Britain in 1930 with the Ted Lewis orchestra, were amazed to find themselves lionized by fans who knew more about their recording careers than they knew themselves.

Louis Armstrong and Duke Ellington were among the greatest favorites with foreign audiences. Their constant success on records paved the way for a continuous pilgrimage of jazz stars to Europe during the 1930's: Armstrong in 1932, Ellington with his whole band in 1933, Cab Calloway, Lucky

Millinder, Coleman Hawkins and many more, found on overseas jaunts a keenness of understanding and enthusiasm they had seldom encountered at home.

Meanwhile, in the United States, despite the economic crisis, the increasing interest in livelier forms of musical expression had enabled a number of big new bands to enjoy a fair degree of commercial success. Glen Gray's Casa Loma Orchestra, originally a group of Canadian musicians, achieved a wide popular following by alternating commercial popular songs with jazz tunes. The jazz consisted mainly of trite two-bar "riffs" and the improvised solos were mediocre, but the Casa Loma band succeeded in its fumbling way in auguring the shape of things to come, for its success was in effect a foretaste of the swing era.

The early 1930s produced a flock of great Negro bands, most of them led by men who were talented both as arrangers and as instrumentalists. Among them were Benny Carter, Don Redman and Luis Russell. The Savoy Ballroom, soon to become known internationally as the "home of happy feet," rocked to the persuasive drums and superb ensemble of Chick Webb. Earl Hines reigned at the Grand Terrace Ballroom in Chicago. Duke Ellington crashed the gates of Hollywood to appear in *Check and Double Check,* an early talking picture. Louis Armstrong, on location in Los Angeles, fronted a band led by Les Hite, which featured a teen-aged drummer named Lionel Hampton. Kansas City jazz was brewing in the bands of Benny Moten and Andy Kirk. Of all these, the only band to achieve the commercial stability afforded by a sponsored radio program was Don Redman's. It was hoped that in setting this precedent he was paving the way for many other Negro bands. Unfortunately this did not prove to be the case.*

Because of the limitations imposed on the Negro artist, it was perhaps natural that the next major step in the progress of jazz should be taken by a white band. By 1934 the Dorsey Brothers were able to start their own band, with an approach that kept closer to real jazz than that of any previous white unit since Pollack's.

During the same year Benny Goodman, who, like the Dorseys, had made a very successful living for several years as a studio musician, but had also led various jazz groups in record dates, started a series of hour-long broadcasts for the National Biscuit Company. Using three trumpets, two trombones, four saxophones and four rhythm instruments (piano, guitar, bass and drums), Benny assembled a radio band the like of which had never been heard. Within a few months, after some shifts in personnel that enabled him to take his band on the road to cash in on the national prominence his broadcasts had brought him, he had lined up such men as Bunny Berigan, Jess Stacy and Gene Krupa, as well as a library of arrangements by Benny Carter, Deane Kincaide, Will Hudson and Fletcher and Horace Henderson. It was Fletcher's arrangements of *King Porter Stomp* and *Sometimes I'm Happy,* recorded by the Goodman band for Victor in July of 1935, that earned Goodman his famous style identification. Fletcher provided Benny with much of his best material during the next few years.

Goodman and Henderson accomplished something unique: they were able to deliver current popular songs to the public with the conventional vocal chorus sung (by Helen Ward) in a style that made subtle use of syncopation, expressing in ensemble terms the ideas that had been voiced by the great jazz soloists. They achieved a smooth ensemble sound without losing contact with jazz.

Goodman's success was not immediate. He made a poor impression at Billy Rose's Music Hall in New York, and in the early bookings when his band went on the road. But while he was on his way to California, the records he had made were building an audience of eager youngsters for him, and his engagement at the Palomar Ballroom in Los Angeles, for which many had predicted dire results, was an overnight sensation.

The music "swung." In 1932 Duke Ellington, by recording his composition *It Don't Mean a Thing If It Ain't Got That Swing,* had issued a manifesto. As the word "swing" gained increasing currency it became a new name for jazz. "Swing music" was born and a new jazz generation had begun.

Simultaneously with the rise of swing music, a comparable development had taken place in the small-band field. In the New York block of West Fifty-second Street between Fifth and Sixth Avenues, where during speakeasy days Art Tatum had played at the original Onyx Club for an audience composed mainly of musicians from the radio stu-

* The role played by racial discrimination in charting the course of jazz is discussed in the chapter "Jazz in American Society."

dios, a sprinkling of clubs dedicated to jazz appeared. At the new Onyx, at the Famous Door and other small, intimate clubs, the music was provided by such men as Wingy Manone, Bunny Berigan, Eddie Condon, Red McKenzie, the Five Spirits of Rhythm, Billie Holiday, and a new star, Teddy Wilson, who for a while was the intermission pianist at the Famous Door. Fifty-second Street, in addition to providing a miniature replica of the swing craze initiated by Benny Goodman, played a vital role in launching the new fad as a concert attraction.

If the swing era was born with the thunderous success of the Goodman band in California in the fall of 1935, it can be said to have enjoyed its baptism at the Imperial Theatre in New York on Sunday evening, May 24, 1936, when Joe Helbock, the manager of the Onyx Club, decided to bring respectability to the trend by presenting the first official "Swing Music Concert." Though Goodman and Duke Ellington were absent, the personnel at the Imperial that night constituted to a large extent a Who's Who of the swing era. The participants included Bob Crosby, fronting the big orchestra that pioneered in the attempt to turn Dixieland jazz into a vehicle for a full-size band; Tommy Dorsey, with a so-called "Clambake Seven" contingent from the new big band he had formed on breaking up with his brother Jimmy; violinist Stuff Smith, xylophonist Red Norvo and trumpeter Bunny Berigan with their swing sextets; Glen Gray's Casa Loma orchestra, and groups from the bands of Paul Whiteman and Louis Armstrong.

Perhaps the least impressive item on the printed program announced the appearance of "Arthur Shaw's String Ensemble." Shaw, then a radio studio musician and almost unknown to jazz fans, had decided to make a revolutionary move by backing his jazz clarinet with a string quartet. To the astonishment of Helbock, of the audience and above all of Shaw himself, the group's performance of Artie's *Interlude in B Flat* was the hit of the evening. As Shaw recalled in his autobiography *The Trouble with Cinderella,* "I had no idea that this slight difference in instrumentation would have caused any such commotion as it did. . . . Accordingly I scouted around and eventually put together my first band."

Thus, within a few months of his unexpected triumph at the Imperial Theatre, Artie Shaw created the first major schism in the swing field. Benny Goodman, after a year of unchallenged supremacy, had a rival. The rivalry became more intense when Shaw, after abandoning his first jazz-with-strings orchestra, formed a band with the conventional brass-reeds-and-rhythm constitution.

By the time this move was made, several other leading instrumentalists had entered the rapidly growing swing market. Tommy Dorsey had secured a niche for himself with his swing versions of classical melodies and other novel ideas. Jimmy Dorsey was making headway with a capable band of his own. Woody Herman had reorganized the remnants of the old Isham Jones band into a coöperative outfit whose work hovered between Benny Goodman's brand of swing and Bob Crosby's overgrown Dixieland.

The Negro bands were not as much involved in this competition as they would be today if swing were in the ascendancy. However, through the media of records and late-night, unsponsored radio, much of the best music of the swing age was being performed by Duke Ellington, Jimmie Lunceford, Teddy Hill, Chick Webb and the newly arrived sensation from Kansas City, the Count Basie band.

The year 1936 saw the arrival not only of many important big bands, but also of a subsidiary jazz movement that enjoyed national popularity for several years: boogie-woogie.

The term boogie-woogie was generally used to denote a style of jazz played on the piano with a rolling, eight-beats-to-the-bar left hand rhythm. It had been played for years at "rent parties" (which might be described as benefits for the landlord) and honky-tonks in Kansas City and Chicago when John Hammond, intrigued by a record he had unearthed by the name of *Honky Tonk Train Blues,* started a search for the man who had composed and recorded it, Meade Lux Lewis. After a long investigation he found Lewis washing cars in a Chicago garage, restored him to the music world by rerecording *Honky Tonk Train Blues,* and soon found that he had inadvertently begun a whole new trend.

Meade Lux Lewis, Pete Johnson and Albert Ammons were the first and best boogie-woogie pianists to achieve some degree of prominence. Before long the style found its way, like innumerable jazz innovations of Negro origin, into the white jazz world. Bob Zurke, playing the *Yancey Special* with Bob Crosby's band, was acclaimed by the public with far greater interest than it had ever shown in Meade Lux Lewis, who had created the composition, or in Jimmy Yancey, on whose bass rhythm pattern he had constructed it.

As boogie-woogie and swing became national topics of conversation, jazz made its long-delayed transition from unknown quantity to acknowledged art form in America. Amazing though it seems in retrospect, until the middle 1930s there was hardly ever a mention of jazz in any national American magazine; *Down Beat* did not come into existence until 1934, and *Metronome* at that time was dedicated mainly to commercial music; there was nowhere for an American jazz fan or musician to turn if he wanted to read about jazz, except the growing backlog of books and periodicals in foreign countries. In the swing era and right up to the early 1940s, jazz, with very occasional exceptions, was generally ignored—even as a subject for magazine features. Not until 1939 did any American publisher deem this native American art form worthy of a documentary book.

Jazz was gaining ground on the record front. Starting in 1935, Teddy Wilson and Billie Holiday made a long and memorable series of sessions for Brunswick and Vocalion, usually featuring superior commercial songs performed in a jazz vein; Lionel Hampton made all-star sessions with a broad variety of groups for Victor; Count Basie's orchestra and Art Tatum, among others, made their most famous dates for Decca. In a more commercial vein, Fats Waller's good-humored vocals and impeccable piano earned consistent popularity in recordings of pop songs for Victor.

In those days there were only three record companies of any consequence in the entire United States—the American Record Corporation, which owned the Columbia, Brunswick and Vocalion labels, and other subsidiaries; Victor, with its Bluebird subsidiary; and Decca. The need for a separate label specializing in jazz without any commercial concessions was filled in 1938 and 1939, when the Commodore, H.R.S. (Hot Record Society) and Blue Note labels were founded.

The late 1930s found most of the important jazz experimentation concentrated in New York City. It was at the Onyx Club that John Kirby produced with his sextet a soft, subtle brand of swing music that enabled him (often with his wife, singer Maxine Sullivan) to break down many racial taboos and achieve a degree of popularity unprecedented among Negro combos. It was at Carnegie Hall in New York that Benny Goodman violated convention by presenting a jazz concert in 1938. Also at Carnegie Hall, two concerts called *From Spirituals to Swing,* in 1938 and 1939, brought such stars as Count Basie, Joe Turner, and the boogie-woogie pianists to the concert stage for the first time.

As the power and acceptability of swing music grew, and the popularity of its exponents grew with it, many sidemen from the top bands broke away to form swing bands of their own. Harry James and Gene Krupa, on the strength of popularity acquired as members of the Benny Goodman band, started their own units in 1938. Glenn Miller, long a respected arranger for the Dorsey Brothers and many other bands, failed in his own first efforts as a leader but enjoyed a phenomenal success from 1939 on. Erskine Hawkins, the raucous trumpeter whose record hit *Tuxedo Junction* became an even greater success later in the Glenn Miller version, became the new king of the Savoy Ballroom.

By 1939 the market was flooded with swing bands. Many of them, like Harry James', came to rely more on insipid commercial performances than on real swinging jazz for their success. Even a second-rate band could by now give a passable imitation of the Goodman or Lunceford ensembles. The only unique sounds and the only completely inimitable orchestral units in jazz seemed to be those of Duke Ellington and Count Basie. Jazz, to some extent, had reached a stalemate as the 1930s drew to a close.

The answer to the problem came slowly, imperceptibly, from a variety of sources—from Kansas City, where an alto saxophonist named Charlie Parker was defying melodic and harmonic convention in his improvisations; from Oklahoma City, where a youngster named Charlie Christian seemed to be expressing new concepts of time and phrasing as he played a novel instrument known as the electric guitar; from the Count Basie band, where Lester Young's tenor saxophone expressed a cool, lagging style that contrasted with the customary brilliance always identified with this instrument through its long-reigning king, Coleman Hawkins;

and from a club in Harlem called Minton's Play House, where a bunch of young rebels gathered together when their regular jobs were through and worked out new ideas. Among these innovators were a trumpeter from Cab Calloway's band named Dizzy Gillespie, a pianist, Thelonious Monk, a drummer, Kenny Clarke, and a handful of others.

In California in 1940 Oscar Moore, guitarist with the King Cole trio, ended the group's first Decca record, *Sweet Lorraine*, on a ninth chord with a flatted fifth (an unheard-of departure then, an overworked cliché today). At Cafe Society in New York, Kenneth Kersey, pianist with the then popular Red Allen sextet, found his way from a tonic to a dominant chord through an unconventional progression of minor sevenths. Jazz was fighting its way out of a harmonic and melodic blind alley.

Rhythmically it was fighting too; little by little the steady pounding four-to-the-bar that had seemed necessary to the rhythm section of every band gave way to a subtler, more varied punctuation in which the musicians implied the beat instead of hitting the listener over the head with it.

Eventually all these ideas and all these people converged, in Harlem and on Fifty-second Street, and these characteristics were slowly woven together. As musicians gathered outside the clubs along Fifty-second Street to discuss the music of Charlie Parker, who had arrived in town with Jay McShann's blues band, or of Dizzy Gillespie, by this time working in Benny Carter's sextet, they would use an onomatopoeic expression to describe a typical phrase played by these musicians: "rebop" or "bebop," they would say. Eventually the word became shortened and "bop" was accepted as the name for the new branch of jazz that had been born of the desire for progress and evolution.

At the other extreme, a movement had started that was to have no less profound an impact on jazz: the "grass roots" attempt to take the music back to its origins, to reduce it to the least common denominator and retain its basic simplicity as folk music.

Much of the impetus for this movement came from California. Lu Watters started his Yerba Buena Jazz Band in 1939 in San Francisco; Bunk Johnson, retrieved from the rice fields in Louisiana, provided with a new horn and a new set of teeth by traditionalist jazz enthusiasts, enjoyed some of his greatest successes on the West Coast, and Kid Ory, with the help of an Orson Welles radio series, returned to the limelight in Hollywood as leader of his Creole Jazz Band.

While the traditionalists moved further to the right and the modernists shifted to the left, the middle ground was left open for many successes of the early 1940s: Benny Goodman's big band, with arrangements by Eddie Sauter, and his sextet with Cootie Williams and Georgie Auld; Lionel Hampton's exciting new big band, formed at the end of a four-year association with the Goodman Quartet and Sextet; Charlie Barnet's sincere, exciting, Ellington-inspired ensemble. Jack Teagarden had a fine big band that never achieved the recognition it deserved.

During this period the organized jam session, as opposed to the informal sessions musicians had arranged among themselves in earlier years, became a recognized popular factor in jazz. Eddie Condon, no longer merely a guitarist running from one small band to another, was an organizer, a promoter, a manager, with an acute sense of humor and the ability to gather around him a hard core of believers in his theory that Dixieland was the only true jazz.

At the same time there were the artists who did not concern themselves with factionalism: the timeless Red Norvo, now changing over from xylophone to vibraphone and always heading a superb little band; Stuff Smith, the madly swinging violinist of Onyx Club fame; and pianist Mary Lou Williams, free-lancing along the Street. And there were the great jazz voices of the day: Billie Holiday, Mildred Bailey and Ella Fitzgerald; Joe Turner and Jimmy Rushing.

The progress of jazz may well have been impeded by the ban on all recording imposed by the musicians' union in August 1942. Not until the fall of 1943 did the jazzmen return to the studios. Earl Hines' band, a virtual nursery of bop musicians in 1943, had been unable to record, but Coleman Hawkins, an old-style jazzman who had been immediately attracted to the new movement, gathered a group of virtuosi around him, among them Dizzy Gillespie, Max Roach, Budd Johnson and Oscar Pettiford, for what turned out to be the first of countless hundreds of bebop record sessions.

Hawkins was involved in another precedent-setting event in 1944 when he was one of thirteen jazz stars who appeared in the first concert of its kind ever held at the Metropolitan Opera House. The winners of a poll of jazz experts conducted by *Esquire* magazine, they were, in addition to Hawkins, Louis Armstrong, Roy Eldridge, Barney Bigard, Jack Teagarden, Art Tatum, Al Casey, Oscar Pettiford, Sid Catlett, Red Norvo, Lionel Hampton, Billie Holiday and Mildred Bailey. The affair provided the Belgian jazz critic Robert Goffin with a title for his book *Jazz: From the Congo to the Metropolitan.* Whether the first half of his title was correct or not, there was no question about the second.

The period from 1944 to 1947 was notable mainly for the many great jazz groups that paraded in and out of the Fifty-second Street clubs; for the tremendous acclaim accorded to Bunk Johnson, George Lewis, Kid Ory and other revitalized New Orleans pioneers; and for the incessant small-band recording undertaken by an ever-increasing number of independent jazz disc companies. It was noteworthy in a negative sense for the first evidences of a decline on the big band front.

Billy Eckstine, having earned a big following as the ballad singer with Earl Hines' band, formed an orchestra of his own in which almost every leading bop musician played from 1944 to 1946, but was unable to make a financial success of it. (Sarah Vaughan, his vocalist, later became an important new influence in jazz-inflected popular singing.) Stan Kenton, experimenting first with a staccato sax-section style and later with other unusual orchestral sounds, had the only band that arose during these years to achieve any lasting recognition.

The one large jazz orchestra that enjoyed consistent success both financially and musically during the middle 1940s was Woody Herman's, since known as the "First Herd." Sparked by the arrangements of Ralph Burns and Neal Hefti, by the personality of Chubby Jackson and by the originality of such soloists as Bill Harris and Flip Phillips, the Herman band had its own sponsored radio series for a while.

In California, the most important jazz phenomenon of those years was the decision of a young impresario named Norman Granz to start a series of jazz concerts. Sensing that the element of excitement was a key to success in events of this kind, he accentuated the use of such devices as the "battle of jazz" between two tenor saxophonists or two trumpeters, and the release of record albums of music actually recorded during the concerts, an unprecedented procedure. Granz' initiative changed the jazz concert from the rarity of 1945 to the commonplace of today, thus creating an incalculable amount of work for many leading musicians.

Most of the big news of the next few years was made by small bands. While Dizzy Gillespie struggled to keep his big band together, a pianist who had arrived from Chicago, Lennie Tristano, began to stir excited talk among musicians with his radically different improvisations. Tristano's music was not bop; it was a departure beyond bop, in which the choice of notes involved a subtler and more complex harmonic knowledge. Tristano gathered around him a cult of faithful followers, many of whom turned down profitable offers from prominent bandleaders in order to remain in New York studying Tristano's theories.

Tristano, however, was ahead of his time. Even Bud Powell, most brilliant of all the pianists produced by the advent of bop, had not yet been able to find a commercial niche and was unknown except to a handful of musicians and fans. Bop and its creators underwent a period of financial and esthetic frustration; Charlie Parker, in California, ran himself into a physical collapse and was away from the jazz scene for many months. To make matters more difficult, another recording ban was imposed throughout 1948.

Of the musicians who had identified themselves with bop (especially Charlie Ventura, who had gone out on a limb by deliberately branding his vocal-and-instrumental combo blend as "Bop for the People"), very few were able to remain unaffected by the turn of events when the American public, sated with the use of the word "bop" and its false identification in periodicals with such physical manifestations as goatees, berets and horn-rimmed glasses, decided the whole thing was a worn-out fad and would have no more of it. Musicians who had been proud of their association with bop hastily removed it from their billing, while playing exactly the same kind of music. Dizzy Gillespie began to stress singing and comedy to enable himself to maintain a public for his superlative bop trumpet playing. Charlie Parker began to record old popular songs accompanied by a string section.

Miles Davis found the best solution. A trumpeter and arranger who had branched out from a Gillespie style to develop a quiet, introverted and completely original instrumental personality, he was heard, during the year after the recording ban ended, at the head of a nine- or ten-piece band that included a French horn and tuba; most of the arrangements were by Gerry Mulligan, John Lewis and Gil Evans. The soloists included Mulligan, Lee Konitz and the foremost bop trombonist, J. J. Johnson.

The records Davis made with these groups in 1949-50 marked the beginning of the era of "cool jazz."

While many bop musicians play what might be called cool jazz, and while the term has also been used to describe the style of Lennie Tristano, cool jazz to most musicians and students denotes the understated, behind-the-beat style typified by the arrangements and soloists on the Davis records, and by such soloists as Stan Getz on tenor sax, Paul Desmond on alto and Bobby Brookmeyer on trombone.

In addition to cool jazz, the late 1940s were noteworthy for the launching of several popular pianists. Erroll Garner, playing in an unclassifiable and completely original style, the British immigrant George Shearing, leading a quintet that indulged in a modified brand of bop, and Oscar Peterson, an engagingly swinging modern pianist from Canada, all scored hits with musicians and public alike.

As the Fifty-second Street clubs closed down one by one during the post-war slump, a new setting for jazz was found in several cities when owners of a number of night clubs, mostly larger than the cubbyholes of Fifty-second Street, found they were able to fill their establishments by offering a program of modern jazz without providing any space for dancing. At the Royal Roost, Bop City and Birdland in New York, at the Blue Note in Chicago and at similar spots in other major metropolitan areas, jazz fans sat and listened while big bands, small combos and singers found an important new outlet for their ideas.

The advent of the large jazz club coincided with the wedding of jazz with Latin-American rhythms. Jazz musicians, finding that they could break the four beats of a bar into a wide variety of eighth-note formulas (and produce the rhythms with a number of unfamiliar percussion instruments such as the bongos, conga drum and timbales) eagerly incorporated many Afro-Cuban and Latin-American rhythms into their performances. Nat "King" Cole, a pianist and instrumental trio leader who had risen to national fame as a ballad singer, added a bongo drummer as a fourth member of his regular jazz unit; Dizzy Gillespie took the brilliant Cuban percussion artist Chano Pozo on the road with his band. Machito, leader of a popular Afro-Cuban band, appeared at Birdland with such men as Flip Phillips and bop trumpeter Howard McGhee as guest soloists.

The use of bongos and conga drums in jazz was characteristic of the search for "new sounds" that marked the advent of the 1950s. Anxious to tear themselves away from the standard instrumentations that had remained almost unchanged for years, jazzmen turned to instrumental tone colors that had seldom or never before been employed in their music.

The flute, rarely used for jazz improvisation in the past, came into general use from 1953 when Frank Wess of the Basie band, Bud Shank, Herbie Mann and many others, all originally saxophonists, devoted much of their time to it. The Hammond organ, with which Fats Waller had toyed in 1940, was taken up by Count Basie, later by Bill Davis, Bill Doggett and the technically astonishing Jimmy Smith. Oscar Pettiford, one of the first and best of the modern jazz bassists, played pizzicato jazz 'cello from 1950, but few other bassists have followed his example.

The 1950s also saw the adoption to jazz use of the French horn, by such able exponents as John Graas and Julius Watkins; the oboe, by Bob Cooper, Phil Bodner and others, and even the harmonica, by Toots Thielemans and Eddie Shu. In addition, large string sections were incorporated into jazz orchestras by Dizzy Gillespie, Stan Kenton and several other groups recorded by Norman Granz.

While jazz expanded instrumentally, the simple small group formations underwent other changes. Gerry Mulligan, a well-known baritone saxophonist, started a small revolution in 1953 when his quartet revealed that a jazz combo could sound complete and effective without a piano. A Milhaud student named Dave Brubeck, leading a quartet that moved swiftly from San Francisco to national prominence

The Original Dixieland Jazz Band in London, 1919. L. to R.: Russell Robinson, Larry Shields, Nick La Rocca, Emil Christian, Tony Spargo (Sbarbaro) *(The Record Changer)*

King Oliver's Creole Jazz Band, 1923. Standing, L. to R.: Baby Dodds, Honoré Dutrey, Bill Johnson, Louis Armstrong, Johnny Dodds, Lil Hardin. Seated: Joe King Oliver *(The Record Changer)*

King Oliver's Dixie Syncopators, 1926. George Field, trombone; Bert Cobbs, tuba; Bud Scott, banjo; Paul Barbarin, drums; Darnell Howard, clarinet, alto; Joe King Oliver, cornet; Albert Nicholas, clarinet, alto; Bobby Shoffner, trumpet; Barney Bigard, clarinet, tenor; Luis Russell, piano (*Courtesy Jazz Magazine*)

Kid Ory's Original Creole Jazz Band, ca. 1920, with Kid Ory, trombone; Mutt Carey, trumpet (*Courtesy Jazz Magazine*)

Above: Louis Armstrong (indicated by arrow) in the Waifs' Home in New Orleans, about 1912 *(The Record Changer)*

Left: Armstrong with his mother, Beatrice, and sister, Mama Lucy *(The Record Changer)*

Louis Armstrong *(Columbia Records)*

Ella Fitzgerald, Louis Armstrong, at Louis' 57th birthday celebration, Newport, 1957

Wolverine Orchestra, about 1924. L. to R.: Howdy Quicksell, banjo; Tommy Gargano, drums; Paul Mertz, piano; Don Murray, clarinet; Bix Beiderbecke, cornet; Tommy Dorsey, trombone *(The Record Changer)*

Frankie Trumbauer (*Courtesy Marshall Stearns*)

Baby Dodds, 1949 (*Duncan Schiedt*)

Fats Waller *(Down Beat)*

The Fletcher Henderson orchestra, ca. 1926. L. to R.: Howard Scott, trumpet; Coleman Hawkins, tenor sax; Louis Armstrong, trumpet; Charlie Dixon, banjo; Fletcher Henderson, piano; Buster Bailey, clarinet; Elmer Chambers, trumpet; Charlie Green, trumpet; Bob Escudero, tuba; Don Redman, saxes *(Courtesy Jazz Magazine)*

Jelly Roll Morton's Red Hot Peppers, ca. 1926. Andrew Hilaire, drums; Kid Ory, trombone; George Mitchell, trumpet; John Lindsay, bass; Jelly Roll Morton, piano; Johnny St. Cyr, banjo; Omer Simeon, clarinet *(Courtesy Jazz Magazine)*

James P. Johnson, 1950 (*Duncan Schiedt*)

Bunk Johnson, George Lewis and Alcide Pavageau *(The Record Changer)*

Sidney Bechet

George Lewis *(Jean-Marie)*

Albert Ammons *(Courtesy Claude Jones)*

Eddie Lang *(Metronome)*

Red Nichols (*Capitol Records*)

Meade "Lux" Lewis (*Francis Wolff*)

Pee Wee Russell (*Otto F. Hess*)

Edmond Hall (*Albert A. Freeman*)

Red Allen, CBS' *The Sound of Jazz*

Bessie Smith (*Carl Van Vechten*)

The Bennie Moten orchestra, 1930. Standing, L. to R.: Vernon Page, bass; "Lips" Page, Ed Lewis, trumpets; Harland Leonard, alto; Ed Durham, trombone; Woodie Walder, sax; Leroy Berry, guitar; Jimmy Rushing, vocals; Bennie Moten, piano; and Bus Moten (with baton), accordion. Seated, L. to R.: Jack Washington, leaning on couch, sax; Bill "Count" Basie, piano; Booker Washington, trumpet; Thamon Hayes, trombone; and Willie Mac Washington, drums (*Down Beat*)

Adrian Rollini (*Metronome*)

Irving Fazola and Bobby Haggart (*Metronome*)

The Mills Brothers, Lionel Hampton and Les Hite, 1931 (*Courtesy Les Hite*)

Left: Muggsy Spanier (*Down Beat*)

Below left: Don Redman

Below right: Bunny Berigan (*Down Beat*)

in 1954, applied his classical knowledge and keen harmonic ear to a new kind of improvisation.

Around the same time a coöperative group known as the Modern Jazz Quartet, with the composer and pianist John Lewis as its chief mentor, began to examine traditional classical forms and combined its soft, subtle brand of bop-derived swing with extra-jazz elements that placed small group jazz on a new and provocative emotional level, with a strong intellectual appeal.

Small-band jazz was especially active in California in the mid-1950s, when a long series of record sessions described as "West Coast Jazz," but actually an outgrowth of the innovations Miles Davis made in New York City in 1949, appeared on a number of new record labels.

A development that reached important proportions in the late 1950s was the realization by many modern musicians that in learning to run so fast and so soon they had neglected to walk; as a consequence, searching for some of the traditional jazz sources they had neglected and combining them with a modern technical approach, they created a series of performances based on the blues and other early simple forms. Though the themes in most instances were harmonically primitive, the improvisational passages generally incorporated most of the melodic and rhythmic qualities that have been a part of all modern jazz since the advent of bop. This refreshing combination of old and new elements was described by most musicians as "funky," and the improvised jazz, both in these performances and in more complex works played by similar groups, became part of an aggressive and stimulating style commonly designated as "hard bop". The best-known protagonists of this evolution were the composer and pianist Horace Silver, the Art Blakey group known as The Jazz Messengers, the Adderley brothers' quintet and several other small combos, mostly of New York origin. Identified with hard bop, though not necessarily with funk, were the tenor saxophonists Sonny Rollins and John Coltrane, both of whom, representing a new generation, typified a revolt against the cool jazz developments of Stan Getz and his imitators a decade earlier.

A still more adventurous path was opened up in 1959 by Ornette Coleman, an alto saxophonist, who seemed to be establishing a new improvisational procedure that departed violently from the conventional concept of improvising on harmonic changes established by the rhythm section. By 1960 many musicians had taken sides, firmly defending or bitterly opposing the innovations of Coleman; it was still too early to determine whether his work and that of his partner, the trumpeter Don Cherry, would accomplish for the jazz of the 1960s what Parker and Gillespie had for that of the '40s.

Contemporaneous with these new movements, though of little or no musical importance, was the rise to national popularity in the late 1950s of rock 'n' roll. Representing nothing more than the baser manifestations of rhythm and blues music, but expanded into the white area among both exponents and audiences, rock 'n' roll consisted largely of technically crude and harmonically dull performances by inferior singers, out-of-tune vocal groups and instrumentalists willing to prostitute their art to the financial interests of the "big beat." On the fringe of the rock 'n' roll movement were a few genuinely gifted artists, notably Ray Charles, who in his singing stemmed directly from the classic Negro blues traditions while in his instrumental work, as pianist and saxophonist with his own group, he reflected the funky tendency. The greatest damage afflicted by rock 'n' roll can be blamed on good musicians like Lionel Hampton, who, taking advantage of the tremendous appeal of music that was all quantity and no quality, became guilty of subverting both his own style and that of the fine musicians who worked for him.

In general, by the mid-1950s jazz had attained a degree of world-wide recognition that would have seemed impossible to any of the pioneers who had to fight for its acceptance even on a domestic level. Since Don Redman's European tour in 1946, which broke the ice for American postwar jazz in person overseas, almost every big band and small combo had appeared with great success abroad: Louis Armstrong had caused riots in Australia, Japan and most of Western Europe, Norman Granz' Jazz at the Philharmonic unit had been acclaimed in a dozen countries, and the influence of these visiting stars had been reflected in many excellent performances of authentic modern jazz by foreign musicians, notably in Sweden, where many American jazzmen teamed up with outstanding Swedish musicians to produce several first-class records.

In 1956 the United States Government for the

first time took official cognizance of jazz. Realizing that the global interest in America's foremost musical export might be turned to patriotic advantage, the State Department authorized the American National Theater Academy to send a big band under Dizzy Gillespie on a tour of the Near and Middle East. The experiment was so successful that during the next few years several similar trips were partially or wholly government-subsidized for Benny Goodman, Wilbur DeParis, Woody Herman and others.

Another important new development in the mid-'50s was the emergence of the jazz festival as a medium for drawing summer audiences to sequences of open air concerts at which substantial numbers of leading jazz attractions were presented. The first major American jazz festival took place at Newport, R.I. in 1954. By 1960 the success of the Newport initiative had become so obvious that its activities were expanded from two to five days; and festivals had been presented under Newport's auspices in several other cities. Other promoters arranged similar events with varying degrees of success, the most noteworthy being the Monterey, California festivals, launched in 1958, and the indoor festival sponsored by *Playboy* Magazine in the Chicago Stadium in the summer of 1959, which attracted 70,000 spectators at five performances in three days.

The jazz festivals were probably both cause and effect of a phenomenal upsurge in the general interest in jazz during the late 1950s. While concerts and festivals multiplied, attention in the press reached an undreamed-of level as newspapers and periodicals that had neglected or derided jazz for several decades gradually recognized the long-obvious need for serious, analytical coverage of jazz events. Regular departments devoted to the subject were instituted in the *New Yorker, New York Sunday Times* and *The Saturday Review,* as well as in various magazines aimed at hi-fi enthusiasts. *Playboy* started a series of annual polls, the first of which, when the results were published in February 1957, showed vote totals that were staggering when compared with those of the music magazines in which jazz polls previously had been conducted. Ralph J. Gleason, whose jazz column had appeared regularly since 1950 in the San Francisco Chronicle, was read in dozens of newspapers in which his articles were syndicated from 1959.

The attention given jazz on the academic level belatedly became realistic as credit courses in jazz were established at several institutions of higher learning. At the Music Educators' National Conference in St. Louis in April 1956, the potential value of jazz in all curricula for music students was outlined to the conference by Father Norman O'Connor and George Wein, both of Boston U., and by Dave Brubeck and George Avakian. As Avakian later commented in *Down Beat,* "they could have been flip, or obviously polite, about paying lip service to an unscrubbed but unavoidable stepchild. Instead, they were genuinely interested . . . it was obvious that jazz already had made a great impression on the thinking of our leading music educators."

The academic strides made by jazz in 1956-58 were without precedent and had the greatest possible significance for the future. The most important development was the foundation of an actual school of jazz as part of the summer activities at Music Inn in Lenox, Massachusetts. The first three-week course was given in August 1957 with 34 students enjoying tuition by a faculty comprising such figures as John Lewis, Dizzy Gillespie, Max Roach, Ray Brown, Oscar Peterson, Bill Russo, Jimmy Giuffre and Marshall Stearns.

As a corollary of the recognized need for a scholarly approach to jazz, an interest on the part of book publishers developed rapidly between 1955 and 1960. During this five-year period more books on jazz were published, both in the U. S. and overseas, than in the entire lifetime of jazz up to that point.

The skillful use of jazz as an integrated component in motion pictures was another aspect of the importance of jazz in the late 1950s. Until that time there had been practically no attempt to incorporate jazz into films in any but the most superficial manner. The new trend was first observed when a group of West Coast jazzmen played a significant part, aurally and visually, in the successful Frank Sinatra picture *The Man With The Golden Arm.* The intermittent use of jazz in sound-track music to underline the moods of the plot was similarly and successfuly managed in *The Sweet Smell Of Success* and other Hollywood productions. The idea was expanded and, in the opinion of some observers.

more effectively used in several French productions such as *No Sun In Venice,* for which John Lewis provided the music. In addition to providing background music, jazz provided the basic theme for a series of feature films. Louis Armstrong's *Satchmo The Great* in 1957 was a documentary devoted to the trumpeter's overseas tours. Most of the other vehicles, such as *St. Louis Blues* (supposedly based on the life of W. C. Handy), *The Benny Goodman Story* and *The Gene Krupa Story,* were unsatisfactory as biographies, though at least they reflected an increased awareness of the public interest in such subjects.

The use of jazz in television, previously limited to a few short-lived musical series, provided another new substantial outlet during 1958, when several nationally-sponsored, major shows with jazz as subject were presented by NBC and CBS. Though these ventures diminished in number after the excitement of the first year, jazz found a different foothold in TV as the use of background scores in the jazz idiom played by all-star groups of California musicians on a long-run detective show, *Peter Gunn,* seemed to stimulate the use of jazz on several other major series.

With jazz finding recognition and exposure in so many new areas, the artistic scope of jazz inevitably continued to widen. Though many musicians still played in the Dixieland and other traditional jazz styles (by 1960 even the once avant garde styles of the Gillespie generation had been absorbed into the mainstream of jazz and were virtually counted among its traditions), there were many attempts to bring about a rapprochement between jazz and "classical" music. Extended forms, as used by John Lewis, Gunther Schuller, Teo Macero and other musicians, both from inside and outside jazz, along with the use of atonalism and twelve-tone rows, reduced the line between jazz and other music forms at times almost to invisibility. The joint appearance of jazzmen and classical musicians at concerts, once a rare oddity, by 1960 had become a fairly common event. The Modern Jazz Quartet was combined with the Beaux Arts String Quartet to perform specially written works; Howard Brubeck's *Dialogues For Jazz Combo And Orchestra* was performed by the Dave Brubeck Quartet with the New York Philharmonic. Many of these new developments were founded on a healthier and sounder knowledge of the essence of jazz, and of classical forms, than earlier attempts such as those of George Gershwin or even of Igor Stravinsky, whose *Ebony Concerto* for Woody Herman in 1946 had not been considered completely successful by critics on either side of the falling fence.

The use of ambitious and often lengthy jazz compositions, once restricted by the virtual non-existence of jazz concerts and by the time limitation of the three-minute record, was further facilitated during the 1950s by the emergence of the LP (long playing) record. Until 1949 the vast majority of jazz recordings had been restricted to three or four minutes. By the end of the 1950s all jazz of any importance was available on LP records running from fifteen to twenty-five minutes per side; and the quantity of jazz being recorded had reached a staggering, all-time high. There were about as many minutes of recorded jazz made available every week during 1960 as during an entire average year in the early 1940s. Because, on records and in other media, the market for jazz by now was greater than at any previous time, there was a great reduction in the degree to which musicians were forced to work in fields they found musically unsympathetic. If a jazzman had something to offer as a soloist or composer, the chances by now were very good that before his career had gone far he would find many outlets and could earn a living commensurate with his talents.

Jazz, by the onset of the 1960s, had earned unprecedented artistic recognition as well as economic security. It had taken a long time, and there were still several areas in which an improvement in the esthetic approach to the music was desperately needed. But if the millenium was not yet here, jazz, at the end of its sixth decade, recognized at last as America's one true native contribution to the arts, was clearly within reach of the two goals towards which it had been striving with so little success for many frustrating years: security and maturity.

Chronology

The starting date for the following chronology was set at the turn of the century; this was the stage at which ragtime, the first trend conspicuously related to jazz, was flourishing. Negro folk music, spirituals, brass band music and other forms were of course prevalent before this date.

The music listed includes (a) ragtime and jazz compositions, (b) songs that have been popular at one time or another through jazz performances. They are listed under the year of first popularity via publication or recording; in a few cases the date of composition may have been some years earlier. The compositions are not selected in terms of commercial success but are examples of the material used by jazzmen.

1899: Buddy Bolden band playing in New Orleans streets and amusement parks; Eubie Blake playing ragtime in Baltimore; Scott Joplin's *Original Rags, Maple Leaf Rag* published in Sedalia, Mo.

Births: Duke Ellington 4/29.

Music: *Banjo Rag Time; Belle of The Creoles*

1900: Bunk Johnson touring with P. G. Loral circus; King Oliver in children's brass band.

Births: Wilbur DeParis 1/11; Walter Page 2/9; Tommy Ladnier 5/28; Louis Armstrong 7/4; George Lewis 7/13; Don Redman 7/29; Ethel Waters 10/31.

Music: *The Voodoo Man, Blackville Strutters Ball* (Bert Williams-Geo. Walker).

1901: Births: Paul Barbarin 5/5; Edmond Hall 5/15.

Music: *Chocolate Creams Cake Walk; Hunky Dory Characteristic Cake Walk March*

1902: Jelly Roll Morton plays in Tenderloin District, New Orleans.

Births: Jimmie Lunceford 6/6; Buster Bailey 7/19.

Music: *Naked Dance* (Tony Jackson); *The Rag Time Dance* (Joplin); *Bill Bailey, Won't You Please Come Home?*

1903: Scott Joplin's ragtime opera, *A Guest of Honor,* presented in St. Louis.

Births: Bix Beiderbecke 3/10; Ben Pollack 6/22; Jimmy Rushing 8/26.

Music: *St. Louis Rag* (Turpin); *Ida.*

1904: National Ragtime Contest in St. Louis.

Births: Eddie Lang; Pete Johnson; Jimmy Dorsey 2/29; Glenn Miller 3/1; Bing Crosby 5/2; Fats Waller 5/21; Pinetop Smith 6/11; Count Basie 8/21; Joe Venuti 9/1; Eddie Condon 11/16; Coleman Hawkins 11/21.

Music: *Red Devil Rag; The St. Louis Tickle.*

1905: Births: Meade Lux Lewis; Red Nichols 5/8; Jack Teagarden 8/20; Tommy Dorsey 11/19; Earl Hines 12/28.

Music: *My Gal Sal.*

1906: George Baquet with Superior Band.

Births: Barney Bigard 3/3; Frank Teschemacher 3/14; Pee Wee Russell 3/27; Bud Freeman 4/13; J. C. Higginbotham 5/11; Johnny Hodges 7/25; Vic Dickenson 8/6; Muggsy Spanier 11/9.

Music: *Dill Pickles Rag; Chinatown, My Chinatown.*

1907: Buddy Bolden committed to State Hospital 6/5; Scott Joplin moves to New York; Freddy Keppard organizes band w. Alphonse Picou; Fate Marable plays on Miss. riverboats.

Births: Chick Webb 2/10; Jimmy McPartland 3/15; Benny Carter 8/8; Edgar Sampson 8/31.

Music: *Kansas City Rag* (James Scott).

1908: Births: Red Norvo 3/31; Dave Tough 4/26; Cootie Williams 7/24; John Kirby 12/31.

Music: *Sensation Rag; Memphis Rag*

1909: Births: Bunny Berigan; Gene Krupa 1/15; Ben Webster 2/27; Benny Goodman 5/30; Lester Young 8/27; Cozy Cole 10/17; Jonah Jones 12/31.

Music: *Tabasco-Rag Time Waltz; Sapho Rag; Put On Your Old Grey Bonnet.*

1910: "Blues" coming into general use as musical term; Oscar Celestin Orch. at Tuxedo Dance Hall, New Orleans.

Births: Big Sid Catlett 1/17; Django Reinhardt 1/23; Harry Carney 4/1; Mary Lou Williams 5/8; Artie Shaw 5/23; Art Tatum 10/13; Sy Oliver 12/17; Chu Berry 9/13.

Music: *Some of These Days; Steamboat Bill.*

1911: Bunk Johnson with Frank Dusen's Eagle band; Scott Joplin opera, *Treemonisha,* presented in NYC; Kid Ory brings band to New Orleans; Bill Johnson organizes Original Creole band; Jimmie Noone with Clarence Williams.

Births: Roy Eldridge 1/30; Jo Jones 7/10; Mahalia Jackson 10/26; Buck Clayton 11/12; Freddie Green 11/31.

Music: *Alexander's Ragtime Band, Everybody's Doing It Now* (Irving Berlin).

1912: Freddie Keppard to Los Angeles.

Births: Stan Kenton 2/19; Gil Evans 5/13; Don Byas 10/21; Teddy Wilson 11/24; Irving Fazola 12/10.

Music: *Memphis Blues* (W. C. Handy); *Scott Joplin's New Rag; Dallas Blues.*

1913: Tuxedo Dance hall flourishing in New Orleans Tenderloin; Sidney Bechet with King Oliver.

Births: Lionel Hampton 4/12; Woody Herman 5/16; Bob Crosby 8/23.

Music: *Junk Man Rag* (Luckey Roberts); *Peg O' My Heart; You Made Me Love You.*

1914: ASCAP founded.

Births: Kenny Clarke 1/9; Billy Eckstine 7/8; Eddie Sauter 12/2.

Music: *St. Louis Blues* (W. C. Handy); *They Didn't Believe Me; Ballin' The Jack.*

1915: Papa Laine's Ragtime Band at Lambs Cafe, Chicago.

Births: Bobby Hackett 1/31; Billie Holiday 4/7; Harry Edison 10/10; Billy Strayhorn 11/29; Pete Rugolo 12/25.

Music: *Jelly Roll Blues* (Morton); *By Heck.*

1916: Duke Ellington plays first professional job.

Births: Harry James 3/15; Bill Harris 10/28.

Music: *Pretty Baby* (Tony Jackson); *Roses of Picardy; I Ain't Got Nobody; Nola.*

1917: Original Dixieland Jass Band at Reisenweber's; first Victor Records 2/24; Storyville area closed in New Orleans; Fate Marable starts own bands for Miss. riverboat excursions; W. C. Handy to NYC; King Oliver, Jimmie Noone at Lincoln Gardens in Chicago.

Births: Nat Cole 3/17; Dave Lambert 6/19; Buddy Rich 6/30; Charlie Shavers 8/3; Dizzy Gillespie 10/21; Tadd Dameron.

Deaths: Scott Joplin 4/11.

Music: *Indiana; Darktown Strutters' Ball; Tiger Rag; Dixie Jass Band One Step (Original Dixieland); Livery Stable Blues; At The Jazz Band Ball.*

1918: Births: Ella Fitzgerald 4/25; Norman Granz 8/6; Chubby Jackson 10/25; Joe Williams 12/12.

Music: *Frog-i-more Rag* (Morton); *After You've Gone; Hindustan; Ja-da; Smiles.*

1919: Original Dixieland Band in London; Kid Ory in California; Sidney Bechet in Europe with Will Marion Cook.

Births: Charlie Christian; Lennie Tristano 3/19; George Shearing 8/13; Art Blakey 10/11.

Music: *Dardanella; Royal Garden Blues; Swanee.*

1920: Big Bill Broonzy to Chicago; Mamie Smith, first blues singer on records: *Crazy Blues* a hit.

Births: John Lewis 5/3; Shelly Manne 6/11; Charlie Parker 8/29; Thelonious Monk 10/10; Dave Brubeck 12/6.

Music: *Avalon; Margie; The World Is Waiting For The Sunrise; Whispering.*

1921: New Orleans Rhythm Kings at Friars' Inn; James P. Johnson makes first solo jazz piano session for Okeh; Kid Ory band record debut in LA.

Births: Jimmy Blanton; Jimmy Giuffre 4/26; Tal Farlow 6/7; Erroll Garner 6/15; Tony Scott 6/17; Chico Hamilton 9/21; Illinois Jacquet 10/30.

Deaths: Tony Jackson 4/21.

Music: *Loveless Love; The Sheik; Wabash Blues; Wang Wang Blues; I'm Just Wild About Harry.*

1922: Louis Armstrong with King Oliver; Miff Mole with Original Memphis Five; Duke Ellington makes first, unsuccessful, trip to NYC; Coleman Hawkins with Mamie Smith's Jazz Hounds; Friars Society Orch. record for Gennett.

Births: Carmen McRae 4/8; Charles Mingus 4/22; Kai Winding 5/18; Ralph Burns 6/29; Oscar Pettiford 9/30; Neal Hefti 10/29.

Music: *Chicago; China Boy; Stumbling; Way Down Yonder In New Orleans.*

1923: First recordings by: King Oliver, Bessie Smith, Ma Rainey; Fletcher Henderson organizes 10-piece band for Club Alabam, NYC; Coleman Hawkins record debut with the band; Duke Ellington settles in New York.

Births: Milt Jackson 1/1; Osie Johnson 1/11; Buddy De Franco 2/17; Thad Jones 3/28; Percy Heath 4/30; Philly Joe Jones 7/15; Fats Navarro 9/24; Barney Kessel 10/17; Serge Chaloff 11/24.

Music: *The Pearls* (Jelly Roll Morton); *Dipper Mouth Blues (Sugar Foot Stomp)* (Oliver).

1924: Louis Armstrong joins F. Henderson; Fats Waller makes record debut; Ethel Waters introduces *Dinah;* Bix Beiderbecke with the Wolverines, record debut for Gennett, March; Gershwin's *Rhapsody In Blue* introduced by Paul Whiteman at Aeolian Hall 2/12.

Births: J. J. Johnson 1/22; Sonny Stitt 2/2; Sarah Vaughan 3/27; Shorty Rogers 4/14; Dinah Washington 8/29; Terry Gibbs 10/13; Paul Desmond 11/25.

Music: *Tea For Two; The Man I Love; Everybody Loves My Baby; King Porter Stomp; Nobody's Sweetheart; Shine; South.*

1925: First record by Louis Armstrong Hot Five, Chicago, November 12; first record by Duke Ellington's Washingtonians.

Births: Max Roach 1/10; Oscar Peterson 8/15; Zoot Sims 10/29; Al Cohn 11/24.

Music: *Carolina Shout* (James P. Johnson); *Sometimes I'm Happy; Who.*

1926: First "Golden Era" of jazz recording begins; first record date by Red Nichols' Five Pennies, 12/8; Ben Pollack organizes band in California, personnel including Benny Goodman; *Melody Maker* founded in London; Jean Goldkette band starts series of recordings with Bix, Trumbauer, et al.

Births: Gerry Mulligan 4/6; Jimmy Cleveland 5/3; Miles Davis 5/25; John Coltrane 9/23; Ray Brown 10/13; Don Elliott 10/21.

Music: *Muskrat Ramble; Sweet Georgia Brown; Birth of the Blues; East St. Louis Toodle-oo; Snag It.*

1927: First classic Chicago jazz session recorded by Red McKenzie and Eddie Condon 12/9; Jimmie Noone at Apex Club, Chicago; Charlie Johnson at Smalls' Paradise; Duke Ellington enlarges band, opens at Cotton Club 12/4; first use of voice as orchestral instrument: Adelaide Hall records *Creole Love Call* with Duke Ellington 10/26; Elmer Snowden band in Harlem; Earl Hines with Louis Armstrong in clubs and on records; Don Redman directing McKinney's Cotton Pickers; Jack Teagarden in New York; Trumbauer recordings with Bix.

Births: Stan Getz 2/2; Ruby Braff 3/16; Johnny Dankworth 9/20; Lee Konitz 10/13.

Music: *Blue Skies; Struttin' With Some Barbecue; Old Man River; Black & Tan Fantasy.*

1928: Pinetop Smith records *Boogie Woogie,* Chicago, 12/29; Sidney Bechet joins Noble Sissle in Paris; Benny Goodman records first session as leader; Earl Hines' big band debut at Grand Terrace, Chicago, December; Johnny Hodges joins Duke Ellington; *Hot Chocolates* at Connie's Inn with Waller-Razaf score; Luis Russell band at Savoy Ballroom, Harlem.

Births: Maynard Ferguson 5/4; Art Farmer 8/21; Horace Silver 9/2; Cannonball Adderley 9/15.

Music: *How Long Blues* (Leroy Carr); *West End Blues; It's Tight Like That; Basin St. Blues.*

1929: Louis Armstrong on tour with Luis Russell band.

Births: André Previn 4/6; Sonny Rollins 9/7; Bob Brookmeyer 12/19; Chet Baker 12/23.

Deaths: Pinetop Smith 3/14.

Music: *Honeysuckle Rose, Ain't Misbehavin'; Black & Blue* (Waller); *Rent Party Blues, Wall Street Wail* (Ellington); *Stardust* (Carmichael).

1930: Jimmy Dorsey, Muggsy Spanier in Britain with Ted Lewis; Louis Armstrong fronting Les Hite band; Duke Ellington records *Mood Indigo* 10/17; first Lionel Hampton vibes recording, with Louis Armstrong 10/16.

Births: Annie Ross 7/25; Clifford Brown 10/30.

Deaths: Blind Lemon Jefferson; Jimmy Harrison 7/23.

Music: *Handful of Keys* (Fats Waller); *I Got Rhythm* (Gershwin); *Rockin' Chair* (Carmichael).

1931: Duke Ellington records first extended work, *Creole Rhapsody,* for Brunswick and Victor; Don Redman forms band; first Mildred Bailey record date 11/24.

Births: Phil Woods 11/2; Nat Adderley 11/25.

Deaths: Buddy Bolden; Bix Beickerbecke 8/7.

Music: *When It's Sleepy Time Down South; Lazy River; Out Of Nowhere; All Of Me.*

1932: Louis Armstrong makes first visit to Europe; Art Tatum to New York with Adelaide Hall.

Deaths: Frank Teschemacher 2/29.

Music: *It Don't Mean A Thing; Night And Day; Keepin' Out of Mischief Now.*

1933: Duke Ellington band visits Europe; Bunk Johnson retires from music, settles in New Iberia, La.; Benny Carter forms band, hires Teddy Wilson; Billie Holiday makes record debut with Benny Goodman 11/27; Bessie Smith makes final record date 11/24.

Births: Quincy Jones 3/13.

Deaths: Eddie Lang 3/26.

Music: *Moten Swing; Blue Lou; Don't Blame Me; Yesterdays; Sophisticated Lady.*

1934: Coleman Hawkins to Europe, tours with Mrs. Jack Hylton's band; Dorsey brothers organize band; Benny Goodman starts radio series for National Biscuit Company; *Down Beat* Magazine founded; Buck Clayton in Shanghai with Teddy Weatherford; Chick Webb, Jimmie Lunceford bands begin series of Decca recordings; Quintet of Hot Club of France makes debut; Fats Waller starts series of combo records; Ethel Waters' stage hit: *As Thousands Cheer.*

Births: Victor Feldman 4/7.

Music: *Stompin' At The Savoy* (Sampson); *Solitude* (Ellington); *Dream Of You* (Oliver).

1935: Gene Krupa joins Benny Goodman; first Goodman Trio records 7/13; Goodman band enjoys first big success in California; Savoy Ballroom, Harlem, at peak as jazz center with Chick Webb, Teddy Hill et al; Ella Fitzgerald with Chick Webb, makes record debut 6/12; Bob Crosby starts orchestra with "big band Dixieland" style; Teddy Wilson & Billie Holiday start joint record dates for Brunswick; Count Basie at Reno Club, Kansas City, discovered by John Hammond; Tommy & Jimmy Dorsey split, Tommy starts own band; Duke Ellington records second extended work, *Reminiscing in Tempo.*

Music: *Porgy & Bess* score; *Blue Moon; I Can't Get Started; East of the Sun; In A Sentimental Mood; Truckin'.*

1936: Many small jazz clubs flourishing on 52nd Street: Stuff Smith-Jonah Jones at Onyx, Wingy Manone at Famous Door; first swing music concert, Imperial Theatre, 5/24: Artie Shaw introduces string ensemble; first Count Basie combo date with Lester Young, Chicago, 10/9; boogie woogie piano vogue, Meade Lux Lewis rediscovered by John Hammond; Woody Herman forms band, records for Decca; Lionel Hampton joins Goodman; Jo Jones, Buck Clayton join Basie; Mildred Bailey teams with new Red Norvo band.

Records: first jazz concertos, Ellington's *Echoes of Harlem* feat. Cootie Williams, *Clarinet Lament* feat. Barney Bigard.

Film: *Pennies from Heaven* (Armstrong, Crosby).

Music: *For Dancers Only; Christopher Columbus; Honky Tonk Train Blues; I'm Gonna Sit Right Down and Write Myself A Letter; These Foolish Things; The Music Goes Round & Round.*

1937: Dizzy Gillespie, with Teddy Hill band, to France and England; Charlie Parker with Jay McShann; Maxine Sullivan's *Loch Lomond* a 52nd Street sensation; Benny Carter leads international band in Holland; Mary Lou Williams in New York with Andy Kirk band from Kansas City; Harry James with Goodman.

Records: Basie's full band makes first date 1/22; George Shearing makes record debut in London; Goodman's *Sing Sing Sing.*

Deaths: George Gershwin 7/11; Bessie Smith 9/26.

Music: *One O'Clock Jump; Sent for You Yesterday; Swingin' The Blues; Caravan; South Rampart Street Parade.*

1938: Benny Goodman Carnegie Hall concert 1/16; Gene Krupa, Harry James leave Goodman, start own bands; first *Spirituals to Swing* concert staged by John Hammond at Carnegie; John Kirby organizes sextet; Artie Shaw hires Billie Holiday; Big Sid Catlett joins Louis Armstrong; Fats Waller, Art Tatum in London; Louis Jordan forms combo.

Records: Shaw's *Begin the Beguine* 7/24; Tommy Dorsey *Boogie Woogie* 9/22; Chick Webb-Ella Fitzgerald *A-Tisket a-Tasket* 5/2; Eddie Condon heads first Commodore dates.

Death: King Oliver 4/10.

Music: *Blue and Sentimental; Prelude to a Kiss; Love Walked In; Flat Foot Floogee; You Go To My Head.*

1939: Jimmy Blanton, Billy Strayhorn, Ben Webster join Ellington; Charlie Christian joins Goodman, Teddy Wilson leaves to form own band; Sy Oliver leaves Lunceford, joins T. Dorsey; Glenn Miller band nationally popular; Charlie Parker to New York, at Monroe's Uptown House; Billy Eckstine joins Earl Hines; Joe Sullivan organizes interracial sextet for Cafe Society; Jack Teagarden forms big band.

Records: Coleman Hawkins *Body & Soul;* Erskine Hawkins *Tuxedo Junction;* Billie Holiday *Strange Fruit;* Muggsy Spanier Ragtime Band dates; Charlie Barnet *Cherokee.*

Deaths: Tommy Ladnier 6/4; Chick Webb 6/16; Ma Rainey 12/22.

Music: *Tain't What You Do; Wham Rebop Boom Bam; Flyin' Home; Relaxin' at the Touro; All the Things You Are.*

1940: First revivalist records in New Orleans, cut by Kid Rena; Minton's Play House becomes jazz center as Teddy Hill breaks up band and operates club; Lionel Hampton leaves Goodman, forms own band; Cootie Williams leaves Ellington 11/15; Lester Young leaves Basie 12/13.

Records: first King Cole Trio Decca date, Hollywood, 12/6; Fats Waller plays Hammond organ on combo dates.

Death: Johnny Dodds 8/8.

Music: *Cotton Tail, In A Mellotone, How High The Moon.*

1941: Stan Kenton band makes debut at Balboa Ballroom 5/30; Cootie Williams, Peggy Lee, Big Sid Catlett with Goodman; swing era begins to fade as many musicians are drafted; Gil Evans with Claude Thornhill; Charlie Parker record debut with Jay McShann.

Deaths: Jelly Roll Morton 7/10; Chu Berry 10/3.

Music: *Flamingo; Perdido; Let Me Off Uptown; I'll Remember April; Blues In The Night.*

1942: Ray McKinley, Bob Crosby, Glenn Miller, disband and enter service; Dave Tough, Claude Thornhill in Artie Shaw Navy band; Max Roach with Charlie Parker at Monroe's; national recording ban in effect 8/1.

Records: Bunk Johnson's first session 6/11.

Deaths: Charlie Christian 3/2; Bunny Berigan 6/2; Jimmy Blanton 7/30.

Music: *Don't Get Around Much Anymore; Why Don't You Do Right; C Jam Blues.*

1943: Dizzy Gillespie, Charlie Parker, Sarah Vaughan with Earl Hines; Duke Ellington presents *Black, Brown & Beige* at band's first Carnegie Hall concert 1/23; Kid Ory with Bunk Johnson in Los Angeles; Art Tatum forms trio with Tiny Grimes, Slam Stewart; Dinah Washington joins Lionel Hampton band, makes own record date 12/29.

Death: Fats Waller 12/15.

Music: *As Time Goes By; That Old Black Magic; You'd Be So Nice To Come Home To.*

1944: First Metropolitan Opera House jazz concert staged by *Esquire* 1/18; Norman Granz produces short film *Jammin' The Blues,* presents first jazz concert at Philharmonic, Los Angeles, 7/2; Billy Eckstine organizes all-star bop band; Boyd Raeburn leads modern orch. with Oscar Pettiford, Gillespie et al; Erroll Garner heard in 52nd Street clubs; Stan Getz, Anita O'Day with Kenton.

Records: Coleman Hawkins organizes the first bop record date, with Gillespie, Budd Johnson, 2/16; Billie Holiday *Lover Man* 10/4; first Sarah Vaughan session 12/31.

Deaths: Jimmie Noone 4/19; Glenn Miller ca. 12/16.

Music: *'Round Midnight; Woody 'n You; I'm Beginning To See The Light; Artistry In Rhythm, Eager Beaver, Blowin' The Blues Away.*

1945: Bop vogue at height on 52nd Street; Miles Davis to New York, studies at Juilliard; Woody Herman's first "Herd" reaches musical peak with Bill Harris, Flip Phillips, Ralph Burns, Neal Hefti, Dave Tough, Chubby Jackson; Ted Heath band organized; June Christy joins Kenton; Gillespie tours with first big band; Charlie Shavers joins Tommy Dorsey.

Records: First Gillespie-Charlie Parker combo date, Feb.

Music: *Billie's Bounce; Now's The Time; Night In Tunisia; Groovin' High; Hot House; 52nd Street Theme; Caldonia; Bijou; Apple Honey.*

1946: Kai Winding, Shelly Manne join Kenton; Red Norvo with Woody Herman, band introduces Stravinsky's *Ebony Concerto;* Fats Navarro, later Miles Davis, with Eckstine band; Claude Thornhill reorganizes band; Eddie Condon opens club in Greenwich Village.

Records: Ellington's *Just Squeeze Me, Transblucency, Happy Go Lucky Local.*

Music: *One Bass Hit; Oop Bop Sh'Bam; Yardbird Suite; Ornithology; Confirmation.*

1947: Louis Armstrong breaks up big band, forms sextet with Teagarden, Bigard; Woody Herman organizes Second Herd with "Four Brothers" sax team; Stan Kenton breaks up first band; John Lewis' *Toccata for Trumpet & Orchestra* introduced by Gillespie band at Carnegie Hall.

Film: *New Orleans* (Armstrong, Holiday, Herman, Ory).

Death: Jimmie Lunceford 7/13.

Music: *Relaxing at Camarillo; Robbins' Nest; Cubana Be & Cubana Bop* (Russell); *Deep South Suite* (Ellington).

1948: 52nd Street era ends as last remaining clubs close; Louis Armstrong combo plays jazz festival at Nice; Eddie Condon starts own TV series; national recording ban 1/1 to 12/15; Earl Hines breaks up band, joins Louis Armstrong; Stan Kenton concert at Hollywood Bowl; Gillespie band tours Scandinavia, Gillespie and Gil Fuller write *Swedish Suite;* Royal Roost becomes New York's modern jazz center.

Deaths: Dave Tough 12/6; Chano Pozo 12/2.

Music: *Lemon Drop; Early Autumn; Godchild; Well You Needn't; Chasin' The Bird; Manteca.*

1949: Cool jazz trend develops; George Shearing quintet organized Jan.; Cozy Cole joins Armstrong; Paris Jazz Festival with Miles Davis, Charlie Parker, Max Roach; Gene Ammons, Oscar Pettiford, Milt Jackson join Woody Herman; first Oscar Peterson Carnegie Hall concert for Norman Granz; Howard Rumsey inaugurates jazz policy at Lighthouse, Hermosa Beach, Cal.; Birdland opens 12/15.

Records: First jazz LPs released; Miles Davis band on Capitol; Lennie Tristano sextet dates with Lee Konitz; first Dave Brubeck records.

Deaths: Irving Fazola 3/20, Bunk Johnson 7/7, Leadbelly 12/6.

Music: *Move; Jumpin' With Symphony Sid; In the Land of Oo-Bla-Dee; Crosscurrent; Lady Bird; Israel.*

1950: Count Basie breaks up big band, heads septet with Clark Terry, Buddy De Franco, Wardell Gray; Dizzy Gillespie breaks up big band; Woody Herman organizes Third Herd; first Mahalia Jackson concert at Carnegie Hall; Stan Kenton tours with *Innovations in Modern Music* 40-piece orchestra; Horace Silver joins Stan Getz; Red Norvo Trio with Charles Mingus, Tal Farlow.

Death: Fats Navarro 7/7.

Music: *Bags' Groove; Twisted; Venus De Milo; Intuition.*

1951: Dave Brubeck organizes quartet with Paul Desmond; Swedish modern jazz earns acceptance via LPs in US; Duke Ellington gives concert at Metropolitan Opera House, Jan.; Oscar Pettiford, Howard McGhee take combo to Korea; Count Basie reorganizes big band; Louis Bellson, Willie Smith join Ellington; Wild Bill Davis starts Hammond organ trio trend.

Records: Sonny Rollins records first session as leader, 12/17.

Deaths: Big Sid Catlett 3/24; Jimmy Yancey 9/17; Mildred Bailey 12/2.

Music: *Harlem* (Ellington); *City of Glass* (Graettinger); *Coral Reef* (Hefti); *Farmer's Market* (Art Farmer); Swedish folk song introduced by Stan Getz as *Dear Old Stockholm; Straight No Chaser* (Monk).

1952: Gerry Mulligan organizes quartet; Sauter-Finegan band organized; Jazz at the Philharmonic tours Europe; Charlie Ventura with Gene Krupa in Japan; Mahalia Jackson's first European concerts.

Records: Modern Jazz Quartet debut 12/22.

Deaths: John Kirby 6/14; Fletcher Henderson 12/29.

Music: *Lullaby of Birdland* (Shearing); *La Ronde, Vendome* (Lewis); *Sure Thing, Why Not* (Hefti).

1953: Lionel Hampton to Europe with Clifford Brown, Jimmy Cleveland, Art Farmer, Quincy Jones, Gigi Gryce; Johnny Dankworth forms big band; Dorsey Brothers reunited; Institute of Jazz Studies founded; Frank Wess and others bring flute into general jazz use; Norman Granz takes JATP to London for benefit show, first British visit by US jazz group in 16 years; segregated musicians' unions merge in Los Angeles.

Deaths: Django Reinhardt 5/16; Tiny Kahn 8/19; Larry Shields 11/21.

Music: *Bernie's Tune; Young Blood; Walkin'.*

1954: Count Basie, Woody Herman make first European tours; Jazz Club USA tours Europe with Billie Holiday, Buddy De Franco, Red Norvo, Beryl Booker; J. J. Johnson, Kai Winding team to form quintet; first Newport Jazz Festival 7/17; Joe Williams joins Basie 12/25.

Film: *The Glenn Miller Story.*

Death: Oscar Celestin 12/15.

Music: *Muskrat Ramble* revived as pop song; *Solar* (Davis); *Airegin, Oleo* (Rollins); *Misty* (Garner).

1955: Duke Ellington band combines with Symphony of the Air for premiere of *Night Creature;* Cannonball Adderley in New York, makes record debut; Dorsey Brothers' own TV series; Stan Kenton in *Music '55* TV series; Art Blakey's Jazz Messengers include Horace Silver, Kenny Dorham; Miles Davis forms quintet incl. John Coltrane.

Records: *Stan Getz At The Shrine.*

Films: *The Benny Goodman Story; Pete Kelly's Blues.*

Deaths: Charlie Parker 3/12; Wardell Gray 5/25; James P. Johnson 11/17.

Music: *Stablemates* (Golson); *The Duke* (Brubeck); *Blüe Lights* (Gryce); *Django* (Lewis); *Jordu* (Duke Jordan); *Joy Spring* (Clifford Brown).

1956: First U.S.-Britain band exchange: Ted Heath tours U.S., Stan Kenton tours England and Continent; first U.S. Government-sponsored jazz: Dizzy Gillespie forms new big band, tours Near & Middle East, Latin America under State Department auspices; Louis Armstrong makes first British tour in 21 years; Nat Cole starts own TV series; Benny Goodman tours Far East; Horace Silver forms quintet.

Records: Teddy Charles Tentet; Miles Davis Quintet records *Cookin'-Relaxin'* sessions.

Deaths: Clifford Brown, Richie Powell in car crash 6/26; Adrian Rollini 5/15; Frankie Trumbauer 6/11; Tommy Dorsey 11/26; Art Tatum 11/4.

Music: *A Drum is a Woman* (Ellington); *Symphony for Brass & Percussion* (Gunther Schuller); *Whisper Not* (Golson); *Fontessa* (Lewis); *The Preacher; Opus De Funk; Doodlin'* (Silver).

1957: School of Jazz inaugurated at Music Inn, Lenox, Mass.; Jack Teagarden, George Lewis, Gerry Mulligan, Eddie Condon tour Britain; Wilbur de Paris combo tours Africa; Farmingdale High School band a hit at Newport; first national all-jazz TV shows, December; Basie band plays Waldorf-Astoria; Sonny Rollins forms own combo.

Records: Miles Davis, Gil Evans begin series of LP collaborations; Shelly Manne-André Previn *My*

Fair Lady LP starts jazz show tune album trend; first Ray Charles LP; Charles Mingus LPs earn widespread interest; *Brilliant Corners* (Monk).

Films: *Sweet Smell of Success* (Chico Hamilton); *Satchmo The Great* (Armstrong); *No Sun In Venice* (John Lewis, MJQ).

Deaths: Jimmy Dorsey 6/12; Serge Chaloff 7/16; Walter Page 12/20.

Music: *Such Sweet Thunder* (Ellington); *Miles Ahead* (Davis-Evans); *Revelations* (Mingus); *Lament* (J. J. Johnson); *I Remember Clifford* (Golson).

1958: Numerous local and national jazz TV shows including NBC educational series; International Band at Newport and Brussels World Fair; Eddie Condon opens new club on East Side, Feb.; first Monterey, Cal. Jazz Festival Oct.; Lambert, Hendricks & Ross vocal trio organized; Ella Fitzgerald-Duke Ellington concert at Carnegie Hall; Woody Herman tours Latin America for State Department; Savoy Ballroom closed; Miles Davis in France, records sound track for film; poetry readings with jazz in night clubs and on records.

Records: *The Blues Is Everybody's Business* (Manny Albam); first Ornette Coleman LP; Duke Ellington-Mahalia Jackson, *Black, Brown and Beige; Sing A Song of Basie.*

Film: St. Louis Blues (Nat Cole).

Deaths: W. C. Handy 3/28; Big Bill Broonzy 8/14; Julia Lee 12/8.

Music: *Little Niles; Hallelujah, I Love Her So.*

1959: Dwike Mitchell & Willie Ruff introduce modern jazz to USSR; first *Playboy* Jazz Festival, Chicago Stadium, August; Thelonious Monk heads band at Town Hall concert; Ornette Coleman & Don Cherry at Lenox, later in NYC; success of *Peter Gunn* series starts jazz score trend in TV detective shows; first tours of U.S. and Europe under Newport sponsorship; Newport Youth Band founded.

Records: Many *Porgy & Bess* LPs including Miles Davis-Gil Evans; Louis Armstrong-Ella Fitzgerald.

Films: *I Want to Live* (Mulligan); *Anatomy of a Murder* (Ellington); *666* (Teo Macero); *Odds Against Tomorrow* (John Lewis); *Sapphire* (Johnny Dankworth); *The Five Pennies.*

Deaths: Boyce Brown 1/30; Baby Dodds 2/14; Lester Young 3/15; Sidney Bechet 5/14; Billie Holiday 7/17; Omer Simeon 9/17.

Music: *Moanin'* (Bobby Timmons); *Fables of Faubus* (Mingus); *New York, N.Y.* (George Russell).

1960: *The Comedy,* described as a "Jazz Entertainment," with the Modern Jazz Quartet and four ballet dancers, introduced in Paris, then tours Continent and U.S.; Madison Square Garden's first annual jazz festival sponsored by N.Y. *Daily News;* Art Farmer, Benny Golson co-leaders of new Jazztet; Quincy Jones tours Europe with big band; Herbie Mann to Africa for U.S. State Department, leading Afro-Cuban combo; Gerry Mulligan, after appearing in several films, organizes 13-piece band; new Cannonball Adderley quintet a commercial hit; George Russell forms sextet; riot at Newport curtails jazz festival.

Films: *Jazz on a Summer's Day* (filmed at 1958 Newport festival).

Music: *This Here* (Bobby Timmons); *Little Susie* (Ray Bryant); *Blues in Orbit* (Duke Ellington).

The anatomy of jazz

Any analysis of jazz must take into account a priori its simultaneous existence on two levels. The music is either improvised (spontaneously created by one or more musicians with a foreknowledge only of the harmonic outline) or it is written (arranged or orchestrated for a small group or large ensemble). The balance between these two levels has tended more and more heavily toward the second as jazz has evolved; nevertheless, improvisation remains the governing factor, in that it remains a part, in greater or lesser degree, of almost every performance generally classified as jazz. More significantly, the principles underlying jazz improvisation must be borne in mind by the creator of any written music; it has often been said that jazz writing is an extension of jazz improvisation, just as all music traced back to its ultimate origins is an outgrowth of folk music.

Because of this relationship between ad lib creation and documentation in jazz, the bulk of this chapter will be devoted to the nature and content of improvisation. Historiographic treatments of the subject have tended (until the relatively recent emergence of such musician-critics as Billy Taylor, André Hodeir and John Mehegan) to lack any real understanding of the complex nuances to be found in the techniques of jazz improvisation. Unless these subtleties can be committed to paper with a reasonable degree of accuracy and analysed by a musician with some empirical experience as an improvising jazzman, both the music and the analysis may at times seem interchangeable with an inspection of Broadway-style "pop" music, to which jazz bears a strong though superficial resemblance.

The fabric of jazz, like that of all music, comprises these basic elements: melody, harmony, rhythm and tone. From the melodic standpoint most jazz is not essentially different from many other types of music, notably the folk music of the United States, Britain and the Continent. Harmonically, since it uses the same major and minor scales (in the diatonic system) employed for most classical music from the seventeenth century, it has no character that does not derive from a much earlier source. Tonally, though in its early years there were crude attempts to obtain synthetic distortions, the sounds of jazz overlap with those of every other musical territory.

This leaves rhythm as the sole area in which jazz has a character largely distinct from that of any other music. It is through his unprecedentedly subtle use of such devices as syncopation and rubato that the jazzman established the identity of his music. Many non-jazz musicians, and aspiring jazzmen in countries remote from the heart of the trend, which is essentially American, have succeeded in capturing surface qualities in terms of harmony, melody and tone; if there is any lack of authenticity, it is usually through some rhythmic deficiency that it can be determined. (This technical gap, once enormous and seemingly insuperable, is narrowing so fast that in 1959 the American jazz musician Willie Ruff, reporting in *Down Beat* on a visit to the Soviet Union, wrote of an 18-year-old cornetist in Leningrad: "If you closed your eyes you'd swear it was Louis Armstrong.")

Although it is comparatively simple for the experienced listener to distinguish synthetic from real jazz, the definition of the term itself has defied the efforts of experts for several decades. Ask any ten musicians or critics to define the word "jazz" and you will get ten vastly different answers; and because of the accelerating changes in its nature the same respondents may offer a heavily modified definition a few years from now. Our values are as ambiguous as our definitions. A performance that seemed twenty years ago to represent the ultimate in jazz creativity may today sound rhythmically lackluster and melodically uninspired. Today's innovation is tomorrow's cliché; yesterday's precedent is today's platitude. Nevertheless, there are a few fixed standards; the amazing advances in the technique of the average musician, though they have been a means to many important new musical ends, are not of course per se indications of musical progress, nor do they invalidate records made in the late 1920s by Earl Hines, Louis Armstrong and a few others that have a fundamental and almost timeless beauty.

Though jazz has evolved from a largely unlettered and natural folk music into a product of highly skilled artisans, it has retained the elusive essence that separates it from so-called popular music. Admittedly the borderline is thin; the presence not long ago of a jazzman like Pete Fountain in the orchestra of Lawrence Welk, who represents the antithesis of everything jazz stands for, tends to confuse the issue, as does the nomination by Louis Armstrong of Guy Lombardo's orchestra as his all-time favorite. To Armstrong, who in his big-band days tried feverishly to duplicate the sound of Lombardo's reeds in his own saxophone section, this was the band that helped fight the vicious inroads of bop; to most critics and musicians, of course, Lombardo's music has even less bearing on jazz than the rock 'n' roll and other pap fed daily to the American public.

EXAMPLE 1

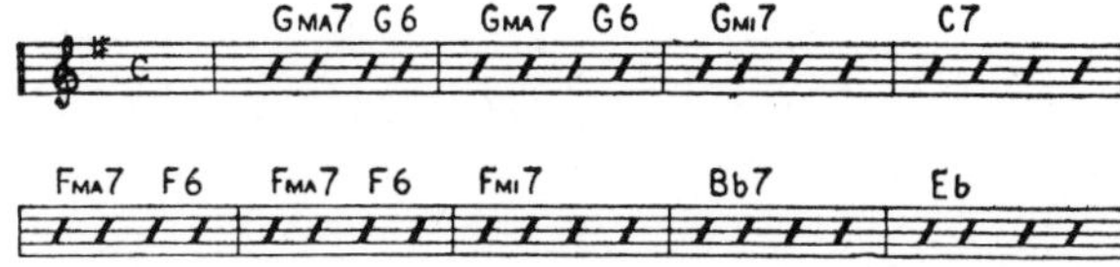

Hand a copy of Example 1 to a Guy Lombardo musician and he will either shake his head in confusion or at best will offer a series of unswinging arpeggios. Hand the same example to a classical musician and he will find it utterly meaningless. Yet the same set of noteless symbols, offered to any jazz musician, can be recognized instantly and will be translated into a passage of unmistakable jazz improvisation. Though it does not include a single note of music and consists simply of chord names and diagonal strokes (each representing one beat in a four-beat measure), no literate jazzman could fail to see in it, at first glance, the first nine measures of *How High The Moon,* or of Charlie Parker's *Ornithology* and other tunes based on the same harmonic pattern. To the jazz musician these themes are not merely the sequences of notes found on the sheet music; they are a harmonic ski-trail along which thousands of musicians have traveled. The improvised bases of jazz usually are not melodies but chord structures; the uninitiated listener who complains of the lack of a melody will eventually realize that a new and far more complex melody has been created, founded not on the missing theme, but on a harmonic routine that is identical with that of the unplayed tune.

Beginning in the late 1950s there was a tendency among some younger jazz musicians, notably those under the influence of Charles Mingus and of Ornette Coleman, to seek new paths avoiding adherence to a set harmonic pattern. Though it is very probable that atonality may become an important part of jazz improvisation, in 1960 at least 99% of the jazz being performed everywhere in the world was based on the tonal harmonic concept, and on the conventional diatonic major and minor scales. The frequent use of the flatted third and flatted seventh has given these notes a special status and in the opinion of some experts qualifies them as members of a "jazz scale" (Ex. 2).

EXAMPLE 2

The chords shown in Example 3, shown in root position and all placed arbitrarily in the key of B Flat, are the most important basic guideposts to improvisation.

EXAMPLE 3

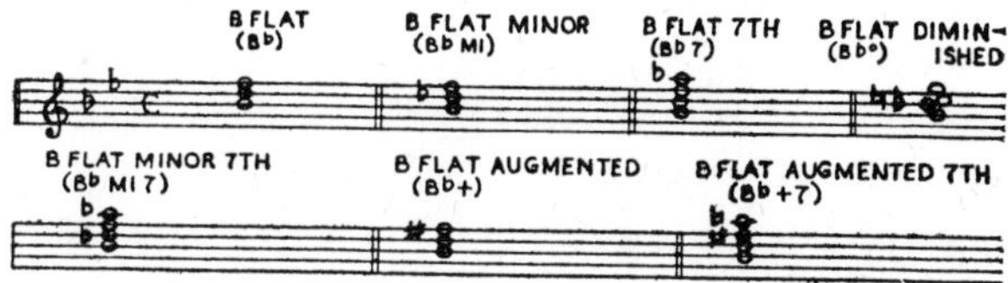

In order to give a slight idea of how jazz has expanded in its use of melody, harmony and rhythm, I have taken the simplest and most popular of all harmonic bases, the traditional twelve-measure blues in B Flat, to show some aspects of a vital trinity of elements: syncopation, improvisation and inspiration. Example 4 shows the barest bones of the blues, using in the bass nothing but triads (an inversion in Measures 7 & 8) and in the right hand a skeletal melody composed of quarter, half and whole notes. As is customary with the blues, the first four measures are based on the chord of the tonic or first note of the scale (here, a B Flat chord); the fifth through the eighth are based on the subdominant or fourth note of the scale (i.e., an E Flat chord here); the ninth and tenth measures are founded on the dominant, or fifth note of the scale (here, F) and the two final measures return to the tonic.

As a first modification of this crude melody, Example 5 shows how the use of flatted thirds and sevenths gives the melody its first hint of a jazz character. Example 6 shows a more complex melody that could be built by drawing on the seven types of chord shown in Example 3 (with additional variety provided by the use of passing tones to link the notes based on these chords).

These chords, of course, would still be very confining for a jazzman concerned with harmonic and melodic expansion. To the major and minor chords he might add a sixth, seventh or ninth; a ninth and/or eleventh and thirteenth could be

added to the seventh chords (in B Flat the major seventh would be A as distinct from the "blue" seventh, which would actually be the minor seventh, A Flat). Some of the effects of these further changes can be seen in Example 7.

During the 1920s jazz had barely struggled to the relatively simple technical level of Examples 6 and 7. Even during the 1930s only Duke Ellington and a handful of other writers (and scarcely any improvising jazzman) dared step beyond the harmonic boundaries implicit in these examples. Bassists continued to play mainly the root and fifth of each chord, pianists and guitarists played various inversions and slight variations of the chords and the horns in the band might voice the notes of the chords to provide an additional element guiding the soloist in his improvisation. Between 1939 and 1942 a reaction against this harmonic stagnation began to brew when a few musicians dared to add not only the ninth, eleventh and thirteenth to the seventh chords, but also an augmented eleventh (that is, E Natural in the key of B Flat, better known as a flatted fifth). Unless used incidentally as a passing tone this chord would have seemed dissonant to the ears of the average listener in earlier years; but it soon earned acceptance in what came to be known as "bop" circles. While soloists incorporated flatted fifths into their improvisations, their constantly improving fluency enabled them also to make use of such devices as grace notes and double time. The latter, employed in 1939 by Coleman Hawkins in parts of his famous *Body and Soul* improvisation, simply meant constructing the melodic line as if the rhythm section were playing at twice its actual tempo.) Such innovations, basic though they may sound in this brief description, altered the basic character of jazz solo work so strikingly that they were hailed as a musical revolution; the bebop movement of which these were primary characteristics was praised by some musicians as a step out of a blind alley and damned by others as a collection of wrong notes and a departure from the true spirit of jazz. The fourth measure in Example 8 shows how the flatted fifth can be incorporated into our sample theme; the use of double-time and of grace notes will be seen in the first and second measures respectively.

During the years of the bop revolution there were other developments that brought into frequent use various extensions and alterations in the use of the basic sets of seven chords. Such chords as raised ninths (e.g. D Flat against a B Flat 7th) and flatted ninths (B Natural against B Flat 7th) came into more extensive use on accented beats instead of being restricted to weak beats, or to passing tones and chords as hitherto. First the musicians' ears, then the fans', finally the general public's and even the critics', became accustomed to these developments; as they were slowly incorporated into the mainstream of jazz, musicians like Lennie Tristano and Dave Brubeck entered the scene with fresh and challenging approaches.

Tristano's concept of jazz improvisation was concerned as much with the horizontal as with the vertical developments. ("Vertical" is the adjective applied to music written, played or studied in terms of the notes of each chord as they are played simultaneously. It is so called because these notes may be found by looking at any part of the scores from top to bottom. Similarly "horizontal" or "linear" denotes the relationships of the notes or chords as they are

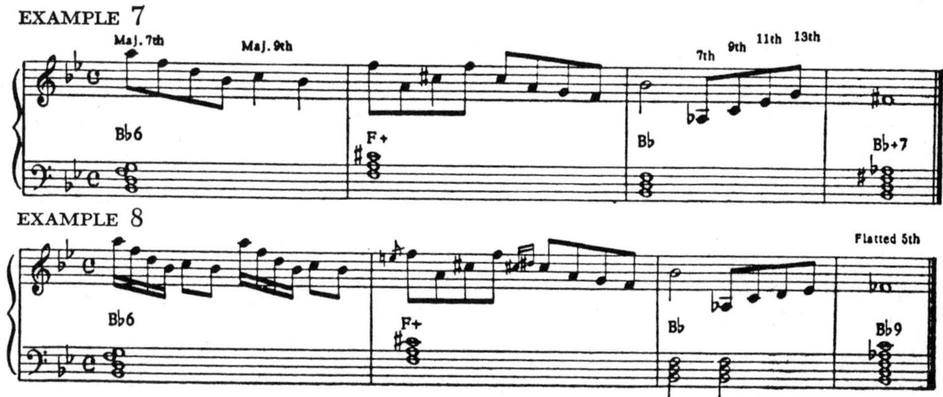

played one after the other, read horizontally across the manuscript.)

Although Dizzy Gillespie, Charlie Parker and Bud Powell had done much, both in their improvising and their compositions, to deliver jazz from predominantly vertical thinking to smoother-flowing, continuous melodic lines, Tristano and his disciples, among them Lee Konitz and Warne Marsh, concentrated even more completely on the horizontal relationship of the notes, as opposed to their relationship simply to the sequence of chords implied by them. Dave Brubeck's new concepts, though still vertical rather than linear in effect, often were conceived in unusual frames of reference; they became more important in the late 1950s when he began to experiment with time signatures not normally used in jazz.

measures, all of which can be accomplished in any time signature. At present most ears and feet are still inclined to feel a binary time as the most natural to jazz, but the now rapidly increasing interest in escape from this limitation may augur a change of attitude and of psychological reaction.

Example 9 shows how our sample blues can be converted into a three-four jazz theme. An even more unlikely time signature, 5/4, was used as the basis for a twelve-measure blues theme, *Bass Reflex*, in the author's 1956 *Hi Fi Suite*, possibly the first 5/4 jazz record. Example 10 shows this theme as played by Dick Hyman; as can be seen in every measure except 9 and 10, syncopation is strongly in evidence—the three chords in measure 1 are anticipations of the second, third and fifth beat respectively, etc.

EXAMPLE 9

Brubeck was among the many who, during the middle and late 1950s, revolted against the long-established dictum that a binary time (any pulse in two beats or multiples of two) was indigenous and essential to all improvised jazz. From the earliest jazz days until 1955 practically all jazz was in 4/4 (common) time or in 2/4; the only variations were in the multiples and divisions of four—for instance, Dixieland often had two main accents to the bar and boogie-woogie piano generally used eight. The author instigated and supervised several recordings demonstrating that jazz could and should be played in 3/4 (Benny Carter's *Waltzing the Blues*, 1936; Bobby Hackett and an all-star band in *Jammin' The Waltz*, 1938, and the writer's own *Bebop Waltz* recorded by Eddie Shu in 1949), all of which failed to constitute a trend; however, during the 1950s there was a gradual increase in experiments of this type, including Thelonious Monk's 6/4 version of *Carolina Moon* in 1952, big band waltzes by Woody Herman and Johnny Richards (later by Duke Ellington) and a series of compositions by Randy Weston, Sonny Rollins, John Graas and many others, all of which ultimately established what should have been clear all along: it is not the 4/4 beat that gives jazz its rhythmic character, but the shifting accents, the syncopation and rubato, the rhythmic and tonal nuances *within* each measure and through the

Up to this point, in attempting to provide at least a few clues in answer to the question "What is jazz?" I have concentrated chiefly on the harmonic aspects. An inspection of the various stages in the development of the sample blues theme will reveal that even Examples 7 and 8 lack an indispensable jazz element. They are completely without syncopation and rubato, which so often help to generate the elusive, intangible quality known as "the beat."

The beat is something too subtle for completely accurate notation. Its presence or absence in countless performances has been the subject of disputes among musicians and critics ever since jazz began.

The title of Duke Ellington's 1931 composition *It Don't Mean a Thing If It Ain't Got That Swing* has been used as a watchword among jazzmen ever since its publication. Another song title that provides a slogan no less applicable to the endless search for the beat is *'Tain't What You Do (It's the Way That You Do It)*, a dictum established by Sy Oliver and Trummy Young when they wrote and recorded the song by that name in the Jimmie Lunceford orchestra in 1939.

Billy Taylor, an outstanding modern jazz pianist, explained this essential doctrine in an enlightening manner. If he were handed a manuscript and told that it was a Beethoven sonata, he points out, he would read and play the music very differently

EXAMPLE 10 *Bass Reflex* (from *Hi-Fi Suite:* MGM Records E 3494) FEATHER

Courtesy of Henry Adler Music Co.

from the manner in which he would read and play the identical sheet of manuscript if he were under the impression that it had been written by a well-known jazz musician.

It is in the analysis of jazz from the rhythmic standpoint that confusion and disagreement most frequently arise concerning the question of what is and is not jazz. A melody like Duke Ellington's *Mood Indigo* provides a perfect example. Based almost entirely on whole, half and quarter notes, it has no qualities that are inherently jazz. The use of "blue notes" in seventh, ninth and augmented chords is a custom clearly of jazz origin, but now common to performances by bands and singers in the popular, non-jazz field. Thus *Mood Indigo* played by, say, André Kostelanetz, may be said not to be jazz, yet *Mood Indigo* played by Ellington's own orchestra is jazz. The reasons are (a) the jazz beat instilled by the accompanying Ellington rhythm section, (b) the use of tonal effects, such as trumpet and trombone muted by rubber plungers, long associated with jazz, (c) the psychological association of Ellington's name with jazz, (d) the "'Tain't what you do" principle.

The dogma that "jazz is where you find it" is especially applicable to the rhythmic aspects of this music. To one listener a performance may seem to have all the essential jazz qualities, while to another the same performance may be the antithesis of jazz. The rhythm section of a commercial dance orchestra or a radio studio band has, for some listeners, far more finesse, variety and rhythmic interest, from the jazz standpoint, than the steady four-to-the-bar pounding that characterized a typical rhythm section on a pioneer jazz record of the 1920s.

Rhythm in jazz is principally a matter of how the notes are *placed* and of how they are *played.*

Returning to our original blues theme, we find in Example 11 a placement of the notes that gives them a more naturally swinging quality. The first and second Fs and the two B Flats are both played an eighth note sooner than they were in Example 6. The phrasing in the fourth measure has been changed to replace the original feeling of straight eighth notes with one of rhythmic variety.

Example 12 shows how the same phrase might have been played according to the jazz standards of two or three decades ago. The extensive use of dotted eighths and sixteenths to replace passages in eighth notes later came to be considered "corny"; younger jazzmen used dotted eighths followed by sixteenths sparingly. The new preference leaned toward sequences of even eighth notes; thus the placement of the notes sometimes became less important than the manner in which they were articulated. The use of staccato and legato, of crescendo, diminuendo, sforzando and other dynamic effects, became more than ever relevant to the degree of swing inherent in a solo or arrangement. An example of this trend away from syncopation may be found in Lennie Tristano's *Crosscurrent,* recorded on Capitol EAP 1-491. Here the manner in which the notes of the melody line are accented is almost entirely responsible for the rhythmic jazz quality of the theme; there is virtually no syncopation.

Contrasting sharply with this approach is the use of syncopation as shown in Example 13, composed by the writer to demonstrate the extensive use of rhythmic anticipation. Recorded by Osie Johnson's Quintet under the title *Johnson's Whacks* on the Bethlehem label (BCP 66), it consists entirely of phrases in which anticipation of one or more notes creates rhythmic character.

Example 14 shows the same theme in what might be called a *reductio ad absurdum,* with all the syncopation removed. Example 13 can easily be made to swing when played by jazzmen with a natural feeling for the beat; it is almost impossible to make Example 14 swing if it is played exactly as written.

The extensive use of rubato in jazz is of more recent origin that that of syncopation. Rubato

literally means "robbed"; musically, it refers to the practice of dwelling on, and (often almost imperceptibly) prolonging, prominent melody tones or chords, requiring an equivalent acceleration of less prominent tones, which are thus robbed of a portion of their time value. A good example of the modern application of rubato in jazz may be found in the composition *Boplicity*, recorded by Miles Davis and his orchestra on Capitol T 762.

Although the use of syncopation and rubato can thus be pointed out, there are many qualities in jazz—rhythmic, harmonic, melodic and tonal—that defy notation or accurate definition. The use of notes that are barely played—"felt" rather than heard—"growl" effects, mutes and rubber plungers on trumpets and trombones, and the use of glissandi (frequently employed by Johnny Hodges in his melodic alto sax solos) and the "smear" (a downward glissando at the end of a note) cannot in themselves be considered jazz qualities, as can easily be proved by asking a non-jazz musician to demonstrate them. Yet when combined with the rhythmic, melodic and harmonic factors described here, they came to be accepted many years ago as essential components of jazz.

It is important to bear in mind that the musicians' own definition of jazz fluctuates frequently. Many of the more advanced performances by commercial TV and radio orchestras today, though now thought of as pop music, would have sounded like first-class swing music (i.e., new jazz of 1935) to 1935 ears.

Although the examples shown up to this point have given some idea of the harmonic and rhythmic nature of jazz, the reader must take into account that certain nuances of phrasing and dynamics essential to inspired jazz improvisation are virtually impossible to notate. In these shadings, as much as in the adherence to the harmonic requirements, lies the potential difference between a genuine jazz solo and one that the jazzman classifies as corny; between the workmanlike performance and the *chef d'oeuvre;* between the cold granite of mathematical extemporization and the fulfilling warmth of improvisatory genius.

There are three kinds of melodic improvisation. In the first and simplest, the original written melody is respected completely; the only change lies in the lengthening or shortening of some notes, repetition of others, use of tonal variations and dynamics to bring out its values in conformity with the personality of the interpreter. In the second, the melody remains completely recognizable but its phrases are subject to slight additions and changes; here and there a note is added or subtracted and perhaps a whole phrase is transmuted, but to the layman listener the original melody remains perceptible throughout, either in the actual statement or by indirection. In the third type of improvisation the soloist departs entirely from the melody; in fact, rather than using it as a point of departure, he uses instead the chord pattern of the tune. To the trained ear of the jazz musician it will still be apparent on what basis he is improvising.

This third category, which may be called full improvisation, is in turn composed of three subdivisions. There are the notes that are decided upon completely impromptu; the notes that are predetermined to the degree that they follow a natural sequence (possibly as part of an arpeggio, chromatic sequence or scalar run), and third, the notes that are played automatically, without real cerebration, because they happen to lie under the fingers and perhaps because they are part of a previously used sequence at the back of the performer's mind. Often a sequence of these notes may constitute a musical cliché; often, too, they will be a direct quotation from some other and completely irrelevant work. The cliché is not an evil per se, provided it is used occasionally, and with discretion and humor. Louis Armstrong plays countless phrases that have become clichés in his own work and in that of his imitators; Dizzy Gillespie can be recognized frequently by his use of phrases he has been playing for a decade. It has long been the belief of Duke Ellington that there is no such thing as complete improvisation, that a certain degree of predetermination governs the hands and mind of every musician. This theory is at least partly in accord with the analytic concept of the various types of improvisation as outlined above.

Another factor that controls the notes selected by the improvising jazzman is, of course, his personality and the environment and background from which it evolved. No two musicians will react alike to any given set of chords, any prearranged melodic pattern or even any group of words to be set to music. To illustrate this point, in what might be called a "Rorschach in rhythm" test, I presented three jazzmen, each of a different era, with a sample line of lyrics and asked them to interpret it spontaneously in music. The line used as the basis for this test was:

You told me that you loved me but you told me a lie

Louis Armstrong's reaction was simple and logical:

EXAMPLE 15

You told me that you loved me but you told me a lie

Armstrong based the entire phrase on the major triad, the only chord implied being the tonic.

Roy Eldridge produced this interpretation:

EXAMPLE 16

You told me that you loved me but you told me a lie

Curiously, Eldridge placed the accent on *you* in the second part of the phrase, instead of using *but you* as a pick-up. His main melodic thought did not differ from Armstrong's in any significant respect, but the final G Sharp clearly implied a change from the tonic chord to a C augmented 7th, leaving the way clear for a logical continuation.

Dizzy Gillespie, confronted with the same line, commented: "That sounds like the blues to me!" and played:

EXAMPLE 17

You told me that you loved me but you told me a lie

Here the melody, though simple, was piquant in its use of grace notes; and instead of staying within the confines of the major triad, as had Armstrong and (but for the last note) Eldridge, he used the sixth (D) at two points and the second (G) at another.

Jazz improvisation most often constitutes a reaction to certain chord sequences (and sometimes to melodies based on those sequences), just as the above samples are a melodically free reaction to the rhythmic pattern suggested by a line of lyrics. In order more fully to illustrate the extemporaneous musical emotions that have always been the core of most jazz, I have selected a representative (and still available) recorded solo by each of the three musicians participating in the above experiment.

The Armstrong example chosen dates back to the year of his creative zenith, 1928, during his memorable partnership with Earl Hines, whose piano in its overwhelmingly effective interaction with Armstrong's horn made *Muggles* one of the most definitive records of its period. Listeners wishing to follow the solo while examining this analysis will find it on Columbia CL 853.

The Roy Eldridge improvisation shown here can be heard in an LP entitled the *Anatomy of Improvisation* on Verve MGV 8230. Like *Muggles* this is based on the regular 12-measure blues pattern but is taken at a much faster tempo. The sample shown here occurs about one minute and 55 seconds from the start of the track, immediately following 36 measures by Gillespie. Eldridge spars gingerly for the first two measures, playing the chromatic triplets (fourth through fifth) that became a jazz cliché in the swing era and were constantly used by Fats Waller and Basie. Swinging up to the flatted seventh to establish that this is, after all, a blues, he uses a naturally rhythmic pattern (quarter, triplet eighths and four eighths) to swoop down to the C, which also represents a phase of jazz harmonic thinking rarely encountered before the 1930s, since it is a thirteenth built on the 7th of the subdominant. Armstrong would rarely have used a thirteenth except in proceeding from the dominant (F 7) to the tonic (B Flat).

After a three-beat pause, Eldridge builds the tension again with a rising phrase, then descends with a group of syncopated notes (the C followed by two B Flats), returns to the quarter-triplet-and-eighths pattern in Measure 8, and throughout Measures 9, 10 and 11 maintains a continuous pattern of eighth notes but avoids the impression of playing a scale by hitting the E Natural instead of moving directly to the F in Measure 10, and similarly avoids the monotony of repeating the unadorned E Flat 7th sequence of notes by using the thirteenth again (C). It is interesting to observe that while Eldridge plays notes that may seem to imply an E Flat 7th pattern through bars 10 and 11, Oscar Peterson's piano accompaniment furnishes an F 7th and a B Flat. At this rapid tempo any series of fast-moving eighth notes is protected from conflict with the underlying chords; the overall horizontal patterns must conform with that of the blues, but the arbitrary passing chords of the rhythm section move too quickly to call for complete conformity.

The extraordinarily fast-changing mood pattern of which Dizzy Gillespie's imagination and technique render him capable can be discerned in the sixteen measures reproduced from *Jessica's Day,* heard in the second chorus immediately after the theme and interlude, one minute and 35 seconds from the start. Like the Eldridge example, this performance can be heard on the *Anatomy of Improvisation* LP (Verve MGV 8230).

Gillespie establishes a "funky" mood by repeating the tonic and subjecting it to tonal variations through the use of the half-depressed valve effect and grace notes. After thus establishing tension during the two measure break, he offers simplicity and relaxation in Measures 3 and 4 of the chorus (though even simplicity, for him, includes what is virtually a pair of grace notes, the C and B Flat preceding the G). Then, in effect, Gillespie says "All right, you've heard what this is—it's one of those

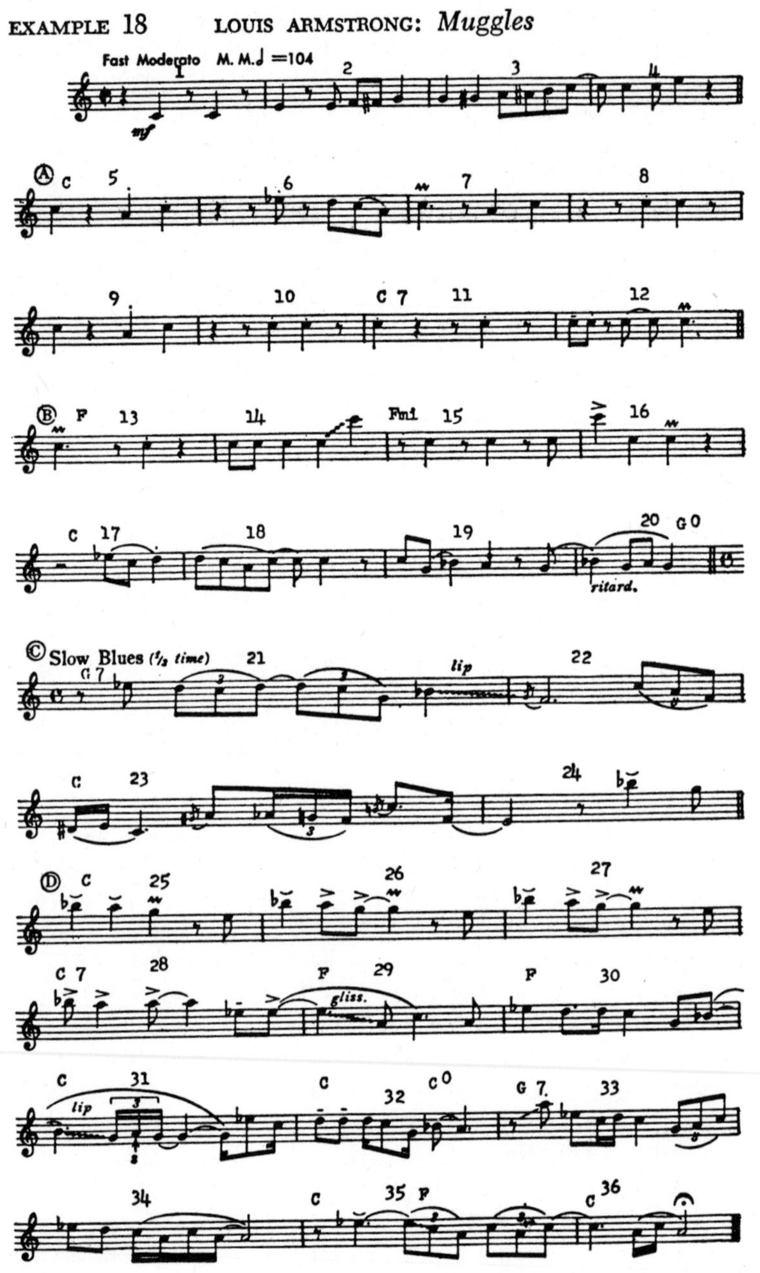

tunes with the conventional B Flat, G, C, F base, a *We Want Cantor* affair—so now we'll try to make something of it." Then comes the flurry of sixteenth notes, but given rhythm balance through the use of syncopation (third beat of Measure 5) and a triplet on the first beat of Measure 6. This serves as a warm-up for an even busier upward sweep in which the tension mounts; notice that the rise is diatonic, except that the flatted seventh (A Flat) and flatted third (C Sharp) are used. After this surge, a three beat pause for breath and thought (Measures 9-10) leads to another concept in which a buoyant mood is established, this time not by the multi-noted fury of the preceding phrases but through a concept

EXAMPLE 19 ROY ELDRIDGE: *Trumpet Blues*

built symmetrically around a simple thought based on the three quarter notes at Measure 11, repeated at Measure 13 in the same descending pattern but with a different formation and an octave lower. Measure 15 is a superb example of the obliqueness of Gillespie's approach to a chord. The root of the F Minor 7th is preceded by notes on either side of it (E Natural and G); the accent of the third beat corresponds with the dissonant E Natural and E Flat against the B Flat 7th chord before the consonant D is reached; and on the fourth beat the B Natural and A Natural are neighboring notes on either side of the B Flat that opens the next measure. The naturally swinging 16th measure (dotted quarter, eighth, two sets of triplets) leads smoothly into a series of sarcastic comments on the return to harmonic home base: Fs fingered naturally, producing the normal tone, alternate with E Naturals fingered at half-valve, with the squeezed sound, before Gillespie concedes to the inevitable and returns to the tonic.

The above three examples are representative of pure jazz extemporization. Although it is generally agreed that improvisation has always been the life blood of jazz (some critics still claim that true jazz cannot be written down), an orchestrated performance can qualify as jazz provided it retains the same rhythmic feeling, the same concepts both in writing and in performance, that are inherent in improvised jazz. If Guy Lombardo's band were to play a Count Basie arrangement, chances are that the result at times would sound like jazz, but it would be awkward and clumsy jazz, lacking the basic rhythmic feeling that the arranger had when he had written the score, or that jazz musicians would have if they played it.

Following are some samples of written jazz exactly as they appeared on the score sheets of prominent arrangers. Example 21 is an excerpt from a blues theme for a small band (ten pieces) orchestrated by Ralph Burns and entitled *Donner,* from the *Winter Sequence Suite* (in *The Swinging Seasons* on MGM E3613).

The main thematic line here has a basic simplicity in that it is built almost entirely on three notes, for the first eight bars. Variety is achieved by syncopation, and by the use of a main phrase that is six beats in length and is played twice in the first

EXAMPLE 20 JOHN (DIZZY) GILLESPIE: *Jessica's Day*

three bars to create a three-against-two effect. While the trumpet and saxophone play the theme in unison, the French horn and tuba add a second line. In the second twelve-bar chorus (four bars of which are shown at the end of this example) the trombone is added and the overall sound of the orchestration has a contrapuntal effect.

Example 22 is an excerpt, scored entirely in concert key, from a blues theme for a large band (twenty-one pieces), composed and orchestrated by Pete Rugolo and entitled *Mixing the Blues,* from his album *Adventures in Rhythm* (Columbia CL 604). The orchestra consists basically of three sections. One is the reed section—saxophones doubling on clarinets, flutes, etc. Second is the brass—four trumpets, four trombones, and two French horns. Third is the rhythm—piano, guitar, bass, drums, tuba, with a second drummer doubling on xylophone.
Ex. 22

In the passage shown, the first section is play-

EXAMPLE 21
Donner
Trumpet
Horn
Trombone
Tuba
Alto
Tenor
col Trpt.
Baritone
col Alto
Piano
Bb Cm Eb E° Bb Bb7 Eb Ebm
Bass
Drums
EXAMPLE 21 (continued)
(col Trpt.)
(col Alto)
Dm7b5 G7 Cm7 Cm7b5 F+7b9 Bb Cm7 Bb F7
etc.

EXAMPLE 22 *Mixing the Blues*

EXAMPLE 22 *(continued)*

ing one melodic theme, the trumpets are playing a second and the trombones a third. (The baritone sax at this point is moving with the tuba to provide a rhythmic counterpoint.) At the fourth measure the French horns join with the xylophone to provide a "fill-in" phrase before the three themes resume in Bar 5.

This is a complex operation, but close inspection will reveal that it is neither overorchestrated nor overpretentious, for the basic blues format is still retained (notice how the D Naturals in Bar 1 are replaced by D Flats in Bar 5, to conform with the regular blues pattern, moving from a B Flat to an E Flat ninth chord in accordance with time-honored blues tradition). And of the three simultaneous themes, only that played by the trumpets is voiced; the others are in unison. The trombones' theme, though it looks complicated because of the profusion of notes in a double-time effect à la bop, actually forms a simple melodic contour, as can be observed by playing or singing it very slowly.

The relationship between improvised and orchestrated jazz has occasionally been pointed up with valuable clarity through literal translation of the first into the second. Occasionally a memorable jazz solo has so impressed an arranger that he has been impelled to adapt it to use by a full orchestra. Bix Beiderbecke's solo on *Singin' The Blues* was the first example; Fletcher Henderson's arrangement used the Bix solo note for note. Illinois Jacquet's famous two-chorus solo on *Flyin' Home* (later played by the whole saxophone section of the Lionel Hampton band) is perhaps the best known. A more recent instance is presented here in an excerpt from *Stockholm Sweetenin'*, the Quincy Jones composition.

The reader is advised to study the original ad lib trumpet solo by Clifford Brown (Prestige LP 7055) before examining its rebirth as part of an orchestration played by the Quincy Jones orchestra (ABC-Paramount 149). The adaptation is introduced by unison trombones, backed by the saxophones; at the seventh measure Brown's improvised line is taken over by saxophone, flute and muted trumpet, with punctuations by the trombones (Example 23). Jones wrote in his album notes, "I consider this one of Brownie's best-constructed solos on record and it serves as a stimulating, inspired composition." That improvisation in effect is composition, an axiom often neglected by jazz students, has never been more clearly shown than in this instance of an orchestrated solo.

In all the musical examples I have cited, with the exception of the waltz and 5/4 excerpts, the beat implied is in the regular 4/4 time. One element not taken into account, because it is not germane to jazz per se, is the infusion of Latin-American or Afro-Cuban rhythms. A commonplace in modern jazz from the early 1950s, this process of cross-fertilization expanded the rhythmic horizons in terms of eighth-note subdivisions. For instance, some jazz performances written in 4/4 time are played in groups of eight eighth notes in which the first, fourth and sixth are accented; in other performances all but the fifth of these eight notes may be accented.

The reader will have observed by now that the aspect of jazz hardest to define and notate is its rhythmic nature; by the same token, a feeling for these rhythms is the quality most difficult to develop in a musician to whom the world and values of jazz are unfamiliar. The crucial distinction between a line of eighth notes, or a series of dotted eighths and sixteenths, the way a jazzman would play them, and the same notes as they might be interpreted by a symphony musician, could perhaps be subjected to an acute mathematical analysis, but the easier and commoner way to define the distinction would be simply to say that the former digs or feels it and the latter, in many instances, fails.

A curious instance can be found in the case of a musician named Donald Shirley, a gifted pianist whose classical training and technique cannot be gainsaid. Because he has worked in jazz clubs and plays the same tunes that are featured by jazzmen it has been assumed by some listeners that he is a jazz pianist; the fact is, though, that the indefinable beat common to Tatum, Peterson, Powell and every other real jazz pianist is lacking in Shirley. An enlightening comparison may be made by studying two versions of *They Can't Take That Away From Me*, played respectively by Shirley on Cadence 1001 and by Billy Taylor on Prestige 7015. The difference is very slight on the surface yet very deep at its core. Shirley's interpretation is academically beyond reproach. Taylor's is not only technically excellent: it also swings.

EXAMPLE 23

Stockholm

Arranger: Q. JONES

1st Violins
1st Sax
2nd Sax
3rd Sax
4th Sax
5th Sax
2nd Trumpet
3rd Trumpet
4th Trumpet
1st Trombone
2nd Trombone
3rd Trombone
Guitar
Bass
Drums
Piano

Only through constant listening can the novice understand these distinctions; ultimately they will provide him with an answer to the perpetual question: "What is jazz?" With the help of the foregoing illustrations and careful examination of the corresponding records and of others recommended in this book, the initiate, ultimately, will arrive at the stage that has been reached by so many others who have been studying jazz ever since the Original Dixieland Band added the word to the dictionary: he will be able to explain a little while understanding a lot.

Jazz in American society

The truism that jazz was the product of red-light districts and has worked its way up to Carnegie Hall, that it is a most important ambassador of good will and a potent propaganda weapon for the U.S., went through an endless valley of repetition in the late 1950s—and remained true. Partly because of the reluctance with which it was accepted in the upper social strata, and partly because of its racial backgrounds, there has remained a curious ambivalence in the status of jazz; ironically, it is an ambivalence that is felt far less jarringly overseas than in the country of its origin.

Nothing is more typical of the Hollywood-to-Broadway concept of our mores than the classic scene in which the jive-talking jazz musician, having worked his way into the chic town house to mix with the elite, ruins the social equilibrium of the moment with some gauche remark, or spills his gin in the duchess' lap. There has always seemed to be, and to the scenario writer there always will be, a naturally comic paradox in the juxtaposition of jazz, a "lowbrow" music, and the higher echelóns of white American society. Yet today's truths are that jazz in some of its present manifestations is a highly intellectualized music, that modern musicians, far removed from their counterparts of the 1930s, today are acutely aware of their role in music and society; that many have college degrees and are skilled in classical music, and that a fair number have even followed the neurotic patterns of their social "betters" by becoming the patients of psychiatrists.

To gain a clear perspective of jazz in its present relationship to American society it is necessary to examine two interrelated phenomena: Jim Crow and the narcotics problem. The former must be inspected first because it will immediately throw light on the other.

Though there is room for considerable disagreement concerning the exact proportions, it has always been clear that a very large percentage of the greatest jazz musicians have been Negroes. It is indisputable, too, that no matter what his economic condition at any stage of his life, the Negro musician is subjected to psychological pressures that the white American will never have to endure. Many a Negro has turned to jazz as an emotional outlet and a livelihood who, had he been born white with the same intellectual potential, might have become a doctor or an engineer. Even before he was able to think of music in terms of a career, the Negro found in music a solace and relief from the tyranny of slavery, an outlet in which he was more likely to be encouraged than punished. Many years later, when he observed the limits of his chances for success (or even for entry) in many leading professions, he found in music, particularly in folk music, forms that called for less formal education, the hope of a fruitful life and the possibility at least to some extent of skirting the bitter alleys of Jim Crow.

Though Jim Crow and music have been partners for more than a half century in a shotgun wedding, with Uncle Sam in charge of the arsenal, the alliance has been an uneasy one from the start. It was observed in a history of the Fisk Jubilee Singers, more than eighty years ago, that "people who would not sit in the same church pew with a Negro, under the magic of their song were able to get new light on questions of social equality."

During the early years of ragtime, of brass band

music and folk blues and other forms that soon crystallized into jazz, there was little social intermingling between whites and Negroes, though from the start there were light-skinned Negroes who "passed" in white bands. Generally, at least through the 1920s, Negroes and whites lived apart, worked and played apart; that two separate bloodstreams were flowing in the veins of jazz can be confirmed by a comparison of the early records of Duke Ellington or Louis Armstrong with those of Ben Pollack and Red Nichols. A Jim Crow society had produced Jim Crowed music. In later years the blood lines tended to reunite, though even today there are many white jazz musicians (particularly in Los Angeles) who tend to work only with other white musicians, and some Negro combo leaders (notably in New York) who use this policy in reverse in their hiring of sidemen.

Despite the contrary impression foolishly given in novels (Garson Kanin's *Blow Up a Storm*) and motion pictures *(The Gene Krupa Story)*, there was, until as late as 1935, when Benny Goodman hired Teddy Wilson, no such thing as an official public appearance, in the same group, of a Negro and a white musician. Even in the seclusion of a recording studio it was a rarity; of the thousands of jazz sides recorded from 1917, when jazz recording began, not more than a couple of dozen were interracial, and then usually only to the extent of one or two Negro guest artists playing with a white group; a white jazzman recording under Negro leadership was even rarer—only four or five instances in 15 years.

After the Goodman initiative (inspired by John Hammond) there were a few token efforts during the next decade: Billie Holiday's eight months with the Artie Shaw band in 1938, Joe Sullivan's mixed sextet at Cafe Society in 1939; June Richmond with the Jimmy Dorsey band, Flip Phillips with Frankie Newton's combo in 1940; Lena Horne's four months with Charlie Barnet's band in 1941, and the long association of Roy Eldridge with the Gene Krupa band from 1941 (pointedly ignored and replaced by a morass of anachronisms in the Krupa film biography).

Miss Horne's experiences with Barnet as reported in her autobiography are typical: "Every time we'd walk down the street together . . . we'd run the gamut of cold eyes and hot tongues. White people would nudge each other in amazement . . . it was just as humiliating for me when we passed other Negroes. I was acutely uncomfortable in restaurants . . . I'd taste the food on my plate suspiciously, wondering if someone in the kitchen had . . . deliberately put something in my order to keep me from coming back."

Soon after, the band played a college date at which Barnet was forbidden to let Miss Horne sing —not in Mississippi, but in New England. "Then," she wrote, "I learned we had a string of bookings which would take us South . . . Even if by some chance they would let me sing, I wouldn't be able to stand it. My nerves were completely gone. I couldn't sleep, I couldn't eat. And sometimes when I'd glance down, I'd see that my hands were shaking."

It is not a long step from Lena Horne's ordeal in 1941 to the scene outside Birdland in 1959 when Miles Davis, after being ordered by a policeman to move along, and refusing on the grounds that he was working there, was brutally assaulted by a detective, had to have several stitches in his head, and wound up in a police station, himself charged with assault! After a long, expensive and tiring series of legal maneuvers, the charges against Davis were dropped.

Jazz has always lived in this twilight world, the world of an American society that professes pious ideals in its constitution and promptly violates them through state laws or unwritten but firmly maintained social taboos.

A subtler irony lies in the willingness of ignorant white officials to be fooled in the matter of racial identification. Lucky Millinder, one of the first Negro leaders to use white sidemen, gave this account of a trip with his mixed band in the early 1940s:

"Usually the evening was half over before anybody noticed anything, and then it was too late for them to do much about it. In some towns I knew the Chief of Police, which helped. Often the musicians would have to pass for Puerto Ricans. I remember one night, when I had a drummer who looked unmistakably Jewish, the cop kept asking questions while the band was playing. After the set he walked up and looked the drummer straight in the eye for quite a while. Then he said, 'Yeh, he's a nigger all right,' and walked away satisfied. We never had a major incident, though we came pretty close a couple of times."

In many of the Southern towns where the Millinder band played, interracial appearances were legally proscribed.

The integration record of the principal jazz orchestras has varied greatly from band to band. Benny Goodman has usually mixed his orchestras and combos freely; at the Waldorf-Astoria in 1957 his sidemen included Buck Clayton, Budd Johnson, Kenny Burrell and Israel Crosby. Tommy Dorsey, who hired Sy Oliver as staff arranger in 1939 and occasionally presented him as vocalist, had Charlie Shavers as a band member off and on from 1945 until Dorsey's death in 1956; Paul Gonsalves played with the band briefly in 1953.

Charlie Barnet used Negro sidemen consistently from 1941, when he hired Dizzy Gillespie for a few weeks; during the 1940s he was responsible even more often than Goodman for the presentation of an integrated ensemble.

Les Brown and Bob Crosby have always maintained all-white personnels. Woody Herman at one juncture showed signs of mixing his band indiscriminately (in 1949-50 he had Gene Ammons, Ernie Royal, Shadow Wilson, Milt Jackson, Oscar Pettiford) but abandoned the practice as a result of some discouraging experiences, and did not resume it until 1959.

Count Basie has used white sidemen from time to time: Georgie Auld, Serge Chaloff and trumpeter Al Porcino were with him for short periods in 1950, Buddy De Franco was a member of the Basie Septet for a full year in 1950-1 and Johnny Mandel played trombone in the big band for five months in 1953.

Duke Ellington hired the non-Negro Juan Tizol, a Puerto Rican, in 1929, but by the peculiar standards of American racism he was a borderline case. The first definite break was the use of Louis Bellson on drums, in 1951-3, followed by another white drummer, Dave Black, in 1953-5. During these periods Ellington, who had often described his contribution to jazz as representative of "Negro music" but who by now was more concerned with its value simply as music, experimented with several other white sidemen. Notable among them was Tony Scott, who quit the band after a month, despite Ellington's protests, in 1953, and whom Duke has since described wistfully as "the only musician who was ever forced out of my band by race prejudice." Scott admitted that the hostile attitude of one or two band members was not conducive to his staying.

Dizzy Gillespie has had a long and honorable racial record. As far back as 1942 he had Stan Levey playing drums with him in Philadelphia; throughout the early years of bop, white musicians intermittently formed a part of his personnel. The big band he formed in 1956 for the State Department-sponsored tours had from one to seven white musicians at one time or another.

If integration was slow to develop on the bandstand it must be remembered that it was even slower to develop in the audience. Cafe Society, the Greenwich Village club that flourished as a jazz center for several years, paved the way, from its opening in 1938, by encouraging integration both in its clientele and entertainment; yet in the early 1940s there were still a few sleazy jazz clubs on 52nd Street that employed Negro groups while refusing to admit Negroes as customers. During World War II there were organized attempts by MPs and others to keep white GIs away from Harlem; subtle anti-mixing propaganda, some of it in the tabloid newspapers, led to the closing for several months of the Savoy Ballroom, once the best-known Harlem center of big band jazz.

Despite these concerted efforts to create friction and ensure separation, jazz musicians and fans tended to get to know one another socially during the 1940s. Little by little the mixed combo, once an exception, became the rule. Today most of the remaining all-white and all-Negro combos retain their monochromatic format more through chance or social relationships among the members than through any active desire to protect racial solidarity. Some Negro leaders understandably hire Negro sidemen because, realizing that the opportunities for the white musician still are much broader, they feel that he may need the job less than a Negro musician of equal skill. Some white leaders hire only white sidemen simply because they live in the same neighborhood or attend the same parties or play golf together. But as the social obstacles disintegrate, professional and economic barriers are slowly fading away.

A survey of combos during the past decade shows that Louis Armstrong has invariably had one or two white musicians in his sextet, and that all the others of any consequence have at one period mixed their personnels: the Shearing Quintet, the Brubeck

Quartet, the groups of Eddie Condon, Jimmy McPartland, Charlie Ventura, the Mastersounds, Lennie Tristano, Miles Davis, Stan Getz, Gerry Mulligan, Chico Hamilton, Charlie Parker, Buddy De Franco, Red Norvo, Terry Gibbs. There was a precedent-setting example of interracial leadership when Jay Jay Johnson and Kai Winding led their quintet in 1954-6; but after they went their own ways Kai Winding organized a septet that maintained an all-white personnel.

The stubbornest barrier of all fell in 1952. Helen Merrill, unmistakably blonde, sang for three months with Earl Hines' Sextet (her white saxophonist husband also was a member of the combo). The following year Lionel Hampton, who has made free use of white musicians, took on Janet Thurlow, an inconspicuous brunette who doubtless was assumed by Southern audiences not to be white; for it is inconceivable to the white cracker mentality that a red-blooded, white, true-blue American girl singer would of her own volition join a Negro band.

The result of the freer association of white and Negro artists on a professional level (and of the greater social mixing occasioned by such factors as the gradual opening up of hotels to Negro patrons in many cities) was, predictably, a breaking down of stylistic lines. Less and less, with the passing of the postwar years, could actual "white jazz" and "Negro jazz" be said to exist. Roy Eldridge, returning from a long sojourn in Europe and influenced by the confused racial attitude still manifest in critical circles in France, made a bet with the author that he would be able, in a blindfold test, to distinguish white musicians from Negroes. At the end of the test he admitted that he had been wrong.

Eldridge at that time, embittered by his experiences with white bands, vowed never again to play in one; the traumatic, nerve-wracking events that are part of a Negro's life in a predominantly white orchestra were described in an interview with this writer for *Down Beat:*

"We arrive in one town (with Krupa) and the rest of the band checks in. I can't get into their hotel, so I keep my bags and start riding around looking for another place where someone's supposed to have made a reservation for me. I have a heavy load of at least a dozen pieces of luggage . . . when the clerk sees that I'm the Mr. Eldridge the reservation was made for, he suddenly discovers the last available room has been taken. I lug all that luggage back into the street and start looking around again.

"By the time that kind of thing has happened night after night, it begins to wear on my mind; I can't think right, can't play right. At the Palladium in Hollywood I had to watch out who I could or couldn't sit at the tables with. If they were movie stars who wanted me to come over, that was all right; if they were just the jitterbugs, no dice. And all the time the bouncer with his eye on me, just waiting for a chance . . . on top of that, I had to live way out in Los Angeles while the rest of the guys stayed in Hollywood. It was a lonely life . . . one night the tension got so bad I flipped. I could feel it right up to my neck while I was playing *Rockin' Chair;* I started trembling, ran off the stand, and threw up. They carried me to the doctor's. I had a 105 fever; my nerves were shot. . . ."

At Norfolk, Virginia, barred from the washroom the other musicians were using, Roy was handed a bucket of water. Riding on the Norfolk ferry with some musicians on the top deck he was told: "We don't allow no niggers up here." When a complaint about this remark was made to the captain, he commented: "Well, if you can stand him, it's all right with me."

"Just as if I had leprosy," said Eldridge.

In Youngstown, Ohio there was no room in the hotels, no service in the restaurant; even Krupa's offer to let him use one of the twin beds in his own room could not console him. Eldridge abruptly left town; it was a week before he could be talked into rejoining the band.

In 1944, working with Artie Shaw, Eldridge ran into the same problems. No food, even in a small Mexican restaurant in Del Mar, California, where the white musicians walked out with him in sympathy. No admission to the local dance hall even though his name was up in lights outside as a featured attraction with Shaw.

"When I finally did get in, I played that first set, trying to keep from crying. By the time I got through the set, the tears were rolling down my cheeks. . . . I went up to a dressing room and stood in a corner crying and saying to myself why the hell did I come out here again when I knew what would happen?

"Man, when you're on the stage you're great, but as soon as you come off, you're nothing. It's not worth the glory, not worth the money, not worth anything."

Despite the later willingness of Eldridge to admit the fusion of white and Negro styles, there remains a persistent legend that jazz still must be the subject of a dichotomy in every analytical discussion. Ironically, the belief of the condescending white southerner that the Negro has instinctive musical gifts (which in the southerner's mind places him in a class with the well-trained poodle) is shared by many foreign jazz audiences; this has resulted in an attitude diagnosed, in an acute monograph by Barry Ulanov, as "Crow Jim." According to this theory jazz, as the property of the Negro, can only be played by whites to the extent that they have assimilated the "Negro idiom." As recently as 1953 it was impossible for any white American musician (even Benny Goodman) to win a French jazz poll.

The automatic assumption of the Negro's supremacy may, indeed, smack of poetic justice; it can easily be understood why many jazzmen, visiting France and other countries where this attitude is prevalent, have decided to take advantage of it by making their homes there. But to the more mature musician, who would rather be accepted as a man than lionized as a Negro, it is uncomfortable to observe some of the manifestations of Crow Jim.

A substantial number of well known jazzmen in the 1940s and '50s seemed to find their answer, and perhaps resolved the need for a sense of belonging, by embracing Mohammedanism. Their conversion to Islam was an attempt to escape Jim Crow, to become a member of an exotic sect, perhaps enabling them to gain access to a few "white" hotels in border states where the wearing of a fez might lead to confusion and nervous kowtowing; but on a less casual basis there was a deep psychological significance behind the move. It enabled them to become members of a private club, a Crow Jim organization with its own values, its own truths and its own rejection of white American society's rigid tenets.

Some of the musicians involved in this movement devoted little time, after the initial stages, to the religious aspects of Mohammedanism, doing little more than adopting a Moslem name. Others, completely sincere, found in the religion a soul-satisfying answer to their problems. Ahmad Jamal is so passionately dedicated to the movement that he becomes incensed when reminded that he was ever Fritz Jones; spiritually, he asserts, he was always Ahmad Jamal. In the midst of a highly successful career as pianist and leader of a trio, he interrupted his activities to visit the Near East and inspect the land of his adopted (or, as he would put it, his real) ancestors. But in the final analysis the inclination to Islam may prove to have been simply one more product of prejudice. With the disappearance of Jim Crow Jamal could again become Fritz Jones, Sahib Shihab might once more be Edmund Gregory and possibly Yusef Lateef would resume life as William Evans.

The Crow Jim implications inherent in the Mohammedan movement can be found in a completely different form among the writing of several leading jazz experts. Ever since the 1930s, a surprisingly large number of European jazz critics have evidenced a blind spot on the race question (which, oddly enough, is considered with far greater objectivity by the American writers). Joachim-Ernst Berendt, Germany's foremost critic, printed a series of genealogical tables in the original edition of his *Das Jazzbuch* showing the relationships of various styles. In each chart there were two main lines, one marked "schwarz", the other "weiss." In a later edition Berendt partially recanted and the segregated charts were removed. André Hodeir, the distinguished French critic and musician, claims to have found a greater relaxation among Negroes which he says manifests itself not only in their jazz performances but in the events at the Olympic Games, a theory not likely to be upheld by any scientist or anthropologist. But the height of impudence was reached when another French critic, in a book of biographies, branded as "of the white race" those few white musicians who were considered worthy of inclusion, while the Negro musicians were unidentified by race—a reversal of an equally obnoxious racial labeling still seen in some parts of the United States when crime stories involving Negroes are reported. (In the American edition of that book the race labels were removed.)

The final proof of the absurdity of this race-oriented view of jazz lies in its arbitrary method of segregation. By what scientific standards, for instance, do these writers assign the saxophonist Willie Smith to the Negro side of the fence when by any but the most Hitlerian of standards he is white? In which branch of their family tree do they place the guitarist Kenny Burrell, paler and whiter than many swarthy Latin-American performers who are accepted as white? And if blood lines are related to natural talent, is Miles Davis, a very dark-skinned Negro, more authentically a jazzman than the saxophonist Jackie McLean, who may have had seven white great-grandparents? The Crow Jim proponents are in a ridiculously untenable position, just as are the white-supremacists who enact laws in each state "determining" what percentage of "Negro blood" (there is of course no such thing) decides a citizen's racial status.

Dizzy Gillespie, in a TV interview with Mike Wallace in 1957, was questioned: "I would like your opinion of the Negro's success in jazz. Is it because, as some people say, the Negro has more music, more rhythm, more beat in him than the white people?" Gillespie replied: "I don't think God would give any one race of people something that the other one couldn't get if they had the facilities . . . you probably could take a white kid and subject him to the same things that one of us was subjected to, and he'd probably stomp his feet just like we do. *It's not a matter of race, but environment.*"

Gillespie's sophisticated attitude is not yet general among Negro musicians. Some, in a partly unconscious revolt against the dominance of white society (and resentment at the early success of inferior white musicians who have imitated them), have hotly endorsed the Crow Jim theory. One distinguished Negro combo leader has made speeches on New York bandstands clearly implying that in order to feel the emotions of jazz one must be of African descent. The hostility toward white musicians is part of a syndrome that has developed as the Negro jazzman, becoming more acutely conscious of his own role in the music and his esthetic potential, developed a concomitant awareness of the discrimination to which he has been subjected. Trying hungrily to grab whatever scraps of democracy have been left on the white plate, he avoids Harlem and moves to a "white" neighborhood, denounces Louis Armstrong as an Uncle Tom, dresses in Brooks Brothers clothes or else defiantly walks on the bandstand in a sweatshirt, uses the Crow Jim theory as a psychological crutch, and clings desperately to an art he feels he can call his own in a society that has tried so often to steal from him and suppress him.

The typical bourgeois white American feels little or no sympathy for those motivations and actions because he has never been close enough to understand them. It is a mystery to him how a musician who makes thousands of dollars a week, imports expensive foreign cars and lives like an amateur Rubirosa can possibly feel any discrimination. Apparently it takes the eyes of a Negro, or a more than normally perceptive white, to observe that the bland, nondescript orchestras of Lawrence Welk and Ray Anthony have had their own regularly sponsored TV series while this privilege was never accorded to Ellington or Basie; that Kate Smith, Ernie Ford, Rosemary Clooney and dozens of other white singers have similarly found the commercial sponsorship for which the Ella Fitzgeralds, Sammy Davises and Sarah Vaughans search in vain. (The answer is not simply that performers of quality are undesirable in the context or that mediocrity is better suited to the mass media: on the contrary, the Basies, Fitzgeralds and Davises make frequent, highly successful television appearances, but always on programs headed by others.) Similarly, the white American feels nothing more than perhaps a superficial compassion on reading that in 1959 the Bell Telephone Company's representatives, in a program under its sponsorship, tried to stop Miss Fitzgerald from using her white guitarist, then kept him out of camera range, as part of a fixed policy against showing interracial groups; that a dozen incidents of this kind take place daily all over America, drops of water that sooner or later could wear away the most granitic resistance, little psychic agonies that no garageful of Dual Ghias can erase.

Counterposed against the attitude of the Crow Jim critics is the position taken by Stan Kenton, who on reading the results of the 1956 *Down Beat* critics' poll sent the magazine a telegram expressing his "complete and utter disgust" with the results and sarcastically deducing that there was now a "new minority group, white jazz musicians." Kenton's telegram brought a flood of protesting mail; his chauvinistically pro-white attitude seemed as indefensible as that of the Crow Jim critics. It is not true that Kenton was motivated by actively anti-Negro feelings, however; his band had included Negro musicians occasionally. Nothing was proved on either side except that the color question remains inflammatory even when it should not be an issue at all.

The race situation today is very slowly receding from the foreground as a musical factor in jazz, though economically it still presents many problems. (Early in 1960 Dave Brubeck canceled $25,000 worth of bookings in Southern colleges when he was asked to hire a white bassist to replace Eugene Wright.) Whatever restrictions are still put on Negro musicians usually are the result of outside pressures. Few white jazzmen harbor any real prejudice; most have a limitless admiration for their Negro contemporaries and in recent years have fraternized freely with them.

Musically, as the pianist Billy Taylor pointed out in a magazine article, "jazz is no longer the exclusive medium of expression of the Negro. As the Negro has become more articulate and outspoken, his music has reflected his growth. And in each stage of its development, jazz has become more and more the medium of expression of all types of Americans and, to a surprising degree, musicians from other lands and other cultures."

Though the broadening of the Negro performer's horizons and the gradual diminution of Jim Crow may have elevated jazz in social acceptance, the decades during which it lived partly underground, unrecognized as a serious art form and unstable as a means of livelihood, left scars that may take decades to heal. The gravest of these is the problem of narcotics.

There have been many conflicting stories in the lay and musical press concerning the use of narcotics among jazz musicians. The newspapers still tend to jump at any opportunity to link jazz and dope; all too often they have ample justification. The movie and TV writers are apparently so blatantly uninformed that on innumerable occasions they have depicted jazzmen as "addicted" to marijuana, a non-addictive narcotic. Yet, musicians and their spokesmen tend to lean backward a little too far in complaining that the adverse publicity is unfair and that the whole profession is being denigrated because of the actions of "a very small minority."

It is not a very small minority. Of the 23 individuals listed as winners in a recent *Down Beat* poll, at least nine were known narcotics users, five of them with a record of arrest and conviction. The proportion is even greater among proponents of certain types of jazz, notably "hard bop," whose principal soloists include an alarmingly high percentage with police records as heroin addicts. Heroin not only hastened the death of Billie Holiday, Charlie Parker, Fats Navarro and many other first-rank artists; it has also resulted in the jailing of so many musicians that the federal hospital-prison at Lexington, Kentucky, has been able to produce its own all star addict orchestra under the direction of Tadd Dameron, a respected composer-arranger serving a long sentence there.

To argue that our antiquated narcotics laws are to blame for this situation is to confuse cause and effect. Certainly it would make more sense, for example, to spend a fortune in government funds to crush the Mafia's power in the U.S., and thus eliminate the heroin traffic entirely, than to squander money endlessly treating as criminals the weak-willed addicts, who, after serving their sentence, are likely than not to return again to their habit. However, to understand the problem more completely, we must first attempt to inspect the original reasons for use.

In their climb up the social ladder during the jazz upsurge of the 1950s, jazzmen were thrown into close contact with millionaire art patrons, jazz-inclined clergymen and debutantes, and innumerable other groups to whom they had never been exposed. These contacts in many instances were natural and successful, but the background of the musicians on occasion created a gulf that could not be crossed. The social environment of the musician has made him peculiarly vulnerable; years of confinement to smoky night clubs, surrounded by liquor, often by racketeer-backed club owners and underworld fringe elements, inevitably made the excessive use of liquor, and the contact with narcotics, too easy and too tempting. It is not until the social forces that brought the musician to this stage can be erased that there will be any completely unselfconscious social mixing of all jazzmen with groups outside their own private world.

The reasons for the prevalence of narcotics in any area are complex. In a study by Gary Kramer in *The Jazz Word* (Ballantine Books) it was pointed out that "certain oppressive features of life in slum neighborhoods . . . weigh heavily on a significantly large number of individuals living there. When the pressures become unbearable, these individuals become vulnerable to drug use and/or the associated pathologies of street corner society, all of which stimulate and promote one another: prostitution, sexual irregularities, gambling, rackets, gang warfare, anti-authority behavior, etc."

As Kramer and many other writers explain, the constant frustrations in the daily life of the American Negro make him unusually susceptible; it is not surprising that the crime and narcotics rates are appallingly high in Negro neighborhoods. It may be that narcotics found their way into jazz as an indirect consequence of poverty and discrimination. However, the answer is not quite that simple. One finds on the police blotters the names of musicians (many of them white) from middle class families, who have had little or no major frustration to contend with. Moreover, non-musicians with the same social background have not turned to narcotics. Clearly it is too pat an explanation to ascribe the presence of dope-peddlers around the jazz clubs, and the brisk business they do, purely to racial or economic factors.

Kramer emphasizes one possible answer: "It seldom happens that one begins using drugs on one's own initiative. It is usually done at the urging of someone you love or respect." Indeed, it seems fundamental that as long as there are individuals whose will power is weak and whose desire for the feeling of belonging to an exclusive "in-group" is strong, there will be willing customers for narcotics, willing teen-age musicians ready to do what their idol does. They may have heard from his own lips a denial that there is any relationship between his artistry and his habits, but they feel they will continue to be outsiders until they have tried, "just one time for kicks," what their favorite musician once tried under the same circumstances and is now obliged to try several times a day. (The "just one time," of course, can lead in short order to a helpless dependence on the drug.)

So we find among the users not only psychopathological subjects and social misfits, but youngsters who, had they not been brought into contact with narcotics by the chance of their association with jazz, would have gone on to lead perfectly normal lives. When Miles Davis was arrested on a narcotics charge some years ago this came as a complete shock even to those who thought they knew him well. The son of a well-to-do family, whose father had sent him from the Middle West to study at Juilliard, Davis for years was considered one of the finest examples of a modern jazzman whose private life was exemplary, who did not even smoke or drink. Even if the charges were true, propinquity, not Davis, would have been the villain. In the 1940s the prevalence, availability and fad status of narcotics in some jazz circles constituted as clear and present a danger as the desire of many musicians to introduce neophytes to it.

To an easily-led youngster during the first years of the bop movement heroin was no more avoidable than measles. The same could have been said in the 1930s of marijuana, and before that of Prohibition liquor. The difference, of course, is that while bathtub gin and reefers can come to dominate one's life to the point of psychological dependence, there is no actual physical addiction. But heroin makes such abject slaves of its users that everything in their lives is focussed on the means of obtaining it; everything else, including music and sex, become trivial; it is the great destroyer of jazz. Withdrawal, of course, involves unspeakable physical agony. Marijuana's greatest danger lies in the probability that its users, once they have developed a tolerance, will look for bigger and better kicks. A high proportion of heroin addicts started as marijuana smokers. A case can be made out against marijuana on this basis, and on the grounds that "pot," though not as dangerous as heroin, can turn a man into a nervous wreck. (But so can liquor, cigarettes or coffee.) Moreover, like heroin, marijuana has been shown in scientific tests to lack the power to improve coördination. Contrary to what they believe when they are under the influence of either marijuana or heroin, and contrary to the picturesque beliefs of some of the public, narcotics users do not play as well when they are "high." Charlie Parker, one of the few jazzmen ever willing to admit this, once told me: "I never play better than when I am cold sober."

A serious effect of the use of drugs, quite apart from the medical, is its creation of a sub-society in which all the users are "hip" and the rest of the world is "square." Heroin addicts tend to hire or recommend one another for jobs, so that a leader who hires one junky may soon find himself with a whole band of them. For the addict, the presence of a fellow-user not only brings a mental communion but ensures the presence at all times of a ready supply of dope. The addict can conceal his habit convincingly, and usually becomes a skilled liar. One famous jazzman a few years ago looked at me intently and said: "Thank God I kicked the habit. I would never want my son to say his father was a junky." It was obvious that he was full of heroin when he made the statement (those of us who have been around junkies are not so easily lied to); since that time he has been through the pathetic cycle of cure and readdiction that will surely mark whatever years are left for him.

Once involved with heroin, the user can never again be psychologically free. Even if he avoids heroin itself he will find refuge in heavy use of marijuana or other escapes, from alcohol to pep pills. The percentage of real, lifelong cures, when one rules out these other stimulants, is infinitesimal.

The damage that was done in the early days will take many years to undo. Jazz today is enjoying economic and artistic success without precedent in its history; simultaneously the opportunities for the Negro musician, despite the persistence of ugly conditions such as those outlined earlier, are better than ever before and are continuing to improve. If the seed had not been planted long ago when it could grow so readily in jazz soil, the evil of narcotics would not be an apparently necessary crutch in our present social scheme. No longer does the worthy jazzman have to complain of public apathy, of back-door treatment, of having to work in a "square" band because of the shortage of better jobs. Heroin and marijuana are still with us in jazz for two closely related reasons. First, because jazz to some degree still operates near some of the fringes of the underworld where narcotics are easily available. The book *Brotherhood of Evil* by Frederic Sondern Jr. shows in searing detail the power of the Mafia in controlling and perpetuating the drug traffic. Second, because the presence of and easy access to narcotics many years ago has implanted the problem in the social structure of jazz much like a contagious disease, one that it will take many years to eradicate. It is a little naive to assume, as some observers have, that by making heroin legally available at low cost to certified addicts, as in England, we could wipe out the evil overnight. By now our proportion of addicts is so high that the plan might not even prove practicable; in any case, it might take a full generation before the medical profession by this method could, through the tapering-off process, effect any drastic permanent reduction in the addiction rates. Narcotics originally assumed their hold on jazzmen as a group because of the need to escape from social and racial pressures, from the unbearable realities of artistic oppression; ironically, now that these pressures are abating, it is from the narcotics themselves that the musician often tries desperately to escape.

Certainly it is necessary to create new hospitals, to revise our laws and to treat the addict as a sick person in every sense. These moves, however, deal with effects and not with causes, overlooking the responsibility of the addict himself, who did not "catch" the dope habit as one catches influenza but stuck the needle in his own arm. None of the clinics and panel discussions can ever change this. But until the causes of narcotics addiction have been destroyed at the source, jazz will continue to be faced with a brutal and ineradicable hazard in its search for acceptance on every level of our society.

While the role of jazz on the American social scene inevitably has been intermingled with the problems of Jim Crow and narcotics addiction, in recent years it has been associated no less directly in the public mind with the so-called "beat generation." If very little space is devoted here to this topic, the reason should be obvious: jazz and the beat generation are a hundred coffee-houses apart. Because Jack Kerouac happened among other eccentricities to develop a confused and well-intentioned affection for jazz, his followers have taken the same position. With very rare exceptions jazzmen are not "beat"; their renunciation of society's conventions has a largely different set of ground rules. Although it has become fashionable for the beat to hang around a couple of jazz clubs in New York and San Francisco, the musicians have little in common with them and their mores. The level of understanding of jazz of the pseudo-hip may be measured by that of their leader, who in *On The Road* held up the jive-talking figure of Slim Gaillard, a novelty singer and comedian, as an example of authentic American art.

Observations about jazzmen, like all generalizations, must be qualified. There is no "average" jazzman; today's musician ranges from the simple, unlettered folk artist (found most often among the survivors of the country blues element, and the older Dixieland musicians) to the most elegant, college-bred, classical-music-grounded intellectual. Politically he may be thoroughly informed and possibly will have developed a strong inclination to the left; or he may be so deeply absorbed in music that he has remained completely apolitical. (Unless he is one of the rare white musicians with an active anti-Negro prejudice or a highly successful status-seeking studio musician it is most unlikely that he will have any right wing tendencies. The number of pro-McCarthyites among leading jazzmen could have been counted, in the Senator's heyday, on the fingers of one thumb.)

In summing up the position of the jazzman in American society, it is important to bear in mind the pitfalls of generalizing. To pretend that most jazz musicians are just like the boy next door in Des Moines would be absurdly naive. As a man with an unusually deep need for self-expression, who has found his outlet through an art that is still in flux and has only lately found firm roots in its own native soil, he is certain to feel emotions and to evolve attitudes that may seem strange to many of his fellowmen. More often than not his sensitivity may erect a wall between him and the individual to whom the music is not much more than pleasant entertainment. It may be because of his unusual feeling toward an art form, and perhaps toward life and society, that he leaves home to go on the road with a band. This does not preclude the possibility that he may later seek the normal social patterns of everyday life and even a respectable suburban existence.

Today this seems to be the trend among the financially successful New York and Hollywood jazzmen, scores of whom have bought comfortable middle-class homes on Long Island or in New Jersey, and in the outlying Los Angeles areas. Where his social life once was restricted to his immediate peers, today he may rub elbows with royalty and the prominent Americans who lionize him at the jazz festivals. He may move into a circle of intellectuals who read (or write for) *The Saturday Review*, or a clique of Madison Avenue advertising agency executives, or into a number of other social avenues that were long unknown or closed to him. Whatever his race or color, he has a chance to enjoy a richer social life than did his father, the Dixieland trombonist in the cellar club, or his grandfather, the ragtime pianist in the red light district. In short, after waiting at the back door of American life for more than a half-century, the jazz musician finally is gaining admittance—having first found his way to the main entrance.

Giants of jazz

The following list is a reference guide to the most important names in jazz. Selected after consultation with numerous musicians, the list names artists who were considered worthy of inclusion not only in terms of artistic accomplishment but also on the basis of their influence on other performers. In several instances there may be some dispute about the esthetic contribution of a musician named, but in no case can there be any question concerning his impact and influence.

Each list was limited to twelve names. The list was shorter in several instances when it was found that fewer artists have made a contribution of sufficiently far-reaching significance.

Although the periods of maximum influence overlapped frequently, an attempt has been made to list the names approximately in chronological order of their greatest era of influence.

The period covered runs from the birth of jazz to 1955. In the case of musicians who had risen to prominence since 1955 it was impossible to judge their ultimate importance in correct perspective. Taken into account in all listings was the greatly accelerated flow of influence after 1920 through the communications media of phonograph and radio.

TRUMPET

King Oliver
Louis Armstrong
Bubber Miley
Bix Beiderbecke
Cootie Williams
Roy Eldridge
Charlie Shavers
Dizzy Gillespie
Miles Davis

TROMBONE

Kid Ory
George Brunis
Miff Mole
Tommy Dorsey
Jimmy Harrison
Jack Teagarden
J. C. Higginbotham
Trummy Young
Bill Harris
J. J. Johnson

ALTO SAXOPHONE

Benny Carter
Johnny Hodges
Paul Desmond
Charlie Parker
Lee Konitz

TENOR SAXOPHONE

Coleman Hawkins
Bud Freeman
Lester Young
Illinois Jacquet
Stan Getz
Sonny Rollins

BARITONE SAXOPHONE

Harry Carney
Gerry Mulligan

CLARINET

Alphonse Picou
Leon Rappolo
Johnny Dodds
Jimmie Noone
Frank Teschemacher
Pee Wee Russell
Barney Bigard
Benny Goodman
Artie Shaw
Buddy De Franco

PIANO

James P. Johnson
*Jelly Roll Morton
Earl Hines
Fats Waller
Pinetop Smith
Art Tatum
Teddy Wilson
Count Basie
Erroll Garner
Bud Powell
*Thelonious Monk
Horace Silver

*Mainly influential as composer.

GUITAR

Johnny St. Cyr
Lonnie Johnson
Eddie Lang
Django Reinhardt
Al Casey
Charlie Christian
Billy Bauer
Barney Kessel

DRUMS

Baby Dodds
Gene Krupa
Dave Tough
Chick Webb
Sid Catlett
Cozy Cole
Jo Jones
Buddy Rich
Kenny Clarke
Max Roach
Art Blakey
Shelly Manne

BASS

Pops Foster
John Kirby
Jimmy Blanton
*Charles Mingus
Oscar Pettiford
Eddie Safranski
Ray Brown

VIBRAPHONE

Lionel Hampton
Red Norvo
Milt Jackson
Terry Gibbs

MALE SINGERS

Blind Lemon Jefferson
Leadbelly
Louis Armstrong
Jack Teagarden
Fats Waller
Joe Turner
Jimmy Rushing
Nat King Cole

FEMALE SINGERS

Bessie Smith
Billie Holiday
Ella Fitzgerald
Dinah Washington
Mildred Bailey
Anita O'Day
Sarah Vaughan

VIOLIN

Joe Venuti
Ray Nance
Stuff Smith

COMPOSER-ARRANGERS

Don Redman
Fletcher Henderson
Duke Ellington
Benny Carter
Glenn Miller
Eddie Sauter
Billy Strayhorn
Sy Oliver
Tadd Dameron
Ralph Burns
Pete Rugolo
Gil Evans

*Mainly influential as composer.

BIG BANDS

Fletcher Henderson
Duke Ellington
McKinney's Cotton Pickers
Glen Gray (Casa Loma)
Benny Goodman
Jimmie Lunceford
Bob Crosby
Count Basie
Woody Herman
Stan Kenton

SMALL COMBOS

King Oliver
Original Dixieland Band
New Orleans Rhythm Kings
Louis Armstrong
Red Nichols
Benny Goodman
John Kirby
Nat King Cole
George Shearing
Lennie Tristano
Dave Brubeck
*John Lewis (Modern Jazz Quartet)

MISCELLANEOUS

Sidney Bechet (soprano saxophone)
Chano Pozo (Afro-Cuban percussion)
Adrian Rollini (bass saxophone)

The votes of ten leading jazz critics, along with that of the author, produced the following list in answer to the question: "Judging your selections in terms of artistic achievement and overall influence on the course of jazz, who in your opinion have been the five most important figures in the history of jazz to date?"

DUKE ELLINGTON

LOUIS ARMSTRONG

CHARLIE PARKER

LESTER YOUNG

COUNT BASIE

Duke Ellington was the only figure named by every voter. All but one named Louis Armstrong and all but two nominated Charlie Parker.

Introduction to biographies

The first edition of *The Encyclopedia of Jazz* contained over a thousand biographies; the *New Encyclopedia of Jazz* has more than two thousand. Obviously this does not mean that the number of important jazz musicians has doubled in five years. As I pointed out in the original edition, it might be claimed that only six or seven hundred of the original thousand had made any deeply significant contribution to jazz history. The reasons for the greatly increased number of references are several: the addition of numerous early jazz figures (including early blues singers) on whom information was previously unavailable; the inclusion of many important foreign musicians; the accelerating rate of the emergence of new names due to the enormous increase in the output of LP records; and, most important, the desire to make this the most valuable and comprehensive work of its kind.

As before, I found it extremely difficult at times to draw the thin, vague lines that separate jazz from popular music, from folk music, from rhythm-and-blues or rock-and-roll, from Latin-American music, from classical, concert, chamber music—not only are the definitions hard to determine, but the cross-breeding between forms has become such a common occurrence in recent years that no two experts, given the task of assembling a list of nominees for inclusion, would be likely to overlap in more than 75% of their suggestions. Again, though, it can be claimed that no lastingly important artist of any jazz school who had made his mark by presstime has been omitted.

Once again there will be found brief mention of some popular dance bandleaders whose connection with jazz is tangential and sporadic. Again the selection among popular singers was often arbitrary. Because of the almost limitless confusion in the definition of a jazz singer, only those vocal performers were included whose associations, either by sheer chance or through the attention of a particular critic, had brought them into the jazz orbit, nominally if not musically.

Among the rock 'n' roll artists the vocal quartets and ballad singers were completely ignored; a number of the solo vocalists and instrumentalists were included. Because of their intermittent association with jazz, Perez Prado and several other figures in the field of Latin-American and Afro-Cuban music are also listed.

As for those whose place was unquestionably in the jazz area, the biographies attempted to answer the following questions: (1) what was this artist's background, (2) what have been his most important associations, (3) on what long playing records can he be heard. In the case of the more important artists, a brief delineation of the nature or quality of his work, either in my own view or in that of other critics, was also included.

The listing of poll victories requires a little amplification here. The fact that a musician at one time was acclaimed a winner in a *Down Beat, Metronome, Playboy, Esquire* or *Record Changer* poll does not necessarily give any indication of relative artistic importance. These listings are included solely for the record, as a matter of historic interest.

The annual *Down Beat* polls began in 1936, with only ten categories; these were gradually increased with the addition of such divisions as Small Combo, Vocal Group, Miscellaneous Instrument, Vibes, etc., until by 1955 there were twenty-two categories. From 1940 to 1949 bandleaders were ineligible for votes in the various instrumental categories; thus in 1941, though Benny Goodman and Coleman Hawkins were still tremendously popular, they could not compete in the clarinet and tenor sax departments because they happened to be bandleaders at the time. *Down Beat* instituted a second poll, starting in 1953, conducted not among its readers but among a selected group of some twenty critics.

The *Metronome* polls began in 1937 and were originally designed to build an imaginary All Star Band: thus some early winners were selected for their ability to lead a reed or brass section, or sit obscurely in a fourth saxophone chair, rather than for their talent as jazzmen. *Metronome* has had no band or combo divisions except from 1945-9 and since 1953.

The *Playboy* poll, by far the biggest in terms of votes cast, has appeared annually since 1957. It represents the opinions of many thousands of the magazine's readers.

The four *Esquire* polls did not involve the readers. A board of experts selected Gold and Silver Award winners in 1944; Gold, Silver and New Star Award winners in '45. In '46 and '47 the New Star voting was placed in the hands of a board of musicians, including winners of the previous polls.

The Record Changer ran only one poll: an "All Time, All Star" readers' ballot in 1951.

In many of the biographies in the following pages, the musicians' own favorite performers on their own instrument have been listed wherever possible; in the case of composers their preferred composer has been named. This was done not only to give some idea of the artists' own musical tastes, but also to reflect in some measure their personal place in the jazz scene; for it stands to reason that if a trumpet player lists, say, Miles Davis as his favorite, he himself is not likely to sound like Roy Eldridge; conversely, if an arranger names Sy Oliver as his idol, it is improbable that his own writing will reflect the influence of a modernist such as Gil Evans.

Because of the chaotic state of the recording industry, in which the flood of new releases has coincided with the regrettable withdrawal from circulation of many previously available items, I have not attempted the impossible task of listing each musician's complete discography, which would become out of date by publication time. In the case of major figures whose LPs seem likely to remain on the market for some time, I have listed the catalogue numbers of most of their LPs. For all other musicians I have simply listed a few representative samples. In the cases of a few musicians overseas whose records were not available in the US at presstime, foreign labels have been listed.

During the 1950s a number of records or excerpts from early jazz performances were reissued on various labels, here and abroad. A main reason was the negligence of the major companies, to whom the masters belonged, in failing to make this material available on their own labels. Although they include many works by artists who have little or no representation elsewhere, no mention has been made of them in the biographies, nor in the chapter on recommended records; first, because they were pirated from the products of other companies and therefore could not be pressed from the masters, the result being inferior sound quality; second, because they were used in this manner without the artists' knowledge or consent. To draw attention to them would encourage a policy that has long been subject to criticism; moreover, fortunately, Columbia is now making much of the same material available on its own label and other companies to whom the performances belong are expected to follow suit.

In 1956, in announcing the results of its annual poll, *Down Beat* stated: "Writing for jazz groups has gone too far beyond simply arranging tunes or simple riffs for bands . . . thus the category formerly called arranger was this year changed to composer."

The author shares this view. Any jazz arranger is, *ipso facto*, a composer. Therefore *The New Encyclopedia of Jazz* has adopted this policy: artists who were listed in *The Encyclopedia of Jazz* as arrangers are now credited as composers. In the case of those who do not orchestrate or are not composers in the generally accepted jazz sense the word "songwriter" is used.

The phrase "Fav. own rec." (used because "Own fav. rec." might be slightly ambiguous) refers to the artist's own selection of an outstanding performance among his or her own recordings.

To the traveling jazzman, the inability to plant deep roots is an occupational hazard; consequently the artists' addresses have only been included where there seemed to be a reasonable degree or likelihood of permanence.

The long biographies are of course all concerned with major figures; minor artists are treated briefly. However, there is no attempt at consistency between these two extremes. The brevity or length of a musician's biography cannot always be construed as a measure of his importance.

Many of the biographies have been considerably extended to cover important events in the artists' lives since the first editions appeared, or to amplify or correct items chronicled earlier, in which inevitably there were some errors of omission and commission. However, none of the biographies has been significantly shortened, so it can be stated with assurance that the reader will find in this section virtually everything that appeared in the original *Encyclopedia of Jazz* along with a great volume of new material.

Finally, a word of explanation is required on the alphabetical arrangement which has been designed to facilitate reference. The artist's name, last name followed by first, is printed in bold capital letters, after which his nickname, or the name by which he is most commonly known, appears in parentheses. Where the artist has changed his name completely, the name by which he is now known appears first, in alphabetical order, and his earlier name in parentheses. In several cases, the listings would seem to be out of alphabetical order in that an "Alfred" may appear after a "Charles." In such cases, the artists are best-known by their nicknames, "Red," "Duke," etc., and their listings are inserted where they will be most easily found.

Abbreviations

ABC *American Broadcasting Co.*
ABC-Par. *ABC-Paramount Records*
acc. *accompanied, accompanying, accompanist*
addr. *address*
AFM *American Federation of Musicians*
Alad. *Aladdin*
All. *Allegro*
Amer. Mus. *American Music*
Ap. *Apollo*
app. *appeared, appearing*
A & R *artists and repertoire*
arr. *arranged, arranger, arrangement*
ASCAP *American Society of Composers, Authors and Publishers*
Atl. *Atlantic*
Audio. *Audiophile*
Aud. Fid. *Audio Fidelity*
b. *born*
Bat. *Baton*
BBC *British Broadcasting Corporation*
Beth. *Bethlehem*
BN *Blue Note*
bro. *brother*
Bruns. *Brunswick*
ca. *about*
Cad. *Cadence*
Cam. *Camden*
Carn. *Carnival*
Cap. *Capitol*
Cav. *Cavalier*
CBS *Columbia Broadcasting System*
cl., clar. *clarinet*
Classic Edit. *Classic Editions*
Col. *Columbia*
coll. *college*
Comm. *Commodore*
comp. *composed, composer, compositions*
cons. *conservatory*
cont. *continued*
Contemp. *Contemporary*
Cor. *Coral*
Ctpt. *Counterpoint*
Crit. *Criterion*
d. *died*
Deb. *Debut*
Dec. *Decca*
Del. *Delmar*
Des. *Design*
dj *disc jockey*
Dix. Jub. *Dixieland Jubilee*
Doo. *Dooto*
educ. *education, educated*
Elek. *Elektra*
Em. *EmArcy*
Empir. *Empirical*
Eso. *Esoteric*
Evst. *Everest*
Fant. *Fantasy*
fav., favs. *favorite, favorites*
feat. *featured, featuring*
Fels. *Felsted*
Folk. *Folkways*
GNP *Gene Norman Presents*
Gold. Cr. *Golden Crest*
Harm. *Harmony*
Imp. *Imperial*
imp. *important*
incl. *includes, including, included*
JATP *Jazz at the Philharmonic*
Jub. *Jubilee*
KC *Kansas City, Missouri*
LA *Los Angeles, California*
Lib. *Liberty*
Lond. *London*

LPs *Long-playing records at 33 1/3 revolutions per minute*
MCA *Music Corporation of America*
Merc. *Mercury*
MJQ *Modern Jazz Quartet*
Mod. *Modern*
mos. *months*
Mot. *Motif*
mus. dir. *musical director*
NBC *National Broadcasting Company*
NJF *Newport Jazz Festival*
NO *New Orleans, Louisiana*
NYC *New York City*
orch. *orchestra*
Per. *Period*
Phil. *Philharmonic*
pl. *played, plays, playing*
Pres. *Prestige*
quart. *quartet*
quint. *quintet*
Rain. *Rainbow*
r & b *rhythm and blues*
rec. *recorded, recordings*
Reg. *Regent*
Rep. *Replica*
repl. *replaced, replacing*
ret. *returned, returning*
River. *Riverside*
Rondo. *Rondolette*
Roul. *Roulette*
Sav. *Savoy*
sch. *school*
SF *San Francisco, California*
SFJ *San Francisco Jazz*
Sig. *Signal*
Som. *Somerset*
South. *Southland*
Spec. *Specialty*
st. *started*
Star. *Starlite*
Stcft. *Stere-o-craft*
Stin. *Stinson*
Story. *Storyville*
stud. *studied, studying*
symph. *symphony*
Trans. *Transition*
tpt. *trumpet*
trom. *trombone*
UA *United Artists*
U., Univ. *University*
Ur. *Urania*
Vang. *Vanguard*
Vict. *Victor*
vln. *violin*
War. Bros. *Warner Brothers*
w. *with*
West. *Westminster*
Wor. Pac. *World-Pacific*
WW *World Wide*
yrs. *years*

Biographies

A

AARON, ALVIN (Abe), *baritone & tenor sax* (also *misc. woodwinds*), b. Toronto, Ont., 1/27/10. Stud. clarinet, soprano sax w. father, a concert bandleader, in Milwaukee. Pl. w. theatre band in Milwaukee, 1930-42; lead alto w. Jack Teagarden's big band, '42. Moved to Hollywood, 1943, did radio work w. Horace Heidt, 1944; Skinnay Ennis, '45-7. Lead alto & jazz clar. w. Horace Heidt, '48-9, then spent ten years w. Les Brown, touring Far East in 1950, England and Continent in '51. Many LPs w. Brown (Coral, Capitol); jazz date w. Billy Usselton, playing bass clarinet (Kapp); LP of Bechet comps. w. Brown (Cap.).

Addr: 19338 Lorne St., Reseda, Cal.

ABDUL-MALIK, AHMED, *bass;* also *oud* & other Oriental instruments; b. Brooklyn, N.Y., 1/30/27. Began stud. violin at seven at Vardi's Cons., then joined a group during junior high school and pl. for Greek, Syrian and Gypsy weddings. Father was from Sudan; used to sing and play Oriental music. Grad. from High School of Music and Performing Arts, pl. w. All City High School Symphony Orch. Worked w. Art Blakey 1945 and 1948; Don Byas in '46; Sam Taylor '54; Randy Weston '57; Thelonious Monk '57-8; various groups which pl. Oriental music from '56-8. Presented program of Oriental music at Nonagon Art Gallery, NYC in '57; app. on Dave Garroway show April '58. Own LP: *Jazz Sahara* (River.); LPs w. Randy Weston (Dawn, River.), Jutta Hipp (Blue Note), Th. Monk (River.).

Addr: 749 Lafayette Ave., Brooklyn, N.Y.

ABNEY, JOHN DONALD (Don), *piano;* b. Baltimore, Md., 3/10/23. Studied privately in Baltimore, later at Manhattan Sch. of Mus. in NYC. Pl. French horn in Army band. Prof. debut w. Bubby Johnson band in Baltimore. Joined Eddie Gibbs trio at Village Vanguard, NYC, 1947; Snub Mosely band, '48; Wilbur De Paris, '48-9. After working as a single at Sherry Netherland Hotel, 1950-1, he became accompanist for the Billy Williams Quartet. Also worked w. Bill Harris-Kai Winding combo, '51; Chuck Wayne, '52, Sy Oliver band, Louie Bellson group, and accompanied Thelma Carpenter. Toured with Ella Fitzgerald as her accompanist and as part of JATP unit, 1945-5. Left Ella fall '57 to free-lance in NYC. Acc. Carmen McRae, '59. Capable modern stylist and excellent accompanist. Favs: Cole, Tatum, Larkins. LPs w. Benny Carter (Verve), Louie Bellson (Verve), Marilyn Moore (Beth.), Oscar Pettiford (Beth.).

Addr: 66 Chase St., Hempstead, L.I., N.Y.

ABRAMS, LEE (Leon Abramson), *drums;* b. New York City, 1/6/25. Raised in Brooklyn. Army 1943-6, then a year with Roy Eldridge; various 52nd Street jobs with Coleman Hawkins, J. J. Johnson, Eddie Davis et al. With Andy Kirk orch. and Eddie Heywood trio, 1948. Toured w. Hot Lips Page, then back w. Heywood; Illinois Jacquet, late '51-early '52; Lester Young to '53, then free-lanced in NYC. LPs w. Al Haig (Eso.), Wynton Kelly (Blue Note); *The Birdlanders* (Per.).

ABRAMS, RAY (Raymond Abramson), *tenor sax;* b. New York City, 1/23/20. Brother of Lee Abrams. Studied with father, who played violin, clarinet; local jobs with Brooklyn combos, then worked for Clark Monroe at latter's Uptown House (with Ch. Parker, who had just arrived in New York) and 78th St. Taproom in early '40s. Played in Dizzy Gillespie's first big band, 1946; toured Europe w. Don Redman, '46. With Andy Kirk, '47-8; back w. Gillespie, '49; toured w. Hot Lips Page, '49, then various small combos incl. Roy Eldridge, Slim Gaillard, Bill Harris, Paul Gayten r & b group, etc. LPs w. Clarke (Vict.), Gillespie (Rondo.); *Hot vs. Cool* (MGM).

ACE, JOHNNY (John M. Alexander, Jr.), *singer;* b. Memphis, Tenn., 1932; d. Houston, Tex., 12/25/54. Father was a minister; had fast rise to fame w. rhythm & blues hits, incl. *My Song* in 1952. Died playing Russian roulette after Houston concert.

ACEA, JOHN ADRIANO, *piano;* b. Philadelphia, Pa., 10/11/17. Free-lanced from late '30s as trumpeter w. Jimmy Gorham, Sammy Price, tenor sax w. Don Bagley, also worked often as pianist. Army 1944-6; to NYC '47, pl. at Minton's w. Lockjaw Davis; w. Dizzy Gillespie big band 1950, then a year w. Illinois Jacquet, a year acc. Dinah Washington. After working w. Cootie Williams, rejoined Jacquet June '53, toured Europe with him Oct. '54. Later free-lanced around NYC. Comp. *Little Jeff* (rec. w. Jacquet). Favs: Tatum, Powell. LPs w. Joe Newman (Vang.), Jacquet (Verve).

Addr: 75 Lasalle Street, New York City, N.Y.

ADAMS, PARK (Pepper), *baritone, tenor, alto sax, clarinet;* b. Highland Park, Ill., 10/8/30. Raised in Rochester, N.Y. Began gigging there on tenor and clar. In Detroit, switched to bari. and in 1947 was working in Lucky Thompson's band w. Tommy Flanagan for two months. Then gigs in Detroit while he worked in auto plants. Into Army and to Korea, 1951-53, w. some playing in Spec. Serv. shows. Back to Detroit w. James Richardson at the Bluebird working w. visiting stars for two years, then w. Kenny Burrell's group. Came to NYC Jan. '56; w. Stan Kenton briefly that year; later w. Maynard Ferguson, then w. Chet Baker. Gigs and studio work on West Coast. Won new star award in *Down Beat* Critics' Poll, '57; ret. to NYC early '58. W. Benny Goodman, fall '58, spring '59. Local gigs, incl. stay at Five Spot w. own group feat. Donald Byrd, '58; co-led group at same club w. Byrd, '59. "The only new baritone saxophonist with any real class."—Ralph Gleason. Favs: C. Hawkins, Chu Berry, Harry Carney, and Detroit pianist Barry Harris. Own LPs: on Interlude; *Pepper-Knepper Quintet* (Metrojazz), *10 to 4 At The Five Spot* (River.), *Critics' Choice* (Wor. Pac.); LPs w. Q. Jones (ABC-Par.), Lee Morgan (Blue Note), L. Vinnegar (Contemp.), Gene Ammons, Jerry Valentine (Pres.), *Roots* (New Jazz), A. K. Salim (Savoy), Chet Baker, Thelonious Monk, J. Thielemans (River.), Shorty Rogers (Vict.), Benny Goodman (Col.), *The Soul of Jazz* (WW), The Mitchells (Metrojazz).

Addr: 314 E. 6th St., New York 3, N.Y.

ADDERLEY, JULIAN EDWIN (Cannonball), *alto sax* (also *tenor, trumpet, clarinet, flute*); b. Tampa, Fla., 9/15/28. Father a jazz cornetist; whole family musical. Studied brass and reed instruments at high school in Tallahassee 1944-8, forming first jazz group with band director Leander Kirksey as advisor. From 1948-56 Adderley was band director at Dillard High School in Ft. Lauderdale, Fla. During this time he also had his own jazz group in south Florida 1948-50. Serving in the Army '50-2, he became leader of the 36th Army Dance Band. In '52 he had his own combo in Washington, D.C., where he was studying at the U.S. Naval School of Music; later he led another Army band at Ft. Knox, '52-3. The nickname Cannonball evolved from "Cannibal," a name given by high school colleagues in tribute to his vast eating capacity. "Cannonball" first attracted attention when he sat in with Oscar Pettiford at the Bohemia, NYC in the summer of '55. Shortly after, he signed with EmArcy records. In the spring of '56, he and his brother Nat (see below) started touring with their own combo which broke up in late '57. Then joined and remained w. Miles Davis until Aug. '59 when he toured with George Shearing's big band as featured soloist. In Oct. reformed own group w. brother.

Cannonball, who names Charlie Parker and Benny Carter as his favorites, sounds like a twin of the former on faster tempi and reflects, at least tonally, the influence of the latter on slow ballads. He feels his music is "an orderly chronological evolution" from bop. During his two years with Davis, his style underwent a change reflecting the influence of Davis and John Coltrane. Tied for new star w. Phil Woods in "Musicians' musicians" poll, *Enc. Yearbook '56;* new star award in DB critics' poll '59. Own LPs on Riverside, Mercury, Savoy, Blue Note; LPs w. Miles Davis (Col.), Dinah Washington, Sarah Vaughan (Merc.), Philly Joe Jones (River.), Paul Chambers (Vee-Jay).

Addr: 112-19 34th Ave., Corona 68, L.I., N.Y.

ADDERLEY, NATHANIEL (Nat), *cornet;* also *trumpet, mellophone, French horn;* b. Tampa, Fla., 11/25/31. Brother of Cannonball Adderley (q.v.). Started as child singer; when his voice began to change, took up trumpet, 1946, switched to cornet '50. His career roughly paralleled that of his brother, incl. service in 36th Army Band '51-3. He was in Lionel Hampton's band July '54-May '55, mainly in Europe and Israel. Toured with brother's combo '56-7, J. J. Johnson combo '57-8; mainly with Woody Herman in '59 (incl. tours of Britain, Saudi Arabia) before rejoining Cannonball in Oct. '59. Adderley states that his brother, who started as a trumpet player, gave him his early training, along with their father and band director Leander Kirksey. A rapidly developing modern soloist reflecting the influences of his favorites: Gillespie, Miles Davis and Clark Terry. Own LPs: River., Savoy, Em.; LPs w. Cannonball Adderley (Savoy, Merc., River.), J. J. Johnson (Col.), Sonny Rollins (Metrojazz), Tony Bennett (Col.), Philly Joe Jones (River.); Lionel Hampton (Em.).

Addr: 112-19 34th Avenue, Corona, L.I., N.Y.

ADDISON, BERNARD, *guitar;* b. Annapolis, Md., 4/15/05. Stud. privately in Washington, where he was schoolmate of Claude Hopkins. Early dates in Phila. w. Rex Stewart; to NYC w. Sonny Thompson, then five years at Smalls', as sideman then leader, in mid-'20s. Worked with Art Tatum, first in Milton Senior band, then acc. Adelaide Hall, 1930. Pl. w. Russell Wooding, Fats Waller, 1931-2; F. Henderson, '33-4; Adrian Rollini, '35; three years touring US and Europe as acc. for Mills Bros. Many recs. in 1930s w. James P. Johnson, B. Miley, Red Allen, C. Hawkins, Mezzrow, B. Holiday, and own date on Bluebird. After Army, USO tour w. Snub Mosley '45; later, much time in Canada, and in recent years on tour acc. Ink Spots. Now studying classical guitar. Was highly regarded rhythm guitarist in '30s. LP w. Eubie Blake (20th-Fox).

Addr: 161-26 128th Ave., Jamaica 34, L.I., N.Y.

ADLER, LARRY, *harmonica,* also *piano, composer;* b. Baltimore, Md., March 1914. App. in Ziegfeld's *Smiles* 1931, he soon became a national name and was seen in films; in one, *Many Happy Returns,* he was acc. by Duke Ellington orch. Scored big hit in London '35. After living in England through 1950s, returned home '59 and toured in clubs acc. by Ellis Larkins, also teamed with Dizzy Gillespie for TV etc. Specializes in classical and pop performances on harmonica and is exceptional technician; enjoys working with jazz musicians. Own LPs: Decca, Audio-Fidelity.

Addr: c/o Audio Fidelity Records, 770 Eleventh Ave., New York City.

AKIYOSHI, TOSHIKO, *piano, composer;* b. Dairen, Manchuria, 12/12/29. Stud. classical piano 1936-45; to Japan with family '46. Took up jazz '47, when she joined Yamada in Fukuoka. In Tokyo w. Mori orch., and Tokyo Jive Combo; Shin. Matsumoto and his combo, Blue Coats orch. '49; Victor All Stars and Six Lemons, '50. Own combo from Aug. '51. Oscar Peterson visiting Japan with N. Granz' JATP unit, heard her in Nov. '53; Granz promptly recorded her with Peterson's rhythm section. Toshiko broke up her combo Sept. '54, formed octet for radio and TV series. She won Japanese magazine awards as Japan's leading jazz pianist. In Jan. '56 she arrived in Boston, to study at the Berklee Sch. on a scholarship, also privately with Margaret Chaloff. As a protegee of Geo. Wein she appeared at his Storyville Club and at NJF as well as occasionally in NYC. While at Berklee '56-9 she had many of her compositions performed by the student and faculty orchestras. In November '59 she was married to Charlie Mariano.

Toshiko has developed a superlative mastery of the Bud Powell style. There is nothing delicately feminine in her work, which is fiery, powerfully articulated and exceptionally fluent. As a composer she has written and orchestrated *My Elegy* and *Silhouette,* both recorded in the Berklee School's own *Jazz in the Classroom* series, as well as many attractive original works on her own LPs.

Fav. pianists: Powell, Peterson, John Lewis. Fav. composers: Ralph Burns, John Lewis. Own LPs: Metrojazz, Storyville, Verve.

Addr: 403 Grand Ave., Leonia, N.J.

ALBAM, EMMANUEL (Manny), *composer;* b. Samana, Dominican Republic, 6/24/22. To NYC at age of six weeks. Stud. cl. at Stuyvesant High Sch. Prof. debut w. Don Joseph Quintet on alto, 1940. Later played (usually baritone sax) and wrote for many bands, incl. Muggsy Spanier, 1941; Bob Chester, '42; Geo. Auld, '42-5; Boyd Raeburn '43-5. After Army service, '45-6, pl. w. Herbie Fields, Bobby Sherwood; Sam Donahue in '47, Ch. Barnet '48-9. From 1950 he gave up playing to concentrate on writing and by 1955 was one of the busiest jazz arrangers in New York, scoring dozens of albums. A first-class modern writer with strong swing-era jazz roots, he has continued to study (w. Tibor Serly in '59-60) and is still expanding his already considerable scope. Influences and favs: Al Cohn, B. Brookmeyer, B. Holman, Q. Jones, Buster Harding, Tadd Dameron et al; Bach, Bartok, Stravinsky. Own LPs: Vict., Coral, Dot, Merc.; arrs. for Woody Herman, Stan Kenton (Cap.), Terry Gibbs (Em.) *Drum Suite* (Vict.); two tracks in *Something New, Something Blue* (Col.); Joe Viola (Berklee).

Addr: c/o Charlap, 244 West 48th St., New York 36, N.Y.

ALBANY, JOSEPH (Joe), *piano;* b. Atlantic City, N.J., 1924. Stud. accordion. Moved to Los Angeles, working there with Leo Watson 1941; was also in the Benny Carter band that included J. J. Johnson, Max Roach; in New York at the Pied Piper 1944 with Max Kaminsky, Rod Cless; rec. in '45 w. Geo. Auld; pl. w. Charlie Parker-Howard McGhee 1946; record date w. Lester Young '46; later free-lanced mainly in LA area. Was working in a small club in San Francisco 1960. Albany is something of a legend in modern jazz; he was evidently one of the first important bop pianists despite his never having been acknowledged by critics at the time of his emergence. According to Orrin Keepnews his sound is basically a funky, blues-oriented one, "momentarily suggestive of Thelonious Monk at times, but fundamentally Joe's own." Own LP: River.

ALCORN, ALVIN ELMORE, *trumpet;* b. New Orleans, La., 9/7/12. Worked w. A. J. Piron 1930-1 and '37; toured with Don Albert's band from Texas '32-7; Sidney Desvignes, '41-50, also briefly w. Tab Smith in mid-'40s. From '47 was active as decorator for real estate company; also pl. w. Papa Celestin, '51; Octave Crosby, '51-4; Kid Ory, '54-6, touring Europe with him in '56. Also worked with Bill Mathews in Las Vegas, '55. College concert tour sponsored by Rev. Alvin Kershaw, '56; sound track for *Benny Goodman Story* w. Ory. Dates with Geo. Lewis, '58; Bill Mathews, Paul Barbarin, '59. Favs: Armstrong, Red Allen, Benny Carter. LPs w. Raymond Burke, Jack Delaney (South.), Ory (GTJ), O. Crosby (Jazz Man), Geo. Lewis (Verve).

Addr: 1606 General Ogden Street, New Orleans 18, La.

ALESS, TONY (Anthony Alessandrini), *piano;* b. Garfield, N.J., 8/22/21. Gigged with Bunny Berigan at 17, later w. Johnny McGhee, Teddy Powell, Vaughn Monroe '40-2, Army to '44, briefly w. Charlie Spivak, then replaced Ralph Burns in Woody Herman's band '45. Left '46, taught three years at New York Conservatory, then into radio work; was a year on staff at WNEW, replaced Elliot Lawrence on daily CBS Jack Sterling show, Feb. '54. Still working as a radio staff musician in NYC. Own LP, *Long Island Suite* (Roost); LPs w. Seldon Powell (Roost), Stan Getz (New Jazz), Woody Herman (MGM, Harmony).

Addr: 31-20 69th St., Jackson Heights 77, N.Y.

ALEXANDER, ROBERT (Bob), *trombone;* b. Roxbury, Mass., 11/23/20. Originally inspired by Tommy Dorsey. Stud. in high school in Portland, Me., 1936. Joined Fenton Bros. orch., '40; Joe Marsala and commercial dance bands in New York, '41-2, Coast Guard, '42-5, then joined Jimmy Dorsey. After 5 months w. Eddy Duchin in '49, took up free-lance studio work in NYC. Favs: Kai Winding, Bill Harris, Tommy Dorsey. LP: *Progressive Jazz* (Grand Award).
Addr: 82 Hazelton Terrace, Tenafly, N.J.

ALEXANDER, ELMER (Mousie), *drums;* b. Gary, Ind., 6/29/22. Father played violin. Stud. in Chicago at Ray Knapp School 1948, in NYC w. Sam Ulano. Played w. J. McPartland '48-50, Marion McPartland '52-3, Sauter-Finegan '53-5, Johnny Smith '55-Feb. '56, Benny Goodman to early '57 incl. Far East tour; Bud Freeman Trio at Condon's '58; joined Condon's own group June '59. Favs: Buddy Rich, the late Joe Timer. LPs w. Johnny Smith (Roost), Geo. Romanis (Decca), B. Goodman (Col.), Bud Freeman (Dot), Sauter-Finegan (Victor), M. McPartland (Savoy).
Addr: 111 Elm Drive, Levittown, L.I., N.Y.

ALEXANDER, VAN, *composer, piano;* b. New York City, 5/2/15. Mother was a concert pianist who played on NBC in the early days of radio. Studied orchestration and comp. w. Otto Cesana. First prof. arr. *Keepin' Out of Mischief* for Chick Webb 1936. Wrote arr. of *A-Tisket, A-Tasket* for Ella Fitzgerald '38, then started own orch. which stayed together until '43, playing theaters like the Paramount, State and Capitol in NYC. Moved to California where he has been active in TV and movies conducting and writing. TV: Mickey Rooney '54, Gordon McRae '55, Lux Spectacular '57, Guy Mitchell '58. Films: *Baby Face Nelson, The Big Operator, Girls Town, Private Lives of Adam and Eve.* Most imp. infl: Victor Young. Favs: Billy May, Pete Rugolo. Own LP: *Home of Happy Feet* (Cap.); LPs for Dakota Staton, Kay Starr (Cap.).
Addr: 424 S. Rexford Drive, Beverly Hills, Calif.

ALLEN, DAVID, *singer;* b. Hartford, Conn., 7/19/23. Father pl. French horn; mother was singer. St. singing prof. in high school, influenced by Bing Crosby. Sang w. Jack Teagarden 1940; w. Army '42, served w. First Division and won Purple Heart. After discharge, joined Van Alexander Orch., then w. Henry Jerome (whose band incl. Al Cohn, Tiny Kahn et al, w. Johnny Mandel arr.). Sang on radio stations and then w. Boyd Raeburn, w. Mandel arr. Moved to West Coast, cont. radio work and rec. for Discovery w. Johnny Richards under Dick Bock's supervision. Out of music for a while, then, with Bock's encouragement, began rec. 1958, again w. Mandel's arr. Essentially a popular ballad singer, he is greatly admired by many leading jazzmen. LPs on Wor. Pac., War. Bros.

ALLEN, EDWARD (Ed), *trumpet;* b. Nashville, Tenn., 12/15/1897. Raised in St. Louis. Piano, cornet from 1907. Prof. debut at 16 in St. Louis roadhouse. Two years w. Ch. Creath on Streckfus Lines riverboats, then own band in St. Louis w. Gene Sedric, Walter Thomas, Pops Foster, Johnny St. Cyr. To Chicago '24, pl. w. Earl Hines in after hours club; to NYC w. Joe Jordan in Ed Daily's Black & White Show. Many records w. Clarence Williams in mid-20s. Pl. w. Leroy Tibbs at Connie's Inn '27-9. Free-lanced around NYC in '30s; quartet at Tony Pastor's in early '40s; working at taxi dance hall on 14th Street since 1945. LPs w. Bessie Smith (Col.); w. Clarence Williams in *History of Classic Jazz* (River).
Addr: 260 West 143rd Street, New York City, N.Y.

ALLEN, GENE (Eugene Sufana), *baritone sax, bass clarinet* etc.; b. East Chicago, Ind., 12/5/28. Pl. w. Louis Prima, 1944-7; Gene Williams, '48; C. Thornhill, '48-50; Tex Beneke, '51-3; Sauter-Finegan, '53-5; T. Dorsey, '56-7; Benny Goodman '58 incl. Brussels World Fair; Roxy Theatre NYC '59, also many gigs with Nat Pierce band at Birdland etc. '59-60. Feat. on *Hey Lulu, Finegan's Wake, Alright Already* w. Sauter-Finegan (Vict.), Goodman (Col.).
Addr: 246 West 73rd Street, New York 23, N.Y.

ALLEN, HENRY JR. (Red), *trumpet, singer;* b. Algiers, La., 1/7/08. His father, who led a brass band that played in and around New Orleans for more than 40 years, died in 1952. Henry Jr., who as a child marched in his father's band, played with Geo. Lewis in '23, John Handy '25, and on riverboats with Fate Marable '26. After working with Fats Pichon in '27 he joined King Oliver in Chicago, later playing more riverboat dates, then joining a band led by Oliver's ex-pianist, Luis Russell, in '29 in NYC. He became well known among musicians through OKeh records with Russell.

Allen worked with Fletcher Henderson, 1933; the Blue Rhythm Band, '34-6; Louis Armstrong's big band, '37-40. He then formed his own sextet, which earned great popularity during engagements at Cafe Society, Kelly's Stable in NYC etc. and remained together, with occasional personnel changes, until the early 1950s. From April 1954 Allen was active mainly as a member of the Dixieland-style house band at the Metropole, NYC. In 1957 he was seen at the NJF and on the CBS-TV show *The Sound of Jazz.* In the fall of 1959 he toured Europe as a sideman with Kid Ory.

Red Allen in his heyday, the mid-1930s, was a jazz trumpeter of great significance. His searing, poignant, sometimes raucous style showed unprecedented tendencies toward linearity; more than any hot jazz trumpet artist before him he seemed to think in terms of long, flowing melodic lines and to play with a sense of continuity that had much in common with the work a few years later of Harry Edison with Basie.

Own LPs on Vict., *Jazz At The Metropole* (Beth.), *At Newport* (Verve); three tracks in *Trumpeters Holiday* (Epic), one track in *Upright And Lowdown,* two tracks in *The Sound of Jazz* (Col.); LPs w. Spike Hughes (Lond.), Jelly Roll Morton (Comm.), Lionel Hampton (Vict.).
Addr: 1351 Prospect Avenue, Bronx, N.Y.

ALLEN, STEPHEN VALENTINE PATRICK WILLIAM (Steve), *piano, songwriter, singer;* b. New York City, 12/26/21.

Self-taught; does not read music. Gigged as pianist while studying at Drake U. After several years as a successful disc jockey in LA, settled in New York 1951 and became nationally famous as TV comedian. A competent swing pianist, most effective playing blues, he did much to expand national interest in jazz through his use of top bands and soloists on his program, and through occasional work as a journalist in *Down Beat* etc.

Allen played the title role in the film *The Benny Goodman Story*, released Jan. '56 (the sound track was recorded by Goodman); he headed the first nationally sponsored network TV jazz show on NBC, 12/30/57. He was the narrator on a three-record historical album, *The Jazz Story*, produced in collab. with the author, released '59 on Coral. He has written hundreds of pop songs, jazz instrumentals etc., incl. *An Old Piano Plays the Blues, Meet Me Where They Play The Blues.* LPs of jazz interest incl. *Jazz for Tonight, Let's Dance* (Coral), *All Star Jazz Concert* Vols. I & II (Decca), others on Dot, Hanover incl. *The Discovery of Buck Hammer.*

Addr: 1558 North Vine Street, Hollywood 28, Cal.

ALLEY, VERNON, *bass;* b. Winnemucca, Nev., 5/26/15. Clarinet, piano at Sacramento, SF colleges. St. w. Wes Peoples band '37; Saunders King '37-9; own band '39-40. Lionel Hampton '40-2; Count Basie '42; Navy band '42-6, then had own band off and on mainly in SF, also own TV show and disc jockey shows in SF. Film: *Reveille with Beverly* w. Basie. LP w. Stan Wilson (Verve), Jimmy Witherspoon (Hifijazz).

Addr: 766 Seventh Avenue, San Francisco, Cal.

ALLISON, MOSE JOHN JR., *piano, singer;* also *trumpet;* b. Tippo, Miss., 11/11/27. Started on piano at 6 w. private teacher, later trumpet and had Dixieland group in high school. Stud. Louisiana State U. Early listening was to Armstrong, Nat Cole, and blues singers Sonny Boy Williamson, Tampa Red, John Lee Hooker, and many others. Army, 1946-7. First came to NYC in 1951, again in '56. Played for a year off and on w. Stan Getz, 1956-7; Gerry Mulligan '58. Pl. at Vanguard, NYC and Great South Bay Festival w. own trio '58, Showboat in Wash., D.C. '58, '59. From Feb. to April '59, played in Paris, Stockholm and Copenhagen w. local rhythm sections. Three extended engagements w. Al Cohn-Zoot Sims at Half Note, NYC '59. One of the few young pianists infl. by early jazz roots. Favs: Sonny Boy Williamson, Ellington, Monk, Gillespie. Own LPs on Prestige & Col.; LPs w. Al Cohn, Cohn-Sims (Coral, UA), Stan Getz (Verve).

Addr: 40-45 75th St., Elmhurst 73, N.Y.

ALMEIDA, LAURINDO, *guitar;* b. Sao Paolo, Brazil, 9/2/17. Played radio staff jobs in Rio de Janeiro and led own orch. at Casino da Urca there. Came to US 1947, gained quick recognition as featured soloist w. Kenton band. Later worked with trio around Hollywood. Plays unamplified Spanish concert guitar, finger style. Scored backgrounds for motion pictures, *Maracaibo* and *Cry Tough.* Own LPs on Wor. Pac. (feat. Bud Shank), Cap., Cor.; LPs w. Stan Kenton, Four Freshman (Cap.), Pete Rugolo (Col.) Herbie Mann (Verve).

Addr: 6488 Mary Ellen Ave., Van Nuys, Calif.

ALMERICO, ANTHONY (Tony), *trumpet;* b. New Orleans, La., 8/16/05. Stud. music in Jesuit high school and st. playing in a dime-a-dance hall. Worked various local engagements and toured the US. Has been leader since 1936. Also active as radio announcer. First came to prominence acc. Lizzie Miles on her albums for Cook. Fav: Louis Armstrong. Own LPs on Dot, Cook.

Addr: 5363 Bancroft Dr., New Orleans 22, La.

ALPERT, HERMAN (Trigger), *bass;* b. Indianapolis, Ind., 9/3/16. Attended Ind. Univ. Worked w. Alvino Rey, then joined Glenn Miller Oct. '40 and remained with him throughout career of both civilian and Army Miller bands. After discharge worked briefly w. Tex Beneke, Woody Herman; did radio series w. Benny Goodman, then staff work w. CBS including several years on Garry Moore show. Many recordings including sessions with Louis Armstrong, Roy Eldridge, Ella Fitzgerald, Tony Mottola, Ray McKinley. Cited by Geo. Simon (Met.) as one of greatest bassists, with exceptional tone and fine beat. Own LP, *Trigger Happy* (Riverside); LPs w. Glenn Miller, Sauter-Finegan, Mundell Lowe (Vict.), Bernie Leighton (Merc.), Jackie Paris (Bruns.).

Addr: Cedar Gate Rd., Darien, Conn.

ALVAREZ, ALFRED (Chico), *trumpet;* b. Montreal, Canada, 2/3/20. Raised in Los Angeles. 10 years of study on violin, piano. Pl. w. Stan Kenton, 1941-51, except for Army service, '43-6, and a few months w. Ch. Barnet, Red Norvo in late '40s while Kenton was disbanded. Since 1952 has been operating piano store in LA, also associated w. Latin bands as songwriter and trumpeter. Feat. on early Kenton records including *Nango, St. James Infirmary, Machito, Harlem Holiday.* Fav: Armstrong. LPs: Kenton (Cap., Dec.).

Addr: 1819 Weldon Pl., Las Vegas, Nev.

ALVIN, DANNY, *drums;* b. New York City, 11/29/02, d. Chicago, Ill., 12/6/58. Father of guitarist Teddy Walters. Played w. Sophie Tucker at Reisenweber's in NYC 1919. Settled in Chicago in early '20s and worked there and in NYC w. numerous Dixieland groups; rec. with Sidney Bechet, George Brunis, Buck Clayton, Wild Bill Davison, Wingy Manone, Joe Marsala. Own LP: Stepheny; LPs w. Art Hodes, Mezz Mezzrow (Blue Note), George Zack, Wild Bill Davison (Comm.).

ALVIS, HAYES, *bass;* b. Chicago, Ill., 5/1/07. Drums, then tuba in high school ROTC. With Lionel Hampton and Sid Catlett, was one of drum corps in *Chicago Defender* Boys' Concert Band. Drums w. Jelly Roll Morton 1927, tuba w. Earl Hines '28, to NYC w. Jimmie Noone; switched to bass fiddle '30. W. Blue Rhythm band '31, Duke Ellington '35-8, Joe Sullivan, Benny Carter '39, Louis Armstrong '40-1; Army '43-5; Cafe Society w. Dave Martin et al to '48. Free-lanced and gigged w. Sy Oliver etc., ran a successful interior decorating business, then became a merchant seaman on S.S. *United States.* Ret. to NYC, May '58 and joined Wilbur De Paris. Rec. on tuba w. Ellington: *Truckin';* also bass on many dates w. Cootie Williams and Ellington in late '30s. LPs w. De Paris (Atl.).

Addr: 470 West 159th St., New York 32, N.Y.

AMBROSE, BERT, *leader;* b. London, England, 1897. Popular mainly in 1930's as leader of what was then the leading British swing band, feat. arrs. by Sid Phillips, cl. solos by Danny Polo. Own LP: *Hors d'Oeuvres* (Lond.).

AMBROSETTI, FLAVIO, *alto saxophone;* b. Lugano, Switzerland, 10/8/19. Stud. w. private teachers and at music school in Lugano, first on piano. Inspired by hearing Coleman Hawkins in Switzerland in late '30s, Ambrosetti pl. w. many Swiss combos; visited Paris 1949 w. Hazy Osterwald band. Has pl. many Italian jazz concerts and festivals, also TV and radio shows in France, Switzerland and Italy. Fav: Charlie Parker. LP: one track on *San Remo Festival* (Verve).

AMMONS, ALBERT, *piano;* b. Chicago, Ill., 1907, d. 12/5/49. Early associate of Pinetop Smith, Meade Lux Lewis. Played at DeLisa and other clubs around Chicago. Had own band '34-8, moved to NYC and was featured in boogie-woogie performances mostly at Carnegie Hall, Cafe Society; usually teamed w. Pete Johnson. Played at Truman inaugural. Was one of the most powerful and effective of boogie-woogie pianists. Own LPs on Blue Note, Vict. Comm., Dec.; also in *Spirituals To Swing* (Vang.).

AMMONS, EUGENE (Gene), *tenor sax;* b. Chicago, Ill., 4/14/25. Son of Albert Ammons. Played w. King Kolax '43, but first gained prominence w. Billy Eckstine's band '44-47. Replaced Stan Getz in Woody Herman band '49. In '50 formed group w. Sonny Stitt which feat. their tenor battles. In '52, group broke up; Ammons has since led his own combo, based mostly in Chicago. He periodically travels to NYC to record. Influenced by Lester Young and originally considered in the "cool" school, but later made entry into r & b field w. sweet ballad and "honking" styles before returning to jazz. British critic Alun Morgan said of him, "Ammons has regained his position as an inventive soloist whose big tone gives him a commanding personality."

Own LPs on Prestige, EmArcy; LPs w. Billy Eckstine (EmArcy), Count Basie (Victor), Bennie Green (Vee-Jay, Blue Note), Woody Herman (Capitol).

AMRAM, DAVID WERNER III, *composer, French horn;* b. Philadelphia, Pa., 11/17/30. Cousin of conductor Otto Klemperer. St. on piano, tpt., stud. at Curtis Inst. Pl. w. National Symph. in Washington '51-2; formed jazz sextet w. Spencer Sinatra. Army, Aug. '52; 7th Army Symph. in Germany '53-4. After discharge went to Paris and during '55 pl. w. Henri Renaud, Bobby Jaspar, made rec. debut w. Lionel Hampton. Back in NYC fall '55, gigged w. Sonny Rollins, C. Mingus, O. Pettiford; own combo at Five Spot Jan.-Mar. '57. By 1959 he had become almost inactive in jazz and spent much time composing and arr. scores for TV shows, NY Shakespeare Festival and many Broadway and off-Broadway productions. His jazz score for a short film *Echo of an Era* won a prize at Brussels World Fair '58. Wrote music for TV play *Turn of the Screw* starring Ingrid Bergman '59. Favs: Julius Watkins, Gunther Schuller, Jim Buffington. Own LP: Amram-Barrow Quartet, *Jazz Studio 6* (Dec.); LPs w. Oscar Pettiford (ABC-Par.), Lionel Hampton (Em.); *Baritones And French Horns* (Pres., 16 rpm); K. Dorham (River.).

Addr: 114 Christopher Street, New York 14, N.Y.

ANDERSON, WILLIAM ALONZO (Cat), *trumpet;* b. Greenville, S.C., 9/12/16. Studied brass instruments at orphans' home in Charleston, S.C. Inspired by Louis Armstrong, took up jazz, toured with Carolina Cotton Pickers '32-6, Sunset Royal orch. '36-41, then w. Lucky Millinder, Erskine Hawkins. First prominent as composer and soloist on *How 'Bout That Mess* with Doc Wheeler's Sunset Royals. Joined Lionel Hampton in summer of '42, then with Duke Ellington Sept. '44-7. Led his own band for three years, rejoining Ellington in '50. A good musician with a tone and style hovering between Louis Armstrong and Harry James, but has spoiled many of his performances with high note effects and poor musical taste. Left Duke again '59.

Featured on *Coloratura* from *Perfume Suite* with Ellington also *Bluejean Beguine* (own comp.), *Happy Go Lucky Local, The Eighth Veil* w. Duke, and many other Ellington LPs. Own LP, *Cat On A Hot Tin Horn,* (Merc.).

Addr: 638 N. 57th St., Philadelphia, Pa.

ANDERSON, ERNESTINE IRENE, *singer;* b. Houston, Tex., 11/11/28. Joined Russell Jacquet orch. in Texas, 1943. Toured w. Johnny Otis '47-49, Lionel Hampton '52-53. Record debut w. Gigi Gryce Nov. '55. Toured Scandinavia w. Rolf Ericson combo in summer '56. Was an immediate success in Sweden. Her album, *Hot Cargo* recorded in Sweden with the Harry Arnold band, was later released in the US. This, and the strong support of critic Ralph Gleason, helped bring her recognition on the West Coast and then nationally. Her style is swingingly assertive on rhythm songs, soulfully sensitive on ballads. Won new star award, DB Critics' poll '59. Own LPs on Mercury; LP, w. Gigi Gryce in *Nica's Tempo* (Savoy).

Addr: 250 West 74th St., New York 23, N.Y.

ANDERSON, IVIE, *singer;* b. Gilroy, Cal., 1904, d. Los Angeles, 12/28/49. Principally remembered as featured vocalist w. Duke Ellington from Feb. 1931 to Aug. 1942. Seen in film *Day At The Races* w. the Marx brothers '37. Best records w. Duke: *It Don't Mean a Thing* (Col.), *I Got It Bad* (Vic.). LPs w. Duke Ellington (Col., Vict.); *All Star Blues* (Tops).

ANDERSON, JOHN, JR., *trumpet, composer;* b. Birmingham, Ala., 1/31/21. Stud. alto horn and trumpet in high school and later at Los Angeles Conservatory of Music and Westlake College of Music. Four years in

Navy band, World War II; worked w. T. Bradshaw '41, free-lanced w. B. Carter, Jerry Fielding, Perez Prado, E. Bostic and others, 1946-57. Led own combos LA area which included B. Collette, C. Counce, Britt Woodman. Joined Count Basie, Aug. '59. Fav. own solos: *Buzzin' Cool* and *Crow's Nest* on Motif w. Max Albright. Favs: H. Edison, Gillespie, C. Shavers. LP w. B. Collette (Dig).

ANDRE, WAYNE, *trombone;* b. Manchester, Conn., 11/17/31. Father pl. sax; began stud. w. private teacher in Hartford 1946; w. Charlie Spivak '50-1; in service '51-5; w. Sauter-Finegan July '55-Dec. '56; Woody Herman Jan.-July '56; Kai Winding July '56-May '58. Attended Manhattan School of Music and free-lanced around NYC after leaving Winding. Favs: Urbie Green, Carl Fontana. LPs w. Winding (Col.), Art Farmer (UA).

Addr: Boston Hill Road, Andover, Conn.

ANDREWS, ERNIE, *singer;* b. Phila., Pa., 12/25/27. Family moved to LA before he was ten. St. singing in church choir. App. in amateur contest led to his rec. for G&G Records, *Soothe Me,* etc. W. Harry James orch. for four months in 1959. Competent pop singer. Own LPs on GNP, Roulette.

ANDRUS, CHARLES E. JR. (Chuck), *bass;* b. Holyoke, Mass., 11/17/28. Stud. Manhattan School of Music. Formed jazz group in Springfield, Mass. w. Joe Morello, Phil Woods, Sal Salvador *et al.* Worked w. C. Barnet '53, C. Thornhill '54, '55; T. Gibbs part of '54, B. Peiffer, '56. Freelanced in NYC since. Fav. own solo: *Royal Garden Blues* w. Don Stratton. Fav: Ray Brown. LPs w. Stratton (ABC-Par.), Peiffer (EmArcy), Jim Chapin (Classic Edit.).

ANTHONY, BILL, *bass;* b. NYC, 3/28/30. Mother st. him on piano; stud. cello and bass w. Clyde Lombardi. Worked w. Buddy De Franco big band 1950, Geo. Auld quintet in '51, Charlie Spivak '52, Jimmy Dorsey '53, Gerry Mulligan '54, Stan Getz '55, C. Thornhill '56, Cass Harrison '58 and other small combos. Favs: Oscar Pettiford, Ray Brown. LPs w. Stan Getz (Verve), Tony Fruscella (Atl.), Zoot Sims, Dick Garcia (Dawn), Johnny Williams (Em.).

ANTHONY, LEO (also known as Lee Roy), *baritone sax;* b. Dover, Ohio, 8/19/25. Brother of Ray Anthony. Raised in Cleveland. Alto w. local bands; w. Ray Anthony '46-53, then had own band, aimed at pop and r & b market. Feat. w. Ray on *Cook's Tour, Jersey Bounce, Dragnet* (Cap.).

Addr: 6500 Yucca St., Hollywood 28, Cal.

ANTHONY, RAY (Raymond Antonini), *trumpet, leader;* b. Bentleyville, Pa. 1/20/22. Raised in Cleveland as one of six brothers. Father, who led family band, started him on trumpet at 5. Led own high school band; joined Al Donahue 1938. Was w. Glenn Miller from Nov. '40 to July '41. Then six months w. J. Dorsey. In Navy '42-6, leading own band in Pacific for two years. Started own civilian band '46, earning great popularity after '49 when he signed w. Capitol Records. Band included brother, Leo, on baritone sax. Anthony plays Harry James-style trumpet and his arrangements are aimed at the popular rather than the jazz market. Biggest hit record: *Dragnet,* Aug. '53. Was married to actress Mamie Van Doren. LPs on Cap.

Addr: 9155 Sunset Blvd., Los Angeles 46, Calif.

ANTON, ARTHUR (Artie), *drums, conga, timbales;* b. NYC, 9/8/26. Stud. 1942 w. Irving Torgman; majored in music at NYU '43-4, '46-7. Navy '44-6. Played w. Herbie Fields '47 and '51. Sonny Dunham, Bobby Byrne, '48; Tommy Reynolds, Jerry Wald, Art Mooney, Bud Freeman '52; Ralph Flanagan, '53; Jerry Gray, Charlie Barnet '54, then free-lanced in LA. Non-music jobs incl. vacuum cleaner salesman, private detective. Best solo performances are on LP (Cap). Favs: D. Tough, Gus Johnson, J. Giuffre, Art Mardigan, Tiny Kahn. Other LPs w. Jack Millman (Dec.).

Addr: 935 North Pass, Burbank, Cal.

APPLEYARD, PETER, *vibes, drums;* b. Cleethorpes, England. 8/26/28. St. on piano at 14; prof. debut as drummer w. British bands. Two years w. RAF, then 3 yrs. in Bermuda pl. drums at Princess Hotel. Moved to Canada '51, took up vibes, pl. w. many groups in Toronto. With Calvin Jackson from '54, later had own quartet, visiting US occasionally from '58 for jobs at East Side NYC clubs. Own LP: Audio-Fidelity. LP w. Calvin Jackson (Col.)

Addr: c/o Peter Dean. 15 West 55th Street, New York 19, N. Y.

ARCHEY, JAMES (Jimmy), *trombone;* b. Norfolk, Va., 10/12/02. New York debut w. Edgar Hayes 1926, then Arthur Gibbs, Joe Steele and in '28 w. King Oliver. Stayed with same group under Luis Russell leadership '37, then w. Willie Bryant '38-9, Benny Carter '39-42, Claude Hopkins '44-5, Noble Sissle '46-9; to France w. Mezz Mezzrow '48, w. Bob Wilbur '48-50; toured Europe with own sextet in '52, again w. Mezzrow in '54-55. Also free-lance work mostly w. Dixieland bands around NYC until summer '55. From Sept. '55 at Club Hangover in San Francisco w. Earl Hines. LPs w. Sidney Bechet (Blue Note); *Creole Reeds, Ragtime,* Wild Bill Davison (River.), *New Orleans Jazz* (Savoy).

ARMSTRONG, LILIAN HARDIN (Lil), *piano, composer;* b. Memphis, Tenn., 1903. Studied for concert career at Fisk University, but while still in teens joined Freddie Keppard in Chicago. Joined King Oliver in 1920; married Louis Armstrong, then second trumpeter in the band, '24, led own band in Chicago with Louis '25, and was on many of Louis' "Hot Five" records.

After her divorce from Armstrong in '32, she remained in NYC, working as an accompanist and w. many groups. From '37-40 she led various all-star bands for a series of Decca sessions. Other bands that she pl. w. were Ralph Cooper '31, Red Allen and Zutty Singleton '40; acc. to Lonnie Johnson '41. In '52 she went to Europe, gigging in France and England w. Peanuts Holland, Michel Attenoux and Sidney Bechet, and as a solo nightclub artist. Back in US, played long series of dates at Red Arrow, Stickney, Ill. from late '50s. A documentary record, personally narrated by Lil Armstrong and containing colorful reminiscences of her life in Chicago and NYC, was released under the title *Satchmo and Me* (River. 12-120). LPs w. Armstrong (Col., River.).

Addr: 421 E. 44th St., Chicago, Ill.

ARMSTRONG, DANIEL LOUIS (Satchmo), *trumpet, singer, leader;* b. New Orleans, 7/4/00. His mother, from Butte, La., granddaughter of slaves, was married at 15 to a turpentine worker in NO. When Louis was five, his parents separated and he lived with his mother at Liberty and Perdido Streets in New Orleans' Third Ward.

Louis' singing career began several years before he started to play. When he was about seven, he and a group of friends would sing on the streets for pennies and nickels; he recalls that he always enjoyed singing, for pleasure and for money. Then on the night of Dec. 31, 1913, he celebrated by running out in the street and firing a gun he had borrowed from his mother without her knowledge. Arrested and sent to the Waifs' Home in New Orleans, he was given a cornet to play in the institution's band and soon was playing picnics and parades, studying his horn with Peter Davis of the Waifs' Home.

After his release from the home he worked in a variety of jobs and was befriended by Joe (King) Oliver, who was his sole musical influence and mentor. Later, when Oliver was leading his own band in Chicago, he sent for Louis to join him as second cornetist, in July 1922. By this time Louis had had considerable experience in Oliver's previous job as a member of the Kid Ory band.

It was in Chicago that Armstrong, who had been married briefly in New Orleans to Daisy Parker, met Lilian Hardin, Oliver's pianist, who on Feb. 5, 1924 became the second Mrs. Armstrong. In Oct. 1924 Louis, then working with Lilian in Ollie Powers' Dreamland band, left to join the Fletcher Henderson band at the Roseland Ballroom in New York. After an extensive road tour with the band through the spring and summer of 1925, Louis left to return to Chicago and to Dreamland, where Lil now had her own band.

Early in 1926 Louis joined the "symphonic jazz" orchestra of Erskine Tate at the Vendome Theatre. A few months later he began doubling in Carroll Dickerson's orchestra at the Sunset Cabaret, where he was billed as "Louis Armstrong, World's Greatest Trumpet Player." The proprietor of the Sunset was Joe Glaser, who for almost all of the past 30 years has been Armstrong's manager.

It was during this period that he began to make records under his own name (Louis Armstrong's Hot Five or Hot Seven); the first tune he recorded as a leader was *My Heart,* Nov. 12, 1925. From then until Dec. 1928 a series of classic sides was recorded, most of the later ones prominently featuring Earl Hines, the pianist with whom he had worked in Dickerson's band. These were the records that earned Armstrong a world-wide reputation. By 1929, when he returned to New York, he was the idol not only of the Negro public that had known him for several years but also of white musicians and fans at home and abroad. His technical facility was exceptional; his limited reading ability had improved. Most important, the emotional intensity and basic simplicity of his solos, especially when he played the blues, had no parallel in jazz. In addition to Hines, his partners on these memorable records included Johnny and Baby Dodds, Kid Ory and Zutty Singleton.

Back in New York, Louis fronted the Dickerson band at Connie's Inn in Harlem and doubled into a featured role with Leroy Smith's band in the revue *Hot Chocolates* at the Hudson Theatre on Broadway. It was in this show that he introduced *Ain't Misbehavin',* his first popular-song hit performance, written for the show by Fats Waller.

This was the pivotal point in Armstrong's career. From this time on he fronted a big band, and used popular songs rather than blues or original instrumentals for his material. For six months in 1930 he toured, backed by Luis Russell's orchestra; during his initial stay in California, which lasted almost a year (1930-31), Les Hite provided a band for him. Russell teamed with him again during the late 1930s. Most of the large orchestras Louis fronted from this time until 1946 fell far short of his own musical standards.

After his California trip Armstrong formed a new band in Chicago, and in June 1931 took it to New Orleans for his first visit since he had left home nine years earlier. Meanwhile, the phenomenal reception of his records overseas led to his first European trip. In June 1932 he was headlined in the show at the London Palladium. It was during this visit that P. Mathison Brooks, editor of the London *Melody Maker,* unwittingly gave him his nickname "Satchmo" by garbling an earlier nickname, "Satchelmouth."

The following year Armstrong went back to Europe for a long Continental tour, remaining until January 1935, fronting various mediocre bands that were assembled for him in Europe. In 1936 he went to Hollywood to take part in the film *Pennies from Heaven* with Bing Crosby. During the next few years, his transition from the status of musicians' idol to that of personality-entertainer saw many changes in the matter and manner of his presentations. Novelty songs such as *Ol' Man Mose, You Rascal You* and *Brother Bill* were among his biggest request numbers. His singing played an increasingly dominant role. Recording for Decca from Oct. 1935, he was heard not only with his own band but with various white bands, with vocal groups, in duets with pop singers and even with Hawaiian orchestras. The greater his impact on the public, the less important were his musical settings and the less durable his musical contributions.

One of his rare opportunities to appear before the public with a small, improvising jazz group came in Jan. 1944 when, celebrating his first victory in the *Esquire* poll, he appeared with fellow-winners in the first jazz concert ever held at the Metropolitan Opera House in New York City.

In 1947 Armstrong was assigned a major acting rôle in a shoddy, inept film entitled *New Orleans*. Instead of assembling another big band after the assignment was completed, he took his place at the head of a sextet featuring Jack Teagarden, trombone; Barney Bigard, clarinet; Dick Cary, piano; Sid Catlett, drums, and Arvell Shaw, bass. This belated use of a small group was an immediate success and he made it his permanent setting, using later such sidemen as Earl Hines, Joe Bushkin, Joe Sullivan, Marty Napoleon and Billy Kyle, piano; Bob McCracken, Edmond Hall, Peanuts Hucko, clarinet; Trummy Young, trombone; Dale Jones, Milt Hinton, Jack Lesberg, Mort Herbert, bass; Cozy Cole, Kenny John, Barrett Deems, Danny Barcelona, drums.

The mounting interest in Armstrong as a symbol of American jazz led to more frequent appearances abroad. Some of the trips he made after World War II included: Nice, France, jazz festival, 1948; European tours, 1949 and '52; Japanese tour, 1954; Great Britain (first visit in 21 years) and Ghana, 1956; British West Indies, spring 1957. During a six-month European tour in 1959 Louis made three films in Germany (*La Paloma; The Night Before the Première; Auf Wiedersehen*) and one in Denmark (*A Girl, A Guitar and a Trumpet*). At the end of the tour Armstrong was stricken while in Spoleto, Italy, by what at first was wrongly diagnosed as a heart attack. After making daily front page headlines around the world, he reaffirmed his iron constitution, a few weeks later playing in New York, his power and assurance undimmed.

Armstrong during the 1950s enhanced his reputation in the popular music field through recordings with elaborate orchestral settings including large string sections, under the direction of Gordon Jenkins, Russ Garcia and others. Since his Decca affiliation he has recorded on a free-lance basis for Columbia, Verve, Audio-Fidelity and other labels. His Verve records include several albums in partnership with Ella Fitzgerald, Oscar Peterson et al.

In 1939 Armstrong made a stage appearance in the short-lived but delightful Shakespeare travesty *Swingin' The Dream,* in which he played the role of Bottom. Though this was his only effort as an actor on Broadway, he has had major comedy parts in some of the films that have used him through the years. These have included *Goin' Places, Artists and Models, Every Day's a Holiday, Pillar To Post, The Strip, Glory Alley, A Song is Born, The Glenn Miller Story, The Five Pennies, High Society, Jazz on a Summer's Day.* A film and record commemorating some of his travels, produced by Edward R. Murrow and entitled *Satchmo the Great,* were released in 1957. A four-volume album, *Satchmo, A Musical Biography,* in which Louis' spoken narrations introduced newly recorded versions of some of his pre-1935 recordings, was also released in 1957.

Louis has appeared at Newport and most of the other major jazz festivals. He has won the following polls, among others: Record Changer All Time All Star poll, 1951, as trumpeter and vocalist; Esquire Gold Award, 1944 (trumpet, vocal); 1945 (vocal), 1946 (vocal), 1947 (trumpet, vocal); also *Down Beat* International Critics' Poll 1953 et seq.; *Down Beat* Hall of Fame award; *Melody Maker* readers' and critics' polls; and polls conducted by *Jazz Hot* (France), *Jazz Echo* (Germany), *Muziek Express* (Holland), etc. In a poll announced Aug. 1959 by *Music U.S.A.* naming the readers' choices for the ten greatest jazz musicians of all time, he finished in fifth place, evidence that younger jazz fans have little sense of history.

It is difficult, admittedly, to see in correct perspective Armstrong's contribution as the first vital jazz soloist to attain worldwide influence as trumpeter, singer, entertainer, dynamic show business personality and strong force in stimulating interest in jazz. His style, melodically and harmonically simple by the standards of later jazz trends, achieved in his early records an unprecedented warmth and beauty. His singing, lacking most of the traditional vocal qualities accepted outside the jazz world, had a rhythmic intensity and guttural charm that induced literally thousands of other vocalists to imitate him, just as countless trumpeters through the years reflected the impact of his style. By 1960 Armstrong, set in his ways, improvised comparatively little; but he retained vocally and instrumentally many of the qualities that had established him, even though entertainment values, by his own admission, meant more to him than the reactions of a minority of musicians and specialists.

Louis Armstrong's recordings include many made in 1924, when he accompanied Ma Rainey and other blues singers. In that year also he recorded with Fletcher Henderson's band. There were other early sessions with Bessie Smith, Chippie Hill, Clarence Williams et al, the Hot Five and Hot Seven sessions 1925-8, his own big bands on Okeh 1929-31, on Victor 1931-3, French Polydor 1934, Decca 1935-46, Victor 1946-7, then back to Decca until 1954, when he continued to make occasional dates for Decca but appeared on other labels as noted above. The best demonstration of his early years can be found in the four-volume *Louis Armstrong Story* on Columbia (see below).

Own LPs: *Satchmo Sings* (Dec. 8126), *Satchmo's Collector's Items* (8327), *Jazz Classics* (8284), *Louis and the Angels* (8488), *Louis and the Good Book* (8741), *New Orleans Nights* (8329), *Pasadena* (8041), *Satchmo At Symphony Hall* (2-Dec. DX-108

8037/8), *Satchmo in Style w. Jenkins* (Dec. 8840), *Satchmo on Stage* (Dec. 8330), *Satchmo Serenades* (Dec. 8211), *At the Crescendo* (2-Dec. 8168/9), *w. Eddie Condon at Newport* (Col. CL-931), *Plays W. C. Handy* (Col. CL-591), *Satch Plays Fats* (Col. CL-708), *Ambassador Satch* (Col. CL-840), *Young Louis Armstrong* (Riv. 12-101), *Louis Armstrong: 1923* (12-122), *Louis Under The Stars* (Verve 4012), *Meets Peterson* (8322), *Ella and Louis* (4003, 4017, 4018), *Town Hall Concert Plus* (Vict. LPM 1443), tracks w. own band in *Guide To Jazz* (LPM 1393), *Pennies From Heaven* (1443), *Playboy Jazz All Stars* (Playboy), *Satchmo the Great* (Col. CL 1077), *Porgy & Bess* with Ella Fitzgerald (two LPs: Verve MG V 4011-2); also some tracks on *History of Classic Jazz* Vos. 3 & 4 (Riverside SDP 11), *Kings of Classic Jazz* (Riverside 12-131), Bessie Smith (Col. CL 855), w. Johnny Dodds-Sidney Bechet on *Introduction to Jazz* (Decca 8244).

The Louis Armstrong Story, four LPs including the most important sides from 1925-31, are on Col. CL 851-854. *Satchmo—a Musical Autobiography,* four LPs with illustrated booklet, with recreations of early hits, and reminiscences narrated by Armstrong, on Decca DX 155. *Satchmo & Me,* reminiscences by Lil Armstrong of Louis' early years, documentary without music, Riverside 12-120.

For books see bibliography.

Addr: c/o Associated Booking Corp., 745 Fifth Avenue, New York 22, N.Y.

ARNOLD, BUDDY (Arnold Buddy Grishaver), *tenor sax, clarinet, oboe;* b. NYC, 4/30/26. St. on soprano and alto saxes. Played w. Joe Marsala, Geo. Auld 1943; Will Osborne, Bob Chester '44; Army band '44-6. After discharge played w. Herbie Fields, Buddy Rich; entered Columbia U., took courses in music and economics. Played w. Geo. Williams, Claude Thornhill, then left music for 1½ yrs. Toured w. Buddy DeFranco orch. during '51, Jerry Wald '52, later w. Tex Beneke, Elliot Lawrence, Neal Hefti. Early solo on *Just Goofin'* with Gene Williams (Mercury). Favs: Al Cohn, Zoot Sims, Sonny Rollins. Showed great promise, making own album for ABC-Par. in '56 but has been in obscurity since. Other LP w. Phil Sunkel (ABC-Par.).

ARNOLD, HARRY (Harry Arnold Persson), *leader, composer;* also *saxophones, clar.;* b. Hälsingborg, Sweden, 8/7/20. Father pl. valve trombone. Stud. alto sax, clar. 1937-8. St. arr. '38 without benefit of formal study. Learned through "analyzing works from different composers between Basie and Ravel." Own 12-piece band at Amiralen, a dance hall in Malmo, April '42-Apr. '49. To Stockholm as tenorman, arr. w. Thore Ehrling's band. Took own band back to Malmo to play weekends between '52 and Oct. '54. Composer-conductor-arranger for Europa Films, Stockholm since then. Organized 17-piece band for weekly (except in summer) radio broadcasts Oct. '56. Fav. arrs: Sy Oliver, Quincy Jones; although Arnold no longer plays his first infl. was Benny Carter. Own LPs on Mercury, Atlantic, Jazztone.

Addr: Hässelbytorg 2, Stockholm, Sweden.

ARNOLD, KOKOMO, *singer, guitar;* b. Jackson, Miss., 1909. Heard on a series of Decca records 1935-8, the first of which, *Milk Cow Blues,* enjoyed considerable success. Samuel B. Charters, in *The Country Blues* (Rinehart), wrote: "Kokomo was a fine guitar player, using a bottle neck on his little finger in a frenzied rhythmic style." Arnold also sang in an earthy, persuasive manner. He was out of the music business after 1939.

ARODIN, SIDNEY, *clarinet;* b. New Orleans, 3/29/01, d. 2/6/48. Featured in many small groups in New Orleans and Chicago but best known as co-composer of *Lazy River,* later popularized through Hoagy Carmichael; recorded w. Abbie Brunis (Col. '26); Johnny Miller (Col. '28); Jones and Collins (Vict. '29); Louis Prima (Bruns. '34).

ASH, MARVIN (Marvin Ashbaugh), *piano;* b. Lamar, Colo., 10/4/14. Raised in Kansas. Early exp. w. local bands incl. Wallie Stoeffer. In early '30s worked w. Connie Conrad, Herman Waldman, Jack Crawford. Settled in Tulsa 1936, did local staff radio work. To LA, '42, pl. at Hangover Club, also w. Wingy Manone et al. Own LPs: Dec., Cap.; one track in *History of Jazz, Vol. 2* (Cap.).

Addr: 15741 Addison, Encino, Cal.

ASH, VICTOR (Vic), *clarinet, saxophones;* b. London, Eng., 3/9/30. Stud. w. priv. teacher 1945. Played w. Kenny Baker '51-3, Vic Lewis '53-5; acc. Hoagy Carmichael, Cab Calloway on British visits '55, leading own quartet. Won *Melody Maker* critics' poll '52 and readers' poll '57. Toured USA with own combos Nov. '57 and Sept. '58; USA w. Vic Lewis band Feb. '59. Toured Britain fall '59 as only British group on concert unit of Newport Jazz Festival. Series of religion-plus-jazz TV shows, *Sunday Break,* '59. Own LP of mood music (MGM); others LPs in England for Pye-Nixa. Fav. own solo: *Hoagy* w. own quartet (Nixa). Favs: S. Getz, J. Hamilton.

Addr: 36 Yale Court, Honeybourne Road, London N.W.6., England.

ASHBY, DOROTHY JEANNE, *harp, piano;* b. Detroit, Mich., 8/6/32. Father, self-taught guitarist, instr. her in harmony. Stud. Cass Tech. High, Wayne U.; mus. educ. major. Gave piano recitals; bought harp in '52; first job on harp in Phila. club Nov. '53. Concerts w. Louis Armstrong, Woody Herman '57, also many night clubs in Detroit and NYC. Has written book on playing of jazz and modern harmony for harp and 'cello. Tasteful performer with more jazz feeling than most harpists. Favs: O. Peterson, B. Taylor, Shearing. Own LPs: New Jazz, Prestige, Regent.

Addr: 9327 Richter Street, Detroit 14, Mich.

ASHBY, IRVING C., *guitar;* b. Somerville, Mass., 12/29/20. Started on ukulele at seven. Attended New England Cons., Boston. With Lionel Hampton '40-42; Eddie Beal, etc. in LA; replaced Oscar Moore in King Cole

Trio, Oct. '47. W. Cole through '50, making European trip with him. W. Oscar Peterson trio in JATP '52, touring overseas in first such trip by Norman Granz' unit. Since that time teaching and freelancing in LA. LPs w. JATP (Verve), Lester Young (Intro), Ernie Freeman (Imperial), Jackie Davis (Capitol), Louis Jordan (EmArcy), Wardell Gray (Modern).

Addr: 1764 W. 24th St., Los Angeles 18, Calif.

ASMUSSEN, SVEND, *violin;* b. Copenhagen, Denmark, 2/28/16. Made professional debut in '33, formed quartet patterned after Joe Venuti's "Blue Four" '34; record debut, 1935. Popular throughout Scandinavia mainly as a vaudeville star, he sings, does comedy, plays several other instruments. Records are mostly in the popular vein, but some critics have called him one of the top jazz violinists. Made a brief visit to US in '55 but did not perform professionally. Own LPs on Col., Epic, Bruns., Angel.

ASSUNTO, FRANK JOSEPH, *trumpet, leader;* b. New Orleans, 1/29/32. Two sisters both play woodwinds, piano; brother Fred plays trombone. Stud. w. father. Organized "Dukes of Dixieland" band in Jan. 1949 for Horace Heidt talent show; after short tour w. Heidt, played around NO and remained at the Famous Door for four years. In the late '50s the Dukes became nationally popular, via TV, LPs, clubs, featuring a highly commercial blend of musicianship and showmanship; in 1958 they became the first jazz group to be heard on a stereo disc. Favs: Armstrong, Hackett, Berigan. LPs w. Dukes of Dixieland on Aud. Fid., Roul.

ASSUNTO, FRED J., *trombone;* b. New Orleans, 12/3/29. Brother of Frank Assunto (q.v.), with whose career his own has run parallel. Member of Frank Assunto band since its inception. Favs: J. Teagarden, Santo Pecora, Jac. Assunto. LPs: see Frank Assunto.

Addr: 1301 Nicholas Ave., New Orleans, La.

ASSUNTO, JACOB (Papa Jac), *trombone, banjo;* b. Lake Charles, La., 11/1/05. Father of the Assunto brothers, Frank and Fred, whose Dukes of Dixieland combo he joined Aug. 1955. Formerly directed Redemptorist High School band. LPs w. Dukes of Dixieland on Aud. Fid., Roul.

ASTOR, BOB (Robert E. Dade), *leader, trumpet, drums;* b. New Orleans 10/5/15. Worked w. local groups around NO and East Texas oil fields; formed first big band in LA, where he also worked as disc jockey, night club manager and MC. Although his band never recorded, Astor was important in NYC in the early 1940s as one of the first employers of many subsequently celebrated musicians, among them Neal Hefti, Les Elgart, trumpets; Corky Corcoran, Zoot Sims, Illinois Jacquet, tenor saxes; Shelly Manne, Teddy Charles, Irv Kluger, drums; George Williams, Marty Napoleon, Leo DeLyon, piano. In recent years, Astor has been a booking agent for Shaw Artists.

Addr: Shaw Artists Corp., 203 N. Wabash Ave., Chicago, Ill.

AUER, JOSEF (Pepsi), *composer, piano;* b. Munich, Germany, 6/14/28. Stud. w. Hans Kray. Played US military clubs 1945. Pianist w. Freddy Christmann quartet '54-6, then took over group for a year. W. Freddy Brocksieper '57-8; toured w. German All Stars '58. Since April '58, in Frankfurt as pianist-arranger w. Frankfurt All Stars (incl. Emil Mangelsdorff, Joki Freund, Peter Trunk). Has written arrs. for Kurt Edelhagen. Regular broadcasts on Frankfurt radio. Records w. German Jazz Festival '55, Albert Mangelsdorff. Favs: H. Silver, B. Powell.

Addr: Viktor Scheffelstr. 3, Munich 23, Germany.

AULD, GEORGIE (John Altwerger), *tenor, alto, soprano saxes;* b. Toronto, Ontario, Canada, 5/19/19. Moved to Brooklyn, N.Y., '29. Won Rudy Wiedoft scholarship on alto, '31. Tenor, '35, after hearing a Hawkins rec. Own band at Nick's; w. Bunny Berigan, '37-8; Artie Shaw, '38-9. Took over Shaw band, '40, then led new group of his own. W. Jan Savitt briefly, then Benny Goodman, mid-'40, for a year. Rec. famous Goodman sextet sides w. Charlie Christian, Cootie Williams, Count Basie. Rejoined Shaw, '41-2; Army, '43. Own big band, '44-6. Semi-inactive for next few years, working at various small clubs with own combos. Style had changed progressively; by 1948 Auld was in spirit of modernists. In '49, led 10-piece band, also appeared as actor in Broadway play *The Rat Race.* Led quintet, 1950-1, featuring Frank Rosolino, Tiny Kahn. After group broke up, began rec. for Coral, doing ballad standards with vocal-group backgrounds. Living in Hollywood, he opened own night club, the Melody Room, 1954. Later had band with Lunceford style arrs. by Billy May. Ret. to NYC in '58 to do studio work and rec. Numerous app. on Art Ford's TV *Jazz Party.* Auld is a highly expressive and sensitive musician whose style can be adapted to any mood and context. Own LPs on Em., Savoy, Coral, Bruns., Cap., All., Gr. Award, Roost; LPs w. B. Goodman (Col.), Artie Shaw, Count Basie (Vict.), Barney Kessel (Contemp.), Dinah Washington, Maynard Ferguson (Em.), B. De Franco (Verve), *Saxes, Inc.* (War. Bros.).

Addr: 1360 York Avenue, New York City.

AUSTIN, CLAIRE (Augusta Marie Austin), *singer;* b. Yakima, Wash., 11/21/18. Stud. piano in Tacoma; drama at Whitemire studio in Seattle, 1935-6. After graduation from high school, played night clubs in Seattle, Spokane, Portland. During war years, did floor show vocals in Cincinnati, Chicago. Ten months at Italian Village in SF, '52; month at Tin Angel in SF, '54. Held various jobs as bookkeeper, stenographer, worked for Division of Accounting, State of Cal. in '55. Has made lecture-concert appearances w. Dr. S. I. Hayakawa. Recorded with Turk Murphy, '52; Kid Ory, '54; Bob Scobey and all-star group, '55-6. Her style shows an intelligent absorption of the early blues tradition with a timbre recalling Bessie Smith. Own LPs: Good Time Jazz, Contemporary.

Addr: 609 East 12th Street, Davis, Cal.

AUSTIN, LOVIE (Cora Calhoun), *piano, composer;* b. Chattanooga, Tenn., 9/19/1887. Daughter Patricia is singer. Studied piano at Roger Williams Univ. in Nashville and Knoxville Coll. Acc. singers in Chicago, many vaudeville tours, sessions with "Blues Serenaders." Worked as pianist in pit bands, Monogram Theater for 20 years, Joyland Theater for 9 years. During World War II, she was an inspector in a war plant for two years. Also had her own traveling shows and theaters. From late '40s employed as pianist at Jimmy Payne's dancing school, also serving as assistant trainer for St. Anslem's Kindergarten. Fav: Duke Ellington; impt. infl: Tommy Ladnier. First rec. w. Ida Cox '23 (Paramount). LPs: w. Ida Cox in *The Great Blues Singers;* Ma Rainey, Johnny Dodds (River.).

Addr: 5940 Michigan Ave., Chicago, Ill.

AUSTIN, SYLVESTER (Sil), *tenor saxophone;* b. Dunnellon, Fla., 9/17/29. Private teachers in St. Petersburg, 1943 and New York City, '44. First major job w. Roy Eldridge for three months in '49; then 2½ years w. Cootie Williams. After working w. Tiny Bradshaw '52-4 he organized his own group and has since successfully toured US, Latin America and West Indies. First big hit was *Slow Walk* for Mercury in '56. Although his success has been in the rock 'n' roll field, his favorite saxophonists are Hawkins, Parker, Young, Stitt; his ambitions are "to worry less about commercial music" and to form a Basie-type big band. Fav. own solo: *Ping Pong* w. Bradshaw (King). Own LPs: Mercury.

Addr: 178-19 119th Road, St. Albans, L.I., N.Y.

AUTREY, HERMAN, *trumpet;* b. Evergreen, Ala., 12/4/04. To NYC 1926 with revue, but did not settle there until 1933. Worked w. Ch. Johnson at Smalls '33-4, Fats Waller off and on '34-41, playing on most of his records; also first trumpet w. Fletcher Henderson '35; Claude Hopkins band '38-9; joined Stuff Smith '42, then took over group himself on West Coast. In late '40s free-lanced mostly in Canada w. own group; in early '50s jam sessions at Jimmy Ryan's, Stuyvesant Casino, NYC. In late '50s, led own combo in Canada, and in Brooklyn; gigs w. Lester Lanin, Conrad Janis, Frank Cary and at Eddie Condon's. LPs w. Waller (Vict.), Buster Bailey (Felsted), Geo. Wettling (Stere-o-craft).

Addr: 760 Tinton Avenue, Bronx 56, N.Y.

B

BABASIN, HARRY, *bass, cello;* b. Dallas, Texas, 3/19/21. Raised in Vernon, Texas; w. Jimmy Giuffre, Herb Ellis, Gene Roland at N. Tex. State College; mid-western bands, then NYC with Krupa, Boyd Raeburn, Ch. Barnet. To Cal. '45, worked with Raeburn, Benny Goodman. Was first to play pizzicato jazz cello, on '47 Dial date w. Dodo Marmarosa. Toured w. Woody Herman '48, then free-lanced in Hollywood w. radio, TV bands etc. Started Nocturne Record Co., since defunct. Formed own group, "The Jazzpickers," '56 and rec. w. varying personnels incl. himself on cello w. vibes, etc. Film: *A Song Is Born* '54. Own LPs w. Jazzpickers (Merc.); LPs w. Laurindo Almeida (Wor. Pac.), Barney Kessel (Contemp.), dates w. many other West Coast groups.

Addr: 12486 Wingo St., Pacoima, Calif.

BADINI, GERARD, *clarinet, tenor sax;* b. Paris, France, 4/16/31. Self-taught. Prof. debut at Monte Carlo Sporting Club 1952. In 1954, concerts at Salle Pleyel, Paris; Festival Hall, London; Continental tour w. S. Bechet. Radio, TV, with J. Dieval in Germany, Scandinavia, Yugoslavia, etc. Many recs. w. Claude Bolling, Gerard Pochonet, Michel Attenoux. Fav. own solo: *Caravan* w. Bolling. Fav: B. Goodman. Very capable swinging soloist. Feat. w. Bolling on Omegadisk LP.

Addr: 12 Rue Parent de Rosan, Paris 16, France.

BAGGE, ERIC LARS OTTO (Lars Bagge), *piano, composer,* also *bassoon, trumpet;* b. Stockholm, Sweden, 5/7/35. First job on trumpet w. school band at thirteen; prof. debut on piano 1941. Played w. Lars Gullin '55; Ib Glindemann in Copenhagen '56; two trips as pianist on board the *Stockholm* to N.Y. '56-7; Carl-Henrik Norin Orch. '57-9; also bassoonist in Gävle Symphony Orch. '58-9. Recently working as music teacher in Katrineholm. Has recorded w. Rolfe Billberg and Lars Gullin for Sonet; also w. Norin and Billberg for HMV and Monica Zetterlund for Swedish Columbia. Favs: Bud Powell and Bill Evans.

Addr: 7 Katrineholm, Sweden.

BAGLEY, DONALD N. (Don), *bass;* b. Salt Lake City, Utah, 7/18/27. Graduated from LA City College; studied bass w. Arthur Pabst, composition w. Dr. Wesley La Violette. Started w. Hollywood Teenagers 1944. Worked w. Shorty Sherock, Wingy Manone, '45; Dick Pierce, '48; Stan Kenton, '50-4, then formed own trio. Featured w. Kenton on *Bags And Baggage, Study For Bass,* and *Bags.* Joined Les Brown '57, making Far East tour w. Bob Hope. Continued writing and playing w. band; heard on Steve Allen TV series 1959-60. Film: *Visit To A Small Planet* '59. Favs: George Duvivier, Red Mitchell, Ray Brown. Own LPs on Dot, Regent; LPs w. Kenton (Cap.), *Down Beat Jazz Concert* (Dot).

Addr: 8440 Canby Ave., Northridge, Calif.

BAILEY, ERNEST HAROLD (Benny), *trumpet;* b. Cleveland, Ohio, 8/13/25. Father pl. sax as hobby, mother piano. Stud. music at Central High School in Cleveland, flute first then trumpet. Prof. debut w. Bull Moose Jackson in Buffalo 1941. Went to LA w. Scatman Crothers '44. Pl. w. Jay McShann '47, Dizzy Gillespie '48 incl. European trip, Lionel Hampton '49-53. Remained in Sweden after pl. there w. Hampton. W. Harry Arnold's band on Swedish radio '57-9. Made film in Germany w. Oscar Pettiford '59. Ret. to

US '59 and joined Quincy Jones' orch. in Nov. of that year. First infl: Tommy Enoch, Freddie Webster; favs: Miles Davis, Art Farmer. LPs w. Hampton (MGM), Harry Arnold (Merc., incl. fav. own solo, *Meet Benny Bailey*), Stan Getz (Verve).

BAILEY, WILLIAM C. (Buster), *clarinet;* b. Memphis, Tenn., 7/9/02. Studied under Franz Schoepp of Chicago Symph., who also taught Benny Goodman. Played with W. C. Handy orch. 1917, Erskine Tate in Chicago '19-22. From '23-4 made big name in jazz, working mostly w. Fletcher Henderson (also toured Europe w. Noble Sissle and worked from time to time w. Carroll Dickerson, King Oliver and others). W. Lucky Millinder '34-6, John Kirby '37-46, Wilbur De Paris to '49, Red Allen & own groups '51, Big Chief Russell Moore Sept. '52-Feb. '53, pit band *Porgy and Bess,* NYC '53-4, Red Allen '54 in Boston and at Metropole NYC. Continued to play at Metropole w. Allen and also made symphony app. w. Leon Barzin, Everette Lee, Dmitri Mitropoulos. Pl. at NJF '57, '59, Great South Bay Festival '57, Shakespeare Fest. in Canada '58. Bailey was the first academically trained clarinetist to make a name as an outstanding jazzman. His characteristics are a fluent technique, a thin tone, and a style sometimes called cold, but always highly personal. Own LP on Felsted; LPs w. Kirby (Col.), *Jazz At The Metropole* (Beth.), two numbers w. Wingy Manone in *A String Of Swingin' Pearls* (Vict.); *Golden Era of Jazz* (Design), Juanita Hall (Ctpt.); Fletcher Henderson (River.), Dickenson-Thomas (Atl.).

Addr: 341 Washington Ave., Brooklyn 5, N.Y.

BAILEY, SAMUEL DAVID (Dave), *drums,* b. Portsmouth, Va., 2/22/26. Raised in Philadelphia where he received first training at home with musical family. Moved to NYC 1947; studied at Music Center Conservatory under G.I. Bill. First job w. Herbie Jones band '51-53; gigged w. Al Sears, J. Hodges, L. Donaldson, C. Mingus, H. Silver, Mulligan et al. Worked frequently w. Gerry Mulligan '55-9, making four European tours with him; during one tour, March '59, made soundtrack for Italian movie in Milan w. Lars Gullin et al. Played w. Ben Webster, NYC '58; Billy Taylor '59, Art Farmer-Benny Golson Jazztet fall '59. Skilled and tasteful performer, Bailey is one of the best small group drummers in modern jazz. Favs: Blakey, Roach, Ed Thigpen, A. Taylor, Philly Joe Jones, Elvin Jones, Ron Jefferson. LPs w. Mulligan (Merc., Verve, Wor.-Pac., Col.), Lou Donaldson (Blue Note), Bob Brookmeyer (Wor.-Pac.), Art Farmer (UA), Lee Konitz (Verve); *The Subterraneans* soundtrack (MGM).

Addr: 1164 East 223rd St., Bronx 66, N.Y.

BAILEY, DONALD ORLANDO, *drums;* b. Phila., Pa. 3/26/34. Got first musical inspiration from brother Maurice, who pl. tenor and drums. Largely self-taught. Gigs around Phila. w. Jimmy DeBrest. W. Jimmy Smith trio from 1955. Favs: Blakey, Roach, Philly Joe Jones, Art Taylor. LPs w. Jimmy Smith, Sonny Rollins (Blue Note).

Addr: 3220A McMichael St., Phila., Pa.

BAILEY, MILDRED (née Mildred Rinker), *singer;* b. Tekoa, Wash., 2/27/07, d. 12/12/51. Her brother, Al Rinker, teamed w. Bing Crosby as one of the original rhythm boys of Paul Whiteman's band. Joining Whiteman in 1929, she became one of the first girl band vocalists, remaining w. him for several years, during which time she married Red Norvo, who was also with the band. From '36-9 she and Norvo were joint leaders of a band. Later she worked mainly as a solo act; had her own CBS radio show in the mid-'40s. Won *Esquire* award '44 (Silver), '45, '46 (tied for Gold). Partly of American Indian origin, she was inspired by Bessie Smith, Ethel Waters and other early blues singers and was the first non-Negro girl singer accepted in jazz. Her unique, rather high-pitched tone and sense of jazz phrasing, especially on blues and ballads, and her association on records with the accompaniment of Red Norvo, Teddy Wilson, John Kirby, earned her a lasting place in jazz history.

Beginning 10/5/29, when she made her debut on *What Kind O' Man Is You* w. Ed Lang's Orch. on Okeh, she recorded prolifically, mainly for Victor 1931, Bruns.-Voc.-Col. '33-40 (often w. Norvo Orch.), Decca '41-2, Crown '45, Majestic '46, and a few later sides for Victor & Decca. An LP is available on Regent; many sides are due for reissue on Col., Decca.

BAILEY, OZZIE, *singer;* b. New York City, 11/6/25. Began stud. voice in 1951; later coached by Luther Henderson until joining w. Duke Ellington March, '57. Experience was gained through work at parties and in small clubs. Feat. w. Ellington on the TV spectacular, *A Drum Is a Woman,* CBS, '57, and on the album of the same name for Col. Toured Europe w. Ellington fall '58. Expressive voice, effective on ballads; not a jazz singer. LPs w. Ellington (Col.), Luther Henderson (MGM).

BAILEY, PEARL, *singer;* b. Newport News Va., 3/29/18. Began as dancer; sang in NYC nightclubs in early '40s, then toured as band vocalist w. Cootie Williams '43-4. Starred in Broadway musical *St. Louis Woman* '46. In late '40s became nationally known as comedienne, though much of her work retained many jazz qualities. Married Louis Bellson Nov. '52. Film: *Carmen Jones,* 1954. Broadway musical, *House of Flowers,* 1954-55. Scored a big hit with her appearance in a Bob Hope film, *That Certain Feeling* '56; in nightclub app. at the Waldorf-Astoria NYC, as well as on many television shows. Acc. by Bellson's band in club and theatre work. Film: *St. Louis Blues* '58. Own LPs on Coral, Merc., Roul., Voc.

Addr: Apple Valley, Calif.

BAKER, CHESNEY H. (Chet), *trumpet, singer;* b. Yale, Okla., 12/23/29. Family moved to Calif. 1940. Began musical training at Glendale Jr. High. Trumpet in marching and dance bands; drafted '46. Pl. in 298th Army Band, Berlin, Germany. Discharged '48. Theory and harmony at El Camino College, LA. Re-enlisted '50 in order to join Presidio Army Band in San Francisco. Sat in nightly at Bop City there. Discharged

'52, pl. dates on the Coast w. Charlie Parker, joined Gerry Mulligan and gained national prominence. Left in '53 to form own group for clubs and records. Spent Sept. '55 to Apr. '56, touring European continent, Iceland and England. Toured US w. Birdland All Stars, Feb. '57 then in Scandanavia and Italy w. own combo. Semi-inactive since then, working with quartet or quintet of varying personnel from time to time. Still working mainly in Italy during 1959-60. Light, pure sound, stylistically descendant from Miles Davis; as singer, weak-voiced but appealing to feminine audiences. Won *DB* Critics' Poll '53 as new star; *DB* poll '53-4, *Met.* poll '54-5, London *Melody Maker* poll '55, German *Jazz Echo* poll '56, '58, *Playboy* poll '58. Own LPs on Wor. Pac., Col.; LPs w. Mulligan (Wor. Pac., GNP.), Stan Getz (Verve).

BAKER, EDWARD, JR. (Eddie), *piano;* b. Chicago, Ill., 10/13/27. Stud. piano and comp. American Conservatory, 1937-41, and w. Bill Russo '48-56. Became interested in jazz after hearing M. Roach, Bud Powell, L. Young, D. Gordon. Worked in Chi. w. Miles Davis '50, Illinois Jacquet '51, Paul Bascomb, Bill Russo, Sonny Stitt, Wilbur Ware. European tour w. Russo '55; acc. Billie Holiday for four weeks in Honolulu, summer '56; backed Roy Eldridge at Bee Hive, Chi. '56. Wrote *L'Affaire Bugs* for Russo's *World of Alcina* LP on Atl. Favs: J. Lewis, B. Powell, Monk, H. Silver. Fav. arr: Lewis, G. Russell, Russo. LPs w. Russo (Atl.), Max Roach (Argo).

Addr: 314 So. Sacramento Blvd., Chi. 12, Ill.

BAKER, DAVID N. (Dave), *trombone;* also *piano, bass, tuba, bass trom.;* b. Indianapolis, Ind., 12/21/31. Stud. tuba and trom. at Arthur Jordan Cons. and Indiana U. where he got a master of music education degree. Pl. with several local groups 1948-53; w. Tony Papa in Chicago '53; back to Indianapolis playing w. local groups. W. Stan Kenton briefly '56; Maynard Ferguson '57; own big band '58-9. Awarded the *Down Beat* Hall of Fame scholarship to Berklee School of Music '59; att. School of Jazz in Lenox, Mass. Aug. '59. Favs: Bill Harris, J. J. Johnson, Slide Hampton, Frank Rosolino. Fav. arr: John Lewis, Gil Evans, Al Cohn, Bill Holman. One of the best-equipped and most promising of younger trombonists.

BAKER, KENNETH (Kenny), *trumpet;* b. Withersnea, Yorks, England, 3/1/21. Learned piano at home; took up cornet at 12 in local brass band. Began pl. w. Lew Stone in London, 1939; also worked w. Maurice Winnick, J. Hylton, Ambrose, Sid Millward. From '46-9 was lead trumpeter and arr. for Ted Heath. Studio and film work '49-51, incl. sound tracks for *Red Shoes, Genevieve,* etc. Leads his own group, Baker's Dozen, but works mainly as a soloist in TV, etc. Won *Melody Maker* Readers' Poll of Britain's Best, '57. L. Armstrong, B. Berigan were early influences. Fav. own solo: *Dark Eyes* w. Heath (Decca). On all Heath LPs for Decca/London. Own LPs on Nixa, Polygon, Br. Columbia.

Addr: 63 Witley Ct., Woburn Place, London, W.C. 1, England.

BAKER, LA VERN, *singer;* b. Chicago, Ill., 1928. Starting professionally in early teens, she worked as singer and dancer in Chicago clubs during '40s and early '50s; toured Europe in 1953. Her record of a novelty nonsense song, *Tweedlee Dee,* released in '54, elevated her overnight from $125-a-week obscurity to $1,500-a-week national fame as a rhythm and blues attraction. Originally known as "Little Miss Sharecropper," she was later billed "LaVern Baker, the Tweedle Dee Girl." From the jazz standpoint she is one of the better rock-and-roll performers, with a relaxed rhythmic style that rises above the level of her material. Records for Atlantic, mostly single releases; also LPs incl. *La Vern Baker Sings Bessie Smith.*

Addr: c/o Atlantic Records, 157 W. 57th St., NYC 19.

BAKER, McHOUSTON (Mickey), *guitar;* b. Louisville, Ky., 10/15/25. Began pl. bass 1945; switched to homemade guitar. After exp. as sideman, leader, studio musician on many recs., he teamed w. Sylvia Vanderpool; they had great success in r & b field as "Mickey & Sylvia." The team became "Mickey & Kitty" in '59 when Kitty Noble joined Baker's act. Has own guitar school. Fav: Ch. Christian. Own LPs: Atl.; LP w. Louis Jordan (Merc.), w. Sylvia: Vik.

Addr: 238 West 101st St., New York 25, N.Y.

BAKER, HAROLD (Shorty), *trumpet;* b. St. Louis, Mo., 5/26/14. With Erskine Tate, Fate Marable, Eddie Johnson in early '30s, Don Redman '35-7, Teddy Wilson's big band '39-40, Andy Kirk '40, Mary Lou Williams (to whom he was married) '42. On and off w. Duke Ellington, Jan.-Apr. '38 and Nov. '43 to Dec. '51, incl. European tour '50. Free-lanced in East, club dates w. Teddy Wilson, Ben Webster '52; joined Johnny Hodges orch. '54. Rejoined Ellington May '57. Left the band again Sept. '59, formed own quartet. Fine tone, capable section leader and solo man. Own LP on King; LPs w. Ellington (Col.); *Jazztime USA* (Bruns.).

Addr: Hotel Alvin, 52nd Street & Broadway, New York 19, N.Y.

BALES, BURTON F. (Burt), *piano;* also *mellophone, bar. sax;* b. Stevensville, Mont., 3/20/16. Private piano lessons 1928, theory and arranging at Tamalpais High School, '34. St. Piano playing in speakeasies, '31, Santa Cruz, Calif. Jazz experience w. Lu Watters '42. Army, '43. Joined Bunk Johnson '43, Dude Martin, '44; own group and solo work '45-9; re-joined Watters '49, then worked w. Turk Murphy at Hangover Club in SF '49-50. Played w. Bob Scobey '50 and '53, Marty Marsala '54, but has worked mostly as single and w. own groups since '50. Soloist at Pier 23 Club, SF for several years in late '50s; appeared w. Lizzie Miles at Monterey Jazz Festival '59. Favs: Jelly Roll Morton, Fats Waller, J. P. Johnson, Joe Sullivan, Don Ewell, Ralph Sutton. Won dj poll on west coast for ragtime piano '43. Record debut '49 on GTJ, in trio w. Ed Garland

and Minor Hall. Own LPs on ABC-Par., GTJ; LPs w. Turk Murphy, Bob Scobey, Bunk Johnson (GTJ).

Addr: c/o Musicians Union No. 6, San Francisco, Calif.

BALL, RONALD (Ronnie), *piano;* b. Birmingham, England, 12/22/27. Local bands at 15; to London '48, rec. w. Tony Kinsey, Ronnie Scott, Vic Feldman and other jazz combos. Immigrated to US in Jan. '52. Stud. w. Lennie Tristano. With Chuck Wayne trio Aug. '52; Lee Konitz quint. '53-5. Moving to West Coast he worked w. Warne Marsh quint. '56-7; own trio w. Red Mitchell, Dennis Budimir fall '57. In '58 he worked w. the Buddy Rich and Kai Winding combos, joining the Gene Krupa quart. in Oct. '58, app. with him at clubs and jazz festivals. He was also w. Roy Eldridge briefly in '59. Fleet, impressive modern soloist. Own LP on Sav.; w. Warne Marsh (Imp., Kapp); Ted Brown (Vang.), *Hot vs. Cool* (MGM), L. Konitz (Atl., Story.).

Addr: 185 E. 2nd St., New York 9, N.Y.

BALLARD, GEORGE (Butch), *drums;* b. Camden, N.J., 12/26/18. With Cootie Williams '42, Louis Armstrong '46, Eddie Davis at Minton's; own band in Philadelphia '47-8; Mercer Ellington '48, Count Basie '49; toured Europe w. Duke Ellington, supplementing the other drummer, Sonny Greer, '50. With Ellington again for a few months '53. During the late '50s, led his own small band in Phila. and other Eastern cities incl. Canada. Backed Nina Simone, Dinah Washington, Sonny Stitt, etc. at Showboat in Phila. Rec. on Cap. w. Cootie Williams, *No Variety Blues* w. Armstrong (Vict.), *Slider* w. Basie (Vict.). LPs w. Eddie Davis (Roul.), Ellington (Cap.), Basie (Vict., Cam.).

Addr: 1882 Plum St., Philadelphia 24, Pa.

BANK, DANIEL BERNARD (Danny), *baritone sax;* also *reeds, flute;* b. Brooklyn, N.Y., 7/17/22. Played with Ch. Barnet 1942-4; B. Goodman '45; J. Dorsey, Paul Whiteman '46-7; Artie Shaw, Tommy Dorsey, and back several times with Barnet; extensive free lance work in NYC '50-'60, more often as section man than as soloist. Featured on *Dancer* in *The Swinging Seasons* (MGM); *Cu-ba* w. Barnet (Cap.). Other LPs w. Sauter-Finegan (Vict.), Rex Stewart (Grand Award), Ralph Burns (Decca).

Addr: 570 East Second St., Brooklyn 18, N.Y.

BAQUET, GEORGE, *clarinet;* b. New Orleans, La., 1883; d. Phila., Pa., 1/14/49. Played w. brass bands around the turn of the century incl. the Onward Band, Imperial Orch. Worked w. John Robichaux 1904, Superior Band 1906, Magnolia and Olympia bands 1908-14, then toured w. Bill Johnson's original Creole Orch. In Los Angeles, Chicago and New York until 1918. Settled in Phila. and remained there until his death. Reputed to be the first to play the famous solo on *High Society,* he was one of the first known clarinetists of jazz; inspired Jimmie Noone and Sidney Bechet. Rec. w. Bessie Smith (Col. '23), Jelly Roll Morton (Vict. '29).

BARBARIN, PAUL, *drums;* b. New Orleans, La., 5/5/01. Father, Isadore, pl. mellophone and alto horn in brass band. Began on clarinet at the age of fifteen, then took up drums. Pl. w. Silver Leaf Orch. '18. Then w. Luis Russell; Amos White '24. To Chicago w. King Oliver '25. Ret. to NO '27, worked w. Fats Pichon, A. Piron. To NYC '28, joined Luis Russell, returning to NO '33. Toured w. Louis Armstrong '35-39, then ret. to NO again. W. Red Allen '42, Sidney Bechet '43; then in Mardi Gras parade band and w. other NO outfits; w. Art Hodes at Jazz Ltd., Chi. '53. Own band at Childs, NYC Jan. '55, Beverly Cavern in LA, May '55. App. on *Today* ('56) and *Wide, Wide World* ('58) TV shows. In June '59, two weeks as guest drummer at Basin Street, Toronto, Can. Own LPs on Atlantic, Riverside.

Addr: 2605 St. Anthony St., New Orleans 19, La.

BARBER, JOHN WILLIAM (Bill), *tuba;* b. Hornell, N.Y., 5/21/20. Stud. Juilliard. B.M. and M.M.E. from Manhattan School of Music. Worked w. KC Philharmonic, ballet and theatre orchs. Army 1942-45. W. Ch. Ventura, Claude Thornhill, Miles Davis, 1940s; Sauter-Finegan, Pete Rugolo, 1950s. Birdland and Apollo Theatre w. Gil Evans '59; Newport Festival w. G. Shearing '59. Also pl. first season of Nassau-Suffolk Symphony Orch. Believed to be first musician to play modern jazz (both solo and section work) on tuba. LPs w. Miles Davis (Cap., Col.), Gil Evans (Wor. Pac.), Pete Rugolo (Col.), *Music For Brass* (Col.), *The Swinging Seasons* (MGM), Ralph Burns (Decca), Urbie Green (ABC-Par.).

Addr: 25 Scott Drive, Huntington Station, N.Y.

BARBER, DONALD CHRISTOPHER (Chris), *trombone, leader;* b. London, Eng., 4/17/30. First pl. violin, sop. sax; stud. trom., bass at Guildhall School of Music. St. first band '49; helped org. band w. Ken Colyer '53, took it over himself '54. Barber's position in Eng. is comparable w. Turk Murphy's in US; though attacked by many critics as musically worthless, his band has enjoyed a phenomenal success in the past couple of years and has pl. to packed houses in concert halls all over Europe. On the strength of his hit recording of Sidney Bechet's *Petite Fleur,* featuring Monty Sunshine on clarinet, Barber's band came to the US in Feb. '59 for concert appearances. Back in US Sept.-Oct. '59, app. at Monterey Jazz Festival. Film: Band pl. musical background for *Look Back In Anger* '59. LPs on Atl., Colpix. Laurie.

BARBOUR, DAVID MICHAEL (Dave), *guitar, songwriter;* b. New York City, 5/28/12. Banjo, then guitar in small groups including Wingy Manone '34, Red Norvo '35-6. In late '30s made many record dates w. Louis and Lil Armstrong, Mildred Bailey, Teddy Wilson, Bunny Berigan etc. Worked with name bands including Artie Shaw '39, Benny Goodman '42. Goodman's singer was Peggy Lee; during their marriage ('43-52), Barbour accompanied her on many Capitol records and they wrote popular songs such as *Mañana* and *It's a Good Day.* Inactive as jazz guitarist in recent years, except for a few weeks in Cuba w. Woody Herman Dec. 1949, Barbour has led groups on record dates for Nellie Lutcher, Jeri Southern, and others. Appeared in acting role opposite Claudette Colbert in *Secret Fury* '51; except for occasional record dates, Barbour has since been in retirement in Malibu, Cal.—a regrettable waste of a fine talent. LPs w. Peggy Lee, J. Teagarden (Cap.).

Addr: 11618 Cowia, Brentwood, Calif.

BARCELONA, DANIEL (Danny), *drums;* b. Honolulu, 7/23/29. Self-taught. Trombonist Trummy Young, then resident in Hawaii, took Barcelona out of high school into his orch. in 1948. After working w. Young for three years, he formed his own sextet, the Hawaiian Dixieland All Stars, and toured the Far East. In 1955 he visited the Far East again as a member of an international revue. Pl. club engagements in Waikiki, etc. until Sept. '57, when he left for US. In Feb. '58 Trummy Young, now a member of Louis Armstrong's band, recommended him for a job w. Armstrong, whom he then joined, replacing Barrett Deems. Favs: Krupa, Buddy Rich, Max Roach. LPs w. Louis Armstrong (Col., Decca), Teddy Buckner (Dix. Jub.).

Addr: c/o Associated Booking Corp., 745 Fifth Ave., New York 22, N.Y.

BAREFIELD, EDWARD EMANUEL (Eddie), *clarinet, saxes, arranger;* b. Scandia, Iowa, 12/12/09. Piano at 10, alto sax at 13, by ear until 17. Broke into music bus. w. Edgar Pillows in Des Moines, '26. W. Va. Ravens '27; in '30 stud. clarinet at cons. in Chi.; in '31 w. Teddy Wilson, Art Tatum; '32, lead alto w. Bennie Moten; '33, McKinney's Cotton Pickers, then Cab Calloway; to NYC and then to Europe w. Cab in '34. Les Hite '37; joined F. Henderson '38; fall '38 Don Redman at Savoy. Calloway again '39, then Ella Fitzgerald's Orch.; '40, small combos around NYC incl. Coleman Hawkins & own; Benny Carter '41. 1942-6 staff member and arr. at ABC. 1947, Duke Ellington at Hurricane, also *Endorsed By Dorsey* show, WOR; '48-9, conductor and arr. for band in *Streetcar Named Desire.* With Sy Oliver at Zanzibar '50. To Brazil and Uruguay w. Calloway in '51. Later free-lanced in NYC, continued to work off and on for Calloway, as mus. dir. for his revues incl. Miami and Las Vegas '57, Latin America '58; Copper Door on Broadway, NYC, fall '59. Toured Europe w. Sammy Price combo '58. Fav. musician: Benny Carter. Fav. own solo: *Moonglow* w. Calloway (Vict.). LP: *Swing Goes Dixie* w. Roy Eldridge (Verve).

Addr: 861 Macy Place, Bronx 55, N.Y.

BARKER, DANIEL (Danny), *guitar, banjo;* b. New Orleans, La., 1/13/09. Grandfather was Isidore John Barbarin, horn player with Onward Brass Band. His uncle, Paul Barbarin, interested him in music, taught him drums; he also took a few lessons on clarinet with B. Bigard, but soon switched to ukulele, guitar and banjo, later stud. w. Bernard Addison. Played w. Jones-Collins Astoria group and many local bands. To NYC, 1930, worked w. Harry White, Dave Nelson, Lucky Millinder, Cab Calloway, James P. Johnson, Benny Carter; also acc. and wrote tunes for his wife, singer Blue Lu Barker, and r & b records. Reverted from guitar to banjo, pl. w. Barbarin '54-5, then settled in NYC, free-lancing in single and duo work in clubs. LPs: *Sound of Jazz,* also Bunk Johnson, Jimmy Rushing (Col.), Dickenson-Thomas (Atl.), Chu Berry (Comm.), Sir Ch. Thompson (Apollo), *Lavern Baker Sings Bessie Smith* (Atl.), *Magic Horn* w. G. Wein (Vict.), Mary Osborne (Warwick). Own banjo LP on Period. Barker is prominently featured in autobiographical passages in *Hear Me Talkin' To Ya* (Rinehart).

Addr: 495 West 130th St., New York 27, N.Y.

BARKER, WARREN, *composer, conductor;* b. Oakland, Cal., 4/16/23. Father played organ in church and in silent movies. Studied piano and trumpet while in High School; music at UCLA and w. Mario Castelnuovo-Tedesco. Played in Air Force band '43-6. Active since '47 in radio, movie, and TV scoring, mainly in pop field, though he earned some jazz association for his work on the 77 *Sunset Strip* show and the best-selling album of music from this series in '59. Own LP: 77 *Sunset Strip* (War. Bros.)

Addr: 2099 Centella Place, Newport Beach, Calif.

BARKSDALE, Everett, *guitar;* b. Detroit, Mich., 4/28/10. Started on alto, guitar, bass; early exp. w. dance schools. Pl. w. Erskine Tate, Chicago; ten years w. Eddie South through 1930s. Early '40s w. Benny Carter, Herman Chittison, then several years w. Leon Abbey. Also CBS staff work, w. Jubilaires on Arthur Godfrey show, '42-4. Art Tatum trio '49-55. Spent most of '56 as music director and arr. for Billy Kenny and the Inkspots in Europe and Canada. Rejoined Tatum in Sept. '56 and pl. last engagements before Tatum's death. Since then active in studio work, rec., and local NYC gigs such as doubling on bass w. Buddy Tate '58-9. LPs w. Tatum (Cap.), Louis Armstrong (Decca), Red Allen (Vict.), Dickie Wells, Buddy Tate, Rex Stewart (Fels.), Sarah Vaughan, Dinah Washington (Mercury), Chris Connor (Beth.), Dickenson-Thomas (Atl.).

Addr: 10 West 135th St., New York 37, N. Y.

BARNES, GEORGE, *guitar;* b. Chicago Heights, Ill., 7/17/21. Studied with father. Toured Middle West with own quartet 1935-9, then NBC staff to Chicago. Worked with Bud Freeman at College Inn, Chi., '42, then Army to 1946. ABC radio in Chi. to Nov. 1951, when he moved to NYC to do TV and recording work. Has worked more in pop than jazz field. LPs w. Lawson-Haggart (Decca), Garry Moore (Col.), Ernie Royal (Urania).

Addr: 12 Southfield Rd., Glen Cove, L.I., N.Y.

BARNET, CHARLES DALY (Charlie), *alto, tenor, soprano saxes, leader;* b. New York City, 10/26/13. Scion of a wealthy family, whose urgings that he become a corporation lawyer were stubbornly resisted, he led his own band on a transatlantic liner at 16. He crossed the ocean 22 times, later went to the South Seas and

Latin America. First prominent in jazz circles as leader of band at Paramount Hotel, NYC, 1932, and on Red Norvo records (Col. '34). Achieved greatest fame w. hit record of *Cherokee,* rec. for Victor-Bluebird 7/17/39. A volatile tenor stylist and Hodges-influenced alto man, he also played soprano sax leading the reed section. His 1939-41 band was a fine swing outfit feat. arrs. by Billy May and Barnet, many Ellington tunes. Barnet played the Apollo theatre in Harlem in 1933 and was among the first white leaders to feature Negro stars extensively, among them Lena Horne '41; Trummy Young, Peanuts Holland, Oscar Pettiford '43. In later years he formed and disbanded numerous large and small groups, feat. artists incl. Frances Wayne and Neal Hefti, Ralph Burns, B. De Franco, Fran Warren, Kay Starr and dozens of first-rate jazzmen. A colorful personality, married six times, Barnet often made newspaper headlines and was one of the most talked about figures in jazz in the late 1930s and early '40s. He won the Met. poll 1941-4. Rec. affiliations: Melotone '33, Bluebird '34-42, Decca '42-6, Apollo '46-7, Cap. '49-50, Abbey '52, Clef-Verve '53-57, Everest '58-60. Barnet entered personal management in Hollywood '58. Since that time he has also played gigs and recorded with pick-up groups. Own LPs on Verve, Cap., Decca, Camden, Vict.; LPs w. Red Norvo (Epic), *Metronome All Stars* (Harmony, Vict.).

Addr: 8546 Hillside Ave., Los Angeles 46, Calif.

BARRETTO, RAY, *conga drums;* b. New York City, 4/29/29. Became interested in jazz overseas during Army service 1946-9 when he met European musicians. From '49-53 jammed around Harlem, playing w. Lou Donaldson, Donald Byrd et al. Began pl. professionally '54 with Tito Puente, Jose Curbelo and Pete Terrace; has pl. with many jazz and Afro-Cuban groups. LPs w. Red Garland, Gene Ammons (Pres.), Lou Donaldson (Blue Note).

Addr: 920 Prospect Ave., Bronx 59, N.Y.

BARTH, BEN CALDWELL (Benny), *drums;* b. Indianapolis, Ind., 2/16/29. Stud. at Butler U.; pl. with Lennie Niehaus, Conte Candoli. Joined Buddy and Monk Montgomery and Richie Crabtree to form the Mastersounds (q.v.) 1956. Names Gene Krupa, Dave Tough, Jo Jones and Sid Catlett as influences. LPs w. Mastersounds (Wor. Pac.), Virgil Gonsalves (Omega); *Drums On Fire* (Wor. Pac.).

BASCOMB, WILBUR ODELL (Dud), *trumpet;* b. Birmingham, Ala., 5/16/16. One of the original Ala. State Coll. students who came to NYC in 1935 w. Erskine Hawkins, he was feat. with the band until '44, playing the trumpet solos (often wrongly attributed to Hawkins) on *Tuxedo Junction, Gin Mill Special,* etc. Had his own band with brother Paul for a year, '44-5, then own combo on 52nd St.; a year w. Duke Ellington 1947 (feat. on *Women,* Col.). In early '50s led his own quintet at Tyler's Country Club, Rahway, N.J. Since '55 numerous theatre dates, also one-nighters w. Jackie Wilson for Universal Attractions.

Addr: 457 West 164th St., New York 32, N.Y.

BASCOMB, PAUL, *tenor sax;* b. Birmingham, Ala., 2/12/10. Like his brother Dud, he was feat. for many years with the Erskine Hawkins band, his best known solo being *Sweet Georgia Brown.* Since the late 1940s he has toured with his own combo, which has enjoyed considerable success in r & b circles. He recorded w. Count Basie in '41. Many rec. dates late '50s, incl. Dinah Washington (Merc.) in '56; Little Esther, the Flamingos, etc. and own group for State and Mercury. Feat. since 1957 at Esquire Club in Chi.

Addr: 7438 So. Champlain, Chicago 19, Ill.

BASIE, WILLIAM (Count), *leader, piano, organ, composer;* b. Red Bank, N.J., 8/21/04. Stud. music with mother. Played piano from childhood, picking up rudiments of ragtime from early Harlem pianists and studying organ informally with Fats Waller. Prof. debut in New York as accompanist to vaudeville acts; replaced Waller in an act called Katie Crippen and her Kids; also worked with June Clark, Sonny Greer and others.

While traveling with the Gonzel White vaudeville show on the Keith Circuit, he found himself stranded in Kansas City when the outfit broke up. He played at a silent movie theater for a while, then spent a year with Walter Page's Blue Devils, 1928-9. The band included Jimmy Rushing.

After this band broke up Basie and some of the other members joined Bennie Moten. This band stayed together until Moten's death in 1935. The band continued under the leadership of Moten's brother Buster, but Basie, starting a new group of his own and working at the Reno club, soon had the best of Moten's personnel working for him.

The band gradually built up in quality and quantity of personnel; broadcasting from the club on a small local station it was heard by John Hammond, who decided the band must be brought to New York. The band enlarged its personnel further, came to New York in 1936 and made its first recording session for Decca in Jan. 1937. By the following year it had become internationally famous. The qualities that established it were Basie's simple, somewhat elliptical piano style and the rhythm section that supported it (from March 1937 this consisted of Freddie Greene, guitar, Jo Jones, drums, and Walter Paige, bass); the blues singing of James Rushing, and the styles of the principal soloists—Lester Young and Herschel Evans on tenor saxes, Earl Warren on alto, Buck Clayton and Harry Edison on trumpets, Benny Morton and Dickie Wells on trombones, among others; also the arrangements, some written by Eddie Durham and various men in the band, others spontaneously developing "head" arrangements.

Through the 1940s, despite the occasional loss of key soloists, Basie consistently maintained a band whose contagious rhythmic pulsation and superlative team spirit, combined with a succession of inspired

Duke Ellington (*Herman Leonard*)

Johnny Hodges (*J. C. Bernath*)

Jimmie Lunceford (*Courtesy Claude Jones*)

Ben Webster (*Herman Leonard*)

Duke Ellington's orchestra, at Birdland, 1951. Trumpeter next to drummer Louis Bellson is Harold Baker; saxophones are Paul Gonsalves, Jimmy Hamilton, Willie Smith, Russell Procope, Harry Carney; trombones; Quentin Jackson, Juan Tizol, Britt Woodman *(Bob Matthew)*

Django Reinhardt with Duke Ellington in New York, 1948 *(Bill Gottlieb)*

Duke Ellington (*Columbia Records*)

Trummy Young (*Down Beat*)

Barney Bigard; Velma Middleton in background (*Down Beat*)

Benny Carter (*Otto F. Hess*)

Jonah Jones (*Capitol Records*)

Stuff Smith and Stephane Grappelly (*Herman Leonard*)

Jimmy and Tommy Dorsey *(Courtesy Claude Jones)*

Tommy Dorsey and Jack Teagarden (*Otto F. Hess*)

While a student at the University of Colorado, Glenn Miller did some of his earliest professional work playing at a small club in Denver

Glenn Miller on his way to a one-night stand with the band, about 1939

Artie Shaw (*David B. Hecht*)

Count Basie's orchestra, 1940. Trumpets, L. to R.: Buck Clayton, Ed Lewis (hidden), Al Killian, Harry Edison; trombones: Vic Dickenson, Dickie Wells, Dan Minor; saxes: Buddy Tate, Tab Smith, Jack Washington, Lester Young. Rhythm: Walter Paige, bass; Basie, piano; Jo Jones, drums; Freddie Greene, guitar (*M. Smith*)

Count Basie, Mezz Mezzrow and Earl Hines in Paris (*Jean-Marie*)

Count Basie (*Victor Tanaka*)

Harry Edison
(Down Beat)

Bobby Hackett
(Capitol Records)

Buck Clayton
(Robert Parent)

Mildred Bailey and Red Norvo, ca. 1937 (*Fred Hess and Son*)

52nd Street, 1938: Pete Brown, Maxine Sullivan and Buster Bailey at the Onyx Club (*Down Beat*)

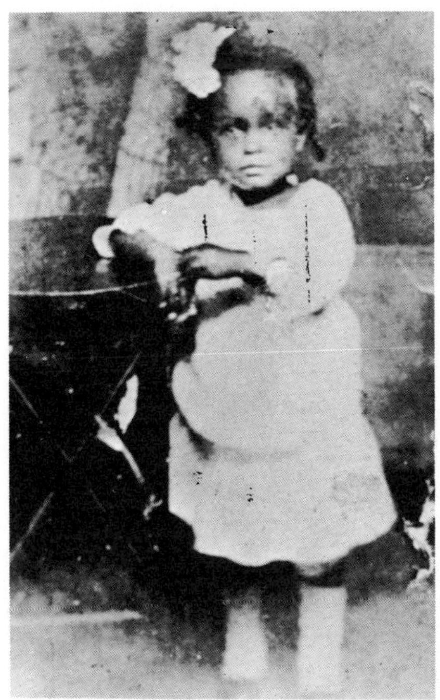

Billie Holiday, 1918 (*Courtesy Greer Johnson*)

Billie Holiday (*Bert Block*)

Benny Goodman orchestra at the height of its fame, 1937, seen here in one of its Hollywood motion picture appearances. Rhythm section comprises Harry Goodman, bass; Jess Stacy, piano; Allan Reuss, guitar; and Gene Krupa, drums. Trumpets are L. to R.: Harry James, Ziggy Elman, Chris Griffin, trombones: Murray McEachern, Red Ballard; saxophones: Vido Musso, Hymie Schertzer, Arthur Rollini, George Koenig (*Metronone*)

Part of Benny Goodman's Sextet, 1941: Cootie Williams, Georgie Auld, Goodman, Charlie Christian, Dave Tough (*Otto F. Hess*)

Dave Tough (*Courtesy Claude Jones*)

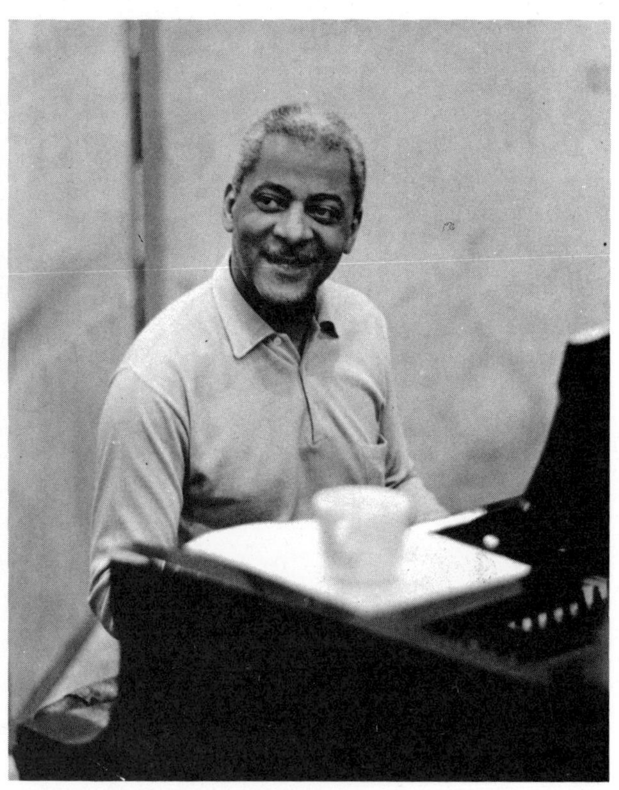

Teddy Wilson (*Columbia Records*)

Charlie Christian and Gene Krupa (*The Record Changer*)

Gene Krupa, NBC's *Timex Show;* Steve Allen, Woody Herman and Jack Teagarden in background

Benny Goodman

Teddy Wilson, Arvell Shaw, Benny Goodman and Red Norvo, NBC's *Swing into Spring*

Peggy Lee, Benny Goodman, Lionel Hampton, Ella Fitzgerald celebrating Goodman's 25th anniversary as a bandleader, 1959 (*Photo by Popsie*)

John Hammond (*Columbia Records*)

Joe Turner (*Metronome*)

Big Bill Broonzy

Eddie Condon; Edmond Hall in background (*Columbia Records*)

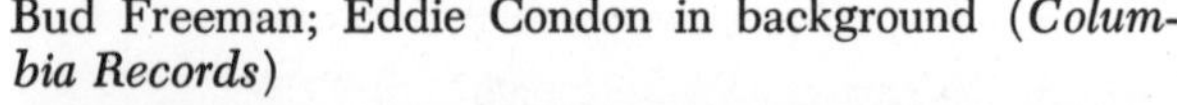

Bud Freeman; Eddie Condon in background (*Columbia Records*)

Hot Lips Page (*Herman Leonard*)

soloists, remained unique in jazz. During these years the band featured a number of outstanding tenor sax men, including Don Byas, Buddy Tate, Lucky Thompson, Illinois Jacquet and Paul Gonsalves. Al Killian, Joe Newman and Emmett Berry were among the trumpet stars; the trombone section included Vic Dickenson and J. J. Johnson. (Basie also used girl singers, usually for the pop ballads; the first and best was Helen Humes.)

Except for a period in 1950-1, when economic conditions compelled him to tour with a septet (the personnel included Clark Terry, Wardell Gray and Buddy de Franco), Basie has led a big band continuously for the past two and a half decades and has gained a global reputation for his undying allegiance to the beat, his loyalty to the blues as a basic form, and his ability to produce, year after year, records of unflaggingly high caliber. In 1954, when the band made its first tour of Europe, and '55, when Basie completed his twentieth year as a leader, many new stars were featured, among them Thad Jones and Joe Wilder on trumpets; Benny Powell and Henry Coker on trombones; Frank Foster and Frank Wess on tenors. Most of the arrangements were by Ernie Wilkins and Neal Hefti, with additional scores by Johnny Mandel, Frank Foster, Manny Albam and others. The band toured overseas with tremendous success, visiting the Continent for the first time Sept. '56, and making the first of several tours of Britain Apr. '57. During a second British tour, Oct.-Nov. '57, Basie's became the first U.S. band ever to play a Royal Command performance for the Queen. Basie also set a precedent by playing 13 weeks in the roof ballroom of the Waldorf-Astoria Hotel, NYC, June-Sept. '57, the first big Negro jazz band ever to play the Waldorf.

In addition to frequent foreign tours, US concert tours and appearances at the major jazz festivals, the band has appeared many times each year at Birdland on Broadway.

The Basie orchestra has won the following polls: *Esquire* Silver Award '45; *Down Beat* readers' poll '55, '57-9; *Metronome* poll '58-60; DB Critics' Poll '54-7; *Playboy* All Stars' All Stars '59; as pianist, won Met. poll '42-3; in '58 he was elected to DB Hall of Fame.

Basie recorded for Victor as a sideman with Page and Moten from 1929 (these records have long been unavailable). His first session as a leader, cut with a quintet in Chicago Oct. '36, is now under Lester Young's name on an Epic LP. The band's affiliations were with Decca (Jan. '37-Feb. '39); the Columbia-Vocalion-Okeh group from Mar. '39 until Aug. '46 (many sides now on Col. and Epic LPs); RCA Victor '47-9; Columbia '50-1; then with Norman Granz' labels (Clef, Verve) until fall '57, when the band signed with Roulette.

LPs: Basie & Orch. (Dec. 8049), *April In Paris* (Verve 8012), *Band of Distinction* (Verve 8103), Basie (Roulette 52003), Basie-Eckstine (Roulette 52029), *Basie In London* (Verve 8199), *Basie One More Time* (Roulette 52024), *Basie Rides Again* (Verve 8108), *Basie Roars Again* (Verve 8018), *Basie's Back In Town* (Epic 3169), *Blues by Basie* (Col. CL-901), *Breakfast Dance & Barbecue* (Roulette 52028), *Chairman of the Board* (Roulette 52032), *Count* (Camden 395), *Basie's Basement* (Camden 497), *Count* (Vervo 8070); with Tony Bennett (Col. CS 8104, Roulette 25072), Davis Trio & Joe Newman (Roulette 52007), *The Greatest* (Verve 2016), *Hall of Fame* (Verve 8291), *Jumpin' at the Woodside* (Brunswick 54012), *King of Swing* (Verve 8104), *Memories ad Lib* with Joe Williams (Roulette 52021), *One O'Clock Jump* (Col. CL-997), *Basie Plays Hefti* (Roulette 52011), *Sing Along with Basie* with Lambert, Hendricks & Ross (Roulette 52018), *Swingin' Count* (Verve 8090), with Joe Williams (Verve 8063), with Lester Young (Epic SN-6031). Other LPs with Benny Goodman (Col. OSL 160, CL 500), Metronome All Stars (Harmony 7044, Camden 426), Illinois Jacquet (Verve 8085), Lester Young (Savoy 12068, 12071), *Spirituals to Swing* (Vanguard 8253-4), *A Night at the Apollo* (under pseud. "Band of the Year"; Vang. 9006).

Addr: 174-27 Adelaide Lane, St. Albans, L.I., N.Y.

BASSO, GIANNI, *tenor saxophone;* b. Asti, Italy, 5/24/31. Stud. music in Turin but started playing professionally in Germany and Belgium 1946-9. Later settled in Milan, worked in commercial bands but often appeared in jazz concerts. Close friend of Oscar Valdambrini, whose career his own has paralleled since '54. Arrigo Polillo comments: "He is by far the best tenor man in Italy; started imitating Stan Getz of the cool days, later developed his own style." LPs on Verve.

BATEMAN, CHARLES (Charlie), *piano;* b. Youngstown, Ohio, 9/12/21. Played w. Edmond Hall at Cafe Society Uptown 1946-8, then dates w. Sy Oliver, Lucky Millinder, Gene Ammons, Sonny Stitt; South American tour with Panama Francis '54. Worked w. Aaron Bell trio in upstate New York '54-6, around NYC until early '58. Devoting time to teaching since, gigging occasionally. App. w. Buffalo Phil. '38, Concord Symph. '55. Fav: Art Tatum. LPs w. Aaron Bell (Herald), Sonny Stitt (Pres.).

Addr: 108-55 Ditmars Blvd., East Elmhurst 69, L.I., N.Y.

BATES, ROBERT (Bob), *bass;* b. Pocatello, Idaho, 9/1/23. Mother an organist; three brothers all pl. bass. Stud. tuba, trumpet, trombone at school; legit. bass in NYC and SF, 1944-8. While in coll. at Boise filled bass chair in local band. Worked w. Sonny Dunham, 1947; Jack Fina, '48-9; Two Beaux and a Peep Trio, 1950-3, then worked w. Dave Brubeck '53-5. Inactive in jazz since then. Rec. debut w. Jack Sheedy's Dixieland band, SF '49. Favs: Blanton, Ray Brown, Red Mitchell. LPs w. Brubeck (Col.).

Addr: 5222 Marathon Ave., Los Angeles 29, Calif.

BATES, JAMES BERNARD (Jim), *bass, piano, composer;* b. Boise, Idaho, 11/16/30. Stud. w. brothers Bob and Norman, both ex-Brubeck bassists. Worked w. casual bands, jazz combos around SF, 1949-51; Army '51-3; from '54 w. commercial bands, etc. around LA. Favs: Blanton, Ray Brown, Red Mitchell. LP: *Linear Sketches* w. Julius Wechter Quartet (Jazz: West).

BATES, NORMAN LOUIS, *bass;* also *piano, sax;* b. Boise, Idaho, 8/26/27. Mother, Emily Bates, prof. pianist, organist. Brothers Bill, Bob, Jim all musicians. Stud. at home, inspired by D. Ellington. Bass w. J. Dorsey 1945, Raymond Scott '46; Henry King, C. Cavallaro '47; Dave Brubeck Trio '48-9. Piano and bass w. Jack Sheedy Dixieland band '50; Air Force '51-5. Bass w. Wally Rose Dixieland band '55, then repl. his brother Bob in Brubeck Quartet until Feb. '58, when he returned to San Francisco and led own trio at Fack's. Favs: Blanton, Red Mitchell. LPs w. Brubeck (Fant., Col.), Wally Rose (Col.).

Addr: 2335 45th Avenue, San Francisco, Cal.

BAUDUC, RAYMOND (Ray), *drums;* b. New Orleans, 6/18/09. Studied w. father and brother Jules, whose job he took over as first prof. engagement. To NYC w. Dorsey Bros., Joe Venuti-Eddie Lang 1926; record debut '26 on Pathé w. Memphis Five. W. Freddie Rich Hotel Astor Orch. '26-8; Ben Pollack '29-34, Bob Crosby '35-42, acquiring greatest fame with Crosby through record of *Big Noise From Winnetka,* a duet w. bassist Bob Haggart, during part of which he pl. drumsticks on Haggart's bass strings. Led own band, recorded for Capitol; w. Jimmy Dorsey '47-50, then w. Jack Teagarden until '55 when he and Nappy Lamare formed their own group which has toured the US frequently. Bauduc has long been a symbol of the Dixieland revivalist movement in southern Calif. Own LPs on Cap.; LPs w. Bob Crosby (Coral), Bing Crosby (Decca), Jack Teagarden (Beth.).

Addr: 4909 Holly Blvd., Bellaire 101, Texas.

BAUER, WILLIAM HENRY (Billy), *guitar;* b. New York City, 11/14/15. Started on banjo, mostly self-taught. Joined Jerry Wald on guitar in '39; then Carl Hoff, Dick Stabile, Abe Lyman. Joined Woody Herman early '44. When Herman disbanded in '46, returned to NYC and played w. Benny Goodman, Chubby Jackson and most importantly, Lennie Tristano. In 1953-4, played with Bobby Byrne's band on Steve Allen TV show. Since that time, mainly free-lancing in radio, TV, transcriptions and recording. Pl. Brussels World's Fair w. Benny Goodman '58; app. w. Lee Konitz at Half Note, NYC '59. Excellent rhythm man and facile, inventive soloist; influenced by Tristano. Favs: Charlie Christian, Chuck Wayne. Won DB poll '49-50, Met. poll '49-53. Own LP on Verve; LPs w. Konitz (Verve, Atl., Pres.), Jay and Kai (Savoy), Al Cohn (Vict.), Charlie Parker (Verve), Bobby Hackett-Jack Teagarden (Cap.), Woody Herman (MGM, Col., Ever.).

Addr: 121 Green Way, Albertson, L.I., N.Y.

BEAL, EDDIE, *piano, composer;* b. Redlands, Calif., 6/13/10. Stud. piano w. mother; violin at school. Percussionist w. school symphony. Came to LA as drummer 1931, but switched to piano after a year, playing with the bands of Charlie Eccles, Earl Dancer, Teddy Weatherford (in Shanghai, '34-6). Several years free-lancing around LA, incl. many records w. Herb Jeffries. Army '41-3. Then played with Spirits of Rhythm, Billie Holiday; recorded hit, *Candy Store Blues* w. Toni Harper. Played double piano w. Earl Hines on soundtrack for film *The Strip.* Active in recent years as songwriter and music publisher, he wrote *Softly,* recorded by Georgia Carr, and *Scoot,* recorded by Stan Kenton. LPs w. Red Callender (Metrojazz, Modern), The Platters, The Diamonds, etc. (Merc.).

BEAN, WILLIAM FREDERICK (Billy), *guitar;* b. Philadelphia, Pa., 12/26/33. Mother pl. piano; father guitarist; sister is prof. vocalist. Stud. privately 1945-6 and '51-2. Gigged with many commercial groups around Phila.; joined Ch. Ventura July '56; left him and moved to Cal. Jan. '58, rec. and app. with many combos in LA incl. Paul Horn, Buddy Collette, Buddy De Franco, Calvin Jackson; three wks. on road w. Les Elgart; Bud Shank Quartet. Facile and impressively inventive modern guitarist. Fav. own LPs: *Take York Pick,* guitar duets w. J. Pisano (Dec.). Other LPs: *Makin' It* w. Pisano (Decca), *Slippery When Wet* w. Shank (Wor.-Pac.), *Plenty of Horn* (Dot); Ch. Ventura (Tops, Baton).

BEAN, FLOYD R., *piano composer;* b. Ladora, Iowa, 8/30/04. Played w. Bix Beiderbecke at Linwood Inn in Davenport, 1923; w. Bunny Berigan in Cy Mahlberg band '26; w. Jack Jenney in Earl Hunt band '30. On combo in Davenport '33 and in Chicago '43-4 and '48. Wide experience w. both commercial bands and jazz groups. Best known associations are w. Jimmy McPartland, Bob Crosby '39; Wingy Manone '40; Boyd Raeburn '43; arr. and second piano w. Jess Stacy '45; Paul Mares and Sidney Bechet in '48, all in and around Chicago. After working w. Sid Catlett and Miff Mole, he toured w. Muggsy Spanier '51-2. Joined Georg Brunis '53, remaining w. him through '57 at 1111 Club in Chi. W. Bob Scobey '58, then rejoined Brunis at Preview Lounge in Chi, '59. App. w. him at Playboy Jazz Festival '59. Fav. and greatest influence: Earl Hines. LPs w. Muggsy Spanier (Em.), Jimmy McPartland in *Chicago Jazz Album* (Decca).

Addr: 4878 N. Magnolia, Chicago 40, Ill.

BEAU, HENRY JOHN (Heinie), *composer, clarinet;* b. Calvary, Wisc., 3/8/11. From large musical family. St. on piano at parochial school, then on clar. under father's instruction. Began arr. very early for family orch. which toured the Midwest. To Milwaukee 1939 w. Nick Harper's orch.; later w. Johnny "Scat" Davis, Red Nichols; w. Tommy Dorsey '40-43. Settled in Hollywood as free-lance arr. and musician, working in radio, TV, movies and rec. LPs w. Peggy Lee, Paul Weston, Frank Sinatra (Cap.); Harry Zimmerman

(HiFiRecord); Ted Nash (Col.). Own LP: *Moviesville Jazz* (Cor.), for which he wrote and arr. all compositions.

Addr: 4836 Agnes Ave., N. Hollywood, Calif.

BECHET, SIDNEY, *soprano sax, clarinet;* b. New Orleans, La., 5/14/97; d. Paris, France, 5/14/59. Borrowed his brother Leonard's clarinet at age six, and two years later became a protégé of George Baquet, clarinetist w. John Robichaux's orch. Around the same time he sat in w. Freddie Keppard's band, and by the time he was 17 he had pl. with Jack Carey, Buddy Petit, and the famous Eagle Band of New Orleans, to which Bunk Johnson introduced him about 1912. From '14 to '16 he toured Texas and other southern states w. Clarence Williams and Louis Wade. In '16, back in NO, he worked w. King Oliver's Olympia Band before migrating to Chicago to work w. Tony Jackson, Freddie Keppard and others. Late in '19, after moving to New York and jobbing around for several months, he joined Will Marion Cook's Southern Syncopated Orch., a concert group, which went to Europe, pl. in England and on the continent. Bechet and the band were the subjects of an enthusiastic report by conductor Ernest Ansermet, Bechet becoming probably the first individual jazzman to be seriously considered by a distinguished musician in the classical field.

After Cook's band broke up Bechet joined Bennie Peyton, played in Paris until '21, then returned to NYC. In the early '20s, devoting more of his time to soprano sax and reducing his clar. activities, Bechet made his first and since celebrated records w. Clarence Williams' Blue Five, as well as many other sessions feat. Mamie Smith, Rosetta Crawford and other blues singers, usually under Williams' direction. He worked briefly w. Duke Ellington, one of his greatest admirers, in '25, before ret. to Europe w. the Black Revue; visited Moscow w. Tommy Ladnier, then in '27 led the show band in a new version of the revue. In '28 he joined Noble Sissle's band in Paris and from then until '38 (when he left the music business temporarily and had a tailor shop in NYC), he pl. with Sissle off and on in the US and Europe, often leaving to form bands of his own. After leading a trio at Nick's in Greenwich Village, Bechet app. at many Town Hall concerts w. Eddie Condon during the early '40s, went to Chicago w. a band feat. Vic Dickenson, Sid Catlett. From the late '40s he spent most of his time in Europe, living in France. He returned to the US in '51, and for two months in the summer of '53, recording for Blue Note and Storyville.

The only jazz artist to achieve fame through the use of the sop. sax., Bechet maintained a colorful style with a heavy vibrato and created forceful melodic lines. In France he transcended jazz fame to become a national vaudeville figure, an entertainer and personality in the Maurice Chevalier class. He won the Rec. Ch. All Time, All Star poll, 1951. Own LPs: Blue Note 1201, 1202, 1203, 1204, 1207, GTJ 12013, Col. CL 836, Bruns. 54037, 54048, Wor. Pac. 1236; *Jam Session* w. Spanier (Rondo. A24); tracks in *Creole Reeds* (River. 12-216), *Dixieland At Jazz, Ltd.* (Atl. 1261), *Great Jazz Reeds* (Cam. 339), *Guide To Jazz* (Vict. LPM 1393), *Lower Basin Street* (Cam. 321); w. Noble Sissle in *Encyclopedia of Jazz on Records, Vol. 2* (Decca 8384); w. *New Orleans Feetwarmers* in *Spirituals To Swing* (Vang. 8523/4).

BECK, PIETERNELLA (Pia), *piano, singer;* b. The Hague, Holland, 9/18/25. No formal study, but family played various instruments. Ran away from home at 18 to play w. Miller Sextet; did USO shows. Formed own trio late '49; to US '52 and almost every year since, also Latin America and West Indies in '58 and many other tours all over Europe, Africa, Asia. Operates two night clubs in Holland. Her trio was voted best small combo in Holland and she has extended her activities to writing articles and composing. Fav. own rec. *I'm Feeling Like a Stranger in This Big Town.* Favs: O. Peterson, E. Garner, Mary Lou Williams; Ella Fitzgerald, Sarah Vaughan. Own LP: Epic.

Addr: The Flying Dutchman, The Hague, Holland.

BECKENSTEIN, RAYMOND, (Ray), *saxophones, clarinet;* also *flute, piccolo, violin;* b. Brooklyn, N.Y., 8/14/23. Says he grew up "with Terry Gibbs, Al Cohn, Tiny Kahn and several kids who became lawyers." On road w. Johnny McGhee 1939—fired (says "I couldn't handle the baritone sax"); during 1940s was w. many dance bands: Lew Gray, Lee Castle, Dick Himber, Bobby Sherwood. In recent years has been very active in NY recording. LPs w. Geo. Handy, John Carisi (Victor); flute on vocal albums w. Ralph Burns Orch.; jazz alto w. Urbie Green (ABC Par.), Hal Schaefer (UA). Favs: Lester Young, Ch. Parker.

Addr: 8305 98th St., Woodhaven, L.I., N.Y.

BECKETT, FRED LEE, *trombone;* b. Tupelo, Miss., 1/23/17; d. 1945 in military service. Began pl. trombone in high school w. school band. Moved to Kansas City, then joined Johnson's Crackerjacks in St. Louis 1934. With Andy Kirk and Prince Stewart, '37; Nat Towles, '37-8; Tommy Douglas, '38-9; Harlan Leonard '39-40; Lionel Hampton '40-44. Rec. several excellent solos w. Leonard incl. *My Gal Sal, Skee, A La Bridges.* Noted for tone and range; considered by J. J. Johnson to have been the first great modern trombonist.

BEIDERBECKE, LEON BISMARCK (Bix), *cornet, piano, composer;* b. Davenport, Iowa, 3/10/03; d. 8/7/31, Long Island. High school in Davenport, then to Lake Forest Academy near Chicago for a year. Mostly self-taught on piano and cornet from early childhood. In 1923 he was the star of the Wolverines, with whom he made his first records and came to New York to play at Roseland. In 1925, while with Charlie Straight's commercial orchestra, he spent much spare time listening to, and sitting in with, the pioneer Negro artists in Chicago, among them King Oliver, Louis Armstrong and Jimmie Noone. In 1926 Bix went to St. Louis for a job with Frankie Trumbauer's orchestra at the Arcadia Ballroom. After working with Jean Goldkette in Detroit, he joined Paul Whiteman's band, with whom he was featured from 1928 to '30, with many absences (including one while the band made its famous early sound film *King Of Jazz*) owing to illness. The last year of his life was spent in Davenport and New York, gigging with Glen Gray's Casa Loma Orch. and others; he died of pneumonia and was buried in Davenport.

Bix Beiderbecke was appreciated only by a handful of musicians and fans during his lifetime. It was not until years after his death that he began to acquire the status of a legend, partly through Dorothy Baker's novel *Young Man With A Horn,* which was inspired by (but *not* based on) his life story. Bix was known chiefly as a cornetist with an exquisite tone and legato style of improvisation. He was probably the first white musician ever to be admired and imitated by Negro jazzmen: Rex Stewart and others learned to play his most famous ad lib solo (the Trumbauer record of *Singin' The Blues*) note for note. Originally inspired by a white trumpeter named Emmett Hardy, and by Armstrong, Joe Smith and others, Bix has himself had many followers, the best known of whom are Bobby Hackett and Jimmy McPartland. As a pianist and composer, Bix was one of the first jazzmen to be inspired by Debussy's harmonic ideas. Though often surrounded by musicians of inferior stature and by over-commercialized arrangements, notably in the Whiteman band, Bix nevertheless left a legacy of performances unmatched in subtlety and finesse blended with a sensitive jazz feeling.

A more detailed story of Bix, together with almost all his best records, can be found on three 12-inch Columbia LPs, CL844 (*Bix and His Gang*), 845 (*Bix and Tram*), 846 (*Whiteman Days*). A suite of piano compositions by Bix is played by Ralph Sutton on Commodore 30001. *Shades of Bix,* played by Jimmy McPartland, is on Bruns. BL58049. Other Beiderbecke LPs: River. 12-123 (*Wolverines*), 12-127 (four nos. in *On The Road Jazz*).

BEILMANN, PETER ROBERT (Pete), *trombone;* b. Lancaster, Pa., 11/8/05. Stud. at 12; local bands to 1922, then on road. Rec. debut 1924 in Camden, N.J. while touring w. Oliver Naylor jazz septet. Pit band in Lancaster 1926, then to NYC, free-lancing. Spent 3½ years w. Bernie Cummins to 1934, then 7½ years w. Ted Weems. Settled in LA 1941; pit band, many radio shows w. John Scott Trotter et al, rec. w. Wingy Manone. Joined Red Nichols March 1958. Favs: Teagarden, Mole. LPs w. Nichols (Cap.).

Addr: 4220 Colfax Ave., North Hollywood, Cal.

BELDINY, ALFRED ROSARIO (Al), *drums, singer;* b. Brooklyn, N.Y., 11/28/34. Father a prof. mus., pl. vln., banjo, mandolin etc. Prof. debut w. Frankie Carle. Has worked w. Ray Eberle, Paul Bley, Larry Sonn; many dates w. Don Elliott. LPs w. Elliott, Rolf Kuhn et al at Newport (Verve); *Jazzville No. 2* (Dawn). Has occasionally doubled as singer with several bands. Fav: orig. Gene Krupa, recently Roach, Blakey, Philly Joe Jones.

Addr: 1240 Herkimer St., Brooklyn 33, N.Y.

BELL, GRAEME, *piano, leader;* b. Australia, 1914. Started playing New Orleans style jazz in Melbourne 1943. From '47, toured band successfully in Britain, France, Belgium, Holland. After several months of running an art gallery, he formed a new band late in '59. LPs on 10" for Angel not available.

BELL, SAMUEL AARON, *bass;* b. Muskogee, Okla., 4/24/22. Majored in music teaching at Xavier U. in NO. In navy '41-6; joined Andy Kirk '47, then home for a year teaching music in high school in Muskogee. Master's degree in music education at NYU 1950. Plays euphonium, trumpet, piano, several other instruments. Played w. Ed Wilcox, Lucky Millinder, Herman Chittison, Teddy Wilson, Lester Young, Eddie Heywood, Johnny Smith, Dorothy Donegan, Mat Mathews. Had own trio at Concord Hotel in upstate New York, Dec. '54-May '56, w. Charlie Bateman, piano and Charlie Smith, drums. Led pit band for Broadway show, *Compulsion* '57-8; TV shows and rec. dates in NYC. Briefly joined Billy Taylor trio, fall '59; w. Duke spring '60. Fav: O. Pettiford. Own LPs w. orch. on MGM, w. trio on Vict., Herald; LPs w. Jimmy Rushing, Buck Clayton (Vanguard), Charlie Shavers (Beth.).

Addr: 444 S. Columbus Ave., Mt. Vernon, N.Y.

BELLETTO, ALPHONSE JOSEPH (Al), *alto, baritone sax, clarinet;* b. New Orleans, 1/3/28. Began playing clar. in high school and was jobbing around NO as soon as he had his first sax. Own group while att. Loyola U. where he earned Bach. of Mus. Ed degree; also has Master's degree in mus. from La. State U. Worked w. Sharkey Bonano, Leon Prima, W. Manone, Dukes of Dixieland. Started own sextet Dec. '52; worked in leading jazz clubs. The group was incorporated into Woody Herman's band Jan.-Nov. '58, incl. State Dept. tour of So. America, and again for a few months in '59. Favs: Ch. Parker, Basie, Kenton. Own LP: Capitol; LP w. Jerri Winters (Beth.).

BELLSON, LOUIS (Louis Balassoni), *drums, composer;* b. Rock Falls, Ill., 7/26/24. Father owner of music shop. After winning several amateur drum contests in high school, came to NYC and won contests run by Gene Krupa for best drummer under 18. Worked w. Ted Fio Rito, Benny Goodman before entering Army '43; spent another year with Goodman after discharge, then w. Tommy Dorsey '47-9; sextet with Charlie Shavers, Terry Gibbs '50; then in Calif. w. Harry James until, with Willie Smith and Juan Tizol, he quit James to join Duke Ellington, March '51. With Duke, became known as an arranger, wrote such arrangements as *Hawk Talks, Skin Deep, Ting-a-Ling.* Left Ellington Jan. '53, shortly after his marriage to singer Pearl Bailey. Since then has toured, mostly with her, leading own group for nightclub and theatre dates. Rec. with various groups for Norman Granz' labels. An extraordinary technician, Bellson conceived the idea, in '46, of using two bass drums. He was credited with revitalizing the Ellington band during his two years w. Duke. Visited Europe w. JATP, Feb. '55; feat. w. Dorsey Bros. orch. Aug. '55-Aug. '56. Then free-lanced as drummer, composer, arranger, incl. score for Broadway show in '58. Continued to tour w. wife, forming a big band in March '59. Own LPs on Verve; LPs w. Ellington (Col.), Ella Fitzgerald-Louis Armstrong, Art Tatum, Buddy De Franco-Oscar Peterson, Armstrong-Peterson (Verve); one track in *Hi-Fi Drums* (Cap.).

Addr: Apple Valley, Calif.

BENEKE, GORDON (Tex), *tenor sax, leader;* b. Fort Worth, Texas, 2/12/14. With Ben Young, 1935-7; Glenn Miller, 1938-42, then in Navy band. On returning to civilian life he led what was first called "The Glenn Miller Orchestra directed by Tex Beneke"; later Miller's name was dropped. Beneke, who won the DB poll on tenor in 1941 and '42, Met. poll '41-2, was one of the most popular soloists in Miller's band during the height of its fame, though his role was completely omitted from the *Glenn Miller Story* film. For records, see Glenn Miller. Own LPs on Camden; LPs w. Met. All Stars (Harm., Cam.).

Addr: 3504 Buffalo Drive, St. Louis 23, Mo.

BENFORD, THOMAS P. (Tommy), *drums;* b. Charleston, W. Va., 4/19/05. Mother played piano, organ; father, tuba and drums. Early experience with band led by brother, Bill, and w. Gus and Gene Aiken. Pl. w. Marie Lucas, Jelly Roll Morton, Edgar Hayes, Charlie Skeete, Fats Waller, also subbed w. Duke Ellington for a month. To Europe in 1932 w. Eddie South; worked in Paris w. Freddie Taylor '36-7, Willie Lewis '38-41. Toured Germany & Switzerland w. Jimmy Archey '52; pl. in Canada w. Muggsy Spanier '54. From '56-9 spent summers at Cape Cod w. Leroy Parkins, Bob Pilsbury bands; ret. to NYC Sept. '59, working at Central Plaza and Jimmy Ryan's. Favs: Catlett, Rich. Rec. extensively in Europe w. Eddie South, Coleman Hawkins, Benny Carter.

Addr: 1188 East Tremont Ave., Bronx 60, N.Y.

BENJAMIN, JOSEPH RUPERT (Joe), *bass;* b. Atlantic City, N.J., 11/4/19. Raised NYC; stud. violin w. Hall Johnson. Worked for several years as music copyist for Jimmie Lunceford, Billy Moore, Jr. et al. A protege of Geo. Duvivier. He played bass w. Mercer Ellington, 1946; Billy Taylor, Artie Shaw, Fletcher Henderson '50; second bass w. Duke Ellington at Met. concert Jan. '51; also several years off and on w. Lena Horne, Sy Oliver and Ellis Larkins. On tour w. Sarah Vaughan May '53-June '55. Toured US and Europe during 10 months w. Gerry Mulligan '57. Duo w. Ellis Larkins '58; Dave Brubeck Quartet May-July '58; clubs w. H. Edison, B. Webster, T. Glenn et al, and extensive recording work in NYC. Seen in Broadway musical *The Nervous Set* '59. Fav: Blanton. LPs w. Budd Johnson (Felsed), J. Mundy (Epic), S. Vaughan (Merc.), C. McRae (Kapp), Brubeck (Col.), Dizzy Gillespie (Atl.), Roy Haynes (Em.), Dick Katz (Atl.).

Addr: 120-14 Farmer's Blvd., St. Albans 12, L.I., N.Y.

BENNETT, BETTY, *singer;* b. Lincoln, Neb., 10/23/26. Mother, a pianist, had jazz band in 1920s. 12 yrs. of piano study in Hamburg, Iowa, 2 yrs. legitimate voice study. Sang w. Geo. Auld 1943. While in WAVES, 1945, was MC of CBS show, *WAVES on Parade.* Worked w. Claude Thornhill '46, Alvino Rey, '47, Charlie Ventura, Kenton All-Stars '49, Woody Herman small band '50, Charlie Barnet '52. Formerly married to André Previn, who has played, arr. and conducted for her records. An excellent pop singer, she made her solo debut in an album for Trend (now on Kapp), Hollywood '53. Favs: E. Fitzgerald, early S. Vaughan, Martha Raye. Own LPs: Atlantic, UA, Kapp (incl. fav. own rec., *Time After Time*). LP w. Ventura: *It's All Bop To Me* (Victor).

Addr: 1522 No. Beverly Drive, Beverly Hills, Calif.

BENNETT, MAX, *bass;* b. Des Moines, Iowa, 5/24/28. Raised in Kansas City and Oskaloosa, Ia. Studied at U. of Iowa. Worked w. Herbie Fields 1949, Georgie Auld, Terry Gibbs, Charlie Ventura. Army Sept. '51-Sept. '53. Toured w. Stan Kenton '54, then settled in LA, working w. own small group and at Lighthouse; backed Peggy Lee. Joined acc. unit for Ella Fitzgerald '57, touring Europe w. her in JATP '58. W. Terry Gibbs band '59. Own LPs on Beth.; LPs w. Bill Holman (Coral), Terry Gibbs (Merc.), Conte Candoli/Stan Levey in *West Coasting,* Ch. Mariano (Beth.), Bob Cooper (Contemp.).

Addr: 5707 Melvin Ave., Tarzana, Calif.

BENSKIN, SAMUEL (Sammy), *piano, composer;* b. New York City, 9/27/22. Debut w. Bardu Ali 1940; Bobby Burnet at Cafe Society, '41; Stuff Smith, '42, then Al Cooper, Gene Sedric, Benny Morton, Don Redman. Own trio around New York, then solo at 52nd St. clubs. Acc. singers Roy Hamilton and Titus Turner. Joined Three Flames Aug. 1954. Single thereafter, also appeared in *Time of Your Life* at City Center, Jan. 1955. Acc. Roy Hamilton '55; coached singers incl. Diahann Carroll. Pl. w. Stan Rubin early '58; Al Hibbler May-Oct. '58, then rejoined *Time of Your Life* for perfs. at Brussels World's Fair. Back w. Hibbler to Aug. '59, briefly w. Dinah Washington; continued to coach singers, arrange, produce records. First class accompanist. Rec. early solo on BN and dates w. Benny Morton, E. Barefield, B. Holiday, John Hardee. LPs: Josh White (ABC-Par.), Hibbler (Dec.).

Addr: 1311 Needham Ave., Bronx 69, N.Y.

BENTON, WALTER BARNEY, *tenor sax;* b. Los Angeles, Calif., 9/9/30. Father pl. saxophone, sister piano. Studied C-melody sax in junior high school. Started pl. local jobs at USO. W. 21st Army Band, Ft. Lewis, Washington, Oct. 1950-Nov. '52; 289th Army Band, Yokahama, Japan, Jan. '53-July '53; Perez Prado '54-7, incl. tour of Japan, Korea, Okinawa, Philippines, Sept.-

Dec. '56; free-lance in LA, then own group from March '59. Favs: Lucky Thompson, Milt Jackson, Ch. Parker. LPs w. Kenny Clarke (Savoy, incl. own fav. solo on *Blues Mood*), Clifford Brown in *Best Coast Jazz* (Em.), Quincy Jones (ABC-Par.), Perez Prado (Vict.).

Addr: 2936 11th Ave., Los Angeles, Calif.

BERIGAN, ROLAND BERNARD (Bunny), *trumpet;* b. Fox Lake, Wis., 1909; d. New York City, 6/2/42. As youth, played violin, trumpet in grandfather's orchestra. College dance bands at Univ. of Wisconsin, then name bands incl. Hal Kemp, Rudy Vallee, Freddie Rich; Dorsey Bros. 1934; Benny Goodman '35-6; Tommy Dorsey '37. Left Dorsey to form his own big band, which he led with limited success until 1940, when he rejoined Tommy Dorsey for six months before leading another band until his health broke down and he died of pneumonia.

Berigan's career paralleled that of Bix Beiderbecke in many ways; his individuality of style, his compromises in playing with commercial bands, his losing battle with alcohol and his disintegration and death all followed a similar pattern. His playing had a lyrical beauty that was especially effective in the lower register. Among his first big hit records were *Sometimes I'm Happy* and *King Porter Stomp* with Goodman. His biggest hit was *I Can't Get Started With You,* on which he both sang and played. His chorus on *Marie* with Dorsey was widely admired and imitated. He won the *Metronome* poll in 1937 and '39.

Though he made many records as a sideman during the 1930s, many of them have not been made available on LP. They included sessions with Red Norvo, Billie Holiday, Bud Freeman and others. Own LPs on Epic, Victor; LP w. Red Norvo (Epic), T. Dorsey, Goodman (Vict.).

BERMAN, SAUL (Sonny), *trumpet;* b. New Haven, Conn., 4/21/24; d. New York City, 1/16/47. From 1940 to early '45 pl. w. Louis Prima, Sonny Dunham, T. Dorsey, G. Auld, Harry James, B. Goodman. Joined Woody Herman Feb. '45, and from then until his death from a heart attack he was a sparkplug in Herman's band, a modern soloist of grace and warmth whose great possibilities can still be heard on the few records he left. His best solo on record with Woody was *Sidewalks of Cuba* (Col. CL592, *The Three Herds*). Own LP on Esoteric; LPs w. Woody Herman (MGM), *Jazz Concert* (Grand Award), *The Jazz Scene* (Verve).

BERNAL, GILBERT (Gil), *tenor sax, etc.;* b. LA, 2/4/31. Mainly self-taught. Met Lionel Hampton through former high school English teacher and toured w. the band 1950-2. Aside from this, has always fronted his own combo, but worked w. Spike Jones as featured singer and soloist '56. Of Castilian, Spanish-Gypsy origin, Bernal, whose parents were born in Mexico, has many other interests incl. boxing, sketching, short story writing. Favs: Ch. Parker, early Lester Young. LP w. Dan Terry (Col.).

Addr: c/o Arena Stars, 366 N. Camden Drive, Beverly Hills, Calif.

BERNHART, MILT, *trombone;* b. Valparaiso, Ind., 5/25/26. Tuba at 10, trombone at 12. Studied w. Forrest Nicola in Chicago, Donald Reinhardt in Phila. At 16 joined Boyd Raeburn at Bandbox in Chicago. With Buddy Franklin, Jimmy James, '43; Teddy Powell in Hollywood, Dec. '43, until inducted into Army Aug. '44. After discharge July '46, joined Stan Kenton and was w. him off and on until Sept. '51, also playing w. Boyd Raeburn in summer of '47; Benny Goodman, Sept. '48 to Jan. '49. First rec. solo was *Peanut Vendor* w. Kenton. Member of staff orch., Columbia Pictures '55-58. Very active in TV '59-60, playing for *Richard Diamond, M. Squad, Staccato,* etc. Favs: Bill Harris, Joe Howard. Own LP on Decca; LPs w. Kenton (Cap.), Pete Rugolo (Col.), Shorty Rogers (Vict.), Maynard Ferguson (EmArcy), Jack Marshall (Cap.); *Peter Gunn* (Vict., Dot), *The Man With The Golden Arm* (Decca).

Addr: 1714 N. Evergreen St., Burbank, Calif.

BERNSTEIN, ARTHUR (Artie), *bass;* b. Brooklyn, N.Y., 2/4/09. Originally a lawyer, took up bass as sideline, became prof. 1930, working w. Red Nichols, Dorsey Bros., Benny Goodman; innumerable record dates through 1930s. California studio work since early 1940s. Won DB award on bass, 1943. LPs w. Benny Goodman (MGM, Col.), Met. All Stars (Cam.), *Spirituals To Swing* (Vang.).

Addr: 7055 Cantaloupe, Van Nuys, Calif.

BERNSTEIN, ELMER, *composer;* b. New York City, 4/4/22. Stud. piano at Juilliard, comp. w. Aaron Copland and several others, incl. Stefan Wolpe. Wrote dramatic background scores for Army Air Force radio shows. Did background for United Nations shows, 1949, as a result of which he was selected by Columbia Pictures to do motion picture work. Has been associated w. such films as *Sudden Fear* '52, *Man with the Golden Arm* '55, *The Ten Commandments* '56, *Sweet Smell of Success* '57. Bernstein states that his aim is to integrate jazz in film scores and serious comp. Favs: Aaron Copland; Kenton, Armstrong, Basie. Own LPs: *Sweet Smell of Success, Blue and Brass* (Decca).

Addr: 12127 Iradelle St., No. Hollywood, Calif.

BERNSTEIN, LEONARD, *piano, composer, conductor;* b. Lawrence, Mass., 8/25/18. Grad. Harvard U. 1939. Stud. Curtis Inst. of Music, Philadelphia with Fritz Reiner. Bernstein's non-jazz background will not be dealt with here; however, throughout his career he has had a peripheral association with jazz and a stronger one with popular stage music. In the late 1930s he served as pianist for a night club act, The Revuers. His Second Symphony, *The Age of Anxiety,* showed a slight jazz influence. His music for Broadway shows has included scores for *On the Town,* 1944; *Wonderful Town,* 1952; *West Side Story,* 1957. Beginning in '53 at Brandeis U., later at the Hollywood

Bowl, 1955, etc., he took part in forum discussions on jazz. From '55-60 he frequently discussed jazz on television. In Oct. '55, on the NBC-TV show *Omnibus,* he conducted the premiere of his piece for jazz orchestra: *Prelude, Fugue and Riffs.* He has commissioned such jazz composers as Teo Macero ('57) and Bill Russo ('58) to write works for performances by the New York Phil., of which he was appointed conductor in '58. LP: *What Is Jazz?* (Col.).

Addr: c/o New York Phil. Society, 113 W. 57th St., New York 19, N.Y.

BERRY, LEON (Chu), *tenor sax;* b. Wheeling, W. Va., 9/13/10; d. 10/31/41, Conneaut, Ohio, in auto crash. After playing with Cecil Scott, Benny Carter and Teddy Hill in the early 1930s, he was prominent with Fletcher Henderson (1935-6), partnered with Roy Eldridge as one of the band's top soloists. Played with Cab Calloway's band from July 1937 until his death. Many rec. sessions in late '30s w. Lionel Hampton, Mildred Bailey, Gene Krupa, Wingy Manone. Soft sound and lush, mellow tone; was rated by fellow-jazzmen as one of the top three tenor men along with Hawkins and Lester Young. He won DB poll, 1937, Met. poll '37, '39. His most famous solo was *Ghost of A Chance* with Calloway (Col.). Own LP on Epic; *Pres and Chu* (Jazz.); LPs w. Lionel Hampton (Vict.), Red Norvo (Epic).

BERRY, CHUCK, *singer;* b. St. Louis, Mo., 10/18/26. Majored in music at high school; pl. guitar, saxophone and piano. Popular artist in rock-'n-roll field. Rec. for Chess. Film: *Jazz on a Summer's Day.*

BERRY, EMMETT, *trumpet;* b. Macon Ga., 7/23/16. Raised in Cleveland, stud. w. symphony musician. Joined Chicago Nightingales in Toledo, 1932. Jobbed around Albany, N.Y. '34-6, then joined Fletcher Henderson and was with his band or Horace Henderson's until 1940. With Teddy Wilson '41-2, Raymond Scott at CBS '42-3, Lionel Hampton, Benny Carter '43, John Kirby '44, Eddie Heywood '45, Count Basie '45-50, Jimmy Rushing '51, Johnny Hodges '51-4, Earl Hines, Cootie Williams, '55. Toured France, N. Africa w. Sam Price for Jeunesses Musicales Jan.-May '56, then 6 wks w. I. Jacquet, F. Henderson reunion band at Great South Bay festival '57. Started retail music business in NYC Dec. '58, but still active as musician, touring Europe w. Buck Clayton Sept.-Oct. '59. Admirable soloist in swing-era style. Fav. own solo: *Jappa* w. Hodges (Verve). Own LP: Col.; LPs w. Jo Jones, J. Rushing and *Night at Count Basie's* (Vang.); *Sound of Jazz* (Col.), Hodges (Verve), B. Clayton (Col.), Basie (Victor), Bobby Donaldson (World Wide), Illinois Jacquet in *The Angry Tenors* (Savoy), Ed Hall (Comm.); *Trumpets All Out* (Savoy).

Addr: 50 West 106th Street, New York 25, N.Y.

BERT, EDDIE, *trombone;* b. Yonkers, N.Y. 5/16/22. Joined Sam Donahue '40; Red Norvo '41, on road w. Norvo combo incl. Shorty Rogers; Woody Herman '43; Herbie Fields '46; Kenton '47; back w. Woody 50; Bill Harris' three-trombones combo '51; Kenton '51; Herbie Fields, Ray McKinley '52; Les Elgart '54; Ch. Mingus Nov. '55-Jan. '56; Tony Aless-Seldon Powell group '56; Lena Horne, Benny Goodman '57; Goodman at Newport Festival and *Swing Into Spring* TV show '58; Urbie Green, Th. Monk Orch. '59; Monday nights at Birdland w. own group, gigs and records w. Elliot Lawrence '55-59. In Aug. '59, featured guest soloist and conductor at Fifth Annual Caracas Jazz Club Concert, Caracas, Venezuela. Rec. M.M. from Manhattan Sch. of Mus. '57; is substitute mus. teacher in public sch. between gigs. Rec. first solo w. Norvo '42, *Jersey Bounce* on Col. Own LPs on Somerset, Savoy; LPs w. *Met. All Stars* (Verve), E. Lawrence (Fant.), *Jay & Kai Plus 6,* Bob Prince-Teo Macero, *LeGrand Jazz* (Col.), Sal Salvador (Decca), T. Monk (River.), *Trombones Inc.* (Warn. Bros.), Al Cohn (Vict.).

Addr: 41 Ehrbar Ave., Mt Vernon, N.Y.

BERTON, VIC, *drums;* b. Chicago, Ill., 5/7/1896; d. Hollywood, Cal. 12/26/51. Father was theatre violinist and teacher. Vic, a child prodigy, was hired as regular pit drummer for the Alhambra theatre in Milwaukee at the age of 7. While in his teens, he stud. w. Josef Zettleman of Chicago Symphony. During the 1920s, in addition to playing w. Paul Whiteman, Vincent Lopez and innumerable other commercial dance bands, Berton rec. regularly w. Red Nichols and popularized the use of "hot tympani," using a pair of machine kettledrums to play bass parts for novelty effects. He is said to be one of the first drummers, if not the first, to have transferred the cymbal from a place fixed to the bass drum to its subsequently standard position as a separate instrument to be played by hand. Berton also composed (with fellow drummer Art Kassel) *Sobbin' Blues,* 1922; and was responsible for bringing Bix Beiderbecke and the Wolverines to NYC in 1924. From the late '30s he gave up dance band work to become a Hollywood studio musician. He was a feat. soloist in several concerts with the LA Phil., and was chosen by Igor Stravinsky as percussionist for West Coast performances of *L'histoire du soldat.* LPs w. Red Nichols (Bruns., River.).

BEST, DENZIL DE COSTA, *drums, composer;* b. New York City, 4/27/17. Father pl. tuba in military band. Piano at 6. Trumpet 1940 w. Joe Gordon, Chris Columbus. Sat in on tpt., piano at Minton's w. Joe Guy, Kenny Clarke, Monk. After long illness '40-1, gigged on piano & bass, took up drums '43. With Saxie Payne, Eddie Williams, Harvey Davis, Leon Gross; nine months w. Ben Webster. Later Coleman Hawkins, Illinois Jacquet; toured Sweden w. Chubby Jackson Dec. '47. Joined George Shearing's Quintet in '49, remaining until a serious auto accident forced him into retirement in '52-3. He was an important contributor to the success of the Shearing group, his manner of brushwork being an identifying sound. After recuperating he played w. Artie Shaw's new Gramercy 5, '54. Toured w. Erroll Garner '56-7. His activity curtailed by an illness that affected his hands, Best remained in NYC, played w. Lee Evans and Cecil Young in '58-9, and gigged w. Nina Simone and Tyree Glenn in '59. As a composer he contributed some of the most attractive melodic lines to the early bop years, his best-known tune being *Move.* Others were *Dee Dee's Dance, Wee (Allen's Alley), Nothing But D. Best, 45° Angle.* LPs w. Shearing (MGM), Phineas Newborn (Vict.), Jack Teagarden (Urania); *52nd St.* (Interlude).

Addr: 411 West 156th St., New York, N.Y.

BEST, CLIFTON (Skeeter), *guitar;* b. Kinston, N.C., 11/20/14. Stud. w. mother, a piano teacher. Prof. debut w. Abe Dunn's local band in early 1930s. Worked mainly w. Slim Marshall in Philadelphia 1935-40. Joined Earl Hines late '40. Navy '42-5; Played w. Bill Johnson combo '45-9. USO tour of Japan and Korea w. Oscar Pettiford '51-2. Since then, has free-lanced in NYC w. own trio and w. Paul Quinichette, Jesse Powell, Kenny Clarke. Rec. solos on *Swingin' the Blues* w. Quinichette; *Best By Test* w. Sir Charles Thompson. Has also had considerable experience as arr., esp. w. Navy band. Underrated and first-class modern guitarist. LPs w. Modern Jazz Sextet (Verve), Sir Charles Thompson, Mel Powell (Vang.).

BEST, JOHN McCLANIAN JR. (Johnny), *trumpet;* b. Shelby, N.C., 10/20/13. Mother pl. piano; sister and brother musical. Stud. piano for one year when six, then stud. trumpet first year high school. First jobs in college orch. at Davidson, U. of North Carolina and Duke U., where he pl. w. Duke Blue Devils. W. Les Brown '35-6; Charlie Barnet '37; Artie Shaw '37-9; Glenn Miller '39-42. In the Navy, '42-5, pl. w. Artie Shaw and Sam Donahue. After discharge worked w. Benny Goodman '45-7, on radio w. Bob Crosby and Jerry Gray '47-53; w. Billy May '50-55 and many West Coast studio dates. Worked at Honeybucket in San Diego w. Bart Hazelet '59. LPs w. Glenn Miller, Artie Shaw (Vict.), *Texas, USA* (Col.), Benny Goodman (Col.).

Addr: P. O. Box 337, Pauma Valley, Calif.

BETTS, WILLIAM THOMAS (Keter), *bass;* also *drums;* b. Port Chester, N.Y., 7/22/28. Began stud. drums in grade school and continued through high school. Switched to bass upon graduation in 1946. After one year w. private teacher began playing local jobs. With Earl Bostic April '49-Sept. '51; Dinah Washington Nov. '51-Nov. '56; brief stay w. Adderly brothers before settling in Washington, D.C., '57. Has lived there since, playing w. Charlie Byrd at the Showboat, taking time off to tour w. Woody Herman in England and Saudi Arabia, '59. Favs: Ray Brown, Blanton, Pettiford; Infl: Miles Davis, John Coltrane. LPs w. Byrd (Offbeat, Savoy), Cannonball Adderley, Dinah Washington (Merc.), Woody Herman (Evst., Roul.).

Addr: 610 Jefferson St., NW, Washington, D.C.

BICKERT, EDWARD ISAAC (Ed), *guitar;* b. Hochfeld, Manitoba, 11/29/32. St. on guitar in Vernon, B.C., 1943; pl. dance dates with father, a fiddler, and mother, a pianist. Moved to Toronto, worked w. local groups incl. Norm. Symonds Octet, Ron Collier Quintet at Stratford Festival '56 and '57; also w. Collier, Phil Nimmons and Moe Koffman at Canadian Jazz Fest. '59. Visited US in Nov. '56 and gigged at Birdland, also colleges in upstate NY Oct. '57. Film: *The Young and the Beat.* One of Canada's most promising young jazzmen. Favs: Segovia, Tal Farlow; names J. Giuffre as major influence. LPs w. Moe Koffman (Jubilee), Phil Nimmons (Verve).

Addr: 171 Birkdale Road, Scarborough, Ontario.

BIGARD, LEON ALBANY (Barney), *clarinet;* b. New Orleans, 3/3/06. A reluctant musician despite his family's wish that he become one, he took up music only after trying other careers first. Studied w. Lorenzo Tio on clarinet, later doubled on tenor sax; played w. Octave Gaspard and Albert Nicholas, then went to Chicago, where he joined King Oliver, 1925. From 1926 to '28 he worked for Charlie Elgar, rejoined Oliver and came to NYC with him, then played with Luis Russell. In Jan. 1928 he joined Duke Ellington, remaining with him until July 1942. During his 14 years with Ellington he became world-renowned as one of the most original of jazz clarinetists (and one of the few to play the old Albert system clarinet instead of the now generally used Boehm fingering). Settled in Calif., joined Freddie Slack '43-4, led own combo, pl. w. Kid Ory. In '46 he joined Louis Armstrong and, except for a short period in '52, remained until '55, incl. visits to Europe, Japan. Ret. to LA and has since led his own groups there and in Las Vegas. Rejoined Armstrong May '60. Cozy Cole Nov. '58-March '59. Films: *New Orleans* w. Armstrong '47; *St. Louis Blues* '57. Won Esq. Silver Award 1944, '46, '47. Own LPs on Liberty; *Duke's Men* (Epic); LPs w. Ellington (Vict., Cam., Bruns.), Armstrong (Decca, Col.), Eddie Heywood (Coral); *History Of Jazz* (Cap.). Own EP w. strings on Atl.

Addr: 3445 Vinton Ave., Los Angeles 34, Calif.

BIG MAYBELLE—See SMITH, Mabel

BILLBERG, ROLF GUNNAR, *alto sax;* also *tenor sax, clarinet;* b. Lund, Sweden, 8/22/30. Clarinet in military band, Uddevalla 1948. Was concert clarinetist but after hearing Parker and Tristano turned to jazz. Pl. w. Simon Brehm '54, Lars Gullin '54-5, Ib Glindemann in Copenhagen '56, all on tenor sax. Switched to alto in '57, pl. in Germany and France at American clubs. From Sept. '57 working w. Carl-Henrik Norin in Nalen, Sweden. Film: soloist on sound track for Swedish *Line 6.* Favs: Lee Konitz, Ch. Parker; imp. infl: Lars Gullin. LP w. Gullin (Em.).

Addr: Hagavagen 63, Solna, Sweden.

BILLINGS, FRANK R. (Josh), *drums;* b. Chicago 1904, d. New York City 1957. Parents both doctors. He was a better-than-average artist and enthusiastic fan of Chicago's Austin High Gang. When this group went to NYC in 1928, Billings and Mezz Mezzrow were left behind. They followed later and joined the others in a reorganized Mound City Blue Blowers in which

Billings played drums (actually a suitcase equipped with wrinkled wrapping paper, which produced soft effects when stroked with whisk brooms—for the bass effects, he kicked the case with his heel). He maintained his friendship with the Chicago musicians but found a job as band boy w. Ray Noble in the mid-30s. Later became a lithographer in Chicago, moving back to NYC when Eddie Condon opened his club in Greenwich Village. Rec. for Okeh and Victor.

BISHOP, WALTER JR., *piano;* b. New York City, 10/4/27. Son of the noted ASCAP songwriter. Air Corps 1945-47, then to Art Blakey's Messengers, and smaller Blakey group at Minton's. Later w. Andy Kirk, Oscar Pettiford, Terry Gibbs, Kai Winding, Charlie Parker, Miles Davis. Non-music day job '53-5. Own trio at Cafe Bohemia for short time thereafter. Inactive for several years, ret. to music as leader on Monday nights at Birdland during spring and summer '59. W. Allen Eager, Philly Joe Jones fall '59. One of the early Bud Powell disciples. LPs w. Miles Davis, Hank Mobley, also *The Brothers* (Pres.), Ch. Parker (Verve), Milt Jackson, Phil Urso (Savoy), Art Blakey (Beth.), Jackie McLean (Blue Note).

Addr: 133 West 113th St., New York 26, N.Y.

BIVONA, GUS, *clarinet, alto sax, flute;* b. New London, Conn., 11/25/17. Stud. alto in Stamford, Conn., 1934. After working locally w. Frank Dailey's orch., went to NYC in '37. Played w. Hudson-DeLange '37, Bunny Berigan '38, Teddy Powell '39, feat. as clar. soloist. After leading own band in Larchmont, N.Y., he worked for B. Goodman '40, Jan Savitt, and Les Brown '41. In service '42, led own band in Navy Air Force. Played w. T. Dorsey '45, Bob Crosby '46; since '47 on staff at MGM Studios. Associated w. Steve Allen in 1958-9, playing w. him at Roundtable, NYC, on Allen's TV show, and recording an album of his tunes. Fav: B. Goodman. Own LP on Merc.; LPs w. Steve Allen (Merc.), Glen Gray, Four Freshman (Cap).

Addr: 15902 Gault St., Van Nuys, Calif.

BJORKSTEN, GUNNAR O. (Hacke), *tenor sax;* also *flute;* b. Helsinki, Finland, 2/27/34. Mother is a piano teacher. Studied clarinet first, then alto sax, finally tenor. Played w. Kenneth Fagerlund band 1950. Since '54, has had own septet at Walen in Stockholm. Won Orkester Journalen "golden record" for best Swedish rec. of year '56. Favs: Getz, Sims, Konitz. LP w. Tommy Potter on East-West under the name Woody Birch.

BLACK, DAVID JOHN (Dave), *drums;* b. Philadelphia, Pa., 1/23/28. Studied at Mastbaum School of Music. As house drummer at Blue Note in Philadelphia, he worked with Charlie Parker, Georgie Auld, Buddy De Franco, etc. from '48. Joined Duke Ellington Oct. '53 and toured with the band until '55. In recent years has been working w. Bob Scobey. Fav: Buddy Rich. LPs w. Ellington, feat. on *Tan Your Hide* (Cap.); this selection is also included in *Hi-Fi Drums* (Cap.).

BLAIR, LEE L., *banjo, guitar;* b. Savannah, Ga., 10/10/05. Self-taught except for a few lessons from Mike Pingatore. Started in dancing school w. Ch. Skeete, Billy Kato. Rec. w. Jelly Roll Morton '28 and '30; feat. on *Kansas City Stomps.* Left Morton to join Luis Russell at Connie's Inn; toured with this band when it was under Louis Armstrong's name '35-40. During '50s he was with Wilbur De Paris; feat. on *Banjoker* (Atlantic). Rec. w. Pee-Wee Erwin '59. Inactive of late except for occasional gigs, he has a chicken farm in upstate New York. Favs: Elmer Snowden, banjo, Ch. Christian, guitar.

Addr: 711 Jerusalem Avenue, Bellmore, N.Y.

BLAKE, ARTHUR (Blind Blake), *singer, guitar;* b. prob. Jacksonville, Fla., ca. 1890. Featured in a series of Chicago recordings on Paramount 1926-9, some of which incl. Johnny Dodds. Later toured with show, returned to Jacksonville and is believed to have died there a year or two later. Samuel B. Charters wrote in *The Country Blues* (Rinehart): "He was a good guitar player and singer . . . despite a rather nasal quality to his voice. He played in a rhythmic dance style with considerable melodic inventiveness." LP: one track w. Charlie Spand in *Jazz, Vol. 10* (Folk.).

BLAKE, EUBIE, *composer, pianist, leader;* b. Baltimore, Md., 2/7/1883. Tuition w. Llewellyn Wilson, conductor w. Baltimore Colored Symphony. Also studied Schillinger. Won national piano contest, became big café attraction. In 1915 he and Noble Sissle joined forces as a vaudeville team; later they wrote many hit songs together, notably *I'm Just Wild About Harry.* Also associated with Sissle through Jim Europe's 369th Infantry band, which toured country after World War I (under Sissle's leadership after Europe's death). Many of Blake's songs became national hits, among them *Memories of You, You're Lucky To Me, Love Will Find a Way, Lovin' You the Way I Do.* During World War II he toured for several years as a USO entertainer. He has occasionally resumed his partnership with Sissle for clubs, benefits and on a 20th-Fox LP, *The Wizard Of The Ragtime Piano,* released under Blake's name in '59.

Addr: 284-A Stuyvesant Ave., Brooklyn 21, N.Y.

BLAKEY, ART (Moh. name: Abdullah Ibn Buhaina), *drums;* b. Pittsburgh, Pa., 10/11/19. Studied piano at school; took up drums when the drummer with a band in which he was playing became sick. Joined Fletcher Henderson, '39; w. Mary Lou Williams' first band at Kelly's Stable, '40; then a year w. own group at Tic-Toc in Boston. With Billy Eckstine for duration of band 1944-7, then around NYC w. own groups and others. Lucky Millinder in '49; Buddy De Franco's quartet '51-3. Own groups and as sideman at Birdland Monday sessions '54. Formed Jazz Messengers '55, personnel incl. Kenny Dorham, tpt., Hank Mobley, ten. sax, Horace Silver, pno., Doug Watkins, bass. Since then has toured successfully in US and Europe. Some of the men who have played with his quintet during the '50s: Donald Byrd, Bill Hardman, Lee

Morgan, tpts.; Jackie McLean, alto sax; Johnny Griffin, Benny Golson, Wayne Shorter, ten. sax; Sam Dockery, Junior Mance, Bobby Timmons, Walter Davis, pno. While in France, Nov.-Dec. '58, the group recorded the sound track for the film *Les Femmes Disparaissent* (*The Disappearing Women*). Pl. at Newport and Randall's Island '58-9. "Blakey is perhaps the most emotionally unbridled drummer in jazz, and there are times when his backgrounds resemble a brush fire"— Nat Hentoff. Won DB Critics' poll New Star award '53. Favs: Max Roach, Sid Catlett, Cozy Cole. Own LPs on Blue Note, Col., Wor. Pac., Jub., Beth., Elek., Atl., LPs w. Thelonious Monk, Miles Davis (Blue Note, Pres.), Buddy De Franco (MGM), Benny Golson (New Jazz) and numerous others; *Drum Roll* (Em.).

BLAKKESTAD, WILLIAM T. (Bill), *drums;* b. Minneapolis, Minn., 2/17/29. From musical family; stud. drums at MacPhail School of Music in Minneapolis 1941; pl. in school bands and dance bands. With Bob Davis' group '53-8. Favs: Buddy Rich, Art Blakey. LPs w. Davis (Zephyr, Steph.)

Addr: 600 N. Lilac Drive, Minneapolis 22, Minn.

BLAND, JACK, *guitar;* b. Sedalia, Mo., 5/8/1899. With Dick Slevin, a kazoo-playing soda clerk in St. Louis and Red McKenzie, started the combo known as the Mound City Blue Blowers. Isham Jones got them their first record date, on which they played *Arkansas Blues* and *Blue Blues;* rec. in Chicago 2/23/24, it was a sensation and reputedly sold a million records. Later that year, with guitarist Eddie Lang added, the group visited England. Bland later became a close associate of Eddie Condon, playing guitar on a number of records for which Condon was banjoist. He recorded w. Geo. Wettling 1940; Art Hodes 1944. LP w. Wettling in *Chicago Jazz* (Decca).

BLANTON, JIMMY, *bass; b.* St. Louis, Mo., 1921; d. 7/30/42. Played with Jeter-Pillars & Fate Marable orchs. in St. Louis, where Duke Ellington heard him in 1939. From the fall of '39 until two years later, when he contracted tuberculosis and left to spend the rest of his brief life in California, Blanton exercised an incalculable influence in transforming the use of the string bass in jazz. Before his day it had rarely been used for anything but quarter-notes in ensemble or solos. Blanton improvised as if the bass were a horn, phrasing fluently with frequent eighth- and sixteenth-note runs, using harmonic and melodic ideas that were unheard of on the instrument. The clarity of his tone, the definition and timing of his notes, made earlier exponents seem like amateurs. Oscar Pettiford, Ray Brown and almost all the other top bassists acknowledge Blanton's position in jazz history as the pioneer, the first true master of this cumbersome vehicle. LPs w. Duke Ellington on Victor LPM 1092, 1364, 1715.

BLAZE, RALPH LEWIS, *guitar;* b. New Brunswick, N.J., 4/11/22. Self-taught. Pl. w. Gene Krupa 1948-50; Stan Kenton '50-2, then settled in Salt Lake City, where he led a quartet at his own night club, the Cinegrill, to May '54; later rejoined Kenton, toured Europe with him '56. Since leaving Kenton has had own quintet working throughout Orange County, Calif. Is talented sculptor; made mobiles for Lighthouse, Hermosa Beach. Favs: Almeida, Johnny Smith. LPs w. Kenton, *Cuban Fire, Contemporary Concepts* (Cap.).

Addr: 1574 Brande Ave., Anaheim, Calif.

BLEY, PAUL, *piano, composer;* b. Montreal, Quebec, Canada, 11/10/32. Violin at five; piano at eight, junior diploma at McGill Conservatory at 11. Led high school band; own quartet at Chalet Hotel, Montreal, 1945-8. First jazz break came when he joined forces with Ozzie Roberts & Clarence Jones, bassist and drummer of the Oscar Peterson trio, after Peterson left for the US in 1949. Played nearly a year at the Alberta Lounge, then left for New York, where he took composition and conducting courses at Juilliard. Returned to Canada 1952, did weekly TV show for Jazz Workshop of Montreal, also made movie short dealing with jazz history, in which Stan Kenton appeared. Began to acquire US jazz reputation from '54, playing NYC clubs; midwestern colleges '55, night clubs in Los Angeles '56-8 incl. group w. Ornette Coleman & Don Cherry late '58. Many college concerts in Cal. '57-9. Back in East, fall '59, started new quartet. With Ch. Mingus, Jan. '60. Own LPs: Mercury, Debut, GNP.

Addr: 55 East 9th Street, New York 3, N.Y.

BLOCK, SIDNEY SANFORD (Sandy), *bass;* b. Cleveland, Ohio, 1/16/17. Moved to Brooklyn, stud. violin, switching to bass in high school, 1934. Worked as sideman in various big bands in the '30s and '40s, incl. Van Alexander, A. Rey, J. Wald, T. Dorsey. Since then has worked w. various groups, incl. C. Shavers quartet, and is currently mainstay in New York recording studios. Fav. own record: *Then I'll Be Happy* w. T. Dorsey. Fav: T. Dorsey. LPs w. Hazel Scott (Decca), Teddi King, T. Dorsey (Vict.).

Addr: 1824 E. 15th St., Brooklyn 29, N.Y.

BLONS, HARRY, *clarinet, tenor sax;* b. St. Paul, Minn., 11/29/11. Began w. private teacher in St. Paul, 1927. Played w. local groups in '30; later w. H. McIntyre '37-8; on tour w. Red Nichols '39; Red Dougherty '39-42. Formed own Dixieland combo '49; joined Doc Evans Sept. '54; back w. own group '55. Fav. own solo: *Singin' The Blues* on Merc. Favs: Jack Teagarden, B. Goodman, I. Fazola, Ed Hall, O. Simeon. Own LPs: Merc., Zeph., Audio.

Addr: 1471 Grand Ave., St. Paul, Minn.

BLYTHE, JIMMY, *piano;* b. 1899; d. ca. 1936. While in Chicago during the 1920s he recorded piano solos and many accompaniments to vocalists, mostly for Paramount, incl. Ma Rainey sessions; also recorded w. Jimmy Bertrand's Washboard Wizards (incl. J. Dodds), Vocalion, 1927; J. C. Cobb and his Grains of Corn (Vocalion, 1928-9); Memphis Night Hawks (Vocalion, 1932); Bumble Bee Slim, 1934-5. LP: one track w. State Street Ramblers in *History of Classic Jazz* (River.).

BO DIDDLEY (Ellas McDaniel), *guitar, singer;* b. McCombs, Miss., 12/30/28. Parents moved to Chicago when he was an infant. Faced his first audience at the age of ten on a street corner as leader of a combo comprising two guitars and washboard. No formal training. Professional debut 1951 at 708 Club in Chi. Scored hit in r & b circles on Chess and Checker labels with such tunes as *Bo Diddley* and *I'm A Man* '55. App. in rock 'n' roll concert in Carnegie Hall.

Bo Diddley, a singer and electric guitarist capable of producing some of the earthiest and most authentic sounds since the earliest days of primitive blues artists, is one of the few performers in the so-called rock 'n' roll field blessed with genuine artistic value.

Addr: c/o Shaw Artists Corp., 565 5th Ave., New York 17, N.Y.

BODNER, PHILIP L. (Phil), *saxophones, clarinet, flute, oboe;* b. Waterbury, Conn., 6/13/19. Moved to New Jersey as a youngster. Stud. clarinet at age 8, then saxophone. Started pl. w. local bands in Paterson while still in high school. To NYC 1939 where he began the first of many different studio jobs. Took up flute in '40. After Army service '42-5, resumed his career in NY studios and recordings. Oboe in '48. Favs: Getz, Artie Shaw; Bob Bloom, oboe; Julius Baker, flute. LPs w. Billy Taylor (River.), Metropolitan Jazz Quartet, (MGM), L. Feather: *Hi-Fi Suite* (MGM), *Jingles All The Way* (Lib.); Chris Connor (Atl.), Joe Williams (Roul.).

Addr: 91 Central Park West, New York 23, N.Y.

BOLDEN, CHARLES (Buddy), *cornet;* b. New Orleans, 1868; d. New Orleans, 11/4/31. He is believed to have been one of the first and most powerful musicians ever to play what was subsequently called jazz. A barber by trade, he led a band in which Bunk Johnson played from 1895-99. Samuel Charters, in his book *Jazz: New Orleans* says of him: ". . . he was so popular he sometimes had six or seven bands going in one night, and he'd go from one to another playing his specialties, *Make Me A Pallet On the Floor, Bucket's Got A Hole In It* and *Funky Butt, Funky Butt, Take It Away.*"

The sound of his horn, according to those who heard him play, was comparable to that of John Peel. In 1906, he began suffering periods of derangement; the last job he is known to have played was a funeral with the Allen Brass Band in 1907. He was committed to the East Louisiana State Hospital on June 5, 1907 where he spent the rest of his life. Since his career predated the making of commercial records of his kind of music, there is nothing left of him but legend.

BOLDEN, WALTER LEE, *drums;* b. Hartford, Conn., 12/17/25. Studied at Julius Hartt's Sch. of Mus., Hartford, 1945-7. Played w. Stan Getz '50-1; Horace Silver, Howard McGhee '52; Mat Mathews '53; Teddy Charles '54, then various combos in and around NYC incl. T. Scott. Toured w. Lambert, Hendricks and Ross, pl. w. Don Abney, Sims-Cohn '59. Favs: Roach, Blakey, Kenny Clarke. LPs w. Gerry Mulligan (Pres.), Tony Scott (Coral), Stan Getz (Roost).

BOLLING, CLAUDE, *leader, piano, composer;* b. Cannes, France, 4/10/30. Stud. in Nice and Paris; prof. debut playing for US Army in Nice 1945. Paris jazz festival '47; worked at Club St. Germain in Paris '49-52. Was w. L. Hampton in France; formed own big band in '56 for records. Rec. in Paris w. Rex Stewart, Roy Eldridge, Mezzrow, L. Hampton, Albert Nicholas, and w. own combo and band. Main influence Ellington; favs: Tatum, Hines. Own LP: *Rolling with Bolling* (Omegadisk), *French Jazz* (Bally).

Addr: 12 bis Rue Pergolèse, Paris 16, France.

BOLVIG, PALLE S. P., *trumpet, composer;* b. Copenhagen, Denmark, 11/25/32. Formal training, 1949-51; since '51 has been w. Ib Glindemann Orch. as lead trumpet & arr. except for summer '58 when he pl. w. Newport International Band at NJF and Brussels World's Fair. Was in staff orch. for *Hidden Fear,* John Payne movie filmed in Copenhagen. Fav: Maynard Ferguson; fav. arr: Bill Holman. LP w. International Band (Col.).

Addr: Vermundsgade 10, Copenhagen, Denmark.

BONANO, JOSEPH (Sharkey), *trumpet, singer;* b. Milneburg, La., 4/9/04. In 1920s worked w. Johnny Miller, Jean Goldkette and local New Orleans bands. Early records w. Brownlee's Orch. on Okeh, 1924; J. Miller, Col., '28; Monk Hazel, Bruns., '28. With advent of swing era, acquired some popularity as pseudo-Armstrong type trumpeter and singer along lines established by Wingy Manone and Louis Prima. Made three sessions with pickup Dixieland groups in NYC for Vocalion, 1936. In recent years, own combo mostly in New Orleans, but did play Child's Paramount, NYC, Feb. '55 and later toured the US, playing at numerous hotels in the Hilton chain as part of their shows. Led group at Roundtable, NYC, Sept. '59. Own LPs on Roul., South., Cap.

Addr: 40 Swallow St., Lake Vista, New Orleans 24, La.

BOND, JAMES E. JR. (Jimmy), *bass, tuba;* b. Philadelphia, Pa., 1/27/33. St. on bass in junior high school; bass and tuba at Mastbaum High. Grad. from Juilliard 1955; while in school had pl. with Gene Ammons, Louis Bellson, Charlie Parker et al. W. Chet Baker July, '55-Sept. '56; Ella Fitzgerald Oct. '56-Jan. '57; Buddy De Franco Mar. '57 and various small combos '58-9. Favs: Oscar Pettiford, Ray Brown. LPs w. Chet Baker (Wor. Pac.), Fred Katz (Dot), L. Marable (Jazz: West).

BONNEMERE, EDWARD VALENTINE (Eddie), *piano;* b. New York City 2/15/21. Church pianist in Harlem while in school; Army '42-5; w. Claude Hopkins at Zanzibar, '46. Won jazz piano scholarship on WOV '47; master's degree at NYU in music education; taught school until Feb. '54. Began specializing in Latin music around '53, featured on Roost recordings. Favs: Shearing, Cole, Previn. Own LP on Roost.

Addr: 1475 Gaylord Terrace, West Englewood, N.J.

BOOKER, BERYL, *piano;* b. Philadelphia, Pa., 6/7/22. Self-taught; never learned to read music. Local combos incl. own groups; to NYC w. Slam Stewart trio 1946. With Slam off and on to 1951, also toured as accompanist for Dinah Washington. Formed trio with Bonnie Wetzel, Elaine Leighton, June 1953; toured Europe w. *Jazz Club USA* show Jan. '54. Trio broke up summer '54. She then worked with small groups, often fronting her own trio, teaming up occasionally w. Slam Stewart. In '59 she again acc. Dinah Washington for several months, incl. engagement in Stockholm during July. Rec. 10 inch LPs (no longer available) for Em., Cadence.

BOSE, STERLING BELMONT, *trumpet;* b. New Orleans, 1906. Recorded w. Arcadia Serenaders, 1924-6. Worked w. Jean Goldkette 1927, then w. Victor Young, WGN Chicago; Ben Pollack 1930. To NYC '31; toured w. Joe Haymes '35-7, then w. Ray Noble, Benny Goodman, Glenn Miller, Bob Crosby and four months at Nick's in the early '40s. He played briefly w. Bob Zurke, six months w. Jack Teagarden, then back to Nick's; concerts w. Eddie Condon at Town Hall, etc. in the mid-forties. In June '58, Bose was found dead of a self-inflicted bullet wound in St. Petersburg, Fla., where he had pl. since '50. Rec. w. Jack Teagarden '31, Ben Pollack '33, Vic Berton '35, Mound City Blue Blowers '36, Bob Crosby '38. LPs w. T. Dorsey, *Clambake Seven* (Vict.).

BOSTIC, EARL, *alto sax, composer;* b. Tulsa, Okla., 4/25/13. Clarinet, alto in high school & boy scout bands. Studied harmony, theory, and various instruments at Xavier Univ., New Orleans, then toured w. Charlie Creath-Fate Marable, Marion Sears, Clyde Turpin. In NYC, played w. Edgar Hayes, Don Redman, Leon Gross, Hot Lips Page, Cab Calloway; arranged for Paul Whiteman, Louis Prima, Ina Ray Hutton; played trumpet, guitar, alto w. own band at Mimo Club, Harlem, 1941. After two years with Hampton's band, started again on own in 1945, recording first with big band for Majestic, then with smaller group for Gotham. Later, on King records, became extraordinarily successful, not in jazz circles but with rhythm-and-blues audiences, with whom his extroverted, loud-toned alto solos are big favorites. Hits include *Temptation, Flamingo, Sleep, Moonglow, Cherokee, You Go To My Head;* as songwriter, *Let Me Off Uptown* (rec. by Krupa), *The Major & The Minor* (rec. Alvino Rey), *Brooklyn Boogie* (rec. Louis Prima). Elected to Playboy All Star Band '59 in reader's poll, he appeared at Playboy Jazz Festival, Chi. Aug. '59. Own LPs on King.

Addr: 4585 Don Milagro Dr., Baldwin Hills, L.A., Calif.

BOSWELL, CONNEE (orig. Connie), *singer;* b. New Orleans, La. ca. 1912. Stricken by polio in infancy, she has always worked from a wheelchair. Stud. 'cello at four, later piano, sax, trombone. With sisters Martha and Helvetia (Vet), formed vocal and instrumental trio. From 1931 they sang on dozens of successful records and were precursors in their field of the Andrews Sisters, McGuire Sisters etc. After her sisters married and retired, Connee continued as a single. The Dorsey Bros., B. Goodman, Red Nichols, Don Redman and other name bands of the '30s played on the Sisters' records. "Connee's style was a clean break from the on-the-beat and rather formal style of pop singing in vogue before her arrival; her swing and sure sense of time were and continue to be a big influence on female singers."—Dom Cerulli, *Down Beat.* One singer on whom Miss Boswell had a strong (and probably the only) influence is Ella Fitzgerald. Own LP: *Connee Boswell & Orig. Memphis Five in Hi-Fi* (Vict.); *Connee* (Dec.)

Addr: 101 Central Park West, New York City.

BOTHWELL, JOHNNY, *alto sax;* b. Gary, Ind., 1919. Inspired by Johnny Hodges, bought alto sax; sideman with Gene Krupa, T. Dorsey, Woody Herman, Sonny Dunham. Was key figure in Boyd Raeburn band of 1944-5 progressive era. Had own big and small bands off and on through 1950, then out of music business. LP on Bruns. w. own big band no longer available.

BOWMAN, DAVID W. (Dave), *piano;* b. Buffalo, N.Y. 9/8/14. Studied at Hamilton, Ontario, Cons. and Pittsburgh Mus. Inst. Started w. Ken Steele in Hamilton, then Jack Hylton '36-7. With Bobby Hackett at Nick's '37-40, Jack Teagarden '40, Muggsy Spanier '41, and free-lance radio work until '51. ABC staff to '54 when he joined Bud Freeman trio. Later moved to Florida and was free-lancing there in late '50s. Fav: Tatum; imp. infl: Hines, Stacy. LPs: w. Bud Freeman (Harm., Beth.); George Wettling (Weathers); four tracks in *A String of Swingin' Pearls* (Vict.).

BOWN, PATRICIA ANNE (Patti), *piano;* b. Seattle, Wash., 7/26/31. Sister, a classical pianist, is married to comp. Gerald Valentine. Trained for classics herself, Patti won local contest, stud. privately and at U. of Wash. Played with many local bands from late '40s. Grad. from U. of Seattle '55; came to NYC Sept. '56, worked cocktail lounge jobs in the East. A childhood friend of Quincy Jones, whose orch. she joined Oct. '59 for European tour with Harold Arlen's show *Free and Easy.* A powerfully swinging, independently-thinking pianist. Own LP: Columbia. LPs w. Quincy Jones (Mercury).

Addr: 117 Christopher Street, New York City, N.Y.

BOYD, NELSON, *bass;* b. Camden, N.J., 2/6/28. Feat. in late 1940s w. Coleman Hawkins, Tadd Dameron, Ch. Barnet, Dizzy Gillespie. With Gillespie again in '56, touring the Middle East with him. Rec. *Half Nelson* w. Charlie Parker (Savoy). LPs w. Gillespie (GNP, Verve), Parker, Dexter Gordon, Fats Navarro (Savoy).

BRADFORD, PERRY, *leader, singer, piano;* b. Atlanta, Ga., 2/14/1893. Started band 1910; to NYC 1912. Led band off and on until 1928 and was prominent from 1923 as leader of recording groups that made numerous sessions, sometimes w. Bradford singing, sometimes backing Alberta Hunter and other singers.

Musicians on these records included Louis Armstrong, Buster Bailey, James P. Johnson, Fats Waller, Don Redman.

BRADLEY, WILLIAM ACKERSON (Bill), *drums;* b. New York City, 2/15/38. Son of Will Bradley. Took up drums 1952; rapidly gained acceptance on entering profession in spring '54, playing Birdland, Basin St., etc. with Johnny Smith, Tony Scott, Kai Winding, G. Wallington. Pl. w. Woody Herman, Jan. to Apr., 1956. Favs: Art Blakey, Philly Joe Jones. Own LP, *House Of Bradley,* on Epic; LP w. Tony Fruscella (Atl.).

BRADLEY, WILL (Wilbur Schwichtenberg), *trombone, composer;* b. Newton, N.J., 7/12/12; raised Washington, N.J. To NYC 1928; with Milt Shaw, Red Nichols, then CBS staff '31-4, Ray Noble '35-6, studios to late '39, when he and Ray McKinley formed a band jointly, earning great popularity with a commercialized popular brand of boogie-woogie arrangement, best known of which included *Beat Me Daddy Eight To The Bar, Scrub Me Mama With A Boogie Beat,* and the band's theme, *Strange Cargo.* After the band broke up in '42, Bradley returned to radio and recording work, occasionally fronting a band for a dance date or record session. He has also done some classical writing, including a trombone sonata for American Composer's League, several large string works, a brass suite, and a number of works performed by Dean Dixon on Radiodiffusion, Paris. On staff NBC, also free-lance in TV, radio and rec. Interests himself in silversmithing, gem cutting, wood sculpture and painting. Fav. own solo: *April In Paris* (Col.). Own LPs on Epic, Gr. Award, Vict., *Gold On Silk* (Everest); LP w. Don Redman (Uran.).

Addr: 134 W. 58th St., New York, N.Y.

BRADSHAW, EVANS, *piano;* b. Memphis, Tenn., April, 1933. Began pl. piano at age of 9, by 12 was in father's band. He and Phineas Newborn grew up together and were close friends. Moved to Flint, Mich. '53, where he spent his time working in an auto factory during the day, playing jobs w. his trio at night. It was there he was heard by a talent scout who told Riverside Records about him. He made a session and was hired for engagements by the Village Vanguard and Birdland in NYC. Feat. at Detroit Jazz Fest. 1959. Own LPs on Riverside.

BRAFF, REUBEN (Ruby), *trumpet;* b. Boston 3/16/27. Self-taught, worked w. Pee-Wee Russell, Bud Freeman, Urbie Green, Edmond Hall, Joe Sullivan, George Wettling, Gene Ramey. Played at Brandeis U. Jazz Seminar '53; NJF several times since '54; Toronto, Boston Festivals '59; had acting and playing role in Rogers & Hammerstein musical, *Pipe Dream,* '55-6. Braff's case is a striking illustration of the failure of critical acclaim to bring success to an artist of obvious merit. He has been called "rich, warm, deeply rooted in basic jazz" (John Wilson), "heatedly tender, richly swinging, and melodically flowing and imaginative" (Nat Hentoff), "well-stirred mixture of Armstrong, Berigan, and Will Bill Davison' (Whitney Balliett), and has been similarly embraced by innumerable critics both at home and abroad, yet in 1960 he reported that he had been almost continuously out of work for five years. Possibly because he is a younger musician playing in a basically older style, it has been extremely difficult for him to find work in night clubs. Almost the only area in which he has remained occasionally active is that of recordings.

Braff won the *Down Beat* Critics' Poll as new star '55. Fav: Louis Armstrong. Own LPs: UA, Verve, Epic, Vict., Story., Vanguard, ABC-Par., War. Bros.; LPs w. Mel Powell (Van., Col.), Benny Goodman (Cap.), *The Magic Horn* (Vict.), Buck Clayton (Van., Col.), Vic Dickenson (Van.).

Addr: 3016 Johnson Ave., Riverdale, N.Y.

BRANDT, HELMUT, *baritone sax, composer;* also *tenor, clarinet*; b. Berlin, Germany, 1/1/31. First mus. educ. in Berliner Domchor (church choir) at 9; violin lessons from '41, sax and guitar at cons. for two years. Prof. debut '50; own quintet from Jan. '54, pl. concert tours etc. Member of RIAS Berlin radio dance band from Jan. '59. Rec. w. own combo for Metronome, Jazztone. Favs: Getz, Konitz, Desmond, Mulligan; fav. comps. Gil Evans, Bob Graettinger.

Addr: Am Vierling 1, Berlin-Zehlendorf, Germany.

BRANNON, HUMPHREY J. (Teddy), *piano, arranger, composer;* b. Moultrie, Ga., 9/27/16. Cousin is Babs Gonzales; stud. piano from age nine in Linden, N.J. where family had moved. Played w. local dance bands during high school, then w. a night club band in Newark 1937-42. Was leader of this group for a while. With Benny Carter '42-4; w. various combos along 52nd Street in '45-6. Had own trio '47-50; then w. Roy Eldridge, Buddy Rich, Bennie Green until he joined Johnny Hodges in '52. With Illinois Jacquet '54-7; joined Jonah Jones '58. At various times he also accompanied various singers, incl. Dinah Washington, The Ravens, Ruth Brown et al. Fav: Oscar Peterson; names Teddy Wilson, Garner, Nat Cole, Benny Carter as important influences. LPs w. Jonah Jones (Cap.), Bennie Green (Pres.).

Addr: 2195 7th Ave., New York 27, N.Y.

BRAUD, WELLMAN, *bass;* b. St. James, La., 1/25/1891. Violin at 12; played in string trio at Tom Anderson's in NO, bass in Chicago 1917. With Sugar Johnny's band, Charlie Elgar '20. To Europe w. James P. Johnson '22 in *Plantation Days* show. With Will Vodery, Wilbur Sweatman '23. Toured for three years w. burlesque show, then joined Duke Ellington '26, and was important figure in the band until he left in '35. Took over direction of Spirits of Rhythm '35-6; own trio in Sheepshead Bay restaurant '37-41; in later years was active as businessman in Harlem, running pool hall and playing occasional gigs and record dates. Toured Europe with Kid Ory fall '56. Now retired and living in Brooklyn. Fav: Hinton. Rec. w. Lil Armstrong, Jimmie Noone '37, Jelly Roll Morton,

Louis Armstrong, Sidney Bechet '40, Baby Dodds '45. LPs w. Ellington (Cam., Bruns.).

BREDL, OTTO, *trombone;* b. Munich, Germany, 11/29/28. Stud. bassoon at Academy. Played at American clubs in Munich 1945-9. Radio stations as soloist w. Kurt Edelhagen '49-57; with Eddie Sauter '57-8, then first trombone with Edelhagen. Fav: Teagarden.

Addr. Berrenratherstr. 177, Cologne, Germany.

BREGMAN, BUDDY, *composer, conductor;* b. Chicago, Ill., 7/9/30. Brother of composer Jule Styne. Gave first piano recital at age of 12 in Chicago. Stud. harmony, composition, arranging at Chicago Conservatory, also learned many instruments incl. piano, clar., sax, flute. Later attended UCLA and stud. in LA w. Mario Castelnuovo-Tedesco. Living on West Coast, has orchestrated and conducted for NBC, CBS shows starring Jack Haley, Gary Crosby et al. Won "Emmy" nomination from Academy of Television Arts and Sciences for his scoring of NBC color show, *Anything Goes.* Wrote score for film, *Step Down to Terror,* 1956. Mus. dir. for Ella Fitzgerald and many other jazz artists on Verve '56-7. LPs on Verve.

Addr: c/o N. Goodman, 218 N. Canon Dr., Beverly Hills, Calif.

BREHM, SIMON, *bass;* b. Stockholm, Sweden, 12/31/21. Has toured mostly w. own band, also worked for various visiting stars incl. Hot Lips Page, Teddy Wilson, Tyree Glenn. Paris Jazz Festival, 1949. Gave up music to concentrate on business, running Karusell Record label in Stockholm from mid-'50s.

BRICE, PERCY, *drums;* also *conga, bongos;* b. New York City, 3/25/23. Stud. violin, piano under Works Projects Administration. First name band job w. Luis Russell Oct. 1944. Also worked w. Benny Carter, '45-6; concerts for Fran Kelley at UCLA; Mercer Ellington band '47, then rhythm-and-blues work w. Eddie Vinson, Tab Smith, Cootie Williams, Tiny Grimes. In '53-4 he worked w. Lucky Thompson, Oscar Pettitford and had own combo at Minton's Play House. With Billy Taylor trio June '54-Oct. '56, then joined George Shearing, remaining until June '58. Free-lanced in NYC w. Herbie Mann, Kenny Burrell, Martha Davis and Spouse until April '59 when he joined Sarah Vaughan. To So. America w. her Aug. '59. Numerous festivals in US and Canada w. Taylor, Shearing, Vaughan. Film: *The Big Beat* w. Shearing '58. An expert jazz drummer, serious and ambitious musician. Favs: Roach, Rich, Clarke, Blakey. Fav. own solo: *How High The Moon,* Billy Taylor's *Town Hall Concert* (Prestige). LPs w. Taylor (Pres., ABC-Par.), Shearing (Capitol).

Addr: 794 East 158th St., Bronx 56, N.Y.

BRIGGS, LILLIAN, *singer, trombone;* b. Allentown, Pa., 6/3/35. Vln. at ten, piano at 14; trombone in high school band. After working as truck driver and welder, formed own all-girl band; later played w. Joy Caylor in all-girl orch. In 1955 she rec. a jump blues, *I Want You to Be My Baby,* on which she sang and played. It was an immediate hit and she has since been a successful show business personality w. an emphasis on rock 'n' roll and has toured in Australia, Latin America and Europe.

BRIGHT, RONNELL, *piano;* b. Chicago, Ill., 7/3/30. Began stud. piano at 6, intending to become a concert pianist. Stud. at University of Ill., Juilliard, Roosevelt University. Began playing jazz piano while in Navy band in 1953. Worked in Chicago w. bassist Johnny Pate. Worked w. Rolf Kuhn and own trio around NYC, '57; repl. Jimmy Jones as acc. for Sarah Vaughan, '58. Capable modern soloist and expert accompanist. Favs: O. Peterson, N. Cole, E. Garner, J. Lewis. Own LPs: Vang., Reg.; LPs w. Rolf Kuhn (Vang.).

Addr: 3234 Wilson Ave., Bronx 69, N.Y.

BRIGNOLA, NICHOLAS THOMAS (Nick), *baritone sax;* also *tenor, soprano, bass saxes, clarinet, flute;* b. Troy, N.Y., 7/17/36. Grandfather pl. tuba w. John Philip Sousa band; whole family musical. Mainly self-taught on all instruments; stud. theory at Ithaca Coll. and Berklee School. Pl. with Reese Markewich 1957-9; Cal Tjader quart., Mastersounds in San Francisco '58. Worked w. own group in Albany fall '59. Ambition: to become one of the top five baritone sax players in jazz. Main influence: Ch. Parker. LPs w. Reese Markewich (Mod. Age), *Jazz in the Classroom, Vol. 2* (Berklee).

Addr: 138 Third St., Troy, New York.

BROKENSHA, JOHN JOSEPH (Jack), *vibes, drums;* b. Nailsworth, Adelaide, South Australia, 1/5/26. Father legitimate percussionist, gave him early tuition. As a child had xylophone act in radio and vaudeville. Australian Symph. Orch. 1942-4, Air Force, '44-6; own group touring in concert groups, broadcasts, etc. '47-53. Worked in Canada '54 where the Australian Jazz Quintet (at that time Quartet), of which he is a member, was formed. Made records in Australia w. Rex Stewart. Tours to Australia for ABC '58, Australia & New Zealand w. Sammy Davis & Stan Freberg '59. Currently at WXYZ-TV in Detroit. Fav. own solo, *September Song* w. Australian Jazz Quintet (Bethlehem). Favs: Milt Jackson, Red Norvo. LPs w. AJQ on Beth.

Addr: 214 Geneva, Highland Park, Michigan.

BROOKMEYER, ROBERT (Bob), *valve trombone, piano, composer;* b. Kansas City, Kansas, 12/19/29. Played clarinet and trombone; piano at KC conservatory, then entered Army. Joined Tex Beneke's band as pianist 1951; later worked, mostly on piano, with Ray McKinley, Louis Prima, Claude Thornhill (on second piano and trombone), Jerry Wald, Terry Gibbs, also a month with Woody Herman in '52. Joined Stan Getz quartet for a year '53, then Gerry Mulligan quartet spring '54 incl. Paris Jazz Festival. Toured France and Italy w. Mulligan sextet, spring '56, England w. quartet again, Apr. '57. Own group briefly; then joined Jimmy Guiffre trio, Nov. '57, remaining until end of '58. Free-lanced in NYC '59; toured with Mulligan's big band in 1960. Like Mulligan's his playing is infused with both traditional and modern elements and his solo work fits well in a variety of settings. Won DB Critics' poll, New Star Award on trombone '53. Film: *Jazz On A Summer's Day.* Favs: Teagarden, Harris, Swope, J. J. Johnson; fav. pianists: Basie, Ellington, Tatum, Jelly Roll Morton, Bill Evans. Own LPs on Wor. Pac., Pres., UA, Verve; *Ivory Hunters,* piano duets w. Bill Evans (UA); LPs w. Mulligan (Wor. Pac., Verve, Merc.), Phil Sunkel (ABC-Par.), Jimmy Guiffre (Atl.), Zoot Sims (Dawn, Story.), Al Cohn (Coral), *Jazz Soul of Porgy and Bess* (UA), Phil Urso (Savoy), Teddy Charles (Beth.), George Russell (Decca).

Addr: 306 West 4th St., New York 14, N.Y.

BROOKS, JOHN BENSON, *composer, piano;* b. Houlton, Me., 2/23/17. Mother had scholarship at Peabody Conservatory. He received instruction on several instruments from neighbors, friends and at school. Attended New England Conservatory and Juilliard. Had own band in Boston, 1939; worked w. Eddie DeLange '40; Boyd Raeburn, T. Dorsey, J. Dorsey, L. Brown *et al* in '30s and '40s. Introduced a folk jazz combo at a Town Hall concert by the Weavers in 1950 and recorded similar works for Vik. Wishes to unify folk, New Orleans, Kansas City, mainstream and avant garde jazz into a single style. In '59 devised own method of composing and improvising with 12 tones. Own LP, *Alabama Concerto* (River.).

Addr: 535 Hudson St., New York, N. Y.

BROOKS, STELLA, *singer;* b. Seattle, Wash., 10/24/15. Started singing in San Francisco in early '30s; to NYC '37. Concerts at Town Hall 1946; rec. acc. by Frank Newton, S. Bechet, Geo. Brunis, Joe Sullivan, 1946. Made occasional café appearances in '50s, NYC.

BROONZY, WILLIAM LEE CONLEY (Big Bill), *singer, guitar;* b. Scott, Miss., 6/26/1893; d. Chicago, Ill., 8/14/58. His mother, born in slavery, died in 1957 at the age of 102. Raised in Arkansas; to Chicago 1920, working as redcap. First records on Paramount, 1926; played guitar acc. Cripple Clarence Lofton, Bumble Bee Slim; later became widely known as blues singer himself and was top selling male blues vocalist on Perfect & Vocalion in late 1930s. During this time he had a farm in Pine Bluff, Ark., but came to Chicago every few months to record. In 1938 critic John Hammond brought him from the farm to Carnegie Hall for the *Spirituals to Swing* concert, and again in '39. In the late '40s Broonzy worked as a janitor at Iowa State College, but frequently went to Chicago, where he appeared in Studs Terkel's *I Come For To Sing* Monday soirées. He visited England in '51 and became very popular there and on the Continent. Returned to England in '52, when he sang w. Mahalia Jackson, and again in '55 and '57. In late '54 he had his own tavern at 36th and Cottage Grove in Chicago. A serious lung operation curtailed his career in '57 and in '58 he succumbed to cancer. Broonzy's records established him as one of the great singers in the earthiest blues tradition and an outstanding primitive guitarist. His best records, such as *Just A Dream* (Voc.), are out of print. Autobiography, *Big Bill Blues,* as told to Belgian jazz writer Yannick Bruynoghe, was pub. by Grove Press '57. Own LPs on EmArcy; tracks in *Spirituals To Swing* (Vang.).

BROTHER MATTHEW—See BROWN, Boyce.

BROWN, BOYCE, *alto sax;* b. Chicago, Ill., 4/16/10; d. Hillsdale, Ill., 1/30/59. An associate of the early school of Chicagoans—Bix, Muggsy, Tesch, Condon & Co.—Brown worked with Don Carter and other bands, once went to NYC with Benny Meroff, but remained almost always around Chicago, something of a legend, revealing in his few rare recordings a strange, provocative style. He made one session with Paul Mares for Col., 1935, one with Wild Bill Davison, 1940, both unobtainable. The revelation, early in 1956, that he had entered a monastery in 1953 and had become a member of the Servite Order, earned widespread publicity. Together with Father Hugh Calkins, who played piano at sessions with him in the monastery, he earned more publicity than had ever been accorded him in his years as a lay jazzman. In Apr. '56 Brown, known as Brother Matthew, took part in a New York television jam session, and in the LP listed below, royalties from which were turned over to missions of the Servite Order in South Africa. Less than three years later, he died of a heart attack at the Servite Seminary. Own LP, *Brother Matthew With Eddie Condon's Jazz Band* on ABC-Par.; LP w. Jimmy McPartland in *Chicago Jazz* (Decca).

BROWN, CHARLES, *singer, piano;* b. Texas City, Tex., 1920. Pl. piano for church choir at age 11. Grad. Prairie View College 1942, then taught school. Pl. and sang w. Johnny Moore's Blazers mid-40s; had own trio later. Own LP: *Drifting Blues* (Score).

BROWN, CLEO, *pianist, singer;* b. Meridian, Miss., 1909. Studied classics; to Chicago 1919, debut at 14, toured Canada and US; learned boogie-woogie from her brother Everett, a friend of Pinetop Smith. Best-known for series of sides with rhythm acc. (incl. Gene Krupa) made for Decca in 1935. Her version of Pinetop's *Boogie-Woogie* was one of the first to become popular. In semi-obscurity on West Coast for past decade; one session for Capitol 1949. The series of records she made for Decca in the '30s is no longer available.

BROWN, CLIFFORD, *trumpet;* b. Wilmington, Del., 10/30/30; d. 6/26/56 in auto accident. Father gave him trumpet 1945 when he entered senior high school. Stud. jazz harmony, theory, trumpet, piano, vibes, bass w. Robert Lowery in Wilmington. Gigs in Philadelphia, '48, w. such men as Miles Davis, Fats Navarro. Latter encouraged and influenced him. Won scholarship to Maryland State Coll. in '49, arr. for coll. band. Hospitalized after car crash, June '50 to May '51. Toured w. Chris Powell r & b group on trumpet and piano, '52-3, Tadd Dameron '53; w. L. Hampton, Aug.-Dec. '53; free-lanced in NYC '53; to Cal. w. Max Roach. Won New Star Award in '54 DB critics' poll after being hailed by DB for his inspired, technically exceptional solos, which combined the best qualities of both Davis and Navarro. Many musicians and critics felt that if he had lived, Brown would have gone on to be one of the two or three top trumpeters in contemporary jazz. Own LPs on Blue Note, Prestige, EmArcy; LPs w. Max Roach (EmArcy, GNP), Sonny Rollins (Pres.), Art Blakey (BN).

BROWN, LAWRENCE, *trombone;* b. Lawrence, Kans., 7/3/05. Raised in Pasadena, Cal., where he studied piano, violin, tuba, alto, trombone. First public appearance before Mother's Day crowd of 6,000 at Aimee Semple McPherson Temple in Los Angeles. W. Ch. Echols, Curtis Moseby in LA, then first rec. while w. Paul Howard (Vict.) '27-30. With Les Hite's band (along with Lionel Hampton) while it backed Louis Armstrong '31. Joined Duke Ellington '32, left '51 to tour w. Johnny Hodges. After leaving Hodges, he free lanced in NYC '55-6, then joined CBS staff early '57. Brown toured Europe w. Ellington in '33, '39, '50, acquiring international fame as a smooth, melodic stylist. He rejoined the Ellington orchestra in June 1960. He won the Esq. Silver Award '44-5. Own LP on Verve; LPs w. Duke Ellington (Col., Vict.), Jimmy Rushing (Vang.), Joe Turner (Alt.), Ruby Braff (Epic), Johnny Hodges (Verve), Rex Stewart (Gr. Award), Met. All Stars (Harm.), Louis Armstrong (Col.), Lionel Hampton (Vict.), Frankie Laine & Buck Clayton (Col.); one track w. Rex Stewart in *History of Jazz, Vol. 3* (Cap.); feat. on *Opiate d' Amour* w. Jackie Gleason (Cap.).

Addr: 100 Hirliman Road, Teaneck, N.J.

BROWN, LESTER RAYMOND (Les), *leader;* b. Reinerton, Pa., 3/14/12. As child, studied on father's soprano sax. Cons. of Music in Ithaca, N.Y., 1926-9; Duke Univ. '32-5, where "Duke Blue Devils" were formed. Made first rec. for Bluebird, but band broke up Sept. 1937. Free-lance arr. for Larry Clinton, Isham Jones; started new band 1938 and gradually, through '40s, built up its name as good swing band operating mainly in pop field. Many radio, TV shows and other engagements with Bob Hope, incl. European tour 1951. Toured US Army bases in England '57. Seen and heard on Steve Allen TV show '59-60. Nicknamed the "Band of Renown," it has featured arrs. by Ben Homer (who wrote band's biggest hit, *Sentimental Journey*), Frank Comstock; solos by Dave Pell, Don Fagerquist, Geoff Clarkson. Doris Day was vocalist 1940 and '43-6. Brown himself plays alto and clarinet, but has never been featured as soloist. Best LP of jazz arrs.: *Party At The Palladium* (Coral); other LPs on Coral, Cap., Col., Kapp.

Addr: c/o Associated Booking Corp., 8619 Sunset Blvd., Los Angeles 46, Calif.

BROWN, MARSHALL RICHARD, *leader, composer-arranger, educator, valve trombone;* b. Framingham, Mass., 12/21/20. Father a vaudeville magician; mother pl. piano in silent movies. Pl. guitar at nine, valve trombone at 16, self-taught. BS *cum laude* in mus. at NYU, 1949; MA at Col. U. '53. Org. own band while in high sch. '37. While in Army '42-5, pl. and arr. w. Bernie Leighton. Staff arr. at Adirondacks summer hotel '49; band dir., East Rockaway High Sch. '49-51; Farmingdale High Sch. '51-7. Org. & dir. Farmingdale band, heard at NJF '57; International Band, NJF '58; Newport Youth Band, NJF '59.

Brown has enjoyed great success as a pop. songwriter, his hits incl. *Seven Lonely Days, The Banjo's Back In Town* and a big success in France, *Tout au Bout de la Semaine*. He wrote the score for a U.S. Steel Hour music drama in '56. Named "outstanding educator of the year" by Westlake Coll. of Mus. '57. Brown's main infl., he says, were Charlie Parker in jazz, John Dewey in education. Own LPs w. International Band (Col.), Youth Band (Coral).

Addr: 103 East 86th St., New York 28, N.Y.

BROWN, JAMES OSTEND (Pete), *alto, tenor saxes;* b. Baltimore, Md., 11/9/06. Piano, violin first; sax at 18. To NYC 1927 with Banjo Bernie orch. Ch. Skeets, 1928-34; own combo at Brittwood in Harlem; best known through intermittent partnership with Frankie Newton, first in original John Kirby band '38, also on Newton's Bluebird records and in his band at Kelly's Stable. Rec. dates w. Joe Marsala, Jimmie Noone, Buster Bailey et al.; own dates on Decca and series for Savoy 1942-5. Widely admired in late '30s for his humorous, staccato, wheezy-toned alto style. In early '40s heard on tenor, mostly in Brooklyn, also w. Slim Gaillard at Birdland. App. w. Coleman Hawkins at Newport Festival '57. LPs w. Coleman Hawkins (Vict., Verve), Sammy Price (Jazz.), Champion Jack Dupree (Alt.); *Jazz Kaleidoscope* (Beth.), *Alto Altitude* (EmArcy).

Addr: 141 W. 53rd St., New York 19, N.Y.

BROWN, RAYMOND MATTHEWS (Ray), *bass;* b. Pittsburgh, Pa., 10/13/26. Studied piano, bass; fin. high school 1944; eight months ea. w. Jimmy Hinsley & Snookum Russell. Came to NYC, joined Dizzy and pl. w. small group and later first big band. Left to form own trio, married Ella Fitzgerald in '48 and acc. her in all engagements incl. JATP. (Divorced 1952.) Thereafter became regular member of annual JATP tour. Since '51 w. Oscar Peterson Trio. Toured Europe w. JATP '57 and in the spring of '58. Member of the faculty at School of Jazz, Lenox, Mass., '57. Won Esq. New Star Award '47, Met. poll '55-60, DB poll '53-59, DB Critics poll '54, Playboy poll '58-60, Playboy All Stars poll '59-60. Own LPs; *Bass Hit* (Verve 8022), *This Is Ray Brown* (Verve 8290); LPs w. Peterson, JATP Vols. 5-11, B. De Franco, B. Webster, B. Powell, *Jam Session* 1, 2, 5, 6, 7, S. Stitt, Getz-Mulligan, C. Parker, L. Hampton, L. Armstrong (Verve); S. Rollins, *The Poll Winners* (Contemp.), D. Gillespie (Savoy).

Addr: 7220 Mt. Vernon St., Pitts., Pa.

BROWN, RICHARD (Rabbit), *singer, guitar;* b. New Orleans, La., ca. 1880; d. New Orleans, 1937. Prominent as a country blues singer in the streets of New Orleans before and during World War I, Brown is not known to have recorded before 1927, when his *James Alley Blues* was cut locally for Victor.

BROWN, RUTH, *singer;* b. Portsmouth, Va., 1/30/28. Sang spirituals at local church, where her father was choir director. Sang w. Lucky Millinder in 1948, but was fired. Soon after, Blanche Calloway discovered her in Washington, D.C.; brought her to NYC, '49, and she became an overnight hit in r & b circles. Unusual broken-note style similar to that of Miss Cornshucks and other southern artists. Own LPs on Atl.

BROWN, ALEXANDER (Sandy), *clarinet;* b. Izatnagar, India, 2/25/29. Self-taught. Own band in England since 1946, except for two years in service. Occasional solo work w. Humphrey Lyttelton, Chris Barber. Is a qualified architect and acoustic physicist. Rec. for Tempo, Pye-Nixa, Col. Fav. own solo *The Last Western* (Engl. Col.). Favs: J. Dodds, Eddie Miller, Giuffre, Pee Wee Russell.

Addr: 97 Canfield Gardens, London N. W. 6., England.

BROWN, SCOVILLE TOBY, *clarinet;* b. Chicago, Ill., 10/13/15. Stud. Chi. Mus. Coll. 1938-9; also w. Simeon Bellison '43-4, Leon Russianoff '54. Worked with Louis Armstrong, '32-4; Don Redman, '39-40; Fats Waller, '40-2; Army, '43-5; alto w. Claude Hopkins at Zanzibar, '45; Teddy Wilson show on CBS, Lucky Millinder etc. in NYC. Had own cocktail unit '48-52 and again '58-60; played Dixieland sessions at Stuyvesant Casino and Central Plaza '52-5; joined Lionel Hampton Jan. '56 and toured US, Europe and the Middle East with the band in '56 and '57. Pl. at Lake Champlain Valley fest. '59; joined Muggsy Spanier '59. Favs: Reg. Kell, Goodman, De Franco, Shaw. LPs w. Armstrong (Victor); *Flamenco Jazz* w. Hampton (Victor).

Addr: 313 West 102nd Street, New York 25, N.Y.

BROWN, THEODORE G. (Ted), *tenor saxophone;* b. Rochester, N.Y., 12/1/27. Father jazz banjoist. Stud. banjo w. him, 1933; violin, '37; at 14, stud. clar. & tenor w. uncle. Moved to Cal., 1941; several more years of study. USO tour '45; Army bands '46-7; gigs in Hollywood '47-8, then moved to NYC to study w. Lennie Tristano. Took day job in office, rarely working in music for several years. Pl. w. Tristano, Lee Konitz combos, late '55; to Hollywood, with Warne Marsh quintet Sept. '56-Apr. '57. Back in NYC, played club dates. Favs: Early Lester Young; Ch. Parker, W. Marsh, Konitz, Z. Sims, Rollins. Fav. own solos in *Jazz of Two Cities* w. Marsh (Imp.). Own LP on Vanguard, 1956; also w. Marsh in *Modern Jazz Gallery* (Kapp), Ronnie Ball (Savoy), Konitz-Giuffre (Verve).

Addr: c/o Fichera, 243 East 38th St., New York 16, N.Y.

BROWN, TOM, *trombone;* b. New Orleans, La., 1890; died N.O., 3/25/58. Began with "kids" band at 8 on violin, later switched to trombone; many young white New Orleans players were in and out of his groups. Took the first Dixieland band w. Ray Lopez, cornet; Gussie Mueller, clar.; Bill Lambert, drums; Arnold Loyocano, piano and bass to Chicago in 1915. Worked in vaudeville w. "The Five Rubes" and w. various groups, incl. Yerkes Marimba orch., Happy Six, Ray Miller, Johnny Bayersdoffer, Norman Brownlee and others. During the years before his death he owned a radio and music shop and gigged around New Orleans w. "Red" Bergan, Johnny Wiggs and others. Recorded for Comm. w. J. Wiggs and w. own group for Jazzology.

BROWN, VERNON, *trombone;* b. Venice, Ill., 1/6/07. Raised in St. Louis where he played w. Frank Trumbauer and Bix Beiderbecke at the Arcadia Ballroom in 1926. W. Jean Goldkette in Chi. '28, Joe Gill in Texas '31. Best known for his work w. Benny Goodman '38. W. Artie Shaw '40; Muggsy Spanier big band '41-2; since then, radio and TV staff work at ABC in NYC. Has taken leave of absence at different times to go on tours w. Goodman, such as the one to Europe in the spring of '58. Also pl. Newport Fest. w. Goodman '58. Occasional jazz work on records w. Cozy Cole, Bud Freeman and concerts in NY area w. Billy Butterfield. Capable Teagarden-inspired trombonist. LPs w. Goodman (Col., Vict.), Bud Freeman (Em.), Steve Allen (Coral), Wild Bill Davison (Comm.).

Addr: 93 Parkway Drive, Roslyn Heights, L.I., N.Y.

BRUBECK, DAVID W. (Dave), *piano, composer;* b. Concord, Calif., 12/6/20. Mother a pianist, two brothers music teachers. Started piano at four, taught by mother; 'cello at nine. Piano with local hillbilly, Dixieland and swing bands from age 13. Had 12-piece band 1941-2 while at College of Pacific, where he majored in music. Studied composition at Mills College in Oakland, Calif., under Darius Milhaud. While in Army, kept up study of composition under Arnold Schoenberg; had own ETO band in Europe, '44. On release from the Army, Brubeck continued studies off and on with Milhaud, also piano in '49 with Fred Saatman. He formed an experimental octet in '46, a trio in '49, quartet from '51. Took part in *Lyons Busy,* a jazz series with Jimmy Lyons over KNBC '50.

The earliest Brubeck records, originally made in '49 for Coronet, are still available on Fantasy, the label for which he recorded until '54, when he was also heard on Columbia. After causing a local stir in San Francisco, his group rose swiftly to the top among modern jazz combos and was soon nationally known. His quartet toured in concert work and occasional night club dates in '55, appeared at the Newport Jazz Festival July '58, and toured with great success in England, on the Continent, in Poland, and through the Middle East in '58. In the Fall of '59, the group again visited Great Britain. Toured Australia March 1960. Brubeck's US tours included the *Jazz For Moderns* show in Fall of '58, '59.

Brubeck's piano style, sometimes heavy in touch and extremely complex harmonically, was the subject of much disagreement among critics and musicians, some of whom felt that his was not a naturally swinging jazz technique. However, the addition to his repertoire of a series of highly attractive compositions (many of them in waltz time and in other meters unconventional in jazz), and the presence of Joe Morello in the Quartet from late '56, lent considerable added interest to the group's performances. In December '59, the Quartet joined with Leonard Bernstein and the New York Philharmonic in the premiere performance of *Dialogue For Jazz Combo And Symphony,* composed by his brother Howard Brubeck.

Brubeck has won the following awards: as pianist, *Down Beat* Critics poll '53, *Metronome* poll '55-6; for combo, *Met.* poll '54, 56, *DB* poll '53-5, '59, *Playboy* poll '57-60; Musician of the Year, *DB* '55. Favs: Tatum, Waller, Garner, M. McPartland, T. Wilson. Fav. comp.: Duke Ellington. Fav. own solos: *On The Alamo* (Col.), *Over The Rainbow* (Fantasy), *Blue Rondo A La Turque* (Col.). Own LPs: *Brubeck-Desmond* (Fan. 3229), *Brubeck & Desmond at Wilshire-Ebell* (3249), *Jazz at College of Pacific* (3223), *Jazz at Oberlin* (3245), *Jazz at Storyville* (3240), *Jazz at the Blackhawk* (3210), *Octet* (3239), *Quartet* (3230), *Reunion* (3268), *Solo Piano* (3259), *Trio* (2-3204/5); *Brubeck Time* (Col. CL-622), *Dave Digs Disney* (1059), *Gone With The Wind* (1347), *In Europe* (1168), *Jazz Goes To College* (566), *Jazz Goes To Junior College* (1034), *Jazz Impressions of Eurasia* (1251), *Jazz Impressions of USA* (984), *Jazz: Red Hot and Cool* (699), *Newport 1958* (1249), *Plays Brubeck* (878), *Storyville 1954* (590), *W. Jay & Kai at Newport* (932), *Time Out* (1397).

Addr: 6630 Heartwood Drive, Oakland 11, Calif.

BRUBECK, HOWARD, *composer;* b. Concord, Cal., 1916. Not a jazz musician, he is listed here because his *Dialogues for Jazz Combo and Symphony Orchestra* was performed at Carnegie Hall Dec. 1959 by the N.Y. Philharmonic (conducted by Leonard Bernstein) in conjunction with his brother Dave Brubeck's quartet. Now living in La Mesa, Cal., he is Chairman of the Music Dept. at Palomar Jr. College.

BRUNIS, GEORG (orig. name George Brunies), *trombone;* b. New Orleans, La., 2/6/00. As youngster worked w. Jack "Papa" Laine and brother, trumpeter Abbie Brunies. To Chi. 1919 w. New Orleans Rhythm Kings, with whom he made first record '22. Toured w. Ted Lewis '23-35. Since then has worked w. various small Dixieland units. Led his own band in Chicago at the 1111 Club, Blue Note, etc. Brunis, who changed his name on the advice of a numerologist, is a pioneer tailgate stylist; also known as comedian who can manipulate trombone slide with foot. Pl. Playboy Jazz Festival Aug. '59. Own LP, *Meet Me In Chicago* (Merc.), also on South. Comm.; LPs w. Ted Lewis (Col.), Muggsy Spanier (Vict.), Bix Beiderbecke (River.), *Brunies Bros. Dixieland Band* (Amer. Mus.), Eddie Condon, Wild Bill Davison (Comm.).

Addr: 5550 Kenmore Ave., Chicago 40, Ill.

BRYAN, MIKE, *guitar;* b. Byhalia, Miss., 1916. Self-taught; worked around Memphis 1934; to Chicago 1935, joined Red Nichols; own band in Greenwood, Miss., '38-9. Best known for work with Benny Goodman, 1940-1 and '45-6; also briefly w. Artie Shaw 1941; in Army '42-5. Retired from music in recent years. Good section man, rarely heard in solos. LPs w. Goodman (Col.).

BRYANT, RAPHAEL (Ray), *piano;* b. Philadelphia, Pa., 12/24/31. Mother, sister play piano; brother Tommy pl. bass. Started on bass in junior high school. Professional debut through Jack Fields of Blue Note Club in Phila. After working w. Billy Krechmer band 1951-3, became house pianist at Blue Note accompanying Charlie Parker, Miles Davis and many other jazz men. His trio became the backing unit for Carmen McRae in '57, app. at NJF with her. W. Jo Jones trio '58. In '59, played a variety of gigs w. Sonny Rollins, Charlie Shavers and Curtis Fuller, all in NYC. Own trio at Vanguard, NYC, Dec. '59. Unusually adaptable modern pianist with strong roots in the traditions of jazz. Favs: Tatum, Wilson. Own LPs on New Jazz, Pres., Epic; LPs w. Jo Jones (Vang., Evst.), Miles Davis, Sonny Rollins, Jerry Valentine, Coleman Hawkins, Arthur Taylor, Hal Singer, Tiny Grimes (Pres.), Art Blakey (Blue Note, Col.); Cliff Jordan, Lee Morgan (Blue Note); Budd Johnson (Fels.), Dizzy Gillespie (Verve), Benny Golson, Oliver Nelson (New Jazz).

BRYANT, THOMAS (Tommy), *bass;* b. Philadelphia, Pa., 5/21/30. From musical family: mother has church choir, brother Ray plays piano; sister plays and sings. Began stud. at age 12; later at Mastbaum High. Pl. with small groups around Phila.; worked w. Billy Krechmer there and w. various jazzmen who came to town. With Elmer Snowden 1949-52; in Army '54-6, where he played w. band. Had own trio off and on '57; w. Jo Jones '58, Charlie Shavers summer '59. Favs: Oscar Pettiford, Slam Stewart. LPs w. Dizzy Gillespie (Verve); Jo Jones (Vang., Evst.).

BRYANT, WILLIAM STEVEN (Willie), *leader;* b. New Orleans, 8/30/08. Not an instrumentalist, but was active 1933-Feb. '39 and '46-8 as leader of a good swing band whose members at one time included Benny Carter, Teddy Wilson, Ben Webster, Cozy Cole, Taft Jordan, Jimmy Archey. Bryant sang with the band, which recorded for Victor and was best known for its theme, which he wrote, *It's Over Because We're Through.* He has mainly been known in recent years as disc jockey and nightclub emcee.

BUCK, JACK, *trombone, piano;* b. Keokuk, Ia., 10/6/11. Raised partly in SF, where he worked w. Ellis Kimball, Griff Williams; after touring w. Williams, worked in Oakland dance hall for several years, made record debut w. Frisco Jazz Band, 1946 on Pacific label, later played trom. and piano w. Bob Scobey. Appeared on regular TV series in SF, *Clancy's Corner* feat. Clancy Hayes, vocalist and banjoist with Scobey. Favs: Jack Teagarden, Kid Ory, Geo. Brunis. LPs w. Bob Scobey, Albert Nicholas, Darnell Howard (GTJ).

BUCKNER, MILTON (Milt), *piano, Hammond organ, composer, leader;* b. St. Louis, Mo., 7/10/15. Early exp. w. McKinney's Cotton Pickers in Detroit and Jimmy Raschell. Was with Lionel Hampton from 1941-8 and

'50-2. After first departure, had own big band which recorded for MGM; since '52 has played organ with own trio. As Hampton pianist, Buckner became famous as the *Hamp's Boogie-Woogie* soloist and as the first to popularize the "locked-hands" jazz piano style (both hands playing parallel chord patterns), since widely imitated. Was also one of first to play rhythm-and-blues on Hammond organ. Own LPs on Cap., Savoy; LPs w. Hampton (Decca, GNP), Dinah Washington (Em.).

Addr: 454 No. Salford St., Phila., Pa.

BUCKNER, THEODORE GUY (Ted), *alto sax;* b. St. Louis, Mo., 12/14/13. Brother of Milton Buckner, with whom he worked in Jimmy Raschell's band from 1935. Prominent in the Jimmie Lunceford band from '39-'43, he was feat. in solos on the band's records of *Down By The Old Mill Stream, Margie, By The River St. Marie* and *Ain't She Sweet.* Later had own band in Detroit for several years, toured with Todd Rhodes, returned to Detroit and reorganized own group. Played on singer Johnnie Ray's first records. LPs w. Lunceford (Col., Decca).

BUCKNER, JOHN EDWARD (Teddy), *trumpet;* b. Sherman, Texas, 7/16/09. Raised in Calif., he worked w. Lionel Hampton, Benny Carter and Horace in the 1930s. Feat. off and on w. Kid Ory from '49 to '53. Since Feb. '54 has led his own band at Beverly Cavern in LA. Has been a movie stand-in for his fav., Louis Armstrong. Other films: w. Fats Waller in *King of Burlesque;* seen and heard in prologue to *Pete Kelly's Blues* '55. Distantly related to Ted Buckner (see above). Own LPs on Dix. Jub.; LPs w. Kid Ory (Col.), George Brunis (South.).

Addr: 764 East 42nd Pl., Los Angeles 11, Calif.

BUDDLE, ERROL LESLIE, *tenor sax, bassoon, bar. sax, clar.;* b. Adelaide, Australia, 4/29/28. Stud. saxes and clar. at Adelaide College of Music 1936-41, bassoon at Sydney and Adelaide Conservatories '50-52. Radio studio work in Adelaide '46-7; Jack Brokensha quartet and other combos '47-50. Led own all-star group in weekly jazz concerts in Sydney '50-52. Arrived in Canada Oct. '52, played first bassoon w. Windsor Symph. and tenor w. local jazz bands. Worked w. Johnny "Scat" Davis on Detroit TV summer '54; own combo in Detroit, w. Elvin Jones on drums, July to Nov. '54. Joined Australian Jazz Quartet Dec. '54. Ret. to Australia, Sept. '58 and has free-lanced there since. Voted Musician of the Year by Australian *Music Maker* 1952. Also first-place winner on ten. sax. Fav. own solo, *These Foolish Things* on Bethlehem. Favs: Stan Getz, Sonny Stitt, Zoot Sims. Buddle is the first musician in jazz to make extensive use of the bassoon in ad libbing. LPs: Australian Jazz Quartet, Joe Derise (Beth.).

BUDIMIR, DENNIS MATTHEW, *guitar;* b. Los Angeles, Calif., 6/20/38. St. on piano in 1947, then guitar. Pl. occ. gigs from age of 14. W. Ken Hanna '55; Keith Williams '57-8; Harry James Mar.-Oct. '58, then joined Chico Hamilton. Favs: Tal Farlow, Jimmy Raney. Intends to study classical guitar. LPs w. Harry James (Capitol); Chico Hamilton (Warner Bros.).

Addr: 2415 Hitchcock Dr., Alhambra, Calif.

BUDWIG, MONTY REX, *bass;* b. Pender, Neb., 12/26/29. Parents pl. piano, alto in band together. Stud. at high sch. in LA. Early experience w. Anson Weeks 1950; Vido Musso '51 and various jobs around SF. During three years in Air Force went to band school, pl. in service band. In LA '54, worked w. Barney Kessel, Zoot Sims combos, then 14 months w. Red Norvo trio '54-5. With Woody Herman combo in Las Vegas fall '55, then w. Herman's big band '56-7; with Shelly Manne combo '58-60. Fav. own solo: *Bass Face* w. Herman (Cap.). Favs: Blanton, Ray Brown, Red Mitchell. LPs w. Kessel, L. Niehaus, S. Manne (Contemp.), Tal Farlow (Verve).

Addr: 1947 W. 93rd Street, Los Angeles 47, Cal.

BUFFINGTON, JAMES LAWRENCE (Jim), *French horn;* b. Jersey Shore, Pa., 5/14/22. Self-taught; father played trumpet, piano. Picked up Fr. horn in school, later got Master's degree at Eastman School of Music. Gigged in N.Y. during 1950s, especially w. O. Pettiford. Participated in Miles Davis-Gil Evans series for Columbia. Fav. own record: *A Touch of Modern* w. Stu Phillips (MGM). Was one of the first soloists to play jazz Fr. horn. Fav: John Barrows. LPs w. Phillips (MGM), Lou Stein (Epic), Miles Davis (Col.); *Know Your Jazz* (ABC-Par.).

Addr: 245 W. 104th St., New York 25, N.Y.

BUNCH, JOHN L. JR., *piano;* b. Tipton, Ind., 12/1/21. Stud. harmony and popular piano at 11; pl. with a band at 12. Was prisoner of war in Germany during World War II; grad. Indiana U. 1950, where he stud. speech. Back to music in '56 after working in factories, offices, and as a salesman. Joined Woody Herman Aug. '56 for one year; w. Benny Goodman Sept. '57-Jan. '58; Maynard Ferguson Mar.-Nov. '58; Urbie Green for club dates around NYC. Has also led trio. Own quartet at Randall's Island Jazz Fest. '59. Favs: Teddy Wilson, Fats Waller, Erroll Garner, Bud Powell; Duke Ellington is fav. all-around musician. LPs w. Woody Herman (Verve); Maynard Ferguson (Roul.); Rex Stewart, Urbie Green (Vict.).

Addr: 350 W. 55th Street, New York 19, N.Y.

BUNKER, LAWRENCE BENJAMIN (Larry), *drums, vibes;* b. Long Beach, Cal., 11/4/28. Accordion, piano and drums at high school. Army 1946-8, then first prof. job w. bop septet on Mississippi riverboat. During two years gigging in Calif. on piano, picked up vibes; joined Howard Rumsey at Lighthouse, Jan. '51. With Art Pepper, Geo. Auld, '52, back to Rumsey in fall. With Gerry Mulligan, Jan.-Sept. '53; six months on daily Bob Crosby TV show to Mar. '54, also briefly with Barney Kessel, Stan Getz. Often worked w. Peggy Lee unit '55-'60, and during this time began to concentrate on vibes. One of the most gifted musicians identified with the West Coast jazz scene. LPs w. Gerry Mulligan (Wor. Pac., GNP), Art Pepper

(Savoy), Hamp Hawes (Pres.), John Graas (Decca), Jack Millman (Lib.), *Jazz City Workshop* (Beth.).

Addr: 1217 West 47th St., Los Angeles 37, Calif.

BUNN, THEODORE (Teddy), *guitar;* b. Freeport, L.I., N.Y., 1909. Best known through 1930s as key figure (with Leo Watson) in Spirits of Rhythm, novelty vocal-instrument group that enjoyed great popularity at the Onyx Club and recorded for Decca. During that time he also made numerous sessions with Jimmie Noone, Johnny Dodds, Trixie Smith, Milt Herth (Dec.), Tommy Ladnier, Mezzrow (Vic.), etc. Free-lancing on west coast since 1941, with Edgar Hayes, etc. Plays non-amplified guitar on most records, in unique single-string and chord style. Solo session on Blue Note, 1939. LPs w. Sidney Bechet (Blue Note).

BURKE, RAYMOND N. (Barrois), *clarinet, soprano and tenor saxes;* b. New Orleans, La., 6/6/04. Self-taught; whole family musical. Featured locally w. Sharkey's Kings of Dixieland, Johnny Wiggs' New Orleans Kings, Dukes of Dixieland, Geo. Hartman's New Orleans Jazz Band, Geo. Girard and His New Orleans Five. etc. Favs: Harry Shields, Leon Rappolo. LPs w. George Girard (South.), Johnny Wiggs (GTJ, Gold. Crest).

Addr: 905 N. Rampart St., New Orleans, La.

BURKE, JOSEPH FRANCIS (Sonny), *leader, composer;* b. Scranton, Pa., 3/22/14. Violin, piano from age five. All-state fullback during high school days. Mus. studies at Duke U., Durham, N.C., where he, Les Brown and Johnny Long all led student bands. Took 15-piece college band for summer booking on trans-atlantic liner. Worked in department store in Detroit, then became free-lance arr. for Buddy Rogers, Joe Venuti, Xavier Cugat. To NYC '38; toured w. own band '39-'40; through Glenn Miller, got job as arr. for Ch. Spivak until '42. Three years as arr. for Jimmy Dorsey. During '50s was recording dir. and band leader for Decca in LA; had big hit w. own arr. of *Mambo Jambo.* Arr. *King Porter Stomp* for Jimmy Dorsey (Decca), *Everything I Have Is Yours* for Billy Eckstine (MGM). Fav. arrs: P. Rugolo, N. Riddle, J. Graas, S. Rogers. Own LP: *Let's Mambo* (Decca 8090).

Addr: 342 N. Rockingham Ave., Los Angeles 49, Calif.

BURKE, VINNIE (Vincent Bucci), *bass;* b. Newark, N.J., 3/15/21. Mostly self-taught. Violin at five, then guitar, gigging locally. Worked in war plant 1942-5; during this time, lost use of finger in milling machine accident; gave up guitar and became bassist. Worked w. Joe Mooney, Tony Scott; three years w. Cy Coleman trio, briefly w. Sauter-Finnegan, a year w. Marion McPartland. Records and night clubs w. Gil Mellé in mid-fifties. House bassist on Art Ford's *Jazz Party,* WNTA-TV, May-Dec. '58. W. Vic Dickenson at Arpeggio, NYC summer '59. Own LPs: ABC-Par., Jub.; LPs w. Johnny Mehegan-Eddie Costa, Mike Cuozzo (Sav.), Don Elliott (ABC-Par.), Chris Connor (Beth.), Gil Mellé (Pres.), Tal Farlow (Verve).

Addr: 10 Brookdale Ave., Newark, N.J.

BURLAND, GRANVILLE ALEXANDER (Sascha), *composer, singer, guitar;* b. New York City, 10/25/27. Att. Yale U.; served in Marines; stud. piano at David Mannes Mus. Sch., guitar w. B. Galbraith. Active since 1950 producing, writing and sometimes singing and playing commercial "jingles" for radio and TV, Burland was a pioneer in bringing jazz ideas and leading jazz musicians to vast audiences through these media, using, for instance, Osie Johnson as singer for Nestle and Flit commercials; Art Farmer, Billy Taylor, Quincy Jones to play or write for other such jingles. Also wrote opening theme for *What's My Line* TV show; wrote and sang jazz novelty songs with Don Elliott (Hanover Records) under name "Nutty Squirrels." Favs: Q. Jones; B. Galbraith, G. Van Eps, B. Kessel. LPs: *Nutty Squirrels* (Hanover), *Jingles All The Way* (Lib.).

Addr: 285 Central Park West, New York 24, N.Y.

BURLEY, DAN, *piano, journalist;* b. Lexington, Ky., 1907. Lived in Chicago from 1917 and played at many rent parties and clubs during the '20s, becoming a friend and associate of most of the early boogie-woogie pianists. His career, however, was in journalism: he was with the Associated Negro Press, then spent several years in New York in the '40s as theatrical editor of the *N.Y. Amsterdam News.* In the '50s he was associated with *Ebony* in Chicago. In 1945 he recorded a session of piano duets with the author. In 1946 he assembled a group (incl. Brownie McGhee) for a Circle Records session calling it "Dan Burley & His Skiffle Boys." The term "skiffle," thus established by Burley, later gained wide currency in England in association with a brand of traditionalist music practiced mostly by amateur or semi-professional musicians. Burley also rec. *Hamp's Salty Blues* and *Ridin' on the L & N* with Lionel Hampton for Decca in 1946.

BURNES, LEROY (Roy), *drums;* b. Emporia, Kans., 11/30/35. Private lessons from eight years through high school. Later stud. w. teacher in Kansas City. Went to New Orleans 1954, pl. with Billy Williams society band; later w. George Girard. Came to NYC '55 and pl. in society bands. Gigged at Metropole '56; w. Woody Herman '57; Benny Goodman '57-9, with whom he toured Europe '58. After leaving Goodman, he gigged around NYC. App. on Goodman's "Swing into Spring" TV shows. Ambition is to have own small group. Favs: Buddy Rich, Kenny Clarke, Philly Joe Jones. LPs w. Goodman (Col.), Roland Hanna (Atco), Teddy Wilson (Verve).

Addr: 28 Perry Street, New York, N.Y.

BURNS, RALPH, *composer, piano;* b. Newton, Mass., 6/29/22. Piano at 7; New England Conservatory 1938-9; local bands from early teens. To NYC '40 with band led by Nick Jerret (brother of singer Frances Wayne); joined Charlie Barnet for a year. After six months with Red Norvo, 1943, joined Woody Herman as arranger early '44 and has worked for him ever since; also played piano with him for first year. Occasional jobs as pianist incl. Ch. Ventura, Bill Harris, 1947; accompanist on Mildred Bailey's last tour, 1951; pianist and mus. director for Fran Warren, '53-4. Toured Europe as soloist with Herman, spring '54, then remained for several months playing at Bricktop's in Rome. From '55-'60 he was intensively active in NYC, scoring for commercial record dates, films and TV but rarely playing piano and only occasionally working in the jazz field. He wrote music for Benny Goodman's *Swing Into Spring* show on NBC '58.

Burns won the *Esquire* New Star award '46, *Down Beat* award '52-3, *Metronome* award '53. His work, irrespective of tempo and mood, always remained firmly rooted in jazz, though often seeking new forms and harmonic development. His outstanding works for Herman were *Summer Sequence* and *Lady McGowan's Dream* (Harm.), *Bijou* (Harmony, MGM, Evst.), *Early Autumn* (Cap., Verve). Own LPs: *Ralph Burns Among The JATP* (Verve 8121), *Jazz Recital* (Verve 8098), *Jazz Studio 5* (Decca 8235), *Very Warm For Jazz* (Decca 9207), *The Masters Revisited* (Decca 8555), *Bijou* (Beth. 68), *Porgy And Jazz* (Decca 9215); LPs w. Woody Herman (Harm. 7093), Sonny Berman (Eso. 532).

Addr: 124 West 55th St., New York 19, N.Y.

BURRELL, KENNETH EARL (Kenny), *guitar;* b. Detroit, Mich., 7/31/31. Three brothers, all musicians. Never studied except 1½ yrs. of classical guitar 1952-3. Bachelor of Music degree Wayne U., Detroit '55. Played w. Candy Johnson Sextet '48, Count Belcher, '49, Tommy Barnett '50, own combo and Dizzy Gillespie '51, then had own groups until Mar. '55, when he briefly repl. Herb Ellis in the Oscar Peterson trio. Moved to NYC and free-lanced with own group and other combos '55-6. Worked w. Benny Goodman '57. Own combo intermittently since '57. Own trio at NJF '59. Described by John S. Wilson as "a loose, loping guitarist who manages to swing along on almost consistently interesting lines." Burrell also sings and plays bass. Ambition: to become a college music teacher. Favs: Charlie Christian, Django Reinhardt, Oscar Moore. Own LPs: Blue Note, Pres., Vang.; LPs w. Thad Jones, Kenny Dorham, Paul Chambers, Jimmy Smith (BN), Frank Foster (Savoy), *All Night Long, All Day Long, Earthy,* Gene Ammons, *Interplay,* C. Hawkins (Pres.), *The Cats* (New Jazz), *Jazz For Playboys,* A. K. Salim, *Jazzmen: Detroit,* Frank Wess (Savoy), *One World Jazz* (Col.).

Addr: 142 West 46th St., New York 36, N.Y.

BURROUGHS, CLARK, *singer;* b. Los Angeles, 3/3/30. Att. Powers High Sch., Loyola U. Worked as actor before becoming member of the Hi-Lo's (q.v.).

Addr: 1626 N. Vine, Hollywood, Calif.

BURTON, JOE, *piano;* b. Chicago, Ill., 5/28/28. Moved to NYC at 7 mos. Stud. at Chicago Cons.; St. Paul's Coll. in Gary, Ind. and Chicago; Eastman College in Rochester, N.Y. Pl. club dates around NYC, later in Chicago and Calif. W. Mal Hallett 1945 in Montreal; pl. Embers NYC '56; acc. Jane Russell, Anita O'Day. Favs: Bud Powell, Lennie Tristano. Own LPs on Coral, Regent.

BUSH, LEONARD WALTER (Lennie), *bass;* b. London, England, 6/6/27. Prof. debut at 17; has gigged and/or recorded with Victor Feldman, Ronnie Scott, Tony Crombie, Dizzy Reece; played w. Louis Armstrong at Hungarian Relief concert in London '56. Working with Jack Parnell's studio band for ATV 1956-60. Favs: Ray Brown, Tommy Potter.

Addr: 157 Gloucester Place, London, N.W.1, England.

BUSH, LOUIS F. (Joe Fingers Carr), *piano, composer;* b. Louisville, Ky., 7/18/10. Stud. Cincinnati Cons. Had own combo, Lou Bush's Tickletoe Four, at 12. Left home at 16; toured w. Clyde McCoy, Henry Busse, George Olsen, many other name bands during late '20s and '30s. Last band was Hal Kemp; after latter's death Bush settled in LA '41. Army '42-5. While working as an A & R executive at Capitol Records in LA ca. '49 he started recording corny ragtime solos under the "Fingers Carr" pseudonym; they rapidly achieved nation-wide popularity. A novelty performer rather than a jazz artist. Fav: Tatum. Own LPs: Cap.

Addr: 1344 N. Beverly Drive, Beverly Hills, Calif.

BUSHELL, GARVIN P., *clarinet;* also *saxophone, oboe, flute, bassoon;* b. Springfield, Ohio, 9/25/02. Mother was voice teacher; father a composer; uncles pl. w. circuses. St. on piano in Ohio, then other instruments in Paris, New York and Berlin. Toured Europe w. Sam Wooding 1925-27; pl. bassoon w. Chicago Civic Orch. '50. App. at Great South Bay Jazz Festival '58; replaced Omer Simeon w. Wilbur De Paris band, Sept. '59. Extensive reminiscences by Bushell app. in *Jazz Review,* Jan.-Feb. '59. Fav: Benny Goodman. Rec. w. Bessie Smith, Bunk Johnson, Cab Calloway, Chick Webb et al. LPs w. Bessie Smith (Col.), Rex Stewart (Uran.).

Addr: 574 St. Nicholas Ave., New York, N.Y.

BUSHKIN, JOSEPH (Joe), *piano;* b. New York City, 11/17/16. Early experience from 1935 with Louis Prima, Bunny Berigan, Joe Marsala, Muggsy Spanier; also record dates 1936-9 with Eddie Condon, Sharkey Bonano, Lee Wiley. First solo session on Comm. '40. Joined Tommy Dorsey '40; Army Jan. '42, played trumpet in Army band, later asst. to David Rose, *Winged Victory* Air Force show; then to S. Pacific, Japan. Joined Benny Goodman, spring '46; free-lance TV etc. '47; acting, playing role in *Rat Race* on B'way '49; own quartet at Embers, NYC, '51; joined Louis Armstrong, spring '53, but soon reorganized own group. Numerous records w. Condon, other Dixieland groups, but plays in neutral swing style; acquired society following in early '50s, recorded with Tallulah Bankhead; featured as singer on radio, TV. In the late '50s he went into voluntary semi-retirement, vacationing in Europe, appearing on occasional TV shows, etc. As songwriter, he is best known for *Oh! Look At*

Me Now. Favs: Tatum, Peterson, Wilson. Own LPs: Cap., Epic; LPs w. Eddie Condon, Max Kaminsky (Comm.).

Addr: 435 East 52nd Street, New York 22, N.Y.

BUTERA, SAM, *tenor sax;* b. New Orleans, La., 9/17/27. Father pl. accordion at Italian weddings. Stud. from 1935. On road w. Ray McKinley, '46; named teenage instrumentalist of year by *Look* Magazine '46. Own group in NO, '47-54. Featured soloist w. Louis Prima since 1954, mainly as entertainer, though he is a capable jazz tenor man in r & b oriented style. Many r & b records on Vict., Groove, Cadence; own LP and many with Prima on Capitol; since '59 w. Prima on Dot.

Addr: 2920 Mandeville St., New Orleans, La.

BUTLER, FRANK, *drums;* b. Kansas City, Mo., 2/18/28. St. on drums in high school in Omaha, Nebr., then on USO shows and w. jazz groups in KC. Joined Dave Brubeck in 1950 in San Francisco; w. Edgar Hayes '51-3; own group '53; Duke Ellington '54. Worked w. Perez Prado and Curtis Counce '56. App. on TV *Stars of Jazz* show in Hollywood and on TV series w. Prado. Favs: Jo Jones, Art Blakey, Max Roach, Philly Joe Jones. LPs w. Curtis Counce (Contemp.).

BUTTERFIELD, CHARLES WILLIAM (Billy), *trumpet;* b. Middleton, Ohio, 1/14/17. Prominent with Bob Crosby, 1937-40; Artie Shaw, '40-1; Benny Goodman '41-2 (solo on *La Rosita,* Col.); CBS and ABC studios '42-5; Army '45-6. Toured w. own band and rec. for Cap. '46-7, then back to free-lance NYC studio work. W. Goodman at NJF, etc. '58. Resident of Rescue, Va., gigging and teaching locally, '59-60. Pure-toned horn in swing era style, akin to B. Hackett. Own LPs on Vict., West., Essex; as "Gus Hoo" in *New York Land Dixie* (Vict.); LPs w. Steve Allen (Decca), Peanuts Hucko (Gr. Award), one track w. Turk Murphy in *Jazz Omnibus* (Col.); Tommy Reynolds (King), Stan Rubin (Coral), Artie Shaw (Vict.), Benny Goodman (Col.), Lou Stein (Jub.), Bob Crosby (Decca, Coral).

BUTTERFIELD, DON, *tuba;* b. Centralia, Wash., 4/1/23. Army 1942-6, then stud. at Juilliard. Prof. debut w. Goldman Band. CBS, NBC studio work, many jobs w. symph. orchs., recs. w. Jackie Gleason; was briefly w. C. Thornhill orch. Has been with Radio City Music Hall orch. for many years, though active in jazz as well, doing Jazz Composers' Workshop series w. Teddy Charles, Ch. Mingus '55-6; org. own sextet and rec. for Col. '55, presenting it at NJF '58. Butterfield is one of the few musicians with technical command and imagination enough to make the tuba meaningful in jazz. Own LP: Atl. Prominent on LPs w. Art Farmer and *Brass Shout* (UA), J. Cleveland (Merc.), *Sonny Rollins & Big Brass* (Metrojazz), *Top & Bottom Brass* w. Clark Terry (Riv.), *Gold on Silk* w. Rayburn Wright (Evst.), Teddy Charles (Atl.), Gil Mellé (Blue Note); also many classical albums.

Addr: 68-43 Nansen St., Forest Hills 75, L.I., N.Y.

BYARD, JOHN A. JR. (Jaki), *piano, composer;* also *saxophones, trumpet, trombone, guitar, drums;* b. Worcester, Mass., 6/15/22. Mother played piano, father baritone horn in marching band. Studied piano between ages of 8 and 10. Got into business through Entertainment Club at Worcester Boys Club. Pl. w. local orchs. 1938-41; Army '41-6. To Boston as sideman w. various local bands. W. Earl Bostic '49-50, Jimmy Tyler in Larry Steele's *Smart Affairs* '50-2. Solo pianist at Stable in Boston '53-5, also tenor sax w. Herb Pomeroy '52-5, alternating in these capacities until '59 when he joined Maynard Ferguson. Favs: Fats Waller, Rube Bloom. Rec. w. Bostic (*Blip Boogie* on King), Ch. Mariano. LPs w. Ferguson (Roul.).

Addr: 130 Brookway Road, Roslindale 31, Mass.

BYAS, CARLOS WESLEY (Don), *tenor sax;* b. Muskogee, Okla., 10/21/12. Mother pl. piano, father clarinet. Own group at college '30; w. Eddie Barefield in LA '35. Worked w. Don Redman, Lucky Millinder, Eddie Mallory; Andy Kirk '39-40. Count Basie 1941 and at Yacht Club w. Coleman Hawkins. With Dizzy's quintet '44 at Onyx. Europe '46, w. Redman. Remained and toured continent; made European tour w. D. Ellington 1950. Settled in France and after living there for several years moved to Holland. Has made numerous tours of the Continent; recordings w. Quincy Jones and other visiting American musicians as well as w. local jazzmen. Known for big sound of Hawkins school but with added modern characteristics, rhythmically and harmonically. Won Esq. Silver Award '46. Own LP on Regent; LPs w. Eddie Heywood (Coral), Charlie Christian (Eso.), Count Basie (Epic), Coleman Hawkins (Em.), Q. Jones-E. Barclay (UA).

BYERS, WILLIAM MITCHELL (Billy), *composer, trombone;* also *piano;* b. Los Angeles, Calif., 5/1/27. Pl. w. Hollywood Canteen Kids 1942-3, then free-lance movie studio work, a year at Harvard and 15 months in the Army '44-5. After 3 years writing for movies, pl. w. Georgie Auld, Buddy Rich '49, then to NYC w. Benny Goodman writing and playing, followed by Charlie Ventura big band. Replaced Johnny Mandel on staff at WMGM, NYC as arranger, conductor, trombonist, pianist. Then wrote for Max Liebman's *Show of Shows* etc. After extensive free-lance work in NYC, he went to Paris in Feb. '56 to work for producer Ray Ventura on various record and motion picture projects, returning to NYC in Nov. '57. Later free-lanced as arr.; as trombonist pl. w. Yves Montand one-man show, also w. Johnny Richards orch. '59. To Europe as assistant to Quincy Jones w. *Free And Easy* '59-60. Favs: Earl Swope, Jack Jenney; Al Cohn, Johnny Mandel. Own LP: Vict., also own band in *Lullaby of Birdland* (Vict.); LPs w. Al Cohn, Manny Albam (Vict.), Johnny Richards (Coral), Kenny Clarke (Epic), Hal McKusick (Pres.), Jim Chapin (Classic Edit.), Ralph Burns (Decca), Don Elliott

(Beth.), *Jazz On The Left Bank* (Epic), Georgie Auld (Savoy).

Addr: 140 West 69th St., New York 23, N.Y.

BYRD, CHARLES L. (Charlie), *guitar;* b. Suffolk, Va., 9/16/25. Began stud. at 10 w. father, also a guitarist. Started playing for high school dances; later worked w. Sol Yaged 1947, Joe Marsala, Barbara Carroll '48, Freddie Slack '49. Took up classical guitar '50; has pl. recitals in Washington, D.C. area. Studied w. Andres Segovia in Siena, Italy '54. Pl. at Showboat in Wash. '57-9, app. regularly on Mutual's *Bandstand USA*. Comp. and pl. music for play, *The Purification,* by Tennessee Williams; also for Agriculture Dept. films. W. Woody Herman, spring '59 for engagement at the Roundtable NYC and tour including England, Saudi Arabia. "He has re-established that the Spanish guitar can play swinging jazz."—John A. Tynan, *Down Beat.* Favs: C. Christian, Segovia. Won DB critics' poll as new star '59. Own LPs on Savoy, Off Beat, Everest, River.; Washington (classical); LPs w. Woody Herman (Roul.).

Addr: 6435 Barnaby St., N.W., Washington, D.C.

BYRD, DONALD, *trumpet;* b. Detroit, Mich., 12/9/32. Father a Methodist minister and musician. Stud. Cass Tech High, Wayne University, and Manhattan School of Music. Played w. Air Force bands 1951-3. Geo. Wallington combo at Bohemia, NYC Aug. to Oct. '55. Joined Art Blakey's Messengers Dec. '55. Acclaimed by New York musicians as jazz soloist with great future, he came into demand for free-lance recording work during '56. With Max Roach, summer '56; in 1957 he was part of a group which gigged around NYC and recorded under various leaders, incl. Red Garland, A. Taylor, J. Coltrane or L. Donaldson, and G. Joyner. He also worked w. Gigi Gryce in the Jazz Lab quintet. In early 1958 he was w. Pepper Adams at the Five Spot Cafe in NYC. Has also played w. S. Rollins, C. Hawkins, L. Hampton, T. Monk, and own quintet. In July-Nov. '58, he played at festivals in Belgium and on Riviera, toured Sweden, took part in one German and two French films. Favs: Dizzy Gillespie, Miles Davis. Own LPs: Blue Note, Savoy, War. Bros.; LPs w. Art Blakey, Michel Le Grand (Col.), Sonny Clark, Sonny Rollins, Horace Silver, Jackie McLean (Blue Note), Kenny Drew, Pepper Adams, Thelonious Monk (River.), André Hodeir, *Top Brass* (Savoy), George Wallington (Sav., Pres., New Jazz), *Jazz Eyes* (Reg.), *The Young Bloods, All Day Long, All Night Long, All Morning Long, Three Trumpets, Two Trumpets, Two Guitars,* Arthur Taylor (Pres.), w. Gigi Gryce in *Jazz Lab* (Riv., Col., Verve), Lionel Hampton (Aud. Fid.).

Addr: 594 Teasdale Place, Bronx 56, N.Y.

BYRNE, ROBERT (Bobby), *trombone;* b. Columbus, Ohio, 1918. Father a noted music teacher. Studied harp, piano, piccolo, flute, trombone, 'cello, percussion. Joined Dorsey Bros. at 16; when brothers split, took over Tommy's work and remained with Jimmy Dorsey to Oct. '39, then had own band for three years. Army Dec. '42-Sep. '45. Free-lance in NYC in late '40s; led Dixieland combo on Steve Allen's nightly TV show '53-4. Inactive in jazz in recent years. Own LPs: Gr. Award; one half of *Dixieland Jazz,* tracks in *Musical History of Jazz* (Gr. Award).

Addr: 216 Ivy Lane, Teaneck, N.J.

C

CACERES, ERNESTO (Ernie), *clarinet, baritone sax;* b. Rockport, Tex., 11/22/11. Stud. w. Mexican Prof. Bolanos. Clar. first, then guitar and saxes. Worked w. brother Emilio's band, then to NYC. Joined Bobby Hackett 1937, J. Teagarden '38, B. Zurke, '39, Glenn Miller '40, Johnny Long '42, B. Goodman and T. Dorsey '43, W. Herman '44; Army service band '45, B. Butterfield '47, then own combo. Daily TV series w. Garry Moore '50-56. With Hackett at Henry Hudson Hotel '56-7. Fluent swing-style soloist, feat. on *Long Tall Mama, Volga Boatmen* w. Miller (Vict.), *Lover Come Back to Me* w. Condon (Dec.), *Easy to Remember* w. Butterfield (Cap.), *Creole Blues* w. Geo. Williams (Coral). LPs w. Hackett, Teagarden (Comm.), Condon (Dec.), J. McPartland (Bruns.), Metronome All Stars (Cam.).

CAIN, JACQUELINE RUTH (Jackie), *singer;* b. Milwaukee, Wis. 5/22/28. To Chicago '46; met Roy Kral (q.v.) and their careers ran parallel: they were w. Ch. Ventura early '48 to Apr. '49, were married June '49, had their own sextet, then free-lanced, had own TV series in Chicago, and were back w. Ventura during most of '53. Worked as night club duo after that. Best known for light, humorous, bop-influenced unison vocals with Kral, she is also a fine ballad singer. Has also studied 'cello and flute. LPs: ABC-Par., Story., Bruns.; LPs w. Ventura on Reg., Em., Decca, Bruns, GNP, Vict.

CALDWELL, ALBERT (Happy), *tenor sax;* b. Chicago, Ill., 7/25/03. Studied clarinet w. Buster Bailey. Joined Bernie Young's Creole Jazz Band, 1922; Mamie Smith's Jazz Hounds, '23; Willie Gant, '24; played with many Harlem bands in later '20s and '30s incl. Fletcher Henderson, Ch. Johnson, Fats Waller, Cliff Jackson, Louis Metcalf, Arthur Gibbs, Tiny Bradshaw, Hot Lips Page, Elmer Snowden. Worked w. Metcalf at Metropole '56, sessions on Long Island and weekends with him since. Very active in Masons as master of his lodge, he has a dance band which plays for various fraternal, social and political affairs. Rec. *Knockin' A Jug* w. Louis Armstrong 1929; also sessions w. Eddie Condon '29; Bubber Miley '30; Red Allen '36; Mezzrow '37; Jelly Roll Morton '39. LP w. Louis Armstrong (Col.).

Addr: 207 West 131st St., New York 27, N.Y.

CALLENDER, GEORGE (Red), *bass, tuba;* b. Richmond, Va., 3/6/18. Studied at Bordentown, N.J., trumpet, alto horn, tuba, bass, harmony, arr. Joined Banjo Bernie in Atlantic City, 1933, while in high school; to Calif., w. Louis Armstrong (rec. debut with him Nov. '37). King Cole Trio, Lester Young, '42; own trio to '45; L. Armstrong (incl. film *New Orleans*) '46; Erroll Garner '47; own trio in Honolulu '47-50; Jerry Fielding '51-3. Made r & b dates under own name for Vict., Decca, Exclusive. Wrote pop hit, *Primrose Lane,* in '59. Active in free-lance studio work in LA during '50s incl. *Life of Riley, You Asked For It.* App. at Monterey Jazz Fest. '59. Highly regarded among jazzmen. Own LPs: Metrojazz, Crown; LPs w. Tatum, Webster, De Franco, Hampton (Verve), J. Fielding (Kapp), John Graas (Merc.), Billy May, Nat Cole, George Shearing (Cap.).

Addr: 2200 Clyde Ave., Los Angeles 16, Calif.

CALLOWAY, CABELL (Cab), *singer, leader;* b. Rochester, N.Y., 12/24/07. Raised in Baltimore, then moved to Chicago, where he took over the leadership of the Alabamians '28, bringing them to NYC the following year. Calloway then took over the Missourians; the band recorded under that name for Victor '29, and under Calloway's name for Perfect from '30. In '31 Cab recorded *Minnie the Moocher,* which made him a national name as a novelty "scat" singer, nicknamed "the hi-de-ho man." Though discounted as a jazz performer by most musicians and critics, he was important as leader of a big band that lasted until mid-'48. Its alumni incl. Ben Webster, Chu Berry, Eddie Barefield, Dizzy Gillespie, Cozy Cole. He was seen in *The Singing Kid* with Al Jolson, *Big Broadcast of 1933, Stormy Weather, Sensations of 1945* and other movies. He travelled to Montevideo with a big band in Feb. '51, and retained a band during most of that year, but mainly fronted small combos from '48 until June '52, when he took the role of Sportin' Life in *Porgy and Bess,* touring Europe and the US until Aug. '54; he then resumed nightclub work, usually as a solo act, though he has occasionally fronted a band assembled for him by Eddie Barefield. Own LPs: Epic; three nos. feat. Chu Berry (Epic); *Porgy & Bess* cast album (Col.).

Addr: 1619 Broadway, New York 19, N.Y.

CAMERON, JAY, *baritone sax;* b. NYC, 9/14/28. Stud. alto in Hollywood, '43-7. Played w. Ike Carpenter '46-7, Rex Stewart in France and Italy '49, various bands in Germany, Belgium, Scandinavia '50-4. Spring of '55 w. Sadi orch. at Rose Rouge, Paris, then joined Henri Renaud July '55 for 4 months. Back in US, pl. w. Woody Herman from Jan. '56 to July '56, then briefly w. Chet Baker, Dizzy Gillespie. W. Maynard Ferguson from Nov '57 to Nov. '58. Free-lance in NYC '59, occ. pl. gigs w. own group; w. Slide Hampton '60. Favs: Cecil Payne, Lars Gullin, Pepper Adams. LPs w. Maynard Ferguson (Roul.), André Hodeir (Savoy), Woody Herman (Cap.), Slide Hampton (Strand).

Addr: 316 E. 6th St., New York 3, N.Y.

CAMPBELL, JAMES L. (Jimmy), *drums;* b. Wilkes-Barre, Pa., 12/24/28. Self-taught, he began playing while in the Army in 1947. First prof. job. w. Lee Vincent in '50; later worked w. R. Flanagan '52, Tommy Tucker, Don Elliott, Ralph Marterie, Sal Salvador, Claude Thornhill and Tex Beneke. Rejoined Elliott '56; also pl. w. Maynard Ferguson's "Birdland Dream Band" that year. Then worked w. Kai Winding, Elliot Lawrence, Bernard Peiffer, Johnny Smith and Johnny Richards. W. Woody Herman, making State Dept. tour of So. America May-July '58 and European-Saudi Arabian tour Feb.-April '59 with him. Joined Stan Kenton, summer '59. Favs: Tough, Blakey, Lamond, Roach. LPs w. Bob Corwin (River.), Don Elliot (ABC-Par.), Sal Salvador (Beth., Decca), Tal Farlow (Verve), Frank Socolow (Beth.), Johnny Richards (Cap., Roul.), Woody Herman (Roul., Evst.).

Addr: 150-24 75th Ave., Flushing 67, N.Y.

CANDIDO (Candido Camero), *bongo, conga drums;* b. Regal, Havana, Cuba, 4/22/21. Never studied. Started on bass and guitar, then took up bongos and later conga drums. 6 years w. CMQ Radio in Havana, also 6 years w. Armando Romeu at Tropicana Club in Havana, '47 to '52. To US Oct. '52; after 6 weeks at Clover Club in Miami w. *Night In Havana* show, came to NYC. Dizzy Gillespie took him to the Downbeat Club, where he sat in w. Billy Taylor; as a result he worked there a year. Toured w. Stan Kenton in fall of '54. Free-lanced in NYC '56-57; w. Dizzy Gillespie's combo '58. Much work on TV and in clubs, both in the US and Venezuela, Puerto Rico and Dominican Rep. Rec. w. almost every big name in jazz, pop and Latin fields incl. Shearing, Kenton, Gillespie, Dinah Washington, Tito Puente, Machito. Own LPs on ABC-Par.; LPs w. Gene Ammons, Billy Taylor, Bennie Green (Pres.), Duke Ellington, Art Blakey (Col.), Kenny Burrell (Blue Note), Dinah Washington (Em.).

Addr: Alamac Hotel, Broadway at 71st St., New York, N.Y.

CANDOLI, SECONDO (Conte), *trumpet;* b. Mishawaka, Ind., 7/12/27. Stud. w. brother, Pete, 1940; pl. in local groups around South Bend. Joined Woody Herman briefly at 16, then ret. to high school. Graduated Jan. '45, rejoined Herman. Army Sept. '45-Nov. '46. To Scandinavia w. Chubby Jackson Dec. '47. With Kenton '48, Ventura '49, Herman '50. Rejoined Kenton '52 and remained until he disbanded early '54. Own group in Chicago, then joined combo at Lighthouse, Hermosa Beach, Cal. Also has free-lanced extensively in LA doing TV series, concerts and albums. Film: *Bell, Book and Candle.* Though accused by John S. Wilson and other critics of lacking any conception of continuity, Candoli at his best is a bristling, aggressive modern soloist. His hundreds of LPs include: own LPs on Beth., Interlude; LPs w. Stan Getz

(Verve), *West Coast Wailers* (Atl.), Red Mitchell (Beth.), Pete Candoli (Merc., Dot), Ch. Ventura (Decca, GNP, Verve, Vict.), Stan Levey (Beth.), Howard Lucraft (Decca), Kenton (Cap.), Frank Morgan (GNP), Howard Rumsey (Contemp.), Herb Geller (Em.), Shelly Manne (Savoy), Jack Montrose (Pac. Jazz), Woody Herman (Atl.), Birdland Stars (Vict.); three tracks in *Rhythm Plus One* (Epic).

Addr: 1310 No. Olive Drive, Los Angeles 46, Calif.

CANDOLI, WALTER JOSEPH (Pete), *trumpet, composer;* b. Mishawaka, Ind., 6/28/23. Bass, Fr. horn at 12. Tpt. w. Sonny Dunham 1940; Will Bradley '41; B. Goodman, R. McKinley '42; T. Dorsey '43-4; F. Slack, Alvino Rey, Ch. Barnet, Teddy Powell, W. Herman '44-6; T. Beneke '47-8. Inactive for long period owing to injured lip. Later did West Coast studio work, also pl. w. Les Brown, S. Kenton. With Peggy Lee '53; own band '54-5. Has occasionally teamed w. brother Conte. Powerful solo and section man and good arranger. Won Esq. New Star award '46. Film: *Bell, Book and Candle.* Own LPs: *The Brothers Candoli, Bell, Book and Candoli* w. Conte (Dot), *Jazzin' Around* (Merc.); LPs w. Herman (Harm., MGM), *The Man With The Golden Arm* (Decca), Ray Brown (Verve), Kenton (Cap.), Bob Cooper (Contemp.), Pete Rugolo (Merc.).

Addr: 2151 Sunset Crest Drive, Los Angeles 46, Calif.

CANNON, GUS, *banjo, jug, singer;* b. Red Banks, Miss., 9/12/1883. Worked for many years in cotton farming, but played banjo at parties from 1898 and is believed to have made a cylinder recording for Victor circa 1901. Later lived in Memphis and played medicine shows every summer. Recorded for Paramount '27 and made a series of Victor sides in '28 and '29 with a group he called the Jug Stompers. Cannon continued to work in Memphis and was playing and singing there in '59.

CANO, EDWARD JR. (Eddie), *piano;* also *trombone, bass;* b. Los Angeles, Cal., 6/6/27. Grandfather pl. in Mexico City Symphony; father pl. bass, guitar. Stud. bass w. grandfather, piano & trom. w. private teacher. Army, 1945-6. Pl. w. Miguelito Valdes, 1947-8; acc. Herb Jeffries, led own combo, '48-9; with Bobby Ramos, '49-53; Tony Martinez, '53-5, then back w. Jeffries & own group. Versatile pianist who aims at closer relationship between harmony & melody of jazz, rhythm of Latin music. Favs: P. Jolly, Lou Levy, Tatum, Garner. Fav. own solo *I Can Groove You* in own LP *Cole Porter & Me,* rec. 1956 for Victor. Also LPs w. Les Baxter, Cal Tjader.

Addr: 2946 Vaquero Ave., Los Angeles, Cal.

CAPP, FRANK, *drums, vibes;* b. Worcester, Mass., 8/20/31. Stud. drums in school at Worcester, then at Boston U. Replaced Shelly Manne w. Stan Kenton in 1951; w. Neal Hefti '52, Billy May '53, Peggy Lee '53-4. Also w. Dorothy Dandridge, Betty Hutton, Ella Fitzgerald '56. Pl. and rec. w. Marty Paich, Art Pepper, Dave Pell, Australian Jazz Quartet, Jack Millman. Staff work at Warner Bros. '57. Later free-lanced in Cal. w. André Previn and others; to NYC w. Previn fall '58. Gigs w. Benny Goodman '59. LPs w. Jack Millman (Lib.), Marty Paich, *Tenors West* (GNP), Australian Jazz Quartet, Jazz City Workshop (Beth.), The Mitchells (Metrojazz), Dave Pell (Vict.), Billy Usselton (Kapp), Benny Goodman (Chess).

Addr: 934 Pass Ave., Burbank, Calif.

CAREY, THOMAS (Mutt), *trumpet;* b. New Orleans, La., 1892; d. Los Angeles, Calif., 9/3/48. Took up music 1912, first as drummer, then studied cornet with brother Jack Carey, in whose band he played until '14 when he joined Kid Ory. Arriving in Chicago in '17 w. Johnny Dodds, he followed King Oliver into the Dreamland. Back in NO he worked with Wade Whaley in '18, moved to Calif. and rejoined Ory. For the next 22 years he worked as a pullman porter, mailman, etc., occasionally working in music with Ory, with whom he was officially reunited in '44 in a network broadcast promoted by Orson Welles. He came to NYC in '47 and worked with Edmond Hall and other New Orleans musicians. At the time of his joining Ory in SF, "He was such a sensation with muted effects he had learned from Oliver, that Oliver was passed over as a Mutt Carey imitator when he played San Francisco a year later."—Samuel Charters in *Jazz: New Orleans.* LP w. Kid Ory (Good Time Jazz).

CARISI, JOHN E. (Johnny), *composer, trumpet;* b. Hasbrouck Heights, N. J., 2/23/22. Stud. trumpet, theory in high school, composition w. Stephan Wolpe, 1948-50, tpt. w. Carmine Caruso, '53-4. After working w. Babe Russin, George Handy, Herbie Fields and several pop dance bands '38-43, entered Glenn Miller's US Air Force Band; also pl. in Ray McKinley, Lou Stein contingent '43-6. Later pl. tpt. w. Skitch Henderson, Claude Thornhill, Charlie Barnet; arr. for Vincent Lopez and various jazz combos. Had works for chamber groups performed at various concerts incl. music symposium at Yale U. Best known in jazz circles as comp. of *Israel,* recorded by Miles Davis on Cap. Also wrote *Lestorian Mode* for Brew Moore (Savoy). Favs: Miles Davis, Dizzy Gillespie, Billy Butterfield; fav. arrs: Gil Evans, George Russell, Gerry Mulligan. Own LP: Columbia; LPs as arr: Davis (Cap.), Moore in *Lestorian Mode* (Savoy), Urbie Green (ABC-Par.).

Addr: 1 East 198th St., Bronx 58, N.Y.

CARLISLE, UNA MAE, *singer, composer, pianist;* b. Xenia, Ohio, 12/26/18; d. NYC 12/12/56, after a long illness. First prominent in Cincinnati radio work; discovered by Fats Waller, she emulated his piano style and made a series of Waller-patterned combo records while in England, 1938. Sang on Fats' rec. of *I Can't Give You Anything but Love* in US '39; recorded w. own all-star combos for Bluebird '40-1, incl. Lester Young, Benny Carter, John Kirby. Wrote and rec. her biggest hit songs, *Walkin' by the River* '40, and *I See a Million People* '41. Toured night clubs through '40s; had own TV and radio series in late

'40s and '51-3; rec. for Col. w. Don Redman, Bob Chester, '50. Ill, retired to Ohio, '54 and remained inactive until her death. The majority of her rec., done for Bluebird-Vict. are unobtainable now.

CARLSON, FRANK L., *drums;* b. New York City, 5/5/14. Best known as drummer with original Woody Herman band, 1937-42. During that time he also rec. w. Glenn Miller (his brother Tony was bassist w. Miller). Later settled in LA doing studio work with N. Riddle, Skip Martin, Benny Goodman, Sonny Burke and LA Philharmonic. LP w. Herman (Decca).

Addr: 13801 Calvert St., Van Nuys, Cal.

CARMICHAEL, HOAGLAND HOWARD (Hoagy), *songwriter, vocalist, piano;* b. Bloomington, Ind., 11/11/1899. Was associated in 1920s with many jazzmen including Dorsey brothers, Louis Armstrong, Clarence Williams, w. all of whom he worked. Led own all-star recording band w. Bix, Benny Goodman, and others on Victor sessions in 1930. Mainly a radio, TV and movie personality and popular singer rather than a jazz artist, Carmichael is best known as a writer of popular songs, incl. *Stardust, Rocking Chair, Lazy River, Georgia On My Mind.* Own LPs on Wor. Pac., Kapp, Decca, Golden Record; LP w. Paul Whiteman (Gr. Award).

Addr: 9126 Sunset Blvd., Los Angeles 48, Cal.

CARNEY, HARRY HOWELL, *baritone sax;* b. Boston, Mass., 4/1/10. Private teachers. Started professionally 1925 w. Bobby Sawyer, Walter Johnson, Joseph Steel, Henry Sapro in Boston, where Duke Ellington heard him and obtained his parents' permission to take him on the road with the band in 1926. By the time he had neared the end of his third decade with the band Carney had been acknowledged by jazz fans all over the world as the first, and for a long time almost the only, great jazz soloist on baritone sax. His rich, virile tone and compellingly individual style gave the Ellington band a unique tonal quality that now has become the sole throwback to the band's original distinctive sounds. Carney has also been heard occasionally on bass clarinet, clarinet and alto sax. He won the Esq. Silver Award '45, '47, DB reader's poll '44-8, also '52, Met. poll '44-8, DB Critics' poll '53-4, '56, tied w. Mulligan '59, Musicians' poll in *Encyclopedia Yearbook* '56. Own LP on Verve; LPs w. Ellington (Col., Vict., Cap., Beth.) (on *Ellington at Newport '58*, Col. CL 1245, he and Gerry Mulligan play a duet on *Prima Bara Dubla); The Jazz Scene* (Verve), *The Sound Of Jazz* (Col.), *Holiday In Sax* (EmArcy), *Billy Taylor* (Argo), Hodges-Ellington in *Back to Back* (Verve). In addition, Carney has made many dates w. recording bands under the leadership of B. Goodman, Sonny Greer, Lionel Hampton, J. Hodges, H. James, Jimmy Jones, Timme Rosenkrantz, Rex Stewart, Cootie Williams, Sandy Williams and Teddy Wilson. Very few of these are available on LP.

Addr: 450 West 147th St., New York, N.Y.

CARPENTER, ISAAC M. (Ike), *leader, composer, piano;* b. Durham, N.C., 2/11/23. Played w. college bands from 1936; extensive concert piano studies at Duke U. After graduation he joined Johnny "Scat" Davis, worked w. Denny Beckner and Johnny Long. Featured with the Boyd Raeburn band during its first period of jazz prominence, '44-5, he left in the summer of '45, then worked w. his own octet along the East Coast. In March '47 he assembled a band in Hollywood, Calif., his headquarters ever since. Disbanded in '56, worked w. Ice Capades as solo pianist '56-7, own small groups '58-9. Band at first had heavy Ellington influence, later emphasized pop music approach. Films: *Rhythm and Rhyme, Holiday Rhythm.* LP: Score.

Addr: 6431 Primrose, Los Angeles 28, Cal.

CARR, JOE FINGERS: see BUSH, Lou.

CARR, LEROY, *singer, piano;* b. Nashville, Tenn., 1899; d. Memphis, Tenn., June 1935. After working for several years in day jobs, he began to play week-ends at a dance hall, accompanying a singer, 1922; a few years later, he took up singing himself. He moved to Chicago early '28 and a few months later his record of *How Long Blues* was released on Vocalion and was an immediate hit. From then until '34 he recorded about 100 blues, including several versions of *How Long.* His final record date was made in Chicago, '35 on Victor's Bluebird label. Carr's blues style had a great impact during the period of his recordings. More urbanized than that of the country blue guitarist-singers, it was copied by innumerable other blues singers throughout the '30s.

CARROLL, BARBARA (Barbara Carole Coppersmith), *piano;* b. Worcester, Mass., 1/25/25. New England Conservatory; USO tour with girl trio; in NYC, led trio 52nd St. with Chuck Wayne, Clyde Lombardi. First rec. w. Eddie Shu (Rainbow, 1949). Was first feminine disciple of Bud Powell bop piano school; began to acquire society following 1952, when she began a long series of engagements at the Embers with trio (Herb Wasserman, Joe Shulman). Acting & playing role in *Me & Juliet* on B'way, 1953. Modified her style in direction of pop music but still retains jazz qualities. Married Sept. '54 to bassist Joe Shulman, who died in 1957. Heard at festivals and clubs, '58-60. Own LPs on Verve, Vict., Kapp, Atl.

Addr: 360 East 55th St., New York 22, N.Y.

CARROLL, JOE (Bebop), *singer;* b. Philadelphia, Pa., 11/25/19. Best known as comedy vocalist with Dizzy Gillespie, whom he joined in '49 and left shortly after a European tour w. him in '53. His recordings w. Dizzy include: *Jump-Did-Le-Ba* for Victor, '49, *Honeysuckle Rose* for Capitol, '50, and a series on Dee Gee label '51-2, also his own sessions for Pres. '52, Vogue (in Paris) '53. Patterned his style after that of the late Leo Watson. Own LPs on Epic, Reg.; LPs w. Gillespie (Vict., Atl., Savoy).

CARRUTHERS, EARL MALCOLM (Jock), *baritone sax;* b. West Point, Miss., 5/27/10. Music at Fisk University, then w. Benny Moten '28, Dewey Jackson '29-30, Fate Marable '31, and best known as soloist w.

Jimmie Lunceford from '32 until Lunceford's death in '47. Solos include: *I Love You, Harlem Shout, Organ Grinder's Swing.* LPs w. Lunceford (Decca, Col.).

CARRY, GEORGE DORMAN (Scoops), *alto sax, clarinet;* b. Little Rock, Ark., 1/23/15. Mother has degree in music, brother Ed is orch. leader in Chicago. Degree from Chi. Music Coll. where he stud. harmony, theory, clarinet from '23-32. Got into bus. w. Iowa Univ. orch. Lucky Millinder's Cotton Club orch. '33, Ed Carry '34, Fletcher Henderson '36, Roy Eldridge '37, Art Tatum '38, Earl Hines '39, Horace Henderson '40, Earl Hines '41-7. In '47 took up law and is now practicing in Chi. Among his clients is Local 208 A.F.M. Pl. lead alto on all Hines' rec. during period w. band. Fav. own solo: alto on *Jelly Jelly* (Vict.).

CARSON, NORMA, *trumpet;* b. Portland, Ore., 1922. Worked w. Ada Leonard, Sweethearts of Rhythm, Vi Burnside; from 1952 free-lanced in Phila; married to tenor player Bob Newman. Inspired by Gillespie and Davis, she revealed considerable talent in the *Cats vs. Chicks* LP on MGM, but has remained in relative obscurity.

Addr: 902 Brant Ave., Clark, N.J.

CARTER, BENNETT LESTER (Benny), *alto sax, composer, trumpet, clarinet, tenor sax;* b. New York City, 8/8/07. Mainly self-taught; stud. piano w. mother and sister. Early influences incl. Bubber Miley and a cousin, trumpeter Cuban Bennett. Went to Wilberforce U. to study theology, but instead of attending classes there he left to play w. Horace Henderson's Wilberforce Collegians. Worked briefly with Duke Ellington; then w. Charlie Johnson at Smalls, and the bands of Fletcher Henderson, Chick Webb and McKinney's Cotton Pickers.

By 1933 Carter, already greatly respected by fellow-jazzmen, was able to launch his own big band, which he kept together intermittently for a couple of years. He also organized an all-star band for the visiting British composer-critic Spike Hughes; the records made with Hughes are available on a London LP. Sidemen in Carter's regular band were Wilbur De Paris, Chu Berry, Sid Catlett, Teddy Wilson et al. In 1934 Carter worked for a while as sideman with Willie Bryant's band, playing trumpet. He then left for Paris to join Willie Lewis' band on trumpet and alto, 1935. At the instigation of the author he came to England, to work as staff arranger for Henry Hall's BBC house radio band for a year. In the summer of 1937 he played a season at a Dutch seaside resort leading a big interracial and international band, the first successful unit of its kind in jazz history. Before returning to the US in May, 1938 he also spent some time in Scandinavia and France. Back in New York, he re-formed a band; sidemen from time to time included Vic Dickenson, Eddie Heywood, Jonah Jones, Tyree Glenn. In late 1941 he formed a sextet which stayed together for a few months, with Dizzy Gillespie and Jimmy Hamilton. In 1943 he formed a band in California; members at one time or another were Max Roach, Hal Schaefer, J. J. Johnson, Buddy Rich, Joe Albany, Henry Coker. Back in NYC for a series of sides on the now defunct De Luxe label; however, since the mid-'40s he has spent almost all his time living in Hollywood, writing sound track music for movies and occasionally fronting a small group for club work. He was seen as well as heard in some films, among them *The View from Pompey's Head, The Snows of Kilimanjaro.* A new assignment 1958-9 brought him to national audiences w. the TV series *M Squad,* for which he played backgrounds and wrote much of the original music. Other film assignments incl. *The Five Pennies, The Gene Krupa Story.*

Benny Carter is admired as much as any saxophonist in jazz. As an alto man he ranked w. Johnny Hodges as one of the two vital influences in the '30s. Endowed with superb tone and flawless technique, and reflecting unflagging inspiration, he continued to evolve and progress; by 1960 he was even more elegant and consistently swinging than in earlier days. As a trumpeter, too, though he has played the instrument only occasionally, he achieved a rich tone and highly personal legato style that can be heard to advantage on the Contemporary LPs. One of his earlier trumpet specialties was *I Surrender Dear,* on Capitol. His small-toned but smooth clarinet work was heard on *All of Me* (Victor) and with Lionel Hampton's group in *Shoe Shiner's Drag* (Victor). On trombone, his only recorded solo was *All I Ever Do Is Worry* w. Julia Lee (Cap.). While in England he played piano on one or two sides. He also used to sing, but w. less success. As a composer-arranger, he was represented in the libraries of F. Henderson, B. Goodman and many top swing bands, though most of the best examples of his writing can be found on his own LPs. An arranger in the classic big band tradition, he was and is a master of scoring for saxophone sections. In recent years he has continued to study arranging and has done much writing for strings.

Benny Carter today is a jazzman about whom virtually everyone who has ever heard him has been warmly enthusiastic, and who continues to work successfully, though without large-scale international acclaim or economic success, as a writer and instrumentalist.

Many of the best Carter records are no longer available on LPs. He rec. for Columbia-Vocalion, 1933-4; British Vocalion '36-7; Amer. Vocalion '39-40; Okeh, Decca, '40; Bluebird (Victor subsidiary) '40-1; Capitol '43-5; De Luxe '46; free lance for several years, then Victor '53; Clef-Norgran (Verve) '54-7; free-lance, often for United Artists, '58-60.

Own LPs: *Cosmopolite* (Verve 8160), *Alone Together* (Verve 8148), *Moonglow* (Verve 2025), *Urbane Jazz* (8208); *Aspects* (UA 4017), *Fabulous* (Aud. Lab 1505); *Jazz Giant* (Contemp. 3555), *Swingin' The Twenties* (3561).

LPs as sideman: w. Abbey Lincoln (Lib.), Barbara Dane (Dot 3177), Tatum (Verve 8227), Ben Webster (Verve 8020), Quincy Jones (ABC-Par. 186), Al Hibbler (Bruns. 54036); arr. for Billy Daniels (Verve 2072).

Addr: 2752 Hollyridge Drive, Hollywood 28, Cal.

CARTER, BETTY (Lillie Mae Jones), *singer;* b. Flint, Mich., 5/16/30. Stud. piano at Detroit Cons. of Mus; won amateur show 1946. Prof. debut as singer '46. Toured w. Lionel Hampton '48-51. Has since worked mainly in night clubs, often in New Jersey, also theatres w. Miles Davis '58-9. Once known as "Betty Be-Bop" Carter, she has a musicianly and piquant rhythmic style. She has also occasionally written arrangements. Fav: Billie Holiday. Own LPs: Epic, Peacock; one track w. King Pleasure (Pres.).

Addr: 125 N. 17th Street, East Orange, N.J.

CARTER, BOB (Robert Kahakalau), *bass;* b. New Haven, Conn., 2/11/22. Parents were Keith Circuit vaudevillians; father, later a teacher of Hawaiian music, taught Bob guitar and bass. Prof. debut w. father's orch.; local bands around Boston, '37-40. Toured w. various units, 1940-2; own trio in Boston, '44. After Army service '44-5, was prominent on 52nd St.; worked w. Tony Scott, Gillespie, Parker, Stuff Smith, Shavers, etc. Toured w. Ch. Ventura '47-8 and '53-4. Worked w. B. Goodman '49 and '50. Began stud. comp. and arr. in '55; stud. w. Wesley LaViolette in Calif. '56, pl. and writing for Red Norvo, Bob Harrington and Shelly Manne. Then to Honolulu where he worked w. all kinds of orch., pl. Hawaiian, Japanese, Korean and Filipino music. Ret. to NYC, July, '58. W. Bobby Hackett '59. No special favs., but was inspired orig. by Walter Page. LPs w. Red Norvo (Vict.), Bob Harrington (Imp.), Buddy Weed (Coral), Lou Stein (Epic), Bob Alexander (Gr. Award), Johnny Smith (Roost), Ch. Ventura (Bruns.).

Addr: 347 West 55th St., New York 19, N.Y.

CARTER, RONALD LEVIN (Ron), *bass;* also *cello, violin, clarinet, trombone, tuba;* b. Ferndale, Mich., 5/4/37. One of eight children, all of whom have studied musical instruments. St. on cello in school at age 10 and soon after began pl. chamber concerts. Switched to bass at Cass Tech. High in Detroit. Pl. bass in local group '55. Led own groups in Rochester, N.Y. while earning a B.M. at Eastman School of Music '56-9. Pl. and rec. w. Eastman Philharmonia under dir. of Howard Hanson. Joined Chico Hamilton, Sept. '59. Favs: Ray Brown, P. Heath, P. Chambers.

Addr: 45 West 139th St., New York 37, N.Y.

CARVER, WAYMAN ALEXANDER, *composer, flute;* also *saxophones, clarinet;* b. Portsmouth, Va., 12/25/05. Uncle, D. D. Copeland, was dir. of municipal band and pl. flute, piano, trumpet; father, Wayman, Sr. pl. clar.; daughter pl. flute, piano. Took up flute at 14, later pl. w. college dance band. W. Benny Carter 1933-4, Chick Webb, Ella Fitzgerald '34-39. Now is associate Professor of Music at Clark College in Atlanta, Ga. where he also directs the school band. Pl. occasional dates w. a local combo as clarinetist. Notable as first jazzman to make extensive use of flute w. Webb's "Little Chicks" contingent. Favs: D. D. Copeland (flute), Benny Carter (sax. & clar.). Rec. w. Dave Nelson, Benny Carter, Spike Hughes, Webb, Fitzgerald. Fav. own solo on *Sweet Sue* w. Webb. LP: w. Webb in *Five Feet Of Swing* (Decca); Spike Hughes (London).

Addr: 186 West Lake St., Atlanta, Ga.

CARY, RICHARD DURANT (Dick), *piano, trumpet, alto horn, mellophone, composer;* b. Hartford, Conn., 7/10/16. Studied violin from 1920-30; composition w. Stepan Wolpe '47-52. Violin w. Hartford Symph. while in high school. Pianist at Nick's '42-3, w. Benny Goodman, Glen Gray '43; Army '44-6; Billy Butterfield '46; Jean Goldkette '47; first pianist in reorganized Louis Armstrong combo '47-8; Jimmy Dorsey '49; staff work at WPIX '49-50, also mellophone and arranger for Eddie Condon TV series. Trumpet at Eddie Condon's '54. W. Bobby Hackett, Sept. '56-Nov. '57 both as chief arr. and instrumentalist, in successful engagement at the Henry Hudson Hotel in NYC. Joined Max Kaminsky, Mar. '58, playing trombone, alto horn, and arranging. App. at Great So. Bay '58, where his *Georgia Sketches* was played. Formed own experimental group out of the nucleus of Hackett band, Jan. '59. Mus. Dir. for Friendship House concert in Wash., D.C., Mar. '59. Has written originals for the Dorsey brothers as well as a symphonic work for Rochester Symph. A talented and versatile musician, long identified w. Dixieland, Cary enlarged his scope considerably in the '50s. Fav: Roy Eldridge, tpt.; Art Tatum, piano; Eddie Sauter, arr.; Don Elliott, mellophone. Own LPs on Stereocraft, Golden Crest; LPs w. Armstrong (Vict.), Eddie Condon (Col., MGM), Bobby Hackett (Cap.), Jimmy McPartland (Epic), Barbara Lea (Pres.), Ed Hall (Rae-Cox).

Addr: 821 6th Ave., New York 1, N.Y.

CASEY, ALBERT ALOYSIUS (Al), *guitar,* b. Louisville, Ky., 9/15/15. Started on violin. First prominent in NYC w. Fats Waller combo, touring and rec. off and on 1934-42. Many rec. dates incl. Mezzrow, Teddy Wilson, Billie Holiday, James P. Johnson. Most famous solo w. Waller was *Buck Jumpin'*. Won Esq. Gold Award '44-5; seen at '44 Esq. concert at Met. Opera House. In Calif. '45, rec. own session for Capitol, later freelance in New York and in recent years has been featured soloist w. King Curtis All Stars in and around NYC. A gifted and technically accomplished musician, made his mark in jazz just before the electric guitar era; though equally impressive on the amplified instrument, he has long been neglected in jazz circles. LPs w. Waller (Vict.); *52nd Street Jazz* (Coral), one no. w. own group in *History of Jazz, Vol. 4* (Cap.); w. Earl Hines in *Dinah Washington Sings The Blues*

(Gr. Award); Teddy Wilson (MGM), *Saturday Night Swing Session* (Ctpt.), Ed Hall (Comm.).

Addr: 452 St. Nicholas Ave., New York 27, N.Y.

CASTAGNINO, WILLIAM (Bill), *trumpet;* b. San Francisco, Cal., 5/31/24. Worked with Ch. Barnet, Chuy Reyes, various Latin bands in LA; joined Woody Herman '54, toured Europe with him and worked with the band off and on through '57, also w. Jerry Fielding '56, Perez Prado '57. Since '58, small combo work as leader and sideman in LA, Chevrolet TV series, etc. Castagnino is a licensed mortician and has been active in this field since early '58. LPs w. Herman (Cap., Verve).

Addr: 1132 S. Trenton Street, Los Angeles 15, Cal.

CASTLE, LEE (Lee Castaldo), *trumpet, leader;* b. New York City, 2/28/15. Trumpet at 15; private teachers. First prominent job w. Joe Haymes 1935; Artie Shaw '36, Tommy Dorsey '37. In '38 Dorsey sent him to study with Dorsey's father for a year on the family farm at Lansford, Pa. Later played w. Red Norvo, Dick Stabile, Glenn Miller, Jack Teagarden, Will Bradley. Had own band off and on in '38 and throughout '40s. Joined Dorsey Brothers Orchestra '53 as featured soloist. With their deaths became leader and part owner of the orch. Films: *Stage Door Canteen, The Girls They Left Behind* w. Benny Goodman; short for Universal w. the Dorseys. TV w. Dorsey band: *Stage Show,* Patti Page Show, George Jessel Show, NBC Bandstand. One of Louis Armstrong's most fervent disciples; outstanding tone and forthright style. Own LPs: *Dixieland Heaven* (Joe Davis); one solo in *The Mellow Moods of Jazz* (Vict.); *Jimmy Dorsey's Greatest Hits w. Lee Castle, Jimmy Dorsey On Tour* (Epic), *Dorseys in Hi-Fi* (Col.), *Tribute to J. Dorsey* (Frat.).

Addr: 17 Longmeadow Road, Yonkers, New York.

CASTRO, JOSEPH (Joe), *piano;* b. Miami, Ariz., 8/15/27. Brother & sister musical. Raised in Pittsburg, Calif., where he pl. many gigs as leader and sideman from age 15. After att. San Jose State Col., was in Army 1946-7, pl. in Army band and combo. Ret. to college, then formed group that worked along West Coast from Seattle to San Diego and went to Hawaii regularly. Pl. Palladium, London, '52; w. own groups on coast from '53 (sideman incl. Chico Hamilton, Red Mitchell); acc. June Christy '58-9. A hard-swinging, jubilant modern soloist whose reputation by 1960 had still not measured up to his talent. Fav: Art Tatum. Names M. Ravel, Ch. Parker as major influences. Own LPs: *Mood Jazz, Groove Funk Soul* (Atl.); two tracks w. Teddy Edwards in *Sonny Rollins at Music Inn* (Metrojazz).

CATHCART, CHARLES RICHARD (Dick), *trumpet;* b. Michigan City, Ind., 11/6/24. Father pl. cornet; 3 brothers have all been prof. musicians. Started on clar. at 4 yrs., switched to tpt. at 13. Later stud. w. Geo. Wendt and Louis Maggio. First job w. Bob Barnes at Indiana U. Worked w. Ray McKinley, Alvino Rey, 1942, USAAF Radio Orchestra '43-6, Bob Crosby Feb.-Dec. '46. After 3 yrs. of studio work, mostly at MGM, he played in Ben Pollack's combo '49-50, Ray Noble '50-51, Frank DeVol '51-53; since '51, has worked off and on with his own jazz combo, best known as Pete Kelly's Big 7, incl. '51 radio show, *Pete Kelly's Blues,* '55 film bearing same name and as musical dir. and soloist for TV series based on same character '59. Other films: *Dragnet* '54, *Battle Stations* '55; dubbed solos for Billy May in *Nightmare* '55. Cathcart, who has been compared with Bix, states that his favs. are Armstrong, Hackett and Butterfield. Own LPs connected w. Pete Kelly on Vict., Col., Warn. Bros.; *Bix MCMLIX* (Warn. Bros.); LPs w. Paul Weston (Col.), Billy May (Cap.).

Addr: 12329 Huston St., No. Hollywood, Calif.

CATLETT, SIDNEY (Big Sid), *drums;* b. Evansville, Ind., 1/17/10; d. Chicago, Ill., 3/24/51. To NYC 1930 w. Sammy Stewart, then w. Benny Carter '33, McKinney's Cotton Pickers '33-4, Jeter-Pillars '34-5, Fletcher Henderson '36, Don Redman '36-8, Louis Armstrong '38-42; also briefly w. B. Goodman '41. Worked w. Teddy Wilson then led own group in Calif. '44-5, NYC '46. Rejoined L. Armstrong '47-9, then free-lanced mostly in Chicago, until he died of a heart attack. Won Esq. Gold Award 1944-5. Considered one of the greatest modern jazz drummers of the '30s and early '40s, Catlett was one of the few who survived the transition era initiated by the bop drummers of the middle '40s. He was highly respected by jazz men of every school. LPs w. Louis Armstrong (Vict. LPM 1443), Dizzy Gillespie (Rondolette 11), Charlie Ventura (Verve 8132); History of Jazz, Vol. 4 (Cap. T796), Ed Hall (Comm. 30012), Eddie Condon (Comm. 30010).

CATLETT, GEORGE JAMES (Buddy), *bass;* also *saxophone, clarinet;* b. Long Beach, Calif., 5/13/33. Cousin pl. guitar, brother saxophone. Studied saxophone and clarinet first in Seattle, Wash., then bass. Became prof. w. Bumps Blackwell orch. as saxophonist. In '58-9 was member of house band at Melody Lounge in Denver, Colo., backing such visiting stars as Ben Webster, Sonny Stitt, Anita O'Day, Conte Candoli, etc. W. Cal Tjader '59, then to NYC where he joined Quincy Jones; toured Europe w. him in *Free and Easy.* Favs: Blanton, Pettiford, Ray Brown, Duvivier, Hinton.

CATTOLICA, VINCE, *clarinet;* b. San Francisco, Calif., 11/10/23. Cattolica, who is blind, stud. piano and violin before taking up clar. Pl. w. Jack Sheedy, Wally Rose and Earl Hines; later joined Marty Marsala's band in SF. Has a wide range of taste in jazz from Coleman Hawkins to Charlie Parker. Fav: Goodman. LP w. Burt Bales, *Jazz From The San Francisco Waterfront* (ABC-Par.).

CAVANAUGH, WALTER PAGE, *piano, singer;* b. Cherokee, Kans., 1/26/22. Father a ragtime teacher. St. playing for dances at 12; w. Ernie Williamson band 1938-9, then moved to LA, gigged w. Bobby Sherwood. While in Signal Corps, teamed w. guitarist Al Viola, bassist Lloyd Pratt; formed in May '43 as The Three

Sergeants, the group stayed together after discharge in '45 and for a few years was one of the more popular King Cole Trio-oriented combos. Toured AAF bases in Europe '49. Films: *Romance on the High Seas; Lullaby of Broadway; Big City; A Song is Born.* Favs: Tatum, Garner, Cole, B. Powell. LPs: Capitol.

Addr: 4333 Bakman Avenue, No. Hollywood, Cal.

CELESTIN, OSCAR (Papa), *cornet, leader;* b. Napoleonville, La., 1/1/1884; d. New Orleans, 12/15/54. Came to NO 1906; played in Henry Allen Sr.'s Excelsior Brass Band '08; led own Tuxedo Band '10. Recorded w. own groups in New Orleans on Okeh, Col. 1924-9. The depression forced him into retirement; worked in shipyard during World War II. Reorganized band and recorded for DeLuxe '47. Special performance before Pres. Eisenhower '53. In '54 the Jazz Foundation in New Orleans purchased a bust of Celestin which was presented to the city-owned Delgado Museum commemorating his role as a jazz pioneer. Own LP on Southland.

CESANA, OTTO, *composer, teacher;* b. Brescia, Italy, 7/7/1899. Family moved to San Francisco, 1905. Stud. piano from 1909, later organ, harmony and orchestration w. many teachers. Comp. and arr. for Hollywood movie studios and for radio programs. Gave concert of original works at Town Hall, NYC, 1941. Has written a *Symphony in Jazz* and claims to have been influenced by jazz, though his work is better judged by classical standards and involves no jazz improvisation. In late '50s he returned to Italy. LPs: Col., Cap.

CHALOFF, SERGE, *baritone sax;* b. Boston, Mass., 11/24/23; d. Boston, 7/16/57. Father pl. w. Boston Symph., mother teacher at New England Cons. Stud. piano, clar; self-taught on baritone, inspired by H. Carney and Jack Washington. Pl w. Tommy Reynolds '39; Stinky Rogers '41-2; Shep Fields '43; Ina Ray Hutton '44; Boyd Raeburn '45; changed ideas after hearing Ch. Parker and while w. Geo. Auld and J. Dorsey, '45-6, evolved as first major bop baritone man. Joined Woody Herman '47 and was key man in his famous "Four Brothers" band. Later worked mainly in Boston, teaching at Jazz Workshop. His fine conception, execution and tone earned him several awards as the No. 1 baritone man: Met. poll '49-53 and DB poll '49-51. Own LPs: Cap.; four tracks in *Lestorian Mode* (Savoy); LPs w. Woody Herman (Cap., Col.), Sonny Berman (Eso.) two tracks in *Advance Guard of the '40s* (Em.), *Metronome All Stars* (Harm., one track in History of Jazz, Vol. 4 on Cap.).

CHAMBERS, HENDERSON CHARLES, *trombone;* b. Alexandria, La., 5/1/08. Pl. w. band at Morehouse Coll., Atlanta. Then w. Neil Montgomery, 1931; Doc Banks '32; Speed Webb '33, Zack Whyte '34, Al Sears in Kentucky '35-6, T. Bradshaw '37-8; Chris Columbus in NYC '38-40; Louis Armstrong '41-44, Don Redman '45; various groups at Cafe Society incl. Ed Hall '46-8. Toured w. Lucky Millinder '50-2; Jerry Fielding '54; gigs and recs. w. Sy Oliver; to Miami w. Cab Calloway; subbed w. Duke Ellington '57; many gigs w. Dixieland groups in NYC. W. Mercer Ellington at Birdland '59. Powerful style and tone. Favs: Bobby Byrne, Benny Morton. LPs w. Mamie Webster (Cub), Buck Clayton (Col.), Mel Powell (Vang.).

Addr: 246 West 150th St., New York 30, N.Y.

CHAMBERS, PAUL LAURENCE DUNBAR, JR., *bass;* b. Pittsburgh, Pa., 4/22/35. Started on bar. horn and tuba around Detroit, '49, working w. Kenny Burrell and other combos until Apr. '54. He then left Detroit w. Paul Quinichette, working w. him for about 8 months. In '55 he was heard with the combos of Benny Green, Joe Roland, Jay Jay Johnson and Kai Winding, Geo. Wallington. With Miles Davis since late '55. Chambers, who has a phenomenal technique and whose improvisations are equally exciting arco and pizzicato, is one of the most talented new bassists to enter the jazz scene in recent years. Benny Golson said of him: "He's reached a maturity on his instrument that most guys don't get until they are well into their thirties." Won New Star award in DB Critics' poll '56, "Musicians' Musicians" poll, *Enc. Yearbook* '56. Favs: Blanton, Pettiford. Own LPs on Blue Note, Jazz West, Vee-Jay; LPs w. Miles Davis (Pres., Col.). Lee Morgan, Kenny Burrell, Curtis Fuller, Sonny Rollins, Johnny Griffin, Bud Powell (Blue Note), Red Garland, John Coltrane (Pres.), Kenny Drew, Clark Terry (River.), Benny Golson (River., New Jazz).

Addr: 106 Steuben St., Brooklyn 5, N.Y.

CHAMBLEE, EDWARD LEON (Eddie), *tenor sax;* b. Atlanta, Ga., 2/24/20. Father gave him a sax on his 12th birthday and during law study at the U. of Chicago he worked as a musician. In Army bands from 1941-46; after discharge had own combo in which Osie Johnson played. Toured Europe w. Lionel Hampton '54. In '57-8 was married to Dinah Washington, whom he had known when they both attended Wendell Phillips High School in Chi. With Cozy Cole, '59-60. Own LPs on Merc.; LP w. Dinah Washington on Merc.

CHAPIN, JAMES FORBES (Jim), *drums;* b. New York City, 7/23/19. Piano at 6, clar. at 10; left college at 18 to take up drums. Many commercial jobs from '38; main jazz work w. R. Norvo, '43; Barbara Carroll trio briefly '51, w. Herman Sept.-Dec. '51, T. Dorsey Feb. '52. Many Monday night gigs w. own group at Birdland '54-6. NY and Florida w. Marshall Grant '58-60. Wrote book *Advanced Techniques of the Modern Drummer* and made companion records on Music Minus One label. Favs: Roach, Jo Jones, Rich, Morello. Own LPs: Classic Editions; LPs w. Art Harris (Kapp).

Addr: 50 Morningside Drive, New York City, N.Y.

CHARLES, DENNIS, *drums;* b. Saint Croix, V.I., 12/4/33. Came to US in 1945. Self-taught, his primary infl. has been Art Blakey. Pl. w. calypso and mambo bands, then w. Cecil Taylor in mid-'50s, Gil Evans in late '50s. LPs w. Taylor (Verve, Contemp.), Steve Lacy (Pres.), Evans (Wor. Pac.).

CHARLES, RAY, *piano, singer, composer;* also *saxophone;* b. Albany, Ga., 9/23/32. Accident left him blind at 6; stud. music at school for blind in St. Augustine, Fla. Left school at 15 and began playing w. various local bands in Fla.; two yrs. later organized a trio in the King Cole style, and played on a sponsored television show in Seattle, Wash. Formed own band in 1954 and its first job was as acc. to singer Ruth Brown. The group gradually acquired a style of its own under Charles' careful planning and rehearsal. Its records not only became rhythm and blues and rock-'n'-roll hits but were greatly admired by many jazz artists. In late '57 his first LP was released, consisting of instrumentals, including jazz standards, pop and gospel melodies in a modified modern jazz style. Charles' vocal and piano style is very strongly influenced by the contemporary gospel idiom. As an arr., he also shows a keen appreciation of modern jazz, even in some of his simple blues recordings, and he certainly broadened the market for such music. He sings blues in an authentic fashion with great energy, emotion, and an often subtle rhythmic sense. Favs: Tatum, B. Powell, N. Cole, O. Peterson. Won DB Critics' poll, New Star Award as singer '58. Own LPs on Atlantic.

Addr: c/o Shaw Artists Corp., 565 Fifth Ave., New York 17, N.Y.

CHARLES, TEDDY (Theodore Charles Cohen), *vibes, composer,* also *piano;* b. Chicopee Falls, Mass., 4/13/28. Mother was pianist in silent movie theatres. Stud. percussion at Juilliard '46 and gigged on vibes and drums w. Bob Astor. Piano, vibes w. Randy Brooks '48; Benny Goodman band Nov. '48; Chubby Jackson's big band Feb. '49 (made his record debut w. Jackson on Col.); Buddy DeFranco sextet '49 (rec. for Cap.). Toured w. Artie Shaw's last big band '50, then formed quintet w. Jackie Paris. In '51-2, worked for Anita O'Day, Oscar Pettiford, DeFranco's big band, also briefly w. Roy Eldridge, Slim Gaillard. Since then, has led his own groups whenever possible; stud. with Hall Overton and started experimental writing and recording in New Directions series. Won DB critics' poll, New Star Award '54. Led "tentet" at Newport '56, wrote *Word from Bird* for Stuttgart Light Music Festival '56. Has since toured w. own small combos, also worked as music dir. for Prestige '56-7, Jubilee '58, Bethlehem '58-9. In spare time has worked as salvage diver on plane wrecks, also owns sailboat chartering to skin divers.

Charles' main influences were Parker, Bud Powell and Monk; in recent years he has broadened his scope considerably and has developed into one of the most challenging and original of modern jazz writers. Own LPs: *Collaboration West, Evolution, Olio* (Pres.), *Salute To Hamp* (Beth.), *Tentet, Word from Bird* (Atl.), *Three for the Duke* (Jub.), *Viberant* (Elek.). LPs as arr.: Mary Ann McCall (Jub.), *Something New, Something Blue* (Col.), Sam Most (Beth.); LPs w. *The Prestige Jazz Quartet,* Teo Macero (Pres.), *Metronome All Stars '56* (Verve).

Addr: 4 W. 93rd St., New York 25, N.Y.

CHEATHAM, ADOLPHUS ANTHONY (Doc), *trumpet;* b. Nashville, Tenn., 6/13/05. In 1926 joined a Middle Western band led by John Williams, husband of Mary Lou Williams. Worked in Chicago w. Albert Wynn, later in Phila. w. Bobby Lee. After jobs w. Wilbur De Paris and Chick Webb, toured in Europe for a year w. Sam Wooding, recording with him in Spain and France '30. Was w. Cab Calloway off and on 1932-9, McKinney's Cotton Pickers '33, Teddy Wilson 1939-40, Benny Carter '40-1 and Teddy Hill '41, then became teacher. Was w. Eddie Heywood in '44. In '50 began pl. w. many Latin bands incl. Marcelino Guerra, w. whom he visited France '50; Perez Prado to Buenos Aires '52. In '53-4, free-lanced in Boston, mostly at Mahogany Hall. Since then has divided his time between Jimmy Ryan's and Machito. Made African tour w. Wilbur De Paris '57; to Venezuela, Puerto Rico w. Machito '58; Africa w. Herbie Mann '60. App. on *Sound of Jazz,* CBS-TV '57. LPs w. Machito (Roul.), De Paris (Atl.), Billie Holiday, Eddie Heywood (Comm.), Juanita Hall (Counter.), Pee Wee Russell (Story.).

Addr: 50 W. 106th St., New York 25, N.Y.

CHERRY, DONALD E. (Don), *trumpet;* b. Oklahoma City, Okla., 11/18/36. Moved to LA at 4; began trumpet in junior high and stud. harmony in high school. Gigged around LA from '51 w. Red Mitchell, Dexter Gordon, Wardell Gray et al. Signed by Atl. records w. Ornette Coleman and was sponsored by the company to attend the School of Jazz in Lenox, Mass. Aug. '59. Came to NYC fall '59 w. Coleman. Plays a small "pocket trumpet" in an unconventional style resembling Coleman's. LPs w. Coleman (Contemp., Atl.).

CHEVALLIER, CHRISTIAN, *piano, composer, leader;* b. Angers, France, 7/12/30. Father a pianist, mother a singer. Stud. Nantes Cons. 1936-44. Worked w. New Orleans style band at Kentucky Club '49; D. Byas at Tabou, '50. In '54-5 pl. w. Geo. Daly, Michel de Villers at Rose Rouge. Formed group w. Sadi, Bobby Jaspar et al. Elected best French arr. in *Jazz Hot* poll '55; in '56 Stan Kenton award, Django Reinhardt award and Charles Cros Academy award. Own big band from '56, w. which he recorded his own score for film *Rendez-vous à Melbourne.* Active lately in pop field, writing for musical comedies, etc. Cond. radio symphony orch. in own work at Palais de Chaillot Oct. '59. Favs: John Lewis, G. Mulligan. LP: *French Toast* (Angel).

Addr: 278 Rue de Vaugirard, Paris 15, France.

CHIASSON, WARREN, *vibes;* b. Sydney, N.S. Canada, 4/17/34. Stud. guitar, violin, trombone; 4½ years w. military band incl. European tour Feb.-Nov. '55. Xylophone at college; vibes from '57. While on leave from Army, came to NYC to sell a song, met Geo. Shearing's manager; joined Shearing July '59. Much radio and TV work in Halifax, N.S. '57-9. Inspired by

Dave Pike, Milt Jackson, Teddy Charles, Cal Tjader. LP w. Shearing (Capitol).

Addr; c/o John Levy, 1650 Broadway, New York 19, N.Y.

CHILDERS, MARION (Buddy), *trumpet;* b. St. Louis, Mo., 2/12/26. Self-taught. School band in Belleville, Ill. Auditioned for Stan Kenton Dec. '42 and was with the band seven times between Jan. '43 and '54. Between engagements with Kenton, worked w. Benny Carter '44, Les Brown '47, Woody Herman '49, Frank Devol '50 and '51. Tommy Dorsey '51-52, Geo. Auld, Ch. Barnet '54. Free-lance in LA and Las Vegas since. First rec. w. Kenton, *Artistry In Rhythm* Nov. '43. Fav. own solos: *Solo For Buddy, Autumn In New York* w. Kenton (Cap.). Own LP: Lib.; LPs w. Kenton (Cap.).

CHISHOLM, GEORGE, *trombone;* b. Glasgow, Scotland, 3/29/15. Gigged around Glasgow; worked w. Teddy Joyce '36; w. Benny Carter in Holland '37, Ambrose '38; rec. w. Coleman Hawkins '37; pick-up group and records under own name '37-9; at that time, was rated first great British trombonist, in Teagarden-infl. style. Joined BBC show band '52. Has led own groups on broadcasts, records and TV shows. Also sideman w. Kenny Baker and in '59 w. Jack Parnell. In winter of '58 did Hungarian relief concert w. Louis Armstrong at London Festival Hall.

The accidents of birth and continued residence in Great Britain have prevented George Chisholm from attaining the recognition he has long deserved as one of the half dozen most inventive and emotionally mature trombonists in jazz, regardless of style or country. Although he had evolved in technique and acquired more modern harmonic ideas, he remained in 1960 basically what he had been for more than 20 yrs., a superlative musician with an ageless style. Favs: Bill Harris, L. Armstrong, B. Hackett. LPs: one track w. own group in *A Scrapbook of British Jazz* (Lond.); *One World Jazz* (Col.).

Addr: 5 Oakwood View, Southgate, London N. 14, England.

CHITTISON, HERMAN, *piano;* b. Flemingsburg, Ky., 1909. Began w. Zack Whyte, Cincinnati, 1928, then toured as acc. for Stepin Fetchit; to NYC, acc. Adelaide Hall, Ethel Waters; to Europe '32, worked with Louis Armstrong in Paris '34; Willie Lewis '35-9, then to Egypt for two years. In US, 1941, formed trio and became well known through lengthy engagement at the Blue Angel, smart East Side club, and through weekly broadcasts as the pianist in the CBS *Casey, Crime Photographer* show. Extended run at In Boboli restaurant, NYC in late '50s. Diligent pianist in Tatum-influenced, semi-pop vein. Own LP on Rivoli. LP w. Jack Teagarden in *Boning Up on Bones* (Em.).

Addr: 363 Grand Ave., Brooklyn 5, N.Y.

CHRISTIAN, CHARLES (Charlie), *guitar;* b. Dallas, Texas, 1919; d. New York City, 3/2/42. Raised in Okla. City; studied w. father, played bass in Alphonso Trent's band, guitar in combos around Oklahoma, Jeter-Pillars orch. in St. Louis. John Hammond heard him and recommended him to Benny Goodman, whom he joined in Sept. 1939; he contracted tuberculosis in '41 and spent his last months in a New York hospital. Won DB poll '39-41, Met. poll '41-2, "Greatest Ever" in *Enc. Yearbook* "Musicians' Musicians" poll '56.

During his stay with Goodman, Christian became famous as the first modern jazzman to feature single-string solos on electric guitar. "Christian has a direct connection with bebop. He played up at Minton's in Harlem in those first experimental sessions which yielded, in the early '40s, the altered chords, the fresher melodic lines, the rows of even beats and contrasting dramatic aspects of bop. Some of the participants in the early after-hours affairs credit Charlie with the name 'bebop', citing his humming of phrases as the onomatopoeic origin of the term. All of the musicians who played with him then, as all of us who heard him, insist on his large creative contribution to the music later associated with Parker and Gillespie." —Barry Ulanov, *A History of Jazz in America.*

Christian's work as a precursor of bop is strikingly illustrated in some sessions recorded by a fan, Jerry Newman, at Minton's and Monroe's Uptown House, available on Esoteric 548 as *The Harlem Jazz Scene, 1941.* While with Goodman, Christian only made two tunes with the band, *Honeysuckle Rose* (available on Col. CL 524) and *Solo Flight.* However, with the sextet he can be heard extensively on Col. CL 652 and CL 500. LPs w. Lionel Hampton (Vict. LJM 1000); Metronome All Stars on Camden 426 and Harmony 7044; *Spirituals To Swing* (Vang. 8523/8524), Benny Goodman (MGM 3E9).

CHRISTIAN, EMILE JOSEPH, *trombone;* also *bass;* b. New Orleans, La., 4/20/1895. Brothers, Frank and Charles Christian, pl. trumpet, trombone. Stud. tpt. w. Frank; self-taught on tbn. while playing with Bert Kelly in Chicago 1917. From there, joined the Original Dixieland band at Reisenweber's in NYC '18, traveling with the band to London the following year. Leaving the band 1920, joined Phil Napoleon's Memphis Five briefly; returned to Europe and stayed 20 years, working all over the Continent with various bands as well as in Bombay, India; Eric Borchard orch. in Berlin '24; Leslie Sterling in Paris; then to Germany '27-30, working with Lud Gluskin. Stayed in Europe during 1930s, incl. Belgium '34, Norway '35, Denmark '36; played in Bombay, '35-6, during several years of intercontinental touring as the only white member of Leon Abbey's orch. In New Orleans, has remained locally active, working with George Girard, Leon Prima and other combos. Fav: Tommy Dorsey. Own LP: Southland; w. Johnny Wiggs in *Recorded in New Orleans, Vol. 2* (GTJ), *Dixieland of Old New Orleans* (Golden Crest).

Addr: 926 Music Street, New Orleans, La.

CHRISTIE, RONALD KEITH, *trombone;* b. Blackpool, Eng., 1/6/31. Began study at 14 in Blackpool, later at Guildhall School of Music, London. Worked w. H. Lyttleton, 1949-51; own groups w. brother Ian '51-53, then w. J. Dankworth '53-55; T. Whittle's combo '55-6; free-lanced in London clubs '56-7; joined T. Heath '57, and was present on the latter's tours of the U.S. and Canada. Favs: Armstrong, Teagarden, Parker, A. Cohn. LPs w. T. Heath (Lond.); *Third Festival of British Jazz* (Lond.).

Addr: 38 Peel St., London, W.8, England.

CHRISTY, JUNE, *singer;* b. Springfield, Ill., 11/20/25. Née Shirley Luster; later worked as Sharon Leslie. Local bands 1938; society bands around Chi. incl. Boyd Raeburn in his pre-jazz days, Benny Strong, Denny Beckner. Joined Stan Kenton '45 and scored immediate hit with record of *Tampico.* Married Kenton's tenor sax man Bob Cooper in '46. After Kenton broke up band in '49 she worked as a single, but has frequently teamed with him for concert tours incl. Europe in fall of '53. Toured with Ted Heath show in US, '57 and '58; with Bob Cooper toured Europe '56; Europe and S. Africa '58.

Although completely ignored by many books that analyze jazz, June Christy is unquestionably a jazz singer, and certainly one whose impact had great significance during the late 1940s. At first almost indistinguishable from Anita O'Day, her style, which has suffered at times from imperfect intonation, slowly grew into a personal one involving extensive rhythmic and melodic alteration of the themes. Won DB award as top female band vocalist '46-7-8 and '50; Met. poll '47. Fav: Sarah Vaughan. Own LPs: Capitol. LPs with Kenton (Cap.); *Nat Meets June* w. *Metronome All Stars* (Harm.).

Addr: 3548 Stonewood Drive, Sherman Oaks, Cal.

CHURCHILL, SAVANNAH, *singer;* b. New Orleans, La., 8/21/19. Moved to Brooklyn when she was six. Sang in choirs before entering show business; w. Benny Carter in the 1940s. Rec. w. Carter on Cap. '43; under her own name for Manor '45 w. Don Byas, Jay Jay Johnson.

CINDERELLA, JOSEPH R. (Joe), *guitar, drums;* b. Newark, N.J., 6/14/27. Father, a music publisher and banjoist, introduced him to music. Stud. at the Essex Conservatory. In '46, while in the special service branch of the Army, pl. w. Warne Marsh, C. Candoli, Don Ferrara. During 1955 gigged around N.Y. w. G. Gryce, D. Byrd. Worked w. Vinnie Burke in '55-6, then w. Gil Mellé; made *Jazz '59* concert tour with latter, group incl. brother Don Cinderella on bass. Fav. own solo: *Adventure Swing* in *Primitive Modern* w. Gil Mellé on Pres. Favs: C. Christian, D. Reinhardt. LPs w. Vinnie Burke (Beth.), Gil Mellé (Pres.).

Addr: 174 E. 16th St., Paterson, N.J.

CIRILLO, WALLACE JOSEPH (Wally), *piano, composer;* b. Huntington, Long Island, N.Y., 2/4/27. Navy 1944-6. Studied at N.Y. Cons. of Modern Music '48-'50. Local jazz concerts from early '52; then worked in Chicago; Birdland w. Joe Barone quintet June '52; Chicago w. Chubby Jackson-Bill Harris group June '53. Since '54 has been heard in concerts and on record dates w. John La Porta, Charlie Mingus, featuring many original compositions. A graduate of Manh. Sch. of Mus., he had composed numerous jazz and symphony chamber works, and three symphonies. Active as piano and composition teacher '59-60. Favs: Tatum, Tristano. Own LPs: Savoy. LPs w. John La Porta, *Jazz Workshop* (Debut); *Conceptions* w. La Porta (Fant.); Johnny Mathis (Col.).

Addr: 77 Knollwood Ave., Huntington, L.I., N.Y.

CLARK, WILLIAM E. (Bill), *drums;* b. Jonesboro, Ark., 7/31/25. Worked w. Lester Young, Mary Lou Williams, Lena Horne, Hazel Scott, also briefly w. Duke Ellington in Feb. 1951. With George Shearing in '53-5, Ronnell Bright trio w. Jackie Paris, Rolf Kuhn quartet '56-7, Mary Lou Williams '57-60. LPs w. Ronnell Bright, Rolf Kuhn (Vang.), Jackie Paris (East-West), Muriel Roberts (Dot), Mary Lou Williams, Dizzy Gillespie (Atl.), Shearing (MGM), Lester Young (Verve).

Addr: 125 West 138th St., New York 30, N.Y.

CLARK, WALTER JR. (Buddy), *bass;* b. Kenosha, Wis., 7/10/29. Stud. piano, brass instruments, bass in Kenosha; general music courses at Chicago Musical College 1948-9. Doubled on trom. and bass in first jobs. Worked in Chicago w. Bud Freeman, Bill Russo combos, '50; on the road w. Tex Beneke '51-4. Moved to LA, worked w. Bob Brookmeyer, Kenny Drew groups '54, traveled w. Les Brown orch. '55-6. Night clubs w. Peggy Lee group '56, Red Norvo '56, Dave Pell '57, free-lance in LA '58. Played at Monterey Jazz Festival w. Med Flory Sept. '58. Worked w. Jimmy Giuffre '59 incl. European tour. Ambition: To divide time between jazz, symphony and motion picture studio work. Favs: Ray Brown, Red Mitchell, Percy Heath. Movies: Soundtrack for *Sweet Smell of Success, The Subterraneans.* LPs w. Gerry Mulligan-Johnny Hodges (Verve), Bill Holman (Andex), Peggy Lee (Decca), Bob Brookmeyer, Konitz-Giuffre (Verve), Mel Lewis, Marty Paich (Inter.).

Addr: 4141¼ Cahuenga Blvd., N. Hollywood, Calif.

CLARK, ALGERIA JUNIUS (June), *trumpet;* b. Long Branch, N.J., 3/24/01. Moved to Philadelphia in 1908; aunt taught him piano when he was 10. Learned bugle while w. a boys' group; later stud. trumpet w. private teacher and pl. in a brass band. Worked as Pullman porter and while in New Orleans listened to much local jazz. Toured TOBA circuit after World War I; pl. with Willie The Lion Smith at Conner's in Brooklyn '22. Pl. in Charlie Smith's band at Smalls '23-5; in New York and Chicago clubs for a number of years. A member of Sugar Ray Robinson's entourage in recent years, long inactive in music. Rec. w. Duke Ellington for Bruns. '27.

CLARK, CONRAD YEATIS (Sonny), *piano;* b. Herminie, Pa., 7/21/31. Moved to Pittsburgh at 12, stayed until 19. Played bass and vibes in high school band; went to the West Coast w. his brother in 1951; worked w. Wardell Gray, then was in a band w. O. Pettiford in San Francisco. With B. De Franco quartet late '53-6, incl. European tour, Jan., Feb. '54. Throughout '56 was w. H. Rumsey's Lighthouse All-Stars. Returned East, Apr. '57, as acc. to Dinah Washington, and has since free-lanced in NYC. Own LPs on Blue Note; LPs w. C. Fuller, C. Jordan, J. Griffin, J. Jenkins (BN), Rollins (River.), Chaloff (Cap.), De Franco (Verve), Rumsey (Contemp.), Bennie Green (Enrica).

CLARKE, GEORGE, *tenor sax;* b. Memphis, Tenn., 8/28/11. Stud. under Jimmie Lunceford at Manassas High Sch. in Memphis and joined Lunceford's band, remaining until 1933. Pl. w. Guy Jackson in Buffalo '33-4; Stuff Smith, Lil Armstrong, '35; back with Stuff Smith '39. Own group in Buffalo '42. Back to NYC '54 to join Cootie Williams, with whom he toured Europe Jan. '59. Favs: Hawkins, Webster, Byas, Eddie "Lockjaw" Davis. LPs w. Jonah Jones (Beth.), Wild Bill Davis (Evst.), Cootie Williams (Vict.).

Addr: 540 West 146th St., New York 31, N.Y.

CLARKE, KENNETH SPEARMAN (Kenny, "Klook") (Moh. name Liaqat Ali Salaam), *drums;* b. Pittsburgh, Pa. 1/9/14. Father played trombone, brothers drums, bass. Studied piano, trombone, drums, vibes and theory in high school. Five years with Leroy Bradley; Roy Eldridge 1935. To St. Louis with Jeter-Pillars Orch.; to NYC, joined Edgar Hayes, made first record with him and toured Finland, Sweden '37. With Claude Hopkins for eight months, then with Teddy Hill '39-40. Later he took remnants of Hill band into Minton's; also toured for a few months with Louis Armstrong; in Ella Fitzgerald's band and with Benny Carter '41-2. Year and a half in Chicago with Red Allen; then had own band at Kelly's Stable, NYC, also fronted by Coleman Hawkins. In Army '43; trombone with stage band in Paris. Out of Army, joined Dizzy Gillespie for eight months '46. Then worked with Tadd Dameron, but rejoined Gillespie for European trip, January '48. At the end of tour spent several months in Paris, recording and teaching. Ret. to US, worked at Royal Roost with Dameron and other groups. Toured with Billy Eckstine concert unit '51. In April '52 he helped organize the Modern Jazz Quartet, remaining with them until February '55. Then free-lanced in New York at Cafe Bohemia, etc. while recording extensively. Went to France, summer '56 to join Jacques Hélian band and has since worked in Paris with such visiting Americans as Bud Powell, Miles Davis *et al.* Clark was the first drummer to evolve from the old sock-cymbal style into a subtler approach; using the top cymbal for steady rhythm, he used the bass drum for unexpected punctuations, integrating drums with arrangement and soloists. He was one of the top figures, with Gillespie and Parker, in the foundation of bop. Favs: Max Roach, Sid Catlett.

Own LPs, *Plays Andre Hodeir* (Epic LP 3376), *Clarke-Wilkins Sextet* (Savoy 12007), *Bohemia After Dark* (Savoy 12017), *Sextet* (Sav. 12006), *Klook's Clique* (Sav. 12065), LPs w. The Modern Jazz Quartet, *The Quartet* (Sav. 12046), *MJQ* (Pres. 7059), LPs w. Miles Davis (Col., Cap., Pres., BN), Charlie Christian (Eso.), Dizzy Gillespie (Rondo.), Sidney Bechet (Wor. Pac.) and many others.

CLARK, MAHLON BRYAN, *clarinet, saxes, flute;* b. Portsmouth, Va., 3/7/23. As a child, sang, danced, played piano, guitar; clarinet at 13. Joined Dean Hudson band at 16 for a year, then w. Will Bradley, Ray McKinley bands; Maritime Service '42-5. Settled in Calif., free-lanced in radio, then joined staff at Paramount studios 1946. Expelled from AFM for activities with newly formed Musicians' Guild, he became a member of the Board of Directors in the latter organization. Film: playing and acting in *The Rat Race.* Favs: Goodman, De Franco. Rec. w. Ray Linn, also own dates for now defunct Jewel label; heard on many Sinatra sessions.

Addr: 5525 Round Meadow Road, Calabasas, Calif.

CLAXTON, ROZELLE, *piano;* also *organ;* b. Memphis, Tenn., 2/5/13. Mother, father, four sisters, three brothers all played piano. Stud. organ, took piano lessons at the age of eleven; oldest sister taught him to read music. Pl. house parties when he was twelve. Sideman w. Clarence Davis' Rhythm Aces. W. C. Handy took over band in 1931. Pl. gigs w. band while in high school where he stud. arr. W. Harlan Leonard in KC '36. Rec. w. Ernie Fields, Decca '39. Acc. Pearl Bailey at Chez Paree in Chi. '58. W. Franz Jackson '59. Has arr. for Hines, Lunceford, Norvo, Basie, Andy Kirk. Holds M.M. from Chi. Cons. Favs: Tatum, Hines, Waller, Wilson, James P. Johnson.

CLAY, JAMES EARL, *tenor sax, flute;* b. Dallas, Texas, 9/8/35. Studied alto in high school; became professional when school director took him on gigs. Made first rec. date w. Lawrence Marable for *Jazz:West* in LA '57. Ret. to Dallas '58; in service '59. Fav: Sonny Rollins. LPs w. Red Mitchell (Contemp.), own track in *Solo Flight* (Wor. Pac.).

Addr: 113 Cliff St., Dallas Texas

CLAY, WILLIAM ROGERS CAMPBELL (Sonny), *drums, leader;* b. Phoenix, Ariz., 5/15/99. Pl. drums at eight; stud. various instruments. Went to Calif. where he pl. drums w. Kid Ory and Jelly Roll Morton. Had own band until World War II. Rec. for Voc., Sunset.

CLAYTON, WILBUR (Buck), *trumpet, composer;* b. Parsons, Kansas, 11/12/11. Father pl. trumpet, bass, led church orch. and taught Buck piano. At 19 he pl. in church orch. Went to Calif. at 21, played taxi dances, then own 14-piece band in LA, later taken over by Teddy Weatherford, with whom he worked at the Canidrome in Shanghai '34-6. Back in US, he replaced Hot Lips Page in the Count Basie band, then on its way to NYC, and remained with Basie until '43. Army, '43-6, then toured with JATP, free-lanced in NYC and toured France in '49 and '53. Feat. w. Joe Bushkin quartet in NYC '51-3. Led various groups for concerts around NYC, also with B. Goodman at Waldorf-Astoria '57; concert tour w. Teddy Wilson fall '57; toured Europe with own combo in Newport

Jazz Festival show fall '59. He was seen in the film *The Benny Goodman Story* 1956, though in fact he was never a part of the original Goodman band; also in *Jazz On A Summer's Day,* released 1960.

Buck Clayton's unique vibrato, well modulated open sound and highly individual use of the cup mute were some of the vitally distinctive sounds of the great Basie band in the late '30s, and during the same period were heard in hundreds of recordings under the names of Teddy Wilson, Billie Holiday, the Kansas City 5, 6 and 7 etc. Clayton won Esq. Gold Award '45 as best musician in armed forces.

As a writer, Clayton works skillfully in a modernized swing-era style; some of his best known arrangements are *One O'Clock Jump* and *Hollywood Hangover* for Ellington; *Down for Double, It's Sand Man, Taps Miller, Red Bank Boogie, 7th Ave. Express* for Basie, *Jackpot* for Harry James, and many for his own Columbia LPs. Own LPs: *The Hucklebuck* and *Robbins' Nest* (Col. CL 548), *How Hi The Fi* (Col. CL 567), *Buck Clayton Jams Benny Goodman Favorites* (Col. CL 614), *Jumpin' At The Woodside* (Col. CL 701), *All The Cats Join In* (Col. CL 882), *Cat Meets Chick* (Col. CL 778), *Jazz Spectacular* w. Frankie Laine (Col. CL 808), *Buck Clayton All Stars at Newport* (Col. CL 933), *Buck Meets Ruby* (Vang. 8517), *Buckin' The Blues* (Vang. 8514), *Harry Edison Swings Clayton* (Verve 8293), *Songs For Swingers* (Col. CL 1320); LPs w. Basie (Decca 8049, Bruns. 54012, Col. CL 901, Epic 3169), *Lester Young Memorial* (Epic SN 6031), Harry James (Col. CL 655), Mel Powell (Col. CL 557); *Spirituals To Swing* (Vang. 8523/8524), Dickenson-Thomas (Atl. 1303).

Addr: 145-31 Glassboro Ave., Jamaica 35, L.I., N.Y.

CLESS, ROD, *clarinet;* b. Lenox, Iowa, 5/20/07; d. New York City, 12/8/44. First prominent in Chicago ca. 1927 w. Bud Freeman, later working w. Frankie Quartel, Louis Panico, Charlie Pierce. In many small combos in Chicago on alto and clarinet. Recorded w. Jack Teagarden 1933 in Chicago for Columbia. In NYC, recorded w. Muggsy Spanier for Bluebird 1939; Art Hodes 1940 and '42; Max Kaminsky, Yank Lawson 1944. LP w. Max Kaminsky (Comm.).

CLEVELAND, JAMES MILTON (Jimmy), *trombone;* b. Wartrace, Tenn., 5/3/26. Father was a plumber. After Army service 1944-6 he attended Tennessee State U. and was heard at Carnegie Hall w. the college band. Joined Lionel Hampton '49, left late '53 and freelanced in NYC. He won DB Critics' Poll New Star Award in '55. Off and on w. Johnny Richards band at Birdland, etc. '57-60, also gigs and recs. w. D. Gillespie; part of regular group on educational TV series *The Subject Is Jazz,* NBC, Mar.-June '58; gigs w. G. Mulligan '59, and innumerable record dates. Toured Europe w. Quincy Jones band in the musical *Free and Easy,* '59-60.

Cleveland's modern and highly technical style has led to disagreement among critics. Whitney Balliett in *The Sound of Surprise* (Dutton) calls him "a masterly trombonist who rips off phenomenally rapid, burr-like strings of notes"; Nat Hentoff has written that "his technique is extensive and under firm, functional control," while John S. Wilson complains of his "nervous, jabbing trombone" and believes that "his inclination to insert pointless stutters makes his solos needlessly officious" (*The Collector's Jazz, Modern:* Keystone). Own LPs: Mercury; LPs w. Quincy Jones, Cannonball Adderley, Clark Terry, Dinah Washington (Merc.), Gil Evans (Wor. Pac., New Jazz), Specs Powell (Roul.), Q. Jones, O. Pettiford, B. Taylor, Candido, Lucky Thompson (ABC-Par.), Milt Jackson (Atl.), Leonard Feather-Dick Hyman (MGM), Art Farmer (UA, Pres.), Hampton (Contemp.), Gigi Gryce (Savoy), *Three Bones And A Quill* (Roost), Johnny Richards (Cap., Roul., Coral).

Addr: 204 West 82nd Street, New York 24, N.Y.

CLINTON, LARRY, *composer, leader;* b. Brooklyn, N.Y., 8/17/09. Mother a concert soprano. Self-taught as arranger and trumpeter; pl. briefly w. Ferde Grofe '32, arr. for Isham Jones, Claude Hopkins '33; Dorsey Bros. '34, Glen Gray '35-6, T. Dorsey, B. Berigan '37; had own successful swing band '38-41 and '48-50; Air Force '42-6. In publishing and recording business in '50s; A & R director for Kapp Records in NYC '58-9. Clinton's most popular records were *Dipsy Doodle, My Reverie, Deep Purple, Shadrack, Johnson Rag, Martha, Hezekiah.* Favs: Fletcher Henderson, Igor Stravinsky. LPs: Kapp, Camden, Victor.

Addr: 56 Old Brick Road, Roslyn Heights, N.Y.

COBB, ARNETT CLEOPHUS, *tenor sax;* b. Houston, Texas, 8/10/18. Piano w. grandmother, also studied violin, C-melody sax, trumpet. Professional debut 1933 w. Frank Davis; Chester Boone '34-6, Milton Larkins '36-42. Replaced I. Jacquet in Lionel Hampton's band '42; left in '47 to form own band; inactivated by serious illness the following year. Reorganized band '51 and toured for several years but was inactivated after serious injuries in an accident. He later returned home to Houston, where he had his own 16-piece band in '59-'60. Own LPs: Pres.; *Very Saxy* (Pres.); one track in *Saxomania* (Apollo); LPs w. Lionel Hampton (Decca).

COBB, WILBUR JAMES (Jimmy), *drums;* b. Washington, D.C., 1/20/29. Stud. drums at Armstrong High, 1946 and pl. in school's marching band. Pl. with Charlie Rouse, Leo Parker, Frank Wess, Rick Henderson, Billie Holiday and Pearl Bailey in Washington, then left town w. Earl Bostic in '51 for a year. W. Dinah Washington off and on for five years, after which gigged around NYC before joining Cannonball Adderley Jan. '57. Worked w. Stan Getz and Dizzy Gillespie after Cannonball broke up group Jan. '58, joined Miles Davis summer '58. Studying vibes and other percussion inst. Favs: Max Roach, Kenny Clarke, Art Blakey, Philly Joe Jones, Buddy Rich. LPs w. Cannonball Adderley, Dinah Washington (EmArcy); Miles Davis (Col.), Paul Chambers (Vee-Jay).

Addr: 584 East 164th St., Bronx 56, N.Y.

COE, ANTHONY GEORGE (Tony), *alto sax, clarinet, composer;* b. Canterbury, England, 11/29/34. Was reporter on *Kentish Gazette* before taking up music. Pl. w. Joe Daniels' Hotshots, Nat Gonella and Al Fairweather. With Humphrey Lyttelton since May 1957, incl. American tour, Sept. '59. Has played clarinet w. London Philharmonic in Canterbury Cathedral. Hobbies are chess and occultism. Favs: Parker, Hodges, Webster, Armstrong. LPs w. Lyttelton (Lond.).

Addr: 74 Fordwych Road, London, N.W. 2, England.

COGGINS, GILBERT LLOYD (Gil), *piano;* b. New York City, 8/23/28. Started playing as a youngster but did not take the piano up seriously until after his discharge from the Army. Played with Miles Davis, also Lester Young in early '50s. Sold real estate in '54. Favs: Art Tatum, Bud Powell, Nat Cole, Hank Jones, George Shearing. LPs w. Miles Davis (Blue Note); Jackie McLean (Jub.), Ray Draper-John Coltrane (New Jazz).

COHN, ALVIN GILBERT (Al), *composer, tenor sax;* also *baritone sax, clarinet, bass clar.;* b. Brooklyn, N.Y., 11/24/25. Private clarinet, piano lessons; never studied tenor. Joe Marsala big band 1943, then G. Auld off and on until end of '46. Alvino Rey, Buddy Rich, '47; Woody Herman Jan. '48 to April '49; w. Artie Shaw for a few months, after which he retired from music business. Returned in spring of '52 w. Elliot Lawrence, subsequently free-lancing, mainly as an arranger. In the '50s, wrote for Jack Sterling's CBS radio show and Hit Parade, Andy Williams, Pat Boone and Steve Allen TV shows. In '55-6 was under contract to RCA Victor, working on innumerable record albums, as tenor saxophonist, arranger, or both. In '57 banded together w. Zoot Sims in quintet. Group did not achieve any permanence until '59 when they pl. several lengthy engagements at the Half Note, NYC and the Randall's Island Jazz Festival. A swinging, modern, Basie-oriented arranger and tenorman of the Lester Young school, Cohn is much admired by his contemporaries. Fav. tenors: Zoot Sims, Sonny Stitt, Charlie Parker. Fav. arr: Johnny Mandel, Neal Hefti. Own LPs on Dawn, Savoy, Coral, Vict.; LPs w. Sims on Vict., Coral, UA; LPs w. *The Brothers, Earthy, Tenor Conclave,* Miles Davis (Pres.), Manny Albam (Coral), Elliot Lawrence (Fant.), Gerry Mulligan (Wor. Pac.), Candido, J. Raney (ABC-Par.), Dick Cary (Steft.), *Jazz Soul of Porgy And Bess* (UA), Irene Kral (UA), *Saxes, Inc.* (War. Bros.); Cond. *Aztec Suite* for Art Farmer (UA).

Addr: 244 West 48th St., New York, N.Y.

COKER, HENRY, *trombone;* b. Dallas, Texas, 12/24/19. Studied piano and harp in high school and at Wiley College in Washington, Tex. Joined Nat Towles '37. From '38 to '45, lived in Honolulu, playing w. Hawaiian bands. Came to Calif., joined Benny Carter for a year, then Eddie Heywood sextet; free-lanced around Calif. Was w. I. Jacquet off and on from '49; out some time owing to long illness. Joined Count Basie Feb. '52. Rec. solos: *Paper Moon* w. Heywood; *Hot Rod* and *Flyin' Home* w. Jacquet; *Straight Life, Peace Pipe* w. Basie. LPs w. Basie (Verve), Eddie Heywood (Decca), Frank Foster (Sav.), Tadd Dameron (Pres.), *Metronome All Stars* (Verve).

Addr: 1800 7th Ave., New York 26, N.Y.

COKER, JERRY, *tenor sax;* b. South Bend, Ind., 11/28/32. Parents both jazz musicians. Has stud. piano, clarinet, flute, bassoon, tenor and composition. Played w. Fred Dale's Indiana Univ. band. Joined Woody Herman fall, '53, left in mid-'54 to settle on West Coast. Favs: Getz, Sims, Cohn. Own LP, *Modern Music From Indiana University* (Fant.); LPs w. Woody Herman (Verve, Col.), *Intro To Jazz,* Mel Lewis (SFJ).

COLE, EDWIN LE MAR (Buddy), *piano, organ;* b. Irving, Ill., 12/15/16. Raised in Hollywood, Cal. Theatre organist 1934, then played with dance bands incl. Frankie Trumbauer, 1939-40; Alvino Rey, '41-2. A successful studio musician and conductor during past decade, in Hollywood. Not related to Nat Cole, but played piano on many of Nat's vocal records in which the solos were wrongly assumed to be by Nat, among them *Nature Boy.* Seen in the movie *A Star is Born.* Own LPs on War. Bros.; LPs w. Lionel Hampton (Decca), Nat Cole (Cap.).

Addr: 4905 Gentry, No. Hollywood, Calif.

COLE, WILLIAM (Cozy), *drums;* b. East Orange, N.J., 10/17/09. Stud. privately as child; at school made drumsticks in manual training. Inspired by Sonny Greer. Made first records with Jelly Roll Morton, 1930. Joined Blanche Calloway '32, for three years; Benny Carter off and on for 1½ years, Willie Bryant '35-6; Stuff Smith '36-8. His first big break came in Feb. '39 when he joined Cab Calloway's band and was featured on what he considers his best recordings: *Crescendo in Drums, Paradiddle, Ratamacue,* etc., on Voc.-Okeh. Joined Raymond Scott on CBS radio staff '42-5. Featured on Broadway stage in *Carmen Jones* and *Seven Lively Arts,* '45-6; played several months w. Benny Goodman during this period. Free-lanced in NYC until '49, when he joined L. Armstrong for 4½ years. Left Nov. '53, started drum school w. Gene Krupa, Mar. '54, and continued to work very successfully as one of the most prolific recording artists in history. In the jazz field he was one of handful of drummers (Sid Catlett and Dave Tough were perhaps the only others) to please every school and work with jazzmen of every style. Outside jazz, he enlarged his scope by studying at Juilliard from '42-5, also w. Saul Goodman of NY Philharmonic. Acquired knowledge of piano, clarinet, vibes, tympani, etc. He was featured in *The Glenn Miller Story* and other films w. Armstrong, with whom he toured Europe '49 and '52. From 1955-8 he appeared regularly at the Metropole, NYC, also toured Britain and Continent w. J. Teagarden, Earl Hines, fall '57. A freak hit record of

Topsy, made by Cole with a small combo on a 45 rpm disc for the new Love label, gave Cozy Cole's name commercial value in '58 and enabled him to tour with his own combo. Cole won the Esq. Silver Award 1944. Favs: Krupa, Jo Jones, Rich, Bellson.

LPs: *Cozy's Caravan* (Fels. 7002), *Concerto For Cozy* (Savoy 14010), After Hours (Gr. Award 33-334); LPs w. Louis Armstrong (Decca 8037, 8038, 8041, 8330), Lionel Hampton (Vict. LJM 1000), Dizzy Gillespie (Rondolette 11), *Drum Roll* (Em. 36071), w. Earl Hines in *The Jazz Greats* (Em. 36048).

Addr: c/o Krupa & Cole Drum School, 261 W. 54th St., New York 19, N.Y.

COLE, NAT (King) (Nathaniel Coles), *singer, piano;* b. Montgomery, Ala., 3/17/17. Raised in Chicago, he made his record debut at 19 in a sextet led by his brother, bassist Eddie Cole, on Decca. Formed his own band, which left Chicago to tour in vaudeville with the *Shuffle Along* revue. After the show broke up in Los Angeles Cole worked as a solo pianist in night clubs, then in 1939 formed the original King Cole trio, with Oscar Moore, guitar, and Wesley Prince, bass. They recorded for Decca in 1940 and '41, playing small clubs in Hollywood and New York. The group featured unison vocals, and occasional solo singing by Cole. After making sessions for two obscure companies, the trio moved to Capitol and had its first national hit in *Straighten Up and Fly Right,* recorded Nov. 1943.

Starting with *The Christmas Song,* recorded Aug. 1946, Cole began to add string sections, etc. to augment the trio for his vocal records. By 1949 he was recording mainly with big band accompaniment; his piano became subjugated more and more to his singing, and in the early 1950s he was a national figure in the popular music scene, his jazz associations almost forgotten and the "King Cole Trio" name dropped, even though he continued to use a guitarist and bassist, and his own drummer on most night club jobs.

Cole, in '50-'60, was an international show business name, appearing at smart supper clubs, occasionally making concert tours, and singing for audiences in Cuba, Australia, and Latin America. He took singing and acting roles in a number of motion pictures, among them *Small Town Girl, The Blue Gardenia, Hajja Baba, The Nat King Cole Story,* a short feature based on his career; *Istanbul, China Gate, St. Louis Blues.* In the last, he played W. C. Handy. Cole's was the first Negro jazz combo to have its own sponsored radio series (Wildroot Cream Oil '48-9). In '56-7 he was the only Negro artist to have his own series on network TV; he abandoned the show protesting the agencies' failure to find a national sponsor.

Because of his unique tonal quality, Cole can enrich even the poorest of the Tin Pan Alley songs he chooses to sing. His was the first jazz-grounded male voice since Louis Armstrong to gain world-wide popular acceptance. As a pianist, Cole played delightfully in a Hines-influenced style, but by the late '50s made only occasional token appearances as a pianist. He has won the following awards: As a pianist: Esq. Gold Award '46; Esq. Silver Award (tie) '47; Met. Poll '47-9. As singer: Esq. Silver Award '46-7. Trio won Small Combo award, DB poll, '44-7, Met. Poll '45-8. Own LPs: *After Midnight* (Cap. W 782), *Instrumental Classics* (Cap. T 592), *The Piano Style of Nat "King" Cole* (Cap. W 689), *In The Beginning* (Decca 8260), *St. Louis Blues* (Cap. W 993), *10th Anniversary* (Cap. W 514); many vocal LPs on Cap.; one track in *Metronome All Stars* (Harm. 7044); LPs w. Lester Young (Verve 8164), JATP, Vol 3 (Verve); w. Int. Jazzmen in *History of Jazz,* Vol. 3 (Cap.).

Addr: c/o H. Plant, Suite 110, 449 S. Beverly Dr., Beverly Hills, Calif.

COLEMAN, WILLIAM JOHNSON (Bill), *trumpet;* b. Paris, Ky., 8/4/04. To NYC 1926 w. Cecil Scott; later worked w. Ch. Johnson. W. Lucky Millinder in Europe June-Oct. '33. Benny Carter and Teddy Hill bands '34-5. Back to France Sept. '35; w. Willie Lewis '36-8, also in Bombay w. Leon Abbey Nov. '36-Apr. '37. Formed co-op group that pl. in Alexandria, Egypt, 1939, playing for wedding reception of Shah of Iran and Farouk's sister. Back to US March '40, pl. w. Benny Carter. With Teddy Wilson at Cafe Society '40-1; joined Andy Kirk Oct. '41 at Famous Door; toured South w. N. Sissle '42. NYC trio work '43-4; to Calif. w. John Kirby early '45. To Philippines w. USO show Dec. '45. Worked for month in Japan '46. Joined Sy Oliver band '46-7; returned to France Dec. '48 and, except for trips to US in '54 and '58, has remained in Europe, touring w. own groups in France and Germany etc. Has been at Trois Mailletz in Paris since '54 but has taken many leaves of absence to play dates all over Continent and N. Africa. Two French films, *Respectful Prostitute* and *Printemps à Paris;* many TV, radio shows and rec. dates for HMV, Pathé, French Col. etc.

Bill Coleman was one of the great unrecognized jazzmen of the late 1930s. His best records, made with the Dickie Wells and Fats Waller combos on Victor, reveal a mellow, gentle tone and a beautifully legato swinging style. In the 1940s he rec. w. Wilson, the Capitol Intl. Jazzmen, Buck Clayton. LPs w. Teddy Wilson, pl. behind singer Eddy Howard in *Yours* (Harm.), *International Jazzmen* in *History of Jazz, Vol. 2,* Django Reinhardt (Cap.).

Addr: 54 Rue Monsieur le Prince, Paris 6, France.

COLEMAN, CY (Seymour Kaufman), *piano;* b. New York City, 6/14/29. Started with private teachers at 4; attended New York College of Music. Gave recitals at 6 in Steinway and Town Halls. Began as single at Stage Door Canteen and Sherry-Netherlands bar. Formed trio, played at Bop City, at which time he decided jazz was the music he wanted to play. Generally known as a cocktail pianist, he has more and more reflected the influence of the jazz idiom. App. at East Side clubs like the Arpeggio in the late '50s. Wrote song *Witchcraft.* Favs: Tatum, Garner, B. Taylor, R. Freeman. Own LPs on Jub., West., Seeco.

Addr: c/o Richman, 151 East 50th St., New York 22, N.Y.

COLEMAN, EARL, *singer,* b. Port Huron, Mich., 8/12/25. Moved to Leland, Miss. at the age of two. Childhood friend of Jimmy Grissom, later singer w. Duke Ellington. To Indianapolis '39, sang w. Ernie Fields, Bardu Ali. W. Jay McShann '43; Earl Hines, King Kolax '44. Joined McShann again in '45, to Calif. While there, recorded *This Is Always* and *Dark Shadows* with Ch. Parker. Inactive for several years. W. Gene Ammons '54. Resumed recording 1960. A fine ballad singer, he was much admired by Parker; sings good blues. Fav: Billy Eckstine. Own LP, *Earl Coleman Returns* (Prestige); LP w. Sonny Rollins (Pres.).

COLEMAN, GEORGE, *tenor sax, alto sax;* b. Memphis, Tenn., 3/8/35. Toured w. several r & b combos incl. B. B. King; gigged around Chicago w. Ira Sullivan, John Gilmore, Bill Lee. In NYC pl. w. Kenny Burrell at Birdland. Joined Max Roach '58; left '59 and free-lanced in NYC. W. Slide Hampton '60. Favs: Parker, Rollins, Coltrane, Stitt, Golson. LPs w. Roach (Time, Em.), Lee Morgan, Jimmy Smith (BN), Slide Hampton (Strand), *Down Home Reunion* (UA).

COLEMAN, ORNETTE, *alto saxophone, composer;* b. Ft. Worth, Texas, 3/19/30. Largely self-taught, Coleman was influenced by his cousin, a music teacher. Began on alto at 14; switched to tenor 1946. Gigged around Ft. Worth until '49, then left for brief stint with carnival. Toured w. Clarence Samuels r & b group, then settled in New Orleans, working mostly at day jobs. Back to Ft. Worth '50, then joined Pee Wee Crayton's r & b band, left it in LA and jobbed locally. After a couple of years back in Ft. Worth he again went to LA; while working as elevator operator he studied harmony and theory textbooks, and developed a completely new style, virtually atonal, divorced from the conventional concept of improvisation based on chord patterns. Signed with Atlantic Records, who sponsored his attendance at the School of Jazz, Lenox, Mass., Aug. '59. To NYC fall '59; soon was the subject of much controversy. Julian Adderley, examining him in *Down Beat,* wrote: "I am sure there is a place in jazz for an innovator of this type," but admitted that "75% of jazz musicians dismiss Ornette's whole thing . . . he is an innovator of the first water; but he is certainly no messiah." John Hammond, though crediting Coleman with "considerable talent," felt he had been "over-touted . . . he's going to become more and more of a bore," and critic Ralph Berton compared enthusiastic reactions to Coleman with the story of the emperor's clothes. At the same time, John Lewis stated: "Coleman is doing the only really new thing in jazz since the innovations in the mid-'40s of Gillespie, Parker and Monk." Own LPs: Atlantic, Contemporary.

Addr: c/o Atlantic Records, 157 West 57th Street, New York 19, N.Y.

COLES, JOHN, *trumpet;* b. Trenton, N.J., 7/3/26. Mainly self-taught; st. playing in 1939. Pl. with military band in '41; w. Slappy and His Swingsters '45-8; w. Eddie Vinson '48-51; formed group w. Philly Joe Jones et al '51, then w. Bull Moose Jackson '52. With James Moody 1956-8; Gil Evans' band for club and record dates '59. Fav: Miles Davis. LPs w. Evans (Wor. Pac.); Moody (Argo).

Addr: 2419 West York St., Philadelphia, Pa.

COLLETTE, WILLIAM MARCELL (Buddy), *saxes, flute, clarinet, composer;* b. Los Angeles, Calif., 8/6/21. Studied piano for two years, later alto sax; had own band at age 12. Joined Ralph Bledsoe 1939; Woodman Bros. '39-40. Own band '40-1; Cee Pee Johnson Orch. '41-2, Les Hite '42. In Navy '42-5, led naval and dance band. Worked w. Lucky Thompson, Ch. Mingus '46; Treniers, Edgar Hayes '47; Jerry Brent, Louis Jordan '48; Benny Carter '48-9; Gerald Wilson '49-50; then four years in radio and TV w. Jerry Fielding Orch. (on Groucho Marx show, etc.). Took leave of absence from Marx show to go on tour w. Chico Hamilton quintet, spring '56. Left Hamilton Oct. '56 to form own group which in '59 incl. Gerald Wilson, trumpet; Al Viola, guitar; Red Callender, bass; Earl Palmer, drums. Teaches reeds, composing and arranging. Films: comp. score for *George Washington Carver Story* (Artisan Prod.). An extremely versatile and talented performer; among the top two or three flutists in jazz. Favs: Lucky Thompson, Ch. Parker, Harry Klee, Abe Most. Own LPs on ABC-Par., Contemp., Dooto, Challenge, Inter., Music & Sound, *The Swingin' Shepherds* (Merc.); LPs w. Chico Hamilton (Wor. Pac.), Jimmy Giuffre (Atl.), Barney Kessel, Red Norvo (Contemp.), Quincy Jones (ABC-Par.), Red Callender (MGM).

Addr: 5177 Pickford St., Los Angeles 19, Calif.

COLLINS, BURTON I. (Burt), *trumpet;* b. Bronx, N.Y., 3/27/31. Moved to Philadelphia at nine, stud. trumpet at 14. Worked w. Neal Hefti 1955; Woody Herman, Dizzy Gillespie, Claude Thornhill '56, then w. Johnny Richards whenever he organized a big band for dates from '56 on; also w. Urbie Green and Elliot Lawrence. Names Harry James as early influence, Clifford Brown as favorite. LPs w. Johnny Richards (Capitol, Coral, Roul.); Woody Herman (Evst.).

Addr: 252 W. 71st St., New York 23, N.Y.

COLLINS, RICHARD (Dick), *trumpet, composer;* b. Seattle, Wash., 7/19/24. Whole family musical for many generations. As child, was mascot of band led by father, pianist Fred Collins. Studied at San Jose w. Red Nichols' father and in Paris with Darius Milhaud 1947-8. Worked with Dave Brubeck, Ch. Barnet, Alvino Rey; Woody Herman, Feb. '54 to Oct. '56. Joined LA union, Nov. '56 and free-lanced until joining Les Brown in April '57. Has made several tours to Europe, Africa and Asia w. Brown '57, '58. Scored dance-drama presentation of Tennessee Williams' *At Liberty* performed at Idyllwild Arts Festival '58. Own LPs: Vict; LPs w. Woody Herman (Cap., Verve), Les

Brown (Coral, Cap.), Dave Brubeck, Ch. Mariano, *The Herdsmen Play Paris* (Fant.).

Addr: 3817 Elm Ave., Long Beach 7, Calif.

COLLINS, JOHN ELBERT, *guitar;* b. Montgomery, Ala., 9/20/13. Studied music with mother, Georgia Gorham, who recorded for Black Swan and worked as demonstration pianist for W. C. Handy. Toured with her band, incl. Dan Grissom on alto, Truck Parham on bass, 1932-5; joined Art Tatum '35; Roy Eldridge in Chicago '36-9 and New York '40. Worked in NYC w. Lester Young, Dizzy Gillespie, Benny Carter, Fletcher Henderson, then in Army 1942-6. Slam Stewart quartet '46-8, Billy Taylor trio '49-51. Joined Nat Cole Sept. '51. Won *Esquire* New Star award 1947. One of the most underrated of Christian-inspired guitarists, he was kept in obscurity in the '50s as a result of his constant touring w. Cole, for whom he worked in a background role, never taking solos. Fav: Barney Kessel. LPs w. Cole (Cap.), Billy Taylor (Atl.), Beryl Booker (Merc.), Art Tatum (Bruns.).

Addr: 2023 South Curson Ave., Los Angeles 16, Calif.

COLLINS, LEE, *trumpet;* b. New Orleans, La., 10/17/01, d. Chicago, 7/3/60. Studied w. father. Began at 15, playing dances and parades in NO w. Papa Celestin. To Chicago, joined King Oliver 1924, replacing Louis Armstrong. Recorded w. Jelly Roll Morton '24 (*High Society, Tiger Rag,* etc.). Best known for records w. Jones & Collins Astoria Hot Eight '29. Later worked w. Luis Russell, Dave Peyton, Zutty Singleton, Dodds brothers; Mezzrow, incl. tour of France w. Mezz '51. Accompanied many blues singers, and led own combo, frequently at Victory Club on Chicago's Clark St. In the late '50s, inactive due to serious illness. Considered by traditional jazz students to be one of the leading descendants of the Buddy Bolden-Bunk Johnson brand of jazz pioneers. LPs w. Jack Delaney (South.), *Great Jazz Brass* (Cam.), Jelly Roll Morton (River.).

COLLINS, RUDOLPH ALEXANDER (Rudy), *drums;* b. New York City, 7/24/34. Stud. trombone first at Seward Park High; drums at Wurlitzer Sch. of Mus. while still in high school; later stud. w. Sam Ulano '53-7, Charlie Tappin. Prof. debut in 1952 pl. club dates & local dances. W. Hot Lips Page, Cootie Williams '53, Eddie Bonnemere '53-6; Johnny Smith at Birdland, Jay & Kai at Newport Fest., Roy Eldridge at Bohemia, all in '56; six months at Town Hill, Brooklyn w. Austin Powell '57-8. In '58 also app. w. Cab Calloway, Timmie Rogers; one-nighters in Canada w. Carmen McRae. Concerts w. Cecil Taylor '59. Joined Herbie Mann Sept. '59, making African tour w. him '60. Favs: Roach, Jo Jones, P. J. Jones, Persip. LPs w. Jay & Kai (Col.), Cecil Taylor (UA), Pete Brown in *Jazz Kaleidoscope* (Beth.).

Addr: 900 Home St., Bronx, N.Y.

COLLINS, LESTER RALLINGSTON (Shad), *trumpet;* b. Elizabeth, N. J., 6/27/10. Father a minister. Raised in Lockport, N. Y. Played in band organized by Charlie Dixon, fronted by Cora LaRedd. In '30s pl. w. Webb, Benny Carter, Teddy Hill (with whose band he visited England and France in '37), Count Basie ('39); Cab Calloway 1941 and '45-6. r & b dates w. Sam Taylor '55 and various combo jobs in NYC area. LPs: *For Basie; Basie Reunion* (Prestige); Vic Dickenson (Vang); *Like Who?* (United Artists), *Spirituals To Swing* (Vang.).

Addr: 412 West 148th Street, New York 31, N.Y.

COLTRANE, JOHN WILLIAM, *tenor sax;* b. Hamlet, N.C., 9/23/26. Father, a tailor, played several instruments as hobby. Stud. E-flat alto horn, clar., then saxophone in high school; later at Granoff Studios and Ornstein School of Music in Philadelphia. Prof. debut with cocktail combo in Philadelphia, 1945. Navy band in Hawaii '45-6. Toured w. Eddie Vinson r & b band '47-8; Dizzy Gillespie '49-51; Earl Bostic, '52-3; Johnny Hodges '53-4; Miles Davis '55-7. Joined Thelonious Monk and pl. with him at Five Spot, NYC summer and fall '57, also working around NYC area with Red Garland, Donald Byrd, etc. Rejoined Davis Jan. '58, remaining off and on until April '60.

Coltrane's style has led to violent disagreements. Some musicians have accused him of groping, in a style he has yet to consolidate, and of playing strings of meaningless notes; John S. Wilson, the critic, has written that "he often plays his tenor sax as if he were determined to blow it apart, but his desperate attacks almost invariably lead nowhere." Yet Dom Cerulli in *Down Beat* called him "the most individual young tenor I've heard in recent years," and John A. Tynan describes him as "an impassioned, compulsive musical personality." Though Whitney Balliett described him as "a student of Sonny Rollins," actually, as Ira Gitler has pointed out, Coltrane and Rollins are parallel figures, each an important and fast-growing influence on young jazzmen.

Favs: Dexter Gordon, Stitt, Rollins, Getz. Own LPs on Pres., BN, Atl.; LPs w. Davis (Pres., Col.), Monk (River.), Ray Draper (Jub.), Paul Chambers (BN, Jazz: West), Sonny Clark, Johnny Griffin (BN), Tadd Dameron, Mal Waldron, Arthur Taylor, *Tenor Conclave, Cattin'* w. Quinichette, *Interplay, Wheelin' and Dealin',* Gene Ammons (Pres.), Michel Le Grand (Col.), George Russell (Decca), Wilbur Harden (Savoy).

Addr: 203 W. 103rd St., New York 25, N.Y.

COLUMBUS, CHRIS (Joseph Christopher Columbus Morris), *drums;* b. Atlantic City, N.J., 6/17/03. Father of the Count Basie drummer, Sonny Payne. Worked w. own band and Louis Jordan combo in '40s; Bill Davis trio in early '50s, then had own group. LP w. Davis (Epic).

Addr: 1716 Arctic Avenue, Atlantic City, N.J.

COLYER, KEN, *trumpet;* also *guitar;* b. Gt. Yarmouth, Norfolk, England, 4/18/28. Brother Bill Colyer plays washboard. Taught himself to play harmonica 1939, trumpet '45 while at sea. Formed and led Crane River Jazz Band '49; w. Christie Bros. Stompers '51. Since

'53 has played w. his own group, Ken Colyer's Jazzmen, in England and in Denmark '53, Germany '54 and again in '59, Gibraltar '56, NYC and various New England towns '57. Favs: Mutt Carey, Bunk Johnson, King Oliver, Percy Humphrey, Lee Collins. Own LP: London.

Addr: 99 The Drive, Hounslon, Middlesex, England.

COMFORT, JOSEPH G., *bass;* also *trumpet, trombone, tuba, baritone horn;* b. Los Angeles, Cal., 7/18/19. Entire family musical, all in classical field. Stud. tbn. w. father; played other brass instrs. while in Army. Self-taught on bass. Played w. Lionel Hampton 1946-7; Phil Moore '47; Nat Cole '48-51, touring Europe in '50; Oscar Moore '52, Perez Prado '53, Harry James '54, Billy May '55; Nelson Riddle '56-60, playing on all Riddle's F. Sinatra LPs. TV series: Sinatra (ABC, 57), *M Squad* w. Benny Carter '59-60. Excellent jazz bassist whose work has been ignored because so much of it is in pop field. Orig. infl: Blanton. Favs: R. Brown, O. Pettiford, P. Chambers. LPs w. Cole: *This is Nat Cole; To Whom It May Concern* (Cap.); other LPs incl. *Harry James in Hi Fi* (Cap.), *B. Collette's Swinging Shepherds* (Mercury), *Geo. Auld In Land of Hi Fi* (Merc.); fav. own solo on *Mood for Max* (Motif).

Addr: 2902 Edgehill Drive, Los Angeles 18, Cal.

CONDON, ALBERT EDWIN (Eddie), *leader, guitar;* b. Goodland, Ind., 11/16/04. Self-taught on ukulele and banjo, he was raised in Momence and Chicago Heights, Ill., and from the age of 15 worked as a semi-professional musician with groups including Hollis Peavey's Jazz Bandits. Living in Chicago during the '20s, he became closely associated with a group of young musicians who were making their start in jazz, among them Gene Krupa, Frank Teschemacher, Bud Freeman, Joe Sullivan, Jimmy McPartland. He also began an informal partnership w. Red McKenzie (q.v.); the first records by the McKenzie-Condon Chicagoans, including the above-mentioned musicians, were recorded in Chicago, Dec. 9, '27, and later became acknowledged as classics in the foundation of what was known as Chicago style jazz.

Condon went to NYC in '28, played for a while w. Red Nichols but worked most frequently with McKenzie, guitarist Jack Bland, and suitcase-drummer Frank Billings. This group was known as the Mound City Blue Blowers. Condon worked intermittently during the '30s in small combos along 52nd street, occasionally in bigger bands such as Bobby Hackett's, and briefly with Artie Shaw. His real importance as a jazz figure took shape around '39, when he became known as a promoter of jam sessions and jazz concerts. In the early '40s these sessions expanded into a series of concerts at Town Hall in New York. Condon also opened a night club of his own in Greenwich Village in '46 and began his own TV jazz series in '48. Meanwhile he had become a fashionable personality, patronized by prominent figures from the book, magazine, and art worlds and publicized widely in many articles that identified him as a one-man crusade for jazz. In 1947 his autobiography, *We Called It Music,* co-authored by Thomas Sugrue, was published by Henry Holt.

In '54 and '56, his group played the Newport Jazz Festival; in '57 he successfully toured Great Britain. His club closed Dec. '57; in Feb. '58, he moved the club to the upper East Side.

Condon's relentless campaign for Dixieland music was of value in bringing public recognition to the talents of Bobby Hackett, Joe Bushkin, and scores of other musicians who were associated with him off and on during the '40s. Though he himself has been the first to belittle his own talents as a guitarist (he won the *Down Beat* poll in '42-3), it was through his efforts as a proponent of his own school that he initiated countless listeners into a more active interest, not only in his own music, but in all types of jazz. Own LPs on Col., Decca, Comm., Bruns., MGM; LPs w. Brother Matthew (ABC-Par.), Jimmy McPartland (Epic), Wild Bill Davison, Max Kaminsky (Comm.).

Addr: Eddie Condon's, 330 East 56th St., New York, N.Y.

CONDON, LESLIE RICHARD (Les), *trumpet;* b. London, England, 2/23/30. Pl. trumpet in Air Force Military Band 1948. Worked w. Vic Lewis '53; Tony Crombie '54-6; Tubby Hayes '56; Tony Kinsey '54-9. Pl. with Woody Herman's Anglo-American band '59. Favs: Dizzy Gillespie, Miles Davis, Fats Navarro, Clifford Brown. Rec. with Crombie, Kinsey, Vic Lewis.

Addr: 12 Ducarel House, Hemans St., London S.W. 8, England.

CONNIFF, RAY, *composer, trombone;* b. Attleboro, Mass., 11/6/16. Stud. w. father; played w. Dan Murphy '34; Hank Biagini '36; Bunny Berigan '37-8; Bob Crosby '39-40; Artie Shaw, Harry James and other name bands during '40s. Arr. many pop songs and comp. instrumentals, mostly simple riff tunes for James. In Aug. '54, went to work as staff trombonist at NBC in NYC. Signed as arr.-cond. w. Columbia Records '55 and discontinued pl. trombone. Since that time has been responsible for successful pop LPs under his own name and many singles for Johnnie Ray, Guy Mitchell and Johnny Mathis. LPs w. Art Hodes (BN) and Bobby Hackett (Bruns.) never reissued on 12 inch.

Addr: 17348 Weddington St., Encino, Calif.

CONNOR, CHRIS, *singer;* b. Kansas City, Mo., 11/8/27. Father was violinist. Played clarinet for 8 years in school. Began singing w. Univ. of Mo. band, then w. jazz group in KC, led by Bob Brookmeyer. To NYC '49, joined Claude Thornhill, then Jerry Wald; she was with Wald when June Christy heard her and recommended her to Stan Kenton. After leaving Kenton in July '53, she went to work as a single in night clubs. Within three years, as a result of her LPs on Bethlehem, she had attained great popularity among the younger jazz fans. The reaction among musicians and critics has been less than unanimous. Many jazzmen have found her agreeable to record with and believe that she is unquestionably a jazz singer. But

Martin Williams has said: "I question the expressive range, content, and specifically musical quality that is usually achieved in this style." John S. Wilson has written of the "flat hoarse manner" which, he alleges, Miss Connor derived from June Christy, and has criticized her "strained, mannered, quivering work"; but he has admitted that "when she is not forcing herself or being self-consciously hip she can be a pleasant pop singer." Own LPs: Atl., Beth.

Addr: c/o Atlantic Records, 157 West 57th St., New York 19, N.Y.

COOK, HERMAN (Junior), *tenor sax;* b. Pensacola, Fla., 7/22/34. Father and older brother play trumpet. St. on alto sax in high school, then switched to tenor. Worked w. Gloria Bell, June-Dec. 1957; Dizzy Gillespie two months '58; joined Horace Silver May '58. Received early encouragement from Gigi Gryce. Favs: Wardell Gray, Sonny Stitt, Sonny Rollins et al. LPs w. Silver, Kenny Burrell (Blue Note).

Addr: 1800 7th Ave., New York 26, N.Y.

COOK, WILL MARION, *composer, conductor, violinist;* b. Washington, D.C., 1/27/69; d. NYC, 7/19/44. Stud. at Oberlin Coll., later in Europe. Began comp. for stage shows which feat. Bert Williams. Created music for the Negro show *Clorindy* in 1898 which app. in London and NYC. Org. all-Negro orchestra which toured Europe and U.S. Comp. include *I'm Coming Virginia, Mandy Lou, Mammy* et al.

COOK, JOHN (Willie), *trumpet;* b. East Chicago, Ind., 11/11/23. Worked with King Perry '40, Claude Trenier '41, own combo '42, Jay McShann '43, Earl Hines Dec. '43-48 off and on, Ed. Wilcox '48, Dizzy Gillespie '48-50. After playing with Gerald Wilson's band in LA, went to St. Louis to study, then joined Duke Ellington Nov. '51. Remained until spring '57, rejoining for European tour, fall '59. Fav: Clark Terry. Opening solo on *Jam With Sam* (Col.), LPs w. Ellington (Col., Cap.), Billy Taylor (Argo).

COOPER, BOB, *tenor sax, oboe, composer;* b. Pittsburgh, Pa., 12/6/25. Clarinet in high school 1940, tenor sax '41 w. private teachers. With Stan Kenton '45-51, Jerry Gray '53, Shorty Rogers, Pete Rugolo '54. Joined Lighthouse All Stars '54 and has pl. with them ever since, taking leave to tour Europe '56, Europe-Africa '58 w. June Christy (his wife since '46), Bud Shank, Claude Williamson. In '59 became part owner of Lighthouse Records Inc. On TV, played for Richard Diamond show. Film: *Mad At The World.* Comp. score for *A Building Is Many Buildings* (Graphic Films). Remained virtually the only jazz musician to effectively use the oboe for improvisation. As a tenor man, originally inspired by Don Byas, Lucky Thompson but in the '50s switched over to reflect his new favs., Zoot Sims, Stan Getz, Sonny Stitt. Own LPs on Contemp., Light.; LPs w. Shank (Wor. Pac.), Howard Rumsey, B. Kessel, Spud Murphy (Contemp.), Shorty Rogers (Vict.), Stan Kenton, Four Freshmen (Cap.), Jimmy Giuffre (Atl.), Buddy Rich (Verve).

Addr: 3548 Stonewood Drive, Sherman Oaks, Calif.

COOPER, GEORGE (Buster), *trombone;* b. St. Petersburg, Fla., 4/4/29. Stud. trombone in high school; pl. with 16-piece band in Fla. Came to NYC 1950, stud. at Hartnett School until '52, then joined Lionel Hampton for three years, making a European tour w. him in '53. In Paris w. Curly Hamner 1959. Fav: J. J. Johnson. LPs w. Prestige Blues-Swingers (Pres.); A. K. Salim (Sav.); Lionel Hampton (Col.).

COPELAND, RAY M., *trumpet, composer;* b. Norfolk, Va., 7/17/26. Four years tpt. study at Wurlitzer School of Music. Further studies with Prof. Middleton, concert tpt. artist. Started gigging around Brooklyn with local groups. Joined Cecil Scott at Savoy Ballroom, NYC in 1945. After working w. Chris Columbus at Small's Paradise throughout '46, toured w. Mercer Ellington band '47-8 and w. Al Cooper's Savoy Sultans '48-9. In '50, took day job with paper company, remaining there for 5½ years and gigging in spare time w. Andy Kirk, Lucky Millinder, Lucky Thompson, Sy Oliver et al. Played lead tpt. on Frankie Laine-Buck Clayton session for Columbia, October, '55. W. Lionel Hampton, Randy Weston '57-8, Tito Puente '58, Oscar Pettiford '58, Johnny Richards, Gigi Gryce '58-9. Since Sept. '58 has played with the Roxy Theatre Orchestra. Also has own fourteen-piece band which plays occasional gigs for clubs and civic organizations. Film: heard on sound track for *Kiss Her Goodbye* w. Johnny Richards. Favs: Ernie Royal, Clifford Brown, Joe Wilder, Jimmy Nottingham. LPs w. Thelonious Monk (Pres., River.), Johnny Richards (Cap., Coral, Roul.). Oscar Pettiford (ABC-Par.), Specs Powell (Roul.), *Sightseeing In Sound* w. Roxy Orchestra (Craft.), Cat Anderson (Merc.), *Top Brass* (Savoy), Randy Weston (UA).

Addr: 106-59 Roscoe St., Jamaica 33, N.Y.

COPPOLA, JOHN, *trumpet, composer;* b. Geneva, N.Y., 5/11/29. Attended school in Oakland, Calif., where he began stud. trumpet. Played w. Charlie Barnet 1950, Stan Kenton '51, Billy May '52, various small combos around San Francisco '53-5; joined Woody Herman, Aug. '55. Favs: Dizzy Gillespie, Louis Armstrong, Miles Davis, Harry Edison et al. LPs w. Stan Kenton, Billy May, Woody Herman (Capitol).

CORB, MORTIMER G. (Morty), *bass;* b. San Antonio, Tex., 4/10/17. Began stud. guitar, then bass in LA in 1947. Played w. Jan Savitt, '47, Louis Armstrong '47, Benny Goodman '51, Jack Teagarden '53, Bob Crosby '56-8. Pl. in service band in South Pacific '45. Four years on Bob Crosby's TV show. Pl. on *Pete Kelly's Blues* radio show. Own LP, *Strictly from Dixie* (Tops); LP w. Bob Crosby (Coral).

Addr: 4343 Babcock Ave., No. Hollywood, Calif.

CORCORAN, GENE PATRICK (Corky), *tenor sax;* b. Tacoma, Wash., 7/28/24. Discovered by Jimmie Lunceford. Joined Sonny Dunham band just after his 16th birthday. In Oct. '41 became a featured soloist w. Harry James; earned much prominence through many movie and radio appearances w. James. He joined Tommy Dorsey in May '48; had his own group in

'49, but returned to the James band later in '49 and again in '51 and '54. Upon leaving James Nov. '57 after a European concert tour, he returned home to work with his own combo, mainly in Seattle with occasional trips to LA. Hailed as a prodigy during his early years with James, he placed second in DB poll '43 and '44. Favs: Webster, Hawkins, Getz. Own LPs: *Sound of Love* (Epic), *Sound of Jazz* (Celestial). Many LPs w. James incl. *Wild About Harry, James in Hi Fi* (Cap.) and earlier sets on Col.; w. Lionel Hampton (Decca).

Addr: 864 So. Prospect St., Tacoma, Wash.

CORWIN, ROBERT (Bob), *piano;* b. Hollis, L.I., N.Y., 10/2/33. Father pl. piano in silent movies; brother played w. many big bands. Stud. w. Lennie Tristano, then worked w. Don Elliott, Flip Phillips, Jimmy Dorsey, Warren Covington for short periods. Appeared w. Don Elliott quartet on radio and TV shows; worked off and on w. Chet Baker, Phil Woods, Anita O'Day 1958; at Eddie Condon's as a single, '58-9. Fav: Art Tatum. Own LPs on Riverside; LPs w. Don Elliott (ABC-Par.), Phil Woods (Epic), Herbie Mann (UA).

COSTA, EDWIN JAMES (Eddie), *piano, vibes;* b. Atlas, Pa., 8/14/30. Stud. piano w. brother, then w. private teacher; self-taught on vibes. After high school, left for NYC; at 18 joined Joe Venuti. Two years in Army, then clubs w. Sal Salvador, Tal Farlow, K. Winding, Don Elliott; Newport festival '57 and many night clubs jobs w. own trio, also off and on w. Woody Herman '58-9. Sometimes uses an unusual octave-unison style on piano; he is equally effective as vibes soloist. Won DB Critics' Poll new star award '57. Own LPs: Dot, Coral, Jub.; *Eddie Costa, Mat Mathews and Don Elliott At Newport* (Verve); LPs w. Hal McKusick (Coral, Pres.), Don Bagley (Reg.), Mike Cuozzo (Jub., Savoy), Tal Farlow (Verve), *The First Modern Piano Quartet* (Coral), Betty Glamann (Merc.), Lenny Hambro (Epic), Andre Hodeir (Savoy), *A Pair of Pianos* w. John Mehegan (Savoy), Joe Puma (Jub.), Sal Salvador (Beth., Cap.), Woody Herman (Roul.); Spirit of Charlie Parker (WW).

Addr: 153-10 75th Avenue, Flushing 67, L.I., N.Y.

COSTA, JOHN, *piano, composer;* b. Arnold, Pa., 1/18/22. Stud. w. Oscar Levant's teacher, and at Carnegie Tech. 1945-51. B.A. in composition. Pl. w. Tommy Reynolds '40-42; solo work in Pittsburgh area, later regularly on KDKA-TV and twice-a-year stints at the Embers in NYC. Says he aims to "encompass rhythms of Waller and Tatum with the sounds of Hindemith and Stravinsky." Has written several classical works. Own LPs on Coral.

Addr: 1607 Fairmont Ave., New Kensington, Pa.

COSTANZO, JACK JAMES, *bongo, conga drums;* b. Chicago, Ill., 9/24/22. Started as dancer in contest-winning team w. wife Marda Saxon, touring in early '40s. Served in Navy; after discharge, '45, taught dancing in Beverly Hills Hotel. Bobby Ramos heard him playing bongos on jam session and gave him job w. his orch. Jan. '46. Later worked w. Lecuona Cuban Boys, Chuy Reyes, Desi Arnaz, Rene Touzet; toured and recorded w. Stan Kenton '47-8. Joined Nat Cole Feb. '49, remained until Sept. '53, has since worked with acts incl. Peggy Lee, Frances Faye, Judy Garland, Betty Grable. TV app. on *Staccato*, Danny Thomas show. Films: *Mary Lou* (as dancer), *Thrill in Brazil, Small Town Girl;* own big band for *Bernadine* (20th Cent. Fox); spot in *Visit To A Small Planet* '59. Many records w. Kenton best of which he believes are *Peanut Vendor, Monotony, Abstraction, Bongo Riff.* Own LPs for GNP, Zephyr, Liberty; LPs w. Kenton, Cole (Cap.).

Addr: 1312 No. Harper St., Los Angeles 46, Calif.

COUNCE, CURTIS LEE, *bass;* b. Kansas City, Mo., 1/23/26. Started at 15 w. Nat Towles, w. whom he worked from 1941 to Dec. '44. Settled in LA, studied composing and arr. w. Lyle (Spud) Murphy, worked 4 years w. Edgar Hayes combo, several years off and on w. Benny Carter, also w. Wardell Gray, Billy Eckstine, Bud Powell. In '54 was featured on countless West Coast jazz recordings; joined Shorty Rogers, made concert tour w. him. With Buddy De Franco '56; join. Stan Kenton and toured Europe w. him March-May '56. Formed own group Aug. '56. Pl. and teaching bass in LA since then. Monterey Fest. '59 w. Coleman Hawkins. Films: *Sweet Smell of Success, St. Louis Blues, Five Pennies, Carmen Jones.* Fav: Blanton. Own LPs on Contemp., Dooto; LPs w. Teddy Charles (Pres.), Shorty Rogers (Vict., Atl.), Maynard Ferguson, Herb Geller (Em.), Stan Kenton (Cap.), Chet Baker-Art Pepper (Wor. Pac.), Spud Murphy (Contemp.).

Addr: 1919 West 35th St., Los Angeles 18, Calif.

COURTLEY, BERT, *trumpet;* b. Manchester, England, 9/11/29. Self-taught, began pl. in 1946. Toured Scandinavia '47; pl. with most big bands in England incl. Geraldo, Eric Delaney, Vic Lewis, Cyril Stapleton. Had own band for eight months in '56; worked with Don Rendell '57-8. Pl. with Woody Herman's Anglo-American band April, 1959. Has done radio and TV work, and rec. w. Rendell, Ronnie Ross, Vic Lewis.

Addr: 14 St. Olaves Walk, London S.W. 16, Eng.

COUSINEAU, ROBERT PATRICK (Cus), *drums;* b. Calif., 1923. Grandfather was a banjo and violin player. Listening to a Chick Webb recording started his interest in drums. Stud. at College of the Pacific; later in the Army; then at Westlake School of Music in Los Angeles. Pl. with Boyd Raeburn, Jimmy Dorsey, Jack Sheedy, Marty Marsala. Favs. include Dave Tough, Sid Catlett and Sonny Payne. LP w. Burt Bales, *Jazz from the San Francisco Waterfront* (ABC-Par.).

COVINGTON, WARREN, *trombone, leader;* b. Philadelphia, Pa., 8/7/21. Stud. trombone in Philadelphia suburb; first job w. Isham Jones in 1939, subsequently w. Mitchell Ayres, Horace Heidt until '43, when he joined Coast Guard. In *Tars and Spars* show while in service; joined Les Brown after discharge for five months, then w. Gene Krupa. From '46-56 was on CBS staff in NYC. Led a group called The Commanders '46-7.

Assumed leadership of Tommy Dorsey's band in Feb. '58 after the latter's death, taking it on the road and making records. Tommy Dorsey was early influence. Own LPs w. Dorsey Band on Decca.

Addr: 1939 Valentines Road, Westbury, L.I., N.Y.

COX, IDA, *singer;* b. Knoxville, Tenn., 1889. One of the most successful blues recording artists, she made a series of Paramount sides from '23, accompanied by Lovie Austin's Blues Serenaders, Fletcher Henderson and others. In '30s she toured her own tent show successfully in the South. Her husband, piano-organist Jesse Crump, worked and recorded with her. In '39 John Hammond brought her to NY for the "From Spirituals to Swing" concert. Soon after, she made a series of sides for Vocalion-Okeh accompanied by James P. Johnson, Charlie Christian, Lionel Hampton and others. LP: two tracks in *Great Blues Singers* (River.), *Spirituals To Swing* (Vang.).

CRABTREE, RICHARD ARTHUR (Richie), *piano;* b. Sidney, Mont., 2/23/34. Has worked w. C. Candoli, Scat Davis, Monk Montgomery's Mastersounds. Favs: Parker, Gillespie, Miles Davis, B. Powell. LPs w. Mastersounds (Wor. Pac.).

CRAWFORD, JAMES STRICKLAND (Jimmy), *drums;* b. Memphis, Tenn., 1/14/10. Self-taught. First heard by Jimmie Lunceford when the latter was a physical education instructor and Crawford a student in Manassas High School in Memphis. Toured w. Lunceford 1929-42, then went to work in a defense plant. Briefly on 52nd St. w. Ben Webster, then to Army Oct. '43, working in Army under Walter Gross, Sy Oliver; out in '45. Several years at Cafe Society w. Edmond Hall and other combos. During the '50s was occupied by work in the pit bands of many Broadway shows incl. *Alive and Kicking, Pal Joey, Mr. Wonderful, Jamaica* and *Gypsy.* One of the most versatile and successful drummers in NYC, he is best remembered as one of the main sparkplugs of Lunceford's band in its heyday. Has made rec. w. Goodman, Basie, Oliver, Gillespie, as well as Bing Crosby, Mary Martin, Rosemary Clooney and all the Jackie Gleason albums on Cap. LPs w. Lunceford (Decca, Col.), Goodman (Cap.), Mel Powell (Vang.), Juanita Hall (Counter.), Hazel Scott (Decca), Eddie Heywood (Em.), Dickenson-Thomas (Atl.), Ed Hall (Rae-Cox), Linton Garner (Enrica).

Addr: 3420 Netherland Ave., Bronx 63, N.Y.

CREATH, CHARLIE CYRIL, *trumpet, leader;* b. Ironton, Mo., 12/30/90; d. Chicago, Ill., 10/23/51. Led a band in St. Louis and on Mississippi riverboats from 1916-40. Many famous musicians pl. in his bands from time to time, incl. Pops Foster, Zutty Singleton, Lonnie Johnson et al. Rec. for Okeh.

CRIMMINS, ROY, *trombone;* b. London, England, 8/2/29. Stud. tpt. 1948; tbn. '49. Worked w. Dickie Hawdon '50, Mick Mulligan '51, Freddy Randall '53, Mick Mulligan again in '53-'54, Alex Welsh '54. Frequent continental tours and record dates w. Welch. Main influence: Teagarden.

Addr: 125 Hartfield Road, Wimbledon, London S.W. 19, England.

CRISS, WILLIAM (Sonny), *alto sax;* b. Memphis, Tenn., 10/23/27. Went to LA '42. Pl. w. Shifty Henry after school hours; finished school winter '46; worked w. Sammy Yates, Johnny Otis, Howard McGhee, Al Killian, and small Eckstine group at Billy Berg's; then w. Gerald Wilson. Joined Norman Granz' JATP Nov. '48, made several concert tours, incl. one w. Billy Eckstine in early '50s. Free-lanced in LA until West Coast tour w. Stan Kenton *Jazz Showcase* '55. Own groups in LA '56-7; Chi., NY and other Eastern cities w. Buddy Rich '58; reformed own small group in LA '59. App. twice on Boby Troup's *Stars of Jazz* TV show. Favs: Benny Carter, Charlie Parker. Plays in a bluesy bop style strongly infl. by Parker. Own LPs on Verve, Imp., Peacock; LPs w. Ralph Burns (Decca), Wardell Gray (Pres.), *Hollywood Jazz Concert* (Sav.).

Addr: 10306 East Mary Ave., Los Angeles 2, Calif.

CROMBIE, ANTHONY JOHN (Tony), *drums, composer, leader;* b. London, England, 8/27/25. Mother was silent movie pianist. Self-taught. As sideman toured with Lena Horne, Carmen McRae, Annie Ross et al; formed own band Sept. '54 and led it until '56; reorganized big band Oct. '59. Original score & arrs. for 39 TV films in series *Man from Interpol,* also for several films incl. *Teenage Killer, The Nudist Story.* Mus. dir. of Gloucester Music Co. Own LP: *Sweet Beat* (Ember). Other LPs released in England on Top Rank, Decca, Columbia.

CROSBY, GEORGE ROBERT (Bob), *singer, leader;* b. Spokane, Wash., 8/23/13. Younger brother of Bing Crosby. Began career as singer with Anson Weeks orchestra. Joined Dorsey Bros. '35, then took over the remnants of Ben Pollack's orchestra to front a big swing band specializing in orchestrated Dixieland. The nucleus of this group, many of whom continued to record together under the leadership of Crosby and others long after the band broke up in '42, included Yank Lawson, trumpet; Eddie Miller, tenor sax; Nappy Lamare, guitar and vocals; Bob Haggart, bass; Ray Bauduc, drums. Gil Rodin, a member of the reed section, was the director. In World War II Crosby served with the Marines. In the late '40s and throughout the '50s he was mainly active as a radio and TV personality, reviving the band often on records and using some of the original sidemen. He won great popularity with his daily Club 15 show on CBS and a weekly NBC variety show. Own LPs: *Bob Cats* (Decca 8061), *Bob Cats Ball* (Cor. 57005), *Bob Cats in Hi-Fi* (Cor. 57170), *Bobcats Blues* (Cor. 57060), *Bobcats on Parade* (Cor. 57061), *In Hi-Fi* (Cor. 57062), 1936-1956 (Cor. 57089); *Petite Fleur* (Dot 3170), *Porgy & Bess* (3193), *South Pacific Blows Warm* (Dot 3136).

Addr: 9028 Sunset Blvd., Los Angeles 46, Cal.

CROSBY, HARRY LILLIS (Bing), *singer, songwriter;* b. Tacoma, Wash., 5/2/04. Att. Gonzaga Coll., Spokane. While stud. law there, teamed w. Al Rinker and formed group, playing drums and singing. Toured in vaudeville, to LA 1927, joined Paul Whiteman band, where he and Rinker soon were teamed with a third singer, Harry Barris; as the Rhythm Boys, the trio soon achieved national popularity. After making the film *King of Jazz* w. Whiteman, Crosby left the band to work as a single. As screen actor, starred in many films from '31. Is part-writer of many songs incl. *When the Blue of the Night Meets the Gold of the Day,* his theme for many years on CBS radio series in the '30s; *Love Me Tonight, Ghost of a Chance, From Monday On.*

Though the Rhythm Boys were considered a "hot" vocal trio in their day and Crosby certainly has had jazz associations, he is of course basically a pop music figure. Jazzmen with whom he was teamed on records included Bix Beiderbecke, Frankie Trumbauer on Okeh, 1928; Dorsey Bros., Okeh '29; Duke Ellington (as a member of the Rhythm Boys in *Three Little Words,* Victor, Aug. '30, and solo in *St. Louis Blues,* Col., Feb. '32); Don Redman, Bruns. '32; Louis Armstrong, Dec. '36 (*Pennies from Heaven* medley, Decca); Jack Teagarden '41, Bob Crosby '42, Louis Jordan '44, Eddie Heywood '45, all on Decca, and later several sessions with Dixieland bands incl. Bob Scobey (Vict.), and the Bob Haggart, Bob Crosby and Eddie Condon bands (Decca). Rec. one number w. Rhythm Boys on Paul Whiteman 50th Anniversary Album (Grand Award).

Addr: 9028 Sunset Blvd., Los Angeles 46, Cal.

CROSBY, CHARLES, *drums;* b. Memphis, Tenn., 11/25/31. From musical family; stud. with private teacher in Memphis beginning 1947. Pl. in high school band w. pianist Phineas Newborn; also worked w. pianist Evans Bradshaw. Pl. with B. B. King '48-53; had own combo in Columbus, Ohio from '53-7; pl. with Rusty Bryant combo for a while '57, then joined Joe Alexander in Cleveland. Fav. Art Blakey. LP w. other Memphis musicians: *Down Home Reunion* (UA). Rec. with B. B. King (Chess).

Addr: Majestic Hotel, 2291 E. 55th St., Cleveland, Ohio.

CROSBY, ISRAEL, *bass,* b. Chicago, Ill., 1/19/19. Started on trumpet; switched to bass 1934, and was heard in mid-'30s w. Albert Ammons, Fletcher and Horace Henderson, coming into prominence through records w. small bands. Joined Ahmad Jamal '51; left in '53 to pl. w. Benny Goodman band and sextet through '54. Rejoined Jamal '56. Greatly admired by John Hammond under whose supervision he made his first featured solo, *Blues Of Israel* w. Gene Krupa. LPs w. Jamal (Argo), Jimmy Yancey (Atl.), Jimmie Noone in *Gems of Jazz* (Decca), Georgie Auld (Grand Award), Bill Russo (Atl.).

CROTTY, RONALD O. (Ron), *bass;* b. San Francisco, 1929. Was member of early Dave Brubeck groups, recording with Brubeck Trio and Quartet. Also worked in San Francisco with Wally Rose, Virgil Gonsalves, Brew Moore, Earl Hines. While in Army, played w. many British jazzmen during service in England. Favs: Blanton, R. Brown, R. Mitchell, Heath, Chambers. Own trio on *Modern Music from San Francisco* (Fant.) LPs w. Brubeck (Fant.).

CROW, WILLIAM ORVAL (Bill), *bass;* b. Othello, Wash., 12/27/27. Played trumpet in 4th grade; baritone horn, alto sax, drums in later school bands and valve trombone and drums in Army dance bands. After discharge, worked as society drummer, took up bass in summer of '50 (had also played trombone in Bumps Blackwell, Buzzy Bridgford orchs. in Seattle). Drums w. Mike Riley '51; bass and trombone w. Glen Moore '52; bass w. Teddy Charles, Stan Getz, '52; Claude Thornhill '53; Terry Gibbs '53-4; Jerry Wald, Marian McPartland, '54. Joined Gerry Mulligan Jan. '56, pl. w. sextet, then quartet until Feb. '57. Rejoined Marian McPartland for year beginning May '57, then w. Mulligan again July '58-Aug. '59. While w. Mulligan pl. all over Europe '56; '59. Did lighting for off-Broadway show, *Anatol* NYC '58; record and book reviews for *Jazz Review* '58-9. Favs: Pettiford, Ray Brown, Heath, Ware. LPs w. Getz (Verve), Al Haig (Eso.), Marian McPartland (Cap.), Mulligan (Em., Wor. Pac., Col.) Bob Brookmeyer (Story., Wor. Pac.), Jimmy McPartland (Epic), *Jay and Kai at Newport* (Col.).

Addr: 22 Cornelia St., New York 14, N.Y.

CRUMP, JESSE (Tiny), *piano;* b. Paris, Texas, 1906. Left Dallas 1919, spent 13 years on the road w. TOBA vaudeville circuit. Blues writer and accompanist for many Ida Cox records on Paramount. Had first Negro band to play at Pickwick Hotel radio station in KC. Accompanied Billy McKenzie on Paramount records in Chicago, 1929-30. Worked mostly around Muncie, Ind., 1937-52; settled in San Francisco, working w. Marty Marsala and as solo pianist in traditional jazz clubs in recent years. LPs w. Bob Scobey (Verve), two tracks w. Ida Cox in *Great Blues Singers* (River.).

CUESTA, HENRY FALCON, *clarinet, alto sax;* b. McAllen, Tex., 12/23/31. From musical family, he is a cousin of Ernie and Emilio Caceres. First stud. violin w. father 1940; st. playing w. small groups at 14. Att. Del Mar Coll. of Music for three years; pl. in Corpus Christi Symp. Orch. '50-3; after service in Army, pl. in Midwest hotel bands, then joined Jack Teagarden June '59. LP w. Teagarden (Roul.).

Addr: 2025 Violeta Courts, Corpus Christi, Tex.

CULLEY, WENDELL PHILIPS, *trumpet;* b. Worcester, Mass., 1/8/06. W. Noble Sissle 1931-37; Lionel Hampton '44-9; Count Basie '52-Aug. '59. Mostly a leadman, he was heard in solos w. Hampton on *Airmail Special* and *Midnight Sun.* LPs w. Hampton (Decca), Basie (Verve, Roul.).

Addr: 295 Convent Ave., New York 31, N.Y.

CULVER, ROLLAND PIERCE (Rollie), *drums;* b. Fond du Lac, Wis., 10/29/08. Two brothers pl. drums but not prof., sister pl. piano, wife piano, vln., trombone. Took up drum in 1930. St. in high school band and orch.; app. in theaters as tap dancer. Pl. w. Wally and Heinie

Beau in Wis. '30-40. Joined Red Nichols '41, then w. Joe Sanders, Jimmy Joy '42-4. Rejoined Nichols '45 and has been w. him since. App. in over twenty films for 20th Century Fox incl. *Say One For Me* w. Bing Crosby '59. Claims that Gene Krupa has influenced him most, but Buddy Rich is fav. drummer. Has rec. w. Phil Harris, Vict., Kay Starr, Cap. LPs w. Nichols (Cap.); fav. own solo on *1954 New Orleans All Stars* (Dix. Jub.).

Addr: 4351 McConnell Blvd., Los Angeles 66, Cal.

CUOZZO, MIKE, *tenor sax;* b. Newark, N.J., 1925. Played in many name bands 1943-9 including Tommy Reynolds, Joe Marsala, Shep Fields, Elliot Lawrence. Since then, has free-lanced around New Jersey and worked in building and contracting. Own LPs on Jub., Savoy; LPs w. Mort Herbert (Savoy).

CUPPINI, GILBERTO (Gil), *drums;* also *piano;* b. Milan, Italy, 6/6/24. Father was drummer, accordionist. Stud. piano first in 1935, harmony from '39; medicine, surgery at U. of Milan. Inspired to become musician by Benny Goodman Quartet. Took up drums '46; prof. debut '47 in Switzerland. Pl. w. Hazy Osterwald around Europe '49, Gorni Kramer '50, own group at Taverna Mexico, Milan '55; on radio-TV Italiana '56; was w. Armando Trovajoli's big band '57. Pl. at Newport Fest. w. Int. Youth Band '58; Lee Konitz, Teddy Wilson '58. From '56 has app. annually at San Remo Jazz Fest. Favs: originally Gene Krupa, now Max Roach, Philly Joe Jones. LPs w. Int. Youth Band (Col.), San Remo Fest. (Verve).

Addr: 43 Viale Piave, Milan, Italy.

CURRY, RICHARD (Dick), *drums;* b. Greenfield, Ind., 1900. Began playing w. Clarence Miller in 1916; w. Charles Elgar '17-23. Toured w. "Plantation Days" show two years, incl. six months in Europe. Joined Darnell Howard '28; Jimmy Bell '31. In recent years has been w. Franz Jackson's group in Chicago.

CUTSHALL, ROBERT DEWEES (Cutty), *trombone;* b. Huntington County, Pa., 12/29/11. Started as symphony trombonist in Pittsburgh. Joined Charlie Dornberger 1934, Jan Savitt '39, Benny Goodman '40. Army '42-46, then back w. Goodman to Dec. '46. Free-lanced '47; w. Billy Butterfield at Nick's '48. Became regular at Eddie Condon's '49. Made tour of England and Scotland w. Condon Jan.-Feb. '57. Rec., radio, TV in NYC in the '50s. Favs: Teagarden, Bradley. LPs w. Condon (Col., Sav., MGM), Wild Bill Davison (Col.), Brother Matthew (ABC-Par.).

Addr: 93-29 86th Drive, Woodhaven 21, L.I., N.Y.

D

DAHL, JAMES RUSSELL (Jim), *trombone;* also *valve trombone, baritone horn;* b. Mahnomen, Minn., 5/2/30. Father played bass; mother plays organ, brother trumpet; sister teaches piano. Stud. music in high school and junior college in Coleraine, Minn.; tuba his first instrument. On the day he was discharged from Army joined Clyde McCoy. W. Claude Thornhill '55. Heard most often as a member of Johnny Richards orchestra from '57; also w. Nat Pierce at Birdland, Dec. '59. Studio work at ABC and CBS. Favs: Bill Harris, Bob Brookmeyer. LPs w. Gene Quill (Roost), Richards (Cap., Roul.), Chubby Jackson (Evst.), Specs Powell (Roul.), Jackie Gleason (Cap.), Manny Albam (Coral, Dot).

Addr: 56 West 54 St., New York 19, N.Y.

DAHLANDER, NILS-BERTIL (Bert), *drums;* b. Gothenburg, Sweden, 5/13/28. Stud. violin, piano; later stud. at Juilliard. Worked w. Thore Ehrling radio band and w. own quartet; in 1954 went to U.S. for year and a half, playing first for house band at Beehive in Chicago, then a year w. Terry Gibbs combo. Back in Europe, touring w. Chet Baker, '56. In U.S. again Feb. '57, rejoined Gibbs, then settled in NYC as member of Teddy Wilson Trio, August '57, appearing at numerous night clubs and jazz festivals '57-60. A modern drummer with exceptional finesse and taste, infl. by Max Roach. Own LP, *Skal!* (Verve); also *United Notions* w. Toshiko (Metro.) and many LPs w. T. Wilson.

Addr: 1216 First Ave., New York 21, N.Y.

DAILY, PETE, *cornet;* b. Portland, Ind., 5/5/11. Played baritone horn in grade school; switched to tuba after borrowing one from a girl in high school band. Later took up cornet and worked in Chicago for a decade, starting '30, with Art Van Damme, Boyce Brown, Bud Freeman et al. Close friend and musical influence was the late Frank Melrose. Worked his way to Calif. in '42 with Mike Riley; joined Ozzie Nelson's band, then served in the merchant marine for a year. Started own combo on West Coast '46, and earned great regional popularity as Dixieland leader. Own LPs on Cap.; four tracks in *Jazz Band Ball* (GTJ).

DALLAS, FRANCIS DOMINIC JOSEPH (Sonny), *bass, singer;* b. Pittsburgh, Pa., 10/27/31. Father pianist, vocalist, brother pl. trombone. Started singing prof. at age of eight. Stud. bass w. Herman Clements in Pitt. 1949. Pl. w. Charlie Spivak, Ray Eberle, Claude Thornhill, Les Elgart '53-4. Came to NYC March '56, worked w. Bobby Scott, Zoot Sims, Sal Salvador; Phil Woods-Gene Quill '57-8, George Wallington '58-9, Mary Lou Williams, Lennie Tristano '59. Did NJF tour w. Tristano, fall '59. Favs: Red Mitchell, Pettiford, Chambers. LPs w. Phil Woods (Epic), Sal Salvador (Beth.), Mary Lou Williams (Roul.).

Addr: 132-47 41st Ave., Flushing, L.I., N.Y.

DAMERON, TADLEY EWING (Tadd), *piano, composer;* b. Cleveland, Ohio, 2/21/17. Learned jazz rudiments from brother Caesar, who played alto sax locally. The late Freddie Webster gave him his professional start as a pianist; then w. Zack White, Blanche Calloway. By 1940, in Chicago, he had become an arranger.

Came to NYC w. Vido Musso; later joined Harlan Leonard in KC, writing arrangements for many of that band's Bluebird records. After war-plant work, wrote for Lunceford, Auld, Sarah Vaughan; helped organize Babs' Three Bips and A Bop. Wrote *Soulphony* for Dizzy Gillespie's Carnegie Hall concert '48; led own quintet featuring Allen Eager and Fats Navarro at Royal Roost, NYC '48. In '49 went to Paris jazz festival with Miles Davis quintet; then to England as arranger for Ted Heath. Back to US, w. Bull Moose Jackson '51-2. Formed own band '53, pl. summer season in Atl. City w. Clifford Brown, Benny Golson. Dameron's career has been interrupted by narcotics problems; in 1958 he was given a long jail sentence and since then has been confined to the Government institution at Lexington, Ky. He was one of the first arrangers to make effective use of the devices of bop. Won Esq. New Star Award as arranger '47. Compositions include: *Hot House, If You Could See Me Now, Good Bait, Lady Bird, Our Delight.* Own LPs: *Fontainebleau* (Pres. 7037), *Mating Call* w. Coltrane (Pres. 7070), *Clifford Brown Memorial* w. 1953 band (Pres. 7055); LPs w. Fats Navarro (Blue Note, Savoy), Dexter Gordon (Savoy).

D'AMICO, HENRY (Hank), *clarinet;* b. Rochester, N.Y., 3/21/15. Violin first, then clar. in school band in Buffalo. First jobs on lake boats between Buffalo and Chicago. Worked w. Red Norvo '36-9; Bob Crosby '40, also w. Richard Himber, Tommy Dorsey, and own band. With Raymond Scott at CBS '43. Since '44, house musician at ABC network in NYC, '44-'55; since then recordings, clubs, TV, and radio around NYC. Own LP: Golden Crest; LPs w. Steve Allen (Coral), Wingy Manone (Decca), Charlie Shavers (Beth.).

Addr: 70-07 37th Ave., Jackson Heights, L.I., N.Y.

DANE, BARBARA, *singer, guitar;* b. Detroit, Mich., 5/12/27. Classical voice training 1940-5; stud. piano from age eight, self-taught on guitar. Sang folk songs on radio in San Francisco, where she was elected "Miss TV of San Francisco" 1951; soon had own series, *Folksville USA,* first televised folk music show. Night club debut w. Turk Murphy '56. Sang at NJF and several other jazz festivals '58-9. With J. Teagarden combo at Detroit Jazz Festival '59. Timex TV Jazz Spectacular in Jan. '59 with Louis Armstrong, who wanted her to tour Europe with him as vocalist; the plan was canceled at the last minute. Miss Dane is an anomaly, an artist steeped in the folklore aspects of jazz and thoroughly familiar with the backgrounds of early blues singers, many of whom she knows well personally. Her style, often evoking Bessie Smith, and her entire approach are so incompatible with her social background that she was the subject of a unique feature article entitled *White Blues Singer* in Ebony Magazine Nov. 1959. Living in Los Angeles with her husband, silversmith Byron Menendez, and their three children, she has sung only intermittently, but her attractively anachronistic work has been widely acclaimed by critics. Own LPs: Dot, Barbary Coast.

Addr: 2144 Rockledge Road, Hollywood 28, Cal.

DANKWORTH, JOHNNY, *alto sax;* b. London, England, 9/20/27. Played in ship bands on many transatlantic crossings and was strongly influenced, during NYC visits, by Charlie Parker and other early boppers. Played w. Tito Burns and others before forming own septet in March '50. Started own big band '53. Won British *Melody Maker* poll for several years as best alto, best combo leader, and best musician of the year.

In July 1959 his band made its first US visit, playing with great success at the NJF, at Birdland (the first British group ever allowed to play in a New York night club) and at Lewisohn Stadium.

Dankworth not only is one of the best jazz instrumentalists produced by Great Britain, but also ranks as one of his country's foremost composer-arrangers. His band is unique in that it has no regular saxophone section, substituting a special section of soloists along with the regular brass and rhythm teams. Dankworth is married to the talented singer Cleo Laine, with whom he has recorded and performed frequently.

Own LPs: Verve, Top Rank. LPs: *Cool Europe* under pseud. King John I (MGM), *London Broil* (Angel), *New Sounds from the Old World* (Blue Note), Cleo Laine (MGM).

Addr: 4 Denmark Street, London W.C.2., England.

DARENSBOURG, JOSEPH (Joe), *clarinet, soprano sax;* b. Baton Rouge, La., 7/9/06. Father was cornetist-leader of brass band. Stud. clar. w. Alphonse Picou; also violin, piano. Pl. in NO w. Buddy Petit; worked w. Fate Marable on riverboats and many New Orleans style bands incl. Gene Mayl, Pete Daily, Teddy Buckner; ten years w. Kid Ory st. in 1944, when he replaced Jimmie Noone. Great success with own group in Los Angeles in late '50s; had hit record, *Yellow Dog Blues,* '57; made several app. on *Stars of Jazz* TV show and was seen at Hollywood Bowl Dixie Jubilee '59. Fav. own solos: *Sweet Georgia Brown, Yellow Dog Blues* (Lark). Modest about his admirable musicianship, but says: "I am the best amateur cook in the world." Own LP: Lark.

Addr: 12763 Magnolia Blvd., North Hollywood, Cal.

DARIN, BOBBY, *singer, songwriter;* b. Bronx, N.Y., 5/14/36. Grad. from Bronx High Sch. of Science; one year at Hunter Coll. Achieved national prominence after app. on Dorsey Bros. TV show March 1956. First record *Dealer in Dreams,* his own comp., Decca, spring '57. Soon after this he signed w. Atco and has been exceptionally popular with teenagers, singing much rock-'n'-roll, though he is a better than average singer, and has some jazz feeling. Comps. include *Love Me Right, Delia, By My Side.* LPs on Atco.

Addr: c/o Atlantic Records, 157 W. 57th St., New York 19, N.Y.

DAROIS, PHILIP NERI, *bass, tuba;* b. Lynn, Mass., 2/23/19. Stud. at school in Charlotte, N.C., later with private teachers and at Loyola U. Local bands in Charlotte and Boston; Dean Hudson, '40-2, then 4 years in Army, pl. in symphony, dance, military bands. Briefly back w. Hudson '46, then w. Ray Eberle, Johnny Blowers. Living in New Orleans, worked w. Leon Prima, Louis Prima and own combo '47-9. From 1950 on was almost continuously w. Peter Toma orch. at Roosevelt Hotel, also staff job at local TV station to '56, jazz TV work from time to time, and w. Pete Fountain and His Three Coins. Feat. w. S. Pecora in NO travelog film for Col. Pictures. Favs: B. Haggart, W. Page. LPs w. A. Hug (Golden Crest, GTJ), Jack Martin (Patio), Monk Hazel (Southland).

Addr: 2418 Pressburg St., New Orleans, La.

DASH, ST. JULIAN BENNETT, *tenor sax;* b. Charleston, S.C., 4/9/16. Attended Ala. State Teachers' Coll., where Erskine Hawkins discovered him. He has been w. Hawkins' band on and off since 1938 and has played solos on many sides incl. *No Soap, Bicycle Bounce, Double Shot.* Has also formed his own recording groups for sessions on Signature, Mercury, Coral etc. Fav: Chu Berry. LPs w. Buck Clayton (Col.).

Addr: 522 West 157th St., New York, N.Y.

DAVENPORT, CHARLES (Cow Cow), *piano, singer;* b. Anniston, Ala., 1894; d. Cleveland, Ohio, 12/2/55. Studied theology, but was expelled from seminary for playing ragtime piano. Toured carnival and vaudeville '14-30, scoring biggest successes after teaming with singer, Dora Carr. Later settled in Chicago, took out a unit called Cow-Cow's Chicago Steppers. Stranded in Florida '35, decided to give up show business. Settled in Cleveland 1937; worked for WPA. Came to NYC once in '40s but had no success as a musician. Believed to be one of the first pianists to experiment with boogie-woogie ideas. As song writer, claims authorship of *You Rascal, You; Mama Don't Allow It;* name dropped from authorship of *Cow-Cow Boogie* when he sold it outright in '42. Selections in 10 inch LPs on Bruns., River., no longer being issued. One track of Davenport can be heard in *History of Classic Jazz* (River.).

DAVERN, JOHN KENNETH (Kenny), *clarinet;* also *saxophones;* b. Huntington, L.I., N.Y., 1/7/35. Played with Alfredito 1952; Ralph Flanagan '53-4; Jack Teagarden '54; Phil Napoleon '55; Pee Wee Erwin '56; Empire City Six '57; own Salty Dogs, Billy Butterfield, Pee Wee Erwin again '58. After working w. Herman Autrey at Henry's in Brooklyn, Jan.-June '59, rejoined Erwin at Nick's, NYC in July. Has app. on TV w. Erwin, NJF w. Phil Napoleon '59. Infl. and favs: L. Armstrong, Pee Wee Russell. Own LP on Elektra; LPs w. Erwin (UA), Charleston All Stars (Grand Award), Empire City Six (ABC-Par.).

Addr: 1815 Riverside Drive, New York 34, N.Y.

DAVIES, JOHN ROSS TWISTON, *trombone, alto sax;* also *guitar, banjo, trumpet, clarinet,* etc.; b. Wivelsfield, Sussex, England, 3/20/27. Self-taught. Banjo, guitar w. Mick Mulligan's Magnolia band, 1948-9; trombone w. Crane River band (incl. brother, Julian, on tuba) '49-50; Steve Lane '52-3; Cy Laurie '54-5; tbn. & alto w. Sandy Brown '55-6.

Addr: 1 Walnut Tree Cottage, Burnham, Bucks, England.

DAVIS, ARTHUR (Art), *bass;* b. Harrisburg, Pa., 12/5/34. Stud. bass and tuba in high school; later in NYC at Manhattan and Juilliard schools of music. Symph. experience both in Harrisburg and NYC. Had own band, then joined Max Roach 1958. LPs w. Roach (Merc.).

Addr: 623 Reilly St., Harrisburg, Pa.

DAVIS, ROBERT NELSON (Bob), *piano;* also *bass, guitar;* b. Minneapolis, Minn., 7/26/27. Mother a pianist who traveled w. road bands. St. on drums in high school in Minneapolis, and w. family band at 13. With Herbie Fields 1950-1; had own group, pl. club dates in Minneapolis, Chicago. Favs: Bud Powell, Oscar Peterson, Art Tatum. Own LPs, *Jazz from the North Coast* (Zephyr), *Jazz in Orbit* (Steph.).

DAVIS, EDDIE (Lockjaw), *tenor sax;* b. New York City, 3/2/21. Self-taught; eight months after buying horn, worked at Clark Monroe's Uptown House in Harlem. Cootie Williams band '42-3, then Lucky Millinder, Andy Kirk, Louis Armstrong. Own combo, mainly at Minton's '45-52. Joined Count Basie May '52, remaining until July '53. Fronted own group w. various rhythm sections until Feb. '55 when he inaugurated own trio w. organist Shirley Scott. They have stayed together since then, excepting period from Oct.-Dec. '57 when Davis visited Britain and France w. Basie. In '58-9 the trio did several long engagements at Basie's club in NYC. Favs: Hawkins, Evans, Webster. Rec. solos on *Paradise Squat, Bread* w. Basie. Own LPs on Pres., Roul., Roost., King; LPs w. Basie (Verve, Roul.) Bennie Green in *Trombone By Three* (Pres.), *Battle of Birdland* w. Sonny Stitt (Roost), Arnett Cobb, *Very Saxy* (Pres.); Gene Krupa (Verve), Fats Navarro (Savoy).

Addr: 171-11 Foch Blvd., Jamaica, L.I., N.Y.

DAVIS, JACKSON (Jackie), *organ;* b. Jacksonville, Fla., 12/13/20. Began stud. piano at seven; later at Florida A & M and Temple U. Has acc. many vocalists incl. Dinah Washington, Ella Fitzgerald, Nat Cole et al; has had own group since Army discharge in 1946 except '57-8, when he was feat. with Louis Jordan. Favs: George Wright, Doug Duke, Wild Bill Davis, Bob Wyatt, on organ; Art Tatum, piano. Own LPs on Kapp and Cap.

Addr: c/o Phelps Newberry, Jr., 1200 Philadelphia Nat'l. Bank Bldg., Philadelphia 7, Pa.

DAVIS, KAY (Kathryn Elizabeth Wimp), *singer;* b. Evanston, Ill., 12/5/20. Voice major and piano studies at Northwestern U. 1938 to '43. After a year of recital work around Chicago she joined Duke Ellington, who featured her almost exclusively on wordless vocals, using her voice as an instrument in the style he had introduced on records in 1927 w. Adelaide Hall. She made Universal shorts with the band, toured England and the continent in 1948 with Ellington and Ray Nance, and visited France with the entire band in 1950. Leaving Ellington in June 1950, she married Edward Wimp, retired from music and settled in Chicago.

Her contributions—notably *Transblucency, Minnehaha, On A Turquoise Cloud, Creole Love Call*—were among the most pleasant aspects of the Ellington band personality during the '40s. LPs w. Ellington (Col., Vict., Rondo.).

Addr: 7700 S. Michigan Ave., Chicago, Ill.

DAVIS, LEMUEL ARTHUR (Lem), *alto sax;* b. Tampa, Fla., 6/22/14. Prominent during 1940s on 52nd St.; worked w. Nat Jaffe, Coleman Hawkins, Rex Stewart, Eddie Heywood. While w. Heywood composed *Tain't Me* (rec. for Comm.). Later worked around Brooklyn w. Teacho Wiltshire and own group during '50s. Rec. on Savoy, Pres. LPs w. Buck Clayton, Mel Powell (Col.), Eddie Heywood (Decca, Comm.), Billie Holiday (Comm.), Eddie Safranski (Savoy).

DAVIS, MILES DEWEY JR., *trumpet, fluegelhorn, composer, leader;* b. Alton, Ill., 5/25/26. Family moved to East St. Louis in 1927. Well-to-do parents: father, a prominent dentist and substantial landowner, gave him a trumpet for his 13th birthday. Played in high school band; with Eddie Randall in St. Louis '41-3. An early influence, whom he heard and met locally, was Clark Terry; he also met Gillespie and Parker when the Billy Eckstine band passed through town. His father sent him to New York to study at Juilliard in '45 and before long he was working in the small 52nd Street clubs with Ch. Parker and Coleman Hawkins; he also toured with the Benny Carter band and in '46-7 spent five months on the road with Eckstine. Back in NYC in '48, he led two bands at the Royal Roost: one was with Parker, Kai Winding and Allen Eager, the other a nine-piece group that later became internationally known through a series of Capitol recordings.

The Capitol band (its only appearances outside the recording studios were the two-week engagement at the Royal Roost in Sept. '48 and one week, a year later, at the Clique Club) employed an instrumentation never before heard in jazz, including a French horn as well as trumpet, trombone, tuba, alto and baritone saxes, piano, bass and drums. The band was the outgrowth of extensive discussions among Davis and members of the big band often led by Claude Thornhill, two of whose arrangers (Gil Evans and Gerry Mulligan) and several of whose instrumentalists (Lee Konitz, Mulligan et al) were involved in the recordings, along with John Lewis, Johnny Carisi, Max Roach and others. With Davis as leader and focal figure in this experiment, the band and the skilful scoring, along with Davis' withdrawn, understated horn, became symbols for what was then believed to be a transition from the aggressive qualities of bebop into a new era of "cool" jazz. Davis has stated that he had always wanted to play with a lighter sound: tonally and rhythmically the Capitol band marked the first successful attempt to crystallize his personal qualities.

Despite the recognition it earned among a small group of New York musicians, this band had no commercial success at all, and some of its records were not even released for several years. Davis continued to work with a small combo, appearing at the Paris Jazz Festival in '49, gigging around NYC in '50-1 and touring in '52 in a group with Zoot Sims and Milt Jackson. He led his own quintet or sextet off and on through 1960, but during this time a reunion with Gil Evans, involving a considerable extension of the earlier orchestral concept, brought him far wider recognition. Fronting a 19-piece orchestra in an album called *Miles Ahead,* Davis found a new and perfect setting for his lyrical, sensitive and hauntingly melodic solos. Beginning with this album Davis was heard frequently playing the fluegelhorn, which lent his work an even richer and more probing sound than the trumpet. Firmly established as a major figure in jazz history, he earned a big following abroad, especially in France, where he provided the background music for a 1958 film *L'Ascenseur Pour l'Echafaud (Elevator to the Gallows),* released here on the *Jazz Track* LP.

Davis has been the subject of many scholarly analyses. The French critic André Hodeir wrote of him that "Whereas the lyricism of a Charlie Parker, in his great moments, seemed to want to open the gates of delirium, Miles' lyricism tends rather toward a discovery of ecstasy. This is particularly perceptible in slow tempos." Bill Coss found in his playing "the almost fragile, though never effeminate, tracing of a story line that is somewhat above and beyond him, of almost-blown-aside, pensive fragments that are always persuasively coherent." Favs: Armstrong, Eldridge, Gillespie, Hackett, James, Terry, F. Webster.

Davis has won the following awards: *Esquire* New Star Award '47; *Metronome* poll '51-3, '58-60; *Down Beat* poll '55, '57-9; *Down Beat* Critics' Poll, '55 (tied w. Gillespie), '59; *Playboy* poll '60. Own LPs on Columbia: *Porgy And Bess* (CL 1274), *Kind Of Blue* (CL 1355), *Jazz Track* (CL 1268), *Miles Ahead* (CL 1041), *Milestones* (CL 1193), *'Round About Midnight* (CL 949); on Prestige: *Musings of Miles* (7007), *Miles* (7014), *Miles And Horns* (7025), *Miles And Milt* (7034), *Collectors' Items* (7044), *Dig* (7012), *Blue Haze* (7054), *Walkin'* (7076), *Cookin'* (7094), *Relaxin'* (7129), *Bags' Groove* (7109), *Modern Jazz Giants* (7150), *Workin'* (7166); *Birth of the Cool* (Cap. T 762); Vols. 1 & 2 (Blue Note 1501, 1502); two tracks w. own group, four w. Lee Konitz in *Conception* (Prestige 7013); LPs w. Cannonball Adderley (Blue Note 1595), Sarah Vaughan (Col. CL 745), *Metronome All Stars* (Cam. 426); Charlie Parker (Savoy, 12000, 12001, 12009, 12014, 12079, Dial 2210, Verve 8010); w. *Metronome All Stars* in *History of Jazz. Vol. 4* (Cap. T 796).

Addr: 881 10th Ave., New York 19, N.Y.

DAVIS, RICHARD, *bass;* b. Chicago, Ill., 4/15/30. Private lessons 1945-54; Vandercook Coll. '48-52. Pl. w. Youth Orch. of Chicago '46-8; Chicago Civic Orch., De Paul and Roosevelt orch. and Sinfoniettas '48-54; local dance band led by Eddie King, Walter Dyett '52-3. Pl. w. Ahmad Jamal '53-4; Don Shirley '54-5. In addition to musical activities, for a while he managed his father's restaurant business. Since leaving Shirley, has worked w. Benny Goodman, Sauter-Finegan, Ch. Ventura, but mainly w. Sarah Vaughan in late '50s, making tours of Europe and So. America w. her. During her vacation period, he worked w. Kenny Burrell '59. An excellent classical musician with exceptional bowing technique. Favs: Serge Koussevitsky, James Vhrel (Chicago Symphony), Oscar Pettiford. LPs w. Don Shirley (Cadence), Sarah Vaughan (Em.), Sam Most (Beth.), Paul Knopf (Playback), Ch. Ventura (Baton).

Addr: 1427 Nelson Ave., Bronx 52, N.Y.

DAVIS, SAMMY JR., *singer;* also *drums, vibes, etc.;* b. New York City, 12/8/25. On the road from infancy with uncle (Will Mastin) and father; was an official part of their vaudeville act from age four. Seen in movie *Rufus Jones for President* w. Ethel Waters 1931. Except for Army service '44-5, was part of Mastin trio until father and uncle retired from show business in late '50s. Rec. debut '49 for Cap.; soon gained wide acceptance as astonishingly accurate mimic for other singers. Rec. for Decca since '53, made new reputation as fine rhythmic vocalist in own style. Starred in Broadway musical *Mr. Wonderful* '56. His films include *Porgy and Bess* '59. A capable drummer, who has on occasion subbed in the Herman and Hampton bands, he also plays vibes, trumpet and other instruments. Own LPs on Decca, Design.

Addr: c/o William Morris Agency Inc., 1740 Broadway, New York, N.Y.

DAVIS, THOMAS MAXWELL, *tenor sax, composer;* b. Independence, Kansas, 1/14/16. Stud. violin, alto sax in Wichita, Kan., where he led his own band for 4 years. Switched to tenor while w. Gene Coy in Seattle. To LA 1937, pl. w. Fletcher Henderson. Worked three years in burlesque theatre; to San Diego w. Happy Johnson. Wrote arrangements for J. Lunceford off and on in early '40s. Played early JATP concerts. Spent 8 years as a & r man at Aladdin records in LA, writing, playing and directing r & b sessions until early '54, when he switched to Modern records. Recorded w. Horace Heidt, Ella Mae Morse, June Christy; many r & b dates w. Jesse Price, Geechie Smith, etc., on Capitol in mid-'40s. Feat. soloist on *Idaho* w. Ray Anthony (Cap.). Fav: Coleman Hawkins; fav. arr: Sy Oliver. Own LP: Aladdin.

Addr: 1458 East 82nd St., Los Angeles, Cal.

DAVIS, WALTER JR., *piano, composer;* b. East Orange, N.J., 9/2/32. Played around Newark, N.J., then to NYC w. Max Roach in 1952, making first records with him on Debut. With Dizzy Gillespie '56, incl. State Dept. tour of Europe and Middle East; European tour w. Donald Byrd, Art Taylor '58. Joined Art Blakey '59. Favs: Tatum, Bud Powell. Own LP: Blue Note; LPs w. Jackie McLean (Blue Note), Arthur Taylor (New Jazz), Gillespie (Verve).

Addr: 256 So. Clinton St., East Orange, N.J.

DAVIS, WILLIAM STRETHEN (Wild Bill), *organ, piano, composer;* b. Glasgow, Mo., 11/24/18. Played guitar and piano at school and in Milt Larkins' orch. '40. Pianist and arranger w. Louis Jordan '45-8. Began to specialize in Hammond organ '49 and by '50 had started a whole trend among jazz pianists, many of whom followed the fashion he had started by doubling on organ. Davis has a forceful style that earned him wide acceptance in r & b rather than jazz circles. From '51 toured with his own trio featuring guitar and drums. Arr. *April In Paris* for Count Basie. Own LPs: Epic, Evst., Imp.; LP w. Arnett Cobb (Pres.).

Addr: 114-18 179th St., St. Albans, L.I., N.Y.

DAVIS, WILLIAM E. (Will), *piano;* b. Chicago, Ill., 2/17/26. Father pl. clarinet. Stud. in Roanoke, Va. under private teacher, later at Detroit Cons. Pl. w. Snookum Russell and Paul Bascomb bands. W. Howard McGhee in Chi. 1946; in Detroit w. Milt Jackson, Sonny Stitt, Wardell Gray. At Crystal Bar w. own trio backed Coleman Hawkins, Lester Young, Charlie Parker and Miles Davis '53. Not yet widely known outside Detroit, but a potentially exciting talent in "funky" modern piano. Favs: Billy Kyle, Sir Charles Thompson, Bud Powell, Art Tatum, John Lewis. Rec. w. "Lord Nelson" (Sonny Stitt) for King '48. Own LP: Sue.

Addr: 8251 Carbondale, Detroit, Mich.

DAVISON, WILLIAM (Wild Bill), *cornet, leader;* b. Defiance, Ohio, 1/5/06. Pl. banjo, mellophone in high school band. Made record debut w. Chubb Steinberg orch. on OK, Apr. 1924. To Chicago '27, pl. w. theatre bands; from '33-40 had own groups in Milwaukee, also worked often in Chi. In NYC from '40, worked a year as leader at Nick's, then w. combo in Katherine Dunham show. Army '43-5; w. Art Hodes at Village Vanguard, then worked at Condon's club, with occasional leaves of absence, from '46 until '57. Since '57 he has visited Europe annually, fronting local Dixieland bands in Germany, Switzerland, Austria, and has led own quartet in US. One of the most colorful products of the Chicago jazz scene of the late '20s, Davison has what John S. Wilson has called "the cockiest, sassiest, even blowsiest trumpet style in jazz." Favs: Armstrong, Hackett. Own LPs: River., Col., Comm., Reg., Savoy, Dix. Jub.; LPs w. Sidney Bechet (Blue Note), Brother Matthew (ABC-Par), Eddie Condon (Col.), Bud Freeman (Em.), Tony Parenti (River.), George Wettling (Kapp), Garry Moore, *My Kind of Music* (Col.).

Addr: 22 Central Park South, New York 19, N.Y.

DAWSON, ALAN, *drums;* also *vibes;* b. Marietta, Pa., 7/14/29. Studied at Charles Alden Drum Studio in Boston 1947; drums first, then vibes two years later. Worked w. Frankie Newton '49, Sabby Lewis '50, Serge Chaloff '51; Army dance band '51-2, during which time he made app. on Elliot Lawrence TV show. Joined Lionel Hampton, Aug. '53 upon discharge from the Army, made European tour w. him. Stud. theory at Berklee school. Currently an instructor at that school; also pl. in Cambridge at coffee house w. John and Paul Neves. Own drum method book published in '60. Favs: Jo Jones, Catlett, Roach, Haynes. LPs w. Joe Viola, Berklee Faculty (Berklee), Quincy Jones (Merc.).

Addr: Berklee School of Music, 284 Newbury St., Boston, Mass.

DAWUD, TALIB AHMAD (Al Barrymore), *trumpet;* b. Antigua, B.W.I., 1/26/23. Father played trumpet w. concert bands; mother pl. piano and sang. Stud. banjo and organ in West Indies; father taught him trumpet. Stud. music at Benjamin Franklin High School and Juilliard. Formed own group in NYC, playing local gigs. Joined Tiny Bradshaw 1940, later w. Louis Armstrong, Benny Carter, Andy Kirk, Jimmy Lunceford, Roy Eldridge et al. Worked w. Dizzy Gillespie's big band '47-8 and again '57-8. Married singer Dakota Staton '58; owner of African imports shop in NYC, inactive in music, '59. Fav: Dizzy Gillespie.

DEAN, VINNIE (Vincent DiVittorio), *alto sax, flute;* b. Mt. Vernon, N.Y., 8/8/29. Pl. w. Shorty Sherock, Johnny Bothwell 1946, Charlie Spivak '47-8, Charlie Barnet '49, Elliott Lawrence '51-2, Stan Kenton '53, Eddie Bert combo '54. In mid-fifties pl. w. Carl Erca at Log Cabin in Armonk, N.Y. and managed own record store in Mt. Vernon which he later sold. In '59 he played a variety of jobs w. Benny Goodman, George Williams, Elliot Lawrence, Urbie Green, Hal McKusick, and led his own quartet at the Paddock in Yonkers. Has own recording studio, licensed booking agency and publishing company. Made record debut w. Charlie Spivak. Fav: Ch. Parker. LPs w. Kenton (Cap. incl. *Prologue* in *The Kenton Era*), *Winter Sequence* (MGM), Ch. Barnet (Evst.), Tony Bennett (Col.).

Addr: 39 Davenport Ave., New Rochelle, N.Y.

DE ARANGO, WILLIAM (Bill), *guitar;* b. Cleveland, Ohio, 9/20/21. Ohio St. U. Local groups '39-42; Army, '42-4. A year w. Ben Webster on 52nd St. NYC, then own group feat. Terry Gibbs in NYC and Chi; retired to Cleveland '48 and except for a record session for Mercury in NYC '54 has been in obscurity since then, despite a fleet, modern style that placed him among the vanguard of bop guitarists in the '40s. Won Esq. New Star Award '46. LPs w. Charlie Ventura (Em., Reg.), Ike Quebec in *The Angry Tenors* (Savoy).

Addr: 392 East 326th St., Willoughby, Ohio.

DEARIE, BLOSSOM, *singer, piano;* b. East Durham, N.Y., 4/28/26. Worked w. vocal groups in mid-1940s, incl. Blue Flames w. Woody Herman band and Blue Reys w. Alvino Rey; also pl. cocktail piano on many jobs. Went to Paris in 1952, singing in clubs there w. Annie Ross and forming a vocal group, The Blue Stars, for which she wrote some of the arrangements. Their jazz vocal version of *Lullaby of Birdland,* sung in French, was a big hit, both in France and the U.S. While in Paris, married Belgian tenor saxophonist Bobby Jaspar. Ret. to NYC, summer '56 and has since app. in night clubs like the Upstairs at the Downstairs, Versailles, singing to her own accompaniment. Own LPs on Verve; LP w. The Blue Stars (Em.).

Addr: 138 W. 10th St., New York, N.Y.

DE BREST, JAMES (Jimmy or Spanky), *bass;* b. Phila., Pa., 4/24/37. Worked locally w. Jimmy De Preist, Lee Morgan; joined Art Blakey, July '56, remaining w. him until Apr. '58. Gigs in Phila. until Nov. '58 when he joined Jay Jay Johnson. Favs: Heath, Pettiford, Brown, Ware. LPs w. Blakey (Col., Wor. Pac., Elek., Beth., Jub.), Ray Draper (Pres.), Jay Jay Johnson (Col.).

Addr: 315 E. 6th St., New York, N.Y.

DEDRICK, LYLE F. (Rusty), *trumpet, composer;* b. Delevan, N.Y., 7/12/18. Brother, Arthur, played trom. w. Red Norvo. Attended Fredonia State Teachers College; studied privately with Paul Creston and Stephan Wolpe. Worked w. Dick Stabile 1938-9, Red Norvo '39-41, Claude Thornhill '41-2. After Army service '42-5, he spent 3 months in Ray McKinley's band then rejoined Claude Thornhill '46-7, after which he settled in New York doing NBC-TV shows, records, etc., and arranging for Richard Maltby and others. Though not well-known as a jazzman, he has an exceptional tone and pleasant ad lib style. Favs: Louis Armstrong, Bunny Berigan, Miles Davis, Don Elliott. Own LPs: Ctpt.; *Counterpoint for Six Valves* w. Don Elliott (River.); LP w. Benny Payne (Kapp.).

Addr: 3 Tenth St., Carle Place, L.I., N.Y.

DEEMS, BARRETT, *drums;* b. Springfield, Ill., 3/1/14. At 15 joined Paul Ash; own groups on and off through '30s; Joe Venuti orch. '38-44; Red Norvo '48, Ch. Barnet '51, Muggsy Spanier '52. With Louis Armstrong May '54-Feb. '58. Own group at Brass Rail, Chi. '59-60. Film: *Rhythm Inn,* Universal '51. Book: *Drummer's Practice Routine* (publ. Martin Dixon, Miami). LPs w. Armstrong (Col., Decca).

DE FAUT, VOLTAIRE (Volly), *saxophones, clarinet;* b. Little Rock, Ark., 3/14/04. Stud. violin at six, clar. and sax at 14. Attended school in Chicago; pl. with New Orleans Rhythm Kings; w. Jean Goldkette in late 1920s. Did radio work '30-40, then in Army. Lived in Chicago in recent years. Rec. in '24 w. Jelly Roll Morton, Merritt Brunies on Autograph; Muggsy Spanier's Bucktown Five on Gennett. Latter rec. are now incl. in *Chicago Jazz* (River.).

DE FRANCO, BONIFACE FERDINAND LEONARDO (Buddy), *clarinet;* b. Camden, N.J., 2/17/23. Father a piano tuner. Clarinet at 12; won prize in Tommy Dorsey amateur contest; jammed at Billy Krechmer's sessions in Phila. Joined Scat Davis late '39; w. Gene Krupa '41-2; Ted Fio Rito '42; Charlie Barnet '43-4; Tommy Dorsey '44-6; settled in Calif., then joined Boyd Raeburn. Ret. to Dorsey Sept. '47-Sept. '48. Then numerous jobs w. small combos in NYC and Chi. Count Basie's septet in '50; own big band in '51; then own quartet in '52. Toured Europe w. Jazz Club USA in Jan. '54. After 1955, when De Franco settled in Calif., the popularity he had enjoyed as the first artist to bring modern jazz to the clarinet declined with unusual rapidity, partly because of his reluctance to leave Calif. He appeared in a mediocre film, *Wild Party,* in 1956. He recorded Nelson Riddle's *Cross Country Suite,* teamed with the composer and a large orchestra, and performed it with him at the Hollywood Bowl. In 1958-9 he undertook a brief recital tour and appeared at the Tri-State Music Festival in Enid, Okla. and the Rose Festival in Portland, Ore.

De Franco is a musician with a phenomenal technique, great scope, tone, fire and imagination. His poll winning achievements were accomplished with relatively little help from the critics, many of whom criticized his work as over-technical, mechanical, cold and unemotional. Musicians know better. The best measure of De Franco's talent is the list of those who voted for him in the "Musicians' Musicians" Poll conducted for the *Encyclopedia of Jazz* in 1956. His supporters included Count Basie (one of De Franco's warmest admirers before, during, and since Buddy's tenure in the Basie group), Teddy Charles, Jimmy Cleveland, Nat Cole, Bobby Hackett, Woody Herman, Horace Silver, Billy Taylor, and Lester Young. As they observed, De Franco's work is not the result of mere cerebration and automatic key pushing; it represents one of the high points in modern jazz improvisation.

De Franco won the *Down Beat* poll annually from 1945-54; DB critics poll in '53, and tied in '54; the Metronome poll from '50 through '55.

From the standpoint of pure improvisation the outstanding De Franco LPs are those he made with Art Tatum (Verve 8229) and with Oscar Peterson (Verve 8210). Own LPs: MGM 3396, *Autumn Leaves* (Verve 8183), *Broadway Showcase* (Verve 2033), *Cooking the Blues* (Verve 8221), *Bravura* (Verve 8315), *Cross-Country Suite* (Dot 9006), *Gershwin Song Book* (Verve 2022), *I Hear Goodman & Shaw* (Verve 2108), *In a Mellow Mood* (Verve 8169), *Jazz Tones* (Verve 8158), *Mr. Clarinet* (Verve 8159), *Odalisque* (Verve 8182), *Plays Artie Shaw* (Verve 2090), *Plays Benny Goodman* (Verve 2089), *Sweet & Lovely* (Verve 8224), *Wailers* (Verve 8175). LPs w. Lionel Hampton: *Air Mail Special* (Verve 8106), and others w. Hampton quintet (Verve); in *Hot vs. Cool* (MGM 3286, one track).

Addr: 3921 Hillcrest Drive, Los Angeles 8, Calif.

DE HAAS, EDGAR O. (Eddie), *bass;* also *guitar;* b. Bandoeng, Java, Indonesia, 2/21/30. Ukulele, 1940; played guitar in Hawaiian groups during Japanese occupation '42-5. Came to hear jazz through Rob Pronk, '46. Self taught; moved to Netherlands and took up bass in '51, joining Pia Beck. Toured Continent w. Wally Bishop, '52-3; France and N. Africa w. Bill Coleman and Martial Solal combos, '54-5; Henri Renaud '55; Iceland, Scandinavia, Italy, Germany w. Chet Baker '55-6. After leading own trio '56-7 he immigrated to US Feb. '57, worked w. Terry Gibbs, Sal Salvador, Miles Davis, B. Peiffer '57; K. Winding, B. Goodman, Toshiko, Blossom Dearie, Chris Connor '58-9. Orig. infl. Ch. Christian; favs. Pettiford, Ray Brown. LPs: *Swinging States* w. Winding (Col.), Chris Connor (Atl.); many dates in France w. Mezzrow, Dave Amram, Chet Baker et al.

Addr: 185 East 3rd St., New York, N.Y.

DELANEY, ERIC, *drums;* b. London, England, 5/22/24. From a musical family, he began pl. piano in school, drums w. private tutor in 1934. Stud. tympani at Guildhall School of Music '46-7. Studio recording and concert work '47-54. App. w. *Musical Express* Poll Winners concert '55-7. Favs: Bellson, Blakey, Woodyard, Krupa, Webb. Fav. own solo: *Mainly Delaney* (Merc., Nixa). Own LP: Merc.

Addr: 13 Alders Close, Edgeware, Middlesex, England.

DELANEY, JACK MICHAEL, *trombone;* b. New Orleans, La., 8/27/30. Studied Southeastern Louisiana College. Played w. Johnny Reininger 1949-51, Sharkey Bonano, '51-3, Tony Almerico '53-4, then rejoined Bonano. Also worked as staff member of WDSU—TV station in New Orleans. W. Sharkey Bonano '55-56; Tony Almerico '56-8. Since '58 w. Leon Kelner, "house band" in the Blue Room of Roosevelt Hotel. Fav: Jack Teagarden. Own LP on Southland; LPs w. Bonano (Cap., GTJ, South.), Almerico (Cook, Crescent City, South.), Lizzie Miles (Cook, Cap.), Los Angeles Dixieland Jubilee Concert '54 (Dix. Jub.), Monk Hazel (South.).

Addr: 1609 Oleander St., Metairie, La.

DENNIS, MATTHEW LOVELAND (Matt), *singer, composer, arranger, piano;* b. Seattle, Wash., 2/11/14. Led school band in San Rafael, Calif. Sang, played w. Horace Heidt 1933; formed band fronted by Dick Haymes; worked as arranger and vocal coach for Margaret Whiting, Martha Tilton. As staff arranger-composer in early 1940s w. Tommy Dorsey, wrote many of his biggest hit songs. After 3½ years in AAF, did radio work as arr. for top shows 1946-8, then settled in Los Angeles and worked there as single in supper clubs. Also annual visit to NYC clubs such as Living Room. Own color TV series on NBC, summer '55 incl. many jazz guest stars; also app. on Revlon Spectacular, Patti Page show '59, Dave Garroway Today show at different times '56-9. Pl. at Del Commodoro Hotel, Havana, Cuba '57. Most popular of his songs among jazz singers and musicians incl. *Everything Happens To Me, Angel Eyes, Let's Get Away From It All, Will You Still Be Mine? Violets For Your Furs.* Films: *Jennifer, The Bigamist.* Own LPs on Vict., Kapp, Jub.; LP w. Dave Garroway (Vict.).

Addr: 340 No. Camden Drive, Beverly Hills, Calif.

DENNIS, WILLIE, *trombone;* b. Philadelphia, Pa., 1/10/26. Mainly self-taught. Has played with bands of Elliot Lawrence, Claude Thornhill, Sam Donahue; traveled to Brussels w. Benny Goodman band and to Latin America w. Woody Herman '58. Also heard with many jazz combos incl. Howard McGhee, Ch. Ventura, C. Hawkins, L. Tristano, K. Winding. From 1956 made numerous appearances w. Ch. Mingus in Calif. and NYC. At Birdland and other clubs with

Buddy Rich Quintet '59. An adaptable musician who has shown himself equal to the considerable demands of the Mingus groups. LPs w. Ronnie Ball (Savoy), Mingus (Col.), Woody Herman (Everest, Verve), Elliot Lawrence (Vik), Buddy Rich (Mercury), Morgana King (Camden).

Addr: P.O. Box 31, Radio City Station, New York 19, N.Y.

DE PARIS, SIDNEY, *trumpet;* b. Crawfordsville, Ind., 5/30/05. To Washington w. Sam Taylor '24; Ch. Johnson orch. in NYC '26; McKinney's Cotton Pickers '31; Don Redman '32-6; then free-lancing with various groups around NYC, also w. Benny Carter '40-1, and Wilbur De Paris combo off and on since '43. LPs w. Wilbur De Paris (Atl.); four tracks w. Art Hodes in *Gems of Jazz,* Vol. 5 (Decca); w. Sidney Bechet (Blue Note), one track w. Bechet in *Great Jazz Reeds* (Cam.).

DE PARIS, WILBUR, *trombone;* b. Crawfordsville, Ind., 1/11/00. Studied w. father. Began career 1919 w. small band in Philadelphia. In '20s worked w. most of name Negro bands incl. Leroy Smith, Orig. Blue Rhythm band; to Europe w. Noble Sissle '31. In '30s w. Benny Carter; Teddy Hill in Europe '37; Louis Armstrong '38-41. In '40s w. Ella Fitzgerald, Roy Eldridge; Duke Ellington '45-7. After leaving Ellington reformed band he and brother Sidney had originated in '50s. For fifteen weeks, beginning March '57, toured Africa under auspices of State Dept. while Sidney maintained the group at Ryan's. App. on many TV programs incl. NBC's *The Subject Is Jazz* Apr. '58. Films: *The Small Hours, The Pirate, Windjammer.* Own LPs on Atlantic; LP w. Tony Scott (Coral).

Addr: 55 West 19th St., New York 11, N.Y.

DE PREIST, JAMES ANDERSON (Jimmy), *drums, tympani, composer;* b. Phila., Pa., 11/21/36. Nephew of Marian Anderson. Studied piano at age ten, drums in Phila. school system and privately w. Jules Benner. Pl. w. All Philadelphia High School orch., had own dance band during four years of high school. Became interested in jazz in senior year through Shelly Manne 78s. Formed own quintet while at U. of Penn. Won Music Soc. of Amer. award as best college jazz group in East, app. on Steve Allen show '56. Cond. and arr. for first Modern Music Festival at U. of Penn. '56. Group pl. college concerts and Red Hill Inn '57-8. Army, under six-month program, Aug. '58-Jan. '59. Randall's Island Jazz Festival, Phila. Jazz Fest. '59. Director of Contemporary Music Guild which put on a concert series in '59-60. Own ballet score, premiered at Phila. Academy of Music, Feb. '60. Favs: Max Roach, Mel Lewis; comp: Johnny Richards, John Lewis.

Addr: 764 So. Martin St., Phila., Pa.

DESMOND, PAUL (Breitenfeld), *alto sax;* b. San Francisco, Cal., 11/25/24. Father, once organist for silent movies, later worked with Fanchon & Marco, Paul Ash, Raymond Paige, as arranger. Paul studied clarinet at SF Polytechnic High and SF State. Joined Jack Fina '50, Alvino Rey '51, Dave Brubeck '51. Won DB critics' award as new star on alto '53, following rapid rise to fame through his many records w. Brubeck. Very light sound, clear tone, and swinging style, with very personal melodic lines, established him as one of the most important alto men of the '50s. In addition to his albums with Brubeck, he has recorded one outside LP a year (see below). With Brubeck, he toured with great success in England, on the Continent, including Poland, and through the Middle East in the Spring of '58; toured England again with NJF show Fall '59. Favs: Parker, Konitz, Pete Brown. Desmond has won the following polls: *Down Beat* poll '55-9; *Metronome* poll '55-60. Playboy Poll '57-60. Own LPs: War. Bros. 1356, Fant. 3235, one half on Fant. 3220; *Desmond-Mulligan Quartet* (Verve 8246); LPs w. Brubeck (q.v.).

Addr: 27 Deming, San Francisco 14, Calif.

DESVIGNES, SIDNEY, *cornet;* b. New Orleans, 9/11/1895; d. Pacoima, Cal., 12/2/59. Played at 101 Ranch Cafe in NO red light district; also w. Excelsior Brass Band, Maple Leaf Orch., and as second cornet to Louis Armstrong w. Fate Marable on riverboats, moving up to first cornet chair when Armstrong left to join King Oliver. Desvignes worked other riverboat jobs until '27, worked in NO '28-9, but was inactive after '32, moving to Calif. and later operating a restaurant. He is said to have made one obscure record date but there is little real information on the nature of his work.

DEUCHAR, JAMES (Jimmy), *trumpet, mellophone, composer;* b. Dundee, Scotland, 6/26/30. From musical family, studied trumpet and played in local jazz band. Joined Johnny Dankworth combo in London 1950; left '51; played w. J. Parnell '52, R. Scott '53-4, T. Crombie '55; toured w. L. Hampton '56; rejoined R. Scott and toured US w. him '57; then joined K. Edelhagen at radio station Cologne, Germany. One of Britain's best modern trumpets, Deuchar also contributed significantly, as a Dameron-influenced arranger-composer, to the libraries of Scott and others. Own LP: Contemporary.

DEVENS, GEORGE (Debella), *vibes, drums;* b. Bronx, N.Y., 8/24/31. Studied drums with Henry Adler, vibes with Phil Kraus, theory and harmony at High School of Music and Art. Worked with local groups until '54 when he joined George Shearing quintet. After leaving Shearing '55 he entered the commercial field, recording jingles, etc. and joined CBS as staff musician '58. Played on sound track of film *Island In The Sun.*

Addr: 17 Warren Place, Plainview, L.I., N.Y.

DE VILLERS, MICHEL, *baritone & alto saxophone;* b. Villeneuve sur Lot, France, 7/13/26. Self taught, from age 14, by listening to records. St. on alto. Pl. w. Django Reinhardt Quintet 1946. Toured Germany w. Don Byas, Bill Coleman, '47. Took up baritone '50. Rec. w. Buck Clayton, B. Coleman, Lucky Thompson, Reinhardt, Jonah Jones, K. Clarke and most leading French jazzmen. Has had regular radio series as disc jockey, also regular broadcasts w. Jack Diéval and own band. Won French critics' and fans polls as best French baritone. Favs: Parker, Stitt, alto. He is considered one of France's most interesting and original soloists.

Addr: 109 Ave. Pierre Brossolette, Montrouge, Seine, France.

DEVITO, FRANK ALBERT, *drums;* b. Utica, N.Y., 8/14/30. Stud. locally in 1942, then with Jim Chapin in NYC, 1948. Inspired by seeing Leo Gorcey in drum sequence in picture *Blues in the Night,* he made professional debut at 12. Played w. Bob Astor 1947, Ben Ventura '48, Buddy DeFranco '49 and '51, then w. Glen Gray and Hal McIntyre. Featured w. Terry Gibbs Quartet off and on '53-5. In '56-7 w. Nelson Riddle backing Frank Sinatra, then Dave Pell Octet. W. Betty Hutton night club act '57-9. Currently free-lance in LA area for records and TV, he has worked w. De Franco on many different occasions since '51. Film: *Wild Party* w. De Franco '56. Favs: Roach, Rich, Krupa. LPs w. Gibbs (Bruns.), De Franco (Verve), Steve Allen (Em.), Julius Wechter (Jazz: West).

Addr: 1850 N. La Brea, Hollywood 46, Calif.

DIAL, HARRY, *drums;* b. Birmingham, Ala., 2/17/07. Raised in St. Louis. In 1920s worked w. Charlie Creath and Fate Marable on riverboats; w. Dewey Jackson, Norman Mason; in Chicago from '28 w. Clifford King, Jerome Pasquale. Worked w. Louis Armstrong '33; Sam Wooding '34. Recorded w. Alex Hill, Fats Waller '34. Played maracas on Ella Fitzgerald-Louis Jordan date '45. Since '51 working as safe deposit manager at Chemical Corn Exchange bank in NYC, also working gigs w. own band occasionally; from July '55 part of Les Boone trio at Lucky's in Brooklyn.

Addr: 545 Edgecombe Ave., New York, N.Y.

DICKENSON, VICTOR (Vic), *trombone;* b. Xenia, Ohio, 8/6/06. Local bands around Columbus from 1922, joined Speed Webb '27, then with Zack Whyte, Blanche Calloway, Benny Moten. First prominent in jazz circles with Claude Hopkins' band '36-9. Featured w. Benny Carter '40; Count Basie, March '40 to June '41; then w. Hot Lips Page, Sidney Bechet, Frankie Newton. Moved to Calif. Inactive for some time owing to illness but played with Eddie Heywood '43-5. Returning East, he free-lanced with many bands around Boston and NYC. Dickenson established himself during the '40s as one of the great individualists of the trombone, playing with a sometimes humorous, always intensely rhythmic style on fast numbers and with great warmth and personality on slower tunes. Although equally admired by jazzmen of new and old schools he worked mostly with Dixieland groups from the late '40s on, incl. Red Allen at Metropole '58. One quartet at Arpeggio, NYC, summer '59. TV app: *The Magic Horn, The Sound of Jazz* '57. Won *Esquire* Silver Award '46-7. Own LPs: Vang., Des., *Mainstream* (Atl.); LPs w. Ruby Braff (Vict., Vang.), Eddie Condon (Col.), Lester Young (Epic, Alad.), Eddie Heywood (Decca, Comm.), *The Jazz Giants '56* (Verve), Jonah Jones (Beth.), LaVern Baker (Atl.), Jimmy Rushing, Count Basie, Buck Clayton (Vang.), Rushing (Col.), Ed Hall (Comm.).

Addr: 1312 Stebbins Ave., Bronx, N.Y.

DI NOVI, EUGENE (Gene), *piano;* b. Brooklyn, N.Y., 5/26/28. Pl. w. Henry Jerome 1943, J. Marsala '44; B. Raeburn, B. Rich '45-6; solo at Three Deuces NYC, and w. Chuck Wayne, Stan Hasselgard '47-8; Anita O'Day, Chubby Jackson '49. Peggy Lee off and on '51-5, Tony Bennett '52-3. Solo at Show Spot NYC '53-4. From '55 until Aug. '59 was accompanist to Lena Horne, incl. job in pit band for her Broadway show *Jamaica* '57-9. With Benny Goodman at Basin St. Nov. '59, then free-lanced in NYC. Fav: Tatum. Rec. w. Marsala, Aaron Sachs, Artie Shaw, Chubby Jackson. LPs w. Brew Moore in *In The Beginning . . . Bebop* (Savoy), Lester Young (Aladdin), Benny Goodman (MGM).

DI PIPPO, ANGELO, *accordion;* b. Providence, R.I., 9/6/29. Father and five brothers amateur musicians. Began stud. accordion 1938; grad. from college '51, then came to NYC to study and play '52. Toured Europe summer '50 with college group; worked clubs in NYC '57-8; appeared at Newport Jazz Festival summer '58. Favs: Art Van Damme, Leon Sash. Own LP on Apollo.

DISTEL, SACHA, *guitar, singer;* b. Paris, France 1/29/33. Nephew of noted bandleader and producer, Ray Ventura. Stud. piano at 5; guitar from 1948. Started in college band; won amateur contest. Worked w. Bernard Peiffer, 1952; Henri Renaud, Sandy Mosse, Bobby Jaspar '53, also w. Martial Solal, Barney Wilen, Rene Urtreger, Kenny Clarke. Recently featured as singer though best known as outstanding modern jazz guitarist. Favs: Ch. Parker, K. Burrell, J. Raney, Tal Farlow, Ch. Christian. LPs w. Lionel Hampton, Bobby Jaspar (Em.), John Lewis (Atl.); own LP for Fr. Versailles label.

DIXON, ERIC, *tenor sax, flute;* b. Staten Island, N.Y., 3/28/30. Studied w. Peter Luisetti from 1946. Prof. debut in '50. W. Johnny Hodges '54, Cootie Williams '55, Bill English in late '50s in NYC. Favs: Paul Gonsalves, Eddie Davis. LPs w. Bennie Green (Pres.), Mal Waldron (New Jazz).

DIXON, JOSEPH (Joe), *clarinet, reeds;* b. Lynn, Mass., 4/21/17. Stud. clarinet at 8 w. local bandmaster in Malden, Mass., later w. symphony clarinetist in Boston. Stud. harmony at New England Conservatory. Had small combos for high school dances; worked w. Bill Staffon, 1934; in house band at Adrian Rollini's after hours room; T. Dorsey, 1936-7 (feat. w. Clambake Seven); G. Arnheim, 1937 (S. Kenton was in band); Bunny Berigan, 1938. During '40s worked at Condon's; w. Miff Mole at Nick's. Had own quintet in New York area in late '50s. Fav: own record: *I'm Coming Virginia* and *Carolina in the Morning* w. Brad Gowans (Vict.). Favs: D. Murray, I. Fazola, Goodman, De Franco, T. Scott. LPs w. T. Dorsey (Vict.); Miff Mole (Stepheny).

Addr: 214 Bayfield Blvd., Oceanside, L.I., N.Y.

DODDS, WARREN (Baby), *drums;* b. New Orleans, La., 12/24/98; d. Chicago, 2/14/59. Early associate of Louis Armstrong, Papa Celestin, King Oliver, playing NO and Mississippi riverboats until '21, when he went to SF w. Oliver. Worked with Lil Armstrong, Willie Hightower, and was frequently associated w. his brother, Johnny Dodds, until the latter's death in '40. With Jimmie Noone '41, Bunk Johnson '44, Mezz Mezzrow in France, then with Bob Wilber, and later in Chicago w. Lee Collins. Made many records w. Jelly Roll Morton, Johnny Dodds, Sidney Bechet, and with own group. Considered by Louis Armstrong and his other contemporaries to be the outstanding exponent of early NO drums. He won R. Ch. All Time, All Star poll, 1951.

Baby Dodds has been widely praised by musicians and students of the early jazz years. Jazzmen from Louis Armstrong to Max Roach have praised him; German critic Joachim-Ernst Berendt called him "one of the greatest figures in New Orleans jazz" and Nat Hentoff wrote (in *Jazz Makers*): "Increasingly overlooked have been the intrinsic values of Baby's style; his developed insights into the basic nature of jazz drumming; elements in his work that . . . helped to form certain aspects of modern jazz percussion." Opinion about Dodds is less than unanimous; *The Heart of Jazz* by Grossman & Farrell stated that under the right conditions Dodds had no superior, but conceded that he had "an occasional tendency to overexuberance that is sometimes damaging in ensembles." George Simon observed in *Metronome:* "Dodds, when he plays for the band instead of the crowd (which is very seldom) is the great drummer I'd always heard he was. But . . . he goes through all sorts of antics and gyrations, constantly messing up the beat with all sorts of explosions and tom-toms, cowbells, rims etc., that detract tremendously." These qualities, along with a lumpish use of the bass drum, are discernible even in some of Dodds' records, recorded when no crowd was present. Own LP: *Talking* and *Drum Solos* (Folkways FP 30); *Baby Dodds No. 2* (Amer. Music); LPs w. J. Dodds (Epic 3207), Albert Nicholas in *Creole Reeds* (River. 12-216), Louis Armstrong (Col. CL 851, CL 852, River. 12-122); Bunk Johnson (River. 12-119, Amer. Mus. 638, 647), George Lewis (Amer. Mus. 638, 645).

DODDS, JOHNNY, *clarinet;* b. New Orleans, 4/12/1892; d. Chicago, 8/8/40. Brother of Baby Dodds. Self-taught; worked various non-music jobs, playing first full-time music engagement w. Kid Ory in 1911. Remaining w. Ory until 1918, he then went on tour w. Billy Mack, working w. Mutt Carey, and made his first trip to Chicago. After returning home and working w. Ory again, he went back to Chicago in 1920 to join King Oliver, spending four years with him in the famous band that pl. at the Lincoln Gardens, in addition to playing in Calif. in 1921. From about 1926, Dodds was heard frequently on records w. Louis Armstrong, Jelly Roll Morton, Oliver and w. various groups under his own name. In the late 1920s, Dodds led his own orch., mostly at Kelly's Stable in Chicago. His musical career came to a virtual halt between 1930 and '38, when both he and his brother fell on hard times and had to drive taxis for a living. Dodds came to NYC in Jan. 1938 to take part in record session for Decca; he recorded again in Chicago shortly before his death, which was caused by a cerebral hemorrhage.

Johnny Dodds has been ranked by many students of New Orleans jazz w. Jimmie Noone among the top clarinetists of this school. In Charles Edward Smith's *Jazz Record Book,* it was claimed that "Those who appreciated exceptional warmth of tone and freedom in improvised ensembles will insist that Dodds never made a bad record . . . his playing was always on such a high, uncompromisingly hot plane that his excellence was often taken for granted." The late Eugene Williams, a prominent critic of New Orleans jazz, called him "unsurpassed on his instrument among Crescent City jazzmen." André Hodeir, however, has described Dodds as musically deficient and called his technique rudimentary. Dodds won the R. Ch. All Time, All Star poll '51. Own LPs: *New Orleans Clarinet* (River. 12-104), *Johnny Dodds and Kid Ory* (Epic 3207); single nos. in *Great Jazz Reeds* (Cam. 339), *Guide To Jazz* (Vict. LPM 1393); LPs w. Armstrong (Col. CL 851, CL 852, River. 12-122), King Oliver (Epic 3208); *History of Classic Jazz* (River. SDP 11).

DODGE, JOSEPH GEORGE (Joe), *drums;* b. Monroe, Wis., 2/9/22. Raised in San Francisco, stud. w. SF symphony drummer. Army '42-Jan. '46, then formed group w. Paul Desmond '47, toured w. Nick Esposito '48-9. Day job at bank '50-3, working occasionally w. Jack Sheedy Dixieland combo. Toured w. Dave Brubeck Dec. '53-Sept. '56. Since then has again worked day job and gigged on weekends with band at Oakland ballroom etc. Favs: Roach, Blakey. LPs w. Brubeck (Col.).

DODGION, JERRY, *alto sax, flute;* b. Richmond, Calif., 8/29/32. Started on alto in junior high school. Worked with local bands around Richmond and San Francisco. Pl. w. Gerald Wilson band, 1954-5; w. Benny Carter, Las Vegas, '55; Vernon Alley Quartet in SF, '55-6. Joined Red Norvo quintet March '58, visiting Australia with him in Frank Sinatra show, April '59 and touring Europe w. Norvo as part of the Benny Goodman group, Oct. '59. LPs: Benny Goodman (MGM); *Beauties of 1918* w. Charlie Mariano (Wor. Pac.); two quartet nos. w. Vince Guaraldi in *Modern Music From San Francisco* (Fant.); solo on *Do Nothing Till You Hear From Me* w. Dinah Shore-Norvo.

Addr: c/o Norvo, 420 Alta Ave., Santa Monica, Calif.

DOGGETT, WILLIAM BALLARD (Bill), *organ, piano, composer;* b. Philadelphia, Pa., 2/16/16. Piano w. Jimmy Gorman; his own band 1938; Jimmy Mundy, Lucky

Millinder '40. Piano and arranger w. Ink Spots '42-4. Later worked w. Louis Jordan and was greatly influenced by Bill Davis, whom he replaced in this band. Took up organ '51, accompanied Ella Fitzgerald on *Smooth Sailing, Rough Riding, Airmail Special.* Records, and tours, w. own Hammond organ combo. During the middle and late '50s, Doggett enjoyed great commercial success as a rhythm and blues attraction on a series of hit records, playing in an aggressive style comparable with that of Wild Bill Davis. Won *Cashbox* award as top r & b performer, '57-9. Own LPs: King; LPs w. Illinois Jacquet: other side of *Rex Stewart Plays Duke Ellington* (Gr. Award); four tracks w. Ike Quebec in *The Angry Tenors* (Savoy).

DOLNEY, WILLIAM (Bill), *drums;* b. Bronx, N.Y., 9/27/31. Stud. drums w. Henry Adler in NYC; joined Alvino Rey June 1949 and went to West Coast with him. W. Charlie Barnet June '52; Jack Montrose '56. Joined Buddy Collette Nov. '56. Fav: Kenny Clarke. LPs w. Buddy Collette (Contemp., ABC-Par.); Jack Montrose (Vict.).

Addr: 408 La Paloma Ave., Alhambra, Calif.

DOLNY, JOSEPH, *composer, trumpet;* b. Cleveland, Ohio, 3/14/24. Stud. tpt. at 11. St. arranging 1944 while in service, but did not study until '51 when he att. Westlake Coll. in LA. Pl. w. Bobby Sherwood, '46; Buddy Rich, '47; had small group called the Quintones, '47-50; pl. w. C. Thornhill, '50, J. Wald '51; then did radio and TV work. More recently w. Jerry Gray, Ray Anthony, Harry James. Had had one of best rehearsal groups in LA for some time. Many arrs for Si Zentner, Ralph Mendez et al. Favs: Miles Davis, Gil Evans. Own LP: Era.

Addr: 1508 Sanborn Ave., Los Angeles 27, Cal.

DOLPHY, ERIC ALLAN, *alto sax, clarinet, flute, bass clarinet;* b. Los Angeles, Calif., 6/20/28. Began stud. clar. 1937 in LA. Worked w. George Brown, Gerald Wilson, Buddy Collette; w. Eddie Beal '56; Chico Hamilton '58-9. Favs: Buddy Collette, Charlie Parker. LP w. Chico Hamilton (Warner Bros.).

Addr: 1593 W. 36th St., Los Angeles, Calif.

DOMINIQUE, ANATIE (Natty), *trumpet;* b. New Orleans, 8/2/1896. Studied w. Emanuel Perez and worked w. latter's Imperial band. After World War I, worked in Chicago w. Jimmie Noone for two years, Carroll Dickerson four years, and various clubs around Chicago w. Johnny and Baby Dodds, Geo. Filhe. Retired and became redcap at airport, emerging occasionally to play w. Baby Dodds and others. Recorded in '20s w. Jelly Roll Morton, Johnny Dodds; also in '40 w. Dodds and Noone. LPs w. Johnny Dodds (River.), Baby Dodds (Amer. Mus.).

DOMINO, ANTOINE (Fats), *piano, singer, songwriter;* b. New Orleans, La., 2/26/28. Father played violin and an uncle had worked w. Kid Ory and Oscar Celestin. Began picking out tunes on piano at home and when he was 10 was playing for pennies in local bars, but during early youth did factory work. Re-learned piano after an accident to his hand. His reputation among musicians led a record scout to a roadhouse where he was playing and he was signed to almost immediate success during the rock-'n'-roll craze. Has toured widely w. own group since, playing in clubs, for dances and in theatres throughout the U.S. Appeared in the film *The Girl Can't Help It.* Even on the pop material he performs, he manages to show himself an authentic blues singer; has also composed several fine blues. Many LPs for Imp.

Addr: c/o Shaw Artists Corp., 565 Fifth Ave., New York 17, N.Y.

DOMNERUS, ARNE, *alto sax, clarinet;* b. Stockholm, Sweden, 12/20/24. Started w. Thore Ehrling and Simon Brehm bands; played at Paris Jazz Festival, '49. Since '51 he has had his own combo, members of which have included Lars Gullin, Gunnar Svensson and other leading Swedish jazzmen from time to time. Though best known as Sweden's foremost alto star, he is also a capable clarinet soloist. LPs: *Swedish Modern Jazz* (Cam.), *Swedes From Jazzville* (Epic); w. George Wallington in *Swingin' In Sweden,* Harry Arnold-Quincy Jones (EmArcy), Clifford Brown (Pres.).

DONAHUE, SAM KOONTZ, *tenor sax, trumpet, arranger, leader;* b. Detroit, Mich., 3/8/18. While in school was offered first prof. job at newly legalized beer garden in River Rouge, Mich. Own band, 1933-8; played w. Gene Krupa 1938-40; w. Harry James, Benny Goodman '40. Own band in NYC and on Bluebird, Okeh records '40-2; then entered Navy, where he took over leadership of Artie Shaw's Navy band, 1944-5. This outfit played a battle of music against Glenn Miller's AAF orch. in London; Donahue became big wartime favorite through broadcasts in Britain. After discharge, had own band again and acted as teacher at Hartnett Studios, NYC, until '51, when he spent six months back in the Navy. After this, he worked w. Tommy Dorsey, and in Jan. '54 was chosen to front the Billy May band on tour which he did through '56. From '57-9, he led his own band, appearing at Birdland and the Blue Note '57. Own LPs on Cap., Prescott; LPs w. Billy May (Cap.), Jerry Fielding (Kapp).

Addr: PO Box 1149, Lake Worth, Fla.

DONALDSON, ROBERT STANLEY (Bobby), *drums;* b. Boston, Mass., 11/29/22. Many musicians in family incl. eldest brother Don, who was mus. dir. for Fats Waller in late 1930s. Played with Tasker Crosson and other local bands 1939-41. Army 1941-5, played in service band with Russell Procope in NYC. Toured with Cat Anderson '46; studied at Schillinger House '47; worked with Paul Bascomb, Willis Jackson, also at Cafe Society with Edmond Hall from 1950-2. Gigged with Sy Oliver, Lucky Millinder, Andy Kirk; 1953-4 with Buck Clayton in Basin Street; Benny Goodman; Red Norvo at Metropole, Dorothy Donegan, Eddie Condon, and many other combos. Heard with Max Kaminsky, Teddy Wilson '58, then joined Eddie Heywood. Favs: Jo Jones, Shadow Wilson, Buddy Rich. Own LPs: World Wide, Gold. Cr., Savoy; LPs w.

Herbie Mann-Bobby Jaspar (Pres.), Mel Powell, Buck Clayton-Ruby Braff (Vang.), Heywood (Merc., Vict.), *Spirit of Charlie Parker* (WW).

Addr: 52 Wellesley St., Hempstead, L.I., N.Y.

DONALDSON, LOU, *alto sax;* b. Badin, N.C., 11/1/26. Son of a preacher and a music teacher. Studied with mother, took up clar. at 15. Attended college at Greensboro, obtained much of musical training while in Navy, then completed training at Darrow Institute in '50 and sat in w. Parker, Stitt et al. Came to NYC and began recording for Blue Note, first w. Horace Silver, then under own name. Forced to work r & b gigs by necessity, he has also led his own jazz group in the East; mainly in NYC clubs like the Five Spot, Half Note, The Play House, Smalls. Critic John Wilson has said of him: "He mixes a warm, full tone, remarkable dexterity and a roaring sense of swing but has little resort to stylistic crutches . . . unlike most other neo-Parkerites, he can project a ballad with deeply felt expression." Own LPs on Blue Note; LPs w. Art Blakey, Jimmy Smith, Milt Jackson, T. Monk (Blue Note), Gene Ammons (Pres.).

Addr: 471 Swinton Ave., Bronx, N.Y.

DONEGAN, DOROTHY, *piano;* b. Chicago, Ill., 4/6/24. Studied at Chicago Cons., Chi. Mus. Coll., USC. Church organist in Chi., then pl. cocktail lounges; to Hollywood to appear in *Sensations of 1945* film. To NYC '45, did Broadway play, *Star Time,* then toured with it. Popular in night clubs such as the Embers since then, first pl. boogie woogie and swinging the classics, recently in more modern jazz style. Much of her appeal, however, is based on her visual antics. Favs: Tatum, V. Horowitz. Early records on Continental, Decca, Vict. Own LPs: Jub., Roul., Cap.

Addr: 676 St. Nicholas Ave., New York 30, N.Y.

DORHAM, McKINLEY HOWARD (Kenny), *trumpet;* also *tenor sax;* b. Fairfield, Texas, 8/30/24. Mother and sister played piano, father guitar. Piano at seven, trumpet in high school in Austin, Tex. Professional start through Wiley College band (Wild Bill Davis was also a member). Army '42 where he was on boxing team. Joined Russell Jacquet '43, Frank Humphries '44, Dizzy Gillespie '45, Billy Eckstine '46, Lionel Hampton '47, Mercer Ellington '48. W. Charlie Parker '48-50, app. w. Bird at Paris Jazz Festival '49. Freelanced in NYC, '51-5, then joined Art Blakey's Jazz Messengers '55. Formed own Jazz Prophets in early '56. In June '56 replaced Clifford Brown in Max Roach quintet. On faculty of School of Jazz, Lenox, Mass. summers '58-9. Own group at Five Spot, NYC late '58. Own rehearsal band '59. Films: sound track work for *A Song Is Born* MGM; composed the score, acted and played in French film, *Witness In The City* '59; app. in French *Dangerous Liaisons* '59. Made LP as vocalist for River. '58. Favs: Miles Davis, Dizzy Gillespie. A sure-fingered, assertive hornman whose flowing style has left its influences far enough behind to be an immediately recognizable, independent voice. Own LPs: Blue Note, River., ABC-Par., New Jazz; LPs w. Max Roach (Em., Argo), Sonny Rollins, Hank Mobley, Tadd Dameron, J. J. Johnson (Pres.), Art Blakey, Lou Donaldson, Monk, Silver (Blue Note), Herb Geller (Jub.), Charlie Parker (Verve), Ernie Henry, Matthew Gee (River.), Oliver Nelson (New Jazz).

Addr: 1242 Sterling Place, Brooklyn, N.Y.

DOROUGH, ROBERT LROD (sic) (Bob), *piano, singer, composer;* b. Cherry Hill, Ark., 12/12/23. Stud. clar. at Plainview, Texas high school and Texas Tech.; comp. and piano at N. Texas State Coll. Two yrs. acc. & arr. for Sugar Ray Robinson in US, Canada, France. Five months at Mars Club, Paris, '54-5. Own trio in NYC, '55-6; Chicago, '57, then had various combos in and around LA. Has a curious, nervous and attractive swinging vocal style and is competent modern pianist. Favs: Powell, Silver, D. Jordan, J. Lewis. Fav. singers: Teagarden, Armstrong, Mama Yancey. Own LP: Beth.; LPs w. Sam Most (Beth; incl. own fav. solo *Hushabye*); *Jazz Canto* (Wor. Pac.).

Addr: 518 Frontenac, Los Angeles 65, Cal.

DORSEY, JAMES (Jimmy), *clarinet, alto sax;* b. Shenandoah, Pa., 2/29/04; d. 6/12/57. Father, a music teacher, taught him cornet first. Made first appearance at eight, playing in father's brass band at local parades. Two years later Dorsey Sr. gave Jimmy a tenor sax and then an alto; he took up clarinet later but never formally studied it. At 17, worked with Scranton Sirens and Jean Goldkette; at 18, broadcast with the Dorsey Novelty band over Baltimore's first radio station. During the '20s he toured with the Calif. Ramblers, Paul Whiteman and Red Nichols; became outstanding jazz figure on alto sax, comparable with Lee Konitz or Charlie Parker today. After playing in many commercial radio bands, Jimmy formed an orchestra with brother Tommy, which incl. Glenn Miller, Ray McKinley and Bob Crosby; this lasted from '33-5, when Tommy left to form his own band. Jimmy went on to big commercial success with a unit featuring vocals by Bob Eberly and Helen O'Connell, hitting his commercial peak in the early '40s. His theme was *Contrasts.* Film: *The Fabulous Dorseys,* 1947, with Tommy. In '53 he gave up his band to join Tommy's orch. which he continued to lead after Tommy's death until illness forced him to turn it over to Lee Castle.

Ironically, a single record that Jimmy Dorsey made some months before his death for the Fraternity label, *So Rare,* had risen rapidly in public acceptance and was his first hit in several years.

Though generally not highly rated as a jazz musician in the later stages of his career, Dorsey was a fine technician and once had an influential solo style. He won the *DB* poll on alto '37-9, *Met.* poll '39-41. Own LPs on Decca, Lion, Frat., Col., Epic; w. Dorsey Bros. in *Five Feet of Swing* (Decca) and on Design, Col.; LPs w. *Jazz of The Roaring Twenties* (River.), Ted Lewis, Red Norvo (Epic), Paul Whiteman (Gr. Award).

DORSEY, THOMAS (Tommy), *trombone, leader;* b. Shenandoah, Pa., 11/19/05; d. Greenwich, Conn., 11/26/56.

In early years he was equally well-known as both trumpet and trombone player, recording several hot jazz solos on trumpet in '27. His career closely followed that of Jimmy Dorsey (q.v.); by '30 he was one of the most successful free-lance radio and recording artists on trombone, recognized both for his exceptional tone and legato style on ballads and for his fine solos on faster tempi. *I'm Getting Sentimental Over You* was first recorded Sept. 24, '32 by a pick-up recording group under the Dorsey brothers; in '35, when Tommy quit Jimmy to form a band of his own from the remnants of Joe Haymes' orchestra, this became his theme number. Among those who worked in the Dorsey orchestra were Bunny Berigan, Pee Wee Erwin, Charlie Spivak, Yank Lawson, Charlie Shavers and Ziggy Elman, trumpets; Johnny Mince, Buddy De Franco, clarinets; Bud Freeman, tenor sax; Joe Bushkin, piano; Dave Tough, Louis Bellson, drums; and many popular singers such as Frank Sinatra, Jo Stafford, Connie Haines, Pied Pipers, Lucy Ann Polk; arrangers included Sy Oliver, Paul Weston, and Axel Stordahl.

After the brothers were reunited in '53, the Dorsey Brothers orch., led mainly by Tommy, but with Jimmy prominently featured, earned national publicity in '55-6 through the Dorseys' own TV program, *Stage Show*, on CBS. During this period, the band worked frequently at the Statler Hotel, NYC.

Dorsey died suddenly at his country home. Death was caused by strangulation due to food particles. In the fall of '57 an orch. designed as the Tommy Dorsey band, under the direction of trombonist Warren Covington, was organized and toured dance halls throughout the US.

Dorsey's biggest selling record was *Boogie-Woogie*, reputed to have sold four million. Some of his records were of a semi-jazz nature, made occasionally with a small contingent from the band which he called the Clambake Seven. Many of his biggest hits such as *I'll Never Smile Again* belong strictly in the popular music field. Won *DB* poll '36-9, *Met.* poll '37, '39-46. Own LPs: Vict., Decca, Col., Voc.; w. Dorsey Bros. in *Five Feet of Swing* (Decca 8045) and on Design, Col.; LPs w. *Jazz of the Roaring Twenties* (River. 12-801); nos. w. all star group in *A String of Swingin' Pearls* (Vict. LPM 1373); Paul Whiteman (Gr. Award).

DOUGLAS, THOMAS (Tommy), *clarinet and reed inst.;* b. Eskridge, Kans., 11/9/11. Educ. at Boston Cons., Boston, Mass. 1924-8, where he was an associate of Johnny Hodges, Harry Carney, Otto Hardwicke. Worked w. George E. Lee, Jelly Roll Morton, Jap Allen and Bennie Moten '27-31; had own large orchestras from '30-42, one of which became the nucleus of Harlan Leonard's Rockets in '36. Musicians who pl. in his bands include Paul Webster, Eddie Tompkins, Jo Jones, Charlie Parker, Fred Beckett, Ted Donnelly et al. In recent years has led combos around Missouri. Favs: Hodges, Carney, Buster Smith, Buster Bailey, Omer Simeon, Ed Hall. Rec. for Capitol under own name and w. Julie Lee; also w. Lee on Merc. LP: one number in *History of Jazz, Vol. 3* (Cap.).

Addr: 1111 E. 22nd St., Kansas City, Mo.

DOUGLASS, WILLIAM (Bill) *drums;* b. Los Angeles, Calif., 2/28/23. Stud. at Westlake College of Music. Has worked w. Benny Goodman, Ben Webster, Benny Carter, Art Tatum mostly around Los Angeles, and has accompanied June Christy, Lena Horne, Kay Starr and other singers. Teaching at "Drum City" and free-lancing in Hollywood 1960. Favs: Jo Jones, B. Rich, C. Cole, S. Catlett. LPs w. Cal Tjader, Gus Mancuso (Fant.), Art Tatum-DeFranco, Tatum-Webster (Verve), Harry Babasin (Merc.), Gerry Wiggins (Dig, Spec.), Red Norvo (Lib., Tampa, Vict.), Red Callender (MGM).

DOWDY, BILL, *drums;* b. Benton Harbor, Mich., 8/15/33. Began pl. drums in high school and worked in a trio on weekend gigs and radio programs. After grad. joined Rupert Harris' band, then in Army until 1954. Went to Chicago and stud. drums at Roosevelt U. gigging around w. blues bands and pl. w. Johnny Griffin, J. J. Johnson and others who passed through. In '56 formed The Four Sounds in South Bend, Ind.; group later became The Three Sounds and worked around Washington, D.C., then to NYC Sept. '58. Group comprised Dowdy, drums; Andrew Simpkins, bass; Gene Harris, piano. LPs w. The Three Sounds, Lou Donaldson (Blue Note), Nat Adderley (Riverside).

DRAKES, JESSE, *trumpet;* b. New York City, 10/22/26. Studied at Juilliard 1944. Played w. Savoy Sultans '45, then w. J. C. Heard, Sid Catlett, Eddie Heywood, Gene Ammons combos. From '49-55, heard mostly w. Lester Young. Own combo in Wash., D.C. '55; also w. Harry Belafonte, Louis Bellson '55. Back w. Young '55-6. Pl. w. Duke Ellington, March '56. Pl. w. band at Eden Roc hotel, Miami Beach '59. LPs w. Young (Savoy, Verve).

Addr: 112 West 117th St., New York, N.Y.

DRAPER, RAYMOND ALLEN (Ray) *tuba;* b. New York City, 8/3/40. Father, Barclay, played tpt. w. name bands; mother concert pianist. Got into High School of Performing Arts after auditioning on tuba. Jazz Unlimited sessions with own group at The Pad and Birdland, winter '56-7. Documentary film w. All City High Sch. Symphony, '57. Comp. *Fugue For Brass Ensemble* played at NYU; working on symphony. He toured w. Max Roach combo in '58-9. Fav: Bill Barber. Own LPs on Pres., Jub.; LPs w. Jackie McLean (Jub., Pres.), Max Roach (River., Merc.).

Addr: 50 West 106th Street, New York 25, N.Y.

DRASNIN, ROBERT JACKSON (Bob), *flute, reeds;* b. Charleston, W. Va., 11/17/27. Raised in Los Angeles where he stud. reeds and flute. Had own combo in college at UCLA. During 1950s worked w. L. Brown, A. Rey, T. Dorsey et al. Grad. work in comp. at UCLA, 1954-7; associate conductor UCLA Symphony. With Red Norvo quint. '56-8. Fav. own solo: *Get Out of Town* w. Norvo (Lib.). Favs: Goodman, Shaw,

Parker, Gillespie, Getz. LPs w. Norvo (Vict., Lib., Tampa).

Addr: 7873 Ranchito Ave., Van Nuys, Calif.

DREARES, ALBERT ALFRED (Al), *drums;* b. Key West, Fla., 1/4/29. Father pl. tpt. Stud. at Hartnett Cons. in NYC 1949. Toured w. Paul Williams band '53-4. Pl. w. Teddy Charles, '55; Ch. Mingus, Randy Weston, '56; Freddie Redd, Kenny Burrell, '57; Gigi Gryce, '58, Jerome Richardson, Phineas Newborn, '59; also w. own and other small combos around NYC. LPs w. Weston, Redd (Riverside), Bennie Green (Blue Note). Greatly influenced by Fats Navarro, whom he knew when they were children in Key West. Favs: Art Blakey, Philly Joe Jones.

Addr: 561 Bainbridge St., Brooklyn, N.Y.

DREW, JOHN DEREK, *bass;* b. Sheffield, Yorkshire, England, 12/23/27. Stud. piano as child, took up bass in Liverpool at 16; private teacher. To London, pl. w. show and pop bands incl. 2 yrs. w. Billy Ternent on BBC etc. Immigrated to US 1954. Worked w. Les Elgart, went to West Coast; w. Gene Krupa '56 as first bassist to augment trio to quartet; also w. Stan Getz '56. App. and rec. w. Neal Hefti, Nat Pierce bands. 1957 season with Miami Symphony, also w. Barbara Carroll trio. Free-lanced in NYC incl. acc. Peggy Lee '58; Marian McPartland, Sauter-Finegan et al in NYC, '59. Orig. infl.: Blanton. Favs: Ray Brown, Red Mitchell, M. Hinton. Polished, swinging modern bassist. LPs w. Toshiko, *United Notions* (Metrojazz); w. Krupa, *Drummer Man* etc. (Verve), Dave McKenna (Epic), Joe Saye (Merc.), Bobby Scott (Verve), Benny Carter pl. Cole Porter (UA), B. Carroll (Kapp), Hefti (Epic), Dick Garcia-Tony Scott (Dawn).

Addr: 29 West 65th Street, New York 23, N.Y.

DREW, KENNETH SIDNEY (Kenny), *piano;* b. New York City, 8/28/28. Studied classical piano privately from the age of five; gave recital at age eight. Further studies at Music and Art High. Prof. debut as accompanist at Pearl Primus' dance school. First rec. w. Howard McGhee Jan. 1950 for Blue Note. Worked w. Coleman Hawkins, Lester Young, Charlie Parker '50-1, Buddy De Franco '52-3. Settled in Calif., working w. own trio in LA and SF. Returned to East in March '56 as acc. to Dinah Washington. Two months w. Art Blakey in spring '57, then free-lanced in NYC w. Coltrane, D. Byrd, Griffin, etc. Joined Buddy Rich June '58 and remained w. him until March '59. Own trio at Cork 'N Bib, Westbury, L.I. during summer, then own trio in Miami, Pensacola, Fla. fall '59.

Own LPs on Verve, River., Judson, Jazz:West; LPs w. Johnny Griffin, Ernie Henry, Chet Baker, Jean Thielemans (River.), Sonny Rollins, Sonny Stitt (Pres.), Art Farmer (New Jazz), John Coltrane (Blue Note), Sonny Criss (Imp.), *Best Coast Jazz* (Em.), Paul Chambers (Jazz:West).

Addr: 1534 Nelson Ave., Bronx 52, N.Y.

DROOTIN, BENJAMIN (Buzzy), *drums;* b. Russia, ca. 1920 (does not know exact date); to US at five, raised in Boston. Father, two brothers all musicians. Toured w. Ina Ray Hutton '40, Al Donahue '41-2. To Chi., worked w. Jesse Stacy, Wingy Manone. To NYC '47, 4½ years w. E. Condon, then w. B. Hackett, B. Butterfield, J. McPartland et al. Back to Boston, worked for G. Wein at Mahogany Hall etc. '53-5, then settled in NYC '55, playing w. Ralph Sutton, Wild Bill Davison, Pee Wee Erwin, Condon, Ruby Braff; frequently w. Bobby Hackett '57-60. LPs w. Hackett-Teagarden (Cap.), Braff (Verve, Epic, ABC-Par., Vict.), Condon (Savoy).

Addr: 5614 Netherland Ave., Riverdale 71, N.Y.

DUKES OF DIXIELAND. A group under the direction of Frank and Fred Assunto (q.v.), known during their New Orleans high school days as the Basin Street Four, Five or Six, and later during several months on the road with Horace Heidt, as the Junior Dixie Band. Their engagements included a 44-month stay at the Famous Door in New Orleans. Playing a synthetic brand of Dixieland jazz, of minor musical interest, the Dukes of Dixieland rose to national popularity in 1958-9, largely on the strength of their LPs, one of which was the first stereo jazz disc ever released. LPs: numerous volumes on Audio-Fidelity, also on Roulette, RCA Victor.

DUKOFF, ROBERT (Bob), *tenor sax;* b. Worcester, Mass., 10/11/18. Raised in Sioux City, Iowa. Pl. w. Carl Hoff, Johnny McGhee, Jerry Wald; Benny Goodman 1941-2; Sonny Dunham, Abe Lyman, Jimmy Dorsey. Studio work in Calif. '44-9; later in business, manuf. sax mouthpieces. Records for Vict. and occasional gigs in late '50s. Own LPs: Vict., Cam.

Addr: 6720 S.W. 57th Terrace, Miami, Fla.

DUNCAN, HENRY JAMES (Hank), *piano;* b. Bowling Green, Ky., 10/26/96. Stud. Central High School, Louisville, Fisk U., Nashville. Had own combo in Louisville incl. Jimmy Harrison, trom. Coming to NYC, he worked w. Fess Williams at the Savoy Ballroom and w. Charles "Fat Man" Turner at the Arcadia Ballroom, 53rd and Broadway. Toured U.S. w. Fats Waller's big band. Opened Mar. 2, 1947 at Nick's in Greenwich Village and remained there until May '55; then at Metropole in trio w. Zutty Singleton, Louis Metcalf to Aug. '56, after which he returned to Nick's; was still there in '60. LPs w. Tony Parenti (Jazztone); Wild Bill Davison (Jazzology).

Addr: 112-46 Dillon Street, Jamaica 33, L.I., N.Y.

DUNHAM, ELMER LEWIS (Sonny), *trumpet, trombone, leader;* b. Brockton, Mass., 1914. Popular in 1930s as featured soloist w. Glen Gray, he led his own band in the '40s; also pl. w. Bernie Mann, Tommy Dorsey in '51. Won *Met.* poll '37. LP: Met. All Stars (Cam.).

Addr: 70 Orange St., Brooklyn 1, N.Y.

DUNLOP, FRANCIS (Frankie), *drums;* b. Buffalo, N.Y., 12/6/28. Brother plays piano, father played guitar. Began stud. piano at nine at Buffalo Youth Center. After a year switched to drums and stud. with member of the Buffalo Symphony. First prof. job on drums at

16; later pl. with small groups around western N.Y. from 1948-50. W. Big Jay McNeely for a short time, then led own combo for a year after returning from Army '53; w. Skippy Williams' band '54, then w. Sonny Stitt, Charlie Mingus, Thelonious Monk, Sonny Rollins. Toured w. Maynard Ferguson's big band summer '58-Jan. '60. Joined Duke Ellington March '60. One of the most promising modern drummers. Favs: Max Roach, Philly Joe Jones, Lex Humphries. LPs w. Maynard Ferguson (Roul.); Wilbur Ware (River.).

DUNN, JOHNNY, *trumpet;* b. Memphis, Tenn., 1900; d. 1938. To NYC w. W. C. Handy orch. 1917; later w. Perry Bradford, Mamie Smith, own band, and Carroll Dickerson in Chicago. In late '20s and early '30s toured Europe w. Plantation orch. and Noble Sissle. Dunn was among the first trumpeters to make extensive use of the "wa-wa" muted style. He was heard on a number of Col. records with his Original Jazz Hounds from '21.

DUPREE, (Champion Jack), *piano, singer;* b. New Orleans, La., 7/4/10. Parents killed in a fire; he was in Colored Waif's Home for Boys until age 14, when he was taken in by a family. Learned piano from a pianist in a barrelhouse club; st. playing professionally in 1930. During Depression turned to boxing to make a living, hence the nickname "Champion." Went to Indianapolis in '40 for last boxing match and remained there several years, singing and playing piano in clubs. Began rec. for Okeh, cutting over 20 sides '40-1. Came to New York around '44, rec. for various labels incl. Joe Davis, Apollo, Continental, King et al. Dupree refers to himself as one of the last of the barrelhouse piano players, whose blues portray the life of both the urban and Southern rural Negro. He says, "My songs tell about my experiences in life or what I saw in the lives of other people." Own LP: *Blues from the Gutter* (Atl.).

DURAN, EDWARD, LOZANO (Eddie), *guitar;* b. San Francisco, 9/6/25. Brothers, Carlos, bass and Manual, piano, play w. Cal Tjader. Stud. piano in 1932, took up guitar in '37. Stud. for 7 months, but mainly self-taught. As child, sang in amateur hours with brother Manual in Fanchon & Marco reviews, winning first prizes. Aside from 2 yrs. in the Navy, has spent most of his time in SF where he has worked w. Freddie Slack. Flip Phillips, Charlie Parker, Stan Getz, George Shearing, Vince Guaraldi, Red Norvo, and Earl Hines. Own LP: Fantasy; LPs w. Vince Guaraldi, Ron Crotty, Cal Tjader, Earl Hines (Fant.).

Addr: 1370 Broadway, San Francisco, Calif.

DURHAM, EDDIE, *composer, guitar, trombone;* b. San Marcos, Texas, 8/19/06. Prominent in '30s, when he played w. Benny Moten, Willie Bryant, Jimmie Lunceford (arr. *Pigeon Walk, Lunceford Special, Blues in the Groove*), Count Basie (arr. *Out the Window, Topsy, Time Out*). Wrote several arrangements for Glenn Miller '39 including *Slip Horn Jive, Glen Island Special, Wham.* Was among first jazzmen to play electric guitar. In '40s led own group, also musical dir. of Sweethearts of Rhythm, and other bands. Only sporadically active during '50s, though his compositions, particularly *Topsy,* enjoyed a substantial revival. LPs: two tracks w. own group in *Kansas City Jazz* (Decca); LP w. Count Basie (Bruns.).

Addr: 2006 Amsterdam Ave., New York 32, N.Y.

DUTREY, HONORE, *trombone;* b. New Orleans, La., 1890; d. Chicago, Ill., 2/21/37. Brothers Pete and Sam pl. violin and clarinet respectively. With King Oliver 1907, then w. Buddy Petit, John Robichaux, Jimmie Noone. Navy '17, then to Chicago where he pl. w. Oliver from '19-24. Later worked w. Carroll Dickerson, Johnny Dodds and briefly w. Louis Armstrong '27. Rated highly among traditional trombonists by students of early jazz. He rec. w. Oliver, Dodds, Richard M. Jones, Armstrong: LP. *Louis Armstrong:1923* (River.).

DUTTON, FREDERIC M. (Fred), *bass;* also *bassoon;* b. San Jose, Calif., 4/26/28. Grandmother was well-known concert pianist in Chicago circa 1900. Extensive studies incl. San Jose State College '47-'55 (interrupted by Army service '51-3); Master's degree in Musicology, Stanford U. '57; later worked on PhD thesis in Europe. Dutton played bass and bassoon in the first Dave Brubeck Quartet in '51. Also worked w. Chamber Jazz Sextet '56-8; Joe Castro Trio Jan.-Sept. '58. In Europe '59. Played w. Romano Mussolini, later w. Hans Koller, appearing w. him on TV shows in Baden-Baden. Favs: L. Vinnegar, P. Chambers, R. Brown, S. La Faro. LPs w. Brubeck (Fant.), Chamber Jazz Sextet (Cadence).

Addr: 20200 La Paloma, Saratoga, Calif.

DUVIVIER, GEORGE B., *bass, composer;* b. New York City, 8/17/20. Studied violin at Conservatory of Music and Art, composing and arranging at NYU. Played w. Coleman Hawkins 1941; joined Lucky Millinder and sold first arr. to Jimmie Lunceford '42. Army '43-5, then w. Lunceford band as arranger until leader's death. Wrote and arr. originals w. Sy Oliver on MGM '47. Joined Nellie Lutcher '50, made two European tours w. her. Toured w. Terry Gibbs, Don Redman, Bud Powell, Pearl Bailey, Billy Eckstine but mainly with Lena Horne, with whom he had made several extended European trips, when not free-lancing in New York. Admitted to ASCAP '57. Favs: Blanton, Ray Brown; fav. arrs: Rugolo, Rogers, Hefti. LPs w. Chico Hamilton (Wor. Pac.), Count Basie-Joe Williams, (Roul.), Bud Powell (Blue Note, Verve), *Jazz Soul of Porgy and Bess* (UA), Candido (ABC-Par.), Mundell Lowe (Cam.), Eddie Davis, Arnett Cobb, *Very Saxy* (Pres.), *Saxes Inc.* (War. Bros.), Lena Horne (Vict.), Sy Oliver (Decca), Don Redman (Golden Crest), *One World Jazz* (Col.).

Addr: 445 W. 153rd St., New York 31, N.Y.

E

EAGER, ALLEN, *tenor, alto saxes;* b. New York City, 1/10/27. Studied clarinet at 13 for a year. On the road at 16 w. Bobby Sherwood; later w. Sonny Dunham, Shorty Sherock, T. Dorsey and Johnny Bothwell (small group). Played w. assorted groups on 52nd St. incl. his own quartet in 1945. Spent most of '48 at Royal Roost w. Tadd Dameron. In late '40s and early '50s w. Buddy Rich's orch. several times. Gave up music for a while in early '50s, teaching skiing and horseback riding, playing only occasionally. Had own quartet in Boston and NYC for short time in '53. Pl. sessions in Greenwich Village during '54-5 at Open Door, etc.; also w. Oscar Pettiford. Spent two years in Paris where he started pl. alto, returning to the US in Nov. '57. Since then he has been intermittently active in music. Eager was a charter member of the "cool school" and one of the most prominent tenor men in the early days of bop. Fav: Young, Rollins, Cohn, Sims, Getz, Parker. LPs w. Fats Navarro (Blue Note), Gerry Mulligan (Pres., Wor. Pac.), *The Brothers* (Pres.), Tony Fruscella (Atl.), *Saturday Night Swing Session* (Ctpt.), *Advance Guard of The Forties* (Em.), *In The Beginning . . . Bebop* (Savoy).

EARDLEY, JON, *trumpet;* b. Altoona, Pa., 9/30/28. Father pl. trumpet w. Paul Whiteman, Isham Jones; now heads finance company in Altoona. Jon pl. outdoor circuses and fairs every summer from ages 15 to 22. Started pl. jazz while stationed in Wash., D.C. when in AAF '46-9. Pl. w. Buddy Rich, then came to NYC after discharge in '49. Pl. w. Gene Williams '49-50. Back to Altoona for three years. Returned to NYC '54. Appeared at Open Door sessions in Greenwich Village. Joined Gerry Mulligan in the fall of '54, touring Europe w. him in early '56. In the late '50s Eardley was inactive in music. LPs: *Down East* (Pres.), Gerry Mulligan (Em., Wor. Pac.).

EAST, ROY, *alto sax;* also *clarinet, flute, baritone, tenor;* b. Northampton, England, 5/5/30. Stud. alto, clar. privately in Northampton, 1944; flute in London '55, and at Trinity College. East has a twin brother who plays the same instruments, working in London shows and clubs. Discovered by columnist Tony Hall while visiting London in '52, worked with name bands incl. Oscar Rabin '54-5; Vic Lewis '55-6; New Jazz Group w. Dizzy Reece '57; Vic Ash '58-9; back w. Lewis for American tour Feb. '59. Rec. for the author's international *One World Jazz* project in London, June '59. An alto player of exceptional intensity; though he names Duke Ellington as a main influence and Parker as his favorite, his phrasing and tone often recall Phil Woods. LPs: *One World Jazz* (Col.).

Addr: 118 A Elgin Crescent, London W. 11, England.

EATON, JOHN CHARLES, *piano, composer;* b. Philadelphia, Pa., 3/30/35. Extensive studies; pl. Poconos resorts from age 9. W. Clem Wiedenmyer '49-53; Stan Rubin '54-5, also own group '53-6 while stud. at Princeton. Favs: Powell, Tristano, Hines. Own LP: *College Jazz: Modern* (Col.).

ECKHARDT, WALLACE W., *bass;* b. St. Louis, Mo., 12/14/24. Brother also plays bass. Studied French horn in high school. Joined Sammy Gardner '55. Favs: Chubby Jackson, Eddie Safranski. LPs w. Gardner (Roul., Evst., Mound City); *Alabama Jubilee* (Mound City), *Windy City Six* (Delmar).

Addr: 6805 West Park, St. Louis 10, Mo.

ECKSTINE, BILLY (Mr. B) (William Clarence Eckstein), *singer;* b. Pittsburgh, Pa., 7/8/14. Educated in Washington, D.C. at Armstrong High and Howard U., he worked as singer and emcee in night clubs, first for a year and a half in Buffalo, then in Detroit; later in Chicago for two years at the Club de Lisa, etc. Through Budd Johnson, he was hired as vocalist with Earl Hines' band in 1939; he and Johnson were largely responsible later for the addition of Charlie Parker, Sarah Vaughan and others to the band. After becoming a big attraction with Hines (he also played occasional trumpet), Eckstine left in 1943 and went into night club work as a solo act. In the spring of '44 he decided, again with Budd Johnson, to put together a band of his own featuring stars of the then crystallizing bop movement.

Between June 1944, when the band played its first date, and the period in 1947 when he decided to abandon it in favor of what turned out to be a short-lived small combo, Eckstine led an orchestra that was years ahead of its time. The personnel included, at one time or another, Dizzy Gillespie, Fats Navarro, Miles Davis, Kenny Dorham on trumpets; Gene Ammons, Dexter Gordon, Lucky Thompson on tenor saxes, Charlie Parker on alto, Leo Parker on baritone; John Malachi on piano; Art Blakey on drums; Tommy Potter on bass; arrangements by Budd Johnson, Tadd Dameron and Jerry Valentine; vocals by Sarah Vaughan; Eckstine himself sang and played valve trombone.

From 1948 on, Eckstine was immersed in the commercial waters of popular ballad singing, but his flirtation with jazz had been a vitally significant one. Even though his band (recording for National) was so poorly recorded and balanced that there is no adequate evidence left of its exceptional musical ability, Eckstine nevertheless, because of his faith in bop and in the stars it produced, gave employment and encouragement to many of them during the transitional era and was, in effect, himself a pivotal figure in jazz history. Won Esq. New Star Award '46, DB poll '48-'52, Met. poll '49-54. Own LPs on Merc., MGM, Lion, Reg.; *Basie/Eckstine Inc.* (Roul.).

Addr: c/o William Morris Agency, 202 No. Canon Dr., Beverly Hills, Calif.

EDELHAGEN, KURT, *leader, piano;* also *clarinet, saxophone;* b. Herne, Westphalia, Germany, 6/5/20. Father, an amateur violinist began giving him lessons at age 8. Studied piano for five years, then clarinet at 14. Graduated from "Folkwang-Schule" in Essen at age 21. Member of advanced class for classical conducting when called into Army 1941. After World War II, led own combo at British club in Herne '45. Own big band from May '46, playing at US clubs in Bad Kissingen '46, Heidelberg, Munich '47, Frankfurt '48. Regular broadcasts on Armed Forces Network. Since then featured on German networks in Nurnberg, Baden-Baden and Cologne. Founded first school of jazz on a university level at Cologne "Staatliche Hochschule Für Musik"; band pl. first performance of Liebermann's *Concerto For Jazz Band and Symphony Orchestra* '55. His band, which in recent years has had an international flavor, feat. such men as Derek Humble, Rob Pronk and Dusko Gojkovic, has pl. all over Europe. Won the *Jazz-Echo* poll from '53 as best German jazz orchestra. Favs: Basie, Kenton; fav. pianists: Tatum, Peterson. Recs. for Bruns. and Polydor in Germany. LPs: *Jazz From Germany, Salute To The Girls* w. Caterina Valente (Decca).

Addr: Junkersdorf bei Koln, Am Frankenhain 28, Germany.

EDGEHILL, ARTHUR, *drums;* b. Brooklyn, N.Y., 7/21/26. Stud. drums in 1948 at Parkway Music Inst.; on road w. Mercer Ellington summer '49, then ret. to study at Parkway until '52. Pl. with Ben Webster '53; Horace Silver '54; Kenny Dorham's Jazz Prophets and Gigi Gryce '56. With Dinah Washington '57-8, then joined Eddie Davis-Shirley Scott trio. Favs: Kenny Clarke, Max Roach, Art Blakey, Philly Joe Jones. LPs w. Shirley Scott, Mal Waldron, Arnett Cobb, Eddie Davis (Pres.); Kenny Dorham (Blue Note, ABC-Par.).

EDISON, HARRY (Sweets), *trumpet;* b. Columbus, Ohio, 10/10/15. Early experience w. Alphonso Trent; w. Lucky Millinder in NYC 1937; joined Count Basie, Sept. '37 and was with him almost continuously until Basie's big band broke up in '50; then worked w. Buddy Rich's band. Later made international tour as single w. Josephine Baker, played w. JATP, worked w. Benny Carter on film sound tracks and led own combo off and on in Hollywood. Club dates and extensive rec. activity there '57, also tours w. Pearl Bailey and Louis Bellson early '58. First visit to NYC in several years when he acc. Pearl Bailey at the Waldorf-Astoria in Feb. '58. Worked regularly w. Frank Sinatra on TV show, records. Formed his own quintet late '58, working in NYC and touring with it. His virile, extroverted style, somewhat of the Roy Eldridge school, was a major influence during his years w. Basie. He was seen in the Norman Granz film, *Jammin' The Blues.* Own LPs on Verve, Roul.; LPs w. Basie (Decca, Vict., Bruns., Col.), Lester Young (Epic); Buddy Rich, Billie Holiday, Illinois Jacquet, Buddy De Franco, B. Webster, R. Brown, W. Herman, *Tour De Force* (Verve), J. Giuffre, S. Rogers (Atl.), Cy Touff (Wor. Pac.), B. Kessel (Contemp.), *Session At Midnight* (Cap.), Red Norvo (Vict.), L. Feather-D. Hyman (MGM), M. Albam (Coral); Lambert, Hendricks & Ross (Col.), *Spirituals To Swing* (Vang.), Bill Potts (UA).

EDWARDS, ARTHUR W., *bass;* b. Ft. Worth, Tex., 2/9/14. Stud. bass in high schools in Ardmore, Okla., Oklahoma City, and Wiley College, Marshall, Tex. Worked in Chicago, Denver, Los Angeles w. Bud Scott '43-5; Horace Henderson '47-53. Was w. T. Buckner from '54. Fav: O. Pettiford. LP w. T. Buckner (Dix. Jub.).

Addr: 217 W. 54th St., Los Angeles 37, Calif.

EDWARDS, EDWIN BRANFORD (Eddie), *trombone;* b. New Orleans, 5/22/1891. Free-lanced locally until the formation of the Original Dixieland Jazz Band (for details, see La Rocca). Had own band at Silver Slipper, NYC, 1925-7, worked w. society bands in New York through most of '30s and '40s; toured with reorganized Dixieland band for Katherine Dunham show, 1943-4. Still active in 1960 doing club dates in NYC with own jazz sextet. Favs: Miff Mole, Higginbotham, Teagarden. LP: Commodore (revival of ODJB).

Addr: 6 Amsterdam Avenue, New York 19, N.Y.

EDWARDS, THEODORE MARCUS (Teddy), *tenor sax, songwriter;* b. Jackson, Miss., 2/26/24. Father pl. trombone, reeds, violin; grandfather pl. bass. Stud. in Jackson, 1936, and in Los Angeles under Merle Johnston, 1949. Alto and clarinet w. Doc Parmlee, 1936. Don Dunbar, '38; Paul Gayten, '40; moved to Detroit '42, worked w. Hank Jones, Tweed Beard et al. Own band in Alexandria, La., and Tampa, Fla. After playing w. Ernie Fields, Roy Milton, joined Howard McGhee and switched to tenor sax. Worked in Calif. w. Benny Carter, Gerald Wilson; a year at the Lighthouse in Hermosa Beach, '49-50; a year at Bop City, SF. Many jazz concerts in Calif. W. Max Roach '54, Benny Carter '55, own group in LA, SF '55-60, also w. Leroy Vinnegar '58. App. at Monterey Fest. '58. As songwriter has had three tunes recorded by Jimmy Witherspoon. Fav. own solo: *Up In Dodo's Room* w. McGhee. LPs w. Max Roach (GNP), Leroy Vinnegar, Helen Humes (Contemp.), Joe Castro (Atl.), Jimmy De Michael (Challenge), *Blowing The Blues* (Wor. Pac.), Jimmy Witherspoon (Wor. Pac.); two numbers w. own group in *Sonny Rollins At Music Inn* (Metrojazz).

Addr: 3103 S. Dalton Ave., Los Angeles 18, Calif.

ELDRIDGE, DAVID ROY (Little Jazz), *trumpet, fluegelhorn, singer, drums;* b. Pittsburgh, Pa., 1/30/11. Stud. with elder brother, the late Joe Eldridge, who played violin and alto. Drums at six; first gig New Year's Eve 1917 w. brother. Early exp. with carnivals; in Little Rock w. Oliver Muldoon '27, then had own band as "Roy Elliott" for eight months. After a few months w. Horace Henderson's band he went home and studied again with his brother; worked briefly w. Zach Whyte, then w. Speed Webb, whose band he later took over in Flint, Mich.

Eldridge came to NYC Nov. 1930, worked in Cecil

Scott's band and later with the Elmer Snowden and Ch. Johnson bands at Smalls. He then played with Teddy Hill, with the show band for Connie's Hot Chocolates; in 1934 he was with a band led by him and his brother and later that year with McKinney's Cotton Pickers. In 1935 he was back with Teddy Hill's band at the Savoy ballroom, he and Chu Berry being the principal soloists. He and Chu were later heard in the Fletcher Henderson band 1936-7. He had his own band at the Three Deuces in Chicago, then in 1938 quit the music business to study radio engineering. After a few months he returned, working in the Mal Hallett band, '38, and leading his own band at the Arcadia Ballroom NYC '39-40.

Eldridge rose to national prominence as featured trumpeter and singer with Gene Krupa's band from Apr. 1941 until 1943, when the band broke up. He was on CBS staff in NYC with Paul Baron's orch. '43-4, playing on the Mildred Bailey radio series; toured with Artie Shaw's band '44-5, then had various groups of his own. He was back with Krupa for a few months in '49. In 1950 he joined the Benny Goodman sextet for a European tour and remained on the Continent for 18 months, playing concerts w. Bechet, Ch. Parker and others.

During the 1950s an association he had begun during the early years of Norman Granz's tours became a regular engagement, and in the middle and late 1950s he toured the U.S. and Europe annually with either Jazz at the Philharmonic or, later, a smaller Granz show starring Ella Fitzgerald and Oscar Peterson. In the late '50s Eldridge also appeared frequently in clubs with a quintet co-starring Coleman Hawkins.

Though he has stated that Rex Stewart and Red Nichols were important influences in his formative years, it was not long after Roy Eldridge arrived in New York that he became an original stylist and major influence himself. He was as vital a figure in the development of trumpet jazz during the '30s as Armstrong had been in the '20s and as Gillespie was to be in the '40s or Miles Davis in the '50s. He was described by Barry Ulanov as "a biting, driving brass man, almost without equal for sheer power from the earliest years of swing to the present . . . few individuals on any instrument can match him for staying power, from style to style, from decade to decade."

In the late 1950s Eldridge alternated between fluegelhorn and trumpet. He is an adequate performer on piano, bass and drums. As a singer he has a personable, gruff quality; his best known vocal record was *Let Me Off Uptown,* a duet with Anita O'Day, on Krupa's 1941 record.

Eldridge has been a prolific recording artist since the '30s, when he cut many sessions with Henderson, Hill, B. Holiday, T. Wilson, Putney Dandridge, Chu Berry, Mildred Bailey, G. Krupa. He recorded with his own groups for Vocalion '37, Varsity '40, Decca '44-7, and through the '50s for the N. Granz labels (Clef, Verve); also sideman dates w. Ch. Barnet, C. Hawkins et al. He also made sessions in Paris and Stockholm.

Considered the foremost jazz trumpeter in jazz in the early and mid-'40s, Eldridge won the *Down Beat* poll '42, '46; Metronome poll '44-6; *Esquire* Silver Award '45.

Own LPs: *Little Jazz* (Verve 8068), *Rockin' Chair* (Verve 8088), *Dale's Wail* (Verve 8089), *Swing Goes Dixie* (Verve 1010), *Roy's Got Rhythm* (Em. 36084); three nos. in *Trumpeters Holiday* (Epic 3252); one no. in *Encyclopedia of Jazz on Records, Vol. 3* (Decca 8400); LPs w. Art Tatum (Verve 8064); Dizzy Gillespie: *Trumpet Kings* (Verve 8110), *Trumpet Battle* (Verve 8109); Gillespie & Harry Edison: *Tour De Force* (Verve 8212); Chu Berry (Epic 3124); w. Teddy Wilson & Fletcher Henderson in *The Jazz Makers* (Col. 1036); Gene Krupa (Cam. 368, Col. CL 641, CL 753, CL 611, Verve 2008, 8069); Artie Shaw (Vict. LPM 1201, LPM 1241); Ralph Burns (Verve 8121), Herb Ellis (Verve 8252), *Peterson-Eldridge-Stitt-Jo Jones At Newport* (Verve 8239), *Only The Blues* w. Sonny Stitt (Verve 8250); *Metronome All Stars* (Harm. 7044), w. Met. All Stars in *Mr. B. With A Beat* (MGM E3176); Lester Young (Verve 8316), Ben Webster (Verve 8318).

Addr: 194-19 109th Avenue, Hollis 12, L.I., N.Y.

ELGART, LARRY, *leader, alto sax;* b. New London, Conn., 3/20/22. Mother a concert pianist; brother, Les Elgart. Lead alto w. Ch. Spivak at age of 17 on recommendation of Hymie Shertzer. Formed band with brother which was heard under latter's name from '53 to middle of '58. Then took over leadership when Les moved to Calif. Primarily a dance band with an emphasis on honest reproduction of sound, Elgart's orchestra has featured various jazzmen from time to time. Own LPs on Vict., Decca.

Addr: 667 Madison Ave., New York, N.Y.

ELGART, LES, *trumpet, leader;* b. New Haven, Conn., 8/3/18. Played trumpet w. Berigan, McIntyre, Spivak, etc. in 1940s, then led own band. Not a jazz musician but has used some modern jazz stars as sidemen. LPs on Col.

Addr: 295 Central Park West, New York 24, N.Y.

ELIZALDE, FRED, *piano, composer, leader;* b. Manila, Philippines, 1907. Went to school at Cambridge in England and formed band w. brother Manuel in 1926. Opened at Savoy Hotel in London '28 w. group of American and British musicians incl. Adrian Rollini. The band broke up in '29. Elizalde studied classical music in Spain, and under Maurice Ravel in France. He ret. to England for a series of jazz recordings in '32. Since then he has lived in the Philippines, operating the radio station in Manila and occasionally ret. to England for classical concerts. LP: one track w. his band in *A Scrapbook of British Jazz, 1926-1956* (Lond.).

ELLINGTON, EDWARD KENNEDY (Duke), *composer, leader, piano;* b. Washington, D.C., 4/29/99. His father, a butler, later was a Navy blueprint maker; the family was always modestly well-to-do. Ellington studied piano from 1906. His nickname was given him arbitrarily by a young neighbor. At Armstrong High, Washington's leading Negro manual training school, he became absorbed in art and won a poster contest sponsored by the NAACP. He continued to study music at school and with Henry Grant, a private teacher, but learned even more from listening to the ragtime pianists around town. He turned down a scholarship to Pratt Inst. in Brooklyn, played gigs and painted commercial signs, and by June 1918, when he married Edna Thompson, he was doing very well, supplying bands for parties and dances. His sidemen were Toby Hardwicke on bass and saxes, Arthur Whetsol on trumpet, Sonny Greer on drums and Elmer Snowden on banjo.

The only period in Ellington's life marked by real poverty was his first sojourn in New York, when he, Greer and Hardwicke came to join a pseudo-symphonic band led by Wilbur Sweatman. After a short and unhappy stay with this unit they struggled unsuccessfully for some months; Duke soon went back to Washington but in the spring of '23 was induced by Fats Waller to move back to Manhattan. Duke and his Washingtonians worked for Ada Smith, better known in later years as the "Bricktop" of European cafe society; and under Snowden's leadership at Barron's in Harlem. Ellington became the official leader, and Fred Guy took over the banjo chair, when they landed their first downtown job at the Hollywood, Broadway and 49th St., later known as the Kentucky Club. It was here that some of the first important orchestral ideas and solo styles began to develop as the group acquired such men as Bubber Miley, trumpet; Joe Nanton, trombone; Harry Carney, saxes; Rudy Jackson, clarinet and tenor; and from '26 on the definitive rhythm section which remained unchanged for a decade: Duke, Fred Guy, Greer and Wellman Braud. During this time the band began to record as Ellington's Kentucky Club Orch.

Ellington wrote his first revue score, for a show called *Chocolate Kiddies,* in '24; though the show never got to Broadway it ran for two years in Germany. After four years off and on at the Kentucky (with time out for summer trips to New England and short stints at the Flamingo and other clubs) the band made its decisive move into the big time when on 12/4/27 it began an engagement at the Cotton Club on Lenox Ave., remaining there until '32, with time out in '30 for a trip to Calif. to appear in the film, *Check and Double Check,* with Amos and Andy. During the Cotton Club years, when the band was frequently broadcast nationally from the club and was recording regularly under Duke's own name and under various pseudonyms, the Ellington name became internationally synonymous with the highest qualities of both orchestral and improvised jazz. Soloists who joined the band in that era included Barney Bigard, clarinet; Johnny Hodges, alto and soprano sax; Cootie Williams and Freddie Jenkins, trumpets.

Ellington's first big hit in the popular music field was *Mood Indigo,* first recorded in Oct. '30 under the title *Dreamy Blues.* Early Ellington orchestral characteristics included the use of what he originally called "jungle style" effects, through the use of plunger mutes, in which Miley, C. Williams and Nanton were the most talented specialists. Much of the success of the band, however, was attributed to Ellington's unique selection of tonal colors, through orchestral voicings that could never be duplicated because the individual timbre of each man in the orchestra was itself essential to the overall effect.

The Ellington band made its first trip to Europe in '33, enlarged to include six brass (Cootie, Jenkins, Whetsol, Nanton, Juan Tizol, Lawrence Brown) and four reeds (Hardwicke, Hodges, Bigard, Carney). After enjoying an unprecedented reception throughout England and the Continent, Ellington returned home to further popular successes.

His biggest hits in subsequent years included: *Solitude,* first recorded '33, *Sophisticated Lady* '33, *In a Sentimental Mood* '35. These, however, were mere single-line melodies that earned him acceptance with the lay public, while his most respected efforts among musicians were the works in which the orchestration was as important as the melody itself; among these were *Daybreak Express, Rude Interlude, Stompy Jones, Harlem Speaks, Ducky Wucky, Blue Ramble, Blue Harlem,* etc. Most of his greatest records during the band's first successful decade were of works either composed by Ellington alone or co-composed with members of the band (e.g., *Rockin' in Rhythm* by Ellington and Carney).

A unique characteristic of the Ellington band throughout the 1930s was the constancy of the personnel, which enabled Ellington to achieve an ensemble unprecedented in its precision and coordination. In 1939 there were three important changes: Billy Strayhorn had been added as assistant arranger, Jimmy Blanton had joined the band on bass and Ben Webster on tenor sax. From this time until August 1, 1942, when a recording ban went into effect, Ellington produced what was later regarded by many musicians as his most consistent series of superb performances. Among them were Strayhorn's *Take the A Train,* which became the band's theme, *Chelsea Bridge* and *Johnny Come Lately;* and Ellington's own originals: *Warm Valley, Harlem Airshaft, Jack the Bear, Bojangles,* etc. (seven of the best 1940 performances were reissued on Victor LPM 1715). In this period, too, the band participated in the revue *Jump for Joy* in Hollywood, which produced several excellent performances of songs in a semi-pop vein from Duke's score. Outstanding was *I Got It Bad and That Ain't Good,* generally regarded as Ivie Anderson's best recorded performance. During these years the band was enriched by the new talents of Ray Nance on trumpet and violin, and the frequent presence of Billy Strayhorn on piano.

The period 1943-1950 was significant for a series of annual concerts, initiated by Ellington at Carnegie Hall in January 1943, when he presented the brilliant *Black, Brown and Beige,* his first attempt at extended composition, running about fifty minutes in its original form. Owing to the recording ban, this was never recorded, except for extracts which later appeared in a Victor album (reissued on LPM 1715), but it was widely discussed as the most important step of its kind in combining the essential elements of jazz into a major work suitable for concert hall performance. Duke gave subsequent recitals in Carnegie Hall at which he introduced several other long works, among them *Deep South Suite, Blutopia, Blue Belles of Harlem, Liberian Suite, New World A-Comin', Tattooed Bride.* Another work of this kind, a suite entitled *Harlem,* was played at an Ellington concert in the Metropolitan Opera House in January, 1951. Ellington's band was combined with the Symphony of the Air for the premiere of his *Night Creature* at Carnegie Hall in Mar. 1955.

During the 1940s, the band's personnel fluctuated much more than it had in previous years. Outstanding instrumentalists heard during these years included: Rex Stewart, Taft Jordan, Harold Baker, trumpets; Jimmy Hamilton, clarinet; Oscar Pettiford, bass; Kay Davis, Herb Jeffries, Al Hibbler, vocals. In the summer of 1948, Duke toured England and France as a vaudeville act with Kay Davis and Ray Nance, accompanied by local musicians. In 1950, the entire band toured Continental Europe, the personnel now including Ernie Royal and the late Al Killian on trumpets; Quentin Jackson on trombone; and Butch Ballard as second drummer.

In the early 1950s, changes in the band became even more frequent, the most significant being the return of Juan Tizol and the addition of Willie Smith on alto sax and Louis Bellson on drums, all three having left Harry James to join Duke in May 1951. Bellson contributed several arrangements but was mainly important to the band in the unprecedented drive he lent to the rhythm section and the renewed spirit imparted to the band as a whole.

By 1953, Bellson and Smith had left the band, there were no more new works to be presented at annual Carnegie Hall concerts, and many of Ellington's public performances indicated a slackening in morale and teamwork; but it remained one of the two or three top bands in jazz, usually achieving its peak moments when playing revised arrangements of some of the old works.

In 1955 Johnny Hodges rejoined the band after a four-year absence; during the next five years the band underwent a vital renaissance. Encouraged by a highly successful appearance at Newport in '56, by a new contract with Columbia Records, and by a color TV spectacular built around him (*A Drum is a Woman,* CBS, May '57) Ellington resumed writing prolifically and regained much of his lost popularity. A suite written with Strayhorn and inspired by characters from Shakespeare *(Such Sweet Thunder)* was premiered at Town Hall in '57; an album was recorded for Verve combining Ella Fitzgerald with Ellington's songs and the orchestra; they celebrated its release with a joint Carnegie Hall concert, Apr. '58. In Oct. '58, on his first European tour in eight years, Ellington took his band to Britain for the first time since 1933. The band toured Europe again in the fall of '59. During this entire period ('55-60) there were increasingly frequent appearances at all the major jazz festivals including Newport, *Playboy* (Chicago), Great South Bay. In '59, for the first time, Ellington wrote (and the band recorded) the score for a film, *Anatomy of a Murder.*

By 1960 Ellington could look back on a career during which, in 33 years as a nationally known figure, he had constantly shown the paths that music could follow in searching for new horizons, new forms and exciting orchestral developments without ever losing track of the fundamental qualities of jazz *qua* jazz. His countless innovations included the wordless use of a voice as a jazz instrument, in '27 (Adelaide Hall); the circumvention of the three-minute record time, which he accomplished by expanding two early works to cover two and four sides respectively on 78-speed discs (*Creole Rhapsody,* '31; *Reminiscing in Tempo,* '35); the use of a miniature concerto form to build compositions around a jazz soloist (*Clarinet Lament* for B. Bigard, *Echoes of Harlem* for Cootie Williams, both '35); and the creation of new works for special jazz concert premieres. These and numerous other Ellington concepts were so widely imitated that they are now commonplace and are taken for granted.

Despite his modest repudiation of any importance as a pianist, Ellington has also made a valuable contribution here, playing discreetly within his technical limitations and occasionally recording a series of pleasant, unpretentious solos. One of his major influences was Willie (The Lion) Smith; others were Fats Waller, Luckey Roberts, James P. Johnson and several more mentioned by him in his article in this book.

Though it is through his songs that he has become one of the major world figures in the music of the 20th century, Ellington's chief significance, in the view of most musicians and critics, lies in his career as the leader of and writer for an orchestra. He and his band have always been considered interdependent to an extent that was without precedent and may well remain without successor. In showing to what heights a large jazz orchestra could aspire, he achieved a reputation not likely to be duplicated or forgotten. Certainly by 1960 it was clear that he had made a more extensive and more important contribution than had any other figure in the history of jazz.

Duke Ellington, a full-length book by Barry Ulanov, was published in '46 by Creative Age, later taken over

The John Kirby Sextette, seen here during its halcyon years, about 1940, was known as "the biggest little band in America." L. to R.: O'Neil Spencer, drums; Charlie Shavers, trumpet; John Kirby, bass; Buster Bailey, clarinet; Russell Procope, alto sax; Billy Kyle, piano (*Down Beat*)

Louis Jordan (*Down Beat*)

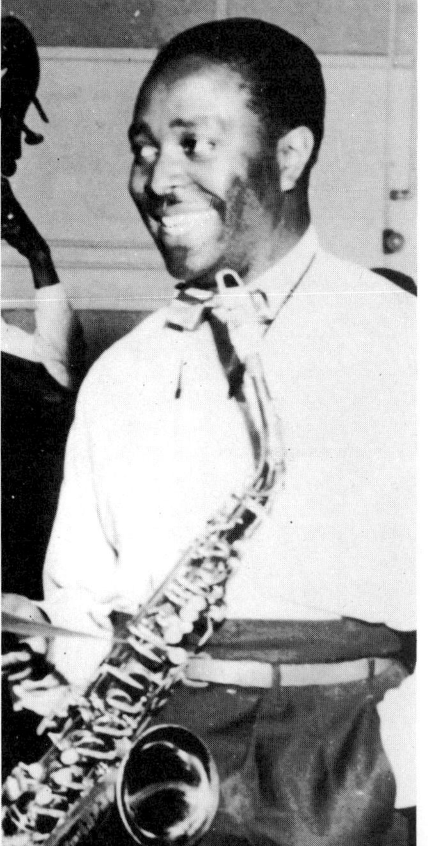

Slam Stewart (*Metronome*)

Mary Lou Williams (*Bill Gottlieb*)

Ella Fitzgerald and Chick Webb, ca. 1938 *(Seymour Rudolph)*

Ella Fitzgerald (*Jean-Pierre Leloir*)

Art Tatum (*Down Beat*)

Leadbelly

The original King Cole Trio, ca. 1939, with Oscar Moore, guitar; Wesley Prince, bass *(Metronome)*

Baby Dodds, Jimmie Noone, Roy Eldridge at a jam session, Chicago, 1940 *(Down Beat)*

Jimmy Blanton

Lionel Hampton and Charlie Barnet (*Leonard Feather*)

Roy Eldridge, Harry James and Cootie Williams at a Metronome All-Stars record session (*Otto F. Hess*)

Coleman Hawkins and Roy Eldridge at Newport (*Bert Block*)

Cab Calloway's orchestra, 1941. Trumpets, L. to R.: Dizzy Gillespie, Lammar Wright, Jonah Jones; Danny Barker, guitar; trombones: Keg Johnson, Tyree Glenn, Quentin Jackson; Jerry Blake, clarinet; saxophones: Hilton Jefferson, Andrew Brown, Walter "Foots" Thomas (*Metronome*)

Jo Jones (*Slade*)

Sidney Catlett

Sister Rosetta Tharpe (*Jean-Marie*)

Tommy Dorsey and his vocalist Frank Sinatra, 1941

Bing Crosby and Les Brown (*Dave Pell*)

Cozy Cole practicing backstage at the Metropole *(Leonard Feather)*

Milt Hinton *(Chuck Stewart)*

Lester Young and mother, Lisetta (*Courtesy Jazz Hot*)

Lester Young (*Columbia Records*)

Lester Young at his final record session, Paris, 1959 (*Daniel Filipacchi*)

Esquire All-Stars, Commodore Records, 1943. L. to R.: Art Tatum, Al Casey, Coleman Hawkins, Sidney Catlett, Cootie Williams, Edmond Hall, Oscar Pettiford; Leonard Feather who supervised session

Earl Hines' big band, opening at the Apollo Theatre, April 23, 1943. Trumpets, L. to R.: Dizzy Gillespie, Benny Harris, Gail Brockman, Shorts McConnell; pianos: Earl Hines and Sarah Vaughan; saxophones: A. Crump, Andrew Gardner, Scoops Carry, John Williams, Charlie Parker. Trombone next to drummer Shadow Wilson is Benny Green. Jesse Simkins, bass; Julie Gardner, accordion *(Courtesy Benny Harris)*

52nd Street, 1943: L. to R.: Coleman Hawkins, Benny Harris, Don Byas, Thelonious Monk, Denzil Best (*Down Beat*)

Stan Kenton and Duke Ellington

Sy Oliver

George Russell; Mrs. Russell in background *(RCA Victor)*

June Christy and Bob Cooper (*Ralph Poole*)

Sarah Vaughan

Charlie Parker and Jay McShann, 1939

Billy Eckstine and Charlie Parker at Birdland, 1950 (*Down Beat*)

Tommy Potter, Charlie Parker and Miles Davis (*Down Beat*)

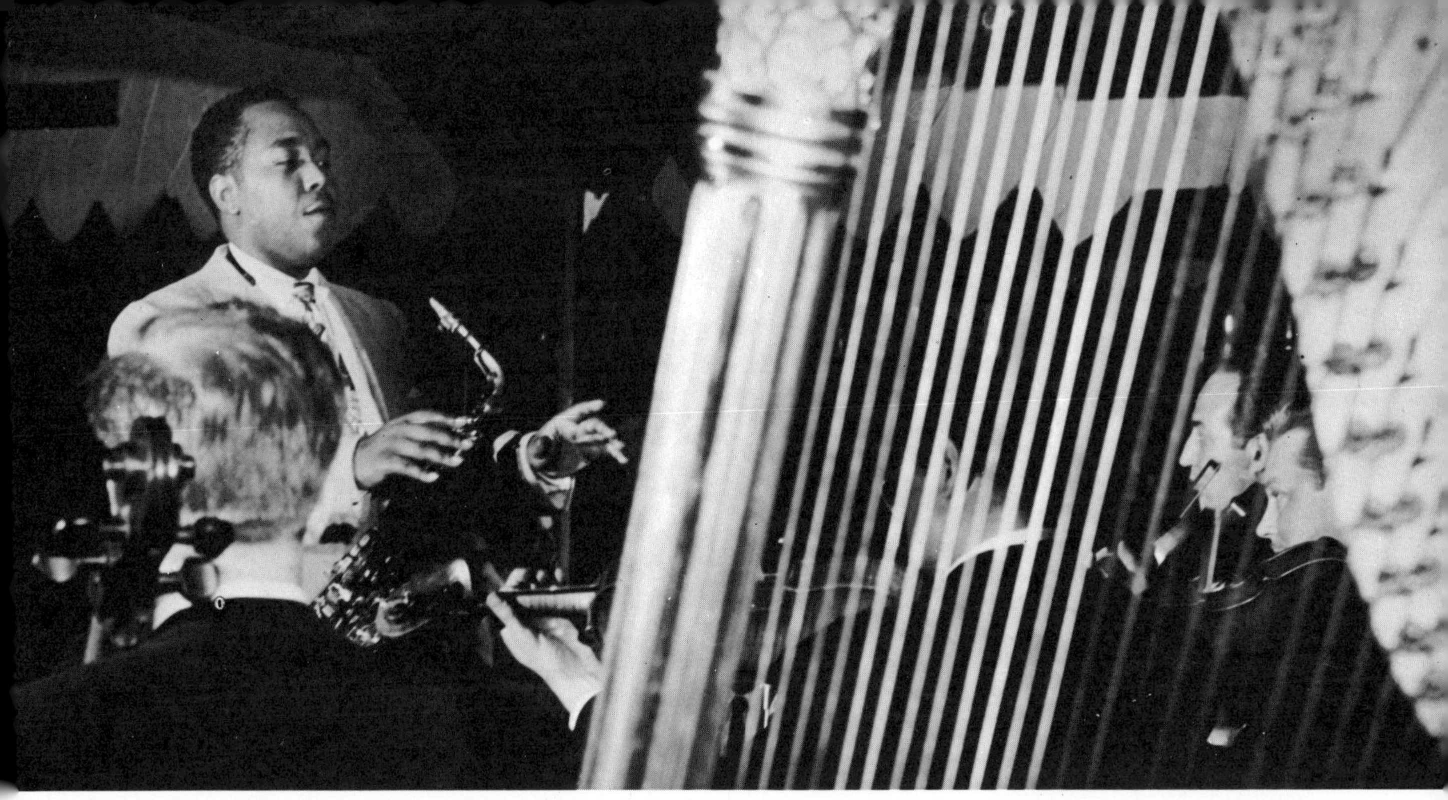

Charlie Parker leading his string ensemble (*Al Fairweather*)

Charlie Parker, Miles Davis, Allen Eager and Kai Winding at the Royal Roost, ca. 1948 *(Herman Leonard)*

Thelonious Monk
(Tony Scott)

Miles Davis and Bud Powell
(J. C. Bernath)

by Farrar, Straus & Young. An anthology of British writing on Duke, *Duke Ellington: His Life And Music* was published by Roy (Phoenix Edition) '59. A chapter on Ellington by the author appears in *The Jazz Makers* (Grove Press).

Ellington has won the following awards: *Esquire* Gold Award, arr. and band, '45-7; band won *Down Beat* poll '42, '44, '46, '48; *Metronome* poll '45; *Down Beat* Critics' Poll '53, '58-9; *Down Beat* poll as composer '57-8; *Down Beat* Hall of Fame '56. Fav. soloist, *DB* poll '48.

Own LPs: one side of *The Birth of Big Band Jazz* (River. 12-129); *Early Ellington* (Bruns. 54007), *The Music of Duke Ellington* (Col. CL 558), *In A Mellotone* (Vict. LPM 1364), *The Duke And His Men* (Vict. LPM 1092), *At His Very Best* (Vict. LPM 1715), *At Newport* (Col. CL 934), *At The Bal Masque* (Col. CL 1282), *At The Cotton Club* (Cam. 459), *Back To Back* w. Johnny Hodges (Verve 8317), *Black, Brown and Beige* (Col. CL 1162), *Cosmic Scene* (Col. CL 1198), *A Drum Is A Woman* (Col. CL 951), *& Orchestra* (Rondo. 7), *Ellington '55* (Cap. T521), *Ellington Indigos* (Col. CL 1085), *Ellington Jazz Party* (Col. CL 1323), *Ellington Showcase* (Cap. T679), *Ellington Sidekicks* (Epic LN 3237), *Ellington Uptown* (Col. CL 830), *Historically Speaking* (Beth. 60), *Masterpieces* (Col. CL 825), *Music of Ellington* (Col. CL 558), *Newport 1958* (Col. CL 1245), *Plays Ellington* (Cap. T 477), *Such Sweet Thunder* (Col. CL 1033), *At Newport* (rev. Buck Clayton, Col. CL 933), *Blue Rose* w. Rosemary Clooney (Col. CL 872), *Blue Light* (Col. CL 663), *Dance To The Duke* (Cap. T 637), *Ella Fitzgerald Sings The Duke Ellington Song Book* (Verve 4008, 4009), *Liberian Suite* (Col. CL 848), *Festival Session* (Col. CS 8200).

Addr: 1619 Broadway, New York 19, N.Y.

ELLINGTON, MERCER KENNEDY, *trumpet, composer, leader;* b. Washington, D.C., 3/11/19. Son of Duke Ellington. To NYC, studied alto, trumpet. Attended Col. U., Juilliard, studied Schillinger at NYU. First band, which he formed in '39, included Dizzy Gillespie, Clark Terry, Calvin Jackson and arrangements by B. Strayhorn (before he started arranging for Duke). Army '43-5, mostly in band under Sy Oliver, then led own band to '49 including Wendell Marshall, Butch Ballard (both later with Duke), and Carmen McRae. Worked w. Duke's band for several months in 1950 playing E flat horn, also ran Mercer record label '50-2; left music, worked as a salesman '53; toured with Cootie Williams as road manager and trumpet '54. Worked as general assistant to Duke Ellington '55-9, then resumed playing and led his own big orch. at Birdland Oct. '59. A talented composer-arranger, he assembled a series of all-star groups including most of the Duke Ellington band for two LPs released on Coral in 1958-9. His comps. include *Things Ain't What They Used to Be, Blue Serge, Moon Mist, The Girl in My Dreams.* Own LPs: *Stepping Into Swing Society* (Coral); *Colors in Rhythm* (Coral); LP w. Ellington (Col.).

Addr: 113-02 175th Street, St. Albans 12, L.I., N.Y.

ELLIOTT, DON (Don Elliott Helfman), *mellophone, vibes, trumpet, bongos, singer;* b. Somerville, N.J., 10/21/26. Piano at six, accordion at eight, baritone horn and mellophone in high school bands, then trumpet in dance bands. Harmony at Juilliard 1944-5. Trumpet in Army band, also gunner on B-29. Out late '46. Started on vibes and studied arranging at U. of Miami '47. Jan Raye Trio '48, then joined Hi, Lo, Jack & the Dame as singer '48-9. WMCA staff job on trumpet, vibes; George Shearing Quintet July '50 to Feb. '51, then w. Teddy Wilson at Embers, Terry Gibbs Quintet, and briefly w. Benny Goodman '52; Buddy Rich, early '53. Free-lanced, mainly in NYC, often leading own quartet, '54-60; had commercial hit in Nov. '59 in vocal duo with Sascha Burland on "Nutty Squirrels" jazz novelty recs. (Hanover). Seen on B'way stage 1960 in *Thurber Carnival,* for which he wrote music and led quartet. Though he has spread his many talents so thin that he has never enjoyed complete acceptance in any one area, Elliott is a capable musician with a sense of humor and has shown excellent technique on all the instruments he plays. Own LPs: ABC-Par., Beth., River., Decca, Design, Savoy, Vang.; *Eddie Costa, Mat Mathews and Don Elliott at Newport* (Verve); LPs w. Bob Corwin (River.), Terry Gibbs in *Jazztime, USA* (Bruns.), Shearing (MGM), Billy Taylor (ABC-Par.), L. Feather-D. Hyman (MGM), Ruby Braff (Epic).

Addr: 41 Central Park West, New York 23, N.Y.

ELLIS, DONALD JOHNSON (Don), *trumpet;* b. Los Angeles, Calif., 7/25/34. Mother is church organist. Had own dance bands in junior high and high school; stud. trumpet, B.M. in comp. at Boston U. Worked w. Ray McKinley after college graduation in 1956; pl. in U.S. Army jazz bands '57-8 in Germany. Briefly w. Charlie Barnet '58; with Maynard Ferguson '59. Names several trumpet players as his influences: Dizzy, Fats Navarro, Clark Terry, et al. Says he is "trying to combine an older style of trumpet playing with advanced harmonic and rhythmic ideas."

Addr: 8 W. 102nd St., New York City.

ELLIS, MITCHELL HERBERT (Herb), *guitar;* b. McKinney, Texas, 8/4/21. Attended North Texas State College. Joined Glen Gray's Casa Loma orch. in '44; later worked w. Jimmy Dorsey and acquired first prominence as member of Soft Winds instrumental-vocal trio, recording for Majestic and composing jointly several tunes including *Detour Ahead, I Told Ya I Love Ya Now Get Out.* Replaced Barney Kessel in Oscar Peterson trio '53, toured w. trio in JATP, visiting Europe several times and remaining with Peterson until Nov. '58. During most of '59 he worked in Ella Fitzgerald's acc. unit. Ellis is one of the greatest modern jazz guitarists, swinging effortlessly and warmly at all tempos and to exceptionally moving effect on the blues. Own LPs: Verve; LPs w. Peterson, Flip Phillips, Ben Webster, Armstrong, Lionel Hampton; JATP Vols. 16 & 17, *Giuffre Meets Ellis* (Verve).

Addr: 5452 Delta Street, San Gabriel, Cal.

ELMAN, ZIGGY (Harry Finkelman), *trumpet;* also *trombone, clarinet, saxes, leader;* b. Philadelphia, Pa., 5/26/14. Raised in Atlantic City from 1918. House mus. at Steel Pier, Atl. City, mainly on tbn., 1930-6. Best known as feat. trumpeter w. Benny Goodman '36-40, his biggest hit being *And the Angels Sing*. After working w. T. Dorsey 1940-7 (except for absence in service '43-6) Elman settled in LA, led his own band at the Palladium and on MGM Records. Studio work and band gigs '54-5; ill while *The Benny Goodman Story* was being filmed, he was seen doing *And the Angels Sing* but the trumpet work for this passage was recorded by Manny Klein. Since then, has done commercial TV work w. Dinah Shore, Bing Crosby et al; feat. in Paul Weston LPs (Col). Elman was a florid, brash soloist whose incorporation of Yiddish "fralich" elements into his solos w. Goodman gave him a strong identity in the late '30s, carrying over into the '40s when his popularity earned him the *Down Beat* poll victory '40-1, '43-5 and '47; *Met.* poll '41-3, as #1 trumpet. Favs: Harry James. Own LPs: MGM; LPs w. Goodman, Lionel Hampton, Tommy Dorsey (Vict.), Goodman (MGM), Jess Stacy (Atl.), *Golden Era of Jazz* (Savoy); one no. in *Great Jazz Brass* (Cam.); discusses jazz in *Escapade Reviews The Jazz Scene* (Lib.).

Addr: 5759 Columbus Avenue, Van Nuys, Cal.

ENEVOLDSEN, ROBERT MARTIN (Bob), *valve trombone, tenor sax, bass;* b. Billings, Mont., 1/11/20. Grandfather a violin teacher in Denmark, both parents active in music. B.M. at U. of Mont. '38-42; Army '42-6; settled in Salt Lake City, studied composition at U. of Utah. Played clarinet in Utah symphony for two years. Migrated to LA early '51 and has been heard on records with numerous jazz groups. Bass w. Bobby Troup Trio '54-5. Like Don Elliott, Enevoldsen plays too many instruments too well to have gained full recognition or strong identification with any one. LPs w. Mulligan (Cap.), Shelly Manne, Howard Rumsey, Lennie Niehaus (Contemp.), Shorty Rogers (Vict.), *Jazz For Cops And Robbers* w. Leith Stevens (Coral), Bob Troup (Lib., Vict., Beth.), Tal Farlow (Verve).

Addr: 16423 Kinzie St., Granada Hills, Calif.

ENNIS, ETHEL, *singer;* b. Baltimore, Md., 11/28/34. Began stud. piano at seven; pl. in clubs and for friends while in high school; won local TV amateur singing contest in 1950 and began pl. night clubs in Baltimore, Cleveland etc. Joined Benny Goodman summer '58 for European tour. A small-voiced night club singer; not a jazz artist despite her associations with jazzmen. Own LPs: *Change of Scenery, Have You Forgotten* (Cap.); *Lullabies for Losers* (Jub.).

ERICSON, ROLF, *trumpet;* b. Stockholm, Sweden, 8/29/27. To US '47. Worked w. Benny Carter, Ch. Barnet, Elliot Lawrence, Ch. Ventura, Benny Goodman, and several months w. Woody Herman. Returned to Sweden '50, worked w. Arne Domnerus orch. Back to US '52. Worked w. Ch. Spivak, Stan Kenton, then w. Howard Rumsey at Lighthouse in Calif. Toured Sweden with own all star American combo, summer '56; spent most of '56-8 on West Coast working w. Harry James, Les Brown and at the Lighthouse. Joined Stan Kenton '59. Own LP on Merc.; LPs w. Curtis Counce (Dooto), Harold Land (Contemp.), Lighthouse All Stars (Contemp.).

Addr: 5007 W. 118th Place, Hawthorne, Calif.

ERRAIR, KENNETH EDWARD, *singer, trumpet;* b. Detroit, Mich., 1/23/28. No formal training. In Navy 1946-7, pl. in first dance band below the Antarctic Circle in Byrd Expedition, also did benefit concert in Alaska. Began working in Detroit clubs '49, pl. trumpet, then as singer in '50. Four Freshmen came through Detroit needing a replacement, and he joined them in '53, left in '56. Married actress Jane Withers. After leaving Freshmen, was heard as solo performer. Own LP: *Solo Session* (Cap.); LPs w. Four Freshmen (Cap.).

Addr: 19700 Devonshire, Chatsworth, Calif.

ERVIN, BOOKER TELLEFERRO JR., *tenor sax;* b. Denison, Tex., 10/31/30. Pl. tbn. 1939-44 in high school, Denison; stud. tnr. at Berklee Sch. of Mus., Boston, '50; pl. on Okinawa '51-2 while in Air Force. Toured w. Ernie Fields '54-5; pl. in Dallas, Denver, '56-7, then in Pittsburgh; to NYC May '58. Joined Ch. Mingus, Nov. '58. Also pl. w. John Bunch at RIJF '59, Roland Hanna '59. Forceful and persuasive modern soloist. Fav: J. Coltrane. Infl. by Lester Young, Dexter Gordon, Sonny Stitt. LPs w. Ch. Mingus (Atl., UA, Col.).

Addr: 316 East 6th St., NYC.

ERWIN, GEORGE (Pee Wee), *trumpet, leader;* b. Falls City, Neb., 5/30/13. Raised in KC, where father played trumpet in territory bands and gave him first horn and lessons. Joined Eddie Kuhn 1927, Joe Haymes '31, Isham Jones '33, Freddie Martin '34. While w. Ray Noble '35, did *Let's Dance* broadcast w. Benny Goodman, replacing Bunny Berigan. Joined Goodman again Jan. '36, Tommy Dorsey Mar. '37, remaining off and on to '39 when he joined Raymond Scott Quintet. Had own big band '41-2, then freelanced in radio until '49, when his own Dixieland sextet made its debut at Nick's, NYC. He was there most of the time throughout the 1950s and in '60. Fav: Berigan. Own LPs on UA, Gr. Award, Cadence, Uran., Command, Evst., Bruns.; LPs w. T. Dorsey (Vict.), Bobby Byrne (Gr. Award).

Addr: 1393 6th Ave., New York 19, N.Y.

ESTES, GENE PAUL, *vibes, drums;* b. Amarillo, Tex., 10/3/31. Father a prof. drummer. St. with children's bands. Pl. drums w. Will Osborne, 1950; Air Force dance band in Washington, '51-4. Later pl. drums and vibes w. Jack Teagarden, Paul Horn, Fred Katz; vibes

w. Harry Babasin, Billy Bean, John Pisano. ABC staff work and many West Coast TV shows incl. *Peter Gunn*. Own LP: Carlton; LPs w. Bean-Pisano (Decca), F. Katz (War. Bros., Wor. Pac.). Favs: Milt Jackson, Cal Tjader, Jo Jones.

Addr: 12329 Califa St., North Hollywood, Cal.

EUELL, JULIAN THOMAS, *bass;* b. New York City, 5/23/29. Took up bass in '44. Army '45-7. In '47 stud. at 3rd St. Settlement House, pl. w. S. Rollins, J. McLean, Art Taylor; gave up playing, worked in post office '49-52. Gigged w. Benny Harris '52-4. Stud. w. Ch. Mingus, Fred Zimmerman, '53; a year in mus. dept. at Col. U. '54-5. Jobbed w. Joe Roland '55, Freddie Redd trio '56; Gigi Gryce quintet '56-7, Phineas Newborn '57. Stud. at NYU '51-4, att. Col. U. to receive BS in sociology; active in youth work in Newark, N.J. from Jan. '58-fall '59. During this period semi-active in music, playing w. Mal Waldron '58, '59; Randy Weston '59. Then returned to jazz on a full-time basis. Highly regarded by Mingus, he is generally credited with less than his actual talent. Fav: Pettiford. LPs w. Waldron (Pres., New Jazz), Coltrane-Quinichette (Pres.).

Addr: 1611 Park Ave., New York 29, N.Y.

EUROPE, JAMES REESE (Jim), *leader;* b. Mobile, Ala., 2/22/81; d. New York City, 5/10/19. Moved to Washington, D.C. before he was ten and stud. violin w. assistant dir. of U.S. Marine Band. Came to NYC 1904 and got job as pianist; in 1910 org. the Clef Club, a clearing house for Negro musicians. Had concert at Carnegie Hall '14 featuring 125 singers and musicians. Toured US with Vernon and Irene Castle 1914; rec. for Victor and worked NYC clubs. Was Lieutenant in Army, org. 369th Infantry Regiment Band. Had a successful tour of France '18; ret. to US in 1919 and was stabbed to death in a night club altercation. Though a few jazzmen worked for him, Europe had no direct relationship to jazz.

EVANS, WILLIAM J. (Bill), *piano, composer;* b. Plainfield, N.J., 8/16/29. Stud. piano, violin, flute. Had own group w. brother at 16, incl. Don Elliott. Degree from Southeastern Louisiana Coll.; pl. w. Mundell Lowe and Red Mitchell. Six months w. Herbie Fields 1950, followed by a year in Army. After discharge in '54, worked w. Jerry Wald, Tony Scott. From Feb. until Nov. 1958 he was with the combo of Miles Davis, who says: "I sure learned a lot from Bill Evans. He plays the piano the way it should be played." Recently he has studied at Mannes School of Music in NYC, led his own trio and free-lanced. On faculty at School of Jazz, Lenox, Mass., summer 1959. He was prominently heard in the sound track of John Lewis' score for the film *Odds Against Tomorrow*, 1959. An intellectual, skilled and serious musician, Evans has never lost touch with an essential need to swing. He is a pianist and composer of great distinction, whom Julian Adderley has credited with "rare originality and taste." Own LPs: Riverside; *Ivory Hunters* w. Brookmeyer (UA); LPs w. Miles Davis (Col.), Art Farmer, Bill Potts, *Odds Against Tomorrow* (UA), Konitz-Giuffre (Verve), George Russell (Decca), Eddie Costa (Coral); w. Gunther Schuller in *Modern Jazz Concert* (Col.).

Addr: 310 West 106th St., New York 25, N.Y.

EVANS, PAUL WESLEY (Doc), *cornet;* b. Spring Valley, Minn., 6/20/07. Played violin, piano, drums, sax, but was cornetist with band at Carleton Coll., Minn., from which he graduated 1929; gave up sax entirely for cornet in 1931. During 1930s taught school for a year, raised champion cocker spaniels, returning to music full-time 1939 w. Red Dougherty. Heard in many jazz concerts w. Bunk Johnson, Eddie Condon, etc. in '40s; led combo 1940-1 incl. Joe Sullivan; has toured with own group in recent years, most often around Minnesota, where he has great following as Dixieland leader. Own LPs on Audiophile, Soma; *Dixieland At Jazz Ltd.* (Atl.).

EVANS, GIL (Ian Ernest Gilmore Green), *composer, piano;* b. Toronto, Canada, 5/13/12 of Australian parentage. Raised in British Columbia, state of Washington, and Stockton, Calif. Self-taught. From 1933-8 he led his own band in Stockton; when this group was taken over by Skinnay Ennis he remained with it as arranger until 1941.

Except for an Army stint from '43-6, Evans was with the Claude Thornhill orchestra from 1941-8. His arrangements for the band during this period, which employed French horns as well as the conventional brass, reed and rhythm sections, showed more originality in their variety of tonal textures than anything else that was then being created in either the dance band or the jazz field; nevertheless he was completely ignored by the critics and unknown to the public.

Toward the end of this period, however, Evans became one of the key figures in a group of musicians who were eager to experiment with similarly heterodox ideas in the form of a smaller group for jazz performances. The informal workshop that included Evans, Miles Davis, Gerry Mulligan and John Lewis eventually produced a series of significant records under the name of Davis (q.v.). Evans orchestrated *Moondreams* and *Boplicity* for this group (heard in *Birth of the Cool,* Capitol T 762).

Evans never played any instrument professionally until 1952, when he took up piano seriously. He free-lanced as an arranger in NYC in comparative obscurity; the only writer to acknowledge him in print was Andre Hodeir, who in 1954 wrote: "*Boplicity* is enough to qualify Gil Evans as one of jazz's greatest composer-arrangers."

After a 1957 reunion of Evans and Miles Davis, which produced *Miles Ahead,* a Columbia album by a 19-piece band, the other jazz critics belatedly jumped on the bandwagon and suddenly Evans found himself the subject of innumerable scholarly analyses. Soon he was in constant demand for record dates. By 1958 he was a recording bandleader in his own right; he collaborated with Davis on further albums; in '59 he led his own band at Birdland, in one of his rare public appearances.

In the recordings under his own name Evans has made frequent use of a soprano saxophone (played by Steve Lacy). No matter what the instrumentation or size of the groups for which he has written, he extracted from each a fullness and orchestral variety compared to which the average swing band arrangement of the 1930s seemed like the work of a child playing with blocks. Despite the complexity of his work on every level—melodic, rhythmic, tonal and especially harmonic—Evans, like Duke Ellington, has remained firmly rooted to jazz and as a consequence has succeeded in taking the music a step further along the path to orchestral maturity. Own LPs: *New Bottle, Old Wine* (Wor. Pac. 1246), *Great Jazz Standards* (Wor. Pac. 1270), *Big Stuff* (New Jazz 8215); arrs. for Miles Davis: *Miles Ahead* (Col. CL 1041), *Porgy And Bess* (Col. CL 1274), *Birth of the Cool* (Cap. T 762), Claude Thornhill (Harm. 7088), Helen Merrill —*Dream of You* (Em. 36078), Don Elliott—*Jamaica Jazz* (ABC-Par. 228); two originals for Hal McKusick in *Jazz Workshop* (Vict. LPM 1366); one arr. for *Teddy Charles Tentet* (Atl. 1229).

Addr: Whitby Apts., 325 West 45th St., New York 36, N.Y.

EVANS, HERSCHEL, *tenor sax;* b. Denton, Texas, 1909; d. New York City, 2/9/39. Worked w. Benny Moten and w. Lionel Hampton's early Calif. band; attained prominence as alternate tenor soloist w. Lester Young in the Count Basie band, w. which he played from 1936 until his death. Considered one of the finest soloists of the warm-toned Coleman Hawkins school, and a direct influence on tenormen like Buddy Tate, Illinois Jacquet and Arnett Cobb, he scored his biggest success w. Basie's record of *Blue and Sentimental.* Comp. *Texas Shuffle, Doggin' Around.* While w. Basie rec. sessions w. Mildred Bailey, L. Hampton, Harry James, Teddy Wilson. LPs w. Basie (Bruns., Decca), *Spirituals To Swing* (Vang.), w. Harry James in *$64,000 Jazz* (Col.).

EWELL, DONALD TYNAN (Don), *piano, composer;* b. Baltimore, Md., 11/14/16. Brother, Ed Lynch, pl. trombone w. Casa Loma band. Stud. at Peabody Cons. With the Townsmen, local swing band, 1936-40; flute, piccolo etc. w. military bands during war. Bunk Johnson, spring of '46; Doc Evans '47; S. Bechet '48; M. Spanier '49; Miff Mole '49-50; Geo. Brunis '51, then various Dixieland and modern combos in Chi. incl. own group. Eddie Wiggins '52; Lee Collins '53; Kid Ory '53-5; single at Hangover in SF, then with Jack Teagarden from summer of '56 almost continuously through '60. Plays excellent interpretations of the styles of his favorites: James P. Johnson, Jelly Roll Morton, Fats Waller. Own LP: GTJ; LPs w. *Dixieland At Jazz Ltd.* (Atl.), Miff Mole (Argo), Turk Murphy (Col.), Albert Nicholas in *Creole Reeds* (River.), Kid Ory (GTJ), Jack Teagarden (Cap., Roul.).

EXINER, WILLIAM, *drums;* b. Brooklyn, N.Y., 11/22/10. Worked w. band pl. opposite Stuff Smith at Onyx Club in mid-1930s; w. Hudson-DeLange orch. '37; Mal Hallett '38-9; Jan Savitt '39-40; Georgie Auld '41-2, then in Army. Joined Harry James '46; Peggy Lee '47-9; Claude Thornhill '50-3; Barbara Carroll '54. Joined Tony Bennett mid-54. Simple, underrated modern drummer. Favs: Catlett, Cole, Jo Jones. LPs w. Peggy Lee (Cap.); Tony Bennett (Col.), C. Thornhill (Harm.).

Addr: 147-32 72nd Road, Flushing 67, N.Y.

F

FAGERQUIST, DONALD A. (Don), *trumpet;* b. Worcester, Mass., 2/6/27. With Mal Hallet 1943; Gene Krupa '44-5, again in '48, later had own combo backing Anita O'Day. Also worked w. Artie Shaw, Woody Herman, Les Brown. Joined staff of Paramount film studios in LA, Jan. '56. LPs w. *Jazz Studio 2* (Decca), Shelly Manne (Contemp.), Les Brown (Coral, Cap.), John Graas (Decca), Mel Tormé (Beth.), *West Coast vs. East Coast* (MGM), Dave Pell (Atl., Cap., Kapp), Gene Krupa (Col.).

Addr: 7261 Ponce Ave., Canoga Park, Calif.

FAGERSTEDT, CLAES-GORAN, *piano;* b. Stockholm, Sweden, 11/18/28. Pl. w. Nisse Skoogh, 1948; own band, '49-53; Thore Jederby, '53; Lars Gullin off and on from '54; Jazz Club '57; own group '57-60. Rec. w. Gullin, Jazz Club '57 on Sonet label. Favs: B. Powell, T. Monk, Bill Evans. Swedish critic Carl-Erik Lindgren says of Fagerstedt (who is a textile salesman and part-time musician): "He is more or less a leader of a clique of Swedish jazzmen who favor men like Coltrane, Rollins and Silver instead of earlier influences. He discovered Bernt Rosengren."

Addr: Multragatan 36, Vällingby, Sweden.

FAIRWEATHER, ALEXANDER (Al), *trumpet;* b. Edinburgh, Scotland, 6/12/27. Self-taught. Played with Sandy Brown, 1948-53 and '54-7; Cy Laurie, '53-4; own sextet '58-60. Recs. for Tempo, Pye-Nixa, Engl. Col. Favs: Armstrong, Edison, Eldridge.

Addr: 44 Peel Road, Wealdstone, Middlesex, England.

FARLOW, TALMADGE HOLT (Tal), *guitar;* b. Greensboro, N.C., 6/7/21. Worked as sign painter; picked up guitar in 1943; inspired by Charlie Christian. First major job w. trio led by pianist Dardanelle. To NYC with Marjorie Hyams trio '48; played with Buddy De Franco sextet '49, Red Norvo trio '50-3, Artie Shaw's Gramercy 5 '53-4; back with Norvo May '54-Oct. '55, then went into semi-retirement, emerging occasionally for trio dates at Composer, NYC etc. One of the most inventive and facile of modern guitarists, Farlow introduced a specially made fingerboard more than an inch shorter than the standard length, for looser tuning and softer sound. He won the DB critics' poll New Star Award '54. Favs: Christian, J. Raney. Own LPs: Verve; LPs w. Norvo (Decca, Savoy, Fant.), Artie Shaw, B. De Franco (Verve).

Addr: 16 Peninsula Avenue, Sea Bright, N.J.

FARMER, ADDISON GERALD, *bass;* b. Council Bluffs, Iowa, 8/21/28. Twin brother of trumpeter, Art Farmer. Stud. bass with Fred Zimmerman; piano and theory at Juilliard and Manhattan School of Music. Has worked w. Jay McShann, Art Farmer, Benny Carter, Howard McGhee, Gerald Wilson, Teddy Charles, Lucky Thompson, Ch. Parker, Miles Davis. Record debut in L.A., 1949 w. Teddy Edwards. Free-lanced in NYC several years w. many groups, incl. Art Farmer-Gigi Gryce, Teddy Charles, Stan Getz and Mose Allison, before joining a group formed by his brother and Benny Golson Oct. '59. Favs: O. Pettiford, R. Brown, P. Heath. LPs w. Mose Allison, Gene Ammons, Teo Macero, *Prestige Jazz Quartet,* Mal Waldron (Pres.), Art Farmer (Pres., New Jazz, Contemp., UA), Stan Getz (Verve).

Addr: 20 West 95th St., New York 25, N.Y.

FARMER, ARTHUR STEWART (Art), *trumpet;* b. Council Bluffs, Iowa, 8/21/28. Raised in Phoenix, Ariz. He and twin brother, Addison, went to LA in 1945. Worked w. Horace Henderson, Floyd Ray, then came East w. Johnny Otis. Free-lanced in NYC '47-8 and studied w. Maurice Grupp. Ret. to West Coast '48 and pl. w. Benny Carter; w. Wardell Gray '51. Joined Lionel Hampton for a year in the fall of '52, touring Europe w. him in '53. Settled in NYC fall '53 and gigged w. Gigi Gryce. Formed quintet w. Gryce in late '54 which stayed together, off and on, until midway in '56. Joined Horace Silver, Aug. '56, then Gerry Mulligan '58, app. w. the latter in the films *I Want To Live, The Subterraneans.* In late '59, Farmer and tenor man Benny Golson formed their own group, the Jazztet. A lyrical, highly sensitive performer, he is one of the most adaptable of contemporary trumpeters; he has managed to fit, successfully, the styles of such diverse groups as George Russell, Silver and Mulligan. Won DB Critics' poll '58. First rec. w. Jay McShann, Gerald Wilson '49. Own LPs on Pres., New Jazz, ABC-Par., UA, Contemp.; LPs w. Mulligan (UA, Col.), Silver, Sonny Clark (Blue Note), Gene Ammons, Wardell Gray, Gil Melle, Bennie Green, *Earthy, Three Trumpets* (Pres.), Mal Waldron (New Jazz), Jimmy Cleveland (Em.), Gigi Gryce; *Trumpets All Out* (Savoy), Sandole Bros. (Fant.), Benny Golson (River., Contemp.), Hal McKusick (Decca, Coral), Manny Albam (Coral), *Alabama Concerto* (River.), *Modern Jazz Concert* (Col.), George Russell (Decca, Vict.), Bill Potts (UA).

FARROW, ERNEST (Ernie), *bass;* also *drums, piano;* b. Huntington, West Va., 11/13/28. Stud. piano first in NYC under uncle, Charles Lewis. St. playing w. own little band in high school. With Terry Gibbs '54, Stan Getz '55, Yusef Lateef from '56; also own trio at Blue Bird in Detroit, '58, Red Garland trio '60. Favs: Blanton, Ray Brown, Pettiford, Junior Raglin. LPs w. Gibbs, Johnny Williams (Merc.), Lateef (Pres., Savoy, Verve).

Addr: 9453 Ravenswood, Detroit 4, Mich.

FATOOL, NICHOLAS (Nick), *drums;* b. Milbury, Mass., 1/2/15. W. Don Bestor, Joe Haymes, '37; Geo. Hall, '38; Benny Goodman '39-40, Artie Shaw '40-1. Later worked w. Claude Thornhill, Jan Savitt, Alvino Rey; settled on West Coast, played w. Harry James and did studio work incl. Bing Crosby show, 1956-8; *Pete Kelly's Blues,* '59; concerts w. Bob Crosby band '57-9. Has taken part in Frank Bull-Gene Norman Dixieland Jubilees for past 13 years. LPs: *Coast Concert* w. Bobby Hackett (Cap.); *Dixieland Jubilee* (Decca); Matty Matlock, Pete Kelly (War. Bros.), Glen Gray (Cap.); Benny Goodman (MGM, Col.; *Spirituals To Swing,* Vang.).

Addr: 7003 Haskell Ave., Van Nuys, Calif.

FATTY GEORGE (Franz Pressler), *clarinet;* b. Vienna, Austria, 4/24/27. Mother pl. guitar in folk music trio. Started on alto sax in Vienna 1942, then seven years of clarinet studies in Konservatorium and music high school. Turned prof. in '45 at Russian clubs, later pl. for GI clubs. To Germany '47 opened jazz club. In late '50 pl. w. Special Service band in Nurnberg. Opened Fatty's Jazz Casino in Innsbruck '52. Back to Vienna '55, pl. there and touring Germany, Switzerland, France and Italy. Opened Fatty's Saloon in Vienna '58. Has app. at jazz festivals in San Remo, Italy, Bath, England among others. Favs: originally infl. by Goodman, he now cites Ch. Parker, Ed Hall, Gillespie, Hodges, Hucko, Miles Davis as well. Rec. on German labels.

Addr: Fatty's Saloon, Petersplatz 1, Vienna 1, Austria.

FAZOLA, IRVING, *clarinet;* b. New Orleans, 12/10/12; d. 3/20/49. Played in NO w. Candy Candido, Louis Prima. In NYC w. Ben Pollack '35, Gus Arnheim '36, Glenn Miller '37-8, Bob Crosby Mar. '38 to Aug. '40. Later w. Claude Thornhill; Muggsy Spanier '41-2; Teddy Powell, Horace Heidt. Retired to NO, working w. local bands off and on until his death. Was considered almost the only clarinetist to combine NO influences with the newer elements of the Benny Goodman swing era. Several free-lance record dates w. Billie Holiday, Sharkey Bonano, etc. Won DB poll '40-1. Own LP: eight tracks in *New Orleans Express* (EmArcy); one track in *Great Jazz Reeds* (Cam.); LP w. Bob Crosby (Decca).

FEATHERSTONHAUGH, RUPERT EDWARD LEE (Buddy), *baritone saxophone;* also *tenor, clarinet;* b. Paris, France, 10/4/09. Stud. at school in Sussex, England. Debut w. Pat O'Malley combo in Hendon, 1927. Prominent as a tenor soloist in the 1930s, he recorded with Spike Hughes, '30-31; toured w. Louis Armstrong band '32; rec. w. Valaida Snow, '35 and Benny Carter, '37. Had own sextet for BBC Radio Rhythm Club and HMV recordings, '43-5, and in trip to Iceland, '46, then was semi-inactive in jazz, working as auto salesman. In recent years, playing baritone, had own pianoless quintet for Pye-Nixa Records and jazz club gigs, 1956-8; toured Middle East for British War Office w. quintet, '57. Almost alone among British jazzmen of his generation he has developed into a first-class (and greatly underrated) modern stylist. Fav: Mulligan. No LPs in US.

Addr: 39 Haringey Park, Crouch End, London N.8., England.

FELD, MOREY, *drums;* b. Cleveland, O., 8/15/15. Self-taught. Played w. Ben Pollack '36; Joe Haymes '38; Benny Goodman '44-5; Eddie Condon '47; Billy Butterfield '52; Bobby Hackett '53; Peanuts Hucko '54; ABC staff orchestra '55-'60. Made record debut '40 w. Jess Stacy combo; many sessions in mid-'40s w. Slam Stewart, Red Norvo et al. Film: *Sweet and Lowdown* w. Goodman. Favs: Buddy Rich, Don Lamond. Own LP on Kapp; LPs w. Goodman (Col.).

Addr: 350 West 55th St., New York 19, N.Y.

FELDMAN, VICTOR STANLEY (Vic), *vibes, drums, piano, composer;* b. London, England, 4/7/34. Mainly self-taught through listening to brothers; played gig on drums at age seven and was hailed as child genius. Record debut at eight. Took up piano at nine. Stud. at London Coll. of Mus.; vibes at 14 w. Carlo Krahmer. Own trio w. two brothers 1941-7; guest star w. Glenn Miller AEF band '44; played w. Vic Lewis, Ted Heath; to Switzerland w. Ralph Sharon '49. Paris Jazz Festival '52; to India w. Eddie Carroll '53-4. Won five magazine awards as Britain's number one vibes man. Left for US Oct. '55; toured w. Woody Herman, Jan. '56-June '57. Settled in Los Angeles, worked w. Lighthouse All Stars Oct. '57-Aug. '59. Stud. arr. w. Marty Paich '59. Won DB Critics Poll as new star on vibes '58. A brilliant musician, by '59 he was in constant demand for choice studio jazz work incl. regular TV shows such as *Peter Gunn* w. Hank Mancini, etc. Favs: Milt Jackson, Norvo, vibes; Tatum, John Lewis, piano; Sid Catlett, Tiny Kahn, Max Roach, Buddy Rich, Kenny Clarke, Art Taylor, drums; Ellington, Mulligan, J. Lewis, arrangers. Own LPs: Contemporary, Interlude; LPs w. Hank Mancini (Vict.), Bert Dahlander (Verve), Shelly Manne, Leroy Vinnegar, Jimmy Deuchar, Bob Cooper (Contemp.), Howard Rumsey (Omega Disk), *Esprit De Jazz* w. Terry Gibbs & Larry Bunker (Inter.), Buddy De Franco, Mel Tormé (Verve), Woody Herman (Cap.), Herb Geller (Jub.), Dempsey Wright (Andex).

Addr: 19355 Pacific Coast Highway, Malibu, Calif.

FERGUSON, ALLYN M., *piano;* b. San Jose, Calif., 10/18/24. Father pianist and trombonist w. dance bands. Stud. trumpet with Loring Nichols (Red's father) at 4 years; piano at 7. Played prof. since 14, working w. various dance bands on West Coast. Holds both B.A. and M.A. in music. Organized Chamber Jazz Sextet in 1956. Acc. Kenneth Patchen's readings on Cad. Worked w. Skinnay Ennis '59, then reformed Chamber Jazz Sextet. Own LPs on Cadence.

Addr: 8066 Woodland Lane, Los Angeles 46, Calif.

FERGUSON, MAYNARD, *leader, trumpet, valve trombone, baritone horn;* also *saxes, clarinet, oboe, French horn;* b. Montreal, Canada, 5/4/28. Stud. at French Cons. of Mus. in Montreal. Had own band in Verdun, Quebec, '43-7. First seen in U.S. '48 w. Boyd Raeburn, also solo act at Cafe Society playing saxes, several brass instruments; later w. J. Dorsey orch. Left Canada permanently July '49, pl. w. Ch. Barnet. Joined Stan Kenton Jan. '50 and remained with him, except for one absence of a few months, until summer of '53, building big following with fantastic technique and screaming high-note style.

After three years of free-lancing in LA, working with every type of group from studio orch. to hillbilly bands, Ferguson led the Birdland Dream Band in NYC Aug. '56 and another all-star band in LA Dec. '56. From March '57 he led a permanently organized 13-piece band. With arrs. by Willie Maiden, Bill Holman, Slide Hampton et al, it soon achieved great popularity in the East, appearing regularly at Birdland; toured in *Jazz for Moderns* show fall of '58 and '59.

Ferguson is an anomaly in modern jazz. Although it was his forays into the stratosphere that helped win him the DB poll on trumpet in '50-1-2, it was only after he began to reveal a more balanced style, playing solos in the normal register and doubling effectively on valve trombone, that he began to earn acceptance among critics. Respected by Miles Davis and most fellow-musicians, he has shown greatly improved taste in recent years and his band, which ran second only to Basie's in the '59 DB readers' poll, has revealed a library of often valid and brilliantly scored music, though suffering from a lack of shading and a tendency toward excessive volume. Own LPs: Roulette, EmArcy; LPs w. Kenton (Cap.), Pete Rugolo (Merc., Col.), Georgia Auld (Em.), *Jam Session* (Em.), Johnny Richards (Beth.), as "Tiger Brown" w. Jack Millman (Decca).

Addr: 530 West End Avenue, New York 24, N.Y.

FIELDING, JERRY (Joshua Feldman), *leader, arranger;* b. Pittsburgh, Pa., 6/17/22. Studied piano, clarinet, sax; to West Coast at seventeen w. Alvino Rey band as arranger. Later wrote for T. Dorsey, Ch. Barnet, Kay Kyser and was mus. dir. on Groucho Marx and Mickey Rooney TV shows; also worked on "Life of Riley" show. Toured with own semi-jazz dance band 1954. Own LPs: Decca, Kapp, Hanover.

Addr: c/o E. H. Gordon, 9399 Wilshire Blvd., Beverly Hills, Calif.

FIELDS, HERBERT (Herbie), *saxes, clarinet;* b. Elizabeth, N.J., 5/24/19; d. Miami, Fla., 9/17/58. Juilliard '36-8. Worked w. Raymond Scott, Leonard Ware trio, and others; served in Army, leading band at Fort Dix '41-3. Later had own civilian band but gave it up in '44 and joined Lionel Hampton for a year. From early

'46, had own band, recording for Vict. Won Esq. New Star Award on alto in '45. Originally a jazz musician, later specialized in commercialism. Fields, relatively inactive in the late Fifties and despondent over reversals in his career, committed suicide. Own LPs: RKO-Unique; one half of *Blow Hot, Blow Cool* (Decca); LPs w. Woody Herman (Bruns.), Lionel Hampton (Decca), Metronome All Stars (Cam.).

FIELDS, CARL DONNELL (Kansas), *drums;* b. Chapman, Kansas, 12/5/15. Stud. drums in Chicago, 1930. In late '30s played in Chicago w. Johnny Long, Jimmie Noone, Walter Fuller; w. King Kolax '40, Roy Eldridge '41, also own band. With Ella Fitzgerald '41, then to NYC w. Benny Carter. Worked w. Edgar Hayes, Charlie Barnet, also w. Parker, Gillespie, at Minton's '42. Navy '42 to '45; after discharge, joined Cab Calloway, then gigged w. Eddie Condon, Willie "The Lion" Smith and Roy Eldridge. With Sidney Bechet at Jimmy Ryan's '47, Dizzy Gillespie '49, own group at Cafe Society Downtown '51. Toured Europe w. Babs Gonzales and Mezz Mezzrow '53; living in Europe since '54. LPs w. Lionel Hampton (Em.), Dizzy Gillespie (Savoy).

FINEGAN, WILLIAM J. (Bill), *leader, composer, piano;* b. Newark, N.J., 4/3/17. Parents, sister, brother all play piano (not prof.). Stud. privately and at high school; later at Paris Cons. His first break came through Tommy Dorsey, who, after buying his arr. of *Lonesome Road,* played it for Glenn Miller, who offered Finegan a job in late 1938. After working as staff arr. for Miller until 1942, he joined Dorsey, arr. for him intermittently for the next 10 years. From 1948-50 he lived in France and England, studying much of the time. He joined forces with Eddie Sauter in 1952 to form the Sauter-Finegan band, which remained together until March '57. Sauter and Finegan collaborated again in '59, doing commercial jingle work for TV and radio. Finegan wrote many of Dorsey's best arrangements during the '40s.

Never prof. active as a soloist, Finegan says his best work on record is a chest solo on the Sauter-Finegan record *Midnight Sleigh Ride* ("I beat on my chest to simulate the sound of a sleigh horse running on hard-packed snow; this is probably my finest effort on wax—or snow.") Arrs. for Dorsey incl. *The Continental, Wagon Wheels, Hollywood Hat, Bingo, Bango, Boffo* and *Pussy Willow.* Arrs. for Miller incl. *Little Brown Jug, Song of The Volga Boatmen, Sunrise Serenade, Serenade In Blue, Rhapsody In Blue.* Fav. arrs: Sauter, Sy Oliver, Gerry Mulligan. LPs: Sauter-Finegan (Vict.); *Jingles All The Way* (Lib.).

Addr: 425 E. 63rd St., New York 21, N.Y.

FISCHER, HORST, *trumpet;* b. Chemnitz, Germany, 6/8/30. Stud. violin 1937-45; trumpet '44-6. Played w. Ernst Knauth '47, Karl Walter '48-9, Leipzig radio band '49-51. First trumpet and soloist w. Erwin Lehn Stuttgart radio dance band from April '51; own big band on Philips Records '57. Several movie tracks. Favs: C. Candoli, M. Ferguson, C. Baker, M. Davis, C. Brown. Rec. w. Erwin Lehn, own group, etc.

Addr: Neustadt Krs. Waiblingen, Korberstrasse Neubau, Germany.

FISHKIN, ARNOLD (Fishkind), *bass;* b. Bayonne, N.J., 7/20/19. Raised in Freeport, L.I. Childhood friend and neighbor of Chubby Jackson. Violin at 8, bass at 14. Bunny Berigan big band '37. Jack Teagarden '40-1. Then played w. Les Brown until Army service '42-6. After release, played w. Dick Stabile, Jerry Wald. Joined Lennie Tristano trio (w. Billy Bauer) in Freeport. To West Coast w. Ch. Barnet. Played in Hollywood w. the Butch Stone band, which also included Stan Getz, Shorty Rogers. Back in NYC, worked w. Tristano; into free-lance radio '50; later joined ABC staff. Favs: J. Blanton, R. Brown. LPs w. Lee Konitz (Pres., Atl.), Johnny Smith (Roost), one track w. Tristano in *History of Jazz, Vol. 4* (Cap.).

Addr: 10 Southfield Road, Glen Cove, L.I., N.Y.

FITCH, MAL, *singer, piano, composer;* b. Cleveland, O., 1927. Stud. with Cleveland Philharmonic conductor and others; 2 yrs. at Bethany College. Entered service '45, later continuing studies until '50. During Army career was leader of 2nd Army Band at Ft. Meade, Md., '46-8, also acting as disc jockey on Armed Forces station. Formed duo with wife, Betty, a singer, working in Dallas hotel for more than a year. With Crew-cuts, popular vocal group in mid-'50s as pianist and arr., Fitch showed attractive vocal style recalling at times some of the characteristics of Nat Cole and Bobby Troup.

FITZGERALD, ELLA, *singer;* b. Newport News, Va., 4/25/18. Discovered while singing at amateur show in Harlem 1934. Joined Chick Webb's band; made her first record (*Love and Kisses*) w. Webb, June 12, '35. She remained with him until his death, then took over leadership of the band for a year. Afterwards, she appeared as a solo act in nightclubs and theaters. During her years with Webb, she built up a tremendous reputation among musicians and other singers for her bell-like clarity of tone, flexibility of range, and rhythmic brilliance of style, all of which were equally effective on ballads and rhythm tunes. Her biggest hit was the novelty song *A-tisket, A-tasket,* which she recorded with Webb, May 2, '38. From '46, she worked frequently with Norman Granz, appearing on his annual tours and visiting Europe and Japan with JATP unit. By this time, she had become the favorite female singer of virtually all her contemporaries. Many of her records used vocal material of the lowest grade and she had to rise above it to give consistently compelling performances. This situation changed late in '55 when, ending her 20-year affiliation with Decca, she began to record for Norman Granz on his new Verve label. Under the personal management of Granz, she began to play choice hotel jobs, etc., and to earn even wider general recognition. Her first featured film appearance, in *Pete Kelly's Blues,* gave her added attention in late '55. During '57 she set several new precedents, appearing at the Copacabana in NYC, and presenting her own concert at the Hollywood Bowl. In April '58, she gave a Carnegie Hall concert with Duke Ellington to celebrate the release of a four-LP set on Verve titled *Ella Fitzgerald Sings the Duke Ellington Song Book;* also on B. Goodman's *Swing Into Spring* TV show on NBC. She continued to visit Europe annually, teamed with the Oscar Peterson Trio as a concert attraction.

Among the many awards won by Ella Fitzgerald are: *Esquire* Gold Award '46 (tie), Silver Award '47; *Metronome* poll '54, '56 (tie), '57-60; *Down Beat* poll '37-9, '53-9; *Down Beat* Critics' poll '53-9; Playboy poll '57-60.

From '48-'52 she was married to bassist Ray Brown. Favs: she admires many contemporary pop and jazz singers, but names Connee Boswell as her original inspiration and influence.

Own LPs: *Lullabies of Birdland* (Decca 8149), *Best of Ella* (2-Decca DX 156), *Ella & Her Fellas* (Dec. 8477), *First Lady of Song* (Dec. 8695), *Sweet and Hot* (Dec. 8155), *Pete Kelly's Blues* (Dec. 8166), *Ella Sings Gershwin* (Dec. 8378); *Billie, Ella, Lena, Sarah* (anthology) (Harmony 7125). Following are all on Verve: *Cole Porter Song Book* (4001-2); *Rodgers & Hart Song Book* (4002-2); *Ella & Louis* (4003); *Like Someone In Love* (4004); *Ella & Louis Again* (4006-2); *Duke Ellington Song Book* (four LPs) (4010-4); *Porgy & Bess* with Armstrong (4011-2); *Ella Sings Irving Berlin* (4019-2); *Swings Lightly* (4021); *Here Come the Girls* (anthology) (2036); *Metronome All Stars 1956* (anthology) (8030); *Jazz at the Hollywood Bowl* (anthology) (8231-2); *Ella and Billie at Newport* (8234); *Ella at Opera House* (8264); *One O'Clock Jump* (8288); *Sweet Songs for Swingers* (4032); *Gershwin Song Books* (five LPs) (4029); *Hello Love* (4034).

Addr: 3971 Hepburn Avenue, Los Angeles, Calif.

FLANAGAN, RALPH, *composer, leader, piano;* b. Lorain, Ohio, 4/7/19. Arranged for Sammy Kaye, Hal McIntyre, Charlie Barnet, Alvino Rey. Started touring w. own band March '50; became very successful in popular field. His records only occasionally have a jazz flavor. LPs: Cam., Vict., Imp.

Addr: M.C.A., 7630 Biscayne Blvd., Miami 38, Fla.

FLANAGAN, TOMMY LEE, *piano;* b. Detroit, 3/16/30. Clarinet at 6; piano at 11; prof. debut 1945 w. Dexter Gordon; later w. Lucky Thompson, Milt Jackson, Rudy Rutherford '46-8. Was w. Billy Mitchell before and after Army service '51-3. Joined Kenny Burrell '54; to NYC Feb. '56, worked w. O. Pettiford to May, subbed for Bud Powell at Birdland; acc. Ella Fitzgerald July-Aug.; toured w. J. J. Johnson Sept. '56-Sept. '57; Miles Davis to Dec. '57; back with J. J. Jan.-Oct. '58. Own trio at Composer, NYC; w. Tyree Glenn at Roundtable, then with Harry Edison quintet '59-60. The best pianist since Hank Jones to be produced by the Detroit area. Own LP: Prestige; LPs w. Miles Davis (Pres.), Burrell (Blue Note, Pres.), Thad Jones (UA, Period), S. Rollins (Pres.), Milt Jackson (Atl.), *The Cats* (New Jazz), Wilbur Harden (Savoy), Curtis Fuller (UA).

Addr: 251 West 101st Street, New York 25, N.Y.

FLAX, MARTY (Martin Flachsenhaar), *baritone sax;* b. New York City, 10/7/24. Has worked w. Woody Herman, Louis Jordan, Raymond Scott, Lucky Millinder, Perez Prado. After playing some dates w. Les Elgart in 1956 he joined the band assembled by Quincy Jones for Dizzy Gillespie and toured Middle East and So. America for State Dept. w. him. Made Woody Herman State Dept. tour of So. America '58. Led own group at Cafe Society '57; w. Claude Thornhill '59. LPs w. Gillespie (Verve), Bobby Scott (Belltone), Woody Herman-Tito Puente (Evst.), Sam Most (Van., Beth.).

Addr: 30-70 48th St., Long Island City, N.Y.

FLEAGLE, JACOB ROGER (Brick), *composer, guitar;* b. Hanover, Pa., 8/22/06. Stud. Peabody Institute, started as banjoist in Fla. 1923; to NYC in vaudeville band act. Later played guitar with dance bands incl. Roy Ingram, Orville Knapp, Hal Kemp. Around 1926 he began a long association and close friendship w. Rex Stewart, who was then in Fletcher Henderson's band; played and arranged on most of Rex's record dates from 1937 to '44. During the '30s he arranged occasionally for Chick Webb, Jimmie Lunceford; Fletcher Henderson recorded his *Pixie From Dixie,* 1941. Led his own band at Arcadia Blrm. NYC '34-5. Continued to lead his own "rehearsal band," which played privately for "kicks" but never appeared in public, from 1935-49. Since 1946, has headed successful music copying office in NYC.

Addr: Music Writing Service, 113 West 57th St., New York 19, N.Y.

FLEMMING, HERB (Niccolaiih El-Michelle), *trombone, singer;* b. Puente, Cal., 4/5/04. Stud. 'cello, Fr. horn, bass, etc. Dobbs Sch., Dobbs Ferry, N.Y.; St. Cecelia Academia, Florence; Univ. di Roma. One of the most widely traveled musicians in jazz, he was with Jim Europe's 15th Inf. Band in World War I, later toured extensively in N. Africa, Latin America, Russia, the Orient, and every European country. Rec. debut ca. 1921 w. Perry Bradford, Johnny Dunn. Band affiliations incl. Sam Wooding, Noble Sissle, Lucky Millinder, Earl Hines, Fats Waller, Bardu Ali, usually doubling as vocalist. Lived in Cal. 1941-51, working as US Treasury Int. Revenue agent '43-9. Pl. w. Dixieland group at Metropole, NYC, '54-8; Central Plaza gigs '53-9, also semi-classical and pop vocal jobs. Films: *No Time for Romance, Pillow to Post.* LP: *Jazz at the Metropole* (Beth.); EP w. Panama Francis (MGM).

Addr: 3311 Wilson Avenue, Bronx 69, N.Y.

FLORES, CHARLES WALTER (Chuck), *drums;* b. Orange, Cal., 1/5/35. Raised in Santa Ana, Cal. Stud. w. Shelly Manne in early '53. Worked w. Ike Carpenter in Bal boa and w. Maynard Ferguson; latter recommended him to Woody Herman, with whom he toured '54-5, later free-lanced in LA, mainly w. Bud Shank. Favs:

Lamond, Blakey, Bunker. LPs w. Herman (Verve, Col., Cap.), Al Cohn, Dick Collins (Vict.), Bud Shank, Cy Touff (Wor. Pac.), Claude Williamson (Beth.); feat. on two tracks in *Hi-Fi Drums* (Cap.).

Addr: 824 East 1st St., Santa Ana, Calif.

FLORY, MEREDITH IRWIN (Med), *alto, tenor saxophones, composer, singer;* b. Logansport, Ind., 8/27/26. Father a teacher. Studied clarinet privately. After serving in Air Corps got BA in Philosophy at U. of Indiana 1950, then joined Claude Thornhill on clarinet. Later played w. Art Mooney; lead tenor w. Woody Herman, summer '53. Sang and played w. Tommy Tucker, also had own band in NYC '54. Moved to Calif. Jan. '56 and organized a rehearsal band in LA which was a big success at the first Monterey Jazz Festival '58. Flory appeared on the Ray Anthony television show '56-'57 as singer; *Music For Fun,* ABC-TV as singer. W. Woody Herman at Monterey Jazz Festival '59. Own LPs: *Jazzwave* (Jub.); four tracks in *West Coast Jazz Gallery* (Cap.); LPs w. Urbie Green (Vang.), Dick Collins (Vict.).

Addr: 6044 Encin Ave., No. Hollywood, Calif.

FLYNN, FRANK JOSEPH, *vibes, drums;* b. NYC, 12/4/16. Began stud. drums, vibes and arr. in Huntington Park, Calif., 1933; pl. in high school dance band. Worked w. Slim Martin orch. '36; arr. for Ben Pollack and others '37. With Ted Fio Rito as drummer, vocalist, arr. '38-42; in Air Force '42-5, leading dance band; own trio '45-7 incl. brother Bill, who plays bass. From '47-53 worked various radio shows and in movies; '53-9 worked in pictures, CBS staff, etc. Favs: Red Norvo, vibes; Ray McKinley, Buddy Rich, Alvin Stoller, drums. LPs w. Frank Sinatra, Nelson Riddle (Cap.); Ella Fitzgerald (Verve).

FONTANA, CARL CHARLES, *trombone;* b. Monroe, La., 7/18/28. Stud. w. father, Callie Fontana, a saxophonist, pl. in his band 1941-5. Prominent in jazz w. Woody Herman '50-2. Was with Al Belletto '52-3 and '57-8; Lionel Hampton summer '54; Hal McIntyre '54-5; Stan Kenton '55-6; Kai Winding '56-7. Since inactive in jazz, working in show bands in Las Vegas. When he shared solos with Urbie Green in Herman's trombone section he was rated a promising new find. Tied for new star in DB Critics' poll '53. LPs w. Herman (Verve), Kenton (Cap.), Bill Perkins (Wor. Pac.), Max Bennett (Beth.), Winding (Col.).

FORD, JAMES M. (Jimmy), *alto sax;* also *singer, clarinet;* b. Houston, Tex., 6/16/27. Studied alto in Houston; played tenor with Tadd Dameron at Royal Roost 1948. After a long absence, returned to the music scene and joined Maynard Ferguson's band 1957, touring with him until March 1960. An erratic but potentially brilliant musician, one of the most fluent of modern Parker counterparts. Favs: Ch. Parker, Sonny Stitt. Rec. debut with Red Rodney (Prestige); also LPs w. Ferguson (Roulette).

FORD, MARY (nee Colleen Summers), *singer, guitar;* b. Pasadena, Calif., 7/7/24. Married 12/29/49 to Les Paul, she has worked with him on hit records, vaudeville tours, TV, etc. For further details see Les Paul.

FORESYTHE, REGINALD, *composer, arranger, piano;* b. London, Eng., 5/28/07; d. London, 12/23/58. Began pl. piano at eight; later pl. for dances and as acc. for singers. Worked w. various film companies in Calif. in 1920s; to Chicago in '30, where he wrote *Deep Forest,* Earl Hines' theme song. Ret. to London and appeared at the Cafe de la Paix in '33 with a 10-piece band. In '34 ret. to NYC and was guest artist w. Paul Whiteman. During this trip he made a number of rec. on Columbia w. American musicians Benny Goodman, Toots Mondello, Hymie Shertzer, John Kirby et al. Ret. to London '35 and appeared at the "400" Club with own orch., as well as in a British movie. Served as intelligence officer in RAF during World War II, after which he pl. in various clubs in and around London. One of the most original arrangers of his time, he was among the first to make use of woodwinds in jazz. Comp. include *Dodging a Divorcee, Serenade to a Wealthy Widow* et al.

FORREST, JAMES ROBERT JR. (Jimmy), *tenor sax;* b. St. Louis, Mo., 1/24/20. Mother now organist at St. James AME Church in St. Louis. Played in high school from 1929 and with family band; worked around St. Louis w. Dewey Jackson, Fate Marable, Jeter-Pillars in 1930s. To NYC for first time in 1940 w. Jay McShann. With Andy Kirk 1941-7, then had own combo in St. Louis. Repl. Ben Webster w. Duke Ellington for nine months, 1949-50. Since then, has had own group, also played w. Harry Edison 1958-60. Scored big hit in r & b circles with *Night Train,* a record inspired by Ellington's *Happy Go Lucky Local.* Favs: Gray, Ammons, Gordon. LPs w. Edison (Verve), Jerry Valentine, *Outskirts Of Town* (Pres.), Bennie Green (Enrica), Edison-Clayton (Verve).

FOSTER, FRANK BENJAMIN, *tenor sax, composer;* b. Cincinnati, Ohio, 9/23/28. Sax, clar. in high school & Wilberforce U. To Detroit 1949; w. Wardell Gray, then to Army '51, released May '53; upon recommendation of Ernie Wilkins and Billy Eckstine got job w. Basie July '53. Arrs for Basie: *Shiny Stockings, Down For The Count, Blues Backstage, Did'n You;* also six arrs. in *Count Basie Swings, Joe Williams Sings* (Verve). According to John S. Wilson his work at its best can be "rounded and gracious, projected with vitality and vigor" but is at times "pushing and strident." Ira Gitler, on the other hand, calls him "a strong swinger out of Sonny Stitt and Wardell Gray who is very underrated." Favs: Sonny Stitt, Don Byas. Own LP: *Wail Frank, Wail* (Pres.); LPs w. Basie (Verve, Roul.), *Jazz Studio 1* (Decca), T. Monk (Pres.), Donald Byrd (Savoy), Milt Jackson (Atl.), Tony Scott (Vict.), Matthew Gee (River.), Thad Jones (Per.), *All Day Long* (Pres.), *No Count* (Savoy), one track each in Montage, and *Jazz Is Busting Out All Over* (Savoy); *Arthur Taylor* (New Jazz), *The Saxophone Section* (WW).

Addr: c/o Mrs. Graves, 337 West 138th St., New York 30, N.Y.

FOSTER, HERMAN, *piano;* b. Philadelphia, Pa., 4/26/28. Began pl. piano in grammar school; st. prof. in Asbury Park, N.J. in 1949; did factory work '51-2; back to music playing gigs w. Eric Dixon and Lou Donaldson '53. Played various clubs in Harlem '56-7 w. Seldon Powell, Lord Westbrook, Bill English. Favs: Oscar Peterson, Art Tatum, Erroll Garner, Hampton Hawes. LPs w. Lou Donaldson (Blue Note).

Addr: 121 East 106th St., New York 29, N.Y.

FOSTER, GEORGE MURPHY (Pops), *bass;* b. on a plantation in McCall, La., north of New Orleans, 5/19/1892; family moved to NO 1902. Started on cello. Foster left home in '14, playing river boats, working w. Charlie Creath in St. Louis. Also worked w. King Oliver, Bunk Johnson, Freddie Keppard, Kid Ory, Fate Marable, Dewey Jackson. With Oliver at Savoy NYC, '28, then w. similar personnel under Luis Russell ('29-35) and Louis Armstrong ('35-40). Formed duo w. guitarist Isidore Langlois. Out of music business, subway worker '42-5, but recorded w. Bechet in NO '44. Worked a year in Boston, then w. Art Hodes at Stuyvesant Casino '46. Pl. on *This Is Jazz* radio series w. Rudi Blesh on WOR. Toured France w. Mezzrow '48; in Boston w. Bob Wilber and others '49-51. With Jimmy Archey in Europe, '52, and at Ryan's NYC, '53, also many jobs w. various bands in Boston. After a year of inactivity in '55, he left NYC in Dec. of that year to tour Europe and North Africa w. Sammy Price returning to NYC May '56. To San Francisco June '56, working w. Earl Hines at Club Hangover since then. Foster, who was among the first to popularize the string bass in jazz, also played tuba occasionally from '22-8. He won DB poll '36 on bass, also R. Ch. All Time, All Star poll '51. Fav. own rec.: *Mahogany Hall Stomp,* w. Armstrong. LP w. Sidney Bechet (Blue Note).

Addr: 3255 Sacramento Street, San Francisco 15, Calif.

FOTINE, LARRY (Lawrence Constantine Fotinakis), *piano, composer;* b. Camden, N.J., 4/27/11. Mother pl. piano in theaters, grandfather led brass band and pl. trumpet and clar. Stud. piano three months, self-taught arr. St. own orch. 1932; joined Sammy Kaye as arr. '40-6; Blue Barron, Art Mooney as arr. Org. own orch. '48; toured US with it until '54, then moved to Calif. Arr. for Lawrence Welk '56; formed Beale Street Buskers '56 for record dates. Ambition is to write a show based on Dixieland music. Associated with a light, commercialized brand of Dixieland jazz. LPs w. Beale Street Buskers (Bel Canto, Dixieland).

Addr: 15038 Haynes Street, Van Nuys, Calif.

FOUNTAIN, PETER DEWEY JR. (Pete), *clarinet, saxes;* b. New Orleans, La., 7/3/30. Father played drums and violin with jazz bands around Biloxi, Miss. Started on clarinet in school band, 1942; played with Junior Dixieland Jazz Band, '48-9; Phil Zito, '49-50; Basin Street Six, '50-4; since then, featured with his own group, Pete Fountain and his Three Coins. Has worked mainly in New Orleans but also made several trips to Chicago for jobs at Jazz Limited and the Blue Note, '49-53. Disbanded his own group to join Lawrence Welk April '57 and was featured as leader of a Dixieland combo within Welk's band on the latter's ABC-TV series, Left Welk Jan. '59, returning to New Orleans and genuine jazz. Favs: Irving Fazola, Eddie Miller. Own LPs: Coral, South.; LPs w. Al Hirt (Verve), Tony Almerico (Dot), *Basin Street Six* (Merc.), Jack Delaney (South.), Sharkey Bonano in *Recorded In New Orleans* (GTJ), Lawrence Welk (Coral).

FOUR FRESHMEN, *instrumental and vocal group;* the original personnel comprised Don Barbour, guitar and vocal, b. 4/19/27; brother, Ross, drums and trumpet, b. 12/31/28; Ken Errair, trumpet, bass, French horn, vocals, b. 1/23/28; Bob Flanigan, trombone, bass, b. 8/22/26. In April '56 Errair was replaced by Ken Albers, who plays trumpet, mellophone and takes the bass voice parts. The group was originally organized in Indianapolis at the Arthur Jordan Cons. of Mus. After enjoying considerable success throughout the midwest, they were discovered by Stan Kenton, who helped arrange their record debut. While rec. for Capitol in Hollywood, the group made its local debut at Jerry Wald's Studio Club and was signed for a motion picture debut in *Rich, Young and Pretty.* Won DB poll as top vocal group 1953-6, '58; Playboy poll '57-60; Met. poll '56, '59. LPs: Cap.

Addr: c/o General Artists Corp., 1270 6th Ave., New York 20, N.Y.

FOURNIER, VERNEL ANTHONY, *drums;* b. New Orleans, 7/30/28. Stud. parade drum in grammar school at age of 10. First prof. job w. Dooky Chase at 13. Played w. Alabama State Collegians while in college there 1945-6; w. King Kolax in Chicago '46-8; from '49-53 worked w. Teddy Wilson, Tom Archia, Dallas Bartley, Buster Bennett, Paul Bascomb; w. Norman Simmons '53-5 in house band at Bee Hive in Chicago. Joined Ahmad Jamal '56. Considered by John Hammond to be one of handful of top contemporary jazz drummers. Favs: A deceased Chicago drummer, Ike Day; Max Roach. LPs w. Johnny Pate, Lorez Alexandria (King); Ahmad Jamal (Argo, Epic).

Addr: 215 E. 71st Street, Chicago, Ill.

FOWLKES, CHARLES BAKER (Charlie), *baritone sax;* b. Brooklyn, N.Y., 2/16/16. Studied alto, tenor, clar., vln. Six years w. Tiny Bradshaw. L. Hampton '44-8, then worked w. Arnett Cobb and managed wife, singer Wini Brown. Joined Count Basie '53. Fav: Harry Carney. LPs w. Basie (Verve, Roul.), J. C. Heard (Argo), one track in *Jazz Is Busting Out All Over* (Savoy); Buck Clayton (Col.), Osie Johnson (Beth.).

Addr: 314 Quincy St., Brooklyn 16, N.Y.

FRANCIS, DAVID ALBERT (Panama), *drums;* b. Miami, Fla., 12/21/18. Grandfather was choirmaster of St. Ann's Church in the Bahamas. Booker T. Washington School band 1930; joined Geo. Kelly Cavaliers '34; Florida Collegians '38; Tab Smith in NYC Aug. '38;

Billy Hicks, Roy Eldridge, '39; Lucky Millinder '40; Willie Bryant Sept. '46; Cab Calloway Jan. '47 (w. Cab to Panama, Cuba, Uruguay); left Cab late '52, worked briefly w. D. Ellington, Ch. Shavers, Slim Gaillard, free-lanced in NYC; took own band to Montevideo Mar. '54. In the mid and late '50s, studio work at major networks in NYC; house drummer for Dixieland sessions at the Central Plaza. Bought grocery store '59. Fav: Chick Webb. LPs w. Woody Herman (Verve), Charlie Shavers (Beth.), *Swingin' On Broadway* w. Ray Conniff (Col.), Sil Austin-Red Prysock (Merc.).

Addr: 1968 Morris Ave., Bronx 53, N.Y.

FRANZELLA, SAL JR., *clarinet, composer; b. New Orleans,* 4/25/15. Father was clarinetist in old French Opera Co. in New Orleans. Stud. w. Jean Paquay, who also taught Fazola, T. Parenti. Joined musicians' union at 12; played in Saenger Theatre at 15. After many local band and radio jobs, went on road w. Benny Meroff '36; Isham Jones '37. Joined Paul Whiteman '38; NBC staff NYC, '41-7; then studio work in California. Guest soloist w. Buffalo Symphony, etc. Began serious concert work on clarinet, bass clarinet, alto, 1955. Favs: B. Goodman, J. Mince, A. Shaw, Abe Most.

Addr: 13807 Valerio St., Van Nuys, Calif.

FREE, RONALD GUY (Ronnie), *drums;* b. Charleston, S.C., 1/15/36. Father started him on drums at eight. He later played with high school band and with local groups from the age of thirteen. Came to New York in 1956; played for *Shoestring Revue.* Met Oscar Pettiford and worked with him. Two weeks with Woody Herman; Sal Salvador and Ray Eberle, '58. With George Wallington, '59; Mose Allison '58-'59. *Great South Bay Jazz Festival* '58, *Jazz '59* concert tour with Allison. Joined Lennie Tristano, Aug. '59. Favs: Art Blakey, Philly Joe Jones, Kenny Clarke. LPs w. Allison (Prestige), *Konitz Meets Giuffre* (Verve).

FREEDMAN, ROBERT (Bob), *composer, alto* and *baritone sax, piano;* b. Mount Vernon, N.Y., 1/23/34. Pl. with Serge Chaloff and Vido Musso 1955; w. Woody Herman '57; Herb Pomeroy '57-8. Comp. and arr. for Toshiko, Herb Pomeroy, Maynard Ferguson and Berklee School LP *Jazz in the Classroom.* Taught at Berklee School; now concentrating on comp. and arr. Comps. can be heard in LPs by Pomeroy (UA), Ferguson (Roul.).

Addr: 142 Washington St., Medford, Mass.

FREEMAN, LAWRENCE (Bud), *tenor sax;* b. Chicago, Ill., 4/13/06. In early '20s was associated with Austin High School clique in Chicago w. Frank Teschemacher, Jimmy and Dick McPartland. In Paris with Dave Tough, 1928. During the next 15 years, divided his time between the jazz and popular fields, playing with Art Kassel, Roger Wolfe Kahn, Ben Pollack, Red Nichols, Joe Haymes. In '35 he was featured w. Ray Noble's first American band, then joined Tommy Dorsey '36-8, Benny Goodman '38. In '39 he recorded w. his own group, known as the Summa Cum Laude orch., and from this period on was heard mostly with various small units. In Army '43-5 (to Aleutians with band); took trio, including Joe Bushkin, to Brazil '47; spent year in Chile and Peru '52-3. Since then many jobs in NY area incl. a stay at Eddie Condon's w. his own trio '58. Appeared at NJF and RIJF in late '50s. Freeman, whose tone has been compared with that of Lester Young, though his style is highly personal, was the first tenor sax man to be accepted in the Dixieland circles of which Eddie Condon was the key figure. In the early '50s, he became interested in modern jazz forms and spent some time studying with Lennie Tristano, but his own style remained basically unchanged, as a study of the many records to which he has contributed excellent solos will show. Won Met. poll '37, DB poll '38. Own LPs on Dot, Beth., *Midnight At Eddie Condon's* (Merc.), Harm., Vict.; LPs w. Condon (MGM), J. McPartland (Epic), *Chicago Style Jazz* (Col.), *A String Of Swingin' Pearls* (Vict.), *Great Jazz Reeds* (Cam.), Geo. Wettling (Weathers).

Addr: 55 East 10th St., New York, N.Y.

FREEMAN, RUSSELL DONALD (Russ), *piano;* b. Chicago, Ill., 5/28/26. Cousin of composer Ray Gilbert, singer Joanne Gilbert. Studied classical music in LA 1934-8. With Howard McGhee, Dexter Gordon, '47; Art Pepper, Wardell Gray, '52; Lighthouse All-Stars, Shorty Rogers, '53; Chet Baker '54. Joined Shelly Manne '55 and has been with him since; also worked on occasion w. Benny Goodman in '58, '59, making European tour with him in Oct. '59. In a & r capacity for Wor. Pac. Records in '57-'58. Assisted w. underscoring for *I Want To Live* '58, *Porgy & Bess* '59. Favs: Art Tatum, Bud Powell, Joe Albany, Horace Silver. Incisive, swinging style made him West Coast favorite, much in demand for records. Own LPs: *Double Play* w. Andre Previn (Contemp.), *Quartet* w. Chet Baker, own trio (Wor. Pac.); various tracks in *Jazz West Coast, The Blues, Pianists Galore, Solo Flight, Have Blues, Will Travel* (Wor. Pac.); LPs w. Chet Baker (Col., Wor. Pac.), Shelly Manne (Contemp.), Bill Perkins, Cy Touff (Wor. Pac.), Art Pepper (Jazz: West, Tampa, Intro), Maynard Ferguson, Pete Rugolo (Em.), Med Flory (Jub.).

Addr: 7953 Cherrystone Blvd., Van Nuys, Calif.

FREEMAN, STANLEY (Stan), *piano, singer, composer;* b. Waterbury, Conn., 4/3/20. Army 1943-6. Toured w. Tex Beneke band '46. Freeman is best known as a concert pianist (Gershwin concert w. NY Philharmonic, June '51), and as a night club comedian (worked in London June '52) but has occasionally revealed himself as a talented jazz pianist in solos such as *Just Friends* w. Charlie Parker (Verve). For several years he was featured in a popular duo w. Cy Walter. Own LPs on Epic, Col.; LP w. Charlie Parker (Verve).

Addr: 214 East 78th St., New York 21, N.Y.

FREUND, JOKI, *tenor sax;* also *piano, tuba;* b. Frankfurt am Main, Germany, 9/5/26. Started on accordion in 1935. Turned prof. on tenor sax after the end of World War II. Active as leader of his own quintet in jazz clubs and all German jazz festivals. Played Polish jazz festival, 1957, San Remo in Italy, '58. Did TV show w. Donald Byrd, Arthur Taylor and Doug Watkins in Baden-Baden, '58. Made film w. Oscar Pettiford, also worked w. Albert Mangelsdorff on Radio Frankfurt. Breeds carrier pigeons as hobby. Favs: Coltrane, Getz. LP: W. Jutta Hipp in *Cool Europe* (MGM).

Addr: Schulstrasse 18, Schwalbach/TS, Germany.

FRIEDMAN, DONALD E. (Don), *piano;* b. San Francisco, Calif., 5/4/35. Began stud. piano in 1940; first job after participating in local jam sessions. Worked briefly w. Dexter Gordon, S. Rogers, B. Collette '56; w. Buddy De Franco '56-7; July-Sept. '57 w. Chet Baker, then w. Ornette Coleman in Vancouver. Came to NYC '58. Worked w. Pepper Adams '58, trio w. Teddy Kotick on Staten Island last part of '58, first part of '59, then joined Dick Haymes as accompanist. Favs: Parker, B. Powell. LP w. Buddy Collette (Contemp.).

Addr: 1541 1st Ave., New York 28, N. Y.

FRIGO, JOHN VIRGIL, *bass, violin;* also *trumpet;* b. Chicago, Ill., 12/27/16. Stud. with Nathan Oberman, Ludwig Becker. Tuba, bass viol, in high school. Member of Four Californians cocktail unit, 1934-40. In Chico Marx band 1943-5 as musician, comedian; singer in Mel Tormé group. Bass, violin w. Jimmy Dorsey band, '45-7; then left, with Dorsey pianist Lou Carter and guitarist Herb Ellis to form the Soft Winds Trio, a delightful instrumental and vocal group. Their compositions, *Detour Ahead* and *I Told Ya I Love Ya, Now Get Out* earned some popular success. Since '52, Frigo has free-lanced in Chicago on TV and records mostly, with pianist Dick Marx, incl. trio at Mr. Kelly's '57-9. Won Chicago Emmy Award as lyricist for best radio and TV commercials, June '59. Exhibited 22 pastels in Chi. Gold Coast Art Festival, Aug. '59. Frigo is one of the few modern musicians to experiment successfully with ad lib violin. Fav: Ray Brown; no fav. on violin. Own LP on violin for Mercury; LPs w. Dick Marx (Coral, Bruns.), Dave Remington (Jub.), Buddy Greco (Coral).

Addr: 2801 Sheridan Road, Chicago 14, Ill.

FRILEY, VERNON (Vern), *trombone;* b. Marshall, Mo., 7/5/24. Played w. Ray McKinley 1946-7, later w. Woody Herman, Sauter-Finegan, Les Brown, also recorded w. Chico O'Farrill. Free-lancing in Hollywood '55-60; two years at Paramount Pictures. Many TV shows incl. jazz on *M-Squad.* Solos: *Borderline* w. McKinley, *Azure-te, Nina Never Knew* w. Sauter-Finegan, *Four Others* w. Herman. LPs w. McKinley (Cam., Savoy), Sauter-Finegan (Vict.), Herman (Verve).

Addr: 822 Mason, Canoga Park, Calif.

FRUSCELLA, TONY, *trumpet;* b. Orangeburg, N.J., 2/4/27. Lived in orphanage until age of 14; stud. with Jerome Cnuddle. At 18, entered Army and played in 2nd Division Band. Later worked w. Lester Young, Gerry Mulligan, Stan Getz, playing at Newport Jazz Festival in 1954 w. Mulligan. In the late '50s Fruscella was relatively inactive. Favs: Joe Thomas, Phil Sunkel, Dizzy Gillespie, Don Joseph. Own LP on Atl.; app. in *East Coast Scene* (Coral); LP w. Stan Getz (Verve).

FRYE, DONALD (Don), *piano;* b. Springfield, Ohio, 1903. Stud. privately. Worked locally w. Lloyd & Cecil Scott, then to NYC with them, pl. Savoy Ballroom etc. Later worked w. Fred Moore, Pete Brown, the orig. John Kirby sextet, Lucky Millinder, and long engagements at Village Vanguard and Jimmy Ryan's, latter as intermission pianist for more than ten years. Infl. by Fats Waller, Art Tatum. LPs w. Danny Barker (Period) etc.

FULLER, BLIND BOY (Fuller Allen), *singer, guitar;* b. Rockingham, N.C., 1903; d. Durham, N.C., 1940. Blinded in an accident circa 1925, he sang on the streets of various North Carolina towns. In '34 he met Sonny Terry; they later teamed for a series of recordings. Fuller recorded regularly from '35 until his death; many of his performances used obscene lyrics but his style gave them artistic validity. The records, on Vocalion and Decca, have long been unavailable.

FULLER, CURTIS DUBOIS, *trombone;* b. Detroit, Mich., 12/15/34. Played baritone horn in high school 1949, later switched to trombone. In Army band '53-5 w. Cannonball Adderley, Junior Mance. Played w. Kenny Burrell, Yusef Lateef in Detroit '55-6; to NYC '57, worked briefly w. Miles Davis. Six months w. Lester Young '58; Dizzy Gillespie, Gil Evans, Benny Golson '59, Golson-Art Farmer '59-60. Favs: J. J. Johnson, Cleveland, Brookmeyer, Urbie Green. Fluent, Johnson-influenced trombonist. Own LPs: UA, Blue Note, Pres.; LPs w. Bud Powell, Sonny Clark, John Coltrane (Blue Note), Benny Golson (River., New Jazz); *Monday Night At Birdland* (Roul.), Yusef Lateef, Wilber Harden (Savoy), Paul Quinichette (Pres.), Blue Mitchell, Philly Joe Jones (River.), Art Farmer (UA), Gil Evans (Wor. Pac.).

Addr: 1104 Findlay Ave., Bronx 56, N.Y.

FULLER, WALTER GILBERT (Gil), *composer;* b. Los Angeles, Cal., 4/14/20. Studied at NYU, then ret. to West Coast, writing for Les Hite and Floyd Ray. Came East w. Ray '38, later worked for Jimmie Lunceford, Tiny Bradshaw. One of the first arrangers to work in bop idiom, he wrote for Eckstine, helped to assemble and direct Dizzy Gillespie's band; was co-composer and arr. of *One Bass Hit, Ray's Idea, Things To Come, Manteca, That's Earl Brother* and *The Swedish Suite* premiered at Carnegie Hall '48; *Fuller Bop Man, Tropicana* for James Moody (Blue Note). Own big band date for Disc., *The Scene Changes,* etc. Has owned several music pub. firms; authored bop arr. method book. Retired from music, went into real estate business, '51. Returned to music early '55, working briefly for Stan Kenton, and has free-lanced in NYC since then.

Addr: 229 West 105th St., New York 25, N.Y.

FULLER, GERALD (Jerry), *clarinet;* b. Santa Maria, Cal., 3/15/29. Took up clarinet in fifth grade; grad. high sch. 1948, joined Jimmy Zito band '49; Will Osborne '50; U.S. Army '51-3, in Korea with 2nd Div. Band. With Pete Daily's Chicagoans '53-4; own trio for three months in Hollywood, Cal., then spent four years with Jack Teagarden sextet from Apr. '55, incl. US State Dept. tour of Asia in '58. Joined Dukes of Dixieland Apr. '59. Though identified with Dixieland bands, is a swing-style soloist with superior technique and some modern characteristics. LPs w. Teagarden (Cap.), Dukes of Dixieland (Audio-Fid.), Pete Daily (Jazz Man).

Addr: 832 B S. Pine St., Santa Maria, Calif.

FULLER, JESSE, *singer, guitar;* b. Georgia, March 1897. Fuller has worked as a prof. tap dancer, singer and blues guitarist but is not a full-time musician. He used to be a construction worker and also worked in Hollywood during the silent picture days playing a small part in *The Thief of Baghdad* w. Douglas Fairbanks. Recently he has been running a shoe shine parlor. He has also been heard playing a home made, one-man-band instrument, the fotella. He has performed at folk and jazz festivals in California and in early 1960 was heard in England. In the late '50s he began recording; an LP was released on Good Time Jazz. Fuller names no musical influences and says "I have been my own favorite on my own instrument."

Addr: 1679 11th St., Oakland 20, Calif.

FULLER, WALTER (Rosetta), *trumpet, singer, leader;* b. Dyersburg, Tenn., 2/15/10. Father played mellophone in brass band. Prof. debut at 14 w. medicine show. To Chicago 1925, played w. Sammy Stewart; working at Savoy Ballroom, NYC '29. After working w. Irene Edie combo in Chicago, joined Earl Hines '31 and, except for a period w. Horace Henderson in '37, remained with him until '41 when he formed his own group. While w. Hines he made two records which earned him considerable popularity, *Rosetta* and *After All I've Been To You.* His combo opened in San Diego, Calif. '46 and he has been there ever since; he is also a member of the Board of Directors of the San Diego Musician's Union. Film: *Submarine Command* w. William Holden. Fav: Louis Armstrong.

Addr: 571 So. San Miguel, San Diego 13, Calif.

G

GAILLARD, BULEE (Slim), *guitar, piano, vibes, singer;* b. Detroit, Mich., 1/4/16. First prominent when teamed on guitar with Slam Stewart as a duo. Their record of *Flat Foot Floogie,* one of the big hits of '38, brought them national recognition. Slim later branched out on his own, and has since been best known as comedian-leader of a small group. His talent as a jazzman is limited, but in the mid-'40s he made a series of records for various small labels that included Dizzy Gillespie, Charlie Parker, and others. Gaillard has been seen in the following movies: *Hellzapoppin, Star Spangled Rhythm, Almost Married, Sweetheart of Sigma Chi, Go, Man, Go.* Own LPs on Verve, Dot; w. Charlie Parker (Savoy).

Addr: Rm. 906, 1619 Broadway, New York 19, N.Y.

GAINES, CHARLES (Charlie), *trumpet;* b. Philadelphia, Pa., 8/8/00. Played w. brass band; w. Wilbur Sweatman NYC in 1919. Rec. with Clarence Williams; played various club dates w. Charlie Johnson, Earl Walton, Leroy Smith in '20s. Rec. with Fats Waller; had own band in Philadelphia after '30. Rec. w. Louis Armstrong for Victor '33; in Detroit since '30s.

GAINES, ROY, *guitar;* b. Houston, Tex., 8/12/34. First pl. piano, then began on guitar in 1947. Won amateur contest in Houston, worked in a local club, then left for Calif. to join Roy Milton's group. After ten months, joined Chuck Willis, 1955, remained until Willis' death, '58. Came to New York and led a small band pl. at clubs, also making record dates. He was infl. by blues singers such as John Lee Hooker, T-Bone Walker; likes Django Reinhardt, Tiny Grimes, Tal Farlow. LPs w. Jimmy Rushing (Van.).

GALBRAITH, JOSEPH BARRY, *guitar;* b. Pittsburgh, Pa., 12/18/19. Self-taught. Worked w. Red Norvo, Teddy Powell, Babe Russin, '41; Claude Thornhill '41-2 and '46-7; also w. Hal McIntyre '42. Army '43-6; NBC and CBS staff work since 1947. From '55-'60, he built a unique reputation as perhaps the most recorded guitarist in the New York scene, participating in hundreds of popular and jazz LPs. Favs: Christian, Raney, Farlow. Own LP on Decca; LPs w. John Benson Brooks, Coleman Hawkins (River.), Betty Glamann (Beth., Merc.), Tommy Shepard, Hal McKusick, *Manhattan Jazz Septette* (Coral); Don Elliott, Ralph Burns (Decca), Claude Thornhill (Harm.), John Lewis (Atl.), Tony Scott, Hal McKusick, George Russell (Vict.), Wild Bill Davison (Col.), Hank Jones (Gold. Cr.), Tal Farlow (Verve).

Addr: 198-19 Dunton Ave., Hollis 23, L.I., N.Y.

GAMBRELL, FREDERIC, JR. (Freddie), *piano;* also *violin, guitar, bass, trumpet, tuba* etc.; b. Washington, D.C., 3/21/36. Violin at 11, Calif. State Boarding School, Berkeley. No formal piano studies. Lost his sight at 17. Played obscure night club jobs until 1958, when he led duo w. Ben Tucker at Jazz Workshop, SF, then at Sticky Wicket in Santa Cruz, where he also sang, played guitar and lectured on jazz. Rec. first LP Apr. '58 and was hailed by some critics as important new talent, while others found him diffuse and over-technical. Fav: Art Tatum. Fav. own solos: *Blues Reservation; Yesterdays.* Own LPs: World Pacific.

Addr: 1600 Golden Gate Avenue, San Francisco, Calif.

GAMMAGE, EUGENE SHELTON (Gene), *drums;* b. Atlanta, Ga., 1/30/31. No formal training. Air Force 1948-52;

bought drums with discharge pay; prof. debut in Charleston, S.C., then moved to Los Angeles May '53. First jazz exp. w. Teddy Charles at the Haig '53; 3½ months w. Hamp Hawes '55; Barney Kessel '56; several times w. André Previn since '55; with Oscar Peterson in Las Vegas, Nov. '56 and again in Chicago etc. late '58. Orig. infl. by Max Roach, later by K. Clarke, Philly Joe Jones, Art Blakey, Elvin Jones. LPs: *My Fair Lady* w. O. Peterson (Verve); *The Gellers* (Mercury); Pat Moran (Audio-Fid.), Jack Sheldon (Jazz: West).

Addr: 1217 West 47th Street, Los Angeles, Calif.

GANLEY, ALLAN, *drums;* b. Tolworth, Surrey, England, 3/11/31. Interested in jazz from age ten; started practicing drums at 16, turning prof. after two years in the RAF, at age 20. Worked w. Jack Parnell 1953, Ambrose '54, Johnny Dankworth '55, New Jazz Group w. Derek Smith, Dizzy Reece '57. Formed own group '58 which became known as The Jazzmakers in Nov. of that year when Ronnie Ross joined. Toured US w. Ronnie Scott '57 and w. The Jazzmakers in NJF tour Sept. '59. Favs: Roach, Rich, Haynes. Own comp.: *Duffle Coat,* rec. w. Victor Feldman on Contemp. LPs: *The Jazzmakers* (Atl.); many on British labels.

Addr: 15, Brondesbury Road, London, N. W. 6, England.

GARCIA, RICHARD JOSEPH (Dick), *guitar;* b. New York City, 5/11/31. Great-grandfather played command performance for King of Spain; grandfather and father both guitarists. Started playing by ear at 9; one year's study 1944-5. Terry Gibbs, hearing him at jam session in Greenwich Village, recommended him to Tony Scott, with whose combo he first played in 1950. While with George Shearing quintet, Feb.-Dec. 1952, toured US and Honolulu, recorded *Lullaby of Birdland,* etc. Free-lanced around New York, worked with Joe Roland '55, back with Tony Scott off and on '55-6. Rejoined Shearing summer '59. Fav. own recs: *Jazzville USA, Vol. II* (Dawn) w. own quartet. Favs: Farlow, Kessel, Raney. Garcia is an extraordinarily gifted guitarist, fleet in technique and unusually fluent in phrasing and style. Own LP on Dawn; four tracks w. Joe Puma in *The Four Most Guitars* (ABC-Par.); LPs w. Shearing (MGM), Milt Buckner (Cap.), Lenny Hambro (Col.), Joe Roland (Beth.), Tony Scott (Vict.), five tracks w. John Glasel (ABC-Par.).

Addr: 325 West 76th St., New York 23, N.Y.

GARCIA, RUSSELL (Russ), *composer, trumpet, French horn;* b. Oakland, Cal., 4/12/16. Oakland High, San Francisco State College; private studies w. Edmund Ross, Mario Castelnuovo-Tedesco and others. Trumpet and arr. with high school and local dance bands; later played with Horace Heidt, Al Donahue, Al Lyons at Orpheum Theatre in LA; NBC staff work in Hollywood. Motion picture scores for Universal-International, Warners, Disney, etc. Although mainly concerned with the field of popular music, Garcia has provided appropriate accompaniments for many jazz soloists and for semi-jazz as well as for pop singers. Own LP: Beth.; also four tracks w. own band in *Modern Jazz Gallery* (Kapp); arrs. for Buddy DeFranco, Oscar Peterson, Anita O'Day (Verve), Frances Faye, Herbie Mann-Sam Most (Beth.).

Addr: 1570 North Gower, Los Angeles 28, Calif.

GARDNER, SAMUEL LEROY (Sammy), *clarinet;* also *oboe, flute, saxophone, trumpet, trombone, violin, tuba;* b. St. Louis, Mo., 6/4/26. Studied clarinet in Kirkwood, Mo. school system. Played jobs in high school. Army 1944-7, then attended St. Louis Institute of Music where he received a Bachelor of Music in Education. Taught in St. Louis county public schools '51-8. Then formed Mound City Six. Appeared on Arthur Godfrey TV show July '58; own TV show in St. Louis for two years. Played at the Roundtable, NYC Sept. '59, then extended stay at the Tiger's Den, St. Louis. Favs: Benny Goodman, Edmond Hall. Own LPs: Roul., Evst., Mound City.

Addr: 5537 Cates Ave., St. Louis 12, Mo.

GARI, RALPH (Ralph Garofalo), *alto sax; clar., flute, piccolo, English horn;* b. New Castle, Pa., 7/15/27. Stud. in New Castle, Pittsburgh and NYC. Pl. w. Eddie Rogers in NYC 1945; Frankie Carle '49; settled in Las Vegas '50, working in concert and jazz groups; organized own quartet '54, pl. at El Rancho Vegas. Gari's work, though clever and complex, is not of the type usually considered to be legitimate jazz. Own LP: EmArcy.

Addr: 1916 Howard St., Las Vegas, Nev.

GARLAND, EDWARD B. (Montudie), *bass;* b. New Orleans, 1/9/1895. Pl. bass drum, tuba w. marching bands in parades from 1908. Worked w. Excelsior band and Frankie Dusen's Eagle band 1910, Imperial and Security bands '11; left NO in '14, working in Chicago at DeLuxe Cafe, later w. Emmanuel Perez, Freddie Keppard, Ch. McCurtis; King Oliver, '16-21. Migrating to Cal. w. Oliver, he worked in LA taxi dance halls. Led own One Eleven band '29-33. After many years in obscurity he was heard on bass w. Kid Ory in the New Orleans revival on the West Coast from '44; worked w. San Francisco combos incl. Earl Hines at Hangover, '55-6; Beverly Tavern and 400 Club in LA '57-8; with Turk Murphy '57; to France w. Kid Ory '57. Film: *Imitation of Life,* '59. Fav. own record: *Muskrat Ramble* w. Ory (Good Time Jazz). Favs: Arvell Shaw, Pops Foster. LPs w. Ory (GTJ), Claire Austin (GTJ).

Addr: 1221 West 45th Street, Los Angeles 37, Cal.

GARLAND, JOSEPH COPELAND (Joe), *composer, tenor* and *bass saxes;* b. Norfolk, Va., 8/15/07. Studied Aeolian Cons. in Baltimore. Played w. Elmer Snowden, Leon Abbey in '20s; Lucky Millinder, Edgar Hayes, Don Redman in '30s; Louis Armstrong in '40s, taking over directorship from Luis Russell in '41. In '50s, semi-retired from music, working as a housing inspector in NYC. Best known as composer of *Leap Frog* (theme of Les Brown's band), and *In the Mood,* which he adapted from a traditional blues line. In '59,

Garland occasionally led a big band on weekends in New Jersey; personnel incl. Clyde Bernhardt, Charlie Holmes, June Coles and Louis Metcalf.

Addr: 159-26 Harlem River Drive, New York 39, N.Y.

GARLAND, WILLIAM M. (Red), *piano;* b. Dallas, Tex., 5/13/23. Started on clar., stud. with Prof. A. S. Jackson and alto saxophonist Buster Smith. Discovered by Hot Lips Page when the latter was passing through Dallas. Has worked with many name jazz-men since 1945, among them Charlie Parker, Coleman Hawkins, Roy Eldridge, Charlie Ventura, Billy Eckstine Band, Sonny Stitt, Ben Webster, Eddie Davis, Bennie Green, Lou Donaldson, Hot Lips Page; w. Miles Davis in '56-7. Pl. around New York area w. D. Byrd, Coltrane, Art Taylor et al, rejoined Davis '58. Formed own trio '59 with which he toured country. "He has brought back some long absent elements to jazz piano, made them acceptable to the ultra-modernists, and proved over again the sublime virtue of swing and a solid, deep groove."—Ralph J. Gleason, *DB.* Favs: Tatum, B. Powell, H. Jones. Own LPs: Prestige; LPs w. Miles Davis (Pres., Col.), J. Coltrane, A. Taylor, *Tenor Conclave* (Pres.), Art Pepper (Contemp.).

Addr: c/o Shaw Artists, 565 5th Ave., New York, N.Y.

GARNER, ERROLL, *piano, songwriter;* b. Pittsburgh, Pa., 6/15/21. Father also pianist; Erroll, who did not study and has never learned to read music, was a schoolmate of Dodo Marmarosa and an early associate of Billy Strayhorn. Started with local bands in '37; he came to NYC at the age of 23 and took a series of jobs along 52nd street at the Three Deuces, Tondelayo's, etc. After being featured in nightclubs and on records with the Slam Stewart trio, he went out on his own, working mostly with a bassist and drummer. He appeared at the Paris Jazz Festival in '48. From '45-9, Garner made a tremendous number of records for scores of companies on a free-lance basis before signing exclusively for Columbia, whom he left in '54 to join Mercury, rejoining Columbia in '56. In the late '50s Garner enjoyed tremendous public success. He made his first European tour Dec. '57 to Feb. '58. In '58 he became the first jazz artist ever to be booked by impresario S. Hurok. His best-known composition, *Misty,* enjoyed great popularity during '59.

Garner achieved recognition with the general public through a style that was found palatable by many non-jazz-minded people. His main ingredients were the use of spread chords and melodic variations on popular themes; and, on faster tempi, a delayed-action, single note, right-hand style accompanied by a guitar-like strumming of chords with the left hand. He has won the following awards: Esq. New Star '46, DB poll '49, '56-8; Met. poll '58-60; DB Critics' poll '57; *Playboy* poll '58-60; *Playboy* All Stars' All Stars '60. Own LPs: Col. CL 883, 535, 939, C2L-9, 583, 617, 667, 1014, 1060, Em. 36001, 36026, 36069, Merc. 20055, 20090, 20063, Atl. 1227, Savoy 12022, 12003, 12008 (rev. Billy Taylor), Rondo. 15, Roost 2213 (rev. Art Tatum); LP w. Woody Herman (Col. CL 651).

Addr: Carnegie Hall Apts., New York 19, N.Y.

GARNER, LINTON, *piano, composer;* also *trumpet, alto & bass horn;* b. Greensboro, N.C., 3/25/15. Brother Erroll, sisters Martha, Ruth, Berniece all play piano. Stud. piano in Pittsburgh 1923; trumpet '24. Pl. tpt. through high school and in local bands that incl. Art Blakey, B. Eckstine. Gave up trumpet '35, returned to piano; stud. reading, theory. Pl. w. Larry Steele revue, Burns Campbell; worked in Rochester, N.Y. for two years, then at McVann's Club in Buffalo until '40, when he joined a band from Pittsburgh which was later fronted by Fletcher Henderson '41-3. Army, '43-5; piano & arranger for Eckstine band '46-7. Accompanist for comedian Timmie Rogers '47-55, also wrote arrs. for D. Gillespie '50, Earl Coleman and others, and acc. dancer Teddy Hale and many other acts. Rec. sessions as sideman w. Fats Navarro, Allen Eager, Babs Gonzales, Eckstine. Very capable modern musician, playing in style unlike Erroll's. Ambition: "To play well enough to have my brother really enjoy my playing"; to compose and arrange extensively in jazz field. Own LP: Raecox.

Addr: 53 N. Willow Street, Montclair, N.J.

GARRISON, ARVIN CHARLES (Arv), *guitar;* also *bass;* b. Toledo, O., 8/17/22, d. Toledo, 7/30/60. Grandmother prof. pianist. Self-taught, started on ukulele at 9, guitar while at church social. Pl. lodge dances at age 12, high school dances until 18. Formed own combo, played at Kenmore Hotel in Albany, N.Y. 1941. Joined Don Seat band in Pittsburgh. Started own trio which played on both coasts '41-8. From '46 it was known as the Vivien Garry Trio in the name of the bassist to whom he was married. In the '50s, Garrison was living and playing in Toledo. Recs. Vict., Musicraft, Sarco, Guild, Black and White, Metro and Exclusive; Vic Dickenson on Signature, Charlie Parker on Dial. Original inspiration: Django Reinhardt. LP w. Earle Spencer on Tops incl. fav. own rec. *Five Guitars In Flight.*

GARRISON, JAMES EMORY (Jimmy), *bass;* b. Miami, Fla., 3/3/34. Moved to Philadelphia at the age of 10. Started on clarinet in high school, switching to bass in his senior year. After graduation began gigging around Philly w. young local band incl. Bobby Timmons and Al Heath. From 1953-8 played w. Louis Judge and others; from '55-8 also drove a truck by day. To New York '58 where he has pl. since w. Philly Joe Jones, Lennie Tristano, Tony Scott, Benny Golson, Curtis Fuller, Kenny Dorham and Bill Evans. Back w. P. J. Jones '60. Favs. and imp. infl: Percy Heath, Ray Brown. LPs w. P. J. Jones (River.), Jackie McLean (Blue Note), Tony Scott (Hanover), J. R. Monterose (Top Rank), Konitz-Marsh (Verve).

GASKIN, LEONARD, *bass;* b. Brooklyn, N.Y., 8/25/20. Stud. piano, then bass in high school and w. private teachers. Worked at Monroe's in Harlem w. D. Jordan, M. Roach in 1943; D. Gillespie '44; E. South, C. Shavers, C. Parker '45-6. Joined E. Condon, Oct. '56; made British tour '57. Still w. Condon; also studio work in radio, TV, recording. Favs: O. Pettiford, G. Duvivier. LPs w. R. Bright (Reg.), B. Freeman (Vict.), Condon (War. Bros., Col.), Miles Davis (Pres.).

Addr: 65 Lefferts Pl., Brooklyn 16, N.Y.

GAYLOR, HAROLD WALDEN (Hal), *bass;* b. Montreal, Can., 7/9/29. Father and sister musicians; began pl. clar. in school and in Royal Canadian Navy Band. Stud. bass at McGill Cons. 1949 and began pl. prof. jobs. Won first place on TV shows over CBC '56; w. Chico Hamilton '57-8; joined Kai Winding Sept. '58. Fav: Ray Brown. LPs w. John Pisano, Billy Bean, Fred Katz (Decca); Chico Hamilton (Wor. Pac.).

Addr: Linden House, Greenwood Lake, N.Y.

GEE, MATTHEW JR., *trombone;* b. Houston, Tex., 11/25/25. Father pl. bass; brother Herman, trombone. Began on trumpet, then baritone horn and at age 11, trombone which he was infl. to play by hearing Trummy Young. Stud. at Alabama State and later in NYC at Hartnett Studios. Pl. w. Coleman Hawkins, then, after Army service, worked w. Dizzy Gillespie in 1946, pl. baritone horn and trombone. Joined Joe Morris; worked w. Gene Ammons-Sonny Stitt. Solos on own comp. *Wow!* rec. w. Morris (Atl.) and Ammons (Pres.). After eight months w. Count Basie, joined Illinois Jacquet fall '52, touring Europe w. him Oct. '54. In mid-'50s worked numerous dates in Brooklyn clubs; w. Sarah Vaughan Show to Europe '56; Gillespie again briefly in '57. Monday nights at Birdland; "house" band at Apollo Theater '59. Joined Duke Ellington Oct. '59. One of the best and most underrated of the bop-influenced trombonists. Favs: J. J. Johnson, Bennie Green. Own LP on River.; LPs w. Jacquet (Verve), Lou Donaldson (Blue Note).

Addr: 228 W. 17th St., New York, N.Y.

GELLER, HERBERT (Herb), *alto sax;* b. Los Angeles, Cal., 11/2/28. Saxophone at 8; later stud. clarinet, piano. While at high school heard Benny Carter at a local theatre and was first influenced by him. Later influenced by Charlie Parker and pianist Joe Albany. Joined Joe Venuti 1946; Jimmy Zito '48. Came to NYC '49. With Jack Fina's orch. (sax section included Paul Desmond). Later worked 8 months w. Claude Thornhill, settled in NYC, and married pianist Lorraine Walsh. Gigged w. Jerry Wald, Lucky Millinder, 1950, then returned to Calif. w. Billy May's band '51. Played and recorded w. Howard Rumsey's Lighthouse group, Shorty Rogers, Maynard Ferguson, Dan Terry, Bill Holman, Chet Baker, 1953-4. From '54 until her death, his wife, the late Lorraine Geller, occasionally gigged and recorded with him locally. In '58-9, Geller was seen on the East coast and worked with the bands of Benny Goodman and Louis Bellson. He is a soloist with considerable verve and inspiration, never guilty of the blandness that has been associated with so many West Coast performers. Won DB Critics' poll as new star '55. Own LPs: EmArcy, Jubilee, Atco; LPs w. Bellson (Verve), *Saxes, Inc.* (War. Bros.), Shorty Rogers (Vict.), John Graas (Decca), Manny Albam (Coral), Quincy Jones (ABC-Par.), Maynard Ferguson (Em.), Benny Goodman (Col.).

Addr: 2984 Goodview Trail, Los Angeles 28, Calif.

GELLER, LORRAINE WINIFRED WALSH, *piano;* b. Portland, Ore., 9/11/28; d. Los Angeles, Calif., 10/10/58. Toured w. Anna Mae Winburn's Sweethearts of Rhythm, 1949-52; free-lanced around NYC w. Bonnie Wetzel; married alto saxophonist Herb Geller and settled in Los Angeles, working w. Shorty Rogers, Maynard Ferguson, Zoot Sims, '53-4; Herb Geller Quartet '54-5 and intermittently until her death. Also app. as accompanist to Kay Starr '57, comedian Lenny Bruce. W. Bill Holman & Mel Lewis at Monterey Jazz Fest. '58. Excellent soloist showing influences of her favorites: Tatum, Bud Powell, Horace Silver. Fav. own solo: *Alone Together* in Emarcy LP. Own LP on Dot; LPs w. Herb Geller (Em.).

GENTRY, CHARLES T. (Chuck), *saxophones, clarinets;* b. Belgrade, Neb., 12/14/11. Brother prof. musician. First stud. clar. in high school, later at Colorado State Teachers Coll. Pl. w. Ken Baker in LA 1935-9; Vido Musso '39; Harry James '40-1; Benny Goodman '41-2; Jimmy Dorsey '42-3; Glenn Miller Air Force Band '43-4; Artie Shaw '44-5; Jan Savitt '45-6; NBC staff orch. '46-9; radio and TV work '50-53; joined orch. at 20th Century Fox Studio '54. Best known for baritone sax work and as reliable section man. Favs: Harry Carney, Gerry Mulligan. LPs w. Pete Rugolo (Merc.); Lyle Murphy (Contemp.), Franz Waxman, (Decca).

Addr: 18231 Karen Drive, Tarzana, Calif.

GERSH, SQUIRE (William Girsback), *bass;* b. San Francisco, Calif., 5/13/13. Worked w. various commercial groups; was part of the San Francisco "revivalist" movement when he worked w. Lu Watters, B. Scobey, T. Murphy, Mutt Carey, B. Johnson. W. Louis Armstrong Oct. '56-Jan. '58, including South American tour Oct. '57. Toured Europe w. Kid Ory Aug-Nov '59. Favs: Several New Orleans bassists and Jimmy Blanton. LP: *Satchmo* w. Armstrong (Decca).

Addr: 562 Ashbury St., San Francisco, Calif.

GERSHMAN, NATHAN (Nat), *'cello;* b. Philadelphia, Pa., 11/29/17. Brother violinist. Stud. privately, then at Curtis Institute of Music, Philadelphia. Worked w. Cleveland Symph. 1940-7; moved to NYC until '53, doing free-lance recordings and TV work, then to LA. Joined Chico Hamilton early '58, appearing w. him at many jazz festivals '58-9. Favs: Emanuel Luerman, Frank Miller in classical music; Chico Hamilton. LPs w. Hamilton (Warner Bros.).

Addr: 3822 Legion Lane, Los Angeles 39, Calif.

GERSHWIN, GEORGE, *composer, piano;* b. Brooklyn, N.Y., 9/26/1898; d. Beverly Hills, Cal., 7/11/37. Wrote first musical show *La La Lucille,* 1919. First song *Swanee.* His *Rhapsody in Blue,* first performed by

Paul Whiteman in a concert in Aeolian Hall 2/12/24, was followed by *Concerto in F* '25; *American in Paris* '28; *Second Rhapsody* '31; *Cuban Overture* '34; *Porgy and Bess* '34-5. Gershwin's symphonic works made only superficial use of jazz devices and are now not generally considered to be an important part of jazz history; his main importance to jazzmen has been the use of the chord patterns (and frequently the melody) of many of his popular songs as the basis for jazz improvisation and orchestrations. An excellent example of the former is *Oscar Peterson Plays Gershwin* on Verve. An album of Gershwin playing his own works is on Heritage 0073. The release in 1959 of a motion picture version of *Porgy and Bess,* resulted in a rash of LP recordings of the songs from Gershwin's opera. An account of Gershwin's life, *A Journey To Greatness* by David Ewen was published by Henry Holt and Co., 1956.

GETZ, STANLEY (Stan), *tenor sax;* b. Philadelphia, Pa., 2/2/27. Started on bass in NYC, then bassoon; James Monroe High in Bronx. Pl. in All City Orch. At 15 w. Dick "Stinky" Rogers; back to school, then into bands again at 16 w. Jack Teagarden, Dale Jones, Bob Chester; a year w. Kenton '44-5; then briefly w. Jimmy Dorsey, Benny Goodman. Worked w. Randy Brooks, Buddy Morrow, Herbie Fields. Moved to Calif. '47. Worked there w. Butch Stone, also own trio at Swing Club in Hollywood. In Sept. '47, joined the new Woody Herman band in rehearsal and remained until early '49. Getz, Zoot Sims, Serge Chaloff, Herbie Steward (later Al Cohn) comprised celebrated "Four Brothers" in the tune of that name rec. by Herman that gave the band its identifying sound. Getz rose to prominence w. Herman's rec. of *Early Autumn.* Led a quartet w. Al Haig on piano. In '51 he toured Scandinavia. In '52 did NBC studio work in NYC but soon returned to leading his group, usually a quintet. While on a visit to Stockholm in the fall of '55, Getz was taken seriously ill and for the next six months he did not work, recuperating in Scandinavia and Africa. On his return to the US, he resumed touring night clubs w. a quartet. He was feat. in motion picture, *The Benny Goodman Story* '56. Toured w. JATP fall '57 and spring '58; during this time he also app. at jazz clubs and in concert w. his own groups and as a single. In '58 he settled in Copenhagen, working jobs all over the Continent. One of the great interpreters of ballad material, a sound style-setter in the post-bop "cool" era and a fine technician, he was internationally recognized as the top tenor sax man of the 1950s. Favs: Lester Young, Herb Steward, Zoot Sims, Al Cohn, Charlie Parker. Won Met. poll '50-60; DB poll '50-9; DB Critics' poll '53-56, '57-8; Playboy poll '57-60. Playboy All Stars' All Stars '60; *Encyl. of Jazz* "Musicians' Musicians" New Star Award. Own LPs: *Imported From France* (Verve 8331) *At The Shrine,* (2-8188-2), *And The Cool Sounds* (8200), *Award Winner* (8296), *Getz Meets Mulligan* (8249), *In Stockholm* (8213), *More West Coast Jazz* (8177), *Plays* (8133), *Quintet No. 3 Interpretations* (8122), *Soft Swing* (8321), *Stan Getz '57* (8029), *Stan Meets Chet Baker* (8263), *Steamer* (8294), *West Coast Jazz* (8028); *At Storyville,* Vol. 2 (Roost 2225), *Quintet at Storyville* (2209), *Sound* (2207), *The Brothers* (Prest. 7022); *Long Island Sound* (New Jazz 8214). LPs w. Chet Baker (Verve 8623), Herb Ellis (Verve 8252), J. J. Johnson (Verve 8265), Cal Tjader (Fant. 3266), Dizzy Gillespie (Verve 8141), *For Musicians Only* (Verve 8198), *Sittin' In* (Verve 8225), Gerry Mulligan (Verve 8249), Oscar Peterson (Verve 8251), Modern Jazz Society (Verve 8131), *The Brothers* (Pres. 7022), Johnny Smith (Roost 2211); own group on several tracks in *Lestorian Mode* (Savoy 12105), *Opus De Bop* (Savoy 12114), w. Kai Winding in *Loaded* (Savoy 12074); Woody Herman (Harm. 7093, Cap. T324, Col. CL 592).

GIBBS, EDWARD LEROY (Eddie), *bass, guitar, banjo;* b. New Haven, Conn., 12/25/08. Raised in NYC from age of 10. Studied banjo at music schools; guitar under Elmer Snowden 1932. After playing w. Billy Fowler, Charlie Johnson, and Eubie Blake, he toured Europe and US w. Edgar Hayes 1937-8. With Eddie South combo '40-1. During '40s worked w. Dave Martin, Luis Russell, Claude Hopkins in NYC and had own trio at Village Vanguard. Took part in two Broadway shows, *The Pirate* and *Beggars are Coming to Town.* After working w. Cedric Wallace trio, switched back from guitar to banjo, which he has been playing since Mar. 1952 to Mar. '55 w. Wilbur De Paris. Took up bass Feb. '59, studying w. Bass Hill, and continued gigging in NYC area w. Henry Goodwin, Cecil Scott et al. LPs w. Wilbur De Paris (Atl.).

Addr: 527 Manhattan Ave., New York 27, N.Y.

GIBBS, TERRY (Julius Gubenko), *vibes;* also *piano, drums;* b. Brooklyn, N.Y., 10/13/24. Father played violin, bass, on Jewish radio shows; brothers and sisters all musical. Studied brother's xylophone; later took up drums, tympani; won Major Bowes contest at 12 and toured w. Bowes unit. Drums w. Judy Kayne (Dave Pell was in band). Army for three years. Club dates w. Bill De Arango; first record *Meeskite* on Sav. w. Allen Eager. Six weeks w. T. Dorsey; toured Sweden w. Chubby Jackson Dec. '47; Buddy Rich until Sept. '48; then w. Woody Herman for one year. Left to form own band, gave it up in '50 to form sextet w. Louis Bellson and Ch. Shavers. Formed own band again and did Mel Torme TV show for 10 months. Then out w. Benny Goodman Sextet, June '51. He toured with his own quartet for several years, often featuring vibes duets (first with Don Elliott, later with Terry Pollard). From '57 on he was active mainly in LA, where he organized a big band early '59. He was frequently associated, in TV and recording work, with Steve Allen, appearing in Allen's jazz combo at the Roundtable, June '58.

Gibbs has always played with tremendous vitality and a natural beat that established him as the bop era's equivalent of Lionel Hampton. He won the *Metronome* poll '50-5, *Down Beat* poll '50-4. Favs: Milt Jackson, Teddy Charles, Lionel Hampton. Own LPs: *Swingin'* (Em. 36103), *Terry Gibbs* (Em. 36047), *Mallets-A-Plenty* (Em. 36075), *Vibes On Velvet* (Em. 36064), *Plays The Duke* (Em. 36128), *More Vibes On Velvet* (Merc. 80027), *Launching A New Sound In Music* (Merc. 60112), *Terry* (Bruns. 54009; four tracks in *Swing . . . Not Spring* (Savoy 12062); *Esprit De Jazz* w. Larry Bunker, Victor Feldman (Interlude 507); *Newport '58* (Em. 36141), *Jazztime, U.S.A.* (Bruns. 54000), *Jazztime, U.S.A.*, Vol. 2 (Bruns. 54002); LPs w. Herman (Cap. T 324), Goodman (Col. CL 552), Steve Allen (Merc. 80004).

Addr: 23011 Bigler St., Woodland Hills, Calif.

GIBSON, ALBERT ANDREW (Andy), *composer;* b. Zanesville, O., 11/6/13. Took few lessons on violin, then self-taught on trumpet, which he pl. w. band from Cumberland, Md. led by Lou Redman, brother of Don; also w. Zack Whyte band 1932-3, playing and writing. After working w. Blanche Calloway, McKinney's Cotton Pickers, settled in NYC, pl. w. Lucky Millinder off and on for a few years, then gave up playing; on Duke Ellington's recommendation in 1937 began writing for Ch. Barnet, working for him intermittently for ten years; also for Basie '38-42. In Army '42-5, was in Europe and led own band; on discharge, moved to Calif. and rejoined Barnet. Back to NYC '48, free-lanced; joined King Records 1955 as arr. and later became a & r exec. there. One of the better and less-publicized composer-arrangers of the late swing era years. Arrs. for Basie incl. *Tickle Toe, Louisiana, The World is Mad, Shorty George, Jump for Me, Let Me See, Apple Jump, Hollywood Jump;* for Barnet *Shady Lady, Bunny, Charleston Alley, Blue Juice.* Favs: Ellington, Hefti, Oliver. Own LP: Camden.

Addr: c/o King Records, 146 West 54th St., New York 19, N.Y.

GIFFORD, HAROLD EUGENE (Gene), *composer, guitar;* b. Americus, Ga., 5/31/08. Pl. w. Blue Steele, 1928-9. Best known as arr. (also in the early years banjoist and guitarist) with the Casa Loma Band, first in 1929 when it was known as Jean Goldkette's Orange Blossom Orch., and from 1930-9 under Glen Gray. Gifford's early form of "riff" music, typified by his *Black Jazz, White Jazz, Maniacs' Ball, Casa Loma Stomp,* etc., was very popular in the early '30s; he also wrote the successful ballad *Smoke Rings.* Many of his arrs. were played by Fletcher Henderson and other bands of swing and pre-swing days. He led his own band (incl. B. Berigan) on Victor session, 1935. Gifford, who has also worked as draftsman-engineer, radio technician and operator, audio consultant, stevedore and teacher of theory and counterpoint, wrote for Bob Strong '43-4; Tommy Reynolds '44-5; CBS staff in New Orleans '45; USO tours '45-6; back w. Glen Gray '48-9; then free-lance. LPs: two nos. in *A String of Swingin' Pearls* (Vict.); also see Glen Gray.

Addr: c/o ASCAP, 575 Madison Ave., New York 22, N.Y.

GILBERT, LESLIE ERIC (Les), *alto sax, clarinet;* b. Sheffield, England, 3/29/15. Father former pianist, brother plays trumpet, son is trombonist. Studied violin at eight, then clarinet and tenor at 15; switched to alto 1932. Worked as jazz violinist; to London '33, became lead alto player with Piccadilly Hotel Orch. '35. With Eddie Carroll '37-8; Jack Hylton '38-9; on staff of BBC until drafted Dec. '40. After discharge in '46 joined Ted Heath, making many tours, records, TV, radio shows. Favs: Hymie Shertzer, Johnny Hodges, Jimmy Dorsey, Benny Carter, Lee Konitz, Herb Geller. LPs w. Heath (London).

Addr: 110 B Chase Side, London N. 14, England.

GILLESPIE, JOHN BIRKS (Dizzy), *trumpet, composer, singer, leader;* b. Cheraw, S.C., 10/21/17. His father, who died when Dizzy was ten, was an amateur musician; through him Dizzy obtained a working knowledge of several instruments. He started on trombone at 14, trumpet a year later, studying harmony and theory (but never trumpet) at Laurinburg Inst. in N. Carolina. From '35 he lived in Philadelphia, playing his first major job with Frank Fairfax (Ch. Shavers was in the trumpet section with him).

Dizzy was in those days emulating the style of Roy Eldridge, whose place he took in the Teddy Hill band early in '37, visiting France and England the same summer. After free-lancing around New York in '39 and working with Mercer Ellington, he joined Cab Calloway in the fall of '39 and during the next two years was one of the three instrumental stars prominently featured with Cab's band (the others were Chu Berry and Cozy Cole). By this time his style had developed some of the characteristics later known as bop, and he had begun arranging. After leaving Cab, he worked briefly w. Ella Fitzgerald and Benny Carter bands, toured w. Ch. Barnet and then w. Les Hite early in '42. During the following year he worked w. Calvin Jackson, Lucky Millinder, Earl Hines (early '43). For a few months he worked with small groups on 52nd street and w. John Kirby at the Aquarium. Then he joined Billy Eckstine's new big band June '44. Later that year Gillespie's name and the word bop acquired great prominence among musicians, and in early '45, after fronting a combo at the Three Deuces, Gillespie toured w. his first big band. Toward the end of '45 he formed a small combo in California. He reorganized a big band in '46, toured Scandinavia in Jan. and Feb. of '48 and broke up the big band early in '50. He visited Europe in Mar. '52, and in Feb. '53 with a quintet.

Although it has been the subject of much dispute whether Gillespie or Parker was the primary influence in shaping the bop revolution in jazz, the truth seems to be that their ideas and those of several others were interdependent and that each drew upon the others' ingenuity. The result was a melodic, harmonic, and rhythmic advancement of jazz, the incorporation of many subtleties that call for a more developed technique than had hitherto been at the disposition of most jazzmen. Even his detractors (including Louis Armstrong) pay respect to Gillespie's superb musicianship and technical facility.

In later years, after the novelty of bop as a fad had worn off, Gillespie commercialized his music by singing frequently and by emphasizing comedy, but his command of the instrument was unimpaired. Venturing into the record business, he started his own record label, Dee-Gee, in Detroit '51, the catalogue of which was later taken over by Savoy. From late '53 on he recorded for Norman Granz, for whom he had participated in JATP on several concert tours.

A new big band, organized for Gillespie by Quincy Jones, made a tour of Pakistan, Lebanon, Syria, Turkey, Yugoslavia and Greece Mar.-May '56, subsidized by the US State Dept. This was the first time the US government had ever accorded official recognition and economic aid to jazz. Except for time out on tour with JATP, Gillespie kept the band together until Jan. 1958; in the fall of '56 he went on a second goodwill tour for the State Dept., this time in Latin America. He was heard mainly as leader of a quintet '58-60, touring with the NJF show in Europe fall '59.

Gillespie won the *Esq.* New Star award 1945, Silver Award '47, *Met.* poll '47-50, *DB* poll '56, *DB* Critics' Poll '54, '56-7, tied w. Davis '55. Own LPs: *Groovin' High* (Savoy 12020); Rondolette 11; *The Dizzy Gillespie Story* (Savoy 12110), *The Champ* (Sav. 12047), *School Days* (Reg. 6043); GNP 23; *At Newport* Verve (8242), *Birk's Works* (Verve 8222), *Dizzy Gillespie And Stuff Smith* (Verve 8214), *Big Band* (Verve 8178), *Diz And Getz* (Verve 8141), *Dizzy In Greece* (Verve 8017), *Duets With Rollins & Stitt* (Verve 8260), *Jazz Recital* (Verve 8173), *For Musicians Only* (Verve 8198), *Jazz From Paris* (Verve 8015), *Manteca* (Verve 8208), *Trumpet Battle* (Verve 8109), *Trumpet Kings* (Verve 8110), *World Statesman* (Verve 8174), *Have Trumpet, Will Excite* (Verve 8313), *Ebullient Mr. Gillespie* (Verve 8328), *Sonny Side Up* (Verve 8262), *At Home And Abroad* (Atl. 1257), *Concert In Paris* (Roost 2214), *Dizzy Gillespie, 1941* (Ctpt. 548), *Bird And Diz* (Verve 8006), *Tour De Force* (Verve 2812), w. *Mary Lou Williams At Newport* (Verve 8244); LPs w. JATP, Vols. 1, 2, 5, 10, 11 (Verve), *Sittin' In* (Verve 8225), *Jam Session #6* (Verve 8054), #7 (8062), #8 (8094), #9 (8196), *Krupa and Rich* (Verve 8069), *Jazz Concert* (Gr. Award 316), *Hot Vs. Cool* (MGM 3286), Charlie Parker (Savoy 12079).

Addr: 3468 106th St., Corona, L.I., N.Y.

GIRARD, GEORGE, *trumpet;* b. New Orleans, La., 10/7/30; d. NO, 1/18/57, after long siege of cancer. Began playing prof. after grad. from high school, 1946, first w. Johnny Archer on nation-wide tour, then back in New Orleans w. Phil Zito, Basin Street Six, Joe Mares et al. Formed own group in '54 to play at Famous Door in NO. Pl. the annual Dixieland Jubilee in Los Angeles, fall '54. Was active in music until Jan. '56, when he had operation; played again 4 months, spring '56, before illness forced him to retire permanently. Last rec. date for Dr. Edmond Souchon, who organized Good Time Jazz/New Orleans Jazz Club date, Apr. 14, 1956. LPs: portions of *New Orleans Dixieland* (South.), *Recorded In New Orleans, Vol. 1* (GTJ); one number w. Armand Hug in *History of Jazz, Vol. 1* (Cap.).

GIUFFRE, JAMES PETER (Jimmy), *composer, clarinet, tenor* and *baritone sax;* b. Dallas, Texas, 4/26/21. Started on clarinet at nine; tenor sax at 14; Bach. of Mus. at No. Texas St. Teachers' Coll. '42, one semester for Master of Music at USC '46. Later eight years of comp. w. Dr. Wesley La Violette in LA. Clar. and tenor w. Official AAF Orch. '44. Pl. tenor on *Porgy and Bess* w. Dallas Symph. '46; w. Boyd Raeburn briefly, then J. Dorsey for six months in '47; Buddy Rich '48, writing and playing; w. Woody Herman '49; Garwood Van and Spade Cooley '50; w. Lighthouse All Stars '51-2; Shorty Rogers' Giants from Sept. '53 through '55.

From early '56 Giuffre became increasingly active in LA, writing music for many record dates and heading his own trio, which later appeared in the East. He has continued to lead a group intermittently, playing a subdued, improvisational chamber music, using American folk sources as well as jazz. Since '57 he has been on the faculty of the summer School of Jazz at Lenox, Mass. In the late '50s his tenor playing showed an increasing awareness of Sonny Rollins. In addition to writing basic jazz material for his trio, and various recording groups, he has written a number of ambitious works for larger orchestras including *Pharoah* and *Suspensions,* under the direction of Gunther Schuller on Columbia's *Music For Brass* (CL 941) and *Modern Jazz Concert* (WL 127) respectively. Among his better-known works for jazz groups are *Four Brothers,* written for Woody Herman in '49; *Four Mothers, Four Others,* etc.

Although he rarely explored the full possibilities of the instrument, preferring to confine himself to the lower register, Giuffre earned wide popularity as a clarinetist in the late '50s and won the following polls: *Down Beat* '57; *Down Beat* Critics' as new Star '55, new star baritone sax '56; Metronome poll on clar. '58-9. Film: *Jazz On A Summer's Day* '60. Own LPs: Verve, Atl., Cap.; LPs w. Bob Brookmeyer (Wor. Pac.), Teddy Charles (Pres.), Herb Ellis, Ray Brown (Verve), *Jazz Composer's Workshop* (Savoy), Lennie Niehaus, Shelly Manne (Contemp.), *Modern Jazz Quartet At Music Inn* (Atl.) Shorty Rogers (Cap., Vict., Atl.), *Lighthouse All Stars* (Contemp.); *Jimmy Giuffre Meets Herb Ellis, Sonny Stitt Plays Jimmy Giuffre Arrangements* (Verve); *The Jimmy Giuffre 4, Anita O'Day Sings Jimmy Giuffre Arrangements* (Verve).

Addr: c/o Verve, 451 No. Canon Drive, Beverly Hills, Calif.

GLASEL, JOHN (Johnny), *trumpet;* b. New York City, 6/11/30. Stud. Yale U. and Yale Sch. of Music. Grad. 1951-2 w. Bach. Mus. & Bach. Arts degrees. First prof. experience w. Bob Wilbur '45; pl. w. New Haven Symph. From '53-5, worked w. chamber groups, subbed at Radio City Music Hall; jazz work w. "The Six" at Ryan's. W. Ray McKinley "Glenn Miller" orch. May-June '56. Pit orchs. for *Bells Are Ringing* Oct. '57-Mar. '59, *Once Upon A Mattress* May-Oct. '59. Pl. w. Bill Russo's orch. July-Aug. '59. Favs: Armstrong, Gillespie. Own LP: ABC-Par.; LPs w. Dick Cary (Gold. Crest), Jerri Adams (Col.), *The Six* (Beth.).

Addr: 38 West 73rd St., New York 23, N. Y.

GLENN, EVANS TYREE, *trombone, vibes;* b. Corsicana, Texas, 11/23/12. With Tommy Mills in Wash., D.C. '34-6. In NYC played w. Eddie Barefield '36-7; Eddie Mallory, Benny Carter, '37-9, Cab Calloway '40-6. Toured Europe w. Don Redman '46, then spent five years in Duke Ellington's orchestra. Entered radio-TV field; staff musician and occasional actor at WPIX, NYC from '52. Replaced Tiny Kahn on Jack Sterling's show, daily on CBS radio since Aug. '53; also, in late '50s, often heard in NYC clubs with own quartet. On trombone, he has used the "wah-wah" plunger style original with Ellington's Joe (Tricky Sam) Nanton; on vibes he purveys an innocuous, pleasant brand of swing music. Own LPs: Roulette. LPs: *Liberian Suite* w. Ellington (Col.); *Seven Ages of Jazz* (Metrojazz), Cozy Cole (Gr. Award).

Addr: 308 West Englewood Avenue, Englewood, N. J.

GLOW, BERNIE, *trumpet;* b. NYC, 2/6/26. Grandfather was prof. musician. Stud. trumpet at nine with private teachers, later at High School of Music and Art, NYC. Worked two weeks, while in high school, w. Louis Prima for theater date; on tour w. Richard Himber 1943; Raymond Scott CBS house band '44-5; Artie Shaw '45-6; Boyd Raeburn '47; Woody Herman '47-9. On staff at WMGM '50-5; since then doing free-lance recording, radio and TV work. Mainly known as dependable section man; not jazz soloist. LPs w. numerous groups on a variety of labels incl. Woody Herman (Cap.), Bill Potts (UA).

GOJKOVIC, DUSAN (Dusko), *trumpet;* b. Jajce, Yugoslavia, 10/14/31. Stud. at mus. sch. in Belgrade '48-53; pl. w. Radio Belgrade dance orch. '51-5. To Germany: rec., concerts, tours w. German All-Stars; named by critics as best of year at '56 Frankfurt Jazz Festival. Since Apr. '57 w. Kurt Edelhagen band at Radio Cologne. Worked briefly w. Chet Baker in Storyville Club in Frankfurt. Pl. w. International Youth Band at Brussels World's Fair and Newport Festival '58. W. Albert Mangelsdorff, Bernt Rosengren and Rudy Jacobs, formed a group called the Newport International Septet, pl. at Storyville in Frankfurt '59. Has made movies w. Caterina Valente and Edelhagen. Favs: Gillespie, Armstrong, M. Davis, Clifford Brown, Eldridge. LPs w. Int. Band (Col.), Caterina Valente (Decca).

Addr: Maybachstr. 28, Cologne, Germany.

GOLD, SANFORD, *piano;* b. Cleveland, Ohio, 6/9/11. Studied privately. Own sextet in Cleveland for several years; to NYC 1935, conducted for ice shows, etc., then joined Babe Russin at Hickory House. W. Abe Lyman, Raymond Scott, 1938-40; trio w. Dave Barbour at Lincoln Hotel '41, followed by a year of staff work at CBS. Army 1943-6. After discharge, made records w. Don Byas and other 52nd Streeters of the day; also a year playing and recording w. Mary Osborne trio. Staff job at NBC 1949-54, free-lanced in NYC from summer '54. Almost the only pianist of his age to have moved with the times, he developed into an excellent Bud Powell-influenced soloist. Favs: Bud Powell, Tatum, H. Silver. Own LP: Prestige. LPs w. Johnny Smith (Roost), Don Byas (Regent); w. Al Cohn in *Mr. Music; East Coast-West Coast Scene* (Victor).

Addr: 150 West 55th Street, New York 19, N. Y.

GOLDIE, DON (Donald Elliott Goldfield), *trumpet;* b. Newark, N. J., 2/5/30. Father pl. with Paul Whiteman for more than 15 years; mother a concert pianist. Stud. violin, piano, then trumpet at age ten. Won scholarship when 11; stud. with private teachers. Father had own orch. after Whiteman disbanded; pl. first job w. father at 14. In Army 1951-4; pl. with Joe Mooney '56-8; Neal Hefti '59; joined Jack Teagarden June '59. In addition to bearing both musical and physical resemblance to Billy Butterfield, Goldie is noted for extraordinarily accurate vocal imitations of Louis Armstrong. Favs: Butterfield, Armstrong, Berigan et al. LPs w. Hefti (Cor.), Teagarden (Roul.).

GOLDKETTE, JEAN, *leader, piano;* b. Valenciennes, France, 3/18/99; raised in Greece, studied in Russia; to US 1911. Had own band in Detroit during '20s. Played major part in organizing, booking other bands, incl. McKinney's Cotton Pickers, original Casa Loma orch. Though not a jazzman himself, employed Joe Venuti, Eddie Lang, Bix Beiderbecke, Frank Trumbauer, Danny Polo, Jimmy McPartland, and the Dorsey brothers during his bandleading career. Later became an agent, managing the Charioteers, but had own band again in '45 and '47. Active as concert pianist '55, he later became President of the National Actors Foundation, a non-profit organization dedicated to encouraging new talent. There was a 10 inch LP of Goldkette's band on Label "X" but this adjunct of Victor is no longer issuing records.

Addr: c/o Linden, 1623¾ Hillhurst, Los Angeles 27, Cal.

GOLSON, BENNY, *tenor sax, composer;* b. Philadelphia, Pa., 1/25/29. Began stud. piano at 9, switched to sax at 14. Attended Howard U. in Washington. Worked around Philadelphia; left w. Bull Moose Jackson in 1951 (band incl. Tadd Dameron, who encouraged his interest in arranging). Joined Dameron's group in 1953; later the same year w. L. Hampton; w. J. Hodges, 1954; E. Bostic '54-6. Joined D. Gillespie's big band in '56 and toured S. America. With Gillespie until band broke up in '58; joined Art Blakey in Feb. and remained w. him until Feb. '59. Formed own quintet July '59, pl. on both coasts. In fall '59 combined w. Art Farmer to co-lead The Jazztet. Originally influenced by Lucky Thompson and Don Byas, Golson's playing was touched by John Coltrane in '58. One of the most important new composers in jazz to emerge in the '50s, his compositions like *Stablemates, Whisper Not* and *I Remember Clifford* have been widely recorded and played. Fav. instrumentalists: Coltrane, Byas, Thompson, D. Gordon, Hawkins, Stitt, Getz. Fav. arr: Dameron, Q. Jones, Gryce, Wilkins. Own LPs on River., New Jazz, Contemp., UA; LPs w. Art Farmer (UA), Art Blakey, Lee Morgan (Blue Note), Lem Winchester (New Jazz), Dizzy Gillespie (Verve), James Moody (Argo), Jimmy Cleveland (Em.), Sahib Shihab (Savoy), Philly Joe Jones (River.), George Russell (Decca), Clifford Brown (Pres.).

Addr: 55 West 92nd St., New York, N. Y.

GOMEZ, PHILIP LOUIS (Phil), *clarinet;* b. Mazatlan, Mexico, 8/24/19. Started in LA, played w. Ken Baker; Ben Pollack, Sonny Dunham, Will Bradley 1941-2. In service '43-5. With Jan Savitt and many West Coast Dixieland groups. '52-4 w. Muggsy Spanier; joined Kid Ory early '55, remaining w. him through European tour '57. Fronted own band w. Ory sidemen '58. W. Jerry Colonna '59, backing him on his tours w. band known as Phil Gomez' Swingin' Kings. Favs: Fazola, Goodman, De Franco. Own LP: *Dixieland Mambo* (Omegadisk); LPs w. Ory (GTJ, Verve), Jerry Colonna (Merc.), Muggsy Spanier (Weathers).

Addr: 13533 Morrison St., Sherman Oaks, Calif.

GONZALES, BABS, *singer;* b. Newark, N.J., 10/27/19. With Tadd Dameron, organized vocal group, Babs' Three Bips and a Bop, in '46. Later active as disc-jockey, also manager and vocalist w. James Moody; promoter of various modern jazz ventures. Recorded series of novelty items with leading bop musicians for Cap. '49. Composed *Oo-pa-pa-da.* Own LPs: Hope, Jaro; LP w. James Moody (Em.).

GONSALVES, PAUL, *tenor sax;* b. Boston, Mass., 7/12/20. Raised in Pawtucket, R. I. Started on guitar in 1936; later, on tenor, was prominently featured with Sabby Lewis' band in Boston during the early '40s. In Army '42-5; joined Count Basie '46. Worked briefly w. Dizzy Gillespie big band '49-50, then joined Duke Ellington and has remained with him except for a few weeks w. T. Dorsey in early '53. Extroverted tenor out of Hawkins-Webster school. Own LP: Argo; LPs w. Clark Terry (River.), *Sittin' In* (Verve), Dinah Washington (Merc.), Ray Charles (Atl.), Billy Taylor (Argo), Count Basie (Cam., Vict.); also see Ellington.

Addr: 50 West 106th St., New York, N. Y.

GONSALVES, VIRGIL, *baritone saxophone, clarinet;* b. Monterey, Cal., 9/5/31. Stud. SF State Coll. Pl. w. Alvino Rey 1950; J. Fina '51; T. Beneke '52; own sextet in SF and free-lancing locally. App. at Monterey Fest. '58. Favs: Mulligan, Konitz, Getz. Own LPs on Liberty, Omega.

GOODMAN, BENJAMIN DAVID (Benny), *clarinet, leader;* b. Chicago, Ill., 5/30/09. One of a large and poor family, he studied at Hull House in Chicago and by 1919 had acquired some proficiency on the clarinet. He was about 12 when he appeared onstage with Benny Meroff in Chicago doing an imitation of Ted Lewis, then the prevailing clarinet favorite. Ben Pollack, who heard him at that time, later sent for him to join the band at the Venice ballroom in Los Angeles. His first recorded solo, *He's the Last Word,* recorded with Pollack's orchestra in Chicago 12/17/26, reveals his early style, which was influenced by Frank Teschemacher, Jimmie Noone, and Leon Rappolo.

While with Pollack, Goodman recorded a few combo sides as a leader: one 1928 date (now available on Brunswick LP 54010) offers his only recorded solos on alto and baritone saxophones. After leaving Pollack in '29 he became a very successful free-lancer in NYC in pit band, radio and recording work. In the spring of '34 he led his first regularly organized band, which was featured on a regular radio series over NBC called "Let's Dance." After playing at Billy Rose's Music Hall and at the Roosevelt Hotel in NYC, and recording first for Columbia and later (April '35) for Victor, Goodman took his band on the road. Most of his engagements up to and during this first tour had very little success, but by the time the band reached Los Angeles, its recordings had paved the way for a wildly enthusiastic reception. The swing era, in effect, had begun.

The arrangements by Fletcher Henderson (also by Horace Henderson, Benny Carter, Deane Kincaide, Edgar Sampson and others), and the solos by Goodman, Bunny Berigan, and Jess Stacy, as well as drumming by Gene Krupa and the vocals by Helen Ward, were important elements in the band's popularity, which by '36 had reached phenomenal proportions. Although in the next few years many other bands cashed in on the swing fad and rivaled Goodman's reputation, he and his orchestra remained a peak attraction almost continuously until mid-'44, when he disbanded.

The history of the Benny Goodman combos began in the summer of '35 with the recording of the first session by the Benny Goodman trio (Goodman, Krupa, Teddy Wilson). By taking Wilson on the road the following spring for personal appearances with the trio as an adjunct to the band, Goodman broke down racial taboos for the first time in jazz history on a large national scale. In August '36, Lionel Hampton made his first session with Benny in Hollywood and the trio became a quartet. In October '39, the addition of Charlie Christian on guitar and the inclusion of Arthur Bernstein on bass made Goodman's small group a sextet for the first time. From that point on, and with many different personnels, Goodman's small combos, from trio to septet size, played a vital part in his career. One sextet appeared with him at the Center Theatre in *Swingin' the Dream* in the fall of '39; another played onstage with him in '44 in the *Seven Lively Arts*. Goodman reorganized the big band in '45 and continued to front it off and on until '50, when he took a sextet, including Roy Eldridge and Zoot Sims, on a European tour. After that year he limited his activities to occasional appearances with a small group, except for one brief tour fronting a big band in the spring of '53, during most of which Krupa fronted the band, Goodman being ill.

In 1955 Goodman and a specially assembled band recorded the sound track for a film, *The Benny Goodman Story,* in which Steve Allen played the role of Goodman. Heavy with anachronisms and Hollywood clichés, the picture was not the artistic or even commercial success it could and should have been. It did, however, induce Goodman to emerge from his semi-retirement and reassemble a band, which he fronted at the Waldorf-Astoria Hotel in NYC Feb. '56. He continued to lead a band off and on, undertaking a partially State Dept. sponsored trip to the Far East in the winter of '56-7; a well publicized event was his appearance at the royal palace in Bangkok, when he took part in a jam session with the jazz-loving King Phumipol Aduljej of Thailand.

Goodman sent out another band in the US under his name in the fall of '57, but it was led by Urbie Green and he did not generally appear with it. Another band was formed in the summer of '58 and Goodman took it to the Brussels Fair. In the spring of '58 and '59 he was also seen starring in his own TV show *Swing Into Spring.*

During more than three decades as a jazz celebrity, Goodman earned a multiple niche: instrumentally he showed great technique and an inspired, definitive solo style that inspired a whole school of jazz clarinetists from 1935 on; as a bandleader he adopted an unprecedented policy, converting both standard and popular songs to the idiom that came to be known as swing and thus starting a new era in jazz. No less important was his achievement on the social level when, encouraged by the enthusiasm of his friend and patron John Hammond, he became the first white bandleader to incorporate Negroes into his entourage. Hammond's sister, Alice Duckworth, married Goodman in 1941.

Sidemen who have been featured with Goodman at one time or another include Harry James, Bunny Berigan, Ziggy Elman, Buck Clayton, Cootie Williams, Roy Eldridge, Billy Butterfield, trumpets; Joe Harris, Jack Lacey, Vernon Brown, Lou McGarity, Cutty Cutshall, Trummy Young, Kai Winding, trombones; Toots Mondello, Hymie Shertzer, Skip Martin, alto saxes; Arthur Rollini, Bud Freeman, Vido Musso, Jerry Jerome, Wardell Gray, Georgie Auld, Stan Getz, Zoot Sims, tenor saxes; Claude Thornhill, Frank Froeba, Fletcher Henderson, Johnny Guarnieri, Mel Powell, Joe Bushkin, pianos; Allen Reuss, George Van Eps, Mike Bryan, Dave Barbour, Steve Jordan, guitars; Dave Tough, Sid Catlett, Nick Fatool, Morey Feld, Louis Bellson, drums; Harry Goodman, John Simmons, Clyde Lombardi, Slam Stewart, Harry Babasin, basses; Red Norvo, Terry Gibbs, Teddy Charles, vibes; Martha Tilton, Peggy Lee, Patti Page, Dick Haymes, Art Lund, vocals. Hundreds of other musicians worked off and on with Goodman, some for recording sessions only, others on tours.

Goodman has had a concurrent but less publicized career as a classical clarinetist since 1938. He recorded with the Budapest string quartet; and in 1939 commissioned Bela Bartok to write *Contrasts,* which he recorded in 1940 for Columbia, with Joseph Szigeti; he also commissioned concertos of Aaron Copland and Paul Hindemith.

In addition to being heard in the biographical movie, Goodman was seen in several pictures including *Stage Door Canteen, A Song is Born, Powers Girl, The Big Broadcast of 1937, Hollywood Hotel, Sweet and Lowdown;* he recorded a soundtrack for Walt Disney's *Make Mine Music.*

Goodman has won the following awards: as clarinetist, *Playboy* poll every year since its inception in 1957; *Esquire* Gold Award every year the poll was held ('44-7); *Down Beat* poll as fav. soloist '43-7, '49; *Metronome* poll '40-9; *Down Beat* Critics' poll '54 (tie), '56.

Own LPs: *B. G. In Hi-Fi* (Cap. W565), *B. G.—1927-1934* (Bruns. 54010), *Benny Goodman and his Orchestra* (Col. CL 534), *The Benny Goodman Band* (Cap. T 409), *Combos* (Cap. T 669, Col. CL 500), *Fletcher Henderson Arrangements* (Col. CL 524), *Eddie Sauter Arrangements* (Col. CL 523), Sextet and Orch. with *Charlie Christian* (Col. CL 652), *The Benny Goodman Story, Vols. 1 & 2* (Decca 8252, 8253), *The Benny Goodman Trio Plays for Fletcher Henderson Fund* (Col. CL 516), *Trio, Quartet, Quintet* (Vict. LPM 1226), *Benny In Brussels, Vols. 1 & 2* (Col. CL 1247, 1248), *Carnegie Hall Jazz Concert* (Col. OSL 160), *The King Of Swing* (1937/38 Jazz Concert No. 2—Col. OSL 180), *The Golden Age of Benny Goodman* (Vict. LPM 1099), *The Golden Age of Swing* (Vict. LPT 6703), *The Goodman Touch* (Cap. T 441), *The Great Benny Goodman* (Col. CL 820), *Mostly Sextets* (Cap. T 668), *The New Benny Goodman Sextet* (Col. CL 552), *Peggy Lee Sings With Benny Goodman* (Harm. 7005), *Plays Selections Featured In The Benny Goodman Story* (Cap. S 706), *This Is Benny Goodman* (Vict. LPM 1239), *The Vintage Goodman* (Col. CL 821), *Happy Session* (Col. CL 8129), *Benny Rides Again* (Chess 1440), *The*

Benny Goodman Treasure Chest (MGM 3E9), *The Sound of Music* (MGM E3810); LPs w. Ted Lewis (Epic 3170), Billie Holiday (Col. CL 637), Red Norvo (Epic 3128), *Metronome All Stars* (Cam. 426, Harm. 7044); *Spirituals To Swing* (Vang. 8523/4).
Addr: 200 East 66th St., New York 21, N. Y.

GOODMAN, THOMAS ALAN (Tommy), *piano, composer;* b. Brooklyn, N.Y., 12/3/24. Extensive studies from 1931-51 incl. Juilliard, Eastman, Yale (w. Paul Hindemith), Paris Cons. Rec. debut w. Benny Goodman (not related) on *Blue Skies* (Col. 1946). Pl. w. Bud Freeman 1953, Louis Bellson 1954, also gigged and rec. w. The Six, '54-5. Fav: Mel Powell, T. Wilson, Tatum.
Addr: 85 Riverside Drive, New York 24, N. Y.

GOODWIN, HENRY CLAY, *trumpet;* b. Washington, D.C., 1/2/10. Mother, Blossom Harrison, played honky-tonk piano. Studied at Armstrong High and w. private teachers: drums, tuba, then trumpet. First major job was European tour w. Josephine Baker 1925, w. S. Bechet, Claude Hopkins. To Buenos Aires w. Paul Wyer '26. In NYC, worked w. Cliff Jackson '29; to Europe in '33 w. Lucky Millinder, Willie Bryant, '33; Ch. Johnson '34-6; Cab Calloway '36; Europe again w. Edgar Hayes '37-8. Rec. w. Slim Gaillard '40; S. Bechet '41; worked with Cecil Scott 1942-4; rec. w. Art Hodes '46. Jazz Festival at Nice '48; Bob Wilber '49-50; Jimmy Archey '51-2 (also toured Europe). In recent years has been free-lancing around NYC in various Dixieland sessions at Metropole, etc. Also w. George Stevenson '59. LP w. Bechet in *Creole Reeds* (River.).
Addr: 9 Croydon Road, Amityville, N. Y.

GORDON, ROBERT (Bob), *baritone sax;* b. St. Louis, Mo., 6/11/28; d. Calif., 8/28/55. Stud. at Westlake Coll., LA 1948-9. Played w. Shorty Sherock, Lee Williams, Jimmy Palmer '46; Alvino Rey '48-51, Billy May '52, Horace Heidt '52-3, George Redman '54. In '55 he was killed in an auto accident while on the way to play a concert in San Diego with Pete Rugolo's band. Won award as New Star in *DB* Int. Critics Poll '55. LPs w. Jack Montrose (Wor. Pac., Atl.), Lennie Niehaus, Duane Tatro (Contemp.), Maynard Ferguson (Em), Pete Rugolo (Col.), Jack Millman; *Blow Hot, Blow Cool* (Decca); one no. w. own group in *Jazz West Coast* (Wor. Pac.).

GORDON, DEXTER, *tenor sax;* b. Los Angeles, Cal., 2/27/23. Father was doctor whose patients included Duke Ellington, Lionel Hampton. Studied harmony, theory, clarinet at 13; alto at 15. Quit school '40, took up tenor; joined Harlem Collegians, local band. With Lionel Hampton Dec. '40 for three years. Back to LA w. Lee Young, Jessie Price; six months w. Louis Armstrong in '44. First rec. solo was *Blowing The Blues Away* during 18 months w. Billy Eckstine's band. To NYC w. Charlie Parker at Spotlite; own group at Three Deuces. To West Coast summer '46; two months in Honolulu w. Cee Pee Johnson. Ret. to NYC late '47, gigged around 52nd St., then back to West Coast, where he worked w. small groups off and on. Gordon, strongly influenced by Lester Young, later was one of the first to transfer the characteristics of bop to the tenor and himself became an influence on important players of the '50s such as John Coltrane and Sonny Rollins. Own LPs: Savoy, Dooto, Beth.; LPs w. Wardell Gray (Pres., Reg.), Billy Eckstine in *Advance Guard of the '40s* (Em.), Stan Levey (Beth.), Fats Navarro (Savoy).

GORDON, JOSEPH HENRY (Joe), *trumpet;* b. Boston, Mass., 5/15/28. Studied w. Fred Berman, New England Conservatory. Worked as sandwich-boy on Boston-Albany railroad 1947; gained entry to music field by selling newspapers around local clubs. Had own combo at Savoy '47, then worked w. Sabby Lewis, Georgie Auld. Later w. Ch. Parker, Ch. Mariano, Lionel Hampton, Art Blakey, Jimmy Tyler, Don Redman. Joined Dizzy Gillespie '56 and toured the Middle East with him, March-May. Formed own group in Boston after leaving Dizzy in summer of '56, then joined Herb Pomeroy's band at the Stables, remaining until may '58. Moved to LA and worked gigs w. Harold Land, Dexter Gordon, Benny Carter, Barney Kessel before joining Shelly Manne in Nov. '58. Also one night a week at Lighthouse. Film: *The Proper Time* w. Manne '59. Favs: Gillespie, Eldridge. LPs w. Manne (Contemp.), Benny Carter (UA), Barney Kessel (Contemp.), Gillespie (Verve), Barbara Dane (Dot).
Addr: 124½ Surf St., Santa Monica, Calif.

GOTTUSO, ANTHONY (Tony), *guitar;* b. New York City, 2/2/17. Played w. Paul Whiteman, Artie Shaw, other namebands; TV and radio work in NYC since mid-1940s. Featured guitarist on Rusty Draper rec. *Gambler's Guitar*. Feat. in occasional solos on Steve Allen NBC-TV show, 1954-5. Inactive in jazz in recent years. LP w. Artie Shaw (Epic).
Addr: 74 Glenwood Road, Tenafly, N.J.

GOURLEY, JAMES PASCO JR. (Jimmy), *guitar;* b. St. Louis, Mo., 6/9/26. Father was founder of Monarch Cons. of Mus. in Hammond, Ind. Guitar at 10; pl. in school band w. Lee Konitz on tenor '41. Toured w. commercial bands in La., '43-4; Navy, '44-6. Replaced J. Raney in Jay Burkhart band in Chicago, stayed two years, then w. Vido Musso, Anita O'Day, Gene Ammons, Sonny Stitt, Jackie Cain-Roy Kral and other Chi. combos. Lived in Paris, Apr. '51 to Nov. '54, studying, playing; worked mainly w. Henri Renaud. One year at the Tabou; own quartet at the Ringside. Many rec. dates in Paris w. Zoot Sims, Konitz, Gryce, Clifford Brown, Brookmeyer, Renaud, Roy Haynes et al. Back in Chicago, rec. w. Chubby Jackson '56; also various local jobs before resuming residence in Paris Dec. '57. Six months w. Art Simmons at Mars Club. Own group as house band at Blue Note backing visiting American soloists. Talented modern soloist. Fav: Raney. LP w. Chubby Jackson (Argo).
Addr: 45 Rue Monsieur Le Prince, Paris 6, France.

GOWANS, ARTHUR BRADFORD (Brad), *trombone, clarinet, composer;* b. Billerica, Mass., 12/3/03; d. Los Angeles, 9/8/54. Played clarinet in Tommy De Rosa's NO jazz band replacing Sidney Arodin, then switched to cornet and to Joe Venuti's band '26. Later that year he joined Jimmy Durante's jazz band; following this he was with Mal Hallett's orchestra for two years. In subsequent years made many records w. Red Nichols. Concentrated later on trombone, recording w. Bobby Hackett, Wingy Manone, Joe Marsala, Bud Freeman, Ray McKinley, Art Hodes, Eddie Condon. He invented a combination slide and valve trombone which he called a "valide." For several years before his death he lived on the West Coast, playing his last engagement w. Ed. Skrivanek's sextet in Las Vegas for a year April '53. As a clarinetist and trombonist Gowan was considered a disciple of Larry Shields and Eddie Edwards of the original Dixieland jazz band. He wrote many effective arrangements for quasi-Dixieland bands such as Bud Freeman's Summa Cum Laude orchestra. Own LP on Vict.; LPs w. Art Hodes in *Gems of Jazz* (Decca), Bud Freeman in *A String of Swinging Pearls* (Vict.), Eddie Condon, Max Kaminsky (Comm.).

GOZZO, CONRAD JOSEPH, *trumpet;* b. New Britain, Conn., 2/6/22. Stud. w. father, who is still a trumpet teacher. Repl. one of his father's students in Isham Jones band, 1938. Worked w. Tommy Reynolds, Red Norvo, Johnny Scat Davis, Bob Chester, 1939-41; Claude Thornhill 1941-2, then three months w. Benny Goodman. In Navy w. Artie Shaw band '42-5, then rejoined Goodman. After a year with Woody Herman until the breakup of the first Herman Herd in Dec. '46, he worked w. Boyd Raeburn, Tex Beneke; settled in Los Angeles '47, played 4½ years on Bob Crosby broadcasts. Mainly a superb section man, but was feat. w. Herman on *Stars Fell On Alabama,* and on *Mean To Me* in the MGM Carnegie Hall concert LP; has also made all Billy May sessions. Solo on *Fortune & Dreams* w. Kay Starr (Cap.). Own LP: Vict.

Addr: 743 Uclan Drive, Burbank, Calif.

GRAAS, JOHN, *French horn, composer;* b. Dubuque, Iowa, 10/14/24. Started on the horn in high school, where he won national solo contest; scholarship to Tanglewood, where he played under Koussevitsky. First horn with Indianapolis Symphony 1941-2; Claude Thornhill Orch. '42; own band in Army '43-5; Cleveland Symphony '45-6; Tex Beneke '47-8; concert tours with Stan Kenton '49-50. Studied composition with Lennie Tristano, Shorty Rogers, and Rogers' teacher, Wesley La Violette. Since 1950, free-lancing in Hollywood; many TV shows, also wrote movie scores for RKO, Warner's, etc., and toured with Liberace. Had strict classical background but says he felt inhibited when symphony conductors imposed their interpretations upon the instrumentalist. Graas won Met. poll, 1955, in Miscellaneous Instruments division. His ambition to follow jazz in its newer developments, and to apply the same fluidity of improvisation to the French horn that had been common to other jazz instruments, was realized from '53 in a series of recordings that established him as a jazz pioneer on his instrument. Graas's compositions vary from unpretentious swinging jazz to a technically brilliant though sometimes over-heavy incorporation of European classical influences. Own LPs on Decca, Merc., Kapp; LPs w. Kenton, *Modern Sounds* w. Shorty Rogers & Gerry Mulligan (Cap.), Pete Rugolo (Col.), Bob Cooper (Cap.).

Addr: 9020 Willis Ave., Van Nuys, Calif.

GRAETTINGER, ROBERT, *composer;* b. Ontario, Cal., 10/31/23; d. Los Angeles, Cal., 3/12/57. Stud. sax at nine; first prof. job at 16 w. Bobby Sherwood, playing and writing. After similar jobs w. Benny Carter, Johnny Richards, Alvino Rey and Jan Savitt, he started full time composing. Joined Stan Kenton 1947; first original rec. by Kenton was *Thermopylae.* Graettinger's *City of Glass,* a symphonic work, was performed by Kenton in '48, expanded and rec. in '51. Other comps. rec. by Kenton: *This Modern World, House of Strings, Incident in Jazz* (Capitol). Graettinger was an extraordinarily gifted modern writer; his work bore little or no relationship to jazz.

GRAH, WILHELM JOSEF (Bill), *vibraphone;* also *piano, drums;* b. Cologne, Germany, 6/24/28. Father is pianist-conductor Willi Grah; brother, bassist Heinz Grah, has worked with him for several years. Piano lessons 1936; st. on vibes '47, stud. drums in Luxemburg '51. Formed own student band '46, pl. for Allied Forces. Worked w. Nachtfalter Quintet '49-53; vibes and piano w. Fatty George '54; own group since then. Rec. w. own group and w. Lionel Hampton, F. George. Favs: Hampton, Tatum. Won German jazz polls as country's best vibraphonist '55-7.

Addr: Fischerstiege 1-7, Vienna 1, Austria.

GRAHAM, WILLIAM (Bill), *baritone, alto sax;* b. Kansas City, Mo., 9/18/18. Raised in Denver. While at Denver U. gigged w. own band incl. P. Quinichette. Stud. for two years at Tuskegee Inst. in Alabama. Army to 1945, then att. Lincoln U. in Missouri. Worked w. Basie, Millinder, E. Hawkins, Ed Wilcox. With D. Gillespie's large and small bands off and on '46-52; then formed own combo which pl. for two years at Snookie's in NYC. Toured w. Basie Feb. '55-Sept. '57; Duke Ellington Jan.-Mar. '58; own group '58-9; with Mercer Ellington at Birdland fall '59. Recently teaching music at public school in NYC. While with Ellington he played Johnny Hodges' parts and was feat. on LP of *Black, Brown & Beige* (Col.). Other LPs w. Basie (Verve), Gillespie (Atl., Roost).

Addr: 2170 Madison Avenue, New York 37, N. Y.

GRAHAM, KENNY (Kenneth Thomas Skingle), *composer, tenor sax, clarinet, flute;* b. London, Eng., 7/19/24. From musical family, began playing banjo at 5, sang in church choir, played w. Ambrose, J. Parnell et al. Formed own group called the Afro-Cubists in early '50s and worked in Eng. and on Continent until '58 when he was confined to a hospital for a year. Has since given up playing and concentrated on composing and arranging for Ted Heath, Humphrey Lyttelton, etc. Also musical dir. for rec. sessions by Big Bill Broonzy and Josh White in Eng. Comp. *Beaulieu Suite* for Ted Heath's app. at Beaulieu Jazz Fest. '59. Favs: Ellington, Gillespie. Own LP: *Moondog and Suncat Suites* (MGM); LP w. Heath: *Australian Suite* (Lond.).

Addr: 135 Haverstock Hill, London N. W. 3, Eng.

GRANZ, NORMAN, *producer;* b. Los Angeles, Cal., 8/6/18. Attended UCLA, worked as part-time quotation clerk w. LA Stock Exchange. Following Army service 1941-4, worked as film editor at MGM studios. After running a series of informal jazz concerts (starting 7/2/44) at the LA Philharmonic Auditorium (from which his famous concert unit, "Jazz At The Philharmonic," derived its name), he took a group of musicians on a limited tour of the western states and Canada in the fall of '45. The show worked its way up the West Coast, then collapsed in Canada. After several of his albums, recorded at JATP concerts, had been released on records, he was able to embark on a successful tour. In addition to the albums, he supervised a short film, *Jammin' The Blues,* photographed by Gjon Mili, which won an Academy Award nomination for the best short feature of the year (1944). Granz produced his own records, but in 1944-5 he released them on the Philo and Asch labels, and from 1948 to 1951 on Mercury. In 1951, having recalled the rights to all his recordings, he transferred the entire catalogue to his own Clef label, supplementing this w. the Norgran label in '54. In the late '40s, in addition to his tours, Granz began to spend more and more time making studio recordings of jazz artists. His most ambitious venture was the *Jazz Scene,* an experimental album by various large and small groups in '49. In early '57, he consolidated all his record releases under the Verve label.

In the late '50s Granz greatly expanded his concert activities, particularly in Europe, where he sponsored extended tours by Duke Ellington, and other artists in addition to JATP. The latter unit no longer toured the US after '57, though a more compact show starring Ella Fitzgerald and Oscar Peterson continued to tour annually. Granz's first Broadway stage production, in the fall '59, was a one-man show by Yves Montand, who was backed by a small combo featuring Jimmy Giuffre and other jazzmen.

Though not a musician, Granz was important as an employer of jazz talent, with which, during the '40s, he proved that the selling of excitement, by means of jazz, was a commodity with vast commercial potential. By the early '50s, he had built up a virtual empire, controlling the activities of many outstanding jazzmen, distributing his records throughout the world, touring the JATP unit in Europe, Hawaii, Japan, and Australia, and booking tours for several other concert units in addition to his own. In these capacities, he proved to be perhaps the most important factor in the propagation of jazz during his first decade as a promoter. His most widely imitated innovation was the recording of jazz at concerts, when all previously released jazz discs had been made in recording studios.

GRAPPELLY STEPHANE, *violin;* b. Paris, France, 1/26/08. W. Django Reinhardt, he was a principal member of the quintet of the Hot Club of France, 1934-9. From '40 on, lived and worked principally in England. During late '30s recorded for French Swing label w. visiting American stars incl. Eddie South, Bill Coleman. From 1948 to '55 appeared at Club St. Germain des Prés in Paris. Worked in St. Tropez May to Oct. '55, nine months at Hotel Claridge in Paris, '56. Grappelly has also pl. all over Europe, appearing at Knokke, Belgium and Cannes Jazz Festivals. Own LPs: Verve, EmArcy; LPs w. Eddie Barclay-Quincy Jones (UA), *One World Jazz* (Col.).

Addr: 10, Rue Dorchampt, Paris 18, France.

GRAY, GLEN (Spike) (Glen Gray Knoblaugh), *leader;* b. Roanoke, Ill., 6/7/06. Played alto sax in the Orange Blossom Band, a 10-piece group that played at the Casa Loma Hotel in Toronto in 1928. The group was incorporated in NYC in 1929 as the Casa Loma Orch. and began recording in November 1929, earning great popularity (especially in college circles) in the early '30s. It is said to have been the first big white band with a deliberate jazz policy, though its arrangements and soloists did not stand the test of time. From the mid '30s the band was billed under Gray's name, recording regularly for Decca until 1942 and for Mercury 1946. LPs: Harmony; selections in *Encyclopedia of Jazz on Records, Vol. 2* and *Five Feet of Swing* (Decca); recreations of the Casa Loma band on Capitol.

GRAY, JERRY, *composer, leader;* b. Boston, Mass., 7/3/15. Father taught him violin, accordion, solfeggio. Led own band 1931; arr. for Sonny Kendis. Toured with Artie Shaw 1936-9, first as violinist, then as arranger; scored Shaw's best-selling record *Begin the Beguine.* Joined Glenn Miller as chief arranger 1939; wrote such popular arrangements as *Pennsylvania 6-5000, String of Pearls, Sun Valley Jump, I Dreamt I Dwelt in Harlem, The Spirit is Willing.* Staying with Miller in AAF band, he was awarded bronze medal in 1946 for keeping orch. together after Miller's death. Later led own orch. in Hollywood and on tour. LPs: Decca, Lib., Tops, Voc.

Addr: 13724 Valley Vista, Sherman Oaks, Calif.

GRAY, WARDELL, *tenor sax;* b. Oklahoma City, Okla., 1921; d. Las Vegas, 5/25/55. St. on clar. in Detroit; stud. at Cass Tech. Worked w. Jimmy Rachel, Benny Carew. Joined Earl Hines '43, stayed two years, then settled on West Coast. With Vernon Alley, Benny Carter, Billy Eckstine, and Gene Norman jazz concerts. In '48 to NYC w. Benny Goodman Sextet; then at Royal Roost w. Count Basie's band and Tadd Dameron's group. Nov. '48 w. Benny Goodman's big band. Was back with Basie in small and big bands 1950-1, but spent most of his last few years free-lancing around the West Coast and Midwest, making frequent recordings. A descendant of the Lester Young school, he later came under the influence of Charlie Parker, showing a fuller tone and more aggressively swinging style closer to Sonny Stitt than the Stan Getz of that period. Comp: *Twisted.* Own LPs on Pres., Modern, Savoy, Reg.; three tracks in *Tenors, Anyone?* (Dawn); LPs w. Fats Navarro (Blue Note), Count Basie (Col.), Frank Morgan (GNP), *Jam Session* (Verve).

GREB, RONNIE (Ronald David Grabowski), *drums;* b. Duryea, Pa., 10/19/38. Began stud. at 14 w. private teacher; later w. Gene Krupa and Cozy Cole at their school, NYC. Joined Jack Teagarden Dec. 1957, went on State Dept. world tour w. him Sept. '58-Jan. '59. Favs: Buddy Rich, Shelly Manne. LP w. Teagarden (Roul.).

Addr: 2023 Voorhies Ave., Brooklyn 35, N. Y.

GRECO, ARMANDO (Buddy), *piano, composer, singer;* b. Philadelphia, Pa., 8/14/26. Two brothers both musicians. Studied w. father, a music critic, who had own radio show in Phila. Led trio 1944-9; w. Benny Goodman as pianist, singer, and arranger 1949-52, touring England and France with him in '50. Then formed own trio for night clubs and records, sometimes app. as a single. Good modern pianist; aims at career as singer in movies. Favs: Tatum, Shearing, Calvin Jackson. LPs: Coral, Kapp.

GREEN, BENNIE, *trombone, composer;* b. Chicago, Ill., 4/16/23 of a musical family, incl. brother, Elbert, once tenor sax w. Roy Eldridge. After high school and local gigs, joined Earl Hines in 1942; drafted Nov. 1943, spent two years in 343rd Army Band in Illinois. Rejoined Hines after discharge in May 1946, stayed until Jan. '48, then worked briefly with Gene Ammons and joined Charlie Ventura, with whom he earned great popularity in night club and concert work. Toured with Hines' small combo '51-3, then toured for several years with his own quintet but was only sporadically active after '57. One of the most facile and inspired of modern trombonists. Favs: T. Dorsey, B. Byrne, J. J. Johnson, L. Brown. M. Gee. Own LPs: Decca, Blue Note, Pres., Vee-Jay, Enrica; LPs w. Ventura (Decca, Em., GNP, Vict.), *Jazz Studio 1* (Decca), Miles Davis (Pres.), Sarah Vaughan (Col.), one track w. Coleman Hawkins in *The Anatomy of Improvisation* (Verve).

Addr: 571 East 37th St., Chicago, Ill.

GREEN, BERNARD (Benny), *saxophones;* b. Leeds, Yorkshire, England, 12/9/27. Father, who pl. sax and clar., taught him soprano in 1941; later stud. w. private teacher on tenor. Stud. English lit. and modern history at London U. Pl. bari. sax w. Ronnie Scott '52-5; tenor w. Dizzy Reece '57. In '56 pl. bari. sax w. Stan Kenton during his tour of England. In addition to being an expert craftsman, he is a witty and knowledgeable critic who has contributed to *New Musical Express, Record Mirror* and various English books and magazines. Rec. with Ronnie Scott et al.

Addr: 22 Howard House, Cleveland St., London W. 1, Eng.

GREEN, FREDERICK WILLIAM (Freddie), *guitar;* b. Charleston, S. C., 3/31/11. To NYC to finish school; musically self-taught from age 12. Was working in small Greenwich Village club when John Hammond heard him, recommended him to Count Basie, whom he joined Mar. '37. Has been with Basie almost continuously ever since. Never played solo, never played amplified guitar, but constantly in demand for record sessions, which he made w. Benny Goodman, Benny Carter, Teddy Wilson, Lionel Hampton, Joe Sullivan, I. Jacquet, Lester Young, Billie Holiday, etc. Prominently heard w. John Sellers (Van.). Won *DB* Critics poll '58. Own LP on Victor; LPs w. Buck Clayton (Col.), *Jam Session* (Verve), Joe Turner (Atl.), Jimmy Rushing, *Spirituals To Swing,* Jo Jones (Van.), Al Cohn, Joe Newman (Vict.); also see Count Basie.

Addr: 2171 Madison Ave., New York 30, N. Y.

GREEN, LIL, *singer;* b. Chicago, Ill., ca. 1922; d. 1954. Recorded regularly for Bluebird in Chicago from 1940 and scored big hits w. *Romance in the Dark* and *Why Don't You Do Right,* the latter being later popularized by Peggy Lee. Big Bill Broonzy was usually featured as her accompanist. She toured w. Tiny Bradshaw and appeared at NYC Cafe Society, but worked mostly around Chicago until her death. LP: one track in *Singin' The Blues* (Cam.).

GREEN, URBAN CLIFFORD (Urbie), *trombone;* b. Mobile, Ala., 8/8/26. Father a barber; two elder brothers both trombonists. Studied piano w. mother, took up trombone at 12, and by age 16 was w. Tommy Reynolds and Bob Strong bands. While at professional school in Hollywood, Green worked w. Jan Savitt. After two years w. Frankie Carle and four w. Gene Krupa, he joined Woody Herman Oct., '50, and in his two years w. the band made a reputation comparable with that achieved by Bill Harris in an earlier Herman band. Active in studio and recording work in NYC, he spent a month in Benny Goodman orch. at Waldorf-Astoria Feb.-Mar. '56, was seen and heard in motion picture, *The Benny Goodman Story.* In '57 he fronted the Goodman orch. on a three month tour. Formed own band for college concerts and dances '58. Pl. Birdland w. band Jan., '59. Won DB Int. Critics Poll as New Star '54. Own LPs: ABC-Par., Vict.; LPs w. Woody Herman (Verve), Goodman (Decca, Cap.), Buck Clayton, Jimmy Rushing (Col.), Joe Newman, T. Scott, Manny Albam, Billy Byers (Vict.), Barry Galbraith, Toots Thielemans, Ralph Burns (Decca), Terry Gibbs (Merc.), Herbie Mann (River.), *Session At Riverside* (Cap.), *Manhattan Jazz Septet* (Coral), Jim Chapin (Classic Edit.).

Addr: 35-05 163rd St., Flushing 58, N. Y.

GREENLEE, CHARLES, *trombone, composer;* b. Detroit, Mich., 5/24/27. First musical studies w. American Legion drum and bugle corps, then baritone horn, drums and mellophone in grammar school. Pl. w. local bands while attending Cass Tech. High. W. Floyd Ray '44, Lucky Millinder, Buddy Johnson, Benny Carter '45, Dizzy Gillespie '46 and again in '49-50. Own band incl. Tommy Flanagan, Billy Mitchell, Frank Foster '47. Worked w. Lucky Thompson '48, Gene Ammons '50. During this period he was known as Harneefan Mageed but later renounced Mohammedanism. Retired from music '51; was heard briefly w. Yusef Lateef '57 and returned on a full-time basis w. Maynard Ferguson '59. Comp. *El Sino.* Fav: J. J. Johnson. LPs w. Ferguson (Roul.).

Addr: 245 Carlton Ave., Brooklyn, N. Y.

GREENWOOD, LILLIE (Lil), *singer;* b. Mobile, Ala., 11/18/23. Club dates around Oakland and SF, Calif. from her early twenties. Discovered by Duke Ellington 1958. Appeared w. him at all major jazz festivals '58-'59. A full-voiced, extrovert entertainer; not a jazz singer. Fav: Ella Fitzgerald.

GREER, WILLIAM ALEXANDER (Sonny), *drums;* b. Long Branch, N.J., 12/13/03. Prof. debut w. Harry Yerek during World War I. Met Duke Ellington in Washington, D. C. 1919. Their careers ran parallel almost immediately; Greer was with Ellington from his first days as a bandleader until March 1951. He then played w. Johnny Hodges' band to Sept. '51, later free-lanced in NYC at Metropole, Stuyvesant Casino etc. Went to Bermuda w. Red Allen combo; many app. on Art Ford TV show; 2½ years off and on w. various combos at Embers, NYC, '56-8; Roundtable w. Tyree Glenn '59. When not playing, active as official host at steak house in Astoria, L. I.

Sonny Greer was noted for the personality he lent to the Ellington band, for his elaborate equipment and unique use of chime effects in such numbers as *Ring Dem Bells.* Though rarely heard in solos he was a vital part of the band's character. In the '30s and early '40s he also rec. w. Stewart, Hodges, Bigard and C. Williams contingents from Ellington band; also w. Lionel Hampton and Esquire All Stars. LPs: see Ellington; also w. Hodges (Verve), Hampton (Vict.); own group for one no. in *History of Jazz, Vol. 2* (Cap.).

Addr: 1029 College Avenue, Bronx 56, N. Y.

GREY, ALBERT THORNTON (Al), *trombone;* b. Aldie, Va., 6/6/25. From musical family in which trumpet, piano, organ, sax and clarinet were played. During World War II worked in Navy band w. several name musicians who recommended him to B. Carter, whom he joined on discharge. Subsequently w. J. Lunceford, L. Hampton, A. Cobb, L. Millinder, and recorded with all these bands. With D. Gillespie '56-7; joined C. Basie late '57. Fav. mus: B. Carter. LPs: see Basie; Gillespie; w. Thad Jones (UA); *Dizzy Atmosphere* (Spec.); own LP on Argo.

GRIFFIN, JOHN ARNOLD III, *tenor saxophone;* b. Chicago, Ill., 4/24/28. Mother a singer, father ex-cornetist. Clar. at Du Sable High School, 1941. Pl. w. L. Hampton, 1945-47; Joe Morris, 1947-50; Jo Jones, 1950; Arnett Cobb, 1951; Art Blakey, Mar.-Oct. '57; Thelonious Monk spring through fall '58. Returned to Chicago, working in that area '58-'60, occasionally coming to NYC for record dates. Fav: C. Parker. Good tenor man of hard-bop school. Own LPs on River., Blue Note, Argo; LPs w. Wilbur Ware, Clark Terry, Monk, Nat Adderley, Philly Joe Jones, Blue Mitchell (River.), Art Blakey (Beth., Jub., Atl.).

Addr: 1201 East Madison Park, Chicago, Ill.

GRIMES, HENRY ALONZO, *bass;* b. Philadelphia, Pa., 11/3/35. Stud. violin in junior high school; later tuba at Mastbaum High. Came to NYC, stud. at Juilliard, then went on road w. Arnett Cobb, Willis Jackson et al. Beginning in 1957, pl. with Anita O'Day, Charlie Mingus, Gerry Mulligan, Tony Scott, Sonny Rollins. Soon established himself as one of finest young bassists on East Coast, with extraordinary technique and imagination. Favs: Ray Brown, Oscar Pettiford, Charlie Mingus, Wilbur Ware. LPs w. Lee Konitz (Verve), Tony Scott (Dawn), Gerry Mulligan (Wor. Pac.), Sonny Rollins (Metro.).

GRIMES, LLOYD (Tiny), *guitar;* b. Newport News, Va., 7/7/17. Self-taught on piano, he began playing in amateur shows around Wash., D. C. in 1935. Pl. piano and danced at Rhythm Club in NYC '38. Taught himself guitar; bought electric model and joined Cats And A Fiddle '40, remaining until '41. Jamming at a club in Calif., he met Art Tatum and Slam Stewart and was w. them until '44. Formed own group, the Rocking Highlanders, which was prominent on 52nd Street up to '47, then went to Cleveland. From '51-5 toured midwest w. group, then settled in Philadelphia, working from there. Still plays four-string guitar. Favs: Christian, Snags Allen, Johnny Smith. Own LPs: Pres.; LPs w. Coleman Hawkins, Jerry Valentine (Pres.), Charlie Parker (Savoy), Tatum (Bruns.), Met. All Stars (Cam.).

Addr: 5530 Market St., Phila., Pa.

GROSS, WALTER, *song writer, piano;* b. Brooklyn, N.Y., 1909. At 11 played a week with symphony orch. at Brooklyn theatre. Toured w. name bands incl. California Ramblers, Terry Black, George Hall, Rudy Vallee. During 1930s featured on CBS Saturday Night Swing Club, later became musical director. Army '43-5. A & R head of Musicraft records '45-7; while there he had Sarah Vaughan make the first record of his composition *Tenderly,* which soon became a jazz standard. Featured since the late 1940s as solo pianist in Los Angeles clubs. Own LPs: ABC-Par., Harm.

Addr: 6340 Hollywood Blvd., Los Angeles 28, Calif.

GRUNTZ, GEORGE, *piano;* b. Basel, Switzerland, 6/24/32. Stud. at conservatory in Zurich at 14. Won several first prizes at Swiss amateur jazz festivals. Pl. for 6 months in Scandinavia; back home, had to make living as auto salesman, but since '56 has been doubling as pianist & arr. on Basel radio. Seen at San Remo Jazz Festival annually since '56. After appearing w. the Newport International Band, summer '58, he continued as auto salesman but became much more active in European jazz circles. Played several jazz concerts in combos w. other members of the International Band; to Stockholm to record w. Lars Gullin. Favs: Tatum, Bud Powell, H. Silver. LP w. Newport International Band (Col.).

Addr: Amerikanestr. 16, Basel-Binningen, Switzerland.

GRYCE, GIGI, *alto sax, flute, composer;* b. Pensacola, Fla., 11/28/27. Raised in Hartford, Conn., where he attended music school. Studied later at Boston Conservatory, majoring in classical composition. Started on clarinet, later took up flute, alto, piano. Worked with local bands from '46, leading his own 23-piece group (incl. Horace Silver) at auditorium in Hartford. Studied on Fulbright Scholarship, Paris, '52. Returning, he gigged in NYC with Max Roach, Howard McGhee, worked in Atlantic City w. Tadd Dameron, then spent six months w. Lionel Hampton's band, with which he toured Europe. In '55-8 played clubs and NJF '57, with a group called The Jazz Lab Quintet, co-starring Donald Byrd on trumpet, also composed and arranged for many record sessions. A gifted modern soloist and first class composer-arranger, he has led his own group since '59, app. at the Five Spot, Cork 'N Bib, etc. Favs: Parker, Carter, Konitz.

Own LPs: New Jazz, MGM, Savoy, Jub., Verve, Col., River.; LPs w. Art Farmer (Pres.), Lee Morgan, Thad Jones, Clifford Brown (Blue Note), Oscar Pettiford (Beth., ABC-Par.), Mal Waldron (Pres.), Thelonious Monk (River.), Teddy Charles (Atl.).

Addr: 1265 Broadway, New York 1, N. Y.

GUARALDI, VINCENT ANTHONY (Vince), *piano;* b. San Francisco, Cal., 7/17/28. Working on SF *Daily News* as apprentice in '49, almost lost finger in accident; as a result, decided to switch to music on full-time basis. Is nephew of Muzzy Marcellino, TV mus. dir., and Joe Marcellino, SF bandleader, who helped him get started in music. Played w. Cal Tjader trio in SF '50; Bill Harris-Chubby Jackson orch. '53, Geo. Auld '53, Sonny Criss '55. Toured with Woody Herman '56-7 and again on tour of Britain and Saudi Arabia in '59. Back with Tjader '57-9; joined Lighthouse All Stars Sept. '59. "More than an interesting pianist . . . he can play simple, emotionally pure piano on ballads and get pixieish, funky, hard-swinging on originals and standards."—Ralph Gleason. Own LPs: Fantasy. LPs w. Tjader (Fant.), C. Candoli, F. Rosolino (Interlude), *Blues Groove* w. Herman (Cap.).

Addr: 368 Skyline Drive, San Francisco, Cal.

GUARNIERI, JOHN A. (Johnny), *piano, composer;* b. New York City, 3/23/17. Piano from 1927, studying classical music first; started in dance band business in '37 w. George Hall. Best known for his work w. Benny Goodman '39-40, and Artie Shaw '40-1. While w. Shaw, made Gramercy Five sides on which he became first jazz musician to play harpsichord solo, Sept. '40. Later worked w. Jimmy Dorsey, Raymond Scott, Cozy Cole, and from '43-7 was one of the most recorded artists in jazz, making hundreds of sessions with every type of group. Later he settled into radio and TV staff work w. NBC. Led his own quartet on various shows, also app. on Art Ford's Jazz Party. Descendant of the Guarnerius family of violin makers, he contributed to the jazz of the '40s a derivative, versatile style most frequently imitative of Fats Waller and Teddy Wilson. As a member of ASCAP, he has composed more than 3,500 selections of all types short of rock 'n roll. Own LPs: Coral, Vict., Golden Crest, Cam. LPs w. Slam Stewart, Lester Young (Savoy), Benny Goodman (Col.), *Boning Up On Bones* (Em.).

Addr: 54 Hillside Ave., Glen Ridge, N. J.

GUERIN, ROGER, *trumpet;* b. Sarrebruck, Saar, France, 1/9/26. Stud. vln. 8 yrs, tpt. 12 yrs; first prize tpt. and cornet at Paris Cons. Prof. debut w. Aime Barelli band, 1947. Pl. w. Django Reinhardt, Don Byas, James Moody, Hubert Fol in early '50s; Bernard Peiffer '53; Michel Legrand band '56; also worked w. Christian Chevallier, Fats Sadi, J. Raney, B. Jaspar, K. Clarke, Lucky Thompson; sang for a year w. Blossom Dearie's Blue Stars. To Newport, Brussels w. International Band '58. Replaced Clark Terry in Q. Jones band Mar. 1960. From 1954, first place in annual *Jazz Hot* referendum. The most original jazz trumpet yet produced by France. Favs: Armstrong, Davis. Fav. own solo: *I Love You* in Cole Porter LP w. Legrand. Many LPs, incl. *One World Jazz, Newport Intl. Band* (Col.), *K. Clarke plays A. Hodeir* (Epic).

Addr: Ruelle du Clos, Beynes, Seine-et-Oise, France.

GUITAR, SLIM (Eddie Jones), *guitar, singer;* b. Greenwood, Miss., 12/10/26; d. New York City 2/7/59. Sang in church choir; to New Orleans as youth. No musical training. St. playing guitar 1950, prof. '51, leading trio at local club; later formed band and toured US. Rec. debut for Imperial '52; in '53 began to rec. for Specialty and immediately had a big hit, *Things I Used To Do;* later enjoyed great success with *The Story of My Life.* To Atco Recs. '56, had another hit with *Down Through the Years.* He was a down-home traditional singer whose early material was of a simple rural character. No LPs; some singles still available.

GULDA, FRIEDRICH, *piano;* b. Vienna, Austria, 5/16/30. Stud. piano from age 7 with Prof. F. Pazofsky. Entered State Academy of Music, 1942, stud. with Prof. B. Seidlhofer until '47. In '46 he won international music competition at Geneva. Played at festivals in Prague, '47, Vienna, '48. Many concerts throughout the Continent and South America. Made New York debut in Fall of 1950 at Carnegie Hall and was hailed by critics as one of the greatest new classical piano talents of this generation. Gulda, who has spent many hours visiting jazz clubs during his trips to New York, soon developed a talent for jazz piano and composing. In '56, after sitting in with the Modern Jazz Quartet and other groups, he took a combo into Birdland and appeared with it at the Newport Jazz Festival. Then returned to Austria, pl. and writing in Vienna jazz circles, recording in Berlin, Hamburg; concert tours as classical musician. He is represented by many classical recordings, principally of Beethoven, on the London label. Jazz LPs on Victor.

Addr: Schottengasse 7, Vienna 1, Austria.

GULLIN, LARS, *baritone sax, composer;* b. Sweden, 5/4/28. Was clarinetist in a military band on an island off the coast of Sweden; also active as classical composer, pianist. Went to Stockholm 1948. Took up baritone sax late '49, after hearing Gerry Mulligan. Joined Arne Domnerus '51. Rec. w. numerous US musicians visiting Sweden incl. Zoot Sims, Stan Getz, James Moody. Won *DB* Critics' poll as new star '54, the first overseas musician ever to win a US magazine jazz poll. Active in Italy '58-9. Own LPs: Atl., East-West, Em.; LPs w. Stan Getz (Roost, Verve), Clifford Brown (Pres.), George Wallington in *Swingin' In Sweden* (Em.).

GUSTAFSSON, RUNE URBAN, *guitar;* b. Goteborg, Sweden, 8/25/33. Uncle, who plays guitar, insisted that he study guitar at age 14 to become a ballad and folk singer. Graduated from amateur contests to prof. jobs. Played w. Bert Dahlander 1952, Putte Wickman '54, Hacke Bjorksten '56, back w. Wickman '57. He intends to study arranging and also concert guitar. Favs: Raney, Farlow, Hall, Kessel. LPs in Sweden w. Gullin, Wickman, Domnerus.

GUTESHA, MLADEN (Bobby), *composer, conductor;* also *trombone;* b. Sarajevo, Yugoslavia, 12/16/23. Studied conducting at Belgrade Cons. 1945-59. Self taught on trombone since '41. Pl. trombone in various radio dance orchs. from '43 in Belgrade, Vienna, Trieste. Conducted dance orch. of the Yugoslavian Broadcasting System in Belgrade '47-53. From '55-58, arranger for Erwin Lehn orch. of South German Radio in Stuttgart. Wrote arrs. which feat. visiting American jazzmen: Lee Konitz, MJQ, Miles Davis. Composed a number of scores for Benny Goodman orch.; scores for German TV and movies. Fav. arrs: Michel Legrand, Bill Russo, Bill Holman; fav. trom: J. J. Johnson, Bill Harris. LPs as arr. w. Goodman (Westinghouse, Col.).

Addr: Birkenwaldstrasse 30, Stuttgart, West Germany.

GUY, FRED, *guitar;* b. Burkeville, Ga., 5/23/1899. Prominent as banjoist w. Duke Ellington from early 1920s, switched to guitar '33. He left the band in '47 and Ellington never hired another guitarist. Though Guy was not featured as a soloist, his sound was an important part of the early Ellington rhythm section. After leaving Duke he retired from music and went into business in Chicago as manager of Parkway Ballroom. LPs: see Ellington; one no. w. Sonny Greer in *History of Jazz, Vol. 2* (Cap.).

GUY, JOSEPH LUKE (Joe), *trumpet;* b. Birmingham, Ala., 9/20/20. Raised in NYC. Early experience w. Fats Waller, Coleman Hawkins; joined Charlie Barnet '41; Cootie Williams' big band '42; frequent visitor at Minton's during incubation period of bop. Played on first JATP album during sojourn in Calif. Closely associated w. Billie Holiday, '45-7, playing backgrounds on several of her Decca records. Later moved to Philadelphia. Comparatively inactive in recent years. LPs w. Charlie Christian-Dizzy Gillespie (Esoteric), Billie Holiday (Decca); *Jazz At The Philharmonic* (Stinson).

H

HACKETT, ROBERT LEO (Bobby), *trumpet, cornet, guitar;* b. Providence, R. I., 1/31/15. Son of a blacksmith, sixth of nine children, he quit school at 14 and played his first jobs on guitar, banjo and violin respectively, with a sextet in a Chinese restaurant, a 15-piece band in a ballroom, and Billy Lossez's hotel orchestra. Later played cornet and violin with Herbie Marsh in Syracuse, Payson Re on Cape Cod. After a couple of seasons in Boston and Providence with Teddy Wright and Pee Wee Russell in various clubs, he took over leadership of Herbie Marsh's band in the Theatrical Club in Boston with Brad Gowans writing arrs. Though Hackett's model has been Louis Armstrong, he became identified through this period with Dixieland music of the Bix Beiderbecke style. He soon attracted national attention after critic George Frazier praised him in several reports. Coming to NYC in '37, he played with Joe Marsala, then spent a year at Nick's, later led a large group on 52nd street. By '39 he was on the road for MCA with a big group, but gave it up to join Horace Heidt, with whom he worked for a year. He joined Glenn Miller, playing guitar and occasional cornet, from July '41 until the band broke up the following year. After a year on the staff at NBC and a tour with Brad Gowans in a Katherine Dunham revue, he joined Glen Gray in '44 for two years. Following this he became a house musician at ABC in NYC. He took a leave of absence '51-2 to play a series of nightclub dates, and appeared in public on and off at the Embers, etc. In 1953-5 he earned individual fame through a series of albums and appearances with Jackie Gleason, through weekly TV shows with Martha Wright on ABC, and through numerous other TV and radio jobs.

In 1957-8, Hackett led a sextet at the Henry Hudson Hotel and several jazz festivals, which drew on jazz styles from Dixieland to Monk in its often ingenious arrangements (most of which were by Dick Cary) and manner of playing. In the next few years, he went back to the quartet format, playing in NYC and touring.

Hackett has been an important force in jazz ever since he first came to NYC. His essentially melodic style, most often heard on ballads, has been praised by musicians of every school. In many ways he is a modern parallel of Bix, although he disclaims any direct stylistic derivation. He made his name entirely as a cornetist and trumpeter but has remained a proficient guitarist and can be heard in the rhythm section on a number of records, notably with Glenn Miller. Own LPs: Epic, Cap.; LPs w. Jackie Gleason (Cap.), Louis Armstrong, Glenn Miller (Vict.); as "Pete Pesci" w. Eddie Condon in *Bixieland* (Col.), Lee Wiley (Col.); Hackett-Teagarden, *Jazz Ultimate* (Cap.), Benny Goodman (Col.), Eddie Condon (Comm.).

Addr: 34-21 84th St., Jackson Heights 72, L.I., N.Y.

HADI, SHAFI (Curtis Porter), *tenor sax, alto sax, composer;* b. Philadelphia, Pa., 9/21/29. Piano lessons from grandmother at six; pl. w. high school orch, later w. rhythm & blues bands incl. Paul Williams, Griffin Bros, Ruth Brown. Stud. comp. at Howard U. and U. of Detroit. Joined Ch. Mingus Sept. '56, remained to Jan. '58 and rejoined him Oct. '59. Film: *Shadows* for John Cassavetes. Active as painter: sold series of paintings of scenes from *Porgy & Bess.* LPs w. Mingus (Beth., Atl., Col.); Horace Parlan-Langston Hughes (MGM), Hank Mobley (Blue Note).

Addr: 255 West 108th Street, New York 25, N.Y.

HAFER, JOHN RICHARD (Dick), *tenor sax;* also *alto & baritone saxes, oboe, English horn, flute, bass clarinet;* b. Wyomissing, Pa., 5/29/27. Clarinet in high school. Played w. Ch. Barnet, 1949. Solos on *Really, Oh Henry* and *Overtime* (Cap.). Six months w. Claude Thornhill, then back w. Barnet. With Woody Herman from Aug. '51-Aug. '55, touring Europe w. him in '54 for six weeks. Since leaving Herman, has been active in recording in NYC. Also app. w. Tex Beneke at Statler Hotel for two mos. '55, Bobby Hackett at Henry Hudson Hotel, Nov. '57-Feb. '58, Nat Pierce orch. at Birdland. *Soundflight 56* for 13 weeks on radio w. Larry Sonn orch. in '56. Favs: Lester Young, Getz, Cohn. LPs w. Herman (Evst., Col., Cap.), Ch. Barnet (Cap., Evst.), Nat Pierce (Fant.), Ruby Braff, Urbie Green, Dick Collins (Vict.), Larry Sonn (Coral), Don Stratton (ABC-Par.), Jaye P. Morgan (Vict.).

Addr: 33-45 81st St., Jackson Heights 72, N.Y.

HAGGART, ROBERT SHERWOOD (Bob), *bass, composer;* b. New York City, 3/13/14. Raised in Douglaston, L. I. Played banjo, guitar, piano and trumpet. Came to prominence in '35 as member of Bob Crosby's orch., with which he played throughout its duration, scoring his biggest hit with the *Big Noise From Winnetka,* playing a duet with Ray Bauduc. He won Met. poll '37, '39-44, DB poll 1937-42, '44. After leaving Crosby he settled in NYC, doing commercial radio work. In early '50 he joined forces with trumpeter Yank Lawson for a series of Dixieland albums on Decca. Haggart enjoyed great success as co-writer of many of the Crosby band's most durable hits, among them *What's New* and *South Rampart Street Parade;* he has continued to write arrangements for Crosby's LPs, incl. *South Pacific* and *Porgy & Bess* (Dot). Other Crosby LPs: Decca, Coral. Lawson-Haggart LPs: Decca. Haggart formed own "jingle" writing firm, also wrote score for musical *Mad Avenue.*

Addr: 30 Maple Drive, Great Neck, N.Y.

HAIG, ALAN W. (Al), *piano;* b. Newark, N.J., 1923. Raised in Nutley, N.J. With Coast Guard bands '42-4; then club dates around Boston and briefly with Jerry Wald orch. In '45 he was an important member of the 52nd Street scene, playing in most of the early bop bands under Dizzy Gillespie et al., and on countless record dates. In late '45 he played in Calif. w. Charlie Barnet, subsequently working w. Jimmy Dorsey and w. various jazz groups. In May '49 he went to France w. Charlie Parker's quintet. From '49-51 he worked mostly w. Stan Getz, then became inactive for a couple of years and was in virtual obscurity to Dec. '54 when he joined Chet Baker. Pl. w. Gillespie's big band briefly on two occasions in late '56 and early '57. Worked in Bermuda '59. W. Perry Lopez '60. One of the first and best of the bop pianists. Own LP on Ctpt.; one selection in *Pianists Galore* (Wor. Pac.); LPs w. Stan Getz (Roost, New Jazz), Woods-Byrd, *The Youngbloods* (Pres.), Charlie Parker (Debut, Verve), Wardell Gray (Pres.), Gray & Getz in *Tenors Anyone?* (Dawn), Dizzy Gillespie (Rondo.), Fats Navarro (Savoy).

HAKIM, SADIK (Argonne Dense Thornton), *piano;* b. Duluth, Minn., 7/15/21. Grandfather was music professor, school-teacher; mother and others in family pl. chamber music. Stud. theory w. grandfather; no piano lessons. Left home 1940, gigged in Peoria, Ill., w. Fats Dudley; to NYC from Chicago late '44, pl. w. Ben Webster for 15 months, then w. Lester Young to '48; later worked w. Slam Slewart; in Canada w. Louis Metcalf, and toured w. James Moody orch. '51-4; for next 2 years jobbed around in N.Y. and New Jersey; had own quartet in Mount Vernon, then pl. w. Buddy Tate orch. '56-9. Also pl. and wrote for co-op group in Brooklyn which played a few dances for the Mayor's Committee for Live Music, summer '59. Pl. own comp. *Impulse* on *Look Up And Live* TV show '59. Hakim, whose name was changed in 1947 for religious reasons, was important as one of the first bop pianists. He played, on the famous C. Parker rec. date for Sav., 8 bars on *Ko-Ko* and all the rest of the date, except *Billie's Bounce* and *Now's The Time.* (Dizzy Gillespie was on piano for these.) Also *Dexter's Deck,* etc., w. Dexter Gordon (Sav.), Aladdin dates w. Lester Young, etc. Fav. own solos: *Jumping With Symphony Sid, No Eyes Blues* w. Young. Favs: Tatum, Bud Powell. LPs

w. Parker, Gordon (Savoy), Young (Alad.), Tate (Pres.).

Addr: 162 Vernon Ave., Brooklyn 6, N.Y.

HALCOX, PATRICK (Pat), *trumpet;* also *piano;* b. Chelsea, London, England, 3/18/30. Stud. piano first when very young. Gained experience on trumpet pl. w. amateur bands. W. Chris Barber from 1954, visiting US w. him in '59. Heard in background score for film *Look Back In Anger.* Fav: Louis Armstrong. LPs: see Chris Barber.

Addr: 19 Mount Pleasant Road, Ealing, London W. 5, England.

HALE, CORKY (Merrilyn Cecelia Hecht), *piano, harp, singer* (also *flute, piccolo, 'cello*); b. Freeport, Ill., 7/3/31. Started piano at 3, harp at 8, flute at 10, 'cello at 12. Stud. mostly in home town; a few lessons at Chicago Music Conservatory and 5 summers at Interlochen, Mich. She has worked mainly with commercial groups, started w. Freddy Martin in 1950, Dave Rose in '51, and toured w. Liberace '51-5. Sang and played harp w. Harry James '55; pianist and vocalist briefly w. Ray Anthony early '56. Appeared in motion pictures *The Benny Goodman Story, Sincerely Yours.* The first album on which she was prominently featured w. Kitty White, Dec. '54, revealed her exceptionally modern approach to the harp. Favs: Dorothy Ashby, harp; Oscar Peterson, Billy Taylor, piano. Own LP on GNP; four tracks in *Escape* (GNP); LPs w. Kitty White (Pacifica), Anita O'Day (Verve).

Addr: 8031 Sunset Blvd., Los Angeles 46, Calif.

HALEN, CARL H., *cornet, trumpet;* b. Hamilton, Ohio, 6/10/28. One of the younger members of the "revivalist" school; first played accordion, then switched to trumpet, 1948. Played w. Dixieland Rhythm Kings, 1948-50; Army band '50-2; formed own group in 1953 known as the Gin Bottle 7. Favs: Bix, B. Hackett, Doc Evans. Own LP, *Gin Bottle Jazz* (River.); selections in *Jazz Potpourri, Dixieland Jazz* (Audiophile).

Addr: 345 McAlpin Ave., Cincinnati 20, Ohio.

HALL, ADELAIDE, *singer;* b. New York City, 1909. Toured w. many Negro revues in 1920s, including *Shuffle Along, Blackbirds.* Brought Art Tatum to NYC as her accompanist, '32. From middle '30s spent most of her time in Europe, settling in England. Not a jazz singer, but made important contribution through several wordless vocals assigned to her by Duke Ellington on his early records, such as *Blues I Love To Sing, Creole Love Call,* 1927.

HALL, ALFRED WESLEY (Al), *bass;* b. Jacksonville, Fla., 3/18/15. Raised in Phila. Played 'cello, tuba, starting on bass '32 and working from '33-5 w. local bands. With Billy Hicks in NYC 1936-7; Skeets Tolbert '37-8; Teddy Wilson '39-41; Ellis Larkins at Blue Angel, etc. '42-3; CBS staff work w. Paul Baron on Mildred Bailey show '43-4. From 1945 on worked in B'way pit bands, but was active in jazz '47-50 running own company, Wax Records (catalogue later taken over by Atlantic). Toured w. Erroll Garner, also few weeks w. Count Basie, 1952. Studied TV production and direction for a while. Free-lancing in NYC for most of '50s; subbed for G. Duvivier for seven weeks in pit band of *Jamaica* '58; pl. for Jerome Robbins' *Ballet USA* '58, Yves Montand '59. Rec. w. Harry Belafonte. Orig. infl: John Kirby, Billy Taylor; favs: Blanton, Hinton, R. Brown, Pettiford, Duvivier, Chambers. LPs w. Eddie Condon (War. Bros.), Ellington-Hodges (Verve), Fats Navarro (Savoy), w. Sonny Stitt in *Opus De Bop* (Savoy), Bud Freeman (Beth.), Teddy Wilson (MGM), Barbara Lea (Pres.), Josh White (ABC-Par.), Erroll Garner (Col.), Linton Garner (Enrica), Ed Hall (Rae-Cox).

Addr: 411 West 52nd St., New York, N.Y.

HALL, EDMOND, *clarinet;* b. New Orleans, 5/15/01. Played guitar first, active on clarinet (self-taught) at 17, playing in local bands including Bud Russell, Chris Kelley, Jack Carey. After touring with Buddy Petit, Mat Thomas, Eagle-Eye Shields in the early '20s, he came to NYC in '28, working with Alonzo Ross, Billy Fowler, and Charlie Skeets. When the latter's band was taken over by Claude Hopkins in '30, he remained until '35, playing baritone sax and clarinet. He later worked w. Lucky Millinder '36, Billy Hicks '37-8, Zutty Singleton and Joe Sullivan, '39. Red Allen '40-1, Teddy Wilson, '42-4. Fronted his own band in NYC '44-8, Boston '48-9, Calif. '50. Joined Eddie Condon at Condon's club July '50 and left in '55 to replace Barney Bigard in the Louis Armstrong combo, touring US, Australia, and Europe. Left Armstrong July '58 and went into semi-retirement in NYC. Spent three months in Ghana late '59, playing and teaching. Hall, who plays Albert system clarinet, is perhaps the best equipped technically of all the NO clarinetists. His sharp, reedy tone and warm style are equally effective on fast tunes and blues. He was among the most-recorded jazz artists of the late '30s and '40s, having been heard with all the above-mentioned bands as well as with Lionel Hampton and numerous recording groups. He won the Esq. Silver Award in '45. Own LPs on Rae-Cox, Comm., UA; LPs w. Mutt Carey in *New Orleans Jazz* (Savoy), Wild Bill Davison (River., Comm., Savoy), Vic Dickenson, Mel Powell (Vang.), Bud Freeman (Em.), Jonah Jones, J. Teagarden (Beth.), Jimmy McPartland in *Hot Vs. Cool* (MGM), Eddie Condon (Col.), Louis Armstrong (Col., Decca).

Addr: 889 Stebbins Ave., Bronx 59, N.Y.

HALL, MORRIS EUGENE (Gene), *teacher, tenor sax;* also *alto, clarinet, flute, oboe;* b. Whitewright, Texas, 6/12/13. Stud. C-Melody sax and clarinet. Played C-melody sax in home town theatre orchestra, 1925. Worked with various bands for 10 years incl. Nick Stuart, Bob Strong, Isham Jones; six months in Spain w. Clarence Nemir '35; a few dates w. Ray McKinley late '40s. During depression worked in honky-tonk band in cabaret. Staff arranger and head producer at NBC in Fort Worth '44-7. From fall of '47 until '59 he was on the staff of North Texas State College at Denton,

Texas, where he set up a musical education program leading to a major in dance band work. He was the first educator to put jazz on a formal credit basis of this kind. In '59 he joined the staff at Michigan State University to take care of the jazz interests of students. Hall was dean of the first national dance band clinic sponsored by Stan Kenton. He has contributed a series of articles to the *Encyclopedia Britannica Book of the Year*. Hall has made an important contribution to the acceptance of jazz at the school level. Favs: Hawkins, Lucky Thompson, Lester Young.

Addr: Music Dept., Michigan State University, East Lansing, Michigan.

HALL, HERBERT (Herb), *clarinet, reeds;* b. Reserve, La., 3/28/07. Younger brother of Ed Hall. Started on guitar, then clar. borrowing brother Robert's instrument. Left home 1927 to join band in Baton Rouge; later to New Orleans w. Sidney Desvignes. Worked in Texas w. Don Albert, '29-'45, then came to New York. In '55-6 toured Europe and North Africa w. Sammy Price for Les Jeunesses Musicales de France. Joined Eddie Condon '57. Fav: Ed Hall. LP w. Condon (MGM), Ed Hall (Rae-Cox), Dickenson-Thomas (Atl.).

Addr: 251 E. 148th St., Bronx, N.Y.

HALL, JAMES STANLEY (Jim), *guitar;* b. Buffalo, N.Y., 12/4/30. Bachelor of Music degree from Cleveland Institute of Music; studied guitar privately. Started working in local bands at 13. Moved to LA, March 1955. Worked w. Bob Hardaway quartet, Ken Hanna band, Dave Pell octet. Toured w. Chico Hamilton quintet '55-6; joined Jimmy Giuffre in late '56 and has been w. him since. On faculty at School of Jazz, Lenox, Mass. '57-9. W. Giuffre trio made JATP tour of Europe, June-Aug. '59. Heard in background score for film, *Odds Against Tomorrow* '59. "Hall is a young, no-nonsense guitarist who has much of the spare deliberation of Charlie Christian"—Whitney Balliett. Favs: Farlow, Raney, Kessel, H. Roberts. Own LP on Wor. Pac.; LPs w. Giuffre (Atl.), Chico Hamilton, John Lewis, Bob Brookmeyer (Wor. Pac.), *A Girl And A Guitar* (UA), Jack Montrose (Vict.), Paul Desmond (War. Bros.).

Addr: 11978 Kiowa Ave., Los Angeles 49, Calif.

HALL, MINOR (Ram), *drums;* b. Sellies, La., 3/2/97; d. 10/23/59. Started in 1914 as sub for his brother, Tubby, then Kid Ory '16. In Calif. with King Oliver '21-2, then in Chicago w. Jimmie Noone; later pl. w. Mutt Carey and Winslow Allum. Played an important part in the New Orleans revival w. Kid Ory in the '40s, joining him in '42 and remaining w. him until taken ill during a tour of Europe in '56. LPs w. Ory (Col., GTJ), Don Ewell (GTJ), one track w. L. Armstrong (Vict.).

HALL, ARCHIE (Skip), *organ, piano;* b. Portsmouth, Va., 9/27/09. Stud. with father on organ and piano at eight; later at Martin-Smith School NYC. St. playing in school bands and at rent parties and gigs in Harlem. Led own band 1931-8 in Cleveland; free-lance arr. during big band era late '30s. Arr. for Jay McShann and pl. piano occasionally '40-4. Was sideman and leader on various record sessions in '40s and '50s—some w. brother-in-law Sy Oliver; Thelma Carpenter, Buddy Tate, Don Redman et al. Toured England as leader of 1332nd. Eng. Band during World War II. Fav: Art Tatum. LPs w. Tate (Fels.).

Addr: 375 W. Palisade Ave., Englewood, N.J.

HALL, ALFRED (Tubby), *drums;* b. Sellies, La., 10/12/95; d. Chicago, Ill., 5/13/46. Brother of Minor Hall. Raised in New Orleans, where he played in '13, '15, and '16 with Frank Dusen's Eagle Band, the Crescent Band, and Silverleaf Band respectively. Prominent in '20s with Jimmie Noone, Carroll Dickerson, Louis Armstrong and Boyd Atkins, and in '30s in Chicago with Armstrong, Frankie "Half Pint" Jaxon, and Noone. LP: w. Jimmie Noone in *Gems of Jazz* (Decca).

HALLBERG, BENGT, *piano;* b. Gothenburg, Sweden, 9/13/32. After studying classics, took first dance band job in 1948 w. Thore Jederby. Later worked w. Kenneth Fagerlund '49. Accompanied Stan Getz on latter's Swedish tour '50. Rec. w. all star Swedish group July, '51, and subsequently became known both in Sweden and US as his country's foremost jazz pianist. Unique, light-fingered style, exceptionally effective in single note lines on medium tempi. In Jan. '54, the Swedish jazz magazine, *Estrad,* elected him musician of the year. In the late '50s Hallberg was relatively inactive in jazz, concentrating on commercial studio work. Own LP on Epic; LPs w. Lars Gullin (Em., Atl.), Harry Arnold, Quincy Jones (Em.), Stan Getz (Roost, Verve), Clifford Brown (Pres.).

HAMBRO, LEONARD WILLIAM (Lenny), *alto sax;* also *clarinet, flute;* b. New York City, 10/16/23. First major job w. G. Krupa; Army '41-4; later back w. Krupa, also w. Billy Butterfield, Bobby Byrne, Vincent Lopez, Pupi Campo. Played with and managed Ray McKinley band 1951-2; 1952, on tour with Machito Orch.; pl. lead and jazz alto w. him off and one until '56. Formed own quintet for rec. '54; did studio work and teaching. Joined Glenn Miller orch. led by Ray McKinley in May '56. Hambro's quintet was feat. in band as they toured Europe in '57 and '58. Fav: Charlie Parker. Own LPs: Col., Epic, Savoy; LPs w. Chico O'Farrill (Verve), Ray McKinley (Vict.).

Addr: 147-09 77th Rd., Kew Gardens Hills, L.I., N.Y.

HAMILTON, FORESTSTORN (Chico), *drums;* b. Los Angeles, Cal., 9/21/21. Started on clarinet. Formed band with schoolmates incl. Ernie Royal, Ch. Mingus, I. Jacquet; worked w. Floyd Ray, Lionel Hampton, 1940; Lorenzo Flennoy, Lester Young, '41. During Army service, '42-6, studied drums w. Jo Jones. Toured w. Jimmy Mundy, Count Basie. Went to Hollywood, worked at Billy Berg's as house drummer. In '48 joined Lena Horne, stayed w. her off and on for six years incl. European tour. During this time also did Paramount studio work incl. all feature drumming in film *Road To Bali;* played w. Charlie Barnet; got together w. Gerry Mulligan and helped form original quartet, '52. Toured w. Lena Horne '54-5. In '56 an unusual quintet featuring cello and flute, formed by Hamilton in LA began to acquire a national name. It was featured in the film *Sweet Smell of Success* in '57. The original personnel incl. Buddy Collette, Jim Hall and Fred Katz. Hamilton continued to tour, using a different personnel '58-'60. This group app. in film: *Jazz on a Summer's Day* '60. Favs: Jo Jones, Blakey, Rich, Roach. First rec. w. Slim and Slam (Okeh '41). Own LPs: Wor. Pac., War. Bros.; LPs w. Freddie Gambrell, John Lewis (Wor. Pac.), Gerry Mulligan (Fant., Wor. Pac.), Lester Young (Alad.).

HAMILTON, JAMES (Jimmy), *clarinet, tenor sax, composer;* b. Dillon, S.C., 5/25/17. Raised in Philadelphia. Starting at the age of seven, he studied trombone, piano, trumpet, saxophones. Played w. Teddy Wilson's orch. 1939-41, Benny Carter's sextet '41-2. Replaced Chauncey Haughton in the Duke Ellington band late '42, and has been w. Ellington ever since. Mainly known as an exceptionally schooled, clean-toned clarinetist, he was also featured on tenor sax from the late '40s. His best known solos w. Duke include *Flippant Flurry, Air-Conditioned Jungle, VIP Boogie, Smada, Honeysuckle Rose.* Won Esq. New Star Award 1946. Own LPs on Urania; LPs w. Ellington (Col., Cap., Rondolette, Beth.).

Addr: 2146 Hughes Ave., Bronx, N.Y.

HAMMOND, JOHN HENRY JR., *critic;* b. New York City, 12/15/10. Stud. at Hotchkiss, 1925-9; Yale, '29-31; studied music at Juilliard. Acquired ownership of a theatre on 2nd Ave. at 4th St., N.Y.C., in which he ran Negro shows with Fletcher Henderson, Luis Russell et al., Mar. 1932; in May, persuaded Columbia Records to make session w. Henderson's band. Served as announcer, disc jockey and producer of live jazz shows on WEVD for six months in '32, using mixed bands.

As a writer, Hammond was associated through the 1930s with three British publications: *The Gramophone,* '31-3; *Melody Maker,* '33-7; and *Rhythm,* '37-9. In addition, he was music critic of the *Brooklyn Daily Eagle,* '33-5; assoc. ed. in '34-5 of *Melody News,* a house organ owned by publisher Irving Mills; columnist for *Down Beat,* '34-41, and intermittently since. His other writing affiliations as co-editor and co-publisher, '43; *N.Y. Daily Compass,* '50-2, Sunday *Times,* '52-3; *Herald Tribune,* '55-6; music editor of *Gentry,* '56-7; contrib. *Hi-Fi Music at Home,* '58.

As a recording director, he produced U.S. masters for British release for Columbia and Parlophone, 1933-5; was recording director for Irving Mills in '34; sales manager, Columbia Masterworks, '37; supervised Teddy Wilson, Billie Holiday dates, etc., for Vocalion-Brunswick, '35-8; was associate recording director for Col. '39-43, and again briefly in '46; director of Keynote, '46; and recording director of Majestic, '47. Keynote subsequently merged with Mercury, of which he was vice-president, '47-52; director of jazz classics for Vanguard, '53-8; returned to Columbia as executive producer '59.

Throughout his career, Hammond has always been intensely active in race relations (vice-president of NAACP, member of board since 1937); he covered the Scottsboro trial for *The Nation* and *The New Republic,* 1933 and 1935. He arranged interracial jobs, for public appearances as well as records and radio, in the early 1930's when such things were practically unheard of, and in 1935 was responsible for the formation of the Benny Goodman Trio, the first interracial jazz unit ever to tour the U.S.

Hammond served as the propulsive force for two major phases of jazz, overlapping each other in the late 1930's: the swing era and the boogie-woogie piano craze. He engineered the former through his association with Benny Goodman, with whom he worked closely in the formation of a band first for the *Let's Dance* radio series, later for public appearances. He revived the long-dormant boogie-woogie, never known to the white public, when, after a long search for the artist on a record of *Honky Tonk Train Blues* that had fascinated him, he located the performer washing cars in a Chicago garage, re-recorded the tune and launched him on a successful career. The artist was Meade Lux Lewis. Hammond similarly arranged for the other best boogie-woogie pianists of that time, Albert Ammons and Pete Johnson, most of their affiliations in records, night clubs and concerts.

He produced two memorable concerts, *From Spirituals To Swing,* in 1938 and '39, recordings of which were released in '59 on the Vanguard label.

Hammond discovered and helped along to international acceptance, often at the expense of seemingly endless time and money, an impressive list of great jazz names, among whom the best known are Count Basie, Teddy Wilson, Charlie Christian, Billie Holiday and the musicians already named. A board member of the Newport Jazz Festival, he has continued to offer unofficial sponsorship to younger musicians and to rediscover older ones; many have been heard on Vanguard in the past five years, among them Ruby Braff, Sir Charles Thompson and Ronnell Bright.

A man of intense opinions on almost every subject—he has rarely been heard to express faint praise or mild displeasure at anything or anyone—Hammond has been not only the most important of all jazz writers but by far the most effective catalyst in the development of jazz. A member of a wealthy and socially prominent family, he has used his advantages to effect so much musical, racial and social good that a complete tribute to the work he has done would take a full book; fortunately, such a project is now in progress, as Hammond has been giving material for his biography to Willis Conover and it will be published by Horizon Press Inc.

Hammond has been collecting records since 1920

and now has well over 10,000 78s and several thousand LPs. His main interests are swing, mainstream jazz and the blues, though he has shown enthusiasm for some modern and experimental groups. An accomplished viola player, he has always played privately for pleasure; his Mozart clarinet quintet performance with Benny Goodman in 1935 led to Goodman's interest in classical music. In 1942 he became Goodman's brother-in-law when Goodman married one of Hammond's sisters, Alice.

Addr: 444 East 57th St., New York 22, N.Y.

HAMPTON, LIONEL, *vibraharp, drums, piano, leader;* b. Louisville, Ky., 4/12/13. Raised in Chicago, played drums in *Chicago Defender* Boys' band. Moved to Calif. '28, playing drums with Paul Howard orchestra, Eddie Barefield, and Les Hite. While Louis Armstrong was fronting the Hite band, Hampton picked up vibes; his first recorded solo on this instrument was *Memories of You,* made with Louis Oct. '30. After four years with Hite, Hampton organized his own band to play at Sebastian's Cotton Club in Los Angeles. Benny Goodman heard him, used him on a record date with Teddy Wilson and Gene Krupa Aug. '36, and persuaded him to give up his band and go on the road with Goodman. From then until '40, in addition to touring with the Goodman quartet on vibes (and occasionally subbing in the big band on drums), Hampton made a series of Victor records with pickup recording bands that achieved great prestige among collectors. Featured on these sessions were sidemen from almost every top name jazz band. In Sept. '40 Hampton fronted his own permanent orch. The band was an almost immediate success but did not record in its entirety until Christmas eve '41. The following May Hampton recorded the first big band version of *Flyin' Home,* which he had previously made with the Goodman sextet and with a ten-piece band on Victor. The new record was a colossal success and established Hampton's dominance in the big band field. Throughout the '40s he went from success to success commercially, while hundreds of since-celebrated musicians passed through the ranks of the band, among them such men as Illinois Jacquet, Jack McVea, Dexter Gordon, Arnett Cobb on tenor saxes. The Hampton band, operating on the premise that excitement was the main objective of jazz, gradually reduced the accent on musicianship, and by the early '50s had become as much a rhythm-and-blues as a jazz attraction, with circus overtones; nevertheless, the band remained the medium for the introduction of many great jazz talents.

After taking part in the film *The Benny Goodman Story* '55, Hampton resumed touring and during '56-'60 the band spent a great deal of its time overseas, enjoying a spectacular success in Israel, also touring in Britain, the Continent, North Africa and Australia.

Hampton was the first jazz musician to feature the vibraharp or vibraphone (popularly known as vibes). Although a wonderful beat and tremendous energy are the best-known qualities of his work, some of his finest records have been made at slower tempi and in groups other than his own big band. The orchestra recorded for Decca from '41-7, later was heard on MGM. In '53 Hampton started to record for Clef, mainly with small all-star groups assembled by Norman Granz; many of his LPs since then can be heard on the Verve label, though he has free-lanced. Hampton occasionally plays piano in the "trigger-finger" style he originated, using his two forefingers as if they were vibraphone mallets and playing extremely fast single-note passages; he is also a heavy, enthusiastic drummer. His main place in jazz was made as a dynamic personality, operating best with harmonic and melodic simplicity, with the vibes as his real medium. Won Met. poll '44-6, misc. inst.; Esq. New Star Band Award '45, DB critics' poll '54, on vibes; Playboy poll '57-60, misc. inst. Own LPs: On Verve: *Plays Love Songs* (2018), *Travelin' Band* (8019), *Norman Granz' Jam Session No. 5* (8053), *No. 7* (8062), *No. 8* (8094), *Gene Krupa-Lionel Hampton-Teddy Wilson w. Red Callender* (8066), *The Hampton-Tatum-Rich Trio* (8093), *King of the Vibes* (8105), *Airmail Special* (8106), *Flying Home* (8112), *Swinging With Hamp* (8113), *Hamp* (8114), *Hamp's Big Four* (8117), *Hamp and Getz* (8128), *And His Giants* (8170), *Here Come The Swingin' Bands* (8207), *Genius of Lionel Hampton* (8215), *L. Hampton '58* (8223), *Hallelujah Hamp* (8226), *The High and the Mighty* (8228). Audio Fid. 5913, 1913, *All American Award Concert* (Decca 8088), *Crazy Rhythm* (Em. 36034), *Golden Vibes* (Col. CL 1304), *Wailin' At The Trianon* (Col. CL 711), *Swings In Paris* (Contemp. 3502), *Hamp In Paris* (Em. 36032), *Swings* (Perfect 12002), *Open House* (Cam. 517), *Mooglow* (Decca 8230); Lion 70064; *Jazz Flamenco* (Vict. LPM 1422), *Just Jazz All Stars* (GNP 15), *Just Jazz* (Decca 9055), *Jivin' The Vibes* (Cam. 402), *Jam Session In Paris* (Em. 36035); Harm. 7115; *Apollo Hall Concert, 1954* (Epic LN 3190); LPs w. Goodman (Cap. S 706, Col. CL 500, Col. SL 160, SL 180, MGM 3E9); *Spirituals To Swing* (Vanguard VRS 8523/4), Col. CL 820, Vict. LPM 1099, Decca 8252, 8253; w. Charlie Christian (Col. CL 652).

Addr: 337 West 138th St., New York, N.Y.

HAMPTON, LOCKSLEY WELLINGTON (Slide), *trombone, tuba, composer;* b. Jeannette, Pa., 4/21/32. Raised in Indianapolis. From musical family, began pl. trombone at early age. With Buddy Johnson 1955-6; Lionel Hampton '56-7, incl. foreign tours; toured w. Maynard Ferguson band '57-9. Formed own octet '59. Pl. both slide and valve trom.; plays left-handed. Not related to Lionel Hampton. An outstanding arranger, his best works for Ferguson incl. *The Fugue* and other originals rec. on Roul. Favs: Dizzy Gillespie, Charlie Parker, Max Roach, John Coltrane. Own LP: Strand; LPs w. Curtis Fuller (Blue Note); Ferguson (Roul.), Melba Liston (Metro.).

HANDY, GEORGE (George Joseph Hendleman), *composer, piano;* b. Brooklyn, N.Y., 1/17/20. Mother, a pianist, started him at five. Studied at Juilliard, NYU, also privately w. Aaron Copeland. Joined Michael Loring, 1938. Army 1940, then w. Raymond Scott for six months in '41; began writing about this time. Met Boyd Raeburn late '43 and the following spring played with his band at Lincoln Hotel. Was with band off and on for a year and did his first important writing for Raeburn early '45 and '46—the latter period after he had rejoined the band following a stretch as songwriter at Paramount studios in LA. His arrs. of *There's No You, Tonsillectomy, Dalvatore Sally,* etc. made him the most-talked-about new arranger of the day. After this he lapsed into obscurity in NYC, occasionally emerging to play piano w. Buddy Rich, Bob Chester, also working on piano sonatas and a ballet. His *The Bloos* in N. Granz' *Jazz Scene* album, released in 1949 (rec. in '46) is the only major extended example of his work still available. He emerged briefly in '54, writing for a couple of record dates, but has done little since then to exploit his undeniably great talent. Fav. arr: Johnny Mandel. Handy won Esq. Silver Award '47. He rec. two albums under his own name for Label "X" which are now unavailable. LPs: arrs. for Boyd Raeburn (Savoy), Zoot Sims (ABC-Par.), *The Jazz Scene* (Verve); as pianist w. Zoot Sims (ABC-Par., River.).

HANDY, JOHN, *alto sax, tenor, flute, clarinet;* b. Dallas, Tex., 2/3/33. Moved to Los Angeles for two years '43-4; back to Dallas '44-8. Self-taught on clar. at age 13, then became interested in boxing, and won amateur featherweight championship '47. Began pl. alto '49 when family moved back to Calif. Stud. theory. In Army '53-5, then back to college. From '49 jammed w. musicians in San Francisco, mainly in after hours clubs, pl. tenor almost exclusively. Came to New York '58, worked w. Charlie Mingus, '58-9, Randy Weston '59. Would like to have own group and to establish a music school. LPs w. Mingus (UA, Col.).

Addr: 8 Morningside Ave., New York 26, N.Y.

HANDY, W. C., *songwriter, cornet, leader;* b. Florence, Ala., 11/16/1873; d. New York City, 3/28/58. Stud. at Kentucky Mus. College. Went on the road with touring units; bandmaster of Mahara Minstrels 1896. Although he led his own orch. off and on during the next 25 years, Handy was important mainly as a songwriter and documentor of traditional blues themes. His first well-known song, originally written as a 1909 political campaign song in Memphis for E. H. "Boss" Crump and entitled *Mr. Crump,* was published in 1912 as *Memphis Blues.* His most famous song was *St. Louis Blues,* 1914; others were *Yellow Dog Blues* '14, *Joe Turner Blues* '15, *Beale Street Blues* '16, *Loveless* (or *Careless*) *Love* '21 and *Aunt Hagar's Blues* '22. In the early '20s Handy settled in New York as a music publisher. He gradually lost his sight during the 1930s and was totally blind by the early '40s, but he remained active, conducting business at his Broadway office until a few months before his death. In 1957 a film entitled *St. Louis Blues,* purportedly based on Handy's life with Nat Cole portraying Handy, was rolled off the Hollywood assembly line. It is perhaps fortunate that Mr. Handy did not get to attend a screening. His tunes have been recorded countless times incl. entire LPs such as *Louis Armstrong Plays W. C. Handy* (Col. CL 591) and *The Blues—Mamie Webster Sings W. C. Handy* (Cub 8002).

HANNA, KENNETH L. (Ken), *composer, leader, trumpet;* b. Baltimore, Md., 7/8/21. Studied at Peabody Institute. Pl. trombone and arranged for local bands, later forming own group, disbanding at start of war. Joined Stan Kenton as arranger 1942. Entered service late '42. Trumpet and arr. with Kenton 1946-8. Arranged for Charlie Barnet '49. Back w. Kenton as arranger '50-1. Free-lance arr. Los Angeles '51-3. Own band 1954. Lately active selling and distributing records. Arr. for Kenton: *Somnambulism, How Am I To Know* (Cap.). Own LP on Trend, no longer available. LP: *Jazz For Dancers* (Cap.).

Addr: 16417 Labrador St., Granada Hills, Calif.

HANNA, ROLAND, *piano;* b. Detroit, Mich., 2/10/32. Father a preacher in a Sanctified Church, where Roland was first exposed to rhythm and blues-tinged music. First interest was in classical music; later influenced by friend Tommy Flanagan. Began pl. in bars and clubs in Detroit in the late 1940s; in Army from '50-2, where he pl. with a band. After discharge, pl. in clubs all over the US until '54, when he began stud. at Eastman School; later at Juilliard. Pl. with Benny Goodman's band in its appearances at the Newport Jazz Festival, the Brussels World Fair and the European tour that preceded it, in '58. W. Charlie Mingus at Half Note, then own trio at Five Spot '59. Admits that he is still influenced by Erroll Garner, not in the notes he plays, but in his touch and his concept of rhythm. Own LP: *Destry Rides Again* (Atco); LP w. Benny Goodman (Col.).

HARDAWAY, ROBERT BENSON (Bob), *tenor sax etc.;* b. Milwaukee, Wis., 3/1/28. Father is J. B. "Bugs" Hardaway, creator of movie cartoon characters Bugs Bunny and Woody Woodpecker. Darrell Caulker, film composer, helped him get started in music. First clar. in Air Force band 1946; wrote and cond. *Air Force Frolics* of 1947, which toured Caribbean. Stud. at LA City Coll. '49-50; pl. w. Ray Anthony '52 and '55, Hal McIntyre '53; solo rec. debut in Billy May *Bacchanalia* LP (Cap.). Solos w. Jerry Gray incl. *Thou Swell, Baby's Lullaby, Kettle Drum,* in '55 (Decca). Pl. w. Kenton, Les Elgart, Alvino Rey, Benny Goodman, Mel Torme, Bob Florence, Gus Bivona, Med Flory, Si Zentner; first sax w. Woody Herman '56. LPs w. Anthony, Ken Hanna (Cap.), Florence (Carlton), *Blues Groove* w. Herman (Cap.).

Addr: 5256 Strohm Avenue, No. Hollywood, Cal.

HARDEN, WILBUR, *fluegelhorn, trumpet;* b. Birmingham, Ala., 1925. Pl. with the blues bands of Roy Brown and Ivory Joe Hunter and in Navy band while in service. Replaced Curtis Fuller in Yusef Lateef group in spring of 1957. Migrated to NYC '58 and recorded a series of LPs for Savoy incl. a jazz version of *The King And I.* Favs: Davis, Navarro, Gillespie, Thad Jones, Clifford Brown. LPs w. Lateef (Savoy, Pres., New Jazz).

HARDIN, LIL: see ARMSTRONG, Lillian Hardin.

HARDING, LAVERE (Buster), *composer;* also *piano;* b. Cleveland, Ohio, 3/19/17. Originally self-taught, later studied Schillinger in NYC. Had own band in Cleveland, then joined Marion Sears. Lived in Canada for a year, then came to NYC in '38; was arranger and second pianist w. Teddy Wilson's big band '39-40. Later arranged for many swing bands including Artie Shaw (*Little Jazz*), Cab Calloway (*Smooth One*) and principally Count Basie, for whom his work includes *Rockin' the Blues, Mad Boogie, Hobnail Boogie, Paradise Squat, Nails, Rusty Dusty Blues.* In '54 he wrote vocal background for Billie Holiday; *Confusion* and other originals for Dizzy Gillespie.

HARDMAN, WILLIAM FRANKLIN JR. (Bill), *trumpet;* b. Cleveland, Ohio, 4/6/33. Uncle plays bass w. James Moody. Stud. trombone in junior high school, then worked in local groups. With T. Bradshaw from 1953-5; local gigs w. T. Dameron, C. Mingus '56. Member of Jazz Messengers from Sept. '56 to Aug. '58, then w. Horace Silver to Nov. '58. Since then free-lancing in and out of NYC. App. w. Mingus at NJF '56; Blakey at Randall's Island Fest. '56, '58; Benny Golson and Charlie Rouse in Baltimore Fest., July '59, Lou Donaldson at the Playhouse, NYC, Dec. '59. Favs: C. Brown, M. Davis, D. Byrd, D. Gillespie. LPs w. Jackie McLean, Mal Waldron (Pres.), Messengers (Beth., Jub., Elek., Col., Atl., Wor. Pac.), one track w. Mingus (Beth.).

Addr: 17 Vernon Ave., Brooklyn 6, N.Y.

HARDWICKE, OTTO (Toby), *alto, bass sax;* b. Washington, D.C., 5/31/04. A childhood friend of Duke Ellington, he worked w. him from 1918 in Elmer Snowden's and other local bands, and went with him to NYC in '23. Leaving Ellington in '28, he toured Europe w. Noble Sissle and worked w. Fats Waller, but rejoined Duke in '32, and remained w. him until '45. Soon after this he retired from music to a farm in Maryland. Not mainly a jazzman, he was known in the early Ellington days for his alto and soprano sax work on the original versions of *Black and Tan Fantasy, Birmingham Breakdown,* etc. Later he was featured soloist on the original version of *Sophisticated Lady* (of which he was co-composer) in '33 (Col. CL558). LPs w. Ellington (River., Col., Vict., Bruns.), Sonny Greer in *History of Jazz,* Vol. 2 (Cap.).

HARPER, HERBERT (Herbie), *trombone;* b. Salina, Kansas, 7/2/20. Raised in Amarillo, Texas and in Colorado. After working w. Johnny "Scat" Davis, Gene Krupa, Ch. Spivak, B. Goodman, Ch. Barnet, settled in Hollywood 1947. Worked w. own combo in sessions at Showtime Club and free-lanced in radio, TV, movie and recording. Since '55, occupied mainly in TV at NBC, Hollywood. Served on Board of Directors of Local 47 AFM, '56-8. Favs: Urbie Green, J. J. Johnson, Carl Fontana. Own LPs on Interlude, Tampa; LPs w. Pete Rugolo (Col., Merc.), Maynard Ferguson (Merc.), Bob Florence (Carlton), Ray Brown (Verve), Frances Faye (Beth.), 3 tracks w. Fred Katz (Wor. Pac.).

Addr: 8950 Hollywood Hills Rd., Los Angeles 46, Calif.

HARPER, ROCQUELLE TONI, *singer;* b. Los Angeles, Calif., 6/8/37. Uncle, Buddy Harper, guitarist, played w. Ben Pollack. Featured for years as a child star, she scored her first hit with *Candy Store Blues* on Columbia records in 1947. Later made several records incl. *Blacksmith Blues* w. Harry James; also rec. w. Paul Weston (*Silly Heart*). Films: *Manhattan Angel, Make Believe Ballroom.* Made her album debut on Verve records in 1955. Throughout her youthful recording career, she has shown a strongly jazz-influenced style reminiscent of Ella Fitzgerald's. In '59 she was teamed w. Count Basie's band for three dates. Own LPs: Verve.

Addr: 1751 W. 36th Place, Los Angeles 18, Calif.

HARRINGTON, ROBERT M. (Bob), *piano, vibes, drums;* b. Marshfield, Wis., 1/30/12. Father plays violin. Stud. E-flat bass in high school; played piano w. C. Barnet, 1951-4; G. Auld, 1955-6; B. De Franco, 1956; Vido Musso, 1949-52; played drums w. Red Nichols and Bud Freeman, '54-5. W. Maynard Ferguson '56-7, Ben Webster '57, Buddy De Franco '57-8; also accompanist and arr. for Ann Richards '56-9. Favs: Ellington, Basie, Red Norvo. Own LP: Imperial; LPs w. Harry Babasin (Merc.), Ann Richards (Cap.).

Addr: 417 W. Avenue 43, Los Angeles 65, Calif.

HARRIOTT, ARTHURLIN (Joe), *alto, baritone, tenor sax;* b. Jamaica, B.W.I., 7/15/28. Stud. clar. at boys' school in Jamaica; joined dance band after leaving school. Went to England 1951; pl. at Paris festival w. Tony Kinsey '54; w. Ronnie Scott '55, various small jazz combos in England. One of best though lesser-known among British saxophonists. Toured England w. MJQ, Nov.-Dec. '59. Favs: Charlie Parker, Charlie Ventura. LP: two nos. in *Jazz Britannia* (MGM).

Addr: 154 Portnall Road, London W 9, England.

HARRIS, ARTHUR SIDNEY (Art), *composer, piano, Fr. horn,* etc.; b. Philadelphia, Pa., 4/3/27. Stud. Yale U. 1947-52. Played w. Buddy Williams, Philadelphia, '45; Jeff Stoughton Dixieland Band, New Haven, '50-52; own trio in New Haven, '52. Featured in '55-6 on a series of recordings of a quasi-jazz nature. Favs: Brubeck, Tatum. LPs: Kapp.

Addr: 160 West 73rd St., New York 23, N.Y.

HARRIS, BARRY DOYLE, *piano;* b. Detroit, Mich., 12/15/29. Mother, a church pianist, gave him lessons from age 4. Pl. w. jazz band at amateur show '46. From '54, was house pianist at Blue Bird Club in Detroit, pl. w. visiting stars incl. Miles Davis, Sonny Stitt, M. Roach; for a while pl. at Rouge Lounge w. Konitz, Lester Young et al. Developed own theory of jazz instruction and had numerous students '58-60. Favs:

Powell, C. Parker. A major influence among the newer Detroit jazzmen. Own LP: Argo; LPs w. B. Golson (Riv.), Donald Byrd (Trans.), H. Mobley, Art Farmer-Byrd (Pres.), Thad Jones (Blue Note).

Addr: 6568 Stanford St., Detroit 10, Mich.

HARRIS, BENJAMIN (Little Benny), *trumpet;* b. New York City, 4/23/19. Self-taught. French horn in children's band at 12; took up trumpet 1937. Through Dizzy Gillespie, got jobs w. Tiny Bradshaw 1939, Earl Hines 1941. Though not a major instrumentalist, he was a principal figure in the evolution of bop, mainly as an acolyte who followed Gillespie and Parker, spent many nights at Minton's jamming with them. Worked w. John Kirby 1943, also brief spells w. Coleman Hawkins, Don Redman, Benny Carter, Boyd Raeburn, Don Byas, Herbie Fields. Best known as comp. of *Ornithology, Craze-ology* (rec. by Parker), *Little Benny* (rec. by Harris w. Clyde Hart), *Lion's Den* (rec. by Vic Dickenson). Rec. w. Don Byas, Clyde Hart (Savoy).

HARRIS, WILLARD PALMER (Bill), *trombone;* b. Philadelphia, Pa., 10/28/16. Played trumpet, tenor, and other instruments; did not begin professionally on trombone until he was 22. First major job w. Buddy Williams 1942, then w. Bob Chester and Benny Goodman '43-4. Led his own sextet at Cafe Society Uptown, spring '44. Made his name as a jazzman w. the Woody Herman band '44-6. His best-known recording with that band was *Bijou.* Later worked w. Charlie Ventura combo '47; rejoined Herman '48-50. Starting in '50, he toured annually w. JATP. Fronted small combos off and on during early '50s, while not on JATP tours; lived in semi-retirement in Florida, also working as disc jockey on Miami radio station. Rejoined Herman Jan. '56 for two years, then returned to Fla. Toured Europe w. Benny Goodman in fall of '59.

Harris was the creator of a much-imitated, much-discussed style, the main characteristics being a burry tone and unusual vibrato on slow numbers, savage attack and choppy rhythmic quality on faster tempi. To many musicians, he was the first new original trombone stylist since Teagarden and Higginbotham came to prominence. He won the DB Award '45-54, DB critics' poll '53-4, Esq. New Star Award '45, Esq. Gold Award '46-7, Met. Award '46-55. Own LP: *Bill Harris And Friends* (Fant. 3263); LPs w. JATP, Vols. 5, 6, 9, 10 (Verve); Woody Herman (Harm. 7013, 7093, Lion 70059, Cap. T784, Verve 8255, 2069), Ralph Burns (Verve 8121), Chubby Jackson (Argo 614, 625), Flip Phillips (Verve 8075), Gene Krupa (Verve 8107, 8071), Billy Ver Planck (Savoy 12101), Charlie Ventura (Verve 8132, Reg. 6064), Benny Goodman (MGM 3810); *The Soul of Jazz* (WW 20002).

Addr: 517 Zamora Ave., Coral Gables, Fla.

HARRIS, WILLIE (Bill), *guitar;* b. Nashville, N.C., 4/14/25. Mother taught him the rudiments of harmony on piano and he later played organ in his father's church. When he was 12, an uncle bought him a guitar, but his progress was so limited that he gave up. Entering the Army at 18 in the Engineers Corps, he limited his musical activities to bugling, while he saw overseas service in England and France. After his discharge in Sept. 1945, he studied guitar in Wash., D.C., gradually becoming a fair jazz guitarist as well as learning to play a few classics with a pick. Later, at Columbia School of Music in Washington, Sophocles Papas, who owned the school, encouraged his studies as a classical guitarist. The problem of making a living precluded any further efforts in this direction. In 1950, after some gigging in Washington with jazz groups and teaching at local schools, he joined The Clovers, r & b vocal group, as accompanist. Has been on the road with them ever since. Guitarist Mickey Baker heard him practicing jazz and classics in his dressing room, encouraged him to make some demonstration records. Result was series of LP solos showing remarkable versatility and range of styles. Favs: Oscar Moore, Barney Kessel, Les Paul, Django Reinhardt, Charlie Christian, John Collins. Own LPs on EmArcy.

Addr: 2021 Hamlin St. N.E., Washington 18, D.C.

HARRIS, CHARLES PURVIS (Charlie), *bass;* b. Alexandria, Va., 1/9/16. Studied violin and bass in Baltimore. Pl. w. Pete Diggs orch. while still at school, 1937-9. Toured w. Mac Crockette orch. '39-43, Lionel Hampton '44-9. Joined Nat Cole '51, making European and Australian tours w. him. Favs: Ray Brown, Pettiford, Hinton. LPs w. Hampton (Decca), Cole (Cap.).

HARRIS, GENE, *piano;* b. Benton Harbor, Mich., 9/1/33. Self-taught since age of nine, influenced by Albert Ammons and Pete Johnson, later by Erroll Garner and Oscar Peterson. Formed trio which played week end dates and had a weekly radio program. Joined Army 1951, pl. in 82nd Airborne Division band where he learned to read music. After discharge toured US w. various bands '54-6. In '56, w. drummer Bill Dowdy, *q.v.*, formed The Four Sounds, which in '57 became The Three Sounds, working around Washington, D.C. Came to NYC Sept. '58, playing club dates and recording. LPs: *The Three Sounds,* Lou Donaldson (Blue Note); Nat Adderley (River.).

HARRIS, JOSEPH ALLISON (Joe) *drums;* b. Pittsburgh, Pa., 12/23/26. Studied privately at 15. Worked with Dizzy Gillespie 1946-8 off and on. Arnett Cobb '48; Billy Eckstine '50; Erroll Garner '52; several months w. James Moody '54, otherwise free-lance in NYC incl. house band at Apollo Theatre. Stud. tympani, xylophone w. Alfred Freise and played w. Young Men's Symphony at City Center early '55. After touring Sweden in the summer of '56 w. Rolf Ericson, he decided to settle in Stockholm and has been living and playing there since. Favs: Roach, Blakey, Rich, Saul Goodman. LPs w. Gillespie, George Russell (Vict.), James Moody (Pres.), Tommy Potter (East-West), Teddy Charles (Atl.), Jimmy Cleveland (Em.), Milt Jackson (Savoy).

HARRISON, JAMES HENRY (Jimmy), *trombone;* b. Louisville, Ky., 10/17/00; d. New York City 7/23/31. Raised in Detroit, playing with small combos there and throughout the middle west 1916-21. In NYC, worked with Fess Williams, Elmer Snowden, June Clark, Billy Fowler, and, also, briefly with Duke Ellington in early 1920s. From 1926 until early '31, he worked off and on with Fletcher Henderson; was frequently with Ch. Johnson at Small's Paradise. His last job was with Chick Webb's band for a few months in 1931. He died of ulcers after a short illness.

According to Benny Carter, who was his closest friend and associate in several bands, and other contemporaries who heard him extensively, Harrison was the first truly great jazz trombonist and has never been excelled for warmth, feeling, tone, and style. Some of his most effective records were made with Carter's Chocolate Dandies Group in 1930. As a singer, he liked to imitate the late Bert Williams and made one or two vocals in this style, now unobtainable. His trombone work impressed and influenced Jack Teagarden, Dickie Wells, Tommy Dorsey, and many others. LP: w. Fletcher Henderson in *The Birth of Big Band Jazz* (River.).

HART, CLYDE, *piano;* b. Baltimore, Md., 1910; d. New York City, 3/19/45. Well known from 1937, when he played with Stuff Smith at the Onyx. Worked with Lucky Millinder, Roy Eldridge, John Kirby, Oscar Pettiford. An habitué of 52nd St. and Minton's, he was developing from a swing into a bop style, and was much in demand for record sessions before he succumbed to tuberculosis. He wrote the arrangement for Lionel Hampton's *In the Bag,* original coupling of *Flying Home* on Decca. LPs w. Charlie Parker (Savoy), Dizzy Gillespie (Rondolette), Don Byas (Reg.), Lionel Hampton (Vict.), Lester Young (Savoy).

HARVEY, EDWARD THOMAS (Eddie), *trombone, composer, piano;* b. Blackpool, Lancashire, England, 11/15/25. Mother pl. piano and sang. While stud. engineering, Harvey met Geo. Webb and became founder member of latter's Dixielanders, the first British traditionalist revival band, 1943-6. Served in RAF '46-9. Pl. w. Freddy Randall, '49-50; Vic Lewis 1950; founder member of J. Dankworth combo '50-53 and big band to '55. London jazz club jobs '55-7. Don Rendell combo '57-9. Many arrs. for Humphrey Lyttelton 1957-9; also arrs. for Kenny Baker, Oscar Rabin. LPs w. Dankworth (Verve), Lyttelton (London).

Addr: 4 A Bassett Road, London W. 10, England.

HASSELGARD, AKE (Stan), *clarinet;* b. Bollnas, Sweden, 10/4/22; d. 11/23/48 in auto accident near Decatur, Ill. Raised in Upsala. Rec. in Sweden w. Tyree Glenn, Bob Laine, Simon Brehm. Came to US July 1947 to take course at Columbia U. in art history. Worked w. Benny Goodman Sextet, spring '48, the only clarinet soloist other than Benny himself ever to be featured by Goodman. Might have developed into greatest of all modern clarinetists. Recorded in Hollywood w. own combo incl. Red Norvo (Cap.), released on EP but unavailable now.

HAWES, HAMPTON, *piano;* b. Los Angeles, 11/13/28. Father a clergyman; as a child he listened to spirituals and tried to reproduce the sounds on the piano. Prof. debut while still at LA Polytechnic High. Worked w. Big Jay McNeely '44; Dexter Gordon, Wardell Gray et al; Howard McGhee '50-1; Shorty Rogers and Howard Rumsey combos '51-2; Army '52-4, then had own trio for a couple of years feat. Red Mitchell and was heard throughout the US in night clubs, but went into obscurity as a result of personal problems and was off the scene entirely during much of '58-60. In '57 John Mehegan in *Down Beat* described him as "the key figure in the current crisis surrounding the rhythmic (funky) school of jazz piano." Hawes' style, derived from Charlie Parker and Bud Powell, showed signs of becoming strongly influential until the breakup of his trio. Own LPs: Contemporary; one side of *Piano East/Piano West* (Pres.), three tracks in *I Love Jazz Piano* (Savoy), two tracks in *Lighthouse At Laguna* (Contemp.); LPs w. Ch. Mingus (Jub.), Art Pepper (Savoy), *Baritones And French Horns* (Pres.), Tommy Turk-Sonny Criss (Verve).

HAWKINS, COLEMAN (Bean), *tenor sax;* b. St. Joseph, Mo., 11/21/04. Started at five on piano, later cello; tenor at nine; att. Washburn College in Topeka. Worked w. Mamie Smith's Jazz Hounds on tour, 1922-3, coming to New York with her. Made first records with Fletcher Henderson June 1923, and during his decade with this band became the first (and for a while the only) jazzman to attain fame as a tenor saxophonist, his monopoly on the instrument later being challenged by Bud Freeman, Chu Berry et al. Having earned a world-wide reputation, he left Henderson in '34, worked in England with the bands of Jack Hylton and Mrs. Jack Hylton, then toured the continent on his own, making many records, with Benny Carter, Django Reinhardt and others. Back in US July 1939, he formed a nine-piece band which on Oct. 11 recorded *Body & Soul* for Bluebird. This became his biggest hit and established him as a national jazz name. In 1940 he toured and recorded with his own 16-piece band, then gave it up to work with combos. An early admirer of Dizzy Gillespie and Charlie Parker, he assembled an all-star band for the first bop record session, Feb. 1944 on Apollo. In '44-5 he had his own sextet in Calif. w. Sir Charles Thompson, Howard McGhee, Denzil Best. He later freelanced in the East, toured with JATP, visited Europe in 1950 and again in 1954. In 1957 he was seen at NJF, toured w. JATP in the fall, and was seen on the *Sound of Jazz* CBS show in Dec. In '58-9 he appeared at the *Seven Ages of Jazz* concerts in Wallingford, Toronto etc. From '55-60 heard often at Metropole, NYC. A two-LP set of biographical reminiscences, with Hawkins recalling his life in music, was released on Riverside in '57.

Hawkins' role as a pioneer in his field was one of incomparable importance. He brought to this hitherto-ignored instrument a full-blooded warmth of tone, a buoyancy of rhythmic feeling that put him head and shoulders above the handful of tenor artists who attempted to challenge his dominance in the 1930s. By the early '40s there were innumerable great tenor sax soloists on the jazz scene; by the late '40s it had become the most-used, most-abused instrument in jazz, with the advent of the "honking" and other freak styles appealing to r & b audiences; Hawkins, whose big tone was no longer fashionable after the advent of the Stan Getz "cool school," remained a superb musician whose performances on slow tempi were still vital and compelling. Hawkins won *Esquire's* Gold Award every year the poll was held (1944-5-6-7). He won the *Down Beat* award in 1939 (as a bandleader he was disqualified from winning in later years) and the *Metronome* award 1945-7; DB Critics' poll '59. Film app: *The Crimson Canary.* Own LPs: Uran. 1201, River. 12-117, 118, 12-233, Cap. T 819, Pres. 7149, 7156, Fels. 7005, Wor. Wide 20001, Decca 8127, Savoy 12013, Verve 8261, 8237, 8266, 8240, Vict. LPM 1281; tracks in *Midnight Jazz At Carnegie Hall* (Verve 8189-2), *Tenor Saxes* (8125), *The Jazz Scene* (8060); JATP Vol. 1, 4 (Verve); tracks in *Great Jazz Reeds* (Cam. 339), *Guide To Jazz* (Vict. LPM 1393), *History of Jazz, Vol. 4* (Cap. T 796); LPs w. Tiny Grimes (Pres. 7138), *Very Saxy* (Pres. 7167), Ben Webster (Verve 8318); *Sittin' In* (Verve 8225), *Jazz Concert* (Gr. Award 316), Buck Clayton (Col. CL 701, 614, 933), Thelonious Monk (River. 12-242), Red Allen (Vict. LPM 1509), Feather-Hyman (MGM 3650), *Seven Ages Of Jazz* (MGM 1009); Ruby Braff (Epic 3377), Eddie Heywood (Coral 57095), Spike Hughes (Lond. LL 1387), Don Redman (Gold. Cr. 3017), *Session At Riverside* (Cap. T761), the International Jazzmen in *History of Jazz, Vol. 3* (Cap. T795); *Saxes, Inc.* (War. Bros. W1336).

Addr: 445 West 153rd St., New York 31, N.Y.

HAWKINS, ERSKINE RAMSAY, *trumpet, leader;* b. Birmingham, Ala., 7/26/14. Started a band at Ala. State Teachers College in 1935. Came to NYC the following year, recorded for Vocalion. Achieved great popularity '39-41, playing frequently at Savoy Ballroom and making a series of hit records for Bluebird, biggest of which were *Tuxedo Junction* '39, which became his theme; *After Hours* '40, featuring Avery Parrish, piano; *Tippin' In* '45. Hawkins, a florid trumpet player, always had a competent swinging band, its appeal directed mainly at r & b audiences. In the early '50s he recorded for Coral. He was still leading a band, though one rarely heard by jazz audiences, in '60. LPs: one selection in both *Perfect For Dancing—Fox Trots* and *Perfect For Dancing—Jitterbug or Lindy* (Vict.).

Addr: c/o Circle Artists, 48 W. 48th Street, New York 36, N.Y.

HAWKINS, JELACY (Screamin' Jay), *singer, piano;* b. Cleveland, Ohio, 1929. Adopted from Cleveland orphanage when 18 months. At 6 he began playing a neighbor's piano and in later years continued playing as he pursued a career as a boxer, winning a Golden Gloves contest in 1947, later turning professional. In 1953, after completing Army service, he joined Tiny Grimes as pianist, and later was w. Lynn Hope and Fats Domino. When he went on his own, he began affecting outlandish costumes and a wild stage manner to achieve great success in the rock-'n'-roll field. At base, Hawkins is an authentic blues shouter. Own LP: *At Home with Screamin' Jay* (Epic).

Addr: c/o Gale Agency, 48 W. 48th St., New York 36, N.Y.

HAWKSWORTH, JOHN (Johnny), *bass, piano;* b. London, England, 1/20/24. Stud. in Sheffield, Eng.; Capetown, S. Africa (while in R.A.F.); and in London after the war. Met Buddy Featherstonehaugh while in R.A.F. and joined his group later; then w. Tommy Sampson. Toured Britain, US w. Ted Heath; won first place in *Melody Maker's* Readers' Poll of Britain's Best. Good bassist who earned fan acclaim through comedy showmanship. Favs: Ellington, J. Smith, T. Farlow, O. Peterson, Ray Bryant. LPs w. Heath (Lond.).

Addr: 22 Crundale Ave., Kingsbury, N.W. 9, England.

HAYES, CLANCY, *banjo, singer;* b. Caney, Kansas, 11/14/08. Seventh son of a seventh son in a musical family. Started as drummer in grade school; led own band, The Harmony Aces, as teenager. After playing with his brothers' band in Oakland in 1923, he toured the midwest with a vaudeville show, playing w. Ham Crawford in Phoenix. Moved to San Francisco 1926 and joined NBC staff '28. Built large following in SF and LA, playing and singing w. Sid Lippman, Raymond Paige and many others. Joined Lu Watters 1938, and was a key figure in the old-time jazz revival touched off by Watters' Yerba Buena band. Worked w. Bunk Johnson in SF '44; joined Bob Scobey '49. One of his most popular hits is *Huggin' and a Chalkin',* which he composed. Won DB critics' poll as New Star singer 1954. Own LP on Verve. LPs: w. Bob Scobey (GTJ., Vict.), Bunk Johnson (GTJ), Lu Watters (Verve), Bing Crosby-Scobey (Vict.).

HAYES, EDGAR JUNIUS, *piano;* b. Lexington, Ky., 5/25/04. Stud. at Fisk and Wilberforce U. Debut in 1919 w. Fess Williams. Pl. w. Mills Blue Rhythm Band '31-6, under Baron Lee, Lucky Millinder. Had an excellent swing band 1937-40, touring Scandinavia '38, personnel incl. Kenny Clarke, Joe Garland. Scored national success with this band when he rec. a flashy, florid version of *Star Dust.* Moved to Riverside, Cal., July '42; at the Somerset House, spent 12 years as soloist, the last six acc. by rhythm section. From '54-60 worked as single at Jimmie Diamond's Lounge, San Bernardino, Cal. Member of LA Pianist Club; they have jam sessions once a month and concerts twice yearly. The records made by Hayes on Decca are unavailable.

Addr: 2974 Cridge Street, Riverside, Cal.

HAYES, LOUIS SEDELL, *drums;* b. Detroit, Mich., 5/31/37. Father pl. drums; stud. w. cousin at 11; Wurlitzer

Sch. of Mus. in Detroit '51-2. Worked w. own group in local club at 15; w. Yusef Lateef '56; to NYC, Aug. '56, joining Horace Silver and remaining with him until Sept. '59. With Cannonball Adderley since. Made European tour w. Silver March '59. Favs: Philly Joe Jones, Blakey, Roach, Clarke. LPs w. Silver, Sonny Clark, Cliff Jordan, Bennie Green (Blue Note), Yusef Lateef, Wilbur Harden (Savoy), Curtis Fuller (Pres.), Cannonball Adderley (River.), Cecil Taylor (UA).

Addr: 17 Vernon Ave., Brooklyn 6, N.Y.

HAYES, EDWARD BRIAN (Tubby), *tenor sax;* also *vibes, flute, alto & baritone saxes;* b. London, Eng., 1/30/35. Studied violin at age eight; father played on BBC. Switched to tenor at 12; became prof. at 15; then joined Kenny Baker in 1951. Later pl. w. Ambrose, Vic Lewis, Jack Parnell. Led own octet April '55-Oct. '56. Took up vibes Dec. '56 after encouragement from Vic Feldman. In Apr. '57 formed Jazz Couriers w. tenor man Ronnie Scott, remaining together until Aug. '59. Also toured Germany w. Kurt Edelhagen June '59. Own quartet from Sept. '59. Superior soloist inspired by Parker, Rollins, Getz. Own LPs on Carlton, Imp.; LPs w. Dizzy Reece (Blue Note, Savoy), Jimmy Deuchar, Victor Feldman (Contemp.).

Addr: 8 Kensington Park Gardens, London, W. 11, England.

HAYMER, HERBERT (Herbie), *tenor sax;* b. Jersey City, N.J., 7/24/15; d. in auto crash in Santa Monica, Calif., 4/11/49. Best known as featured soloist w. Red Norvo 1935-7. Later played w. Jimmy Dorsey, Kay Kayser, Woody Herman; moved to Calif. and did studio work. Best records were made w. quintet (Ch. Shavers, Buddy Rich, Nat Cole, John Simmons) issued on Sunset 78s and Monarch 10 inch LP but unavailable now.

HAYNES, ROY OWEN, *drums;* b. Roxbury, Mass., 3/13/26. As a teenager, played in Boston w. Sabby Lewis, Frankie Newton and Pete Brown. W. Luis Russell 1945-7, Lester Young '47-9, Kai Winding '49, Charlie Parker '49-50. Joined Sarah Vaughan '53 and remained w. her until March '58. Gigs w. Phineas Newborn, Miles Davis, Lee Konitz, then at Five Spot, first w. Thelonious Monk for four months, own group until Dec. '58. Pl. w. Lambert, Hendricks & Ross; George Shearing for a month in Hawaii, Lennie Tristano, Kenny Burrell, all in '59. One of the most versatile and tasteful modern drummers. Favs: Blakey, Roach, Clarke, Philly Joe Jones. Own LP: *We Three* (New Jazz); one half of *Jazz Abroad* (Em.); LPs w. Lester Young (Savoy), Bud Powell (Blue Note), Wardell Gray (Pres.), Stan Getz (Pres., Roost), Sarah Vaughan (Em.), Red Rodney (Fant.), Dorothy Ashby (Pres., New Jazz), Monk (River.), John Handy, Phineas Newborn (Roul.), Lee Konitz (Verve), *Open House At The Five Spot* (UA).

Addr: 194-24 Hollis Ave., Hollis 12, L.I., N.Y.

HAYNES, GEORGE (Tiger), *guitar, bass;* b. St. Croix, V.I., 12/13/07. No formal musical training but father and brother taught him at home. First came to prominence when he joined the Three Flames in Sept. 1945 for very successful night club stints; played for several years at Bon Soir, NYC. Had own NBC-TV series for 39 wks. Favs: D. Reinhardt, C. Christian. Own LPs w. Three Flames (Merc., Barbary).

Addr: 587 E. 169th St., Bronx 56, N.Y.

HAYSE, ALVIN COOPER, *trombone;* b. Detroit, Mich., 4/7/21. Played w. Snookum Russell, Kelly Martin, 1940-1; McKinney's Cotton Pickers, '42; Lionel Hampton, '43-6 and '51-5, incl. European tour '54; has also worked with Milt Buckner band, Sabby Lewis. LPs: see Hampton.

HAYTON, LEONARD GEORGE (Lennie), *composer, piano;* b. New York City, 2/13/08. Was prominent as jazzman in late 1920s, recording with jazz groups under Frankie Trumbauer, Bix Beiderbecke, Red Nichols, Joe Venuti, and working with Paul Whiteman. As arranger and leader on Bing Crosby radio show in early '30s, he used such sidemen as Benny Goodman, Artie Shaw, Dorsey Brothers. Toured with own dance band 1937-40. Mus. Dir. at MGM studios in California 1940-53. Married Lena Horne Dec. 1947, and in recent years has been traveling as her mus. dir. Own LPs: Roulette. LPs w. Lena Horne (Vict.), Red Nichols (Bruns.).

Addr: 300 West End Ave., New York 23, N.Y.

HAYWOOD, CEDRIC, *piano;* b. Houston, Texas, ca. 1918. Attended Phyliss Wheatley High School w. Arnett Cobb. He and Cobb joined Chester Boone's band in 1934, then w. Milton Larkins in late '30s, Lionel Hampton in early '40s. Pl. for a short time w. Sidney Bechet in Sprinfield, Ill. '42. In SF from '43 until '48 when he joined Illinois Jacquet, remaining w. him until '51. Then ret. to SF, working w. Saunders King before becoming a permanent member of the Kid Ory band at the Tin Angel '55. Toured Europe w. Ory twice in late '50s. Comp. *Hot Rod* rec. by Jacquet (Vict.). LPs w. Ory (Verve, GTJ).

HAZEL, ARTHUR (Monk), *drums, cornet, mellophone;* b. Harvey, La., 8/15/03. Raised in Gretna and NO. Joined Emmett Hardy 1920; early associate of Abbie Brunis, playing with his Halfway House Dance Orch. 1924-5; rec. w. Tony Parenti '25. Led own Bienville Roof orch. on Bruns. rec. session 1928. In NYC w. Johnny Hyman, Jack Pettis, and own band, 1929-31; later went to Hollywood, worked w. Gene Austin, rec. w. him on cornet. Retired from music during World War II, then resumed as drummer w. Sharkey Bonano on Bourbon St. in NO, and was inactive for some time owing to illness. In '59 he was with Roy Liberto at the Dream Room in New Orleans, Sharkey Bonano in NO, Atlanta, Ga. & NYC. Own LP: South.; LPs w. Jack Delaney (South.), Sharkey Bonano (Cap.).

Addr: 1028 Arabella, New Orleans 15, La.

HEALEY, RICHARD J. (Dick), *alto sax, clarinet, flute;* b. Youngstown, Ohio, 7/5/29. Studied clar. for 2 yrs. Worked with local bands through high school; went on the road after graduation. Joined Bob Astor orch. in 1947, Burt Massengale '48-9, Al Belletto, June '49; Australian Jazz Quartet, Dec., '54. Ret. to Australia Sept. '58 and led pit band for touring show. LPs w. Australian Jazz Quartet, Joe Derise (Beth.).

HEARD, EUGENE M. (Fats), *drums;* b. Cleveland, O., 10/10/23. Stud. piano at Cleve. Inst. of Mus. Worked w. Coleman Hawkins, L. Hampton; TV salesman 2½ years; toured w. Erroll Garner, Dec. '52 until '55, when he returned to Cleveland and a business career. Took over operation of Modern Jazz Room, Cleve., Sept. '59. LPs w. Garner (Col.).

Addr: 10800 Greenlawn Ave., Cleveland, O.

HEARD, JAMES CHARLES (J.C.), *drums;* b. Dayton, Ohio, 10/8/17. First prominent w. Teddy Wilson's big band, 1939-40. Benny Carter 1942; Cab Calloway 1942-5; own sextet '46-7; then free-lance, incl. tours with JATP in US, Europe, and in Japan, where he took up residence in 1953. At various times his group incl. Toshiko on piano and Miyoshi Umeki as vocalist. Until he returned to the US in Nov. '57, Heard was feat. as a single and w. supporting groups in China, the Philippines and Australia. To Cannes Fest. and Brussels Fair w. JATP '58. Worked in NYC since w. Coleman Hawkins & Roy Eldridge at the Metropole, Lester Lanin and own group. Films: four in Japan. One of the best drummers of the swing school, comparable w. Jo Jones, Cozy Cole. Favs: Rich, Jo Jones, Roach. Imp. infl: Chick Webb. Rec. *Congo Blues* w. Norvo, Gillespie, Parker. Own LPs: Argo, Epic; LPs w. Teddy Wilson (MGM); *Jam Session #1 & 2*, Roy Eldridge, Billie Holiday, Dizzy Gillespie-Stuff Smith, JATP, Vol. 9, *Sittin' In* (Verve).

Addr: 511 West 159th St., New York, N.Y.

HEATH, ALBERT (Al), *drums;* b. Phila., Pa., 5/31/35. Father played clarinet in marching band; brothers are Percy and Jimmy Heath (see below). Toured w. Jay Jay Johnson 1958-9. First influence was "Specs" Wright; current favs. Blakey, Philly Joe Jones, Max Roach. LPs w. Johnson (Col.), Adderley Bros., Johnny Griffin, Jimmy Heath (River.), Mal Waldron, John Coltrane (Pres.).

Addr: 175-02 139th Rd., St. Albans, L.I., N.Y.

HEATH, JAMES EDWARD (Jimmy), *tenor sax, composer;* also *alto, baritone saxes;* b. Philadelphia, Pa., 10/25/26. Started in carnivals, then w. Nat Towles band. Pl. w. Howard McGhee 1947-8, incl. visit to France, Dizzy Gillespie '50-1; toured w. Symphony Sid concert unit '52. W. Kenny Dorham for three months, Miles Davis for two months incl. Toronto and French Lick Festivals '59. Gil Evans band at Apollo Theater '59. Comp. and arr. music for Chet Baker *Playboys* album on Wor. Pac. '56. Favs: Rollins, Parker, Stitt. Own LP: River.; LPs w. Miles Davis, J. J. Johnson (Blue Note), Blue Mitchell (River.).

Addr: 1927 Federal St., Philadelphia 46, Pa.

HEATH, PERCY, *bass;* b. Wilmington, N.C., 4/30/23. Raised in Philadelphia. Violin in school orch. Army 1943; 2½ years as fighter pilot in Air Force. After discharge, went to Granoff Sch. of Mus. in Phila., studied bass. Six months later, was working on bass with a trio, the Hollis Hoppers; later became house bassist at Down Beat Club in Phila. Howard McGhee brought him to NYC w. his sextet, late '47, and to the Paris Jazz Festival in May '48. After working with Miles Davis, Fats Navarro, J. J. Johnson, he joined Dizzy Gillespie June 1950, remaining for two years. Then free-lanced in NYC and in 1954, with John Lewis, Kenny Clarke and Milt Jackson, went on tour as member of the Modern Jazz Quartet. Won *Down Beat* critics' New Star award, 1954. One of most-recorded bassists in jazz, admired for his superb tone and technique.

LPs w. MJQ (Pres., Atl., Verve), Miles Davis (Pres., Blue Note), Bill Evans-Bob Brookmeyer, Art Farmer, *Odds Against Tomorrow* (UA), *Grand Encounter* (Wor. Pac.), John Lewis (Atl.), Howard McGhee (Beth.), Charlie Parker (Verve), Thelonious Monk (Pres.), Milt Jackson (Blue Note, Savoy, Atl.), Clifford Brown, Thad Jones, Kenny Dorham (Blue Note), J. J. Johnson (Col.), Sonny Rollins (Pres., River.), Paul Desmond (War. Bros.), Ornette Coleman (Contemp.).

Addr: 175-02 139th Rd., Springfield Gardens, L.I., N.Y.

HEATH, EDWARD (Ted), *leader, composer, trombone;* b. Wandsworth, London, England, 3/30/00, son of leader of Wandsworth Borough Band. At ten, won prize playing tenor horn in brass band contest. Trombone at 14. While working as street musician, was discovered by Jack Hylton, through whom he got first job on Queens Hall Roof, where Hylton was relief pianist, 1922. Played w. Bert Firman 1924-5; Jack Hylton '25-7; Ambrose '27-35; then with Sid Lipton and Geraldo, leaving latter in late '44 when he was assigned by BBC to assemble band for radio series. Band started concerts at London Palladium in 1945; these became regular Sunday event in later years. Meanwhile Heath's band built up a tremendous following throughout England and the continent through hit records, many broadcasts and tours. By early 1950s several former Heath stars had started out on their own, among them Jack Parnell, Ronnie Scott, singers Lita Roza, Dickie Valentine. The success of Heath's LPs in the US resulted in his being brought over for a concert tour in April '56. The band has since visited the US several times with great success. Heath's policy is a modified style of big band modern jazz with many competent jazz soloists and with a high degree of showmanship that has contributed greatly to the band's popularity. LPs: London.

Addr: 23 Albemarle St., London W., England.

HEFTI, NEAL, *composer, leader, trumpet, piano;* b. Hastings, Nebr., 10/29/22. Stud. trumpet at 11; while at high school wrote first arrs. for Nat Towles' band. Played w. Bob Astor 1941; to Cuba w. Les Lieber;

played and wrote for Ch. Barnet, Bobby Byrne, also made several arrs. for Earl Hines. To LA w. Ch. Spivak '43. After working briefly w. Horace Heidt, he joined Woody Herman, Feb. '44 for film *Sensations of 1945*. After staying in California for six months, he rejoined Herman Aug. '44. Played trumpet for most of the next year. His arrs., notably *The Good Earth* and *Wild Root* played an important part in the success of the Herman band during this period. Married Herman's vocalist Frances Wayne Oct. '45. Worked w. Ch. Ventura's big band '46; Harry James '48-9.

From '50-'60 Hefti frequently wrote for Count Basie —originally for Basie's Septet, then for the big band, starting with *Little Pony*. By '60 more than forty of his originals had been recorded by Basie and he was credited with establishing much of the new band's personality. From '52 Hefti intermittently led various bands and combos of his own. He gave up playing trumpet entirely in '53 but resumed in early '60. A skilled, versatile writer, he was in the vanguard of the bop movement as early as '43. During the '50s he was chiefly active in the pop field, leading bands for singers, writing for many major TV shows etc. Fav. own compositions for Basie: *L'il Darlin', The Kid From Red Bank, Duet, Cute* (all on Roulette).

Own LPs on Epic, Coral; arrs for Herman (Harm.), Basie (Verve, Roul.), Whitey Mitchell (ABC-Par.), *The Jazz Scene* (Verve); Frances Wayne (Bruns., Epic), Steve Allen (Coral).

Addr: 161 West 75th St., New York 23, N.Y.

HELM, ROBERT, *clarinet;* b. Fairmead, Cal., 7/18/14. First paying job was in theatre pit band in Dos Palos, Cal., when he was eleven years old. Joined union in '32, playing mostly saxophone, also capable on trumpet, guitar, etc. Moved to SF '35; met Lu Watters and Turk Murphy, w. whom he has worked almost exclusively since '39, first in the Yerba Buena Jazz Band, later w. Murphy's own band. Also six months w. the Castle Jazz Band in Portland, Ore., before Murphy organized his band in '52. Fav: Johnny Dodds. Own LP on River.; one number in *History of Classic Jazz* (River.); LPs w. Turk Murphy (Col., GTJ).

HENDERSON, WILLIAM RANDALL (Bill), *singer;* b. Chicago, Ill., 3/19/30. Prof. debut at age five, singing and dancing in Phil Baker's *Artists and Models* show. While at school, cont. to take juvenile parts in radio and on stage. Sang in Chicago clubs; in service two years, sang and emceed show that toured bases in Europe. Sang in opening show at Blue Note in Chicago. Soon after arr. in NYC, rec. *Senor Blues* w. Horace Silver, a big hit in 1958. Henderson, who had no formal mus. ed., is a singer with a definite jazz affinity. Favs: B. Holiday, Joe Williams, Dick Haymes. First own LP released '59 on Vee-Jay label, also recs. w. H. Silver (Blue Note) and w. all star jazz group on River.

Addr: 150 West 77th Street, New York 24, N.Y.

HENDERSON, BOBBY (Jody Bolden) (Robert Bolden Henderson), *piano, trumpet;* b. New York City, 4/16/10. Studied from 1923. Acc. Billie Holiday ca. '33; in obscurity in upstate N.Y. for years until John Hammond recorded him in 1956. Very much influenced by Harlem "stride" pianists. Appeared at Newport Jazz Festival, 1957. Favs: Tatum, Ellington, Waller, C. Profit, T. Wilson, Basie. Own LP on Vang.; at Newport (Verve); LP w. Basie (Vang.).

Addr: The Kerry Blue, 16 Eagle St., Albany 10, N.Y.

HENDERSON, JAMES FLETCHER (Smack), *leader, composer, piano;* b. Cuthbert, Ga., 12/18/1898; d. New York City, 12/29/52. Majored in chemistry, math. at Atlanta U., came to NYC 1920 to do postgraduate work, but took part-time job playing with W. C. Handy, and in '22 went to work as house pianist w. Black Swan records; also assembled group to acc. Ethel Waters, toured with her. Led his own band at the Club Alabam NYC, 1923, and at Roseland on Broadway the following year and frequently for many years thereafter. Henderson's was the first large band to acquire a wide reputation by playing jazz. In the 1920s he played piano on records with Bessie Smith and innumerable other singers; his band, recording for Vocalion, Columbia, etc., featured at times such men as Louis Armstrong, Joe Smith, Rex Stewart, Bobby Stark, Tommy Ladnier, trumpets; Charlie Green, Jimmy Harrison, trombones; Don Redman, Benny Carter, alto saxes; Buster Bailey, clarinet; Coleman Hawkins, tenor sax; Charlie Dixon, banjo; Bob Escudero, June Coles, bass; Kaiser Marshall, drums. During the 1930s Fletcher often conducted while his brother, Horace, played piano. The band toured with varying success and fluctuating personnel, its stars including Red Allen, Joe Thomas, Roy Eldridge, Dick Vance, Emmett Berry, trumpets; Claude Jones, Keg Johnson, Fernando Arbelo, J. C. Higginbotham, Dickie Wells, Benny Morton, trombones; Edgar Sampson, Russell Procope, Hilton Jefferson, altos; Ben Webster, Chu Berry, tenors; Clarence Holiday, Lawrence Lucie, guitar; John Kirby, Israel Crosby, bass; Walter Johnson, Sid Catlett, drums.

Also during the '30s, Fletcher wrote arrangements for many other bands, among them Isham Jones, the Dorsey Brothers, etc., and he achieved his greatest recognition through such arrangements as *Sometimes I'm Happy, When Buddha Smiles, King Porter Stomp, Blue Skies, Down South Camp Meeting* and *Wrapping It Up* for Benny Goodman. In August 1939, having been semi-inactive as a bandleader for some time, he joined Benny Goodman's orch. on piano for a few months; his most popular record as pianist with the band was *Stealin' Apples*. Henderson continued to lead a band intermittently. From 1944 to '45 he was at the Club de Lisa in Chicago. In '46-7 he was in California, writing arrangements for Goodman, many of which were recorded on Capitol. In 1948-9 Henderson toured as a pianist, accompanying Ethel Waters. After illness and inactivity in the first half of 1950, he wrote the score with J. C. Johnson for *The Jazz Train,* produced at Bop City in NYC, and led the band there. He was leading a sextet at Cafe Society when he suffered a stroke just before Christmas, 1950, and was bedridden during most of the last two years of his life.

Although he led what was often a great jazz orchestra, Fletcher Henderson was poorly represented on records, sometimes through the quality of his material but often through inadequate recording; thus his main legacy to jazz is his work as an arranger. The basic simplicity of his style involved such devices as the pitting of reed against brass section and the use of forthright, swinging block-voiced passages. The style he popularized, which was virtually synonymous with swing and greatly responsible for the rise of swing music, was soon incorporated into the mainstream of popular music. In the 1940s and '50s many commercial radio and TV bands featured arrangements with many Henderson characteristics, by now acceptable enough to the general public to be considered pop music rather than jazz. In '57 and '58, Rex Stewart organized and directed a group of Henderson's ex-sidemen in a reunion band heard at the Great South Bay Festival and on records. Henderson won the *DB* poll as arr., '38-40. LPs: *The Birth of Big Band Jazz* (River. 12-129); one track in *Guide To Jazz* (Vict. LPM 1393); one track in *History of Classic Jazz* (River. SDP 11); one track in *Encyclopedia of Jazz on Records,* Vol. 2 (Decca 8384); one track in *The Jazz Makers* (Col. 1036); LPs w. Bessie Smith (Col. SL 856, 857, 858), Benny Goodman in *Spirituals To Swing* (Vang. 8523/4); *Benny Goodman Presents Fletcher Henderson Arrangements* (Col. CL 524).

HENDERSON, HORACE, *piano, leader;* b. Cuthbert, Ga., 1904. Brother of Fletcher. Studied at Atlanta U. and Wilberforce U. While at latter, formed band which toured during summer vacations, Benny Carter and Rex Stewart being early members. Henderson led a band until 1931, when he joined forces with Don Redman as pianist and arranger. From '33 to '36 he frequently played in Fletcher Henderson's band, and, like Fletcher, wrote arrangements for Benny Goodman, among them *Japanese Sandman, Dear Old Southland, Big John Special, Always, Walk Jennie Walk, I Found a New Baby.* In the late '30s he had his own band, mostly in Chicago, recording for Vocalion-Okeh, with Ray Nance, Emmett Berry and Israel Crosby in the personnel. He arranged for Charlie Barnet (*Little John Ordinary, Charleston Alley,* etc.) in 1941; later toured as pianist and musical director for Lena Horne. He was in Los Angeles in 1944-5 and recorded with small groups for Capitol. In the late '40s and early '50s he worked generally around Chicago with a small band, aiming at the r & b market and recording for Decca and other labels, but offering little of musical interest. Had own combo in Minneapolis club '58.

A Hines-influenced pianist, often called superior to Fletcher as a soloist though lacking his fluency as an arranger, Horace Henderson also wrote for Tommy Dorsey, Glen Gray and others.

HENDERSON, LUTHER, *composer, piano;* b. Kansas City, Mo., 3/14/19. Father a school teacher and actor. Studied at Juilliard. As pianist, won Harlem amateur show 1934. Worked with Leonard Ware '39-44; Navy band at Great Lakes '44-6; w. Mercer Ellington band, also coaching at own studio '46-7. Pianist and mus. dir. w. Lena Horne, 1947-50. Since then has had own coaching and arranging studios, writing for Eartha Kitt, Marge and Gower Champion, etc. Has arranged occasionally for Duke Ellington since 1944 incl. *Indiana* (Vict.). Orchestrated Ellington's compositions, *New World A-Comin', Harlem* and *Night Creature* performed by Symphony of the Air, Oct. '55. Comp.-arr., conductor for TV shows: Playhouse 90's *The Helen Morgan Story;* Polly Bergen '57, Victor Borge '58. Dance arrs. for *Flower Drum Song* '58. Signed w. Columbia Records Feb. '59. Own LPs on Col., MGM; LPs for Carmen McRae (Kapp), Polly Bergen, Andre Kostelanetz (Col.), Anita Ellis (Epic).

Addr: 124 West 79th St., New York 24, N.Y.

HENDERSON, RICHARD ANDREW (Rick), *alto sax;* b. Washington, D.C., 4/25/28. Studied composition at Armstrong High. Led bands in D.C. clubs '46-9. Army '50-2. Duke Ellington March '53 to summer '55. Favs: Carter, Parker, Hodges. Featured w. Ellington on *Frivolous Banta, Stompin' At The Savoy* (Cap.). LPs w. Dinah Washington (Merc.), Ellington (Cap.).

HENDERSON, SKITCH CEDRIC, *piano, conductor;* b. Halstad, Minn., 1/27/18. Studied piano with Malcolm Frost of Portland, Ore., Roger Aubert of Paris; conducting with Albert Coates and Fritz Reiner; harmony with Schoenberg. Early work with territory bands, then theater orchestras; film and radio studios on West Coast 1939-40; pilot in US Air Force '41-5, piano soloist on Sinatra and Crosby radio shows '46. Toured with own dance band '47-9, then resumed radio work. Since '51, he has been under contract to NBC in New York, appearing as pianist, conductor and playing versatile role as leader and comedian on the Steve Allen TV show, *Tonight* 1955-6. Many appearances as guest conductor with New York Phil., Minneapolis Symph., etc. Though not a jazz musician, he has featured such excellent jazzmen as Doc Severinsen in his NBC orch. Favs: Art Tatum, Teddy Wilson. Ambition: To become conductor in opera, concert work. LPs: Seeco, Decca, Vict.

Addr: c/o National Broadcasting Company, RCA Building, New York 20, N.Y.

HENDRICKS, JOHN CARL (Jon), *songwriter, singer;* also *drums;* b. Newark, Ohio, 9/16/21. One of 17 children; of 15 survivors, he is the only one in music professionally. Sang hymns and spirituals with his mother in church. As child, sang at local banquets from 1929 and on radio in Toledo soon after his family moved there in '32. Art Tatum, a friend of the family, accompanied him from time to time. After completing high school, he lived for two years in Detroit, where he sang with the band of his brother-in-law, Jessie Jones, a violinist and trumpeter.

Hendricks was in the Army from '42 to Dec. '46, spending three years in Europe and singing in several European countries incl. France and Belgium where he sang in French. After his discharge, he stud. at the University of Toledo and during this time started teaching himself to play drums. As a drummer he worked for two years in Rochester, N.Y. where he organized what was at that time the only bop combo in town. Back in Toledo he had his own quartet with which he sang and played drums. Moving to NYC in '52, he became intensely active as a songwriter but had little or no success. He recorded a vocal version of *Four Brothers* with Teacho Wiltshire for a small label, since defunct. He worked mainly as an office clerk and as recently as '57 was a shipping clerk for Westminister Records. He did, however, enjoy one success as a writer when his song, *I Want You To Be My Baby,* written for Louis Jordan became a hit when Lillian Briggs recorded it. He was also heard on a King Pleasure record, *Don't Get Scared,* on Prestige, for which he did a vocal version of what had originally been a Lars Gullin instrumental solo.

In 1957, Hendricks teamed with Dave Lambert to produce a new version of *Four Brothers* for Decca. Soon after, Hendricks and Lambert joined forces with Annie Ross to produce a multi-tape recording in which each sang several parts to give the effect of a full band in versions of old Basie recordings for which Hendricks had set lyrics, not only to the ensembles but also to every note of the ad lib solos, taken directly off the records. The album, *Sing A Song Of Basie,* released early in '58 on ABC-Paramount, was so successful that in Aug. '58 the three organized as a permanent unit, teamed with the Basie band itself for a new album (this time without multi-tracking), *Sing Along With Basie,* on Roulette.

The novel technique adopted by Lambert, Hendricks and Ross, never before used by a singing group, added a new dimension to vocal jazz. The trio rose rapidly in popularity, played theatre dates with Basie, and during '59 Hendricks found himself in demand everywhere to write lyrics for countless other songs. He won the DB Critics Poll as New Vocal Star '59 and the trio won the DB Readers' Poll as number one vocal group '59.

John Hendricks by '60 had been adopted as the virtual poet-laureate of modern jazz. In fitting poignant, ingenious and often intensely humorous lyrics to music often so intricate that it would have seemed impossible to write or sing words to it, he showed a talent bordering on genius. As a solo singer he has an engaging and agreeably rhythmic style, but it is as a member of the trio and as a lyricist that he has made his real contribution to jazz. Hendricks, who has never learned to read music, plays a little piano and has written a few instrumental tunes, one of which, *Minor Catastrophe,* was recorded by the Pepper-Knepper Quintet (Metrojazz). Hendricks' favorite artists are Art Tatum, King Pleasure, and drummers Max Roach, Art Blakey, Sidney Catlett; his favorite composers are Quincy Jones, Gigi Gryce and Gil Evans. Own LP: Wor. Pac.; LPs w. Lambert, Hendricks & Ross (Wor. Pac., Col., ABC-Par. Roul.); King Pleasure (Pres.).

Addr: c/o Willard Alexander, 425 Park Ave., New York 22, N.Y.

HENDRICKSON, ALTON REYNOLDS (Al), *guitar, singer;* b. Eastland, Texas, 5/10/20. Studied w. Luis Elorriaga. Lived in Calif. since 1925. Joined Artie Shaw '40; Coast Guard '42-5. Worked w. Ray Linn combo; toured as singer and guitarist for six months w. Freddie Slack; played and sang w. Benny Goodman big band and sextet, also toured and/or rec. w. Boyd Raeburn, Ray Noble, Woody Herman, and other name bands. Active in studio work for movies and TV. Played for *I Want To Live, Staccato, M-Squad, New Orleans Beat,* etc. Signed contract w. Columbia Records '59. Favs: Segovia, Ch. Christian. Own LP, *Out of the Mist* (Lib.); LPs w. Billy May (Cap.), Shorty Rogers-Andre Previn (Vict.), *Guitars Inc.* (War. Bros.), *Gramercy Six* (Edison International), Buddy Bregman (Verve), *I Want To Live* (UA), Benny Goodman (Cap.), Jess Stacy (Atl.).

Addr: 15039 Encanto Drive, Sherman Oaks, Calif.

HENKE, MELVIN E. (Mel), *piano;* b. Chicago, Ill., 8/4/15. Studied at Chi. Coll. of Mus. Played w. various bands around Chi. and on ABC and NBC staffs, then moved to Calif. Pl. w. John Scott Trotter on Geo. Gobel TV show, 1954-5. Since then writing music for TV films incl. *Disneyland* series '55-7. Has occasionally recorded jazz solos in an unusual style, for Collector's Item '39-40, Vict. '46, Vitacoustic '46 and Tempo '48, '53. Own LPs on Contemp.

Addr: 20921 Waveview Drive, Topanga, Calif.

HENRY, ERNEST ALBERT (Ernie), *alto sax;* b. Brooklyn, N.Y., 9/3/26; d. Brooklyn, 12/29/57. Violin at 8, alto at 12. Discovered by Tadd Dameron whose band he joined at Famous Door, 1947. W. Fats Navarro shortly, also various combo gigs w. Ch. Ventura, Geo. Auld, Max Roach and Kenny Dorham. W. Dizzy Gillespie's band '48-9, Illinois Jacquet '50-1. Jam sessions in Brooklyn, then w. Thelonious Monk '56. Henry had been w. Dizzy Gillespie again for about a year when he died in his sleep one morning after playing w. the band at Birdland. Originally influenced by Charlie Parker, he was really beginning to develop on his own in the year before his death. Own LPs: Riverside; LPs w. Fats Navarro (Blue Note, Savoy), Dizzy Gillespie (GNP, Vict., Verve), T. Monk, K. Dorham, M. Gee (River.).

HENRY, HAYWOOD, *saxophones, clarinet;* b. Birmingham, Ala., 1/7/19. Pl. clar. in high school band; w. 'Bama State Collegians, later called the Erskine Hawkins' band. With Hawkins 15 years; in recent years freelanced on all saxes, clar. and flute. App. w. Fletcher

Henderson All Stars at Great South Bay festivals 1957 and '58. Fav: Harry Carney. LPs w. Rex Stewart leading Henderson alumni (UA, Uran.); Stewart (Fels.).

Addr: 555 Edgecombe Ave., New York, N.Y.

HENSEL, WES, *composer, trumpet;* b. Cleveland, Ohio, 6/10/19. Was w. Ch. Barnet 1946, Boyd Raeburn '47. Since 1948 has been w. Les Brown primarily as arr. In '59 pl. lead trumpet w. Jack Cathcart in Las Vegas. Fav. arrangement *You Are Too Beautiful* w. Dave Pell octet. Arrangements for Les incl. *Montoona Clipper, Flying Home, Ebony Rhapsody.* LPs w. Brown (Coral, Cap., Kapp); arrs. for Dave Pell (Atl., etc.).

Addr: 19420 Lorne, Reseda, Calif.

HERBERT, MORT (Morton Herbert Pelovitz), *bass, composer;* b. Somerville, N. J., 6/30/25. After two lessons on trumpet, taught himself bass in high school and began doing local gigs. Worked w. various swing bands during 1940s and '50s; in charge of music for the Navy in Pearl Harbor area '43-46. From Sept. '55 to Jan. '58 was featured at the Metropole in NYC w. Sol Yaged's group and has also gigged w. Sauter-Finegan, Marian McPartland, Don Elliott. Joined L. Armstrong, Jan. '58 and has toured w. him throughout US and overseas. Fav. own solo and arrangement: *I've Got You Under My Skin* in *Night People* (Savoy). Favs: Red Mitchell, P. Heath, C. Lombardi; fav. arrs: E. Sauter, N. Hefti, E. Wilkins. Own LP: *Night People* (Savoy); LP w. Don Elliott (Savoy).

Addr: Congressional Hotel, 483 West End Ave., New York 24, N. Y.

HERMAN, WOODROW CHARLES (Woody), *clarinet, alto sax, singer, leader;* b. Milwaukee, 5/16/13. Sang, danced in local theatres from age of six; started on saxophone at nine. While at high school, played with Joey Lichter's band. Left home 1930 with Tom Gerun's band (singer Tony Martin was also in the band's reed section); tried unsuccessfully to start his own band in '33, then spent a year as sideman with Harry Sosnik, Gus Arnheim. With Isham Jones, 1934-6, featured on tenor sax, clarinet and vocals in first records with Isham Jones Juniors for Decca. When Jones' band broke up, Herman took the key men and organized a group of his own on a cooperative basis. The orchestra rapidly became famous as "the band that plays the blues," though its repertoire also included many pop songs and non-blues instrumentals. Its biggest hit, the fast blues *Woodchopper's Ball,* recorded April 1939, eventually sold a million records. Key men in the band's early days included Saxie Mansfield, tenor; Joe Bishop, flugelhorn and arranger; Tommy Linehan, piano; Frank Carlson, drums; Walt Yoder, bass.

Changing gradually from a semi-Dixieland and blues identification, the band modernized itself in the early '40s with Ellington and Lunceford style arrangements. The addition in 1943 of Chubby Jackson on bass, and in '44 of such men as Neal Hefti and Ralph Burns (both playing and arranging), Bill Harris, Flip Phillips, Billy Bauer and Dave Tough, created a band that, before its break-up in Dec. 1946, earned many honors, some of them without precedent, including its own sponsored network radio show, 1945-6. It was voted best swing band in the 1945 *Down Beat* poll; given Silver Award by critics in '46 and '47 *Esquire* polls; won Met. poll, band division 1946. Herman led another big band, late '47 to '49; took a small group to Cuba in late '49, then reorganized a large orchestra, which at one time or another included Stan Getz, Terry Gibbs, Urbie Green, Red Mitchell, Milt Jackson, Zoot Sims, Al Cohn. The 1947-9 band was known as the "Four Brothers" band (see Getz, Giuffre); the later band, which won the Met. poll '53, was called the "Third Herd." The band made its first European tour in the spring of '54. Starting in late '55, when he led a small group in Las Vegas, Herman had a big band on a less regular basis. After leading a full orchestra throughout '58 (incl. a 10-week tour of Latin America subsidized by the US State Dept. in July-Sept.), he worked in '59 with several small combos, but toured Britain with a specially assembled Anglo-American band in the spring and led another *ad hoc* all star unit at the Monterey Jazz Festival in Oct. His sidemen in the late '50s incl. Vic Feldman, Bill Harris, Vince Guaraldi, Richie Kamuca, Arno Marsh, Nat Adderley, Zoot Sims.

Herman plays alto pleasantly on ballad numbers in a Hodges-derived style. As a clarinetist he is a capable performer, but has never attempted to modernize his style along the lines of the soloists in his bands. His singing at its best reflect many early blues influences. He made his greatest contribution to jazz history by keeping a big band together, often against severe economic odds, and maintaining an uncompromising jazz style, progressing with all the new trends of the '40s and providing an incubator for innumerable soloists and writers of major importance.

Own LPs: *Woodchopper's Ball* (Decca 8133), *The Swinging Herman Herd* (Bruns. 54024), *Summer Sequence* (Harm. 7093), *Bijou* (Harm. 7013), *Carnegie Hall '46* (Lion 70059), *The Three Herds* (Col. CL 592), *Classics In Jazz* (Cap. T324), *Hi Fl-ing Herd* (MGM E 3385), *The Woody Herman Band* (Cap. T 560), *Road Band* (Cap. T 658), *Jackpot* (Cap. T 748), *Blues Groove* (Cap. T 784), *Jazz, The Utmost* (Verve 8014), *Early Autumn* (Verve 2030), *Men From Mars* (Verve 8216), *Woody Herman '58* (Verve 8255), *Love Is The Sweetset Thing* (Verve 2096), *Songs For Hip Lovers* (Verve 2069), *The Herd Rides Again In Stereo* (Evst. SDBR 1003), *Sextet At The Roundtable* (Roul. 25067), *Songs For Tired Lovers* w. Erroll Garner (Col. CL 651); LPs w. Buck Clayton (Col. CL 567), Jimmy Witherspoon (Hifijazz 421).

Addr: 8620 Hollywood Blvd., Los Angeles, Calif.

HEYWOOD, EDDIE, JR., *piano, composer;* b. Atlanta, Ga., 12/4/15. Began studying 1923 with his father, a pianist and well-known combo leader; made prof. debut 1930 in local theatre band. Joined Clarence Love, 1935. To NYC '38, played Harlem clubs. First attracted attention on jazz scene w. Benny Carter '39-40. Played for shows at Village Vanguard; formed own sextet late '43, made name through pop-style arr. of *Begin The Beguine*. Forced to stop playing in '47 owing to partial paralysis of hands, he resumed in '51 and thereafter worked mainly with a trio. His work became increasingly commercial during the '50s, aiming at the pop rather than the jazz market. Won Esq. New Star award '45. Best jazz perfs. are on Coral 57095, *Featuring Eddie Heywood*. Other own LPs: Epic, Vict., Decca, Em., MGM; LPs w. Billie Holiday, Ed Hall (Comm.), Ella Fitzgerald (Decca).

Addr: 10 Jefferson Place, White Plains, N. Y.

HIBBLER, ALBERT (Al), *singer;* b. Little Rock, Ark., 8/16/15. Blind from birth. Early infl. was Pha Terrell of the Andy Kirk band. After winning amateur contests in Memphis, joined Dub Jenkins' band; led own band in San Antonio, Tex., then toured the South w. Jay McShann band (Dec. 1942). After leaving McShann and free-lancing in NYC, he made a national name while touring with the Duke Ellington band, 1943-51, then went out on his own. Much of Hibbler's popularity was achieved by the use of grotesque distortions, described by Duke Ellington as "tonal pantomime" and valid more as entertainment than as jazz or pop singing. He won the Esq. New Star Award as male singer, 1947; DB award as band vocalist, 1948-9. Own LPs on Verve, Bruns., Decca, Atl., Score, Argo; LPs w. Ellington (Vict., Col.), Basie (Verve).

HIGGINBOTHAM, JACK (Jay C.), *trombone;* b. Atlanta, Ga., 5/11/06. Raised in Cincinnati, where he joined Wes Helvey's band 1924-5. Worked in Buffalo w. Eugene Primos and Jimmy Harrison, '26-7; in NYC Sept. '28, joined Luis Russell, leaving in '31 to join Chick Webb for a few months, then w. Fletcher Henderson to '33. With Mills' Blue Rhythm Band (later called Lucky Millinder's orch.) '34-6; Louis Armstrong '37-40, then joined the sextet formed by Red Allen, who had been with him in all the above bands through the '30s. Allen and Higginbotham were teamed throughout most of the '40s; later they worked in Boston and NYC jointly and separately. Higginbotham had his own group in Cleveland, '55, returned to Boston in May for several club jobs, then opened at the Metropole Cafe in NYC with a Dixieland-style group '56 and remained until the summer of '59, except for a European tour in Oct. '58 with Sammy Price. App. at Randall's Island festival with Henderson reunion group.

Though he is completely ignored or given only a passing mention in the leading books on jazz, J. C. Higginbotham was rated by Louis Armstrong, Tommy Dorsey and countless other musicians as a major factor in the development of jazz trombone, the foremost exponent of the gutty, extrovert style characterized by a forceful tone and savage attack. He made many record dates as a sideman in the '30s with Lil Armstrong, Mezzrow, Coleman Hawkins et al. He won the *Esquire* Gold Award 1945, *DB* poll '41-2-3-4, *Metronome* poll '43-4-5. LPs w. Red Allen (Vict. LPM 1509, Verve 8233), Louis Armstrong (Decca 8284), Coleman Hawkins (Vict. LJM 1017), w. Hawkins in *Guide To Jazz* (Vict. LPM 1393), Lionel Hampton (Vict. LJM 1000), *The Big Challenge* w. Cootie Williams and Rex Stewart (Jazztone 1268), Metronome All Stars (Harm. HL 7044, Cam. 426), Fletcher Henderson All Stars: *Cool Fever* (Uran. 2012), *The Big Reunion* (Jazz. 1258), *Jazz At Stereoville* (Uran. 2004), *Callin' The Blues* w. Tiny Grimes (Pres. 7144).

Addr: 152 West 118th Street, New York 26, N. Y.

HIGGINS, BILLY, *drums;* b. Los Angeles, Calif., 10/11/36. Began drums at 12; pl. in r & b combos at 19 for a couple of years. Worked w. Red Mitchell; Ornette Coleman '59-60. LPs w. Mitchell (Contemp.), Coleman (Contemp., Atl.), Teddy Edwards (Metro.), Joe Castro (Atl.).

Addr: 11913 N. Bromont, Pacoima, Calif.

HIGGINS, HAYDN (Ed), *piano;* also *clarinet, bass;* b. Cambridge, Mass., 2/21/32. Mother, a pianist, works in Boston as accompanist. Prof. debut in Chicago night clubs while studying at Northwestern Sch. of Mus. 1950. Dixieland jobs w. George Brunis, Jimmy Ille '52-4; Army '54-6. While in service, went to Puerto Rico, worked w. local Latin bands, conducted and arranged big band on San Juan TV. Won All-Army talent contest in Caribbean area as piano soloist in '55. In Fall of '56 he formed his own trio, which worked regularly at London House and Cloister Inn from May '57. An opponent of labels such as "hard bop", "dixieland", etc., he believes he can express himself without pledging allegiance to any musical faction. Fav: O. Peterson. Own LP: Replica. LPs w. Sandy Mosse, Cy Touff (Argo), Eddie South (Merc.), Paul Severson (Replica).

Addr: 2045 W. Berwyn, Chicago 25, Ill.

HIGUERA, FRED, *drums;* b. Oakland, Calif., 1909. Father a prof. drummer; began stud. drums at seven; pl. first prof. job at 15. Moved to SF 1930, pl. with various hotel, night club and dance hall bands. Played in Army band '43-5; joined Bob Scobey '49. Enjoys Latin music and has stud. all types of Latin rhythms. Favs: Shelly Manne, Max Roach, Gene Krupa, and traditionalists Zutty Singleton, Baby Dodds, Ben Pollack. LPs w. Bob Scobey (Verve, Vict., GTJ).

HILL, ALEXANDER (Alex), *piano, composer;* b. Little Rock, Ark.; d. NYC, 2/1/36. Received earliest training from his mother, had own group, 1924. Worked around Chicago from about 1925 on as pianist and arranger for Jimmie Noone, L. Armstrong and others. In 1930 went to NYC where he arranged for Claude Hopkins, Benny Carter, Andy Kirk, Fats Waller, others. One of the better and less recognized arrangers of the early swing era, Hill had planned to start his own band, but his career was ended when he became a victim of tuberculosis. Hill occas. pl. piano on rec. dates, incl. one session w. E. Condon (*The Eel*, etc., 1933). LP: two nos. in *Piano Jazz, Vol. 2* (Bruns. 54013).

HILL, ROGER (Buck), *tenor sax;* b. Washington, D.C., 1928. Started on soprano sax at 13. Att. Armstrong High where he had same music teacher who taught Duke Ellington. A professional since 1943, Hill also drives a taxicab during the day. Favs: Coltrane, Rollins, Webster, Hawkins, Young. "He plays with a big, firm tone, a direct, uncluttered style and effortless swing."—Paul Sampson, *Washington Post and Times Herald.* LP w. Charlie Byrd, *Jazz At The Showboat* (Offbeat).

HILL, BERTHA (Chippie), *singer;* b. Charleston, S.C., 1905; d. 5/7/50, in auto accident. Made her debut at Leroy's in Harlem; joined Ma Rainey's show as dancer and singer; later, in Chicago, sang with King Oliver at the Palladium Dance Hall. In 1925-6 she made a series of blues records accompanied by Louis Armstrong, Richard M. Jones, et al. In obscurity from about 1930 to 1946, working at many menial jobs until she was rediscovered with the help of Rudi Blesh, who brought her back into the limelight with a series of record sessions for his Circle label in '46, accompanied by Lee Collins, Baby Dodds, Lovie Austin and other jazz figures of the 1920s. She appeared in night clubs 1947, took part in the Paris Jazz Festival '48, and in a Bessie Smith Memorial concert at New York's Town Hall, Jan. '48. A contemporary of Bessie Smith, who was her prototype, she excelled in the same brand of honest, basic blues singing. LP: one no. in *History of Classic Jazz* (River).

HILL, THEODORE (Teddy), *leader, saxes;* b. Birmingham, Ala., 12/7/09. Played tenor with Luis Russell band 1929-31; started own band 1934, playing frequently at Savoy Ballroom in Harlem. Personnel incl. Roy Eldridge, Dickie Wells, Bill Coleman and Chu Berry (Perfect records 1935); Frankie Newton and Cecil Scott (Vocalion '36, Bluebird '37); Dizzy Gillespie (Bluebird May '37). Toured England and France in summer of '37. Inactive as bandleader after 1940, but well known as operator of Minton's Playhouse, often called "birthplace of bop."

Addr: Hotel Cecil, West 118th St., New York, N. Y.

HI-LO'S. Vocal quartet organized in Apr. 1953, discovered by Jerry Fielding, who arranged their first rec. date for now defunct Trend label. Later rec. for Starlite, Col., seen at Hollywood Bowl and in movies; rapidly rose to become most popular jazz-oriented vocal group of kind. See Clark Burroughs, Bob Morse, Gene Puerling, Don Shelton. LPs: Col.

HINES, EARL KENNETH (Fatha), *piano, songwriter;* b. Duquesne, Pa., 12/28/05. Father played trumpet in Eureka Brass band; mother was organist. Stud. piano from 1914 w. Pittsburgh teachers; planned to be concert artist. While in Schenley High Sch. in Pittsburgh, led trio in clubs; first full-time job with singer Lois Deppe in Chicago '22. Toured w. Carroll Dickerson, played w. Sammy Stewart at Sunset Cafe, Jimmie Noone at Apex and for a while, in '27, Louis Armstrong. In Dec. '28 he opened with his own big band at the Grand Terrace in Chicago; from then until '48, when his band broke up and he joined Armstrong, he led his own big band continuously. After leaving Armstrong in '51 he worked with small groups on the West Coast. Settled in San Francisco, '56; toured Britain and Continent w. Jack Teagarden, fall '57. Back in SF, led own band with Muggsy Spanier et al at the Hangover, playing and talking on widely-heard weekly broadcasts for US Treasury Dept., also occasionally touring.

Hines is one of the great pianists of jazz history; his style, amazing to musicians when first noticed in the late 1920s, was virtually unchanged except for added technical polish in 1960. His greatest impact was the result of the series of records he made under the Louis Armstrong Hot Five name (see Armstrong), through which he earned a reputation as "the trumpet style pianist" because of the incisive use of single note lines in his right hand and dynamic effect of octaves and tremolos. His work did indeed have (and still has) an almost brassy quality, rhythmically bright and often quite intricate, especially by the standards of the men who surrounded him in the early days. Hines' style was the source of inspiration for countless jazz pianists during his heyday and it was not until the advent of Teddy Wilson in the mid-'30s that an influence of comparable significance made itself felt in jazz piano.

Hines additionally earned immortality as a bandleader, first during his years of nightly network broadcasts from the Grand Terrace and again in the '40s when the orchestra became a cradle of bebop. In the early years the sidemen included arrangers and tenor saxmen Jimmy Mundy and Budd Johnson; singer-trumpeter Walter Fuller; clarinetists Omer Simeon and Darnell Howard, and such pop singers as Herb Jeffries, Arthur Lee Simpkins and Ida James. The later band included Dizzy Gillespie, Charlie Parker, Bennie Green, Benny Harris, Wardell Gray, Shadow Wilson, Billy Eckstine, Sarah Vaughan. Popular hits during the '30s were *Deep Forest,* Hines' radio theme (co-composed by British writer Reg. Foresythe) and *Rosetta,* Hines' best-known tune. His other early song hits included *My Monday Date,* recorded with Armstrong. His hit records of the '40s included *Jelly Jelly, Boogie-Woogie on St. Louis Blues, Stormy Monday Blues* (all rec. for Victor subsidiary, Bluebird). Hines' own favorites are his records of *Second Balcony Jump, I Got It Bad* and *The Earl.*

Popular before the days of jazz polls, Hines won only one such trophy, the *Esquire* Silver Award in '44. His most important early solos, cut in '28 as piano rolls and issued on a 10 inch Atlantic LP, are no longer available; the best vintage Hines can be heard on

The Louis Armstrong Story, in Vol. 3 of Columbia CL 853.

Own LPs: *Oh, Father!* (Epic 3223), *Earl Hines Trio* (Epic 3501), *Fatha Plays Fats* (Fant. 3217), *Solos* (Fant. 3238); selections in all of the following: *Great Jazz Pianists* (Cam. 328), *Guide To Jazz* (Vict. LPM 1393), *The Best Of The Big Name Bands* (Cam. 368), *The Art of Jazz Piano* (Epic 3295), *The Jazz Makers* (Col. CL 1036). LPs w. Armstrong (Decca 8041), Benny Carter (Contemp. 3561), Barbara Dane (Dot 3177).

Addr: 815 Trestle Glen Rd., Oakland, Calif.

HINTON, MILTON J. (Milt), *bass;* b. Vicksburg, Miss., 6/23/10. Mother still active as music teacher and church organist. Starting on violin at 13, he played bass while at high school in Chicago and was with Eddie South on and off from '31-6, also working w. Erskine Tate. Played w. Zutty Singleton at Three Deuces in Chicago '36; joined Cab Calloway later that year and remained with him until '51, then worked East Side night clubs in NYC with Joe Bushkin, Jackie Gleason, Phil Moore. After two months w. Count Basie, he toured with Louis Armstrong July '53-Feb. '54 including a visit to Japan. In '54 did CBS staff work in NYC with Ray Bloch, Teddy Wilson, Russ Case, and worked w. Jimmy McPartland at Metropole. Benny Goodman combo at Basin Street, Mar. 1955. From '56-'60 appeared only occasionally at concerts, confining his work mainly to intensive studio activity in recording and TV. Long admired for his superb musicianship and tone, he won *Esq.* Silver award in '44 (tied with Al Morgan). Favs: Blanton, Safranski, Pettiford. Own LP: Beth; one feat. track in *After Hours Jazz* (Epic); LPs w. John Benson Brooks (River.), Tony Scott (Bruns., Vict.), Paul Barbarin (Atl.), Chu Berry (Epic), Buck Clayton (Col.), Rex Stewart (Gr. Award), Zoot Sims (Dawn), Ralph Burns (Decca), *Basses Loaded,* Hal McKusick, George Russell, Al Cohn, Joe Newman, Freddie Greene, Manny Albam (Vict.).

Addr: 106-14 Ruscoe St., Jamaica 5, L. I., N. Y.

HIPP, JUTTA, *piano;* b. Leipzig, Germany, 2/4/25. Stud. painting at Acad. of Arts, joined local Hot Club for jam sessions before and during World War II. When Russians occupied Leipzig and closed the Acad. she fled with her family to Munich, pl. w. Ch. Tabor; rec. w. Hans Koller '52. Own quintet in Frankfurt '53-5. Arrived in NY 11/18/55; played at Hickory House for several months in '56 using trio w. Peter Ind, Ed Thigpen. Her style underwent a change from a Tristano to a H. Silver influence and lost much of its individuality, she slipped into obscurity and in '58-60 was working mainly in non-music day jobs. Early work showed great promise. LPs: *Cool Europe* (MGM), own trio, quintet (Blue Note), *Dass 1st Jazz* (Dec.).

Addr: Prescot Hotel, 61st & Broadway, New York 23, N. Y.

HITE, LES, *leader, alto sax;* b. DuQuoin, Ill., 2/13/03. Lived in Los Angeles during '20s and took over leadership of Paul Howard's Quality Serenaders in '30. Louis Armstrong fronted this band for long periods from '30-2, when the personnel included Lionel Hampton on drums, Marshall Royal, Lawrence Brown, etc. Hite remained active as a bandleader until the early '40s and later alumni included trombonist Britt Woodman, guitarist-blues singer T-Bone Walker, bassist Al Morgan. While the band was in the East, in 1942, the personnel included Dizzy Gillespie. Never active as an instrumentalist, Hite later retired from the band business and opened his own successful booking agency. LP: In vol. 4 of *The Louis Armstrong Story* (Col.), what was then Hite's band backs Armstrong.

Addr: 2021 So. Redondo Blvd., Los Angeles 16, Calif.

HITZ, WILLIAM F. (Bill), *clarinet, saxophone, flute;* b. Philadelphia, Pa., 12/22/22. Stud. sax at 12; st. playing dances when in high school. In 1943, pl. with Jack Teagarden; w. Gene Krupa '44-5; later Charlie Ventura, Buddy Rich, Charlie Barnet and Ralph Flanagan. Fav: Buddy De Franco; names Lyle Murphy as imp. influence. Own LP: *Music for This Swingin' Age* (Decca).

Addr: 7001 Glasgow Ave., Los Angeles, Calif.

HIXSON, RICHARD (Dick), *bass trombone;* b. Western Pennsylvania, 5/17/24. Father pl. trombone, mother piano. Took up piano at age 10. Pl. w. local dance bands around Greensburg, Pa. Rec. w. Les & Larry Elgart, Kai Winding, Luther Henderson, Miles Davis' *Porgy and Bess* (Col.), *Trombones Inc.* (War. Bros.).

Addr: 11 Cedar Lane, Croton-On-Hudson, N. Y.

HODEIR, ANDRE, *composer, critic;* b. Paris, France, 1/22/21. Studied violin from 5; later at Nat. Cons., where he won three awards (harmony, counterpoint, mus. history); joined André Ekyan Sextet as violinist 1942, under name of Claude Laurence. As arranger, worked w. Django Reinhardt for movie *Le Village de la Colère,* 1946. Arr. *Autour d'un Récif* for Tony Proteau orch. w. Don Byas, '49; arr. & cond. session for James Moody w. strings, '51; for Bernard Peiffer "concrete music" experiment 1952; for own band, *St. Tropez,* '52; for Bobby Jaspar band *Paradoxe I* and *Sanguine,* '54. Since '54 has worked intermittently with a unit he organized, Jazz Groupe de Paris w. Guerin, Michelot et al. President of Academie du Jazz in Paris, 1954. Was editor of *Jazz Hot* magazine 1947-50; as music critic, has had five books published incl. *Hommes et Problèmes du Jazz,* publ. Flammarion 1954, one of the most sensitive and analytical books on jazz, publ. in USA as *Jazz: Evolution & Essence.* Visited USA, Feb.-May '57, rec. w. American jazzmen. Wrote several film scores incl. *Une Parisienne* (Brigitte Bardot), '57; *Palais Ideal, Chutes de Pierre,* '58. In '57-8 own works were performed at German mus. fest. and w. Modern Jazz Quartet at Cannes Jazz fest. New book *Since Debussy* publ. 1960. Favs: Gil Evans, Ellington.

Own LPs: Savoy; *Kenny Clarke Plays André Hodeir* (Epic).

HODES, ARTHUR W. (Art), *piano;* b. Nikoliev, Russia, 11/14/04. Father and uncle sang in choir in Russia. Family immigrated to Chicago when he was six months old. Stud. at Hull House. First heard jazz through bassist Earl Murphy; later spent much time hanging around Armstrong band. First steady job 1925 at Rainbow Gardens. Went on road in 1926 with Wolverines (Beiderbecke was not in band then). From 1927 he formed a close and long association with Wingy Manone and worked in various combos with Krupa, Teschemacher, Bud Freeman, Spanier and Floyd O'Brien at Liberty Inn, Derby and Harry's New York Bar. Also played in big band fronted briefly by Wingy. Moving to NYC in 1938, he worked almost exclusively with small combos, leading his own groups off and on from 1939. During the '40s he became active in several media as a crusader for traditionalist jazz, running his own disc jockey show on WNYC, and, from Feb. '43 to Nov. '47, his own magazine, *The Jazz Record.* In recent years he has been back in Chicago, working at various clubs with his own combo and presenting jam sessions in the area. Joined staff at Park Forest Cons., teaching pop piano for all ages, July '58. Pl. with Austin High Gang at *Playboy* festival '59. Articles for *Jazz Review, Second Line, Chi. Tribune.* Has written several tunes, incl. *Pagin' Mr. Jelly* rec. by Bob Scobey. Hodes plays in a simple blues style inspired by Morton, James P. Johnson and other early jazzmen. Fav. own solos: *K.M.H. Drag* (Blue Note); *Sweet Georgia Brown* (Em.). Favs: Hines, Tatum and "Many I admired and learned from who are now dead or not playing professionally." Own LPs: Merc., Dotted Eighth; four nos. in *Gems of Jazz, Vol. 5* (Decca), one no. in *History of Classic Jazz* (River.).

Addr: 54 Ash St., Park Forest, Ill.

HODGES, JOHN CORNELIUS (Johnny or Rabbit), *alto sax;* b. Cambridge, Mass., 7/25/06. Started on drums, then took up piano, beginning on sax at 14. Self-taught at first, he worked as a youth for Sidney Bechet, who gave him some schooling and presented him with a soprano sax. Played w. Bobby Sawyer 1925, Lloyd Scott '26, Chick Webb '27. Joined Duke Ellington early '28 and remained with him until March '51, when he formed his own band. This group enjoyed an early success in the r & b market with a Mercury record, *Castle Rock;* however, Hodges gave up the band in '55, worked that summer in NYC in the daily Ted Steele TV show, then rejoined Ellington and resumed his role as a mainstay of the orchestra.

During his early years with Ellington, Hodges gained world renown as a swinging jazz musician; he and Benny Carter reigned jointly as alto sax kings during the early '30s. At this period, Hodges also occasionally played soprano sax. Starting in the mid-'30s, he expanded his fame through a series of slow, melodic solos in which his sweet tone and effective use of glissandi, since widely imitated, became his main identification.

During the late '30s, he made record sessions with his own contingent from the Ellington band, also with groups led by Barney Bigard, Cootie Williams, Teddy Wilson, Lionel Hampton. He won the Esq. Silver Award '44, '46, Gold Award '45; DB poll '40-9; Met. poll '45-7; DB Critics' poll '59.

Own LPs: Epic 3105; three tracks each in *The Duke's Men* (Epic 3108) and *Ellington Sidekicks* (Epic 3237); Verve 8317, 8145, 8180, 8150, 8151, 8179, 8136, 8139, tracks in *Alto Saxes* (8126); LPs w. Eddie Heywood (Coral 57095), Earl Hines (Gr. Award 318), Duke Ellington (Bruns. 54007, Vict. LPM 1092, 1715, 1364, Cam. 459, Rondo. 7, Col. CL 825, 848, 558, 872, 951, 933, 934, 1085, 1245, 8166, 8127); Metronome All Stars (Cam. 426, Harm. 7044), Billy Taylor (Argo 650).

Addr: 555 Edgecombe Ave., New York 32, N. Y.

HOFFMAN, JEAN, *electric piano, singer;* b. Portland, Ore., 9/22/30. From a musical family, she started classical piano at 5, but played largely by ear; started sitting in w. local combos around '53. Working as a single, she added vocals. Married drummer Bill Young and in 1957 they formed a trio. Favs: Bartok, B. Young, C. Parker. Own LP: Fant.

Addr: 245 Bristol Blvd., San Leandro, Calif.

HOGAN, GRANVILLE T. (G.T.), *drums;* b. Galveston, Tex., 1/16/29. Pl. tenor sax in high school. Drums w. Randy Weston and other combos in NYC; in Paris w. Bud Powell 1959. Favs: Kenny Clarke, Max Roach, Philly Joe Jones. LPs w. Kenny Drew, Kenny Dorham (River.); Randy Weston in *New Faces at Newport* (Metro.).

HOLIDAY, BILLIE (Lady Day) (Eleanor Gough McKay), *singer;* b. Baltimore, Md., 4/7/15; d. New York City, 7/17/59. Her father, Clarence Holiday, played banjo and guitar in Fletcher Henderson's band in the early '30s. Billie moved to NYC in '29 with her mother. Within a year she was singing in such Harlem clubs as Jerry Preston's Log Cabin, The Yeah Man, etc. She was discovered by John Hammond and Benny Goodman, and made her record debut with Goodman in Nov. '33. Her international fame began with a series of records she made with Teddy Wilson's orch. July '35-Jan. '39, and with a number of all-star bands under her own name starting in July '36. During those years she was vocalist for a while with the bands of Count Basie '37, and Artie Shaw '38. Throughout the '40s and '50s she toured in theaters and night clubs as a solo attraction. Her only feature film was *New Orleans,* an inferior quasi-jazz musical in '46. She made her first European tour with the *Jazz Club USA* unit Jan. '54 and was again seen in Europe briefly in late '58. During her last few years the many tragedies in her personal life, marked by endless and hopeless battles with narcotic addiction, took a heavy toll on her voice, but almost until the end enough of the original quality remained to enable her at times to recapture at least a shred of the glory of her early years. She made her final appearance at a benefit concert at the Phoenix Theater in Manhattan in June '59 and a few days later was taken to a hospital where, because of the US laws that treat narcotic addiction as a crime, she was arrested on her death bed.

Though the subject of what is and what is not jazz singing has led to many differences of opinion among experts, Billie Holiday's voice had in it elements that were indisputably the essence of jazz. Hers was one of the incomparable voices that jazz produced in the '30s. Some observers likened her to Bessie Smith, and she admitted to a great admiration for Louis Armstrong, but her debt to any earlier artist was minimal. The timbre of her voice, despite its gradual deepening through the years, remained unique even when her intonation began to falter. The coarse yet warmly emotional quality of this sound, and the exquisite delicacy of her phrasing and dynamic nuances, were often given added lustre by the support she gained from her long association with Lester Young and other members of the Basie band on her earlier records, and with the more elaborate but usually effective backgrounds on later records for Decca, some of which included strings. Her greatest successes both artistically and commercially included *Strange Fruit* and *Fine and Mellow,* both recorded '39 for Commodore, and *Lover Man* in '44 for Decca. She won the following awards: Esq. Gold Award '44, '47, Silver Award '45, '46. Met. poll '45-6. Own LPs: Col. CL 637, MGM 3764, Comm. 30008, Col. CL 1157, Decca 8215, 8701, 8702, DXB 161, Verve 8338-2, 8096, 8257, 8074, 8026, 8027, 8099, 8197, 8239, 8302, 8329, one half of *Ella Fitzgerald and Billie Holiday at Newport* (8234), one half of *Jazz Recital* (8098); tracks w. Eddie Heywood (Comm. 30011); Score 4014; one track in *The Jazz Makers* (Col. CL 1036), one in *The Sound of Jazz* (Col. CL 1098); one track w. Benny Goodman in *The Vintage Goodman* (Col. CL 821); *The Unforgettable Lady Day* (two LPs) (Verve MG V-8338-2); *The Billie Holiday Story* (two LPs) (Decca DXB-161).

HOLIDAY, JOE (Joseph A. Befumo), *tenor sax;* b. Agira, Sicily, 5/10/25. Father a clarinetist; family moved to US when he was six months old, settled in Newark, N. J. Has had own group since '45. First recorded for King '50, then Prestige, making first hit with *This Is Happiness.* Favs: Stan Getz, Wardell Gray. Own LP: Decca.

HOLLAND, HERBERT LEE (Peanuts), *trumpet;* b. Norfolk, Va., 2/9/10. Played with Alphonso Trent in the Southwest 1929-33; led own band '33-8, also played brief spells during this period with Willie Bryant, Jimmie Lunceford. Came to NYC 1939, played with Coleman Hawkins; Fletcher Henderson 1940; Ch. Barnet 1941-6. In 1946 he went to Europe with Don Redman; has remained there ever since, touring the continent as a single or with his own combo. Numerous records in Paris with Don Byas, Billy Taylor et al. LPs w. Barnet (Decca), Mezz Mezzrow (Ducretet-Thompson).

HOLLEY, MAJOR QUINCY JR., *bass* (also *tuba, 'cello*), b. Detroit, Mich., 7/10/24. From musical family; stud. violin at seven, later tuba; in Navy band four years, then stud. bass on G.I. bill at Groth School of Music. Worked w. Dexter Gordon and Wardell Gray in Calif.; briefly w. Charlie Parker and Ella Fitzgerald; w. Oscar Peterson '50; worked on BBC-TV in London '54-6; w. Woody Herman '58, touring South America w. him for the State Dept.; Al Cohn-Zoot Sims '59-60. Is expert at bowing bass and humming simultaneously in style of Slam Stewart. LPs w. Oscar Peterson (Verve); Michel Legrand (Col.); Dickie Wells, Vic Dickenson (Felsted).

Addr: 870 Jefferson Ave., Brooklyn 21, N. Y.

HOLMAN, WILLIS LEONARD (Bill), *composer, tenor sax;* b. Olive, Cal., 5/21/27. Raised in Santa Ana. Navy 1944-6. Studied engineering at UCLA '48; counterpoint w. Russ Garcia, and general music studies at Westlake College '48-51. Played w. Ch. Barnet '51, joined Stan Kenton Feb. '52. First composition recorded was *Invention for Guitar and Trumpet* rec. by Kenton on Cap. In 1956-7 he worked mainly with Shorty Rogers in Hollywood. In 1958 he and drummer Mel Lewis had a hard-swinging, East Coast style quintet in the LA area. André Previn has written that Holman is "most assuredly a first-rate saxophonist, but his true instrument is the orchestra, and he plays it with musicianship, honesty and brilliance." Hundreds of records of Holman's work attest to the skilful, swing-conscious nature of his writing; they include a whole LP by the M. Ferguson band (Merc.); own LP (Andex); *Fabulous Bill Holman* (Coral); many Kenton LPs; Demsey Wright (Andex). Film work incl. *Swamp Women* (1956), *Get Out of Town* ('59). LPs as saxophonist: *West Coast Wailers* (Atl.), Shelly Manne (Contemp.), Conte Candoli (Beth.).

Addr: 6923 Mammoth Ave., VanNuys, Cal.

HOLMES, CHARLES WILLIAM (Charlie), *alto sax;* b. Boston, Mass., 1/27/10. Childhood friend of Johnny Hodges. Studied oboe, played with Boston Civic Symphony 1926. To NYC '27. Played w. Chick Webb, then Luis Russell; Louis Armstrong until '40. W. Bobby Burnet '41, Cootie Williams '42-5; toured Far East w. USO show '45-6 w. Jesse Stone. After working w. John Kirby '47, freelanced in NYC. In recent years has been working w. an insurance company, gigging w. Joe Garland's band on week-ends. Was considered one of the better Hodges-styles altos of the '30s. Rec. w. Al Sears for King '52; solo on *Steady Eddie.*

Addr: 400 West 150th St., New York 31, N. Y.

HOLMES, HAROLD, *bass;* also *guitar, tuba, composer;* b. Mobile, Ala., 10/10/13. Mother, sister, brothers all play instruments. Took up tenor banjo at 15. Pl. in Erskine Hawkins' Alabama St. Revelers for a year, then turned prof. With Don Alberts 1937, George Baquet 1938-43, Lucky Millinder '49-50, Ivory Joe Hunter '50-1, Bill Johnson '51-4, then moved to Canada. Fav: Jimmy Blanton. LP w. Pat Riccio (Quality).

Addr: 425 Sherbourne St., Toronto, Ont., Canada.

HOLMES, MARTY (Martin Hausman), *tenor sax;* also *piano, composer;* b. Brooklyn, N. Y., 2/7/25. Stud. violin at age six; st. sax at 15, clar. at 16. Self-taught on piano. Worked with various dance bands in the late 1940s and '50s incl. Jerry Wald, Bobby Byrne, Tommy Reynolds, Neal Hefti and Tito Puente. Formed own octet in '57. Favs: Stan Getz, Zoot Sims. Own LP: *Art Ford's Party for Marty* (Jub.).

Addr: 84-20 Austin St., Kew Gardens, L. I., N. Y.

HOLT, ISAAC (Red), *drums;* b. Rosedale, Miss., 5/16/32. Sister plays classical piano. Took up drums in second year at Crane Tech. High in Chi. Played in teen-age band with Ramsey Lewis and El Dee Young. Pl. in 17th Reg. of 4th Div. Army Band in Germany 1955. W. Ramsey Lewis trio from late '56. LPs w. Lewis (Argo, Merc.), James Moody (Argo), Ken Nordine (Dot).

Addr: 5317 Ellis Ave., Chicago 15, Ill.

HOMER, BEN, *composer;* b. Meriden, Conn., 6/27/17. New England Conservatory 35-7, to NYC '38; wrote for Bob Chester, Jack Teagarden, Raymond Scott, Nat Shilkret, Artie Shaw, Tommy Dorsey. Best known as staff writer with Les Brown for several years beginning 1940, his biggest hit being his own composition *Sentimental Journey.* Since '53, active as minister in Jehovah's Witnesses.

Addr: 18031 Welby Way, Reseda, Cal.

HOOKER, JOHN LEE, *singer, guitar;* b. Clarksdale, Miss., 1917. Father and one brother ministers. Sang in spiritual groups at 14, took up guitar at 16 under tutelage of Will Moore, who was well known in that part of the country. Left Clarksville at 21, went to Knoxville, Tenn. for a while, then moved to Detroit in 1941. Marshall Stearns has called him "one of the few truly authentic exponents of archaic guitar style, a style which may well trace back to Civil War days." Own LPs on River., Vee-Jay.

HOPE, ELMO, *piano, songwriter;* b. New York City, 6/27/23. Parents from West Indies. Was childhood friend of Bud Powell, with whom he spent many hours listening to classical records. Won medals for solo recitals from 1938. Toured for a couple of years with Joe Morris' r & b band; then free-lanced with Clifford Brown, Sonny Rollins et al. Style closely resembles Powell's. In the late '50s he migrated to Calif. where he played w. Harold Land, etc. In the fall of '59 he pl. w. Lionel Hampton at the Moulin Rouge in Hollywood. Own LPs: Pres.; one track in *The Hard Swing; Have Blues, Will Travel* (Wor. Pac.); LPs w. Clifford Brown, Lou Donaldson (Blue Note), *Two Tenors* (Mobley & Coltrane), Sonny Rollins, Jackie McLean, Frank Foster (Pres.), Curtis Counce (Dooto).

HOPKINS, CLAUDE, *piano, leader;* b. Washington, D.C., 8/3/03. AB, Howard University, where his parents were on faculty. To NYC 1924 with Wilbur Sweatman. To Europe late '25 as mus. dir. for Josephine Baker (band incl. S. Bechet). Returned in '27; led own group at Crystal Cavern in Washington. Took over Charlie Skeets band at Cocoanut Grove in Harlem 1930 and moved to Savoy Ballroom; Roseland '31-5; Cotton Club '35-6. During those years, his was one of the most popular Negro bands in the country, with considerable network air time. Band incl. Edmond Hall, Vic Dickenson; Fred Norman, trombonist and arranger; Ovie Alston, Jabbo Smith, trumpets. Broke up band 1940; worked as arranger for Phil Spitalny, Tommy Tucker, Abe Lyman, etc. From '44-7 he was at the Zanzibar on Broadway, leading bands of various sizes. Took novelty quintet on tour '48-9; own combo at Cafe Society '50-1; joined George Wein, in Dixieland combo, Mahogany Hall in Boston '52-3; joined Red Allen at Metropole NYC, 1954-5. Pl. there and at Central Plaza since w. various groups. LPs w. Cozy Cole (Gr. Award), *Red Allen at Newport* (Verve), Juanita Hall (Ctpt.), *Golden Era of Dixieland Jazz* (Design).

Addr: 507 West 152nd St., New York 31, N. Y.

HOPKINS, SAM (Lightnin'), *singer, guitar;* b. Centerville, Texas, 3/15/12. Learned to sing listening to his cousin, Texas Alexander, and to Blind Lemon Jefferson. Worked on farm for many years, playing and singing occasionally; moved to Houston and took up music full time in '46, recording locally and later that year in Los Angeles. During the '50s he worked as an itinerant singer, wandering the streets of Houston, rarely moving out of Texas, though he made several trips to Chicago and New York for record dates. He has recorded about 200 sides for Decca, Mercury and countless independent labels, many of which were big sellers on single releases. Samuel Charters described him as "the last singer in the grand style; he sang with sweep and imagination, using his rough voice to reach out and touch someone who listened to him." LPs: Score, Time.

HORN, PAUL, *saxes, flute, clarinet;* b. New York City, 3/17/30. Mother was Irving Berlin's pianist for many years. Began on piano, took up clarinet, then sax at 12, flute in college. Bach. of Music at Oberlin College 1952; M.A. Manhattan School of Music, 1953. Played lead tenor with Sauter-Finegan Orch., 1956; from Sept. '56 to Feb. '58 was featured with Chico Hamilton Quintet. Free-lance West Coast studio work 1958 to Aug. '59, when he joined local NBC staff. A very fluent, if not always impassioned soloist, whose contribution to the Hamilton group was considerable. Fav. own solo: *Reflections* w. Hamilton (Wor. Pac.) Films: *Sweet Smell of Success; The Rat Race.* Own LPs: Dot, Wor.-Pac. LPs w. Hamilton (Wor.-Pac., Dec.), Fred Katz (Wor.-Pac., Dot, Dec.), B. Collette (Merc.),

Down Beat Jazz Concerts (Dot), Pisano-Bean (Decca).

Addr: 5431 Corteen Pl., No. Hollywood, Calif.

HORNE, LENA, *singer;* b. Brooklyn, N.Y., 6/30/17. Started as dancer at Cotton Club 1934; toured and recorded with Noble Sissle Orch. 1935-6. After four months with Ch. Barnet's band '40-1, she earned great popularity as a singer at Cafe Society and later became a movie personality, starring in *Cabin in the Sky, Stormy Weather,* etc. Mainly a popular rather than a jazz singer, but closely associated with many jazz artists. Her pianists and musical directors have incl. Horace Henderson, Phil Moore, and in recent years Lennie Hayton, whom she married in Paris, Dec. 1947. Her autobiography, *In Person, Lena Horne,* was published in 1950 by Greenberg. After a successful engagement at the Waldorf-Astoria, she app. in the Broadway musical *Jamaica* Oct. '57 to early '59. She continued to sing at leading supper clubs in New York, Las Vegas, etc. Own LPs: Vict., Lion, Tops; LPs w. Charlie Barnet (Cam), one track w. Artie Shaw (Vict.).

HORROX, FRANK (Horrocks), *piano;* b. Bolton, Eng., 2/15/24. Parents amateur musicians; began piano study at 8 w. private teacher, later at Trinity College of Music, where he won three exhibition prizes. At 17 joined Bertini's band as pianist. Was featured soloist and arranger for 8 years w. T. Heath, later leaving to free-lance w. own trio, but continued to arr. for Heath. Fav. own solo and arr: *Love For Sale* w. Heath in *Spotlight on Sidemen* (London). Favs: Peterson, Garner, Tatum, Wilson, Newborn. LPs w. Heath (Lond.).

Addr: 4 Palace Court Gardens, Muswell Hill, London, England.

HOWARD, DARNELL, *clarinet;* b. Chicago, Ill., 1892. Played violin in W. C. Handy's Orch. in Memphis, 1919. Later worked in Chicago with Junie Cobb, Ch. Elgar; toured Europe with James P. Johnson in *Plantation Days* revue '23-4. Went to China with Teddy Weatherford. Played with most name bands in Chicago during '20s and '30s incl. King Oliver, Erskine Tate, Earl Hines 1930-8. During the 1940s he spent some time in Calif., working and recording with Kid Ory. Feat. w. Muggsy Spanier '52-5; with Earl Hines in SF '55-60. A warm-toned clarinetist of the J. Noone school, he was also heard as a jazz violinist during his early Hines years. LPs w. Kid Ory, Don Ewell (GTJ), Barbara Dane (San Francisco), Miff Mole (Argo), Earl Hines (Epic), Baby Dodds (Amer. Mus.).

Addr: Grant Hotel, Bush St., San Francisco, Calif.

HOWARD, FRANCIS L. (Joe), *trombone;* b. Batesville, Ind., 11/3/19. Stud. music in grammar and high school, later at LA City Coll. 1938-9. Played w. various dance bands in LA incl. Stan Kenton, Ben Pollack, Will Osborne, Woody Herman, Gene Krupa. Free-lance radio work in Hollywood '48-55; joined NBC staff orch. there '55. Fav.: Tommy Dorsey. LPs w. Paul Weston (Col.), Glen Gray (Cap.); three tracks w. Fred Katz (Wor. Pac.). Own LPs: *Jazz Highway 20, Swingin' Close In* (Key).

Addr: 15444 Vanowen Street, Van Nuys, Calif.

HOWARD, PAUL, *tenor sax, leader;* b. Steubenville, Ohio, circa 1900. Went to Los Angeles 1913, lived w. uncle who was a music teacher; soon embarked on musical career. First prof. engagement '16 w. Wood Wilson's Syncopators. Org. own group '23 which he kept under various sizes and names, the best known of which was Quality Serenaders, until 1930; rec. for Victor. Pl. with Lionel Hampton '35-6, Eddie Barefield '37; had own group from '39-48. His sidemen incl. Lionel Hampton and Lawrence Brown.

HUBBLE, JOHN EDGAR (Eddie), *trombone;* b. Santa Barbara, Cal., 4/6/28. Father a LA radio trombonist. Debut w. Hollywood Canteen band, and in Ken Murray's *Blackouts* 1943. To NYC '44; high school in Scarsdale w. Bob Wilber who ran combo with him. Later worked w. Buddy Rich, Alvino Rey; Jess Stacy '45; rec. w. Doc Evans on Disc '45; also pl. w. Eddie Condon, Geo. Wettling. Own band off and on w. Johnny Windhurst from '48. Played w. The Six '53-4; later moved to Columbus, Ohio and was more recently working w. small groups in Connecticut; also played w. Muggsy Spanier '59-60. Fav: Teagarden. LP: *Jazz At Storyville* (Savoy).

HUCKO, MICHAEL ANDREW (Peanuts), *clarinet, tenor sax;* b. Syracuse, N.Y., 4/7/18. Private teachers. Came to NYC, summer 1939; worked briefly with Jack Jenney; joined Will Bradley, fall '39. Was also w. Joe Marsala, Ch. Spivak, and Bob Chester before entering Army 1942. Joined Glenn Miller's military band '43, playing in England and France. Discharged in 1945, he played tenor for two months with Benny Goodman, spent a year w. Ray McKinley until April 1947. After radio series with Jack Teagarden on WHN, worked at Condon's from late '47 to August '50, then a year at CBS with Bernie Leighton; staff work at ABC from fall of '51 until '55, then free-lanced in NYC; toured Europe w. Jack Teagarden group fall of '57. Joined Louis Armstrong combo July '58. Hucko plays Goodman-derived clarinet and is one of the most fluent exponents of this style. Own LP on Gr. Award; tracks in *The Mellow Moods of Jazz, Wide, Wide World of Jazz* (Vict.); LPs w. *The Magic Horn* (Vict.), Bobby Byrne (Gr. Award), Lee Castle (Joe Davis), Eddie Condon (Col.), Morey Feld (Kapp), Bud Freeman (Em.), Lawson-Haggart (Decca), Lou Stein (Epic), *Session At Riverside,* Hackett-Teagarden (Cap.).

Addr: 350 First Ave., New York 10, N.Y.

HUDSON, WILL, *composer, leader;* b. Barstow, Calif., 3/8/08. Raised in Detroit. In late '20s wrote many arrs. for McKinney Cotton Pickers, Erskine Tate; later for Ina Ray Hutton, Calloway, Hines, Kirk, Henderson, Redman, Lunceford. Led own swing band jointly w. Eddie DeLange '36-8 and on his own '39-40. Later free-lanced arrs. for music publishers. From '48 stud. comp. at Juilliard; in obscurity and inactive in jazz during '50s. LP: *Songs of Hudson and DeLange* by Johnny Guarnieri (Coral).

Addr: 191 Aster St., Massapequa Park, L.I., N.Y.

HUG, ARMAND, *piano, songwriter;* b. New Orleans, 1910. Stud. w. mother. Prof. debut at 13. Pl. in taxi dance hall in French Quarter at 15. Early associate of Fazola, Monk Hazel. Pl. w. Louis Prima, Sharkey Bonano. Maritime service 1942-5. Feat. as soloist in New Orleans clubs and TV series on WDSU; recorded w. Bonano, Johnny Wiggs. Elected to membership ASCAP Sept. '59. Own LPs: Golden Crest, South., Ace; nos. in *Recorded in New Orleans* (GTJ), *History of Jazz, Vol. 1* (Cap.).

Addr: 1545 Camp Street, New Orleans, La.

HUGHES, LANGSTON, *lyricist, author, poet, playwright;* b. Joplin, Mo., 2/1/02. Won magazine prize 1925 for poem *The Weary Blues.* First play, *Mulatto,* produced on Broadway '35. Wrote lyrics for musical *Street Scene* and has been associated w. several plays on Broadway including *Simply Heavenly* '57. Though best known as the author of many books, Hughes has had frequent contact w. jazz and a number of his poems have been based on the blues structure. In '57, he collaborated w. the author in an album, *The Weary Blues* (MGM) for which he read a number of his poems with jazz backgrounds provided by Charles Mingus and others. He also wrote eleven blues recorded by Big Miller '59 in the album *Did You Ever Hear The Blues?* (UA).

Addr: 20 East 127th St., New York, N.Y.

HUGHES, PATRICK C. (Spike), *composer, bass;* b. London, England, 1908. After pl. bass with Cambridge U. band, he recorded with British jazz groups for Decca in the late '20s and early '30s, climaxing his career in April and May 1933, when, with Benny Carter's help, he assembled an all star band in New York to record a series of his compositions. After this, he retired from jazz but continued for several years as a critic, writing for the London *Melody Maker* under the pseudonym "Mike." The writing on his American records reveals a talent for jazz scoring that was adventurously far ahead of its time. Own LP: Lond.; one selection in *A Scrapbook of British Jazz,* 1926-1956 (Lond.).

HULTCRANTZ, JOHAN TORBJORN, *bass;* b. Stockholm, Sweden, 5/2/37. Mother, a piano teacher, started him at age seven; took up bass at 18 in private studies with Prof. Gullbrandsson. "Sheer love for jazz" made him skip planned university studies. Played w. Lars Gullin 1956, Jazz Club 57, '57; joined Seymour Österwall '59. "Generally considered as the number one, up-coming bassist in Europe"—Carl-Erik Lindgren. Favs: Heath, Chambers, Pettiford. Swedish LPs w. Lars Gullin, Ake Persson, Jazz Club 57, *Swedish Punch.*

Addr: Nyängsvagen 3/4, Bromma, Sweden.

HUMES, HELEN, *singer;* b. Louisville, Ky., 1913. Made her first records at the age of 15 with James P. Johnson. She was best known as vocalist w. Count Basie 1938-42, also rec. with Harry James 1938; made session w. Pete Brown for Decca '42; later settled in California. Scored a big hit with *Be-baba-leba,* a jump blues on Philo (Aladdin) records in 1945. She concentrated mainly on rhythm and blues material after this and was heard in various jazz concerts and clubs. Her work with Basie showed her to be a superior ballad singer with jazz inflections, but her style degenerated in later years into a more commonplace blues-shouting technique. Fortunately she returned to a jazz context in the late 1950s, touring Australia with the Red Norvo trio; she also played several Hollywood clubs with Norvo. She also appeared in the West Coast version of the play *Simply Heavenly.* Appeared at NJF and French Lick Jazz Festival summer '59. Own LPs on Contemp., Col.; w. Red Norvo: *Red Plays the Blues* and *Red Norvo in Hi Fi* (Vict.), NJF album (Col.); two tracks on *All Star Blues* (Tops), *Spirituals To Swing* (Vang.).

Addr: 2091 West Adams Blvd., Los Angeles 18, Calif.

HUMPHREY, PERCY, *trumpet;* b. New Orleans, 1/13/05. Drums at 13; tpt. lessons w. grandfather; led own band 1925. Pl. w. Eureka Brass band; to Chicago w. Kid Howard '29, odd jobs in '30s, retired '39, returning to music '46 and working w. Geo. Lewis '53; leader of Eureka band, with which he rec. in '51. Also rec. w. Geo. Lewis, Paul Barbarin, '54.

HUMPHREY, WILLIE JR., *clarinet;* b. New Orleans, 1901. Grandson of Prof. Jim Humphrey, a cornetist and teacher, many of whose children and grandchildren became well-known musicians. Prof. debut 1918. Pl. w. Excelsior band, King Oliver, Lawrence Duhe, Lee Collins, Dewey Jackson; W.P.A. band during '30s; Paul Barbarin combo from early '50s. LP w. Barbarin (Atl.).

HUMPHRIES, LEX P. III, *drums;* b. Rockaway, N.Y., 8/22/36. Mother plays violin, brother conga drums. No formal study; pl. with Chet Baker in Europe 1956; joined Dizzy Gillespie's combo '58. With Golson-Farmer '60. Fav. Philly Joe Jones. LPs w. Duke Pearson (Blue Note), Gillespie (Verve).

HUNT, WALTER (Pee Wee), *trombone, leader;* b. Mt. Healthy, Ohio, 5/10/07. Mother pl. banjo, father violin. Started career on banjo 1924. Grad. from both Cincinnati Cons. of Music and Ohio St. Pl. w. local bands 1927; w. Jean Goldkette in Detroit 1928-9; Glen Gray's Casa Loma Orch. 1929-42. Merchant Marine '43-5; later formed his own combo. Scored big hit with corny satires on Dixieland music, notably his best-selling *Twelfth Street Rag* 1948, and *Oh!* '53. Own LPs: Capitol; LP w. Glen Gray (Harm.).

Addr: 278 Main St., Kingston, Mass.

HUNTER, ALBERTA, *singer, songwriter;* b. Memphis, Tenn., 4/1/1897. To Chicago at 12; prof. debut at 15 in a club called Dago Frank's, where she stayed for two years. Later she was feat. at Hugh Hoskins', the Panama and the Dreamland; during this last engagement she wrote *Downhearted Blues,* with which Bessie Smith made her phenomenally successful record debut in Feb. 1923. Quitting Chicago for NYC, Miss Hunter joined the Broadway show *How Come?*. After a national tour she went to Europe, where she is said to have introduced blues singing to European audiences. During the 1920s she was heard on many top blues records, her accompanists incl. Louis and Lil Armstrong, Sidney Bechet, Fletcher Henderson, Perry Bradford, and Fats Waller. She spent many years in Europe as singer and actress, and by the end of World War II had flown around the world six times and made 25 trips to European and South Pacific areas, entertaining Generals Eisenhower and MacArthur on USO tours. In 1954-5 she was with the Broadway show *Mrs. Patterson* understudying three major roles.

In '56 she attended the YWCA School for Practical Nurses. After graduation she went to work at Goldwater Memorial Hospital on Welfare Island, NYC, May '57.

Addr: 133 West 138th St., New York 30, N.Y.

HUNTER, LURLEAN, *singer;* b. Clarksdale, Miss., 12/1/28. Worked w. Red Saunders at Club De Lisa, Chicago; heard in numerous Chicago clubs. Came to New York to make first album for RCA Victor, Oct., 1955. Good pop singer, not particularly related to jazz. Favs: Sarah Vaughan, Carmen McRae, Connie Russell. LP: Vict.

Addr: 6227 South Park Ave., Chicago, Ill.

HURLEY, CLYDE L. JR., *trumpet;* b. Ft. Worth, Tex., 9/3/16. Mother, Esther B. Temple, was pioneer radio singer and pianist in Texas. Studied piano briefly, then taught self to play tpt. by listening to Louis Armstrong records. Solo trumpet w. TCU jazz band 1932-6. Joined Ben Pollack in Dallas, '37, went to Hollywood with him and did radio work there until Glenn Miller sent for him. After working w. Miller, '39-40, Tommy Dorsey, '40-1, Artie Shaw, '41, he free-lanced in film studios in '42-3, then was under contract to MGM from '44-9. Joined staff at NBC in Hollywood in '50 remaining until '55, then free-lanced for Columbia records, radio and TV shows, etc. Also has cigarette vending machine business. Films: *The Five Pennies, The Gene Krupa Story.* Hurley played the trumpet solo on Glenn Miller's famous record *In The Mood.* Favs: Bunny Berigan, with whom he recorded in Tommy Dorsey's band, and Louis Armstrong. LPs w. Matty Matlock, Paul Weston (Col.), *Gene Krupa Story* (Verve).

Addr: 4245 Bellaire Ave., North Hollywood, Calif.

HUTCHENRIDER, CLARENCE BEHRENS, *clarinet, saxes;* b. Waco, Texas, 6/13/08. Professional debut with Ross Gorman 1928. Tommy Tucker '29, Austin Wiley '31. Was popular as featured clarinetist with Glen Gray's Casa Loma Orch. 1931-43. After three years w. Jimmy Lytell on ABC radio in NYC, free-lanced in radio; retired, 1951-2, then w. Walter Davidson combo on Long Island. In '58-9 had own trio at Gaslight Club on LI. Own LP on Aamco; w. Glen Gray on Harm., in *Five Feet of Swing* (Decca).

Addr: 189-23 43rd Rd., Flushing 58, L.I., N.Y.

HUTCHINSON, RALPH, *trombone;* b. Newcastle, England, 2/25/25. Father played flute, piccolo w. BBC Symph. Stud. piano '39, tbn. '43; to US '48, worked with Bill Russo '49, Herbie Fields '50; Muggsy Spanier '51-5. Professional golfer, assistant to Carl Hoff (Anita O'Day's ex-husband) '55-8. NBC and CBS staff in Chicago, '58; joined Bob Scobey '59, also briefly reunited w. Spanier. Fav: Bill Harris. LPs w. Spanier (Weathers, Em.), Scobey (Vict.).

Addr: 201 N. Le Claire Street, Chicago, Ill.

HUTTON, INA RAY, *leader, singer;* b. Chicago, Ill., 3/13/16. Sang and danced with Gus Edwards at Palace NYC, 1930, Ziegfeld Follies '34. Best known as leader of all-girl swing band 1935-9. Led male band in 1940s, then fronted new girl group for television. Formerly married to Randy Brooks. In recent years has continued to lead a band intermittently.

Addr: c/o Premier Artists, 1046 N. Carol Drive, Los Angeles 46, Calif.

HYAMS, MARJORIE (Margie), *vibes;* b. New York City, 1923. Featured w. Woody Herman 1944-5; own trio 1945-8. Joined George Shearing Feb. 1949. Married and retired June 1950. LPs: w. Shearing on MGM, Savoy; Herman (Harmony).

HYLTON, JACK, *leader;* b. Great Lever, Lancashire, England, 1892. Pl. organ in theatre around 1913. In Army during World War I; after war was second pianist w. roof garden band, later became leader of the group which took his name in '21. Band became vaudeville show unit, doing stage and radio work. Did many tours of the Continent, revues, movies. Came to America without band '35 and formed a band in Chicago for a few engagements. Ret. to England and in recent years has been a theatrical producer. Hylton's association with jazz was indirect and mostly accidental. He was, however, responsible for Coleman Hawkins' coming to England in 1934.

HYMAN, RICHARD ROVEN (Dick), *piano, composer, organ, clarinet;* b. New York City, 3/8/27. Uncle is Anton Rovinsky, noted pianist and teacher. Extensive classical training. Stud. w. Teddy Wilson under a scholarship won through WOV contest. Navy 1945-6. Columbia U. '46-8. Prof. début at Wells' in Harlem, fall '48, then joined Victor Lombardo orch. With Tony Scott, Red Norvo combos, '49-50; then two months at Birdland with various groups. Toured Europe w. Benny Goodman sextet spring '50. Later worked w. Alvy West combo and on WMCA staff. Made a series of deliberately corny records for MGM 1954-8, pl. piano, harpsichord, organ; some, incl. *Unforgettable, Moritat,* were big hits. After working on staff at NBC he left in fall '57 to free-lance; led own jazz trio at Composer etc. In Dec. '58 became mus. dir. for Arthur Godfrey radio and TV series at CBS.

John S. Wilson has pointed out in *The Collector's*

Jazz: Modern that Hyman is "an unusually able pianist" who can play "almost any kind of jazz at least reasonably well, often very well," and can "play both piano and organ with flowing competence." The author, who agrees with Mr. Wilson, has collaborated with Hyman on many instrumental compositions, as well as on a number of record album and concert ventures since 1955. The collaborations included a series of *Encyclopedia of Jazz* concerts, with Hyman as mus. dir. and the author as narrator; one of these was rec. and released under the title *The Seven Ages of Jazz* (Metrojazz). Other LPs w. L. Feather: *East Coast vs. West Coast Jazz; The Swingin' Seasons; Hi Fi Suite; Oh Captain!* (MGM). Own jazz trio LPs incl. *Gigi, Whoop-Up, Hyman Trio Swings* (MGM), *Swingin' Double Date* (Lion). Other LPs as pianist or arranger: Trigger Alpert, Mundell Lowe, *Counterpoint for 6 Valves* (Riverside).

Addr: 265 Tenafly Road, Tenafly, N.J.

I

IGOE, OWEN JOSEPH (Sonny), *drums;* b. Jersey City, N.J., 10/8/23. Self-taught until the age of 16, when he won a Gene Krupa contest. Later studied w. Bill West; served in the Marines from 1942-6; then played in a band of ex-Marines under Tommy Reed '46-7. Joined Les Elgart '47; Ina Ray Hutton '48; Benny Goodman '49; Woody Herman '50-2; Chuck Wayne Quintet winter '52-3. Joined Ch. Ventura, April '53, and was prominently featured with him during the next two years. Best known featured number was *New Golden Wedding,* with Woody Herman, MGM. W. Billy Maxted at Nick's in late '50s; also member of NBC staff, active as teacher. App. Newport Fest. '59. Favs: Rich, Blakey, Morello. LPs w. Maxted (Cadence, incl. solo on *Big Crash From China*), Ventura (Bruns.), W. Herman (Cap., MGM).

Addr: 169 Vivian Ave., Emerson, N.J.

IND, PETER VINCENT, *bass;* b. Oxbridge, Middlesex, England, 7/20/28. Piano, harmony, at Trinity Coll. Pl. piano w. local bands; took up bass 1947, played w. Freddie Barrat, Tommy Sampson. From 1949 worked on transatlantic boats; stud. w. Lennie Tristano while in NYC. Immigrated to US April '51; did clerical work. Studies and occasional dates w. Tristano until Feb. '54, when he joined Lee Konitz. Opened own rec. studio '57, where he has been teaching, recording and holding sessions. Studying painting since '57; hopes to have own exhibition. Fav: Blanton. Fav. own solo: *Pennies in Minor* in *The Real Lee Konitz* (Atl.). Other LPs w. Tristano (Atl.).

Addr: 32-07 30th Ave., Astoria, L.I., N.Y.

INGE, EDWARD FREDERICK, *clarinet, saxes, composer;* b. Kansas City, Mo., 5/7/06. Private studies from 1919 in St. Louis, Mo., and Madison, Wis. Played w. George Reynolds orch. 1924; Dewey Jackson, Willie Austin '25; Art Sims, Bernie Young, '26; McKinney's Cotton Pickers '29-31; Don Redman '31-9; Andy Kirk '40-3. Settled in Buffalo, leading own combo at clubs in '50s. Inge, who made his record debut on Okeh w. Art Sims, early 1927, was responsible for the arrangement and clarinet solo on *You're Driving Me Crazy* by McKinney's Cotton Pickers (Victor), clarinet solos on Redman's *Chant of the Weed,* and many arrangements for Redman, Kirk, Lunceford, Armstrong.

INGOLFSSON, ANDRES SVERRIR, *alto sax;* also *tenor sax;* b. Iceland, 7/11/35. Started on accordion, pl. school dances when he was 12; clarinet at 13, alto sax at 14, tenor sax in 1958. Became interested in jazz during high school through other young musicians. Made prof. debut '55. Pl. w. Orion Quintet '56, own sextet '58; from June '59 w. K. K. Sextet. First idol was Benny Goodman; present fav: Lee Konitz, also Miles Davis, Gil Evans. Has recorded as a sideman backing Icelandic vocalists on local labels. In '59 won a scholarship to study at the Berklee School of Music in Boston.

Addr: Langholtsveg 204, Reykjavik, Iceland.

IRVIS, CHARLES (Charlie), *trombone;* b. New York City, 1899; d. NYC, ca. 1939. Recorded with Clarence Williams 1923-5; played with Duke Ellington 1924-6; Charlie Johnson '27-8. Also recorded with Jelly Roll Morton, Fats Waller, Bubber Miley '29-30. Worked mostly with Elmer Snowden and Charlie Johnson during the 1930s. LPs w. King Oliver (River.), Duke Ellington in *The Birth of Big Band Jazz* (River.).

ISAACS, CHARLES EDWARD (Ike), *bass,* also *trumpet; sousaphone;* b. Akron, Ohio, 3/28/23. First cousin is Maxine Sullivan. Son, Richard Lett, plays trumpet. Studied trumpet at Central Music School in Akron. Army, 1941 where met Wendell Marshall who taught him bass in exchange for tuba instruction. Pl. w. Tiny Grimes '49. After a short hitch w. Air Force Band, worked w. Earl Bostic '51-3; Mat Mathews, Paul Quinichette '53, Bennie Green '54. Returned to Ohio and formed his own group called the Four Maestros. Married Carmen McRae '56 and headed her acc. trio for two years incl. tour of British West Indies. Own trio backing Lambert, Hendricks and Ross '58-9. Most imp. infl: Wendell Marshall. Fav: Ray Brown. LPs w. Lambert, Hendricks and Ross (Wor. Pac., Col.), Carmen McRae (Decca), Ray Bryant (Pres.), Bennie Green (Decca, Blue Note), Mat Mathews (Coral), Earl Bostic (King).

Addr: 341 Gold St., Akron, Ohio.

ISOLA, FRANK, *drums;* b. Detroit, Mich., 2/20/25. Took up drums after hearing Gene Krupa with Goodman, 1936. Played in high school band; AAF band '43-5; then studied in California and played with Bobby Sherwood, Earle Spencer. In New York 1947; worked w. Johnny Bothwell, Elliot Lawrence; two or three years off and on with Stan Getz; with Gerry Mulligan 1953-4. Free-lance around New York, then ret. to Detroit '57. LPs w. Stan Getz (Verve), Gerry Mulligan (Wor. Pac.), Johnny Williams (EmArcy), Mose Allison (Pres.).

ISRAELS, CHUCK, *bass;* b. New York City, 1936. Attended junior high in Cleveland, where he stud. cello and guitar. Ret. to NYC and went to the High School of Performing Arts. Attended MIT where he was president of the symphony orch. Self-taught on bass from 1955 after developing an interest in jazz through association w. Herb Pomeroy. Stud. music at Brandeis U. Has pl. with vocalists Billie Holiday and Dakota Staton, and in concerts w. Max Roach, Don Elliott, Tony Scott et al. Stud. in Paris and pl. there w. Bud Powell 1959. LPs w. Cecil Taylor (UA).

J

JACKSON, BENJAMIN CLARENCE (Bull Moose), *leader, singer;* b. Cleveland, Ohio, 1919. Sang in church choirs as a child and stud. violin; tenor sax in high school. Made debut w. Freddie Webster; later w. Lucky Millinder 1944-5. After working as a single he org. a group called the Buffalo Bearcats, which became popular with rhythm and blues fans. Semi-retired, running bar in Philadelphia 1958-9.

JACKSON, CALVIN, *composer, piano;* b. Philadelphia, Pa., 5/26/19. Mother a concert singer. Jackson had 17 years of study: 13 with private teachers in Phila., 4 at Juilliard and NYU. First prof. job w. Frankie Fairfax's band. Assistant Mus. Dir. under Geo. Stoll at MGM in Hollywood, 1943-7; later settled in Toronto, where he had own TV and radio shows leading combos, also 21-piece jazz orch. on TV. Back on West Coast '57-60. Mainly a concert artist, he has attempted jazz solos in a Tatum-inspired style. Own LPs on Col.; LP w. Phil Moore (Verve).

Addr: 416 Huron St., Toronto, Ontario, Canada.

JACKSON, GREIG STEWART (Chubby), *bass, songwriter;* b. New York City, 10/25/18. Raised in Freeport, L.I. Clarinet in school band 1934; started on bass 1935. 1937-41, worked with pop bands incl. Mike Riley, Johnny Messner, Raymond Scott, Jan Savitt, Terry Shand, Henry Busse; featured w. Charlie Barnet 1941-3; Woody Herman 1943-6, '48, '50, and off and on since then. Took own quintet to Scandinavia, December 1947. Led his own big band in NYC 1949. Worked in all star groups w. Charlie Ventura 1947 and '51. Settled in Chicago 1953, working with local bands and in radio, also emceeing popular daily children's TV show for over five years. Early in '58 he resumed residence in NYC, again moderated children's show on WABC-TV and free-lanced as trio leader and sideman. Very active as songwriter, collab. with Jose Ferrer, Steve Allen et al.

Chubby Jackson was a major figure in one phase of the jazz revolution of the '40s. Most significantly, though an able bass player, he was important as the catalytic agent or cheerleader whose personality sparked the Woody Herman band at its peak. His personality and comedy gimmicks attracted attention without upsetting the musical value of the group. He has occasionally led his own big bands for LPs (see below). Jackson won the Esquire New Star Award 1945 and Gold Award '46-7; DB poll '45. Own LPs: Argo, Everest; LPs w. Herman (Col., Cap., Verve, MGM, Evst.), Ch. Barnet (Evst.), *Advance Guard of the Forties* (Em.), Ch. Ventura (Verve); two tracks in Louis Armstrong *Town Hall Concert Plus* (Vict.), one track in *Dixieland and New Orleans Jazz* (Cam.).

Addr: 490 West End Avenue, New York 24, N.Y.

JACKSON, CLIFTON LUTHER (Cliff), *piano;* b. Washington, D.C., 7/19/02. Studied privately; first prof. work at dance school in Washington. Came to NYC 1923; joined Lionel Howard's Musical Aces. From 1925 he worked either on his own or supported by a small band. He also accompanied a number of blues singers on records incl.: Viola McCoy, Lena Wilson, Sarah Martin, Clara Smith. He earned great popularity as house pianist at Cafe Society from 1943-51; subsequently worked at Lou Terrasi's and other NYC clubs. Plays in a style that suggests an expert modernization of his favorite pianists, James P. Johnson and Fats Waller. LPs: one track in *History of Classic Jazz* (River.).

Addr: 818 Ritter Place, New York 59, N.Y.

JACKSON, DEWEY, *trumpet;* b. St. Louis, Mo., 6/21/00. St. playing w. Odd Fellows' band at 12; later w. Charlie Creath and Fate Marable on riverboats off and on during 1920s and '30s. Had own band occasionally at this time, pl. in ballrooms. From '41 played club dates in St. Louis.

JACKSON, FRANZ, *tenor sax, clarinet, leader, arranger;* b. Rock Island, Ill., 1912. Stud. clar. and tenor in Chicago high school; comp. and arr. at Chicago Musical Coll. With Carroll Dickerson at the Grand Terrace from 1932-6, then w. Jimmie Noone for a year; w. Roy Eldridge and Fletcher Henderson in late '30s; Fats Waller '40-1; Earl Hines '42; then DeParis brothers. Toured w. USO group, then spent two years in Europe as band manager in late '40s. Formed Original Jass (*sic*) All-Stars '56. Though basically a swing band performer, he earned much local popularity in and around Chicago leading his traditional jazz combo.

JACKSON, MAHALIA, *singer;* b. New Orleans, 10/26/11. Her father worked as a stevedore, as a barber after working hours, and as a clergyman on Sundays. Mahalia sang in her father's choir from the age of five. As a child she heard records of Ida Cox, Bessie and Mamie Smith, but her interest remained with sacred music rather than blues. After attending school through the eighth grade, she went to Chicago at the age of 16, worked as a hotel maid, and packed dates in a factory. She led a quartet of church singers, attracted attention at various Baptist churches. Saving her money, opened a beauty salon, a flower shop, and later bought real estate. Continued to sing at various churches and also from 1945 on Apollo records, through which she began to acquire a national reputation. Her *Move On Up A Little Higher* reached a sale of over a million; her *Silent Night* was an amazing success in Denmark, outselling any other record ever released in that country. As a result, she made a successful continental tour in 1952, visiting Denmark, France, England, singing in concert halls. Starting in 1950 she made a series of appearances at Carnegie Hall. In 1954 she switched from Apollo to Columbia Records and started her own weekly radio program on CBS every Sunday evening.

In addition to her regular appearances in churches and periodic concerts, Miss Jackson was at the Newport Jazz Festival for the gospel afternoon session, July '57; later that summer she was at the Music Barn in Lenox, Mass., for a concert. In Feb. '58 she and Duke Ellington recorded an expanded version of his *Black, Brown and Beige.* They performed it together at Newport in '58. In '59 she sang for President Eisenhower at his birthday in Washington. Film: *Jazz on a Summer's Day.*

Though Mahalia Jackson has been associated mainly with sacred music and has refused many lucrative offers to work in night clubs and bars because of her religious convictions, her singing illustrates the close link between Negro religious music and fundamental blues, both of which have common roots with the origins of jazz. She has listened closely to records by Grace Moore, Caruso, and Lawrence Tibbett, but the deep, rich vibrance of her voice suggests the impact of Bessie Smith, despite the wide disparity in their material. LPs: Col., Apollo, Gr. Award; w. Ellington (Col.).

Addr: 8358 S. Indiana, Chicago 19, Ill.

JACKSON, MILTON (Bags), *vibraharp;* also *piano, guitar;* b. Detroit, Mich., 1/1/23. Studied music at Mich. State. Dizzy Gillespie heard him with a Detroit combo and brought him to NYC 1945. After working with Gillespie, he free-lanced, then pl. w. Howard McGhee, Tadd Dameron, Thelonious Monk; replaced Terry Gibbs in Woody Herman band 1949-50. Rejoined Gillespie, playing piano and vibes '50-2.

From '53-'60 Jackson established his professional and artistic identification as a member of the Modern Jazz Quartet. As the first bop musician to play vibes, he had long been recognized as one of the masters of this instrument in the modern idiom, but his relaxed and subtle sense of timing and his ability to incorporate into his work elements of an early blues feeling and even of gospel music roots could be more readily discerned as the basic character of the Modern Jazz Quartet and its individual members became defined in the middle and late '50s. Some of the character of Jackson's work can be attributed to his adjusting of the vibraphone to produce a slower than normal vibrato: Whitney Balliett has written that he "gets a rich, forceful, quavering tone." Some writers, however, believe that Jackson's personality is inhibited by the context of the Modern Jazz Quartet. British critic Francis Newton observed: "Mr. Milt Jackson must play in the style of the Modern Jazz Quartet when with that group, even though he may not always want to." Jackson's records under his own name, some of them revealing a more aggressive style and a forceful swing consistent with the use of a stronger pulse in the musicians selected for his background, have a more extroverted quality than his performances with the MJQ.

Jackson was appointed to the faculty of the School of Jazz in Lenox, Mass. Aug. '57. He is prominently featured in John Lewis's score for the film *Odds Against Tomorrow* '59. Won Esq. New Star Award '47; Met. poll '56-60; DB poll '55-9; DB Critics' poll '55-9; *Playboy* All Stars' All Stars '59-60; Encyc. poll as "greatest ever" '56. Own LPs: Atl. 1242, 1269, 1294, *Soul Brothers* w. Ray Charles (1279), UA 4022, Savoy 12070, 12080, 12042, 12061, *Opus De Jazz* (12036); Pres. 7003, Blue Note 1509; *Howard McGhee and Milt Jackson* (Savoy 12026); one half of *MJQ* (Pres. 7059), other half has Jackson w. Modern Jazz Quartet; other LPs w. MJQ: Savoy 12046, Pres. 7057, 7005, Atl. 1231, 1265, 1247, 1284, 1299, Verve 8269; LPs w. Miles Davis (Pres. 7034, 7109, 7150), Hank Mobley (Blue Note 1544), Sonny Rollins (Pres. 7029), Thelonious Monk (Blue Note 1510, 1511), Kenny Clarke (Sav. 12006), Dizzy Gillespie (Sav. 12020, 12110, 12047, Rondo. 11, Fats Navarro (Blue Note 1531, 1532), Dinah Washington (Gr. Award 318).

Addr: 192-12 105th Ave., Hollis 12, N.Y.

JACKSON, OLIVER JR. (Bops Junior), *drums;* b. Detroit, Mich., 1934. Studied drums at Miller High and w. Merle Auley. Pl. w. Wardell Gray, later w. the piano trios of Alex Kallao, Dorothy Donegan and Teddy Wilson. With Yusef Lateef from Sept. '57 until migrating to NYC in '58 after which he played at the Metropole w. various groups in '59.

LPs w. Lateef (Savoy, Pres., New Jazz), Will Davis (Sue).

JACKSON, PRESTON, *trombone;* b. New Orleans, 1903. To Chicago 1917; played with Bernie Young, Dave Peyton, Erskine Tate; from 1931-2 with Louis Armstrong in Chicago (solo on *You Rascal You*) and later with Frankie "Half Pint" Jaxon and Zilmer Randolph. Free-lancing in Chicago in 1950s with Natty Dominique and others; w. Lil Armstrong '59. LPs w. Jimmie Noone in *Gems of Jazz* (Decca), Baby Dodds (Amer. Mus.).

JACKSON, QUENTIN LEONARD (Butter), *trombone;* b. Springfield, Ohio, 1/13/09. Piano, violin, organ with private teachers; trombone with his brother-in-law Claude Jones. Worked with Gerald Hobson 1927-8, Wesley Helvey 1929-30, McKinney's Cotton Pickers '30-2, Don Redman '32-40, Cab Calloway '40-5. Toured Europe with Don Redman 1946, then rejoined Calloway. Member of Duke Ellington band from '48 to Nov. 59; specializing in plunger-mute solos à la Tricky Sam Nanton. Solos with Duke: *Fancy Dan, Jam with Sam,* (Col.), *Black and Tan Fantasy,* (Cap.). Joined Quincy Jones, Nov. '59, touring Europe w. him in *Free And Easy* '59-60. LPs w. Ellington (Cap., Col.), Clark Terry (River.).

Addr: Alvin Hotel, Broadway & 52nd St., New York 19, N.Y.

JACKSON, RUDY, *clarinet; b.* Ft. Wayne, Ind., 1901. From a musical family, he stud. clarinet in high school. St. playing w. bands in Chicago 1918: Carroll Dickerson, later King Oliver. With Duke Ellington '26-7, Noble Sissle '31-3, incl. tours of Europe. When Sissle ret. to the States, Jackson went to Bombay, India, where he pl. with various groups incl. Teddy Weatherford. Stayed in India during World War II, then ret. to US. Jackson, who played a thin-toned clarinet and was prominent in some of the earliest Ellington records, was replaced by Barney Bigard. LP w. Ellington (Bruns.).

JACKSON, ANTHONY (Tony), *piano, songwriter, singer;* b. New Orleans, 1876; d. Chicago, 4/21/21. Played at Mahogany Hall and other famed New Orleans bordellos, also worked with Bunk Johnson and Adam Olivier around 1894. After 1905 he travelled extensively and was often heard in Chicago and New York. Between 1917 and his death he led a band, occasional members incl. Freddy Keppard, Lorenzo Tio, Wellman Braud, Sidney Bechet. As a composer, he had his biggest success with *Pretty Baby* 1916; also wrote *The Naked Dance* and *Michigan Water Blues.* All three were recorded for the Library of Congress by Jelly Roll Morton, who was greatly influenced by him. Though he never made any records as far as is known, there is no doubt that Jackson was one of the first important ragtime pianists.

JACOBS, WILLEM BERNARD (Pim), *piano, composer;* b. Hilversum, Holland, 10/29/34. Mother has ballet school; father plays piano for a hobby; brother is Rudy Jacobs (see below). Took up piano in 1940 and has studied intermittently ever since. After winning first place in a jazz competition, decided to turn prof. Since '54 has led his own trio and has acc. such visiting American jazzmen as Stan Getz, Lucky Thompson, Tony Scott. Regular acc. for Rita Reys. Has written background music for documentary and commercial films. Favs: Bud Powell, Bill Evans, Al Haig, Teddy Wilson.

Addr: Wernerlaan 22, Hilversum, Holland.

JACOBS, RUDOLF (Rudy), *bass;* also *tenor sax;* b. Hilversum, Holland, 5/3/38. Also plays clar., piano. St. on alto at 16; soon after bought bass, stud. for 6 months, pl. in trio w. brother on piano. Concerts in Amsterdam w. Herbie Mann, Tony Scott, Bud Shank, Bob Cooper, Lucky Thompson, radio work w. Rita Reys, rec. w. H. Mann, Wes Ilcken. Pl. w. Newport International Band at Brussels World's Fair and NJF '58. Formed group w. Dusko Gojkovic, Albert Mangelsdorff, Bernt Rosengren which pl. at Storyville in Frankfurt, Germany. Rec. on bass and tenor sax w. his brother Pim, a pianist. Favs: Blanton, Ray Brown, Chambers, Pettiford; also Ch. Parker, Bud Powell. LP w. Int. Band (Col.).

Addr: Wernerlaan 22, Hilversum, Holland.

JACQUET, BATTISTE ILLINOIS, *tenor sax;* b. Broussard, La., 10/31/22. Moved to Houston at 6 months. His father was bassist with a railroad company band. Started on soprano and alto sax in late 1930s with Lionel Proctor, Bob Cooper, Milton Larkins bands. Went to West Coast 1941 with Floyd Ray Orch. and there joined Lionel Hampton, in whose band his solo on *Flying Home* attracted wide attention and, in effect, started a whole new school of big-toned, extrovert, erotic tenor sax stylists. He worked with Cab Calloway '43-4, Count Basie '45-6, then alternated between touring with his own band and JATP units. In '55-6 he occasionally enlarged his group to full size for theater dates. In '59 he was heard often at the Metropole. Film: short, *Jammin' The Blues* '44.

Though long identified with freak high notes and other artificial effects, Jacquet at his best (mainly in slower tempi) has shown a fine tone and style seemingly influenced by Herschel Evans and perhaps slightly by Lester Young and Coleman Hawkins. His fast tempo solos, when not spoiled by unmusical gimmicks, are often genuinely exciting and show a fine sense of construction and climax. Own LPs: *Port of Rico* (Verve 8085), *Swing's The Thing* (Verve 8023), *Groovin'* (Verve 8006), *Jazz Moods* (Verve 8084), and his Orch. (Verve 8061, Roul. SR 52035), w. Ben Webster in *The Kid And The Brute* (Verve 8065); other side of *Rex Stewart Plays Duke Ellington* (Gr. Award 33-315); *JATP All-Stars at the Opera House* (Verve 8267), *Jam Session, Jazz At The Philharmonic* (many volumes of each on Verve); *The Angry Tenors* (Savoy 14009); w. Count Basie (Col. CL 754); *Krupa and Rich* (Verve 8069); w. Al Casey in *History of Jazz, Vol. 4* (Cap. T 796).

Addr: 112-44 179th St., St. Albans, L.I., N.Y.

JACQUET, ROBERT RUSSELL, *trumpet, singer;* b. Broussard, La., 12/3/17. Played w. Floyd Ray 1939, stud. Wiley Coll., Texas, '40-4, then went to Calif. w. brother Illinois' band. Had own band at Cotton Club in Hollywood. Rejoined his brother in '46 and has worked w. him intermittently since, incl. tour of Europe in the fall '54. Living and playing in Oakland, Calif. '59. Recs. for King, now unavailable.

JAERNBERG, KURT, *valve* and *slide trombone, composer;* b. Gävle, Sweden, 6/8/32. Father, brother pl. tpt. Started as Army musician, 1946. Pl. in big band at dance hall, the Tivoli in Copenhagen '54. Rec. w. Lars Gullin, Goesta Theselius, Eric Moseholm. Pl. w.

Ib Glindemann band, Copenhagen, June '56-Dec. '57. Appeared w. Newport International Band July-Aug. '58. Returned to America, toured w. Kai Winding Sextet; gigged w. newly formed Bill Russo Orch. Associated w. Newport Youth Band in summer '59, helping to copy much of its library. Returning to Sweden, he organized a Gävle Youth Band, also gigged w. jazz combos in local clubs. Favs: Bill Harris; also Fats Navarro, Lee Konitz. LP w. Newport International Band (Col.).

Addr: Box 3605, Gävle, Sweden.

JAFFE, NAT, *piano;* b. New York City, 1918; d. NYC, 8/5/45. Lived in Berlin from 1921-32. Played w. Charlie Barnet 1938; Jack Teagarden '39-40; prominent for several years on 52nd St. as soloist and w. combos. Led own group incl. Ch. Shavers, Don Byas, shortly before his death. One of the most advanced pianists of his day, combining Earl Hines and modern influences. Recorded w. Louis Armstrong (Decca), Jack Teagarden (Varsity), Ch. Barnet (Bluebird); own sessions on Black & White; Signature. No LPs available.

JAMAL, AHMAD, *piano;* b. Pittsburgh, Pa., 7/2/30. Stud. w. Mary Caldwell Dawson, a noted concert singer and teacher; later w. James Miller. While at Westinghouse High he made prof. debut and on leaving school toured with the George Hudson orch. Worked with a group called the Four Strings in '49-50, then toured briefly as acc. for song and dance team. Started own trio, first known as the Three Strings, playing for some time at the Blue Note in Chi. '51-2, and at the Embers in NYC '52, when John Hammond in *Down Beat* called the trio "unbelievably subtle." Around this time Jamal, who had been known as Fritz Jones, adopted the Mohammedan faith and the group was soon established as the Ahmad Jamal Trio. Intensely dedicated to his religion, he visited North Africa in November '59.

The release in 1958 of an album (*But Not For Me,* Argo) recorded by the trio during an engagement at the Pershing Hotel in Chicago proved to be a turning point in Jamal's career; almost overnight the trio was in national demand, and the record was one of the year's top selling LPs. Jamal's success was greeted with a mixed reaction among musicians and critics. Ralph J. Gleason pointed out that Jamal seemed to be "a sort of refined, effete Erroll Garner . . . there is no density in Jamal's playing as a pianist; it leaves too many spaces for the other members to fill," but he conceded "the Jamal music is beautifully designed for casual listening. It swings thoroughly, is melodic, and light and airy." Whitney Balliett in *The New Yorker* wrote that the style was "vaguely akin to an attenuated version of Count Basie's" and found his work lacking in impact. Jamal has been highly praised by Miles Davis and other musicians who find his elliptical manner delicately charming. Own LPs: Argo, Epic.

Addr: c/o John Levy, 1650 Broadway, New York 19, N.Y.

JAMES, ELMER, *bass;* b. Yonkers, N.Y., 1910. Played tuba with Chick Webb and June Clark 1930-3. String bass with Fletcher Henderson '34, Lucky Millinder '34-6, Edgar Hayes '37-9, Claude Hopkins '40.

JAMES, HARRY HAGG, *trumpet, leader;* b. Albany, Ga., 3/15/16. Parents with circus; raised in circus atmosphere. He studied trumpet with his father, attended high school in Beaumont, Texas, and won a State championship with a solo at the age of 14. Soon after, he played with the Old Phillips Friars, then with Logan Hancock. Herman Waldman, and from 1935-6 with Ben Pollack, with whom he made his record debut September 1936. He joined Benny Goodman Dec. '36 and made such a big hit with the swing public that he was able to leave and form his own band in January 1939. As a bandleader, James scored his biggest hits with non-jazz solos such as *You Made Me Love You.* Much of his work in later years was in this vein, though he continued to play occasional jazz in a style reflecting the influence of his favorites, Muggsy Spanier and Louis Armstrong. Won DB poll 1937-9, Met. poll 1939-46.

In early '50s James was in semi-retirement, living in LA and occasionally touring with the band. After being featured in *The Benny Goodman Story* in '55, he re-organized his band on a more permanent basis. He toured Europe in Oct. '57 and placed more emphasis on jazz in his performances, featuring arrangements by Ernie Wilkins, Neal Hefti and Jay Hill, as a result of which the band, which had a strong Basie flavor, became one of the best big orchestras on the US jazz scene. James is married to Betty Grable. Own LPs on Col., Harm., Cap., MGM; LPs w. Goodman (Vict., Col., MGM, Cap.); tracks in *Great Jazz Brass* (Cam.), *Upright And Lowdown* (Col.), *A String of Swinging Pearls* (Vict.), Metronome All Stars (Cam., Harm.).

Addr: 1606 Vista del Mar, Hollywood 28, Calif.

JANIS, CONRAD, *trombone, leader;* b. New York City, 2/11/28. Father runs art gallery; mother, Harriet Janis, active in jazz through Circle Records, is co-author with Rudi Blesh of *They All Played Ragtime.* Self-taught, Janis played guitar in Broadway play *Dark of the Moon,* took up trombone Jan. 1949. Gigged in California with own band. Won *Record Changer* contest and came East to do TV, forming band here Nov. 1950. Throughout '50 he led a double life as actor and trombonist, appearing in dramatic roles on more than 300 major network shows incl. *Studio One, Danger, The Web, Big Town,* etc. Band appeared with him on some 30 of these shows. At one time or another, in addition to his acting, which began in '41, he has made a living as press photographer, sport car racer, art dealer, and TV writer. He appeared on Broadway in *Visit To A Small Planet* '57-8, *Make A Million* '58-9, but continued to play frequent gigs at the Metropole, Central Plaza, etc. with his own quintet. Favs: Brunis, U. Green, Fontana. Own LPs: Jub., River.

Addr: 60 East 79th St., New York 21, N.Y.

JANKOWSKI, HORST, *piano, composer;* b. Berlin, Germany, 1/30/36. Stud. bass, piano, trumpet in Berlin Music Coll. 1949; grad. '53 as concert pianist. Played w. Kurt Hohenberger orch. '53-4; acc. Caterina Valente '54-5; with Erwin Lehn's Südfunk radio band in Stuttgart '55-60; also toured w. Tony Scott in Yugoslavia '57; soloist w. Benny Goodman at Brussels World's Fair '58; concerts with many visiting US jazzmen. Own sextet pl. background music for film *Die feuerrote Baroness.* Many of his comps. have been played behind iron curtain. Favs: T. Wilson, H. Hawes, R. Freeman, O. Peterson. Writing infl. by Russ Garcia. LPs: John Graas Jazz Symphony (Merc.); Johnny Hodges, *Gershwin and Strings* (Verve). Own combos on several European labels; *Jazz at TV Tower, German Jazz Hurricane* w. Erwin Lehn (Electrola).

Addr: Stuttgart-Ditzingen, Schönblickstrasse 19, Germany.

JANSSON, LENNART JOEL HARALD, *baritone sax;* b. Karlskrona, Sweden, 5/11/32. Stud. cornet in Army at 13, then tpt., drums, clar. Mus. Cons. in Gothenburg and Royal Acad. of Mus. in Stockholm, stud. clar. and piano. Subbed for Harry Arnold in Olle Gordon band in Malmö, 1950; pl. w. Malte Johnson, '52; Seymour Osterwall, '53; Arne Domnerus '54; Carl-Henrik Norin '57; Harry Arnold '57-8; German tour with Kurt Weill '58; free-lance in Stockholm '59-60. Records with Bengt Hallberg, Egil Johansen, Harry Arnold; *Swedish Punch* w. L. Feather. Fav. own solos: *Swedish Punch.* Ambition: to go to US. Best of the new baritone men of post-Gullin school.

Addr: Nykroppavägen 32, Farsta, Sweden.

JASPAR, ROBERT B. (Bobby), *tenor sax;* also *clar., flute;* b. Liège, Belgium, 2/20/26. Grandfather, father, were musicians. Stud. piano in Liège, 1937-9; clar. at 16. Worked for American Army Special Service in Germany. Played w. Henri Renaud in Paris, '50, later w. Bernard Peiffer, Aime Barelli. Had own quintet, '54-6, played at Club St. Germain in Paris; also made many record sessions in Paris w. Jimmy Raney, Henri Renaud, Chet Baker, Bernard Peiffer, Andre Hodeir, David Amram, and sessions under his own name for Vogue and Blue Star. Won first place for tenor sax and for small combo in *Jazz Hot* poll, '55. Came to US April, 1956 and made first American appearance w. Gil Fuller's band at concert in NYC. Pl. w. J. J. Johnson '56, Miles Davis '57. W. Donald Byrd for six months in '58, pl. at Cannes and Knokke Festivals, five months at Chat Qui Pèche in Paris. Ret. to NYC '59; app. as guest soloist w. Bill Evans trio at Showplace. Worked in acc. unit for Chris Connor '60.

Married to American singer, Blossom Dearie. Jaspar is one of the finest jazz musicians produced on the European scene in recent years. His style and sound were originally compared with those of Stan Getz, but since coming to the US, he has also been influenced by Zoot Sims and members of the Parker-descended school. Own LP on Riverside; LPs w. J. J. Johnson (Col.), Hank Jones (Savoy), Herbie Mann in *Flute Flight, Flute Soufflé* (Pres.), *Interplay* (Pres.), Toshiko (Metrojazz), Barry Galbraith (Decca), *Spirit of Charlie Parker, The Soul of Jazz* (WW).

Addr: 138 West 10th Street, New York City.

JAZZPICKERS: see BABASIN, Harry

JEFFERSON, LEMON (Blind Lemon), *singer, guitar;* b. on farm near Wortham, Texas, 1897; d. Chicago 1930. Blind from birth, he was begging on the streets, playing and singing, while in his teens and soon became popular singing for farm parties and picnics. In 1917 moved to Dallas, where he was active for a while as a wrestler. Began recording in '25 for Paramount, and for several years before his death was a successful "Race record" artist. Had a great influence on Leadbelly and Josh White, both of whom acted as his guide at one time. Folklore authorities John and Alan Lomax stated that before 1920 Jefferson and Leadbelly "joined forces, and with Huddie's mandolin and Lemon's Hawaiian guitar made a good living in the saloons and redlight district of East Dallas." Samuel B. Charters, in *The Country Blues* (Rinehart) stated: "Lemon was fat, dirty, dissolute, but his singing was perhaps the most exciting country blues singing of the 1920s." LPs: *Classic Folk Blues* (Riverside).

JEFFERSON, EDGAR (Eddie), *singer;* b. Pittsburgh, Pa., 8/3/18. Stud. tuba in school, also plays guitar, drums. Guided into show business by his father, also an entertainer, he was active for many years as a dancer and singer, appearing at the 1933 Chicago World's Fair with the orig. Zephyrs; w. Coleman Hawkins' band in Chicago, '39; as dancer with the Lanny Ross show '46, and as a member of the team "Billie and Eddie" with Sarah Vaughan show '50. From the early '40s Jefferson made a hobby of setting lyrics to improvised jazz solos, thus pioneering in a technique later adopted by King Pleasure and made nationally popular many years later by Lambert, Hendricks and Ross. He recorded a series of vocals of this type in 1951 for the now defunct Hi-Lo label. From 1953 he was with the James Moody band in the dual capacity of manager-vocalist (it was he who originally set lyrics to Moody's celebrated solo on *I'm In The Mood for Love*). Favs: Cab Calloway, Lester Young, James Moody. Own LP on Triumph; LPs w. James Moody (Prestige, Argo).

Addr: 57 West 90th St., New York 24, N.Y.

JEFFERSON, HILTON, *alto sax;* b. Danbury, Conn., 7/30/03. Started with Julian Arthur, came to NYC with him and played with Claude Hopkins 1927-9. Chick Webb '29-30, McKinney's Cotton Pickers '31, Fletcher Henderson '32-3, then back with Hopkins, Webb et al. Worked chiefly with Cab Calloway from 1940-51; with Duke Ellington for a year to Feb. '53, then gigged with Harry Dial, Noble Sissle. Working in NYC bank since 1954, still gigging in spare time; appeared at NJF '58 with group of ex-Ellingtonians. W. Henderson reunion band at GSBJF '57-8. Featured on *Porgy & Bess Revisited, Showboat Revisited* (War. Bros.); LPs w. Jonah Jones (Merc.), Rex Stewart (Grand Award), Maxine Sullivan (Period), Frankie Laine-Buck Clayton (Col.), Jimmy Rushing (Col.), *Big Reunion* (Jazz.), Henderson Homecoming (UA).

Addr: 449 West 153rd Street, New York 31, N.Y.

JEFFERSON, ROLAND PARRIS (Ron), *drums;* New York City, 2/13/26. Studied at New York School of Music and w. private teacher. Played w. Roy Eldridge 1950, Coleman Hawkins '51, Joe Roland Apr. '55-Feb. '56; Apr.-June '56 w. Oscar Pettiford, Nov. '56-Jan. '57 w. Lester Young, then w. variety of groups incl. Randy Weston, Gil Melle, Horace Silver, Lou Donaldson, Charlie Mingus, Freddie Redd, etc. until March '57 when he joined Les Jazz Modes. Left in May '58 to move to Calif. Has worked in LA w. Sonny Rollins, Art Pepper, Shorty Rogers and Leroy Vinnegar. Acc. Nina Simone from Nov. '59. Favs: Roach, Blakey, Clarke, PJ Jones. LPs w. Joe Roland (Beth.), Freddie Redd (Pres.), Oscar Pettiford (Beth.), Les Jazz Modes (Dawn).

Addr: 1217 West 47th St., Los Angeles 37, Calif.

JEFFERSON, THOMAS (Little Tom), *trumpet;* b. Chicago, Ill., 6/20/20. Started on drums, then French horn and trumpet. First played in Jones' Home (now the Municipal Boys' Home) Band with Peter Davis, wha had taught Louis Armstrong, Kid Rena, and Red Allen. Worked w. Celestin Tuxedo Orch. 1936, later w. Sidney Desvignes, Jimmy Davis, Jump Jackson, John Casimir; also did TV work in New Orleans. Motion picture, *Pete Kelly's Blues.* Favs: Louis Armstrong. Ambition: To front his own band, and to sing and to play like Louis Armstrong. LPs w. Johnny St. Cyr, Santo Pecora (South.), Freddie Kohlman (MGM), George Lewis (Cavalier).

Addr: 2536 Conti St., New Orleans, La.

JEFFRIES, HERB, *singer;* b. Detroit, Mich., 1916. Worked with Howard Bunt, Erskine Tate, Earl Hines, Blanche Calloway. Strictly a ballad singer, not a jazz artist, but earned popularity w. Duke Ellington Orch. 1940-2, scoring his biggest hit with *Flamingo.* LPs: Harm., Vict., Bruns., Olympic.

JENKINS, FREDDY (Posey), *trumpet;* b. New York City, 10/10/06. Started with Horace Henderson, Wilberforce U. Best known as soloist w. Duke Ellington 1928-34, also briefly in 1937. Gave up trumpet owing to illness and has been active in recent years mainly as songwriter. LP w. Ellington (Bruns.).

JENKINS, JOHN, JR., *alto sax;* b. Chicago, 1/3/31. Clarinet at Du Sable High under Capt. Walter Dyett. Six months later switched to alto. From 1949 to 1956 appeared at Roosevelt College sessions run by Joe Segal. Appeared with Art Farmer in Chicago and Cleveland in 1955; own quartet at Bee Hive in Dec. 1955. Came to New York in Mar. 1957, working with Charlie Mingus for a short while and then concentrating on recording. Favs: Parker, McLean, Stitt, Rollins. Own LPs: Blue Note, *Jazz Eyes* (Savoy); LPs w. H. Mobley (Blue Note), J. McLean, P. Quinichette (Pres.), *Bird Feathers* (New Jazz).

JENKINS, PAT, *trumpet;* b. Norfolk, Va., 12/25/14. Trumpet at 15. To NYC 1934. Played w. Al Cooper's Savoy Sultans for eight years, then went into Army. Three years w. Tab Smith after discharge, then formed own group for short time. Joined Buddy Tate '51. LP w. Tate (Fels.).

JENNEY, JACK, *trombone;* b. Mason City, Iowa, 5/12/10; d. Los Angeles, Cal., 12/16/45. After playing with Mal Hallett, Austin Wylie, Isham Jones, did free-lance studio work during '30s; led own band 1939-40; with Artie Shaw '40-2, then studio work in California until his death. Best known for the quiet beauty of his tone and style on sweet melodic variations, of which *Star Dust* was the most extraordinary example. LP w. Red Norvo (Epic).

JEROME, JERRY, *tenor sax, flute, conductor;* b. Brooklyn, N.Y., 6/19/12. Played in college band while studying medicine. Joined Harry Reser's Clicquot Club Eskimos 1935, to earn money to finish education, but never returned to college. Played w. Glenn Miller '36-7, Red Norvo '37, WNEW staff '38, Benny Goodman '38-40, Artie Shaw '40-1. Staff conductor at NBC '42-6; a & r head of Apollo Records '46-8, NBC-TV '49; Mus. Dir. at WPIX-TV in NYC since 1950. Composed jingles for various TV commercials.

Solos on records incl. *Doin' the Jive* w. Glenn Miller; *Please Be Kind* w. Norvo; *Night and Day, Stealin' Apples, Siren Song, Undecided* w. Goodman; *Concerto for Clarinet* w. Shaw; *Gin for Christmas, Munson St. Breakdown,* and *Flying Home* (Victor) w. Lionel Hampton. Favs: Lester Young, Ben Webster. Own LPs on MGM, Cam., ABC-Par.; LPs w. Lionel Hampton (Vict.), Benny Goodman (Col.).

Addr: 1 Snapdragon Lane, Roslyn Heights, L.I., N.Y.

JERRET, NICK (Nicholas Bertocci), *clarinet, leader;* b. Somerville, Mass., 7/29/21. Uncle leads concert group in Rome; sister is singer Frances Wayne. Brought own group (incl. Ralph Burns, Frances Wayne) to NYC 1940. Played w. Vaughn Monroe '43; in service '44; led combos on 52nd St. '45-8, own trio in Boston '49 and early '50s. In '59, Jerrett presented a series of 12 jazz concerts at Boston high schools with a 30 piece band and a small combo from within the band. Also pl. concerts at Cafe Society in Boston '58-9. Interested in hypnotism and the occult sciences. Rec. for National w. Charlie Ventura and w. own group for now defunct Mood label.

Addr: 40 Hopkins Road, Arlington, Mass.

JETER-PILLARS BAND: An orchestra formed in 1934 by James Jeter, an alto saxophonist, and Hayes Pillars, a tenor saxophonist, who had both worked in Alphonso Trent's band. Very popular at one time in St. Louis, the band worked there for almost ten years, playing floor shows and working as a commercial unit. Sidemen from time to time during the '30s and '40s included Walter Page, Sid Catlett, Floyd Smith, Kenny Clarke, later Carl Pruitt and Jimmy Forrest. Despite the presence of such men it was not basically a jazz orchestra.

JOHANSSON, ARNOLD, *trumpet;* also *valve trombone, accordion, misc. saxes, bass, piano;* b. Boxholm, Sweden, 11/10/22. Comes from extremely musical family in which all members either play instruments or sing. Studied accordion at age four. Further musical studies at 14 for three years while in Army. Worked w. Frank Vernon, Malte Johnson, Gothenburg; Thore Ehrling, Stockholm. Now w. Harry Arnold. In 1947 and again in '59 worked on Swedish-American Line ships to NY, Canada and Bermuda. "Arnold Johansson is rated as one of Sweden's most facile musicians and therefore used in practically every thinkable context, mostly in studio work. He is highly thought of among his colleagues but vastly underrated as far as audiences and critics go. He is admired for his ability to change effortlessly between his different instruments."—Carl-Erik Lindgren. Favs: Hackett, Gillespie, Davis.

Addr: Platslagarvägen 2, Bromma, Sweden.

JOHANSSON, JAN, *piano;* also *guitar, composer;* b. Soderhamn, Sweden, 9/16/31. Father had brass band which toured Northern Sweden in the 1920s. Began studying piano at age 11. Became prof. with touring bands at 15. Studied electrical engineering for a while but realized that he had more interest in music. W. Gunnar Johnson Quintet '56-'59, also toured w. Stan Getz in Scandinavia during last half of '58. Since June '59 working w. Oscar Pettiford in house rhythm section of Cafe Montmarte in Copenhagen backing such guest artists as Stan Getz, Don Byas, and other leading European jazzmen. Writes arrangements for many Swedish bands. Fav: Art Tatum. Records w. Gunnar Johnson for Metronome (Swed.), w. Pettiford and Danish vibist Louis Hjulmand on Debut (Dan.). LP w. Getz (Verve).

Addr: Mäster Johansgat, 12 Göteborg Ö, Sweden.

JOHNSON, BLIND WILLIE, *singer, guitar;* b. Marlin, Texas, 1902; d. Beaumont, Texas, 1949. Blinded during childhood, he became an itinerant musician, singing in the streets of various Texas towns. He recorded about 30 numbers for Columbia 1927-9, many of them religious songs that showed a great warmth and intensity. Samuel B. Charters in *The Country Blues* (Rinehart) wrote: "He was one of the finest country guitarists on record, and the interplay between the voice and the guitar was astonishing."

JOHNSON, ALBERT J. (Budd), *composer, tenor sax;* also *alto, clarinet, baritone;* b. Dallas, Texas, 12/14/10. Studied music with daughter of Booker T. Washington. Went on the road as drummer 1924, taking up tenor two years later; went to KC '27, worked w. George E. Lee; led combo in Chicago w. Teddy Wilson until they both joined Louis Armstrong '33. Played w. Earl Hines off and on from Sept. '34 till Dec. '42.

Johnson played a unique role in the development of modern jazz. The only large bands of the early 1940s involved in the transition from swing to bop were those of Earl Hines and Boyd Raeburn in '42-44, Billy Eckstine and Woody Herman in '44-45, and Gillespie in '45-46. The only common thread linking them was Johnson, who wrote music for all five bands and played tenor sax in person or on records with all but Raeburn's. Not only did Johnson pioneer in the installation of modern musicians with some of these bands; he also was responsible for organizing the first bop record date ever cut (a Coleman Hawkins session featuring Gillespie, early in '44). With Gillespie and Oscar Pettiford he was a member of the first organized small bop combo, at the Onyx Club on 52nd Street in early '44. Johnson, who later showed additional talent as a Parker-oriented alto soloist, probably is the most underrated of the catalytic figures who helped bring about the full emergence of bop.

During the 1950s, Johnson remained in NYC most of the time, playing w. J. C. Heard and Cab Calloway and making numerous r&b record dates. In '52 he visited England and played tenor w. Snub Mosley's band in a USO unit. From Feb. '56-June '57 he played and wrote for the Benny Goodman band, working at the Waldorf-Astoria, also touring Asia w. Goodman Dec. '56-Jan. '57. LPs w. Hawkins (Vict.), Ben Webster (Verve), Frankie Laine-Buck Clayton (Col.), Earl Hines (Epic), Sarah Vaughan (Col.), Sam Taylor (Metrojazz), Gil Evans (Wor.-Pac.), Jimmy Rushing (Col.).

Addr: 144-17 Shore Ave., Jamaica 35, N.Y.

JOHNSON, WOODROW WILSON (Buddy), *leader, arranger, piano;* b. Darlington, S.C., 1/10/15. To NYC 1938; played in small night clubs and toured Europe with colored revue until outbreak of war. First break came in November '39 when a Decca official heard him play his composition *Stop Pretending* at Barney Gallant's in Greenwich Village. He recorded it and it became a hit. From that time until 1954, when he switched to Mercury, Johnson was featured continuously on Decca Records, first with a small combo and from 1944 with a 14-piece band, which played frequently at the Savoy Ballroom in Harlem, and became a big r&b attraction in the South. His big band records, especially those with vocals featuring his sister Ella (q.v.), are outstanding for their unique beat and for the melodic variety Johnson's arrangements attain within a narrow blues framework. Own LPs: Mercury.

JOHNSON, WILLIAM GEARY (Bunk), *cornet, trumpet;* b. New Orleans, 12/27/1879; d. New Iberia, La., 7/7/49. Stud. w. Prof. Wallace Cutchey from 1887; pl. w. Adam Olivier orch. ca. 1896; second cornet off and on w. Buddy Bolden for a few years, then road tour w. Holecamp's Georgia Smart Set, a minstrel show, with which he came to NYC 1903. After working with a theatre band in Dallas he went to San Francisco in 1905. Back in NO 1910 w. Billy Marrero's Superior orch. and w. Frankie Dusen's Eagle Band in '11. Left

NO in '14, teaching and playing in Mandeville, then moving to Lake Charles and Baton Rouge. Played minstrel shows, county fairs, honky-tonks; in the 1920s worked w. Gus Fortinet's band in New Iberia and Evan Thomas' Black Eagle band in Crowley, La. He was with the latter group in 1932 in Rayne, La., when he lost his leader (murdered on the bandstand), as well as his horn (destroyed in a fight) and his teeth, which combination of misfortunes led to his retirement to New Iberia, where he hauled sugar cane in the rice fields and was a teacher in the WPA program.

Much of the Bunk Johnson legend (and in retrospect it seems to be 90% legend and 10% fact) was the product of tireless research undertaken by a group of well-meaning but misguided amateurs. Rediscovered in 1937 by Frederic Ramsey Jr. and William Russell, with whom he corresponded frequently for the next few years, he became the focal point of a so-called "New Orleans revival" from '42, when two groups of collectors converged on him to record him for the Jazz Information and Jazz Man labels. In April '43 he left for San Francisco, where he appeared and recorded with the Yerba Buena Jazz Band and worked days as a drug store clerk. In '45 Bunk worked briefly in Boston with Sidney Bechet (whose dentist brother Leonard had made the teeth that enabled him to take up the horn again). He was acclaimed at Stuyvesant Casino in NYC in Sept. '45, playing there until Jan. '46. Surrounded by other New Orleans veterans retrieved from obscurity, he remained a living legend, playing at jam sessions, concerts and record dates until '48, when he went home to New Iberia.

There are numerous accounts, of or by Johnson, in *Hear Me Talkin' To Ya* and other books, of his early days. It is impossible to place much credence in any of the facts and associations claimed by him, since much of the information he furnished was contradicted by his contemporaries. One fact that seems indisputable is that Johnson's claim to have been Louis Armstrong's influence and teacher is false. Armstrong has repeatedly pointed out that though he admired Bunk's purity of tone, King Oliver was his one and only mentor. There is even greater disparity of opinions on the value of Johnson's own work; though it seems very probable that he was an inventive musician in his prime, it was impossible to determine this from a hearing of anything he played after his rediscovery. Unfortunately it was during the latter period that he made his only recordings. Samuel Charters, in his valuable documentary work *Jazz New Orleans,* wrote: "Bunk in these years was a petulant, spiteful man who drank too much and played only when he was in the mood, but he had waited many years for success, and for him, at least, it had come a little too late."

Own LP on Columbia; LPs w. Lu Watters, *Bunk and Lu* (Good Time Jazz), three nos. in *New Orleans Legends*, one in *History of Classic Jazz* (Riverside).

JOHNSON, BUSTER, *piano;* b. Cheyenne, Wyo., 1897; d. ca. 1927. Raised in Illinois. Little is known of this artist, who is said to be one of the first pianists to have used the style once called walking bass (later known as boogie-woogie), and who was once named by Albert Ammons as an early influence. He reputedly recorded four numbers for a small Chicago label a year or two before his death.

JOHNSON, CHARLES WRIGHT (Charlie), *leader, piano, trombone;* b. Philadelphia, Pa., 11/21/1891; d. NYC, 12/13/59. Raised in Lowell, Mass. Originally a trombonist, he came to NYC in 1914, worked as a sideman, but rose to prominence as pianist-leader of a band that made its bow in Atlantic City in 1924 and opened the following year at Smalls' Paradise in Harlem. The original personnel included Sidney De Paris, Jabbo Smith, trumpets; Ch. Irvis, trombone; Ben Whitted, Benny Waters, saxes; Bobby Johnson, banjo; Cy St. Clair, tuba; Geo. Stafford, drums. Johnson enjoyed an almost uninterrupted reign at Smalls' for 15 years, his later sidemen including Benny Carter, Roy Eldridge, Frankie Newton, Bill Coleman, Jimmy Harrison, Dickie Wells, Geo. Stevenson, Edgar Sampson and Sidney De Paris. After the band broke up in 1938 he remained in New York, playing local gigs. The band recorded several sessions for Victor in its early years. LP w. Ellington (River.).

JOHNSON, RICHARD BROWN (Dick), *alto sax, clarinet;* b. Brockton, Mass., 12/1/25. Mother, who holds Master's degree in music, encouraged him to begin study on piano at 5. Started on clar. at 16, alto at 19. Two years at New England Conservatory, Navy band during World War II, gigged around Boston until 1952, then joined C. Spivak and later B. Morrow '55. App. at NJF '57; Boston Arts Fest., Boston Jazz Fest. w. Herb Pomeroy '59. Favs: Ch. Parker, Dave McKenna. Own LPs: River., Em.; LPs w. Eddie Costa at Newport (Verve), Morrow (Merc.).

Addr: 22 Milton St., Brockton, Mass.

JOHNSON, OLLIE (Dink), *piano, drums, clarinet;* b. New Orleans, La., 10/28/92; d. Portland, Ore., 11/29/54. Pl. drums in Biloxi, Miss. as a small boy; later pl. piano in sporting houses there. In Las Vegas 1913-4; joined Freddie Keppard in LA '14. Later pl. drums w. his brother-in-law, Jelly Roll Morton, in LA and about '20 joined Kid Ory, playing clar. and piano. It was this group that made the first Negro jazz record in '21 for Sunshine label. In '46-7 recorded again, mostly on piano. Fav: Jelly Roll Morton.

JOHNSON, ELLA, *singer;* b. Darlington, S.C., 6/22/23. Sister of Buddy Johnson, with whose band she made her first hit record, *Please Mr. Johnson,* in October 1940. She continued to tour and record with the Johnson band. Later hits incl. *When My Man Comes Home* 1942, *That's the Stuff You Gotta Watch* 1944, *Since I Fell For You* 1945. Started her own series of record sessions 1954. Still almost unknown to the white public, Ella Johnson is one of the great individualists of modern blues singing; the combination of her laconic style and her brother's ingenious arrangements and lyrics is unique and delightful. Own LPs and LP w. Buddy Johnson (Mercury).

JOHNSON, GUS, *drums;* b. Tyler, Texas, 11/15/13. Stud. piano, bass & drums at school; Henry Coker was a Dallas schoolmate. First job at nine, in Houston, as child prodigy; local bands in Kansas City through '30s. To NYC w. Jay McShann '41 (band incl. Ch. Parker), then to Army. Back w. McShann, then joined Eddie Vinson. Played w. Hines' last big band; followed Jo Jones in Basie band '48, small Basie group '50, big band through Dec. '54. Free-lanced in NY '55-7; toured w. Ella Fitzgerald '57-9, also briefly w. Woody Herman '59 and extensive free-lance work in NYC. Johnson is one of the most effective drummers ever heard with the Basie band. Favs: Buddy Rich, Jo Jones, L. Bellson. LPs: The Drum Suite (Vict.); LPs w. Charlie Byrd (Savoy), Basie (Verve, Col., Vict.), Zoot Sims (Argo, Dawn, ABC-Par.), Nat Pierce (Coral).

Addr: 1057 E. 219th St., Bronx 69, N.Y.

JOHNSON, JAMES PRICE (Jimmy or James P.), *piano, composer;* b. New Brunswick, N.J., 2/1/1891; d. New York City, 11/17/55. Studied with mother and private teachers. Family moved to NYC and by 1904 he was working professionally, for $9 a week, during summer vacations from school. An early friend and major early influence was Luckey Roberts. Fronted small band at Clef Club toward end of World War I; played solo at Barron Wilkins' cabaret; toured in vaudeville; made piano player rolls for Aeolian Co. Musical director of *Dudley's Smart Set,* his first road show; toured England and the continent with *Plantation Days.*

Back in the US, he went to Hollywood, where he wrote the score for (and took a small part in) the Bessie Smith short *Yamacraw.* He made several other film shorts, toured and recorded both solo and as accompanist to many singers. During the 1930s he retired to home in Jamaica, New York, to devote much time to the writing of concert music based on traditional American Negro themes. His first work was a tone poem begun in 1930; in '32 he completed *Symphony Harlem* in four movements and presented it as ballet music at Harlem's Lafayette Theatre in '37. In 1936 he produced an elaborate "symphonic jazz" treatment of *St. Louis Blues.*

Partially paralyzed by a stroke in 1940, Johnson became semi-inactive. In 1945 he was well enough to work for a while at a Greenwich Village club; that year, too, parts of *Symphony Harlem* were given at an all-Johnson jazz festival at Carnegie Hall. He spent a few months in California in '49, writing the music for a show, *Sugar Hill,* produced in Los Angeles. During the last five years of his life he was completely inactive, a 1951 stroke having left him without the power of speech; he remained bedridden until his death.

Although Johnson today is recognized by jazz scholars as a pianist of vital influence, during his lifetime he was less familiar to the public than was the most celebrated of his informal students, Fats Waller. Johnson and Waller met in 1919 and Fats' style to a great degree was an extension of Johnson's modified, adroit "stride piano," which in turn was a direct outgrowth of ragtime. Johnson was a tremendous influence on Duke Ellington and many other Harlem pianists of the '20s. He enjoyed great success as a composer of popular songs, among them *If I Could Be With You, Old Fashioned Love, Charleston* and *Runnin' Wild.*

LPs: Riverside, Folkways; selections in *Spirituals To Swing* (Vang.). (A 10-inch Decca LP by Johnson of Fats Waller's songs is not currently available.) LP w. Max Kaminsky (Comm.).

JOHNSON, JAMES LOUIS (J.J.), *trombone, composer;* b. Indianapolis, Ind., 1/22/24. Piano at 11, trombone at 14. Original influences were Trummy Young, T. Dorsey, Teagarden, Dickie Wells. Played with Clarence Love, 1941-2; Snookum Russell '42; then toured, often in California, with the Benny Carter band '42-5 (Max Roach was with Carter during this period). After working with Count Basie, '45-6, he jobbed with various small bop combos along 52nd Street, toured with Illinois Jacquet '47-9, gigged with Woody Herman, Dizzy Gillespie; joined Oscar Pettiford Oct. '51 for tour of Korea and Japan under USO auspices.

A slump in steady jobs led Johnson to retire from music in August 1952. From then until June '54 he was a blueprint inspector in a Sperry factory near NYC, gigging occasionally. He then teamed with Kai Winding and from Aug. '54 until Aug. '56 they toured very successfully as the "Jay and Kay Quintet." Each then formed his own group, Johnson taking a quintet on a tour of Sweden, France etc. Johnson and Winding were reunited for a tour of Britain and the Continent in the fall of 1958.

In 1959 Johnson, who had been writing music since the mid-'40s, achieved recognition as a composer. He took part in the performance by the Monterey Festival Workshop Orchestra of *El Camino Real, Sketch for Trombone and Orchestra* and other works. He has continued to write extended pieces and to perform them with larger groups while retaining a quartet or quintet for concert and night club appearances.

J. J. Johnson was, in effect, the founder of the modern generation of jazz trombonists, the first musician to show himself capable of adapting the rigorous demands of bop to this instrument. In the early stages of bop evolution his technique seemed so incredible that many listeners to his records refused to believe that he was not playing a valve trombone to achieve the fast-moving multi-note passages which this type of improvisation sometimes required. Johnson was the pioneer, too, in promulgating on the trombone a tonal quality that soon became standard, one that could lend an air of melancholy to the brightest of tempos. He was as much imitated and idolized as Gillespie and Parker and provided an exact parallel to their work in the development of jazz during the 1940s.

Buddy Rich and Max Roach

Art Blakey (*Jean-Pierre Leloir*)

Oscar Pettiford

Tadd Dameron (*Francis Wolff*)

Dizzy Gillespie, age 17

Dizzy Gillespie (*Slade*)

Lucky Thompson (*Herman Leonard*)

Cecil Payne

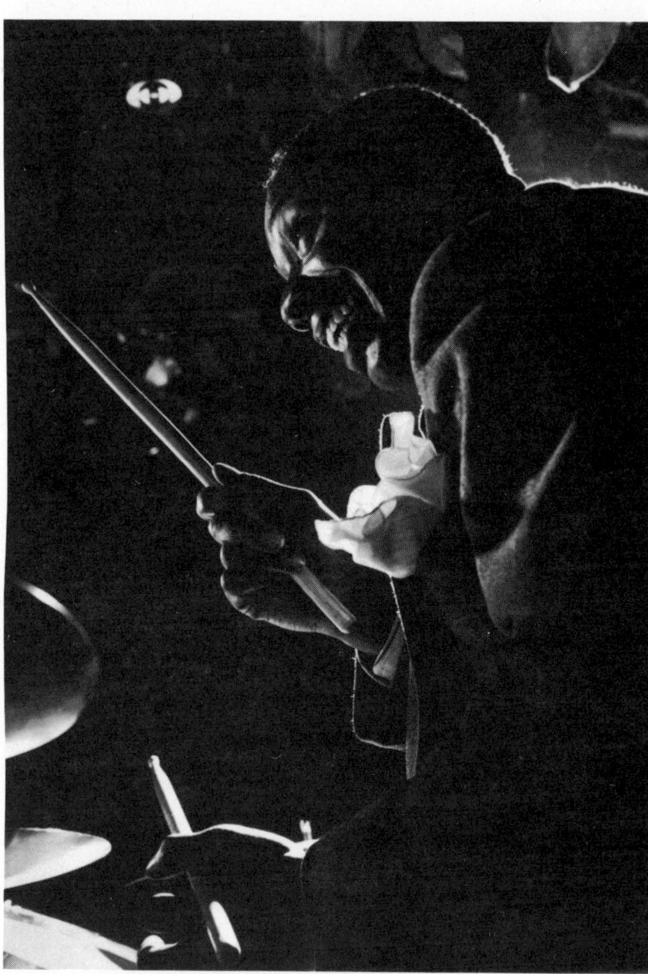

Kenny Clarke (*Herman Leonard*)

Fats Navarro and Illinois Jacquet (*Down Beat*)

At Los Angeles Philharmonic Auditorium, January 1945: Lena Horne congratulates Billy Strayhorn at the Esquire All-American jazz concert. Strayhorn won Silver Award as arranger

Jimmy Raney (*Prestige Records*)

Woody Herman's orchestra, 1946, the "First Herd." Trumpets, L. to R.: Sonny Berman, Cappy Lewis, Conrad Gozzo, Pete Candoli, Shorty Rogers; trombones: Ralph Pfiffner, Bill Harris, Ed Kiefer, Neal Reid; saxophones: Flip Phillips, John La Porta, Sam Marowitz, Mickey Folus, Sam Rubinwitch. Red Norvo is on vibes: Jimmy Rowles, piano; Chuck Wayne, guitar; Don Lamond, drums; Joe Mondragon, bass; Woody Herman, clarinet

Stan Getz, Ralph Burns and Woody Herman, 1949 *(Gene Lester)*

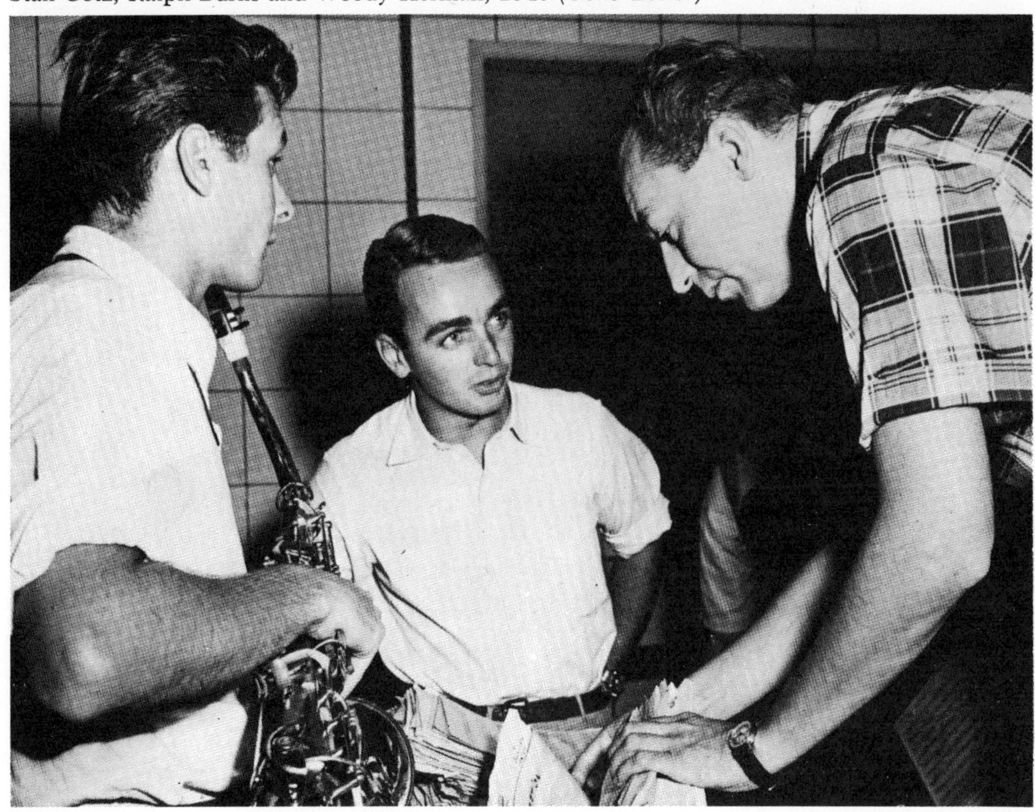

The "Four Brothers" of Woody Herman's 1948 band, reunited on Serge Chaloff's final record session, Vik Records, February 1957: Herbie Steward, Al Cohn, Zoot Sims, Serge Chaloff

Conte Candoli (*Chuck Stewart*)

Ruby Braff, Vic Dickenson, Sam Margolis (*Vanguard Records*)

Mahalia Jackson (*Columbia Records*)

Chubby Jackson (*Arthur Zinn*)

Dinah Washington

Erroll Garner (*Columbia Records*)

The original George Shearing quintet, 1949, with John Levy, Margie Hyams, Chuck Wayne and Denzil Best (*Down Beat*)

Shelly Manne (*Bernie Thrasher*)

Bud Shank

George Shearing at Newport (*Slade*)

Shorty Rogers (*RCA Victor*)

Stan Getz (*Bernie Thrasher*)

Miles Davis band, 1949. Junior Collins, french horn; Bill Barber, tuba; Kai Winding, trombone; Gerry Mulligan, baritone; Miles Davis, trumpet; Al Haig, piano; Lee Konitz, alto; Joe Shulman, bass (*Photo by Popsie*)

Pete Rugolo conducts the Metronome All-Stars, 1948-49, whose music stands make further explanation unnecessary. The drummer is Shelly Manne (*Metronome*)

Rugolo conducts the Metronome All-Stars, 1949-50 (*Metronome*)

Above: Lennie Tristano, Buddy De Franco, Lee Konitz, Eddie Safranski *(Herman Leonard)*

Left: Gil Evans and Miles Davis (*Columbia Records*)

Gerry Mulligan (*Bernie Thrasher*)

Gerry Mulligan and Harry Carney (*Bert Block*)

Lee Konitz and Warne Marsh (*Atlantic Records*)

Joe Morello in India while on State Department-sponsored tour with Dave Brubeck Quartet.

Father O'Connor and Dave Brubeck (*Herman Leonard*)

Chet Baker (*Courtesy Daniel Filipacchi*)

Paul Desmond (*Bert Block*)

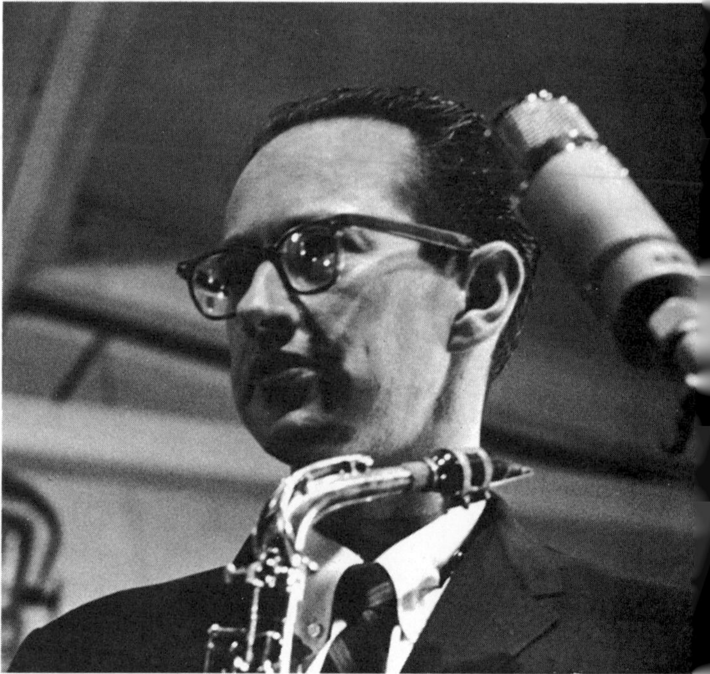

Red Norvo Trio, 1950, with Tal Farlow and Charlie Mingus (*Down Beat*)

Jay Jay Johnson and Kai Winding (*Herman Leonard*)

Bob Brookmeyer

Don Elliott, mellophone (*ABC-Paramount*)

Barney Kessel (*Metronome*)

Cal Tjader

Teddy Charles (*Robert Parent*)

Terry Gibbs (*Herman Leonard*)

Johnson has won the following awards: *Esquire* New Star 1946; Met. poll '56-60; DB Critics' poll '55-9; Playboy poll '57-60; "Musicians' Musicians" poll, Encyclopedia Yearbook of Jazz '56. Own LPs: *J. Is For Jazz* (Col. CL 935), *Dial J. J. 5* (Col. CL 1084), *First Place* (Col. CL 1030), *J. J. In Person* (Col. CL 1161), *Blue Trombone* (Col. CL 1303), *Eminent J. J. Johnson,* vols. 1 & 2 (Blue Note 1505, 1506); w. *Jay & Kai:* Col. CL 742, CL 932, CL 973, Savoy 12010, Beth. 6001, Pres. 7030; w. Stan Getz *At The Opera House* (Verve 8265); four nos. w. own group in *Trombone By Three* (Pres. 7023), one w. own group in *Playboy All Stars* '57; as composer-arranger: *Music For Brass* (Col. CL 941), *Trombones Inc.* (Warner Bros. W 1272); LPs w. Miles Davis (Prestige 7076, Blue Note 1501, 1502, Cap. T 762), Charlie Parker (Roost 2210), Sonny Stitt (Pres. 7024), Coleman Hawkins (River. 12-233); *One World Jazz* (Col. WS 314).

Addr: 131 Garden St., Teaneck, N.J.

JOHNSON, JAMES LEROY JR., (Jimmie), *drums;* b. Philadelphia, Pa., 1/20/30. Father played drums and led own band in 1930s and '40s. Stud. harmony and theory at Mastbaum High School in Philadelphia. Pl. with father's band; joined Duke Ellington March '59. Favs: Jo Jones, Louis Bellson, Max Roach, Buddy Rich. LPs w. Ellington (Col.).

Addr: 4033 Ogden Street, Philadelphia, Pa.

JOHNSON, FREDERIC H. (Keg), *trombone;* b. Dallas, Texas, 11/19/08. Father was cornetist and choirmaster, young brother is Budd Johnson. Keg studied music w. Booker T. Washington's daughter and other private teachers. Quit job with father at Studebaker to join first band. Worked w. T. Holder, Jesse Stone, Geo. E. Lee, 1929; Grant Moore, Eli Rice, Eddie Mallory, '30-1, Ralph Cooper at Regal Theatre Chicago, '31-2. Toured w. Louis Armstrong '32-3, recording his first solo with him on *Basin Street Blues* (Vict.). In NYC 1933, worked w. Benny Carter then toured w. Fletcher Henderson. Joined Cab Calloway at Cotton Club 1934, and remained with him until 1948. With Lucky Millinder 1948-50, also three months w. Gene Ammons 1949. Moved to Los Angeles and played w. Sammy Franklin, Wardell Gray. In recent years contracting small paint jobs, continuing to gig occasionally in NYC. Favs: J. Jenney, J. Teagarden. LPs: W. Cab Calloway, Chu Berry (Epic), Louis Armstrong (Vict. in one no., *Basin St. Blues*).

Addr: c/o Budd Johnson, 144-17 Shore Ave., Jamaica 35, L.I.

JOHNSON, LONNIE, *singer, guitar;* b. New Orleans, 2/8/1889. Stud. guitar, violin as child; pl. in local theatres with brother James during World War I. Seen in revue in London '17-19; riverboats w. Ch. Creath band '20-22. Settled in St. Louis '25; won a blues contest and made rec. debut for OKeh, pl. guitar, piano, violin, kazoo. From then until '32 he was a popular and frequent recording artist for OKeh in Chi. and NYC. He made guitar duets with Eddie Lang (the latter was listed as Blind Willie Dunn); acc. Victoria Spivey, Spencer Williams and other singers, also rec. w. Louis Armstrong (*Savoy Blues, I'm Not Rough, Mahogany Hall Stomp*), Duke Ellington (*Hot and Bothered, The Mooche, Misty Morning*), and the Chocolate Dandies.

In 1932-7 he was in Cleveland w. Putney Dandridge's orch. doing occasional radio work and often taking jobs outside music. He resumed recording in '37 (Decca), also pl. at Three Deuces in Chi. w. Johnny Dodds until '40. From '39 he rec. for Bluebird, also made dates w. Dodds' J. Noone for Decca. In the mid-'40s he took up amplified guitar and emphasized ballads rather than authentic blues. He rec. for King for several years until '52, toured England in '52 and during the next few years was living in Cincinnati. In 1958-60 he was a chef at the Benjamin Franklin Hotel, Philadelphia. Johnson's vocal and instrumental styles were of the urban rather than the rural blues variety but had great authenticity within this field, especially in earlier records. LP w. Armstrong (Col.).

JOHNSON, MANZIE ISHAM, *drums;* b. Putnam, Conn., 8/19/06. Resident of NYC since six weeks old. Stud. piano and violin as child, later studied w. pit drummer at Lincoln Theater. Started playing parlor socials w. Fats Waller, James P. Johnson et al. Best known as drummer w. Don Redman band during most of the period from 1931-40. Also played w. Fletcher and Horace Henderson, Louis Armstrong, Willie Bryant; subbed in Ellington and Lunceford bands; record dates in '30s w. Red Allen, Lil Armstrong, Mezzrow, and in '40s w. Sidney Bechet. Originally inspired by George Stafford and Kaiser Marshall, Johnson was one of the most respected drummers of the early swing years. LP w. Sidney Bechet (Blue Note).

Addr: 923 St. Nicholas Ave., New York 32, N.Y.

JOHNSON, JAMES OSIE, *drums, composer, singer;* b. Washington, D.C., 1/11/23. Studied harmony, theory w. John Malachi and at Armstrong High Sch. where his schoolmates incl. Leo Parker, Frank Wess. Played w. Harlem Dictators '41; Sabby Lewis '42-3; Navy band at Great Lakes, Chicago, w. Willie Smith, Clark Terry et al. '44-5; then night clubs around Chicago and arr. for record dates incl. Dinah Washington's *Fool That I Am, Too Soon To Know,* etc. Toured w. Earl Hines Sextet '52-3; then Tony Scott Quartet; I. Jacquet band, Dorothy Donegan Trio '54. Settled permanently in NYC and has since been one of the busiest free-lance musicians in jazz, app. on countless record dates. Pl. at NJF '57; app. w. Erroll Garner, Cleveland Symph. '57; *Sound of Jazz,* CBS-TV Dec. '57, *Subject Is Jazz,* NBC-TV '58. Won DB Critics' Poll as new star '54. Own LPs: Beth., Vict.; LPs w. Al Cohn, Hal McKusick, Freddie Green, Manny Albam in *The Drum Suite,* Geo. Russell (Vict.), Leonard Feather-Dick

Hyman (MGM), Coleman Hawkins (Pres.), Milt Hinton (Beth.), *Saxes, Inc.* (War. Bros.).

Addr: 194-42 114th Drive, St. Albans 12, L.I., N.Y.

JOHNSON, PETE, *piano;* b. Kansas City, Mo., 1904. Started as drummer in high school band; piano from 1922. Throughout the '20s he was heard in many local clubs, including the Hawaiian Gardens and Piney Brown's Sunset Cafe; at the latter he teamed up with singer Joe Turner, who was working there as a bartender. He appeared with Turner at the *From Spirituals to Swing* concert at Carnegie Hall in '38. During that year he also made numerous records, some w. Harry James, others w. Turner and solo. Appeared and recorded as piano team w. Albert Ammons during the next few years, enjoying great success at Cafe Society, NYC; also formed three-piano team w. Ammons and Meade Lux Lewis (rec. for Col.). His authoritative, vigorous style in the boogie-woogie idiom earned him a reputation as one of the few outstanding performers in this piano style. During the 1950s he lived and played in Buffalo, N.Y.

After he suffered a heart attack in December '58, his playing activity was sharply curtailed. LPs: *Joe Turner and Pete Johnson* (EmArcy); various tracks in the following: *Upright and Lowdown* (Col.), *Giants of Boogie Woogie* (River.), *Jazz Piano* (Gr. Award), *Great Jazz Pianists* (Cam.), *Kansas City Jazz* (Decca), *Spirituals To Swing* (Van.); LPs w. Jimmy Rushing (Van.), Joe Turner (Atl.).

Addr: 171 Broadway, Buffalo 4, N.Y.

JOHNSON, PLAS JOHN, JR., *tenor sax;* b. New Orleans, La., 7/21/31. From musical family; stud. soprano sax w. father in NO. Formed combo w. brother in high school. Heard on many pop rock-and-roll records on West Coast. Favs: Illinois Jacquet, Don Byas, Charlie Parker et al. Own LP on Cap.; LP w. Van Alexander (Cap.), Barbara Dane (Dot).

JOHNSON, ROBERT, *singer, guitar;* b. near Clarksdale, Miss., ca. 1898; d. San Antonio, Texas, 1937. Made a series of recordings for Vocalion in 1936-7. A few weeks after his last record date, in Dallas, he was murdered. Considered to be one of the most brilliant country blues artists, he recorded such performances as *Stones In My Pathway, Hellhound On My Trail, Preachin' Blues,* and *32-20 Blues* for Vocalion.

JOHNSON, WALTER, *drums;* b. New York City, 1905. Went to school w. Bubber Miley, Benny Carter. Followed Ellington into Kentucky Club w. Elmer Snowden, 1927, then pl. Strand Roof w. Billy Fowler. From 1928, worked off and on w. Fletcher Henderson for a decade, also w. Sam Wooding, Leroy Smith et al. With Lucky Millinder in mid-'40s, then several years w. combo at Elks' Rendezvous. After leaving Tab Smith in '54 remained in NYC free-lancing. Heard on many rec. dates w. Benny Carter, '34; Red Allen, '33-6; C. Hopkins, W. Bryant, L. Feather in '40s. Steady, dependable drummer, greatly admired by John Hammond. LP w. Danny Barker (Period).

Addr: 660 St. Nicholas Ave., New York City.

JOLLY, PETE (Peter A. Ceragioli), *piano, accordion;* b. New Haven, Conn., 6/5/32. Father plays and teaches accordion. Started on accordion at age 3, piano at 9. Father helped him get started; after playing with school band and local groups, he settled in LA, working w. Geo. Auld '52, Shorty Rogers '54-6, Buddy De Franco Quartet, '56. Own trio and duo, incl. bassist Ralph Pena, since. Also pl. w. Terry Gibbs. Several app. on *Stars of Jazz* TV show. Films: *Man With The Golden Arm, Wild Party, I Want To Live.*

In addition to being an extremely facile pianist of the Horace Silver school, Jolly has shown promise of becoming almost the only important modern jazz accordionist in the single note solo style. Favs: Horace Silver, Bud Powell, Geo. Wallington. Own LPs on Vict.; LPs w. Shorty Rogers (Vict., Atl.), Cy Touff (Wor. Pac.), Lennie Niehaus (Contemp.), Perkins/Kamuca (Lib.), Terry Gibbs (Merc.), Buddy De Franco (Verve), *I Want to Live* (UA).

Addr: 404 North Roxbury Drive, Beverly Hills, Calif.

JOLSON, ASA (Al), *singer, songwriter;* b. Washington, D.C., 3/26/1886; d. San Francisco, Cal., 10/23/50. Widely publicized as *The Jazz Singer* in the 1927 film of that name, Jolson was not a jazz singer by almost any accepted definition. (Some of the songs he coauthored have been in occasional jazz use as instrumentals, notably *Avalon, Back in Your Own Backyard, Sonny Boy, California Here I Come.*) However, as British critic Francis Newton has pointed out: "Though the jazz lover may have fits at the idea, the reporter can no more deny the right of the late Al Jolson to call himself a jazz singer . . . than the literary critic can deny the right of the average businessman to claim that he writes English."

JONES, BURGHER WILLIAM (Buddy), *bass, tuba;* b. Hope, Ark., 2/17/24. Met Ch. Parker in Kansas City at the age of 17; under his influence decided to enter music. Took up string bass in Navy; worked w. Charlie Ventura in 1947, then moved to LA, gigging in small jazz groups incl. Joe Venuti trio, '49, later joined Ina Ray Hutton. Came to NYC in '50; worked with Gene Williams, Lennie Tristano Quintet, Buddy De Franco, Elliot Lawrence. Joined Jack Sterling morning show on CBS Radio, '52 (others in group were Elliot Lawrence, Tiny Kahn, Mary Osborne) and was still w. Sterling in '60. Favs: Walter Page, Milt Hinton, Jimmy Blanton. LPs w. Al Cohn (Vict.), Elliot Lawrence (Fant.), Phil Woods-Gene Quill (Vict.), Sam Most (Beth.), Johnny Costa (Coral).

Addr: 208 Woodhampton Drive, White Plains, N.Y.

JONES, CLAUDE, *trombone;* b. Boley, Okla., 2/11/01. Private lessons, on trumpet, drums; trombone w. McKinney's Cotton Pickers 1923-9; Fletcher Henderson and Chick Webb intermittently '30-4, Alex Hill

'34, Cab Calloway '36-9; Coleman Hawkins band at Golden Gate ballroom NYC '40; valve trombone w. Duke Ellington '44-9. Briefly back w. Henderson in '50; rejoined Ellington for six months Sept. '51. Since '52, out of music, has been officers' steward on S.S. *United States.* Jones recorded on Jelly Roll Morton's last Victor session, 1939, and on many dates in '30s w. bands listed above; most recs. no longer available. Feat. in one track of *Boning Up On Bones* (EmArcy). LPs: see Ellington.

Addr: 2171 Madison Ave., New York 37, N.Y.

JONES, DALE, *bass, leader;* b. Cedar County, Nebraska, 8/13/02. Spent many years barnstorming through Neb., Okla., Tex. in jazz groups from 1922. Early friend and associate of Jack Teagarden. In late '20s came to NYC, spent several years pl. and arr. w. Will Osborne, later pl. in Jack Teagarden's big band. Settled in Cal.; own combo at H'wood Palladium, and worked w. small Teagarden combo. Spent several months in Louis Armstrong group 1951, and has since rejoined it for brief periods. Own quintet in Las Vegas 1958-60, also dates w. Charlie Teagarden. LPs w. Armstrong: *Satchmo The Great* etc. (Col.).

Addr: Rt. # 1, Box 227 B, Las Vegas, Nev.

JONES, EDWARD (Eddie, or Jonesy), *bass;* b. New York City 3/1/29. Raised in Red Bank, N.J., where he lived two doors away from Count Basie and was friend of family. Started on bass at Howard U. in Washington, 1946. Left to teach music at Beaufort, S.C., '51-2, then spent a year singing and playing in trio by night, working at post office by day. In Aug. '53 he joined Count Basie and remained with the band continuously, except for a brief trip to Sweden with Joe Newman Sextet Oct. '58 while Basie was on vacation. Favs: Ray Brown, Nelson Boyd, M. Hinton. LPs w. Basie: Verve, Roulette. Many other LPs w. combos incl. Osie Johnson (Beth.), Joe Newman (Cor.), Dave Lambert (ABC-Par., Wor. Pac.), Ruby Braff (Epic), Thad Jones (Metrojazz), *Jones Boys* (Period).

Addr: 21 West 87th Street, New York 24, N.Y.

JONES, ELVIN RAY, *drums;* b. Pontiac, Mich., 9/9/27. Brother of Hank and Thad Jones. Self-taught; played in school band. Entered Army in 1946 and played in military band. Released in '49, spent 3 yrs. at the Bluebird in Detroit w. Thad Jones, Billy Mitchell et al. Played Newport Jazz Festival, Summer, '55, w. Teddy Charles, Ch. Mingus. Moved to NYC Spring '56, worked w. Bud Powell trio. Later gigged w. many combos in NYC inc. Pepper Adams-Donald Byrd '58; Tyree Glenn '58-9; Harry Edison '59-60. One of the most resourceful of modern drummers, he has shown an ability to construct complex cross-rhythms, while at the same time keep the basic beat flowing. Favs: Max Roach, Art Blakey, Kenny Clarke, Philly Joe Jones, Roy Haynes.

LPs w. Tommy Flanagan (Pres.), Thad Jones (UA, Savoy, Per., Blue Note), Jay Jay Johnson (Col.), *After Hours, Olio,* Kenny Burrell (Pres.), Sonny Rollins (Blue Note), Miles Davis (Debut), Pepper Adams (Riv., Metrojazz), Gil Evans (Wor. Pac.), Art Farmer (New Jazz, UA).

JONES, HENRY (Hank), *piano;* b. Pontiac, Mich., 7/31/18. Studied with Carlotta Franzell. Local bands in Mich., Ohio, then with George Clarke in Buffalo. To NYC '44, when he was influenced by Al Haig and Bud Powell. Worked with Hot Lips Page and Andy Kirk; accompanied Billy Eckstine, then six months with John Kirby. Two years off and on with Coleman Hawkins, Howard McGhee. Went on tour with JATP in fall of '47. Was accompanist for Ella Fitzgerald on tour of Europe in '48. Left her in '53 and free-lanced in New York. Worked off and on w. Benny Goodman band and combos from Feb. '56 until '58. Jones, whose early influences were Waller, Wilson and Tatum, has been taken somewhat for granted in recent years because most of his work has been concentrated in the commercial recording field in NYC. He is, however, a dependable, flexible and at times inspired modern pianist and has teamed w. Barry Galbraith, Osie Johnson and Milt Hinton to provide, on innumerable LPs, what many musicians consider an ideal rhythm section. Own LPs on Verve, Savoy, Cap., Gold. Cr.; *Keeping Up With The Joneses* (Metrojazz); LPs w. Charlie Parker on *The Bird, Charlie Parker Story #2* (Verve), certain tracks in *The Genius of Charles Parker, #3* (Verve—Al Haig is incorrectly listed as having been on the entire album.); Lester Young, Flip Phillips (Verve), vols. 5-8 of JATP (Verve), Milt Jackson, Cal Tjader, A. K. Salim, Eddie Bert, Cannonball Adderley, Donald Byrd, *Flutes and Reeds, Opus De Jazz, Top Brass* (Savoy), Sonny Stitt (Roost), Artie Shaw (Verve), Jerome Richardson (New Jazz), *Stretching Out* w. Sims-Brookmeyer (UA), Quincy Jones, Jimmy Raney (ABC-Par.), Jimmy Rushing, Jay Jay Johnson (Col.), Coleman Hawkins, Kenny Dorham (Riverside), Illinois Jacquet (Verve), Paul Chambers (Blue Note), Specs Powell (Roul.), Joe Wilder (Col., Savoy), *One World Jazz* (Col.).

Addr: 39 Seventh St., Cresskill, N.J.

JONES, JAMES HENRY (Jimmy), *piano;* b. Memphis, Tenn., 12/30/18. Started on guitar, then played piano w. various Chicago combos. Attracted attention when featured w. Stuff Smith Trio 1943, coming to NYC w. Smith the following year. Worked w. J. C. Heard 1946-7; toured as accompanist for Sarah Vaughan 1947 until April 1952, when illness forced him into retirement for two years. After free-lancing in New York, he rejoined Sarah Vaughan and toured Europe w. her October 1954, West Indies, So. America and Cuba '56. Left her to free-lance in NYC, Jan. '58. Since then has worked w. Ben Webster, Harry Edison, Ruby Braff; backed Anita O'Day at NJF '58, Pat Suzuki NJF '59, also Morgana King, Dakota Staton. Active as an arranger for *Subject Is Jazz* TV series on NBC '58; for Mercer Ellington, Joe Williams, Ernie Andrews, Milt Jackson with strings albums '59. Jones developed a style that is uniquely attractive, composed mostly of gently played, discreetly distributed and harmonically ingenious chords, though occasionally he also plays interesting single-line right hand solos. Own LPs on Atco; four tracks on *Escape* (GNP); LPs w. Vaughan (Col., Merc.), Sonny Stitt (Verve, Roost), Buck Clayton (Col., Vang.), Duke Ellington (Col.), Illinois Jacquet (Verve), Beverly Kenney (Roost), Ben Webster, Harry Edison-Buck Clayton (Verve).

Addr: 176-14 132nd Ave., Springfield Gardens, L.I., N.Y.

JONES, JONATHAN (Jo), *drums;* b. Chicago, Ill., 7/10/11. Stud. music for 12 years and became proficient on saxes, trumpet and piano. On leaving school, joined a carnival and toured the Chatauqua circuit, working often as a tap-dancer and singer; later spent three years in Omaha, coming to Kansas City Nov. 1933 and joining a combo led by Tommy Douglas. Was with Count Basie from late '35, leaving in early '36 to work in St. Louis. After the Basie band settled at the Reno Club in KC, Jones became a permanent member and, except for time out in the Army, remained until 1948. He also appeared with JATP '47, Illinois Jacquet '48-9, Lester Young '50-1, Joe Bushkin '52-3, then spent several years free-lancing around NYC. Toured Europe with Ella Fitzgerald-Oscar Peterson spring '57; JATP fall '57; often had his own trio at New York clubs '57-60, and in Puerto Rico early '60. Originally identified with his light, subtle use of the top cymbal, Jones was hired and admired throughout the '40s and '50s by jazzmen of every school. Not normally given to long solos, he has always shown discretion, taste, frequent flashes of humor and a compellingly driving beat. He was heard on record dates with Harry James, Mildred Bailey, Billie Holiday, Teddy Wilson, Lionel Hampton in '37-8; Benny Goodman Sextet '41, and in recent years with innumerable Basie-type combos as well as Dixieland bands, modern groups and pop vocal sessions. Won DB Critics poll '56.

Own LPs: Vang. 8053, 8525, Evst. 5023; LPs w. Basie (Decca 8049, Bruns. 54012, Verve 8243, Col. CL 901, CL 754, Epic LN 3169), *Lester Young Memorial* (Epic SN 6031); Buck Clayton (Vang. 8514, Col. CL 548, 567, 614, 701), Ruby Braff (Vang. 8504), Sonny Stitt (Roost 2204, Verve 8219), Art Blakey (Blue Note 1554-55, Col. CL 1002), Paul Quinichette (Pres. 7127, 7147), *Peterson, Eldridge, Stitt, Jo Jones at Newport* (Verve 8239); also LPs w. Hawkins (River.), Rushing (Vang., Col.), Young, Eldridge, Tatum, Wilson, JATP (Verve), Nat Pierce (Vang.), *Spirituals To Swing* (Vang.), *One World Jazz* (Col.).

Addr: 401 East 64th St., New York 21, N.Y.

JONES, ROBERT ELLIOTT (Jonah), *trumpet;* b. Louisville, Ky., 12/31/09. Played w. Wallace Bryant on Mississippi riverboats 1929, also w. Horace Henderson '29, Wesley Helvey '30, Jimmie Lunceford '31, Stuff Smith '32-4 and '36-40, McKinney's Cotton Pickers '35; Fletcher Henderson 1940, Benny Carter '40-1, Cab Calloway '41-52. With Joe Bushkin at Embers '52. Toured w. Earl Hines combo '52-3, *Porgy & Bess* pit band '53. Several months in Europe as solo attraction '54. Jonah, one of the most personable and individual trumpet products of the swing era, was heard in many record sessions in the 1930s w. Teddy Wilson, Billie Holiday, Lionel Hampton, Lil Armstrong and others. He was best known as the perennial and perfect foil of Stuff Smith, with whom he often shared comedy vocals. They were reunited briefly in 1953. In the late 1950s he adopted a "muted jazz" quartet policy, playing frequently at the Embers, NYC; by 1958 his LPs w. this group had made a surprise hit in the commercial market and Jones enjoyed a tremendous career renaissance, further fortified by appearances on Fred Astaire's TV shows, '58 and '59. Favs: Armstrong, Gillespie, Berigan. Own LPs: Capitol, Vict.; one side of *Jazz Kaleidoscope* (Beth.); LPs w. Sidney Bechet (GTJ, Blue Note), Lionel Hampton (Cam.), George Wettling (Weathers), Benny Payne (Kapp).

JONES, JOSEPH RUDOLPH (Philly Joe), *drums;* b. Philadelphia, Pa., 7/15/23. Mother, a piano teacher, gave him lessons as child. Played for several years in local combos, backing Dexter Gordon, Fats Navarro and other name jazzmen visiting Phila. With Ben Webster in Washington, 1949. Subsequently free-lanced extensively in NYC, working w. Z. Sims, L. Konitz at Down Beat club, 1952, and w. Miles Davis intermittently since '52 and more or less regularly from '55 to summer '58. Also w. Tony Scott '53, Tadd Dameron '54. Pl. w. Gil Evans '59, then own group at Showplace, NYC and on tour.

"Philly Joe," as he is called among musicians (he is not related to the Jo Jones who played drums w. the old Basie band), has enjoyed increasing prestige in the past couple of years as one of the most dynamic and expert percussionists of the explosive modern school. Ralph J. Gleason has called him "the greatest drummer in jazz today and maybe the greatest drummer since Chick Webb." Whitney Balliett described his solos as "careful, remarkably graduated structures, full of surprises, varied timbres and good old-fashioned emotion."

All-time favs: Cozy Cole, Sid Catlett. Own LPs on Riverside; LPs w. Miles Davis (Pres., Col.), Clifford Brown (Blue Note, Pres.), Tony Scott (Bruns.), Art Pepper (Contemp.), Kenny Drew, Clark Terry, Wynton Kelly, Johnny Griffin et al. (River.), Paul Chambers, Lee Morgan, Hank Mobley, J. R. Monterose, etc. (Blue Note), Jackie McLean, Art Farmer (Pres.), Serge Chaloff (Cap.).

Addr: 120 Bainbridge St., Brooklyn, N. Y.

JONES, QUINCY DELIGHT, JR., *composer, leader;* also *trumpet, piano;* b. Chicago, Ill., 3/14/33. To Seattle at ten; had vocal quartet in church there. Started on trumpet 1947, first lessons w. Clark Terry in Seattle '50, when Clark was in town w. Basie. To Boston '51 on scholarship to Schillinger House (later known as the Berklee School of Music), where he studied before joining Lionel Hampton for two years. After leaving Hampton in Nov. '53, he free-lanced in NYC as arranger for Ray Anthony and for many record dates for Epic, Mercury and others. Inactive as trumpeter '54-6, he took up the instrument again and became musical director, arranger and member of the brass section in the band that toured under Dizzy Gillespie's leadership, starting in the Near East, May '56.

In May '57 he left for Paris; spent next 18 months there composing, arranging and conducting for Barclay Records, visiting Scandinavia in '58. On his return to NYC he resumed his free-lance writing career, writing an album of originals for Count Basie and working prolifically as composer and music publisher. In the fall of '59, at the suggestion of John Hammond, he was hired as musical director for the Harold Arlen blues opera, *Free And Easy.* The all-star jazz orchestra which he assembled for this show went to Europe, opening in Amsterdam December '59 and touring extensively through the Continent during '60.

Quincy Jones was one of the youngest and most brilliant arranger-composers to make his mark in jazz during the '50s. His writing is not exploratory; unlike many of the young writers who have experimented with atonality and extended forms, he has remained within the classic jazz framework; his reputation rests mainly on brief compositions that combine the swinging big band feel of the better orchestras of the '30s with the harmonic developments of the '40s. Jones' first recorded composition was *Kingfish,* recorded by Lionel Hampton on MGM; in it he played one of his rare trumpet solos. His other compositions include *Jessica's Day, Quince, Stockholm Sweetnin'* and *Evening In Paris.* Own LPs: ABC-Par., Merc.; one half of Jazz Abroad (Em.); arrs. for: Count Basie (Roul.), Dizzy Gillespie, Gene Krupa (Verve), Sonny Stitt (Roost), Art Farmer, Clifford Brown (Pres.), Jimmy Cleveland, Helen Merrill, Clark Terry (Em.).

Addr: 55 West 92nd St., New York, N. Y.

JONES, REUNALD SR., *trumpet;* b. Indianapolis, Ind., 12/22/10. Studied w. father & at Mich. Cons. Local bands in Minneapolis, Milwaukee; w. Speed Webb (in section w. Roy Eldridge) 1930; during '30s and early '40s w. Fess Williams, Chick Webb, Willie Bryant, Teddy Hill, Ch. Johnson, Don Redman. In 1946 briefly w. J. Lunceford, Duke Ellington, Erskine Hawkins. Rec. dates w. Lil Armstrong, Mezzrow, many dates w. Sy Oliver. Joined Basie band Feb. '52, toured Europe '54. After leaving Basie in fall of '59, he free-lanced in NYC. Toured England w. Woody Herman April '59; night club and concert work w. George Shearing's big band, fall '59. LPs: *The Jones Boys* (Period), Basie (Verve, Roul.).

Addr: 64 W. 108th St., New York 25, N. Y.

JONES, RICHARD MYKNEE, *pianist, songwriter;* b. New Orleans, 6/13/1889; d. Chicago, Ill., 12/8/45. Studied alto horn, cornet, pipe organ; played in Eureka Brass Band 1902. Was one of the most prominent pianists in New Orleans bordellos 1908-17. Went to Chicago 1919 and worked for Clarence Williams' music publishing company. Later organized many sessions for Okeh Records in Chicago 1925-8, accompanied "Chippie" Hill 1925-6, led own "Jazz Wizards" groups on Okeh, Victor, Gennett, Paramount. Returned to New Orleans 1931-2, but was back in Chicago 1934, recording for Decca in '35, with Herschel Evans, Louis Metcalf and others. Jones, who made his final record date for the now defunct Session label in 1944, was composer of many tunes whose authorship was subsequently much disputed. Among them were *Jazzin' Babies Blues, Trouble in Mind, Riverside Blues, 29th and Dearborn,* and *Red Wagon.*

JONES, SAMUEL (Sam), *bass;* b. Jacksonville, Fla., 11/12/24. Father pl. piano. Second cousin of bassist Al Hall. Pl. drums in school marching band; inspired by Lunceford, Basie, Eckstine bands and early Parker, Gillespie records. Worked around NYC w. T. Bradshaw, Les Jazz Modes, K. Dorham, I. Jacquet, C. Adderley; with D. Gillespie Jan. '58-Feb. '59, Th. Monk Feb.-Oct. '59, then rejoined C. Adderley. Eminently capable modern bassist. Favs: Blanton, R. Brown, Pettiford, Hinton, Al Hall. LPs w. Gillespie (Verve), Bill Evans, N. Adderley, Monk (River.), C. Adderley (River., BN, Merc.), Red Garland (Pres.), K. Dorham (BN, ABC-Par.), Ellington-Hodges (Verve).

Addr: 54 West 106th Street, New York 25, N. Y.

JONES, WILMORE (Slick), *drums;* b. Roanoke, Va., 4/13/07. Stud. w. father. Prof. debut w. John Lockslayer 1925; later came to NYC on scholarship to Damrosch Cons. Pl. w. F. Henderson '35-6; Fats Waller off and on to '42, later w. Eddie South; Louis Jordan '44; Stuff Smith, Hazel Scott, Don Redman; at Jimmy Ryan's w. Wilbur De Paris '54. Active as songwriter, elected to ASCAP 1956. LPs w. L. Hampton, Fats Waller (Vict.), Bechet (Blue Note).

Addr: 425 West 160th Street, New York 32, N. Y.

JONES, CLIFFORD (Snags), *drums;* b. New Orleans, La., 1900; d. Chicago 1/31/47. Pl. with Buddy Petit and others; w. King Oliver 1924. Was long in comparative obscurity in Chicago, except for occ. dates w. Darnell Howard; acc. Bunk Johnson for concerts in Chicago '46.

JONES, THADDEUS JOSEPH (Thad), *trumpet;* b. Pontiac, Mich., 3/28/23. Brother of Hank Jones; together with a third brother, drummer Elvin, they had their own combo in late '30s. Worked in Saginaw with Sonny Stitt; other Mich. bands until Army Dec. 43-Apr. '46. Own band in Okla. City; two years with Billy Mitchell in Detroit, then on road with Larry Steele revue. Joined Count Basie May 1954 and has since gained wide critical acclaim. According to Nat Hentoff: "A modern jazz trumpeter capable of a more satisfyingly brassful and ringing tone than most of his contemporaries, Thad also has an individuality, maturity and continuity of conception that mark him as one of the most important contributors on his horn."

Although he has been featured more, of late, with Basie, Jones does his best playing in a small group. Won *Down Beat* Int. Critics' Poll as new star '56. Own LPs on UA, Blue Note, Savoy, Period; LPs w. Charlie Mingus (Beth.), *Olio, After Hours* (Prestige), Basie (Verve, Roul.), Sonny Stitt (Roost), Feather-Hyman, *East Coast vs West Coast* (MGM), Monk (River.).

Addr: 161 W. 105th St., New York 25, N. Y.

JONES, WILLIAM (Willie), *drums;* b. Brooklyn, N.Y., 10/20/29. Started w. Thelonious Monk; has worked w. Cecil Payne, Joe Holiday, Ch. Parker, Kenny Dorham, Ch. Mingus, Jay Jay Johnson, Lester Young. Favs: Roach, Clarke, Blakey. LPs w. T. Monk, Elmo Hope (Pres.), Mingus (Atl.).

Addr: 77 Lefferts Place, Brooklyn, N. Y.

JOPLIN, SCOTT, *piano, songwriter;* b. Texarkana, Texas, 11/24/1868; d. NYC, 4/11/17. Joplin, who was prominent as a soloist in St. Louis and Chicago during the '90s, played in the Chicago World's Fair 1893. He was best known as composer of *Maple Leaf Rag,* published 1899; called "the king of ragtime composers." Other works included: *Original Rag, Sugar Cane Rag, Wall Street Rag,* and *Tremonisha,* an opera which he produced at his own expense for a single performance in Harlem in 1911. LPs: one track in *History of Classic Jazz;* also in *Ragtime Piano Roll* (River.).

JORDAN, CLIFFORD LACONIA, *tenor sax;* b. Chicago, Ill., 9/2/31. Began on piano when quite young and tenor at 14. Att. Du Sable High Sch. w. Johnny Griffin, John Gilmore, John Jenkins and other musicians. Gigs around Chicago w. Max Roach, Sonny Stitt, and various r & b bands. Left Chi. to go w. Roach, then w. Horace Silver's quint. in 1957. After ten months w. Silver, he left in May '58, free-lanced on the West Coast, ret. to NYC Mar. '59, and worked w. Jay Jay Johnson. Favs: Young, Rollins, Coltrane, Byas, Mobley. LPs w. own group and w. P. Chambers, H. Silver, J. Gilmore (BN).

JORDAN, IRVING SIDNEY (Duke), *piano;* b. Brooklyn, N.Y., 4/1/22. Started w. Steve Pulliam's Manhattan Sextet, which won prize as amateur combo at NY World's Fair, 1939 (Jimmy Nottingham was also a member). Left this group and went to work in 1941 for Clarke Monroe in the sextet which later worked under Coleman Hawkins' leadership at Kelly's Stable, NYC. Worked a year w. Al Cooper's Savoy Sultans. Was playing w. Teddy Walters' trio at Three Deuces when Ch. Parker heard him; then worked for three years off and on for Parker incl. JATP. Later worked w. Stan Getz for about nine months; Roy Eldridge for four months, Oscar Pettiford and other combos around NYC. During the '50s he was heard around the New York area in a variety of groups incl. his own trio. Went to Paris '59.

One of the early bop pianists, Jordan plays in a more subdued, spare style than the Powell-oriented players. Favs: Tatum, Teddy Wilson. Own LPs on Signal; LPs w. Charlie Parker (Roost, Savoy), Stan Getz (Verve), Gene Ammons, Art Farmer, Sonny Stitt (Pres.), Howard McGhee, Oscar Pettiford (Beth.), Cecil Payne (Sig.), *Bird's Night* (Savoy).

JORDAN, LOUIS, *singer, alto sax, leader;* b. Brinkley, Ark., 7/8/08. Studied music w. father from 1915. Played w. Ruby Williams in Hot Springs, Ark., then moved to Philadelphia, where he joined Charlie Gaines 1930. In NYC he worked w. Kaiser Marshall and Leroy Smith; first prominent w. Chick Webb, with whom he was heard on alto sax and as occasional vocalist 1936-8. In 1938 he formed his own group and played at the Elks' Rendezvous in Harlem. In the next few years Jordan's combo, known as the Tympany Five, enjoyed a slow and steady rise to national fame as Jordan featured himself more and more in vocal blues and novelties. His major hits were *Knock Me a Kiss, Gonna Move to the Outskirts of Town,* both recorded 1941; *Five Guys Named Moe* 1942, and *Choo Choo Ch' Boogie* in 1946, the last-named ultimately selling a million records. Jordan recorded duets with Bing Crosby '44, with Ella Fitzgerald '45 and '49, Louis Armstrong '50, etc. Originally limited to r & b circles, he broke into the front lines of show business through a unique combination of visual showmanship, good musicianship, a strong accent on humor and a delightfully original and rhythmic vocal style. Jordan organized a big band for a tour in the fall of 1951 and has occasionally expanded for theatre dates since then, but normally plays with a small group. In the early '50s he was intermittently inactive owing to illness and confined himself to his Arizona home but came back strong in the mid-'50s. His band recorded for Decca from '38 until late '53 when he switched to Aladdin; w. "X" Records '55, then to Mercury. Own LPs: Decca, Merc., Score.

Addr: c/o Ben Waller Enterprises, 1853 Arlington Ave., Station 201 So., Los Angeles 19, Calif.

JORDAN, STEPHEN PHILIP (Steve), *guitar;* b. New York City, 1/15/19. Stud. w. Allan Reuss. Played w. Will Bradley 1939-41; Artie Shaw '41-2; Navy band w. Saxie Dowell '42-5; then w. Bob Chester, Freddie Slack, Glen Gray. With Stan Kenton '48, Boyd Raeburn '49, then left music to work in production dept. at NBC, '50-2. Worked with Benny Goodman off and on '53-6. Since then almost inactive in music; working in tailor shop '59. Able rhythm section guitarist in Freddie Green tradition. Fav: Geo. van Eps. LPs w. Vic Dickenson, Mel Powell, Buck Clayton, Sir Charles Thompson (Vang.), Gene Krupa (Verve).

JORDAN, JAMES TAFT, *trumpet, singer;* b. Florence, S.C., 2/15/15. Baritone horn in school, Norfolk, Va.; finished schooling in Phila. and started on trumpet 1929. After playing w. Doc Hyder in Phila. he joined Chick Webb Sept. 1933 and remained with the band after Webb's death under Ella Fitzgerald's leadership, until it disbanded in 1942. Led own combo '42; w. Duke Ellington '43-7; in Lucille Dixon Orch. Savannah Club '49-53. Featured on records w. Modernaires, Steve Lawrence '54, also many sessions w. Sy Oliver. Pl. w. Benny Goodman in '58, '59 incl. Brussels World's Fair. App. on Steve Allen TV show '58, Jackie Gleason jazz show, TV '58 and rec. w. Gleason '58-9. Shows Armstrong influence in both playing and singing. Solos w. Ellington incl. *Royal Garden Blues* (Vict.), *Trumpets No End, Jam-A-Ditty* (Rondolette). Own LP on Mercury; LPs w. Goodman (Col.), Sy Oliver (Decca), Henderson reunions w. Rex Stewart (Urania, UA), Chick Webb in *Five Feet of Swing* (Decca); *Porgy and Bess* (Aamco).

Addr: 270 Convent Ave., New York, N.Y.

JOSEPH, PLEASANT, *singer, guitar;* b. Wallace, La., 12/21/07. Also known as Cousin Joe, Smiling Joe; raised in New Orleans, where he sang spirituals and blues from childhood. Prominent in NYC in the mid-'40s, when he made a number of record sessions for Savoy, King Jazz, Signature, etc. Returned to New Orleans 1948 and later recorded for Decca. Combines a sense of humor with earthy blues sound and feeling.

JOYNER, GEORGE LEON, *bass;* b. Memphis, Tenn., 6/21/32. Stud. w. mother, a church pianist. Golden Gloves bantamweight boxer at 15; got first bass at 16, played first gig less than 2 wks. later. At Arkansas State '49-52, led college dance band. Tuba in Army band '53-5; part of time in special services w. Phineas Newborn, Wynton Kelly. Electric bass w. B. B. King '55-Mar. '56, then to NYC with Newborn; stud. w. Michael Krasnapolsky, pl. w. Teddy Charles, S. Rollins, S. Stitt et al. In Europe and No. Africa with Idrees Sulieman '59-60. Joyner is also known by the name Jamil Nasser. Favs: Ray Brown, Mingus, Pettiford. LPs w. Red Garland, Gene Ammons (Pres.), Lou Donaldson (Blue Note), Down Home Reunion (UA).

JUG STOMPERS: See CANNON, Gus.

K

KAHN, ROGER WOLFE, *composer, conductor;* b. Morristown, N.J., 10/19/07. Stud. violin at age seven, and mastered 18 instruments. Began comp. at 12; org. own orch. at 15, pl. in various theatres, clubs in NYC. Had booking office and own night club in mid-twenties; became interested in aviation about 1935 and gave up orch. Was a test pilot for aircraft company '41. Several jazzmen pl. in his orch. during '20s, incl. Eddie Lang, Joe Venuti et al.

KAHN, NORMAN (Tiny), *composer, drums;* b. New York City, 1924; d. 8/19/53 of heart attack. As child won prize playing harmonica; took up drums at 15, worked w. Georgie Auld, Boyd Raeburn, was key figure in Chubby Jackson's big band, '49, and later w. Stan Getz' quartet. During '53 did daily CBS radio show w. Elliot Lawrence, playing mostly vibes. Kahn was considered one of the greatest modern drummers. As an arranger, according to his childhood friend Terry Gibbs, he was influential as an inspiration for Al Cohn, Johnny Mandel and others. His arrs. include *Tiny's Blues, Father Knickerbopper,* for Jackson; *Over The Rainbow* for Charlie Barnet; *Leo The Lion* for Woody Herman. LPs w. Stan Getz (Roost), Al Cohn (Savoy), Charlie Barnet (Cap.), Red Rodney in *Advance Guard of the '40s* (Em.), Serge Chaloff in *Lestorian Mode* (Savoy); on Fant. 3219, Elliot Lawrence plays Kahn's arrangements.

KALEEM, MUSA (Orlando Wright), *tenor sax;* also *baritone sax, flute, bass clarinet;* b. Wheeling, W. Va., 1/3/21. Bought an Albert system clarinet in Pittsburgh for four dollars, summer 1937. Left home w. El Rodgers Mystics of Rhythm as tenor saxophonist '39; Eddie Jefferson was head of show. Worked around Pitt. w. Erroll Garner, Art Blakey. Worked w. Mary Lou Williams in NYC and Pitt. '42, then w. Fletcher Henderson '43. Gigged in St. Louis '44, then ret. to NYC where he pl. at Minton's and w. Savoy Sultans, Jimmie Lunceford, Basie, Ellington. Pl. and rec. w. Art Blakey's Messengers '47. During '50s was away from music, working as a seaman. W. James Moody '59. Rec. debut w. Blakey on Blue Note '47. Fav: Don Byas. LPs w. Tiny Grimes (Pres.), Moody (Argo).

Addr: c/o Eddie Jefferson, 57 West 90th St., New York, N.Y.

KALLAO, ALEXANDER (Alex), *piano;* b. Pittsburgh, Pa., 9/1/32; blind since birth. Raised in Detroit, studied with father, a prof. pianist; debut at 15 in Detroit clubs. To NYC 1953. Kallao is a superior technician but not basically a jazz musician, although his appearance at such clubs as the Embers has erroneously given this impression. LPs: Vict., Baton.

Addr: 215 East 86th St., New York 28, N.Y.

KAMINSKY, MAX, *trumpet;* b. Brockton, Mass., 9/7/08. Studied w. Henry Pollack in Boston. Prof. debut 1924; moved to Chicago 1927, working w. Frank Teschemacher, George Wettling, at Cinderella Ballroom. In NYC worked w. Red Nichols '29; pop. orchs. '30-4; T. Dorsey '36, and again in '38; Artie Shaw '37 and '41-3; toured South Pacific w. Shaw's Navy band. From '43, worked mostly Dixieland jobs w. own combo. Kaminsky was also heard on record dates

w. Benny Carter's Chocolate Dandies '33, Eddie Condon '33, Mezz Mezzrow '33 and '34, Bud Freeman '39, also dates during '40s w. Willie The Lion Smith, Sidney Bechet, Art Hodes, Joe Marsala, Jack Teagarden, G. Brunis. After free-lancing around NYC & Conn. in '50s he toured Europe w. Teagarden, fall '57; had own combo at Duane Hotel for six months in '58, also quartets at Roundtable and Metropole; State Dept.-sponsored tour of Far East w. Teagarden, Sept. '58-Jan. '59, visiting 18 countries. Simple, hard-driving Dixieland stylist. Own LP: Comm. LPs w. Bud Freeman (Col., Bruns.), Pee Wee Russell (Atl.), Teagarden (Comm.), Art Hodes (Blue Note), Condon (War. Bros., Comm., Dec.).

Addr: Hotel Bristol, 129 West 48th Street, New York 19, N.Y.

KAMUCA, RICHARD (Richie), *tenor sax;* b. Philadelphia, Pa., 7/23/30. Stud. Mastbaum Sch. Pl. w. Stan Kenton, '51-2; Woody Herman '54-5; Chet Baker, Maynard Ferguson, '57; Lighthouse All Stars, '57-8; Shorty Rogers, Shelly Manne '59. At Monterey jazz fest. w. W. Herman, Oct. '59. Film: *Kings Go Forth.* Early solos included *Young Blood, Prologue* with Kenton; from '57 was frequently and prominently heard in LA sessions, recording at least 40 jazz LPs in 1959 alone. A style that seemed at first highly derivative began to show marked individuality by 1960. Own LPs: Interlude, HiFi Record; LPs w. Kenton (Cap.), Al Cohn (Vict.), Cy Touff (Wor. Pac.), Herman (Cap.), Bill Perkins (Wor. Pac.), Stan Levey, Johnny Richards (Beth.), Manny Albam (Cor.), Shorty Rogers (Vict.), Dempsey Wright (Andex).

Addr: 1032 N. Pass Ave., Burbank, Calif.

KARLIN, FREDERICK JAMES (Fred), *composer, trumpet;* b. Chicago, Ill., 1/16/36. The film *Young Man With A Horn* stimulated him to study trumpet in high school. B.A. from Amherst College, where he led Dixieland group, later 16-piece dance band. Free-lanced in France, Germany, Italy, summer '52. Wrote for Fred Dale '56; WGN house band '57-8. Several months at Jazz Ltd. in Chi. spring '58. In '59 wrote scores for Chubby Jackson, Harry James, Raymond Scott, Bill Russo, Marshall Brown, Benny Goodman. Skilful and promising writer. LPs as writer: *The Sound of Music* for B. Goodman (MGM), *Ballad for Jai* pl. by C. Jackson (Everest).

Addr: 315 Riverside Drive, New York 25, N.Y.

KATZ, RICHARD AARON (Dick), *piano, composer;* b. Baltimore, Md., 3/13/24. Stud. Peabody Inst., U. of N.C. Navy 1943; att. Navy Sch. of Mus. in Washington. Discharged Apr. '46; to NYC, Manhattan Sch. of Mus. Bach. degree '50, majoring in theory, comp. Stud. w. Teddy Wilson, Juilliard, '50, also gigged in Greenwich Village and w. Al Casey on 52nd Street. Worked in his father's adv. agency for several years, doubling in music. Solo at Chez Inez and Ringside, Paris, 1951. Played w. Ben Webster, Chuck Wayne, Don Elliott combos; mainly w. Tony Scott '52-4, recs. and clubs w. K. Winding-J. J. Johnson '54-5. Panelist and soloist at Music Inn, Lenox, '56, '8, '9. Has worked with innumerable combos around NYC incl. Tyree Glenn, Lucky Thompson, Gigi Gryce, Whitey Mitchell. Organized trio to acc. Carmen McRae, Aug. '59. First class modern pianist and composer. Own LP: Atlantic. LPs w. Jay & Kai (Col., Pres.), Raney-Brookmeyer, O. Pettiford (ABC-Par.), Buck Clayton (Col.), S. Rollins (Metrojazz), M. Albam (Dot), Music Inn concert (Atl.), *Jazz Piano International* (Atl.), T. Scott (Bruns.), C. McRae (Beth.), *Saxes, Inc.* (War. Bros.).

Addr: 28 West 12th Street, New York 11, N.Y.

KATZ, FREDERICK (Fred), *composer, 'cello, piano;* b. Brooklyn, N.Y., 2/25/19. Grandfather was violinist; mother played drums; father (Dr. Hyman Katz) played many string instruments. Stud. piano and 'cello under scholarship at Third Street Music Settlement—'cello with pupil of Pablo Casals. Made his living for years as concert 'cellist; while overseas in Army after VE Day, was mus. dir. of 7th Army HQ. After leaving the service, he worked for several years as piano accompanist for Vic Damone, Mindy Carson, Lena Horne, Tony Bennett, Jana Mason et al. As 'cellist, first real jazz job was w. Chico Hamilton quintet 1955-6. Katz is the first musician to put the 'cello to full use both in arco and pizzicato solos. He wrote much of the music for the original Hamilton quintet. Since leaving Hamilton has free-lanced in LA. Own LPs: Wor. Pac., Decca; LPs w. Chico Hamilton (Wor. Pac., Decca), Paul Horn (Dot).

Addr: 3701 Loadstone Dr., Sherman Oaks, Calif.

KATZMAN, LEE, *trumpet;* b. Chicago, Ill., 5/17/28. Aunt a concert pianist. Began playing at 13 in various Chi. clubs, and from '46 was w. big bands incl. Bob Strong, Sam Donahue, C. Thornhill, G. Krupa, J. Dorsey. With Stan Kenton '55-8; Les Brown and local LA work, '58; Terry Gibbs big band '59. Fav. own solo: *Between The Devil & The Deep Blue Sea* w. Med Flory in *Jazz Wave* (Jub.). Favs: Parker, Gillespie. LPs: *Jive for Five* w. Bill Holman (Andex); Pepper Adams (Wor.-Pac.), Jimmy Rowles (Andex), S. Stitt (Verve).

Addr: 14354 Germain, Dennis Park, Calif.

KAWABE, KINICHI (Keiichi Ishitsuji), *composer, trombone;* b. Kitakamata, Tokyo, Japan, 5/3/27. Studied at Tokyo Academy of Music Instrumental School 1945. Orig. wanted to be symphony musician. Joined Ernie Pyle Theatre pit orch. '50. W. Blue Coats orch. '51. Formed Emaniairs orch. w. Atsumo and Ebihara Oct. '52, then own Golden Charioteer orch. April '53, All-Star Giants April '55. Left Giants Aug. '56 to reform Emaniairs. Disbanded Feb. '58 and joined Columbia Recording Orch. Comp. and arr. for radio, TV and Nikatsu movie co., Favs: Frank Rosolino, J. J. Johnson. Rec. for Japanese labels.

Addr: 6, 2-chome Hirakawacho, Kojimachi, Chiyoda-ku, Tokyo, Japan.

KAWAGUCHI, GEORGE, *drums;* also *vibes;* b. Fukakusa, Kyoto, Japan, 6/15/27. Mother, a pianist; father, a violinist, taught him to play guitar and clarinet in Dairen, Manchuria 1940. Has led own groups since '53. Is also a licensed commercial pilot. Has app. in several Japanese movies incl. *Jazzy Girls, Youthful Jazz Girls.* Favs: Chick Webb, Krupa, Hampton. Rec. for Nippon Victor, Nippon Mercury, etc.

Addr: 751 3-chome Higashi Magome, Ota-ku, Tokyo, Japan.

KAY, CONNIE (Conrad Henry Kirnon), *drums;* b. Tuckahoe, N.Y., 4/27/27. At six, stud. piano w. mother; self-taught drums at 10, lessons at 15. Played with Fats Noel, 1939; as full-time prof. made debut in mid-'40s, pl. w. Sir Ch. Thompson, Miles Davis at Minton's, '44-5 and with Cat Anderson's band '45. Followed by Roy Haynes in Lester Young combo '49-50 and worked with him again from '52 to '55; between the two stints with Young, played in the combos of Charlie Parker, Coleman Hawkins, Beryl Booker and Stan Getz. Replaced Kenny Clarke in the Modern Jazz Quartet, 1955, and soon achieved a national reputation among jazz fans for his delicate yet (when required) firmly swinging work. As Whitney Balliett commented in *The New Yorker,* "Few drummers have had as steady and irresistible a beat, or have matched his sensitivity to what is going on elsewhere. Also, he has an uncanny way of combining crispness and delicacy so that his work is startlingly audible yet never obtrusive." Favs: Catlett, Blakey, Roach, Clarke, Manne. LPs w. MJQ (Pres., UA, Atl.); *The Ivory Hunters* (UA), Chris Connor (Atl.), L. Young (Verve), *Modern Jazz Society* (Verve), Randy Weston (Jub.), Joe Newman (Cor.), Dick Katz (Atl.), Paul Desmond (War. Bros.).

KEATING, JOHN, *composer, trombone;* b. Edinburgh, Scotland, 9/10/27. Began stud. piano at 8, taught himself arr. at 15. Took up trombone at 17 w. local teacher. After stint w. T. Sampson, played trombone w. Ted Heath '52-3; in '54 became staff composer-arranger for Heath, giving up trombone. A talented writer, he quit the music business early '58 and has since been working in mus. publ. house, gigging occasionally. Fav. own arr. *English Jazz* (Bally), *Swinging Scots* (Dot). Favs: K. Winding, M. Bernhart, B. Harris. Fav. arr: N. Hefti.

Addr: 51 Woodhill Cres., Kenton, Middlesex, England.

KEENE, BOB (Robert Kuhn), *clarinet, leader;* b. Manhattan Beach, Cal., 1/5/22. Stud. Music at USC; clar. under Lucien Caillet. Worked w. Ray Bauduc 1946; Eddie Miller '46-7; in addition to these jobs, has always had own band since age 17; has also worked as heavy equipment operator, construction superintendent, salesman, executive. Own combo intermittently in LA since '54. Own LP on Whippet.

Addr: Box 599, Torrance, Calif.

KELLENS, CHRISTIAN, *trombone, bass trombone, euphonium;* b. Andenne, Belgium, 1/18/25. St. on harmonica; tbn. self-taught from 1944. Prof. debut w. Fats Sadi. Has pl. w. many bands in Belgium (Franz Lebrun, Jack Sels, the Bob Shots *et al.*); Germany (Kurt Edelhagen); France (Jack Diéval, Henri Renaud, Tony Proteau, Martial Solal); Holland and Scandinavia. Pl. bass tbn. w. Christian Chevallier, euphonium w. Fred Bunge, '56; Aimé Barelli, '56; Edelhagen, '57-8; Newport International band, '58; Belgium w. Sels, Israel w. Jack Diéval, Germany w. Sadi, '59. Foreign languages are his hobby; he once quit music for four years to work as an interpreter. Fav. musicians: Armstrong, Ellington, Basie. LPs w. Edelhagen, Chevallier *et al.;* Int. Band (Col.).

Addr: 678b Route de St. Gerard, Wepion, Belgium.

KELLEY, JOHN DICKMAN (Peck), *piano;* b. Texas, ca. 1900. Kelley is important chiefly as an example of how a legend can take hold; leader of a band in which Jack Teagarden played in 1921-2, he was praised for many years by Teagarden. Although never heard on records and unknown except by repute outside the small Texas clubs where he played, he became the subject of articles in major national magazines, largely because he had turned down offers from numerous name bands. He remained in obscurity and was never persuaded to travel or record. John Hammond, visiting him in 1939, described him as "a great musician and topnotch pianist."

KELLY, GEORGE, *tenor sax,* b. Miami, Fla., 7/31/15. Stud. piano at nine for four years, then began on alto sax. Switched to tenor soon after. Formed a band at 15 in which Panama Francis played. With Al Cooper's Savoy Sultans 1941-4. Did free-lance rec. several years and had own group for a while. Joined Cozy Cole early '59. Favs: Coleman Hawkins, Lester Young. LP w. Rex Stewart. (Fels.).

KELLY, THOMAS RAYMOND (Red), *bass;* b. Shelby, Montana, 8/29/27. Raised in Seattle. Picked up bass simply because of wartime shortage of musicians—had no previous musical training. Started w. Johnny Wittwer, pianist in San Francisco. Worked w. Chubby Jackson's big band '49 (Chubby was fronting), also Ch. Barnet, Herbie Fields, and to Honolulu w. Norvo trio. One year w. Claude Thornhill, then joined Woody Herman Jan. '53. Moved to Seattle, working w. Pat Suzuki on her first vocal job; later was with Maynard Ferguson band, two years with Stan Kenton, then went with Med Flory band, also working as duo with Claude Williamson in LA. Favs: Jimmy Blanton, Red Mitchell. LPs: *Back To Balboa* w. Kenton (Cap.), *Jazz Wave* w. Med Flory (Jub.); Woody Herman (Verve), Dick Collins (Vict.), Lennie Niehaus (Merc.).

Addr: 850 N. Huntley Drive, West Hollywood, Cal.

KELLY, WYNTON, *piano, composer;* b. Jamaica, B.W.I., 12/2/31. Brought to United States at age of 4, raised in Brooklyn; prof. debut early 1943; toured Caribbean w. Ray Abrams combo at 15. Spent several years in r&b field w. Hal "Cornbread" Singer, Eddie "Lockjaw" Davis, and three years as accompanist to Dinah Washington. First attracted attention as a jazz soloist while working w. Lester Young and Dizzy Gillespie combos. Army '52-summer '54. Later rejoined Gillespie, working with his big band; left in Dec. '57 to form own trio. Joined Miles Davis '59. As Orrin Keepnews has observed, Kelly is "a thoroughly experienced musician, his style and approach fully formed and individual . . . he is a jazz composer of considerable wit and originality." Own LPs: River; LPs w. Miles Davis (Col.), Jay Jay Johnson, Hank Mobley, Sonny Rollins, Lee Morgan (Blue Note), A. K. Salim (Savoy), Clark Terry, Philly Joe Jones, Nat Adderley, Ernie Henry, Benny Golson (River.), Dizzy Gillespie (Verve), *Sittin' In* (Verve), Steve Lacy (Pres.), *Dizzy Atmosphere* (Spec.), Johnny Griffin (Blue Note, River.), Paul Chambers (Vee-Jay).

Addr: 586 Lincoln Place, Brooklyn, N.Y.

KENNEDY, CHARLES SUMMER (Charlie), *alto sax;* also *tenor sax, clarinet, flute;* b. Staten Island, N.Y., 7/2/27. Mother pl. violin, sister plays piano, accordion, organ in church. Studied clarinet at age 12 in Weehawken, N.J. Joined Louis Prima '43 through trumpeter Al Porcino. W. Gene Krupa '45-8. Rec. w. Chubby Jackson, Chico O'Farrill in early '50s. Migrated to West Coast. Pl. w. Med Flory at Monterey Fest. '58, Terry Gibbs' big band in Hollywood '59. Films: shorts and a movie w. Gene Krupa for Republic. Fav: Charlie Parker. LPs w. Bill Holman (Coral, Andex), Gibbs (Mercury), Med Flory (Jub.), Gerry Mulligan in *Conception* (Pres.), Krupa (Col.).

Addr: 22016 Leadwell St., Canoga Park, Calif.

KENNEY, RICHARD MATHEWSON (Dick), *trombone;* b. Albany, N.Y., 7/6/20. 'Cello at school at 12; Army band 1942 w. Toots Mondello and the late Paul Villepigue, who helped get him started in NYC. With Johnny Bothwell 1946-7; to California, worked w. Earle Spencer studied at Westlake College; w. Ch. Barnet on and off for three years, then a year w. Kenton '51. W. Woody Herman Sept. '53-July '55. Free-lanced in New England until Feb. '57 when he joined Les Brown. Has made European trips w. Herman, Brown, Pacific tour w. Brown. Fav: Bill Harris. LPs w. Barnet (Verve, Cap.), Herman (Cap.), Brown (Cap., Coral).

Addr: 4525 Murietta Ave., Sherman Oaks, Calif.

KENTON, STANLEY NEWCOMB (Stan), *leader, composer, piano;* b. Wichita, Kansas, 2/19/12. Raised in Los Angeles. Studied w. mother and various private teachers. Wrote his first arrangement 1928. After playing with various local bands he joined Everett Hoagland as pianist and arranger '34, later spent a year with Gus Arnheim and played in the bands of Vido Musso and Johnny Davis. Led his own band at Balboa Beach in '41, recorded for Decca Sept. '41, and again Feb. '42. Original band included Chico Alvarez, trumpet; Red Dorris, tenor sax and vocals; Bob Gioga, baritone sax; Howard Rumsey, Bass; arrangements by Ralph Yaw and Kenton. After the release of *Artistry In Rhythm* (the band's theme), on its first Capitol session Nov. '43, the band began to acquire national reputation. The orchestral trademark in these early years was a staccato reed section style; in '44-5 most of the records were vocals, featuring Anita O'Day, Gene Howard, and June Christy. In '46, when Pete Rugolo joined as arranger, Kenton began to do far less of the writing. After the band's dissolution in April '47, Kenton fronted bands on a less permanent basis, spending most of 1949 in retirement. In Jan. '50 he took out a 40-piece orchestra with strings for a tour, using the slogan "Innovations In Modern Music." For several years he organized in the fall for a concert tour and broke up the band the following summer. In the summer of '55 he fronted a band of NYC musicians for a weekly TV series, *Music '55*. In Mar. '56 he took a new band to England for a highly successful concert tour; it was the first time a US band had played for civilian British audiences since '37, owing to Union restrictions that Kenton was instrumental in breaking down. During the next few years Kenton varied his activities, assembling orchestras with strings for lush, commercially designed LPs, and touring extensively with a band composed mainly of newer musicians in '58-60. Kenton is married to singer Ann Richards.

The value of Kenton's music has varied greatly according to the arrangers he has used. The music has fallen generally into three categories: First, the ambitious concert works, such as those of Bob Graettinger, many of which qualify as modern classical writing, but not as jazz. Second, the simple, short pieces, some of them with vocals, that have attempted to broaden the band's commercial appeal, and do not pretend to be of any significance (examples are: *All About Ronnie, The Creep, September Song*). Third, the swinging arrangements by Shorty Rogers, Gerry Mulligan, Bill Holman, which place the orchestra on the same plane as that of Woody Herman, featuring numerous improvised solos. It is on this third level that Kenton, in the opinion of most critics, made his most valid contribution to jazz. His band has served as a workshop and incubator for many writers and soloists who have achieved their first major exposure through him; moreover, Kenton's own strong personality as spokesman for modern jazz has lent added significance to his efforts. Like Duke Ellington, he is far less important for his piano work than for his other contributions. Originally inspired by Earl Hines, he is rarely heard now in jazz solos. Band won DB poll '47, '50-54; Met. poll '47-9, '54, '56; *Playboy* poll '57-60. Kenton was elected to DB readers' poll Hall of Fame 54.

Own LPs (all on Capitol): *Artistry in Rhythm,* T 167; *Back to Balboa* T 995; *Ballad Style* T 1068; *City of Glass* & *This Modern World* W 736; *Cuban Fire!* T 731; *Duet with June Christy* T 656; *Encores* T 155; *In Hi Fi* W 724; *Innovations in Modern Music* W 189; *The Kenton Era* (four LPs). incl. documentary narrated by Kenton and large illustrated biog. booklet) WDX 569; *Kenton with Voices* T 810; *Lush Interlude* T 1130; *Milestones* T 190; *New Concepts of Artistry in Rhythm* T 383; *Popular Favorites* T 421; *Portraits on Standards* T 462; *Kenton Presents* T 248; *Progressive Jazz* T 172; *Rendezvous* T 932; *Road Show* (with June Christy, Four Freshmen in concert) SB 1327; *Showcase* T 598; *Sketches on Standards* T 426; *Stage Door Swings* T 1166. Also early sides on *The Formative Years* (Decca 8259).

Addr: 1010 S. Robertson Blvd., Los Angeles 35, Calif.

KEPPARD, FREDDIE, *trumpet;* b. New Orleans, 1889; d. Chicago, 7/15/33. Played w. the Olympia Band from about '05, later taking over direction of band. He left NO about '13 w. Original Creole Band, visiting Chicago in '14, and NYC '15-16. The band broke up in '18 and Keppard settled in Chicago, first leading his own band, then working w. Bill Johnson, Doc Cook, Ollie Powers, John Wycliffe and Erskine Tate. Keppard was one of the most significant figures in NO jazz before World War I, but did not make any records until he had passed his peak. According to those who heard him in his early days he was a performer of extraordinary power and conviction. LP: one track in *History of Classic Jazz* (River.).

KERSEY, KENNETH LYONS (Kenny), *piano;* b. Harrow, Ontario, Canada, 4/3/16. Studied w. mother, a music teacher, and at Detroit Inst. of Mus. Art. Started in NYC as trumpet player 1938. Piano w. Lucky Millinder '39; Red Allen '40; Roy Eldridge and Cootie Williams, '41; Andy Kirk '42; Army until Feb. '46. Toured w. JATP '46 to early '49. With Ed Hall in Boston '49-50, Sol Yaged trio '52-4. Working around NYC at Metropole and Central Plaza in late '50s. Was one of most advanced swing pianists of his day in early '40s. Record debut w. Frankie Newton's Cafe Society Band '39 (Voc.). Best known as comp. of *Boogie-Woogie Cocktail,* which he played and recorded w. both Andy Kirk and Red Allen. LPs w. Charlie Shavers (Beth.), Jack Teagarden (Uran.), one track w. Red Allen in *Upright and Lowdown* (Col.), JATP (Verve), *The Harlem Jazz Scene* w. Ch. Christian (Ctpt.), *Jazz At The Metropole,* Bud Freeman, Jonah Jones (Beth.), Sol Yaged (Her.), Andy Kirk (Vict.).

Addr: 521 West 157th St., New York 32, N.Y.

KESSEL, BARNEY, *guitar;* b. Muskogee, Oklahoma, 10/17/23. Self-taught. Joined Chico Marx orch. (dir. by Ben Pollack) 1943. In '44 appeared in film short, *Jammin' The Blues.* Worked w. Charlie Barnet '45, then Hal McIntyre, Artie Shaw. After free-lancing in many top radio shows in LA w. Frank DeVol, etc., he went on tour w. JATP '52-3 as member of Oscar Peterson trio visiting 14 foreign countries. He was music director for Bob Crosby TV show '54; a & r man in charge of pop music for Verve from Feb. '57 to March '58. In Aug. '57 played at annual festival of jazz club in Caracas, Venezuela, app. w. two orchestras and two small groups during his 12-day stay. Occupied mainly with free-lance work in TV, movies, and recording during the latter part of the '50s. Played for *Staccato* show on TV '59-60. Kessel, in his many recordings, has shown himself as a stylistic disciple of Charlie Christian, and perhaps the most distinguished exponent of this style since Christian's death. The German jazz critic Joachim Ernst Berendt has called him "the most rhythmically vital guitarist in modern jazz."

He won the Esquire Silver Award '47; DB poll '56-9; DB Critics' poll '53, '59; Met. poll '58-60; Playboy poll '57-60. Own LPs on Contemporary: *Easy Like* (3511), *Plays Standards* (3512), *To Swing Or Not To Swing* (3513), *Music To Listen To Barney Kessel By* (3521), *Poll Winners* (3535), *Poll Winners Ride Again* (3556), *Some Like It Hot* (3565), *Carmen* (3563); LPs w. Lionel Hampton, *Just Jazz* (Decca); JATP (Verve), Red Norvo (Contemp.), Harry Edison, Billy Holiday, Ben Webster, Stuff Smith, Woody Herman, Buddy DeFranco, Oscar Peterson, Roy Eldridge (Verve), Julie London (Lib.), Jackie & Roy (Story.), *Bell, Book and Candoli* (Dot).

Addr: 5330 Ben Ave., No. Hollywood, Calif.

KIFFE, KARL HERMAN, *drums;* b. Los Angeles, Calif., 7/6/27. Won Gene Krupa drum contest Dec. 1943. Leader of Hollywood Canteen Kids '43, then worked as single in Ken Murray's *Blackouts.* Joined Jimmy Dorsey, July '45. Worked w. Ted Weems, Butch Stone, Georgie Auld '48-50; back w. J. Dorsey, July '50 until Feb. '53. Three months w. Tex Beneke, then free-lanced in NYC w. Ch. Barnet, Jimmy McPartland. Subbed w. Stan Getz for a short time '56; also w. Charlies Shavers, Zoot Sims '56. W. Woody Herman, July-Nov. '57; Red Norvo, March '58-Jan. '59; June Christy, June-Aug. '59. Since then w. Jack Cathcart at Flamingo Hotel in Las Vegas. Fav: Jo Jones. LPs w. Don Stratton (ABC-Par.), Pee Wee Russell (Ctpt.), bongos w. Georgie Auld in *Jumpin' Bands* (Savoy), w. J. Dorsey in *The Swingin' Dorseys* (Decca).

Addr: 1713 Princeton St., Las Vegas, Nevada.

KILLIAN, ALBERT (Al), *trumpet,* b. Birmingham, Ala., 10/15/16; d. Los Angeles, Cal., 9/5/50, murdered by a psychopathic landlord at his Los Angeles home. First prominent on records with Slim Gaillard in 1939; worked w. Don Redman, Claude Hopkins, '40; Count Basie, '40-4; also Ch. Barnet in '43 and '45-6, Lionel Hampton in spring '45. After touring with JATP, joined Duke Ellington Dec. '47, remaining with him until shortly before his death, incl. European tour

'50. Took high note parts w. Duke incl. own comp. *Y'Oughta,* but was also excellent modern jazzman in normal register. LPs w. Jazz at the Philharmonic (Verve); Basie (Epic); Barnet (Dec.), Ellington (Col.).

KINCAIDE, DEANE, *composer, clarinet, saxophones;* b. Houston, Texas, 3/18/11. Arranged and played w. Ben Pollack 1932-5, Bob Crosby '36-9, Woody Herman '37; also Tommy Dorsey, Ray Noble, Muggsy Spanier. W. Ray McKinley band in late '40s. Pl. w. McKinley's small group in Las Vegas, Chi. and NYC '56, also w. Frank Signorelli at Nick's but has occupied himself mainly w. arranging. His arrs. for the Bob Crosby orch. were among the first and most successful efforts to translate Dixieland jazz into big band terms. Arr. for Steve Allen TV show, NBC Bandstand '57-9; arr. and co-ordinated music for Garry Moore TV show. Arrs. for Glenn Miller orch. under McKinley, Benny Goodman Brussels trip. Active in radio/TV jingle field from '55. Own LP: *The Solid South* (Evst.); LPs as arr. w. Wild Bill Davison (Col.), *The Fabulous Dorseys* (Col.); as arr. & player w. Bob Crosby (Dot, Coral), Dave Garroway (Vict.).

Addr: 380 Old Long Ridge Road, Stamford, Conn.

KING, MORGANA, *singer;* b. Pleasantville, N.Y., 6/4/30. Father played guitar and sang. Stud. at Metropolitan School of Music. Appeared at Basin Street and other NYC clubs from 1956-60 incl. upstairs at the Roundtable '59. One of the best jazz-inclined pop singers of recent years. Ambition: To become dramatic actress. Own LPs on EmArcy, UA.

KING, TEDDI, *singer;* b. Boston, Mass., 9/18/29. On graduating from high school she joined the Tributary Theatre and was drafted into singing part as mermaid in *Peter Pan.* Won singing contest sponsored by Dinah Shore in Boston theatre; spent a year singing for USO and Amer. Theatre Wing. Stud. classical singing for three months, jazz piano six months. Sang w. Geo. Graham, Jack Edwards bands; rec. debut w. Nat Pierce on now defunct Motif label. Toured w. Geo. Shearing quintet, July '52-Mar. '53; rejoined Shearing for Caribbean tour May '53. Single work in night clubs since fall of '53. "Jazz influenced . . . uniquely versatile entertainer . . . most impressive vocal equipment in pop music . . . intonation and diction are flawless."—Nat Hentoff. Own LPs on Vict., Coral; w. George Shearing in *Cool Canaries* (MGM).

KINSEY, ANTHONY (Tony), *drums;* also *piano;* b. Birmingham, England, 10/11/27. Father plays violin, mother piano. Piano lessons at age 7 in Birmingham. Mainly self-taught on drums. Studied w. Bill West in NYC while working on transatlantic liners. Help from a Birmingham drummer by the name of Tommy Webster. Worked w. Johnny Dankworth Seven; backed Oscar Peterson, Ella Fitzgerald, Lena Horne, Sarah Vaughan. Own group at London's Flamingo Club from 1953. Pl. Paris Jazz Fest. in '54 and has made tours of Germany and Belgium. Fav: Kenny Clarke; infl: Charlie Parker, Duke Ellington. Rec. for English Decca, poetry and jazz EP for Parlophone.

KIRBY, JOHN, *leader, bass;* b. Baltimore, Md., 12/31/08; d. Hollywood, Cal., 6/14/52. Started on trombone, then tuba, playing w. Fletcher Henderson 1930-3. String bass w. Chick Webb from late '33 to '35; back w. Henderson '35-6; Lucky Millinder '36. In 1937 he formed his own sextet. Originally the band included Frankie Newton and Pete Brown, but the personnel identified with its years of fame comprised Charlie Shavers, whose muted trumpet and arrangements were the prime factor in its success, Russ Procope on alto, Buster Bailey clarinet, Billy Kyle piano, O'Neil Spencer drums, and Kirby. This combo, with its light, breezy sound and unique style, brought a new element of ingeniously orchestrated finesse to small-band jazz. The band acquired a smart enough following to enable it to set several precedents for Negro orchestras, including an engagement at the Waldorf-Astoria in NYC and a network radio series in 1940, *Flow Gently Sweet Rhythm,* co-starring Maxine Sullivan, who was then Kirby's wife.

After 1942 the Kirby vogue slowly declined and the band lost most of its personality as the personnel changed, Billy Kyle's long absence in the Army and Shavers' defection to Tommy Dorsey being major factors. There was a brief revival in 1946, with Billy Kyle back and Sarah Vaughan as vocalist, but by the following year Kirby was working erratically and the sextet was defunct. The original personnel was reassembled (with Sid Catlett replacing Spencer, who had died) for one night, when Kirby gave a Carnegie Hall concert, in Dec. 1950, but the attendance was pathetically small. Kirby moved to California and spent the last year of his life in obscurity while Benny Carter, an old friend, tried to rehabilitate him. He died of diabetes.

As a bassist, Kirby had a light, gentle sound that contrasted with the heavy-handed plucking of earlier jazz bassmen. As a leader, he was perhaps the most important combo director of the 1930s. Among the sextet's greatest successes were *Pastel Blue* and *Undecided,* written by Shavers, and a large number of swing adaptations of classical works, incl. *Anitra's Dance, Humoresque, Sextet from Lucia, Sugar Plum Fairy* etc. Own LP: *Intimate Swing* (Harm. 7124); also one track in *Encyclopedia of Jazz on Records, Vol. 2* (Decca 8384); LPs w. Lionel Hampton (Cam. 402), Billie Holiday (Col. CL 637). On *The Complete Charlie Shavers with Maxine Sullivan* (Beth. 67) the original band, minus Kirby, is heard in some 1955 recreations.

KIRK, ANDREW DEWEY (Andy), *leader;* b. Newport, Ky., 5/28/1898. Raised in Denver, Colo.; one of his music teachers was the late Wilberforce Whiteman, father of Paul Whiteman. Played tuba in Geo. Morrison's orch.

in Denver from early '20s; started as bandleader 1929, working mostly around KC w. Mary Lou Williams as featured soloist and arranger. Kirk originally played bass sax with the band but later only conducted. The group, known as "Andy Kirk and His 12 Clouds of Joy," became nationally known as the result of his best-selling record *Until the Real Thing Comes Along,* featuring vocal by Pha Terrell, 1936; the band recorded regularly for Decca from that year until it broke up early in 1948. Kirk then went to California and formed a new band. Has been in real estate business since '52, from Aug. '58 managing the Theresa Hotel in NYC. Since '55 his jobs in the music business have been limited to occasional appearances with pick-up bands. In its heyday Kirk's band was a smooth, swinging outfit. Its outstanding soloists incl. the late Dick Wilson on tenor, Henry Wells and Ted Donnelly on trombones, and later such men as Don Byas, Howard McGhee and Fats Navarro. LPs: one number in *Encyclopedia of Jazz on Records, Vol. 2,* two numbers in *Kansas City Jazz* (Decca); *A Mellow Bit of Rhythm* (Vict.).

Addr: 555 Edgecombe Ave., New York 32, N.Y.

KLEIN, HAROLD (Harry), *baritone, alto saxes;* b. London, Eng., 12/25/28. Began stud. alto in 1944 and is largely self-taught. Worked for K. Baker '52, J. Parnell '52-3, and in '56 was feat. w. S. Kenton on his European tour. Has recorded extensively w. own group and w. various pick-up bands in Eng. One of the most confident and capable of Brit. jazzmen. Won *Melody Maker* Britain's Best Poll, 1957. Favs: Parker, Hodges, B. Carter. LPs w. V. Feldman (Contemp.).

Addr: 21 Lewis Flats, Amhurst Rd., Hackney, London, E.8, Eng.

KLEINSCHUSTER, ERICH, *trombone;* b. Graz, Austria, 1/23/30. Stud. piano 1946, and tbn. '53 at Cons. in Graz. Prof. debut in radio dance band; featured since '54 in Kleiner Tanzorchester von Radio Graz. A lawyer by profession, he became a full-time musician after working w. Newport International Band at NJF and Brussels World's Fair, summer '58. He then gave up his law practice, gigging locally. Favs: Brookmeyer, Jay Jay Johnson. LP w. Newport International Band (Col.).

Addr: Schoeckelbachweg 39, Graz, Austria.

KLINK, AL, *tenor sax, flute;* b. Danbury, Conn., 12/28/15. First important job with Glenn Miller 1939-42. Solos on *In the Mood* (split w. Tex Beneke), *Boulder Buff.* After Miller band broke up he worked with Benny Goodman and Tommy Dorsey until '45, then WNEW staff early '47. Free-lanced until summer '54, when he joined NBC staff. Bass sax solo on *Goodnight Sweetheart* w. McGuire Sisters. Fav: Lester Young. Own LP on Grand Award; LPs w. Glenn Miller (Vict.), Benny Goodman (Cap.), Steve Allen (Coral), Mundell Lowe (River.), Sauter-Finegan (Vict.), Jim Timmens (War. Bros.).

Addr: 31 Elto Road, Stewart Manor, Garden City, L.I., N.Y.

KLUGER, IRVING (Irv), *drums, vibes;* b. Brooklyn, N.Y., 7/9/21. Stud. violin 1930-4 at Henry St. Settlement School; drums w. Henry Adler; comp. at NYU. St. with Bob Astor; Georgie Auld, '42-3; Bob Chester, Freddy Slack, '43-4; Boyd Raeburn '45-7; Herbie Fields, Bobby Byrne, '47; Stan Kenton '47-8; Tex Beneke, Artie Shaw, '49; *Guys and Dolls* pit band '50-3; Shaw Gramercy 5 '53-4; house band at Moulin Rouge in Hollywood '54. Free-lanced in Hollywood '55-'60; joint owner with Roy Harte of "Valley Drum City" store. TV w. Red Rowe, also seen on *Line Up.* Kluger played on early D. Gillespie records (*Good Bait, Be-Bop,* etc.) commonly attributed to Shelly Manne. Favs: C. Webb, A. Levitt, S. Levey. LPs w. Shaw (Verve), Kenton (Cap.).

Addr: 14007 Van Owen, Van Nuys, Calif.

KNEPPER, JAMES M. (Jimmy), *trombone;* b. Los Angeles, Calif., 11/22/27. Began on alto horn at 5, trombone at 9 w. private teacher and later at Los Angeles City and State colleges. Has worked w. a great variety of big bands: Barnet, Spivak, Herman, Marterie, Thornhill, Kenton et al, and small groups of Ch. Parker, G. Roland, Ray Bauduc, Art Pepper. Joined Ch. Mingus Jazz Workshop '57; with Tony Scott '58; toured w. Kenton March-June '59, then rejoined Mingus. Joined Herbie Mann for African tour '60. Infl. by Parker and by such trombonists as D. Wells, Higginbotham, L. Brown, Dickenson, Knepper has been called by Whitney Balliett "the first original trombonist in the modern idiom since J. J. Johnson". He won DB critics' poll '58 as new star. Own LPs: Bethlehem; Pepper-Knepper Quintet (Metrojazz). LPs w. Langston Hughes (MGM); Mingus (Debut, Atl., Col.), T. Scott *52nd St. Jazz* (Coral).

Addr: 260 Lilypond Avenue, Staten Island, N.Y.

KNIGHT, JOSEPH (Joe), *piano;* b. Brooklyn, N.Y., 5/14/22. Played w. Hot Lips Page 1947-51; w. Earl Bostic '51-2; then w. Lucky Thompson's group and free-lance work around NYC w. Kenny Burrell et al. LPs w. Bennie Green (Blue Note).

KNOPF, PAUL, *piano, composer;* b. New York City, 2/3/27. Parents and brother musical; stud. piano at seven, clar. at 12. Played in dance band in high school. Went to New Orleans after grad. and pl. in clubs there; later in NYC. Creates and performs in an eccentric and provocative style. Fav: Thelonious Monk. Own LPs, *Enigma of a Day* and *The Outcat* (Playback).

Addr: 397 1st Ave., New York, N.Y.

KNOX, BERTELL EMANUAL, *drums;* b. NYC, 6/10/27. Stud. privately w. Specs Wright and in Band Training Unit, Camp Lee, Va., 1946. After discharge worked in Washington night clubs; Howard Theater house band, The Washingtonians, directed by Frank Wess, '49-50; Howard U. Swingmasters, '50-51. Toured w. Pearl Bailey, Ella Fitzgerald, Jackie Davis and Arnette

Cobb, '52-57. With Charlie Byrd at Showboat from '58. Has also worked as US Govt. clerk, '56-60. Infl: Denzil Best, Jo Jones. LPs w. Byrd (Offbeat), Jackie Davis (Cap.).

Addr: 3419 20th St. NE, Washington, D.C.

KOCH, MERLE, *piano, composer;* b. Lexington, Neb., 11/12/14. After stud. and pl. at school, local dance band work. Worked for many years in commercial dance bands; as leader, had quintet in 1938 in Hollywood, Cal. Began to acquire jazz reputation after joining Pete Fountain 4/9/59. Favs: Bob Zurke, Teddy Wilson. Fav. own recs: *Kansas City Stomps* in *Shades of Jelly Roll* LP (Carnival), *China Boy* w. Fountain.

Addr: 600 Bourbon St., New Orleans, La.

KOFFMAN, MOE, *flute, alto sax, composer;* b. Toronto, Ont., 1/28/28. Stud. vln. at 9, alto at 13. Later clar., stud. at Toronto Cons. Won all-Canadian jazz poll '48; to NYC Jan. '50 6 mos. w. Sonny Dunham band, 9 mos. w. Ralph Flanagan, then 6 mos. w. Buddy Morrow, 4 mos. w. J. Dorsey. Settled in NYC, rec. and pl. weekends w. Ch. Barnet, Art Mooney, Tito Rodriguez, Chico O'Farrill. A year on road w. Tex Beneke, year w. Don Rodney at Arcadia Ballroom. Moved back to Toronto Oct. '55; did TV studio work, org. own jazz combo and pl. after-hours jazz club for year and a half. Signed w. Jubilee Records '57; his tune *Swingin' Shepherd Blues* in his first LP became a big hit single record in US. App. at Stratford Ont. festival '58, Canadian Timex TV jazz show '59, Toronto jazz fest. '59. Own LPs: Jubilee.

Addr: 1 Bondhead Place, Thistletown P.O. Box 411, Toronto, Ont.

KOLLER, HANS, *tenor sax;* also *clarinet, baritone, alto;* b. Vienna, Austria, 2/12/21. Stud. cl. 1935 at Vienna Music Academy; diploma '39. Prof. debut on tenor '38 until entered German Army '40. Was one of very few jazzmen who played during Nazi years. Own groups from '47; led first important modern German jazz combo in '50 w. Jutta Hipp, Al Mangelsdorff. Toured Germany w. D. Gillespie '53, w. Lee Konitz-Lars Gullin '54, concerts as soloist w. Stan Kenton '55; own quintet w. Roland Kovac '54-6. Worked in Eddie Sauter's Baden-Baden radio house band '57-8, then free-lanced in Baden-Baden, leading own combos w. O. Pettiford, K. Clarke. Made film short *Jazz Gestern und Heute* for J. E. Berendt.

Orig. infl. by Lester Young, later by Konitz & Tristano, then by Al Cohn, Koller has made many recs., chiefly for German Brunswick. Koller is also an abstract painter. He likes basic, simple swinging jazz and is considered the no. 1 tenor man in Germany, where he has won *Podium* and *Jazz-Echo* polls several times. Own LP: Vanguard. Six tracks by own combo on *Das ist Jazz!* (Decca).

Addr: Baden-Baden, Herchenbachstr. 11, Germany.

KONITZ, LEE, *alto sax;* b. Chicago, Ill., 10/13/27. Early experience with Gay Claridge and other commercial bands in Chicago, followed by a few months w. Jerry Wald. Studied at Roosevelt College, toured w. Claude Thornhill '47-8 and made his first records (*Anthropology, Yardbird Suite*) with this band. He appeared with Miles Davis' Capitol recording group at the Royal Roost, September '48, and recorded with Davis '48-50. During these years he became very closely associated with Lennie Tristano, absorbed a great deal of Tristano's influence and made occasional appearances with him. In November 1951 he spent a week in Scandinavia fronting local combos at concerts. He joined Stan Kenton in August 1952, remaining a little over a year. In '54-5 he led his own combo, mainly in New York and Boston. Played successful series of concerts in Germany late '55 w. Hans Koller, Lars Gullin et al. Active as teacher and performer in NYC, incl. long stay at Half Note Cafe '57-8; working there again in reunion with Tristano '59.

Konitz, according to Barry Ulanov in *A Handbook of Jazz* (Viking) is "well endowed with melodic resourcefulness, a distinctive tone and a subtle sense of time." One of the most uncompromising individualists in jazz, he turned down many offers to join name bands, refusing to adapt his style to a different setting, preferring to remain a part of the clique of avant-gardists surrounding Tristano. His small, languid sound and his clear reflection of the harmonic feeling he had absorbed through Tristano placed his solos among the most valuable and durable sounds of the 1950s. Konitz won the *Metronome* poll '54, *Down Beat* critics' poll '57-8. Own LPs: Pres. 7004; *Lee Konitz With Warne Marsh* (Atl. 1217), *The Real Lee Konitz* (Atl. 1273), *Lee Konitz Inside Hi-Fi* (Atl. 1258; Konitz plays one half of the LP on tenor sax), *Very Cool* (Verve 8209), *Tranquility* (Verve 8281), *An Image* (Verve 8286), *Lee Konitz Meets Jimmy Giuffre* (Verve 8335), *Lee Konitz With Gerry Mulligan* (Wor. Pac. 406); six tracks in *Conception* (Pres. 7013); LPs w. Ralph Burns in *Jazz Recital* (Verve 8098); Miles Davis (Cap. T762), *The Gerry Mulligan Songbook* (Wor. Pac. 1237), Claude Thornhill (Harm. 7088), Lennie Tristano (Atl. 1224); three tracks w. Tristano in *Cool And Quiet* (Cap. T371); *Metronome All Stars* (Harm. 7044, Verve 8030), one track in *History of Jazz, Vol. 4* (Cap. T 796).

Addr: 83 Twig Lane, Levittown, L.I., N.Y.

KOTICK, THEODORE JOHN (Teddy), *bass;* b. Haverhill, Mass., 6/4/28. Guitar at 6; bass in high school. Gigged in New England; to NYC 1948, pl. w. Johnny Bothwell, Buddy Rich, Tony Pastor, Buddy De Franco Sextet '49; Artie Shaw '50; Stan Getz '51-3; off and on w. Ch. Parker. Toured w. Horace Silver Quintet '57-8; after this gigged in NYC area. Rarely heard in solos; excellent rhythm section bassist. Favs: Blanton, Ray Brown, Tommy Potter. LPs w. Charlie Parker (Verve), Stan Getz (Roost, Verve), Silver (Blue Note), Jimmy Raney, Phil Woods, Bob Brookmeyer, *Earthy* (Pres.), Teddy Charles (Atl.), Nick Travis, Tony Scott (Vict.), Bill Evans (River.), Jimmy Knepper (Beth.), *The*

Four Most Guitars (ABC-Par.), George Wallington (Pres., Atl.).

Addr: 8542 151st Street, Jamaica, L.I., N.Y.

KOVAC, ROLAND, *clarinet, saxophone, piano;* b. Vienna, Austria, 11/7/27. From musical family, he began stud. piano in 1933; in Vienna Boys' Choir '35-8; stud. clar. '40-9. Doctor's degree in musicology from U of Vienna '52. Had own combo '45-9; w. Hans Koller off and on; worked in radio, concerts and films. Rec. w. Koller.

Addr: Mariahilferstrasse 127, Vienna 6, Austria.

KRAL, IRENE, *singer;* b. Chicago, Ill., 1/18/32. Brother is Roy Kral; pl. piano and clar. in high school. Began singing at 16 w. Jay Burkhardt; briefly w. Woody Herman, Chubby Jackson; joined vocal group called Tattle Tales, leaving in 1955 to go out as single. Worked w. Maynard Ferguson's band '57-8. Fav: Carmen McRae. Own LPs: *Steveireno; The Band and I* w. Herb Pomeroy (UA); w. Maynard Ferguson (Em.).

KRAL, ROY JOSEPH, *singer, piano, composer;* b. Chicago, Ill., 10/10/21. Army 1942-6. Arr. for concert band touring Midwest, then did studio staff work w. band at WWJ, Detroit. While working in Chicago w. Geo. Davis Quartet, met Jackie Cain. They formed a vocal duo, played several concerts sponsored by Dave Garroway, at one of which they met Ch. Ventura, whose combo they joined early in 1948. Leaving Ventura Apr. '49 they were married June 27th, had their own sextet (three men, three girls) which played Bop City and other jazz clubs 1949-50. Disbanded and settled in Chicago, where they had own TV show; rejoined Ventura for eight months 1953, then came to NYC and continued to work as duo. Resident in Las Vegas 1957-60. Kral comp. & arr. most of the material sung by him and Miss Cain. The duo, basically geared to sophisticated night club audiences but equally acceptable to jazz fans, is unique in its smooth, airy and thoroughly hip approach. Their performances blend witty lyrics and unusual melodies with a light modern jazz feeling. Feat. on TV commercial for Plymouth 1960. Own LPs: ABC-Par., Bruns., Story; LPs w. Ventura: Bruns., Decca, Merc., Reg.

Addr: 1601 Hartke, Las Vegas, Nev.

KRESS, CARL, *guitar;* b. Newark, N.J., 10/20/07. First prominent in Paul Whiteman Orch. during Bix-Trumbauer era, recording with the latter pair in 1927 on Chicago Loopers date, and w. Red Nichols, Miff Mole, Dorsey Brothers, etc. 1927-9. In the '30s he was prominent as a successful radio guitarist and also as a partner in the original Onyx Club on 52nd Street. He recorded guitar duets with Eddie Lang in '32 and Dick McDonough in '34. Kress, who was one of the pioneers of chord-style jazz guitar, has remained in commercial radio and TV work but occasionally appears on records as a rhythmic soloist of merit in the swing idiom. LPs w. Red Nichols (Bruns.).

Addr: 444 Hunt Lane, Munsey Park, L.I., N.Y.

KRUPA, GENE, *drums, leader;* b. Chicago, Ill., 1/15/09. First band he worked with was the Frivolians, a group of youngsters in Chicago around 1921. It was not until years later that he started to study drums (with Edward B. Straight and Roy Knapp). He spent a year at St. Joseph's College in Indiana, a prep. seminary, 1924-5. Krupa made his record debut Dec. 9, 1927 on Okeh with McKenzie-Condon Chicagoans; this was believed to be the first record session on which a bass drum was used. During '27 and '28 he worked in Chicago with the bands of Thelma Terry, a girl bass player, Joe Kayser, Leo Shukin (with Teschemacher, Mezzrow, Joe Sullivan) and the Benson Orch. In 1929 he came to New York with Red McKenzie. Joined Red Nichols at the Hollywood Rest. and played with him in pit bands for several plays. During the early '30s he worked mostly with commercial bands such as those of Irving Aaronson, Russ Colombo, Mal Hallett, and Buddy Rogers, but was also heard as jazzman through frequent record dates with Bix Beiderbecke, Benny Goodman, Adrian Rollini, etc. In March 1935 he joined Benny Goodman; as a main attraction with the Goodman band (he was featured on the best-selling record *Sing Sing Sing*), he became one of the important figures of the swing era and was able to start a successful band of his own in March 1938. The band stayed together until 1943, earning great popularity during its last two years, with the help of Roy Eldridge and Anita O'Day.

Krupa rejoined Goodman for a couple of months in 1943, then toured with Tommy Dorsey Dec. '43-July '44. He led his own big band from '44 until '51. In the fall of '51-'52-'53 he toured as a member of the JATP unit; between these engagements he led his own trio, first with Charlie Ventura (with whom he played Japan 1952), later with Eddie Shu. In '51 he studied with Saul Goodman, tympanist with the N.Y. Philharmonic; in March 1954 he started his own drum school jointly with Cozy Cole. He again toured Europe with JATP May '59.

In Dec. '59 a film was released entitled *The Gene Krupa Story,* allegedly based on the drummer's life. Ludicrously inaccurate even by Hollywood standards, it neglected most of the salient facts and consisted largely of anachronisms, distortions and outright fiction. The title role was played by Sal Mineo but Krupa recorded the sound track.

Gene Krupa was the first drummer in jazz history to attain a position of global renown. His steady, relentless beat and ever-improving technique made him a vital figure in the years of Goodman's triumphs; his tremendous showmanship earned him renewed success as a leader in his own right. He won the Met. poll 1937-45, DB poll 1936-9, '43, '52-3, Esq. Silver Award 1946. Favs: Cozy Cole, Buddy Rich, Dave Black. Own LPs: *Hey! Here's Gene Krupa* (Verve 8300), *Gene Krupa Story* (Verve VS 6105), *Driving Gene* (Verve 8107), *Drum Boogie* (Verve 8087), *Drummer Man* (Verve 2008), *Exciting Gene Krupa* (Verve 8071), *Jazz Rhythms* (Verve 8204), *Krupa & Rich* (Verve

8069), *Krupa Rocks* (Verve 8276), *Plays Mulligan Arrangements* (Verve 8292), *Sing Sing Sing* (Verve 8190), *Trio at JATP* (Verve 8031), *Drummer Man* (ARS 427), *Swingin' With Krupa* (Cam. 340), *Gene Krupa's Sidekicks* (Col. CL 641), *Gene Krupa* (Col. CL 753); LPs w. Teddy Wilson-L. Hampton-R. Callender (Verve 8066), Benny Goodman (Col. OSL 180, OSL 160, MGM 3E9, Vict. LPT 6073, LPM 1226), Red Nichols (Bruns. 54047).

Addr: 10 Ritchie Court, Yonkers, N.Y.

KUHN, ROLF, *clarinet;* b. Cologne, Germany, 9/29/29. Father a variety artist. Stud. concert piano 1938 in Leipzig; clar. '41. Moved to West Germany '52 to join jazz group, heard Goodman and De Franco records and was soon broadcasting w. own quartet on US station RIAS in Berlin and winning European polls. Moved to US May '56; pl. w. Caterina Valente in NYC. Through the encouragement of Friedrich Gulda, John Hammond and agent Willard Alexander, formed own quartet, appearing at NJF '57 and on Birdland concert tour '57. From Sept. '57 to Jan. '58 he was with the band sent out under Benny Goodman's name, playing Goodman's parts and doubling on alto sax. Toured w. Warren Covington (T. Dorsey memorial band) Jan.-Mar. '58. Gigs w. Urbie Green big band '58-9. From March-Sept. '59 was in Germany, Belgium, Switzerland, making several record dates.

Rolf Kuhn had the misfortune to enter the jazz scene at a time when his chosen instrument had suffered an apparently irreparable decline in popularity. Had it not been for these circumstances he might well be a major name in jazz today. Though his idols clearly are De Franco and to some extent Goodman, he has developed an almost unmatched fluency and swing and is certainly one of the finest living jazz clarinetists. Own LP: Vang.; LPs w. Toshiko, *United Notions* (Metrojazz); Eddie Costa Trio at Newport (Verve); Urbie Green (Vict.).

Addr: 26 West 87th St., New York City, N.Y.

KYLE, WILLIAM OSBORNE (Billy), *piano;* b. Philadelphia, Pa., 7/14/14. Studied organ, piano; local bands from 1930. Played w. Tiny Bradshaw, Lucky Millinder, before joining John Kirby, with whom he was prominently featured from 1938-42. After three years in the Army he rejoined Kirby briefly '46, then worked with Sy Oliver and for several years played mainly on commercial recording dates, also long stretches with pit orchs. on Broadway incl. 2½ years with *Guys and Dolls.* Since 1953 has been w. Louis Armstrong. Kyle was noted for his unique single note style, dynamically reminiscent of Earl Hines but melodically quite original and often humorous in spirit. During his years of prominence w. Kirby, he was in demand for record dates and can be heard on sessions w. Lionel Hampton, Jack Teagarden, Rex Stewart, Joe Marsala, etc. LPs w. Armstrong (Col., Decca), Sy Oliver (Decca), one no. w. Kirby in *Encyclopedia of Jazz on Records* (Decca), Jack Teagarden (Atl.), Charlie Shavers (Beth.), Buck Clayton (Col.), *Flow Gently Sweet Rhythm* (Per.).

Addr: 227 West 46th St., New York, N.Y.

KYNER, JUNIOR SYLVESTER (Sonny Red), *alto sax;* b. Detroit, Mich., 12/17/32. St. on C melody sax in high school, switched to alto in 1949. Early experience w. pianist Barry Harris' combo from '49-52. Pl. tenor sax several months in '54 w. Frank Rosolino, then alto w. Art Blakey the same year. Came to NYC w. Curtis Fuller '57. Favs: Charlie Parker, Sonny Stitt, Jackie McLean, John Jenkins, Cannonball Adderley. Own LP: Blue Note; LPs w. Curtis Fuller, Paul Quinichette (Prestige).

L

LACY, STEVE (Steven Lackritz), *soprano sax;* b. New York City, 7/23/34. Stud. w. Cecil Scott, Harold Freeman, Joe Allard, Cecil Taylor in NYC, also at Schillinger School in Boston 1953 and Manhattan School NYC '54. From '52 he followed Cecil Scott around and sat in on various jobs with him, later pl. with the Dixieland groups of M. Kaminsky, J. McPartland, R. Stewart, B. Clayton, C. Shavers, Z. Singleton, Hot Lips Page, gigging w. his own groups. Later gave up all this work to study, practice, and play w. Cecil Taylor's quart. 56-7. In '58-9 he was heard on records and in person w. Gil Evans' orch. The only musician to have attained prominence pl. sop. sax in the modern idiom, he was voted New Star of the Year in the 1957 *Metronome Yearbook.* Favs: Ellington, Monk, S. Rollins, M. Davis, Parker, Pee Wee Russell, J. Coltrane. Own LPs: *Soprano Saxophone* (Pres.), *Reflections* (New Jazz). LPs w. Tom Stewart, W. Mitchell (ABC-Par.), C. Taylor (Trans., Verve), Gil Evans (New Jazz, Wor. Pac.).

Addr: 21 Bleecker St., New York 12, N.Y.

LADA, ANTON, *composer, drums;* b. Chicago, Ill., 9/25/90; d. Santa Monica, Calif., 8/28/44. Had priv. lessons and pl. in Milwaukee Symph. Org. own band in New Orleans called "Louisiana Five" with which he rec. for Col., Edison, Emerson. Went to Hollywood 1941 and did scores for motion pictures.

LADNIER, THOMAS (Tommy), *trumpet;* b. Mandeville, La., 5/28/00; d. NYC 6/4/39. To Chicago as a child; began work w. Charlie Creath on riverboats toward end of W.W.I, later working in Chicago w. Roy Palmer, Lovie Austin, Milton Vassar. After pl. in 1924 w. the band of King Oliver, who was his main musical inspiration, he toured Europe in '25 w. Sam Wooding, pl. in France, Scandinavia, Spain, Germany and Russia; also in Poland w. Louis Douglas' orch. Back in US in '26, he worked w. Billy Fowler, Fletcher

Henderson, then from late '28-30 was in Europe again, first w. Wooding, then w. Noble Sissle, remaining with him through 1931. In '32 he joined forces w. Sidney Bechet, and their "New Orleans Feetwarmers" were heard at the Savoy Ballroom and on Victor records. From '33-8 he was almost inactive in music, ret. in November '38 for several record dates on Bluebird under his own name and w. Mezz Mezzrow. He became ill not long afterward and was unable to benefit from the renewed prominence these records brought him.

Ladnier was considered by some critics to be one of the greatest jazz trumpet men in the Armstrong-Oliver tradition. In his early years ('23-7) he was feat. on records w. Ollie Powers, Ma Rainey, Ida Cox, Lovie Austin, and Bessie Smith. His last records, made Feb. '39, were on a blues date accompanying Rosetta Crawford on Decca. LPs w. Johnny Dodds, Fletcher Henderson, Ma Rainey, *History of Classic Jazz* (River.) *Spirituals To Swing* (Vang.).

LA FARO, SCOTT, *bass;* b. Newark, N.J., 4/3/36. Stud. clar. while attending high school in Geneva, N.Y.; at Ithaca Cons. for a year. Gigged around Geneva on tenor sax for a while; took up bass the summer he grad. from high school, and with the exception of the year at Ithaca Cons. has played nothing else since. Worked in rhythm and blues bands and w. Buddy Morrow 1955; w. Chet Baker '56-7. Spent five months in Calif. practicing, then to Chicago and worked w. Pat Moran and Ira Sullivan. Back to LA, he pl. with Barney Kessell and at Howard Rumsey's Lighthouse. To NYC Apr. '59, toured w. B. Goodman. Own trio in NYC fall '59; also w. Bill Evans. Won *Down Beat* Critics' Poll as New Star 1959. Favs: Chambers, Mingus, P. Heath. Brilliant, extremely promising bassist. LPs w. Victor Feldman (Contemp.), Pat Moran (Audio-Fid.), Cal Tjader-Stan Getz (Fant.).

Addr: 4525 Van Noord, Studio City, Calif.

LAFITTE, GUY, *tenor sax;* b. Saint Gaudens, France, 1/11/27. St. on clar. Prof. debut 1945; led Hot Club of Toulouse orch. to '48; toured w. Big Bill Broonzy '50, Mezzrow '51, Bill Coleman & Dickie Wells '52. Won Grand Prix Django Reinhardt '54, Grand Prix du Disques '57. Own orch. from '56. Many rec. w. Lucky Thompson, Emmett Berry, Lionel Hampton; own trio on French Col. from '56. Main infl. Coleman Hawkins; favs. Herschel Evans, Eddie Davis, Ben Webster. One of the most popular tenor men in France.

Addr: 14 Rue Boulle, Paris 11, France.

LAINE, ROBERT ERIC (Bob), *piano* b. Stockholm, Sweden, 1912. Solo at Stork Club, Nick's etc. Rec. w. Bud Freeman, Wingy Manone, Joe Venuti. To Calif. 1936; joined Ben Pollack '37 and remained with him three years. In service '42-5; later worked as single and accompanist to singers in Los Angeles, Las Vegas and Hawaii. Ret. to Sweden for visits in '53 and '59.

LAINE, FRANKIE (Frank Paul LoVecchio), *singer;* b. Chicago, Ill., 3/30/13. His revival of the song *That's My Desire* made this one of the biggest hits of 1947 and established him as a popular recording star. Though most jazz critics have dismissed or ignored Laine, he is greatly admired by many jazzmen, notably Buck Clayton, who has worked with him off and on. In 1956 Laine and Clayton teamed for an LP, *Jazz Spectacular* (Col.) feat. Clayton's all-star band with Kai Winding, J. J. Johnson, Sir Charles Thompson et al. Other LPs: Col., Merc.

LAINE, JULIAN, *trombone;* b. New Orleans, La., 1908; d. NO 9/10/57. Started pl. in dance halls w. Sharkey Bonano; later w. various bands in NO area. Joined Louis Prima briefly in 1937, then w. Joe Venuti. In Army during World War II, after which he joined Tony Almerico. From 1950 until his death, he pl. with Muggsy Spanier in Chicago and w. Sharkey Bonano in NO.

LAINE, GEORGE VITELLE (Jack or Papa), *leader, drums;* b. New Orleans, 9/21/1873. After studying bass, drums and alto horn, he formed his first band in 1888 and claims to have been one of the first to perform ragtime, imitating early Negro stomps and making a specialty of Scott Joplin's *Shadow Rag.* He also led the Reliance Brass Band before World War I (incl. Nick La Rocca), which was said to be the precursor of the original Dixieland band. In 1951 members of the New Orleans Jazz Club presented Laine, then 77, with a scroll proclaiming him to be, in effect, the first white jazz musician. In '60 he was still living in NO, in retirement, often attending meetings of the NO Jazz Club.

LAMARE, HILTON (Nappy), *guitar, singer, banjo;* b. New Orleans, La., 6/14/10. Started in teens w. Midnight Serenaders. Guitar w. Ben Pollack 1930-5; Bob Crosby '35-42, then settled in LA as free-lance musician, often app. at Hangover Club w. other ex-Crosby sidemen. Since '55 he and Ray Bauduc have co-led a Dixieland band on tour of US. Visited Japan, Korea, Okinawa w. band for four months in '55-6. During the '30s recorded w. Wingy Manone, Louis Prima, Jack Teagarden; in '40s, many dates w. Julia Lee, Nellie Lutcher, Jesse Price. Own LPs on Cap., Merc.; LPs w. Bob Crosby (Coral, Decca).

Addr: 14251 Cohasset St., Van Nuys, Calif.

LAMBERT, DAVID ALDEN (Dave), *singer, vocal arranger;* b. Boston, Mass., 6/19/17. Stud. drums at 10 for a year; no other mus. ed. Pl. three summers in late 1930s as drummer w. Hugh McGuinness Trio in New England. Joined CCC for a year, became tree surgeon in Westchester. Joined Army 1940 and saw much active duty as paratrooper, etc. before discharge in '43. After a year as rhythm singer w. Johnny Long's band, joined Hi, Lo, Jack and the Dame. Teamed w. the late Buddy Stewart in Gene Krupa band '44-5, he recorded *What's This,* the first bop vocal record. Led vocal quart. in Broadway show *Are You With It* '46-7. During height of bop fad, rec. with own group for Capitol and w. Jo Stafford for Columbia. Worked as contractor for vocal groups in cartoons, radio and TV jingles, etc.; also background arr. for Carmen McRae and many other singers. In '57 he teamed up w. Jon Hendricks to arrange a vocal adaptation of Jimmy Giuffre's *Four Brothers.* Soon after, Lambert and Hendricks, in combination w. Annie Ross, rec. their first album. *See Lambert, Hendricks & Ross.*

Dave Lambert was the first to translate the new ideas of bop musicians into effective vocal terms. Though he remained unknown nationally until the establishment of the partnership with Hendricks and Ross, for many years before this he had been making a valuable contribution in both the jazz and popular vocal fields. LPs w. Hendricks & Ross: *Sing a Song of Basie* (ABC-Par.), *Sing Along with Basie* (Roul.) *The Swingers* (Wor. Pac.), *Hottest New Group In Jazz* (Col.).

Addr: 24 Cornelia St., New York 14, N.Y.

LAMBERT, HENDRICKS & ROSS. Formed purely as a recording unit, this vocal group was assembled for an album entitled *Sing a Song of Basie* (ABC-Paramount) early in 1958, and by August had gained sufficient popularity to appear in person at the Randalls Island Jazz Festival. Within a few months the trio, now permanently organized, had become the most sought-after new singing group in jazz. Its unique policy was the setting of lyrics (usually by Jon Hendricks) to material drawn from instrumental records. Not only the ensemble passages but the ad lib solos on these records were given lyrics. The trio added a new dimension to vocal jazz and during 1959 was acclaimed at the Playboy Jazz Festival, at Newport and in a *Jazz for Moderns* concert tour in November. (See Dave Lambert, Jon Hendricks, Annie Ross.) The group won the Down Beat poll '59, the Metronome poll '60 and the Playboy All Stars poll '60.

LAMMI, DICK, *bass;* b. Red Lodge, Mont., 1/15/09. Raised in Astoria, Ore., attending grammar and high school there. Stud. violin at 11, then banjo. Pl. with trio in high school. Joined the Pirates Jazz Band in Aberdeen, Wash. 1927; took up bass after moving to Portland, Ore. and pl. for five years w. Cole McElroy's band and Orpheum Theater band. Moved to SF '36, learned tuba; w. Lu Watters '41 until group disbanded, then joined Bob Scobey. Is student of metaphysics, occult sciences and psychology. LPs w. Bob Scobey, Turk Murphy (GTJ).

LAMOND, DONALD DOUGLAS (Don), *drums;* b. Oklahoma City, Okla., 8/18/20. Raised in Washington, D.C. Stud. at Peabody Inst., Baltimore. Joined Sonny Dunham 1943; Boyd Raeburn '44. Replaced Dave Tough in Woody Herman band '45 and remained with this group until its breakup Dec. '46; back w. Herman's next band '47-9. Through the 1950s free-lanced in NYC, working Steve Allen show, TV with Benny Goodman, many dates and recs. w. Dick Hyman, jazz concerts w. J. Bushkin, Lawson-Haggart, etc. One of the best drummers to rise to prominence in the mid-30s, Lamond combined the heritage of the Dave Tough school with modern elements that have made him one of the best and most adaptable percussion men in the profession. LPs: all Dick Hyman dates (MGM), *The Blues* w. Manny Albam (Cor.), *Porgy & Bess* w. Ralph Burns (Decca); Woody Herman (Cap., Col., Evst., MGM), George Russell (Decca), K. Winding, Johnny Smith (Roost), Chubby Jackson (Jub., Argo), Elliot Lawrence (Fant.) and many, many more.

Addr: 600 Route 9-W, Nyack, N. Y.

LAND, HAROLD DE VANCE, *tenor sax;* b. Houston, Tex., 12/18/28. Self-taught during youth in San Diego, Calif. Pl. with Max Roach-Clifford Brown quint. 1954-5; Curtis Counce '57-8, app. with him on *Stars of Jazz* TV shows in Hollywood. Became known in late 1950s as one of few first-rate "hard bop" jazzmen on West Coast. Favs: Charlie Parker, Bud Powell. Own LP, *Harold in the Land of Jazz* (Contemp.); LPs w. Roach-Brown (Em.), Curtis Counce (Contemp., Doo.)

Addr: 2675 S. Arlington, Los Angeles 18, Calif.

LANG, EDDIE (Salvatore Massaro), *guitar;* b. Philadelphia, Pa., 1904; d. 3/26/33. Stud. violin for eleven yrs., played in school orch. w. Joe Venuti. Switched to banjo while w. Ch. Kerr orch. After a year w. Dorsey bros. in Scranton Sirens, joined Mound City Blue Blowers on guitar, pl. Piccadilly Hotel in London and touring in US. After leading a band w. Venuti in Atlantic City he settled in NYC; rec. duets w. Lonnie Johnson, many rec. dates w. Red Nichols, Venuti et al. Following job w. Roger Wolfe Kahn, 1926-8, he made several vaudeville tours. In the spring of '30 Lang and Venuti joined Paul Whiteman and went to Hollywood to make the *King of Jazz* movie. Left the Whiteman band w. Bing Crosby and for two yrs. was Bing's accompanist, app. with him in *Big Broadcast* movie, 1932. He died suddenly after a tonsillectomy.

Lang was the first guitarist to make an international name as a jazz soloist. His sensitive chord patterns and simple, effective single string work were feat. on many great records w. jazz pioneers of the late '20s. Lonnie Johnson, with whom he rec. under the pseudonym Blind Willie Dunn for Okeh in '29, said "Lang could play guitar better than anyone I knew; the sides I made with him were my greatest experience." He won the Rec. Ch. All Time, All Star poll, 1951. LPs: one no. w. Venuti-Lang All Stars in *Encyclopedia of Jazz On Records,* Vol 1 (Decca 8398); w. Armstrong (Col. CL 854), Beiderbecke (Col. CL 845), Red Nichols (Bruns. 54047).

LANG, RONNY (Ronald Langinger), *alto sax;* also *flute, other reeds;* b. Chicago, Ill., 7/24/27. Started w. Hoagy Carmichael's Teenagers band. Worked w. Earle Spencer, Ike Carpenter; Skinnay Ennis 1947. In '49 began a long tenure as sideman w. Les Brown, interrupted by two years in service. In '58-60 doing extensive work in motion picture studios and TV (pl. for *Peter Gunn* and *Staccato* shows). Solos w. Brown incl. *Midnight Sun, Invitation, One O'Clock*

Jump, Happy Hooligan. Own LP on Tops; LPs w. Hank Mancini (Vict.), Les Brown (Coral), Dave Pell (Cap., Kapp, Vict.).

Addr: 14844 Cantara St., Van Nuys, Calif.

LANIGAN, JAMES WOOD (Jim), *bass;* also *tuba, violin, piano;* b. Chicago, Ill., 1/30/02. Father was semi-prof. flutist, mother prof. accompanist. Studied violin at age 6, then piano. Sat in with an eight-piece band at a west side ballroom for kicks and decided on a musical career. Later he became a member of the Austin High gang. Played w. Husk O'Hare 1925, Bill Paley '25-6, Art Kassel '26-7, Johnny Maitland '27, Ted Fio Rito '27-31, radio staff work '32-3, Carlos Molina '33, Chicago Theater '33-7, Chicago Symphony and NBC staff '37-48, WGN radio and TV '48-52. App. w. Austin High Gang at Playboy Fest. '59. Fav: Johann Sebastian Bach—"the master of pure bass and plenty of rhythm." LPs w. Eddie Condon (Col.), Jimmy McPartland in *Chicago Jazz* (Decca).

Addr: 218 No. Addison Road, Villa Park, Ill.

LA PORTA, JOHN D., *composer, clarinet, saxophones;* b. Philadelphia, Pa., 4/1/20. Clarinet at 9, stud. w. Wm. Dietrich, Joseph Gigliotti; stud. comp. w. Ernst Toch and Alexis Haieff. Played in Youth Symphony cond. by L. Stokowski. BA and MA from Manh. Sch. of Mus., where he later became faculty member cond. jazz workshop.

From 1940 LaPorta worked in the bands of Bob Chester, Dick Himber, Ray McKinley, W. Herman; later stud. and rec. w. L. Tristano. Rec. w. Metronome All Stars '51-2. Taught reeds and comp. at high schools and has many private students. Jazz soloist w. New York Phil. pl. Macero's *Fusion* '58. Worked closely w. Marshall Brown as reed coach of Newport Youth Band '59. Helped by the support of critics Barry Ulanov and Bill Coss, La Porta became a major name as comp. and soloist in the middle and late '50s. In the spring of '58, visiting Venezuela, he pl. and rec. w. local groups. Led quartet at NJF '58. Pl. w. Bernstein & NY Phil. in perf. of T. Macero's *Fusion,* '59. Own LPs: Fant., Debut. Everest. Other LPs: clar. soloist w. Herman on *Ebony Concerto* (Everest), baritone sax on *Salute to Bunny* (Counterpoint); also pl. on *Conceptions, South American Brothers* (Fant.), *Modern Jazz Concert* (Col.), Ch. Mingus (Beth.), A. Levister (Debut), Helen Merrill (Merc.).

Addr: 12 Maple St., Massapequa, L.I., N.Y.

LARKINS, MILTON, *trumpet, valve trombone, singer;* b. Houston, Tex., 10/10/10. Inspired by Bunk Johnson in early '30s, self-taught on trumpet. With Chester Boone '34-6; org. own band in Chicago '36, which became a top territorial outfit in late '30s. Members incl. Eddie Vinson, Illinois Jacquet, Wild Bill Davis, Arnett Cobb. Took up trom. while in the service during World War II. Has had own group at Celebrity Club in NYC in recent years.

Addr: 209 W. 148th St., New York 31, N.Y.

LARKINS, ELLIS LANE, *piano;* b. Baltimore, Md., 5/15/23. Stud. Peabody Cons. of Mus.; Juilliard 1940. Debut at Cafe Society Uptown first w. Billy Moore Trio and then w. own trio. From 43 until '52 he pl. on and off at the Blue Angel in NYC, also working w. Ed Hall Sextet at Cafe Society '45-6. In '59 he toured as accompanist to harmonica soloist Larry Adler. A skilled musician with classical training, he has also been very successful as accompanist for various singers, feat. a softly swinging style rich in right-hand chording. Own LPs: *Manhattan at Midnight, Blue & Sentimental, Soft Touch* (Decca); LP w. Ruby Braff (Van.).

Addr: Room 1107, 1619 Broadway, New York 19, N.Y.

LA ROCA, PETE (Peter Sims), *drums;* b. New York City, 4/7/38. Father played trumpet, mother piano. Stud. at High School of Music and Art, CCNY, Manhattan School of Music. Max Roach, hearing him at a Jazz Unlimited session at Birdland, recommended him to Sonny Rollins, for whom he worked off and on Oct. '57-Feb. '59 incl. European tour. Also worked several times w. Tony Scott during '59. Worked in law office '56-7 and as clerk in New York Public Library during most of '58. One of the most promising young drummers in NYC, he names Philly Joe Jones and Elvin Jones as favs. and main influences. LPs w. Slide Hampton (Strand), J. R. Monterose (Top Rank); Jackie McLean, *New Soil,* incl. fav. own solo in *Minor Apprehension* (Blue Note).

Addr: 229 W. 131st St., New York 27, N.Y.

LA ROCCA, DOMINICK JAMES (Nick), *cornet, leader;* b. New Orleans, 4/11/1889. Pl. w. Papa Laine, then formed Original Dixieland Jazz Band, often called the first white jazz band; the original personnel incl. Larry Shields, clarinet; Eddie Edwards, trombone; Henry Ragas, piano; Tony Spargo (Sbarbaro), drums. They scored their biggest success at Reisenweber's NYC, during World War I. After the band broke up in 1925 La Rocca remained out of the limelight until 1936, when he recorded with a reorganized Original Dixieland group for Victor. He remained active off and on but retired finally from music during the next decade, working in the building business from '38 until '58, when he retired and devoted time to writing songs. La Rocca has often expressed, in print, on TV interviews etc., strong opinions claiming that he was not given enough credit for having introduced jazz; he has stated that certain Negro musicians have been given too much credit. "Many of the so-called historians pass on me as if I never existed, and the ones that did write me have twisted . . . history," he wrote to the author in 1959. In '59 he donated his press clippings to the archives of Tulane U. "so that the honest historians will find the truth." LP: one track in *Dixieland and New Orleans Jazz* (Cam.).

Addr: 2218 Constance Street, New Orleans 13, La.

LATEEF, YUSEF (William Evans), *tenor sax, flutes, oboe;* b. Chattanooga, Tenn., 1921. Started on alto, then tenor while at Miller High School in Detroit in 1937. In NYC in 1946 w. L. Millinder through L. Thompson recommendation. Then w. Lips Page, R. Eldridge and others; toured w. D. Gillespie in 1949. Back to Detroit in 1950 where he formed own group in 1955 and returned to study at Wayne U. From that time, his group worked mainly in Detroit but visited NYC several times in the '57-9 period for recordings and one engagement at the Half Note. Known for use of odd instr., incl. argol, rebob, earth-board, etc. Favs: Gillespie, Parker, Billie Holiday, Stitt. Own LPs on Savoy, Verve, Pres., New Jazz, Argo; LP w. Gillespie (Vict.).

LAWRENCE, ELLIOT (Elliot Lawrence Broza), *leader, composer, piano;* b. Philadelphia, Pa., 2/14/25. Led children's band, Horn & Hardart Radio Hour 1937-41; led U. of Pa. college band, and from Jan. '45 WCAU house band, which he brought to NYC summer '46 (rec. for Col.). Had good semi-jazz dance band '47-50 w. arrs. by G. Mulligan, Tiny Kahn, then went into radio, leading combo for several years on early morning Jack Sterling show. Produced and took part in series of jazz LPs for Vik, '57-8; made transcribed jazz series, *Soundflight,* for Air Force Reserve, '58-60; feat. on CBS radio series *Jazz is My Beat,* '58-9. In summer '59, to Moscow & Leningrad; cond. Moscow TV-radio orch. for US variety show sponsored by State Dept. Though not essentially a jazz artist Lawrence has been instrumental in the creation of much first-rate jazz via radio, TV and records. Own LPs: Fant., Decca, Top Rank.

Addr: 11 Cornwells Beach Road, Sands Point, L.I., N.Y.

LAWSON, HUGH, *piano;* b. Detroit, Mich., 1935. Attended Cass Tech. High and Wayne State U., where he stud. tenor sax as well as piano. Joined Yusef Lateef at Klein's in Detroit, March 1956 and has been with him ever since. Favs: Powell, Monk, Garner. LPs w. Lateef (Savoy, Pres., New Jazz).

LAWSON, YANK (John R. Lausen), *trumpet;* b. Trenton, Mo., 5/3/11. Mother played piano. Studied piano, sax and then trumpet; teachers were Carl Webb, Del Staigers. Started in college dance band at U. of Mo. Worked w. Slaty Randall 1931; Ben Pollack '32-4; trumpet and stockholder in co-operative Bob Crosby band 1935-8; Tommy Dorsey '38-40, rejoined Crosby '41-2. After working w. Benny Goodman for a few months in 1942 he went into radio work in NYC. Featured w. Bobby Byrne on Steve Allen TV show 1953-4. With Bob Haggart, co-led Lawson-Haggart band, a Dixieland recording group that made a series of LPs for Decca during the '50s. Fav: Billy Butterfield. Fav. rec. solo *Stormy Weather* w. Frank Sinatra. Own LPs: Lawson-Haggart (Decca); one track in *History of Classic Jazz* (River.); LPs w. Steve Allen (Decca), Deane Kincaide (Weathers), Bob Crosby (Coral, Dot), Will Bradley in *Dixieland Jazz* (Gr. Award).

Addr: 205 Bay Drive, Harbour Green, Massapequa, L.I., N.Y.

LEATHERWOOD, RAY, *bass, tuba;* b. Itasca, Tex., 4/24/14. Had six lessons on trombone; self-taught on tuba and bass. Pl. with Southern Methodist U. dance band and Mustang Band 1933-6; w. Blue Steele, Joe Venuti and various Midwest bands '37-40; Bob Chester, Tommy Dorsey '40-42. In service '42-5, org. band for ATC, AAF Ferry Command in Calif. After discharge, worked in Calif. clubs, then w. Les Brown '47-51. Began free-lancing in LA '52. Favs: Bob Haggart, Jimmy Blanton, Red Mitchell et al.

Addr: 11640 Addison Street, N. Hollywood, Calif.

LEDBETTER, HUDDIE (Leadbelly), *singer, guitar;* b. Mooringsport, La., 1888; d. New York City, 12/06/49. Raised in Texas, he played accordion and guitar. During period ca. 1903 until World War I he worked around Louisiana and Texas. He led a violent life, was jailed for murder in 1918 under the name of Walter Boyd, and was pardoned Jan. 1925. After working in and near Houston and Mooringsport he was again jailed, for attempted homicide. He served time from Feb. 1930 to Aug. '34; contrary to legend he received a routine discharge and was not pardoned as a result of singing for the Governor of La., as had been widely believed. He later went East and worked as chauffeur for John A. Lomax, the folk music archivist, whose protégé he had become. He later served a year in a New York prison for assault, '39-40. Lomax recorded him for the Library of Congress. During the '40s he was heard in many night clubs, playing his 12-string guitar and singing; in 1949 he visited France for concert work. Much of his work had a unique folk quality, but some of it was synthetically designed to please his audiences: as a fellow-convict once remarked, "he was always ready to perform for the whites." Rudi Blesh wrote in *Shining Trumpets:* "Among the finest Negro work songs recorded outside of the prisons are those sung by Leadbelly."

LPs: *Last Sessions* (Folk. 2941/2), *Legacy* (Folk. 2004, 14, 24, 34), *Memorial* (Stinson 17, 19, 48, 51); tracks in *History of Jazz, Vol. 1* (Cap. T 793), *Singin' The Blues* (Cam. 588).

LEE, CHARLES FREEMAN, *trumpet;* also *piano;* b. New York City, 8/13/27. Stud. at Wilberforce Acad. and pl. w. Wilberforce Collegians in Ohio. Piano with Snooky Young 1950; piano and tpt. w. Candy Johnson '51; trumpet w. Eddie Vinson and Sonny Stitt '52; Joe Holiday '53. Free-lanced in NYC '54-5; with James Moody '56. Back to Ohio for a year, then returned to NYC gigging around town on trumpet and piano incl. various Monday nights at Birdland. Holds a B.S. in Biology from Central State College. Favs: Dizzy Gillespie, Kenny Dorham, Fats Navarro. LPs w. Frank Foster (Pres.), Babs Gonzales (Hope).

LEE, JULIA, *singer, piano;* b. Kansas City, Mo., 10/31/02; d. KC, 12/8/58. Father, a violinist, led string trio; Julia made her debut singing w. him when she was four. At 10, she began stud. piano; from 1916 she sang and played at house parties. First steady job w. band led by elder brother, saxophonist George E. Lee, with whom she toured for 17 yrs. until 1933. After that, and until her death, she worked mainly as single in

KC, occasionally in Chicago, etc. She credited her warm, intimate vocal style to the influence of Jimmy Rushing, Joe Turner and other early KC associates. During the '40s she rec. regularly for Capitol, often accompanied by all-star combos. Favs: Margaret Whiting, Frank Sinatra. Fav. pianist: Frankie Carle. The English writer Jeff Aldam said of her: "So many musicians spoke highly of her that it surprises me she was not more widely admired. On piano she swung more than most men." Own LP: *Party Time* (Cap.); one band in *History of Jazz* (Cap.).

LEE, PEGGY (née Norma Dolores Egstrom), *singer, composer;* b. Jamestown, N. Dak., 5/26/22. Sang in small clubs in Middle West, and in Calif., 1939. Working w. a vocal group in Chicago '41, she was discovered by Mrs. Benny Goodman. Singing w. Goodman band from July '41, she made her first big hit record with him (*Why Don't You Do Right?*) in July '42. After marrying Goodman's guitarist, Dave Barbour, in March '43, she retired for several years, except for occasional records, among which were her own comps. (with Barbour as co-composer and bandleader) *You Was Right Baby, It's a Good Day, Manana, What More Can a Woman Do, I Don't Know Enough About You.* Divorced Barbour '52.

She was seen in the films *The Jazz Singer* and *Pete Kelly's Blues,* receiving an Academy Award nomination in '56 for her remarkable acting and singing role in the latter. Limiting her activities in recent years to TV shows and occasional night club dates, mostly in Las Vegas, she has retained, especially on records with small combos, the emotional and soulful qualities that have led her to be compared with Billie Holiday. One of the most sensitive and jazz-oriented singers in the pop field, she won *Down Beat* poll 1946. Her best performances are in the *Black Coffee* LP on Decca and, teamed w. George Shearing, in *Beauty and the Beat* on Capitol. Early LPs w. Goodman on Col. and w. own groups on Cap.

LEEMAN, CLIFFORD (Cliff), *drums;* b. Portland, Maine, 9/10/13. Stud. locally; pl. with Portland Symph. at 13, then left for vaudeville tour as xylophonist before ret. to school. Joined Dan Murphy in Boston '33; Hank Biagini '35; Artie Shaw '36-9; Tommy Dorsey '39; Charlie Barnet '40-3; Woody Herman '43; John Kirby and Raymond Scott '44; Jimmy Dorsey '45; left the business for two years and went to Maine, ret. '47 w. Glen Gray. Back w. Barnet and Dorsey briefly in '49, then w. Bobby Hackett into Nick's, where he stayed 2½ years, followed by 3 years at Eddie Condon's. Also Hit Parade, and free-lance TV work. Films: *Juke Box Jenny,* w. Barnet; *Sensations of 1945,* w. Herman. LPs w. Yank Lawson-Bob Haggart (Decca), Eddie Condon (Sav.), Joe Glover (Epic), Charlie Barnet (Cam.).

Addr: 21-04 154th St., Whitestone, N.Y.

LEGGE, WADE, *piano;* b. Huntington, W. Va., 2/4/34. Parents both pianists. Raised in Buffalo, where Milt Jackson heard him in 1952 and recommended him to Dizzy Gillespie. w. whom he pl. bass for the first two weeks before switching to piano. Left Gillespie '54 and free-lanced in NYC, incl. Johnny Richards orch. Back to Buffalo in late '50s. LPs w. Gillespie (Roost, Verve), Jimmy Cleveland (Em.), Sonny Rollins (Pres.), Charlie Mingus (Atl.).

LEGGIO, CARMELO JOHN (Carmen), *tenor sax;* also *alto, baritone, clarinet;* b. Tarrytown, N.Y., 9/30/27. Began studying clarinet at 11. Pl. local dances at 13; switched to tenor at 14. Pl. w. Terry Gibbs at Birdland, and in occasional jam sessions there 1950-1. Worked around NYC w. various groups incl. sessions w. Marty Napoleon at Van Rensselaer Hotel. W. Benny Goodman orch. and sextet, Oct.-Dec. '57, Maynard Ferguson '58-9. Own group in Westchester '60. Very fluent and expressive on tenor, apparently Rollins-influenced. Favs: Hawkins, Young, Parker. LPs w. Ferguson (Roul.).

Addr: 65 Tower Place, Yonkers, N.Y.

LEGRAND, MICHEL, *conductor, composer, piano;* b. Paris, France, 2/24/32. Father led variety orch. Stud. music at Cons. of Paris from age 11 to 20. Began prof. work as accompanist for singers; arr. for Dizzy Gillespie w. strings 1952. Did many film scores, music for radio and TV. Visiting NYC in '58, made albums w. Frankie Laine and w. all-star jazz groups. Though mainly associated with French pop music, is excellent jazz writer. Favs: Thelonious Monk, Art Tatum, Oscar Peterson; influenced by Duke Ellington, Count Basie, Dizzy Gillespie and Stan Kenton bands. Own LPs, *I Love Paris, Bonjour Paris, Le Grand Jazz* (Col.).

Addr: 17 Rue Verniquet, Paris 17.

LEHN, ERWIN, *leader, composer, piano, vibes;* b. Grünstadt, Germany, 6/8/19. Pl. in father's orchestra; played and wrote for radio groups; co-leader of Berliner Tanzorchester 1948. Through 1950s, vibist-leader of own combo, also leader of house band at Radio Stuttgart. Has appeared at jazz festivals in Frankfurt since 1955, also several successful engagements in France and Switzerland.

LEIGH, MITCH (Irwin S. Michnick), *bassoon,* etc., b. Brooklyn, N.Y., 1/30/28. Studied High School of Music and Art, NYC; Yale U., BA '51, MA '52. Teamed w. Art Harris for daily radio show and series of recordings in mid-'50s. From late '50s active in the production of TV jingles with his own firm, *Music Makers,* occasionally using jazz musicians such as Count Basie sidemen. Own LP w. Art Harris (Kapp).

Addr: 12 E. 66th St., New York 21, N.Y.

LEIGHTON, BERNARD (Bernie), *piano, conductor;* b. West Haven, Conn., 1/30/21. To NYC 1930, played w. Bud Freeman, Leo Reisman, Enric Madriguera; toured w. Raymond Scott 1940; six months w. Benny Goodman '40-1, then CBS studio work in NYC. Army '43-6; after discharge, resumed studies with Bruce Simonds at Yale, grad. '49. Gave solo classical recital at Carnegie Hall and has been in studio work in recent years, arranging, conducting and playing. Several jazz rec. dates in '46 w. Joe Thomas, Dave Tough et al. Soloist in Drake Room, NYC, '59; *Hit Parade* TV '58-9. Own LPs: Harm., Disneyland; feat. on *First Jazz Piano Quartet* (War. Bros.), Bob Alexander (Grand Award).

Addr: 161 West 54th St., New York 19, N.Y.

LEIGHTON, ELAINE, *drums;* b. New York City, 5/22/26. First contact with jazz at high school, where her schoolmates incl. Shorty Rogers, Stan Getz. Played w. Jackie Cain-Roy Kral group, 1949-50; Sweethearts of Rhythm '53; Beryl Booker Trio '53 and European tour Jan.-Feb. '54. After Booker Trio broke up, free-lanced in NYC; three years with combo at Page 3 Club, '57-9. LPs w. Jimmy Raney (Merc.), B. Booker (Cad., MGM).

Addr: 83 MacDougal St., New York 14, N.Y.

LEONARD, HARLAN, *leader, alto, tenor saxes;* b. Kansas City, Mo., 1904. Worked w. Bennie Moten's orch. from the early 1920s until 1931, when the band's personnel was reshuffled. He then formed an orch. w. Thamon Hayes, under whose name it went to Chicago, but failed to enjoy any success. After it broke up in 1934, Leonard took the remnants of the band and kept it together until '37. Soon after this he took over another orch. that had been formed by Tommy Douglas. It was rated along with Jay McShann as one of the leading outfits in KC. Ch. Parker and Jesse Price were among the sidemen, along w. Tadd Dameron, who wrote the arrangements. In 1940 the band made some excellent recordings for Bluebird (Vict. subsidiary) in Chicago, which have been unavailable for many years. The band remained together until about 1946, after which Leonard left the music business and moved to Calif. He has since been working in LA as an internal revenue agent.

LEONARD, HARVEY, *piano, composer;* b. New York City, 12/31/24. Stud. Juilliard, 1941-2. Harry the Hipster Gibson got him his first job, NYC, 1942. Bands incl. Johnny "Paradiddle" Morris '44-5, Geo. Auld '45-7, and '51; I. Jacquet '46; B. Rich '47-8; Jerry Wald '48-9; B. De Franco '49-50; G. Krupa '51; Ch. Barnet '52; Chuck Wayne '52; Slim Gaillard '53-4. To S. America as ship's musician 1951, '2 and '3. Comp. *The Tiger,* rec. by Willis Conover *House of Sounds* orch. on Bruns. Mus. dir. and arr. for Morgana King since 1956. LPs w. Morgana King (Merc.); *Party for Marty* (Jubilee), Georgie Auld (Allegro).

Addr: 562 West 113th St., New York 25, N.Y.

LE SAGE, WILLIAM (Bill), *vibes, composer, piano, accordion;* b. London, England, 1/20/27. Father was semi-prof. drummer in 1920s. Self-taught on piano from '43. Stud. w. Tristano in NYC '50. Prof. debut '48. Original member of Johnny Dankworth Seven from '50-54 on piano. St. playing vibes in '53. Joined Tony Kinsey, May '54. In '60, *Lilywhite Boys,* a musical written by Le Sage and Kinsey, opened in London. Favs: Hampton, Bud Powell. Five time winner of Melody Maker poll on vibes from '56. LPs w. Kinsey, George Chisholm (Lond.); other LPs on British labels w. own group, Dankworth, etc.

Addr: 48 Cavendish Ave., London W. 13, England.

LESBERG, JACK, *bass;* b. Boston, Mass., 2/14/20. Brother a violinist and conductor long active in Florida. Stud. violin, viola, 1930-7; pl. vln. in Boston speakeasies. Pl. w. Muggsy Spanier, 6 months, 1940; w. Mickey Alpert at Cocoanut Grove, Boston, until it was destroyed by fire 1942. Pl. w. Leonard Bernstein & NYC Symph. 1945-8; Eddie Condon '45-50; has since freelanced extensively; toured Britain, Africa, Australia w. Louis Armstrong spring '56; Europe w. J. Teagarden & Earl Hines fall '57. First-class musician in both classical and jazz fields. Favs: Blanton, Haggart, Safranski. Hundreds of LPs incl. Steve Allen *All Star Jazz Concert* (Dec.); *Hot vs. Cool* (MGM); Wild Bill Davison, G. Brunis (Comm.), M. Kaminsky (Bruns.), Paul Whiteman 50th Anniv. (Grand Award).

Addr: 21 Northfield Rd., Glen Cove, N.Y.

LETMAN, JOHN BERNARD (Johnny), *trumpet;* b. McCormick, S.C., 9/6/17. Stud. tpt., mellophone in Chicago, where he was soloist with Nat Cole combo, 1938; Horace Henderson, Red Saunders, '41-2. Later worked in Detroit w. Ted Buckner, John Kirby. Settling in NYC, pl. w. Phil Moore Four at Cafe Society, '45; Lucky Millinder; Cab Calloway, '46; C. Basie, '51; during '50s gigged around NYC w. many combos and bands. One of the less prominent representatives of the Roy Eldridge-inspired school, he is a capable, swinging soloist. Rec. w. own quartet for Felsted, '59. LPs w. Stuff Smith (20th-Fox), Dickenson-Thomas (Atl.), Freddie Slack (Cap.); Phil Moore (Vict.).

Addr: 580 East 164th Street, Bronx 56, N.Y.

LEVEY, STAN, *drums;* b. Phila., Pa., 4/5/25. Studied piano and arr. in high school. After working briefly w. Dizzy Gillespie in Phila. in 1942, he came to NYC, worked w. Oscar Pettiford at the Onyx on 52nd St. and was soon accepted as one of the first and most important drummers of the bop movement. In the mid-40s he worked on 52nd St. w. Gillespie, Parker, Barney Bigard, Allen Eager, George Shearing; he was also w. big bands led by Ch. Ventura, Georgie Auld, Woody Herman, Freddie Slack. After several years of partial inactivity, he returned as a full-time musician to join Stan Kenton '52, leaving him in March '54 to join Howard Rumsey's group at the Lighthouse in Hermosa Beach, Calif. where he has since played. In the late '50s he turned his photography hobby into an additional source of income, doing album covers, fashion and advertising shots.

Levey combines all the elements essential to a swinging, modern drummer. Fav: Max Roach. Own LPs on Beth., Interlude, *Drummin' The Blues* (Lib.); one track in *Hi-Fi Drums* (Cap.); LPs. w. Stan Getz (Verve, New Jazz), *For Musicians Only,* Ben Webster, Herb Ellis (Verve), Kenton (Cap.), Victor Feldman, *Lighthouse All Stars,* (Contemp.), *West Coast vs. East Coast* (MGM), Dempsey Wright (Andex).

Addr: 210 Larson St., Manhattan Beach, Calif.

LEVISTER, ALONZO H., *composer, piano;* b. Greenwich, Conn., 11/1/25. Stud. Boston Cons. of Music 1946. During early '50s wrote dance scores for Primitive

Dance Group in Mexico, the Modern Dance Group, NYC, worked as acc. at Katherine Dunham school. In '53 did vocal arr. for Debut Records and in '55 the Inter-Racial Fellowship Chorus performed his work at Town Hall. His *Manhattan Monodrama* was rec. in '56. He writes: "My main objective is to write opera using jazz-derived material with a librettist sufficiently American in his feelings and outlook to produce suitable libretti." Wrote opera *Blues In The Subway*, performed at NY theatre. Favs: Bach, Bartok. Own LP: *Manhattan Monodrama* (Debut); arrs. for *Roots* (New Jazz); wrote *Slow Dance* rec. by Coltrane (Pres.).

LEVITT, ALAN, *drums;* b. New York City, 11/11/32. Stud. w. Irv Kluger, L. Tristano. Pl. w. Chuck Wayne, Barbara Carroll combos, '51; Stan Getz '52; Tristano, Konitz, Teddy Charles '53; Paul Bley '54. To Europe '56, played w. Pia Beck in Holland. During long stay in Paris, worked w. leading US and French stars, incl. records w. Sidney Bechet, Martial Solal, Rene Urtreger. Back in US Nov. '58; has since worked w. Toshiko, Jackie McLean, and accompanied Chris Connor and Dick Haymes. LPs w. Stan Getz (Verve), Sidney Bechet (Bruns.).

Addr: 2 Pamrapo Court, Bayonne, N.J.

LEVY, JOHN O., *bass;* b. New Orleans, La., 4/11/12; raised in Chicago. Violin at 8, piano at 15; pl. with Ray Nance in high school. Bass at 17; worked w. Earl Hines, Tiny Parham, Red Saunders. Joined Stuff Smith's trio (w. Jimmy Jones) '43, and came to NYC w. him the following year. In NYC pl. with Ben Webster, Erroll Garner, Phil Moore, Don Byas, Earl Warren. Joined George Shearing '48; in '51 gave up bass playing to become personal manager for Shearing and others. LPs w. Shearing (MGM).

Addr: 1650 Broadway, New York 19, N.Y.

LEVY, LOUIS A. (Lou), *piano;* b. Chicago, Ill., 3/5/28. Stud. at Lee Sims studio w. Lucille Gould, and at Roosevelt College. Prof. debut w. Georgie Auld 1947; acc. Sarah Vaughan '47; toured Scandinavia w. Chubby Jackson, winter '47-8. Worked w. Boyd Raeburn, then Geo. Auld-Shelly Manne-Bill Harris-Chubby Jackson group, '48; Woody Herman '49-50. Shavers-Bellson-Gibbs sextet, '50; T. Dorsey, Auld, Flip Phillips, '51. Retired from music, lived in Minneapolis '51-4, working as advertising salesman for dental survey publication. Back in music Nov. '54, worked as house pianist for several months at Blue Note in Chicago. Acc. for Peggy Lee '55-7, then pl. with Terry Gibbs summer '57; joined Ella Fitzgerald Oct. '57 and remained until Sept. '59, touring US and Europe with her. Brilliant and exceptionally facile bop-derived pianist. Favs: Bud Powell, Art Tatum. Own LPs: *Jazz in Four Colors, Solo Scene, A Most Musical Fella* (Vict.), *Baby Grand Jazz* (Jub.); w. L. Niehaus (Contemp., Merc.), B. Holman (Coral), S. Rogers (Atl. Vict.), Q. Jones (ABC-Par.), S. Getz-G. Mulligan (Verve).

Addr: 4475 Murietta Ave., Van Nuys, Calif.

LEWIS, EDWARD (Big Ed), *trumpet;* b. Eagle City, Okla., 1/22/09. Learned bari. horn from father; first prof. job on trumpet w. Jerry Westbrook 1924. With Paul Banks '25; Bennie Moten '26-31; Thamon Hayes '32-4; Harlan Leonard '34-6; Count Basie '37-47. Retired from music '47 and worked in subways and as taxi driver, occasionally playing club dates. Favs: Joe Smith, Lips Page, Buck Clayton, Harry Edison, Al Killian. Rec. with Basie and Moten.

Addr: 310 W. 153rd St., New York, N.Y.

LEWIS, GEORGE, *clarinet, leader;* b. New Orleans, La., 7/13/00. Self-taught; never learned to read music. Got first clarinet at ten, prof. debut 3/19/14, then spent a year w. group feat. Leonard Parker on tpt. For the next two years he worked in Buddy Petit's Black and Tan band and w. Petit in the Earl Humphrey band; in 1923 had his own band w. Red Allen for a year. Worked w. Chris Kelly, Kid Rena. From '33 he was partially out of music, taking various jobs, with the WPA as stevedore etc., and frequently playing at parades and funerals. Rediscovered in '42 by Bill Russell, Gene Williams and others, he recorded w. Bunk Johnson; from this point on, his experiences ran parallel with those of Bunk (q.v.). In recent years he has toured w. his own group of NO veterans, in England, April '57 and England and the Continent early '59. App. at Newport Jazz Festival '57. Though some critics, both in the US and abroad, have belittled Lewis as superannuated and mediocre, he was described by Rudi Blesh in *Shining Trumpets* as "Perhaps the finest jazz clarinetist since Johnny Dodds." LPs: *Oh Didn't He Ramble* (Verve), *Classic New Orleans Traditions, Jazz at Vespers* (River.), *Concert, New Orleans Stompers* (BN), *On Parade, Singing Clarinet, Dr. Jazz* (Del.), *Ragtime Band* (Jazz Man), *A New Orleans Dixieland Spectacular* (Omega); *New Orleans Rhythm Boys* (South.), w. Kid Shots Madison (Amer.).

LEWIS, JOHN AARON, *composer, piano, leader;* b. La Grange, Ill., 5/3/20. Raised in Albuquerque, N. Mex. Father an optometrist; mother stud. singing w. Mme. Schumann-Heink's daughter. Stud. piano from 1927; anthropology and music at U. of N. Mex. until '42, then in Army until Nov. '45. While in Army, met Kenny Clarke, who later helped start his jazz career. Came to NYC, joined Dizzy Gillespie's big band as arr. and pianist; at this time he att. Manhattan School of Music. His first major work, *Toccata for Trumpet and Orchestra*, was introduced by Gillespie at Carnegie Hall, Sept. '47.

After a European tour w. Dizzy, he worked for two months w. Tony Proteau's band in Paris. On ret. to US he joined I. Jacquet band Oct. '48, remaining for eight months. Later he played and rec. w. Lester Young and Charlie Parker. He was soloist and arr. with the nine-piece Miles Davis Capitol recording group in '49.

He cont. at the Manhattan School, where he included some voice lessons in his curriculum, singing

w. the Schola Cantorum choral group. He took two degrees from the school and later devoted some time to teaching piano and theory.

Although he toured US and Australia in '54 while working for a few months as accompanist to Ella Fitzgerald, Lewis was active mainly from '52 as mentor and chief creative force behind the Modern Jazz Quartet (q.v).

While the MJQ achieved international popularity, Lewis began to take on outside ventures as a composer-arranger, orchestrating his music for specially-organized concert groups in person and on records. Early in '57 the quartet made a series of successful European appearances and rec. the sound track for a French film, released in US as *No Sun in Venice.* Beginning in '57 he served as head of the faculty at the annual summer schools of jazz at Music Inn at Lenox, Mass. In the winter of '57 the MJQ played 88 concerts in four months in the British Isles and on the Continent. In Feb. '58 Lewis conducted members of the Stuttgart Symph. Orch. in a series of his orchestrations for the *European Windows* LP. In 1958 and '59 Lewis was music dir. of the Monterey Jazz Festival.

The enhanced prestige of Lewis and his group by this time had enabled him to eliminate all night club work and to restrict his appearances to such events as recitals in Town Hall, NYC, and other occasional concert and festival dates.

John Lewis' is one of the most brilliant minds ever applied to jazz. Completely self-sufficient and self-confident, he knows exactly what he wants from his musicians, his writing and his career; and achieves it with an unusual, quiet firmness of manner, coupled with modesty and a complete indifference to critical reaction. Though many of his more ambitious orchestral works have only a peripheral relationship to jazz, he believes that the jazz elements in his background have contributed to everything he has done.

As an instrumental soloist, Lewis has been described by Whitney Balliett as "a unique and invariably moving jazz pianist . . . his touch is sure and delicate, his ideas are disarmingly simple and honest. He has a rhythmic sense and enough technique to allow him easy freedom."

Lewis' early arrangements for Gillespie include *Two Bass Hit, Emanon, Stay On It, Minor Walk;* for Miles Davis, *Move, Budo,* and *Rouge.* Some of his writing from this period has been reissued in Gillespie LPs on Victor, Rondolette, and in the Miles Davis *Birth of the Cool* (Cap. T762).

The Harry Belafonte film *Odds Against Tomorrow,* with a score written by Lewis and recorded by a 22-piece orchestra, was released Oct. '59. Gunther Schuller has summarized the importance of this score. ". . . it utilizes jazz music as a purely dramatic music to underline a variety of situations not specifically related to jazz. . . . It can serve its purpose in the film but it can also stand as absolute music apart from the original dramatic situation."

The Quartet was integrated with the Beaux Arts String Quartet in a concert at Town Hall, NYC, Sept. '59. Lewis won the *Metronome* poll as arr. '60.

Own LPs: *Improvised Meditations and Excursions* (Atl. 1313), *John Lewis Piano* (Atl. 1272), *European Windows* (Vict. 1742); w. Sacha Distel: *Afternoon in Paris* (Atl. 1267); w. Bill Perkins, Chico Hamilton et al: *Grand Encounter* (Wor. Pac. 1217); *MJQ at Music Inn,* Vol. 1, 2 (Atl. 1247, 1299), *MJQ* (Atl. 1265), *Concorde* (Pres. 7005), *Django* (Pres. 7057), *Fontessa* (Atl. 1231), *One Never Knows* (*No Sun in Venice*) (Atl. 1284), Mod. Jazz Sextet (Verve 8166), w. Miles Davis (Cap. T762), w. C. Parker (Verve 8010).

Addr: 881 10th Ave., New York 19, N.Y.

LEWIS, MEADE LUX, *piano;* b. Louisville, Ky., 1905. First inspired by Jimmy Yancey in Chicago, Lewis, who had originally studied violin, became a night club pianist and recorded *Honky Tonk Train Blues* for Paramount, 1929. He remained in obscurity for several years and was out of the music business until John Hammond, hearing the record, started a search for him and ultimately found him washing cars in a Chicago garage. He promptly arranged for Lewis to record a new version of the composition. He recorded it for both Decca and Victor in 1936, for Blue Note in 1940, for Clef in 1944. During the late '30s, through Hammond, Lewis became one of the three key figures in the boogie-woogie renaissance. Along with Albert Ammons and Pete Johnson, he appeared at Carnegie Hall and Cafe Society and as part of a three-piano team on Columbia Records. The original *Honky Tonk* has great intensity and excitement in its fiercely insistent bass figures and repetitious right-hand riffs, but the appeal of boogie-woogie in general proved somewhat limited after a great degree of over-exposure in the late '30s and early '40s. In recent years Lewis has been playing in night clubs around Los Angeles. Own LPs: *Barrel House Piano* (Tops), *Cat House Piano, Meade Lux* (Verve), *Out of the Roaring Twenties* (ABC-Par.); w. Ammons & Johnson in *Spirituals To Swing* (Vang.).

LEWIS, MEL (Melvin Sokoloff), *drums;* b. Buffalo, N.Y., 5/10/29. Father a prof. drummer for almost 40 years. Prof. debut at 15. Played w. Lenny Lewis 1946-8; Boyd Raeburn, July-Nov. '48; Alvino Rey to Mar. '49, then a year w. Ray Anthony, 3 yrs. w. Tex Beneke. Back with Anthony for a year, to Aug. '54. Two years w. Stan Kenton, '54-6, except for brief membership in Frank Rosolino quintet and Hampton Hawes trio, early '55. To Europe w. Kenton March '56. Settled in LA Jan. '57. Had quintet w. Bill Holman Feb.-Oct. '58. Joined Terry Gibbs big band Feb. '59; also staff work at ABC studios in Hollywood. Superb timekeeper and swinger; one of a handful of completely first-rate jazz drummers in Calif. Favs: T. Kahn, Jo Jones, Roach, Manne et al. Own LP: Andex; feat. on *Fabulous Bill*

Holman (Cor.), Pepper Adams (World-Pac.), Art Pepper big band (Contemp.), B. De Franco-H. Edison (Verve) etc.

Addr: 6669 Sunnyslope Ave., Van Nuys, Calif.

LEWIS, RAMSEY E. JR., *piano, composer;* b. Chicago, Ill., 5/27/35. Stud. privately at age six, later att. Chicago Mus. Coll. and De Paul U. Formed own trio late 1956. Pl. Chicago night clubs for two yrs., rec. on various dates with Sonny Stitt, Clark Terry, Max Roach, Lem Winchester on Argo. In '59 played Birdland and Randall's Island festival NYC. Considers John Lewis and Oscar Peterson his main influences but names Bud Powell and Art Tatum as favorites. Jack Tracy wrote of his trio in *Down Beat*: "This group could hit the heights of acclaim achieved by such as Shearing, Brubeck and Garner. . . . A rare combination of stimulating music and personal magnetism." Own LPs on Argo, Merc.

Addr: 400 E. 33rd St., Chicago, Ill.

LEWIS, STEVE, *piano;* b. New Orleans, La., 3/19/96; d. NO 1939. Began pl. around 1910 w. the Silver Leaf Orch.; on tour several months '17-18 w. Mack's Merry Makers, then returned and joined Armand Piron's band, where he played until about 1932. From the time he left Piron until his death, he worked as a single or w. Paul Barnes or Earl Fouche around NO.

LEWIS, TED (Theodore Leopold Friedman), *leader, clarinet;* b. Circleville, Ohio, 6/6/92. Active as bandleader, comedian, and vaudevillian since 1910, Lewis was always considered a "corny" musician by jazz standards, but several jazzmen recorded and/or toured w. him in the '20s and '30s, among them Muggsy Spanier, George Brunis, Benny Goodman, Fats Waller, Frank Teschemacher. LPs on Epic, Decca, RKO.

LEWIS, VIC, *leader, trombone, guitar;* b. London, England, 7/29/19. Stud. guitar w. grandfather from age three. As teen-ager had own group w. Carlo Krahmer and George Shearing. A great Dixieland enthusiast, he visited NYC in 1938, sat in w. Bobby Hackett at Nick's. While in RAF, pl. in Buddy Featherstonhaugh's sextet '41-4. Worked w. Stephane Grappelly in London '44-5; sessions w. Ted Heath '45; from '46, led own big band in England and on tours to Continent, South Africa, usually featuring Kenton-style Rugolo arrangements, etc. In '50 he visited US briefly to attend Kenton concert at Carnegie Hall. Brought band for tours of US in '56-7, playing first in rock-'n'-roll concert unit, later at US Army camps. Visited US again '58-9. In '59, in addition to his bandleading activities, he became a booking agent with the Harold Davison agency.

Addr: c/o Harold Davison, Eros House, 29/31 Regent St., London S. W. 1, England.

LIGGINS, JOE, *piano, leader;* b. Guthrie, Okla., 1915. Family moved to San Diego in 1930, and he pl. trumpet in high school there. Went to Los Angeles later and suffered a stroke which put a stop to his trumpet playing. He took up piano, also composition; the title of one number, *The Honeydripper,* was later used as his nickname. During World War II he worked in a war plant; afterwards, he org. his own combo, which was popular in rhythm and blues circles.

LINCOLN, ABRAHAM (Abe), *trombone;* b. Lancaster, Pa., 3/29/07. St. on trombone at age five; taught by father. Played w. California Ramblers, Roger Wolfe Kahn, Paul Whiteman. Has worked on radio, TV and rec. studios in Hollywood for a number of years. Awarded a gold key from City of New Orleans for his rec. activities. Able Dixieland jazzman. Favs: Bobby Hackett, Jack Teagarden et al. LPs w. Hackett, Ray Anthony (Cap.), Matty Matlock (Col.), Bob Scobey (Vict.), Pete Fountain (Coral).

Addr: 14934 Burbank Blvd., Van Nuys, Calif.

LINCOLN, ABBEY (Anna Marie Wooldridge), *singer;* b. Chicago, 8/6/30, tenth of twelve children. Raised in Calvin Center, Mich. While in high school, worked as housemaid, sang and acted at social functions; later, while still in teens, toured Michigan as dance band vocalist. In 1951 moved to Calif., worked local clubs; spent two yrs. in Hawaii, singing under name Gaby Lee. Back in US '54; during next three years scored successes at major Hollywood clubs, changing name to Abbey Lincoln in '56 and cutting her first LP, for Lib. In '57 her first movie, *The Girl Can't Help It,* was released, and she made an LP for River. w. Max Roach and an all-star jazz group. Since then she has played in night clubs, incl. the Astor Club in London, June '59. Toured in leading role in road company of stage show *Jamaica,* summer '59. A superior pop singer who has earned acceptance in jazz circles.

Addr: c/o Riverside Records, 235 W. 46th St., New York 36, N.Y.

LINDBERG, NILS, *piano, composer;* b. Uppsala, Sweden, 6/11/33. Uncle was noted composer-organist Oscar Lindberg. Private lessons at eight, music history at Uppsala U. at 21, comp. and counterpoint '56-60 at Royal Acad. of Mus. in Stockholm. Started w. own band in Dalecarlia '51. Worked w. Benny Bailey, '57; Anders Burman '58; Ove Lind, '59; Putte Wickman, '59-60. Fav. own rec. *It's You or No One* w. B. Bailey. Favs: Tristano, H. Hawes, Powell. His deep interest in Swedish folk music has greatly influenced him as a jazz writer.

Addr: Brantingsgatan 15, Stockholm, Sweden.

LINDSAY, JOHN, *bass, trombone;* b. Algiers, La., 8/23/1894; d. Chicago, 7/3/50. Pl. w. Freddie Keppard, Tuxedo Band 1915-6; Army 1917-8; Joe Robichaux '20-3; to NYC w. Armand Piron '23-4. With King Oliver '24; Willie Hightower '25-8; Carroll Dickerson, Jimmy Bell, etc. in Chicago, '29-30. During the 1920s he worked mostly as a trombonist, but in 1931 he played bass w. Louis Armstrong. Free-lanced in Chicago during '30s and '40s. Rec. w. Piron '23, Jelly Roll Morton '26, Jimmie Blythe '28; Johnny Dodds '28 and '40; Jimmie Noone '34, '35 and '40; Sidney Bechet '40, Richard M. Jones '44, Punch Miller '45, Chippie Hill

'46, and w. Victoria Spivey, Harlem Hamfats, J. H. Shayne. LP w. Morton (Vict.).

LINDUP, DAVE, *composer;* also *tenor sax, piano;* b. Worthing, Sussex, England, 5/10/28. Stud. piano, harmony, comp. from 1940. Prof. debut on tenor with local bands '46. After touring with several bands '48-'52 took up residence in London and built up connections as arranger. Gave up playing in '55 to join Johnny Dankworth's Orch. as staff arranger. Co-authored w. Dankworth *Itinerary Of An Orchestra.* Composed *New Forest, Slow Twain, Caribe.* Favs: Ellington, Strayhorn. LPs w. Dankworth (Verve, Roul., Top Rank).

Addr: 65 Trinity Church Square, London, S.E. 1, England.

LINGLE, PAUL, *piano;* b. Denver Colo., 12/3/02. Started on piano 1908; acc. his father, cornetist Curt Lingle, on the Chautauqua circuit 1915-17, and during this time became interested in Jelly Roll Morton, Scott Joplin and other ragtime pioneers. During the 1920s he worked w. many bands incl. Jimmie Grier 1926; own band in San Francisco '28; pianist for Al Jolson in *Sonny Boy* and *Mammy* at Warner's 1929. During the '30s he was staff pianist at KPO, San Francisco; in the '40s he became a legend, playing in local night clubs, earning the admiration of Bunk Johnson, Leadbelly, Turk Murphy. In '52 he moved to Honolulu, organized a jazz band there and opened his own tuition studio. LP: half an LP in *They Tore My Playhouse Down* (GTJ).

LINN, RAYMOND SAYRE (Ray), *trumpet;* b. Chicago, Ill., 10/20/20. Father played trumpet. Joined society band; toured w. T. Dorsey at 18. Left Dorsey '41, worked w. Woody Herman to '42 and again in '45, also w. Artie Shaw '44, Boyd Raeburn '46. Since 1945, living in LA, free-lancing in movies and TV, radio, also leading own combo. Was one of first West Coast trumpeters to develop bop style. Fav: Gillespie. LPs w. Raeburn (Savoy), Georgie Auld (Em.), Peggy Lee (Cap.), Barney Kessel (Contemp.).

Addr: 17228 Valerio, Van Nuys, Calif.

LISTON, MELBA DORETTA, *trombone, composer;* b. Kansas City, Mo. 1/13/26. Raised in Los Angeles from '37; trombone and harmony at Polytech High Pit band in Lincoln Theatre in LA, '42-4. From '44 she was close associate of Gerald Wilson, first in his own band, later for several months w. Dizzy Gillespie and Count Basie. Toured w. Billie Holiday '49. From '50-4 worked as clerk w. Board of Education. Played a bit part w. Lana Turner in *The Prodigal.* Toured w. D. Gillespie spring '56-Nov. '57, including State Dept. tours of Near East and Latin America, then settled in NYC, leading own all-girl quint. for a few months. In '58-9 she expanded her arranging activities, scoring several sessions for Randy Weston, Gloria Lynne and others. In Oct. '59 she joined Quincy Jones' orch. for an acting and playing role in the Harold Arlen-Johnny Mercer musical, *Free and Easy.* A fine musician, the only outstanding feminine trombonist in jazz, she has developed in recent years into a first-class composer-arranger. Fav: Dorsey, Lawrence Brown. Own LP (Metro.); LPs w. Randy Weston (UA), Gillespie (Verve); arrs. for Gloria Lynne (Evst.).

Addr: 1054 E. 228th Street, Bronx 66, N.Y.

LITTLE, BOOKER, JR., *trumpet;* b. Memphis, Tenn., 4/2/38. Sister sings w. London Opera Company; stud. music at Manassas High School in Memphis, Tenn.; later at Chicago Cons. 1955-8. While in Chicago, Sonny Rollins introduced him to Max Roach; joined Max's group June '58, app. with him at Newport Jazz Festival in July. Then free-lanced in NYC; pl. at Five Spot w. Mal Waldron '59, John Coltrane '60. Favs: Charlie Parker, Dizzy Gillespie. Own LP: UA; LPs w. Max Roach (Em., River.); *Down Home Reunion* (UA).

LITTLE RICHARD (Richard Penniman), *singer;* b. Macon, Ga., 12/25/35. Church soloist at 14. At 15 was singing, dancing and peddling herb tonic for a medicine show. Won talent contest in Atlanta 1952 and in the next few years became a best-selling r & b recording artist. Retired from show business to devote himself to religion 1958, but returned the following year. Own LP: Camden, Specialty.

LITTMAN, PETER, *drums;* b. Medford, Mass., 5/8/35. Very little formal study. Mother is choral dir. for local Temple Beth-El. Began stud. piano at 6; at 16 worked w. Herb Pomeroy and C. Mariano, and has been w. C. Baker on and off since the mid-50s, incl. a tour of the NATO countries in '55. Favs: Philly Joe Jones, Blakey, K. Clarke, R. Haynes. LPs w. Baker (Wor. Pac.).

Addr: 83 Dean St., Belmont, Mass.

LIVINGSTON, JOSEPH ANTHONY (Fud), *composer, saxophone;* b. Charleston, S.C., 4/10/06; d. New York City, 3/25/57. Stud. piano, clar. and sax; w. Paul Whiteman pl. sax and arr. for five years; later w. Freddie Rich, Andre Kostelanetz et al. Important figure in early white jazz, arr. and clar., chiefly w. Red Nichols 1927-9, F. Trumbauer; also in England w. Fred Elizalde. In later years he retired from jazz, worked for mus. publ. and in Hollywood for motion pictures.

LIVINGSTON, ULYSSES, *guitar, electric bass;* b. Bristol, Tenn., 1/29/12. Early exp. in road variety shows and carnivals. Pl. with Benny Carter 1938-9; Ella Fitzgerald '40-2. Has been working in clubs and rec. studios in LA for a number of years. Rec. with various r & b groups. Fav: Oscar Moore; infl. by Eddie Durham. LP: JATP (Stinson).

Addr: 6572 3rd Ave., Los Angeles, Calif.

LLOYD, JEROME (Jerry) (Jerome Hurwitz), *trumpet, piano;* b. NYC, 7/17/20. Stud. piano and gave concert at five at Steinway Hall. St. on trumpet at 13, originally as therapy for collapsed lung. First prof. engagement at 13 and has been a union member since.

Worked w. G. Auld, B. Rich, G. Wallington. Out of music for six years due to attack of arthritis, but ret. with Zoot Sims' group in 1956, staying for a few months; has since gigged occasionally w. Sims and Wallington, though since '49 he has also made his living driving a taxi in NYC. Favs: L. Young, R. Eldridge, Parker, Gillespie, M. Davis. LPs w. Jutta Hipp (BN), Sims (Dawn), Wallington: *The Prestidigitator* (East-West); *Lestorian Mode* (Savoy).

Addr: 75-40 Bell Blvd., Bayside 64, L. I., N. Y.

LOCO, JOE (Jose Esteves Jr.), *leader, arranger, piano;* b. New York City, 3/26/21. Stud. Juilliard, Veterans' School, NYU etc. Orig. a dancer, worked w. Chick Webb band at Apollo, etc. from 1936. Trombone w. NY Amateur Symph. on WNYC. Plays violin, guitar, bass, drums, etc. First job as pianist was w. Machito, 1941-4. Air Force, '45-7. Arr. for Pupi Campo, Vincent Lopez, Tito Puente, Tito Rodriguez. Head of Latin music dept. and staff arr. at Marks Music NYC, '55. Completed mambo symphonette in three movements, March '55. Leader of own trio since '51; popular in Birdland and many other jazz and Latin-Amer. clubs. Own LP: *Loco Motion* (Col.); w. Pete Terrace (Fant.).

Addr: 839 E. Cypress Ave., Burbank, Calif.

LOFTON, CLARENCE (Cripple Clarence), *piano, singer;* b. Kingsport, Tenn., 3/28/96; d. Chicago, Ill., 1/28/56. Moved to Chicago 1917, becoming part of the South Side musical activities. Rec. as accompanist for Paramount, Vocalion in 1920s and '30s, and as soloist in late '30s and early '40s on Solo-Art, Session. Self-taught; his unusual style influenced several younger pianists. He was in obscurity from the '40s until his death, making occasional concert appearances in Chicago. LP: track in *History of Classic Jazz* (River.).

LOMAX, ALAN, *writer, singer, guitar;* b. Austin, Tex., 1/15/15. Educ. in private schools; one year at Harvard, grad. from U. of Texas. With father, John Lomax, went on rec. trips through Southern prison camps, where they discovered Leadbelly. Worked on CBS radio for a number of years, during which time he introduced many new folk singers: Woody Guthrie, Josh White, Burl Ives et al. Spent 1951-8 in Europe, where he recorded folk songs in England, Italy and Spain; albums issued by Columbia and Westminster. Best known as folklorist, but is affiliated with jazz through his interest in and knowledge of its roots: folk music, gospel songs, rhythm and blues. His book, *Mr. Jelly Roll* is published by Evergreen. LP: *Blues In The Mississippi Night* (UA) contains conversations and musical performances by country blues singers, recorded on location by Lomax.

LOMBARDI, CLAUDIO (Clyde), *bass;* b. Bronx, N.Y. 2/13/22. Bought bass at 18, stud. w. Fortier (first bass of N. Y. Phil.) for four years. Pl. w. Red Norvo '42-3; record debut w. Joe Marsala '44. Later worked w. Boyd Raeburn '45; Benny Goodman '45-6; C. Ventura '47-8; Goodman '49; Norvo '51 and '53; then free-lanced in NYC incl. gigs w. Eddie Bert; On staff at CBS '59. Favs: Pettiford, Brown, Mitchell, Mingus. LPs w. Specs Powell (Roul.), Al Caiola (Savoy), Zoot Sims (Pres.), George Wallington (Verve).

Addr: 2465 Crotona Ave., Bronx 58, N. Y.

LONDON, JULIE, *singer;* b. Santa Rosa, Calif., 9/26/26. Parents, both singers, had their own radio show. Self-taught; sang briefly w. trio as teen-ager. Two weeks w. Matty Malneck's orch. in 1943. Gave up singing for acting until Bobby Troup interested Lib. records in making her first album. Her initial release, *Cry Me a River,* was a big popular hit in '55. As actress under contract to major studios, she has made many movies, including *The Great Man, The Girl Can't Help It.* A warm and intimate singer who has frequently used jazz-oriented backgrounds under Troup's supervision. Married Troup 12/31/59. Favs: Ella Fitzgerald, Peggy Lee, Johnny Mercer. LPs on Lib.

Addr: c/o Liberty Records, 1556 N. La Brea Ave., Hollywood, Calif.

LOOKOFSKY, HARRY, *violin, viola;* b. Paducah, Ky., 10/1/13. First stud. violin in St. Louis; app. on KMOX radio there at age 12, and traveled w. youth orch. In 1929 joined Isham Jones as violinist and vocalist in trio; w. Vincent Lopez briefly in '34; w. St. Louis Symph. '34-8. To New York; member NBC Symph. 12 years with time out to spend three years in Maritime Serv. Since then has been with Amer. Broadcasting Co. Fav: Fritz Kreisler, Toscanini, in classical field; Stuff Smith, Charlie Parker in jazz. Was first to make successful use in modern jazz of string quintet, composed entirely of himself (through multi-taping) w. Quincy Jones arrs., on own EP, *Miracle In Strings* (Epic).

Addr: 11 Riverside Drive, New York 23, N.Y.

LOPEZ, PERFECTO MACABATA (Perry), *guitar;* b. Philadelphia, Pa., 2/10/24. St. on mandolin; after three years w. Hawaiian combos entered service 1942. Was in four campaigns overseas w. 13th Air Force. Worked at Down Beat Club, Phila. '45-8; a year w. Freddie Slack, then joined Rocky Coluccio Trio. In NYC, was w. Buddy DeFranco for 6 months, then Billy Taylor Quartet. After a year out of music, pl. with Ellis Larkins' Trio for two years, then joined Johnny Smith Quartet. Toured w. Pete Rugolo Oct. '54, then rejoined J. Smith; with Benny Goodman Octet at Basin Street, NYC, Mar. '55. In recent years has been doing pit band work in various Broadway shows, backing singers such as Miriam Makeba and leading his own trio. Favs: J. Smith, Farlow, John Collins. LPs w. Johnny Glasel (ABC-Par.), Leon Merian (Seeco), Charlie Ventura (Verve).

Addr: Park Savoy Hotel, 158 W. 58th St., New York 19, N.Y.

LOVELLE, HERBERT E. (Herbie), *drums;* b. Brooklyn, N.Y., 6/1/24. Two uncles musicians; stud. drums with one at age 12; also stud. clarinet. In Army during World War II; first prof. job w. Hot Lips Page 1949; w. Hal Singer '50; Johnny Moore's Three Blazers '51.

Next three years played w. various bands at the Savoy Ballroom, NYC. Toured w. Arnett Cobb and Teddy Wilson '54. Briefly w. Earl Hines '55, then w. Billy Williams until '57, when he joined Sam (The Man) Taylor. Favs: Sid Catlett, Max Roach, Art Blakey, Buddy Rich. LPs w. Buck Clayton (Col.), Buddy Tate (Fels.), Sam Taylor (Metro.).

LOVETT, LEROY, *piano, arranger;* b. Germantown, Pa., 3/17/19. 12 years' study, incl. Schillinger. Own band around Phila. In NYC '45, writing for Tiny Bradshaw, Luis Russell. Toured w. Noble Sissle, Lucky Millinder; helped organize bands for Cat Anderson, Mercer Ellington, Johnny Hodges. Left Hodges '52 to concentrate on music publishing. Arranger-leader on Al Hibbler LPs (Verve); worked as record producer for N. Granz in Cal. '56-7; ret. to Phila., org. 13-piece dance band; to Dallas, helped build and direct new swing band for Ted Weems; a & r work for Wynne Records '59-60. Film score: *The Gangster Story,* '59. Own LP: Wynne; LPs w. Hodges, Hibbler (Verve), also wrote r & b dates for Atl. etc.

Addr: 5918 Oxford St., Philadelphia 31, Pa.

LOWE, CURTIS SYLVESTER SR., *baritone & tenor saxes;* b. Chicago, Ill., 11/15/19. Cousin of Sam Lowe, tpt. w. Erskine Hawkins for 20 years. St. on soprano sax at eight in Oakland, Cal. Att. Ala. State Teachers' Coll. for six months. Prof. debut 1940; jobbed around Oakland, Ohio, Illinois, Minnesota. In Navy, '42-5, was in band w. Jerome Richardson, B. Collette, M. & E. Royal. Has been with L. Hampton band several times, in '49-51, '52, '55-7, incl. Europe, Israel in '56. Concerts w. Dave Brubeck Octet summer '52; own quintet in SF '52-3; gigs and records w. Earl Hines '58-9. LP: *Jazz Flamenco* w. Hampton (Vict.).

Addr: 2421 Sixth Street, Berkeley 10, Cal.

LOWE, MUNDELL, *guitar, composer;* b. Laurel, Miss., 4/21/22. Studied with father, a music teacher. Moved to New Orleans at 13, played first jobs there w. Abbie Brunis, Sid Devilla and various Bourbon St. combos. To Nashville '39, spent six months w. Pee Wee King on *Grand Ole Op'ry* radio show. Back on tour in Louisiana and Florida, met Jan Savitt and worked briefly with him before entering Army Jan. '43. While in Army, met John Hammond, who got him job w. Ray McKinley soon after discharge in Dec. '45. Left McKinley May '47, spent two years at Cafe Society w. Dave Martin; a few months w. Ellis Larkins at Village Vanguard, month w. Red Norvo at Bop City, '49. Appeared as actor and guitarist in off-Broadway plays. Joined NBC staff in NYC '50, also working w. Sauter-Finegan orch., own quartet at Embers, and w. Billy Taylor. After leaving NBC June '58 became very active as composer-arranger for own LPs, also writing modern jazz scores for documentary films. Lowe is a skilled and inspired modern guitarist and a rapidly maturing composer. Own LPs: Camden, River.; LPs w. Al Klink (Gr. Award), Ray McKinley (Savoy, Cam.), Eddie Safranski in *Concert Jazz* (Bruns.), Tony Scott (Vict.), Johnny Guarnieri (Coral).

Addr: 240 West 98th Street, New York 25, N.Y.

LUCAS, ALBERT B. (Al), *bass;* also *piano, tuba;* b. Windsor, Ontario, Can., 11/16/16. Mother, Fannie Bradley Lucas, was concert pianist, father pl. bass, brother and sister pl. piano. Studied piano from age six w. mother; learned tuba at 12 from school instructor, started pl. bass at same time. Stud. under Paul Brock in NYC 1935 for two years. St. pl. club dances in Cleveland while still in high school. Came to NYC '33, pl. w. Kaiser Marshall. Then w. Sunset Royals '33-40, Coleman Hawkins at Kelly's Stable '42, Eddie Heywood '43-6, also on 52nd St. w. Garner, Lips Page '45; Duke Ellington, briefly '46, Mary Lou Williams on WNEW '46, Illinois Jacquet '47-53, Eddie Heywood trio '54-6, Teddy Wilson trio '56 in NYC and NJF. Pl. in Europe w. Jacquet, Sarah Vaughan, Hawkins, Mary Lou Williams Oct. '54; British West Indies, Jamaica, Barbados, etc. w. Heywood in Nov. '58. W. Heywood when in NYC, also free-lancing. Favs: Blanton, Walter Page. LPs w. Heywood (Vict., Merc.), Jacquet (Verve, Roul.), Heywood-Holiday (Comm.), Ruby Braff (Vang.), Charlie Byrd, incl. fav. own solo *Foggy Day* (Savoy).

Addr: 109-46 172nd St., Jamaica 33, L.I., N.Y.

LUCIE, LAWRENCE (Larry), *guitar;* also *banjo, mandolin, clarinet;* b. Emporia, Va., 12/18/14. Father pl. violin, brother sax, family band pl. hillbilly style for square dances. Stud. by correspondence 1923, later w. Luther Blake and at B'klyn Cons. in NYC. Subbed a week w. Ellington at Cotton Club '34, then joined Benny Carter. Worked w. Fletcher Henderson '34-5 and, after a year w. Lucky Millinder, again w. Henderson '36-9. Coleman Hawkins' big band '40; Louis Armstrong band '40-45. Leader of own combo from 1946 except for tour w. Louis Bellson band March-August '59. With Cozy Cole, Dec. '59. Film: *Jam Session* w. Armstrong. Pl. rhythm guitar and occasional solos on many rec. dates in '30s and early '40s, incl. Spike Hughes (London), B. Carter, T. Wilson, B. Holiday, Putney Dandridge, L. Millinder, Joe Turner, Jelly Roll Morton, Red Allen, Henderson, Armstrong. Fav. own rec: *Traveling Guitars* by Larry & Lenore (Request), a folk album on which he played all the single string work on guitar, banjo and mandolin. One of the best guitarists to rise to prominence in the '30s, inexcusably neglected by critics and historians.

Addr: 661 Lafayette Avenue, Brooklyn 16, N.Y.

LUCRAFT, HOWARD, *composer, guitar;* b. London, England, 8/16/16. Was active during 1940s as arranger, bandleader and commentator, broadcasting on BBC etc. Arrived in US Sept. '50, settled in Calif., worked mainly as writer and promoter, organizing jam sessions and forums at Hollywood clubs, collaborating with Stan Kenton in the founding and running of Jazz International (see Jazz Organizations section). Produced radio and TV shows for Jazz International, also own shows on KNOB, KPFK and many Armed Forces broadcasts heard extensively overseas. Articles for *Metronome;* West Coast correspondent for London *Melody Maker* and for *The Encyclopedia of Jazz.* Fav. mus: Ellington, Basie, Parker. Own LPs: Decca *Showcase for Modern Jazz* (Decca), *Jazz International* (Merc.).

Addr: Box 91, Hollywood 28, Calif.

LUNCEFORD, JAMES MELVIN (Jimmie), *leader;* b. Fulton, Mo., 6/6/02; d. Seaside, Ore., 7/13/47. Lunceford's education included music studies under Wilberforce J. Whiteman, father of Paul Whiteman; BA at Fisk Univ. and later tuition at N.Y. City College. He became proficient on all reed instruments, playing with the bands of Elmer Snowden, Wilbur Sweatman and others in the middle '20s. His bandleading career began in Memphis in 1927; he began to acquire a reputation in Buffalo, 1930-3. Recorded for Victor in '30 & '34; began his real climb to fame with a great series of sides for Decca, beginning Sept. '34. During the next decade Lunceford's band enjoyed a unique reputation as the best-disciplined and most showmanly Negro jazz orchestra. The oddly swinging style of the arrangements (most of them by Sy Oliver, who played trumpet in the band, and Edwin Wilcox, the pianist), and the personable vocals by Sy Oliver, Willie Smith, and others, were main attractions for jazz fans, while the vocals of Dan Grissom added commercial appeal.

The basic personnel of the band during the key years from 1935-7 included Eddie Tompkins, Paul Webster, Sy Oliver, trumpets; Elmer Crumbley, Russell Bowles, trombones; Eddie Durham, trombone & solo guitar; Willie Smith, Earl Carruthers, Laforet Dent, Joe Thomas, Dan Grissom, saxes; Edwin Wilcox, piano; Al Norris, guitar; Moses Allen, bass; James Crawford, drums. Later members included Trummy Young, trombone and vocalist from November '37; Gerald Wilson, who replaced Oliver in August '39; Billy Moore, Jr., arranger from '39. Lunceford himself conducted the band, never playing any instrument (except flute on the record of *Liza*). After 1942 the band's personnel began to change more frequently and the Lunceford vogue slowly faded. The band remained with Decca until 1945 and recorded for Majestic in '46, but in its later years had to rely on rehashes of its earlier hits. Lunceford succumbed to a heart attack while the band was on tour.

The distinctive Lunceford style, generally identified with Sy Oliver although many other arrangers contributed to this extraordinary library, influenced many bandleaders and arrangers right up to the 1950s; first the bands of Sonny Dunham and Sonny Burke, and frequently the band of Tommy Dorsey (for which Sy Oliver worked for several years), reflected this influence. Albums described as tributes to Lunceford have been recorded by many bands including those of Sy Oliver, George Williams, Billy May. The Lunceford band ranked with those of Ellington, Basie, and Goodman among the few lastingly important big jazz orchestras of the 1930s. LPs: Decca 8050, Col. CL 634.

LUTCHER, NELLIE, *singer, piano;* b. Lake Charles, La., 10/15/15. Her father, Isaac Lutcher, played bass w. Clarence Hart band, in which Bunk Johnson was also heard; Nellie joined this band at the age of 15, playing one-nighters in La. and Tex. From '35 to '47 she worked on her own as a night club act, mostly around Los Angeles. Signed by Dave Dexter for Capitol Records, she became an immediate national hit with *Hurry on Down* and *He's A Real Gone Guy,* her own comps. She has continued to tour and record, but after her initial popularity became a successful businesswoman, buying real estate, etc. in Los Angeles. Her quixotic, humorous vocal and piano styles have many jazz inflections, though her main success has been in the pop field. LPs: *Real* Gone (Cap.), *Our New Nellie* (Lib.).

Addr: 2114 La Salle Ave., Los Angeles 18, Calif.

LUTER, CLAUDE, *clarinet;* b. Paris, France, 7/23/23. Studied trumpet before switching to clarinet. Started with a trio in 1946; won amateur contest 1947 and scored a big hit at the Jazz Festival in Nice, 1948. Until 1953 was featured with own band at Vieux Colombier Club in Paris, also working frequently w. Sidney Bechet from 1950. Luter, apparently inspired first by Johnny Dodds and later by Bechet, assimilated the New Orleans jazz style successfully and earned a position in French jazz comparable with that of Bob Wilber in the late '40s in the US. Rec. with Sidney Bechet, Mezz Mezzrow, and own orchestra.

LYNNE, GLORIA, *singer;* b. New York City, 11/23/31. Mother a gospel singer. Sang in church and won contests as a child; had five years of concert training. Prof. debut 1951 after winning amateur contest at Apollo Theatre. After several years of obscure night club work, much of it for rock 'n' roll audiences, she emerged as a first-class pop artist when, after studying with Raymond Scott in 1958, she began a series of LPs for Everest and worked in clubs catering to jazz and pop fans. Excellent control and soulful style reminding one of her two major influences, Ella Fitzgerald and Mahalia Jackson. Own LPs: Everest.

LYON, JAMES FREDERICK (Jimmy), *piano;* b. Camden, N.J., 11/6/21. Army 1942-6. Solo pianist for two years at Fred Waring's estate, Shawnee on the Delaware. In 1948 came from Phila. with Tal Farlow and Buddy DeFranco to NYC, where they intended to form a trio, but were unsuccessful. Spent a year w. Gene Williams' orch., 1½ years as June Christy's accompanist, later worked for Sam Donahue, Connie Haines, Bobby Byrne; to Nova Scotia w. Benny Goodman sextet. From Jan. '53 led own trio at Blue Angel NYC. Recorded solos on *Rumpus Room, Dancing on the Ceiling* w. Buddy DeFranco (MGM).

Addr: 665 Terrace Drive, Paramus, N.J.

LYTELL, JIMMY, *clarinet;* b. New York City, 12/1/04. Prof. debut at roadhouse owned by uncle. Repl. Larry

Shields in Original Dixieland Jazz Band for two years, then toured with Original Memphis Five. Conducted and played in many musical comedies and radio shows throughout '30s and '40s; mus. dir. at NBC in mid-40s. Rec. with own Dixieland band for Thesaurus Transcriptions, London Records, etc. Mus. dir. for Quality Records 1954. Favs: Goodman, Hucko. LPs w. Joe Glover (Epic), *Connee Boswell and the Orig. Memphis Five* (Vict.).

Addr: Dock Lane; Great Neck, L.I., N.Y.

LYTTELTON, HUMPHREY, *trumpet, leader;* b. Windsor, England, 5/23/21. Started w. George Webb's Dixielanders and had his own band from 1948, which accompanied Sidney Bechet in '49. Joined forces w. musicians from Graeme Bell's Australian jazz band for some recordings in '51. Originally a staunch traditionalist, Lyttelton gradually oriented the style of his group toward a more orchestrated approach, building its personnel up to octet size, which enabled him to simulate the sound of the Ellington contingents that recorded in the late 1930s. In Sept. '59 his band made its first US tour under the auspices of the NJF. A versatile figure and colorful personality—old Etonian, nephew of a viscount, successful cartoonist and talented journalist—Lyttelton at one point was the leading British figure in the revival of New Orleans jazz, appearing at numerous jazz concerts in England and on the Continent. He is the author of two witty and perceptive books, *I Play As I Please,* and *Second Chorus,* for which he also drew the illustrations. They were published in 1954 and '58 respectively, by MacGibbon & Kee, London. He has been a regular contributor to the London *Melody Maker.* Own LP: (Lond.).

M

MACERO, ATTILIO JOSEPH (Teo), *composer, saxophones;* b. Glens Falls, N.Y., 10/30/25. After 4 years in Navy (incl. Navy Sch. of Mus. in Washington, D.C. 1943-4) was discharged in late '46 and spent a year in Glens Falls teaching and playing, also working in flower shop. To NYC '48, entered Juilliard, org. a dance band there which played concerts and broadcast on WOR; also taught privately and in school at Ridgewood, N.J.; pl. club dates w. Larry Clinton et al. Bachelor and Master degrees, Juilliard, 1953. Very active as composer of jazz-influenced, atonal classical works; about 150 concert performances of these were given 1955-60. On staff at Columbia Records as music editor, '57-60. Two grants from Guggenheim for mus. comp. 1957, '8: *Fusion* was performed by N.Y. Phil. under L. Bernstein '58. Own LPs: *What's New* (Col.), *Teo* (Pres.); sideman on *LeGrand Jazz* (Col.); two arrs: for *Something New, Something Blue* (Col.). Eclectic composer whose work is experimental and provocative.

Addr: 100 Park Terrace West, New York 34, N.Y.

MacGREGOR, JOHN CHALMERS (Chummy), *piano, composer;* b. Saginaw, Mich., 3/28/03. Pl. with Jean Goldkette, Irving Aaronson in 1920s. Close friend and associate during 1930s of Glenn Miller, with whom he worked in Smith Ballew orch., and in the Miller band until 1942. In '44 he moved to Calif. and did studio work incl. playing and arr. on sound track for *Glenn Miller Story.* LPs: see Glenn Miller.

MACHITO (Frank Grillo), *leader;* b. Tampa, Fla., 2/16/12. Raised in Cuba, but has been back and forth between US and Cuba frequently since 1929. Though not a jazzman, began to earn big following among jazz fans ca. 1950 as one of the first Afro-Cuban music exponents to incorporate jazz ideas. Featured soloists on his records at that time included Ch. Parker, Flip Phillips, Howard McGhee; more recently he has featured Johnny Griffin, Curtis Fuller, and arrangements by Herbie Mann. LPs: Tico, Seeco, Roulette, Harmony, Verve.

Addr: c/o Bauza, 944 Columbus Ave., New York, N.Y.

MacKAY, STUART, *misc. woodwinds;* b. Montreal, Can., 12/10/09. Stud. Ithaca Conservatory, Univ. of Mich., Columbia U. Played w. Isham Jones in mid '30s, Les Brown, '37-8, Red Norvo, '39-40, Eddy Duchin, '40-2, in service, '42-5. Later with Mark Warnow, Russ Case and various musical comedy bands. Since Aug., '54, working in production department at WTVJ, Miami, Fla. Has experimented off and on with his own groups featuring an unusual instrumentation. Favs: C. Hawkins, Benny Carter, Stan Getz. LP: Vict. (*Reap the Wild Winds*).

Addr: 1475 N.E. 138th St., N. Miami, Fla.

MACKEL, JOHN WILLIAM (Billy), *guitar;* b. Baltimore, Md., 12/28/12. Stud. privately; started on tenor banjo; pl. with Percy Glascoe 1932-5, Bubby Johnson '35-40, in Baltimore; own combo '40-4. Made first records on joining Lionel Hampton '44; has remained w. Hampton since then. Fav. own solo: *Limehouse Blues,* with Hampton (Dec.). LPs w. Hampton (Decca, Verve, Epic, Col., Em., Cam., GNP, Aud. Fid., MGM, Lion, Contemp.).

Addr: 104 W. 49th St., New York 19, N.Y.

MADISON, LOUIS (Kid Shots), *cornet;* b. New Orleans, La., 2/19/1899; d. New Orleans, Sept. 1948. Pl. drums in Waifs' Home band w. Louis Armstrong 1915. Stud. cornet w. Dave Jones, Louis Dumaine and Joe Howard. Second cornet w. Original Tuxedo Orch. 1923, under Papa Celestin; rec. debut '25. Later worked w. Frankie Dusen, Big Eye Louis Nelson, Alphonse Picou; WPA brass band during depression years, Young Tuxedo, Eureka Brass Band in '40s. LP w. George Lewis (Amer. Mus.).

MAGALHAES, JOSE MANUEL, *trumpet;* b. Lisbon, Portugal, 1/31/29. First pl. Fr. horn. Worked in Navy band, 1946-52, playing trumpet and tympani. Two years w. symphony orch. on tympani to '54; for several years has been in tpt. section of band at national radio station, also leading dance band w. three of his brothers playing trumpet, saxes and bass. Pl. w. Newport Int. Band at Brussels World's Fair, NJF '58. Fav. mus: Basie, Ellington, M. Ferguson, Armstrong, Gillespie.

Addr: Rua Candido Figueiredo 70-2, Lisbon.

MAHONES, GILDO, *piano;* b. New York City, 6/2/29. Pl. w. Joe Morris 1948; Milt Jackson at Minton's; Army '51-3. Joined Lester Young Sept. '53 and remained with him until early '56; then gigged around NYC with Les Modes (Julius Watkins-Charlie Rouse), Sonny Stitt and others. Joined Lambert, Hendricks & Ross June '59. LPs w. Bennie Green (Blue Note); Les Modes (Dawn, Atl.), Lester Young (Verve), Lambert, Hendricks & Ross (Col.).

Addr: 47 Clifton Place, Brooklyn 38, N.Y.

MAIDEN, WILLIAM RALPH (Willie), *tenor sax, composer;* b. Detroit, Mich., 3/12/28. Stud. piano at five years; worked w. local bands while in junior high. Began pl. prof. in 1950 w. Will Osborne, then w. Johnny Pineapple and Perez Prado. St. writing for Maynard Ferguson in '52, then joined the band '56. Skilful big-band arranger. Fav: Stan Getz. LPs w. Maynard Ferguson (Em., Roul.).

Addr: 255 W. 85th Street, New York 24, N.Y.

MAINI, JOSEPH JR., *alto sax, tenor sax;* also *clarinet, flute;* b. Providence, R.I., 2/8/30. Father, guitarist; brother, mandolinist (Italian folk music). Stud. alto with Joe Piacitelli, toured w. Alvino Rey, Johnny Bothwell in 1948, Jimmy Zito, '49. During a few weeks spent w. Claude Thornhill in '51, Ch. Parker gave him a tenor sax which Maini still plays. Gigs, record dates and short movie w. Dan Terry, '54. During late '50s gigged in Hollywood w. Jack Sheldon, Lorraine Geller, Terry Gibbs' big band. Fav: Charlie Parker. LPs w. Red Mitchell (Beth.), *Best Coast Jazz* (Em.), Kenny Drew (Jazz: West), Jack Montrose (Vict.), Gibbs (Merc.); w. Jack Sheldon in *The Hard Swing* (Wor. Pac.).

MAKEBA, MIRIAM ZENZI, *singer;* b. Johannesburg, S. Africa, 3/4/32. A Xosa tribeswoman, she sang as a child at benefits for Kilmerton Training Inst. in Pretoria which she attended for eight years. After going from town to town with a group of amateurs she was asked to join a vocal group called the Black Manhattan Brothers; remained with them for 2½ years, then in '57 joined a revue, working as a single and touring for 18 months. She was feat. in a film *Come Back Africa* in '57; at a screening at Venice Film Fest. to which she was invited in '59 the film received a Critics' Award. In '59 she was seen on BBC-TV in London; made US debut Nov. '59 on Steve Allen show. A protegee of Harry Belafonte, she was later heard at US night clubs. She sings in English and Xosa dialect with great charm and a strong suggestion of jazz feeling. Married to singer Sonny Pillay.

MALNECK, MATTY, *composer, conductor, violinist;* b. Newark, N. J., 12/10/04. Att. public schools in Denver, Colo.; stud. violin w. private teacher. Began pl. with dance bands at 16; w. Paul Whiteman 11 years, then had own orch. from 1935 for a while. Since then has been best known as songwriter; tunes incl. *I'm Through with Love, I'll Never Be the Same, Goody Goody* et al.

Addr: 508 N. Elm, Beverly Hills, Calif.

MALONE, KASPER DELMAR (Kas), *bass;* b. Paducah, Ky., 10/25/09. Stud. clarinet, flute, French horn. Toured w. theatre bands in the 1920s; worked in midwestern radio stations in '30s and '40s; toured w. Jack Teagarden '54-6, then moved to Las Vegas and has since gigged w. combos in Arizona and Nevada; also played w. Tucson Symphony. Favs: Slam Stewart, Morty Corb. LP w. Jack Teagarden (Beth.).

Addr: 212 West 31st St., Long Beach 6, Calif.

MALTBY, RICHARD (Dick), *composer, leader, trumpet;* b. Chicago, Ill., 6/26/14. Cornet in school band. Stud. at Northwestern U. and played w. dance bands. Staff orchestra, WBBM, Chi. for several years. Composed *Six Flats Unfurnished,* a best-selling 1942 Benny Goodman record. Discovered by Paul Whiteman. Became network conductor-arranger and moved to NYC '45. Began playing dates as leader of dance band May '55, feat. a modified jazz style and using Al Cohn and other jazz soloists on records. LPs on Col., Cam.

Addr: 106 W. 56th St., New York, N.Y.

MANCE, JULIAN CLIFFORD JR. (Junior), *piano;* b Chicago, Ill., 10/10/28. Stud. Roosevelt Coll., Chicago. Pl. with Jimmy Dale 1947; Gene Ammons '48-9; Lester Young '49-50; back w. Ammons '50-1; Army '51-3 (pl. with Army band at Fort Knox, Ky.); combo at Bee Hive Lounge Chi. '53-4; acc. Dinah Washington on tour '54-5. Worked w. Cannonball Adderley quint. Feb. '56 to Nov. '57; joined Dizzy Gillespie March '58, made European tour with him Sept. '59 and app. with him at numerous jazz festivals. Favs: O. Peterson, B. Powell, Tatum. An assertive, adroit modern soloist of whom Ralph Gleason has said: "He is so steeped in the blues tradition that he carries it along everywhere . . . his solos are beautifully constructed, rhythmically as well as melodically." LPs w. Adderley, Dinah Washington (Em.), Wilbur Ware (River.), Art Blakey (Beth.), Gillespie (Verve), Virgil Gonsalves (Omega).

Addr: 94-01 25th Ave., East Elmhurst 69, L.I., N.Y.

MANCINI, HENRY, *composer, conductor;* b. Cleveland, Ohio, 4/16/24. St. on piccolo at age eight; later pl. piano w. local bands around Pittsburgh. Attended Carnegie Tech Music School and Juilliard; stud. w. Mario Castelnuovo-Tedesco, Ernst Krenek. In service 1941-5; w. Ted Beneke '45-6, then went to West Coast to free-lance. With Universal Pictures as staff comp. '51-7; comp. for *Peter Gunn,* TV detective drama, the first to use modern jazz backgrounds throughout. Scores for films incl. *The Glenn Miller Story, The*

Benny Goodman Story, et al. Names the big bands of the '30s as important influences. LPs: *The Music from Peter Gunn* (Vict.); also other LPs on Vict., Lib.

Addr: 17947 Osborne St., Northridge, Calif.

MANCUSO, RONALD BERNARD (Gus), *baritone horn;* also *piano, bass, trumpet, trombone, vibes, singer;* b. Rochester, N.Y., 1933. One of six brothers, all musicians. St. on drums at 11, then switched to trombone; picked up baritone horn in Army band. Worked w. vocal group in Las Vegas, later gigged in Calif. playing piano, bass, baritone horn. A resourceful, modern soloist, he is the first jazzman to have specialized in the baritone horn. Own LP: Fantasy.

MANDEL, JOHN ALFRED (Johnny), *composer;* also *trombone, bass trumpet;* b. New York City, 11/23/25. Studied w. Stefan Wolpe, Van Alexander, Manhattan School of Mus. and Juilliard; also attended NY Military Academy on scholarship. Trumpet w. Joe Venuti 1943; Billie Rogers' band '44. During the next few years, in addition to studying, he toured as trombonist with bands of Henry Jerome, Boyd Raeburn, Jimmy Dorsey, Buddy Rich, Georgie Auld and Alvino Rey. Settled in NYC, May '49. Pl. w. Chubby Jackson; wrote for Artie Shaw; staff writer for year w. band at WMGM and 18 months w. *Your Show of Shows* on TV. Pl. and wrote for Elliot Lawrence off and on '51-3; toured as trombonist w. Count Basie band June-November '53. Moved to LA, where he pl. bass trumpet w. Zoot Sims at the Haig. Wrote part of score for Martin and Lewis movie, *You're Never Too Young.* Since then has been active as composer for films and TV, including *Markham* and G.E. Theatre on TV '59. Mandel's reputation as one of the most brilliant young arrangers was enhanced in '58 by his underscoring for *I Want to Live,* considered to be the first successful integration of jazz into a movie score. Comp. for Basie: *Straight Life;* for Herman: *Not Really The Blues;* for Stan Getz: *Hershey Bar, Pot Luck;* for Chet Baker: *Tommyhawk.* Fav. trom: Brookmeyer, Earl Swope; arrs: Hefti, Al Cohn, Wilkins. App. as leader or composer-arr. on the following LPs: Cy Touff-Richie Kamuca, Hoagy Carmichael, David Allen, Chet Baker (Wor. Pac.), Gerry Mulligan—*I Want To Live, I Want To Live*—soundtrack (UA), Elliot Lawrence (Fant.), Woody Herman (Cap., Evst.).

Addr: 2565 Glen Green, Hollywood 28, Calif.

MANGELSDORFF, ALBERT, *trombone;* b. Frankfurt am Main, Germany, 9/5/28. Brother Emil is well known alto man. Violin from age 12, then guitar w. local bands. St. on trombone 1951 w. Joe Klimm; later w. Hans Koller, Jutta Hipp and several combos of his own. More recently has been w. Frankfurt All-Stars, Joki Freund Quintet; led own band on Frankfurt radio station. Has won German *Jazz Echo* poll every year since '54. To US as member of Newport International Band '58; later worked w. D. Gojkovic in a group called Newport International Septet, heard at Storyville in Frankfurt. LPs available in US incl. *Das ist Jazz!* (Decca), *Cool Europe* w. Jutta Hipp (MGM), Hans Koller (Wor. Pac.), Joki Freund (Jazz.), Newport International Band (Col.). Made movie, *Jazz Gestern und Heute,* w. Hans Koller, '53. Fav. mus: Jay Jay Johnson, Miles Davis.

Addr: 6 JM Sachsenlager, Frankfurt am Main, Germany.

MANGIAPANE, SHERWOOD, *bass, sousaphone;* b. New Orleans, La., 10/1/12. Self-taught. Worked in New Orleans with Blue Parody Orch., Johnny Wiggs, Papa Laine; several seasons on steamboat w. Dutch Andrus; played with servicemen's combo while in Army in England, 1944. Employed by bank from '32, but has continued to play music as sideline. Fav: Bob Haggart. LPs w. Jack Delaney (South.).

MANN, HERBIE (Herbert Jay Solomon), *flute, saxophones,* etc.; b. Brooklyn, N.Y., 4/16/30. Started on clarinet at nine. Overseas in Army, pl. w. band at Trieste for three years. Clubs and records w. Mat Mathews quintet Jan. '53 to Sept. '54; toured w. Pete Rugolo Oct. '54. Wrote and directed the music for several TV dramas in spring '56; toured Scandinavia as single Sept. '56, also visiting France and Holland. Ret. to US and was active on West Coast during summer '57. Formed own Afro Jazz Sextet in NYC, June '59. Pl. Newport Fest., many sessions at Village Gate. In Dec. '59 left on St. Dept. tour of Africa; there w. his group until May '60. Although he plays bass clarinet and tenor sax, Mann concentrates on the flute and has been recognized as one of the most gifted of the modernists on this instrument. Won *Down Beat* poll '57-9. Favs: Frank Wess (jazz); Wm. Kincaid (classical); Henry Klee (all-around). Own LPs: UA, Verve, Beth., Inter., River., Savoy, Pres., Epic; LPs w. Billy Taylor, Philly Joe Jones (River.), Art Blakey (Blue Note), Mat Mathews (Dawn), A. K. Salim (Savoy), *Just Wailin'* (New Jazz), *Swinging Seasons* (MGM), Buddy DeFranco (Verve).

Addr: 105 West 73rd St., New York 23, N.Y.

MANN, HOWARD L. (Howie), *drums;* b. New York City, 8/4/27. Stud. with father, later w. Henry Adler. Pl. with Elliot Lawrence 1947-51; Hal McIntyre, Jerry Wald '51-2. Has had own group off and on since '52, also pl. dates with Bobby Scott, Chubby Jackson, Dorsey Bros. LPs w. Elliot Lawrence (Col.), Phil Urso (Sav.), Bobby Scott (ABC-Par.).

Addr: 10 Hunt Lane, Levittown, L.I., N.Y.

MANNE, SHELDON (Shelly), *drums, composer;* b. New York City, 6/11/20. Father and two uncles drummers. Alto sax first instrument. Stud. drums w. Billy Gladstone. Got into music business playing on boats to Europe. With Bobby Byrne 1939 (made first record w. him); replaced Dave Tough w. Joe Marsala '40; Bob Astor '41, Raymond Scott '41-2, Will Bradley '42, Les Brown '42. In Coast Guard '42-5. With Stan Kenton '46-7, Chas. Ventura '47, Kenton '47-8, Bill Harris-Shelly Manne Sextet '48, JATP '48-9, Woody Herman '49, Kenton '50-1. Settled in Calif. in '52; played w. Howard Rumsey at Lighthouse in Hermosa Beach '53, Shorty Rogers '54 but worked mainly in movie and recording studios, appearing on literally more than half of the hundreds of jazz records made on the West Coast during this period. After his app. in *The Man With The Golden Arm,* for which he also instructed Frank Sinatra in the drumming sequence, Manne formed his own quintet which toured the East in the spring and summer of '56 but has mainly been occupied with night club engagements on the West Coast. In addition to leading his group, he has continued to free-lance in TV and movies. Pl. for *Peter Gunn, Richard Diamond, Staccato* on TV. Films: played the role of Dave Tough in *The Five Pennies* '58 and *The Gene Krupa Story* '59; scored *T-Bird Gang* '58, *The Proper Time* '59. Won DB poll '47-51, '54, '55-8; Met. poll '49, '52-3, '55-60; Playpoll '57-60, Playboy All Stars poll '59-60.

Because of his popular success and because he seems to have cornered such a large segment of the commercial market for jazz in every medium in the Los Angeles area, there has been a tendency to take Manne for granted; subjective listening, however, confirms that he has remained a superlative musician who can lift an anemic quasi-jazz ensemble to undeserved rhythmic heights and, whether working with a trio or a vast studio orchestra, plays with an intelligence and sensitivity that can add fire, color and impetus to his environment. Favs: Lamond, Roach, Jo Jones, Kahn, Tough. Own LPs on Contemporary, *West Coast Sound* (3507), *Swinging Sounds* (3516), *More Swinging Sounds* (3519), *Shelly Manne & His Friends* (3525), *My Fair Lady* (3527), *Li'l Abner* (3533), *Premiere Recording* (3536), *The Gambit* (3557), *Peter Gunn* (3560), *Bells Are Ringing* (3559); LPs w. Kenton (Cap. WDX 569, W724, T167, T1130), Lighthouse All Stars (Contemp. 3501), Hamp Hawes (Contemp. 3509), Sonny Rollins (Contemp. 3530, 3564), also many others w. Barney Kessel, Red Norvo, etc. on Contemp.; Jimmy Giuffre, Stan Getz, Lee Konitz, Teddy Charles et al on countless labels. Manne has been heard on well over a thousand LPs; the above is merely a representative list.

Addr: 18024 Parthenia St., Northridge, Calif.

MANONE, JOSEPH (Wingy), *trumpet, singer, leader;* b. New Orleans, 2/13/04. At the age of 10 he had his right arm amputated after it was crushed between two streetcars; shortly after this he mastered the trumpet. He toured and recorded with many bands in St. Louis, Chicago, New York; was first nationally known as a jazz figure with the advent of the swing era, recording frequently with small groups under his own leadership from 1934-41. His first big hit was a swing version of *The Isle of Capri,* 1935, on Vocalion. After the early 1940s he headquartered on the West Coast, acting as a sort of court jester to Bing Crosby and frequently making radio appearances with him. Film w. Crosby: *Rhythm On The River* '40. Although principally a comedy personality, Manone is a good performer in an Armstrong-inspired style. He was the first to record the riff that later became famous as *In the Mood,* in an early version which he called *Tar Paper Stomp,* for the Champion label in 1929. His autobiography, *Trumpet on the Wing,* co-authored by Paul Vandervoort II, was published 1948 by Doubleday & Co. In the past few years he has played occasional night club dates in Las Vegas. Own LP: *Trumpet on the Wing* (Decca).

Addr: 1321 Phillips St., Las Vegas, Nev.

MARABLE, FATE, *leader, piano;* b. Paducah, Ky., 12/2/1890; d. St. Louis, Mo., 1/16/47. From 1907 he worked almost continually on Miss. riverboats, forming his own bands for these excursions from 1917. In the years between the two World Wars he built up a distinguished honor roll of alumni, among them Louis Armstrong, off and on 1918-22; Red Allen, Zutty Singleton, Johnny & Baby Dodds, Pops Foster, Emmanuel Perez, Johnny St. Cyr, Mouse Randolph, Earl Bostic, Gene Sedric, Al Morgan and Jimmy Blanton. Both before and after the riverboat decades, Marable worked as a pianist in St. Louis night spots. His bands were never put on records.

MARABLE, LAWRENCE NORMAN, *drums;* b. Los Angeles, Cal., 5/21/29. Distant relative of Fate Marable. Father pl. piano. Prof. debut 1947. Heard around LA for several years in various combos incl. Ch. Parker, Dexter Gordon, Wardell Gray, Stan Getz, Hamp Hawes, Zoot Sims, Herb Geller. Joined Johnny Griffin, Jan. 1959; Geo. Shearing big band, Aug. '59. Favs: Kenny Clarke, Art Blakey. LPs w. S. Stitt, J. Giuffre, Tal Farlow (Verve), W. Gray, H. Hawes (Pres.), H. Geller (Merc.), C. Candoli (Beth.).

Addr: 3459 West Blvd., Los Angeles, Calif.

MARABUTO, JOHN SANTOS JR., *piano;* b. Oakland, Calif., 5/21/25. Began stud. accordion in 1932; trumpet, sax and arr. in high school; st. on piano while in service '43. Played w. various groups after discharge, incl. Rudy Salvini, Brew Moore. Fav: Duke Ellington as a composer. LPs w. Brew Moore (Fant.), Rudy Salvini, Mel Lewis (SF Jazz).

MARDIGAN, ARTHUR (Art), *drums;* b. Detroit, Mich., 2/12/23. With Tommy Reynolds' band '42; Army '43-4, then a year w. Geo. Auld, a year in Detroit, and NYC combo jobs w. Dexter Gordon, Ch. Parker, Allen Eager; also w. Elliot Lawrence, Kai Winding, Woody Herman, '52; Pete Rugolo, '54; free-lancing with small combos mainly in Detroit from '55 on. LPs w. Nick Travis (Vict.), Jimmy Rowles (Lib.), Bill De Arango (Merc.), Wardell Gray (Pres.), W. Herman (Verve), Fats Navarro (Savoy).

MARDIN, MEHMET ARIF, *composer;* b. Istanbul, Turkey, 3/15/32. Self-taught comp.-arr.; grad. Faculty of Economics and Commerce in Istanbul; stud. London School of Economics one year. Some of his compositions were rec. by a band led by Quincy Jones for Voice of America. As a result, he was awarded the "Quincy Jones Scholarship" to the Berklee School in Boston, which he attended in 1958, after which he ret. to

Turkey. Fav: Duke Ellington. Arrs. for Herb Pomeroy (UA).

Addr: Ucler Apt., Ayazpasa, Istanbul, Turkey.

MARES, PAUL, *trumpet, leader;* b. New Orleans, 1900; d. Chicago, 8/18/49. Played on Miss. riverboats 1919; to Chicago 1920. Mares opened at the Friars' Inn late in 1921 as leader of the Friars Society Orch., later known as the New Orleans Rhythm Kings, one of the best known jazz groups in Chicago during the early 1920s. The orchestra was less important for Mares' own solo work than for the fact that its personnel included Leon Rappolo on clarinet, George Brunies on trombone, and, for some time, Ben Pollack on drums. The group recorded for Gennett in 1922-3 and for Okeh and Victor in '25, shortly before its dissolution. Mares was inactive in music during most of the rest of his life, but in Jan. 1935 he used the Friars Society name again for an Okeh recording date. Though the Rhythm Kings' career ran parallel in some respects to that of the Original Dixieland Jazz Band, most of their performances lacked the fire and originality of the latter group. LP w. George Brunis (River.).

MARGOLIS, SAMUEL D. (Sam), *tenor sax, clarinet;* b. Dorchester, Mass., 11/1/23. Influenced by Louis Armstrong, Bud Freeman, Lester Young. Brother is classical critic and comp. Principally self-taught, first on clar., then on tenor. Pl. w. combos around Boston, incl. Vic Dickenson, Shad Collins, Bobby Hackett, Rex Stewart et al. Longtime friend and roommate of trumpeter Ruby Braff; app. w. Braff at NJF '57. Returned to Boston '58. Favs: Bud Freeman, Lester Young, Babe Russin, Ben Webster. LPs w. Braff (Jazz., Vang., Verve, Beth.).

MARIANO, CHARLES HUGO (Charlie), *alto sax;* b. Boston, Mass., 11/12/23. Stud. three years at Schillinger House, Boston. Played w. Shorty Sherock 1948; Larry Clinton; Nat Pierce (with whom he made rec. debut); Chubby-Jackson-Bill Harris combo '53. Toured w. Stan Kenton '53 to end of '55, then 2½ years in LA with Shelly Manne. Returned to Boston, worked w. Herb Pomeroy, then rejoined Stan Kenton May-Nov. '59. Married Nov. 24, 1959 to Toshiko Akiyoshi, with whom he formed a quartet early '60. One of the most fluent and original of modern alto men, he was also heard playing recorder (vertical flute) with Mariano-Dodgion Sextet in *Beauties of 1918* (World-Pacific). Own LPs: Bethlehem, Fant.; LPs w. Kenton incl. *Contemporary Concepts* (Cap.), Manne (Contemp.), Manny Albam, Bill Holman (Coral), John Graas (Decca), Max Bennett (Beth.), F. Rosolino (Cap.).

Addr: 403 Grand Avenue, Leonia, N.J.

MARKEWICH, MAURICE (Reese), *piano, flute;* b. Brooklyn, N.Y., 8/6/36. Began on piano at 8, flute in high school. Formed the Mark V Quintet at Cornell U., incl. bar. saxist Nick Brignola, which won a competition and app. at the New York Jazz Festival at Randall's Island, summer '57. Pl. at Cafe Bohemia NYC '58; Ray Eberle orch. summer '58. B. A. at Cornell U. '58; has since been studying, relatively inactive in music. Favs: H. Silver, T. Flanagan, C. Parker. Own LP: Modernage.

Addr: 175 Riverside Drive, New York 24, N.Y.

MARKHAM, JOHN GORDON, *drums;* b. Oakland, Calif., 11/1/26. Began pl. in high school; w. Charlie Barnet 1950-2; Billy May '53; KGO-TV staff orch. '56-9, also acc. Ella Fitzgerald and Peggy Lee during '58. Joined Red Norvo '59, made Australian tour with him, then in Oct. '59, along with Norvo, went to Europe with Benny Goodman group. Favs: Jo & Philly Joe Jones, Roach, Rich, Tough, Krupa. LPs w. B. May, Nat Cole (Cap.), V. Guaraldi, Brew Moore, C. Tjader, E. Duran (Fant.), Ch. Barnet (Merc.), Benny Goodman (MGM).

Addr: 458 40th Ave., San Francisco, Calif.

MARKOWITZ, IRVIN (Marky), *trumpet;* b. Washington, D.C., 12/11/23. Started at Police Boys' Club. Stud. w. Fred Leonberger. Pl. w. Ch. Spivak 1942-3, J. Dorsey '43-4, Boyd Raeburn '44-5, Woody Herman '46 and '48-9, Buddy Rich '46-7, then free-lanced in Washington and NYC. Favs: Harry Edison, Conrad Gozzo, Ray Linn. LPs: *Porgy And Bess* w. Ralph Burns (Decca), *The Jazz Soul of Porgy And Bess* w. Bill Potts (UA), *House Of Sounds* w. Willis Conover (Bruns.), Woody Herman (MGM), Sonny Berman (Ctpt.).

Addr: 166-31 9th Ave., Whitestone 57, New York.

MARMAROSA, MICHAEL (Dodo), *piano;* b. Pittsburgh, Pa., 12/12/25. Schoolmate of Erroll Garner. Closely associated w. Buddy DeFranco, with whom he played 1940-4 in the bands of Scat Davis, Gene Krupa, Ted Fio Rito, Charlie Barnet, Tommy Dorsey. Was w. Artie Shaw 1944-5 and again 1949-50. Between '45-9 lived in Calif., gigged w. Boyd Raeburn, Lucky Thompson, etc. One of the most brilliant pianists to rise out of the bop era, he has been in obscurity in Pittsburgh for several years, his career often having been interrupted by illness during the past decade. Won Esq. New Star Award 1947.

Many of Marmarosa's recordings have long been unavailable. They include sides under his own name on Dial and Sav.; w. C. Parker on Dial. The recordings he made w. Lester Young are now available on Alad.; he is also w. Ch. Barnet on Decca, Corky Corcoran on Em., Boyd Raeburn and Charlie Parker on Savoy.

MARRERO, LAWRENCE, *banjo, guitar;* b. New Orleans, La., 10/24/00; d. NO, 6/5/59. Started on bass; stud. w. father and brothers. Active from about 1919 w. many local bands incl. Buddy Petit, Manuel Manetta, Emmanuel Perez, John Robichaux, George Lewis, Bunk Johnson, also playing frequently with the last two during the 1940s. After intermittent illness he retired in '55 in NO, where he remained until his death. LPs w. George Lewis (Empir., Jazz., Del., BN, River., Omega).

MARSALA, ANDREW (Andy), *alto sax, clarinet, flute, oboe;* b. Brooklyn, N.Y., 6/30/42. Stud. clar. at 9; alto w.

Marshall Brown at 12; later arr. & comp. w. John La Porta. Marsala, who is not related to veteran jazz clarinetist Joe Marsala, scored the major sensation at NJF in '57 as member of Marshall Brown's Farmingdale High School Band, app. there again the following year as extra attraction w. Newport International Band, and again in '59 as a member of the Newport Youth Band. The Farmingdale band made three LPs, circulated privately but not released to the public. Favs: C. Parker, Paul Desmond, and more recently Julian Adderley, John Coltrane. LPs w. International Band (Col.), Newport Youth Band (Cor.).

Addr: 3 Chapin Road, Farmingdale, N.Y.

MARSALA, JOSEPH (Joe), *clarinet, saxes, leader;* b. Chicago, Ill., 1/5/07. Originally self-taught, but later studied with symphony clarinetist. As youngster played in neighborhood bands with brother Marty on drums. Played in trio at dance school w. Dave Rose on piano ca. '27. Later worked w. Art Hodes, Floyd O'Brien, and many other combos in Chicago speakeasies during prohibition days. Worked for Wingy Manone in '29 and '33, came to NYC to rejoin him early 1935 at Hickory House. In summer of '36 formed own band at Hickory House, one of the first mixed combos seen on 52nd St., w. Red Allen, Eddie Condon, Joe Bushkin. Band later featured Bobby Hackett on guitar and trumpet, and harpist Adele Girard, who married Marsala in '37. He remained at the Hickory House off and on with various combos until 1945, then became semi-inactive, living mostly in Colo. '49-53. Became music publisher in NYC '54. As songwriter he had three big hits, *Little Sir Echo, Don't Cry Joe, And So to Sleep Again.* As a jazzman he was an inspired, liquid-toned clarinetist and an excellent tenor and alto man who never achieved the prominence he deserved.

Own LPs: (Decca, Bruns.); LPs w. various personnel: *Jam Session at Commodore* (Comm.), *Chicago Jazz* (Decca).

MARSALA, MARTY, *trumpet, drums;* b. Chicago, Ill., 4/2/09. Brother of Joe Marsala, with whose band he worked frequently in the '30s and early '40s. Later pl. w. own and other Dixieland groups, mostly on West Coast: Jazz Ltd. in Chicago '54-5; Club Hangover '56, Easy Street '57, Kewpie Doll '58-9, all in San Francisco. Own LP: *Jazz From The San Francisco Waterfront* (ABC-Par.); LPs w. Eddie Condon (Comm.), Kid Ory (Verve).

Addr: 654 Bush St., San Francisco, Calif.

MARSH, ARNO LEROY, *tenor sax;* b. Grand Rapids, Mich., 5/28/28. Very little music tuition; st. w. school band; on road in '46 w. territory band. Feat. w. Woody Herman Dec. '51-Aug. '53, then had own band, worked at Rowe Hotel, Grand Rapids '54. In recent years has been inactive in jazz, working with Western band in Las Vegas and other commercial jobs, though he showed great promise during his tenure with Herman. Favs: Getz, Cohn, Young. LPs w. Herman (MGM, Verve).

MARSH, WARNE MARION, *tenor sax;* b. Los Angeles, Calif. Stud. accordion, then bass clarinet, alto, tenor. Private teachers. First job w. Hollywood Canteen Kids 1944, followed by year and half w. Hoagy Carmichael's Teenagers. Army '46-7; while stationed in N.J. he met Lennie Tristano. After discharge, free-lanced in LA and spent four months on tour w. Buddy Rich. Settled in NYC Oct. '48 and since that time has studied and worked almost exclusively w. Tristano, taking non-music day jobs to support himself since 1950. In '59, Marsh, Tristano, and Lee Konitz were reunited for a series of night club and concert appearances. Rec. w. Met. All Stars 1953 (solo on *How High the Moon*). Comp. *Sax of a Kind* w. Lee Konitz; also wrote *Marshmallow.* Marsh's cool tone and pensive, somewhat cerebral style mark him as a typical product of the Tristano-influenced school. His work can be heard at its most effective on the Tristano sides recorded for Capitol. Fav: Lester Young. Own LPs: *Jazz of Two Cities* (Imp.), *Quartet* (Interlude), Warne Marsh (Atl.); LPs w. Tristano (Atl.), Konitz (Pres., Atl.), Konitz-Giuffre (Verve).

Addr: 40 W. 76th St., New York 23, N.Y.

MARSHALL, JACK WILTON, *guitar, leader, composer;* b. El Dorado, Kans., 11/23/21. Began pl. ukulele at 10; st. working in bands around LA after high school grad. Worked as sideman for MGM movie studios seven years; cond. and comp. for several movies. Many dates as mus. dir. for Capitol, not essentially jazz but often with good jazz feeling. Favs: Django Reinhardt, Segovia. Own LP: *18th Century Jazz* (Cap.); LPs w. Andre Previn, Shorty Rogers (Vict.), Peggy Lee (Cap.).

Addr: 13500 Crewe Street, Van Nuys, Calif.

MARSHALL, JOSEPH KAISER, *drums;* b. Savannah, Ga., 6/11/02; d. NYC, 1/2/48. Pl. with Shrimp Jones 1922, Fletcher Henderson late '22 until '29, later led his own band intermittently; toured Europe '37 w. Bobby Martin. During the '40s he free-lanced w. various bands around NYC, rec. with Art Hodes, Mezzrow, and Bechet. Pl. with Bunk Johnson at Stuyvesant Casino '46. Marshall was considered one of the great drummers of the early days of jazz. LPs w. Louis Armstrong (River.), Bessie Smith (Col.).

MARSHALL, WENDELL, *bass;* b. St. Louis, Mo., 10/24/20. First cousin of Jimmy Blanton, who first interested him in bass. Marshall played for a few months w. Lionel Hampton in 1942, then returned to school (Lincoln U. in Jefferson City, Mo.). After Army service '43-6, he played w. Stuff Smith for a few months, then formed own trio in St. Louis in '47. Coming to NYC, he met Mercer Ellington, who, after using him for four months in his own band, introduced him to his father, Duke Ellington, whom Marshall joined in Sept. '48. He toured Europe with the band in 1950 and was prominently featured on *Duet* with Jimmy Hamilton. Leaving Ellington Jan. '55 he free-lanced very successfully in NYC with innumerable groups, also playing in pit and onstage with *Mr.*

Wonderful '56-7; onstage in *Say Darling* '58-9 and in pit of *Gypsy* '59.

He has recorded several hundred LPs, including many with Ellington (Vict., Cap., Col.), Louis Bellson (Cap., Verve), Art Blakey (BN), Jazz Lab Quintet (Col., Jub.), Hank Jones (Savoy).

Addr: 186-01 Hillburn Ave., St. Albans, L.I., N.Y.

MARTERIE, RALPH, *leader, trumpet;* b. Naples, Italy, 12/24/14. Raised in Chicago. Prof. at 14; many years w. local bands and radio studio work in Chicago. First formed band while in Navy, later led civilian orch. for ABC studio in Chicago and began recording. Org. touring band in 1951 which scored major successes as pop rather than a jazz outfit. Many LPs on Merc.

MARTIN, RALPH LAWRENCE, *piano;* b. Paterson, N. J., 10/28/26. Stud. piano at six; pl. clar. and sax in high school; stud. comp. at Syracuse U. 1946-8, U. of Miami '48-50, Juilliard '50-1. Had own group in Navy '44-6. Since '50 has acc. numerous singers and worked gigs w. various big bands incl. Billy Butterfield, Boyd Raeburn, Ray McKinley, Don Redman. Favs: Bud Powell, Al Haig, Joe Albany, John Lewis et al. LPs w. Louis Bellson (Verve), Sal Salvador (Beth.).

Addr: 2258 Grand Ave., Bronx, N.Y.

MARTIN, LLOYD (Skip), *composer, saxes;* b. Robinson, Ill., 5/14/16. Raised in Indianapolis, Ind. In late 1930s and early '40s pl. with name bands incl. Gus Arnheim, Ch. Barnet, Jan Savitt, B. Goodman, Glenn Miller; also wrote a number of arrs. for Count Basie, incl. *Tuesday at Ten.* Later settled in Calif., moved out of jazz into pop field as conductor and arr. One of his most successful arrs. was *I've Got My Love to Keep Me Warm* for Les Brown's orch. Own LPs: MGM, Somerset.

MARTUCCI, DANTE, *bass;* b. New York City, 6/8/22. Pl. trombone, but for physical reasons had to give it up. Began stud. bass in 1946 at New York Coll. of Music. Worked w. numerous jazz groups, incl. Tony Scott, Johnny Bothwell, Teddy Wilson, Buddy Rich, Gene Krupa, Sal Salvador, Urbie Green et al. Has free-lanced and done radio work around NYC in recent years. Favs: Red Mitchell, Ray Brown, Oscar Pettiford. LPs w. Urbie Green (Blue Note), Sal Salvador, Joe Roland (Beth.).

Addr: 212 W. Kingsbridge Road, Bronx, N.Y.

MARX, RICHARD (Dick), *piano, composer;* b. Chicago, Ill., 4/12/24. Private study from age 5, later at De Paul U. Has worked extensively in Chicago as studio man and pl. in the groups of Chubby Jackson, Thad Jones, R. Burns, F. Katz. Since 1952 has frequently teamed w. bassist John Frigo for Chicago night club duo work. Considers himself most successful as accompanist to singers; also teaches piano and does vocal coaching. John S. Wilson has praised his "solidly based talent . . . polished technique . . . delicate touch and fine sense of shading." Favs: Tatum, O. Peterson, B. Taylor. Own LPs: *Delicate Savagery* (Coral), *Marx Makes Broadway* (Omega); LPs w. Frigo (Cor., Bruns.); *First Modern Piano Quartet* (Coral).

Addr: 7652 E. Prairie Road, Skokie, Ill.

MASTERSOUNDS, THE, A quartet composed of Monk and Buddy Montgomery, Richie Crabtree and Benny Barth, q.v. Popularized in 1957 in San Francisco with the help of critic Ralph Gleason, they began their recording career in Seattle and soon earned national attention through a series of LPs on World Pacific. They appeared at the Monterey Jazz Festival, '58, and Newport, '59. Despite the similarity of their instrumentation to that of the Modern Jazz Quartet, the Mastersounds established an individual personality due to their constant experimentation in seeking new ideas for their arrangements. In early '60, the group disbanded.

MASTREN, CARMEN NICHOLAS, *guitar, banjo;* b. Cohoes, N.Y., 10/6/13. Violin, banjo first; guitar from '31 with local groups. Joined Wingy Manone in NYC '35; T. Dorsey '36-40, then staff work at NBC. Army '43-Dec. '45 incl. Europe w. Glenn Miller AAF band. From early '46, very active in studios, cond. and writing for Morton Downey on his Coca Cola series, rarely playing jazz. In 1953 he again joined NBC staff, pl. there with Skitch Henderson et al. The most popular guitarist in jazz at one time, he won Met. poll '39 and '40, DB poll '37. Own LP: *Banjorama* (Merc.); LPs w. Metronome All Stars (Vict.); w. Delta Four in Steve Allen's *The Jazz Story* (Coral).

Addr: 19-15 24th Road, Astoria, L.I., N.Y.

MATHEWS, BERTA LEAH (Lea), *singer;* b. McAlester, Okla., 8/10/25. Won amateur contest Washington, D.C., 1945. Soloist at Cafe Society NYC, 1950. Concerts w. Willis Conover's House of Sounds, '51-2. Toured w. Woody Herman '54-5. Favs: Ella Fitzgerald, Sarah Vaughan, Billie Holiday.

MATHEWS, MAT, *accordion;* b. The Hague, Holland, 6/18/24. Took up music during Nazi occupation because cultural professions were excused from doing forced labor for Germans during early stage. Later, however, he was sent to a concentration camp, escaped to Holland and had many perilous brushes with the Nazis, hiding for three months in the attic of his mother's house. After the war, a Joe Mooney broadcast on AFN inspired him to try playing jazz on the accordion. He broadcast with a quartet for a year in Luxemburg and was on BBC. Arriving in NYC 3/1/52, he developed ideas for a new sound with his button-key accordion. The result was a quartet with which he recorded in 1953; he was hailed as the first musician to produce modern jazz and an attractive new group sound with the accordion. The group unfortunately had little commercial success and Mathews subsided into obscure though steady commercial work in NYC. He appeared at NJF 1957. Own LPs: Elek., Dawn, Bruns., Verve; LP w. Joe Puma (Dawn).

Addr: c/o Galanti, 840 Broadway, New York City, N.Y.

MATLOCK, JULIAN CLIFTON (Matty), *clarinet;* b. Paducah, Ky., 4/27/09. Raised in Nashville from 1917. Clarinet at 12, then C melody sax. Pl. w. Blue Melody Boys, Tennessee Serenaders, then 5 years w. Beasley Smith orch. After 8 months w. Jimmy Joy, 1928-9, he rejoined Smith briefly, worked w. Tracy Brown in Pittsburgh, then replaced Benny Goodman in Ben Pollack orch. in fall of 1929. After 5 years, Pollack disbanded; in the fall of '34 Matlock and the other key soloists worked for a while as Clark Randall's orch., then were fronted by Bob Crosby. In the ensuing years Matlock enjoyed his greatest success as a principal soloist in the Crosby band. He settled in Los Angeles in 1943 and has since broadcast and recorded w. Crosby, Red Nichols and numerous other Dixieland groups. Own LPs: *Pete Kelly* series on Vict., Col., *Rampart and Vine, Dixieland My Dixieland, Texas, U.S.A., Jam Session Coast To Coast* (Col.), *The Dixieland Story* (War. Bros.); LPs w. Marvin Ash (Decca); one no. w. Ray Bauduc-Nappy Lamare in *History of Jazz, Vol. 1* (Cap.), George Brunis in *Dixieland All Stars* (South.), Jerry Colonna (Lib.), Bob Crosby (Coral, Decca, Cap.), Billy May, Bobby Hackett (Cap.), Bob Scobey (Vict.).

Addr: 4431 Simpson, North Hollywood, Calif.

MATSUMOTO, HIDEHIKO (Sleepy), *tenor sax;* also *flute;* b. Tamashimacho, Okayama Pref., Japan, 10/12/26. Older brother played flute in Hiroshima Phil. Symph. Orch. Took up clarinet in school. Says he got into music business "in order to earn bread." Has been in five or six films; in latest, *Gozen Ichiji No Kao* (*The Face at One O'Clock in the Morning*) he app. as actor, not musician. Nicknamed Sleepy by members of UN Forces stationed in Japan because of his looks. Favs: Ammons, Rollins, Stitt. Rec. on Japanese labels.

Addr: 672 Fuchucho, Fuchu City, Hiroshima Prefecture, Japan.

MATTHEWS, DAVID (Dave), *composer, tenor, alto saxes;* b. McAlester, Okla., 6/6/11. Stud. at Okla. U., Chicago Mus. College. Known as alto man in early years, playing w. Ben Pollack 1935, Jimmy Dorsey '36-7, Benny Goodman '37-9, Harry James '39-41, Hal McIntyre '41-2, Woody Herman '42-3, Stan Kenton and Charlie Barnet '44, then settled in NYC and later in Calif. as arranger. Matthews, who played mostly tenor from 1942, was best known as an Ellington-influenced arranger who often embodied actual passages from Ellington records in arrs. but was capable of excellent original work in the same style, such as *A Tribute to Ellington,* recorded by Barnet on Capitol. It is now on LP. Other LPs: Woody Herman (Bruns.), one track w. Jack Teagarden in *History of Jazz,* Vol. 2 (Cap.).

MATTHEWS, GEORGE, *trombone;* b. Dominican Republic, 9/23/12. Father and uncle pl. guitar. Stud. from 1927-31 at Martin Smith School of Music NYC and began playing w. Tiny Bradshaw, Willie Bryant, Louis Armstrong, Chick Webb, Ella Fitzgerald during 1930s and early '40s. W. Lucky Millinder '45-6; Count Basie '46-9; Since '50 has free-lanced on gigs and rec. Fav: Tommy Dorsey. LPs w. Dickie Wells (Fels.).

Addr: 517 Crown Street, Brooklyn 13, N.Y.

MAXTED, WILLIAM GEORGE (Billy), *piano, composer;* b. Racine, Wis., 1/21/17. With Red Nichols off and on from 1937-40, also w. Ben Pollack, Teddy Powell; two years' study at Juilliard during this time. Replaced Freddy Slack in Will Bradley band 1940-2. After 4 years as a flyer in the Navy 1942-5, led own band at 400 Club on Fifth Ave., NYC, arranged for Benny Goodman and Claude Thornhill; led band jointly w. Ray Eberle 1947-8. Since 1949 has been virtually house pianist at Nick's with various Dixieland combos incl. Bobby Hackett, Phil Napoleon, Billy Butterfield, Pee Wee Erwin; toured w. Erwin during most of 1954. Own combo at Nick's almost continuously from '55 until July '58. Formed new sextet Sept. '58 and toured with it, also returned to Nick's, April-June '59 and Feb. '60. Specializing in boogie-woogie, he plays in a style recalling his idol, Bob Zurke. Own LPs: Cadence; LPs w. Pee Wee Erwin (Cad., Uran.).

Addr: 1 Anding Ave., Merrick, L.I., N.Y.

MAY, E. WILLIAM (Billy), *composer, leader, trumpet;* b. Pittsburgh, Pa., 11/10/16. Prof. debut w. Gene Olsen's Polish-American Orch. 1933. Worked w. Al Howard, Lee River, Barron Elliot '37-8; Ch. Barnet '38-9, Glenn Miller '40-2, then did NBC staff work and arr. for Alvino Rey; later settled in Hollywood, arr. for Phil Harris, Ozzie Nelson, and many other shows, often conducting also. From late '40s did frequent commercial sessions at Capitol incl. the Bozo Children's Album series. In Sept. '51 recorded some sides with own studio band for Capitol feat. novel glissando unison sax section style; their success led him to take a band on the road. In '54 Sam Donahue took over the band and May resumed free-lancing in Hollywood. May, who no longer plays trumpet, is a capable arr. whose best work was done during his Barnet era incl. *In a Mizz, Lament for May, S'posin',* and part of the famous arr. of *Cherokee.* He played an acting role in the film *Nightmare* and wrote the arrangements. His solos, however, were played by Dick Cathcart. Own LPs: *Jimmie Lunceford in Hi Fi, Sorta Dixie, His Big Fat Brass,* and many others (Cap.); LPs w. Anita O'Day, Mel Tormé (Verve).

Addr: 1898 N. Stanley, Los Angeles 46, Calif.

MAY, EARL CHARLES BARRINGTON, *bass;* b. New York City, 9/17/27. Self-taught except for brief studies w. Ch. Mingus 1952. In Maritime service '46-7; worked for insurance co. '49-51. Did not become full-time musician until, after gigging w. Mercer Ellington, he joined Billy Taylor trio in late '51. With Taylor until June '59, then w. Phineas Newborn for two months. Free-lance until '60 when he joined Gloria Lynne as mus. dir. Plays bass left-handed, but with strings in normal tuning. Favs: Blanton, Pettiford, Ray Brown. LPs w. Taylor (Pres., ABC-Par., Roost, Argo), Tony Scott (Bruns.).

Addr: 1965 Amsterdam Ave., New York 32, N.Y.

McBROWNE, LEONARD LOUIS (Lennie), *drums;* b. Brooklyn, N.Y., 1/24/33. Father was drummer who played w. bands in Charleston, S.C. during the 1920s. Pl. drums in street bands '45-7, then stud. bass at N.Y. School of Mus. '48. Received a set of drums as a gift in '51 and subsequently stud. w. Max Roach, Morris Goldenberg, Sticks Evans. First prof. job w. Pete Brown; then worked around Brooklyn w. Randy Weston, Cecil Payne, Ernie Henry, etc. To Montreal w. Paul Bley. W. Tony Scott '56. Rejoined Bley for college tour and worked w. him in LA '57-8. W. Richie Kamuca at Lighthouse May-July '58; various gigs w. Harold Land, Sonny Rollins, Sonny Stitt, Teddy Edwards, Benny Golson-Curtis Fuller in LA & SF '58-9. Formed own group '59. Favs: Roach, Clarke, Blakey, Bellson, Elvin Jones, PJ Jones, Best. Own LP: Wor. Pac.; LPs w. Tony Scott (Vict.), Billie Holiday, Sonny Stitt (Verve), Paul Bley (GNP).

Addr: 94 East Claremont St., Pasadena, Calif.

McCALL, MARY ANN, *singer;* b. Philadelphia, Pa., 5/4/19. Discovered while dancing in chorus, and singing with Buddy Morrow's house band, at Phila. club, she worked briefly w. Tommy Dorsey in 1938. Sang w. Woody Herman '39-41, Ch. Barnet '41-3, then lived in San Diego, Cal., semi-inactive until 1946, when she rejoined Herman. Left him in '50 and worked as a single. Joined Ch. Ventura Jan. '54; after leaving him in '55 she retired until '58. Since then, married to a union executive in Detroit, she has appeared in local clubs. Once a conventional pop singer, she evolved during the 1940s into a very convincing stylist much admired by jazzmen. She rec. for Col. in '48 acc. by Howard McGhee, Dexter Gordon et al.; for Dec., Col. & Cap. w. Herman; also on Dec. w. Artie Shaw, and under her own name on Roost acc. by Al Cohn band. Won DB poll as band vocalist 1949. "One of the few authentic jazz singers"—Nat Hentoff. LPs acc. by Teddy Charles (Jub.), Ernie Wilkins (Regent), Johnny Richards (Coral); LP w. Charlie Ventura (Verve).

Addr: 332 S. Bailey Ave., Maple Shade, N.J.

McCLENNAN, TOMMY, *singer, guitar;* b. Yazoo City, Miss., 1908. Worked on a farm for many years, but was discovered by a talent scout and made some recordings for Bluebird, 1939-41, among them *Bottle It Up And Go, I'm The Guitar King, Highway 51,* and *Whiskey Head Woman.* Described by Samuel B. Charters as "a limited guitar player" whose voice was flat and harsh but who was "one of the most ferocious blues singers to get near a microphone."

McCRACKEN, ROBERT EDWARD (Bob), *clarinet;* b. Dallas, Texas, 11/23/04. Stud. pno., dr., harmony, clar. in Fort Worth. Inspired by Al Nunez; toured w. Eddie Whitley band 1921; with J. Teagarden in Doc Ross band '24. To NYC, pl. w. Willard Robison '27-8; Hogan Hancock in Chi. '28; Joe Gill '32-3; F. Trumbauer '35; J. Venuti '36; Leonard Keller in Chi. '39; Bud Freeman, J. McPartland '39-40; W. Manone '41; B. Goodman '41; Russ Morgan '42-4; Wayne King '45-6; house band at Chez Paree, Chi., '47-8; Lou Breese '49-51; in Europe and Africa with Louis Armstrong '52. On West Coast, worked w. Kid Ory '53-4; Ben Pollack, Jack Teagarden '54, touring US and Canada w. latter '56. W. Pete Daily '57, later back to Ben Pollack's restaurant, rejoining Ory for European tour fall '59. Is property manager for apartment building in LA. LPs w. Ory (Jazzman, Verve).

Addr: 828¾ N. Las Palmas Ave., Hollywood, Cal.

McEACHERN, MURRAY, *trombone, alto sax,* etc.; b. Toronto, Ontario, Canada 1915. Won medals, scholarships on violin, then took up clarinet; tenor at 15; alto w. Geo. Simms in Montreal '32; later trumpet, trombone, tuba and bass w. Simms. To Chicago 1936; did one-man-band act in floor shows. Joined Benny Goodman on trombone May 1936; Glen Gray on trombone and alto sax Oct. '38; Paul Whiteman 1941. Settled in California as studio musician. Solo sound track work in films incl. *Glenn Miller Story, Benny Goodman Story.* Concerts at Laguna Bowl, Santa Monica Aud. w. David Rose. *Pete Kelly's Blues* TV series '59. Rec. trombone solos: *Bugle Call Rag, These Foolish Things* w. Goodman (Vict.), *Sleepy Time Gal, Soft Winds* w. Gray (Decca) alto solos w. Gray on *No Name Jive, Rockin' Chair.* Own LPs: For *Sleepwalkers Only* (Key), *Caress* (Capitol); LPs w. Glen Gray (Decca, Capitol), Ray Anthony, Billy May, Nelson Riddle (Cap.), John Scott Trotter, Jack Webb (War. Bros.), Benny Goodman (MGM).

Addr: 328 Bowling Green Drive, Costa Mesa, Cal.

McFADDEN, EDDIE, *guitar;* b. Baltimore, Md., 8/6/28. Stud. at music schools in Philadelphia, Pa., then pl. with rhythm and blues bands there. Joined Jimmy Smith Jan. 1957. Favs: Charlie Christian, Oscar Moore, John Collins. LPs w. Jimmy Smith (Blue Note).

McFALL, RUBEN, *trumpet;* b. Los Angeles, Cal., 2/1/31. Attended Westlake College of Music. W. Freddy Slack, Vido Musso; year w. Stan Kenton; w. Woody Herman '53-5. Solo on *Baggage Room Blues* w. Woody; wrote and arr. *Mambo The Most.* LPs w. Herman (Verve).

Addr: 330 North Western, Los Angeles 4, Calif.

McGARITY, LOU, *trombone;* also *violin;* b. Athens, Ga., 7/22/17. Took up violin at seven; trombone in high school. Pl. w. Kirk Devore in Atlanta 1936, Nye Mayhew at Glen Island Casino, NYC '37, Ben Bernie 1938-40; Benny Goodman '40-2 and '46-7; Raymond Scott '42-3; then record and radio-TV studio work in NYC; also often featured at Eddie Condon's club. Capable jazz soloist in Teagarden tradition, also occasionally heard in vocals (notably his *Blues in the Night* w. the old Benny Goodman sextet). Played jazz violin on *Tennessee Waltz* w. Lawson-Haggart band. Own LPs on Argo, Jubilee; four tracks in *Strictly From Dixie* (MGM); two tracks in *Mellow Moods of Jazz* (Vict.); LPs w. Neal Hefti (Epic), *New York Land Dixie* (Vict.), Lee Castle (Joe Davis), Peanuts Hucko (Gr.

Award), Deane Kincaide (Weathers), Wingy Manone (Decca), Tommy Reynolds (King), George Wettling (Kapp), Lawson-Haggart (Decca), Benny Goodman (Col.), Eddie Condon, Wild Bill Davison, Max Kaminsky (Comm.).

Addr: 322 East 19th St., New York 3, N.Y.

McGHEE, BROWNIE, *singer, guitar;* b. Knoxville, Tenn., 11/30/15. Father guitarist, singer, dancer; brother guitarist. Father taught him to play. Spent years hitchhiking; talent scout for Okeh Records discovered him in 1938 in Burlington, N.C. Made some records in Chicago, then hitch-hiked back South. Met Sonny Terry and began working w. him in Apr. '39. App. on Broadway in *Cat on a Hot Tin Roof* and *Simply Heavenly,* also did some movie work. One of the more authentic and less sophisticated of the later folk-jazz performers, he has enjoyed considerable success in partnership with Terry. Favs: Tampa Red, Lonnie Johnson, Big Bill Broonzy, Leadbelly. Own LPs on Folkways; w. Sonny Terry (Fant.); in *Seven Ages of Jazz* (Metro.).

Addr: 254 E. 125th Street, New York 35, N.Y.

McGHEE, HOWARD, *trumpet;* b. Tulsa, Okla., 2/6/18. Raised in Detroit, pl. clarinet in school band; switched to trumpet after hearing L. Armstrong. Pl. with Leonard Gay 1939, Jimmy Rachel '40; Club Congo, Detroit '41; L. Hampton Sept. '41; Andy Kirk Nov. '41, recording his own *McGhee Special* (Decca) w. Kirk in 1942. After a year w. Ch. Barnet '42-3, he rejoined Kirk until June '44, then pl. with G. Auld for six months and briefly w. C. Basie. To Calif. w. Coleman Hawkins Nov. '44 to Mar. '45. Led own combo '45-7; JATP '47 and '48; own group at Paris Jazz Festival May '48. Later had own big band for a while, pl. with Machito in jazz clubs; Pacific, Korea, Japan w. O. Pettiford winter '51-2. In late 1950s worked infrequently, with occasional gigs at Birdland NYC.

McGhee, who played clarinet occasionally, also piano and saxes, was one of the most recorded artists of the bop era. His solos showed a commendable flow of ideas, perhaps with fewer surprises and less humor than Gillespie, but swinging constantly. He won DB poll in 1949. Favs: Gillespie, M. Davis. Own LPs on Beth.; LPs w. Fats Navarro (BN), *Dixieland vs. Birdland* (MGM), Wardell Gray (Modern), one track w. Coleman Hawkins in *History of Jazz* (Cap.); *Howard McGhee and Milt Jackson* (Savoy), *Jazz: South Pacific* (Reg.), Flip Phillips (Verve), *Jazztime, USA* (Bruns.), JATP (Stinson), JATP, Vols. 1, 5, 6 (Verve); *Jingles All The Way* (Lib.).

McHARGUE, JAMES EUGENE (Rosy), *clarinet;* b. Danville, Ill., 4/6/07. Stud. piano w. mother, 1920-3, then took up C melody sax; clarinet at 18. To Chicago, worked w. Sig Meyers; replaced Benny Goodman in Seattle Harmony Kings. Pl. w. Maurice Sherman, then toured w. Ted Weems '35-42. Settled in LA, worked w. Eddie Miller; pl. 3rd alto w. Benny Goodman '43, then w. Kay Kyser until '46. In late '40s was feat. w. Pete Daily at Hangover, also w. Pee Wee Hunt (made *12th St. Rag* rec.) and Red Nichols. Own band from 1950; five years at Hangover; two years on Dixie Showboat TV show; alternating between clubs in Palos Verdes and E. Pasadena '57-60. LPs: Dixieland *Jazz #3, Jazz Potpourri #1* (Audiophile); *Dixieland Contrasts* (Jazzman).

Addr: 12310½ Montana Avenue, Los Angeles 49, Calif.

McINTYRE, HAROLD W. (Hal), *alto sax, clarinet, leader;* b. Cromwell, Conn., 11/29/14; d. Los Angeles, Calif., 5/5/59. Had own band 1935-6; joined Glenn Miller and was a key man both in the 1937 band and in the band Miller organized the following year that later became famous. McIntyre, whose fine musicianship was a key factor in the all-important reed section that contributed so much to Miller's success, was completely ignored in the film *The Glenn Miller Story.* After leaving Miller in '41, McIntyre had a dance band that was quite successful until the decline of the big band era in the late '40s; he continued to front it until shortly before his death, which occurred in a fire caused by a cigarette in a Los Angeles apartment. His band had been relatively inactive during the previous year or two. Own LPs: *Dancing in the Dark* (Harm.), *It Seems Like Only Yesterday* (Roul); see also Glenn Miller.

McKENNA, DAVID J. (Dave), *piano;* b. Woonsocket, R.I., 5/30/30. Mother pianist and violinist; father a drummer. Stud. with nuns in Woonsocket, later in Boston w. Sandy Sandiford. Prof. debut w. Boots Mussulli, with whom he also worked in Ch. Ventura combo for several months in 1949. After a year and a half w. Woody Herman, '50-1, he entered the Army and was in Korea for much of the next two years. Discharged in '53, he rejoined Ventura for 18 months, then worked w. Gene Krupa combo for two months in '56. W. Bobby Hackett '59. An original and fertile solo stylist, he showed, in his first LP, his ability to swing without any accompanying rhythm section. Favs: Teddy Wilson, Art Tatum, Nat Cole. Own LPs: ABC-Par., Epic; LPs w. Urbie Green, Don Stratton, Ruby Braff (ABC-Par.), Ch. Ventura (Coral, Tops, Verve), Max Bennett (Beth.), Woods-Quill, Sims-Cohn (Vict.), Dick Johnson (River.), Gene Krupa (Verve).

Addr: 47 Cold Spring Place, Woonsocket, R.I.

McKENZIE, WILLIAM (Red), *singer;* b. St. Louis, Mo., 10/14/07; d. NYC, 2/7/48. Originally a jockey, he was known from 1923 as leader of the "Mound City Blue Blowers" group, playing a kazoo (toy instrument). This group name was used off and on for record sessions directed by McKenzie, in some of which he participated as singer or kazoo player. He was closely associated w. Eddie Condon (q.v.). During the 1930s he was often heard fronting jazz groups along 52nd Street. He was inactive in music during most of the 1940s but returned briefly to make a record session for National in 1947. McKenzie was less important as singer or kazoo player than as a promoter of jazz during its struggling depression years. LPs: McKenzie-Condon sides in *Chicago Style Jazz* (Col.) and a track in Riverside's *History of Classic Jazz.*

McKIBBON, ALFRED (Al), *bass;* b. Chicago, Ill., 1/1/19. Father played tuba, guitar. Stud. bass, piano, Cass Tech. High Sch. Got into music through brother, a guitarist. Started w. local bands of Kelly Martin, Ted Buckner; to NYC '43 w. Lucky Millinder. Tab Smith '45-6; Coleman Hawkins, J. C. Heard '46-7; Dizzy Gillespie '47-9, touring Europe with him early '48; Count Basie '50. From 1951 to Mar. '58 he was with the Geo. Shearing Quintet. With Cal Tjader Mar. '58-Aug. '59. Superb tone and beat marked him as one of the best bassists to come to prominence in the mid-'40s. LPs w. Tjader (Fant.), Billy Taylor (Atl.), Gillespie (Vict.), Shearing (MGM, Cap.), Dakota Staton (Cap.), *Birth of the Cool* w. Miles Davis (Cap.).

Addr: 13279 Vaughn Street, San Fernando, Calif.

McKINLEY, RAY, *drums, singer, leader;* b. Fort Worth, Texas, 6/18/10. Worked w. Smith Ballew 1932; Dorsey Bros. '34-5; Jimmy Dorsey '35-9; then became partner of Will Bradley in latter's band and had several record hits as vocalist with Bradley, notably *Beat Me Daddy Eight To The Bar.* Led his own band 1942; in service, joined Glenn Miller's AAF band, and while in Europe led his own "Swing Shift" contingent from this band. Took over leadership jointly w. Jerry Gray after Miller's death. Led own civilian band 1946-50 featuring arrs. by Eddie Sauter and such soloists as Peanuts Hucko, Vern Friley, Mundell Lowe. From '50-5 led own groups and free-lanced as TV singer in NYC. In May '56 he was commissioned by the widow of Glenn Miller to organize a new band under Miller's name using the original library and style. This band made a highly successful tour of Iron Curtain countries in the spring of '57 and has continued to tour in the US with good popular reaction. An infectiously rhythmic singer and one of the most popular drummers of the late '30s and early '40s esp. in Dixieland circles. Own LPs: Camden, Savoy, Victor; one side of *The Swingin' Thirties* (Gr. Award); LPs w. Will Bradley (Epic), Deane Kincaide (Weathers), Steve Allen, J. & T. Dorsey (Decca).

Addr: 568 Pepper Ridge Rd., Stamford, Conn.

McKINNEY, BERNARD ATWELL (Bernie), *trombone, euphonium;* b. Detroit, Mich., 11/26/32. Three brothers are jazz musicians; another a classical pianist. Studied trombone in elementary school, later at Cass Tech. High. First gig w. Barry Harris, Sonny Stitt. Pl. w. Art Blakey in Phila. '54, Alvin Jackson in Detroit '55-6, Yusef Lateef '58. Moved to NYC, working w. Illinois Jacquet '59, Slide Hampton '60. Favs: J. J. Johnson, Henry Coker. Imp. infl: Barry Harris, Charlie Parker. LPs w. Slide Hampton (Strand), Bill Henderson (Vee-Jay), Yusef Lateef, Pepper Adams (Savoy).

Addr: 310 W. 107th St., New York 25, N.Y.

McKINNEY, WILLIAM, *leader, drums;* b. Paducah, Ky., 1894. After serving in World War I he was drummer and leader in a group called the Synco Septet in Springfield, Ohio. In 1923 he turned the drums over to Cuba Austin and later became leader in absentia and business manager of a larger group, known from 1926 as McKinney's Cotton Pickers. Based at the Greystone Ballroom in Detroit but also heard on tours in the Midwest and other regions, the band was under the musical guidance of Don Redman '27-31 and was considered one of the most polished and individual Negro jazz orchestras of the day. The band was often changed or augmented in personnel for its recording sessions (Victor, '28-33); participants from time to time included Fats Waller, James P. Johnson, Claude Jones, Prince Robinson, Todd Rhodes, Rex Stewart, Joe Smith, Benny Carter, Hilton Jefferson, Coleman Hawkins, Quentin Jackson. One early session was made for OKeh under the name "The Chocolate Dandies." After the band broke up in 1934, McKinney left the music business; he worked at the Ford plant in the '40s and was still living in Detroit in recent years.

McKUSICK, HAROLD WILFRED (Hal), *alto sax, clarinet, composer;* b. Medford, Mass., 6/1/24. Raised in Newton, where Ralph Burns was schoolmate. Pl. w. Don Bestor, Les Brown, 1942; Dean Hudson and briefly w. Woody Herman, '43; Boyd Raeburn '44-5. Settling on West Coast, worked w. Johnny Otis, Alvino Rey, Al Donahue, Buddy Rich, '48; alto, later lead clar. w. Thornhill '48-9; Terry Gibbs Quintet '50-1. Mainly w. Elliot Lawrence '51-6, also gigs w. Don Elliott, recs. w. C. O'Farrill, Med Flory, Al Romero. In late '50s became increasingly active recording commercial jingles for TV and radio; also pl. w. Urbie Green and George Williams '58, and led own septet (four saxes and rhythm) '58-9. A guiding force and collaborator with arranger Geo. Handy in the great Raeburn band of the early '40s, McKusick has grown steadily in stature as a soloist and leader of first-class recording units. Favs: Konitz, Parker, alto; DeFranco, Lester Young, clarinet. Own LPs: Bethlehem, Coral, Decca, Jubilee, Prestige, Victor; also tracks in *Bird Feathers* (New Jazz); LPs w. Al Cohn, Andy Kirk, Geo. Russell, Manny Albam (Vict.), Don Elliott (Decca, Betc.), Elliot Lawrence (Fant.), Terry Gibbs, André Hodier (Savoy), Bobby Scott (Verve), *Saxes, Inc.* (War. Bros.), *Jingles All The Way* (Lib.).

Addr: 310 East 49th Street, New York 22, N.Y.

McLEAN, JOHN LENWOOD (Jackie), *alto sax;* b. New York City, 5/17/32. Father, John McLean, pl. guitar w. Tiny Bradshaw. Pl. w. Sonny Rollins, Kenny Drew, Andy Kirk Jr. in neighborhood band, stud. w. Bud Powell after school. Worked mainly w. Paul Bley, George Wallington and Charlie Mingus 1955-6. W. Art Blakey '56-8; then own quintet w. Ray Draper on tuba and as single. Acting and pl. w. quartet on stage for off-Broadway production, *The Connection* '59-60. Favs: Parker, Rollins. Own LPs on Blue Note, Pres.,

Jub. New Jazz; LPs w. Miles Davis (Pres., Blue Note), Art Blakey (Wor. Pac., Col., Elek.), Mingus (Atl.), Gene Ammons, Mal Waldron, Hank Mobley (Pres.).

Addr: 484 East Houston St., New York 2, N.Y.

McNEELY, CECIL (Big Jay), *saxophones;* b. 1928, Raised in Los Angeles. Mainly known as contortionist in rock 'n' roll field. Has been on numerous tours and pl. night club dates. Own LPs: King.

Addr: 2121 E. 110th St., Los Angeles, Calif.

McPARTLAND, RICHARD GEORGE (Dick), *guitar, banjo;* also *violin;* b. Chicago, Ill., 5/18/05; d. Elmhurst, Ill., 11/30/1957. Studied violin w. father. Member of the Austin High Gang w. brother Jimmy, Dave Tough, Bud Freeman, etc. After replacing his favorite guitarist, Eddie Lang, in the Mound City Blue Blowers, McPartland toured with that group for several years in the mid to late '20s. In his early thirties he suffered a heart attack which forced his retirement from music. He drove a cab in Elmhurst, a Chicago suburb, and made occasional public playing app., the last of which was in 1955 w. Baby Dodds, Jim Lanigan and brother Jimmy in a Sunday afternoon concert. Also pl. Spanish guitar, infl. by Segovia. LP: *Chicago Jazz Album* (Decca).

McPARTLAND, JAMES DUIGALD (Jimmy), *trumpet;* b. Chicago, Ill., 3/15/07. Father a music teacher. Started on violin at 5; cornet at 15. At Austin High, started band with schoolmates incl. brother Dick on guitar, Frank Teschemacher, Bud Freeman. First job was w. Al Haid at Fox Lake, Ill. Record debut while w. Wolverines, 1925. Joined Art Kassel 1926, Ben Pollack 1927-9, making many records with Benny Goodman and other jazzmen during those years. After working in Broadway pit bands 1929-30 and with Russ Columbo '31-2 and Horace Heidt, Smith Ballew, Harry Reser, '33-5, he led his own jazz group from 1936 to '41, sidemen at times incl. Rosy McHargue, clarinet; Joe Harris, trombone; Boyce Brown, alto; Geo. Wettling, drums. Last major job before he entered Army was w. Jack Teagarden. In service, was combat soldier in Normandy invasion; later played in USO unit (see Marian McPartland). Back to US '46, had combo with Marian McPartland, then on own. During 1954, in addition to spending several months leading his own combo at the Metropole in NYC, he visited England and made guest appearances on BBC.

As a result of his successful foray as an actor in *The Magic Horn,* a TV fantasy about jazz musicians, he was given a speaking role in *Showboat* at the Marine Theatre, Jones Beach, New York, summer '57. Since then he has continued to play with his own groups around NYC and on the road. McPartland, who replaced Bix Beiderbecke in the original Wolverines and played many similar jobs during Bix's halcyon years, remains one of the best performers in a Bix-inspired, neutral jazz style that he prefers not to hear described as Dixieland. Own LPs on Bruns., Epic; four tracks each in *Gems of Jazz* & *Chicago Jazz* (Decca); one half of *Hot Vs. Cool* (MGM); one half of *After Hours* (Gr. Award); LPs w. *The Magic Horn* (Vict.), Eddie Condon in *Chicago Style Jazz* (Col.), Bud Freeman (Vict.), Jack Teagarden (Beth.); one track w. Wolverines in *History of Classic Jazz* (River.).

Addr: 41 Webster St., Merrick, L.I., N.Y.

McPARTLAND, MARIAN (née Marian Margaret Turner), *piano, songwriter;* b. Windsor, England, 3/20/20. Great uncle, Sir Frederick Dyson, Mayor of Windsor, played 'cello; many other musicians in family for generations. Five years of violin w. private teacher. Scholarship to Guildhall Sch. of Mus. Debut in piano team w. Billy Mayerl. During war, toured with entertainment unit for ENSA, British equivalent of USO. Went to France with USO unit after invasion. Met Jimmy McPartland, then with USO unit in Army, in Belgium 1944; married in Aachen, Germany, 2/3/45; both took part in show for Gen. Eisenhower in Paris. Came to US March '46; started combo with Jimmy, first using her prof. name Marian Page, later adopting husband's name. Broke up group to form own trio '51, and soon attained firm status in jazz circles, working extensively at clubs like the Hickory House and Composer, NYC; London House, Chicago. A thoughtful, skilled musician; achieves fine mood especially on slow tempi. Own LPs on Cap., Savoy, King; w. Hot Lips Page in *Jazztime, USA, Vol. 3* (Bruns.).

Addr: 41 Webster St., Merrick, L.I., N.Y.

McRAE, CARMEN, *singer;* b. New York City, 4/8/22. Studied piano privately. Discovered by Irene Wilson Kitchings (ex-wife of Teddy Wilson and composer of *Some Other Spring*), she worked w. Benny Carter in 1944, also w. Count Basie. With Mercer Ellington band '46-7, she made her record debut under the name of Carmen Clarke (she was then married to drummer Kenny Clarke). Spent several years as intermission pianist and singer at Minton's and other clubs and as clerk-typist when gigs were scarce, but began to attract musicians' attention as a singer in '53, when she recorded for Stardust and Venus labels; signed w. Decca in '54 and appeared frequently w. Mat Mathews' group. Originally reflecting a Vaughan influence, she progressed to become one of the most original song stylists of the 1950s w. many app. at festivals and in nightclubs. Won *Down Beat* critics' poll as New Star '54. Favs: Vaughan, Fitzgerald, Teddi King. LPs on Decca, Kapp.

Addr: 1466 Dean St., Brooklyn, N.Y.

McRAE, TEDDY, *composer, tenor sax, leader;* b. Philadelphia, Pa., 1/22/08. From musical family, he stud. medicine first, later took private music lessons w. brother and other teachers. Org. band w. brothers around 1928, later pl. with other groups as arr., musical dir., incl. Chick Webb '36-9, Ella Fitzgerald '39-41; own band, '44. Comp. of *Back Bay Shuffle, You Showed Me the Way.* Rec. in 1930s w. Red Allen,

Benny Morton, Putney Dandridge. Formed Enrica and Rae-Cox record companies w. Eddie Wilcox '59.

Addr: c/o ASCAP, NYC.

McSHANN, JAY (Hootie), *leader, piano;* b. Muskogee, Okla., 1/12/09. Prominent in Kansas City during the 1930s as leader of a swinging band that played mostly blues, its attractions including singer Walter Brown and an embryonic Charlie Parker, who was w. McShann off and on from '37 to '41 and made his first records with this band for Decca. In Army '44, McShann was discharged in Nov. and rec. for Capitol w. Julia Lee and all-star local band in KC. In the late '40s he led a smaller group in Hollywood, featuring his own blues and boogie-woogie piano work and recording for Aladdin and Mercury. In the late '50s, he was back in KC, playing piano and organ in clubs. LPs: one track each in *Encyclopedia of Jazz on Records, Vol. 3, The Jazz Story* (Decca).

McVEA, JACK, *tenor sax, leader;* b. Los Angeles, Calif., 11/5/14. Pl. banjo, 1925-7; stud. sax privately '26, prof. debut on alto '27 w. his father, who pl. banjo. Later w. Dootsie Williams at Club Alabam, LA. Joined original Lionel Hampton band on baritone sax, 1940. Pl. w. Snub Mosely '43, then became leader. Scored biggest hit with his song *Open The Door Richard,* which he introduced in 1946 on records and in the movie *Sarge Goes to College.* Many studio dates at MGM. Pl. w. Gillespie, Ch. Parker on Slim Gaillard recs. McVea's band has been consistently popular in r & b rather than jazz circles, but he is a good, hard-swinging soloist. LPs w. Charlie Parker (Savoy), JATP, Vol. 3 (Verve).

Addr: 116 East 68th St., Los Angeles 3, Calif.

MEHEGAN, JOHN F., *piano, teacher;* b. Hartford, Conn., 6/6/20. Stud. violin 1926-33; mainly self-taught on piano. Entered Julius Hartt Mus. Sch. at 18; was refused piano as major and was told he would never play. Majored in comp., theory. After playing with various bands in Mass. he came to NYC 1941 and worked as soloist in N.J. and NYC night spots. Taught jazz privately from '44; assisted Teddy Wilson at Met. Mus. Sch. '45; head of jazz dept. '46. Jazz teacher at Juilliard since '47. Pl. in B'way show *A Streetcar Named Desire.* Mus. dir. at Jacob's Pillow Dance Fest. '47; dance scores for Valerie Bettis et al. Piano course in *Metronome* '52-4. Critic for *NY Herald Tribune* from '57. Appointed to faculty of Columbia Teachers' College '58. Critic, panelist, performer at NJF '58. Two month concert and research tour, South Africa, summer '59. Though he has played many NY clubs, Mehegan achieved prominence as the first and foremost true pedagogue of jazz, author of *Jazz Improvisation,* the first definite text on jazz mechanics, contributor to *Down Beat, Sat. Review* and many other publications. Rec. *Blowtop Blues* w. L. Hampton (Dec.), dates w. Tony Perkins (Vict.); own LPs incl. *How I Play Jazz Piano* and *Reflections* (Savoy), *Casual Affair* (T.J.).

Addr: 233 East 69th St., New York 21, N.Y.

MELDONIAN, RICHARD A. (Dick), *alto sax, tenor sax, flute;* b. Providence, R.I., 1/27/30. St. on clar. at eight; took up sax in 1941; later, flute. Pl. w. own quartet during '44 in Providence club. Has pl. with numerous bands since '49, incl. Freddie Slack, Charlie Barnet, Shorty Rogers, John Kirby, Stan Kenton, Johnny Richards, Noro Morales, Nat Pierce, Elliot Lawrence, Bill Russo. Also has had own band. LP w. Phil Sunkel (ABC-Par.).

Addr: 20-15 Shore Blvd., Astoria 5, Long Island.

MELLE, GILBERT JOHN (Gil), *saxophones;* b. Riverside, Calif., 12/31/31. Private sax teachers; comp., harmony w. George Ortiz; also stud. oboe, clarinet. Living in New Jersey in recent years, leading own combos. App. at NJF 1954, and occasional concert dates in late '50s. Fav. own solo: *Quadrille* on BN. Favs: Getz, Lars Gullin. Own LPs on Pres., BN.

MELROSE, FRANKLYN TAFT (Frank), *piano, composer;* b. Sumner, Ill., 11/26/07; d. near Hammond, Ind., Sept., 1941. Began on violin; largely self-taught as pianist. Early work in Chicago, St. Louis, Kansas City, Detroit, then back to Chicago, where he worked and rec. with the Cellar Boys (Wingy Manone, Bud Freeman) 1928-9. Through his brother, Lester, a talent scout for Amer. Rec. Corp., he made a series of solos, some under the name of Kansas City Frank, also rec. in 1929 w. Johnny and Baby Dodds in the Beale Street Washboard Band. Melrose, who frequently exchanged ideas w. Jelly Roll Morton, was in obscurity during the '30s, working for WPA as a piano teacher in '38. In '40-1 he was at the Derby Club in Calumet City, later at the Yes Yes Club on State Street in Chicago, until the time of his death; he died on Labor Day weekend, his body mutilated and the cause of death unknown. Melrose, who made his last records w. Bud Jacobson's Jungle Kings in March '41, was highly regarded by traditionalist jazz students. LP: tracks in *Piano Jazz, Vol. 2* (Bruns.).

MEMPHIS JUG BAND: See SHADE, Will

MEMPHIS MINNIE, *singer, guitar;* b. Algiers, La., 6/24/00. Popular during 1930s, when she recorded for Bluebird; was married to "Kansas Joe" McCoy, also a guitarist and blues singer. Many country blues students have described her as a female Big Bill Broonzy. Her records during the '40s included *Mean Mistreater Blues, Boy Friend Blues.* She once defeated Broonzy in a blues contest.

MEMPHIS SLIM (Peter Chatman), *piano, singer, songwriter;* b. Memphis, Tenn., 9/3/15. Father pl. guitar and piano, mother sang. Began prof. career in 1931; worked w. Big Bill Broonzy '39-42 in Chicago. Rec. for Blue Bird and Okeh. Works mainly in Chicago, app. in other cities occasionally in concert. Featured at Carnegie Hall in folk music concert April '59; at Newport Folk Festival July '59. Fav: Tatum, Fats Waller; Big Bill Broonzy, Leadbelly, Josh White. One of most authentic blues artists of his generation, he wrote *The Comeback* and *Every Day*, popularized by Joe Williams. Own LPs: *The Real Boogie Woogie* (Folk.); Prestige Bluesville; three nos. in *Folk Song Festival* (UA).

Addr: 6423 Ingleside, Chicago, Ill.

MENDELSON, STANLEY J. JR., *piano;* b. New Orleans, La., 6/23/33. Father played violin, sousaphone. Stud. piano and violin at Loyola U. Got into jazz through Dr. Souchon, Johnny Wiggs and other New Orleans jazzmen. Worked with Melody Lads 1947-9, Johnny Wiggs, '50, Dukes of Dixieland, '51, Sharkey Bonano, '52-6, then rejoined Dukes. Fav: Jelly Roll Morton. LPs w. Dukes of Dixieland (Aud. Fid.), Jack Delaney, Johnny Wiggs, Sharkey Bonano, Raymond Burke (South.).

Addr: 4433 Gen. Pershing St., New Orleans 25, La.

MERCER, JOHN H. (Johnny), *singer, songwriter;* b. Savannah, Ga., 11/18/09. Prominent during 1930s when he made a series of ebulliently swinging vocals incl. *Dr. Heckle & Mr. Jive* w. Dorsey Bros. '33; *Fare Thee Well To Harlem, Christmas Night in Harlem* w. P. Whiteman '34; *Sent for You Yesterday* w. B. Goodman '39. Was a founder of Capitol Rec. '42, often heard on the label, co-starring with Nat Cole, Goodman et al. A good rhythm singer in a semi-jazz vein, he made his major contribution as a songwriter, writing lyrics and sometimes music for many that became jazz standards incl. *Come Rain or Come Shine, That Old Black Magic, Jeepers Creepers, Skylark, Laura, Blues in the Night, Too Marvelous for Words.* Own LP: Capitol; w. Jack Teagarden in Paul Whiteman 50th Anniversary Album (Gr. Award).

Addr: c/o Capitol Records, Sunset & Vine, Hollywood 28, Cal.

MERIAN, LEON (Vahan Leon Megerdichian), *trumpet, leader;* b. South Braintree, Mass., 9/17/23. From musical family; stud. trumpet at 12, harmony at 15. Began playing in clubs at 16, then went w. Sabby Lewis; w. Lucky Millinder 1942-5; Boyd Raeburn '47; Gene Krupa '53; Pete Rugolo '54. Worked as musician in Broadway musicals and for stage shows in theaters. Started own big band 1958. Favs: Bunny Berigan, Roy Eldridge, Dizzy Gillespie, Harry James. Own LP: *Magic Horn* (Decca); LP w. Specs Powell (Roul.).

Addr: 18 W. 69th Street, New York 23, N. Y.

MERRILL, HELEN (née Milcetic), *singer;* b. New York City, 6/21/29. Amateur jobs from 1944. Toured w. Reggie Childs' orch. 1946-7. After marrying Aaron Sachs, 8/12/47 (since divorced), she was inactive, except for occasional club dates w. Jerry Wald et al. Three months w. Earl Hines late '52; rec. for Roost '53, Em. '54-8; Metrojazz and Atl. '59. Toured England and the Continent extensively from June '59. A honey-toned, jazz-tinged original song stylist, she is best suited to slow-tempo ballads and folk material. Favs: Ella Fitzgerald, Jo Stafford, Peggy Lee. LPs: EmArcy, Atco, Metro.

MERRITT, JAMES (Jymie), *bass;* b. Philadelphia, Pa., 1926. Mother was choral dir., piano and voice teacher. Inspired by Ellington rec. feat. J. Blanton. In service 1944-6, then stud. w. Carl Torello of Philadelphia Symph. and at Orenstein Mus. Sch. in Phila. for three years. Began playing prof. '49 on gigs w. Tadd Dameron, Benny Golson, Philly Joe Jones. Went on road w. Bull Moose Jackson, Chris Powell, B. B. King; to NYC '57, joined Art Blakey late '58. Favs: Ray Brown, Charlie Mingus, Oscar Pettiford, Jimmy Blanton et al. LPs w. Art Blakey (Blue Note).

MERRIWEATHER, MAJOR (Big Maceo), *singer, pianist;* b. Texas, 3/30/05; d. Chicago, Ill., 2/26/53. Blues singer and boogie-woogie pianist, who worked chiefly in Chicago w. excursions to Detroit and other cities. He was paralyzed by a stroke in 1946. Made numerous recordings on his own and w. Big Bill Broonzy, Sonny Boy Williamson et al. Records, now out of print, were on Victor, Bluebird, Columbia, Specialty. An excellent survey of his work, by Paul Oliver, appears in *The Art of Jazz* (Oxford).

METCALF, LOUIS, *trumpet, leader;* b. St. Louis, Mo., 2/28/05. Pl. in youths' band w. trumpeter Joe Thomas. Came to NYC in 1923; pl. with Jimmy Cooper's Black and White Revue '23-4. From '24-7 played w. various groups, incl. Charles Johnson, Sidney Bechet, Sam Wooding, Johnny Hudgins, Willie (The Lion) Smith, Jelly Roll Morton. Joined Duke Ellington '27; with Luis Russell, King Oliver '29. After working w. Vernon Andrade at the Savoy, he formed his own band, then went to Montreal, where he spent three years working mostly in vaudeville as singer, dancer and emcee. During the 1930s he played on riverboats out of St. Louis; moved to Canada in 1944 and spent seven years there, leading his own international band in Montreal and on tour. He also had his own club in Montreal. Since '51 he has gigged around NYC as leader and sideman, mainly at the Metropole. Began doubling at the Embers and the Arpeggio summer '59. Feat. on *West End Blues, Call of the Freaks* w. King Oliver; *Savoy Shout* w. Russell; *East St. Louis Toodle-oo, Birmingham Breakdown,* etc. w. Ellington. Also rec. w. various blues singers '25. LP w. Ellington (Bruns.).

Addr: 1143 Noble Ave., Bronx 72, N. Y.

METTOME, DOUGLAS VOLL, *trumpet;* b. Salt Lake City, Utah, 3/19/25. Stud. piano 1930-6, then trumpet w. Wm. Leslie. Inspired by Roy Eldridge's *Rockin' Chair,* took up jazz and had own 12-piece band around Salt Lake City before entering the Army for three years. Has worked with many name bands incl. Billy Eckstine '46-7; Herbie Fields off and on '48-52; Benny Goodman '49, recording with big band and sextet on *Bedlam, Blue Lou, Undercurrent Blues etc.* (Capitol); Woody Herman '51-2, Tommy Dorsey '53, Pete Rugolo '54, Johnny Richards, Dorsey Brothers. Between jobs in early years he worked as painter, door-to-door salesman, laborer, driver. In Nov. 1958 went into retirement for almost a year owing to illness. Main influences were Eldridge, Gillespie, Hackett, Butterfield. Eclectic and potentially brilliant modern jazzman. LPs w. Johnny Richards (Cap.); *East Coast Jazz* w. Urbie Green, *Sam Most Plays Bird, Bud, Monk & Miles* (Beth.).

Addr: 3838 Poplar Ave., Brooklyn 24, N. Y.

MEZZROW, MEZZ (Milton Mesirow), *clarinet, saxes;* b. Chicago, Ill., 11/9/1899. Studied sax in jail in 1917. Played in small bands around Chicago during 1920s, recording with the Jungle Kings and Chicago Rhythm Kings 1927-8 and Eddie Condon '28. In 1929 he worked briefly in Paris. During the 1930s he was active occasionally in music. He assembled a band for a Brunswick record date in 1933 and for sessions on Victor-Bluebird between '34 and '38, but mainly made his living selling marijuana, for which he was jailed from 1940 to '42. During the '40s, he recorded w. Art Hodes, played a few clubs and had his own record label, King Jazz, from '45 to '48. Since 1948 he has spent most of his time in France, recording and touring successfully with small groups, often featuring musicians he has imported from the US.

Mezzrow, though merely a vague name to younger musicians and a laughing-stock to some of his contemporaries (he is dismissed sarcastically as a hanger-on in Eddie Condon's autobiography, *We Called it Music*), has been a highly controversial figure among critics and fans. Often belittled as a mediocre musician who has exaggerated the importance of his role, he was described as the "the Baron Munchausen of jazz" by Nat Hentoff, who observed that he "is so consistently out of tune that he may have invented a new scale system." He is admired by the French critic Hugues Panassié, who has hailed him as the greatest white clarinetist and perhaps the greatest musician of the white race (Mezzrow, however, says he considers himself a "voluntary Negro"). He has fought for the early New Orleans-style jazz in which he believes, and has succeeded, no matter what his personal value as an instrumentalist may be, in renewing interest in a large number of older musicians whom he rescued from obscurity. His own best work as a clarinetist was heard on the session he made for Victor with an all star 10-piece band in 1934 (*Apologies,* etc. on "X" LVA3015, no longer available.).

A highly colored account of Mezzrow's life, including the account of his experience as an opium addict, can be found in his lurid and readable autobiography, *Really the Blues,* co-authored by Bernard Wolfe, published in 1946 by Random House and later reprinted in a pocket edition. LPs w. L. Hampton (Em); LPs w. own groups rec. on BN and Vict. are no longer available.

MICHELOT, PIERRE, *bass;* b. Saint Denis, France, 3/3/28. Piano at 7; bass at 16, stud. w. member of Paris Opera orch. Prof. debut in USO tour. Soon after return to Paris, acc. Rex Stewart, Coleman Hawkins. Recorded for Decca, Blue Star w. Django Reinhardt. Later worked with many US jazzmen in Paris, incl. Chet Baker, Kenny Clarke, for whom he also wrote arrs.; James Moody, Dizzy Gillespie, Zoot Sims, Miles Davis, recording for all of these. Michelot has long been considered the foremost French bassist. Fav: Oscar Pettiford. LPs: *Afternoon in Paris* w. John Lewis (Atl.); w. André Hodeir (Sav.), Sidney Bechet (Wor. Pac.), Kenny Clarke (Epic), Miles Davis (Col.), Jacques Loussier (Lond.).

Addr: 8 Rue d'Heliopolis, Paris 17, France.

MICKY AND SYLVIA—See Baker, Mickey and Vanderpool, Sylvia.

MIDDLEBROOKS, WILFRED ROLAND, *bass, tuba;* b. Chattanooga, Tenn., 7/17/33. Stud. piano, U. of Chattanooga '49. On road with vaudeville show '49-'52; w. Tab Smith combo '52-3. After two years in service, moved to Calif., played w. Eric Dolphy group '55, then w. Art Pepper and Buddy Collette combos; Mel Lewis-Bill Holman group '58. Joined Ella Fitzgerald Nov. '58 and toured Europe w. her in '59 and '60. Favs: Ray Brown, Pettiford. LPs w. Lewis-Holman (Andex), Buddy Collette (Dooto), Frank Rosolino (Bethlehem), Howard Rumsey (Liberty).

Addr: 1740 So. Hauser Blvd., Los Angeles, Calif.

MIDDLETON, VELMA, *singer, dancer;* b. St. Louis, Mo., 9/1/17. Feat. in night clubs as solo act from early 1930s. Joined L. Armstrong's big band as vocalist in '42, and remained w. him when he formed the small combo five years later. Armstrong has been widely criticized by critics at home and abroad for the incorporation in his act of what is basically a comedy performance by Miss Middleton, who is a fair singer but certainly not a major jazz talent. She has, however, enjoyed great popularity with the general public. LPs w. Armstrong: *Armstrong Plays W. C. Handy* (Col.), *Satchmo—A Musical Autobiography* (Decca, 4 vol.).

MILES, BARRY, *drums;* also *vibes, piano;* b. Newark, N. J., 3/28/47. Father a salesman. Took up drums at 3, piano at 5, joined Musicians' Union at 9. Own group at local swimming club every summer; local gigs w. Johnny Smith, Roy Eldridge et al; TV shows for Andy Williams, Ted Steele, Art Ford, 1958, on all three instruments. A modest and astonishingly gifted youngster with a unique natural talent. Favs: M. Roach, S. Manne, A. Blakey, R. Norvo, H. Hawes.

MILES, LIZZIE (Elizabeth Mary Landreaux), *singer;* b. New Orleans, La., 3/31/95. Began singing hymns in Sunday School at 5. Later worked in New Orleans w. King Oliver, A. J. Piron, *et al.* Toured the South w. the Alabama Minstrels and Cole Bros. Circus; sang in Paris for a while; worked w. Fats Waller at Capitol Palace in Harlem. During the '20s her recordings were successful and her accompanists included Oliver, Jelly Roll Morton, Clarence Williams and others. To NYC for appearance on CBS-TV show *Crescendo* 1957. LPs: *A Night In Old New Orleans* w. Sharkey

Bonano (Cap.), *Moans & Blues* and others w. Tony Almerico et al (Cook), Bob Scobey (Verve).

Addr: 1214 N. Tonti, New Orleans 19, La.

MILEY, JAMES (Bubber), *trumpet;* b. Aiken, S. Carolina, 1/19/03; d. NYC, 5/24/32. Raised in NYC. In early 1920s toured w. Mamie Smith, led own band and worked w. Elmer Snowden; from late '25 until Mar. '29, when Cootie Williams replaced him, he was w. Duke Ellington's orch., specializing in "growl" solos, a style in which he pioneered and which was later used by many other brass instrumentalists. After leaving Ellington, he played in France w. Noble Sissle, worked w. Zutty Singleton and led his own band during the last two years of his life. He was also heard on records in 1930 w. King Oliver, Jelly Roll Morton, Hoagy Carmichael, Leo Reisman. Miley's "wa-wa" effects, which brought the sound of the trumpet close to that of the human voice, had great emotional value in the early Ellington records. He was an expert in the use of the rubber plunger for special tonal variations. LPs w. Ellington (Bruns., River.).

MILLER, CLARENCE H. (Big), *singer, bass;* b. Sioux City, Ia., 12/18/23. Stud. bass, then trombone, in school in Kansas. Pl. for shows at Kansas Vocational School in Topeka and began singing. Pl. bass and sang w. Jay McShann 1949-54; had own band two years prior to this. Was a hit at Great South Bay Jazz Festival summer '57; seen often on Art Ford TV series 1958. Favs: Walter Brown, Joe Turner. Own LP: UA; LPs w. Fletcher Henderson reunion band, also w. Bob Brookmeyer (UA).

MILLER, EDDIE, *tenor sax, clarinet;* b. New Orleans, 6/23/11. Joined Ben Pollack at the age of 19 and stayed with him for four years, later working in the Bob Crosby Orch. from 1936 until its breakup in 1942. After a year in service 1943-4, settled in Calif. leading own band and doing studio work. He was active in many of the combos in the Dixieland revival on the West Coast. Worked w. Nappy Lamare 1945-7 and w. Bob Crosby off and on since 1950. Plays tenor in a style somewhat akin to that of Bud Freeman. Won Met. poll 1939-40, DB poll '40. LP: own group in one track on *History of Jazz, Vol. 1* (Cap.); LPs w. Bob Crosby (Coral, Decca, Cap.), Rampart Street Paraders (Col.), Billy May (Cap.), *Pete Kelly's Blues* (Vict., Col.).

Addr: 4904 Ben Ave., North Hollywood, Calif.

MILLER, GLENN, *composer, leader, trombone;* b. Clarinda, Iowa, 3/1/04; d. approximately 12/16/44 after taking off for a flight from England to France in a plane that was never seen again. After early experience w. Boyd Senter and studies at the U. of Colo., he later played w. Ben Pollack 1926-7, Paul Ash 1928, Red Nichols 1929-30. In early 1930s was high-priced studio man in NYC. Played and arranged w. Dorsey Bros. 1934; joined Ray Noble's first American band 1935, and about this time began studies with Joseph Schillinger. It was while with Noble that he discovered the reed section voicing (clarinet over four saxes) that later proved a key factor in the success of his own orchestra.

After an unsuccessful band venture in 1937 with a group that recorded for Brunswick, Miller organized a new band in 1938 and began to record for Bluebird, his sidemen incl. Hal McIntyre, Tex Beneke, Al Klink, Chummy MacGregor, vocalists Marion Hutton and Ray Eberle. During 1939 this orchestra reached phenomenal heights of popularity after a series of hit records, among them *Moonlight Serenade* (the band's theme), *Sunrise Serenade, Little Brown Jug, In the Mood.* From that time until he disbanded to enter the service in 1942, Glenn Miller had a following among young swing fans comparable with nothing since the first Benny Goodman regime in 1935. Miller later assembled a large orch. for the AAF which played in England in 1944, broadcasting regularly to the armed forces everywhere. After his disappearance, the band carried on under the direction of Jerry Gray and Ray McKinley, playing in Paris in 1945. The post-war years brought a series of bands that imitated the Miller style, incl. those of Tex Beneke, Ralph Flanagan, Jerry Gray, Ray Anthony. In the late 1950s a band officially endorsed by the Miller estate went on tour under his name under the direction of Ray McKinley (q. v.).

Although in his early years Miller played jazz trombone, and despite his contribution of many arrangements to swing orchestras through the 1930s, Glenn Miller was more prominent as a symbol of popular music than as a jazz figure. In later years he rarely played solo trombone and did very little arranging himself; his main interest was the achievement of the widest possible public appeal for his orchestra. He was a superb disciplinarian, his ensemble was one of the cleanest, his performances among the most showmanly. (He was an admirer of the musicianship and finesse of the Jimmie Lunceford band.) Miller won DB poll for top "sweet" band, 1940-1; was elected to DB Hall of Fame 1953.

A film entitled *The Glenn Miller Story,* based roughly on his life but containing chronological inaccuracies and omitting some of the key figures, was released in 1953, with James Stewart playing the role of Miller and Joseph Gershenson's orch. simulating the sound of Miller's band. LPs w. Ben Pollack, B. Goodman, Red Nichols on various labels no longer available. Own LPs: on Victor: *Concert* (LPM 1193), *Carnegie Hall Concert* (LPM 1506), *50 Never Before Released Original Performances* (3-LPM 6100), *Marvelous Miller Moods* (LPM 1494), *Sound of Glenn Miller* (LPM 1189), *Glenn Miller Story* (LPM 1192), *This is Glenn Miller* (LPM 1190); also *Original Film Sound Tracks* (2-20th Cent. Fox 100-2), *Solo Hop* (Epic LN 3236).

MILLER, MAX, *piano, vibes;* b. New Philadelphia, O., 11/17/11. High school in East Chicago, Ind.; pl.

banjo in the band, later switching to guitar. Pl. with local bands 1928-35; w. Vincent Lopez '37; musical dir. radio station WIND in Gary, Ind. '37-9. Formed own combo '40, pl. numerous club dates in Chicago areas.

MILLER, ERNEST (Punch), *trumpet, singer;* b. Raceland, La., 12/24/97. Pl. cornet with Jack Carey before and after World War I. While in service pl. with military band under Willie Humphrey, an important early influence. Repl. Louis Armstrong in Kid Ory Band. Left in 1927, went to Dallas w. Mack's Merrymakers, then on to Chicago, where he recorded w. Albert Wynn. Toured in Texas, joined Erskine Tate in Chicago, pl. with Frankie Franco's Louisianians, rec. with Chippie Hill, Tiny Parham. Omer Simeon, Jimmy Bertrand et al. During the '30s he worked w. Hughie Swift, Leonard Reed, Zilmer Randolph and Walter Barnes. In the '40s he acc. Big Bill Broonzy, Tampa Red on records, and made his own dates for Session, Century. Pl. with rock-'n'-roll revue in circus '54-6, then ret. to New Orleans, working as handy man and gigging occasionally. LPs: *Jazz-New Orleans* (Savoy).

MILLINDER, LUCIUS (Lucky), *leader;* b. Anniston, Ala., 8/8/00. Not a practicing musician, but has been active since 1930 as a bandleader, touring Europe 1933 and taking over leadership of Mills' Blue Rhythm Band 1934. From that time until the mid-40s, when he began to front bands only intermittently, Millinder had a host of talented sidemen. In the earlier years they incl. Red Allen, Ch. Shavers, Harry Edison, trumpets; J. C. Higginbotham, Wilbur De Paris, trombones; Joe Garland, Tab Smith, saxes; Buster Bailey, clarinet; Edgar Hayes, Billy Kyle, piano; John Kirby, bass; and many others who subsequently rose to fame.

Sidemen during the 1940s incl. Joe Guy, Freddy Webster, Dizzy Gillespie, trumpets; Sandy Williams, Henderson Chambers, Geo. Matthews, trombones; Lucky Thompson, "Lockjaw" Davis, Bull Moose Jackson, Burnie Peacock, saxes; Ellis Larkins, Bill Doggett, Clyde Hart, Sir Charles Thompson, piano; Trevor Bacon, guitar and vocals; Geo. Duvivier, bass; Panama Francis, drums; Sister Rosetta Tharpe, Wyonie Harris, vocals. During the late 1940s Millinder went into the music publishing business. In the summer of 1952 he became a liquor salesman. He has occasionally led a band since then and appeared as a DJ on WNEW. The important years for his band as a breeding ground of talent were from about 1935 until 1943. LPs on King.

MILLMAN, JACK MAURICE, *composer, trumpet, fluegelhorn;* b. Detroit, Mich., 11/21/30. Father was pianist in Canada. Stud. violin from 1939, bass briefly, then trumpet. Majored in music at Compton Jr. College and Los Angeles City Coll. Pl. with Glenn Henry, Sept. '51 to Feb. '52; a few weeks w. Stan Kenton, then in Army to Mar. '54. Since then has had his own combos and worked briefly w. Perez Prado Dec. '55. Favs: Dizzy Gillespie, Fats Navarro, Miles Davis, Clifford Brown. Ambition: To record a jazz symphony he has written. Own LPs: *Jazz Studio 4* (Decca), *Shades of Things to Come* (Lib.).

Addr: 7719½ Hampton Ave., Hollywood 46, Calif.

MILLS BROTHERS: John Mills, b. Bellefonte, Pa., 2/11/89; and his sons, Herbert Mills, b. 4/2/12; Harry F. Mills, b. 8/19/13; Donald F. Mills, b. 4/29/15, all at Piqua, Ohio, raised in Bellefontaine, O. Father, a barber, joined the act in Jan. 1936 to replace his eldest son, John Mills Jr., on the latter's death. The brothers started singing as youngsters while Herbert was an apprentice barber, Harry a shoeshine boy and Donald was still in school. Playing in small Ohio theatres, they originally specialized in instrumental imitations, with Herbert and Donald as first and second tenors, Harry as baritone and John as bass. During ten months of broadcasting in Cincinnati they came to the attention of Tom Rockwell, who brought them to New York; by the end of 1931 they were nationally famous. They appeared in *The Big Broadcast of 1933* and have since been in many other movies; toured England in 1934, have been overseas frequently since then, and have been teamed on records with Duke Ellington, Louis Armstrong, Ella Fitzgerald, Cab Calloway. For many years their sole accompaniment was a guitar (originally played by John Jr., later by Bernard Addison, Norman Brown and others). Though working generally with conventional pop material they maintained a strong link with jazz through their rocking rhythmic performances. They won DB award for vocal group, 1951-2.

In 1957, John Mills, the father, retired to Ohio after operation which necessitated the amputation of one leg, occasionally coming out for record dates. Otherwise the group continued its appearances as a trio. LPs on Decca, Dot.

MILLS, JACKIE, *drums;* b. Brooklyn, N.Y., 3/11/22. Father was bandleader and pl. violin. Stud. guitar at Wurlitzer Music Co. NYC 1931; switched to drums '32. Had own band at 13, pl. jobs around NYC. Pl. with many name bands in the '40s incl. Charlie Barnet, Teddy Powell, Dizzy Gillespie, Raymond Scott, Glen Gray, Boyd Raeburn, Benny Goodman. Has been w. Harry James off and on since '49. Favs: Jo Jones, Krupa. Rec. with most of the bands mentioned above. LPs w. Harry James (Cap.), Boyd Raeburn (Savoy).

Addr: 12104 Aneta Street, Culver City, Calif.

MINCE, JOHNNY (John Henry Muenzenberger), *clarinet, saxes;* b. Chicago Heights, Ill., 7/8/12. To Tulsa, Okla. 1929 w. Joe Haymes band (later taken over by Buddy Rogers). Was well known as jazzman w. Ray Noble's first US band '34-5 and T. Dorsey '36-41; also two months w. Bob Crosby in '36. Toured w. Irving Berlin *This is the Army* show; discharged late '45. From '46, feat. on radio and later TV with Arthur Godfrey; still with him in '60. Mince was one of the mostly highly regarded jazz clarinetists of the swing era. Favs: Goodman, Dodds, Fazola. Solos w. Dorsey incl. *Old Black Joe, Blue Danube.* LPs w. G. Brunis (Comm.), Godfrey (Col.).

Addr: 4 Darby, Glen Head, L. I., N. Y.

MINGUS, CHARLES, *bass, composer, leader, piano;* b. Nogales, Ariz., 4/22/22. Two older sisters stud. piano, violin. School in LA; stud. solfeggio and trombone, was helped by Britt Woodman. Switched to 'cello, then learned bass w. Red Callender at 16. Stud. w. H. Rheinschagen of N.Y. Phil. for 5 years. Got into music business while in high school w. Buddy Collette. With Lee Young '40, Louis Armstrong '41-3; then stints w. Kid Ory, Alvino Rey; Lionel Hampton '46-8. Made record debut w. Hampton in '47 Bebop album on Decca, featured on own comp. *Mingus Fingers.* With Red Norvo Trio '50-1; Billy Taylor Trio '52-3, then w. various groups incl. Charlie Parker, Stan Getz, Duke Ellington, Bud Powell and Art Tatum. Started own record company, Debut, April '52. Movies: *Higher and Higher* w. Frank Sinatra, *Road to Zanzibar* w. Hope and Crosby. Also first CBS color TV series w. Mel Tormé.

Around 1955-6 Mingus began to mature as a creative composer. Some of his work was documented though much of it was achieved through close and sensitive collaboration with sidemen in the various combos he led. His music aimed always at the further extension of the horizons of jazz and sometimes experimented with atonality and with a wide range of dissonant effects, some of which the more conservative listeners found hard to appreciate at first. Some elements offer a sharp and piquant contrast, with clearly defined folk music roots and a savage, shouting, blues-derived intensity. Not for complacent ears, Mingus' music is the prototype of a new and vital jazz generation of the 1960s just as Parker and Gillespie were of the 1940s.

Mingus tied for New Star award in DB critics' poll on bass '53. Favs: Hinton, Callender; fav. soloist, Pettiford.

Own LPs: Atl., UA, Col., Beth., Jub.; LPs w. Langston Hughes (MGM); *Jazz Composers Workshop, No. 2* (Savoy), Teddy Charles (Atl., Pres.); *Modern Jazz Concert* (Col.), John Mehegan (Savoy), Red Norvo (Savoy).

MIRANDA, SANTOS, *congo, bongos, timbales, drums;* b. Ponce, Puerto Rico, 12/19/28. Prof. début 1948 subbing for a drummer who failed to show up at a dance. One of early jobs was in '52 w. Slim Gaillard; also briefly w. Teddy Wilson, Art Blakey. Along with his cousin, Jose Mangual, became member of Herbie Mann Sextet, formed June '59. Favs: Manne, Blakey, Roach. LPs w. Chris Connor (Atl.), H. Mann (Verve).

Addr: 14 East 116th St., New York City.

MITCHELL, BILLY, *tenor sax;* b. Kansas City, Mo., 11/3/26. Stud. Detroit at Cass Tech. and was an early associate of Lucky Thompson, Sonny Stitt, Julius Watkins, Milt Jackson. After playing w. Nat Towles' orch., came to New York w. Lucky Millinder, '48, worked briefly w. Jimmie Lunceford, Milt Buckner, Gil Fuller, and for five months in '49 w. Woody Herman. Returning to Detroit, had his own combo which at one time or another featured Thad and Elvin Jones, Terry Pollard, and Tommy Flanagan; also worked locally with organist Levi Mann. Toured w. Dizzy Gillespie on State Dept.-sponsored visit to Middle East, Spring '56. Served as mus. dir. of band until he left in late '57 to join Count Basie. Excellent modern tenor stylist. Favs: Stitt, Rollins, Mobley, Hawkins, Young. Own LP on Savoy; LPs w. Thad Jones (Blue Note, UA, Savoy), Milt Jackson (Savoy), Dizzy Gillespie (Verve), Count Basie (Roul.), *Dizzy Atmosphere* (Spec.).

MITCHELL, RICHARD ALLEN (Blue), *trumpet;* b. Miami, Fla., 3/13/30. Began pl. trumpet in high school. Worked w. Paul Williams 1951; free-lanced around NYC '52; joined Earl Bostic, staying until '55. Ret. to Miami after making concert tour w. Red Prysock, Sarah Vaughan, Al Hibbler. Joined Horace Silver '58. Outstanding modern soloist reflecting Clifford Brown influence. Favs: Miles Davis, Clifford Brown. Own LPs: River.; LPs w. Cannonball Adderley, Philly Joe Jones, Johnny Griffin (River.), Red and Whitey Mitchell (Metro.), Horace Silver, Lou Donaldson (Blue Note).

Addr: 1818 N.W. 3rd Court, Miami, Fla.

MITCHELL, DWIKE, *piano;* b. Jacksonville, Fla., 2/14/30. Stud. Philadelphia Music Academy. Toured US and Europe w. Lionel Hampton 1953-5, then teamed up with another Hampton sideman, bassist and Fr. horn soloist, Willie Ruff, to form the Mitchell-Ruff duo which attracted immediate attention in New York night clubs and on records. In June '59 he and Ruff, visiting the Soviet Union ostensibly as members of a choral group from Yale U., gave jazz concerts at Tchaikovsky Conservatory and Bolshoi Hall. As the first modern jazzmen ever to play for Soviet audiences, they made a sensational impression and the event was given international publicity. On returning to the US they made TV, concert, and lecture appearances, performing and discussing their trip. Own LPs w. Ruff on Epic, Roul.; LPs w. L. Hampton (Verve, Col.).

Addr: 1150 Chapel St., New Haven, Conn.

MITCHELL, GEORGE, *trumpet;* b. Louisville, Ky., 3/8/1899. To Chicago 1919. During 1920s played w. Carroll Dickerson, Doc Cook, Lil Armstrong, Dave Peyton, and from 1929-31 w. Earl Hines. Rec. w. Cookie's Ginger Snaps for Okeh 1926, Luis Russell '26, Jelly Roll Morton '26-7, Richard M. Jones '27, Jimmie Noone '28-9, Earl Hines '29, Frankie "Half Pint" Jaxon 1933. LP w. Johnny Dodds (Epic).

MITCHELL, LOUIS, *drums, leader;* b. Philadelphia, Pa., 1885; d. Washington, D.C., 9/12/57. Led one of the first jazz bands in NYC; first Negro to play a London West End Theatre, 1914. Went to Paris 1916; operated Grand Duc club there several years; later pl. with James Reese Europe.

MITCHELL, KEITH (Red), *bass, piano;* b. New York City, 9/20/27. Played piano and alto in Army band, later switched to bass. After discharge, played bass w. Jackie Paris trio and w. Mundell Lowe. Played piano w. Chubby Jackson's big band at Bop City 1949. Bass w. Ch. Ventura for three months, then w. Woody Herman from early '49 to late '51. Hospitalized for over a year with TB; returned April '52 to join Red Norvo, with whom he toured Europe Jan.-Feb. '54. Joined Gerry Mulligan quintet April '54. Mitchell's suppleness of tone and style have made him one of the favorite bass players among contemporary musicians. Tied for DB critics' poll New Star, 1953. He was a member of the Hampton Hawes trio '55-6; led his own quart. '57, and in '58-9 was frequently heard on records, and occasionally in person, w. Andre Previn and Shelly Manne. It is estimated that since 1955 he has taken part in over 1,000 LPs. Own LPs: Beth. *Presenting Red Mitchell* (Contemp.); w. Whitey Mitchell and Blue Mitchell (Metro.); Bill Perkins, Jim Hall (Wor. Pac.), Hampton Hawes, Barney Kessel, Red Norvo, Andre Previn, Ornette Coleman (Contemp.), and others on Vict., Tampa, GNP, Lib., Dot.

MITCHELL, GORDON (Whitey), *bass;* b. Hackensack, N.J., 2/22/32. Father plays pipe organ in local churches; brother, Red Mitchell. Stud. clar., then tuba, then bass in school. After playing w. the Elinor Sherry quart., he spent 1951 and most of '52 w. Shep Fields orch., then entered the service, pl. in the 392nd Army Band. After discharge, June '54, settled in NYC. Has gigged w. various groups incl. Tony Scott, Jay and Kai; toured w. Pete Rugolo fall '54; Ch. Ventura Dec. '54-May '55; Gene Krupa May-Nov. '55, then several months w. house combo at the Cameo, NYC. Led own trio at Village Vanguard briefly June '58; worked w. Johnny Richards, Oscar Pettiford, New York Jazz Quartet, Peter Appleyard. Stud. arr. with Manny Albam. An enterprising and gifted musician, he shows signs of following in the successful footsteps of his brother. Favs: Oscar Pettiford, George Duvivier, Red Mitchell. Own LPs on ABC-Par.; LPs w. Red Mitchell and Blue Mitchell (Metro.); Candido, Tom Stewart, Bobby Scott, Jimmy Raney (ABC-Par.), NY Jazz Quartet (Elek.).

Addr: 420 Sutten Ave., Hackensack, N.J.

MIYAKE, MITSUKO, *singer;* b. Manchuria, 5/13/33. Studied at Nippon Music Cons. 1949. Married jazz critic K. Ohashi '56; he has since guided her career. Won *Swing Journal* readers' and critics' polls '58. Is heard and seen weekly on Japanese radio and TV. Favs: Fitzgerald, O'Day. Rec. LP, *Tokyo Canaries* on Japanese label.

Addr: 1261 2-chome, Nogata, Nakano-ku, Tokyo, Japan.

MIYAZAWA, AKIRA, *tenor sax;* b. Yamagata Mura, Nagano Prefecture, Japan, 12/6/27. Learned to play clarinet in Military Brass Band of the Toyama Army Academy, Tokyo 1944. Pl. w. pianist Shotaro Moriyasu '52, later w. Toshiko. App. at Contemporary Music Festival at Karuizawa, Aug. '54. Heard three or four times monthly on radio and TV. Favs: Parker, Rollins, Monk. LPs for Japanese labels.

Addr: 4929 Yamagata-cho, Higashi Chikuma-gun, Nagano Pref., Japan.

MOBLEY, HENRY (Hank), *tenor sax;* b. Eastman, Ga., 7/7/30. Raised in New Jersey. Studied w. private teacher for a year. Worked w. Paul Gayten 1950, Max Roach '51-3 on and off, Dizzy Gillespie Mar.-Sept. '54, Horace Silver late '54. The group with the latter, under the leadership of Art Blakey, became the Jazz Messengers. Mobley remained with them until Sept. '56 when he left w. Horace Silver to join the latter's new group. In the next four years, he was heard w. Silver, Max Roach, Thelonious Monk and rejoined Art Blakey '59. During this period he also app. at many of the Monday night sessions at Birdland. With Dizzy Reece '60. "Mobley is descended from Charlie Parker but he has a rounder sound and less jagged style than most of the tenormen in this general area, although by no means does he lack emotional power."—Ira Gitler. Fav. Parker. Own LPs on Blue Note, Pres., Savoy; LPs w. Blakey (Blue Note, Col.), Silver (Blue Note, Epic), Jimmy Smith, Curtis Fuller, Kenny Dorham, Johnny Griffin (Blue Note), *All Night Long, Tenor Conclave* (Pres.), Max Roach (Merc., Argo), Art Farmer (New Jazz), Kenny Drew (River.), Lee Morgan (Savoy), *Monday Night At Birdland* (Roul.), Curtis Fuller (UA), Dizzy Reece (Blue Note).

MODERN JAZZ QUARTET. An instrumental unit founded by John Lewis (q.v.). Although group first pl. together Aug. 24, 1951, the Quartet was officially born at a recording session for Prestige, Dec. 22, 1952; it did not become a permanently organized unit until late '54. Its members were Milt Jackson, vibes; Percy Heath, bass; Kenny Clarke, drums (replaced in 1955 by Connie Kay).

The group rose rapidly to international prominence and won the following awards: *Down Beat* Critics' Poll, 1954-9; *Down Beat* Readers' Poll, 1956-9; *Metronome* Poll 1957-60; *Jazz Hot* (Paris) since 1956; *Melody Maker* (London) Readers' and Critics' Polls, 1957; *Jazz Echo* (Hamburg) and many other foreign polls, as No. 1 jazz combo.

The Modern Jazz Quartet drew its success from the broad scope of the compositional concepts of its leader, his unique incorporation of classic forms into jazz contexts, and the unique group unity, coupled with an unprecedentedly gentle approach to the art of swinging. Much of what the group plays, in the opinion of some observers, is not jazz; but almost all of it is musically valid on more general terms.

Film scores: *No Sun in Venice,* 1958; *Odds Against Tomorrow,* 1959. LPs on Prestige, Atlantic, Verve, UA. (See John Lewis for record numbers.)

MOER, PAUL (Paul E. Moerschbacher), *piano, composer;* b. Meadville, Pa., 7/22/16. Theory and comp. at U.

of Miami, grad. cum laude 1951. Played w. Benny Carter, Vido Musso '53; Zoot Sims, Stan Getz '54; Jerry Gray, Bill Holman '55; Paul Horn, Shorty Rogers and many other West coast groups; also arrangements for TV incl. Steve Allen, Bob Hope, Les Brown, Desilu Prods. and for Bob Keene (Del Fi Recs.). Enjoys teaching as well as playing, and of late has expanded his writing activities, which have revealed considerable talent. Favs: Horace Silver, Phineas Newborn. LPs w. Jack Montrose (Wor. Pac., Atl.), *Jazzmantics* w. John Graas (Decca).

Addr: 9323 Kester Avenue, Van Nuys, Cal.

MOLE, IRVING MILFRED (Miff), *trombone;* b. Roosevelt, L.I., N.Y., 3/11/98. Stud. vln. 3 yrs., then trom. First trom. gig Bklyn '14 for silent films, house-painting for father daytimes; later priv. lessons. Formed Orig. Memphis 5 w. Jimmy Lytell, Frank Signorelli et al. Joined S. Lanin, Roseland '19, but contd. rec. freq. w. Memphis 5 under many names (Cotton Pickers, Tennessee Tooters, Orig. Tampa 5, etc.), feat. P. Napoleon, F. Trumbauer, A. Schutt, Red Nichols, V. Berton, R. Bloom et al.

In mid-'20s joined Red Nichols & His 5 Pennies (org. within Don Voorhees' Orch. by Nichols & Berton), and under 30 or more rec. names (Charleston Chasers, Red & Miff's Stompers, and own name) made perhaps 100 sides or more. Later w. Ray Miller, Ross Gorman, R. W. Kahn; on staff WOR w. Voorhees; abt. 10 yrs. NBC, pl. mostly classical music. W. Paul Whiteman '38, B. Goodman '42-3; he then led own Dixieland combo for four yrs. at Nick's. A year's free-lancing was followed by trip to Chi. w. Muggsy Spanier. He settled in Chi. '48 and spent several years pl. w. small groups at Blue Note, Jazz Ltd., and Bee Hive.

During late '50s, back in NYC, pl. many Dixieland sessions, but by '59 was ill, on crutches after several operations, now inactive.

LPs: *Doorway to Dixie* (Argo), *Dixieland Jazz at Jazz Ltd.* (Atl.); LPs w. *Red Nichols Story* (Bruns.), Connee Boswell and Orig. Memphis Five (Vict.).

Addr: 250 W. 88th Street, New York 24, N.Y.

MONDELLO, NUNCIO (Toots), *alto sax;* b. Boston, Mass., 1912. Worked w. Mal Hallett, Irving Aaronson, Buddy Rogers, Ray Noble, Joe Haymes, and Benny Goodman; pl. lead alto w. Benny Goodman in 1934 and rejoined him '39-40. Later went into commercial radio work and was inactive in jazz. Won *Met.* poll '37, '39-44. LPs w. Goodman (Col.), Billy Butterfield (Vict.).

Addr: 325 W. 45th St., New York 36, N.Y.

MONDRAGON, JOSEPH (Joe), *bass;* b. Antonito, Calif., 2/2/20. Self-taught; started career by chance when a band needed a bassist, and continued to work with dance bands around Los Angeles. While in service, pl. many Pacific islands. First prominent in jazz w. Woody Herman 1946. Rec. debut w. Alvino Rey. In recent years has been one of the most-recorded jazz bassists on West Coast. Outstanding tone, technique and style. Fav: Ray Brown. LPs w. Buddy Rich, Buddy De Franco, Harry Edison (Verve), Paul Smith (Cap.), Marty Paich (Tampa), Shelly Manne (Contemp.).

Addr: 23443 Burbank Blvd., Woodland Hills, Calif.

MONK, THELONIOUS SPHERE, *composer, piano;* b. Rocky Mount, N.C., 10/10/20; to NYC in infancy. Studied privately from 1939. At Minton's Play House, the Uptown House and other Harlem clubs Monk was one of a handful of innovators who, in the years before World War II, worked together informally on the harmonic and rhythmic innovations that were to lead to the establishment of bop as a new jazz style. Dizzy Gillespie, Charlie Parker, Bud Powell and Kenny Clarke were a part of the same clique of visionary jazzmen. Monk was a member of Lucky Millinder's band for a while in 1942, when Dizzy Gillespie was with Millinder; he also played and recorded with Coleman Hawkins in '44 and worked briefly with Gillespie, but aside from these jobs he worked almost entirely on his own, or leading a trio or small combo, from the mid-40's until February '59, when for the first time he was presented as the leader of a large orchestra, in a concert at Town Hall in New York City.

After many years of neglect by critics, fans and fellow-musicians, Monk gradually began to acquire popularity in the middle and late '50s. During most of '57 he was featured with a quartet at the Five Spot Cafe in NYC, with J. Coltrane as a sideman. He appeared on CBS-TV's *The Sound of Jazz* Dec. '57. In the spring of '58 he was at the Village Vanguard; in '59, with a quartet featuring Ch. Rouse, he appeared at the Randalls Island, Detroit and other jazz festivals.

Opinions concerning Monk's contribution have varied greatly. It is the author's feeling that although his compositions are his most important gift to jazz, he has extended his mastery of an individual piano technique to the point where his harmonic innovations, coupled with the stark, somber quality of his approach and the uniquely subtle use of dynamics, place him among the most important and influential figures in jazz today.

Many of Monk's compositions have become jazz standards in the past few years. Many of them were originally recorded in a series of sessions for Blue Note and Prestige and have been reintroduced in newer versions under his expanded recording schedule at Riverside. They include *'Round Midnight, Ruby My Dear, Off Minor, Epistrophy, Well You Needn't, Straight No Chaser, Blue Monk.* Monk generally has based his writing on conventionally formalized 12 and 32 bar structures; their strength lies in their melodic originality and the harmonic substructure. Unlike most jazz composers, he does not orchestrate his own work except for small combo dates; for the Town Hall concert Hall Overton wrote the scores.

According to Art Blakey "Monk is the guy who

started it all; he came before both Parker and Gillespie." Critic Martin Williams has said: "Monk is the first major composer in jazz since Duke Ellington." Dom Cerulli has written of Monk's music as "highly personal; now brittle and spastic, now firm and outspoken; but always unified in conception and overall sound." British composer Steve Race has stated that the "angular, nagging piano" of Monk leaves him completely unmoved; he and other musicians believe that Monk's technical limitations prevent him from expressing himself fully. Films: music for *Liasons Dangereuses;* seen in *Jazz on a Summer's Day.* Fav: Bud Powell.

Own LPs on Riverside: *At Town Hall* (300), *Brilliant Corners* (226), *5 By 5* (305), *Misterioso* (279), *Thelonious In Action* (262), *Monk's Music* (242), *Monk Plays Duke Ellington* (201), *Thelonious Himself* (235), *The Unique* (209), *Thelonious Alone in San Francisco* (312). Also *Monk, Vols. I & II* (Blue Note 1510, 1511, *Quintets* (Pres. 7053), *Trios* (Pres. 7027), *Work!* with Sonny Rollins (Pres. 7169). LPs with Clark Terry (River. 271), Art Blakey (Atl. 1278), Gerry Mulligan (River. 247), Rollins (Pres. 7058), *Bird & Diz* (Verve 8006), Miles Davis (Pres. 7109, 7150), Milt Jackson (Blue Note 1509), Ch. Christian/D Gillespie (Ctpt. 548), Gigi Gryce in *Nica's Tempo* (Savoy 12137).

Addr: 243 West 63rd St., New York 23, N.Y.

MONTEROSE, J. R. (Frank Anthony Monterose Jr.), *tenor sax;* b. Detroit, Mich., 1/19/27. Family moved to Utica, N.Y., 1928. Clar. in grammar school band at 13, tenor at 15. Legit. clar. with Utica Jr. Symph. After working w. territory bands 1948-9, he joined Henry Busse in '50. Came to NYC, worked w. Buddy Rich in '52, then worked around Syracuse, N.Y., '52-4. Ret. to NYC w. Claude Thornhill; in '55 he gigged around New York w. Dan Terry, Teddy Charles, et al; in '56 w. Ch. Mingus and Kenny Dorham, later had own group in Albany, N.Y., then free-lanced in NYC; pl. with Terry Gibbs' big band at Apollo Theatre '59. Record debut, Jan. '55 w. T. Charles. Favs: Parker, Rollins, Stitt, Coltrane. Own LPs on Top Rank and BN; LPs w. K. Dorham, Kenny Burrell (BN), T. Charles (Atl., Pres.), Ralph Sharon (Beth., Lond.), K. Dorham (ABC-Par.).

Addr: 319 E. 8th St., New York, N.Y.

MONTGOMERY, CHARLES F. (Buddy), *piano, vibes, composer;* b. Indianapolis, 1/30/30. Brother of Wes and Monk. Self-taught. Started with local group, the Hampton Bros. (incl. Slide Hampton). Leader of quartet during Army service '54 incl. Roy Johnson, bass; led Montgomery-Johnson Quintet '55-7; started playing vibes '57, then helped form Mastersounds (q.v.). When the group disbanded in '60, he joined Miles Davis in February. Fav. own rec. solos: *Getting to Know You, All the Things You Are.* Favs: Tatum, Milt Jackson. LPs w. Mastersounds, Montgomery Brothers (Wor.-Pac.).

Addr: 1885 Golden Gate #6, San Francisco, Calif.

MONTGOMERY, EURREAL (Little Brother), *piano, singer;* b. Kentwood, La., 5/17/07. After working around New Orleans, moved to Chicago, where he has been active for many years, occasionally returning to New Orleans. Primarily known as a blues pianist on records, he worked with many NO style groups in the '40s and and '50s. Was w. Franz Jackson spring '58 at Preview Lounge, Chicago; also pl. at Gate of Horn, Red Arrow. App. at Ravinia Festival 1959. W. Chris Clifton band '59. Own LP on Winding Ball label, also singles on Ebony.

Addr: 4213 So. Wabash Ave., Chicago, Ill.

MONTGOMERY, WILLIAM HOWARD (Monk), *electric bass;* b. Indianapolis, Ind., 10/10/21. Largely self-taught, he has played w. L. Hampton, G. Auld, and A. Farmer. In the fall of 1957, along with his brother, Charles (Buddy) Montgomery (vibes), Richie Crabtree (piano), and Ben Barth (drums), he formed the co-operative unit, The Mastersounds (*q.v.*). He is the only bassist with a major jazz combo to make use of the Fender electric bass, a small instrument that is held like a guitar. The Mastersounds, after being featured in West Coast clubs and on recordings, became nationally popular and were heard at jazz festivals before disbanding in early '60. LPs on Wor. Pac.

MONTGOMERY, THOMAS EDWIN (Tom), *drums, trumpet;* b. Evanston, Ill., 11/27/24. Self taught; played bass for three years with trio, also doubled guitar and piano, but since 1952 has concentrated on drums and trumpet, working with Hal McIntyre 1951-4, Ray Anthony '54, and Al Belletto, Kai Winding-J. J. Johnson, S. Stitt. LPs w. Winding Septet (Col.), Jerri Winters (Beth.), *Half & Half* w. Belletto (Cap.).

Addr: 509 Davis St., Kalamazoo, Mich.

MONTGOMERY, WES, *guitar;* b. Indianapolis, Ind., 3/6/25. Brothers Monk and Buddy were members of the Mastersounds (q.v.). Pl. with Lionel Hampton 1948-50; while with the band made some records acc. Sonny Parker, no longer obtainable. Returning to Indianapolis, he led his own combo. In 1959 he went to San Francisco, where he worked with the Mastersounds and recorded for World Pacific. Described by John S. Wilson as "a guitarist who swings strongly with a mixture of single string and chorded playing," he is highly regarded by musicians and critics. Own LPs: Riverside; LP w. *The Montgomery Brothers* (World-Pacific); one no. in *Have Blues, Will Travel* (Wor. Pac.).

MONTROSE, JACK, *tenor sax, composer;* b. Detroit, Mich., 12/30/28. (Not related to J. R. Monterose, see above). Clarinet, alto sax in high school band, Chattanooga, Tenn. BA at Los Angeles State College '51-3. With Jerry Gray '53, Art Pepper Quintet '54; then pl. and rec. w. Bob Gordon, Red Norvo, Shorty Rogers, et al. A bright, young jazz writer, he believes classical chamber music has influenced his work; aims to write large orchestral works with jazz essence. Fav: Zoot Sims. Solos on *Coronado Clipper, Oomp Chuck* w.

Jerry Gray (Decca). Own LPs: Wor. Pac., Atl., Vict.; LPs w. Red Norvo (Lib.), Shorty Rogers (Vict.), Lennie Niehaus, Shelly Manne (Contemp.), Art Pepper (Savoy), John Graas, Jack Millman (Decca), Mel Tormé (Beth.), Chet Baker (Wor. Pac.).

Addr: 8163 Potter Ave., North Hollywood, Calif.

MOODY, JAMES, *tenor and alto sax, flute, composer;* b. Savannah, Ga., 2/26/25. In Army 1943-6; w. Dizzy Gillespie '47; various groups in Europe '48-51 incl. a series of record sessions in Stockholm and Paris. After returning to US he toured with his own band, featuring a brash, florid ballad style that had become very popular through his record of *I'm in the Mood for Love.* His earlier records, however, show him as a capable jazz soloist, especially on tenor. In recent years he has taken up flute and has been developing rapidly as a modern soloist. In 1958, after several months of voluntary retirement, Moody reorganized his orch., playing dance dates and several concerts incl. Carnegie Hall NYC. Own LPs: Argo, Pres. Em.; LPs w. Gillespie (GNP, Savoy).

Addr: c/o Argo Records, 2120 S. Michigan, Chicago, Ill.

MOONDOG (Louis Thomas Hardin), *miscellaneous instruments, composer;* b. Marysville, Kans., 5/24/16. Raised in Indian country in Wyoming. Infl. by both oriental and occidental music, he came to NYC in 1943 and appeared on the streets, playing primitive rhythms and melodies on homemade instruments such as the oo, the samisen, the utsu and the uni. Became a cult among jazzmen in NYC in early '50s. His brand of music, unclassifiable, is of interest as a cultural phenomenon. In 1959 he announced that he was writing a series of short pieces for symphony orchestra and that he had completed a perpetual calendar from 44 B.C. to 3200 A.D. Own LPs on Prestige; LPs w. Julie Andrews & Martin Green (Angel), *Jazztime USA* (Brunswick).

Addr: 179 East 3rd Street, New York 9, N.Y.

MOONEY, JOE, *singer, Hammond organ, accordion, piano;* b. New Jersey, 1911. Mooney, who is blind, made his debut in local radio act with his brother, Dan, in late 1920s. During '30s made many vocal arrangements; took up accordion 1935; formed sextet which was incorporated into Frank Dailey's band 1937. Later had own quartet w. Russ Morgan orch.; for Modernaires, Paul Whiteman, Larry Clinton, Les Brown et al. In Feb. 1946 he formed his own instrumental quartet, which was hailed by Michael Levin in *Down Beat* as "The most exciting musical unit in the US." The group, featuring ingenious arrangements by Mooney and frequently his own intimate and charming vocals, enjoyed a short vogue in NYC. After it disbanded Mooney took up Hammond organ, which he has played at the Embers, NYC, and other clubs. During the '50s he recorded as vocalist w. Sauter-Finegan Orchestra but was in comparative obscurity, working chiefly in small clubs in Fla. Won DB critics' poll on organ '54. Own LP: Decca; LP w. Sauter-Finegan (Vict.).

Addr: 12801 N.W., First Ave., Miami 50, Fla.

MOORE, RUSSELL (Big Chief), *trombone;* b. Komatke, Ariz., 8/13/13. Studied under uncle at Blue Island, Ill.: piano, trumpet, drums, euphonium. Played baritone with National Guard Band, Chicago 1928-9. Played w. Harlan Leonard '41, Noble Sissle '42, L. Armstrong big band '43-5, Sidney Bechet '46-8. Went to Europe '49 for Paris Jazz Festival; toured the continent '53, and made many records in Paris w. Buck Clayton, Mezz Mezzrow. Was seen in film *New Orleans* w. Armstrong. Joined Jimmy McPartland '54. In late '50s worked w. society leader Lester Lanin as jazz soloist; also app. at jazz concerts at Metropole, Central Plaza, and on college dates. Made two concert tours as leader to South Dakota '59, Arizona '59 under the sponsorship of the National Congress of American Indians to help build morale of Indian students and to raise scholarship funds for deserving young American Indians. Moore is a descendant of the Pima tribe. LPs w. Buck Clayton (Jazztone), Lester Lanin (Epic).

Addr: 47-17 Junction Blvd., Corona 73, L.I., N.Y.

MOORE, WILLIAM JR. (Billy), *composer, piano;* b. Parkersburg, W.Va., 1917. Raised in NYC from 1932, he worked for five years in a butcher shop until Sy Oliver got him a job as his replacement arranging for Jimmie Lunceford, 1939. Moore's brittle, swinging scores, reflecting Oliver's influence, were heard in such first-class Lunceford performances as *Belgium Stomp, What's Your Story Morning Glory, Chopin Prelude No. 7, Bugs Parade, Monotony in Four Flats.* He later arranged for Ch. Barnet (*Skyliner,* etc.), Jan Savitt, T. Dorsey; active as music publisher in late '40s, then went to live in Europe, arranging for French bands and touring since 1953 with the Peters Sisters as mus. dir. and pianist. LPs as arr. w. Lunceford (Col.), Barnet (Verve).

Addr: c/o American Express Co., Paris, France.

MOORE, MILTON A. JR. (Brew), *tenor sax;* b. Indianola, Miss., 3/26/24. Mother bought him harmonica on 7th birthday. Played in high school band at 11. First prof. job w. Fred Ford NO dixieland band in 1942, then w. Will Stump. To NYC '43 and several times in the late '40s; led his own quartet, played few months w. Claude Thornhill (also with Gerry Mulligan and Kai Winding at Roost and Bop City) and made occasional record dates and jam sessions. Capable of excellent work in a Lester Young-inspired style, he has had an erratic career and was for some time in semi-obscurity, appearing occasionally at Open Door in Greenwich Village in '53-4 before migrating to San Francisco, where he worked with local combos. After a serious illness in 1959 he resumed work, playing weekend jam sessions at the Tropics and occasional Matson steamer trips to the Orient. Own LPs on Fantasy; four tracks in both *In The Beginning . . . Bebop* and *Lestorian*

Mode (Savoy); LPs w. Chuck Wayne (Savoy); *The Brothers* (Pres.); Kai Winding in *Trombone By Three* (Pres.), George Wallington (Savoy).

MOORE, DEBBY (Emmaline Maultsby), *singer, whistler, guitar;* b. St. Augustine, Fla., 5/18/28. Stud. voice in NYC w. former Fats Waller arranger Don Donaldson. Soloist w. Earl Hines orch. '54; Great South Bay Jazz Festival w. Rex Stewart '58; toured Japan, Korea for State Dept. '58 and made two movies in Japan. A jazz-inclined singer with an individual sound, she has successfully incorporated blues whistling into her act. Fav: Lena Horne. Early recs. for Tuxedo, RCA Victor. Own LP: Top Rank.

Addr: 41 Convent Avenue, New York City, N.Y.

MOORE, FREDDIE, *drums;* b. Washington, N.C., 8/20/00. Learned drums at age 12; pl. with Charlie Creath in St. Louis; w. King Oliver around 1930; w. small bands in NYC during '40s. Pl. with Wilbur de Paris '52-3; toured Europe w. Mezz Mezzrow '54-5. Rec. w. Art Hodes (BN), King Oliver (Vic.).

Addr: 115 West 141st St., New York, N.Y.

MOORE, MARILYN, *singer;* b. Oklahoma City, Okla., 6/16/31. Parents vaudevillians, and she broke in as part of the act at 3. Didn't sing again until high school, when she worked w. a band, then began in clubs around Oklahoma City; later worked around Chicago. Sang briefly w. W. Herman, then back to Oklahoma City; w. Ch. Barnet in 1952. Married Al Cohn in 1953 (since separated) and was in retirement four years. Made record debut in '57 and was compared to the Billie Holiday of the 1930s. One of the few young singers with a natural jazz timbre and sense of phrasing, she has been seriously handicapped by critical resentment of the resemblance to Billie. Own LP on Beth.; w. Leonard Feather-Dick Hyman in *Oh Captain!* (MGM).

Addr: 32-28 164th St., Flushing 58, L.I., N.Y.

MOORE, OSCAR FRED, *guitar;* b. Austin, Texas, 12/25/16. Prof. debut 1934 with his brother Johnny, also a guitarist. Joined King Cole Sept. 1937 and remained with him for exactly 10 years, during which time he earned acclaim as the first of the modern combo guitarists, playing single-string amplified solos and chord work in a style that was a highly attractive element of Cole's records during the early 40s. After leaving Cole he settled in LA, working mostly with his brother Johnny in a group called The Three Blazers. In 1959 he made a series of pop albums. Tremendously popular in the heyday of the King Cole Trio, Moore won the *Down Beat* readers' poll and the *Metronome* poll as the country's No. 1 guitarist every year from 1945 through '48, also the Esq. Silver Award '44 and '45, Gold Award '46 and '47. LPs w. Cole and in *History of Jazz* (Cap.); *Just Jazz* (Modern), own groups (Sky., Tampa, Verve).

Addr: 7641 Beck Avenue, North Hollywood, Cal.

MOORE, NUMA SMITH (Pee Wee), *baritone sax;* also *clarinet, also sax;* b. Raleigh, N.C., 3/5/28. Studied drums first in high school. Pl. w. Royal Hamptonians at Hampton Institute in Va., later at local clubs in Newport News, Va. Worked w. Lucky Millinder 1950-1, Louis Jordan for 5 months in '51, Illinois Jacquet Jan.-May '52, James Moody May '52-Aug. '56; then w. Dizzy Gillespie's big band. Fav: Charlie Parker. LPs w. James Moody (Pres.).

Addr: 2412 7th Ave., New York 30, N.Y.

MOORE, PHIL, *composer, vocal coach, piano, singer;* b. Portland, Ore., 2/20/18. Stud. piano '22; later at Cornish Cons., U. of Wash. Pl. w. Louie's Rinky Dinks '31; later w. Les Hite, Eli Rice et al in Cal. Says "I was going to be a pianist until I watched Tatum; then I started arranging." Pioneered in "block chord" piano style in 1939 (later popularized by Milt Buckner, Geo. Shearing). Ch. Barnet rec. his comp. *Ogoun Badagris* '39. During '40s, 5 yrs. as staff arr: & cond. at MGM film studios in Hollywood; worked on Mildred Bailey CBS radio series in NYC. In mid-'40s sang and pl. with his Phil Moore Four for 19 months at Cafe Society, NYC, and in films *Broadway Melody, A Song is Born.* Toured US, Europe as acc. for D. Dandridge, L. Horne; coached Julie Wilson, Ava Gardner, Jan Russell, Marilyn Monroe, F. Sinatra. Comp. instr. works played by symph. orchs. Active entirely in pop field since early '50s. His pop hits have incl. *Shoo Shoo Baby, I Feel So Smoochie, Blow Out The Candle.* Fav. own arrs: *Frankie & Johnny* for Lena Horne, *Lotus Land* for Martha Raye, Mary Ann McCall album for Discovery, *Misty Moon Blues* by own orch. on Disc. Favs: Gieseking, Tatum, Meade Lux Lewis. Own LPs: Verve, MGM, Col.

Addr: Carnegie Hall Apts., New York 19, N.Y.

MORALES, LLOYD T., *drums;* b. Norwell, Mass., 6/19/28. Stud. with Symphony percussionist in San Antonio. After starting to play while in Air Force, made prof. debut 1952; joined Les Brown band 1/1/56. LPs w. Brown, also on Kapp w. Bill Usselton, Imperial w. Bob Harrington, Decca w. Jeri Southern. Film tracks for *Mamie Stover, Bop Girl Goes Calypso.* Favs: Lamond, Jo Jones, Manne, Roach.

Addr: 626 Parkham Ave., Los Angeles 26, Cal.

MORALES, NORO, *piano, composer, leader;* b. San Juan, P.R., 1/4/11. Pl. with family orch. as a child; this became official orch. of President of Venezuela. To US 1935; formed own orch. '39 playing in night clubs, theatres and on records. His Latin-American band has included jazz musicians from time to time.

MORAN, PAT (Helen Mudgett), *piano;* b. Enid, Okla., 12/10/34. From musical family; began stud. piano in 1943 at Phillips U. in Enid; later in NYC and at the Cincinnati Cons. of Music. St. as concert pianist, then switched to jazz, formed quart. and went on the road. Favs: Bud Powell, John Lewis, Hank Jones, Horace Silver. Own LPs: Beth., Aud. Fid.

Addr: 1215 W. Oklahoma, Enid, Okla.

MOREHOUSE, CHAUNCEY, *drums, miscellaneous percussion;* b. Niagara Falls, N.Y., 3/11/07. Father played ragtime piano. Stud. piano w. Catholic sisters in Chambersburg, Pa. and played as duo w. father in silent movie theaters, then w. Gettysburg College dance band and later w. the nucleus of Ted Weems band at Ocean City, N.J. After playing w. Weems, 1924, Jean Goldkette '25-7, he was with the Don Voorhees orchestra in the pit for the Broadway show *Rain Or Shine* '28. From '29 on he was in commercial radio, later TV, and also had own adv. agency, writing and making jingles. Morehouse developed a set of chromatic, tuned drums which he has used for Afro-Cuban effects, etc. His importance to jazz lay in his participation in a number of classic records, '26-'30, by Bix Beiderbecke, Frankie Trumbauer, Hoagy Carmichael, Red Nichols, Miff Mole, the Dorsey Brothers, Joe Venuti. He has kept abreast of the times and is enthusiastic about many modern drummers, especially Ed Thigpen. Favs: Krupa, Rich. LPs: *Duke Ellington's Jazz Party, Bix Beiderbecke* (Col.).

Addr: 68-31 Ingram St., Forest Hills 75, N.Y.

MORELLI, FRANK ARTHUR, *baritone sax;* also *flute, alto sax;* b. Detroit, Mich., 3/7/32. Mother played piano and was dancer. Stud. alto sax in high school 1947. Father bought him first horn. Played w. Yusef Lateef in late '50s; own group at Hungry Eye in Detroit '59. Favs: Carney, Pepper Adams, Tate Houston. LP: w. Yusef Lateef (Argo).

Addr: 4284 W. Davison, Detroit 38, Mich.

MORELLO, JOSEPH A. (Joe), *drums;* b. Springfield, Mass., 7/17/28. Partially blind since infancy. Worked locally w. Whitey Bernard; joined Glen Gray 1950. Came to NYC '52, pl. with Johnny Smith at the Embers, also briefly w. Stan Kenton; w. Marian McPartland Trio '53-6, after which time he joined Dave Brubeck and made various foreign tours with the quartet. "A powerful, precise drummer, with a left hand as furious as an electric typewriter . . . brilliant snaredrum work, glistening cymbal patterns, and massive, irregular arrays of bass-drum beats . . ."—Whitney Balliett, *The New Yorker.*

Favs: Krupa, Tough, Lamond, Rich, Bellson. LPs w. Sam Most, Sal Salvador (Beth.), Marian McPartland (Cap.), Dave Brubeck (Col.).

Addr: 414 Grove St., Newark, N.J.

MORGAN, AL, *bass;* b. New Orleans, La., 8/10/08. Clarinet, drums at 9; bass at 10 w. private teachers. Riverboats w. Fate Marable 1926-8; Cab Calloway '30-6; free-lanced in Cal. '37-41; Les Hite band '42; next decade mainly in Boston w. Sabby Lewis, also w. Louis Jordan in '45. Tied w. Milt Hinton for Esq. Silver Award '44. Was occasionally heard as blues singer. Heard on many early recs. w. Jones-Collins Hot Eight, Eddie Condon, Chu Berry, Calloway et al, he was one of the better bass men in the simple quarter-note style of the '30s. LP w. Max Kaminsky (Comm.).

MORGAN, LEE, *trumpet;* b. Philadelphia, Pa., 7/10/38. Father pianist for church choir. Stud. trumpet privately and at Mastbaum Tech.; worked locally from the age of 15 at dances w. own group. Sat in with many name bands at Music City, incl. A. Blakey. Joined Dizzy Gillespie when the latter ret. from his South American tour and stayed with the band until it broke up in Jan. '58. With Blakey's Jazz Messengers since Sept. '58. Style not yet fully matured, but shows exceptional technical command and promises to develop into important musician. Favs: Clifford Brown, Gillespie, Navarro. Own LPs on BN, Sav.; LPs w. Gillespie (Verve), Hank Mobley, John Coltrane, Cliff Jordan (BN), Ch. Persip (Lib.), Art Farmer, Curtis Fuller (UA), Philly Joe Jones (River.).

Addr: 315 E. 6th St., New York, N.Y.

MORGAN, LOUMELL, *piano;* b. Raleigh, N.C., 10/27/22. Began stud. piano at eight w. mother and sister. Joined Tiny Bradshaw after grad. from college; later was w. Slim and Slam. Formed own trio in 1942 in Hollywood, and app. in several movies at Universal. Did radio work there, then came to NYC '46 and was on CBS radio and WOR. Popular as leader or sideman in various vocal-instrumental novelty trios playing pop-style jazz for night club audiences incl. The Three Flames. Fav: Art Tatum. LP w. Three Flames (Barbary).

Addr: 1345 Washington Ave., Bronx 56, N.Y.

MORR, SKIP (Charles Wm. Coolidge), *trombone;* also *drums;* b. Chicago, Ill., 3/28/12. Grandfather pl. drums w. Sousa, in Chi. theaters; father, a pianist, acc. Eva Tanguay, Blossom Seely. St. on drums, self-taught; trombone in high school in Burlingame, Calif. Entered Northwestern U. 1930; formed 14-piece band which incl. Richard Maltby, Joe Rushton. Pl. w. Ted Weems '34, Bill Hogan '35, Henry Busse '36, Lou Breese, Busse again '40. To Hollywood '42, remaining until '50 while working w. Artie Shaw, Ch. Barnet and in studios w. Gordon Jenkins, Ray Noble, Axel Stordahl et al. W. pit band for Ken Murray's *Blackouts.* Worked w. Wingy Manone in SF '50, then joined Marty Marsala there '52. Fav: Teagarden, Jenney, McGarity. LP w. Burt Bales, Marsala (ABC-Par.).

Addr: 170 Janes St., Mill Valley, Calif.

MORRIS, JOSEPH (Joe), *trumpet, leader;* b. Montgomery, Ala., 1922; d. Phoenix, Ariz., Nov. '58. Att. Ala. State Teachers' Coll. Stud. with brother, who pl. guitar w. Erskine Hawkins. Playing one-nighters in Florida, he was heard by L. Hampton and worked w. his band 1942-6, recording own comps. *Chop Chop, Punch & Judy, Tempo's Birthday,* also backgrounds on Dinah Washington's first records (*Evil Gal Blues,* etc.). After working w. Buddy Rich 1946, he formed his own band, which rec. for Decca and Atl. and rose to some prominence in r & b field. He was still working intermittently up to the time of his death. LP: tracks in *Dance The Rock & Roll* (Atl.).

MORRIS, MARLOWE, *piano, organ;* b. Bronx, N.Y., 5/16/15. Uncle, Tommy Morrison, well-known jazzman of 1920s; father a music teacher. Self-taught; encouraged greatly by Art Tatum. Worked w. Eric Henry and

Coleman Hawkins in 1940; record debut w. Lionel Hampton 1940. Army '41-2, then played and arr. for Al Sears band at Renaissance Ballroom NYC. Later toured in USO for Sears. Worked w. Big Sid Catlett in '44, moved to Calif. and appeared in Norman Granz's movie short, *Jammin' the Blues.* Back in NYC, worked w. Doc Wheeler, Eddie South, Tiny Grimes. Has app. mainly as soloist since '46. Took day job w. Post Office '49-50, but has been back in music full-time since then, playing Hammond organ in various Harlem clubs. Recs. with Sid Catlett, Ben Webster on Comm., Session, Tiny Grimes on Blue Note, Lionel Hampton on Vict., none available on LP.

MORRISON, JOHN A. (Peck), *bass;* b. Lancaster, Pa., 9/11/19. Stud. trumpet, drums, bass, New Rochelle High Sch. and Hartnett Sch. of Music. Overseas in Spec. Serv. Band in Italy, 1946. Worked w. Lucky Thompson octet at Savoy Ballroom NYC, Dec. '51-Jan. '53, then toured w. Tiny Bradshaw. With Bill Graham's combo at Snookie's, NYC, Apr. '53-June '54, then gigged w. Horace Silver, Gigi Gryce, Art Farmer. Night club dates w. Jay and Kai quint. Oct. '54-Jan. '55. Briefly w. Duke Ellington Jan. '55; Lou Donaldson Apr. '55, Gerry Mulligan, Aug.-Dec. '55; Johnny Smith quart. '56. Served virtually as house bassist at the Five Spot Cafe '57-9, working w. the combos of Randy Weston and Mal Waldron et al. Toured w. Carmen McRae Nov. '58. Favs: Hinton, Pettiford, Clyde Lombardi. LPs w. Lou Donaldson (BN), G. Mulligan (Merc.), K. Winding-J. J. Johnson (Pres.), Randy Weston (Jub.), Duke Ellington-Johnnie Ray (Col.); feat. on *Blues Walk* w. Donaldson (BN).

Addr: 471 Swinton Ave., Bronx 65, N. Y.

MORROW, BUDDY (Moe Zudekoff), *leader, trombone;* b. New Haven, Conn., 2/8/19. Stud. Juilliard, 1934; immediately afterward joined Paul Whiteman for two years. Featured w. original Artie Shaw band w. strings, '36-7; T. Dorsey '38, then w. Vincent Lopez, Bob Crosby and back w. Shaw. Navy '41-4; after a year w. Jimmy Dorsey, led his own band '45-6, then did studio work in NYC. Began recording w. own band 1950, organized big band for road 1951, and met with great success, often w. pop versions of r & b hit numbers. Fine all-around trombonist and good swing soloist. Own LPs on Merc., Vict., Cam.; LP w. Artie Shaw (Epic).

Addr: 110 W. 55th St., New York 19, N.Y.

MORSE, ROBERT (Bob), *singer;* b. Pasadena, Calif., 7/27/27. Musical family; one brother pl. trumpet for Stan Kenton, another arr. for Johnny Richards. Pl. alto at 6; took up bass in '47. Sang w. brother Burton's band in '46. Rec. with the Encores, Billy May. In 1953 joined Hi-Lo's quartet (*q.v.*). Fav. own solo: *Skylark.* Fav. singer: Billie Holiday. LPs w. Hi-Lo's (Col., Kapp).

Addr: 6470 Deep Dell Place, Hollywood, Calif.

MORSE, ELLA MAE, *singer;* b. Mansfield, Tex., 9/12/24. Mother, a pianist, father pl. drums. After singing w. father's jazz band, joined Jimmy Dorsey, 1939; scored first hit w. Freddie Slack when she rec. *Cow Cow Boogie,* '42. Has worked mostly as single since then, and had several other hits incl. *Mr. Five by Five,* '42, *House of Blue Lights,* '46. After several years' retirement, scored again with *Blacksmith Blues,* '51. Good pop singer whose style reflects her jazz background. Fav: Ella Fitzgerald. Ambition: To become actress in movies and TV. LPs on Cap.

Addr: 2475 Arlington, Reno, Nevada.

MORTON, HENRY STERLING (Benny), *trombone;* b. New York City, 1/31/07. First prominent from 1924 w. Billy Fowler's orch., he pl. with Fletcher Henderson 1927 and again '31-2; w. Don Redman '32-7; Count Basie Sept. '37 until Dec. '39, when he joined Joe Sullivan's sextet at Cafe Society. He remained for several years off and on at Cafe Society w. Teddy Wilson 1940, later w. Edmond Hall and then with his own band '46. Also worked at CBS w. Raymond Scott '44. Worked frequently w. pit bands for Broadway shows incl. *Memphis Bound, St. Louis Woman, Lend an Ear, Regina, Guys and Dolls, Silk Stockings, Shinbone Alley, Jamaica, Whoop-Up.* Played in Radio City Music Hall orch. '59, as well as free-lancing around NYC. Morton became known during the 1930s as one of the most personal trombone stylists with a vibrant, intense jazz solo talent that was heard on records w. Benny Carter and Teddy Wilson in addition to the bands listed above. LPs w. Buck Clayton-Ruby Braff (Vang.), Roy Eldridge (Verve), Charlie Shavers (Beth.), Ruby Braff (Vict.), Fletcher Henderson All-Stars (Jazz., UA, Urania), Eddie Condon, Max Kaminsky (Comm.), Count Basie (Bruns.), *Spirituals To Swing* (Vang.).

Addr: 122 W. 132nd St., New York, N.Y.

MORTON, JEFFREY (Jeff), *drums;* b. Brooklyn, N.Y., 6/2/29. Stud. w. Henry Adler, Lennie Tristano. Pl. w. Chubby Jackson 1949, Tristano '49-50, Max Kaminsky '50-1. Worked as machinist '52-3. With Lee Konitz '54-5. Later moved to California, living in Pasadena. Out of music, Morton is now a sculptor. Favs: Roach, Catlett, Tough. LP w. Konitz (Pres.).

MORTON, JELLY ROLL (Ferdinand Joseph La Menthe), *composer, piano, leader, singer;* b. Gulfport, La., 9/20/1885; d. Los Angeles, Cal. 7/10/41. Started on guitar 1892, piano 1895. From 1902 he played piano in bordellos in New Orleans' Storyville quarter. Spending only part of his time as a professional musician, he was later heard in Memphis, St. Louis and Kansas City, and from 1917 to '22 spent much of his time in California. His career as a recording artist began with a series of solos made in Richmond, Ind., 1923-4, but the principal source of his fame was the long series of sessions made under the name of Morton's Red Hot Peppers for Victor from Sept. 1926 to Oct. 1930, recorded mostly in Chicago and New York and featuring Kid Ory, Johnny and Baby Dodds, Omer Simeon and many other subsequently famous musicians.

During the late 1920s Morton enjoyed his greatest

successes as a musician. He displayed his prosperity with legendary ostentation, wearing a diamond filling in one tooth and covering himself with other indications of new-found wealth. During the 1930s, however, his fame and prosperity ended abruptly and by 1937 he was in comparative obscurity, running a night club in Washington, D.C. Returning to New York, he made a series of records in 1939-40. Soon after, he moved to California and spent the last year of his life there.

The life of Jelly Roll Morton has been documented in phenomenal detail, more than that of any other musician in jazz history. Since literally millions of words have been devoted to the study of his career and contributions, any attempt to condense them here would be useless. The best reference source is *Mister Jelly Roll* (Duell, Sloan & Pearce, 1950) by Alan Lomax, a Morton student who recorded him for the archives of the Library of Congress in 1938.

Because of the many claims he made—notably that he "invented jazz in 1902" and that many famous compositions had been stolen from him—Morton became a controversial figure. His most passionate adherents are the traditionalist jazz critics. George Avakian, while conceding that he was "a strange mixture of genius, musician, poet, snob and braggart," said that his claims were almost all true, that he was an extraordinary pianist, and that "there are many who will assure you that no greater jazzman ever sat down at the keyboard." Ralph de Toledano predicted that "Jelly Roll's music will be with us long after the fifth-rate and frenetic bebop imitations of the modernists have mercifully left us." Max Jones, the British critic, called him "a fine soloist, outstanding orchestral pianist, excellent singer (in the jazz sense), arranger of distinction, and a composer unique in the jazz field."

On the other hand, Duke Ellington once stated: "Sure, Jelly Roll Morton has talent . . . talent for talking about Jelly Roll Morton." W. C. Handy, the object for many years of one of Morton's bitter feuds, frequently reiterated that most of Morton's claims were false. According to critic John Hammond "Morton was very important as a composer, but his tremendous ego and his limited technique got in the way of his producing any real music as a pianist." Mary Lou Williams and other musicians, along with a minority of critics, feel that Morton's rôle was exaggerated out of all proportion by cultists.

Morton's best known comps. incl. *King Porter Stomp, Milenburg Joys, Wolverine Blues, The Pearls, Shoe Shiner's Drag (London Blues), Wild Man Blues, Kansas City Stomps.* He won R. Ch. All Time, All Star poll, 1951. LPs: *Classic Piano Solos* (River. 12-111), *The Incomparable* (River. 12-128), *King of New Orleans Jazz* (Vict. 1649), *New Orleans Memories* (Comm. 30001), 12-volume *Documentary* (River. 9001-12).

MOSCA, SALVATORE JOSEPH (Sal), *piano;* b. Mt. Vernon, N.Y., 4/27/27. Stud. in Mt. Vernon and NYC. Is authorized teacher of the Schillinger System. Stud. piano, comp., cond. at NY Coll. of Mus., also w. L. Tristano. Pl. w. Army band, 1945-7; Saxie Dowell, '47, various society and jazz jobs, '47-51. Intermittently w. Lee Konitz since 1951, also working as part time driving instructor and as music teacher. Own duo at the Den, NYC '59. One of the best disciples of Tristano, whose piano style his own strongly resembles. Favs: Tristano, Tatum, B. Powell. LPs w. Konitz (q.v.).

Addr: 35 Rochelle Terrace, Mount Vernon, N.Y.

MOSLEY, LAWRENCE LEO (Snub), *trombone, slide saxophone;* b. Little Rock, Ark., 12/29/09. Stud. Cutaire Sch. of Mus., Cincinnati. Worked w. Alphonso Trent 1925-31, Claude Hopkins '34-6, Louis Armstrong '36-7, six months w. Fats Waller '37; formed own combo '38 and became popular as "The Man with the Funny Horn," rec. a tune by that name (about a novelty instrument, the slide saxophone, on which he did a specialty). Many tours for USO: South Pacific, 1945; England, France, Germany, '52; won ten citations from US Govt. and Armed Forces for entertaining troops and was awarded honorary membership in 2nd Army Div. in Korea. Members of his group incl. Frank Galbraith, Budd Johnson. Since 1955 feat. with own trio at Frolic on Seventh Ave. NYC. Fav: T. Dorsey. Own LP on Felsted.

Addr: 555 Edgecombe Ave., New York 32, N.Y.

MOSSE, SANFORD (Sandy), *tenor & alto sax, clarinet;* b. Detroit, Mich., 5/29/29. Mother a singer in Detroit, where he took up clar. 1939. Stud. in Chi. w. Buck Wells, '43, later Chi. Mus. College and arr. w. Bill Russo. After working w. Jimmy Dale, Jay Burkhart, moved to Europe, where he pl. w. Henri Renaud, Django Reinhardt, Wally Bishop, 1951-3. Back in US, worked in Chi. w. Russo, Chubby Jackson, also briefly w. bands of Woody Herman, '53; M. Ferguson, '56; B. Rich, '58; R. Eberle, '59. Highly expressive, well-equipped modern soloist. Fav. own solo: *Chubby's Back* w. Jackson (Argo). Favs: Young, Cohn, Sims, Rollins, E. Miller, Getz. Own LP and LPs w. Cy Touff, James Moody, all on Argo.

Addr: 1320 W. Columbia, Chicago 26, Ill.

MOST, ABRAHAM (Abe), *clarinet, alto sax, flute;* b. New York City, 2/27/20. Clarinet at 9. Prof. debut at 16; own quartet at Kelly's Stable 1939, then two years w. Les Brown, followed by 3½ years in Army '42-5. Later worked w. own group and T. Dorsey; settled in Calif. as studio musician, broadcasting w. Les Brown until 1950, when he joined 20th-Century-Fox. In late '50s, headed his own casual band for club dates, etc. Uses plastic reed for jazz work on clarinet. Fav: Goodman. Own LP on Liberty; LPs w. Henri Rene (Imp.), Dick Haymes, Paul Smith (Cap.).

Addr: 17030 Otsego St., Encino, Calif.

MOST, SAMUEL (Sam), *flute, clarinet, alto sax, piano;* b. Atlantic City, N.J., 12/16/30. Private teachers. To NYC '34; Abe Most, his brother, helped him get started. Pl. w. T. Dorsey, Shep Fields, 1948-9; also w. Boyd Raeburn, Don Redman. Piano, flute w. own quartet off and on from '53, also flute w. Mat Mathews, '54; concert tour w. Teddy Wilson, clar. & flute, '57; tour w. Teddy Charles, '58; w. Jackie Cooper at Roundtable, '58. Agile and inventive flutist. Won DB critics' poll New Star award '54. Own LPs: Beth., Vang.; LPs w. Herbie Mann (Beth.), Angelo Di Pippo (Apollo).

Addr: 562 West 113th St., New York 25, N.Y.

MOTEN, BENNIE, *leader, piano;* b. Kansas City, Mo., 11/13/94; d. 1935. Moten was bandleader in KC from about 1922 until his death, recording first for Okeh in St. Louis 1923, with a small group, and later in the East with a larger band from 1926 on Victor. Among those who worked for him were his brother Buster Moten, on accordion; Jimmy Rushing, singer; Ed Lewis, Hot Lips Page, Joe Keyes, trumpets; Dan Minor, Eddie Durham, trombones; Harlan Leonard, Jack Washington, Eddie Barefield, Ben Webster, Buster Smith, saxes; Count Basie, second piano; Walter Page, bass. After Moten's death the remnants of the band were taken over by Count Basie. LPs on label "X" no longer available.

MOTEN, CLARENCE LEMONT (Benny), *bass;* b. New York City, 11/30/16. Not related to Bennie Moten. Stud. music at Washington Irving High Sch., Tarrytown, N.Y., taking up bass 1934, graduated '36. Local band, then to NYC; worked w. Hot Lips Page, Jerry Jerome, '41; Red Allen '42-9; Eddie South and Stuff Smith trios '50-1; Ivory Joe Hunter '52; Arnett Cobb '53-4, then back w. Red Allen at Metropole, NYC. Six months w. Ella Fitzgerald trio '56, then a year w. Wilbur De Paris, incl. African tour in '57. LPs w. Red Allen (Bruns.), *At Newport* (Verve); De Paris (Atl.).

Addr: 208-03 47th Ave., Bayside 61, L.I., N.Y.

MOTIAN, STEPHEN PAUL, *drums;* also *guitar;* b. Providence, R.I., 3/25/31. Began on guitar in Providence 1949. Upon discharge from service in '54, gigged around NYC and stud. at Manhattan Sch. of Music. Worked w. G. Wallington, Jerry Wald, Russell Jacquet '56; Tony Scott '56 and early '57, again in May '58; Oscar Pettiford, May-June '57, Zoot Sims '58, Lennie Tristano, Aug.-Oct. '58, Feb., Mar., Aug. '59, Al Cohn-Zoot Sims '59 at Half Note, NYC and RIJF, Bill Evans '59-60. Favs: Kenny Clarke, Philly Joe Jones, Roach. LPs w. George Russell, Tony Scott (Vict.), Bill Evans (River.), Eddie Costa (Coral, Inter.), Don Elliot (Decca), Cohn-Sims (UA), Warne Marsh (Atl.).

Addr: 14 West 71st St., New York 23, N.Y.

MOTTOLA, ANTHONY CHARLES (Tony), *guitar, composer;* b. Kearny, N.J., 4/18/18. Early training from father, later classical guitar w. Prof. D. Vallilio of Rome. Prof. debut w. Geo. Hall orch. '39-41. CBS staff to '46, then free-lance radio, recording, TV in NYC. Celebrated for composing and playing solo background music on CBS-TV dramatic show *Danger.* Scored and played solo background for film *Violated.* TV and LPs w. Perry Como, Ray Charles Singers. Fine Spanish and electric guitarist. Favs: Segovia, Ch. Christian. Own LPs: Kapp, Camden, Allegro, Command; LPs w. Ray Charles Singers (MGM, Decca).

Addr: 59 Clinton Avenue, Arlington, N.J.

MOZIAN, ROGER KING, *trumpet, leader;* b. New York City, 6/30/27. Own combo in upstate N.Y. "borscht belt" 1941-3. Army '44-5, then extensive Schillinger studies; club dates and tours with Louis Prima, Raymond Scott, Larry Clinton, Carmen Cavallaro, then started playing and arranging mostly with Latin bands incl. Tito Rodriguez. Wrote *Asia Minor* for Machito. Started own band, featuring own Latin and jazz arrangements, April '54. Rec. for Clef. With Decca since '57. In late '50s his band was together only occasionally for college dates in and around NY area. Mozian has occupied himself for the most part with arranging for dance acts and Latin bands such as Tito Puente and Johnny Conquet. LPs: Decca.

Addr: 7 Winthrop Ave., Yonkers, N.Y.

MUCCI, LOUIS RAPHAEL (Lou), *trumpet;* b. Syracuse, N.Y., 1/13/09. Began study of baritone horn at 10, switched to trumpet at 16. Went on road w. Don Gregory's band. With Red Norvo-Mildred Bailey in 1937 when E. Sauter switched to arr. With Glenn Miller '38-9, B. Chester '40-1, Coast Guard band '43-6 (toured Italy). Joined B. Goodman upon discharge, then w. C. Thornhill two years. Has done free-lance and studio work since 1951, and from '57-9 he worked closely with the training of musicians for Marshall Brown's various orchestral projects in connection with the NJF; also appeared and recorded w. Gil Evans' orch.

Addr: 325 W. 45th St., New York 36, N.Y.

MULLENS, EDWARD (Moon), *trumpet, composer;* b. Mayhew, Miss., 5/11/16. Moved to Chicago while still a boy. Played w. Frankie Jaxon, Earl Bostic and Hot Lips Page w. whom he made record debut in 1938. Also worked w. Benny Carter before and after the war, Louis Armstrong, '46-7, Cab Calloway and tenor man Joe Thomas. Joined Lionel Hampton December '49 and was with him almost continuously until late '59 when he joined Duke Ellington. LPs w. Hampton and Ellington.

Addr: 2861 Exterior St., Bronx 53, N.Y.

MULLIGAN, GERALD JOSEPH (Gerry), *baritone sax, composer, piano;* b. New York City, 4/6/27. Raised in Philadelphia, where he earned early experience writing for Johnny Warrington's radio band on WCAU. Came to NYC, joined Gene Krupa, who recorded his *Disc Jockey Jump* in Jan. 1947. Played w. Miles Davis' nine-piece band at Royal Roost 1948, recorded w. him for Capitol and wrote some of the arrangements, notably *Jeru, Boplicity, Venus De Milo, Godchild.* Worked with Elliot Lawrence in 1950 and was featured in jazz combo within the band; Lawrence recorded his *Elevation.* Later he wrote and played w. Claude Thornhill, then moved to California in 1952. In the fall of that year he began experimenting with the idea of a pianoless quartet, the original personnel comprising Chet Baker, trumpet; Chico Hamilton, drums, and Bob Whitlock, bass. Recording for local labels, the group rose with extraordinary rapidity to national eminence among jazz combos. Subsequent sidemen included Bob Brookmeyer on valve trombone, replaced by Jon Eardley on trumpet; Red Mitchell joined the group in 1954 and Frank Isola was the drummer during most of that year. In June 1954 his quartet took part in the Jazz Festival in Paris. Led a sextet 1955-8, with which he played engagements early in '56 in Italy and at the Olympia Theatre in Paris; toured Britain April '57. Appeared as a single in two groups on *The Sound of Jazz* CBS-TV Dec. '57. Appeared regularly at the NJF since its inception in 1954. In April '58 formed a new group featuring Art Farmer on trumpet and appeared on the Timex jazz show, CBS-TV; also in film *Jazz On A Summer's Day.* In 1958 he was seen and heard in the film *I Want to Live.* The group remained together for a year, after which Mulligan and Farmer went to Hollywood to take part in a film, The *Subterraneans.* In March '60, he formed a 13-piece band in NYC.

Has won many polls, incl. *DB* readers' poll each year since 1953; *Metronome* Readers' poll each year since '54; readers' polls in *Melody Maker* (England) since 1955; *Jazz Hot* (France) since 1956, *Jazz Echo* (Germany) since 1956; Muziek Express (Holland) since '58. Won *DB* critics' poll 1957 and tied w. Harry Carney 1959; *Playboy* polls since 1958; first place in New Star division of Musicians' Musicians poll in *Encyclopedia Yearbook of Jazz* 1956.

In addition to creating a combo with a new and provocative tone color, Mulligan enriched the modern jazz palette with some excellent arrangements, always melodically attractive and swingingly orchestrated, for the bands of Kenton (*Young Blood,* etc.), Thornhill and others.

Own LPs: *Paris Concert* (Wor. Pac. 1210), *California Concerts* (Wor. Pac. 1201), *Mainstream of Jazz* (Em. 36101), *Modern Sounds* (Cap. T691), Mulligan Sextet (Em. 36056), *Mulligan Plays Mulligan* (Pres. 7006), Quartet (Wor. Pac. 1207), *Quartet in Boston* (Wor. Pac. 1228), Quartet (Fant. 3220), *Reunion w. Chet Baker* (Wor. Pac. 1241), *Song Book, Vol. 1* (Wor. Pac. 1237), *What Is There To Say?* (Col. CL 1307), Quartet (GNP 26), *Profile* (Merc. 20453), *Jazz Combo from I Want to Live* (UA 4006); also *Gerry Mulligan-Paul Desmond Quartet* (Verve 8246), *Getz Meets Mulligan in Hi-Fi* (Verve 8249), *Teddy Wilson and Gerry Mulligan at Newport* (Verve 8235), *Lee Konitz with the Gerry Mulligan Quartet* (Wor. Pac. 1273), *Mulligan Meets Monk* (River. 12-247), Annie Ross with the Gerry Mulligan Quartet (Wor. Pac. 1253). LPs w. Manny Albam (Coral 57173), Johnny Mandel, *I Want To Live* (UA 4005), Miles Davis (Cap. T762); *Jazz Concerto Grosso* (ABC-Par. 225); one duet w. Harry Carney in *Duke Ellington at Newport* (Col. CL 1245), four tracks w. Brew Moore in *Lestorian Mode* (Savoy 12105), four tracks w. Kai Winding in *Trombone By Three* (Pres. 7023).

Addr: c/o Associated Booking, 745 Fifth Ave., New York 22, N.Y.

MUNDY, JAMES (Jimmy), *composer;* b. Cincinnati, O., 6/28/07. Started on violin at six; played many other instruments but worked mainly as a tenor saxman, first in Chicago 1926-9, w. Erskine Tate, Carroll Dickerson; and principally w. Earl Hines, playing and writing (arrs. incl. *Cavernism, Copenhagen*), 1929-36. Beginning in 1935 he wrote frequently for Benny Goodman, his best-known arrs. incl. *Madhouse, Jam Session, Swingtime in the Rockies,* '35-6; *Jumpin' at the Woodside, One Sweet Letter from You,* '39; *Solo Flight, Air Mail Special, Fiesta in Blue,* '41. Also arr. for Count Basie *Super Chief, Feather Merchant, Louisiana,* etc. Had his own band in NYC Nov. '39-Jan. '40. Arr. for Paul Whiteman '40-2; Army '43-5, then free-lance arrs. for numerous commercial bands in NYC and Hollywood, incl. Gene Ammons-Sonny Stitt. In 1959 he took up residence in Paris, working as a musical director for Barclay Disques. One of the best arrangers produced in the swing era; his best works included *Queer Street* and *Blue Skies* for Basie in 1945. LP: Epic.

Addr: c/o Barclay Disques, 143 Avenue de Neuilly, Neuilly sur Seine, France.

MURANYI, JOSEPH PAUL (Joe), *clarinet;* b. Martins Ferry, Ohio, 1/14/28. Of Hungarian descent; parents sang old Magyar melodies and he had his first playing jobs w. symphonic balalaika orch. Used to play ukulele, alto sax, tarogato. Stud. w. L. Tristano and at Manh. Sch. of Mus. Pl. cl. 3 yrs. w. Air Force band. Gigs w. Danny Barker, Red Onion Jazz Band. Has worked for some years as producer at record companies incl. RCA, Beth., Atl. LPs w. Red Onion Band (Elek., Riv.), Barker (Per.), Shel Silverstein (Elek.).

Addr: 205 West 13th St., New York 11, N.Y.

MURPHY, LYLE (Spud), *composer, saxes;* b. Salt Lake City, Utah, 8/19/08. Clarinet from early childhood; at 14, stud. trumpet w. Red Nichols' father. Clarinet on ship's band between US and China. Sax w. Jimmy Joy 1927-8, Ross Gorman '28. Arr. for Tracy-Brown orch. '29-30. Sax & arr. w. Austin Wylie '30-1, Jan Garber '31-2, Mal Hallett '33, Joe Haymes '34. Many arrs. for Benny Goodman and Glen Gray, 1935-7, incl. *Jingle Bells, Get Happy* for Goodman. Led own band 1938-41; weekly jazz show on WJZ 1940. After settling in Hollywood and doing free-lance arr., he developed his own 12-tone system to make an unexpected and successful return to jazz in 1954-5. Students of his system incl. Curtis Counce, Oscar Peterson, Alvin Stoller, Gerald Wiggins. Favs: Giuffre, Niehaus, other modern musicians. Own LPs: *New Orbits in Sound* (GNP), *12 Tone Jazz* (Contemp.).

Addr: P.O. Box 3031, Hollywood 28, Calif.

MURPHY, MELVIN E. (Turk), *trombone, composer, leader;* b. Palermo, Cal., 12/16/15. Studied harmony, theory, taught self cornet, then trombone. Worked as trombonist and arranger with Mal Hallett, Will Osborne; played and sang with Merle Howard. Helped with organization of the Lu Watters band and made his record debut with this group for Jazz Man label 1941; enjoyed great popularity around San Francisco through the 1940s with Watters. In 1951 he played with Marty Marsala, also on and off from 1947 had his own band for recordings and night clubs. In 1954 he became a nationally known jazz name through Columbia records, and came to NYC, playing at Childs Restaurant.

In Oct. '55 Murphy's group played a three-day jazz festival in New Orleans; the performance was recorded and released on Col. CL 793. The group appeared at NJF July '57, enjoyed a tremendous success at the Bourbon Street club NYC, then returned to SF where for a while he had his own club, Easy Street. He has continued to work successfully in night clubs catering to traditionalist jazz fans, always using a combo without drums and featuring banjo.

Murphy, who names as his favorite musicians Kid Ory, Roy Palmer, Jelly Roll Morton (as an arranger) and Sauter & Finegan, along with "many of the progressive school," has been an outspoken opponent of the conventional neo-Dixieland jazz of the Eddie Condon variety, preferring to use lesser-known material in place of the usual standard tunes. He described his ambition, in 1954, as the furthering of his studies with the object of writing for musical fields outside his own. Own LPs on Good Time Jazz, Col., Verve.

Addr: 729 Chestnut St., San Francisco 11, Calif.

MURTAUGH, JOHN, *saxophones;* b. Minneapolis, Minn., 10/30/27. BM from U. of Mich. 1950. Pl. w. C. Thornhill '51, T. Beneke '52, Les Elgart '54-5; has been active in pop field, with house band at Copacabana etc. Favs: Parker, Young, Hawkins. Fav. own solos on *Bobby Scott with Two Horns* (ABC-Par.).

Addr: 67 Palm Lane, Westbury, L.I., N.Y.

MUSSO, VIDO, *tenor sax;* b. Carrini, Sicily, 1/17/13. Raised in Detroit, Mich. from 1920, moved to LA '30, and worked there w. local bands. First prominent w. Benny Goodman '36-8; Gene Krupa '38; Harry James '40-1; back w. Goodman '41; Woody Herman late '42; Stan Kenton '45-7. Between these dates he made frequent attempts to become a band leader, but most of the ventures were short-lived. In recent years he has been free-lancing in Calif., usually leading his own combo. Using a full tone in the Hawkins style and playing in a somewhat fulsome manner, Musso earned considerable popularity during the '40s and won the *Down Beat* poll in '43, '46, and '47. LPs w. Goodman (Vict., MGM, Col.), Kenton (Cap.), Wardell Gray (Mod.); four tracks w. own group in *Loaded* (Savoy).

Addr: 7424 Crenshaw, Los Angeles 43, Calif.

MUSSOLINI, ROMANO, *piano;* b. Carpena (Forli), Italy, 9/26/27. Fourth son of Benito Mussolini. Interested in jazz from childhood, heard US records bought by jazz-fan brothers. After father was killed by partisans in '45 and most of family was killed or fled Italy, he was sent into exile with mother, sister, to Ischia; while seriously ill there, took up piano and accordion as hobby. Self-taught. Originally modeled style on Shearing, later played more percussively in Previn style. Pl. at first Intl. Jazz Fest. in San Remo '56. Turned down many offers to play abroad, cont. to live in Rome in near-poverty after return from exile; works in wood-trade co. for living. Pl. w. Lars Gullin in combo at Viareggio, summer '59; toured Italy w. Gullin, Chet Baker in Caterina Valente show. Rec. for RCA w. Nunzio Rotondo, Lilian Terry.

MUSSULLI, HENRY W. (Boots), *alto, baritone sax;* b. Milford, Mass., 11/18/17. St. on alto and clar. when 12. Pl. w. several bands around Boston incl. Mal Hallett. Replaced Fazola in Teddy Powell's orch. in '42. With Stan Kenton '44, Vido Musso All Stars '47, Gene Krupa '48, Chas. Ventura '49, Kenton '52. Teaching and playing in Mass. '53-4. Pl. alto and baritone on Kenton concert tour, fall '54. Active in late '50s in Boston and Providence, pl. Storyville frequently w. Toshiko and other combos, and w. Herb Pomeroy's band at the Stable; also several concerts in leading New England colleges. Has own school, gives 60 private lessons a week; also ran jazz club in Milford, Mass. '59.

Favs: Hodges, Carter, Parker, Konitz, Mariano, Jimmy Dorsey. Own LP on Cap.; w. Serge Chaloff (Cap.), Pomeroy (Roul.), Toshiko (Story.), Vido Musso (Sav.).

Addr: 6 Pond St., Milford, Mass.

MYERS, HUBERT MAXWELL (Bumps), *tenor sax;* b. Clarksburg, W. Va., 8/22/12. Raised in Calif. from age 9. With Earl Whaley in Seattle 1929; in LA w. Curtis Mosby, Charlie Echols. Went to China w. Buck Clayton and Teddy Weatherford, 1934; stayed in Shanghai 18 months. From '36, heard in LA w. Lionel Hampton, Les Hite; to NYC w. Lee and Lester Young, '42; Jimmie Lunceford band for a short while, Benny Carter 1943 until entered Army. Continued to work off and on w. Carter, but was mainly confined to r & b work, pop record sessions, etc. that failed to give exposure to his exciting, big-toned style in the Hawkins tradition. Fav: Don Byas. LPs w. Benny Carter (Audio Lab); one track w. Benny Goodman in *History of Jazz, Vol. 3* (Cap.).

Addr: 1404 S. Hobart, Los Angeles 6, Calif.

N

NANCE, WILLIS (Ray), *trumpet, violin, singer;* b. Chicago, Ill., 12/10/13. Studied privately. Active as night club entertainer and bandleader from 1932, he played w. Earl Hines 1938; Horace Henderson 1939. Replaced Cootie Williams w. Duke Ellington band in 1940 and has remained in the band ever since, except for an absence of 9 months during 1944 when he led his own trio.

Nance has been known primarily as a comedy personality in the Ellington band. Because of an excessive accent on grotesque visual mannerisms he has obscured the fact that he is one of the most brilliant and versatile musicians in jazz, endowed with a trumpet tone sometimes as soulful as Berigan's, and capable of swinging on the violin like very few other modern jazzmen. He is also a rhythmic vocalist of exceptional talent. Won Esq. New Star Award as violinist, 1945. LPs: see Duke Ellington; also w. Johnny Hodges (Verve), Eddie Heywood (Coral), Earl Hines (Gr. Award).

Addr: Dawn Hotel, 65 St. Nicholas Place, New York 31, N.Y.

NANRI, FUMIO, *trumpet;* b. Saga Prefecture, Japan, 12/24/10. Played in Boys' Brass Band of Takashimaya Department Store, Kobe, 1925. One of his country's first distinguished jazzmen, called by Louis Armstrong "the Satchmo of Japan," he played in Shanghai 1929-30, visited US for six months in '32 and played for Japanese troops in China '42-4, otherwise has been seen mainly in Japan, where a film was produced (*Arashio Yobu Yujo,* or *Friendship Causes a Storm*) based on the story of his life. Seen on Japanese TV quiz shows, many other TV and radio programs incl. *This is Dixie.* Lost his eyesight a few years ago but has recovered it partially; his 30th anniversary in music was celebrated Dec. '58 in big tribute by music profession at Nichigeki Theatre. Favs: Armstrong, Nichols, Beiderbecke.

Addr: 483 Notomicho, Saga-gun, Saga Prefecture, Japan.

NANTON, MORRIS, *piano;* b. Perth Amboy, N.J., 9/28/29. Stud. piano privately, then att. Juilliard 1949-53. Had own trio from 1956, working club dates and rec. Fav: Oscar Peterson. Own LPs: *Flower Drum Song, Roberta* (War. Bros.); w. *Piano Jazz Quartet* (War. Bros.).

Addr: 219 Grant Street, Perth Amboy, N.J.

NANTON, JOSEPH (Tricky Sam), *trombone;* b. New York City, 2/1/04; d. San Francisco, 7/21/48. Started in 1921 w. Cliff Jackson. Frazier's Harmony Five 1923-4; Elmer Snowden 1925; Duke Ellington from 1926 until his death. Nanton, who specialized in the use of the rubber plunger, set a style from his "wa-wa" solos that was comparable with Bubber Miley's trumpet effects, giving the instrument an almost human sound. Nickname was given him by Otto Hardwicke. On some of the earlier Ellington records he played open solos, with a full tone and forceful style. Among his best-known contributions on record were *Black and Tan Fantasy, Echoes of the Jungle, Jack the Bear, Ko Ko, A Portrait of Bert Williams, Chloe,* and the *Work Song* passage from *Black, Brown and Beige.* LPs: see Ellington.

NAPIER, WILLIAM JAMES (Bill), *clarinet;* b. Asheville, N.C., 8/9/26. Parents both in show business. Self-taught. Led own trio in Sausalito, Calif., 1949. Played w. Turk Murphy, '50-2, then with various Dixieland groups, mainly around SF, but also in Chicago and Eastern cities. With Dixieland Rhythm Kings, '52-4; worked at Hangover Club, SF w. Wingy Manone, Joe Sullivan, Marty Marsala, '54; Bob Scobey, '54. Favs: Barney Bigard, Jimmie Noone et al. LPs w. Turk Murphy, Bob Scobey (GTJ, Verve), Gene Mayl (River.).

NAPOLEON, MARTY, *piano;* b. Brooklyn, N.Y., 6/2/21. Played w. Bob Astor 1941, Chico Marx '42, then w. Georgie Auld, Joe Venuti, Teddy Powell, Lee Castle, Ch. Barnet. Replaced his brother Teddy in Gene Krupa band '46. After working w. his uncle Phil Napoleon, he pl. in Charlie Ventura's big band '50, and w. the Big Four (Buddy Rich, Ventura, Chubby Jackson) '51. Replaced Earl Hines in Louis Armstrong combo '52. Made Hawaiian tour w. Armstrong Feb. '52, European tour Sept. '53. In Dec. '55 formed two-piano quartet with brother Teddy, then own group at Metropole, NYC '56-8; w. Coleman Hawkins-Charlie Shavers at same club '58-9. Led own trio '59-60. App. on Timex jazz spectaculars and 18 weeks on Art Ford's Jazz Party on TV. Pl. at Great South Bay, Stony Brook, Randall's Island jazz festivals in late '50s. Fav: Oscar Peterson. Own LPs on Stere-o-craft, Everest; LPs w. Charlie Ventura (Verve), Red Allen (Vict.), *Golden Era Of Dixieland Jazz,* Vol. 2 (Design); four tracks w. Kai Winding in *In The Beginning . . . Bebop* (Savoy).

Addr: 1937 West 11th St., Brooklyn 23, N.Y.

NAPOLEON, PHIL, *trumpet, leader;* b. Boston, Mass., 9/2/01. Famous during 1920s as leader of the Original Memphis Five w. Miff Mole on trombone; Jimmy Lytell, clarinet; Frank Signorelli, piano; Jack Roth, drums. Many records during 1920s with such groups as the Charleston Chasers, the Cotton Pickers and his own Napoleon's Emperors. For many years he also worked w. commercial dance bands such as Sam Lanin's, and w. radio orchestras. From 1949 he was active in jazz again, leading his own combo and using the "Memphis Five" name, at Nick's in Greenwich Village etc. He appeared at NJF in July 1959, coming there from Florida, where he had been living and playing much of the time in recent years. Own LPs: *Dixieland Classics* (Em.).

Addr: 13255 N.E. 4th Ave., North Miami, Fla.

NAPOLEON, TEDDY GEORGE, *piano;* b. Brooklyn, N.Y., 1/23/14. Nephew of Phil Napoleon. St. in same band as Lee Castle in a Chinese restaurant 1943. Toured w. Tommy Tompkins band for three years, then free-lanced around 52nd St. w. Sande Williams society band. In early '40s played w. Johnny Messner, Bob Chester. Joined Gene Krupa in 1944 and was with him off and on until 1958, also working w. Flip Phillips, Bill Harris and various combos in NYC. Toured Japan and Sweden w. Krupa trio '52, Australia '54. Settled in

Florida '59, leading own trio. Fav: O. Peterson. LPs w. Krupa (Verve).

Addr: 1271 N.E. 159th St., N. Miami Beach, Fla.

NASH, RICHARD TAYLOR (Dick), *trombone;* b. Somerville, Mass., 1/26/28. Brother, Ted Nash, gave him his first horn. Started w. Sam Donahue 1947, then w. Glen Gray, Tex Beneke. In service Oct. '50-Oct. '52; to Japan, Korea w. Army band. W. Billy May until July '53, then settled in LA as soloist and part-time arr. on CBS staff until '57. Free-lance since then, pl. for 20th Century Fox and Universal pictures; Peter Gunn, Steve Allen TV shows. Fav: Jay Jay Johnson. LPs w. Ted Nash (Col.), *The Brothers Nash* (Lib.), Hank Mancini (Vict.).

Addr: 8841 Quakertown Ave., Northridge, Cal.

NASH, THEODORE MALCOLM (Ted), *tenor sax, flute, piccolo;* b. Somerville, Mass., 10/31/22. Mother was concert singer. Nash, who had no formal training other than school, went on the road at 17. He was w. Ralph Webster 1939; Joe Hart, Enoch Light '40; Dick Rogers, Johnny Long, Clyde Lucas '41; Horace Heidt '42; Phil Harris '43; Shep Fields '44. Best known as feat. soloist w. Les Brown '44-6 and Jerry Gray '47-52, he has been heard (mostly on records) w. dozens of name bands while living in LA, among them Bob Crosby, Dave Barbour, Pete Rugolo, Ray Anthony. He has also worked frequently on TV (*Peter Gunn, Staccato, I Love Lucy,* etc.) and in movies (*Hole In The Head, Some Came Running, Big Circus*). Member of Board of Directors of three development corporations specializing in subdividing property, building of homes, apartment buildings, etc. Wrote book on high harmonics for saxophone pub. by Leeds Mus. Best known records w. Les Brown; *I've Got My Love To Keep Me Warm, Leap Frog, Twilight Time, Lovers' Leap.* Fav: Getz. Own LP on Col., *The Brothers Nash* (Lib.); LPs w. Hank Mancini (Vict.), Billy May (Cap.), Les Brown (Col.), tracks in *Tenor Sax* (Concord).

Addr: 18056 Karen Drive, Encino, Calif.

NASSER, JAMIL: see JOYNER, George

NAURA, MICHAEL, *piano;* b. Memel, Lithuania (now in Russia), 8/19/34. Self-taught. Stud. sociology, philosophy at Free Univ. in Berlin. Starting playing with quintet at jazz club in Berlin, 1953. Leader of own group since 1956, chosen by German critics as best modern jazz combo in the country. Many broadcasts incl. monthly programs on Norddeutscher Rundfunk, Hamburg. Fav. own solo *Angel Eyes* in *Down To Earth* on Telefunken. Favs: Hank Jones, John Lewis, Carl Perkins.

Addr: Lübeck, Mühlenstr. II, Germany.

NAVARRO, THEODORE (Fats), *trumpet;* b. Key West, Fla., 9/24/23; d. NYC, 7/7/50. Piano at 6, trumpet at 13; little tuition. Played tenor sax for a while, with Walter Johnson's band in Miami. After working with Snookum Russell in 1941-2, he was first heard extensively in the North and East as a member of Andy Kirk's band in '43-4. On Dizzy Gillespie's recommendation, he was hired by Billy Eckstine, with whose band he remained for 18 months. According to Eckstine, "A week or two after he'd joined us, you'd hardly know Diz had left the band. His ideas and feelings were the same and there was just as much swing."

In '47-8 Navarro was with Illinois Jacquet, and briefly with Tommy Reynolds, Lionel Hampton and Coleman Hawkins. He worked sporadically with Tadd Dameron in '48-9, but was semi-inactive for more than a year before his death, gigging now and then at Birdland. Narcotics addiction and tuberculosis were among the causes of his death.

Navarro, in the opinion of most of the fellow-modernists who came up in the bop era of the 1940s, ranked with Gillespie and Davis as one of the gifted and original stylists produced by that phase of the development of jazz. His cleanness of execution and purity of tone were extraordinary, reaching their peak in the series of sides he recorded for Blue Note.

Navarro, who was nicknamed "Fat Girl" (one of his records bore this title), recorded innumerable dates with small bop groups between 1946 and '49, including one unique side with a Benny Goodman Sextet, *Stealin' Apples* (Capitol). His best LPs are Blue Note 1531 and 1532; other own LPs on Savoy; also tracks w. various groups in *In The Beginning . . . Bebop, Opus De Bop* (Savoy); LPs w. Billy Eckstine (Em.), *Saturday Night Swing Session* (Ctpt.), Metronome All Stars (Cam.).

NEIDLINGER, BUELL, *bass;* b. Westport, Conn., 3/2/36. Stud. piano, trumpet, cello; self-taught on bass. Had own band in high school. Att. Yale for a year, became a disc jockey, then came to NYC 1955. Gigged w. Vic Dickenson, Zoot Sims, Tony Scott, Coleman Hawkins. Pl. w. Cecil Taylor at Five Spot '57. With Tony Bennett for six months; later free-lanced around NYC. W. Gil Evans at Birdland 1959. Favs: Ray Brown, Blanton, Percy Heath, Wilbur Ware.

LPs w. Cecil Taylor (Contemp., UA), Steve Lacy (Pres., New Jazz).

NELSON, DAVE, *trumpet, piano;* b. Donaldsonville, La., 1905; d. NYC, 4/7/46. Nephew of King Oliver; came to Chicago w. Oliver but didn't play w. the band except for rec. dates in NYC. With Marie Lucas, Jelly Roll Morton, Richard Jones in 1920s. Had own combo for a while; rec. w. Ida Cox and Ma Rainey. Pl. w. Luis Russell, Jimmie Noone; rec. w. Oliver and w. Oliver's men under title of Dave Nelson and the King's Men for Victor. During '40s until his death he played solo piano and had own combo; also worked as music editor and arr. for publishing firm.

NELSON, LOUIS DELISLE (Big Eye), *clarinet;* b. New Orleans, 1/28/1885; d. New Orleans, 8/20/49. Father a butcher. Stud. w. Lorenzo and Louis Tio. Pl. at Club 28 w. Buddy Bolden. Pl. in string band 1903; was soon adept on harmonica, guitar, bass, banjo and violin as well as clarinet. Pl. w. Golden Rule Orch. 1904; Imperial Band '07, Marrero's Superior Band 1910; repl. Picou in Olympia Band. Later worked for King Oliver ca. 1911, then replaced Geo. Baquet in Freddie Keppard's Original Creole Orch. 1917. Worked in NO in various cabarets during early 1920s but was almost completely out of music for 25 years, though he rec. w. Kid Rena in 1940. In '46 Belgian critic Robert Goffin found him working as a doorman; in an interview w. Goffin he debunked Bunk Johnson's claim to have played with Bolden. Nelson rec. a few sides under the name of Louis Delisle in the late '40s. Though the paucity of recorded evidence makes it impossible to assess his work accurately, he was said to have been one of the foremost clarinetists in the early New Orleans period. LPs: Amer. Mus. (own group); tracks in *New Orleans Legends* (River.).

NELSON, OLIVER EDWARD, *alto & tenor saxes, flute, composer;* b. St. Louis, Mo., 6/4/32. Brother pl. alto w. Cootie Williams in '40s; sister pl. piano w. combo in St. Louis. Stud. piano at 6, saxophone at 11. First job while still in grade school. Worked w. Jeter-Pillars and George Hudson orchs. '47-8; Nat Towles '49; Louis Jordan big band '50-1. While in Marines '52-4, pl. in 3rd Division Band, also in officers' clubs in Japan. Stud. composition and theory at Washington U. '54-7, Lincoln U. '57-8; then to NYC where he pl. w. Erskine Hawkins, Wild Bill Davis and Louis Bellson '59. Has also stud. embalming and taxidermy; worked as streetcar and bus driver in St. Louis. Favs: Parker, Coltrane; comp; Gil Evans, George Russell; imp. infl: Hodges, Byas, Rollins; comp: Strayhorn. A virile, straightforward swinger, he is also touched by Wardell Gray and Jimmy Forrest. Own LP: New Jazz; LP w. Bellson (Verve).

Addr: 111-44 179th St., St. Albans, L.I., N.Y.

NEREM, BJARNE ARNULF, *tenor sax;* also *clarinet;* b. Oslo, Norway, 7/31/23. Father, a tailor, has been an amateur concert clarinetist since 1910. Studied clarinet with father at age 15. Played at several jam sessions and was offered a job w. band in restaurant in '47. With Willy Andresen '47, Karl Westbye '49 in Norway; Thore Jederby '47, Nisse Skoogh '48, Simon Brehm '51, Ernie Englund '54, Ove Lind '58, Aake Persson and Anders Burman '59 in Sweden. Worked on Norwegian-American Line, Oslo to NYC '49. "Originally a tailor, Bjarne Nerem is *the* outstanding tenor player in Scandinavia and enjoys tremendous respect in every field connected with jazz."—Carl-Erik Lindgren. Favs: Lester Young, Stan Getz, Art Tatum. Fav. own solos: *Laura* w. Harry Arnold, *Cocktails For Two* w. Ernie Englund on Metronome (Swed.). LPs w. Arnold (Merc.), Roy Haynes in *Jazz Abroad* (Em.), Stan Getz (Verve).

Addr: Västmannagatan 77, Stockholm, Sweden.

NERO, KURT PAUL, *violin, composer;* b. Hamburg, Germany, 4/29/17; d. Los Angeles, Calif., 3/21/58. Father a violin teacher in New York, founder of Violin Teachers' Guild. Extensive studies incl. scholarship to Curtis Institute, arr. w. Johnny Warrington, conducting w. Fritz Reiner. Worked with dance bands incl. Jan Savitt, 1937 and Gene Krupa, '45; symphony orchs. incl. Pittsburgh Symph. '39; soloist with New York Phil. '45. Leader of US Navy dance band in Washington, '42-4. From '48 until his death, was in commercial radio etc. on West Coast. Active intermittently writing and playing in jazz, he was a licensed pilot and used to say, "I enjoy flying, with or without an airplane." Like Joe Venuti, he was known as much for his quicksilver personality as for his remarkable musicianship. His best known composition was *The Hot Canary.* Favorite violinists were Joe Venuti, Johnny Frigo and Eddie South. After suffering from mental illness for several years, Nero died suddenly in his doctor's office. His LPs, now hard to come by, were on Capitol and Sunset.

NEVES, JOHN, *bass;* b. Mansfield, Mass., 10/22/30. Father pl. guitar, violin. Stud. in Revere, Mass. 1955. Got into music business through brother, Paul, a pianist and violinist. Worked w. Bobby Scott trio; Boots Mussulli in Milford, Mass; three years at Jazz Workshop in Boston w. Herb Pomeroy. While in service pl. in Korea '53. w. George Shearing '58, Paul Neves trio in Cambridge, Mass. '59. Favs: Brown, Heath, Pettiford, Chambers, Red Mitchell. LPs w. Pomeroy (UA, Roul.).

Addr: 22 Blagden St., Boston 16, Mass.

NEWBORN, EDWIN CALVIN, *guitar;* also *piano, flute, piccolo;* b. Memphis, Tenn., 4/27/33. Father is band director; brother, Phineas, pianist; wife, Wanda, trombonist. Stud. Booker T. Washington High Sch. in Memphis; Le-Moyne College. Pl. with Tuff Green's Rocketeers 1951-2; father's band and Roy Milton, '53; again with father '54-6, then worked in quart. formed by brother, Phineas. With Earl Hines '59. Rec. debut in Memphis w. his brother on Peacock label. Favs: Barney Kessel, Tal Farlow. LPs w. Phineas Newborn (Atl.), *Down Home Reunion* (UA).

NEWBORN, PHINEAS JR., *piano;* also *trumpet, ten. sax, vibes, Fr. horn, bar. horn;* b. Whiteville, Tenn., 12/14/31. Father is drummer and leader; mother plays piano, sings. Stud. privately, also at high school and Tenn. State U. Played w. Saunders King, 1947; many local bands in Memphis, '45-50, Lionel Hampton, '50 and '52, Tennessee State Collegians, '50-52, Willis Jackson, '53, Army, '53-5; toured state of Florida making radio and TV appearances for recruiting drive. After many years mainly in rhythm and blues and under his father's influence, he broke away to make what he considered his real start in jazz with his own quartet, '55-6, bringing it to New York for an appearance at Basin Street in May, '56. Newborn has since worked mainly with his own trio, but in Feb. '58 he worked as a duo w. Ch. Mingus, and made a movie with him, John Cassavetes' *Shadows.* In Oct. '58 he toured England and the Continent with the *Jazz from Carnegie Hall* show; in Apr. '59 he made a brief tour of Italy with local sidemen and the Mills Bros.

Newborn for a while in '56 was the darling of several jazz critics, many of whom soon were disillusioned; it was often claimed that he lacked emotional communication, though Nat Hentoff wrote that "he probably has more command of the piano technically than any of his jazz contemporaries" and Ralph Gleason that "he is one of the most impressive pianists to emerge in recent years." In '59-60, under the influence of New York jazzmen, his style became less flamboyant. Own LPs: Atlantic, Victor, Roulette; other LPs: *Down Home Reunion* (UA), *We Three* w. Roy Haynes (New Jazz).

Addr: 62 West 91st Street, New York 24, N.Y.

NEWMAN, DAVID (Fathead), *alto & tenor saxes;* b. Dallas, Tex., 2/24/33. Earned nickname from his music teacher after fumbling an arpeggio. Gigged w. local bands incl. Buster Smith's; soon worked w. Lowell Fulson and other r & b groups, 1952-3; with T-Bone Walker '54, then joined Ray Charles. Used to work mainly on tenor and baritone because of r & b band requirements, but his main instrument is alto. Began to attract attention with Charles in jazz circles, playing Carnegie Hall concert late '57, NJF '58; recorded album under his own name '59. Like Charles himself, Newman has transcended his r & b background to earn a place in jazz as a soloist with a strong beat and funky quality combined with growing elements of individual tone and style. Favs: Parker, Rollins, Stitt. Own LP and LPs with Ray Charles: Atlantic.

Addr: 2306 Lowery Street, Dallas, Texas.

NEWMAN, JOSEPH DWIGHT (Joe), *trumpet;* b. New Orleans, 9/7/22. Father, a pianist, led Creole Serenaders at old Absinthe House, did pioneer radio shows in early 20s. Discovered by Lionel Hampton in Collegians band at Alabama State Teachers College. With Hamp '41-3. Joined Count Basie Dec. 1943, remained with him off and on to 1946, then with J. C. Heard band and Illinois Jacquet 1947. Rejoined Basie Jan. 1952 and has been with him continuously, though in Oct. 1958, while the band was on vacation, he led a sextet of Basie men that played a brief Scandinavian tour. Newman, one of the most talented of modern soloists, played in a style closer to straight bop in the 1940s and has since then evolved what might be called a neutralist-modern approach. Because he has been extremely active on records, the following list is highly selective and includes only records still likely to be available: Own LPs: *Happy Cats, Soft Swingin' Jazz* (Coral), *With Woodwinds* (Roul.), *Salute to Satch,* (Vict.), *Locking Horns w. Zoot Sims* (Roul.); LPs w. Basie (Roul., Verve), Milt Jackson (Atl.), Paul Quinichette (Dawn), Buck Clayton (Col.), Leonard Feather-Dick Hyman (MGM), Tony Scott, Andy Kirk (Vict.).

NEWTON, WILLIAM FRANK (Frankie), *trumpet;* b. Emory, Va., 1/4/06; d. New York City, 3/11/54. First prominent w. Cecil Scott's orch., with which he recorded for Victor 1929. Worked w. Elmer Snowden 1931; Charlie Johnson 1933; Teddy Hill '36-7; also record dates in '36-7 w. Teddy Wilson, Mezzrow, Ch. Barnet, Willie (the Lion) Smith, Buster Bailey, and own band. Was member of original John Kirby sextet 1937. In 1939, he led his own band at Cafe Society and recorded for Vocalion, Blue Note and Bluebird. In 1940 and '41 he continued as a leader in Harlem clubs. Spent much of his time in Boston and also occasionally worked in NYC but was almost inactive in music for some time before his death. Best known in Greenwich Village circles in the late 1930s, Newton acquired a clique of admirers who considered him one of the foremost swing trumpet players. He did some unusual and effective work with a buzz mute.

LPs: three tracks w. own band in *Trumpeter's Holiday* (Epic); w. Joe Turner-Pete Johnson (Em.), Bessie Smith (Col.), Billie Holiday (Comm.), Sidney Bechet (Blue Note).

NICHOLAS, ALBERT (Al), *clarinet;* b. New Orleans, 5/27/00. Teachers included Louis Nelson and Lorenzo Tio Sr. & Jr. Began playing locally with Kid Ory, Buddy Petit and King Oliver during World War I. Served in Navy, then worked w. Luis Russell, Lee Collins ca. 1919-20; Emmanuel Perez, '21; own band at Tom Anderson's '22 w. L. Russell, B. Bigard, P. Barbarin. Rejoined King Oliver '24 in Chicago. Was with Jack Carter orch. '26, playing in China; worked in India and Egypt '27-8. Back in NYC late '28, joined L. Russell, remaining until 1933 and recording for Okeh. Later worked w. Sam Wooding, Chick Webb, '34; Alex Hill, '35. From '35-9 toured with the Russell band under L. Armstrong's direction.

In 1940 he worked briefly at Café Society with the Bobby Burnet Sextet, also pl. w. Eddie Heywood. Out of music '41-5, working in day jobs. Resumed '46, working w. Art Hodes, Bunk Johnson and in LA w. Kid Ory. Led own trio for a while at Jimmy Ryan's.

Nicholas was in Europe from 1953-60, touring and recording w. André Réwéliotty, Claude Luter, the Milan College Jazz Society etc. He was back in the US during the summer of '59, then returned to Paris.

In his early days Nicholas, considered to be one of the best of the New Orleans clarinetists, was heard on many small combo recordings led by Richard M. Jones, Jelly Roll Morton, Fats Waller, Alex Hill, Red Allen, Baby Dodds, Sidney Bechet, Wild Bill Davison, Mutt Carey. LPs: one half of *Creole Reeds* (River.); w. Wild Bill Davison (River., Comm.), Jelly Roll Morton (Comm.), Sidney Bechet (Blue Note), Bob Scobey (GTJ), one no. w. King Oliver in *Introduction To Jazz* (Decca). Many LPs on French labels.

Addr: 206 East 87th St., Chicago, Ill.

NICHOLAS, GEORGE WALKER (Big Nick), *tenor sax;* b. Lansing, Mich., 8/2/22; studied piano, clarinet, sax 1933-9; theory, harmony, Boston Cons. '44-6. Father, a saxophonist, helped him get started with local bands '39-40. Worked w. Kelly Martin at Club Congo in Detroit '42, also three months w. Earl Hines and six months w. Tiny Bradshaw. In Boston w. Sabby Lewis '44-6, then settled in NYC, working w. Claude Hopkins, J. C. Heard, Lucky Millinder '46-7. Toured Europe w. Dizzy Gillespie Jan.-Mar. '48. Led his own combo at the Paradise '53. Gigged around New York '54-7, then three months as soloist in show at Club Harlem, Atlantic City, N. J. '57. Featured soloist w. Shorty Allen group at Elegante in Brooklyn '57-Aug. '59. Featured on Dusty Fletcher record of *Open The Door, Richard* (National), *Manteca* w. Dizzy Gillespie (Vict.), *La Danse* w. Hot Lips Page (Col.). Fav. own solos: *Baby, Baby All The Time, 'Sposin'* w. Frankie Laine. Capable tenor man of the big-toned Hawkins school. Favs: Hawkins, Young, Byas, Webster, Getz. LPs w. Frankie Laine-Buck Clayton (Col.), Bennie Green in *Trombone By Three* (Pres.).

Addr: 114-36 139th St., Jamaica, N.Y.

NICHOLAS, JOE (Wooden Joe), *cornet, clarinet;* b. New Orleans, La., 1883; d. NO, 11/17/57. Uncle of Albert Nicholas. St. on clarinet. Learned cornet under influence of Buddy Bolden and Bunk Johnson. His reputation for power and stamina in street parades led to his own nickname. Pl. with King Oliver 1915; had own band from '18, called Camelia Band or Wooden Joe's Band. During the depression he played occasionally and gave music lessons. Rec. with the Creole Stompers for Paradox in 1944 and for William Russell's American Music in 1945.

NICHOLS, ROBERT JOSEPH (Bobby), *trumpet;* b. Boston, Mass., 9/15/24. Stud. New England Cons. Had own band at 12, and for three years in high school. Joined Vaughn Monroe at 15, stayed with him until Army induction Apr. '43. Overseas with Glenn Miller AAF band. Discharged, joined Tex Beneke Jan. '46; had own combo for six months, fall '47-spring '48; briefly w. Ray McKinley, then Beneke again until auto accident in 1950. Inactive a year, then joined T. Dorsey '51, until fall of '52. Worked w. Roxy Theatre orch. while rec. for Sauter-Finegan, then went on road with latter, '54; featured on their record of *New York 4 a. m.* After the band broke up in '56, gigged with small combo and ret. to Roxy. Fav. own LPs w. Sauter-Finegan: *Under Analysis, Sons of Sauter-Finegan* (Vict.). Favs: Gillespie, Clifford Brown, Armstrong.

Addr: 5505 Woodside Avenue, Woodside, L.I., N.Y.

NICHOLS, HERBERT HORATIO (Herbie), *piano, composer;* b. New York City, 1/3/19. Uncle, Walter Nichols, trumpeter with old Paramount Stompers group. Stud. w. Chas. L. Beck 1928-35. Army, '41-3. An early associate of Thelonious Monk, Nichols was sidetracked into jobs that prevented his modern jazz style from being heard widely. He played during the '40s w. groups led by Snub Mosley, Rex Stewart, Milt Larkins, and w. many rhythm and blues bands. Not until '55, when he made his first solo records for Blue Note, was his harmonically venturesome style fully displayed. He has had virtually no commercial success and has remained in relative obscurity in NYC backing singers at the Page 3 in Greenwich Village. He is co-composer of *Lady Sings The Blues,* recorded by Billie Holiday. Favs: John Lewis; Vladimir Horowitz, classical piano; Duke Ellington, arr. Own LPs: Blue Note. Beth., three tracks in *I Just Love Jazz Piano* (Sav.); LP w. Joe Thomas in *Mainstream* (Atl.).

Addr: 850 Hewitt Place, Bronx 59, N.Y.

NICHOLS, ERNEST LORING (Red), *leader, cornet;* b. Ogden, Utah, 5/8/05. Studied with father, a college music professor. To NYC w. Johnny Johnson orch. 1923. From 1925 until 1932, while working off and on w. Sam Lanin, Ross Gorman, Paul Whiteman, he also led his own pit orch. for such shows as *Strike Up the Band* and *Girl Crazy.* Nichols simultaneously built up a reputation as the most active recording bandleader in early white jazz. In addition to making many sides under such names as the Charleston Chasers, the Red Heads, the Louisiana Rhythm Kings, etc., he began, in Dec. 1926, a famous series of recordings for Brunswick under the name of Red Nichols and his Five Pennies. Early sidemen on these sessions (for which the band, despite its name, usually comprised from 6 to 10 men) included Jimmy Dorsey, Eddie Lang, Miff Mole, Joe Venuti, Arthur Schutt, Vic Berton, Benny Goodman, Lennie Hayton, Fud Livingston, with Glenn Miller frequently present as trombonist and arranger.

During the 1930s Nichols toured with his own big dance band, led theatre pit bands and orchestras on big commercial radio shows, including Bob Hope's first program. Since the late 1930s he has continued to be active as a bandleader, generally with a small group around Los Angeles.

In 1959 a motion picture entitled *The Five Pennies,* purportedly based on a part of Nichols' life but grossly sensationalized, sentimentalized and fictionalized, was enthusiastically accepted by the American public. As a result, Nichols' reputation attained heights it had not reached since the late 1920s. He acquired a loyal following of bankers, brokers, baseball players and assorted Broadway celebrities; playing at such clubs as the Roundtable in New York he successfully appealed to their weakness for nostalgia by offering a bland variation, with slightly more modern voicing, of the music that had been associated with him three decades earlier.

Nichols' place in jazz has been much disputed by the critics. John Tynan (*Down Beat*) observed in 1958: "Red's light, soaring cornet still is strong in lead and solo parts, and the chops sound as firm as ever." Dom Cerulli has praised Nichols' "Bix-toned cornet" but complained of his recent band that though it succeeds in recreating the musical flavor of the '20s, "somewhere along the way the feeling of jazz was lost." Older critics, especially in France, have rejected Nichols entirely as a musician of no importance to jazz. However, as the leader whose records introduced an enormous number of great musicians to a wider public, he had an importance that can hardly be contested.

LPs: *The Red Nichols Story* (Bruns. 54047); other LPs on Cap., Tops, Audiophile; *The Gene Krupa Story* (Verve).

Addr: 1624 Glenment Drive, Glendale 7, Calif.

NIEHAUS, LEONARD (Lennie), *alto sax, composer;* b. St. Louis, Mo., 6/11/29. Sister, Agnes, is a concert pianist. Family moved to LA when he was seven. Stud. until 1951, incl. two years at LA City Coll., three years at State Coll.; BA in mus. teaching. While at college, worked locally w. Jerry Wald '51. After 6 mos. w. Stan Kenton he was in the Army May '52-May '54; rejoined Kenton in fall of '54 and remained until May '59, touring Europe with him in '56. Left band to concentrate on writing. While between jobs w. Kenton he often played w. small groups in LA, usually incl. Bill Perkins. One of the most fluent and facile men to emerge from the West Coast school. Favs: Parker, Konitz. Own LPs: Contemporary, Mercury; LPs w. Duane Tatro (Contemp.), *East Coast-West Coast Scene* w. Shorty Rogers (Vict.), *Jazz For Cops and Robbers* w. Leith Stevens (Coral), Stan Kenton (Cap.).

Addr: 613 N. Kings Road, Los Angeles 48, Cal.

NIMITZ, JACK JEROME, *baritone sax;* b. Washington, D. C., 1/11/30. Clar. at 13, alto w. local bands at 16. With Willis Conover's band in Wash. Joined w. Herman '53; stud. flute, pl. it w. Woody occasionally. In late '50s spent considerable time w. Stan Kenton incl. European tour '56 and major jazz festivals summer '59. Favs: Gerry Mulligan, Lars Gullin. LPs w. Conover (Bruns.), Kenton (Cap.), Herbie Mann (River.), Herman (Verve, Cap.).

NIMMONS, PHILLIP RISTA (Phil), *composer, clarinet;* also *alto sax, piano;* b. Kamloops, Brit. Columbia, Canada, 6/3/23. Parents musically inclined, sister a concert pianist. Stud. piano first. Graduated from Univ. of Brit. Columbia in 1944 with intentions of becoming a doctor but decided to go into music on a full scale. Stud. clarinet in Vancouver and in NYC at Juilliard; composition at Royal Conservatory in Toronto. Pl. w. Ray Norris quintet '43-5. Comp. dramatic music and scores for musical comedies for CBC radio and TV, '50-7. Own group '57-60, pl. radio series on CBS and concerts in Toronto. App. at Stratford Shakespeare Fest., w. Toronto Symph. '57, Toronto Jazz Fest. '59. Films: *A Dangerous Age* '57, *The Young And The Beat* '59. Fav. comp: Stravinsky, Debussy, Ravel, Milhaud, Kenton, Basie, etc.; fav. clar: Goodman, De Franco; most imp. infl: Oscar Peterson. St. music school for students of jazz in Toronto w. Peterson and Ray Brown. Own LP: Verve.

Addr: 40 Shrewsbury Square, Agincourt, Ont., Canada.

NOBLE, KITTY (Katherine Killingsworth), *singer, guitar;* b. Youngstown, Ohio, 7/26/28. St. as vocalist w. Artie Suggs Orch. in NYC. Had own combo, Kitty Noble & Her Kitty Cats, singing and pl. cocktail drums. In early 1959 repl. Sylvia Vanderpool as partner of Mickey Baker in r & b act. Fav: Ella Fitzgerald. LP: *Mickey & Kitty* (Atl.).

Addr: 160 Claremont Ave., New York 27, N.Y.

NOBLE, RAY, *composer, leader;* b. Brighton, England, 1907. Father a noted composer and church organ recitalist. Mus. dir. at HMV studios (English associate of Victor at that time) 1929-34. Came to US late '34 and in '35 led his celebrated all-star American band, in which the sidemen were Glenn Miller, Will Bradley, Charlie Spivak, Pee Wee Erwin, Bud Freeman, Claude Thornhill, Johnny Mince et al. The band is best remembered for its stay in the Rainbow Room in Rockefeller Center. Though not a jazzman himself, Noble often allowed his jazz sidemen solo space. During the 1940s he was confined mainly to commercial radio work in California; during the past few years he has been back in England. His songs include *Cherokee, Goodnight Sweetheart.* LP: tracks in *Best of the Big Name Bands* (Camden).

NOONE, JIMMIE, *clarinet, leader;* b. near New Orleans, La., 4/23/1895; d. Los Angeles, 4/19/44. Took up guitar and clar. 1905, stud. briefly w. Bechet, Lorenzo Tio Jr. Later replaced Bechet in F. Keppard band. Organized band with Buddy Petit, 16; jobbed with Kid Ory, Oscar Celestin, '17. Moved to Chicago, 18; made rec. debut for Gennett in Richmond, Ind., '23. Stud. w. Franz Schoepp in Chicago. Prominent from 1927 at the Apex Club, where Earl Hines was his pianist. This group recorded his most famous numbers, incl. *Sweet Lorraine, I Know That You Know, Sweet Sue, Four or Five Times, Apex Blues* etc. Except for a brief visit to the Savoy Ballroom in '31, Noone remained in Chicago, working irregularly through the 1930s and recording occasionally with pick-up groups. After earning some renewed popularity through his appearance in Decca's 1940 New Orleans jazz album (one of the first jazz albums ever released), he went to the West Coast and joined the Kid Ory band. This group was enjoying its first major success through radio work with Orson Welles when Noone died suddenly.

According to John S. Wilson, Noone "provides the bridge between the New Orleans clarinet and the more recent cosmopolitan style exemplified by Benny Goodman." Certainly he was a strong influence on Goodman, as well as on Joe Marsala, Jimmy Dorsey and many others who tried to emulate his warmly communicative style and tone. In the view of many musicians he was the best all-around musician, in terms of both "soul" and technique, among the early New Orleans jazz clarinetists. LPs: tracks in *Encyclopedia of Jazz On Records, Vol. 1* (Decca 8383), *Gems of Jazz, Vol. 5* (Decca 8043).

NOREN, JACK, *drums;* b. Chicago, Ill., 10/19/29, of Swedish parentage. Worked briefly w. Gene Ammons and other local combos before moving to Sweden with his family in 1946. After playing w. Sam Samson and Thore Jederby he was heard in 1951 with the Rolf

A Jazz at the Philharmonic European tour, 1953. Standing, L. to R.: Norman Granz, Gene Krupa, Ella Fitzgerald, Ray Brown, J. C. Heard, Barney Kessel, Oscar Peterson, Lester Young. Kneeling: Flip Phillips, Charlie Shavers, Willie Smith

Ray Brown (*Clef Records*)

Oscar Peterson (*Verve Records*)

Billy Taylor (*Metronome*)

Marian McPartland

The original Chico Hamilton Quintet, 1956. Buddy Collette, tenor sax; Jim Hall, guitar; Chico Hamilton, drums; Fred Katz, cello; Carson Smith, bass (*William James Claxton*)

Lars Gullin

Above: Arne Domnerus, Aake Persson and Joe Harris, Stockholm, 1959 (*Bengt H. Malmqvist*)

Left: The Jimmy Giuffre Trio. Jimmy Giuffre, tenor, baritone sax, clarinet; Jim Hall, guitar; Ralph Pena, bass (*Capitol Records*)

Jack Teagarden and Anita O'Day (*Bert Block*)

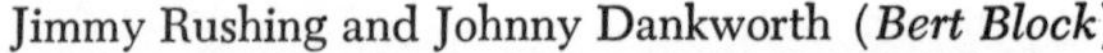

Jimmy Rushing and Johnny Dankworth (*Bert Block*)

Helen Merrill

Toshiko

Turk Murphy

Herb Geller (*Herman Leonard*)

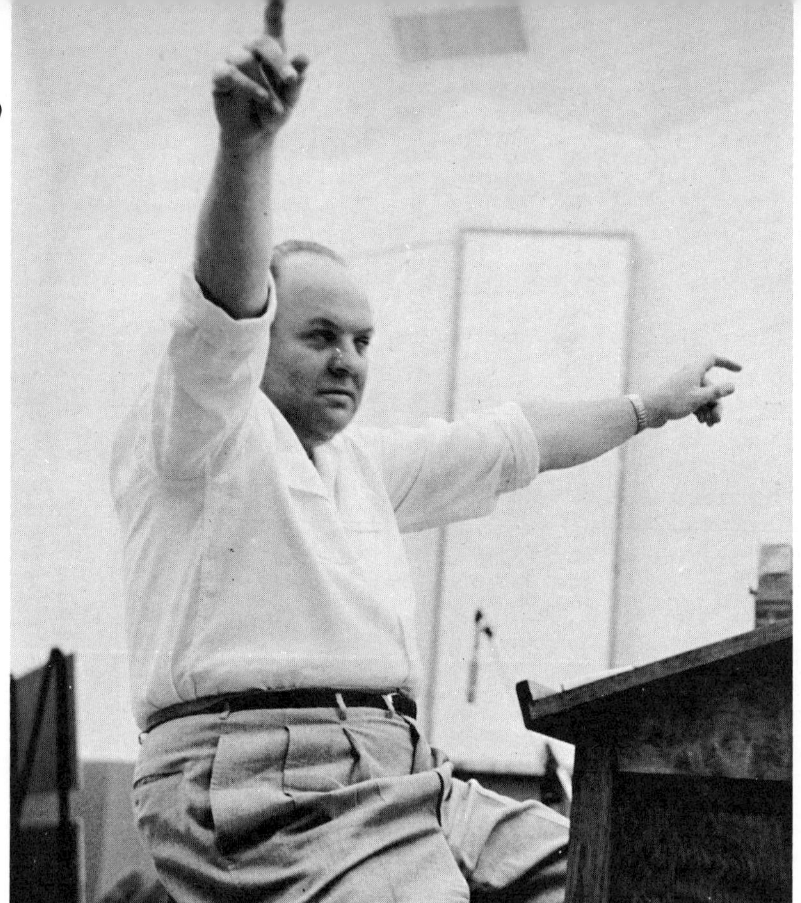

Billy May (*Capitol Records*)

Eddie Sauter and Bill Finegan (*Leo Friedman*)

Ahmad Jamal (*Bert Block*)

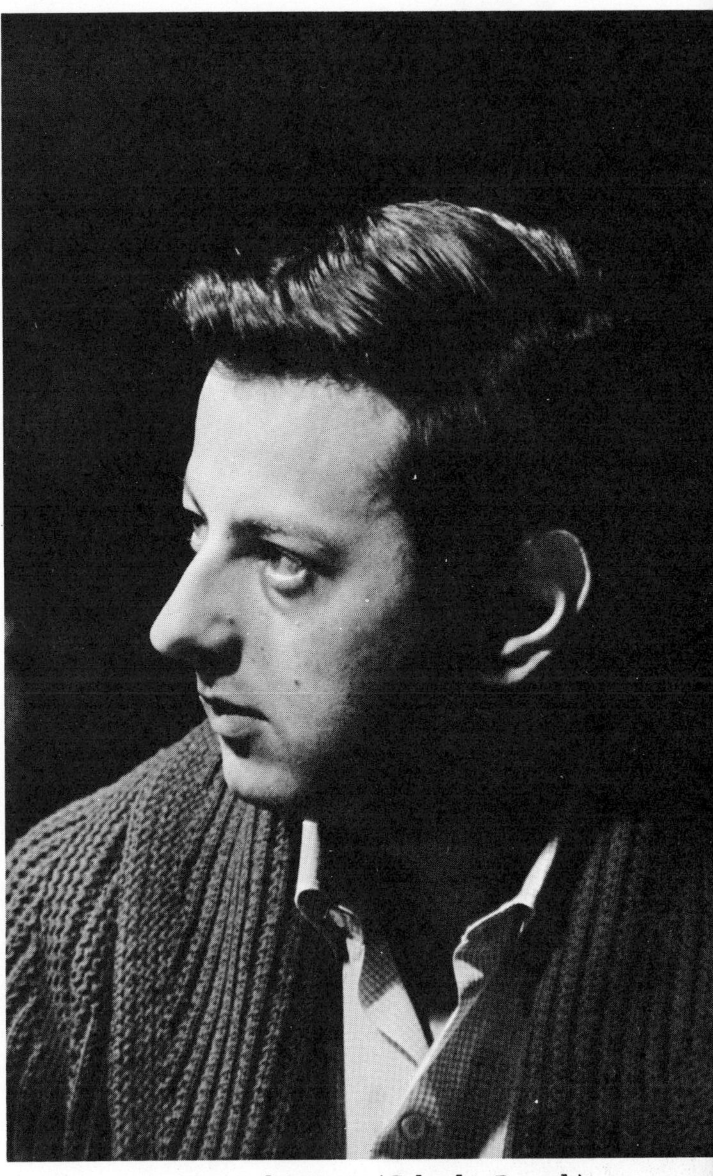

André Previn (*Columbia Records*)

Barbara Carroll (*Robert Parent*)

Tony Scott

Thad Jones (right); Billy Mitchell in background *(Francis Wolff)*

Hank Jones (*Capitol Records*)

Joe Williams (*Herman Leonard*)

Clifford Brown (*Herman Leonard*)

George Wein and Coleman Hawkins *(Bert Block)*

Sonny Rollins and Max Roach (*Bert Block*)

Kenny Dorham (*Bernie Thrasher*)

Sonny Stitt (*Jean-Pierre Leloir*)

John Lewis

Milt Jackson

Mose Allison (*Columbia Records*)

Gunther Schuller (*Columbia Records*)

The Modern Jazz Quartet. Percy Heath, bass; Connie Kay, drums; John Lewis, piano; Milton Jackson, vibes.

Paul Chambers (*Herman Leonard*)

Philly Joe Jones (*Francis Wolff*)

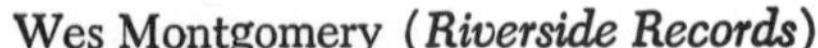

Wes Montgomery (*Riverside Records*)

Marshall Brown (*Bert Block*)

Left: Annie Ross, Dave Lambert, Jon Hendricks *(Columbia Records)*

Middle left: Horace Silver *(Bert Block)*

Middle right: Bill Evans *(Riverside Records)*

Right: Art Farmer and Benny Golson *(Don Schlitten)*

Ray Bryant (*Columbia Records*)

Nat Adderley

Julian "Cannonball" Adderley

Bobby Timmons (*Eric T. Vogel*)

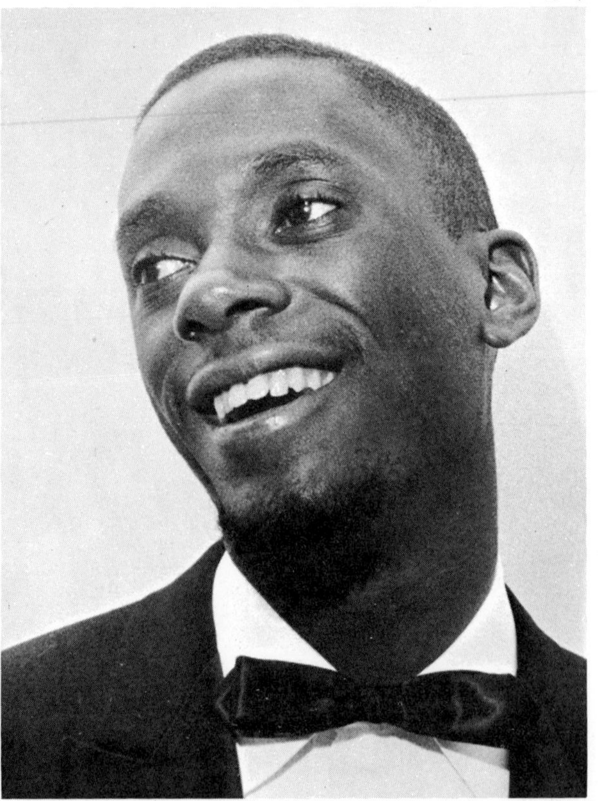

Jimmy Cleveland (*Eric T. Vogel*)

Curtis Fuller and John Coltrane (*Eric T. Vogel*)

John Coltrane (*Don Schlitten*)

Ornette Coleman (*Don Schlitten*)

The Quincy Jones band, as it appeared in the blues opera *Free and Easy,* at the Paris Alhambra, 1960. Back row, L. to R.: Bud Johnson, clarinet; Patti Bown, piano; Floyd Standifer, trumpet; Julius Watkins, horn; Jerome Richardson and Les Spann, flutes; Aake Persson, trombone; Buddy Catlett, bass; Clark Terry, trumpet; Quentin Jackson and Jimmy Cleveland, trombones; Benny Bailey, trumpet; Melba Liston, trombone. Front row: Lennie Johnson, trumpet; Sahib Shihab, flute; Porter Kilbert, alto; Joe Harris, drums; Quincy Jones, leader; Phil Woods, alto.

Ericson-Arne Domnerus combo at the National Ballroom in Stockholm. Accepted as the best modern jazz drummer in Sweden, he was featured on a number of jazz combo dates recorded there in the early '50s, after which he returned to Chicago and worked in night clubs, gigging w. Marty Rubenstein trio '59-60. LPs: Clifford Brown (Pres.).

NORIN, CARL-HENRIK, *tenor sax;* b. Västeras, Sweden, 3/27/20. First prominent with Thore Ehrling's band, he later worked with Simon Brehm and led his own group on numerous record sessions. Originally playing in a style resembling Charlie Ventura's, he later developed a modern and more interesting sound and became one of the best Getz-inspired tenor men in Scandinavia. LP: *Swedes From Jazzville* (Epic).

NORMAN, FRED, *composer;* b. Leesburg, Fla., 10/5/10. Pl. in Washington, D. C. with band led by Elmer Calloway, Cab's younger brother. Prominent as trombonist and arr. w. Claude Hopkins, 1932-8; during this time, wrote for B. Goodman, Isham Jones, Harry James. Staff arr. for G. Krupa 1940-3. Arr. for Jack Teagarden, Bunny Berigan, T. Dorsey, J. Dorsey, and many commercial bands. Mus. dir. at MGM conducting for Leslie Uggams, Diahann Carroll et al 1956. Conducting and arr. albums of Negro spirituals for Carlton Records '59. Music for stage show, *Ol' Man Satan* '59. Own EP on Joe Davis; LPs w. K. Burrell (Merc.), Charlie Margolis (Carlton), Clyde Otis (Merc.), Brook Benton (Merc.).

Addr: 407 Central Park West, New York, N.Y.

NORRIS, ALBERT (Al), *guitar, violin;* b. Kane, Pa., 9/4/08. Started on violin; pl. banjo in Buffalo groups '27-'32; heard there by J. Lunceford, whose band he joined in '32, remaining (with time out for Army service) for most of its existence. Featured on *Cheatin' On Me, Put on Your Old Gray Bonnet, Organ Grinder's Swing, Sweet Sue.* Retired from music and during the '50s worked in NYC for the post office. LPs w. Lunceford (Col., Decca).

NORRIS, WALTER, *piano;* b. Little Rock, Ark., 12/27/31. Stud. from age five to 18, when he left Little Rock. Grad. from high school, then spent 21 months in the service. Went to Los Angeles, worked w. Frank Rosolino, Stan Getz, Zoot Sims, Howard McGhee, et al. LPs w. Ornette Coleman (Contemp.), Jack Sheldon (Jazz: West).

Addr: 1336 Edgecliff Drive, Los Angeles, Calif.

NORVO, RED (Kenneth Norville), *vibraharp, xylophone, leader;* b. Beardstown, Ill., 3/31/08. Took piano lessons at 8; while in high school, took up xylophone and left home at 17 for Chicago, where his career was launched as leader of a 7-piece marimba band called The Collegians. After this group broke up he joined Paul Ash's orchestra, following this stint with a tour in vaudeville as a solo act in which he played *Poet and Peasant* and did a tap-dance. After leading a band in the summer of 1929 in a Milwaukee ballroom he enrolled in the University of Detroit but returned to the music business four months later in Minneapolis, working on Station KSTP, then returned to Chicago to work as a staff musician with Victor Young at NBC. Later, on a radio series with Paul Whiteman over NBC, he met Mildred Bailey, then singing with Whiteman's band. After working together in Chicago they were married and headed for New York with Whiteman. Quitting Whiteman in 1934, Norvo settled in New York and in the summer of the following year fronted his own pianoless octet at the Hickory House on 52nd Street, the personnel including Eddie Sauter on mellophone, Herbie Haymer on tenor sax and Dave Barbour on guitar.

Norvo expanded in 1936 to front a 12-piece band with Mildred Bailey as vocalist, Eddie Sauter remaining as arranger and occasional trumpeter. This band, which recorded regularly for Brunswick from August 1936 until June 1939, was pre-eminent in the purveying of his soft, subtle brand of swing music. Norvo remained active as a band leader from 1940 to '44 but Mildred Bailey worked separately during most of this time. In 1943 he had an all-star combo with Shorty Rogers, Eddie Bert, Ralph Burns and others. During 1943 he switched from xylophone to vibraphone; he has played the latter instrument almost exclusively since then. His next band, in 1944, included Aaron Sachs on clarinet; Remo Palmier, guitar; Clyde Lombardi, bass. He gave up bandleading to join Benny Goodman early in 1945 and spent all of 1946 with Woody Herman's orchestra. In 1947 he settled in California with his second wife, Eve Rogers (sister of Shorty Rogers). Although divorced from Mildred Bailey he continued to record with her occasionally and they remained close friends until her death. After free-lancing for some time in Hollywood, Norvo returned East in 1949, when he led a sextet that included Tony Scott, Mundell Lowe, and Dick Hyman. He adopted a trio format in 1950 with Tal Farlow and Charlie Mingus (later Jimmy Raney and Red Mitchell). His trio records were acclaimed as the most striking examples of subtlety and finesse in modern, chamber-music style jazz. In January 1954 he made his first overseas tour, in the *Jazz Club USA* unit. Continued working on West Coast w. own quintet. Came East to guest w. Benny Goodman on *Swing Into Spring,* NBC-TV Apr. '58. In the fall of '59 his quintet was incorporated by Benny Goodman in a 10-piece band that toured Europe and then pl. at Basin Street East, NYC. Norvo won the following awards: Esq. Gold Award '44 (tie w. Hampton), '45-7; Met. '47-9.

Red Norvo was the first musician to demonstrate the possibility of adapting jazz to the xylophone, hitherto spurned by jazzmen as a novelty instrument. After recording his first solos for Brunswick in April 1933, he commenced, the following year, a long series of recordings with swing groups that have become collectors' items: first with Jack Jenney, Artie Shaw, Charlie Barnet, Teddy Wilson, et al. in 1934, and Bunny Berigan, Jenney, Johnny Mince, Chu Berry, Gene Krupa et al. in 1935, both these sessions on Columbia. Through the years he continued to show not only his own peerless musicianship but also his uncanny ability to select, as sidemen, musicians who were destined to become famous. Own LPs: *Red Norvo And His All Stars* (Epic 3128), *Move* (Savoy 12088), *Red Norvo Trio* (Fant. 3-219), *Red Norvo With Strings* (Fant. 3-218), *Red Norvo* (Rondo. 28), *Red Plays the Blues* (Vict. LPM 1729), *Fi-FIve* (Vict LPM 1420), *Music To Listen To Red Norvo By* (Contemp. 3534), *Windjammer City Style* (Dot 3126); four tracks in *Midnight On Cloud 69* (Savoy 12093); one track in *History of Jazz, Vol. 3* (Cap. T 795); one track in *Encyclopedia of Jazz on Records,* Vol. 4 (Decca 8401); four tracks in *Giants of Jazz, Vol. 1* (Em. 36048); *Norvo Naturally* (Tampa 35), *Vibe-Rations* (Lib. 6012), *Ad Lib* (Lib. 3035); LPs w. Harry Babasin (Em. 36123), Benny Goodman (MGM S3810, Col. CL 500), *Metronome All Stars* (Cam. 426), Woody Herman (MGM E3043, Harm. 7013).

Addr: 420 Alta Ave., Santa Monica, Calif.

NOTO, SAM, *trumpet;* b. Buffalo, N.Y., 4/17/30. Stud. trumpet in grammar school; went on road w. band at 17. Joined Stan Kenton in 1953, making tours of Europe and US. Toured w. L. Bellson-Pearl Bailey show '59. Favs: Fats Navarro, Dizzy Gillespie, Miles Davis, Clifford Brown. LPs w. Stan Kenton (Cap.); Anita O'Day (Verve).

Addr: 381 14th St., Buffalo, N.Y.

NOTTINGHAM, JAMES EDWARD JR. (Jimmy), *trumpet;* b. Brooklyn, N. Y., 12/15/25. Local teachers. Gigged in Brooklyn w. Cecil Payne, Max Roach, 1943; w. Willie Smith's Navy band at Great Lakes, '44-5. Feat. as high-note man with Lionel Hampton '45-7; Ch. Barnet, Lucky Millinder '47; Count Basie, pl. mostly lead trumpet, '48-50. Back w. Millinder for a while, then a year with Herbie Fields. In '51-3 he was heard with such Latin bands as Perez Prado, Noro Morales; then in the pit band of *Hazel Flagg.* CBS staff Feb.-Aug. '54; summer TV series *Music '55* in NYC w. Stan Kenton; back on staff at CBS since late '56. LPs w. Barnet (Everest); *Candido The Volcanic* (ABC-Par.); Tony Scott big band (Vict.); Jimmy Mundy (Epic); Seldon Powell, Sonny Stitt (Roost); Manny Albam (Vict.) and earlier Barnet sides on Verve.

Addr: 80 Carolina Ave., Hempstead, L.I., N.Y.

O

O'BRIEN, FLOYD, *trombone;* b. Chicago, Ill., 5/7/04. In the mid-'20s he was heard w. Earl Fuller, Charlie Cottle, Charles Pierce, Jack Gardner, Gene Krupa, Cato's Imps, the Wolverines, Henri Gendron, Thelma Terry, Joe Kayser. Theatre pit band in Des Moines 1930-1; Floyd Towne in Chicago '32; Joe Venuti, Mezz Mezzrow, Mal Hallett, Smith Ballew, Mike Durso '33-6, NYC; toured w. Phil Harris '36-9; Gene Krupa '39-40, Bob Crosby '40-3. From '43-8, many small bands in Los Angeles incl. Teagarden, Manone, Sherock, Slack; also movie studio work. Since 1948, in Chicago w. Art Hodes, Johnny Lane and own band. In 1950s, also worked as teacher of all brass instruments and as piano tuner. Gigged and recorded again w. Hodes '55-6; with Danny Alvin at Club Basin St., Chi., '57-8; with Smokey Stover on weekend dates and Chess records '59. One of the first white trombonists to emulate the classic New Orleans style, O'Brien was admired from his earliest days for the exceptional warmth of his solo work, and for the high quality of his performances in improvised ensembles.

LPs: *Chicago Jazz* (Decca); *The Golden Era* w. Nichols (Cap.), Al Nicholas (Delmar), Danny Alvin (Stepheny), Natty Dominique (Windin' Ball), Hodes (Merc.).

O'BRIEN, WALTER HOWARD (Hod), *piano;* b. Chicago, Ill., 1/19/36. Mother taught him piano at age six. Studied at Oberlin '54, one semester at Manhattan Sch. of Music. Prof. debut in Conn. '50. Own group at Avaloch in Lenox, Mass., summers of '56-7, Cork 'N Bib, Jazz Gallery '59-60. Favs: Bud Powell, Tatum. LP: *Three Trumpets* (Pres.).

O'BRIEN, KENNETH MICHAEL (Kenny), *bass;* b. New York City, 10/26/28. Played w. Les Elgart 1947; Ch. Ventura '48, also w. Boyd Raeburn, Ch. Spivak, Terry Gibbs, Chuck Wayne, Sal Salvador and many other combos in NYC. Married to drummer Elaine Leighton. Fav: Ray Brown. LPs w. Ch. Ventura (Decca, GNP), Terry Gibbs (Bruns.).

Addr: 125 West 75th St., New York 23, N.Y.

O'DAY, ANITA, *singer;* b. Chicago, Ill., 12/18/19. Worked from 1939 w. Max Miller combo at Three Deuces, Chicago. Joined G. Krupa early 1941, and during the following two years established a great following among jazz fans with a novel, husky-toned style. Her biggest hits w. Krupa included *Let Me Off Uptown,* on which she was featured w. Roy Eldridge, and a wordless vocal on *That's What You Think.* She was featured w. Stan Kenton's band 1944-5; her most popular record w. him was *And Her Tears Flowed Like Wine.* She rejoined Krupa for a few months and then worked on her own in night clubs, her career having been marked by periods of enforced inactivity. In the late '50s she enjoyed a resurgence of popularity, became very active in clubs and on records; was a great success at NJF in '58 and toured Europe w. Benny Goodman Oct. '59. Films: *Gene Krupa Story; Jazz on a Summer's Day.*

Anita O'Day, though her background extends to the latter years of the swing era, has remained a modern singer in every sense of the term and still is a tremendously important influence. The impact of her style has been heard in the work of June Christy, Chris Connor and many other singers during the past twenty years. She won the *Esquire* new star award in 1945, *Down Beat* poll '44 and '45. Own LPs: *Swings Cole Porter* (Verve 2118), *Anita Sings* (Verve 2000), *At Mister Kelly's* (Verve 2113), *An Evening w. Anita O'Day* (Verve 2050), *Lady Is a Tramp* (Verve 2049), *Pick Yourself Up* (Verve 2043), *Anita Sings the Winners* (Verve 8283); w. Kenton: *Kenton Era* (Cap. WDX 569), Krupa: *Drummer Man* (Verve 2008), *Gene Krupa Story* (Verve VS 6105).

Addr: 13674 Taxton, Pacoima, Calif.

ODETTA (Odetta Felious Gordon), *singer, guitar;* b. Birmingham, Ala., 12/31/30. Was in chorus of *Finian's Rainbow* in Los Angeles 1950. Took up guitar and folk singing as hobby and was offered job at the "hungry i" in San Francisco. When she got there, the job had fallen through, but after spending a little time in SF she opened at the Tin Angel and stayed there a year, 1952. Many concerts incl. Yugoslav Hall, NYC, '52; Town Hall, NYC, '58; Newport Folk Festival '59. Specializes in blues, work songs, ballads, and some classical pop songs; says "The separation of these musical forms and interpretations is purely a matter of concept with some awareness of each of these fields." Fav: Leadbelly. Own LPs: Tradition, Vanguard, Fantasy.

Addr: 1252 No. Wells Street, Chicago 10, Ill.

O'FARRILL, ARTURO (Chico), *composer;* b. Havana, Cuba, 10/28/21. Father Irish-born, mother German. St. playing at 19; first studies in composition w. Felix Guerrero in Havana. Stud. law for a year. From 1936-40 in US for studies at Gainesville, Ga. Pl. w. Armando Romeu at Tropicana, other Cuban bands until '48, also arr. from '46. To NYC '48. Studied w. Bernard Wagenaar, Stephan Wolpe, Hall Overton. Met Benny Goodman through Stan Hasselgard, wrote for Goodman band on Cap. (*Undercurrent Blues, Shishkabop*), also arr. for Machito, Miguelito Valdes, Stan Kenton (*Cuban Episode*) and Dizzy Gillespie (*Manteca Suite,* '54). Organized own band in '53 and app. at Birdland and other jazz clubs around the country. Since the late Fifties, living in Mexico where he wrote his First Symphony for performance by Havana Philharmonic. Own LPs: Verve; LPs for Gillespie, Machito (Verve), *Aztec Suite,* Art Farmer (UA).

OFWERMAN, ANDERS IVAR RUNE, *piano;* b. Stockholm, Sweden, 12/24/32. Uncle was famous opera singer. Private piano lessons at age six. After winning several amateur competitions was offered job and turned professional. Played w. Rolf Ericson 1952, Carl-Henrik Norin '54, Hacke Bjorksten '56, Ove Lind '57. Joined Ernie Englund '58. Öfwerman supervises recordings for Gazell, a company in which he has part ownership. Favs: Bud Powell, John Lewis, Art Tatum. LP w. Herbie Mann (Pres.); also records in Sweden w. Lars Gullin, Tony Scott, Leonard Feather, and own trio. Fav. own solo: *Old Spice* w. own trio (Gazell).

OLAY, RUTH, *singer;* b. San Francisco, Calif., 7/1/27. Father a rabbi; mother prof. singer. Started as piano prodigy at four years; stud. piano for nine years. Studied voice w. mother and private teacher; influenced by cantors, also enjoyed music of big bands such as Basie, Ellington, Goodman. Worked as secretary to film writers at Paramount; also followed musical career, singing in clubs. Feat. on Timex CBS-TV jazz show Jan. 1959. Fav: Ivie Anderson. Own LPs: *It's About Time* (Zephyr); *Olay; Easy Living* (Merc.).

Addr: 6506 W. 6th Street, Los Angeles, Calif.

OLDHAM, BILL, *tuba;* also *bass, trombone, baritone sax;* b. Chattanooga, Tenn., 1909, he came to Chicago around 1919. Pl. in local brass bands and joined the Chi. Defender Band in 1925. Pl. with Louis Armstrong '33 and '35, making some records w. him for Victor. Joined Eddie South for a year in 1938. Has Bachelor of Music from Chicago Cons., and has written two symphonies. A member of Franz Jackson's group in Chicago for some time.

OLIVER, JOSEPH (King), *cornet, leader;* b. on plantation near Abend, La., 5/11/1885; d. Savannah, Ga., 4/8/38. His mother was a cook on the plantation. Oliver went to New Orleans as a boy, taking a job as a yard boy. In early childhood, as a result of an accident, he became blind in one eye. After studying trombone briefly with a private teacher he soon switched to cornet. He played in the Melrose Brass Band in 1907, with the Olympia Band under A. J. Piron 1912-14, then in 1915 led a band himself, with Sidney Bechet on clarinet.

Oliver worked with several other bands before leaving New Orleans; among them were the Eagle, Onward and Magnolia bands, and Kid Ory's group. It was Ory who, late in 1917, began billing him as "King" Oliver. During his early years in New Orleans Oliver became an idol of, and strong influence on, the youthful Louis Armstrong. Early in 1918 Oliver migrated to Chicago, where he worked on two jobs, with the bands of Lawrence Duhé and Bill Johnson, remaining with both bands until late 1919. He took over the Duhé band and soon earned great popularity, chiefly at the Royal Garden Café.

In 1922 Oliver sent for Louis Armstrong, who joined the band as second cornetist. The Creole Jazz Band, as Oliver named it, was the finest group of its day and became, in 1923, the first Negro jazz group ever to make a series of recordings. (Except for a couple of numbers by Kid Ory there was virtually no recording of pure Negro jazz until then.) The sidemen with Oliver in the early Chicago years included Johnny and Baby Dodds, Jimmie Noone, Lil Hardin (Armstrong), Kid Ory, Barney Bigard, Albert Nicholas and Honore Dutrey. The first recordings were made for Paramount in Chicago and Gennett in Richmond, Ind., and for

OKeh and Columbia. In 1926-7 his Savannah Syncopators made a number of sides for Vocalion. Oliver's fortunes took a turn for the worse after 1928, the year he moved to New York. Luis Russell, his pianist, took many of his men and formed a new band; Oliver recorded for Victor, Vocalion and Brunswick, using a pick-up group rather than a permanent personnel.

During the next few years, suffering from serious dental trouble, Oliver assigned the trumpet solos to other musicians on many of his records. After a series of catastrophic Southern tours with various bands in the early 1930s he settled in Savannah and lived there in obscurity until his death. The story of Oliver is told in graphic detail in a monograph by Walter C. Allen and Brian A. L. Rust, available from Sidgwick & Jackson Ltd., Bloomsbury Way, London, Eng.

Louis Armstrong makes it quite evident in his autobiography, *Satchmo,* that Oliver was his true idol and his only real musical mentor. Additional biographical details of Oliver's early career can be found in this book. Oliver was responsible, with Armstrong, for the composition *Sugar Foot Stomp* (originally known as *Dipper Mouth Blues*); he also wrote *Canal Street Blues, Snag It, Chimes Blues, West End Blues, Doctor Jazz,* and, with Richard M. Jones, the tune known as *Riverside Blues* or *Jazzin' Babies Blues* which evolved into *Dixieland Shuffle* recorded by Bob Crosby. Own LPs: River. 12-130, Epic LN 3208; also *Louis Armstrong: 1923* (River. 12-122), *Young Louis Armstrong* (River. 12-101).

OLIVER, MERTON A. (Mert), *bass;* b. Herndon, Va., 1/28/17. Self-taught. Worked as bookkeeper 1935-40, cab driver '41. Joined Ralph Hawkins in Washington, 1941; during '40s worked w. Teddy Powell, Sonny Dunham, Georgie Auld, Boyd Raeburn, Buddy Rich, Don Lamond; own trio in Washington '45-6; Jack Jive Scheaffer '46-8. Left Washington, toured w. Woody Herman 1949, Elliot Lawrence '50-1, Ch. Barnet '51, Johnny Smith trio '51-2, T. Dorsey '52. Own band at Coral Room, Washington, '53; w. Willis Conover '53-4; also worked as real estate broker '54. Rec. on Stan Getz Sav. session, 1948 (*Stan's Mood, Stan Gets Along, Fast, Slow*), incorrectly credited to Curly Russell. Favs: Ray Brown, Safranski. LPs: Willis Conover (Bruns.), four tracks w. Stan Getz in *Lestorian Mode* (Savoy).

OLIVER, MELVIN JAMES (Sy), *composer, leader, singer, trumpet;* b. Battle Creek, Mich., 12/17/10. Father was a concert singer; he and Sy's mother both taught music in Zanesville, Ohio. Sy studied trumpet with his father; after graduating from high school in June '38, he pl. w. Zack Whyte's band in Cincinnati. Late in '33 he joined Jimmie Lunceford's orch. and from then until Oct. '39 (when he quit the band to join Tommy Dorsey as arranger) his orchestrations, more than those by any other contributor to the Lunceford library, gave the band the distinctive touch that made its unique reputation. Oliver's writing made use of many simple, swinging effects, frequent staccato phrases that often had a touch of humor, and a brilliant sense of continuity and climax. In addition, he was the band's outstanding trumpet soloist and a vocalist of exceptional charm. His most widely acclaimed arrangements include *Stomp It Off* and *Dream Of You,* '34; *Four Or Five Times, Swanee River, My Blue Heaven, Organ Grinder's Swing, On The Beach At Bali Bali, Me And The Moon, My Last Affair,* '36; *Linger Awhile, For Dancers Only, Raggin' The Scale, Posin', Annie Laurie,* '37; *Margie, Sweet Sue, By The River St. Marie,* '38; *'Tain't Whatcha Do, Cheatin' On Me, Le Jazz Hot, Ain't She Sweet,* '39.

Writing for Tommy Dorsey and also occasionally singing with his band on records, Oliver contributed such originals as *Easy Does It, Swing High, Well Git It, Opus 1.* After leading his own band in the Army '43-5, Oliver resumed writing for Dorsey off and on, led his own band on a radio show entitled *Endorsed by Dorsey,* and from late '40s worked for ten years off and on at Decca as mus. dir., staff arr. and recording supervisor. He led bands occasionally from '47. Worked on LPs for Bethlehem Records '54-55 and for Jubilee '58. TV scores for *The Big Party* etc. Operating arranging service in NYC '59-60. Oliver won Met. poll as arranger '44; DB poll '41-5. Own LPs: *Jimmy Lunceford Arrangements In Hi-Fi* (Decca 8636); also Decca 8740, Dot 3132, 3184; LPs w. Lunceford (Decca 8050, Col. CL 634), Chris Connor (Beth. 56), Tommy Dorsey (Vict. LPM 6003).

Addr: 1619 Broadway, New York 19, N.Y.

ORCHARD, FRANCIS H. (Frank), *valve trombone;* b. Chicago, Ill., 9/21/14. Grandmother ran Orchard Sch. of Mus. Stud. violin age 6 to 12 in Chicago; banjo in St. Louis; trombone and tuba in high school; theory at Juilliard '32-3. Worked w. Stanley Melba '33. Out of music, worked as salesman 1933-41. Joined J. McPartland '41, Bill Reinhardt '42, Max Kaminsky '44, Wingy Manone '45, then free-lanced w. Dixieland groups around NYC for ten years before moving to Dayton, Ohio. LP w. Max Kaminsky (Comm.).

ORE, JOHN THOMAS, *bass;* b. Philadelphia, Pa., 12/17/33. Father pl. 'cello; mother piano. Studied 'cello at New Sch. of Mus. in Phila. '43-6; bass at Juilliard, '52. First job w. Tiny Grimes in '53 for a month; has since worked w. G. Wallington, Lester Young, '54; Ben Webster, Coleman Hawkins '55; Bud Powell, '55 and '57; own trio in Hempstead, L.I., '58; free-lanced in New York area '59-60. LPs w. L. Young, Bud Powell (Verve), Freddie Redd, Elmo Hope (Pres.).

Addr: 697 Putnam Avenue, Brooklyn, N.Y.

ORTEGA, ANTHONY ROBERT, *saxophones, clarinet, flute;* b. Los Angeles, Calif., 6/7/28. Stud. with Lloyd Reese, 1945-8, then worked w. Earle Spencer. After two years in the Army, he toured w. Lionel Hampton's band, '51-3, worked briefly w. Milt Buckner trio in late '53, then led his own combo at the Red Feather in LA, '54. Visited Norway in '54 for concerts and combo jobs. Back in LA, Aug., '54, worked in mambo band; came East in Aug., '55 w. Luis Rivera. Heard off and on w. Nat Pierce, '56-8, and for short periods w. D. Gillespie, E. Lawrence, M. Ferguson. J. Moody; concert w. G. Schuller at Cooper Union. In LA '58, w. P. Bley, Lighthouse All Stars, Claude Williamson. Fav. own solo: *We'll be Together Again* on Herald LP. Own LPs: Beth., Herald. LPs w. Pierce (Cor.), *My Fair Lady* w. Billy Taylor (ABC-Par.), Herbie Mann (Epic), M. Ferguson, D. Washington (Merc.).

ORTEGA, FRANK, *piano;* b. Los Angeles, Calif., 11/27/27. Sang w. Roger Wagner Chorale at 10; stud. piano at 12. Played w. local bands in high school at 14; org. own band at 17, working Club Donavan in Sacramento. Had own band until 1947, then formed trio, working club dates throughout the US. Feat. on 77 *Sunset Strip* ABC-TV '58-9. Essentially a pop pianist rather than a jazz artist. Favs: Duke Ellington, Art Tatum, Count Basie. Own LPs: Imp., Masterseal, Jub.

Addr: 2213 S. Carmona, Los Angeles 16, Calif.

ORY, EDWARD (Kid), *trombone, leader, composer;* also *trumpet, clarinet, piano, banjo, bass, drums, guitar, saxophone, valve trombone;* b. La Place, La., 12/25/1886. As a youngster, organized a quintet with four friends, playing home-made string instruments; bought his first trombone with money made on jobs with this group. Ory sat in with Buddy Bolden's band, studied with private teachers, and in 1911 brought his own band to New Orleans. Mutt Carey, King Oliver and Louis Armstrong, in that order, held the trumpet chair in this band; Johnny Dodds, Sidney Bechet, Jimmie Noone and George Lewis worked for him on clarinet.

Ory moved to California in 1919, studied trombone and composition and led his own band in LA until 1924, when he went to Chicago and worked with the bands of King Oliver 1925-7, Dave Peyton '27, Clarence Black at the Savoy, '27-8, and the Chicago Vagabonds at Sunset Cafe, '28-9; Leon Rene's "Lucky Day" orch., late '29. From '25 to '27 he was also featured, on recordings only, with Lil Armstrong, Ma Rainey, Williams' Stompers, Tiny Parham, Luis Russell, and on a series of "Hot Five" sides with Louis Armstrong, including his own comp. *Muskrat Ramble,* recorded 2/26/26.

Returning to Los Angeles, Ory worked with local bands 1929-30, then retired from music, and from 1930 to '39 ran a successful chicken ranch with his brother. From 1940 on, he returned gradually to music; joining Barney Bigard's combo in 1942, he began to double on bass. After working with Bunk Johnson in 1943 and starring in a broadcast for Orson Welles in 1944, Ory found his star in the ascendancy and worked with great success in San Francisco and Los Angeles, leading his own band, composed mostly of New Orleans veterans, and basking in the rekindled glow of the traditionalist jazz climate. In 1954 his *Muskrat Ramble* enjoyed yet another new lease on life when it was fitted with lyrics and recorded by many pop artists. In 1956 he was seen in an acting and playing role in the film *The Benny Goodman Story.* His band toured Europe with great success in Sept.-Oct. '56 and again in the fall of '59, in addition to appearing at Newport '57, night club work in San Francisco etc.

Ory is the most famous of the original "tailgate" trombone men, using the instrument for rhythm effects, fills and glissandi, but also playing solos in a rough, forceful style. He had a profound influence on many musicians, both in his early years and since the New Orleans jazz revival. Ory was seen with Louis Armstrong in the movie *New Orleans* in 1946, and was reunited with him on records about the same time. Other movies: *Crossfire* '47, *Mahogany Magic* '50. Won Rec. Ch. All-Time, All Star poll 1951. Favs: J. C. Higginbotham, Tommy Dorsey and Zue Robertson. Own LPs: Good Time Jazz 12004, 12008, 12016, 12022; Verve 1014, 1017, 8254, 8233; Col. CL 835; three tracks in *New Orleans Legends* (River. 12-119); *Johnny Dodds and Kid Ory* (Epic 3207); LPs w. Louis Armstrong (Col. CL 851-853).

Addr: P.O. Box 153, San Anselmo, Calif.

OSBORNE, MARY, *guitar, singer;* b. Minot, N. Dakota, 7/17/21. Violin in school symphony; at 15 featured in trio playing violin, guitar, bass, singing and dancing. Inspired by Charlie Christian, whom she heard w. Al Trent's band in Bismarck, she concentrated on electric guitar, played a year on KDKA, Pittsburgh. She toured with the bands of Buddy Rogers, Dick Stabile, Terry Shand, Joe Venuti. Married Ralph Scaffidi, Nov. 1942; worked w. Russ Morgan, Gay Claridge. To NYC 1945; rec. dates w. Mary Lou Williams, Beryl Booker, Coleman Hawkins, (Victor); Mercer Ellington, Wynonie Harris (Aladdin), and own trio on Aladdin, Signature, Decca etc. From Sept. '52 until 1960, featured w. combo on daily Jack Sterling CBS radio show. Exceptional beat and aggressively swinging style established her as a jazz guitarist; she is also a ballad singer of unusual talent. Own LP: Strand; LPs w. Coleman Hawkins (Victor), Tyree Glenn (Roul.), Mary Lou Williams in *Modern Jazz Piano: Four Views* (Cam.).

Addr: 357 Hickory Street, Massapequa, L.I., N.Y.

OTIS, JOHNNY, *drums, vibes, leader, composer;* b. Vallejo, Cal., 1922. Took up drums 1939; self-taught. After working w. Geo. Morrison, Lloyd Hunter and 8 months w. Harlan Leonard, led own band at Club Alabam in LA '45; toured for several years w. great success as r & b attraction introducing many singers incl. Sallie Blair, Little Esther, Mel Walker, Willie Mae Thornton. Daily radio disc jockey show and weekly live-music TV show for past several years in LA; is also president of Dig Records, runs mus. publ. co. and recording studio, promotes dances and concerts. Film: *Juke Box Rhythm.* Own LP: Capitol. Own fav. recs. as drummer: *Paper Moon, After You've Gone, Love Come Back, Jammin' With Lester,* all w. Lester Young (Aladdin).

Addr: 2077 S. Harvard Blvd., Los Angeles 18, Calif.

OVERTON, HALL F., *composer, piano, teacher;* b. Bangor, Mich., 2/23/20. Studied at Juilliard 1947-51 and w. Milhaud on scholarship at Aspen '53. Has played jazz since discharge from Army '46, but is mainly a composer in the contemporary classical sense. A piano sonata and string quartet were presented at Composer's Forum concert NYC '54. His *Symphony For Strings,* commissioned by the Koussevitsky Foundation, was performed at Cooper Union in '56; a string quartet was rec. by the Beaux Arts String Quartet. In jazz he has gigged w. Aaron Sachs, Jimmy Raney and Teddy Charles. Raney, Charles, Mundell Lowe and Wendell Marshall have studied with him. In '59 he arranged Thelonious Monk's compositions for a ten piece orch. which Monk led in concert at Town Hall and at the Randall's Island Jazz Fest. Favs: Powell, Silver, Monk. LPs w. Raney (Pres.), Charles in *Three For The Duke* (Jub.); *Monk Orchestra At Town Hall* (River.).

Addr: 67-38 108th St., Forest Hills, L.I., N.Y.

P

PACE, SALVATORE, *clarinet, saxophones;* b. White Plains, N.Y., 8/10/10. Stud. clar. and started playing w. street marching bands. Crescent City Five in New York, 1924-8, RKO theater band in White Plains, 1929-31. During '30s and '40s, he worked in many commercial dance bands incl. Joe Haymes, '36-7, Al Donahue, '40, Frankie Masters, Teddy Powell, Bunny Berigan, '41, Charlie Spivak, '42. Active in Dixieland jazz work since '49, when he joined Phil Napoleon. From '51-3, he was heard with groups led by Pee Wee Erwin, Billy Butterfield, Yank Lawson, Jimmy McPartland. From '56 until early '58 he was w. Billy Maxted at Nick's; also worked there w. Phil Napoleon Jan.-Apr. '59. Fav. own solo: *After You've Gone* w. Pee Wee Erwin (Cadence). Favs: Goodman, Fazola, De Franco. LPs w. Erwin (Cad., Uran., Bruns.), Billy Maxted (Cad.).

Addr: 41-12 41st Street, Long Island City 4, N.Y.

PAGE, ORAN (Hot Lips), *trumpet, singer, leader;* b. Dallas, Texas, 1/27/08; d. New York City, 11/5/54. High school in Corsicana, Texas; started playing at 12 and was member of children's brass band that also incl. Budd Johnson. Toured w. Walter Page's original Blue Devils 1927-30; Bennie Moten 1931-5 and remained with the band briefly under Count Basie's leadership 1935-6. From 1936 to '41 he had his own band off and on, playing successfully in the East. He joined Artie Shaw in the summer of 1941 for several months and made a number of records w. Shaw, in which he was feat. as singer and trumpeter, notably *Blues in the Night, Take Your Shoes Off Baby* and *Motherless Child.* After leaving Shaw he led various bands and worked as a single in jam sessions around NYC until his death. He played the Jazz Festival in Paris in May 1949, also played Belgian and other continental dates in the summer of '53 and '54. Page was cast in the Armstrong mold both as singer and instrumentalist, performing in a febrile style that was at its most impressive on his many successful blues records. LPs: two tracks w. own group in *Kansas City Jazz* (Decca); LPs w. Chu Berry (Epic), Artie Shaw (Victor), *Jazztime USA, Vol. 3* (Bruns.), *Spirituals To Swing* (Vang.); one track in *Singin' The Blues* (Cam.).

PAGE, WALTER SYLVESTER, *bass;* b. Gallatin, Mo., 2/9/1900; d. NYC, 12/20/57. No relation to Hot Lips Page. Inspired by singing of folk songs and spirituals by his family. Played bass drum with neighborhood band, then horn in high school band and on to bass viol; played with municipal orch.; then with Bennie Moten 1918-23; left to go with road show band. When show closed, band stayed intact under Page as Blue Devils, incl. Count Basie and Jimmy Rushing. Joined Bennie Moten's big band '31; Count Basie '35-43, '46-8. Integral part of fabulous rhythm section that helped make Basie famous. With Hot Lips Page '49, Jimmy Rushing '51-2; then w. Jimmy McPartland at Lou Terrasi's. Played w. Eddie Condon from Nov. '52 until a few months before he died of pneumonia. App. w. Ruby Braff at NJF '57. LPs w. Jo Jones, Nat Pierce, Ruby Braff (Vang.), Joe Turner (Atl.), Roy Eldridge (Verve), Paul Quinichette (Pres.), Eddie Condon (Col.), Count Basie (Decca, Bruns., Epic, Col., Vict.), *Lester Young Memorial* (Epic), Buck Clayton (Col.), Jimmy Rushing (Col., Vang.), *Spirituals To Swing* (Vang.).

PAICH, MARTIN LOUIS (Marty), *piano, composer;* b. Oakland, Cal., 1/23/25. Worked with Gary Nottingham at Sweets Ballroom in Oakland, 1941-3 (Pete Rugolo was the other arranger). Led band in AAF 1943-6. Spent 1946-50 studying under Mario Castelnuovo-Tedesco; Bachelor and Master degrees at LA Cons. Worked briefly w. Bobby Sherwood during this period, resuming full-time career in 1951 w. Jerry Gray. Pl. and arr. w. Shelly Manne '52; wrote library for Dan Terry orch. Arr. and accomp. for Peggy Lee '53. Nine months w. Shorty Rogers' Giants '54. Acc. Dorothy Dandridge in London, spring '56. Film: played and arranged for Walt Disney movie *Lady And The Tramp.* A prominent, capable, frequently recorded member of the West Coast jazz clique. Favs: Art Tatum, piano; Johnny Mandel, arr. Own LPs: GNP, Inter., Tampa, Cadence, Vict., War. Bros.; LPs w. Shorty Rogers (Vict.), John Graas (Decca), Shelly Manne (Contemp.); as arr. Dave Pell (Kapp), Chet Baker (Col.), Mel Torme (Beth., Verve), Ella Fitzgerald, Ray Brown, Anita O'Day, Buddy Rich (Verve), Art Pepper (Contemp.), Stan Kenton (Cap.), Terry Gibbs (Merc.).

Addr: 7701 Hesperia, Reseda, Calif.

PALMER, SINGLETON NATHANIEL, *sousaphone, bass, leader;* b. St. Louis, Mo., 11/13/13. Stud. piano at 12.

Pl. bass w. George Hudson in St. Louis and NYC eight years; two years w. Count Basie, 1948-50. Formed own group in 1950, *Dixie Land Six*, pl. St. Louis clubs. Fav: Tuba player w. Coon-Sanders band. LPs w. Basie (Vict., Cam.).

Addr: 1384 Burd Ave., St. Louis 12, Mo.

PALMIER, REMO (formerly Palmieri), *guitar;* b. New York City, 3/29/23. Planned to be an artist, played club dates to pay for art studies. Became prof. musician Dec. 1942, when he joined Nat Jaffe Trio. With Coleman Hawkins, April 1943; Red Norvo 1944, then led own combo backing Billie Holiday on 52nd St. Played CBS radio series w. Mildred Bailey; joined Phil Moore at Cafe Society, Nov. '44. Left Moore Feb. '45 to join CBS staff and has been there ever since, featured on daily Arthur Godfrey show. One of the most advanced guitarists of the '40s. Recorded w. Barney Bigard '44; *All The Things You Are, Groovin' High* w. Dizzy Gillespie 1945; also Teddy Wilson-Sarah Vaughan date '46. He won the *Esquire* New Star Award 1945, Silver Award 1946. LPs w. Gillespie (Savoy, Rondolette), Red Norvo in *The Jazz Greats* (EmArcy).

Addr: 110 Riverside Drive, New York 24, N.Y.

PARENTI, ANTHONY (Tony), *clarinet, saxes;* b. New Orleans, 8/6/00. As child, played in large orch. organized by his teacher, Prof. Joseph Taverno; started playing jazz 1914, worked on riverboats and in many local clubs; led own band at Bienville Hotel 1921. Came to New York 1927, subbed for Benny Goodman in the Ben Pollack band, worked with Paul Ash and many society bands. From 1930, CBS staff, then at Radio City Music Hall. Toured w. Ted Lewis '36-42; had his own band at Jimmy Ryan's, spent two years at Condon's, then 4½ years in Miami Beach, Fla., mainly with Preacher Rollo's Five Saints. Seven weeks w. Dukes of Dixieland '52. Back in NYC '54, pl. in trio w. Joe Sullivan, Zutty Singleton at Metropole. From '55-60, regular weekends at Central Plaza, daily matinees at Metropole and many one-nighters w. Dixieland combos in NYC and Conn. Timex TV show w. Armstrong, '58. One of the best all-around musicians to emerge from the early New Orleans jazz scene. Own LPs: Riverside, Southland, Jazzology, Jazztone; LPs w. Rollo (MGM), Condon (Dec.), G. Brunis (Comm.).

Addr: 8306 Vietor Ave., Elmhurst, L.I., N.Y.

PARHAM, HARTZELL STRATHDENE (Tiny), *piano, organ, composer;* b. Kansas City, Mo., 2/25/00; d. Milwaukee, Wisc., 4/4/43. Led his own groups and app. as sideman in a variety of Chicago clubs, incl. the Dreamland Cafe, during 1920s. From the '30s worked as organ soloist in theaters and hotels until his death. Rec. w. own band for Vict. '28, '29, w. Johnny Dodds for Paramount '26. LP: one track w. Dodds in *History of Classic Jazz* (River.).

PARHAM, CHARLES VALDEZ (Truck), *bass;* b. Chicago, Ill., 1/25/13. Seven years of vocal training; pl. drums, switched to bass on advice of Sy Oliver. First lessons from Walter Page. Started as valet with a band, pl. w. Zack Whyte in Cincinnati '32-4; also active in late '20s and early '30s as prof. football player with Chicago Negro All Stars, and took a fling at boxing. Worked at the Three Deuces with Roy Eldridge and Art Tatum '35-8; Earl Hines '40-2, J. Lunceford '42-7. Was with M. Spanier combo '50-5 except for few weeks w. Gigi Gryce Jan. '54. Joined Herbie Fields late '56, leaving in June '57 to work with Louis Bellson Quartet; has been w. Bellson off and on since then. Also was w. Dorothy Donegan; made tour of American Indian concerts with Big Chief Russell Moore through the Dakotas, '58. Has also been active as trainer for both child and adult boxers. Rec. early Hines hits incl. *Jelly Jelly;* also was on M. Bailey, R. Eldridge dates in Chi. '37. Fav. own rec. *Fine Brown Frame* w. N. Lutcher. LPs w. Pearl Bailey (Roulette), L. Bellson (Verve), Spanier (Weathers).

Addr: 735 East 65th St., Chicago 37, Ill.

PARIS, JACKIE, *singer, guitar;* b. Nutley, N.J., 9/20/26. Recommended for his first job by the Mills Bros., he played guitar in a trio w. Nick Jerret. Army 1944-6; then studied guitar at Scott School, played and sang with many 52nd St. combos; made solo record debut 1947 on MGM. Joined Lionel Hampton's band and toured with him for several months as singer 1949-50. Gave up playing guitar on jobs and worked as single in night clubs in early and mid-'50s. During the late '50s he took up tap dancing in an attempt to present himself as more of a show business personality. Incorporating this, and his guitar once again, into his act, he appeared in night clubs throughout the US w. comedian Lennie Bruce '59. Won DB critics' poll 1953 as best new male singer of the year. Paris is one of the handful of male singers to come to prominence in the past decade who have retained a true jazz sound, applying this rare quality to skillful interpretations of some of the better ballads and pop songs. Fav: Ella Fitzgerald. LPs: Time, East-West, Bruns.; two nos. in *Jazztime USA, Vol. 3* (Bruns.), one no. in *Advance Guard of the Forties* (Em.).

PARKER, CHARLES CHRISTOPER JR. (Charlie or Bird or Yardbird), *alto sax, composer;* b. Kansas City, Kansas, 8/29/20; d. New York City, 3/12/55. Raised in Kansas City, Missouri. Mother bought him an alto sax in 1931; he pl. baritone horn in school band. Leaving school at 15, Parker very soon fell into company and habits which were to establish the pattern and the limit of his life: he became a narcotics addict. During his first year as a professional musician Parker was held in great contempt by local musicians, but after spending a season at a summer resort with George E. Lee's band he returned to Kansas City with a style that had developed phenomenally and already showed elements of the ideas associated with his most influential years.

Parker was a wanderer, fitfully employed by Jay McShann, Lawrence Keyes and Harlan Leonard in the period of 1937-9. He first came to New York in '39 and for almost a year worked intermittently at Clark

Monroe's Uptown House. On another visit to NYC, in April 1941, he made his first records (with McShann for Decca). Around this time he met Dizzy Gillespie when the latter sat in with McShann at the Savoy Ballroom; the styles of both, however, were already maturing rapidly and it is doubtful that they had any strong influence on one another. They happened to be working along the same lines and were to become known in 1945 as partners and virtual co-founders of the new jazz movement then known as bebop.

Parker's style, already discernible on the McShann records, crystallized after he left the touring band and returned to NYC, where he sat in often at Minton's Play House and worked with the bands of Noble Sissle (with whom he played clarinet and alto for a few months in '42) and Earl Hines (on tenor sax for ten months in '43; during most of this time Gillespie was also in the band). After working briefly with the Cootie Williams and Andy Kirk orchs. he went on the road with the original Billy Eckstine band in '44, playing alto; this was the first big band to make a clear-cut policy of featuring the new jazz style in its solos and arrangements.

In Sept. '44, Parker made his first small combo record date, with Tiny Grimes for Savoy. In Feb. and May '45, under Gillespie's name, seven tunes were recorded by a quintet featuring Parker, Gillespie and a rhythm section. These were the definitive sides that established the new jazz generation on records (they have since been reissued in LPs on Savoy and Rondolette: see below).

Soon after these records were released, Parker and Gillespie became the twin focal points of interest in the then intensely active jazz world of 52nd Street, which was dotted with small clubs that featured them separately or jointly. Although he now enjoyed the respect of a clique of younger musicians, Parker, like Gillespie, had to fight the antagonism of the jazz critics, who were almost unanimously opposed to every new development in jazz; and he had yet to make any impact on the general public. Late in '45 he left for California; working with Gillespie in a small combo at Billy Berg's, he found the local attitude hostile and took refuge in still deeper narcotics involvement. After recording two tunes at a chaotic record session on the night of July 29, 1946, he broke down completely, was arrested and committed to Camarillo State Hospital. After six months there he returned to Los Angeles, recorded two superb sessions for Dial (one featuring Erroll Garner) and went back to work with a quintet. He usually worked in this setting for the next few years, generally in New York and other Eastern cities; he worked intermittently for Norman Granz's JATP unit starting in '46. His sidemen included first Miles Davis, later Red Rodney and Kenny Dorham on trumpet; Duke Jordan and Al Haig, piano; Tommy Potter, bass; Max Roach and Roy Haynes, drums. Parker made his first trip overseas in May 1949, taking part in the Paris Jazz Festival; he visited Scandinavia in Nov. '50. During the last five years of his life he went through several cycles of illness and cure, working irregularly; at one point, only a few months before his death, he appeared at a Town Hall concert and played with a command as great as at any period in his career. Plagued by a complex of illnesses including ulcers and cirrhosis of the liver, Parker suffered from a series of emotional as well as physical problems. On March 4, 1955, he made his final public appearance at Birdland, the club that had been named after him. A week later he died, after a heart seizure, at the New York apartment of a friend.

Charlie Parker is one of the few jazzmen who can be said to have given dignity and meaning to the abused word "genius". It was his desire to devote his life to the translation of everything he saw and heard into terms of musical beauty. Though it was his inspiration, his soul and warmth that earned him an international reputation, and although he had little formal training, he was a man of amazing technical skill, a fast reader and a gifted composer-arranger. His best records were those he made with a small, informal combo, but he was proudest of the series of albums he made, starting in 1950, with a group featuring strings and woodwinds. (The first modern jazz soloist to record in this context, he led the way for dozens of others whose "With Strings" albums followed his.)

In bringing the art of improvisation to a new peak of maturity, Parker had an inestimable influence on jazz musicians regardless of what instrument they played. From the mid-'40s on, it was almost impossible for any new jazzman anywhere in the world to escape reflecting to some degree, consciously or unconsciously, a Parker influence; his work set a new standard on every level: harmonic, tonal, rhythmic and melodic. Acknowledging the jazz world's debt to him, Lennie Tristano once observed: "If Charlie wanted to invoke plagiarism laws, he could sue almost everybody who's made a record in the last ten years."

As a composer, Parker was responsible for the casual creation (usually for record dates) of a series of instrumental numbers designed for unison interpretation by a quintet, all of them displaying the same strikingly original melodic sense that was inherent in his improvised solos. His best known works include *Now's The Time* (later used as the basis for a rhythm-and-blues hit, *The Hucklebuck*), *Yardbird Suite, Confirmation* and *Relaxin' At Camarillo.*

Parker's first official recognition was his New Star award in the 1946 Esquire poll. He won the DB poll '50-4, Met. poll '48-53; DB Hall of Fame '55; DB Critics' poll '53-4; EOJ poll as "greatest ever" '56.

Own LPs: Savoy 12000, 12001, 12009, 12014, 12079, Roost 2210; *Diz' N' Bird* (Roost 2234); Verve 8000-8010; *Jam Session #1, 2* (Verve 8049, 8050), *The Jazz Scene* (8060), JATP Vols. 1, 2, 4, 7 (Verve); LPs w. Dizzy Gillespie: (Savoy 12020, Rondo. 11),

Miles Davis (Pres. 7044); tracks in *Midnight Jazz At Carnegie Hall* (Verve 8189); one track w. Jay McShann in *Encyclopedia of Jazz on Record* (Decca DXF 140) and *The Jazz Story . . . As Told By Steve Allen* (Coral CJE 100); w. *Metronome All Stars* (Cam. 426).

PARKER, JOHN W. JR. (Knocky), *piano;* b. Palmer, Tex., 8/8/18. First learned about jazz from itinerant cotton pickers in Texas, players in Dallas dives, and from following the keys as piano rolls ground out ragtime. Played w. Light Crust Doughboys while at Trinity University in Waxahachie, Tex. After Army discharge joined Z. Singleton-Albert Nicholas trio in Los Angeles area. Gigged around NYC while teaching English at Columbia University and has since embarked on the dual career of English teacher and jazz concert lecturer. Worked w. Inez Cavanaugh at Chez Inez in Paris, '52. Has taught at Kentucky Wesleyan; Peabody Teachers Coll., Nashville, Tenn. and in '59-60 at University of Kentucky. As lecturer he demonstrates styles from Scott Joplin through Brubeck. Fav: Jelly Roll Morton. Own LPs on Audiophile; LPs w. Doc Evans (Soma, Audio.).

Addr: College of Arts & Sciences, University of Kentucky, Lexington, Ky.

PARKER, JOHNNY—see PLONSKY, John

PARKER, LEO, *baritone sax;* b. Washington, D.C., 1925. No relation to Charlie Parker. Studied alto sax in high school. Played w. Billy Eckstine 1944, later w. Benny Carter, Illinois Jacquet, Dizzy Gillespie. Earned some popularity as featured soloist on Sir Charles Thompson's record of *Mad Lad.* Originally inspired by Ch. Parker, he tended later toward a honking style with more r&b than jazz appeal. Since 1948 he has been active only intermittently. LPs w. Dexter Gordon, Fats Navarro (Savoy), Bill Jennings (King); two tracks in *Saxomaniac* (Apollo).

PARLAN, HORACE LOUIS, *piano;* b. Pittsburgh, Pa., 1/19/31. Began piano w. private teachers in 1943. After a childhood attack of polio which left right hand partially paralyzed, Parlan, through the encouragement of his teacher, Mary Alston, and bassist Wyatt Ruther, developed a predominantly left-hand style. Gigged w. local groups in Pittsburgh 1952-7, also brief stint in Washington, D.C. w. Sonny Stitt. Became member of C. Mingus' Jazz Workshop in Oct. '57, worked in New York clubs and on tour. Jobs in NYC with Lou Donaldson '59-60. Favs: H. Silver, B. Powell, J. Lewis. LPs w. Mingus (Beth., Col.). Led own quintet accompanying Langston Hughes in *The Weary Blues* (MGM). LPs w. Bob Gonzales (Hope), Lou Donaldson (Blue Note).

PARNELL, JACK, *drums, leader;* b. London, England, 8/6/23. First prominent in RAF band led by Buddy Featherstonhaugh. After working w. Vic Lewis' Dixieland band, he made a national name as drummer w. Ted Heath, whom he left in 1951 to form a big band of his own. Toured Scandinavia w. Lena Horne 1952. In late '50s his group was heard on a weekly television show. A modern, swinging drummer, one of England's best.

PARRISH, AVERY, *piano;* b. Birmingham, Ala., 1/24/17; d. NYC, 12/10/59. Attended Ala. State College. He became a member of the college band, which later went out professionally under Erskine Hawkins' leadership. With the group for a decade from 1934, he earned his greatest popularity with a much-imitated blues solo, *After Hours,* recorded in June 1940. After suffering paralysis and near-fatal injuries in an accident, Parrish was forced to retire from music. For years before his death, he was in obscurity, working day jobs. Although Parrish's original record of *After Hours* is not available, new versions, based on the original, were recorded in the '50s by many modern pianists incl. Phineas Newborn, Jutta Hipp and Ray Bryant.

PASTOR, TONY (Antonio Pestritto), *singer, leader, tenor sax;* b. Middletown, Conn., 1907. An early associate of Artie Shaw, he worked in many of the same bands, including those of Irving Aaronson and Vincent Lopez. Worked w. Shaw's bands from 1936 until 1940; formed his own orchestra soon after Shaw disbanded in 1940 and led a popular dance band feat. his own Armstrong-inspired vocals. In 1959 he gave up the band and formed a vocal act that incl. his sons Tony Jr. and Guy. Pastor won the *Met.* poll in 1940 on tenor sax. Own LPs: Roulette, Harmony; LPs w. Shaw: Epic, Victor, Camden.

Addr: c/o General Artists Corp., 1270 Sixth Avenue, New York 20, N.Y.

PATE, JOHNNY, *bass;* b. Chicago Heights, Ill., 1923. Stud. piano in early years, took up tuba in seventh grade. Joined 218th AGF Band while in Army, 1944, and stud. bass and arr. Became leader of dance orch. w. Army Band. After discharge in '46, joined Coleridge Davis band in Atlantic City and later Stuff Smith trio in Chicago '47. Worked as staff arr. at Club DeLisa and was house bassist at Blue Note in Chicago. Joined Eddie South, traveling w. him until 1952. Has worked in Chicago since, rec. and club dates. Own LPs (King).

PATTERSON, OTTILIE (Anna-Ottilie Patterson Barber), *singer;* b. Comber, County Down, N. Ireland, 1/31/32. Irish father, Latvian mother. Grandfather pl. bagpipes; many other musical relatives. No vocal training. Working as an art teacher, she became interested in blues as a hobby in 1950 and did not sing prof. until Jan. '55, when she joined the combo of Chris Barber (q.v.). Influenced by folk blues singers, she was the first European artist to sing in this style with conviction and authenticity. Married Chris Barber 11/12/59. Has rec. blues w. Barber, also LP of Irish and pop songs.

Addr: c/o Chris Barber, 37 Soho Square, London W.1., England.

PAUL, LES (Lester Polfus), *guitar;* b. Waukesha, Wis., 6/9/16. Self-taught. Worked in Chicago radio stations 1932-7; w. Fred Waring '38-40; returned to Chicago radio work '41-2, then settled in Calif., where he formed his own trio in '44. During the late '40s he applied his knowledge of engineering techniques to the production of trick recordings made in a studio he had set up in his garage. The unique tonal effects obtained from these multi-taped, multi-speed novelties sold many millions of Capitol records. Paul, who once played in a style resembling that of Django Reinhardt, revealed himself as a good modern jazz guitarist in the last jazz records he made (1946) but has worked exclusively in the pop field in recent years. He married singer-guitarist Mary Ford, partner in his act, 12/29/49. He won the DB poll 1951-3. LPs as jazz artist: JATP, Vol. 3 (Verve); as pop artist: Cap., Decca.

Addr: Deerhaven Road, Mahwah, N.J.

PAVAGEAU, ALCIDE (Slow Drag), *bass;* b. New Orleans, 3/7/1888. Self-taught on guitar, which he played from 1905, and bass, which he took up at the age of 45. Best known as bassist with many groups involved in the New Orleans jazz revival, incl. Bunk Johnson's orch., Geo. Lewis, Herb Morand and other groups in New Orleans. "His amazing tone and forcefulness place him in the front rank of jazz bassists," wrote William Russell in 1944. LPs: see George Lewis, Bunk Johnson.

PAYNE, CECIL McKENZIE, *baritone and alto sax;* b. Brooklyn, N.Y., 12/14/22. Studied alto and clarinet w. Pete Brown. Army 1943-6. Made prof. debut on J. J. Johnson record session, playing alto (*Coppin' the Bop,* etc.). Soon after, while he was working w. Roy Eldridge at the Spotlite on 52nd St., Dizzy Gillespie heard and hired him. He remained w. Gillespie from late '46 until Jan. '49, touring Europe with him in Feb. '48. Free-lanced in NYC w. Tadd Dameron, James Moody and other small combos; toured w. Illinois Jacquet from '52 to Jan. '54. After this, worked with father in real-estate business, gigging in spare time; active chiefly w. Randy Weston '58-60. His big-toned, agile style showed promise that was not fulfilled in later years. Favs: Carney, Chaloff, Mulligan. LPs w. Kenny Burrell (Pres.), Kenny Dorham (Blue Note), Dizzy Gillespie (GNP, Vict.), Randy Weston (Dawn, River.), Matthew Gee (River.), Rolf Ericson, Jimmy Cleveland, Clark Terry, Dinah Washington, Cannonball Adderley (EmArcy), Kenny Clarke-Ernie Wilkins (Savoy), Tadd Dameron (Pres.), *Roots* (New Jazz), Illinois Jacquet (Verve), *Bird's Night* (Savoy).

Addr: 1009 Sterling Place, Brooklyn 13, N.Y.

PAYNE, DONALD RAY (Don), *bass;* b. Amarillo, Texas, 1/7/33. Raised in southern Calif.; started music at high school in Santa Ana. After Army service, 1953-5, lived in Hollywood. Played w. Art Pepper, Joe Maini, Calvin Jackson and Ornette Coleman's first group. Came East Oct. '58. Worked w. Mundell Lowe, Chris Connor and most of '59 in Ralph Sharon's trio accompanying Tony Bennett. Joined Herbie Mann Dec. '59 and toured Africa, Jan-Mar. '60. LP w. Ornette Coleman (Contemp.); also rec. with Harry Babasin, Mundell Lowe.

Addr: 16 West 68th St., New York 23, N.Y.

PAYNE, PERCIVAL (Sonny), *drums;* b. NYC, 5/4/26. Father, Chris. Columbus, is veteran drummer and leader of own quintet. Sonny stud. w. Vic Berton 1936, pl. w. Bascomb brothers '44, Hot Lips Page '44-5, Earl Bostic '45-7. Worked w. bassist Lucille Dixon and her combo for six months, '48, then w. Tiny Grimes until '50, when he began a three-year stint in Erskine Hawkins' orch. Led his own band in Larry Steele Revues, '53-5, then in early '55 joined Count Basie. A flashy and showmanly performer, whose contribution to the Basie band has been disputed, though many feel he is a first rate big band drummer. Favs: Rich, Bellson, Jo Jones, Blakey, Roach. LPs w. Basie (Verve, Roul.), Joe Saye (Em.).

Addr: 1103 Franklin Ave., Bronx 56, N.Y.

PEACOCK, BURNIE, *alto sax, clarinet, etc.;* b. Columbia, Tenn., 6/2/21. Stud. clarinet at 11, sax at 14. Attended Tenn. State College, 1936-8. Local groups in Chicago and Detroit '38-42, incl. Jimmy Rachel's band which featured Wardell Gray, Howard McGhee, Milt Buckner. Played in Navy bands '42-5. With Lucky Millinder, Jimmie Lunceford, '45, Lionel Hampton, '46, Cab Calloway, '47, Count Basie, '48. Subbed as leader for Earl Bostic in '52 when latter was inactive owing to car crash. USO tour for Far East Command, '52. Many records w. Ruth Brown, Bull Moose Jackson and own combos. Favs: Benny Carter, alto; Buddy De Franco, clar.

Addr: 65 University Place, New York, N.Y.

PEARSON, DAVE (David Pearson Barraclough), *drums;* b. Cincinnati, Ohio, 12/29/28. Raised in England. Violin at 10, clar. in Navy; drums from 17. To US with Vic Ash combo Sept. '58; toured Britain with Newport show '59. LPs w. Melody Maker poll winners for Pye-Nixa; Wally Fowkes, Vic Lewis et al. Infl. orig. by Krupa, Rich, now by K. Clarke, Philly Joe Jones.

Addr: 68A Seven Sisters Road, Islington, London N.7, England.

PEARSON, COLUMBUS CALVIN JR. (Duke), *piano;* also *trumpet;* b. Atlanta, Ga., 8/17/32. Mother, a pianist, gave him lessons at five. Took up mellophone, baritone horn and trumpet at 12. Pl. trumpet through high school and college. In Army 1953-4. Pl. in 3rd Army Special Services show w. Wynton Kelly, Phineas Newborn, George Joyner and Louis Smith. Back to Atlanta, Nov. '54, pl. piano again; w. John Peck at Waluhaje Ballroom to '57. Own trio, and quintet w. Louis Smith, at Club Sorrento, Nov. '57-Nov. '58. Came to NYC, Jan. '59. While waiting for union card, worked in religious book store, then gigged w. Steve Pulliam. Joined Donald Byrd, Oct. '59. Favs: Wynton Kelly, Hank Jones. Own LP: Blue Note; LP w. Byrd (Blue Note).

Addr: 1978 Morris Ave., Bronx, N.Y.

PECORA, SANTO (Santo J. Pecoraro), *trombone;* b. New Orleans, 3/31/02. Studied first on French horn. Prof. debut w. Joe Fulco in a local movie theatre. First prominent in jazz as a member of the New Orleans Rhythm Kings, 1924-5, with whom he went to Chicago; rec. with this group for Okeh and Victor, 1925. Later played in many motion picture theatre house bands, and during the 1930s was on the road with such dance bands as Ben Meroff's, Buddy Rogers' and Ben Pollack's. He recorded w. a revived version of the NORK (as Paul Mares' Friars Society Orch.) in Chicago 1935, for Okeh, and made a session in NYC 1936 w. Sharkey Bonano for Vocalion. After spending several years in Hollywood, working w. Wingy Manone and with many combos of his own, he returned to New Orleans in 1942 and has been there off and on ever since, sometimes with Sharkey, often with his own bands. He reached the peak of a major comeback about 1951, working with Sharkey at the Famous Door, but soon after left to form his own band, which stayed together for two years, attempting to cover the pop field as well as jazz with pseudo-Dorsey renditions, etc. In recent years he has been doing odd jobs, recording occasionally for Joe Mares (Southland). Movies: *Rhythm on the River, Blues in the Night.* Pecora for many years was considered one of the best New Orleans trombonists in the "tailgate" tradition. Favs: Bill Harris, Dorsey, Teagarden. Own LPs: Verve, South., three tracks in *Recorded In New Orleans* (GTJ); LPs w. Turk Murphy (Col.), Sharkey Bonano (Cap.), four tracks w. Paul Mares in *Chicago Style Jazz* (Col.), one track w. Armand Hug in *History of Jazz, Vol. 1* (Cap.); Doc Souchon (Gold. Cr.).

Addr: 410 Labarre Drive, Metairie, La.

PEDERSON, PULLMAN G. (Tommy), *trombone;* b. Watkins, Minn., 8/15/20. Stud. many instruments since age of 4, incl. drums, piano, violin. At 17, joined Don Strickland's territory band. During 1940s played w. many dance bands incl. Gene Krupa, '40-5, Red Norvo, Woody Herman, Tommy Dorsey, '43, Charlie Barnet, '44 and '46. Since then, free-lancing in Hollywood, doing all Nelson Riddle and Dave Rose jobs. Simulated all Tommy Dorsey solos in film, *The Gene Krupa Story.* Pederson, who in recent years has stud. w. Mario Castelnuovo-Tedesco, is an expert soloist influenced by his favs. T. Dorsey, B. Harris, L. McGarity, J. Teagarden, F. Rosolino. Ambition: To write operatic and symph. music that will incorporate the color and phrasing of jazz. LPs: *The Gene Krupa Story* (Verve), *Trombones Incorporated; Gershwin With Bongos* (War. Bros.) *Four Freshmen With Trombones* (Cap.).

Addr: 12457 Ventura Blvd., Studio City, Calif.

PEIFFER, BERNARD, *piano, composer;* b. Epinal, France, 10/22/22. Stud. at Marseilles Cons. and at Ecole Normale de Paris. Prof. debut in 1943; worked w. Django Reinhardt, Hubert Rostaing and Andre Ekyan; rec. w. Rex Stewart '47. Working as soloist in Paris clubs, he was hailed by Barry Ulanov in *Metronome* as one of Europe's most original musicians. He emigrated to US Dec. '54, made his first American LP for EmArcy (Mercury) Apr. '56 and later did several dates for Decca. By 1960 Peiffer, who swings in an exultant style unmistakably his own and is technically equipped perhaps as well as any pianist since Tatum, has impressed many musicians with his work; but he had failed to achieve the commercial success gained by many less talented pianists. As John S. Wilson wrote: "He is that rarity among jazz pianists—a legitimately schooled musician with brilliant technique who can transfer much of this brilliance to jazz performances without necessarily falling into the trap of believing that technique is all." Own LPs: Laurie, Decca, Mercury; one side of *Jazz From St. Germain des Pres* (Verve).

Addr: 246 East Johnson Street, Philadelphia 44, Pa.

PELL, DAVID (Dave), *saxophones, clarinets, etc.,* b. Brooklyn, N.Y., 2/26/25. Played w. Bob Astor, Tony Pastor, Bobby Sherwood in early 1940s. Moved to Calif., pl. w. Bob Crosby for two years on the Ford show, then local clubs w. his own group; rec. on own '47. Joined Les Brown '48, leaving in '55 to form own octet out of nucleus of Brown band. Group pl. mostly school dances and concerts in So. Calif., also engagements at Crescendo, Cloisters. Active as a photographer, and as a & r dir. for Tops Records. Produced over 200 albums '56-9, took pictures for covers. Also owns two mus. pub. firms. Went to England '59 to produce sessions, did not play himself. In recent years Pell has specialized in a bland, heavily diluted jazz style that aims to appeal to dancers as well as to jazz fans. Own LPs on Kapp, Atl., Vict., Cap., Coral; LPs w. Brown (Coral).

Addr: 6229 Wilkinson Ave., No. Hollywood, Calif.

PEMBERTON, WILLIAM McLANE, *bass;* b. New York City, 3/5/18. Stud. violin from age eight to 18, then bass for two years. Pl. club dates around NYC; w. Frankie Newton 1941-5. During late '40s and '50s, pl. with Herman Chittison, Mercer Ellington, Alex Kallao, Barbara Carroll, Dorothy Donegan, Art Tatum, Eddie South, Johnny Hodges and Lucky Millinder. Fav: Jimmy Blanton. LPs w. Barbara Carroll, Pete Brown (Verve), Joe Thomas (Atl.), Henderson All Stars reunion band (UA, Uran.).

Addr: 108-01 Fern Place, Jamaica 33, N.Y.

PENA, RALPH RAYMOND, *bass;* b. Jarbidge, Nev., 2/24/27, Father pl. trad. Spanish guitar. Stud. baritone, tuba, Sacramento and SF State Teachers' Coll. Debut in Grass Valley, Calif. w. Jerry Austin '42-4. Heard w. Nick Esposito, '48-9; Art Pepper, V. Musso, C. Tjader, '50; B. May, '51-2; B. Kessel off and on, '53-5; briefly w. Stan Getz, '54; two months w. Ch. Barnet, '54; a year w. Shorty Rogers '55-6. Many dates incl. Music Inn, Lenox, w. J. Giuffre, '56-7; short periods w. Buddy De Franco, '56-9; leader at Sherry's in Hollywood, working w. Hamp Hawes, Carl Perkins. NJF,

Great South Bay Festival '57; led own quartet on *Stars of Jazz* TV show and at concerts around LA. Formed a duo w. Pete Jolly for clubs and records 1959. In his own opinion and the author's, the best work by this talented modern musician can be heard on the Giuffre *Tangents in Jazz* LP (Cap.) Favs: J. Blanton, R. Mitchell. LPs w. J. Millman (Dec.), J. Montrose (Wor.-Pac.); *Man With The Golden Arm* (Dec.), Duane Tatro (Contemp.), Giuffre (Atl.).

Addr: 1139 No. Ogden Drive, Los Angeles 46, Cal.

PEPPER, ARTHUR EDWARD (Art), *alto, tenor saxes;* b. Gardena, Cal., 9/1/25. Studied privately: clarinet at 9, alto at 13. Gigged around Los Angeles in 1943 w. Gus Arnheim, Benny Carter, Lee Young. In Nov. '43 he joined Stan Kenton for 3 months, then spent two years in the Army. After free-lancing in Los Angeles from May '46 to Sept. '47 he rejoined Kenton, remaining with him off and on until early '52. Inactive in 1953, he returned to music in '54, free-lancing in LA with his own combo, but was soon on the sidelines again owing to narcotics problems. Rehabilitated, he gigged in Las Vegas and Los Angeles 1957-60, playing in Latin bands as well as jazz groups. Pepper has an exceptional technique, shows both Konitz and Parker influences, and for years has been one of the best all-around reed soloists in the Los Angeles area. Own LPs: Contemp., Savoy, Reg., Interlude, Intro, Tampa; *Playboys* w. Chet Baker, one side of *Just Friends* w. Bill Perkins (Wor. Pac.); *Mucho Calor* (Andex); LPs w. Stan Kenton (Cap.), Shorty Rogers (Cap., Vict.), Ted Brown (Vang.), *Jazz Composers Workshop* (Savoy), John Graas (Merc., Decca), Howard Lucraft (Decca), Mel Torme (Verve), Shelly Manne (Contemp.).

Addr: 1450 No. Indian, Palm Springs, Calif.

PERAZA, ARMANDO, *bongos, conga drum;* b. Havana, Cuba, 5/30/24. To NYC 1948 as dancer & bongo player w. Afro-Cuban revue. Played w. Machito 1949, Slim Gaillard '50, also w. Perez Prado, Cal Tjader, Dave Brubeck. Joined George Shearing 1954. Fav: Chano Pozo. LPs w. Cal Tjader (Fant.), Machito (Verve), Shearing (Cap., MGM).

Addr: 153 E. 54th St., New York 22, N.Y.

PERCIFUL, JACK T., *piano;* b. Moscow, Idaho, 11/26/25. Began stud. piano at seven; B.S. degree in music educ. from U. of Idaho. Pl. in Army Service Band 1945-6 in Japan. Pl. with small bands around LA; joined Harry James April '58. Fav: Art Tatum. LPs w. Harry James (Cap.).

Addr: 2416 Hassett Avenue, Las Vegas, Nev.

PERKINS, WILLIAM REESE (Bill), *tenor, baritone saxes;* b. San Francisco, Calif., 7/22/24. Raised in Chile and Santa Barbara, Calif. Army 1943-5, then stud. music under GI bill. Did not start full time prof. career until '50. Grad. from Cal. Tech. w. degree as radio engineer. Played w. Jerry Wald. From '52-59 worked mostly w. W. Herman and S. Kenton, incl. European tour w. Herman in spring of '54. Leaving Kenton 1/15/59, he gigged w. Terry Gibbs and Allyn Ferguson in Hollywood, but concentrated on studying engineering and worked for World-Pacific records as engineer, mixer, tape editor. Also, taught at Westlake College of Music. Won DB Critics' poll as new star '55. One of the best tenor men on the West Coast, he was also heard as an effective baritone soloist in the late '50s. Own LPs: *On Stage; Just Friends* w. Kamuca, Pepper (Wor. Pac.), *Tenors Head On* (Lib.); LPs w. Art Pepper (Contemp.), Marty Paich (War. Bros.), Woody Herman (Cap., Verve), Stan Kenton (Cap.), Barney Kessel, Lennie Niehaus (Merc., Contemp.), Bud Shank, John Lewis (Wor. Pac.), Max Roach-Stan Levey (Lib.), Tal Farlow (Verve), *The Brothers* w. Al Cohn, Kamuca (Vict.).

Addr: 248 34th St., Manhattan Beach, Calif.

PERKINS, CARL, *piano;* b. Indianapolis, Ind., 8/16/28; d. Calif., 3/17/58. Not related to singer of same name. Brother, Ed Perkins, is bassist. Self-taught. After working w. Tiny Bradshaw and Big Jay McNeely, 1948-9, he settled in Calif. Dec., '49 and worked mostly as a single, also playing dates w. Miles Davis, '50. Army (saw action in Korea), Jan. '51 to Nov., '52. Spent '53 and Summer '54 w. Oscar Moore trio and worked with him again Sept.-Nov., '55. Own group at Strollers, Long Beach, Calif. '56. Then w. Harold Land, Chet Baker. Talented modern pianist who, at times, played with his left arm parallel to the piano. Favs: Tatum, Hawes, B. Powell, Peterson, Garner. Own LP on Dooto; one track in *Pianists Galore* (Wor. Pac.); LPs w. Dexter Gordon (Dooto), Max Roach-Clifford Brown (GNP), Chet Baker-Art Pepper (Wor. Pac.), B. De Franco (Verve), Curtis Counce, L. Vinnegar (Contemp.), Quincy Jones (ABC-Par.), Illinois Jacquet (Verve).

PERSIANY (orig. Persiani) ANDRE PAUL STEPHANE, *piano, composer;* b. Paris, France, 11/19/27. Father a musical comedy songwriter of 1920s. Prof. debut pl. for US forces in Germany, '45-6. Has recorded in Paris w. Jonah Jones, S. Bechet, Mezzrow, Buck Clayton, Al Nicholas, Bill Coleman, and w. M. de Villers, G. Pochonet, Benny Vasseur and many other groups. During extended stay in NYC, 1956-7, worked w. Dixieland group at Metropole, rec. w. own all-star group for Angel. Orig. infl. Milt Buckner; favs. Ellington, M. Solal. Limited as pianist, by own admission, but is progressing rapidly as composer.

Addr: 65 Rue du Faubourg du Temple, Paris 10, France.

PERSIP, CHARLES LAWRENCE (Charlie), *drums;* b. Morristown, N.J., 7/26/29. Studied under Pearl Brackett in Springfield, Mass. First gigs in Newark, N.J. w. Billy Ford r & b combo and Joe Holiday. Pl. w. Tadd Dameron '53; joined Dizzy Gillespie Sept. '53, toured overseas with him and remained until the big band broke up Jan. '58. Many gigs in '58-9 with Johnny Richards, Phil Woods, Harry Edison; worked with

Harry James band Apr.-May '59. Own group at Birdland Dec. '59. Superior big-band drummer. Favs: Roach, Blakey, Rich. Own group in *Double Or Nothin'* (Lib.); LPs w. Gillespie (Verve), Quincy Jones (ABC-Par.), Hank Mobley, Lee Morgan (Blue Note), Hal McKusick, Phil Woods-Donald Byrd in *The Youngbloods* (Pres.); *Dizzy Atmosphere* (Spec.), *Modern Jazz Sextet* (Verve), George Russell (Decca).

Addr: 69 West 90th Street, New York 24, N.Y.

PERSSON, AAKE, *trombone;* b. Hässleholm, Sweden, 1932. Discovered playing valve trombone in high school band, he was hired by Simon Brehm and in '51 became a national jazz name, acclaimed as Sweden's counterpart of J. J. Johnson and Kai Winding. Has free-lanced on rec. dates and gigs with Sweden's leading jazzmen; left Sweden to tour Europe with the Quincy Jones band in the show *Free and Easy,* fall '59. A mature, independent and exuberantly swinging performer, he is one of the foremost trombonists in contemporary jazz. LPs w. Clifford Brown, Herbie Mann (Pres.), George Wallington in *Swingin' In Sweden,* Roy Haynes & Quincy Jones in *Jazz Abroad* (Em.), Harry Arnold (Merc.), Lars Gullin (Atl.), *Swedes From Jazzville* (Epic), Stan Getz (Verve); *One World Jazz* (Col.).

PETERSEN, ROBERT LEE (Bob), *bass;* b. Davenport, Iowa, 9/15/25. Played in Marine band, '43-6; Chi. Mus. College '46-9; w. Arkansas Symph. '46, Chi. Symphony ('49-'51). With Max Miller Trio '48; backed Anita O'Day, Miles Davis, Stan Getz at Hi-Note, Chi., '49-50. Also worked w. Bud Freeman, Bill Russo in Chi.; w. Jimmy & Marian McPartland's Quartet '49; Hal Otis '50-1; three months w. Eddie South, seven months w. Ch. Barnet '52; four months w. Sauter-Finegan '53; with "The Six" at Jimmy Ryan's '54; to Florida w. Tony Cabot, '54-5, later settled in Miami.

Addr: 6340 N.E. Sixth Court, Miami 38, Fla.

PETERSON, OSCAR EMMANUEL, *piano, singer;* b. Montreal, Quebec, Canada, 8/15/25. Started classical training at the age of 6. At 14 he won a prize in a local amateur contest and soon after was offered a spot on a weekly local radio show. He was featured for several years, starting in 1944, w. Johnny Holmes' orch., one of the most popular in Canada. For some time he enjoyed a big local reputation and received offers from Jimmie Lunceford and others to come to the US, but he remained in Canada, until September 1949, when Norman Granz brought him to NYC for an appearance with JATP at Carnegie Hall. The following year he started recording for Granz, toured the country w. JATP, and rose rapidly to become a national name in the US. He toured Europe w. JATP in '52, '53, '54, led his own trio w. Ray Brown on bass, Irving Ashby, guitar (later succeeded by Barney Kessel and Herb Ellis). In March 1955 he made concert appearances with Ella Fitzgerald in England and Scotland. He has continued to tour Europe and the US annually for Granz. In late '58 he changed the format of his trio when Herb Ellis left; in '59 the new trio, with Ed Thigpen on drums and without a guitarist, was acclaimed by some critics as the best vehicle yet for Peterson's talent.

Sounding at first like an amalgam of Shearing, Garner, Tatum and other influences, Peterson's style soon was found to be clearly distinguishable and marked by the best qualities of both the swing and bop schools. From '53 he was also heard occasionally as a singer in a style almost identical with that of the early Nat Cole. Peterson won the DB award on piano '50-5 and '59; the DB critics' poll '53; Met. poll '53-4.

In addition to the LPs by his own trio on the Verve label, he is featured in hundreds of albums made in 1950-60 (now on Verve) with Billie Holiday, Fred Astaire, Benny Carter, Louis Armstrong, Ella Fitzgerald, Roy Eldridge, Lester Young, Stan Getz, Buddy De Franco et al.

LPs (all on Verve): Famous Composer Song Books: Irving Berlin (2053), Cole Porter (2052), Gershwin (2054), Ellington (2055), Kern (2056), Richard Rodgers (2057), Harry Warren (2059), Harold Arlen (2060), Jimmy McHugh (2061). Other LPs: *In a Romantic Mood* (2002), *Pastel Moods* (2004), *Romance* (2012), *Gershwin Song Book* with Buddy De Franco (2002), *Recital* (2044), *Nostalgic Memories* (2045), *Tenderly* (2046), *Keyboard* (2047), *An Evening With* (2048), *Soft Sands* (2079); *Norman Granz' Jam Session #1* (8049), *#2* (8050), *#5* (8053), *#6* (8054), *#7* (8062); *#8* (8094); *Compendium of Jazz #1* (8194), *#9* (8196); *Peterson Plays Basie* (8092), *Hamp's Big Four* (8117), *Piano Interpretations* (8127); *My Fair Lady* (2119), *Potpourri of Jazz* (2032), *Peterson Quartet #1* (8072), *Alone Together* (8148), *Midnight Jazz at Carnegie Hall* (8189); *Jazz at the Philharmonic* Vols. 8, 9, 10, 11; *Trio at Stratford Festival* (8024), *Little Jazz* (8068), Lester Young with Peterson Trio (8144), De Franco & Peterson Trio (8210), *Tour de Force* (8212), *Jazz at Hollywood Bowl* (8231-2), *With Stitt, Eldridge, Jo Jones at Newport* (8239), *Jazz Giants '58* (8248), Stan Getz with trio (8251), *At Concertgebouw* (8268), MJQ & Peterson Trio at Opera House (8269), *On The Town* (8287), *Louis Armstrong Meets Peterson* (8322), *Songs for a Swinging Affair* (8334), *Fiorello!* (8366), *Swinging Brass* (6119), *Coleman Hawkins & Confreres* (6110), etc.

Addr: 9 Chrysler Crescent, Scarborough, Ontario, Canada.

PETIT, BUDDY, *cornet;* b. New Orleans, La., 1887; d. 7/4/31. Pl. w. Jimmie Noone and Honore Dutrey band 1916; went to Los Angeles to join Jelly Roll Morton in '17, but according to Sam Charters, Morton teased him and the other NO musicians so much they returned home. Led a band called the Young Olympians; his Black and Tan Orchestra began touring in NO area and Texas, also pl. excursions on river boats. Petit never recorded commercially.

PETTIFORD, OSCAR, *bass, cello;* b. Okmulgee, Okla. on an Indian reservation, 9/30/22. His father, Harry "Doc" Pettiford, originally a veterinarian, later formed a family band which included his wife, a music teacher, as well as Oscar and 10 other Pettiford children. Raised mainly in Minneapolis, Oscar started on piano in 1933, picked up bass 3 years later and toured until 1941 with the family band, which enjoyed great success throughout the Midwest.

Ch. Barnet heard Pettiford in Minneapolis Jan. 1943, and hired him to form a two-bass team w. Chubby Jackson. Leaving Barnet in May 1943, he frequented Minton's, played w. Roy Eldridge at the Onyx and was co-leader w. Dizzy Gillespie of the first bebop group to play on 52nd St. During the same year he enjoyed a swift rise to fame among musicians, making his record debut in Dec. '43 with the Esquire All Stars. During '44 he led his own combos on 52nd St.; in 1945 he worked in Calif. w. Boyd Raeburn and Coleman Hawkins. He was w. Duke Ellington from Nov. '45 to March '48 and rejoined him for brief periods several times. From Feb. '49 he was w. Woody Herman for 5 months. While recovering from a broken arm he began to experiment with jazz solos played pizzicato on a 'cello.

He toured with the Louie Bellson-Charlie Shavers combo in 1950; took his own group to Korea and Japan in the winter of '51-2; from '52-8 he free-lanced in NYC, often leading his own sextet and occasionally a 13-piece band. After leaving for England in Sept. '58 on a jazz package concert tour, he settled in Europe and was heard with various groups in '59-60, working with Stan Getz in Scandinavia and with other combos in France, Austria, etc.

At the time of his first emergence to national prominence in the late '40s, Pettiford was virtually unique in jazz, a melodically inventive and technically agile bassist, unequalled since Jimmy Blanton. He showed unusual skill in adapting his style to the 'cello, which he continued to play occasionally. He won the Esq. Gold Award '44-5; Met. poll '45; DB critics' poll '53, '55-7.

Own LPs: *The Oscar Pettiford Orchestra In Hi-Fi* (ABC-Par. 135), *Vol. 2* (ABC-Par. 227), own sextet (Beth. 33), one side of *Bass By Pettiford/Burke* (Beth. 6); *Jazz: South Pacific* (rec. on Guam—Reg. 6001); LPs w. Miles Davis (Pres. 7007, Blue Note 1501, 1502), Th. Monk (River. 12-201, 12-223), Teddy Charles (Jub. 1047), Joe Puma (Jub. 1070), Art Blakey (Col. CL 1002), Kenny Dorham (River. 12-239), Coleman Hawkins (River. 12-233), Sonny Rollins (River. 12-258), Duke Ellington (Rondo. A7, Vict. LPM 1715), Eddie Heywood (Coral 57095), Urbie Green (Beth. 14), Jimmy Cleveland (Em. 36066), Clark Terry (Em. 36007), Joe Roland (Savoy 12039), Lee Konitz (Atl. 1217), Sonny Stitt (Roost 2204), *Swinging Seasons* (MGM E3613), *West Coast vs. East Coast* (MGM E3390).

PETTIS, JACK, *leader, tenor sax;* b. Danville, Ill., 1902. Moved to Chicago; bought a C melody sax at age 16. Pl. with various bands, then went to New York, switching to tenor. Made several records for Victor, Okeh with personnel incl. Adrian Rollini, Joe Venuti, Eddie Lang, Tommy Dorsey, Jack Teagarden, Benny Goodman et al.

PHILLIPS, JOSEPH EDWARD (Flip), *tenor sax;* b. Brooklyn, N.Y., 2/26/15. Studied clarinet, theory with cousin, Frank Reda. Worked as clarinetist in a Brooklyn restaurant 1934-9 and w. Frankie Newton at Kelly's Stable 1940-1. Switched to tenor sax w. Larry Bennett at Hickory House '42-3. Earned a large following playing w. Woody Herman '44-6. After Herman's band broke up he became a permanent member of JATP on its annual tours, winning his largest public acclaim by his frenetic solo on *Perdido*. Beginning in the spring of '52 he visited Europe with JATP annually for several years, also w. Gene Krupa Trio in summer of '52. In the late '50s, retired from the national jazz scene, he lived and played in Florida, emerging to tour with Benny Goodman in Europe in the fall of '59. Though best known for his ability to rouse audiences to a frenzy in the JATP context, Phillips is a fine musician who, on ballads, has shown good taste and an attractive style. He won the Met. poll on tenor in '48; DB poll '48-9; Esq. New Star award '45. Own LPs: Verve; LPs w. Woody Herman (MGM, Harm.), Jam Sessions #1, 2, 5-9, JATP, Vols. 1, 5-11, one track in *The Jazz Scene* (Verve); *Saturday Night Swing Session* (Ctpt.), Ralph Burns, Machito, Buddy Rich, Billie Holiday, Johnny Hodges, *Krupa And Rich* (Verve), Earl Hines (Gr. Award), Benny Goodman (MGM).

Addr: 301 S.E. 12 Street, Cypress Harbor, Pompano Beach, Fla.

PHYFE, EDWIN LLOYD (Eddie), *drums;* b. LaCrosse, Wis., 8/24/29. To NYC as child, later to Larchmont, where he pl. jazz in early '40s w. neighbors J. Glasel, Bob Wilber, Ed Hubble; pl. New Orleans style with them, modern jazz w. Dick Hyman et al. Stud. w. Fred Albright (ex-NBC Symph.) and others. Briefly w. C. Thornhill, otherwise combo work incl. G. Brunis, the McPartlands, B. Butterfield, B. Hackett, N. LaMare, Lee Castle, J. Windhurst, R. Braff, Bud Freeman, M. Napoleon; many sessions at Ryan's, concerts w. Wilber. Pl. w. "The Six," '54-5; moved to Washington, D.C. '56, led house band at Patio Lounge; with Ch. Byrd group '57-8; own trio at Charlie's Café '58-60. Mus. dir. and drummer for film *Dead to the World* '59. LPs w. J. Bushkin (Atl.), *Jazz at Showboat* w. Byrd (Savoy).

Addr: 6615 Hillandale Road, Chevy Chase, Maryland.

PICHON, FATS, *pianist, composer;* b. New Orleans, La., 1906. Stud. piano from age eight to 16, then came to NYC and got summer job in New Jersey. Stud. at New England Cons.; ret. to NYC and worked w.

Elmer Snowden, Fess Williams, Lucky Millinder; arr. for Chick Webb. Ret. to NO in 1931; played on riverboats ten years, then began work as soloist in clubs, particularly Absinthe House, where he had a television show in the '50s. Own LP: Decca.

PICOU, ALPHONSE FLORISTAN, *clarinet;* b. New Orleans, La., 10/19/1878. Started on guitar at 14, clarinet at 15. Played in the Accordiana band 1894, his own Independence band '97, Oscar Duconge '99, Excelsior band 1900, Keppard's Olympia band 1901, later with Bunk Johnson, Emmanuel Perez, Dave Peyton, Wooden Joe Nicholas. Was in Chicago for a while during World War I. During the '20s played with many bands as well as symphony orchs. and jazz groups in NO; after working with the Crescent City orch. '32 was in virtual retirement, but rec. w. Kid Rena in '40 and Papa Celestin '47, both times repeating the famous *High Society* solo (supposedly originated by George Baquet) with which he was most closely associated. In 1960, owner of a bar and store over which he lived, Picou still emerged occasionally to play and march with the Eureka band. LP: *New Orleans Legends* (River.).

Addr: Picou's Bar & Restaurant, 1601 Urselines Avenue, New Orleans, La.

PIERCE, NAT, *piano, composer;* b. Somerville, Mass., 7/16/25. Studied at New Eng. Cons. Turned pro in 1943, working in Boston w. the bands of Nick Jerret, Carl Nappi, Shorty Sherock and Ray Borden. Joined Larry Clinton Nov. '48, then ret. to Boston to form own band, which rec. for now defunct Motif label. Worked on and off w. own band in early '50s. Joined Woody Herman Sept. '51 and remained until '55, when he settled in NYC to free-lance as pianist and arr. Had own big band at various times in '57-59 at Savoy Ballroom, Birdland. Has filled in for Claude Thornhill and Count Basie in their bands. Pl. w. Lester Young, Emmett Berry, Pee Wee Russell. W. Ruby Braff at NJF and RIJF '57. Own trio at Vanguard '59. Arr. for Herman, Basie, Tony Scott, La Vern Baker, Ella Fitzgerald, Quincy Jones. Two weeks in Sweden w. Joe Newman and Basie All Stars Oct. '58. Wrote all the arrs. for *The Sound Of Jazz* on CBS-TV, entire score for off-Broadway play, *The Ballad of Jazz Street.*

Own LPs on Coral; LPs w. Paul Quinichette (Pres.), Jimmy Rushing, *The Sound Of Jazz* (Col.), Pee Wee Russell (Counter., Stcft.), Jo Jones (Vang.), Urbie Green (Vict.), arrs. for Erroll Garner's *Other Voices* (Col.), Woody Herman (Verve, Col., Evst.), Ruby Braff (Verve, Vict., Epic), Lambert-Hendricks-Ross (ABC-Par.).

Addr: 127 West 82nd St., New York 24, N.Y.

PIKE, DAVID SAMUEL (Dave), *vibes;* also *drums, piano;* b. Detroit, Mich., 3/23/38. Began on drums at age of eight; is self-taught on vibes. Started pl. prof. in LA '54. Has worked w. Elmo Hope, Carl Perkins, James Clay, Curtis Counce. W. Paul Bley '57-8. Led own quartets in and around SF '59. Fav. own solo: *Birk's Works* w. Bley on GNP. Favs: Clifford Brown, Milt Jackson, John Coltrane. LPs w. Jazz Couriers (Whippet), Bley (GNP).

Addr: 1700 Lima St., Burbank, Calif.

PINKETT, WILLIAM WARD, *trumpet;* b. Newport News, Va., 4/29/06; d. New York City, 3/15/37. Learned cornet from father; pl. in band at Hampton Inst., later stud. at music cons. in Meridian, Miss. First job w. local groups in Va., then went to Washington, D.C. and joined White Bros. orch. 1926. Moved to NYC, pl. and rec. with numerous groups, incl. Chick Webb, King Oliver, Jelly Roll Morton.

PISANO, JOHN, *guitar;* b. New York City, 2/6/31. Father an amateur guitarist. Began on piano at 10, guitar at 14 w. private teachers. Decided on musical career while w. Crew Chiefs Air Force band, '52-5. Toured with Chico Hamilton Quintet Oct. '56-Oct. '58, then free-lanced in Los Angeles, working several months with Matt Dennis, also dates with Buddy De Franco, Jimmy Giuffre. Film: *Sweet Smell of Success* w. Hamilton. Agile, fast-rising new guitarist. Favs: C. Wayne, J. Raney, Tal Farlow; Andres Segovia. Own LPs: guitar duos w. Billy Bean (Decca). LPs w. Hamilton (Dec., Wor.-Pac.), Fred Katz (Dot, Wor.-Pac., Decca), Paul Horn (Dot). Fav. own solo: *Zen* w. Fred Katz (Wor.-Pac.).

Addr: 2560 Venice Blvd., Los Angeles 19, Calif.

PLATER, ROBERT (Bobby), *alto sax, clarinet, flute;* b. Newark, N.J., 5/13/14. Father played drums. After house rent parties and gigs in Newark, joined Savoy Dictators, 1937-9; Tiny Bradshaw, '40-2. While with Bradshaw, composed and arranged *Jersey Bounce.* Own band in Army to '45, then joined Lionel Hampton and remained with him during much of the following decade, also working w. Cootie Williams, Oscar Estell. Was still w. Hampton in '60. Solos w. Hampton on *September In The Rain* (Decca), *Eli Eli* (MGM). LPs: see Hampton.

Addr: 113 South 11th St., Newark 7, N.J.

PLEASURE, KING (Clarence Beeks), *singer, songwriter;* b. Oakdale, Tenn., 3/24/22. Raised in Cincinnati. Worked at various jobs outside music business but was always interested in singing; after hearing Lester Young's record of *DB Blues* he became interested in developing the idea of setting lyrics to improvised jazz solos. Moved to Hartford, Conn., became prof. 1951 after winning amateur hour at Apollo Theatre NYC, where he sang his own lyrics to a background of James Moody's record *I'm in the Mood for Love.* His own version (*Moody Mood for Love*) became a sensation; though Eddie Jefferson (q.v.) had used the technique earlier, it was Pleasure who started this trend, emulated by Annie Ross, Jon Hendricks and others, of translating ad lib jazz into "vocalese." *Moody Mood for Love* won DB poll as best r & b record of 1953. Because of personal problems Pleasure has been in obscurity since then. Own LP: Prestige.

PLONSKY, JOHN, *trumpet;* b. St. Paul, Minn., 10/15/26. Stud. accordion in LA w. private teacher; later trumpet. Joined Ray Bauduc 1945; w. Nappy Lamare for a while the same year; had own group '46; w. Alvy West '47-52; since then has been free-lancing and writing. Feat. on daily Arthur Godrey radio show as Johnny Parker, '59-60. Fav: Duke Ellington. Own LP, *Cool, Man, Cool* (Gold. Cr.).

Addr: 98-51 64th Ave., Forest Hills 74, N.Y.

POCHONET, GERARD (Dave), *drums;* b. Paris, France, 5/20/24. Stud. drums w. private teacher in 1946; began working in music groups in high school in '42; in prof. combos since '49. Had own group from '53-7 off and on, feat. American musicians who were in France. Worked w. Hazel Scott '51 and '53; Mary Lou Williams '54; w. Guy Lafitte and Andre Persiany off and on '55-8. Favs: Big Sid Catlett, Dave Tough. Emigrated to US April '59.

Addr: 1604 W. North Avenue, Baltimore 17, Md.

POINDEXTER, NORWOOD (Pony), *alto saxophone;* also *tenor sax, clarinet;* b. New Orleans, La., 2/8/26. Stud. clarinet at elementary school, later attended Candell Cons. of Mus. in Oakland, Cal. First prof. job w. Sidney Desvigne at Cave Club in New Orleans 1940. Big-time debut touring w. Billy Eckstine late '47-early '48 and again in '50. Joined Vernon Alley Quartet late '50 in SF; while playing a concert with him, played a phrase he had picked up from Charlie Parker and Neal Hefti, hearing it, used it as the basis for an arrangement for Basie which he called *Little Pony.* (Lyrics were added by Jon Hendricks in 1958.) Poindexter toured with Lionel Hampton '51-2, returned to SF late '52 and at Bop City had his own group, which for two weeks early in '53 was fronted by Ch. Parker. Remained on West Coast touring in various small combos until March '59, when he took a quartet into the Jazz Cellar in SF, remaining there through much of '59-60. First LP cut Oct. '59, *A Good Git-Together* w. Jon Hendricks (Wor. Pac.). Something of a local legend. Poindexter is greatly admired by jazzmen in the Bay area.

Addr: 245 Buchanan St., San Francisco, Calif.

POLLACK, BEN, *leader, drums;* b. Chicago, Ill., 6/22/03. First prominent as drummer w. Friars Society Orch. (New Orleans Rhythm Kings). Rec. for Gennett 1922-3. Formed his own band in Calif., 1925, and during the next 15 years worked frequently in Chicago and NYC, acquiring a long list of distinguished sidemen. His most famous alumni were Glenn Miller, Benny Goodman, Jimmy McPartland, who recorded with him for Victor in the late 1920s; also Charlie Spivak, Matty Matlock, Yank Lawson, Harry James, Freddie Slack, Muggsy Spanier, Ray Bauduc, Dave Matthews, Fazola, who were with him in the 1930s. Pollack, who played drums less and less frequently in subsequent years, confining his role to that of businessman-conductor, assembled a band for Chico Marx to front in 1941, had his own record company (Jewel) in the mid-40s; in recent years he has been running his own restaurant in Hollywood where he plays frequently. Film: *Benny Goodman Story.* Most of the members of his 1934 band later became famous in the Bob Crosby orch. Although not a major musician himself, Pollack was extremely important as a discoverer of talent. Own LP: Savoy.

Addr: 8250 Sunset Blvd., Los Angeles 46, Calif.

POLLARD, TERRY JEAN, *piano, vibes;* b. Detroit, Mich., 8/15/31. Father pl. piano. Never studied music; her first piece was *Star Dust* at age 3½. Got into music business by replacing pianist in a band at her graduation dance. With Johnny Hill '48-9; Emmit Slay Trio '50, '52; Billy Mitchell '52-3; Terry Gibbs '53-7. Miss Pollard and Gibbs enjoyed great popularity as a vibes-duet team; they appeared together on the Steve Allen TV show and toured with the Birdland All Stars. Leaving Gibbs, she settled in Detroit, working locally with Yusef Lateef. A sparkling modern soloist showing Bud Powell and Gibbs influences, she turned down many jobs in 1957-60 in order to remain with her family and consequently has not attained the recognition she deserves. In 1956 she won the DB critics' poll as new star on vibes. LPs w. Gibbs (Merc.).

Addr: 19007 Klinger Street, Detroit 34, Mich.

POLO, DANNY, *clarinet;* b. Clinton, Ind., 1901; d. Chicago, 7/11/49. Played w. Ben Bernie, Joe Venuti, Jean Goldkette in 1920s. Moved to France 1928; after playing w. Arthur Briggs, Ray Ventura, Lud Gluskin, he moved to England and was very popular during the 1930s as featured jazz soloist with the Ambrose band, also rec. w. all-star jazz combos of his own for Decca. Back in the US 1939, he played tenor w. Joe Sullivan at Cafe Society, then worked w. Jack Teagarden and, off and on from 1942 until his death, with Claude Thornhill; also toured w. Dave Barbour 1948. LPs w. George Wettling in *Chicago Jazz Album* (Decca), Coleman Hawkins (Vict.), Thornhill (Harm.).

POMEROY, IRVING HERBERT III (Herb), *leader, trumpet;* b. Gloucester, Mass., 4/15/30. Stud. dentistry at Harvard; theory, composition, piano and trumpet at Schillinger House (later known as Berklee School of Music) in Boston. Worked w. Ch. Parker, Ch. Mariano, etc. in Boston '53; toured w. Lionel Hampton Dec. '53 until April '54. Led own 13-piece band in Boston before joining Stan Kenton in Sept. '54. After leaving Kenton he again became active in Boston, leading a big band or combo as the occasion demanded and appearing with the band at NJF '58. He has also been occupied as a teacher serving on the faculties of the School of Jazz in Lenox, Mass. and Berklee. Though not a permanently organized unit, Pomeroy's band, a modern ensemble with a well-varied library of resourceful arrangements, gained considerable popularity through his lps and concert performances '57-60. Favs: Gillespie, Miles Davis, K. Dorham. Own LPs: Roul., UA; LP w. Serge Chaloff (Cap.).

PORCINO, AL, *trumpet;* b. New York City, 5/14/25. Stud. w. Ch. Colin. During 1940s worked w. many name bands incl. Louis Prima, Gene Krupa, Tommy Dorsey, Jerry Wald, Georgie Auld; Kenton on and off, '47-8; Chubby Jackson's big band '49. Also played w. P. Rugolo, Count Basie, Elliot Lawrence, Ch. Barnet. Was w. Woody Herman several times in '46, '49-50, and toured Europe with him Apr. '54. With Stan Kenton to Dec. '55, then spent nine months in Miami, three in Las Vegas; arrived in LA Jan. '57, organized band with Med Flory and continued rehearsing it for two years but band did little work and dissolved. Weekends with Terry Gibbs' big band from Feb. '59; Monterey Jazz Fest. Oct. '58 w. Flory and Oct. '59 w. Herman. Best known as an exceptionally able lead and section trumpet player. LPs w. Kenton (Cap.), Herman (Col.), *Jazzwave* w. Flory (Jubilee), *Fabulous Bill Holman* (Coral), *Jazz Orbit* w. Holman (Andex), *I Want To Live* w. J. Mandel (UA).

Addr: 11449 Moorpark St., No. Hollywood, Cal.

POTTER, CHARLES THOMAS (Tommy), *bass;* b. Philadelphia, Pa., 9/21/18. Raised in Cape May, N.J. Studied piano and guitar in Jersey City; took up bass in 1940. Worked w. John Malachi in Washington; Trummy Young in Chi. and NYC. W. Billy Eckstine '44-5; John Hardee, Max Roach, etc. in NYC '46-7, Ch. Parker '47-9, also on JATP tours during this time. Six months w. Stan Getz; a few weeks w. Basie in '50, concert tours w. Eckstine. W. Earl Hines '52-3; Artie Shaw Sept. '53 to July '54, Eddie Heywood trio '55, Bud Powell trio '56, tour of Sweden's folk parks w. Rolf Ericson, summer '56; own trio Lamplighter Club, Valley Stream, L.I. '57. Worked w. Tyree Glenn at Roundtable, NYC '58-9, then joined Harry Edison quintet in late '59. One of the first and best bass products of the bop generation. Favs: Pettiford, Ray Brown, Mingus. Own LP, rec. in Sweden, *Tommy Potter's Hard Funk* (East-West); LPs w. Bud Powell (Blue Note), Ch. Parker (Savoy, Roost), Miles Davis, Stan Getz, Wardell Gray, *Four Altos* (Pres.), Artie Shaw (Verve), Pee Wee Russell (Ctpt.), Sam Most (Beth.), Tyree Glenn (Roul.), Gil Evans (Wor. Pac.).

Addr: 314 Jefferson Ave., Brooklyn 16, N.Y.

POTTS, WILLIAM ORIE (Bill), *composer, piano;* b. Arlington, Va., 4/3/28. St. on guitar, then accordion; mainly self-taught. After leaving high sch., toured w. cocktail unit. In 1949, to US Army Band in Washington; during this time was chief arr. for "The Orchestra" presented by Willis Conover. After six years in Army band, worked local clubs w. own combo; in 1954-5 arr. for Tony Pastor, S. Kenton, W. Herman and for rec. dates in NYC. Repl. the late Joe Timer as leader of "The Orchestra". Toured US w. Woody Herman '57 and '59. Ambition: to write film sound tracks "for happy movies, where crime and vice are not associated with jazz," and to expand as symph. composer. After settling in NYC Jan. '59 Potts produced his most important LP to date as arr. and mus. dir. for *The Jazz Soul of Porgy & Bess* (UA). Fav. arrs: Mandel, Mulligan, Cohn, T. Kahn, Holman. Other LPs: *House of Sounds* (Bruns., incl. own fav. comp. *Playground*), The Six (Beth.), Cohn-Perkins-Kamuca (Vict.), Pisano-Bean (Dec.), Chico Hamilton & strings (War. Bros.); piano on *Tribute To Woody Herman* (Crown).

POWELL, BENJAMIN GORDON (Benny), *trombone;* b. New Orleans, 3/1/30. School band at 12; prof. debut New Year's Day '44. Gigs w. Dooky Chase '45, then to Alabama State, where he played w. Collegians. King Kolax '46, Ernie Fields '47, L. Hampton '48-51, then lived in Ottawa, Canada, for a while, singing, playing bongo drums and trombone. Joined Count Basie Oct. '51, playing regular trombone for several years, later switching to bass trombone. An excellent soloist in a Johnson-derived style, he has been featured on many small combo record dates since the late '50s. Favs: J. J. Johnson, Rosolino, B. Green, Dickenson, T. Young. LPs w. Basie (Verve, Roul.), J. C. Heard (Argo), Buck Clayton (Col.), Sir Charles Thompson (Vang.), *No Count; North, South, East, Wess; Trombone and Flute* (Savoy).

Addr: 69 Horatio Street, New York 14, N.Y.

POWELL, EARL (Bud), *piano, composer;* b. New York City, 9/27/24. His father, William Powell, and grandfather were musicians; a brother, William, plays trumpet and violin; another brother, Richie (q.v.), pl. piano with Max Roach in 1954. Leaving school at 15, Bud gigged around Coney Island, worked at Canada Lee's Chicken Coop, and with Valaida Snow and the Sunset Royals. While the first experiments that led to bop were being conducted at Minton's, Powell was a frequent visitor. An incipient bop style was revealed on his first records made while he was w. Cootie Williams' band, 1943-4. After leaving Williams, he was in and out of the 52nd St. scene for several years, but suffered the first of a series of nervous breakdowns in 1945. He worked w. John Kirby, Dizzy Gillespie, Allen Eager, Sid Catlett, Don Byas, and took part in many bop combo sessions for Savoy in the late '40s. From late 1947 he has spent much of his time in mental hospitals around NYC but was seen intermittently with a trio at Birdland and other clubs. In '59 his health greatly improved, and he spent much of the year in Paris, playing at the Chat Qui Pêche. Late in the year he, Kenny Clarke and bassist Pierre Michelot formed a group called The Three Bosses.

Bud Powell's status as the first and foremost of the bop pianists has seldom been disputed. Charged with a fantastic dynamic energy allied with an incredibly fast flow of original ideas, he produced a series of solo albums that made him the idol of almost every young pianist. Technically, he has showed a control and mastery of the keyboard, and tonal individuality in his attack, that no other pianist has quite succeeded in duplicating. Powell counts Duke Ellington, Art Tatum, Count Basie and other jazz veterans among his most ecstatic admirers. As a composer he has contributed several attractive and unusual melodies, among them *Hallucinations* (also known as *Budo*), *Oblivion, Glass Enclosure.*

Own LPs: Blue Note 1503, 1504, 1571, 1598, 4009, Roost 2224, Verve 8115, 8127, 8153, 8154, 8167, 8185, 8218, 8301, Vict. LPM 1423, 1507; LPs w. Sonny Stitt (Pres. 7024), in *Opus De Bop* (Savoy 12114), Fats Navarro (Blue Note 1531, 1532, Savoy 12011); one track in *The Jazz Scene* (Verve 8060); Dexter Gordon (Savoy 12130), Jay Jay Johnson (Savoy 1206), Charlie Parker (Savoy 12000, 12001, 12009).

POWELL, JESSE, *tenor sax;* b. Fort Worth, Texas, 2/27/24. Majored in music at Hampton U. Toured w. Hot Lips Page, 1942-3; Louis Armstrong '43-4; Luis Russell '44-5. To Calif. w. C. Basie, in whose band he repl. I. Jacquet Sept. '46. Own band '48; D. Gillespie big band '49-50 (solo on *Tally Ho,* Cap.); since '50 has free-lanced in NYC, usually leading his own combo and doing r & b work. Was featured at Paris Jazz Festival 1948. Favs: Hawkins, Young, Herschel Evans. Own LP: Jubilee.

Addr: 615 West 150th St., New York City, N.Y.

POWELL, JAMES THEODORE (Jimmie), *alto sax, clarinet, flute;* b. New York City, 10/24/14. From a musical family, stud. vln. at 7; gave Town Hall recital at 14. Piano, harmony, theory at Dewitt Clinton High. Gigged at 17 on alto, w. Frankie Newton. Later w. Fats Waller, Edgar Hayes, Benny Carter ('39-40), Basie ('42-6), combos of S. Catlett, E. Heywood, Lips Page, L. Thompson, I. Jacquet, and Redman, Millinder bands. Toured Near East and Latin America w. D. Gillespie band '56; Latin America w. Machito '58. Member of Reuben Phillips' house band at Apollo Theatre, NYC, '59-60. Good lead alto man. Solo on Basie's *Taps Miller* (Col.). Fav: B. Carter. LPs w. Gillespie (Verve), Red Prysock (Merc.).

Addr: 112 So. 13th Ave., Mount Vernon, N.Y.

POWELL, MELVIN (Mel), *piano, composer;* b. New York City, 2/12/23. Extensive studies with private teachers. At the age of 12 he led his own Dixieland sextet for several months in Nyack, N.Y. Graduating from high school at the age of 14, he worked with various Dixieland combos at Nick's incl. Bobby Hackett, Geo. Brunis, Zutty Singleton, 1939. Played w. Muggsy Spanier in 1940, joined Benny Goodman 1941, and Raymond Scott's CBS band in 1942. Overseas w. Glenn Miller AAF Band '43; after discharge, '45, film and recording studio work in Hollywood, which he gave up to study comp. at Yale. Married actress Martha Scott July '46. After close association w. Paul Hindemith and piano studies w. Nadia Reisenberg, he became music teacher at Queens College. In '54 he played night clubs w. Goodman, composed and recorded w. Vanguard records and did staff work at ABC studios in NYC. He was w. Goodman again at Waldorf-Astoria in Feb. '57. Aside from these engagements he was completely inactive in jazz throughout the '50s, and became comp. teacher at Yale School of Music. He was awarded a Guggenheim Fellowship in comp. '59-'60 and has written many concert works. When in jazz, Powell played a skillful, swinging blend of Teddy Wilson, Hines and his own ideas. Early arrs. for Goodman incl. *The Earl, Mission To Moscow, Clarinade, Jersey Bounce, Darktown Strutter's Ball.* Won Esq. Armed Forces New Star Award '45; DB poll '44-8. Own LPs: Vang., Col.; LPs w. Goodman (Col., Cap.).

Addr: Ponus Ridge Road, New Canaan, Conn.

POWELL, RICHARD (Richie), *piano, composer;* b. NYC, 9/5/31; died, 6/26/56 in auto wreck (see Clifford Brown). Father, William Powell and brother, Bud Powell, both pianists. Stud. City College of New York, 1950-1, also privately with W. F. Rawlins; Jackie McLean, alto sax player, helped him get started. Played at Baby Grand Cafe, NYC w. Jimmie Carl Brown, '49-50. Worked around Philadelphia, '50-1. On the road w. Paul Williams rhythm and blues band, '51-2, and w. Johnny Hodges orch. '52-4. Joined Max Roach-Clifford Brown quintet, '54. An excellent small-group arranger, he did most of the writing foı the quintet. Movie: *Carmen Jones.* Fav. own solos, *I'll String Along With You, My Funny Valentine.* Favs: Bud Powell, Calvin Jackson, Bobby Tucker. LPs w. Brown-Roach, Dinah Washington (Em.), Johnny Hodges (Verve), Sonny Rollins (Pres.).

POWELL, EVERARD STEPHEN POWELL SR. (Rudy); (Moh. name Musheed Karweem), *clarinet, alto sax;* b. New York City, 10/28/07. Stud. privately and in NY Coll. of Mus. With Cliff Jackson at Lenox Club 1928-31; Fats Waller off and on from '34; Europe w. Edgar Hayes '37, then w. Claude Hopkins, Teddy Wilson big band '38-40; Andy Kirk '40; Fletcher Henderson '41-2; Don Redman, Claude Hopkins; Cab Calloway, '46-8; Lucky Millinder, '48-50; briefly w. Ch. Ventura, then w. Jimmy Rushing band '50-2. Also heard w. Arnett Cobb, Erskine Hawkins. Since '54, pl. w. Benton Heath band at taxi dance hall on 14th St. in Manhattan, also gigs and recs. w. Rushing. Well known for his caustically colorful growl clarinet style, he is also a good melodic alto player. Favs: B. Carter, B. Goodman, B. Bigard. LPs w. Waller (Victor), Rushing (Col., Vang.).

Addr: 102 West 138th St., New York 30, N.Y.

POWELL, SELDON, *tenor sax, flute;* b. Lawrenceville, Va., 11/15/28. Stud. Brooklyn and NY Conservatories 1947-9; grad. Juilliard '57. First job with Betty Mays and her Swingtet, '49; Tab Smith at Savoy Ballroom, NYC, '49. Lucky Millinder, Dec. '49 to Jan. '51; Army '51-2, playing w. service bands in Germany and France. Remained in New York on return, playing dates and records w. Sy Oliver, Erskine Hawkins, Neal Hefti, Louis Bellson, Don Redman, '52-5; Friedrich Gulda Sextet at Birdland and NJF, '56; Johnny Richards off and on from '57; NJF w. Don Butterfield '58; Brussels' World's Fair and European tour w. Benny Goodman '58; Woody Herman briefly '59, also concerts w. Jimmy Cleveland and many commercial studio jobs. Extremely fluent style, full but never lush tone; an exceptionally creative artist, one of the best tenor men on the NY scene in the '55-60 period. Favs: S. Stitt, L. Young. Own LPs: Roost; LPs w. Bellson (Verve); J. Richards (Roulette), N. Hefti (Epic), *Saxes, Inc.* (War. Bros.), A. K. Salim (Savoy), *Spirit of Charlie Parker* (WW).

Addr: 89 Carolina Avenue, Hempstead, L.I., N.Y.

POWELL, GORDON (Specs), *drums;* b. New York City, 6/5/22. Played piano and drums with own combo 1938. Drums w. Edgar Hayes '39, Eddie South '39-40, John Kirby '41, Benny Carter '41-2; Red Norvo, also gigs w. Benny Goodman, '42. In 1943 he joined Raymond Scott at CBS; nine months later he was hired as a permanent staff musician for CBS and has worked there since, under Raymond Paige, Leopold Stokowski and innumerable other conductors; heard for several years on Arthur Godfrey's TV and radio shows. He has remained interested and occasionally active in jazz. Powell won Esq. New Star Award '45. Own LP: Roul.; LPs w. Georgie Auld in *Jazz Concert* (Gr. Award), Teddy Wilson (MGM), Erroll Garner (Col.), Charlie Shavers (Beth.), *Saturday Night Swing Session* (Ctpt.).

Addr: 114-41 178th St., St. Albans, L.I., N.Y.

POZO, CHANO (Luciano Pozo y Gonzales), *bongo and conga drums;* b. Havana, Cuba, 1/7/15; d. New York City 12/2/48. As a boy he was intrigued by the rhythms of West African music and from the late '30s belonged to a Nigerian cult, the Abakwa, that provided much of the rhythmic excitement at the local Mardi Gras celebrations. Soon he became a celebrated figure as drummer, dancer and composer: his tunes incl. *El Pin Pin* and *Nague.* Pozo, who lived a turbulent life, came to a violent end when, after a year in the US as a member of the Dizzy Gillespie orch., he was shot and killed at a Harlem bar, the Rio Cafe, for reasons never explained. Pozo's incorporation into the Gillespie band was a major step in the advancement of Afro-Cuban ideas in jazz. Dr. Marshall Stearns in *The Story of Jazz* (Oxford) called him "the greatest of all Cuban drummers." LPs w. Gillespie (Victor, GNP).

POZO, FRANCISCO (Chino), *bongo and conga drums, timbales;* b. Cuba, 10/4/15. Cousin of Chano Pozo. Self-taught; st. on piano, bass. Left Cuba 1937; worked w. Machito '41-3; Jack Cole dancers '43-9, then w. Jose Curbelo, Noro Morales, Tito Puente, Tito Rodriguez, Enric Madriguera; two years each w. P. Prado, Josephine Premice. Toured night clubs w. Peggy Lee, '54-5. Worked with Stan Kenton, '55; Herbie Mann, '56; Jack Cole, '57; Xavier Cugat, Rene Touzet, '59. Favs: Chano Pozo, Candido. LPs w. Machito, Dizzy Gillespie (Verve), Pupi Campo (Seeco), Rene Touzet (GNP), Billy Taylor (River.), A. K. Salim (Savoy).

Addr: 301 West 48th St., New York 36, N.Y.

PRADO, DOMASE PEREZ, *leader, composer;* b. Matanzas, Cuba, 1922 (he himself does not know the exact date). Played with Orquesta Casino de la Playa in Havana; scored his first big success as bandleader in Mexico City 1948, later acquiring an unprecedented following throughout Latin-America, Cuba and eventually in the US, where he was hailed as "King of the Mambo." For a while he fronted a group in the US including several American jazzmen. His relationship to jazz, however, is peripheral. Own LPs: Vict.

Addr: 1608 Argyle Ave., Hollywood 28, Calif.

PRELL, DON, *bass;* b. Santa Monica, Calif., 8/4/29. Stud. bass in junior high; st. playing w. teen-age bands at 14; went on road at 15 w. band. With Ike Carpenter 1948-9; in Army '50-1; Charlie Barnet and Vido Musso '52; Utah Symph. '53-4; Peggy Lee, Frances Faye '55; Bud Shank, late '50s. Favs: Jimmy Blanton, Oscar Pettiford, Red Mitchell, Percy Heath. LPs w. Bud Shank (Wor. Pac.); Claude Williamson (Beth.).

Addr: 1553 Dunsmuir Ave., Los Angeles, Calif.

PRESLEY, ELVIS, *singer, guitar;* b. Tupelo, Miss., 1/8/35. Self-taught. Drove a truck and stud. to be an electrician, also had some experience as furniture maker. Started with Sun Record Co., in Memphis. After first releases scored amazing success locally, RCA Victor bought his contract. His second release for Victor, *Heartbreak Hotel,* sold well over a million records, and by early 1956 he had become the biggest new singing star since Johnnie Ray, enjoying his greatest success with teen-age and pre-teen-age audiences. Presley is a unique phenomenon. In his singing, as in his guitar playing, can be heard the influences of many fields of American music: country and western, rhythm and blues, jazz, and folklore origins in general. He acknowledges two Negro singers, Big Joe Turner and Bill Crudup, as the major influences on his style. After building a national name through films and records, Presley entered the Army in March '58 but on his release in '60 found his popularity undimmed. Own LPs: Vict.

Addr: 1414 Getwell Road, Memphis, Tenn.

PRESS, SEYMOUR (Red), *alto sax, clarinet, flute;* b. New York City, 2/26/24. Stud. sax w. private teacher; in Army band 1943-6; in late '40s and '50s, worked w. Bobby Sherwood, Tony Pastor, Ralph Flanagan, Tommy and Jimmy Dorsey, Benny Goodman. Favs: Benny Goodman, Johnny Hodges, Benny Carter, Charlie Parker. LP w. Don Redman (Gold. Cr.).

PREVIN, ANDRE, *piano, composer, conductor;* b. Berlin, Germany, 4/6/29. Studied at Berlin Royal Cons. & Paris Cons. After arrival in US (1939), studied piano mostly with father, a music teacher; harmony, composition, etc. w. Joseph Achron and Mario Castelnuovo-Tedesco. Jobbed around as arranger and pianist during school; rec. debut 1945 for Sunset. Immediately after high school, hired as arranger at MGM studios; composer-conductor 1948. Then recorded for Vict. w. own groups '49-55. Army Oct. '50-52. Worked w. Shorty Rogers group '53. From '56-60 he took occasional leaves of absence from MGM Studios to return to jazz, leading his trio in night clubs and record dates. In the fall of '56 he conducted a 12-week course in modern American music at U. of Cal. His LP of *My Fair Lady* w. Shelly Manne released early '57 on Contemp. became a best seller and started the entire trend of show-score jazz LPs. Previn went to Paris in summer of '57 to score music for a movie, *Gigi*, for which he won an Academy Award in '59. Other film scores: *Porgy And Bess, The Subterraneans, Bells Are Ringing, Who Was That Lady.*

An astonishing musician whose technique is comparable with that of Oscar Peterson, Previn has remained completely at home in jazz despite his preoccupation with the popular and classical fields. He has listened extensively to Tatum, Peterson, Bud Powell and Horace Silver and plays in an eclectic style that never fails to swing. He was married to singer Betty Bennett, for whom he wrote and conducted both during and after their marriage. Fav. comps: S. Rogers, N. Hefti, J. Mandel. Ambition: to write large-scale work for symphony orch. with jazz soloists. Own LPs: Contemp., Cam., Tops; LPs w. Shelly Manne (Contemp.); *Collaboration* w. Shorty Rogers (Vict.); Dave Pell (Atl.), Barney Kessel, Benny Carter (Contemp.), Pete Rugolo (Merc.), Benny Goodman (Col.), Diahann Carroll (UA), The Mitchells (Metro.).

Addr: 120 El Camino, Beverly Hills, Calif.

PRICE, LLOYD, *singer, leader, guitar, piano;* b. New Orleans, La., 3/9/32. Father was guitarist; mother a gospel singer. Stud. trumpet in high school and formed own combo. Wrote and rec. r & b hit, *Lawdy Miss Clawdy*, 1953; in Army Spec. Serv., where he formed a band which toured the Far East. Out of service, he formed a nine-piece group and made other best-sellers, incl. *Stagger Lee, Personality*, '59. Own LPs on ABC-Par., Spec.

PRICE, SAMUEL BLYTHE (Sammy), *piano, leader;* b. Honey Grove, Texas, 10/6/08. Stud. w. Booker T. Washington's daughter. Prof. debut in Dallas 1923. Was featured as Charleston dancer w. Alphonso Trent's orch. Worked w. Lee Collins 1925; toured TOBA circuit '27-30. Settled in NYC 1938, and was virtually house pianist at Decca for many years, playing both r & b and pop sessions w. Rosetta Tharpe, Trixie Smith, Peter Lind Hayes, Evelyn Knight, etc. In early 1940s led his own "Texas Blusicians" groups for Decca sessions incl. Lester Young; solo appearances at Cafe Society, Famous Door, Eddie Condon's concerts, also in pit band w. Tallulah Bankhead play *Clash By Night.* To Nice Jazz Festival w. Mezzrow 1948. Returned to Texas 1951, for three years. Back in NYC late '54, rec. w. Jimmy Rushing. Toured Europe w. own combo for Jeunesses Musicales De France Dec. '55 to May '56. Since then, has worked frequently at Metropole, NYC. Excellent early-style blues and boogie-woogie pianist. Fav: Tatum. Own LP: Savoy, LP w. Jimmy Rushing (Vang.), Sidney Bechet (Bruns.).

Addr: 48 West 138th St., New York 37, N. Y.

PRICE, VITO (Vito Pizzo), *tenor, alto sax, clarinet;* b. Long Island City, N. Y., 11/23/29. Stud. alto in NYC at 14; joined Bob Chester after grad. from high school in 1947. With Art Mooney '48; Chubby Jackson '50; Tony Pastor '51; US Marine Corps Band '52-3; Jerry Wald '54; own group in Long Island '55; staff musician on WGN, Chicago late '50s. Superior modern tenor man. Favs: Zoot Sims, Sonny Rollins, Stan Getz, Don Byas, Lester Young. Own LP, *Swingin' the Loop* (Argo); LPs w. Chubby Jackson (Argo).

Addr: 561 Arlington Place, Chicago 14, Ill.

PRIESTER, JULIAN ANTHONY, *trombone;* b. Chicago, Ill., 6/29/35. Studied piano at 10 for a year; baritone horn, then trombone under Capt. Walter Dyett at Du Sable High. Pl. w. Sun Ra 1953-4, Lionel Hampton '56, Dinah Washington '57-8. To NYC June '58. Joined Max Roach Jan. '59. Worked w. Slide Hampton in Dec. '59 between engagements w. Roach. Fav: Jay Jay Johnson. Imp. infl: Parker, Rollins, Monk, Gillespie. Own LP: River. LPs w. Roach, Washington (Merc.), Philly Joe Jones, Johnny Griffin (River.).

Addr: 1239A Putnam Ave., Brooklyn, N. Y.

PRIMA, LEON, *trumpet; b.* New Orleans, La., 7/28/07. Brother is Louis Prima; sister, Mary Ann, a nun, pl. organ and piano. First studied piano, private lessons in NO. Influenced to enter music business through association w. Leon Rappolo, Jack Teagarden, Nappy Lamare and Ray Bauduc. Worked w. Peck Kelly at Sylvan Beach, Texas in 1925, later with Pee Wee Russell, Teagarden, Rappolo. W. Louis Prima '40-6, then led his own band in NO until he retired in mid-'50s. Was in night club business until '55, now is active in real estate construction. Favs: Beiderbecke, early Louis Armstrong, Louis Prima. Own LP on Southland.

Addr: 1726 East Lakeshore Drive, New Orleans, La.

PRIMA, LOUIS, *leader, singer, trumpet;* b. New Orleans, 12/7/12. Studied violin for 7 years, then trumpet; at 17, got first job in a New Orleans theatre. With the arrival of the swing era he became a national name; in Sept. '34 he began a long series of records for Brunswick and Vocalion under the name of "Louis Prima and his New Orleans Gang." Sidemen from time to time incl. Geo. Brunis, Sidney Arodin, Eddie Miller, Nappy Lamare, Ray Bauduc. He was later absorbed entirely into the pop music field, leading a large dance band. In 1954, he and his wife, singer Keely Smith, formed a team which became a tremendous night club attraction in New York, Chicago, Hollywood and especially Las Vegas. Film: *Hey Boy, Hey Girl* (Columbia Pictures). Owns own label, Keelou, and also produces records for Dot. Comp. incl. *Sing, Sing, Sing, Robin Hood, Brooklyn Boogie.* Own LPs: Cap., Col., Rondolette; one no. in *The Jazz Makers* (Col.).

Addr: c/o Barbara Belle, 835 No. Clark, Hollywood 46, Calif.

PRINCE, ROBERT HAVEY (Bob), *composer, conductor, vibes;* b. New York City, 5/10/29. Stud. piano at five; harmony and theory w. private teacher at 14. Grad.

Music and Art High School, NYC; B.S. degree from Juilliard. Began by arr. for dance bands and rec. dates; a & r work w. Decca, Columbia, Warner Bros. records. Compositions have been performed at Cooper Union, Town Hall and Carnegie Recital Hall, NYC. Comp. ballet *New York Export: Opus Jazz* for Jerome Robbins, which toured US and Europe, incl. app. at Brussels World's Fair. Names Charlie Christian, Lester Young as first influences. Own LPs, *Saxes, Inc, Charleston 1970* (Warner Bros.); *New York Export: Opus Jazz* w. Leonard Bernstein's *West Side Story* (Warner Bros.); comp. part of *What's New* album (Col.).

Addr: 111-35 76th Ave., Forest Hills 75, N. Y.

PRIVIN, BERNARD (Bernie), *trumpet;* b. Brooklyn, N.Y., 2/12/19. Self-taught. Pl. w. Harry Reser 1937; B. Berigan, T. Dorsey, '38; A. Shaw, '39-40; B. Goodman, '41-2 and '46-8, Ch. Barnet '43; Army, June '43-Jan. '46 (overseas w. Glenn Miller AAF band). Has been on staff at CBS since 1950, playing an occasional solo on Ed Sullivan, Garry Moore, Andy Williams shows. Was feat. on early Barnet rec. *Lois;* and on *Mood Indigo, One O'Clock Jump, Redskin Rhumba, Skyliner* w. Hefti. Own LP: *Dancing and Dreaming* (Regent); LPs w. N. Hefti (Epic), Charlie Parker (Verve).

Addr: 18 Hudson Ave., Mount Vernon, N. Y.

PROBERT, GEORGE ARTHUR JR., *soprano sax, clarinet;* also *alto, baritone sax;* b. Los Angeles, Calif., 3/5/27. Stud. piano at six years of age; mainly self-taught on saxophones and clar. Began pl. with small bands in grammar school; grad. Stanford U. 1948. Joined Bob Scobey '50, staying until '53; w. Kid Ory several months in '54 until he was offered a job in the animation dept. of Walt Disney Studio, where he stayed until 1959, when he became asst. dir. of U.P.A. films. Has worked with the Fire House Five Plus 2 since 1955. Favs: Sidney Bechet and Johnny Hodges on sop. sax; Pete Brown and Hodges, alto; Jimmie Noone, Benny Goodman et al, clar. LPs w. Bob Scobey, Kid Ory, and Fire House Five Plus 2 (Good Time Jazz).

Addr: 9000 Swinton Ave., Sepulveda, Calif.

PROCOPE, RUSSELL, *alto and soprano sax, clarinet;* b. New York City, 8/11/08. Studied violin, alto, clarinet with private teachers. Worked w. Billy Freeman and other local bands from 1926; Chick Webb from 1929-30, Fletcher Henderson 1931-4, Benny Carter '34, Teddy Hill '34-8, touring Eng. and France w. Hill in '37. Was key man in John Kirby combo 1938-45; since Nov. 1945 has been w. Duke Ellington's orch. One of the principal hot alto men of the 1930s, also much admired as a lead and section man, he recorded w. Jelly Roll Morton '39, Timme Rosenkrantz '45, etc. Own LP: Dot; LPs w. Duke Ellington (Beth., Col., Cap.).

Addr: 870 St. Nicholas Avenue, New York 32, N. Y.

PROFIT, CLARENCE, *piano, songwriter;* b. New York City, 6/26/12; d. New York City 10/24/44. Parents both musicians; father was pit pianist for David Belasco's *Lulu Belle.* A child prodigy, Profit played from age three; while attending P. S. 89 (Lenox Ave.) he played classics and jazz at local dances, also broadcast on WHN with a schoolmate, Edgar Sampson. At 18, organized own ten-piece band for Harlem clubs and ballrooms. Recorded w. Washboard Serenaders and Teddy Bunn on Victor. Early in 1931, took octet to West Indies, where grandparents lived; worked in Antigua and St. Kitts. Back to US '37, formed trio feat. Jimmy Shirley, guitar (later Billy Moore, Chuck Wayne) and Ben Brown, bass; pl. at George's, Village Vanguard, Cafe Society, many other clubs until his death. Made a few records for Brunswick, Col., Decca '39-40. Profit played in a harmonically rich, finely textured style that was years ahead of its time; his trio records on Decca (long since cut out of the catalog) were striking examples of his greatly underrated talent. As a songwriter he was best known for *Lullaby in Rhythm* (collab. w. Edgar Sampson).

PRUITT, CARL B., *bass;* also *piano;* b. Birmingham, Ala., 6/3/18. Older brother pl. jazz violin. Began on piano in 1934. St. on bass in Pittsburgh '37. Bought first bass from Walter Page. Pl. in All-City High School Symph. '39. Left Pitts. w. Cootie Williams '44, pl. w. him until June '45. Remained in NYC, working on 52nd St. w. Roy Eldridge's big band; at Le Ruban Bleu w. Cyril Haynes and Maxine Sullivan to Sept. '45. W. Jeter-Pillars touring Japan and Pacific area '45-6; Lucky Millinder '46-8; Mary Lou Williams '48. Off and on w. Earl Hines from '53. Also w. Sauter-Finegan '55; Eddie Grady's Commanders. Fav: Jimmy Blanton; imp. infl. Wellman Braud. Rec. w. Cootie Williams (Cap.). LPs w. Mary Lou Williams (Atl.), Geo. Shearing, Dorothy Donegan (Cap.), Earl Hines (MGM).

Addr: 2384 Paulding Ave., Bronx, N. Y.

PUENTE, ERNEST, JR. (Tito), *vibes, timbales, piano, alto sax, leader;* b. New York City, 4/20/25. Stud. comp. & arr. w. Richard Benda. Played with Noro Morales, Pupi Campo and many other name Latin bands, 1945-9; since then, has led his own group, earning wide popularity both in Latin-American music and jazz circles. Fav. bands: Kenton, Herman, Basie. LP w. Woody Herman, *Herman's Heat & Puente's Beat* (Evst.); other LPs on Tico, Vict.

Addr: 109 East 73rd St., New York 21, N. Y.

PUERLING, EUGENE THOMAS (Gene), *singer;* b. Milwaukee, Wis., 3/31/29. Worked as disc jockey, freelance singer in Milwaukee; org. two vocal groups before moving to West Coast, where he got first major break as leader-arranger for Hi-Lo's quartet (q.v.). Fav. singers Mel Tormé, Four Freshmen.

PULS, STANLEY P., *bass;* b. Appleton, Wis., 1/26/16. Mother pl. piano and organ. Stud. piano 1927-31, then took lessons on bass. Won national music contest '35; went to Chicago '36 and stud. w. bass player of Chicago Symph. until '41. Pl. with a string ens., then began playing jazz. Worked in Los Angeles '55-7 w. Bill Baker trio; joined Jack Teagarden July '57, making the State Dept. tour of the Far East with him. Favs: Red Callender, Red Mitchell. LPs w. Teagarden (Cap., Roul.).

Addr: 7911 Woodman Ave., Van Nuys, Calif.

PUMA, JOSEPH J. (Joe), *guitar;* b. New York City, 8/13/27. Father and two brothers are guitarists. Self-taught. Worked as aircraft mechanic 1944; draftsman '45-7; joined Musicians' Union '48. Worked w. Frank Damone trio, Cy Coleman trio '51; Sammy Kaye '52; Sal George, Joe Roland and Bobby Corwin trios '53; then w. Louis Bellson, Don Elliot, Artie Shaw combos, Les Elgart band, Graham Forbes trio; acc. Peggy Lee '54-5. Own group at Left Bank, NYC '57. W. Lee Konitz quartet, Dick Hyman trio '58; Dick Katz quartet at School of Jazz, Lenox, Mass. '59. Favs: Farlow, Raney. Own LP on Jub.; LPs w. Artie Shaw (Verve), Webster Young (Prestige), Louis Bellson (Verve), Chris Connor, Herbie Mann, Sam Most (Beth.), Don Elliot, *Four Most Guitars* (ABC-Par.).

Addr: 217 North Terrace Ave., Mt. Vernon, N. Y.

PURNELL, WILLIAM (Keg), *drums;* b. Charleston, W. Va., 1/7/15. Father was songwriter and brick mason. Stud. at Sch. of Amer. Mus. in NYC. Pl. w. Chappie Willett at W. Va. State Coll., 1933-4; own trio in NYC '38-9, Benny Carter '39-41, Claude Hopkins '41-2, Eddie Heywood '42-8 and '51-2. Many Dixieland jam sessions in NYC during 1950s. "One of the swingingest, tastiest drummers of them all" (Geo. Simon, *Metronome*). Rec. *Sleep,* etc. w. Benny Carter on Vocalion. LPs w. Heywood (Decca); one track w. Rex Stewart in *History of Jazz, Vol. 3* (Cap.).

PURTILL, MAURICE, *drums;* b. Huntington, L.I., N.Y., 5/4/16. Best known as drummer with the Glenn Miller band during the height of its fame, 1940-2, he had also worked w. Red Norvo '37 to '38 and Tommy Dorsey '39-40. After Miller's civilian band broke up, worked w. Kay Kyser until 1944, when he entered the Navy. On his discharge in '46 he played for a while w. Tex Beneke, then entered free-lance radio and record field in NYC. Fav: Denzil Best. LPs: see Glenn Miller.

Addr: 915 New York Ave., Huntington, L. I., N. Y.

Q

QUEBEC, IKE ABRAMS, *tenor sax;* b. Newark, N.J., 8/17/18. Formerly a dancer and pianist, he started on tenor 1940 w. Barons of Rhythm; later worked w. Frankie Newton, Hot Lips Page, Roy Eldridge, Trummy Young, Sunset Royals, Ella Fitzgerald, Benny Carter, Coleman Hawkins. Worked for Cab Calloway off and on from 1944 to '51. Only sporadically active during the '50s. Quebec was a superior tenor man of the Hawkins school with a big tone and firm, vigorous style. Favs: Hawkins, Webster, Getz. Rec. for Blue Note '59, released on 45 rpm. LP: four tracks in *The Angry Tenors* (Savoy).

QUEENER, CHARLES CONANT, *piano;* b. Pineville, Ky., 7/27/21. To NYC 1940. First major job w. Muggsy Spanier's big band '42; later w. Harry James, Glen Gray, Joe Marsala. After a year w. Benny Goodman '45 he was at Nick's in NYC with various combos '46-9, then free-lanced mostly with Dixieland groups incl. Jimmy McPartland (Metropole, '54), Kaminsky, Hackett, Erwin, Braff. Early in '59 started at the Gaslight Club in NYC with trio incl. Clarence Hutchenrider. Since '57, studying composition w. Paul Creston and writing piano music, quintet for flute & strings and other works. Favs: Peterson, T. Wilson. LPs w. Hackett (Col.), Peanuts Hucko (Epic).

Addr: 8550 Blvd. East, North Bergen, N. J.

QUILL, DANIEL EUGENE (Gene), *alto sax, clarinet;* b. Atlantic City, N. J., 12/15/27. Joined union at 13, worked w. Alex Bartha's house band at Steel Pier, Atlantic City. Later toured with name bands incl. Jerry Wald, Art Mooney, Buddy De Franco, Claude Thornhill, Gene Krupa, Dan Terry. Own combo as co-leader w. Phil Woods in NYC night clubs '57-8, also feat. w. Johnny Richards, Nat Pierce bands. Though lacking the fire of some of the more aggressive, Parker-inspired alto men, Quill during the late '50s developed rapidly, improving his personal style. Favs: Phil Woods, Charlie Mariano, Herb Geller. Own LPs: Dawn, Roost; three tracks in *Rhythm Plus One* (Epic); LPs w. Phil Woods (Pres., Vict.), *Four Altos* (Pres.), Mundell Lowe (River.), Claude Thornhill (Kapp), Johnny Richards (Coral, Cap., Roul.), Jimmy Knepper (Beth.), Quincy Jones (ABC-Par.), Manny Albam (Coral), *Saxes, Inc.* (War. Bros.), Bill Potts (UA).

Addr: 286 West End Ave., New York 23, N. Y.

QUINICHETTE, PAUL, *tenor sax;* b. Denver, Colo., 5/7/21. Studied at Denver U., playing clarinet and alto, then tenor; majored in music at Tenn. State Coll. After gigging around Omaha w. Nat Towles and Lloyd Hunter, he worked w. Shorty Sherock's quintet in Chicago. Joined Jay McShann 1942; Johnny Otis' band in Calif.; Louis Jordan, Lucky Millinder, Eddie Wilcox; J. C. Heard combo at Cafe Society and other small groups in NYC. Recorded and gigged w. Hot Lips Page until 1951, when he joined Count Basie's band. By the time he left Basie early in 1953 he had earned a reputation as "the Vice-Pres", i.e. the closest to Lester Young among the new jazz stars, both in style and tone, though his subsequent work revealed an individual sound and personality. Led own combo off and on in NYC '53-60; pl. w. Benny Goodman Octet '55; led trio at C. Basie's Lounge etc., also gigged w. Nat Pierce band at Savoy, Birdland, TV shows w. Woody Herman. Own LPs: Merc., Pres., Dawn, UA; LPs w. Brookmeyer (UA), Mel Powell (Vang.), B. Holiday (Verve), Basie (Verve), heard in *Blowtop*

Blues on *Dinah Washington Sings the Best in Blues* (Merc.); *LaVern Baker Sings Bessie Smith* (Atl.), *The Herd Rides Again* w. Herman (Evst.).

Addr: 120 East 4th St., New York 3, N. Y.

R

RACE, STEVE, *composer, piano, leader, critic;* b. Lincoln, England, 4/1/21. Studied piano at Royal Acad. of Music, London. Weekly columnist for London Melody Maker since mid-'50s, also contributor to other British publications. Collecting records since 1930s; main interests swing-mainstream, bop, contemporary-experimental. Active as pianist, composer, arranger and conductor; wrote a ballet (*Skyline*) and orchestral works, incl. film music. Staff conductor and mus. dir. for Associated Rediffusion, London, commercial TV contractors. Has also supervised British recording sessions, incl. London dates of Jimmy and Marian McPartland; several BBC disc jockey series, also broadcast in France, Iceland. Many radio, TV shows w. own orch. and quintet. Largely responsible for British acceptance of Brubeck quartet. Made extensive tour of US to hear jazz, summer '59, reporting on trip for *Melody Maker.*

Addr: c/o Television House, Kingsway, London W. C. 2.

RAE, JOHNNY (John Anthony Pompeo), *vibes, drums, timbales;* b. Saugus, Mass., 8/11/34. Father, grad. of U. of Naples and U. of Milan, now a teacher in LA. Mother church org., piano and vocal teacher in Boston. Stud. piano 2 yrs. at New Eng. Cons.; tympani 2 yrs. Boston Cons.; drums, Berklee School. Pl. w. Herbie Lee r & b combo July, 1952-Aug., '53; Al Vega trio, Aug., '53 to Dec., '53 and July, '54-Jan., '55; Herb Pomeroy big band, Dec., '53-Apr., '54; Jay Miglori Jazz Workshop, Apr., '54-July, '54, all in Boston. Joined Geo. Shearing quintet Jan., '55, on recommendation of John Lewis. Leaving Shearing Oct. '56, spent three months w. Johnny Smith Quintet. Worked with quintets of Ralph Sharon, Johnny Eaton, '57; Cozy Cole for six months in '58; four months w. Bambi Lynn-Rod Alexander Dance Jubilee, then joined Herbie Mann's Afro-Cuban combo spring '59. Made African tour w. him '60. Fav: Milt Jackson; other influences: J. Lewis, H. Silver, Th. Monk. LPs w. Shearing (Cap.), Mann (UA, Verve).

Addr: 327 West 56th St., New York 19, N. Y.

RAEBURN, BOYD ALBERT, *leader, composer, saxophones;* b. on ranch near Faith, S. Dak., 10/27/13. Raised mainly in Platte, S. D. Studied privately and at U. of Chi., where he had campus band, won contest. Prof. bandleader from Chi. World's Fair days, using very commercial "Mickey Mouse" type band, slowly moving toward swing policy from late 1930s. To NYC briefly in 1942. Came East again with a few key men early '44, built new, jazz-oriented outfit, opened at Lincoln Hotel Feb. '44. During the next two years the Raeburn band became, along with Woody Herman's band, one of the two main big-band gathering places for young talent of the nascent bop school. Regular sidemen during '44 included Dizzy Gillespie, Sonny Berman, Benny Harris, Trummy Young, Tommy Pedersen, Earl Swope, Don Lamond, Johnny Bothwell, Al Cohn; Ed Finckel, arranger (later Geo. Handy, arr. and piano). Raeburn, who played tenor with the band, switched to baritone in '45, bass sax in '46. From May 1945 the band was in Calif., members incl. Johnny Mandel, Dodo Marmarosa, Harry Babasin. One of Raeburn's most enthusiastic supporters was Duke Ellington, who helped to back the band during this period. On July 9, 1946, Raeburn married Ginnie Powell, former singer with the band, who died in '59 in Nassau.

Back in New York, with Buddy De Franco in the line-up and arrangements by Johnny Richards, Raeburn broke up the band in August 1947. He reorganized in '48 but gave up traveling in '50 and limited his work to occasional dates around NYC with a pick-up band. In May 1952 he entered the furniture business as part owner of the Tropic Shop on Fifth Ave. In '56-7 he gigged and recorded occasionally as band leader, then moved to Nassau, Bahamas where he became interested in various business enterprises and was almost entirely out of the music business. Raeburn's band won the Esq. New Star Award in '47. Own LPs: Savoy.

Addr: P. O. Box 194, Nassau, Bahamas, B. W. I.

RAGLIN, ALVIN (Junior), *bass;* b. Omaha, Neb., 2/16/17; d. Boston, Mass., 11/10/55. Started on guitar. Prominent from Nov. 1941 to Nov. '45 as bassist w. Duke Ellington orch; in obscurity from then until his death. Won *Esquire* New Star award '46. LPs: see Ellington; also w. Rex Stewart in *History of Jazz, Vol. 3* (Cap.).

RAINEY, MA (Gertrude Malissa Nix Pridgett), *singer;* b. Columbus, Ga., 4/26/1886; d. 12/22/39. Began singing in cabarets soon after the turn of the century. William "Pa" Rainey, whom she married, was a member of a troupe known as the Rabbit Foot Minstrels. After many years on the road playing the Negro vaudeville circuits, Ma began a series of recordings for Paramount in 1923, accompanied by Lovie Austin's Serenaders. Her simple, direct blues style was heard on almost 100 sides that brought her belated fame during her peak years, 1923-9. Tommy Ladnier, Joe Smith and Louis Armstrong were among those who accompanied her. Bessie Smith was the most famous protégée and emulator of Ma Rainey, who took her on tour in her show when Bessie was an unknown. From 1930 Ma's fame dimmed rapidly; she was no longer a recording artist, and in 1933, on the death of her mother, she retired from music and settled in Rome, Ga., where she remained until her death. Own LP on River.; two tracks in *Young Louis Armstrong* (River.), one track in *History of Classic Jazz* (River.).

RAMEY, EUGENE GLASCO (Gene), *bass;* b. Austin, Texas, 4/4/13. Played sousaphone w. Geo. Corley 1930 (Herschel Evans was also in band). In 1932 he moved to Kansas City, where Walter Page taught him to play string bass. He worked w. Countess Johnson 1936; Jay McShann '38-44; Luis Russell '44-5; then 52nd St. combos incl. Hot Lips Page, Ch. Parker, Ben Webster. He was w. Count Basie Nov. '52 until early '53; Dorothy Donegan, Art Blakey '54; then gigged w. small groups in New Jersey and NY. Favs: Walter Page, Bob Haggart. LPs w. T. Monk, H. Silver, Lou Donaldson, Sonny Rollins (Blue Note), Fats Navarro, Eddie Davis (Savoy), Lester Young, Teddy Wilson, *Jazz Giants '56* (Verve), Lennie Tristano (Atl.), Stan Getz (New Jazz), Dickenson-Thomas (Atl.).

Addr: 1116 Kelly St., Bronx 59, N. Y.

RANDALL, FREDERICK JAMES (Freddy), *trumpet;* b. London, Eng., 5/6/21. Mainly self-taught. Army, 1940-2. Early associate of Johnny Dankworth, who gigged with him before they both joined a group called Freddy Mirfield and His Garbage Men. After a year w. Mirfield, Randall organized his own group, which toured Germany four times, played concerts successfully throughout England and the Continent, and toured w. Teddy Wilson during the latter's visit to England. In May, '56, Randall brought his septet to the US and played a concert tour of Southern cities on an inter-union exchange arrangement that enabled Louis Armstrong to tour Great Britain. Favs: Armstrong, Bobby Hackett, Billy Butterfield, Charlie Teagarden.

RANDOLPH, IRVING (Mouse), *trumpet;* b. St. Louis, Mo., 6/22/09. Prof. debut on riverboats w. Fate Marable. Moved to Kansas City and worked w. Andy Kirk 1931-3; to NYC w. Fletcher Henderson '34; Benny Carter 1934; Cab Calloway 1935-9, also record dates w. Teddy Wilson 1936, Lionel Hampton 1939. In late '39 he joined the Ella Fitzgerald band, which she had just taken over after Chick Webb's death, and remained with it until it broke up two years later. With Don Redman at Zanzibar NYC, '43; several years at Cafe Society Uptown and Downtown w. Edmond Hall.

In early '50s toured US, Latin Amer. w. Marcelino Guerra, also recs. w. Pearl Bailey for Coral, r & b dates for Victor. Worked with Bobby Medera at Savoy Ballroom '55; with Chick Morrison at La Martinique, NYC, '57-60.

Addr: 53 Hamilton Terrace, New York 31, N. Y.

RANDOLPH, ZILMER T., *composer, trumpet;* b. Dermott, Ark., 1/28/1899. Extensive studies of piano, trumpet, harmony, theory, etc. in conservatories until 1926. Played w. Bernie Young in Milwaukee 1927-31. Best known as arranger and trumpeter from 1931 to '35 w. Louis Armstrong, for whom he composed *Ol' Man Mose.* Settling in Chicago, he arranged for many bands such as Earl Hines, Duke Ellington, Fletcher Henderson, Woody Herman. In late 1940s he built a musical act comprising his son and two daughters, starting his own company to record them. LP w. Louis Armstrong (Vict.).

RANEY, JAMES ELBERT (Jimmy), *guitar, composer;* b. Louisville, Ky., 8/20/27. Father a prominent newspaperman. Studied w. A. J. Giancolla and Hayden Causey; the latter recommended Raney to replace him in Jerry Wald band in NYC 1944. After two months w. Wald he went to Chicago, working there w. Max Miller, Lou Levy and many local combos. Toured w. Woody Herman Jan.-Sept. '48. Worked in trio w. Al Haig for a while, then Buddy DeFranco sextet, and off and on w. Artie Shaw in 1949 and '50. Following 2 months w. Terry Gibbs, he joined the Stan Getz quintet and was responsible w. Getz for the unique combo sound achieved by the group during their two years together.

Starting in March '53 Raney spent a year with the Red Norvo trio, toured Europe with him in Jan.-Feb. '54. After working for three months w. Les Elgart he joined the Jimmy Lyons Trio at the Blue Angel in NYC, remaining there until '60 when he went w. Broadway show, *Thurber Carnival.*

Raney, a superlative musician, is to the guitar what Lee Konitz is to the alto sax. He has written a number of striking compositions among them *Signal, Motion, Lee, Five, Minor.* Favs: Tal Farlow, Ch. Christian. He won the DB critics' poll 1954-5. Own LPs: Pres., ABC-Par., Dawn, one side of *Swingin' In Sweden* (Em.), *Two Guitars* w. Kenny Burrell (Pres.), four tracks in *The Four Most Guitars* (ABC-Par.); LPs w. Stan Getz (Verve, Roost), Red Norvo (Fant.), Bob Brookmeyer (Pres.); *The Street Swingers* w. Brookmeyer (Wor. Pac.), as "Sir Osbert Haberdasher" w. Al Cohn (Vict.); Buddy De Franco (MGM); four tracks w. Stan Getz in *Lestorian Mode* (Savoy), one track w. Artie Shaw in *Encyclopedia of Jazz on Records, Vol. 3* (Decca); Edmond Hall (Rae-Cox), Dick Katz (Atl.).

RAPPOLO, JOSEPH LEON, *clarinet;* b. Lutheran, La., 3/16/02; d. Jackson, La., 10/5/43. Ran away from home at the age of 14 to join Bee Palmer in her vaudeville show; worked w. Emmet Hardy, Peck Kelley and with the Brunis Bros. in New Orleans, sometimes playing guitar and drums as well as clarinet. Rappolo earned his legendary name during his two years with the New Orleans Rhythm Kings, 1922 to early '25 off and on. He returned to New Orleans and worked briefly w. Albert Brunis but was soon committed to a mental home, where he spent the rest of his life.

Rappolo, whose father and grandfather were concert musicians, himself started as a violinist and took up clarinet in emulation of his grandfather. One of the most gifted musicians in jazz at a stage when many of its participants were self-taught and technically limited, Rappolo brought to his performances a soaring, spirited style that made him a musical as well as a personal legend. The series of records made by the Rhythm Kings for Gennett were an inspiration for many later white jazz bands of the 1920s. LP w. NORK (River. 12-102); one track w. NORK in *History of Classic Jazz* (River. SDP 11).

RASKIN, MILTON WILLIAM (Milt), *piano, composer;* b. Boston, Mass., 1/27/16. Pl. w. Wingy Manone 1937, Gene Krupa '38-40, T. Dorsey '42-4, and w. Teddy Powell, Alvino Rey, etc. Settled in LA '44; on staff at MGM Studios during '50s, active as pop songwriter. Solos on *Well Git It, Blue Blazes* w. Dorsey. LPs w. Dorsey (Vict.).

Addr: 517 N. California St., Burbank, Calif.

RAY, JOHN ALVIN (Johnnie), *singer, piano, songwriter;* b. Dallas, Oregon, 1/10/27. Prof. from 1942 on Portland radio; to Los Angeles '44. Discovered by Danny Kessler of Okeh records, 1951, working at Flame Showbar, Detroit; made rec. debut. Soon after, scored national hit w. *Cry* and *The Little White Cloud That Cried,* late '51. Partially deaf, Ray has worn a hearing aid since sixth grade. Though now absorbed into the mainstream of showbusiness and not thought of as a jazz singer, he was strongly influenced by Kay Starr, Billie Holiday and a southern r & b singer called Miss Cornshucks. LPs on Col.

RAZAF, ANDY (Andreamenentania Paul Razafinkeriefo), *songwriter;* b. Washington, D.C., 12/16/1895. Nephew of Queen Ranavalona III of Madagascar. Not a musician or performer himself (though he occasionally recorded as a singer), Razaf was important in jazz tangentially as lyricist for many songs that became jazz standards, and as close friend and songwriting partner of Fats Waller. He wrote for such Broadway night club revues as Connie's Hot Chocolates of 1928, Lew Leslie's Blackbirds of 1930; lyrics for *Honeysuckle Rose, Ain't Misbehavin', Keepin' Out of Mischief Now, Black & Blue, S'posin', Memories Of You, Stompin' at the Savoy, In the Mood, Christopher Columbus* and hundreds of others.

Addr: 3429 Country Club Drive, Los Angeles, Cal.

REARDON, CASPER, *harp;* b. Little Falls, N.Y., 4/15/07; d. New York City, 3/9/41. Worked mostly with symphony orchestras, but was the first to interpret the characteristics of swing music on the harp, recording w. Jack Teagarden in Sept. 1934 and working with him briefly at the Hickory House in '36.

REAY, HOWARD THOMAS WILLIAM, *drums;* b. Seamham Harbour, England, 10/10/30. Stud. Guildhall School of Music in London, served in the RAF, finishing his service as a disc jockey on the British Forces Network in Vienna. Played drums in band at the Elbow Beach Hotel in Bermuda, moving to Canada in 1951. Joined the Calvin Jackson quartet in '53 and remained w. him until early in '57. Since then has been active in studio work in Toronto, also w. Cliff McKay at Flamingo Club in Hamilton, Ont. '58. Pl. jazz gigs a few nights a week '59-60. LP w. Jackson (Col.).

REDD, FREDDIE, *piano, composer;* b. New York City, 5/29/28. Stud. at Greenwich House, NYC. Army 1946-9. In Syracuse w. Johnny Mills '49. Played w. Cootie Williams, Oscar Pettiford, Jive Bombers, '53; Joe Roland, Art Blakey, '54; toured Sweden w. Rolf Ericson summer '56. Led quartet and wrote score for off-Broadway play, *The Connection,* '59, in which musicians were onstage and feat. as integral part of the action. Took up study of tenor sax '59. Described by Ira Gitler as one of the warmer disciples of the Bud Powell school. Fav: Powell. Own LPs: *Piano East/West* (Pres.), *San Francisco Suite* (River.); LPs w. Joe Roland (Beth.), Gene Ammons (Pres.); music from *The Connection* (Blue Note).

Addr: 271 West 150th Street, New York City, N.Y.

REDISKE, JOHANNES, *guitar, composer;* b. Berlin, Germany, 8/11/26. Two brothers are both church organists. Stud. organ, piano, violin, theory; self-taught on guitar. With Berlin AFN house band 1946; own combo from '48. Heard annually at Frankfurt jazz festivals from '53; soloist w. Kurt Edelhagen in Baden-Baden '56, also broadcasts w. Erwin Lehn in Stuttgart '55, '7, '8. His quintet has been heard in many concerts, incl. the first jazz performance ever heard in the concert hall of Berlin's Hochschule für Musik. Comp. and rec. own music for film *Begrenztes Wochenende* '59. Fav. own recs. *Moonlight in Vermont* (Amiga), *Thema in Moll* (Manhattan). LP: one track in *Das ist Jazz* (Decca).

Addr: 30 Windscheidstr., Berlin-Charlottenburg, Germany.

REDMAN, DONALD MATTHEW (Don), *composer, leader, saxes;* b. Piedmont, W. Va., 7/29/00. Father pl. in brass band, mother sang contralto; Redman, a child prodigy, played trumpet at 3, joined a band at 6 and spent much of his childhood studying every instrument in the band as well as harmony, theory, composition. Completing his studies at Boston and Detroit Conservatories, he recorded w. Fletcher Henderson early in '23 and joined the band soon after at the Club Alabam. After three years w. Henderson he was mus. dir. of McKinney's Cotton Pickers '27-31. From '31-40, as leader of his own band (formed with the assistance of Horace Henderson) he had one of the top Negro orchs. of the day and the first to play a sponsored radio series (for Chipso in '32). In '40 he started work as a freelance arr., writing for the *Lower Basin St.* show on NBC, and for Paul Whiteman, Basie, J. Dorsey and numerous pop bands.

Redman again led bands for occasional night club and recording work during the '40s, incl. a European tour in '46-7, but spent most of his time writing. Since 1951 he has been mus. dir. for Pearl Bailey, and for a while he led her band on theatre engagements; he appeared in a small acting role in her starring vehicle *House of Flowers* on Broadway in '54-5. After many years of complete inactivity as an instrumentalist he played on one or two record dates in '58-9, when he cut several albums for Roulette, and one for Urania.

Redman was the first composer-arranger of any consequence in the history of jazz; the first musician with both the inspiration and the academic knowledge for this branch of the music. He was also known in the '20s as a superb instrumentalist, especially on alto sax, also on soprano and baritone. He sang in a delightfully informal, semi-conversational style. His most successful compositions were *Cherry, How'm I Doin'* and his famous band theme of the '30s, *Chant of the Weed.* He was heard on records with Bessie Smith in '24, Louis Armstrong '28, Chocolate Dandies '28-9. Own LPs: Gold. Crest 3017, Roul. 25070, Uran. 1211; LPs w. Louis Armstrong (Col. CL 853), Pearl Bailey (Coral); Fletcher Henderson in *The Birth of Big Band Jazz* (Riv. 12-129).

Addr: 555 Edgecombe Avenue, New York City, N.Y.

REECE, ALPHONSO SON (Dizzy), *trumpet,* b. Kingston, Jamaica, 1/5/31. Father pianist for silent films. Stud. baritone horn at age 11, switched to trumpet at 14. Came to Europe 1948; pl. w. Don Byas, Jay Cameron in Paris '49-50. Later worked in Germany and Holland w. drummer Wallace Bishop, Sandy Mosse and Byas. To London '54, working in clubs and w. Tony Crombie's band. Spent '56-7 in Paris, Portugal and London; in '58 worked in France w. Jacques Hélian's big band. Then he gigged in London clubs, with occasional visits to France before migrating to US, Oct. '59. Greatly admired by Miles Davis, Sonny Rollins, Dizzy Gillespie et al. Fav: Gillespie. Own LPs: *Changing the Jazz* (Sav.), *Star Bright, Blues in Trinity* (BN); LP w. Victor Feldman (Contemp.); London Jazz (Imp.).

Addr: 1069 Colgate Ave., Bronx 72, N.Y.

REED, LUCY (Lucille DeRidder), *singer;* b. Marshfield, Wis., 4/14/21. Worked w. Ray Amicangelo quintet in Iron Mountain, Mich., 1949, Geo. Corsi trio in Milwaukee, and Woody Herman Sextet, '50. Record debut while w. Charlie Ventura's big band, '51. Resident in Chicago, she worked for some time at the Streamliner and at Lei Aloha w. Dick Marx and Johnny Frigo, '53-5, Village Vanguard, NYC, Jan., '56. Fine song stylist in pop vein. Greatly admired by musicians though never commercially successful. Fav. own record: *It's All Right With Me* (Fant.). Fav: Carmen McRae. Own LPs: Fant.

Addr: 4545 N. Clarendon Ave., Chicago 40, Ill.

REESE, DELLA (Dellareese Taliaferro), *singer;* b. Detroit, Mich., 7/6/32. Sang in choirs from 1938; summer seasons w. Mahalia Jackson troupe 1945-9. Stud. Wayne U., had own gospel group. After club work in Detroit, came to NYC, joined Erskine Hawkins. Prominent from '57 as solo artist; many radio shows w. Robt. Q. Lewis, TV w. Jackie Gleason, Ed Sullivan et al. Movie: *Let's Rock,* 1958. A dramatic pop singer rather than a jazz artist. Own LPs on Jubilee, RCA Victor.

Addr: c/o Lee Magid, 224 W. 49th St., New York 19, N.Y.

REHAK, FRANK JAMES, *trombone;* b. Brooklyn, N.Y., 7/6/26. Navy, '43-7. Has played w. Art Mooney, G. Krupa, J. Dorsey, R. McKinley, C. Thornhill, Sauter-Finegan, W. Herman. While with D. Gillespie band '56-7, toured Near East and Latin America. After leaving Gillespie pl. w. Johnny Richards; worked in B'way show *Copper & Brass;* on staff at WNEW; then freelanced incl. much TV and radio commercial work, jazz gigs w. own combo etc. and record dates for over 50 labels. Organized teaching and practice studio on Broadway. Highly respected as one of the most individual of modern trombonists. LPs: own group on one-half of *Jazzville, Vol. 2* (Dawn); André Hodeir (Savoy), Gene Quill (Roost), Al Cohn (Dawn), George Russell (Decca), Melba Liston, The Mitchells (Metrojazz), *Roots* (New Jazz), Bill Potts (UA), *Spirit of Charlie Parker* (WW), *Something New, Something Blue* (Col.), Johnny Richards (Cap.), Dizzy Gillespie (Verve).

Addr: 211 West 53rd St., New York 19, N.Y.

REILLY, DEAN EDWIN, *bass;* b. Auburn, Wash., 6/30/26. Father pl. pno., organ, had dance band in '20s. As child, stud. piano, tpt, bassoon. Took up bass after hearing Jimmy Blanton in person with Ellington; during '50s pl. w. many groups in San Francisco, incl. Geo. Auld, Sonny Criss, Jackie Cain-Roy Kral; two years w. Vince Guaraldi & Eddie Duran at Hungry "i." Joined Jean Hoffman May '57. LPs w. Guaraldi, Duran, Earl Hines (Fantasy); Rudy Salvini, Mel Lewis (San Francisco Jazz).

Addr: 1215 Pacific, San Francisco, Cal.

REINHARDT, JEAN BAPTISTE (Django), *guitar;* b. Liverchies, Belgium, 1/23/10; d. Fontainebleau, France, 5/16/53. Living a typical gypsy life, Reinhardt roamed through Belgium and France in his caravan, picking up a knowledge of violin, banjo and guitar. In Nov. 1928 he was seriously burned in a fire in the caravan and spent most of the next year recovering from his injuries, which put two fingers of his left hand completely out of commission. He quickly developed a new technique to overcome this handicap and managed, with the partly paralyzed hand, to create an original style that was heard first in such bands as André Ekyan's from 1931. In 1934, the Quintet of The Hot Club of France, in which Reinhardt and violinist Stéphane Grappelly were the leaders and featured soloists, made its debut at a concert. The other members were Roger Chaput and Joseph Reinhardt, Django's brother, on guitars; Louis Vola on bass. The quintet worked together off and on until 1939 but was subject to Django's capricious decisions to wander off unpredictably into the country. The group made an international reputation on records; Eddie South, Benny Carter and other visiting jazz musicians recorded with Reinhardt.

During the 1940s, while Grappelly was living in

London, Reinhardt led another quintet, in which Hubert Rostaing played clarinet. Late in 1946 Duke Ellington took Reinhardt on a concert tour; this was his only visit to the US and the reaction was less than a complete success. By this time, Reinhardt was playing electric guitar. He continued to record and tour in France until shortly before his death.

Reinhardt brought a unique style to jazz, one in which the less rhythmic gypsy qualities were so pronounced that his place as a truly first-rank jazz musician is debatable. Beyond dispute, though, is the fact that he was the first overseas musician ever to influence his jazz contemporaries in America. Many of the top American musicians have acknowledged their debt to him and were originally inspired by his style. Reinhardt's most effective performances can be heard mostly on slow tempo numbers, in which his gifts for a rhapsodic brand of melodic improvisation are most apparent. In his later records he seemed to show a bop influence that did not sit too well with his basic style.

Own LPs: *Swing From Paris* (Lond. LL 1344), *Django Reinhardt* (Vict. LPM 1100), Memorial Album, Vol. 1-3 (Per. 1201-1203), *The Best of Django Reinhardt* (Cap. TBO 10226); one side of *Jazz From Paris* (Verve 8015).

RENA, HENRY (Kid), *trumpet, leader;* b. New Orleans, 1900; d. New Orleans, 4/25/49. Played in Kid Ory's band, 1918, then w. Bob Lyons; had own band intermittently after 1924. Led own rec. band in 1940 w. Louis Nelson, Alphonse Picou, Jim Robinson et al. LP: own band in *New Orleans Legends* (River.).

RENAUD, HENRI, *piano, leader, composer;* b. Villedieu, Indre, France, 4/20/25. Stud. violin 1930-1, piano '35-7. Started at small bar in the Latin Quarter, Paris; joined J. C. Fohrenbach's band for summer engagement at St. Jean-de-Luz. After gigging w. Don Byas, Buck Clayton, Roy Eldridge, Hubert Rostaing, he became interested in modern jazz and formed his own small band at the Tabou in Paris, which soon became a favorite hangout for musicians. Early in 1954, while on a visit to New York, he made a series of LPs with Al Cohn and leading US jazzmen. Also rec. in Paris w. Zoot Sims, Lee Konitz, Bob Brookmeyer, Gigi Gryce, Clifford Brown, Dick Collins et al. Visited US again '59 on vacation, playing one Monday night at Birdland w. Philly Joe Jones. Active w. small groups in Paris jazz clubs. His combo won *Jazz Hot* poll '53. Plays cool, understated single-note lines in style showing influence of his favorites: G. Wallington, Al Haig, Th. Monk. LPs w. *The Birdlanders* (Period).

Addr: 12 Rue Du Sergeant Maginot, Paris 6, France.

RENDELL, DON PERCY, *tenor sax, clarinet;* b. Plymouth, Eng., 3/4/26. Parents both prof. musicians; started him on piano at 6 but kept him at it only until he was 10. At 16, he took up alto and was at first largely self-taught, doing his first prof. work at that age. Was w. J. Dankworth's Seven, 1950-3, had own group '54-5, w. T. Heath 6 months in '55, toured Europe w. S. Kenton for 6 weeks in '56; own group again in 1957. Won *Melody Maker* Readers' Poll for Britain's Best, 1957. Fav: L. Young. LPs: own group in parts of *Modern Jazz at Royal Festival Hall* (Lond.), *Jazz Britannia, Cool Europe* (MGM); LPs w. Tony Kinsey, Ted Heath, Ken Moule (Lond.).

REUSS, ALLAN, *guitar;* b. New York City, 6/15/15. First gig on banjo, for $12, at age 12, 12/12/27, after only one lesson. Later stud. w. Geo. Van Eps, who recommended Reuss to replace him in the Benny Goodman band. After touring w. Goodman 1934-8, he joined Paul Whiteman in NYC, then worked with Jack Teagarden 1939-40; Ted Weems '40-1; J. Dorsey '41-2; NBC house band in Chicago, '42-3; back w. Goodman '43; Harry James '43-4; since then has freelanced in movies, TV and radio in Hollywood. During the late '30s Reuss was on numerous record dates with Teddy Wilson, Lionel Hampton, Glenn Miller et al. Fav. own solo: Minor Blues w. Corky Corcoran on Keynote. Won Met. poll, 1944; DB poll, 1944. LPs w. Goodman (MGM, Col.), Lionel Hampton (Cam.), one track w. Coleman Hawkins in *History of Jazz, Vol. 4* (Cap.).

Addr: 2734 Stoner Ave., Los Angeles 64, Calif.

REYNOLDS, THOMAS A. (Tommy), *clarinet, leader, radio producer;* b. Akron, O., 1/17/17. Vln. at 8, concert clar. at 14; stud. at Ohio State U. Pl. w. Isham Jones, 1938-9. Org. band in Cleveland, 1939. Throughout the 1940s led popular swing band, rec. for Col., seen at Meadowbrook, Roseland, New Yorker Hotel, Paramount Th., etc. Gave up touring 1955, became house mus. on WOR-TV, NYC, on Ted Steele show, then became prod. of radio shows, incl. *Bandstand U.S.A.* on Mutual network, two-hour live jazz show, 1956-8. Director of operations at WOR-TV, and occasional gigs as band leader '59-'60. Own LP: King.

Addr: 901 8th Ave., New York, N. Y.

REYS, MARIA EVERDINA (Rita), *singer;* b. Rotterdam, Holland, 12/21/24. Father was a musician; mother a dancer; brother plays alto sax. Got into music business through father. Sang w. Piet van Dijk, then w. Wes Ilcken, to whom she was married until his death in 1957. In addition to singing all over Europe, she has also appeared in Africa '49, US '55-6, England '59. Favs: Holiday, McRae, Fitzgerald. Own LP: Epic.

Addr: Melkpad 2A, Hilversum, Holland.

RHODES, TODD WASHINGTON, *piano, composer;* b. Hopkinsville, Ky., 8/31/00. Stud. at Springfield (Ohio) Sch. of Mus. 1915-17, then four years at Erie Cons. In 1922, organized a small band and called it the Synco Orchestra; went to Detroit, pl. at Arcadia Ballroom; soon the band's name was changed, at suggestion of ballroom manager, to The Cotton Pickers, and the drummer-manager, Wm. McKinney, became nominal leader. As McKinney's Cotton Pickers the band played the Greystone Brm. in Detroit and Roseland in NYC, recording regularly for Victor from

1928, by which time McKinney was no longer playing in the band and Don Redman was the musical director. The group was possibly the No. 1 Negro orchestra of the mid-1920s in terms of general popularity. Musically it ranked with Fletcher Henderson's among the best organized bands and contained many excellent soloists. Rhodes, who has remained active in Detroit, formed a band in '47, rec. for the Sensation and King Labels and was popular in r & b circles with such numbers as *Blues for the Red Boy, Bellboy Boogie, Pot Likker, Rocket 69.* He discovered LaVern Baker, who sang with his band in '52; also gave Johnnie Ray his start at Flame Show Bar in Detroit. Favs: Tatum, Peterson, Shearing, Nat Cole. Most of Rhodes' records are unavailable on LPs. LP: King.

Addr: 739 East Baker, Flint 5, Mich.

RICCIO, PATRICK JOSEPH (Pat), *alto sax;* also *baritone sax, clarinet, flute;* b. Port Arthur, Ont., Canada, 12/3/18. Brother James plays tenor sax, clarinet, guitar and flute, now w. hotel band in Toronto. Took up clar. in Toronto, 1925; alto '39, baritone '47, flute '57. Arranger and musical dir. for RCAF Streamliners 15 piece dance band '41-6, which alternated w. Glenn Miller at Queensbury Club, London '45. Own 12 piece band '56, own quartet '58. App. on Canadian Timex TV show Feb. '59; Can. Jazz Fest. in Toronto, July '59. Won Can. jazz poll on alto '47, baritone '49. Fav: Charlie Parker. Most imp. infl: Lester Young, Jimmy Lunceford Orch. Own LP on Quality incl. fav. own solo on *The Song Is You.*

Addr: 71 Wye Valley Road, Scarborough, Ont., Canada.

RICH, BERNARD (Buddy), *drums, singer;* b. Brooklyn, N.Y., 6/30/17. A natural musician virtually from birth, he started work in his parents' vaudeville act (Wilson & Rich) at the age of 18 months. At 4, he appeared in Raymond Hitchcock's *Pinwheel* on Broadway; at 6 he went to Australia for 18 months, working as a single and managed by his parents. When he was 11 he took out his own band for a year and a half. His jazz career began w. Joe Marsala at the Hickory House in 1938. Subsequent band affiliations: Bunny Berigan 1938; Artie Shaw 1939; Tommy Dorsey Nov. 1939 until '42; Benny Carter 1942. After service in the Marines from 1942 until '44 he rejoined Dorsey until 1946, then he formed the first of several big bands he has fronted.

Starting in 1947 he made several tours w. JATP; in 1951 he was part of a group known as the "Big Four" w. Ch. Ventura and Chubby Jackson. He spent a year w. Harry James 1953-4; back w. Dorsey '54-5; toured Europe w. Harry James Oct. '57. During most of '58-9 he had his own quintet. In addition to his phenomenal technique and dynamically swinging style on drums, Rich is a capable singer, an expert tap dancer and an electric personality. During the late '50s he appeared on TV as an actor and intermittently announced that he was giving up the drums forever to devote himself to a full time singing career; however, he usually returned to the drums after a brief interlude. Inactivated, winter '59-60 by a heart attack, he later resumed singing and playing. Rich has won the following awards: DB poll '41-2, '44; Esq. Gold Award '47; Met. poll '48; DB Critics poll '53-4. Own LPs: *Buddy And Sweets* (Verve 8129), *Krupa And Rich* (Verve 8069), *The Swinging Buddy Rich* (Verve 8142), *The Wailing Buddy Rich* (Verve 8168), *This One's For Basie* (Verve 8176), *Buddy Rich In Miami* (Verve 8285), *Lester Young-Buddy Rich Trio* (Verve 8164), *Hampton, Tatum, Rich Trio* (Verve 8093), *Buddy Rich Sings Johnny Mercer* (Verve 2009), *Buddy Rich Just Sings* (Verve 2075), *Rich Versus Roach* (Merc. 20448); two tracks in *The Jazz Giants: Drum Role* (Em. 36071), one track in *Midnight Jazz at Carnegie Hall* (Verve 8189-2); title track in *Hi-Fi Drums* (Cap. T926); LPs w. Roy Eldridge (Verve 8068), Lionel Hampton (Verve 8117), *Bird And Diz* (Verve 8006), *Jam Session* #3-5 (Verve 8051-53), #7 (8062), #8 (8094), JATP, Vol. 1, 4, 7, 8, 10, 11 (Verve), Tommy Dorsey (Vict. LPM 1432, 1433), Count Basie (Verve 8090), Charlie Ventura (Verve 8165) *Saturday Night Swing Session* (Ctpt. 549).

Addr: 105-07 66th Road, Forest Hills 75, L.I., N.Y.

RICHARDS, ANN (Margaret Ann Borden Kenton), *singer;* b. San Diego, Calif., 10/1/35. Self-taught on piano, with mother's help, at age 10; private singing lessons. Local groups in Oakland and San Francisco, then four months w. Ch. Barnet combo, six months w. George Redman in Hollywood. Eddie Beal recommended her to Stan Kenton, with whom she toured in 1955. Married Kenton summer of '55; a few months later, shortly before winning *Down Beat* poll as No. 1 band vocalist, she gave up career, resuming subsequently for occasional record albums and night club work in LA. One of the best vocalists produced by the Kenton band, she is a superior, jazz-influenced pop singer. Fav. own solo: *Winter In Madrid* w. Kenton. Own LP: Cap.; LPs w. Kenton (Cap.).

RICHARDS, EMIL (Emilio Joseph Radocchia), *vibraphone;* also *xylophone, piano, tympani;* b. Hartford, Conn., 9/2/32. Began studying at 6, first on xylophone. Was at Hartford School of Music, 1949-52. Between 1950-54, was percussionist w. Hartford and New Britain Symphonies and Connecticut Pops Orch. In 1954-5 was assistant leader of Army band in Japan, and worked w. Toshiko Akiyoshi during that time. In 1956 gigged around NYC; joined G. Shearing, Sept. '56, and toured with him until early '59. Moved to LA May '59, pl. marimba in own quintet w. Bill Perkins et al, also worked w. Paul Horn Quintet, Shorty Rogers big band; sound track for movie *The Proper Time* w. Shelly Manne, and misc. studio work. Rapidly developing musician. Fav. own solo: *You Stepped Out of a Dream* w. Shearing (MGM). LPs w. Shearing incl.

In The Night, Shearing on Stage (Cap.); also feat. on *Sounds of the Great Bands* (Cap.).

Addr: 1432 N. Kenmore Ave., Hollywood 27, Calif.

RICHARDS, JOHNNY (John Cascales), *composer;* b. Schenectady, N.Y., 11/2/11. Mother, prof. pianist, was pupil of Paderewski. Stud. theory, etc. in Troy, Syracuse; played violin, banjo, trumpet in vaudeville act, "The Seven Wonders of the World," at age 10 until 12. Saxophone w. band at Phila. theatre at 17, then to England w. Teddy Joyce; spent a year there writing movie scores for Gaumont, 1932-3. To Hollywood, worked as Victor Young's assistant at Paramount and stayed in movie work throughout '30s. Led own dance band 1940-5, playing tenor sax, clarinet, trumpet; early sidemen incl. Paul Smith, later Pete Rugolo, on piano; singer Andy Russell on drums; Bob Graettinger, baritone sax & arr. From 1946, free-lanced as arr. in progressive jazz idiom, incl. *Prelude to Dawn, Soft & Warm, Man With a Horn* for Boyd Raeburn; *Soliloquy, Prologue, Bags & Baggage* for Kenton, and some scores for Ch. Barnet; conductor & arr. for Dizzy Gillespie date w. strings, woodwinds, Oct. 1950. Movie scores in Mexico, '48 and '50. Left Calif. Oct. '52, settled in NYC, arr. rec. dates for Sarah Vaughan, Sonny Stitt, Helen Merrill, Gillespie et al. Occasionally led his own large orchestra in NYC, usually at Birdland '58-'60. Richards writes in a heavy-textured, skillfully orchestrated style that sometimes seems top-heavy in jazz terms though it has resulted in some provocatively colorful music. Favs: Ellington, Rugolo, Graettinger. Own LPs: Coral, Cap., Roul., Beth.; arrs. for Stan Kenton (Cap.), Dizzy Gillespie (Verve, Savoy), Boyd Raeburn (Savoy).

RICHARDS, CHARLES (Red), *piano;* b. Brooklyn, N.Y., 10/19/12. Took up jazz piano after hearing Fats Waller play at parlor socials. Worked w. Roy Eldridge, Bobby Hackett, Sidney Bechet, Jimmy McPartland and four years w. Tab Smith. Rec. debut w. Skeets Tolbert. Spent four months in France and Italy, spring '53, making recs. w. Buck Clayton, M. Mezzrow. Toured w. Muggsy Spanier '53-7, then worked as single in Columbus, O. to Feb. '58 and spent following summer in San Francisco w. Wild Bill Davison, with whom he worked again in '59. Also at Great South Bay festival '57 and '58 in reunion of Fletcher Henderson alumni (rec. on UA). Also on *All About Memphis* LP w. Buster Bailey (Felsted).

Addr: 3944 Paulding Ave., Bronx 66, N.Y.

RICHARDSON, JEROME C., *saxophones, woodwinds, singer;* b. Oakland, Cal., 12/25/20. Alto at 8, stud. music San Francisco State Coll. Local musicians, Ben Watkins and Wilbert Baranco, helped him get prof. start at 14. Local bands to '41; Navy, '42-5, working in Navy dance band under Marshall Royal. Toured w. Lionel Hampton '49-51; Earl Hines '54-5. Has had own quartet at Minton's Play House NYC frequently since '55; pl. w. Lucky Millinder, Cootie Williams; subbed w. Chico Hamilton Quintet for several weeks, and was in pit band at Roxy '54-56; also on *Hit Parade* and other commercial broadcasts from NYC, '56-60. With Quincy Jones '60. First flute solo was *Kingfish* w. L. Hampton (MGM). Richardson, who is also a capable ballad singer, has established himself in recent years not merely as a jack of all trades but as a first class soloist on every instrument he has played. He even made an effective jazz vehicle of the piccolo in *Tweeter,* a comp. in the author's *Hi Fi Suite* (MGM). Favs: F. Wess, flute; Ch. Parker, S. Stitt, S. Getz. Own LPs: New Jazz; LPs w. J. Cleveland, J. Adderley (Merc.), Oscar Pettiford, Jackie Cain & Roy Kral (ABC-Par.), D. Gillespie (Verve), Phineas Newborn (Vict.), Billy Taylor (River.), *All Night Long,* Gene Ammons (Pres.).

Addr: 62 West 91st St., New York 24, N.Y.

RICHMAN, ABRAHAM SAMUEL (Boomie), *tenor sax, clarinet, flute;* b. Brockton, Mass., 4/2/21. Club dates in Boston; to NYC 1942, joined Muggsy Spanier. Pl. w. Jerry Wald '44; Geo. Paxton '45; T. Dorsey '46-52, then free-lance TV, radio and rec. in NYC incl. B. Goodman '53-4. Since then, studio work in NYC; inactive in jazz. Favs: B. Freeman, E. Miller, S. Getz. LPs w. T. Dorsey (Vict.), Neal Hefti (Epic), B. Goodman (Cap.), Steve Allen (Coral), Tommy Reynolds (King), Peanuts Hucko (Gr. Award).

Addr: 27-91 Beatrice Lane, N. Bellmore, L.I., N.Y.

RICHMOND, CHARLES D. (Dannie), *drums;* also *tenor sax;* b. New York City, 12/15/35. Started on tenor at 13, pl. for eight years. Self-taught on drums. Pl. with Charles Mingus Workshop in 1956-7; later w. Chet Baker for several months, then back w. Mingus. Fav: Philly Joe Jones. LPs w. Mingus (Atlantic, Jub., UA, Col.), Baker (Riv.), Jimmy Knepper (Beth.), John Jenkins (BN).

Addr: 2434 7th Ave., New York 30, N.Y.

RIDDLE, NELSON, *composer;* b. Oradell, N.J., 6/1/21. Stud. piano from age of eight to 14, then switched to father's instrument, trombone. Pl. and arr. for Jerry Wald, Charlie Spivak and T. Dorsey. Played w. Army band while in service; joined Bob Crosby after discharge and went w. him to West Coast, where he began work as staff arr. for NBC. Began free-lance arr. in 1950, for such stars as Nat Cole, Frank Sinatra et al. Though very successful in pop field, is first-class swing-style arranger of big band jazz. Own LPs: *C'Mon, Get Happy, Hey, Let Yourself Go, Sea of Dreams, Tender Touch* (Cap.); LPs w. Peggy Lee, Frank Sinatra, Nat Cole, Keely Smith (Cap.), *Cross Country Suite* feat. B. De Franco (Dot).

Addr: 3853 Carbon Canyon Rd., Malibu, Calif.

RIEDEL, GEORG, *bass, 'cello;* b. Karlsbad, Czechoslovakia, 11/8/34. Studied at school in Stockholm 1953-9. Prof. debut with Arne Domnerus band; has since worked in Sweden w. Lars Gullin, Harry Arnold, Gunnar Svensson. Recorded on cello w. various small combos for Metronome Records. Favs: R. Brown, Blanton, Chambers. LPs w. Domnerus (Vict.), Gullin (Em., Atl.).

Addr: Storbergsgatan 19, Hägersten, Sweden.

RITZ, LYLE JOSEPH, *bass, tuba;* also *violin, ukulele;* b. Cleveland, O., 1/10/30. Stud. violin ten years, in Pittsburgh, Occidental College, Carnegie Inst. Also took music courses; pl. with U. of Southern Calif. and Los Angeles Community Symph. Orch. Pl. tuba in Army; met professional musicians incl. Lennie Niehaus and became interested in jazz. Self-taught on bass; pl. as sideman w. Eddie Grady's Commanders; Jerry Fielding; Les Elgart. Favs: Ray Brown, Leroy Vinnegar, Red Mitchell. Own LPs: *50th State Jazz, How About Uke?*—ukulele solos (Verve); LP w. Paul Horn (Wor. Pac.).

Addr: 5706 Whitsett Ave., N. Hollywood, Calif.

RIZZI, TREFONI (Tony), *guitar;* b. Los Angeles, Calif., 4/16/23. Stud. violin for eleven years, then switched to trumpet. Pl. in jam sessions around LA; in Army; and upon discharge pl. with Boyd Raeburn, Milt DeLugg, Alvy West, Les Brown. Has been staff musician on NBC in LA in recent years. Fav: Charlie Christian. LPs w. Les Brown (Cor.), Dave Pell (Kapp, Vict., Atl.), Ted Nash (Lib.), Paul Smith (Cap., Tampa).

Addr: 4471 Don Milagro Drive, Los Angeles, Calif.

ROACH, MAXWELL (Max), *drums;* b. Brooklyn, N.Y., 1/10/25. After finishing school in 1942 he worked w. Charlie Parker at Clarke Monroe's Uptown House. An early visitor to Minton's and to other clubs where he could hear Kenny Clarke, he was greatly influenced by Clarke in developing a style. He made his record debut w. Coleman Hawkins on Apollo, Feb. 1944, working during that year w. Dizzy Gillespie on 52nd St. and later w. Benny Carter in Calif. Back in NYC in 1945 he became the most sought-after young drummer of the newly-born bop movement, working w. Coleman Hawkins, Allen Eager, Miles Davis, Charlie Parker and many other small groups. He visited Paris w. Ch. Parker during the Jazz Festival in May 1949 and toured Europe w. JATP in 1952. In 1954 he was in Calif. w. Howard Rumsey at the Lighthouse, later going on tour with his own quintet, featuring the late Clifford Brown. Roach continued to lead his own combo through '60, with time out every summer from '57 to serve as a faculty member at the School of Jazz at Lenox, Mass.

Max Roach had the widest influence of all the drummers who emerged in the bop era. His use of the top cymbal rather than the bass drum, in an attempt to establish a more legato rhythmic feeling instead of a heavy four-to-the-bar beat, was imitated by countless other percussionists all over the world. Roach has won the following awards: Met. poll '51, '54; DB poll '55; DB Critics' poll '55, '57-9. Own LPs: *Brown And Roach, Inc.* (Em. 36008), *Clifford Brown And Max Roach* (Em. 36036), *Study In Brown* (Em. 36037), *At Basin St.* (Em. 36070), *The Best of Max Roach and Clifford Brown In Concert* (GNP 18), *Max Roach Plus Four* (Em. 36098), *Jazz In ¾ Time* (Em. 36108), *Max* (Argo 623), *On The Chicago Scene* (Em. 36132), *Deeds Not Words* (River. 12-280), *Max Roach 4 Plays Charlie Parker* (Merc. 80019), *Rich Versus Roach* (Merc. 20448), *Max Roach With The Boston Percussion Ensemble* (Merc. 36144); *Drummin' The Blues* w. Stan Levey (Lib. 3064); LPs w. Sonny Rollins (Pres. 7038, 7079, 7020, 7095, 7126, River. 12-258, Blue Note 1542), Miles Davis (Cap. T 762, Pres. 7054), T. Monk (Pres. 7027, River. 12-223, Blue Note 1511), Bud Powell (Blue Note 1503, 1504, Roost 2224, Verve 8153, 8185), Charlie Parker (Savoy 12014, 12079, 1200, 12001, 12009, Roost 2210, Verve 8005, 8010), Coleman Hawkins (Gr. Award 33-316); selections w. Parker-Gillespie, Bud Powell and a featured solo track in *Modern Jazz Hall of Fame* (Design 29); New York, N.Y. (Decca DL 79216).

ROBERTS, HOWARD MANCEL, *guitar;* b. Phoenix, Ariz., 10/2/29. Mostly self-taught on guitar, but studied Schillinger w. Fabian André; also stud. w. Shorty Rogers. Moved to Los Angeles 1950 where he has been very active in movies, TV, and recording work. Has worked in and around LA area with own group and has appeared as sideman w. groups such as Buddy De Franco, Shorty Rogers, Pete and Conte Candoli, Lennie Niehaus, Buddy Collette, Paul Horn and Bud Shank. Outstanding modern soloist in both single-string and chord work. Favs: Segovia, Kessel. Own LPs on Verve; LPs w. Chico Hamilton (Wor. Pac.), John Graas (Decca), Pete Jolly (Vict.), Bobby Troup (Beth.), Frank Morgan (GNP), Pete Rugolo (Col.).

Addr: 5229 Bluebell, No. Hollywood, Calif.

ROBERTS, CHARLES LUCKEYETH (Luckey), *piano,* b. Philadelphia, 8/7/1895. To NYC at 3 as actor in *Uncle Tom's Cabin.* Worked as child acrobat; pl. piano in Baltimore clubs. During the 1920s he was a favorite bandleader in high society, catering to millionaire clientele with his orchestras in New York, Newport, Palm Beach, etc. An early ragtime soloist, he published a number of orig. piano rags from 1913 (*Junk Man Rag, Pork and Beans*) through 1923. In later years he became owner of the Rendezvous, a bar on St. Nicholas Ave. in Harlem, but remained active in music: he had a successful Carnegie Hall concert appearance in 1939, another at Town Hall in '41; one of his more ambitious works, *Whistlin' Pete—Miniature Syncopated Rhapsody,* for piano and orch., was presented at Robin Hood Dell in Phila.

During the 1940s Roberts went in for popular songwriting, enjoying some success with *Moonlight Cocktail* ('41) and *Massachusetts* ('42). One of the most versatile and energetic of all the ragtime pianists of his day, he wrote music for 14 musical comedies, produced before and after World War I. As a society pianist, he was a great favorite of the Duke of Windsor (then Prince of Wales), playing for him frequently and helping to choose his collection of jazz records. He was an important early influence on Duke Ellington, James P. Johnson and many other Harlem pianists of the early 1920s. Own LP: Period.

Addr: 270 Convent Ave., New York 31, N.Y.

ROBINSON, ELI, *trombone;* b. Greensville, Ga., 6/23/11. Began stud. trombone in high school in Charleston, W. Va. Went to Detroit after grad. in 1928; worked in bands for club dates incl. Alex Jackson, Speed Webb, Frank Terry, Zack White, McKinney's Cotton Pickers, Blanche Calloway, Lucky Millinder. With Count Basie '41-7; w. small groups for club dates, rec. '48-54. Joined Buddy Tate '55. Rec. w. Blanche Calloway, Count Basie et al. LP w. Tate (Fels.).

Addr: 31 W. 124th St., New York, N.Y.

ROBINSON, FREDERICK L. (Fred), *trombone;* b. Memphis, Tenn., 2/20/01. Stud. at high school w. same teacher as Buster Bailey, and at Dana's Mus. Inst., Warren, Ohio. Came to Chicago 1927, worked w. Carroll Dickerson and Louis Armstrong; featured on the most famous of Louis' Hot Five sides. During the '30s, worked for two years w. Edgar Hayes' house band at the Alhambra Theatre on 126th St., then at the Arcadia Blrm. w. Charlie "Fat Man" Turner (band later toured theatres w. Fats Waller). Also played w. Benny Carter 1933; Andy Kirk '39-40; several times w. Fletcher Henderson. During 1940s, rec. sessions under mus. dir. Sy Oliver at Decca and free-lanced in NYC. Worked w. Noble Sissle 1950-1; gigged locally '52-3; gave up music to become NYC subway worker, Jan. '54. Rec. w. Jelly Roll Morton for Bluebird 1939: best solos on Armstrong and Morton versions of *West End Blues.* Fav. T. Dorsey. LP w. Louis Armstrong (Col.).

Addr: 304 Madison St., Brooklyn, N.Y.

ROBINSON, JAMES (Jim), *trombone;* b. Deeringe, La., 12/25/1892. Started on guitar. While playing in Army band in France, 1917, he was persuaded by Pops Foster's brother, Willie, to take up trombone. Later worked in New Orleans w. Young Morgan, Kid Rena, Tuxedo Band, etc. In Chicago briefly in 1929, but remained almost unknown outside New Orleans. Worked as longshoreman through most of 1930s, also seven years at Levita taxi dance hall in New Orleans. Rec. w. Kid Rena 1940, and w. Bunk Johnson and Geo. Lewis, in whose bands he played during the 1940s. Described by George Avakian as "tremendous musician." LPs w. George Lewis (Omega, Amer. Mus.), Wooden Joe Nicholas, Bunk Johnson (Amer. Mus.); Bunk Johnson in *New Orleans Legends* (River.).

ROBINSON, PRINCE, *clarinet, tenor sax;* b. Norfolk, Va., 6/7/04. Stud. clarinet at fourteen in Portsmouth, Va. Worked w. Duke Ellington 1926; toured S. America w. Leon Abbey '27. McKinney's Cotton Pickers 1927-34; Blanche Calloway '35-6; Willie Bryant '37-8; Roy Eldridge '38-9; Louis Armstrong '40-4, also w. Lucky Millinder and w. various combos at Cafe Society NYC. From 1947-53 chiefly w. Claude Hopkins combo. Robinson, who made his record debut in the early '20s w. a Clarence Williams group, was one of Coleman Hawkins' rivals for tenor sax supremacy in the '30s; his best solos, he says, were *Cryin' And Sighin'* and *Rainbow Round My Shoulder* w. McKinney's Cotton Pickers. Robinson worked weekends w. Freddie Washington in Bayside, L.I. '54-60, returning to records after a long absence on Andy Gibson date for Felsted, '59. Favs: Hawkins, tenor; Edmond Hall, Goodman, clarinet. LP w. Duke Ellington in *The Birth of Big Band Jazz* (River.).

Addr: 231 West 145th St., New York 30, N.Y.

ROCCO, MAURICE JOHN, *piano, singer;* b. Oxford, Ohio, 6/26/15. Mother was a music teacher. A prodigy and prof. pianist from childhood, he popularized the practice of playing piano while standing up, and is an entertainer rather than a jazz musician, despite the intensity of his fast boogie-woogie performances. Movies: *Vogues of 1938, 52nd Street, Incendiary Blonde* and several shorts. Rec. Decca, Victor, etc.

ROCHE, MARY ELIZABETH (Betty), *singer;* b. Wilmington, Del., 1/9/20. Raised in Atlantic City. To NYC 1939; Savoy Sultans 1941-2. As the first singer to perform the *Blues* sequence in *Black, Brown and Beige* w. Duke Ellington at Carnegie Hall in Jan. 1944, she impressed many listeners as perhaps the finest girl vocalist ever featured with the band. She was with Ellington 1943-4 and again 1952-3. After a couple of years of semi-retirement she recorded for Bethlehem in '55-6 but has since been in obscurity in San Diego. Her blues and ballad work, during her first stint w. Ellington, was far superior to the pseudo-bop singing she featured later. Own LP: Beth.; LP w. Ellington (Col.).

RODIN, GILBERT A. (Gil), *reeds, trumpet, flute;* b. Chicago, Ill., 12/9/06. Studied reeds, flute and trumpet while attending school in Chicago. Joined B. Pollack's orch. in 1927 and was with him until 1935. Helped organize group which became the Bob Crosby orch. in '35 and was long associated with it on alto and as arranger and musical director. Inactive as musician in recent years, working w. Crosby as radio and TV exec. Favs: Eddie Miller, M. Matlock, B. Goodman, I. Fazola. LPs w. Crosby (Coral).

Addr: 445 N. Laurel Ave., Los Angeles, Calif.

RODNEY, RED (Robert Chudnick), *trumpet,* b. Philadelphia, Pa., 9/27/27. Studied at Mastbaum school. On the road at 15, he worked w. Jerry Wald, Jimmy Dorsey, Tony Pastor, Les Brown, Georgie Auld, Claude Thornhill, Gene Krupa. With Woody Herman 1948-9; 8 months w. Charlie Parker 1949-50; Ch. Ventura '50-1. Worked with small combos in Phila. off and on for a few years; with Sammy Davis Jr. show, Oscar Pettiford, '57. In '58-60 enjoyed great success in Phila., building up large following booking groups on society club dates, playing mainly pop music. A chaotic personal life in his early jazz years prevented his full maturity and acceptance as first of the first important bop trumpeters after Gillespie and Davis. Own

LPs: Argo, Signal, Fant.; LPs w. Ch. Parker (Verve, Debut), *Advance Guard of the '40s* (Merc.).

Addr: 2043 N. 62nd St., Overbrook, Pa.

ROGERS, MILTON M. (Shorty), *composer, trumpet, fluegelhorn, leader;* b. Great Barrington, Mass., 4/14/24. Studied trumpet at High School of Mus. & Arts, NYC; comp. and arr. w. Dr. Wesley LaViolette and at LA Conservatory. Spent 6 months in Will Bradley's band in 1942; Red Norvo '42-3; Army May '43 to Sept. '45. Played and arranged for Woody Herman Sept. '45 to Dec. '46, late '47 to late '49, and again in summer of '51. Living in Calif., he played w. Butch Stone and Charlie Barnet in 1947. With Stan Kenton in first "Innovations" tour 1950; after playing trumpet for a year and a half he remained w. Kenton as arranger. Worked w. Howard Rumsey at the Lighthouse, 1953. Seen mostly as leader of own combo in 1954-5. Mus. director, Atlantic Records, Feb. '55; a & r supervisor at RCA Victor from '56. Very active in rec. and film work from '52 on, writing and/or playing. Work often has reflected infl. of Miles Davis; his were among the most swinging works rec. by Kenton and Herman. Arrs. for Kenton incl. *Jolly Rogers, Viva Prado, Art Pepper, Jambo;* for Herman, *More Moon, Keen & Peachy, That's Right.* Films: *Hotsy Footsy* (UPA cartoon), *The Wild One, Private Hell 36, Man with the Golden Arm, Tarzan the Ape Man* etc.

According to John S. Wilson (*The Collector's Jazz: Modern*), Rogers at first was "a crisp, dependable trumpet man," "an arranger with better than average ability," and "a founding father of the West Coast school of jazz," but "soon spread his talents so thin that much of his work was reduced to a set of dreary clichés." However, Wilson says that Rogers at times still shows excellent talent as a writer, and Nat Hentoff, reviewing an LP, observed: "Shorty plays with a consistent feeling for form and supple beat." In addition to his studio work Rogers has gigged with a combo, mainly around LA; in '59 he led a big band at H'wood Bowl Jazz Fest. Fav. arrs: Al Cohn, N. Hefti. No fav. tpts.

Own LPs: Vict. Atl.; one-half of *Modern Sounds* (Cap.); LPs w. Herman (Cap., Harm.), Kenton (Cap.), Johnny Richards (Beth.), Kai Winding in *Loaded* (Savoy), Teddy Charles (Prestige), Jimmy Giuffre (Atl.), *Jazz Composers Workshop* (Savoy), Shank-Rogers-Perkins (Wor. Pac.), Howard Rumsey, Shelly Manne (Contemp.); *Jazz For Cops and Robbers* w. Leith Stevens (Coral).

Addr: 6724 Allott Avenue, Van Nuys, Calif.

ROGERS, TIMMIE (Timothy Louis Aiverum), *singer, tiple, songwriter;* b. Detroit, Mich., 7/4/15. Brother played drums for short time w. McKinney's Cotton Pickers. St. on banjo 1928. Rogers is best known as a comedian, though he is a competent performer on the tiple, a small instrument of the guitar family. In '54 he had his own band, whose members included Buck (of Buck & Bubbles) on piano, Jonah Jones on trumpet, and others. His songs, some of which have been recorded by leading pop artists include *If You Can't Smile and Say Yes, Bring Enough Clothes For Three Days, Fla-ga-la-pa, Back To School Again.* He has toured extensively in night clubs and in vaudeville often in a jazz context and performed in Europe in '36 and '58. He recorded for Majestic, Cameo, Excelsior, etc.

Addr: 555 Edgecombe Ave., New York 32, N.Y.

ROHDE, BRYCE BENNO, *piano;* b. Hobart, Tasmania, 9/12/23. Stud. Adelaide Conservatory, Australia. Worked as pastry cook until 1949, then led own trio in South Australia, '50-3, in radio, clubs, concerts. Moving to US, spent several months in radio and TV work then joined Australian Jazz Quartet. Returned to Australia Sept. '58 and formed own quartet. Intends to ret. to US. Fav: Art Tatum. LPs w. Australian Jazz Quartet (Beth.).

ROLAND, GENE, *composer, trumpet, trombone;* b. Dallas, Tex., 9/15/21. Began stud. at North Texas State Teachers' College, where he majored in music from 1940-2 and roomed w. J. Giuffre and H. Babasin. Later, joined Air Corps, where he and Giuffre formed Air Force band which grew into the Eighth Air Force Orch. Joined S. Kenton, summer '44, as trumpeter-arr.; remained until 1955, except for brief stints both as free-lance arr. and w. L. Hampton, C. Barnet, C. Thornhill, A. Shaw, H. James. Joined W. Herman, Nov. '56; wrote 65 arrangements by Feb. '58, then worked briefly for Dan Terry. Fav. own arrs: *Are You Livin' Ol' Man* (Anita O'Day-Kenton), *Tampico, Sittin' and A-Rockin'* (June Christy-Kenton). Potentially a valuable writer, though very many of his arrs. are based on thin riffs that seem to have been mass-produced. LP: one half of *Jazzville, Vol. 4* (Dawn).

ROLAND, JOSEPH ALFRED (Joe), *vibes;* b. New York City, 5/17/20. Father is chiropodist at Savoy Hotel, NYC. Clarinet at Juilliard 1937-9; led local combos as clarinetist until 1940, when he started doubling on xylophone. Entered service May '42; as radio operator in Air Corps he spent two years in the Aleutians. Soon after his release in Jan. 1946 he bought his first set of vibes, free-lanced around NYC and organized his own group with a string quartet for records. Joined Oscar Pettiford April 1951; replaced Don Elliot w. George Shearing quintet Sept. '51. Left Shearing Feb. '53 and led own combo w. Howard McGhee. Toured w. Artie Shaw's Gramercy 5 Sept. '53 to Feb. '54, then resumed free-lancing in NYC. A gently swinging modern stylist. Favs: Milt Jackson, L. Hampton, T. Gibbs. Own LPs: Savoy, Beth.; LPs w. Artie Shaw (Verve), Geo. Shearing (MGM).

Addr: 1134 College Ave., Bronx 56, N.Y.

ROLLINI, ADRIAN, *vibraphone, bass sax;* b. New York City 6/28/04; d. Homestead, Fla., 5/15/56. Prominent during the 1920s and early '30s as the only jazz bass saxophonist, he was w. Calif. Ramblers for five years; in London w. Fred Elizalde '27-8, and made hundreds of records w. Red Nichols, Joe Venuti, F. Trumbauer, Bix Beiderbecke. During '30s, gave up sax to concentrate on vibes; toured with own non-jazz, pop style trio from '35. During the '50s, living in Florida, he was the proprietor of a hotel. In his early years Rollini earned a niche in jazz history through his admirable bass sax work. LPs: trio (Merc. 20011); one no. w. own group in *Introduction To Jazz* (Decca 8244); w. California Ramblers in *Jazz of the Roaring Twenties* (River. 12-801); Benny Goodman (Bruns. 54010), Red Nichols (Bruns. 54047).

ROLLINI, ARTHUR, *tenor sax;* b. New York City, 2/13/12. Brother of Adrian Rollini. Pl. w. California Ramblers, Paul Whiteman. With Benny Goodman 1934-9. Staff musician at ABC, NYC, 1943-1958. In May '59 opened own laundromat business in Roslyn, L.I., cont. to do commercial rec. and club dates. Solos w. Goodman incl. *Bugle Call Rag, Sent For You Yesterday* (Victor versions). LPs: almost all early Goodmans; also w. Brad Gowans (Vict.).

Addr: 15 Horseshoe Lane, Roslyn Heights, N.Y.

ROLLINS, THEODORE WALTER (Sonny), *tenor sax;* b. New York City, 9/7/29. An older brother played violin, and Sonny took piano lessons briefly when he was nine, but he had no interest in music at the time and the lessons were soon discontinued. He took up alto saxophone while studying music at high school, in 1944. In 1947, after finishing his schooling, he began to gig around New York on tenor sax, which he had been playing for about a year.

Still not sure that he wanted to remain in music, Rollins became more interested late in 1948, when he made his first record date, with Babs Gonzales for Capitol. Soon after, he made sessions with Bud Powell, Fats Navarro, and with J. J. Johnson, who recorded his first composition, *Audubon.*

Rollins worked for a while with Art Blakey in '49, with Tadd Dameron and Bud Powell in '50, and in '50 also made his first trip to Chicago, working with a group led by the late Ike Day on drums. In '51 he spent six months with Miles Davis' unit. After a couple of years of free-lance work around New York he again went to Chicago, working at the Beehive and leaving in Jan. '56 to join the Max Roach Quintet. From the time he left Roach in the summer of '57 he worked with his own combos, usually employing only bass and drums.

Rollins' reputation, established among musicians around New York in the mid-'50s, by 1958 had reached a national level comparable with that of Stan Getz a decade earlier. His influence on other tenor saxophonists was no less profound. Rollins' most clearly evident characteristics are a tone that is hard, sometimes to the point of deliberate harshness; a tendency to make subtle use of musical sarcasm through deliberate melodic distortions; a very personal use of grace notes; and an ability to create, even at amazingly rapid tempos, ideas that show much harmonic imagination. He has also been credited by some writers with having been the first jazz soloist to improvise in terms of the complete, overall pattern of a solo. As Martin Williams has said, "His lines can show a gradual, relaxed building and a developing of continuity and structure that is unique."

Rollins has been, since the late '50s, the storm center of the so-called hard-bop school of jazz. Like many of its adherents, he has rejected any overt show of sentimentality. Some have found more crudity and cynicism than finesse in his work; it has been said that he is not without the talent for poking sly, oblique fun at the listeners and critics who take so seriously every solo he plays. Yet Rollins, when he is not defying the world to seek beauty in him, is capable of the class of improvisation that led such jazzmen as Horace Silver, Bud Powell, Herb Geller and Miles Davis to vote for him in the *Encyclopedia of Jazz* poll as the greatest tenor player ever.

Rollins won the DB critics' poll as new star in 1957; *Playboy* All Stars' All Stars '59. Own LPs: Pres. 7020, 7029, 7038, 7047, 7058, 7079, 7095, 7126, Contemp. 3530, 3564, Blue Note 1542, 1558, 1581, 4001, River. 12-241, 12-258, Metro. 1002, 1011; LPs w. Miles Davis (Pres. 7012, 7025, 7044, 7109), Bud Powell (Blue Note 1503), Max Roach (Em. 36098, 36108, 36078), Monk (Pres. 7053, 7075, River. 12-226), *Modern Jazz Quartet At Music Inn, Vol. 2* (Atl. 1299), Kenny Dorham (River. 12-239).

Addr: 400 Grand Street, New York City, N.Y.

ROMANIS (orig. Roumanis), George Zackery, *composer, bass;* b. Trenton, N.J., 2/11/29. Brother plays sax and clar., arr., comp. Private lessons on bass 1945; self-taught arr. at first, later stud. w. Sy Oliver and Dick Jacobs. Pl. and arr. for Charlie Spivak '49; Ralph Flanagan '50; in Air Force '50-5, pl. and arr. for Air Force Dance Band and Symph. With Johnny Smith off and on since '54. Favs: Gerry Mulligan, Sy Oliver, Count Basie. LPs w. Johnny Smith (Roost); wrote arr. and pl. for Sal Salvador's *Colors in Sound* (Decca). Own LP: *Modern Sketches in Jazz* (Coral).

Addr: 327 Roosevelt Ave., Lyndhurst, N.J.

ROOT, WILLIAM (Billy), *tenor & baritone sax;* b. Philadelphia, Pa., 3/6/34. Father a drummer. Pl. w. Roy Eldridge '51; alto w. Hal McIntyre '52; three months w. Red Rodney, a year w. Benny Green '53-4; two tours w. Stan Kenton; briefly w. Dizzy Gillespie big band '57. Own combo occasionally in NYC and Phila., also dates w. Red Rodney '59-60. Studying electronics, Phila. Wireless Academy. Forceful modern stylist. Favs: Al Cohn, Rollins, Stitt. LPs w. Kenton (Cap.), Rodney (Argo), B. Green (Decca); *A Night at Birdland* (Roulette); *Dizzy Atmosphere* (Spec.).

Addr: 31 East Herman Street, Philadelphia 44, Pa.

ROSE, WALTER (Wally), *piano;* b. Oakland, Cal., 10/2/13. Lived in Honolulu until he was 5, when his family returned to Oakland. In high school he won a contest entitling him to a year's study w. Elizabeth Simpson.

He spent school vacations working as a ship's pianist, traveling around the world for the President Line. After meeting Lu Watters in 1939 he spent the next decade with the Yerba Buena Jazz Band (except for a 3-year hitch in the Navy), then spent a year playing light classics and gypsy music at the Balalaika. He worked w. Bob Scobey 1950-1, then spent several years with Turk Murphy, later working as soloist at various SF clubs. Feat. w. A. Fiedler playing Gershwin's *Rhapsody* on Symphony Pops concert series summer '59. LPs w. Turk Murphy (Col.), Lu Watters (GTJ, Verve).

ROSENGREN, BERNT AAKE, *tenor sax, composer;* b. Stockholm, Sweden, 12/24/37. Accordion at ten, tenor at 15. Toured and recorded w. Jazz Club '57 combo. Stud. harmony for two years and has written many arrangements. Joined Newport International Band summer 1958; later organized a combo, The Newport International Septet which played in Frankfurt, Germany. Went to Holland and played gigs w. Rudolf Jacobs. Fav: Charlie Parker. LP w. Newport International Band (Col.).

Addr: Skansbergsvägen 31, Segeltorp, Sweden.

ROSOLINO, FRANK, *trombone, singer;* b. Detroit, Mich., 8/20/26. Father, mother, brothers, sisters all play instruments. Father started him on guitar at ten; began trombone lessons in 8th grade and continued through high school. Joined Army at 18 and pl. in Army bands for two years in States and Philippines. W. Bob Chester 1946-7, then Glen Gray for six months '47; w. Gene Krupa '48-9, also Tony Pastor end of '49; Herbie Fields '50, Georgie Auld '51, own group in Detroit '52, then to Stan Kenton '52-4. Settled in Calif. to do studio work and rec. A regular at the Lighthouse during last half of '50s. TV: *M Squad.* Films: sang *Lemon Drop* in short for Universal w. Gene Krupa; *I Want To Live* '58. Tied for first, DB Critics' poll New Star Award '53. Own LPs on Cap., Beth., Inter.; LPs w. Kenton (Cap.), *Trombones Inc.* (War. Bros.), *I Want To Live* (UA), Howard Rumsey (Contemp., Lib.), Stan Levey (Beth.), Roach-Levey (Lib.), P. Rugolo (Merc.), S. Rogers (Vict.).

Addr: 11651 Paloma St., Garden Grove, Calif.

ROSS, ANNIE (Annabelle Short), *singer, songwriter;* b. Surrey, England, 7/25/30. To US 1933 with her aunt, singer Ella Logan, and was raised as her foster-daughter in Los Angeles. Appeared in several Our Gang comedies and played Judy Garland's sister in *Presenting Lily Mars,* 1942. Five years later, after studying dramatics in NYC, she left for England, played the lead there in *Burlesque,* teamed with songwriter Hugh Martin in a night club act, then worked in France with the bands of Bernard Hilda, Emil Stern, Jack Dieval. Back to US 1950, studied w. Luther Henderson. Recorded for Prestige 1952, and created a sensation in jazz circles with her "vocalese" version of *Twisted,* comprising a set of neurotic lyrics ingeniously fitted to a tenor sax improvisation on an earlier record by Wardell Gray. She worked with Lionel Hampton's band in Europe for two weeks in the summer of '53, returned to the Paris night club circuit and in '54 sang with the bands of Jack Parnell and Tony Crombie in England; scored a hit in a London revue, *Cranks,* in '56 and later played with it in NYC. After working as a single in local clubs she joined a vocal group on the Patrice Munsel TV series '57-8. During that time she teamed with Dave Lambert and Jon Hendricks to record a multitaped LP, *Sing a Song of Basie* (ABC-Paramount), using the same technique she had employed on *Twisted* of setting lyrics to both the ensembles and solos of instrumental recordings. The technique had been developed originally by King Pleasure and Eddie Jefferson (q.v.).

The success of the album led to the teaming of Lambert, Hendricks and Miss Ross on a permanent basis starting in Sept. '58. During '59 they soared to national popularity, flew to England for a single benefit performance, were a hit at the *Playboy* and Monterey jazz festivals and toured in November in *Jazz for Moderns.* By Dec. '59 Miss Ross has risen from semi-oblivion to third place in the female singer division of the *Down Beat* readers' poll. (She had tied for the critics' poll New Star Award in '53).

Annie Ross' voice is not powerful, but it has a light and attractive personal quality and her ability to simulate instrumental sounds, extraordinary both in concept and execution, is helped enormously by her range, which is twice that of the average jazz singer. Technically, she is the most remarkable female vocalist in jazz since Ella Fitzgerald. As a songwriter, she has shown a flair for combining the humorous with the odd or macabre; *Twisted* and *Jackie* are her best known recorded works. Own LPs: Wor. Pac.; four tracks in *King Pleasure Sings/Annie Ross Sings* (Pres.); tracks in *Singin' And Swingin'* (Reg.); LPs w. Lambert, Hendricks and Ross (ABC-Par., Roul., Wor. Pac., Col.).

ROSS, ARNOLD, *piano, composer, leader;* b. Boston, Mass., 1/29/21. From early '30s stud. extensively on clar., sax, violin, piano. Toured South America, West Indies in ship orchs. 1937-8; pl. Hammond organ w. Frank Dailey '38-9. Joined Jack Jenney '39; Vaughn Monroe '40-2; Army '43-4 (w. Glenn Miller); Harry James '44-7. Free-lanced in Cal. and often acc. Lena Horne, touring Europe with her '52. Pianist, arranger and conductor for Bob Crosby TV show '54-6; Spike Jones TV series '57-8. Also has own trio and was B. Eckstine's accompanist '55; app. and rec. in LA with Dave Pell, Barney Kessel, Nelson Riddle. Own combo at Redondo Beach, Cal., fall '59. A most accomplished, versatile, swinging musician. LPs w. Harry Edison (Wor. Pac.), Buddy Childers (Lib.), B. Kessel (Contemp.), Billy May (Cap.), D. Gillespie (Blue Note); *Jazz at Hollywood Bowl, Jazz At The Philharmonic, Vols. 1 & 2* (Verve).

Addr: 638 West Knoll Drive, Los Angeles 46, Calif.

ROSS, RONALD (Ronnie), *baritone saxophone;* b. Calcutta, India, 10/2/33. To England at 12. Clar. in Grenadier Guards band '51. Toured w. Don Rendell sextet incl. jazz festivals at San Remo and Lyons. Many rec. w. Ken Moule, Ted Heath, Don Rendell, Tony Crombie, Tony Kinsey, Annie Ross, Engl. Decca. While in Stuttgart, Germany, Feb. '58, made session with symphony musicians of *European Windows,* written and conducted by John Lewis, who became one of his greatest admirers and who later took Ross on the Modern Jazz Quartet's English tour in Nov. '59.

With drummer Allan Ganley, Ross formed the Jazzmakers combo Aug. '58 and toured US with it Sept. '59. Ross also toured England as member of Woody Herman's Anglo-American band Apr. '59.

Appearing at the NJF with the Newport International band in July '58, Ross was described by Gerry Mulligan as the first important new challenge on baritone saxophone. Ross, whose lyrical and emotional style has impressed countless musicians both in Europe and the US, won the New Star Award in the 1959 *Down Beat* critics' poll; it was the first such long-distance victory for a British jazzman in any American magazine poll. Favs: L. Young, Mulligan. Own LP on Atlantic; LPs w. John Lewis (Vict.); *One World Jazz* (Col.), Newport International band (Col.).

Addr: 234 Crofton Road, Orpington, Kent, England.

ROTONDO, NUNZIO, *trumpet, composer;* b. Palestrina, Italy, 1924. Son of a musician; stud. mus. St. Cecilia Acad. in Rome. Prof debut late '40s in Rome; rec. debut '50 for Parlophone. Own octet at Salon du Jazz, Paris, '52. Has appeared at all National Jazz Festivals since '50; regularly at San Remo Festival since '55. Orig. inspired by Howard McGhee, later developed personal style, though clearly an admirer of Miles Davis. According to Arrigo Polillo "One of the best jazz musicians in Europe, probably the best trumpet; his tone is very pure and warm, his phrasing personal, at times whimsical." Many records for Italian labels, Col., RCA. LP: two tracks on *San Remo Festival* (Verve).

ROUSE, CHARLES (Charlie), *tenor sax;* b. Washington, D.C., 4/6/24. Stud. clar. w. Sergeant Rice of Howard U. Pl. w. B. Eckstine '44; D. Gillespie '45; Duke Ellington '49-50. Free-lanced in NYC during most of '50s, also working w. Benny Green combo in '55 and serving as co-leader with Julius Watkins of a sporadically active quintet known as Les Jazz Modes, '56-8. Worked with Buddy Rich combo '59, Thelonious Monk '59-60. A fluent, imaginative soloist of the hard bop school. Favs: S. Rollins, S. Stitt, H. Mobley. LPs w. Les Jazz Modes (Dawn, Atl.), Bennie Green (Pres., Blue Note), Art Farmer (Pres.), Fats Navarro (Savoy, Blue Note), Clifford Brown, Donald Byrd (Blue Note); *The Chase Is On* w. Paul Quinichette (Beth.), Monk (River.); *Just Wailin'* (New Jazz), Oscar Pettiford (Beth.), Arthur Taylor (Pres., New Jazz).

Addr: c/o Benskina, 770 St. Nicholas Avenue, New York 31, N.Y.

ROWLES, JAMES GEORGE (Jimmy), *piano;* b. Spokane, Wash., 8/19/18. Educated at Gonzaga U. Studied piano privately. Got start through Ben Webster. Worked w. Slim & Slam, Lee and Lester Young, Billie Holiday 1941; five months w. Benny Goodman '42; Woody Herman '42-3, then into service, pl. in Skinnay Ennis' Army band. Rejoined Herman '46; Les Brown, Tommy Dorsey, B. Goodman, Butch Stone '47; four years on air w. Bob Crosby '47-51. Since then, has free-lanced in Calif. frequently w. Peggy Lee, also w. Dick Stabile, Stan Getz, Chet Baker, Ch. Parker, Benny Carter, Zoot Sims and acc. Josephine Premice, Betty Hutton. Movie studio work at 20th Century Fox; for TV w. *M-Squad, Richard Diamond, Dobie Gillis* '59-60. Fav: Art Tatum. Own LPs on Andex, Liberty; LPs w. Barney Kessel (Contemp.), Bob Brookmeyer, B. DeFranco, Billie Holiday (Verve), *Jive For Five* (Andex), Julie London (Liberty), Bobby Troup (Vict.).

Addr: 11936 Juniette St., Culver City, Calif.

ROWSER, JAMES EDWARD (Jimmy), *bass;* b. Philadelphia, Pa., 4/18/26. Stud. piano at 14; worked as house bassist at Blue Note in Phila. 1954-6; w. Dinah Washington '56-7. Joined Maynard Ferguson Aug. '57, left Aug. '59. W. Red Garland for several months, then rejoined D. Washington. LPs w. Dinah Washington (Em.), Maynard Ferguson (Roul.), Red Garland (Pres.).

ROY, THEODORE GERALD (Teddy), *piano;* b. Duquoin, Ill., 4/9/05. Self-taught; played cornet for seven years. Started in music by assembling a band of musicians all of whom were ten years his senior; worked w. many name bands, mostly in Chicago and New York, incl. Coon-Sanders, Frank Trumbauer, Jean Goldkette, Nat Shilkret, Leo Reisman, Vincent Lopez, Orig. Dixieland, Bobby Hackett, Willard Robison, Miff Mole, Pee Wee Russell. Rec. debut in Chicago 1927, making race records under supervision of Roy Shields. Worked as bartender 1940; in shipyards '41-2; Army '43-5. Free-lance in NYC '46-57, incl. solo stints at Condon's and Henry Hudson Hotel; gigs on Long Island w. Miff Mole, Wingy Manone '58-9. Favs: Jess Stacy, Earl Hines.

Addr: 40-15 81st Street, Elmhurst, L.I., N.Y.

ROYAL, ERNEST ANDREW (Ernie), *trumpet;* b. Los Angeles, Cal., 6/2/21. Studied with private teachers at LA Jr. Coll. Worked w. Les Hite 1937-8; Cee Pee Johnson 1939; Lionel Hampton 1940-2; Navy Oct. '42 to Dec. '45. In San Francisco w. Vernon Alley, Hollywood w. The Phil Moore Four, also w. Count Basie 1946; joined Woody Herman's Second Herd 1947, and remained for two years. After several months w. Ch. Barnet in LA he joined Duke Ellington for four months, touring Europe with him in the summer of 1950. Soon after leaving Ellington he returned to France and spent two years with the Jacques Hélian band, touring the continent and North Africa. Back home in 1952 he spent several months leading a combo w. Wardell Gray in Hollywood; toured w. Stan Kenton, Jan. to Aug. 1953, then settled in NYC, freelancing extensively in mambo, jazz and pop orchestras. Worked w. Kenton again summer '55 on weekly TV series *Music '55*. Pl. w. Neal Hefti at Birdland, but since Oct. '57, when he joined ABC staff in NYC, has confined his work to radio, TV and many record dates. Once thought of as a high note man, Royal revealed later that he is a superlative all-around musician with a jazz solo style at times recalling Edison, Eldridge and Gillespie, whom he names as his major influences. Own LP: Urania; LPs w. J. Cleveland (Merc.), Miles Davis (Col.), Quincy Jones (ABC-Par., Merc.), G. Romanis (Dec.), S. Rollins (Metrojazz), *Jazz Soul of Porgy & Bess* (UA), Geo. Williams' Lunceford tribute (Vict.); *Jingles All The Way* (Lib.), Herman (Cap.).

Addr: 116-03 128th St., South Ozone Park 20, N.Y.

ROYAL, MARSHALL, *alto sax, clarinet;* b. Sapulpa, Okla., 12/5/12. Studied violin as well as reeds; prof. debut at 13. Local bands in Calif.; Curtis Moseby '29; Les Hite '30; was in Hite band through most of '30s, backing L. Armstrong on *Confessin'* and other hits (Col. ML54386); w. Cee Pee Johnson '40; L. Hampton '40-2; Jack McVea, Eddie Heywood, studio work on west coast. Helped Count Basie organize new band '51. Since then one of the pillars of the band as musical director and virtual leader. Fine lead alto, also effective soloist in both sweet and jazz styles. Rec. solos w. Tatum band (Bruns., '31), Hampton Sextet (Vict. '40). LPs w. Basie (Verve, Roul.); *The Saxophone Section* (WW).

Addr: 116-03 128th St., South Ozone Park 20, N.Y.

RUBENSTEIN, BERIL WILLIAM (Bill), *piano;* b. Rochester, N.Y., 11/2/28. Mother pl. piano in sheet music dept. of 5 & 10 cent store. Studied w. private teachers 1933-43 in Syracuse. Joined Syracuse local in '43 and pl. w. dance band around town. Grad. Syracuse U. '51 w. Bach. of Mus., major in Composition. Pl. w. Ray Anthony, Feb. '47-May '47; Buddy Rich, June-Sept. '52; Salt City Five, Nov. '53-Mar. '57; Kai Winding, Sept. '57-July '59; Chris Connor from Aug. '59. Fav. Art Tatum; most imp. infls: Parker, Gillespie, Davis, Rollins, Young, the Basie band.

Addr: 116 Ferris Ave., Syracuse 3, N.Y.

RUBIN, STANLEY NORMAN, *leader, clarinet, saxes;* b. New Rochelle, N.Y., 7/14/33. Daniel Webster School dance band, 1945-6; Fred Breitenfeld's dance band, '47-9. Started jazz band at Princeton, '51; borrowed $1000 from Univ. store to record first album, May '53. After working way across Atlantic as ship's band for Holland-America Line, group enjoyed great success at Maxim's on French Riviera, August '53, then played dates in Italy, Switzerland. Back in U.S., played at Glen Island Casino; big hit at Carnegie Hall college band concert, Nov. '54. In 1955 modified band's Dixieland style to include swing and modern jazz; unit was flown to Monaco Apr. '56 to play at wedding of Prince Rainier and Grace Kelly. His combo, the Tigertown Five, was later incorporated into a big band which he booked for society dances, college proms and concerts, etc. Own LPs: United Artists, Coral, Vict., Jub.

Addr: 2 Arbor Drive, New Rochelle, N.Y.

RUFF, WILLIE, *bass, French horn;* b. Sheffield, Ala., 9/1/31. Bachelor of Music, 1953, Master of Music, '54, Yale U. While still studying, gigged w. Benny Goodman. Worked w. Lionel Hampton during Spring and Summer, '55, then teamed up w. Dwike Mitchell (q.v.). The Mitchell-Ruff duo, featuring Ruff mainly on bass, but with occasional Fr. horn solos, revealed Ruff's high standards of academic musicianship. They were heard at Birdland and other clubs in the late '50s, and in '59 became the first modern jazzmen ever to play in Moscow, in an impromptu concert at the Tschaikovsky Conservatory. Favs: Abe Kniaz (first horn, Wash. Symph.); Ray Brown, O. Pettiford. LPs: Epic, Roulette.

Addr: 87 Kensington Street, New Haven, Conn.

RUGOLO, PETER, *composer, leader;* b. San Piero, Patti, Sicily, 12/25/15. To US at 5. Raised in Santa Rosa, Cal. Father played baritone horn; two sisters, both musicians; BA, San Francisco State Coll.; MA, Mills Coll., where he studied under Darius Milhaud. Played piano in dance bands from high school days, locally and in San Francisco ballrooms.

With Jimmie Grier and Johnny Richards in 1941; Army Nov. '42 until late '45, when he joined Stan Kenton as arranger and became the principal force in shaping the style of Kenton's band of the mid-40s. After leaving Kenton in 1949 he worked for Capitol Records as mus. dir.; settled in Los Angeles 1950 and became increasingly active writing and directing, first for record dates, then also for films and TV. A brief tour in the East leading a big band in the fall of '54 was his only in-person venture. In addition to writing and directing dates for J. Christy, Four Freshmen, Nat Cole, Mel Tormé et al, he was mus. dir. at Mercury Records in LA from 1957. Films incl. *Glory Alley, The Strip, Easy To Love, Latin Lovers, Everything I Have Is Yours, Jack the Ripper.* In TV, wrote theme for *Thin Man* series; scored music for *Richard Diamond series* '58-60.

Pete Rugolo is one of the most accomplished and successful writers in the overlapping fields of jazz and popular music. Though some of his work clearly reflects the Milhaud influence, the jazz essence often has been skilfully incorporated, and a sense of humor is often evident in his work. He won the DB poll 1947, '49-51, '54; Met. poll '49-52. Own LPs: *Adventure in Sounds, Brass* (Merc. 20261), *Reeds in Hi Fi* (Merc. 20260), *Music for Hi-Fi Bugs* (Em. 30682), *Out on a Limb* (Em. 36115), *New Sounds* (Harm.), *Percussion at Work* (Em. 80003), *Rugolo Plays Kenton* (Em. 36143), *Music from Richard Diamond* (Em. 36162); LPs w. June Christy (Cap. T833, 902), arr.

for Ken Errair (Cap. 807); arr. for Stan Kenton: *Kenton in Hi Fi* (Cap. W. 724), *Lush Interlude* (T1130), *Kenton Era* (WDX 569).

RUMSEY, HOWARD, *bass, leader;* b. Brawley, Cal., 11/7/17. Started on piano, then drums; took up bass while attending LA City Coll. While playing in Vido Musso's band he met Stan Kenton, who was then Musso's pianist. Rumsey was a charter member of the original Kenton band of 1941 and was featured on *Concerto for Doghouse* (Decca, 1942). After free-lancing w. various bands around Calif., incl. Freddy Slack, Ch. Barnet, Barney Bigard, he formed his own combo to play at the Lighthouse at Hermosa Beach, Cal., 1949, and has since built up the reputation of this club to make it the best-known California jazz rendezvous. Sidemen who have worked for him there incl. Shorty Rogers, Shelly Manne, Bob Cooper, Max Roach, Jimmy Giuffre, Milt Bernhart, Victor Feldman and Joe Gordon. LPs: Lighthouse All Stars (Contemporary, Liberty); w. Kenton (Cap.).

Addr: c/o The Lighthouse, 30 Pier Ave., Hermosa Beach, Calif.

RUSHING, JAMES ANDREW (Jimmy), *singer;* b. Oklahoma City, Okla., 8/26/03. Father pl. trumpet, mother & brother both singers. Pl. violin, piano by ear. St. music at Douglas High in Okla. City. Got into music business singing in after-hours spots in Calif. '25. With Walter Page's Blue Devils '27-8; Bennie Moten '29; joined Count Basie '35, came to NYC w. Basie's big band '36. In the years that followed he was one of band's mainstays with his intense, high-pitched style of blues singing. Left Basie '50; formed own septet and toured theatres, also pl. Savoy Ballroom NYC from late '50 to '52. Worked as single from June '52, and with the renascence of interest in early blues style enjoyed a great upsurge in popularity, appearing at all major jazz festivals '57-60 and making several highly successful European tours incl. one on his own to England in Sept. '57 and later visits to continent w. Benny Goodman, May '58, Newport show fall '59.

Rushing's voice and the blues have been perfectly mated for three or four decades: his style is authoritative, sensitive and virile, communicating always with unique warmth and conviction. Several experts in recent years have spoken of him as the greatest living male jazz singer.

Rushing was seen in the film *Funzapoppin'* with Olsen & Johnson '44 and in a few major TV shows. He won the *Melody Maker* British critics' poll '57, as No. 1 male vocalist; DB Critics' poll '58-9. Favs: Bing Crosby, Louis Armstrong, Ethel Waters. Fav. own recs: *Sent for You Yesterday, I Want a Little Girl, Goin' To Chicago* w. Basie. Own LPs: *Jimmy Rushing And The Big Brass* (Col. CL 1152), *Rushing Lullabies* (Col. CS 8196), *Jazz Odyssey* (Col. CL 963), *Goin' To Chicago* (Vang. 8518), *Listen To The Blues* (Vang. 8505), *If This Ain't The Blues* (Vang. 8513), *Cat Meets Chick* (Col. CL 778). LPs w. Basie: Decca 8049, Col. CL 754, 901, Verve 8243, Epic SN 6031, Cam. 497; w. Goodman: Col. CL 1247, 1248.

Addr: 32-17 110th Street, Corona, L.I., N.Y.

RUSHTON, JOSEPH AUGUSTINE, JR., (Joe), *bass sax;* b. Evanston, Ill., 4/19/07. Drums, clarinet first, then curved B-flat soprano sax followed by alto, tenor, baritone saxes; bass sax since 1928. Own band around Chicago, 1928-32; briefly w. Ted Weems in '34, also three years w. Jimmy McPartland and many jazz combo jobs w. Bud Freeman et al. After working with Benny Goodman for nine months 1942-3 he settled in Calif. Feb. '43; worked w. Horace Heidt '43-5; Nick Cochran for nine months, various studio jobs, then joined Red Nichols, with whom he has worked since Jan. 1947. Has also held various non-musical jobs incl. Bendix Aviation 1931; airplane co. in Lincoln, Neb., 1937; other aircraft jobs '41-2, '45-6. One of a handful of musicians to make an effective jazz vehicle of the bass sax, he is generally regarded as the most successful since Adrian Rollini gave up the instrument in 1935. LPs w. Red Nichols (Cap., Audio.), Rampart Street Paraders (Col.), one track w. Paul Whiteman in *History of Jazz, Vol. 2* (Cap.).

Addr: 1740 N. Dillon, Los Angeles 26, Calif.

RUSSELL, DILLON (Curly), *bass;* b. New York City, 3/19/20. Played trombone and bass in YMCA Symphony. On the road from 1938; joined Don Redman '41. Made his first records while w. Benny Carter's band in Calif. '43. From 1944, when he participated in first Dizzy Gillespie combo record dates, he was the best-known bassist in and around the bop movement and perhaps the most frequently recorded. Worked mostly around NYC w. Stan Getz, Coleman Hawkins, Ch. Parker, Miles Davis, Bud Powell, up to mid '50s. Toured w. Buddy De Franco's quartet '52. In late '50s was in the comparative obscurity of local r&b gigs. Fav: Ray Brown. LPs w. Horace Silver, Art Blakey (Blue Note), Charlie Parker (Savoy), *Bird And Diz* (Verve), Bud Powell (Verve, Blue Note, Roost), Al Cohn (Savoy), *52nd St.* (Inter.).

Addr: 1248 Teller Ave., Bronx 56, N.Y.

RUSSELL, GEORGE ALLAN, *composer, drums;* b. Cincinnati, Ohio, 6/23/23. Reared by foster parents; real father was prof. of mus. at Oberlin U. First infatuated with jazz as child when he heard Fate Marable on riverboat. Early influence was neighbor, Jimmy Mundy, then writing for B. Goodman. Played drums w. Boy Scout Drum & Bugle Corps. At 15, while at high school, pl. in night club. On receiving a scholarship, joined Wilberforce U. Collegians, who included Ernie Wilkins. Bedded by tuberculosis at 19, learned arranging from fellow-patient at sanitarium. Wrote first arrs. for A. B. Townsend Orch. at Cotton Club in Cincinnati. Joined Benny Carter band on drums and rehearsed first big band arrangement, *New World,* with him in Chicago.

After leaving Carter, Russell wrote show music for Chicago clubs, also some arrs. for Earl Hines. Inspired by Monk's *'Round Midnight,* he came to NYC to absorb new ideas. Was asked by Ch. Parker to play drums in his group, but suffered a health relapse and spent 16 months in a NYC hospital. While there, he formulated the tonal principles based on the Lydian Mode that were to serve as the theoretical foundations of his later writing.

On his release, he wrote the first successful large band work combining American jazz and Afro-Cuban rhythms, *Cubana-Be and Cubana-Bop,* introduced under the author's auspices and played by Dizzy Gillespie's band at the latter's first Carnegie Hall concert, Dec. '47. Later he wrote for Ch. Ventura (*Caravan, Victor*), C. Thornhill, Artie Shaw. The work he considered his most profound up to that time (1949) was *A Bird In Igor's Yard,* rec. by Buddy De Franco's big band for Cap. but never released. His small combo works included *Ezz-thetic* and *Odjenar* rec. by Lee Konitz (Prestige). Latter was named for his wife, Juanita Odjenar, a talented painter.

For some time Russell quit jazz to devote his time to completion of a thesis entitled *The Lydian Concept of Tonal Organization.* This done, in 1953, he resumed occasional jazz activity. In 1956 he wrote an album for RCA Victor; in '58-9 he was on the faculty of the School of Jazz at Lenox, Mass. He was one of three jazz composers commissioned by Brandeis U. to compose a serious jazz work.

Russell is one of the few modern composers whose extended works maintained a firm foothold in jazz while broadening its boundaries in orchestration and form. His Lydian chromatic concept has been called by John Lewis "the first profound theoretical contribution to come from jazz." His writing can be heard on the following LPs, all of which are highly recommended: RCA 1372, 1366; Decca 9209, 9216, Col. WL 127, Atl. 1229. Favs: Ellington, Geo. Handy, Gil Evans, G. Mulligan.

Addr: 121 Bank St., New York 14, N.Y.

RUSSELL, LUIS CARL, *leader, composer, piano;* b. Careening Cay, a small island near Bocas Del Toro, Panama, 8/5/02. Father, Alexander Russell, plays organ for church, directs choir, teaches piano. Luis stud. guitar, then violin, piano at 15, pl. in local theatre and at 16 put on first long pants to play with band in Colón cabaret. At 17 he won $3000 in a lottery and brought his mother and sister to US. Played with Al Nicholas, Barney Bigard, Paul Barbarin in New Orleans, 1920; joined Ch. Cook in Chicago '25 (w. Cook on pipe organ, Freddie Keppard and Jimmie Noone); joined King Oliver at Plantation, Chicago '25; after the club was bombed by gangsters they went to St. Louis, then to the Savoy in NYC, 1927. Led own band at Nest Club NYC, '27, w. Omer Simeon, Bigard, Barbarin, J. C. Higginbotham, Louis Metcalf.

Russell played the Savoy Ballroom, Saratoga Club and Roseland in 1928 and by this time had one of the fastest-rising young Negro bands. After recording and touring briefly with Louis Armstrong in 1929 Russell played the Arcadia Ballroom and Connie's Inn. Members of the band during these years included Red Allen, Charlie Holmes, Teddy Hill, Pops Foster.

After Armstrong returned from a European tour he took over Russell's band and they toured together from 1935 to '43, after which Russell organized a new band, played the Savoy, toured and recorded until 1948, when he quit the music business to open a candy shop. During 1950s ran card, gift and toy shop in Brooklyn; studied Schillinger, classical piano, taught music and pl. weekend club dates w. band. In 1959 he made a visit home (his first in 38 years) to Bocas del Toro, Panama, to visit parents; while there, gave classical piano recital at church benefit. The few records that were previously available on LPs are not currently on the market.

Addr: 528 West 187th St., New York 33, N.Y.

RUSSELL, CHARLES ELLSWORTH (Pee Wee), *clarinet;* b. St. Louis, Mo., 3/27/06. Stud. privately in St. Louis and Muskogee, Okla., Western Military Acad., U. of Missouri. Prof. debut in St. Louis, then to Mexico for a year w. Herbert Berger, later to west coast and St. Louis w. Berger. Early associate of Peck Kelley, Leon Rappolo and other jazz pioneers, then in Chicago in mid-'20s w. Bix Beiderbecke, Frank Trumbauer. Recorded *Feelin' No Pain* w. Red Nichols, Aug. 1927, and from then on with scores of small recording combos.

During the 1930s and '40s Russell was a familiar figure in jazz clubs, playing with so great a variety of combos that complete documentation would be impossible. During the rise of the swing fad in the mid-'30s he was most frequently found along 52nd St. with Red McKenzie, Eddie Condon et al; in 1938 he made one of his rare appearances in a larger group, playing clarinet and (reluctantly) alto saxophone in Bobby Hackett's band.

In the 1940s Pee Wee's regular *pied-à-terre* was Nick's in Greenwich Village. He was heard on records accompanying Lee Wiley as well as with combos led by Miff Mole, Bill Davison, Geo. Brunis, Condon. In 1951, while in San Francisco, he suffered a near-fatal illness; the benefits held for him, and his miraculous recovery, were publicized widely in national magazines. Russell has remained in the forefront of Dixieland jazz, playing mostly in New York and Boston. In the late '50s he was heard at Newport and other jazz festivals. His plaintive tone and style, making unique use of what used to be called a "dirty" tone and of growl effects, was analyzed at length in *The Sound of Surprise* by Whitney Balliett (Dutton). One of the most distinctive musicians of Prohibition-era jazz, he became one of the few constants in a restless scene and four decades after was playing with the same eccentric charm as on his records of the '20s.

Own LPs: *Portrait of Pee Wee* (Ctpt. 565), *Plays Pee Wee* (Stere-O-craft R-105), *Jazz At Storyville, Vols. 1 & 2* (Savoy 12034, 12041); LPs w. Louis

Prima in *The Jazz Makers* (Col. CL 1036), Ruby Braff (Vict. LPM 1513, Verve 8241), Brother Matthew (ABC-Par. 121), Eddie Condon (Col. CL 881, War. Bros. W 1315, Comm. 30010), Bud Freeman (Vict. LPM 1508, four tracks in Vict. LPM 1373), Bobby Hackett (Epic 3106), one track w. Coleman Hawkins in *Great Jazz Reeds* (Cam. 339), one no. w. Yank Lawson in *History of Classic Jazz* (River. SDP 11), George Wettling (Kapp 1028), duet w. Jimmy Giuffre in *The Sound Of Jazz* (Col. CL 1098), Wild Bill Davison (Comm. 30009), Max Kaminsky (Comm. 30013), Red Nichols (Bruns. 54047).

Addr: 37 King St., New York 14, N.Y.

RUSSELL, ISAAC ED. (Snookum), *leader, piano;* also *bass, drums;* b. Columbia, S.C., 4/6/13. Brother Allen leads Do Re Mi Trio. Studied drums first in Columbia, playing in community band at age seven, later joined the city orchestra as pianist. Started on bass in 1933 and from '33 to '39 was sideman w. Hartley Toots of Miami, Fla.; played for coronation celebration of King George VI in Nassau, Bahamas. Led own band '39-'50 in ballrooms, theatres, and in night clubs throughout US. In '59 working at Paddock Lounge in New Orleans. Russell's band was a starting point for many musicians who later went on to stardom incl. Ray Brown, Fats Navarro, and J. J. Johnson. He says, "This is why I'm happy, because I feel like a minor league coach who develops many stars but never made the big league." Recs: *Shy Guy* on Tri-lon and *Basin Street Just Ain't Basin Street Anymore.* Favs: Duke Ellington, Art Tatum, Fats Waller.

Addr: 1260 Foy St., New Orleans, La.

RUSSIN, IRVING (Babe), *tenor sax;* b. Pittsburgh, Pa., 6/18/11. Mainly self-taught except for high school studies. Member of Calif. Ramblers 1926; Smith Ballew Orch. '26-7, then off and on w. Red Nichols, incl. many record dates, 1927-32. During the '30s he played w. Roger Wolfe Kahn, Benny Goodman, Ben Pollack, was on staff at CBS, NYC 1936-8. Joined Tommy Dorsey '39; own band '41; J. Dorsey '42; back w. Goodman several times during '40s, and free-lance work in California. With Bobby Hammack staff orch. on ABC-TV in Hollywood '59-60. One of the first prominent tenor sax stars in jazz, he modernized his style in later years, combining qualities of old and new schools. Seen in film, *The Glenn Miller Story.* Own LP: Dot; LPs w. Glen Gray (Cap.), Red Nichols (Bruns.), Benny Goodman, Billie Holiday (Col.), Jess Stacy (Atl.), *Session At Midnight* (Cap.).

Addr: 6241 Camellia, North Hollywood, Calif.

RUSSO, ANTHONY C. (Andy), *trombone;* b. Brooklyn, N.Y., 7/8/03; d. 9/16/58. Played in Yerkes Happy Six, 1921; organized his own New Orleans Jazz Band, '22-4, then w. Mal Hallett, '25-30, Loew's Theatres '30-1, followed by a decade of radio staff work. With Jimmy Dorsey band, '42-5; back in radio until '48. From '49 until his death, he worked mostly at Nick's in Greenwich Village, NYC, under such leaders as Phil Napoleon, Bobby Hackett, Pee Wee Erwin, Billy Butterfield, Yank Lawson, Jimmy McPartland. Fav. own solo: *Tin Roof Blues* w. Napoleon (Decca). Favs: Will Bradley, Tommy Dorsey, Eddie Kusby, Buddy Morrow, Jack Teagarden, Joe Yukl. LPs w. Pee Wee Erwin (Cadence, Bruns., Uran.).

RUSSO, WILLIAM JOSEPH JR. (Bill), *composer, trombone;* b. Chicago, Ill., 6/25/28. Father a lawyer, mother an artist. High school w. Lee Konitz '41-5. Studied w. Lennie Tristano '43-7; read much music literature, but had no teacher in classical music. Planned to become a lawyer; attended De Paul U., Roosevelt Coll. and U. of Ill. Jobs playing trombone w. Billie Rogers' orch. '43, Orrin Tucker, '44, Clyde McCoy '45. Arranged for Johnny Scat Davis '45-6. From 1948-9 was leader, trombonist, manager and publicist of a rehearsal group, *Experiment in Jazz,* which gave concerts in Chi. and recorded for the now defunct Universal label. From Jan. 1950 he spent five years as arranger with Stan Kenton, also touring with him occasionally as trombonist. To Europe, studying, summer '55, then spent two years in Chi. teaching and composing; completed First Symphony, June '57. Settled in NYC Nov. '57; his second symphony, *The Titans* (Koussevitsky award) perf. by NY Phil. '59. Also wrote ballet for Festival Ballet Co. and has taught comp. at Manh. Sch. of Mus. Formed own orch. '59.

Russo, one of the most literate and articulate men in jazz, as well as a major talent, was responsible for some of the most ambitious experimental works performed by Kenton in the early '50s. Though the NY Phil. performance of *Titans* employed Maynard Ferguson as guest soloist, there was little or nothing in it that showed a direct relationship with jazz. Much of Russo's work is to be judged strictly by the standards of concert music. Russo is a provocative and opinionated writer who has contributed frequently to *Down Beat* and, on classical music, to *The Saturday Review.* Own LPs: *The World of Alcina* (ballet), coupled with one side of jazz septet tracks (Atl.); two tracks in *Something New, Something Blue* (Col.); w. Julian Adderley: *Jump for Joy* (Em.); Lee Konitz: *An Image* (Verve), Stan Kenton: *The Kenton Era* (Cap.).

Addr: 1312 Ritchie Court, Chicago 10, Ill.

RUSSO, SANTO (Sonny), *trombone;* b. Brooklyn, N.Y., 3/20/29. Stud. with father, who plays tpt., violin; and grandfather, a trombonist. Played w. Buddy Morrow, 1947, Lee Castle, '48, Sam Donahue, '49, Artie Shaw, '49-50, Art Mooney, late '50. In '51 and '52 he was heard w. Jerry Wald, Tommy Tucker, Buddy Rich and Ralph Flanagan. Then w. Sauter-Finegan, 1953-5; Dorsey brothers '55-6; since then has worked in Broadway show bands, inactive in jazz. Solos on *Everything I've Got, Scuttlebutt, Lucky Duck* in Neal Hefti album, and many w. Sauter-Finegan. Favs: Tommy Dorsey, Bill Harris, Urbie Green, Jack Teagarden. LPs w. Sauter-Finegan (Vict.), Hefti (Epic), *Brothers Sandole* (Fant.), Mickey Sheen (Her.).

Addr: 21 Argyle Drive, East Islip, L.I., N.Y.

RUTHER, WYATT (Bull), *bass;* also *trombone;* b. Pittsburgh, Pa., 2/5/23. Started on trombone in school band. Stud. at SF Cons. of Mus. '49, Pittsburgh Mus. Inst. '50. Bass w. Dave Brubeck for year and half '51-2; Erroll Garner trio Dec. '52-Apr. '53, five months acc. Lena Horne, then back w. Garner. Organized Canadian Jazz Quartet, Ottawa, '55; music teacher in Ottawa and Hull, '56, Toronto '57; with Peter Appleyard Quartet in Toronto '58; joined Chico Hamilton Sept. '58; toured w. George Shearing '59. Favs: Duvivier, Ray Brown, Hinton. Feat. on *Basses Loaded* (Vict). LPs w. Garner (Col.), Brubeck (Fant.), Hamilton (War. Bros.), Ray Bryant (Epic).

Addr: 57 West 45th Street, New York 36, N.Y.

S

SACHS, AARON, *tenor sax, clarinet;* b. Bronx, N. Y., 7/4/23. Private teachers on clarinet; self-taught on sax. Worked w. Babe Russin 1941; Red Norvo '41-2; Van Alexander '42-3; Norvo '43-4; Benny Goodman '45-6. Inactive owing to illness '48-9, then free-lanced around NYC. Toured w. Earl Hines sextet early '52 to summer '53. Had own combo at Cafe Society; gigged w. Tito Rodriguez. Originally known mainly as a clarinetist, Sachs later showed fresh, individual tenor style as well as considerable talent for small combo arranging. He played on Sarah Vaughan's first rec. session in '44 and on various combo dates in the late '40s. After several years off and on w. Rodriguez he toured with the Louis Bellson big band '59. Formerly married to singer Helen Merrill. Sachs won New Star award on clar. in 1945 Esquire poll. LPs w. Red Norvo (Comm.), Bellson (Verve), Sarah Vaughan (Masterseal).

Addr: 283 E. 171st St., Bronx 56, N.Y.

SADI, FATS (Lallemand Sadi), *vibraphone;* b. Andenne, Belgium, 10/23/26. St. in Belgium ca. 1937 on xylophone, playing in circus. Worked w. Bobby Jaspar in Bob Shots, Liège, '46; Don Byas '47; Nice and Paris jazz festivals '48-9. Later pl. w. Jack Diéval, and at Ringside, Paris, w. Django Reinhardt, with whom he made a movie short. Pl. w. Aimé Barelli '53, Martial Solal '54; own band in Paris '55 w. Jaspar, David Amram et al. Concerts, records and film tracks w. André Hodeir's Jazz Groupe de Paris since '55; with Jacques Hélian late '55 to early '57; own big band in Spain '57. With Michel Legrand '58; concerts w. Edelhagen in Germany '59. Innumerable records with all the above and w. Lucky Thompson, and as singer w. Blossom Dearie's Blue Stars vocal group. One of Europe's freest-swinging jazz vibraphonists. LP w. André Hodeir (Savoy).

Addr: 22 Rue du Moulin, Andenne, Prov. de Namur, Belgium.

SAFRANSKI, EDWARD (Eddie), *bass;* b. Pittsburgh, Pa., 12/25/18. Violin at eight; bass in high school; prof. debut w. Marty Gregor 1937. Came into prominence w. Hal McIntyre Orch., with which he played 1941-5; w. Stan Kenton '45-8. After working w. Ch. Barnet '48-9, he became a studio musician and was on staff at NBC, NYC, through '50-60, leading his own group for a while on a morning radio series and appearing in the house band for the educational TV series *The Subject Is Jazz,* spring '58. An excellent technician, he built a great jazz following during his Kenton years. Won DB poll '46-52; Met. poll '47-54; Esq. Silver award '47. LPs: three tracks in *Concert Jazz* (Bruns. 54027), four tracks in *Loaded* (Savoy 12074); LPs w. Kenton (Cap.), Johnny Smith (Roost), Metronome All Stars (Cam.), Sonny Berman (Eso.), *A Musical History of Jazz* (Gr. Award), *In The Beginning . . . Bebop* (Savoy).

Addr: 53 Coolidge Avenue, Rye, N.Y.

ST. CYR, JOHN ALEXANDER (Johnny), *banjo, guitar;* b. New Orleans, La., 4/17/1890. Father, Jules Firmin St. Cyr, played flute, guitar. John had string trio for four years, then left music, became plasterer. Began long association w. Armand Piron, free-lancing occasionally until 1909; then two years w. Martin Gabriel and later w. Tuxedo Band, Kid Ory, 1914-6; riverboats w. Fate Marable, 1917-9; w. Ed Allen in 1920-2; then back to plastering. Later played in Chicago w. King Oliver, 1923; Jimmie Noone, '24; Charles Cook and five years w. Doc Cook. Back to New Orleans and out of music, 1930, except for occasional gigs. Moved to Los Angeles 1954. Best known for recs. w. Armstrong Hot Five, Jelly Roll Morton in 1926, he won the *Record Changer* All Time All Star poll in '51 on banjo. Own LP: *Johnny St. Cyr and His Hot Five* (South.); LPs w. Louis Armstrong (Col.); *Dixieland Jubilee* (GNP), Johnny Dodds and Kid Ory (Epic), Paul Barbarin (South.), Louis Nelson (Amer. Mus.).

Addr: 4620 S. Wall Street, Los Angeles 11, Cal.

SAL, DIZZY (Edward Saldanha), *piano;* b. Rangoon, Burma, 11/8/34. Three brothers work in band in Kuwait (Persian Gulf). Stud. with father from age four, debut on Rangoon radio at five; concerts at 12. Gigged all over S. India 1949; joined Deccanairs band in Secundarabad, 1941. In 1953 joined India's best known band, led by Ken Mac. Hotel and concert work w. own quartet 1956-8. To US, studied at School of Jazz, Lenox, Mass., summer 1959.

Addr: 14 Wellington St., Richmond Town, Bangalore, India.

SALIM, AHMAD KHATAB (A. K. Atkinson), *composer;* b. Chicago, 7/28/22. Att. DuSable High Sch. w. Bennie Green, Dorothy Donegan, Gene Ammons. Pl. alto w. King Kolax, 1938-9; Jimmy Raschel '41-2; Tiny Bradshaw '43. Jammed at Minton's w. Lester Young, C. Parker *et al.* Stopped playing in '44; wrote for L.

Millinder band for 2 years, later for C. Calloway, J. Lunceford, L. Hampton, Basie. His *Normania* for Basie on Vict. later became famous in new treatment as *Blee Blop Blues.* Inactive 1949-56, in real estate, etc., then returned to write for Tito Puente *et al.*, and in '57-60 did occasional record dates. Fav. arrs: T. Dameron, N. Hefti, E. Wilkins. Own LPs: Savoy.

SALVADOR, SAL, *guitar, composer;* b. Monson, Mass., 11/21/25. Raised in Stafford Springs, Conn. Unaware of jazz until he heard some Charlie Christian records in the early 1940s; he started prof. in '45 w. local bands around Springfield, Mass. To NYC '49. After gigging w. Terry Gibbs and Mundell Lowe, he worked at Radio City Music Hall during the summer '51, then recorded regularly at Columbia in acc. for Marlene Dietrich, etc. Toured w. Stan Kenton, June '52 to Dec. '53. Ret. to NYC free-lancing; led own combo in clubs from Sept. '54 throughout Eastern half of US. Also has had his own *Colors In Sound* big band for various gigs and recording. App. as single at NJF '58. Film: *Jazz on a Summer's Day.* Own LPs on Beth., *Colors In Sound* (Decca); LPs w. Kenton (Cap.), Lenny Hambro (Epic), Don Bagley (Regent).

Addr: 17 Lexington St., Springfield, Mass.

SAMPSON, EDGAR MELVIN, *composer, saxophones;* b. New York City, 8/31/07. Violin w. pvt. teacher from 6; sax at high school. First job in East Side club, in violin-and-piano duo w. Joe Coleman, 1924. Played alto w. Duke Ellington, summer of '27; nine months w. Arthur Gibbs at Savoy Blrm. Ch. Johnson band '28-30; vln. & alto w. Fletcher Henderson '31-3; Chick Webb '33-7. While with Webb he wrote a series of instrumentals that were among the biggest hits of the swing era: *Blue Lou, If Dreams Come True, Stomping at the Savoy, Don't Be That Way, Lullaby In Rhythm.* Benny Goodman recorded all of these; on the last three, Sampson himself wrote the arrs. for Goodman. After quitting Webb he gave up playing, concentrated on arranging for seven years. Played w. Al Sears' band 1944. Switching from alto to tenor sax in 1949, he led his own band at Club 845 in the Bronx, '49-51; in late '40s and early '50s, gigs and rec. w. Latin bands incl. M. Guerra, T. Puente, T. Rodriguez. In late '50s continued to write for Rodriguez and play club dates. Sampson's melodic, swinging scores were among the best examples of big-band writing of the mid-'30s. Rec. w. Charlie Johnson, Lionel Hampton for Vict. Own LP: Coral; LPs as arr: Goodman (Col.).

Addr: 154 Green Street, Englewood, N.J.

SANDOLE, ADOLPHE J., *piano, composer;* b. Philadelphia, Pa., 7/13/25. Prof. debut on baritone sax 1946. Taught music at 20th Century School in Phila., 1947-54; later inactive in music. Representative for intl. correspondence school, 1956. In July 1955 collab. w. brother (see below) for LP. Favs: H. Silver, B. Powell, Al Haig.

Addr: 48 Walnut St., Clifton Heights, Pa.

SANDOLE, DENNIS, *guitar, composer;* b. Philadelphia, Pa., 9/29/17. Self-taught; began rehearsing small group, then w. Ray McKinley 1939-40; Tommy Dorsey, Boyd Raeburn, Gene Krupa, Charlie Barnet, all during '40s. With brother Adolph, comp. and arr. for Fant. LP, *Modern Music from Philadelphia.*

Addr: 243 Rambling Way, Springfield, Pa.

SASH, LEON (Leon Robert Shash), *accordion, vibes, guitar;* b. Chicago, Ill., 10/19/22. Blind since the age of 11. Stud. harmony w. Lew Klatt, arranging w. Mac Gerrard. Made prof. debut at 16 and has toured extensively, leading trios with his wife playing bass, singing and contributing original lyrics. Made novel series of recordings for EmArcy 1954 using voices in place of brass and reed sections. LP: *Toshiko and Leon Sash At Newport* (Verve).

Addr: 5008 Farwell Ave., Skokie, Ill.

SAUNDERS, THEODORE (Red), *drums, tympani, vibraphone;* b. Memphis, Tenn., 3/2/12. Began stud. drums in Milwaukee at St. Benedict the Moor School. Own band in 1937; has worked w. Ellington, Herman, Armstrong. Was popular for many years as bandleader at Chicago's Club de Lisa. Feat. soloist w. Louis Bellson-Pearl Bailey show at Chez Paree, Chi., '59. Active as booking agent. LP: Guy Warren's *Africa Speaks, America Answers* (Decca).

Addr: 7332 Calumet Avenue, Chicago, Ill.

SAURY, MAXIM, *clarinet, leader;* b. Enghien, France, 2/27/28. Father a vaudeville bandleader. Self-taught; vln. for two yrs., then clar. Prof. debut 1949. Acc. S. Bechet, '51; concerts w. R. Eldridge, D. Byas, B. Clayton, Peanuts Holland, Al Nicholas, Bill Coleman, '52-5. Won Grand Prix du Disque, '56; *Jazz Hot* prize '56-9, *Jazz Hot* poll on clarinet '59. Rec. w. own group as "Maxim Saury & His New Orleans Sound." Several films incl. *Bonjour Tristesse, Cherchons la Femme, Music Hall Parade.* One of France's most popular trad. jazz figures, he has toured successfully in several Continental countries: Fav: Barney Bigard.

Addr: 7 Rue Duperre, Paris 9, France.

SAUTER, EDWARD ERNEST (Eddie), *composer, leader;* b. Brooklyn, N.Y., 12/2/14. Educ. Nyack, N.Y., high school and Columbia U. Trumpet and drums from childhood; played on French Line cruises during school vacations. Studied theory at Juilliard. Played w. Archie Bleyer 1932. First prominent playing mellophone and trumpet, as well as arranging, for Red Norvo 1935-9. From 1939 he wrote for the Benny Goodman band, contributing such originals as *Superman* and *Benny Rides Again* as well as highly inventive orchestrations of pop tunes. During the 1940s Sauter also wrote for Artie Shaw (*The Maid With The Flaccid Air,* etc.), Tommy Dorsey, Woody Herman and Ray McKinley.

He joined forces w. Bill Finegan in 1952 to form the Sauter-Finegan orch., which was at first only a recording unit but was later assembled on a permanent basis for night club and TV work. This band, whose leaders both renounced any interest in **jazz** improvisation, used novel tonal effects and clever orchestrations and was popularly received for a while, but broke up in Mar. 1957, when Sauter took a job as leader-arranger at Sudwestfunk radio station in Baden-Baden, Germany. Back in US in '59 he again teamed with Finegan to produce some commercial TV-radio jingles. Sauter's best contributions to jazz were made during his Norvo and Goodman years, when he showed great technical ingenuity and retained a basic swinging beat in everything he wrote. He won Met. poll '47-8. LPs: *New Directions In Music* (Vict. LPM 1227), *The Sound Of The Sauter-Finegan Orchestra* (Vict. LPM 1009), *Concert Jazz* (Vict. LPM 1051), *Adventure In Time* (Vict. LPM 1240), *Under Analysis* (Vict. LPM 1341), *Memories Of Goodman and Miller* (Vict. LPM 1634), *Concerto For Jazz Band and Symphony Orch.* (Vict. LM 1888); *Benny Goodman Plays Sauter* (Col. CL 523).

Addr: 95 Collyer Avenue, New City, N.Y.

SAYE, JOE (Joseph Shulman), *piano, accordion;* b. Glasgow, Scotland, 2/25/23. Lost sight at age of two. Toured w. Roy Fox band playing accordion 1937-8, then spent 8 yrs. in vaudeville. Formed own group, '46. Arrived in US 12/8/55. Occasional club gigs and records '56-7; toured as accompanist to Dakota Staton '58-9, also presenting his trio as "Joe Saye's Scottish Jazz" in leading jazz clubs. Seen on Timex TV show and *Hit Parade* with Miss Staton. Own LPs: Merc., Lond. Favs: O. Peterson, Dwike Mitchell.

Addr: c/o John Levy Enterprises, 1650 Broadway, New York 19, N.Y.

SCHAEFER, HAROLD HERMAN (Hal), *piano, composer;* b. New York City, 7/22/25. Mainly self-taught as pianist; grad. of Music and Art High School, NYC, and stud. arranging w. Mario Castelnuovo-Tedesco. Gigged in the upstate New York "borscht belt" at 13. On graduating from high school, played w. Lee Castle, 1940; Ina Ray Hutton, '41. Several months in Benny Carter band '42, then joined Harry James. Worked w. Boyd Raeburn '43, B. Eckstine '44, later spent 18 months as Peggy Lee's accompanist; arr., conducted for Gloria De Haven and spent several years in film studios as vocal coach and arranger. Returned to NYC '55, led own trio, wrote music for stage shows; since '57 very busy as composer-conductor and album producer for United Artists Records. Orig. works for chamber music group at Town Hall, '57; score for radio show for Nat. Assoc. for Retarded Children, '59. Though sometimes leaning to the tricky and pretentious, Schaefer is a fine musician and has shown great originality both in orchestrations and solo work. Fav: Art Tatum. Own LPs: UA, Vict.; LPs w. wife, singer Lee Schaefer (UA); Benny Carter (UA).

Addr: 285 Riverside Drive, New York 25, N.Y.

SCHILDKRAUT, DAVID (Davey), *alto sax;* b. New York City, 1/7/25. Father pl. clar., bought him his first horn. Stud clar, alto at high school. Prof. debut w. Louis Prima 1941. Off and on w. Buddy Rich combos and bands from '47; also w. Anita O'Day '47; European tour w. S. Kenton summer '53; Pete Rugolo '54, Geo. Handy combo '55; rejoined Kenton summer '59, then had own quartet at Cafe Bohemia, NYC. In addition to free-lancing around NYC, worked as floor mgr. for Woolworth's, '49; office job at Decca '52. Schildkraut, at his best an inspired alto man, was once mistaken for Ch. Parker in a blindfold test. Favs: Parker, Carter. Fav. own solos: *Solar* w. Miles Davis (Pres.); *Case Ace* w. Handy (Label "X"). LPs w. Ralph Burns (Decca), Kenton (Cap.), Eddie Bert (Som.), Davis (Pres.), Johnny Richards (Coral).

Addr: 180 Chester Street, Brooklyn, N.Y.

SCHILPEROORT, PETER (sometimes known as Pat Bronx), *clarinet, baritone sax, leader;* also *piano, guitar, bass, drums;* b. The Hague, Holland, 11/4/19. Piano lessons 1930-2, otherwise self-taught. Prof. debut w. Klaas van Beek radio band '43, after nine years w. various amateur units. In '45, on day of liberation, founded the Dutch Swing College Band, which enjoyed tremendous popularity on the Continent. Remained as leader until '55; after finishing studies at Delft U. was engineer at Fokker Aircraft factory to '58, then led own modern combos. Resumed leadership of Swing College Band Jan. '60. Favs: Bigard, Simeon, Goodman, De Franco, Russell, Mezzrow. LP: Dutch Swing College Band, *Dixieland Goes Dutch* (Epic).

Addr: Klimopstraat 48, The Hague, Holland.

SCHLINGER, SOL, *baritone* and *tenor saxes;* b. New York City, 9/6/26. Stud. w. Bill Sheiner, 1939. Prof. debut w. Henry Jerome '40, playing tenor. While in Shep Fields band, '41-3, toured Europe for USO. Switching to baritone, pl. w. Buddy Rich, '43; T. Dorsey, '43-6; J. Dorsey, '47, and during the next few years was w. Ch. Barnet, Jerry Gray, Herbie Fields, Louis Jordan, Perez Prado. Tenor w. Benny Goodman on concert tour '52 and again in '56 at Waldorf Astoria, NYC. First jazz records w. Al Cohn. Many commercial studio jobs in NYC. LPs w. Al Cohn, Manny Albam (Vict.), Teddy Charles (Atl.), *Porgy & Bess* w. Bill Potts (UA), *Saxes, Inc.* (War. Bros.).

Addr: 961 East 181st St., Bronx, N.Y.

SCHLUTER, WOLFGANG, *vibes;* b. Berlin, Germany, 11/12/33. Stud. tympani, percussion for five years; joined a commercial band on vibes in '55; feat. w. Michael Naura Quintet '56-60. Did TV show with German All Stars Aug. '58. Rec. w. Naura. Fav: Milt Jackson; main influence Cal Tjader.

Addr: c/o Meyer, Lange Reihe 76, Hamburg I, Germany.

SCHNEIDER, ELMER REUBEN (Moe), *trombone;* b. Bessie, Okla., 12/24/19. Father a violinist; three brothers, four sisters, all musically inclined. St. on banjo; trombone at 12. Moved to Calif., 1938. Pl. at Balboa Beach for a year, then w. Ken Baker, Ben Pollack, Gus Arnheim, Will Osborne, Alvino Rey. During two years in service, pl. in Army band w. Ray Bauduc and Gil Rodin. After discharge in '46 rejoined Rey; toured w.

Gene Krupa '47, then settled in LA, worked w. Bob Crosby; Ben Pollack '49 for two years; did radio version of *Pete Kelly's Blues,* also pl. in the movie and later in TV version. Bob Crosby TV show until Aug. '57. Free-lance on records and TV '58; started on staff at ABC w. Bobby Hammack orch. Films: *The Five Pennies, The Gene Krupa Story.* Began stud. in '47 to take up accounting and has had practice since '51, alternating this work with musical activities. Does auditing for mus. union. Favs: Lou McGarity, Teagarden, Ray Sims for jazz; Murray McEachern, Joe Howard for pretty solos. LPs w. Matty Matlock (War. Bros.), Billy May (Cap.), *Pete Kelly's Blues* (Vict., Col.).

Addr: 3244 Bennett Drive, Hollywood 28, Calif.

SCHOEBEL, ELMER, *piano, composer;* b. East St. Louis, Ill., 9/8/1896. Studied guitar, piano, privately. Played for silent movies 1910; vaudeville '12-17; to Chicago '20 w. 20th Century Jazz Band. In Friars' Society orch. '22-3; own orch. at Midway Garden, Chi., '24-5, then to NYC in Isham Jones' band. Back in Chi., pl. w. Louis Panico '26; own band '27; Art Kassel '28. Arranger for Ina Ray Hutton '35, then spent ten years as chief music arr. for Warner Brothers publ. companies in NYC. Resumed as jazz pianist '50-3 in Conrad Janis combo. Acc. Tommy Lyman '54-5, then settled in Florida. Played at St. Petersburg club w. Arnie Mossler band '57-9.

Elmer Schoebel was one of the first important composer-arrangers in jazz. In the early 1920s he prepared many King Oliver, Louis Armstrong and Jelly Roll Morton works for publication. An electrical and mechanical engineer, he invented "tunematic" radio, mfd. in '33 in his own factory. As an ASCAP songwriter he had many hits incl: *Farewell Blues, Bugle Call Rag, Nobody's Sweetheart, Prince of Wails, Spanish Shawl, House of David Blues.* No LPs now available.

Addr: 5561 66th Ave. North, Pinellas Park, Fla.

SCHOONDERWALT, HERMAN, *clarinet;* also *baritone* and *alto saxes;* b. Eindhoven, Holland, 12/23/31. Father was an amateur opera singer. First stud. clarinet in 1938, and started to play in amateur bands the next year. Got into music professionally through his father. Pl. w. Freddy Loggen in Germany for USAF '53; all-star band, incl. Sandy Mosse, on tour of Sweden '55. In '56 pl. in Spain and then formed own group for records. Since '56 has pl. w. the Miller Sextet and been active as a soloist in concerts, radio, TV and films in Holland. Favs: Goodman, DeFranco, Parker. LP: two tracks in *Jazz Behind The Dikes* (Epic).

SCHROEDER, EUGENE CHARLES (Gene), *piano;* b. Madison, Wis., 2/5/15. Mother pl. piano, father trumpet. Stud. piano as Wis. Sch. of Music 1924-7; clar. in high sch. band '30-1. U. of Wis. Mus. School '32. After working w. a few commercial hotel bands and w. Joe Marsala at the Hickory House, he began an association w. Eddie Condon in '43 and has worked with him almost continuously since then, on records, at Condon's club and on his various TV series from '44. Toured Great Britain w. Condon Jan., Feb. '57. Favs: A. Tatum, Tristano. LPs w. Condon (Decca, Col., Comm.); Miff Mole (Bruns.); Wild Bill Davison (Comm.); Bud Freeman (Merc.); Brother Matthew (ABC-Par.), Max Kaminsky (Comm.).

Addr: 4011 79th St., Elmhurst 73, N.Y.

SCHULLER, GUNTHER, *French horn, composer;* b. Jackson Heights, N.Y., 11/11/25. Stud. with first Fr. horn player of Metropolitan Opera and with Robert Schulze of Manhattan School of Music. Two years w. Eugene Goossens' Cincinnati Symph., then 10 yrs. w. the Metropolitan Opera. Although primarily a classical musician, Schuller has an exceptional knowledge and understanding of jazz. On numerous occasions he has worked very closely with John Lewis; has also appeared at jazz concerts, taking a prominent part in the Monterey Jazz Festival Oct. '59. His work, though dismissed by Whitney Balliett in *The New Yorker* as "a strained cross-breeding of jazz and classical music," has drawn into its orbit a group of jazz musicians who feel that such a cross-fertilization can be valid, desirable and logical. One of Schuller's works, *Conversations,* was performed at Town Hall in Sept. '59 by the Modern Jazz Quartet with the Beaux Arts String Quartet. Schuller has written scholarly, analytical articles on jazz for several magazines and books, incl. *Jazz Review.* He also has been an instructor in *Jazz Styles and Composition* at the School of Jazz in Lenox, Mass. LPs as conductor-composer: *Modern Jazz Concert, Music for Brass* (Col.), *Modern Jazz Society* (Verve).

Addr: 610 West End Avenue, New York 24, N.Y.

SCHUTT, ARTHUR, *piano;* b. Reading, Pa., 11/21/02. Stud. w. father, John Gustav Schutt. Planned to be concert pianist. Prof. debut in silent movies at 13; with Paul Specht Orch. 1918. In Philadelphia '21 met Joe Venuti and soon after came to NYC. Pianist in many bands incl. Roger Wolfe Kahn, 2d piano w. Vincent Lopez. From the late '20s he became prominent in jazz through his participation in a number of celebrated record dates w. Trumbauer, Beiderbecke, '27; Red Nichols, '26-8 and '31; Joe Venuti, '27-9; Miff Mole, '27-9; Dorsey Bros., '28-9; Ed Lang, '29; Cotton Pickers, '29; Charleston Chasers, '29-30; Benny Goodman, '31, '34; Adrian Rollini '33. In the '30s and '40s he was on the West Coast as a staff musician at MGM studios; after that he free-lanced around LA. Schutt, who on *All Muddled Up* w. Paul Specht in '22 played what was then considered a precedent-setting ad lib solo chorus, was, according to John Hammond, "the first jazz pianist with a big technique ever to become prominent on records." LP w. Nichols (Brunswick).

Addr: Bungalow Café, 1139 N. La Brea, Hollywood 38, Cal.

SCHWARTZ, THORNEL JR., *guitar;* b. Philadelphia, Pa., 5/29/27. Stud. piano at Landis Inst. Worked w. Freddie Cole 1952-5; Jimmy Smith '55-7; Johnny "Hammond" Smith '58-60. Favs: Tal Farlow, Kenny Burrell.

LPs w. Jimmy Smith (Blue Note), Johnny Smith (New Jazz).

SCOBEY, ROBERT (Bob), *trumpet;* b. Tucumcari, N. Mex., 12/9/16. Raised in Stockton, Cal., where he started on trumpet at 9; moved to Berkeley, where he studied with classical teachers. Worked in radio staff bands, dance orchestra and theatre pit bands around San Francisco; entered jazz field after meeting Lu Watters in 1938. Played with Yerba Buena Jazz Band 1940 to '50 (except for three and a half years in the Army); left to form his own group which worked with great success in Oakland and played at the annual Dixieland Jubilee in LA. Later moved to Chi. Filmed TV commercial for Marlboro cigarettes '59. Fav: Armstrong. Fav. own solo: *Of All the Wrongs.* Own LPs: GTJ, Vict., Verve; LPs w. Lu Watters, Turk Murphy (GTJ), Claire Austin (Contemp.).

SCOTT, BOBBY, *piano, composer, singer;* also *vibes;* b. Bronx, N.Y., 1/24/37. Studied at La Follette Sch. of Mus. in NYC 1945, w. Edvard Moritz, a former pupil of Debussy, '49. Prof. debut '48. By the time he was 15, he had worked w. Louis Prima and other name bands on the road. Worked w. Tony Scott (no relation) '54, Gene Krupa '55. Scored a pop hit as a singer on ABC-Par. w. *Chain Gang.* Did a single at Cafe Bohemia, NYC '57; app. at Great South Bay Jazz Festival '58, New Haven Fest. of Arts '59. In addition to teaching theory and harmony in '59, he resumed studies w. Moritz and is concerned now mostly with composing. Also pl. accordion, cello, bass and clarinet. While in high school had several dozen bouts as amateur boxer. Fav. comp.: Bela Bartok, Roy Harris; fav. pianists: Bill Evans, Dave McKenna. Own LPs on Verve, ABC-Par., Beth.; LPs w. Krupa (Verve).

Addr: 60 West 68th St., New York, N.Y.

SCOTT, ARTHUR BUDD (Bud), *guitar, banjo, singer;* b. New Orleans, 1/11/1890; d. Los Angeles, 7/2/49. While still in teens he played w. Buddy Bolden, John Robichaux, Freddy Keppard, later sang and played on vaudeville tours from 1913. Came to NYC 1915, worked as violinist in pit bands and concert groups; moved to Los Angeles and joined King Oliver's band as banjoist. Scott is the man who originated the now traditional shout of "Oh, play that thing!" in *Dipper Mouth Blues* when he recorded it with Oliver in Apr. 1923. After playing with Oliver on and off until 1927, he worked in Chicago with Erskine Tate, Dave Peyton and Jimmie Noone, then moved to Calif., where he joined Mutt Carey and led his own trio. From 1944 until his death he was closely associated with Kid Ory, appearing along with him and Louis Armstrong in the picture *New Orleans* and recording with him both in Ory's band and under Armstrong. Among Scott's earlier sessions were dates with Johnny Dodds and Jimmy Blythe in 1927, Noone in '28 and Richard M. Jones in '29. LPs w. Ory (GTJ), Armstrong (Vict.).

SCOTT, C. CALO, *cello;* b. Camaguey, Cuba, 3/11/20. To US at age of two; began stud. piano at seven. Pl. sax as a teen-ager and while in Army as member of 17th Special Serv. Band in 1949. After a rheumatic heart forced him to abandon the sax, he began stud. cello in 1951. Pl. gigs around NYC in mid-fifties; w. Vinnie Burke in String Jazz Quartet '57 and w. violinist Bruce Hayden in '58. Fav: O. Pettiford. LPs w. Mal Waldron (New Jazz); Vinnie Burke, *String Jazz Quartet* (ABC-Par.).

Addr: 990 Findlay Ave., Bronx 56, N.Y.

SCOTT, CECIL XAVIER, *tenor sax, clarinet;* b. Springfield, O., 11/22/05. Pl. clar. w. Scott's Symphonic Syncopators (incl. brother Lloyd Scott on drums); Cecil and Lloyd worked together through the 1920s, rec. for Vict. in 1927 under Lloyd's name and in '29 under Cecil's. During the late '20s the band became popular in the East, playing often at the Savoy Ballroom in NYC. Later, Cecil worked w. various Clarence Williams units and w. the Missourians, forerunner of the Cab Calloway band. After working for a while w. Fletcher Henderson, he toured w. Teddy Hill 1936-7, later worked w. Red Allen, Bert Socarras; had his own band again at Ubangi Club NYC, 1942 (incl. singer Ruth Brown). During the '40s he free-lanced with many groups and rec. combo dates w. J. C. Higginbotham, Dickie Wells, Sandy Williams, Art Hodes. Pl. w. Chick Morrison's band at Diamond Horseshoe, 1950-2; Jimmy McPartland '53; jam sessions at Central Plaza, Stuyvesant Casino, etc., from '54; also app. at Jimmy Ryan's '57-8, as both leader and sideman; Great South Bay Festival '57 and '58. Since '54 has been paying regular visits to New York Rehabilitation Center demonstrating use of artificial legs. Visited Canada w. Willie the Lion Smith Aug. '59. Scott's forceful tone and dynamic style typical of the Harlem jazz era of the '30s, has remained equally effective on both tenor and clarinet.

Addr: 440 W. 164th St., New York 32, N.Y.

SCOTT, HAZEL DOROTHY, *piano, singer;* b. Port of Spain, Trinidad, 6/11/20. To US 1924. Mother, multi-instrumentalist, led all-girl band. Hazel made prof. debut at five. Own radio series 1936; sang *FDR Jones* in Broadway show *Sing Out The News* '38. Earned big following at Cafe Society Downtown and Uptown '39-45. Rec. debut in group organized by the writer for Bluebird Dec. '39. Married 8/1/45 to Rep. Adam Clayton Powell Jr. In concert and night club work intermittently '45-57, then took up residence in France for two years. Many of her early recs. were quasi-jazz versions of classics; more recent recs. showed infl. of Tatum, Hines, Wilson and later Bud Powell. Films: *I Dood It, Rhapsody In Blue.* Own LP: Decca.

SCOTT, PATRICK JOHN O'HARA (Johnny), *flute, saxophone;* b. Bristol, England, 11/1/30. Father pl. alto sax and viola. Stud. w. father at age six; piano at ten. While in Army pl. with the Royal Artillery Band and stud. clarinet, harp, sax, piano, and orchestration. After discharge in 1952, pl. with various bands. Began playing flute in '54. With Kenny Baker on radio series '57-8.

Has done mostly studio work recently. Was featured flute player w. Woody Herman's Anglo-American Herd in April '59. Wrote music for a Rex Harrison production *The Bright One,* which was staged in Brighton and London. Favs: Charlie Parker, Art Pepper, Quincy Jones. LPs w. Baker, Ken Moule.

Addr: 16 College Court, Hammersmith, London W. 6, Eng.

SCOTT, LLOYD, *drums;* b. Springfield, Ohio, 8/22/02. Through 1929, career ran parallel with that of his brother Cecil (q.v.); then returned to Ohio, gigging with local bands for a while. Retired from music; since active as night club operator and journalist.

SCOTT, RAYMOND (Harry Warnow), *conductor, composer, piano;* b. Brooklyn, N.Y., 9/10/10. Stud. Inst. of Mus. Art. First prominent while on CBS staff in NYC, 1934-8, he introduced a quintet that earned great popularity playing novelty instrumentals on radio, records and in movies, 1936-8. Mainly a pop unit, the quintet featured very little real jazz. After touring with a full-size band 1939-41, Scott returned to CBS in '42 and was active the following year as conductor of a unique band, the first mixed orchestra to work as a house band and specialize in jazz; its members included Charlie Shavers, Ben Webster, Cliff Leeman, Johnny Guarnieri. Since the mid-'40s Scott has been known for his work in non-jazz fields. A brilliant engineer, he ran his own recording studio, later had his own record label, Audivox; he was also conductor on *Your Hit Parade* and other network TV and radio shows. For several months in '59 he was mus. dir. for Everest Records. Married to singer Dorothy Collins. Scott's best known comps. date from his early years as a leader: *Twilight in Turkey, Powerhouse, Toy Trumpet, Huckleberry Duck* etc. Own LPs: Coral, Evst., tracks in *Ballroom Bandstand* (Col.).

Addr: 140 West 57th Street, New York 19, N.Y.

SCOTT, RONNIE, *tenor sax, leader;* b. London, England, 1/28/27. Pl. w. Cab Kaye, Ted Heath; worked in ship's band crossing Atlantic on the Queen Mary. Later featured w. Tito Burns; Jack Parnell 1952; formed own band '53. Toured US '55. Formed Jazz Couriers '56, pl. in Paris '56, Vienna '59. Opened own jazz night club '59. First British musician to make a national name in England as outstanding tenor sax man in modern field. Own LP: *The Couriers Of Jazz* w. Tubby Hayes (Carlton); LP w. Ted Heath, *Things To Come* (London).

Addr: 14 Edgewarebury Gardens, Edgeware, Middlesex, England.

SCOTT, SHIRLEY, *organ;* also *piano, trumpet;* b. Philadelphia, Pa., 3/14/34. From musical family; stud. piano at Orenstein School of Music in Phila.; took up trumpet in high school and won scholarship. Pl. piano in father's private club w. brother's band. St. organ 1955; worked w. Eddie "Lockjaw" Davis trio 1956-60. Adept, hard-swinging, quasi-modern soloist. Favs: Milt Buckner, Jackie Davis, Jimmy Smith. Own LPs: Pres. LPs w. Eddie Davis (Roul., Pres.), *Very Saxy* (Pres.).

SCOTT, TONY (Anthony Sciacca), *clarinet, saxes, piano, composer;* b. Morristown, N.J., 6/17/21. Father a guitarist and barber; mother played violin. Stud. Juilliard, 1940-2. Own band in Army '42-5. Played w. Buddy Rich, Ben Webster, Trummy Young, Ch. Ventura big band, Sid Catlett and many other combos in late '40s on clarinet, tenor sax; also worked occasionally as pianist for singers. With Claude Thornhill in 1949; arrs. for Billie Holiday, Sarah Vaughan; film score for Lili St. Cyr; spent a month w. Duke Ellington early '53 playing tenor, clarinet and flute. Then played w. Latin bands, gigged as pianist, led own combos at Minton's for several months and was feat. during much of 1954 at the Metropole, NYC. After nine months as musical director for Harry Belafonte in '55, he re-formed his group and worked clubs and festivals until Nov. '59, excepting a seven month tour of Europe and Africa, incl. Iron Curtain countries, in '57. On TV, app. on *The Mythical Bird* on *Camera Three* (CBS), Feb. '57; part of regular group for *The Subject Is Jazz* (NBC), Mar.-June '58. App. NJF '58, French Lick Fest. '59. In Nov. '59 Scott left for the Orient on the first leg of a two year trip that would take him to countries all over the world. He is playing, studying, teaching, photographing, and recording ethnic music.

Originally inspired by Clarence Hutchenrider, clarinetist w. Glen Gray, and by Benny Goodman, Scott developed a style of his own and has been hailed by Nat Hentoff in DB as "our finest contemporary jazz clarinetist," Won DB critics' poll 1953 (New Star), '55, '57-9; DB readers' poll '56, '58-9; *Metronome* poll '60. Favs: Ch. Parker, Ben Webster. Own LPs: Vict., Bruns., ABC-Par., Carlton, Dawn, Coral, Hanover-Signature; LPs w. Sarah Vaughan, Mel Powell (Col.), *Modern Jazz Society* (Verve), Feather-Hyman in *Oh Captain!* (MGM), Trigger Alpert (River.), Milt Hinton (Beth.), Larry Sonn (Coral), Billie Holiday (Verve).

Addr: Rm. 607, 1650 Broadway, New York 19, N.Y.

SEALEY, MILTON RANDOLPH (Milt), *piano,* also *vibes, bass;* b. Montreal, Quebec, Can., 6/2/28. Brothers, George and Hugh, play saxophone. Studied piano at Negro Community Center, McGill Cons., Paris Cons. Prof. start w. brother Hugh's orch. Rec. w. Mezz Mezzrow in Paris 1955; pl. w. Don Byas in Holland '56. Rec. for English Decca in London '56, Montreal '57. Pl. w. Lee Morgan, Lou Donaldson in Philadelphia; own trio at Embers, Left Bank NYC; Dizzy Reece at Jazz Gallery, Jan. '60. LP w. Mezzrow on Ducretet-Thompson. Own LP: London.

Addr: 4926 St. Emilie, Montreal 30, Quebec, Canada.

SEARS, ALBERT OMEGA, *tenor sax;* b. Macomb, Ill., 2/22/10. Mainly self-taught. Played w. Paul Craig in Buffalo, 1927; Chick Webb at Savoy NYC, late '28. Toured w. *Keep Shufflin'* revue and played w. Zack

Whyte. From the early 1930s Sears led numerous bands of his own off and on; first in Buffalo; later in Newport, Ky. (with Helen Humes as vocalist); and at Renaissance Ballroom, NYC. In the early '30s he worked w. Bernie Young and at Smalls' w. Elmer Snowden; retired to Ill. for a while, took business course. In early '40s he played w. Andy Kirk, Lionel Hampton; took own band (incl. Lester Young) on USO tour. Feat. w. Duke Ellington 1943-9, and again intermittently until '51, when he left to become partner and mus. dir. of the Johnny Hodges band, scoring his first big hit as composer of *Castle Rock.* In Oct. 1952 he quit Hodges to settle in NYC as a mus. publisher. Sears' best solos w. Ellington, showing his unusual, choppy phrasing and staccato style, were *Carnegie Blues, I Ain't Got Nothing But The Blues, Liberian Suite, Black, Brown and Beige, Swamp Fire.* Favs: Webster, Hawkins, Byas. LPs w. Ellington (Vict., Rondolette), Hodges (Verve), Rex Stewart in *History of Jazz, Vol. 3* (Cap.).

Addr: c/o Sylvia Music, 1650 Broadway, New York 19, N.Y.

SEBESKY, DONALD J. (Don), *trombone, composer;* b. Perth Amboy, N.J., 12/10/37. Pl. drums as a child, switched to accordion. Stud. trombone w. Warren Covington for three years, and joined his band after grad. from high school. With Kai Winding briefly; Maynard Ferguson, '58-9; Stan Kenton '59-60. Stud. comp. at Manhattan School of Music. Favs: Bob Brookmeyer, Zoot Sims; Bill Holman for comp. LPs w. M. Ferguson (Roul.).

SEDRIC, EUGENE HALL (Gene, Honey Bear), *clarinet, tenor sax;* b. St. Louis, Mo., 6/17/07. Stud. w. private teacher; inspired by father, a popular ragtime pianist known locally as "Con-Con." At 10 he played in a Knights of Pythias band. Prof. debut w. Charlie Creath ca. 1922; played on riverboats w. Fate Marable. Came to NYC 1923 with a burlesque show; joined Sam Wooding and made many tours with him in US, Latin America and Europe during the next decade. After leaving Wooding in 1934, worked briefly w. Fletcher Henderson, then began a long association w. Fats Waller, first on records, then on the road w. Waller's touring band. Upon Waller's death, formed his own band, played Cafe Society, Sherman in Chicago, etc. After a long illness in 1945, he returned to work with the Phil Moore Four. Later he toured with Jimmy McPartland, Bobby Hackett combos; to France 1953, where he worked w. Mezz Mezzrow. Member of Conrad Janis band since August 1953. A highly regarded stylist on both tenor and clarinet, he names Thornton Blue, St. Louis clarinetist, and David Jones, who played C melody sax w. Marable, as early influences. Fav: Coleman Hawkins. LPs w. Fats Waller (Vict., Cam.); tracks in *Battle of the Saxes* (Em.).

Addr: 615 East 168th St., Bronx 56, N.Y.

SEGAL, GERALD (Jerry), *drums;* b. Philadelphia, Pa., 2/16/31. Majored in music at Mastbaum High. Toured w. Benny Green combo, Pete Rugolo band, 1954; gigged in Phila. clubs, joined Johnny Smith quartet, Norma Carson quintet. Pl. w. Terry Gibbs '55-6; Stan Getz during most of '57; also rehearsed and rec. w. Edgar Varèse. Many small combo jobs incl. Mingus, H. Mann, M. Allison, Tristano; mainly w. Bernard Peiffer Trio 1958-60. Also pl. w. commercial bands (Elgart, Thornhill et al). LPs w. Terry Gibbs (Em.), Teddy Charles (Pres., Elek.), Teo Macero, Prestige Jazz Quartet (Pres.), Stan Getz (Verve), Bennie Green (Decca), B. Peiffer (Laurie).

Addr: 309 W. 99th St., New York 25, N.Y.

SEGURE, ROGER, *composer;* b. Brooklyn, N. Y., 5/22/05. Self-taught until 1945, when he studied in NYC; Schillinger system with private teachers. Entered music as acc. for singers, touring America and the Far East w. Midge Williams during the 1930s. From 1938, wrote arrangements for Louis Armstrong, Andy Kirk, Alvino Rey, etc. Many arrangements for J. Lunceford incl. *Whatcha Know Joe, Blue Afterglow;* arr. *Nocturne* for John Kirby. Scored music for film *Blues in the Night* (feat. Lunceford band). Mus. Dir. for Ralph Edwards' TV show 1951; Jerry Fielding orch. '54, then worked at Westlake Coll. of Mus. in LA as teacher, later becoming a high school teacher locally. Favs: Ellington, Finegan, Burns.

Addr: 11956 Hatteras St., North Hollywood, Cal.

SELLERS, JOHN (Brother John), *singer;* b. Clarksdale, Miss., 5/27/24. Raised in Greenville, Miss., by grandmother who used to let out plot of land to travelling tent shows. There he heard Ma Rainey, Ida Cox, and other blues singers of the '20s. Sang in church and was particularly influenced by Leroy Carr's recordings. Moved to Chicago at 10 w. an aunt and did gospel singing, largely under the inspiration of Mahalia Jackson, with whom he toured. During the '50s he became acquainted w. Josh White, Sonny Boy Williamson, S. Price, Tampa Red, and w. Bill Broonzy, who encouraged him. Repl. Broonzy at the Blue Note in Chicago when the latter toured Europe in 1950, and has toured the South and West widely since. Toured and recorded in England in 1957. Own LPs on Vanguard, Monitor.

Addr: 234 W. 65th St., New York, N.Y.

SEMPLE, ARCHIBALD STUART NISBET (Archie), *clarinet;* b. Edinburgh, Scotland, 3/31/28. Led semi-professional combos w. brother, trumpeter John Semple. Prof. debut w. Mick Mulligan 1952-3. Toured w. Freddy Randall '53-5, Alex Welch '55-60. Many records w. own quartet and w. Welch on English Decca, Pye-Nixa, etc. Fav: Pee Wee Russell.

Addr: 6, Marryat House, Churchill Gardens, London S.W.1, England.

SEVERINSEN, CARL H. (Doc), *trumpet;* b. Arlington, Ore., 7/7/27. Father, now a dentist, played violin, cornet. Doc won many state and national contests as cornetist, studying w. father and later w. Benny Baker. Worked w. Ted Fio Rito 1945. Ch. Barnet off and on '47-9; Sam Donahue '48; T. Dorsey on and off since late

1949; Noro Morales, Vaughn Monroe, '50. While on staff at NBC, NYC, seen in jazz solos on Steve Allen TV show, 1954-5. Member of small group for NBC-TV series, *The Subject Is Jazz,* March-June '58. First class soloist whose steady studio work has limited his jazz recognition. Favs: C. Terry, F. Navarro, M. Davis, B. Butterfield. LPs w. Barnet (Cap.), Steve Allen (Coral), Toshiko (Metrojazz), Deane Kincaide (Evst.).

Addr: 80 Stuyvesant Ave., Larchmont, N.Y.

SHADE, WILL (Son Brimmer), *singer, guitar;* b. Memphis, Tenn., 2/5/1898. Played in the streets of Memphis and worked with medicine shows. Made record debut Feb. 1927 on Victor and between this time and 1934, when he made his last recordings for Okeh, his Memphis Jug Band was heard in a series of successful sessions; Shade's partner from '28 was Charlie Burse, another country blues artist, from Decatur, Ala., and their duets became very popular in Chicago and through the South. During the '50s Shade was in Memphis, working in odd jobs and occasionally singing.

SHANK, CLIFFORD EVERETT JR. (Bud), *alto, baritone sax, flute, composer;* b. Dayton, Ohio, 5/27/26. Clarinet at 10, sax at 14, flute at 21. Univ. of N. Car. '44-6; stud. comp. and arr. w. Shorty Rogers, after moving to Cal. '47. Pl. w. Ch. Barnet '47-8; Alvino Rey, Art Mooney '49; Stan Kenton '50-1; later began long association w. Howard Rumsey at Lighthouse, Hermosa Beach, Cal. Toured Europe w. Bob Cooper March-June '56 and again March-May '58, incl. North and South Africa on latter trip. For past few years has worked LA clubs w. own quartet. He won DB critics' poll as New Star on alto, '54. Favs: Konitz, Pepper. A warmly communicative flutist and sensitively improvising jazzman on alto, he has also developed into a first-rate modern composer. Film sound track: *Slippery When Wet,* '59, available on own World-Pacific LP. Own LPs: Wor. Pac.; other LPs w. Lighthouse All Stars, S. Manne (Contemp.), Chet Baker, Laurindo Almeida (Wor. Pac.), Rugolo (Col., Merc.), Kenton, Bob Cooper, Giuffre (Cap.), S. Rogers (Vict., Atl.), Buddy Collette (Merc.), Gerry Mulligan (Cap.).

Addr: 12347 Valleyheart Dr., Studio City, Calif.

SHANNON, TERENCE (Terry), *piano;* b. London, England, 11/5/29. Began pl. at age seven. Since 1955 has pl. w. many British bands and groups. Was a founding member of the Jazz Couriers. Favs: Horace Silver, Bud Powell, John Lewis, Sonny Clark. LPs w. Jazz Couriers (Carlton), Dizzy Reece (Blue Note).

SHARON, RALPH, *piano, composer;* b. London, England, 9/17/23. Stud. w. mother, an American. Prof. debut w. Ted Heath; later was pianist in Frank Weir's orch. in which Geo. Shearing played accordion. Own sextet at London Stork Club. Won *Melody Maker* poll for 4 years as Britain's No. 1 pianist. To US fall '53; pl. at Embers, later acc. Chris Connor; mus. dir. and pianist for Tony Bennett '57-60, writing all arrs. for Bennett's LPs w. Basie, also series of instrumentals for Basie. Own LPs: Rama, Beth., Lond., Argo; LPs w. Chris Connor (Beth.), Tony Bennett (Col.).

Addr: 185 East 3rd Street, New York 9, N. Y.

SHAUGHNESSY, EDWIN THOMAS (Ed), *drums;* b. Jersey City, N. J., 1/29/29. Only child of a musical family. Started on piano; later began playing a set of drums collected by his father in lieu of a bad debt, 1943. Sid Catlett was an early friend and influence. Played w. Geo. Shearing at Three Deuces 1948; Bobby Byrne '48; Ch. Ventura '48 to '50. Toured Europe w. Benny Goodman sextet. April 1950; joined Tommy Dorsey late '50. With Lucky Millinder, March '51. From about this time he remained in NYC to do studio work, recording and night club combo work. Worked w. Charlie Mingus, Duke Ellington, Elliot Lawrence, Johnny Richards. Festivals: Newport '56-8, Randall's Island '58, Great South Bay '58. In late '50s began studying piano and composition. Took up cornet and peck-horn '59. Left studios and organized own small group. Favs: Tough, Catlett, Lamond. LPs w. Trigger Alpert (River.), Teddy Charles, *Music Man* w. Jimmy Giuffre (Atl.), Teo Macero, T. Charles in *Something New, Something Blue* (Col.), Mundell Lowe (Cam.), Al Klink (Gr. Award), Charlie Ventura (Decca, GNP), Chuck Wayne (Savoy), Johnny Richards (Coral).

Addr: 325 West End Ave., New York 23, N.Y.

SHAVERS, CHARLES JAMES (Charlie), *trumpet, composer;* b. New York City, 8/3/17. First musical experience as banjoist. After working w. Frank Fairfax in Phila. in 1935, he was heard in NYC w. Tiny Bradshaw and Lucky Millinder, 1936, then shot up to national jazz fame as principal soloist and arranger with the John Kirby combo. He remained with the band until 1944, but during the last year worked mainly w. Raymond Scott at CBS while occasionally doubling w. Kirby. From 1945 to '49 he toured w. Tommy Dorsey's band, which he rejoined briefly on several occasions, most recently in 1953. In mid-1950 he ran a sextet jointly w. Louis Bellson and Terry Gibbs. Toured w. JATP in '52 and '53; visited Europe with the unit Feb. '53. In 1953 and '54 he worked occasionally w. Benny Goodman. He was back w. the Tommy Dorsey band until Dorsey's death in Nov. '56. He has since fronted his own combos in NYC, worked at the Metropole and free-lanced on numerous record dates.

Shavers is one of the few trumpet players of the swing era who brought to jazz a completely original and unmistakable style and tone. Despite occasional ventures into showmanship for its own sake, he showed himself capable of a wide variety of genuine jazz moods in which a touch of humor could often be detected. As an arranger he molded the whole personality of the Kirby band with his deft handling of the limited voicings offered by trumpet, alto sax and clarinet. He enjoyed several successes as a songwriter, notably *Undecided* and *Pastel Blue.* He won the Esq. Silver Award 1946; DB poll 1948. Own LPs: Beth. 27, 67,

MGM 3765; LPs w. Steve Allen (Coral 57018), Eddie Condon (Em. 36013), Leroy Holmes (MGM 3325, 3554), Coleman Hawkins (Pres. 7156), Hal Singer (Pres. 7153), Gene Krupa (Verve 8087, 8071, 8107), Louis Bellson (Verve 8186), Charlie Ventura (Verve 8132), *Trumpets All Out* (Savoy 12096), Lionel Hampton (Decca 9055), Georgie Auld (Gr. Award 318), Benny Goodman (Cap. W565), w. Georgie Auld in *Jazztime USA* (Bruns. 54001), *The Fabulous Dorseys In Hi-Fi* (Col. C2L 8), T. Dorsey (Vict. LPM 6003), Bill Potts (UA 4032).

Addr: 31-28 101st St., East Elmhurst 69, L.I., N.Y.

SHAW, ARTIE (Arthur Arshawsky), *clarinet, composer, leader;* b. New York City, 5/23/10. Raised in New Haven, Conn., from 1916. While in high school, took up saxophone and gigged with quartet. Professional debut with Johnny Cavallaro, with whom he played saxophones and later clarinet. Lived in Cleveland for three years, played with Joe Cantor, Austin Wylie. Played in Irving Aaronson's band 1929-31; free-lanced in NYC, working at CBS and making numerous record dates, then retired from music for a year. In the summer of 1935, appearing in a swing concert at the Imperial Theatre NYC, he played one of his own compositions accompanied by a string quartet. The sensation caused by this first use of strings in swing music led to the formation of his first big band, which featured brass, strings, rhythm and one saxophone (Tony Pastor). The venture was short-lived; in the spring of '37 Shaw formed a new band with the conventional swing instrumentation of the day—five brass, four saxes and four rhythm.

His record of *Begin The Beguine* with this band, recorded 7/24/38, made him a national figure and, inadvertently, a rival for Benny Goodman's "King of Swing" crown. In Dec. 1939, confused by an excess of success, Shaw abandoned the orchestra and fled to Mexico. Throughout the 1940s he had various bands off and on, including one with a large string section, 1940-1, and a Navy band that toured the South Pacific, '43-4. Periodically he announced his disgust with jazz, his final retirement from music and his intention to become a professional writer. *The Trouble With Cinderella,* his semi-autobiographical, semi-philosophical book, was published in May 1952 by Farrar, Straus and Young. Late in 1953 he formed a new "Gramercy 5" (a name he had used for his smaller recording combos since 1940), dissolving it the following summer. Took up residence in Spain and was completely inactive in music '55-'60.

Throughout his career Shaw's many marriages kept him on the front pages frequently. He was married first to Jane Carns (annulled), then to Margaret Allen, Lana Turner, Betty Kern (daughter of the late Jerome Kern), Ava Gardner, Kathleen Winsor, Doris Dowling, and Evelyn Keyes. For an intricate, introspective examination of Shaw's life in complete detail, reference to *The Trouble With Cinderella* is highly recommended. Won the *Esquire* Armed Forces Gold Award '44.

Own LPs: Band—Vict. LPM 1570, LPM 1217, LPM 1201, LPM 1648, Cam. 465, 959, LPM 1244, Decca 8309, Epic LN 3150; w. strings, Epic LG 3112; Gramercy Five, Vict. LPM 1241, Verve 2014, 2015; *Modern Music For Clarinet* (Col. ML 4260); LP w. Red Norvo (Epic 3128).

SHAW, ARVELL, *bass;* b. St. Louis, Mo., 9/15/23. Tuba in high sch. Bass w. Fate Marable on riverboats '42. Navy '42-5, then two years w. L. Armstrong big band, briefly w. small band. Left in '50 to study harmony and comp. at Geneva Cons. Back w. Louis '52; radio work w. Russ Case Jan.-Apr. '54, then to Armstrong again until spring '56, when he app. with him in the film *High Society.* In '57 worked w. Russ Case at CBS and w. T. Wilson Trio. In '58, again w. Wilson, also w. Benny Goodman, incl. European tour in May. Stayed in Europe through Sept., playing festivals in Cannes and Knokke. Rec. w. Sidney Bechet in Brussels and Cannes. Back in US, rejoined Wilson. Favs: Blanton, Safranski, Red Mitchell, M. Hinton. Many LPs incl. w. T. Wilson (Col., Cap., Verve); almost all Armstrong LPs from 1946-56, incl. *Satchmo at Pasadena, Satchmo, a Musical Autobiography* (Decca), *Ambassador Satch, Armstrong Plays W. C. Handy, Satch Plays Fats* (Col.), w. B. Goodman (Col.).

Addr: 214 W. 96th St., New York 25, N.Y.

SHAW, HANK (Henry Shalofsky), *trumpet;* b. London, England, 6/23/26. Pl. w. Oscar Rabin, 1942; Vic Lewis, '48; worked w. Maynard Ferguson and Oscar Peterson while in Montreal '49. Jack Parnell band '52, Ronnie Scott '54; *Jazz from London* unit, '56; Joe Harriott Quintet '59-60. Rec. w. Harry Roy for Pye-Nixa, '53; Ronnie Scott (Esquire), Harriott for Brit. Columbia '59.

Addr: 4 Lee Court, London N. W. 6., England.

SHAW, JOAN (Joan DeCosta), *singer, songwriter;* b. Newport News, Va., 1/29/30. Uncle, Bootsie Swan, was famous comic, singer, dancer. Began singing in local night clubs when 15; w. Paul Williams, 1948-9. Has worked many club dates and recorded for MGM, ABC-Par., Sav., and other labels. Has written and recorded many original tunes. Though often limited in her work to rhythm-and-blues and pop performances, she is an excellent jazz-oriented singer. Favs: E. Garner, B. Booker.

Addr: 2480 N. W. 55th Terrace, Miami, Fla.

SHEARING, GEORGE ALBERT, *piano, composer;* b. London, England, 8/13/19. Blind from birth; stud. at Linden Lodge Sch. for Blind. Pl. jazz in clubs after hearing Fats Waller, T. Wilson recs. At a Rhythm Club jam session he was heard by the author, who set his first rec. date (1937) and later arr. for his immigration to US. After playing in 17-piece blind band led by Claude Bampton, worked as soloist. Also feat. for two years with Ambrose orch. Won *Melody Maker* poll as top Brit. pianist for 7 years. Pl. accordion in

Frank Weir orch. '47. In Dec. '46 made three-month visit to US (one rec. date for Savoy); back to US, Dec. '47, spent much of '48 at Three Deuces, 52nd St., first as soloist, then w. combos.

In Jan. '49, while leading a quartet at Clique Club (incl. B. De Franco) he rec. for Discovery with a quintet assembled for him by the writer. Group was soon organized on permanent basis for clubs. Orig. members were Margie Hyams, vibes; Chuck Wayne, guitar; Denzil Best, drums; John Levy, bass (now Shearing's manager). First big hit was *September in the Rain* (MGM). Shearing's use of locked-hands style, his way of blending with guitar and vibes, gave the group a sound that made it the most popular in the US for several years. In '54 he added a conga drummer; in summer '59 he formed a big band and toured with it briefly, then resumed the combo format. Shearing is best known internationally as composer of *Lullaby of Birdland.* Written in 1952 as a theme song for the night club and its radio shows, it became the best known standard jazz tune of postwar years, often performed even in the Soviet Union. Shearing in late '50s made several guest appearances with symph. orchs. playing classical works. Filmed educational TV series w. Father O'Connor in Boston '57. Film: *Jazz on a Summer's Day.* Won DB small combo award '49-'52; Met. poll on piano '51-2, combo '53. Own LPs: Lond. LL1343; MGM 3265, 3266, 3216, 3175, 3293, 3122, 3264; Cap. T 648, T 720, T 737, T 858, T 909, T 943, T 1038, T 1082, T 1124, T 1003; w. Teddi King, Billy Eckstine in *Cool Caravan* (MGM 3393); tracks in *Midnight On Cloud 69* (Savoy 12093), *Great Britains* (Sav. 12016); w. Metronome All Stars in *History of Jazz,* Vol. 4 (Cap. T 796).

Addr: Old Tappan Road, Old Tappan, N.J.

SHEEN, MICKEY (Milton Scheinblum), *drums;* b. Brooklyn, N. Y., 12/13/27. Stud. piano at nine, then switched to drums at 12. Began pl. club dates at 13, joined Local 802 at 16. Att. High School of Music and Art NYC, where he led dance band; stud. theory and harm. in school and w. private teacher. In Army 1946; New York U. '47-8. Stud. Schillinger system. Sideman w. various groups in late '40s and '50s, incl. Sol Yaged, Cy Coleman, Coleman Hawkins. With Chubby Jackson and Marty Napoleon, formed "The Big Three" for club and rec. dates. Own LP: *Have Swing Will Travel* (Her.); LPs w. Charlie Shavers (Beth.), Sol Yaged (Her.), The Big Three (Ever.).

SHELDON, JACK, *trumpet;* b. Jacksonville, Fla., 11/30/31. Learned to play at age 12 while att. Cranbrook School in Detroit. Prof. debut in Jacksonville 1944 w. bands of Gene Brandt, Tiny Moore. Moved to LA in '47; stud. at LA City College for two years. Joined Air Force at 19 and pl. w. Air Force Bands in Texas and Calif. Discharged in '52, pl. several months at Lighthouse, then gigged in around LA w. Jack Montrose, Art Pepper, Wardell Gray, Dexter Gordon, Jimmy Giuffre, Herb Geller. W. Curtis Counce '56; Dave Pell at the Crescendo in Hollywood, Stan Kenton '58; Mel Tormé in Las Vegas. Joined Benny Goodman for European tour, fall '59. Mother runs swimming school specializing in teaching small children; Sheldon is an instructor there when not busy w. music. Fav: Dizzy Gillespie. Own LP on Jazz: West; single selection in *The Hard Swing, The Blues, Jazz West Coast, vol. 2* (Wor. Pac.); LPs w. Curtis Counce (Contemp.), Jimmy Giuffre (Atl., Cap.), *I Want To Live* (UA), Mel Tormé (Verve), Benny Goodman (MGM).

Addr: 5311 Hollywood Blvd., Hollywood, Calif.

SHELTON, DON, *singer;* also *alto, tenor saxes, flute, clar., bass clar.;* b. Tyler, Texas, 8/28/34. Studied w. father, a saxophonist; also in Navy School of Music, Wash., D. C. 1952-5. Prof. start as singer on Rusty Draper show, CBS in Calif. Worked around LA w. Bob Florence and numerous other bands. Joined Hi-Lo's June '59. Favs: Peggy Lee, Cole, Sinatra. LPs w. The Hi-Lo's (Col.).

Addr: 11543 Venice Blvd, Los Angeles, Calif

SHEPARD, THOMAS M. (Tommy), *trombone;* b. Chicago, Ill., 3/31/23. Stud. privately on trombone; harmony w. Bill Russo and at Midwestern Cons. Pl. with Ben Bernie at 18; in Army 1942-6; worked at Chicago's Chez Paree '47-8; w. ABC in Chicago '48-53. W. Stan Kenton one year; back to ABC, then joined CBS. Favs: Urbie Green, Jay Jay Johnson, Frank Rosolino et al. Own LP: *Shepard's Flock* (Cor.); LPs w. Bill Russo (Atl.), Stan Kenton (Cap.), Chubby Jackson (Argo).

Addr: 3750 Lake Shore Drive, Chicago 13, Ill.

SHEPPARD, HARRY, *vibes, drums;* b. Worcester, Mass., 4/1/28. Stud. drums in high school and in Navy band; stud. composition at Berklee School in Boston. Began working club dates after high school. Wrote for and sang in vocal group called Four Hits and a Miss. At Metropole NYC 1956-8 as sideman w. Cozy Cole, Roy Eldridge, Coleman Hawkins. Had own group one year. Appeared on Steve Allen TV shows and Art Ford's Jazz Party. On tour w. Cozy Cole early '59. Favs: Lionel Hampton, Milt Jackson et al; names Oscar Peterson and Miles Davis as major influences. LP w. Chubby Jackson (Evst.).

Addr: 335 East Market St., Long Beach, N. Y.

SHERMAN, RICHARD ANTHONY (Dick), *trumpet, composer;* b. New York City, 11/13/27. Stud. at Juilliard and w. Sammy Silen. On road w. Johnny Richards, B. Goodman, C. Barnet, Kenton; writing for Elliot Lawrence. House band at Roxy, 1956-8. LPs w. Al Cohn-Zoot Sims (Vict.), *Jazzville No. 1* (Dawn).

Addr: 4530 Broadway, New York 40, N. Y.

SHEROCK, SHORTY (Clarence Francis Cherock), *trumpet;* b. Minneapolis, Minn., 11/17/15. High school in Gary, Ind.; cornet from childhood, winning children's contest. While in Ben Pollack's orch. 1936, he played the jazz solos (Harry James was the other trumpeter). Worked w. Jimmy Dorsey 1936-8, Bob Crosby '39, G. Krupa '40-1, Tommy Dorsey '41, then w. Raymond

Scott, Bob Strong, Alvino Rey. After a year with Horace Heidt he led his own band '45-7, then rejoined Jimmy Dorsey briefly. During the '50s he became a successful free-lance musician in Los Angeles. His early solos on *Slow Down, Alreet,* etc. w. Krupa showed effective Roy Eldridge influence. LPs: *The Home of Happy Feet* w. Van Alexander, *Session At Midnight* (Cap.).

Addr: 22552 Criswell St., Canoga Park, Calif.

SHERRILL, JOYA, *singer, songwriter;* b. Bayonne, N.J., 8/20/27. Worked briefly w. D. Ellington, fall 1942; joined band in '44 while still in high school after she wrote words to Strayhorn's *Take the A Train.* Remained w. Ellington four years and then went out as a single. Rejoined Duke for his CBS-TV spectacular and recording of *A Drum Is a Woman,* '57. Made tour of night clubs and U. S. military camps in Germany, England and France, June to Aug. '59. Dramatic role in Broadway play, *The Long Dream* '60. An ebullient, jazz-sensitive popular singer, one of the best to emerge from the Ellington ranks. Favs: E. Fitzgerald, L. Horne, Pearl Bailey. Own LPs: Col., Des.; LPs w. Ellington (Col., Vict.).

Addr: 18 Spinney Hill Dr., Great Neck, L. I., N. Y.

SHERTZER, HERMAN (Hymie), *alto sax;* b. New York City, 4/2/09. Violin at 9, sax at 16. Auditioned for B. Goodman in 1934: was required to double on vln. for a job w. Billy Rose at Music Hall. Stayed w. Goodman until '38 and, after a year w. T. Dorsey, rejoined him until 1940, then spent another year w. T. Dorsey; had his final name band fling in '42 w. Goodman. Settling in NYC for radio and rec. studio work, he became an NBC staff musician. Primarily a section man and an excellent lead alto, he played an important role in such celebrated Goodman performances as *Sing, Sing, Sing, Stompin' at the Savoy,* etc. In late '30s also played on record dates w. L. Hampton for Vict., T. Wilson-Billie Holiday for Bruns. Favs: B. Carter, Hodges, J. Dorsey. Own LP: Disneyland; LPs w. Goodman (Vict., Col.), Hampton (Vict.).

Addr: 277 West End Ave., New York 23, N. Y.

SHERWOOD, ROBERT J. (Bobby), *guitar, trumpet, composer, leader,* etc.; b. Indianapolis, Ind., 5/30/14. Parents were vaudevillians; Bobby, who was self-taught, played banjo in vaudeville at age 7. Guitar and trumpet from 1927. On Eddie Lang's death, Sherwood replaced him as Bing Crosby's accompanist and took part in Bing's earliest Decca sessions. After three years w. Crosby he joined the MGM staff in Hollywood and spent several years as a musician in various studios, also recording w. Artie Shaw and other bands. With success of his first record as a bandleader on Capitol (his own semi-Dixieland number *Elks' Parade)* he went on the road as a bandleader from 1942 to '49.

Living in NYC, he then worked as disc jockey, emcee and actor on many radio and TV shows incl. those of Milton Berle, Bert Parks, Jerry Lester. In Nov. '54 he demonstrated his unique versatility by recording a trick multitape recording for Coral in which he played 4 vocal and 4 trumpet parts as well as mellophone, vibes, trombone, piano, guitar, bass and drums. Fav: Andres Segovia. Own LPs: Jubilee; nos. by band in *Classics In Jazz* (Cap.).

Addr: Room 415, 119 West 57th St., New York 19, N. Y.

SHIELDS, HARRY, *clarinet;* b. New Orleans, 6/30/99. Brother Larry, of Original Dixieland Band, showed him how to play. Around 1916-19 pl. w. Alfred Laine, Emmett Hardy, Sharkey Bonano. Never learned to read music; cont. local jobs until he retired in 1942. Began pl. again 1951 w. Bonano, Dukes of Dixieland and Geo. Girard; rejoined Sharkey, pl. w. him in NYC 1959. Many records for Southland, Tempo, Imperial, Good Time Jazz w. Bonano et al. Fav: Larry Shields.

Addr: 4416 Gen. Pershing St., New Orleans, La.

SHIELDS, LARRY, *clarinet;* b. New Orleans, La., 5/17/93; d. Hollywood, Calif., 11/22/53. Member of the Original Dixieland Jazz Band (for details see La Rocca). After working for a while with the reassembled ODJB outfit in the late 1930s, Shields retired from music. Best remembered for his solo work on *Tiger Rag,* he was considered by many admirers to be the most talented soloist with the pioneer combo. LP on label "X" no longer available.

SHIHAB, SAHIB (Edmund Gregory), *alto* and *baritone sax, flute;* b. Savannah, Ga., 6/23/25. Stud. w. Elmer Snowden 1935-9; Boston Cons. '41-2. Got his prof. start w. Luther Henderson '38-9. Worked w. Larry Noble in Savannah '39-41; toured w. Fletcher Henderson '44-5, making his rec. debut w. him. Joined Roy Eldridge '45; Ray Perry in Boston '45-6; Phil Edmund, Boston '46-7; Buddy Johnson, NYC '47-8; Thelonious Monk, Tadd Dameron, other combos in NYC, '47-9; Art Blakey '49-50; Dizzy Gillespie '51-2, and off and on since then; I. Jacquet '52-5, touring Europe with him late '54. Between jobs worked as elevator operator '48, shipping clerk, real estate salesman, '50. In late '50s, free-lanced in NYC and worked w. Dakota Staton's accompanying unit. Excellent musician, product of bop era; aims to study arranging, more instruments, join radio house band. Favs.: Carter, Willie Smith, Parker, alto; Carney, Mulligan, Cecil Payne, baritone. Own LP on Savoy; LPs w. *Four Altos* (Pres.), w. Roy Haynes in *Jazz Abroad* (Em.), Thelonious Monk, Milt Jackson (Blue Note), Howard McGhee (Beth.), A. K. Salim (Savoy), Philly Joe Jones (River.).

Addr: 321 West 108th St., New York 25, N. Y.

SHIRLEY, DONALD (Don), *piano, composer;* b. Kingston, Jamaica, B.W.I., 1/29/27. Stud, first w. mother. At age 9 was invited to study w. Mittolovski at Leningrad Conservatory. Shirley, who comes from a fantastically learned family including innumerable uncles, brothers and other relatives most of whom are doctors as well as gifted musicians, himself has a B.A., M.A., and Ph.D. in psychology from Harvard Univ., and in

1952 earned a degree as Ph.D of Liturgical Art at Catholic University. Although George Shearing, Duke Ellington and Nat Cole, great admirers of Shirley, encouraged his entry into jazz, he is primarily a classical musician and has made numerous symphonic orchestra appearances. Igor Stravinsky said of him, "His virtuosity is worthy of gods." Own LPs: Cadence.

Addr: Carnegie Hall, West 57th St., New York 19, N. Y.

SHIRLEY, JAMES ARTHUR (Jimmy), *guitar;* b. Union, S. Car., 5/31/13. Raised in Cleveland, Ohio; stud. w. father. Played w. Frank Terry in Cincinnati, '34; own quartet (3 guitars, bass) '35-6; Clarence Profit trio '37-41, then own trio in Phila. Toured w. Ella Fitzgerald & The Four Keys, '42-3. Rejoined Profit shortly before his death in '43, then began a long association w. Herman Chittison, in whose trio he was featured (often at the Blue Angel, NYC) in 1943-4, '48, '51 and '54. Also had his own trio off and on and worked w. Phil Moore Four, Toy Wilson trio; acc. to Bill Williams' vocal quartet '50; Vin Strong '53. Shirley became known through the unique sound he obtained by using a "vibrola" attachment, giving his guitar a new sound. Rec. *Lucky So & So* w. Ella Fitzgerald; *Don't Take Your Love From Me* w. Artie Shaw; *Groovy Thing* w. Earl Bostic; *Jimmy's Blues* (Blue Note); albums w. Sid Catlett, Ram Ramirez, Chittison. LP w. Coleman Hawkins (Bruns.).

SHOFFNER, BOB, *trumpet;* b. Bessie, Tenn., 1900. Moved to St. Louis and app. with Charlie Creath; joined King Oliver in Chicago 1925, staying a year. He lost his lip but began practicing again in late '27 and resumed his career. Played w. Earl Hines, McKinney's Cotton Pickers; rec. with Jelly Roll Morton. Has been w. Franz Jackson in Chicago in recent years.

SHORT, ROBERT E. (Bob), *tuba;* also *trombone, cornet;* b. 8/26/11. Pl. with J. Teagarden's big band 1945; Castle Jazz Band '46-50; Turk Murphy '51-4, then rec. and played w. Bob Scobey. Rejoined Murphy Aug. '58. Fav. own solo: *See See Rider* w. Murphy (Col.). LPs w. Murphy (GTJ, Col., Roul.), Scobey (GTJ, Vict., Merc.), Castle Jazz Band (GTJ).

Addr: 719A Chestnut St., San Fancisco, Calif.

SHORT, ROBERT WALTRIP (Bobby), *singer, piano;* b. Danville, Ill., 9/15/26. School in Chicago. Self-taught musically. A child prodigy, he was in vaudeville from the age of 10. Featured at the Blue Angel in NYC, the Haig in LA, and the Gala in Hollywood. Short worked also at clubs in Paris and London, 1952-3, and acquired a reputation among society people for his interpretation of sophisticated lyrics. Although this has been his main appeal, some of his work is of interest from a jazz standpoint. LPs: Atl.

Addr: c/o Winkler, 215 S. La Cienega, Beverly Hills, Cal.

SHORTER, WAYNE, *tenor saxophone;* b. Newark, N.J., 8/25/33. Four years of mus. ed. at NYU. Army 1956-8; worked briefly w. Horace Silver during this time. After discharge Oct. '58, came to NYC to free-lance. Played a few weeks w. Maynard Ferguson July-Aug. '59, then joined Art Blakey. One of the most promising of the younger Rollins-influenced tenor men. Favs: Rollins, Coltrane, C. Hawkins. Own LP: Vee-Jay; LP w. Blakey (Blue Note).

Addr: 152 Pennsylvania Ave., Newark, N. J.

SHREVE, RICHARD G. (Dick), *piano, bass, trombone;* b. Kansas City, Mo., 8/16/28. Father, a doctor, pl. Dixieland trombone in KC; pl. piano w. his band '45. Stud. music 6 yrs. at Okla. U. Several months w. Les Brown '56; settled in LA, pl. w. Buddy Childers, Buddy Collette '56, then w. Howard Rumsey at Lighthouse from '57. Fav: Tatum. LPs w. Collette (ABC-Par.), Rumsey (Lib., Contemp.), M. Roach-S. Levey (Lib.).

SHU, EDDIE (Edward Shulman), *tenor sax, alto, clarinet;* also *trumpet, harmonica, composer, singer;* b. Brooklyn, N. Y., 8/18/18. Studied violin and guitar as a child. Joined Cappy Barra's harmonica band at 17; toured w. vaudeville units for Major Bowes, Benny Davis. Took up sax as hobby and within a month pl. his first gig. While in Hawaii w. harmonica duo on USO tour he enlisted in Army, Nov. 1942. Pl. clarinet and trumpet in military bands; did ventriloquist act for GIs throughout central Pacific.

After discharge in Nov. '45 he worked club dates as ventriloquist, pl. w. the bands of Ben Ribble (as ballad singer), Tadd Dameron; George Shearing '48; Johnny Bothwell, Buddy Rich, Les Elgart; six months w. Lionel Hampton '49-50; Ch. Barnet '50-1; Chubby Jackson '52; own band at Basin Street, NYC '53-4. Joined Gene Krupa's trio '54 and remained w. him until Jan. '58. Pl. in Cuba until Castro revolution incl. app. on Casino de la Allegria TV show. Since then working in Miami. A variable musician, Shu at his best is a first-class jazzman on every instrument he plays. Own LP on Beth.; LPs w. Krupa (Verve).

Addr: 1471 N.W. 64th Way, West Hollywood, Fla.

SHULMAN, JOSEPH (Joe), *bass;* b. New York City, 9/12/23; d. New York City 8/2/57. Self-taught. Pl. w. Scat Davis 1940; briefly w. Les Brown '42; US and overseas w. Glenn Miller AAF band '43-4 (rec. w. Django Reinhardt in Paris); discharged '45, joined Buddy Rich '46. In '47 he was w. Claude Thornhill, one of several members of that band who took part in the significant Miles Davis Capitol recordings. He later toured theatres w. Peggy Lee-Dave Barbour unit, '48 & '50; Lester Young '49; briefly w. Tristano, Bushkin et al in NYC; mainly w. Barbara Carroll Trio from '51 until his death; married Barbara Carroll '54. Shulman was greatly admired by many musicians, incl. Duke Ellington, with whom he once recorded. Favs: Ray Brown, Simmons, Hinton. LPs w. Barbara Carroll (Vict., Atl.), Miles Davis (Cap.), Lester Young (Verve).

SIGNORELLI, FRANK, *piano;* b. New York City, 5/24/01. Stud. with a cousin, Pasquale Signorelli. A pioneer of jazz, Signorelli worked in the Original Dixieland Jazz Band, the Original Memphis Five, and w. Paul Whiteman, Bix Beiderbecke, Joe Venuti, Eddie Lang, and Red Nichols. An important jazz figure in the '20s and early '30s, he has also had great success as a songwriter and became a member of ASCAP in '33. His biggest hits were *I'll Never Be the Same, Stairway to the Stars,* and *A Blues Serenade.* He has also written many piano solo pieces such as *Park Avenue Fantasy, Midnight Reflections, Caprice Futuristic.* In the late 1950s the Original Memphis Five, with some of the old personnel, including Signorelli, was revived for occasional radio and TV shows. Favs: Bob Zurke, Fats Waller. Own LPs: *Piano Moods* (Davis); *Ragtime Duo* (Kapp); w. Phil Napoleon (Em.).

Addr: 326 Avenue S, Brooklyn 23, N. Y.

SILVER, HORACE WARD MARTIN TAVARES, *piano, composer;* b. Norwalk, Conn., 9/2/28. Stud. sax in high school, piano privately with a church organist. Played local gigs on tenor sax and piano. While he was at the Sundown in Hartford w. Harold Holdt, Stan Getz heard him and hired him to tour with the Getz quintet. After a year w. Getz 1950-1, he made his home in NYC, working frequently w. Art Blakey 1951-2. Worked w. Terry Gibbs, Coleman Hawkins, 1952; Oscar Pettiford, Bill Harris, Lester Young, '53, and many other small combo jobs in the East. In addition to a distinctive touch and style, originally inspired by Bud Powell but more recently itself a source of inspiration and imitation, Silver showed great talent as a composer, recording many original works with his own quintet, which he has led since Sept. 1956. He won the DB New Star award on piano in the 1954 Critics' poll.

Own LPs on Blue Note: *Horace Silver & The Jazz Messengers* (1518), *Trio* (1520), *Six Pieces of Silver* (1539), *The Stylings of Silver* (1562), *Further Explorations* (1589), *Finger Poppin'* (4008), *Blowin' The Blues Away* (4017); *Silver's Blue* (Epic 3326). LPs w. Art Blakey (Blue Note 1507, 1508, 1521, 1522, Col. CL 897); Miles Davis (Pres. 7054, 7076, 7109, Blue Note 1502), Milt Jackson (Pres. 7059, 7003), Sonny Rollins (Blue Note 1558), Art Farmer (Pres. 7085, 7031), Kenny Dorham (Blue Note 1535), Lou Donaldson (Blue Note 1537), Gigi Gryce (Savoy 12137), Al Cohn (Savoy 12048), Phil Urso (Savoy 12056), P. Chambers (Blue Note 1534), Lee Morgan (Blue Note 1538, 1541), Hank Mobley (Blue Note 1540, 1544, 1550).

Addr: 23 West 76th Street, New York 23, N. Y.

SIMEON, OMER VICTOR, *clarinet, alto sax;* b. New Orleans, La., 7/21/02; d. New York City 9/17/59. Stud. w. Lorenzo Tio Jr. Worked in Chicago w. Ch. Elgar 1923-7; King Oliver '27; Erskine Tate '28-30; Regal Theatre house band '31; Earl Hines '31-7; Horace Henderson '37-8; Walter Fuller and Hines, '39-40; Coleman Hawkins, '40; J. Lunceford '42-7; after Lunceford died, stayed with the band under Ed Wilcox to '50. Free-lanced, NYC and Boston w. Bud Freeman, Bobby Hackett. Was almost continuously with the Wilbur De Paris combo from Oct. '51 until his death.

Simeon made many sessions w. recording combos incl. King Oliver 1927-8; Morton '26-8; Clarence Williams '28; Richard M. Jones, Alex Hill '29; Paul Mares '35; L. Hampton '38; Kid Ory '44-5. One of the best of the New Orleans clarinetists, he was heard to advantage on alto and bar. sax in his big band years. Favs: Noone, Dodds, Buster Bailey. LPs w. De Paris (Atl.), Paul Mares in *Chicago Style Jazz* (Col.), Kid Ory (Col., GTJ), Ed Hall (Rae-Cox).

SIMMONS, JOHN JACOB, *bass;* b. Haskell, Okla., 1918. Made prof. debut in San Diego and Los Angeles night clubs; discovered by John Hammond, he took part in the celebrated Teddy Wilson quartet date (with Harry James, Red Norvo), Sept. 1937, playing *Just a Mood,* etc. Later worked w. Jimmy Bell, Frank Derrick, Johnny Letman, Roy Eldridge, and briefly w. Benny Goodman in the summer of 1941. Joined Louis Armstrong's big band 1942; Eddie Heywood '45; Illinois Jacquet '46; Erroll Garner '50-2; sporadically active since then. LPs w. Art Tatum-Roy Eldridge, *Jam Session # 3 & 4,* Buddy Rich-Harry Edison (Verve), Matthew Gee (River.), Maynard Ferguson (Em.), Erroll Garner (Atl.), Tadd Dameron, John Coltrane (Pres.), Eddie Heywood-Billie Holiday (Comm.), Phineas Newborn (Roul.).

SIMON, MAURICE JAMES, *tenor sax;* also *baritone sax;* b. Houston, Tex., 3/26/29. Started under infl. of brother and sister, both musicians; pl. w. Anderson Lacy and Russell Jacquet bands in Texas, 1943-4. Moving to Los Angeles, worked w. Gerald Wilson; Joined Illinois Jacquet 1/1/49 for a year, playing baritone, then back to LA, where he and his brother Freddie had a group until 1953. Three months w. Amos Milburn, four months with C. Basie in 1953; later was around NYC with Cootie Williams. Formed group to back Billy Williams Quartet 1956; since then has done cabaret work backing Cab Calloway, Wild Bill Davis; in 1959 featured in Earl Grant's act at Copa, NYC, etc. LPs w. Davis: *My Fair Lady* (Everest); also sessions with R. & I. Jacquet for King, RCA. Plays in exciting, extroverted Jacquet-inspired style.

Addr: 2618 Dalton Ave., Los Angeles, Calif.

SIMONE, NINA (Eunice Waymon), *singer, piano;* b. Tryon, N.C., 2/21/33. One of eight children, all of whom sing or play an instrument. Left home for Philadelphia at 17, studying and teaching piano; later stud. at Juilliard. Worked for four years as accompanist to singers, then began to sing herself. Rose to national prominence with hit record of *Porgy* '59. Appeared at Playboy Jazz Festival. Originally influenced by Marion Anderson, later by Armstrong, Holiday, Vaughan, L. Jordan, Kitty White, she is less a jazz singer than the area of her acceptance would appear to indicate. Her recordings include several piano solos, of limited jazz interest. Own LPs: Beth., Colpix.

Addr: 336 Riverside Drive, New York 25, N.Y.

SIMONETTA, MICKEY, *drums, composer;* b. Chicago, Ill., 8/26/26. Stud. drums and percussion inst. privately and at Midwestern Cons. Pl. with Lennie Tristano and Bill Russo late 1940s; stud. at De Paul U; worked w. various singers and groups in Chicago: Jeri Southern, Erroll Garner et al; worked on NBC-TV. Favs: Shelly Manne, Don Lamond, Buddy Rich on drums; Bill Russo, Pete Rugolo, comp. LPs w. Bill Russo (Atl.); Jeri Southern (Decca).

Addr: 3937 W. Flournoy St., Chicago, Ill.

SIMPKINS, ANDREW, *bass;* b. Richmond, Ind., 4/29/32. Stud. clarinet at 10; piano at 14; pl. both through junior and senior high and two years at Wilberforce U. Became interested in bass just before entering Army in 1953, pl. it while in service. After discharge in '55, worked w. a number of small combos, then met Gene Harris and Bill Dowdy, becoming part of The Three Sounds. Favs: Ray Brown, Oscar Pettiford, Milt Hinton. LPs w. The Three Sounds, Lou Donaldson (Blue Note), Nat Adderley (River.).

SIMPSON, MIKE, *saxophones, clarinet, flute;* b. Winters, Tex., 9/1/16. Self-taught, began pl. with dance bands around Dallas in 1931; w. Art Kassel, Gene Krupa in '30s; worked at Chicago Theater '38-41; in Navy '42-5. Back to Chicago Theater '46-50 as arr. and sideman. On staff at CBS-TV in Chicago. Own LP, *Big Mike Simpson* (Con.-Disc); also date w. Jimmy Woode (Argo).

Addr: 5866 N. Kenneth, Chicago 30, Ill.

SIMS, RAY C., *trombone, singer;* b. Wichita, Kansas, 1/18/21. Brother of Zoot Sims. Started w. Jerry Wald, Bobby Sherwood; w. Benny Goodman 1947; Les Brown '49-58. Joined Harry James '58. Plays in a style similar to that of Bill Harris. LPs: see Brown; James (MGM); w. Frank Sinatra in *Swing Easy* (Cap.).

Addr: 143 W. 118th St., Hawthorne, Calif.

SIMS, JOHN HALEY (Zoot), *tenor sax, alto sax, clarinet;* b. Inglewood, Cal., 10/29/25. Clar. in grade sch. Pl. w. Kenny Baker '41; Bobby Sherwood '42-3; Sonny Dunham, Bob Astor, '43; Benny Goodman, Sid Catlett, '44. In Army 1944-6, then back with Goodman; Bill Harris Sextet at Cafe Society Uptown, 1946 (this group recorded under Joe Bushkin's name on Comm.). Best known as one of the "Four Brothers" sax team with Woody Herman, 1947-9. After this, free-lanced around New York for several years, also toured Europe 1950 with B. Goodman Sextet and '53 with Stan Kenton. Free-lanced in Calif. '54-5; in '56 began doubling on alto sax, toured Europe w. G. Mulligan sextet in spring. Toured w. Birdland All Stars early '57; formed a group w. Al Cohn summer '57 and has often teamed with him in clubs since then. To Europe w. Benny Goodman May '58 and w. *Jazz at Carnegie Hall* package Sept. '58, staying on continent for several months after the tour. Has occasionally rejoined Woody Herman. A consistently warm and fluently improvising musician, originally Young-inspired, with a light, personal sound and a pervasive beat. Favs: S. Stitt, Al Cohn. Own LPs: Argo, ABC-Par., River., Pres., Dawn; LPs w. Cohn on Vict., Coral, UA; LPs w. Herman (Cap., Col.), Kenton (Cap.), Goodman—*Benny In Brussels* (Col.), *The Brothers, Tenor Conclave, Down East* (Pres.), *Porgy And Bess, Stretching Out* (UA), Trigger Alpert (River.), Jutta Hipp (Blue Note), Chet Baker (Col.), Clifford Brown in *Arranged By Montrose* (Wor. Pac.), Gerry Mulligan (Em., Wor. Pac.), Ralph Burns (Decca), Miles Davis (Pres.), Elliot Lawrence (Fant., Top Rank), Joe Newman (Roul.), *Saxes, Inc.* (War. Bros.).

Addr: 102 Bedford St., New York, N.Y.

SINATRA, FRANCIS ALBERT (Frank), *singer;* b. Hoboken, N.J., 12/12/15. Sang w. Harry James 1939; Tommy Dorsey '40-2; started career as single in '43 and soon became an international name as movie, record and TV star. Though he is not basically a jazz performer, his quality of phrasing and beat have a tremendous appeal to jazz musicians. He has won the following awards: *Encycl. of Jazz* "Musicians' Musicians" poll; DB readers poll '42-3, '46-7, '54-9; Met. poll '43-48, '56-60; DB Int. Critics poll '57; Playboy poll '57-60; Playboy All Stars' All Stars poll '59-60. Own LPs on Cap., Col.; LPs w. T. Dorsey (Vict.), Met. All Stars (Harm.); cond. on *Tone Poems of Color* (Cap.).

Addr: c/o Lefkowitz & Berke, 465 S. Beverly Dr., Beverly Hills, Calif.

SINGER, HAROLD (Hal), *tenor sax;* b. Tulsa, Okla., 10/8/19. Violin at eight. Clarinet and saxophone in high school. Rec. degree in agriculture from Hampton Inst. Became prof. musician pl. w. bands around Okla. City during summer vacations. W. Ernie Fields in 1938, Nat Towles, Lloyd Hunter '39, Tommy Douglas in KC from late '39 to '41, then Jay McShann until '42. In NYC '42-7 w. Lips Page, Roy Eldridge, Don Byas, Red Allen and Sid Catlett on 52nd St. W. Lucky Millinder, Duke Ellington '48. r&b hit w. *Cornbread* on Savoy enabled him to take own group on the road. Toured US until May '58 when he became a regular at the Metropole, NYC. Favs: Byas, Hawkins, Webster, Jacquet, Rollins. Own LP on Prestige; LP w. Dickenson-Thomas (Atl.).

Addr: 126 Riverside Drive, New York 24, N.Y.

SINGER, LOUIS CHARLES (Lou), *composer;* b. New York City, 2/26/12. Stud. at Juilliard, Columbia U. and New York U.; was child prodigy on piano at five. Became interested in jazz after grad. from music schools; arr. for W. C. Handy's publishing firm, later at Mills Music. Has orchestrated for many bands incl. Duke Ellington, Woody Herman et al. Staff arr. at CBS for *Flow Gently Sweet Rhythm* and *Duffy's Tavern,* both w. John Kirby. Comp. many pop songs. Favs: Art Tatum, Teddy Wilson; Charlie Shavers, Fletcher Henderson, Duke Ellington as arr.

Addr: 9958 66th Ave., Forest Hills, L.I., N.Y.

SINGLETON, ARTHUR JAMES (Zutty), *drums;* b. Bunkie., La., 5/14/1898. School in New Orleans. Mainly self-taught, he played w. Steve Lewis, Big Eye Louis Nelson, 1920, then w. Tuxedo Band, John Robicheaux, Maple Leaf Band, and w. Charlie Creath and Fate Marable. In Chicago from 1925, worked w. Doc Cook, Dave Peyton, Jimmie Noone, '25-26; Clarence Jones, Carroll Dickerson, '27-8. Later in Chicago and New York w. Louis Armstrong, Alonzo Ross, Fats Waller, Vernon Andrade. With Roy Eldridge at Three Deuces, Chicago, '35-6; Bobby Hackett, Sidney Bechet and other combos at Nick's, etc. in NYC in late '30s. From 1941 he lived in California, appearing in the films *Stormy Weather* '43 and *New Orleans* '46 and working w. Nappy Lamare and other combos. From Nov. '51 to early '53 he was in Europe w. Mezzrow et al. Back in New York, '53-5, he played Dixieland jam sessions at Stuyvesant Casino etc. and in '59 had his own trio at the Metropole. Considered by traditionalist jazz fans to rank with Baby Dodds among the all-time leaders in his field, Zutty made his most famous records as a member of Louis Armstrong's Hot Five but has also contributed to sessions by Jelly Roll Morton (1929 and '39-40), Sidney Bechet, Pee Wee Russell, Lionel Hampton, Wingy Manone, Jack Teagarden, Fats Waller, Mildred Bailey, Buster Bailey, Joe Marsala, Red Allen, Slim Gaillard, Art Hodes, Joe Sullivan, etc. and sessions under his own name for Decca, 1935 and '40; Capitol, 1944.

LPs: own trio for one track in *History of Jazz, Vol. 1* (Cap.), Louis Armstrong (Col., Vict.), w. Jack Teagarden in *History of Jazz, Vol. 2* (Cap.), Jelly Roll Morton (Comm.), Charlie Parker (Savoy).

Addr: Hotel Alvin, 52nd St. & Broadway, New York 19, N.Y.

SISSLE, NOBLE, *leader, songwriter;* b. Indianapolis, Ind., 7/10/1889. Protégé of Jim Europe, in whose band he was drum major in World War I. After Europe's death during an American tour by the band after the war, Sissle took over leadership. Leading a commercial orchestra during the 1920s and '30s, and occasionally after that, he was never a jazz musician. Those who worked for him happened to include Sidney Bechet, Tommy Ladnier, Lena Horne and Buster Bailey, and some songs from the shows he wrote with Eubie Blake (*Shuffle Along,* 1921; *Chocolate Dandies,* 1924) were used by jazzmen. Own LP w. Eubie Blake on 20th Fox. See BLAKE, Eubie.

Addr: 935 St. Nicholas Avenue, New York, N.Y.

SKIDMORE, JAMES RICHARD (Jimmy), *tenor saxophone;* b. East Ham, London, England, 2/8/16. Own band, 1952; also pl. w. Geo. Shearing '42-5; Ralph Sharon '50-2, and w. Jack Parnell, Vic Lewis, Geo. Chisholm. Joined Humphrey Lyttelton, March 1956, visiting US with him fall '59. Favs: Chu Berry, L. Young, Lucky Thompson. Feat. on Vic Lewis rec. *Come Back to Sorrento.* LPs w. Lyttelton (London).

Addr: 7 Beech Drive, Boreham Wood, Herts, England.

SLACK, FREDDIE, *piano, composer, leader;* b. La Crosse, Wis., 8/7/10. Prominent from 1936 when he was heard w. Jimmy Dorsey, he was principal soloist in the Will Bradley-Ray McKinley band 1939-41, known almost exclusively for his boogie woogie work. He later led his own band intermittently, mostly in Calif. Own LP on EmArcy; LP w. Will Bradley (Epic).

Addr: 9803 Vidor Drive, Los Angeles 35, Calif.

SLAPIN, WILLIAM, *saxophones, piccolo, flute;* b. Cincinnati, Ohio, 9/6/29. Stud. clarinet first, then other inst. at Cincinnati Cons. of Music 1947-9; Mannes College of Music NYC '56. Pl. tenor w. Buddy Morrow '47; Hal McIntyre '49; Ray Anthony '51; w. Sauter-Finegan '55, mostly flute and piccolo; back to tenor w. Benny Goodman, whom he accompanied on the State Dept. tour of the Far East in '56; w. Johnny Richards and free-lance rec. since then. Favs: Zoot Sims, tenor; Sol Schlinger, bari. sax; Julius Baker, flute. LPs w. Johnny Richards (Cap., Roul.).

Addr: 207 Valley Road, River Edge, N.J.

SMITH, BESSIE, *singer, songwriter;* b. Chattanooga, Tenn., 4/15/1894; d. Clarksdale, Miss., 9/26/37. Born and raised in the most brutal of southern Negro poverty, she was in her teens when the touring unit known as Ma Rainey's Rabbit Foot Minstrels passed through Chattanooga and Ma Rainey, herself a pioneer blues singer, took Bessie on the road with the show. For several years she worked in honky tonks, carnivals and traveling tent shows. She was discovered and elevated to national success by Frank Walker, recording director for Columbia, who had heard her in an obscure club in Selma, Alabama. Anxious to record some authentic "country" Negro blues in contrast to the urban blues of Mamie Smith and others that had been popular up to that time, he sent pianist-composer Clarence Williams to find Bessie and bring her to NYC. She recorded her first session, accompanied by Williams, on Feb. 17, 1923. The Negro public in both the North and South accorded an unprecedented reception to the record. By the end of her first year as recording artist Bessie Smith had sold over two million records, was the headliner in Milton Starr's Negro vaudeville circuit, and was on her way to becoming the most successful Negro entertainer in the country.

In the years of her greatest fame, from 1924 to '27, she recorded frequently, accompanied by the great jazz artists of the day. Louis Armstrong, Joe Smith, Don Redman, James P. Johnson, Charlie Green and Fletcher Henderson were among those who participated in some of the most memorable sessions.

Married to Jack Gee, a Philadelphia policeman who at that time was handling her affairs, Bessie began slipping in about 1928 for a variety of reasons, among them the changing public taste, drastic revisions in the type of material she was recording, and her own increasing addiction to alcohol. By 1930 she was virtually washed up as a recording artist and the following year stopped recording entirely. She continued to tour in vaudeville, starring in her own show *Midnight Steppers* in 1929; and was seen in a Warner Bros. short, *St. Louis Blues;* in Nov. 1933, as a nostalgic tribute, John Hammond arranged what proved to be her final record session, accompanied by Frank Newton and an all-star band. She continued to struggle through the years, with only moderate public acceptance, until, one night in Sept. 1937, just before Hammond was to leave for Mississippi to bring her to NYC for another session, she was in an automobile crash. According to some reports, she was refused admission to a hospital because of her color and bled to death while being taken to another.

In her lifetime Bessie Smith, known as the "Empress of the Blues," was a big, tall, handsome woman who exercised a majestic control over her audiences. George Avakian described her as "a mistress of vocal inflection and an artist of impeccable taste . . . with a huge, sweeping voice which combined strength and even harshness with irresistible natural beauty." In the 1920s her audience was the American Negro public. During her declining years she was discovered by students of jazz and folk music; after her death her value as artist rather than as mere entertainer achieved full recognition. Shortly after she died John Hammond wrote: "To my way of thinking, Bessie Smith was the greatest artist American jazz ever produced; in fact, I'm not sure that her art did not reach beyond the limits of the term 'jazz.' She was one of those rare beings, a completely integrated artist capable of projecting her whole personality into music." She won R. Ch. All Time, All Star poll, 1951.

A documentation of the Bessie Smith story by George Avakian appears on the liners of four 12-inch LPs which include many of her greatest records: Col. CL 855 (w. Louis Armstrong), CL 856 (*Blues To Barrelhouse*), CL 857 (w. Joe Smith and Fletcher Henderson), CL 858 (w. James P. Johnson and Charlie Green). She has single tracks in the following albums: *The Jazz Makers* (Col. CL 1036), *History of Classic Jazz* (River. SDP 11), *Great Blues Singers* (River. 12-121). In 1958 LPs of songs made famous by Bessie Smith were released: *Dinah Washington Sings Bessie Smith* (Em.), *Lavern Baker Sings Bessie Smith* (Atl.), *The Legend of Bessie Smith* sung by Ronnie Gilbert (Vict.), *Juanita Hall Sings the Blues* (Counter.).

SMITH, HENRY (Buster), *alto sax, clarinet;* b. Ellis County, Tex., 8/26/04. Largely self-taught, he began working w. local bands in Dallas. In 1926 he joined Walter Page's Blue Devils and when Page, Jimmy Rushing and Hot Lips Page left that group to join Bennie Moten, he kept leadership of the Blue Devils, took it on the road, but was soon back in Kansas City, joining Moten. When C. Basie took a small group from the remnants of this band after Moten's death, Smith was part of it at Reno Club, KC, 1936, and contributed a portion of the book. However, when Basie went North, Smith, who had no faith in the enterprise, remained in KC and the Southwest playing w. Andy Kirk, Claude Hopkins and various other groups; later came to NYC as arr. for Basie, B. Carter et al. In '41 Smith returned to Dallas and has been there since w. own small combo. According to many musicians, C. Parker's favorite was Buster Smith; in '37 Parker had been a part of Smith's KC group. He once said, "Buster was the guy I really dug." Until his rediscovery by critics in late '50's Smith had been heard only rarely on recs. w. Pete Johnson, Snub Mosley, Ed Durham. Favs: Parker, Hawkins, Webster, Tatum. Fav. own solo: *Moten Swing* w. Durham in *Kansas City Jazz* (Decca). Own LP: Atlantic.

SMITH, CARSON RAYMOND, *bass;* b. San Francisco, Cal. 1/9/31. Bass in jr. high sch. at 13. Worked w. commercial bands, then ten months w. Gerry Mulligan; a year w. Chet Baker '54; Russ Freeman '55; Chico Hamilton '56-7; recordings etc. around LA and toured w. Stan Kenton '59. LPs w. Chico Hamilton, Chet Baker, Gerry Mulligan, Dick Twardzik (Wor. Pac.).

Addr: 5421 San Vicente Blvd., Los Angeles 19, Cal.

SMITH, CHARLES (Charlie), *drums;* b. New York City, 4/15/27. Raised on Long Island, N.Y. Started gigging 1947; joined trio acc. Ella Fitzgerald (w. Hank Jones, Ray Brown) '48. Has worked w. numerous combos in the East incl. Erroll Garner, Benny Goodman, Oscar Peterson, Artie Shaw, Joe Bushkin, Slam Stewart; also briefly w. Duke Ellington. W. Billy Taylor trio '52-4, Aaron Bell trio '54-6. Jobbed around NYC since w. Bell, etc.; mainly w. Wild Bill Davison '59. LPs: own trio on half of *Jazzville, Vol. 3* (Dawn); LPs w. Billy Taylor (Pres.), Aaron Bell (Herald).

SMITH, DEREK G., *piano;* b. Stratford, England, 4/17/31. Stud. from 1938, led local band '44. Worked for insurance co. for several years before entering RAF and again after discharge in '51, also playing club dates with Kenny Graham et al. Became full-time musician '54 w. Johnny Dankworth band. After 16 months w. Dankworth, worked for a year with a small combo, then emigrated to US April '57. Resumed insurance work, also demonstrated sheet music at Macy's before reentering jazz. Many gigs in trio w. Mel Zelnick and John Drew. Incisive, confident style and good technique mark him as promising newcomer. LPs: three tracks on *Jazz Piano International* (Atl.).

Addr: 410 West End Ave., New York 24, N.Y.

SMITH, ELSIE, *tenor sax, clarinet;* b. New Iberia, La., 12/9/32. Stud. in LA from 1947. St. w. Frances Gray '51; toured w. Lionel Hampton '52-3; w. Fred Skinner on West Coast '53-4; own group, '55-6, then rejoined Hampton Sept. '56. Favs: Getz, Webster, Byas, De Franco.

Addr: 2923 S. Genesee Ave., Los Angeles, Calif.

SMITH, FLOYD (Wonderful), *guitar;* b. St. Louis, Mo., 1/25/17. Son of a drummer, he stud. music locally at the Victor Hugo School after early instruction on ukulele in 1932. Played banjo w. Eddie Johnson and Dewey Jackson for 2 years, then w. Jeter-Pillars orch., with whom he made first records for Bruns. After an appearance w. Sunset Royal Entertainers at Harlem's Apollo Theatre, joined Andy Kirk's band, Jan. 1939, rec. w. Kirk *Floyd's Guitar Blues*, first jazz elec. guitar record of note, and stayed until May '42, when he entered the service. Worked w. Wild Bill Davis, Ravens, and w. various St. Louis groups. Most recently w. drummer Chris Columbus' group. Rec. w. Kirk (Decca), Davis (Everest, Epic). Fav: Segovia.

Addr: 1701 Pendleton Ave., St. Louis, Mo.

SMITH, HOWARD, *piano, composer;* b. Ardmore, Okla., 10/19/10. Spent much of his youth in Canada. To NYC 1933. Pl. w. Irving Aaronson, Isham Jones; Benny Goodman at Music Hall '34; Ray Noble's first US band; rec. w. Red Norvo '36, Glenn Miller '37. Toured w. Tommy Dorsey Apr. '37 to Feb. '40. Best known as pianist on Dorsey's *Boogie Woogie* (arr. Deane Kincaide). Arr. for Dorsey: *Nola.* Since 1940, on staff at CBS, NYC. Garry Moore TV show etc. LP w. Dorsey (Vict.).

Addr: 2 Beekman Place, New York, N.Y.

SMITH, CLADYS (Jabbo), *trumpet, singer, leader;* b. Claxton, Ga., 1908. Prominent in 1920s w. Cecil Scott, Charlie Johnson and Erskine Tate, he recorded w. Duke Ellington in 1927, w. Fats Waller and the Louisiana Sugar Babes '28. From '28-35 he led his own group off and on in the midwest; from '35-8 he was w. Claude Hopkins.

SMITH, JAMES OSCAR (Jimmy), *organ;* b. Norristown, Pa., 12/8/25. Both parents pianists. At age of 9 won a Major Bowes Amateur Show, appeared as pianist on Philadelphia radio programs. In 1942 teamed with his father in song and dance routine for local night club work. Served with Navy in the Pacific; later had his first formal training in Philadelphia, stud. string bass at Hamilton School of Music, '48, and piano at Ornstein School '49-50. Joined a group called Don Gardner and His Sonotones, '52, first playing piano, then organ. Formed his own trio, Sept., '55.

Jimmy Smith was perhaps the most extraordinary new instrumental jazz star to rise to prominence in '56. His relationship to previous jazz exponents of the Hammond organ parallels those of Ch. Christian and Jimmy Blanton to earlier guitarists and bassists. He uses a far greater variety of stops and has a unique gift for astonishing improvisations at fast tempi, producing unique tone colors and showing phenomenal technique with both hands and feet. His New York debut leading his trio at the Bohemia, early '56, was considered by many musicians an event of unprecedented interest. He subsequently appeared at the Newport Jazz Festival, Birdland and other jazz spots with great success. Many LPs, all on Blue Note.

Addr: c/o Blue Note Records, 47 West 63rd Street, New York 23, N.Y.

SMITH, JOE, *trumpet;* b. Ripley, Ohio, 6/28/02; d. New York City, 12/2/37. After working around St. Louis with small combos, he came to NYC and was hired by Fletcher Henderson, for whom he worked off and on during the '20s, sometimes in Henderson's full band; also acc. many blues singers, among them Bessie Smith, Ma Rainey and Ethel Waters. He worked w. Bennie Moten's band for a while and was w. McKinney's Cotton Pickers intermittently from 1929-34, but after his health broke down in the 1930s he worked infrequently; most of the last four years of his life were spent in a Long Island hospital. A spirited, sensitive artist whose tone and warmth of style led some listeners to compare him with Bix Beiderbecke, he ranked with Tommy Ladnier among the most underrated trumpet players of the '20s. LPs w. Bessie Smith (Col.), Fletcher Henderson (River.).

SMITH, JOHN HENRY, JR. (Johnny), *guitar;* also *trumpet, violin;* b. Birmingham, Ala., 6/25/22. Self-taught. To Portland, Me. at 13; prof. debut pl. hillbilly music. Fenton Bros. band '39; trio in Boston '40-1; Army '42-6, pl. tpt. in Air Force band, vln. & viola in concert group, guitar w. Eugene Ormandy & Phila. Orch. NBC staff in NYC '47-53, pl. guitar, tpt. w. pop & symph. orchs. While at NBC, started jazz quintet and rec. *Moonlight in Vermont,* voted one of two top jazz recs. of '52 in DB poll. Heard often at Birdland leading own groups '53-60. Won DB poll '54; Met. poll '54-5; DB critics' poll as new star '53. Favs: Segovia, J. Raney, T. Farlow, C. Wayne. Own LPs: Roost; LPs w. Benny Goodman (Col.); as Sir Jonathan Gasser in *Jazz Studio 1* (Decca).

Addr: 9-22 College Place, College Point 56, L.I., N.Y.

SMITH, JOHN ROBERT (Johnny), *organ, piano;* b. Louisville, Ky., 12/16/33. Studied piano w. private teacher at age 13. St. pl. prof. at 15 w. Kenny Hale. Later w. Paul Williams and Chris Columbus. Favs: Wild Bill Davis, Art Tatum. Own LPs on New Jazz.

Addr: 1051 E. 125th St., Cleveland, Ohio.

SMITH, KEELY (Dorothy Jacqueline Keely Smith Prima), *singer;* b. Norfolk, Va., 3/9/32. Sang on Joe Brown's children's show, later with Norfolk bands. Joined Louis Prima 1948 and has been with him ever since; married Prima 7/13/53. Popular jazz-influenced comedienne-vocalist, seen with Prima in Las Vegas night clubs etc. Films: *Hey Boy, Hey Girl* (for which she and Prima wrote part of score); *Thunder Road.* Best known rec. w. Prima, *That Old Black Magic,* won NARAS award. Heard on Capitol recs. until May '59, when they switched to Dot. Own LPs and LP w. Prima (Capitol, Dot).

Addr: 554 Barbara Way, Las Vegas, Nev.

SMITH, EDWARD LOUIS, *trumpet;* b. Memphis, Tenn., 5/20/31. Began stud. trumpet 1944, later pl. in high school band. Scholarship to Tennessee State U. where he majored in music. Pl. with the Tennessee State Collegians in Carnegie Hall concert. Postgrad. work at

U. of Michigan, where he stud. trumpet under Prof. Clifford Lillya. In Army, Jan. 1954-5; played in the Third Army Special Services unit. In 1955 he began teaching instrumental music at Booker T. Washington High School in Atlanta, Ga. Toured with Horace Silver combo for three months in '58, then returned to teaching school. Was praised by some critics as promising new star in neo-bop style on release of his first record. Favs: F. Navarro, Clifford Brown, C. Parker. Own LPs: Blue Note; LPs w. Kenny Burrell (Blue Note); *Down Home Reunion* (UA).

Addr: 361 Ashby Street N.W., Atlanta, Ga.

SMITH, MAMIE, *singer;* b. Cincinnati, O., 9/16/1890; d. New York City, 10/30/46. Believed to have been the first Negro singer to have made phonograph records (1920), she was best known for *Crazy Blues.* In the early 1920s she toured with an accompanying band that included Coleman Hawkins, Bubber Miley and Perry Bradford; the group was known as Mamie Smith's Jazz Hounds. The dozens of songs (mostly blues) recorded by her for Okeh have long been unavailable.

SMITH, MABEL (Big Maybelle), *singer;* b. Jackson, Tenn., 1924. Sang blues as a child; also was member of Sanctified Church choir. Won vocal contest at 9 in Memphis Cotton Carnival. First sang w. Dave Clark in Memphis; later w. T. Bradshaw, 1947-50, then as a single. Does a great deal of pop material as well as blues, but whatever she does comes out in the traditional blues shouting style. Is very successful in rock-'n'-roll concerts and on records, first for Okeh, currently with Sav. Her appearance at the 1958 Newport Festival was featured in the film *Jazz on a Summer's Day.*

Addr: c/o Associated Booking Corp., 745 Fifth Ave., New York 22, N.Y.

SMITH, PAUL THATCHER, *piano, organ;* b. San Diego, Cal., 4/17/22. Father played trumpet; mother was vaudeville star. Stud. in San Diego with organist Royal Brown. Left home as ward of Johnny Richards, in whose band he played in 1941. Joined Ozzie Nelson, 1942. During Army service, 1943-5, played in band under Ziggy Elman and was also stationed in Germany as MP. Feat. w. Les Paul trio, '46-7; accompanist to Andrews Sisters, 1947. Toured w. Tommy Dorsey, '47-8. After settling in Hollywood, 1949, he recorded with own trio, also many pop dates, radio and TV. Favs: Peterson, Shearing, Stan Freeman. Own LPs: Cap., Savoy, Tampa; LPs w. Dizzy Gillespie (Savoy), Anita O'Day (Verve).

Addr: 17737 Alonzo Place, Encino, Cal.

SMITH, CLARENCE (Pinetop), *piano, singer, songwriter;* b. Troy, Ala., 6/11/04; d. Chicago, Ill., 3/14/29. While in his teens he moved to Birmingham, and at sixteen to Pittsburgh, working in Negro night clubs and theatres as pianist, comedian and tap-dancer. For several years he played vaudeville on the TOBA circuit as a soloist and in a unit w. Ma and Pa Rainey, Butterbeans and Susie and other popular acts. He made his first record date Dec. 1928 for Brunswick in Chicago and his second and last shortly before he died in a brawl in a Chicago Masonic Hall. It was not until six years after his death that his original piano solo with monologue, *Pinetop's Boogie Woogie,* was recorded by Cleo Brown and achieved great popularity. According to Dave Dexter, "Smith pioneered boogie woogie, developed the richly rhythmic eight-to-a-bar manner of playing, and recorded some of the greatest examples in history." LP: three tracks in *Piano Jazz, Vol. 1* (Bruns.).

SMITH, HEZEKIAH LEROY GORDON (Stuff), *violin, singer, songwriter, leader;* b. Portsmouth, Ohio, 8/14/09. Raised in Cleveland; studied with his father. He began his career with a musical unit in 1924; worked w. Alphonse Trent's orch. in Dallas, 1926-9; had his own band, mostly around Buffalo, N.Y. from 1930 and became one of the new heroes of the swing era when he brought a sextet into the Onyx Club on 52nd St. late in 1935, registering with the general public through a nonsensical novelty song, *I'se A Muggin',* with which he made his record debut on Vocalion 2/11/36.

Stuff, who broke all the traditional violin rules, played an amplified violin, gave the rhythmic beat precedence over academic accuracy, and frequently sang, in a hoarsely attractive voice. During the 1940s he worked mostly with a trio. In the '50s, though still working, mainly in small clubs and occasionally on TV, he experienced little or none of the resurgence of popularity enjoyed by other great jazzmen of the 1930s and was largely unappreciated by all but musicians. His unique style, which made him the first real barrelhouse-jazz violinist, was imitated by the few jazz violinists who appeared later. He composed *Time and Again* (rec. by Sarah Vaughan), *Desert Sands, Skip It, Midway* etc. Critics Inez Cavanaugh and Timmie Rosenkrantz described Stuff as the "palpitating Paganini," and as "one of the unique musicians of our time, completely unorthodox in style and technique; one of the great jazzmen who dared to be different." He won Esq. Silver Award 1946. Own LPs incl. *Stuff Smith With Dizzy Gillespie* (Verve); 20th Cent. Fox; LPs w. Nat Cole (Cap.), one track in *Jazztime, U.S.A., Vol. 2* (Bruns.), Dizzy Gillespie (Savoy).

Addr: 2039 Claudina St., Los Angeles 16, Calif.

SMITH, TALMADGE (Tab), *alto sax, tenor sax, leader;* b. Kingston, N.C., 1909. Started on C melody sax at thirteen. Prof. debut w. Carolina Stompers 1929; worked w. Fate Marable, Dewey Jackson, Eddie Johnson in early '30s. First prominent as jazzman while w. Lucky Millinder 1935-9. Count Basie, 1940-2; Millinder '42-3, then formed own combo, with which he had considerable success from the late 1940s as a rhythm and blues attraction, playing with a full, lush tone and style and capable of generating a fine beat. LPs: three tracks w. Frankie Newton in *Trumpeters Holiday* (Epic); Count Basie (Epic).

Addr: 5237 Mossitt Street, St. Louis 13, Mo.

SMITH, WARREN DOYLE, *trombone;* b. Middlebourne, W. Va., 5/17/08. From musical family, stud. piano at age seven; went to Texas at 12; learned to play father's cornet and sax. Toured w. a small band and at 16 joined Harrison's Texans. Went to Chicago in the late twenties; joined Abe Lyman '29-35, then w. Bob Crosby '37-40. Jobbed around Chicago until '45, then went to Calif. where he pl. with Pete Daily. Pl. with Duke Ellington's orch. at the Aquashow on Long Island summer '55. Rec. with Crosby.

Addr: 14749 Hesby St., Sherman Oaks, Calif.

SMITH, WILLIAM McLEISH (Willie), *alto sax, clarinet, singer;* b. Charleston, S.C., 11/25/08. Started on clarinet at ten. While attending Fisk Univ. in Nashville, Tenn. he met Jimmie Lunceford, in whose orch. he played from 1930 to '41. After working with Ch. Spivak in 1942 he entered the Navy and headed an impressive group of star jazzmen stationed at Great Lakes in Chicago. Discharged late in '44, he joined Harry James, with whom he remained until March 1951, when he joined Duke Ellington. Late in 1952 he worked w. Billy May; soon after, he toured with JATP, visiting Europe with the unit early in 1953. He later settled in Calif. and rejoined Harry James. He won *Esquire* Armed Services Award 1945, Silver Award 1947.

To many critics and musicians Willie Smith ranked with Johnny Hodges and Benny Carter as one of the three great alto saxmen of the 1930s. His buoyant, happy tone and rhythmic style, employing fewer glissandi than Hodges, was one of the most distinctive characteristics of the Lunceford band. He has also shown talent as a clarinetist (notably on Lunceford's *Sophisticated Lady, Rose Room* and *What's Your Story Morning Glory*) and occasional vocalist (*Wham, Put It Away, Rhythm Is Our Business* with Lunceford). LPs w. JATP, *Alto Saxes, The Jazz Scene,* Gene Krupa (Verve), Nat Cole (Cap.), Harry James (MGM, Col., Cap.), *Session At Midnight* (Cap.), Red Norvo (Vict.), *Jam Session* (Verve).

Addr: 3485 3rd Ave., Los Angeles 18, Calif.

SMITH, WILLIAM HENRY JOSEPH BERTHOL BONAPARTE BERTHOLOFF (Willie the Lion), *piano, composer;* b. Goshen, N.Y., 11/23/1897, of Jewish and Negro parentage. Father died in 1901; Willie later took the name of his stepfather, Smith. Prof. debut in Newark, N.J. 1914; toured Europe 1917. During World War I he stayed at the front for 33 days with the 350th Field Artillery, scoring several direct hits; it was for his bravery here that he earned his nickname. He had his own band at Leroy's in Harlem in 1920. During the 1920s he toured Canada and the US, working mostly as a single. He played at the original Onyx Club on 52nd St. in prohibition days and spent a year at Pod's and Jerry's, a famous Harlem club.

He remained almost unknown to the public until 1935, when he began recording regularly for Decca with his combos; later in a series of trio sides w. Milt Herth. During the 1940s he continued to free-lance in NYC clubs, playing w. Max Kaminsky at the Pied Piper in Greenwich Village, 1944. He toured Europe and N. Africa 1949-50. Appeared at the Newport Festival in '58 and was a regular at the Central Plaza sessions in NYC during the '50s.

The Lion, whose cigar and bombastic talk were from his earliest years as much of a legend as his musicianship, is one of the true originals of jazz piano history. His lacy, charming melodies sometimes contrast with stride passages of great intensity. Duke Ellington, who has always considered him a unique and peerless phenomenon, once dedicated a composition to him: *Portrait of the Lion.*

Own LPs: Gr. Award, Uran., Dot, Comm.; LPs w. Feather-Hyman, *The Seven Ages of Jazz* (Metrojazz); *The Jazz Story w. Steve Allen* (Coral).

Addr: 300 West 151st Street, New York 30, N. Y.

SMYTH, GLORIA, *singer;* b. Hackensack, N. J., 3/8/34. Started singing in 1951, appearing w. Erskine Hawkins at the Apollo Theater, NYC. Sang in Bermuda '54, Miami '55, Oahada '56, Howard Theater, Wash., D.C., '57, Las Vegas '58, Mister Kelly's in Chi. and Vanguard, NYC '59. Most imp. infl: Ella Fitzgerald. Favs: Lena Horne, Pearl Bailey. Recs. for Sierra, Wor. Pac.

Addr: 172 Stanley Place, Hackensack, N.J.

SNOWDEN, ELMER CHESTER (Pops), *saxophones, guitar, banjo;* b. Baltimore, Md., 10/9/00. Started locally w. Eubie Blake. Had own combo in Washington, D.C., in 1921 w. Sonny Greer, Otto Hardwicke, which travelled to NYC in '23 on the promise that F. Waller would join them. When he did not, D. Ellington was sent for and the group became "The Washingtonians." During the late '20s and early '30s, in NYC, he led successful groups w. many famous jazzmen. At the Bambille in Harlem ('27), he had Count (then Bill) Basie, Claude Hopkins, J. Lunceford, Bubber Miley, Frankie Newton, "Tricky Sam" Nanton, C. Webb and B. Carter. At the Hot Feet Club in Greenwich Village ('28-9), he had Waller, Garvin Bushell, Hardwicke, Webb and others.

During 1930 at The Nest, he feat. Rex Stewart, Jimmy Harrison, Prince Robinson, Joe Garland, Freddy Johnson. From '31-33 he led a very famous band at Smalls' Paradise, which feat. S. Catlett, R. Eldridge, Gus Aiken, D. Wells, Bushell, Al Sears, Hardwicke. This group made several short films for Warner Bros. He was also in the band of Ford Dabney for *Keep Shufflin'* in '28 and w. Eubie Blake for *Blackbirds of* 1930.

From 1923 on he rec. for almost every label in NYC under a variety of pseudonyms: "Sepia Serenaders" for Vict. and Bluebird, "Red Hot Eskimos" for Col., for the Canadian label Ajax, w. a variety of blues

singers, etc. He is still active; visited Canada in '56 and has appeared at the Central Plaza, Jimmy Ryan's and The Metropole in NYC. Fav. own records: *West Indian Blues* (Viola McCoy, Vocalion), *I Ain't Got Nobody* (Bessie Smith, Col.), *Breaking the Ice* (Sepia Serenaders, Bluebird). Favs: Eddie Peabody, banjo; J. Smith, T. Farlowe, O. Moore, guitar.
Addr: 699 N. Broad St., Philadelphia, Pa.

SOCOLOW, FRANK, *tenor sax, clarinet;* b. Brooklyn, N. Y., 9/18/23. Stud. clarinet w. Leon Russianoff at 13. Played w. Jack Melvin, 1941; Geo. Auld, '42, later w. Ted Fio Rito, Roy Stevens, Van Alexander, Shep Fields; Boyd Raeburn, '44; Buddy Rich; Chubby Jackson's big band and combo, touring Scandinavia with him winter 1947-8; Artie Shaw, '49-50, then freelanced around NYC, app. mostly w. Johnny Richards orch. in late '50s. Film: *Visit To A Small Planet* w. Jerry Lewis. Film sound track: *Kiss Her Goodbye w.* Johnny Richards. Favs: Sims, Lester Young, Getz, Al Cohn. Own LP on Beth.; LPs w. Richards (Coral, Cap.); *Bird's Night* (Savoy), *Something New, Something Blue* (Col.).
Addr: 5400 Fieldston Road, Riverdale 71, N.Y.

SOLAL, MARTIAL, *piano, composer;* also *clarinet, saxophone;* b. Algiers, N. Africa, 8/23/27. St. on piano in Algiers at 7 and decided in 1940 to take up jazz. Settling later in Paris, he pl. at the Club St. Germain for several years, working w. Jay Jay Johnson, K. Clarke, L. Thompson, Don Byas and other visiting American stars. Has won several awards, incl. the Prix Django Reinhardt, Grand Prix du Disque, and Prix Jazz Hot. With Bernard Peiffer's departure to the US, Solal immediately earned the position of outstanding pianist in Paris. Has recently been writing music for films. Fav. own solo: *The Squirrel,* w. K. Clarke (Epic). Favs: A. Tatum, Bud Powell. LPs w. S. Bechet (Wor. Pac.), L. Thompson (Dawn), K. Clarke (Epic), *Jazz on the Left Bank,* w. Billy Byers, Dick Mills et al (Epic), *One World Jazz* (Col.).
Addr: 201 Rue de Temple, Paris 3, France.

SOLOMON, JOHANN (Hans), *tenor and alto saxes, clarinet;* b. Vienna, Austria, 9/10/33. Stud. clar. w. Hans Koller, Karl Kowarik, then played in American-sponsored youth club in Vienna. Later pl. w. Dr. Roland Kovacs, Friedrich Gulda; guest soloist w. Lionel Hampton at concert, 1954; also jammed w. many visiting U.S. jazzmen. Feat. in concert of modern music w. Vienna Symphoniker, 1958. Won poll on alto in German magazine *Podium* for past 3 years. Rec. w. Hans Koller, Johannes Fehring. Sound tracks for many Austrian movies; 12 jazz shows w. Gulda for Vienna Radio; several TV shows in Vienna, one w. Johnny Ray. After appearing w. the Newport International Band at NJF and Brussels World's Fair, summer '58, he returned to Vienna for jazz and commercial night club work on tenor. Favs: Konitz, Parker, Getz, Mulligan, Davis. LP w. Newport International Band (Col.).
Addr: Vienna 9, Sechsschimmelgasse 4/19, Austria.

SOMMER, THEODORE (Teddy), *drums, vibes, percussion;* b. New York City, 6/16/24. Stud. violin six months at age of seven; began drums w. private teacher at 14; stud. comp. and percussion at Manhattan School of Music 1947-50. Pl. with children's band in Catskills; w. Ina Ray Hutton briefly '46; in Chicago '50-3 w. band at Hotel Sherman; Les Elgart '54-5 playing one-nighters; w. Neal Hefti briefly '55. Since '55 has done free-lance TV work and recording in NYC. Has written an album for percussion. Favs: Don Lamond, drums; Milt Jackson, vibes; Alfred Friese, tympani. LPs w. Woody Herman (Cap.), Pete Rugolo (Col.), Candido (ABC), Tito Puente, *Drum Suite* w. Ernie Wilkins (Vict.); Joe Puma (Beth.).

SONN, LAWRENCE (Larry), *composer, trumpet, piano;* b. Long Island, N.Y., 1/17/24. Stud. Juilliard. Worked w. Teddy Powell, Bobby Byrne, Vincent Lopez. Had his own orch. for 8 years in Mexico, frequently playing before 80,000 people in the world's largest bullfight arena. Ret. to NYC and organized new band July '55, with which he has been intermittently active in the East. Fav. own solo: *La Virgen de la Macarena* (*The Brave Bulls*) rec. by Columbia in Mexico. Favs: Ch. Shavers, Billy Butterfield. Own LPs: Coral.
Addr: 229-03 Grand Central Pkway., Bayside 64, L.I., N.Y.

SOUCHON, EDMOND II, M.D. (Doc), *guitar, banjo, singer;* b. New Orleans, 10/25/1897. Father played guitar, French horn. Dr. Souchon, who obtained an informal musical education from Negro guitarists around New Orleans and the Gulf Coast, is a prominent and successful surgeon, practicing at Mercy Hosp. and Hôtel Dieu; this has been his profession since 1923, but avocationally he has been intensely active in New Orleans jazz since 1946, notably as key figure in New Orleans Jazz Club and editor of its publication, The Second Line. He donated to the NO Public Library 4000 records and books, with which they opened what was probably the first public library for jazz study in the US. Favs: Snoozer Quinn, Ed Lang, Lonnie Johnson. Own LP: South.; LPs w. *The Six and Seven-Eighths String Band* (Folk.); vocals on *Recorded in New Orleans, Vol. 2,* (GTJ), *Dixieland of Old New Orleans* (Gold. Cr.) w. Johnny Wiggs; Merle Koch (Carn.).
Addr: 2400 Canal, Suite 301, New Orleans 19, La.

SOUTH, EDDIE, *violin;* b. Louisiana, Mo., 11/27/04. Extensive studies from age ten w. private teachers, later at Chicago Coll. of Mus. and in Paris, Budapest. Pl. w. Jimmy Wade, Charlie Elgar and Erskine Tate orchs. in early 1920s; toured Europe w. his own combo '27-31 and '37-8. In almost two decades of night club work, South constantly displayed matchless artistry. Probably the finest musician to play authentic jazz violin, he would have been perfectly equipped to dedicate himself completely to a concert career, but because this field did not become sufficiently inclusive until recently he was never afforded adequate exposure for his talents.

In '45-6 he was heard daily with the studio band at WMGM, NYC; in the '50s he occasionally did TV shows w. Dave Garroway; Fran Allison, Herb Lyons, WGN, Chicago. His best records from the jazz standpoint were made in France in '37 when he was teamed w. Django Reinhardt and Stephane Grappelly. Own LPs on Mercury.

Addr: Mansfield Hotel, 6434 Cottage Grove, Chicago, Ill.

SOUTH, HENRY P. (Harry), *piano, composer;* also *drums, vibes;* b. London, England, 9/7/29. Stud. arranging during year spent in hospital. Pl. w. Basil Kirchin 1953-4 as pianist & arr. Staff arr. w. Ronnie Scott 1954; arr. & piano w. Tony Crombie '55; Tubby Hayes '56-7; Joe Harriott '58-9. Has also worked w. Dizzy Reece Quintet '57, and short stints w. Jimmy Deuchar, Harry Klein, Tony Hall All Stars et al. Main infl: J. Deuchar. Favs: Powell, Silver, Monk, Red Garland, Hank Jones. Many orig. comps. rec. by Ronnie Ross, Humphrey Lyttelton and bands named above. Rec. w. Hayes (Savoy), Deuchar (Tempo), Crombie (Eng. Decca), Harriott (Pye-Nixa), etc.

Addr: 57 Westside, Wandsworth Common, London S.W. 18, England.

SOUTHERN, JERI, *singer, piano;* b. Royal, Neb., 8/5/26. Fifteen years of classical piano study from age five. Prof. debut 1944 in Omaha hotel. After several years as intermission pianist in Chicago night clubs she began to attract attention as vocalist around 1950. She sings in a languid, casual style in which understatement is the keynote. Scored her first record hit with *You'd Better Go Now,* her initial Decca release. Tied for New Star Award, DB critics poll 1953. Own LPs: Decca, Roulette, Capitol.

Addr: c/o Premiere Attractions, 1046 North Carol Drive, Hollywood, Calif.

SOWDEN, JOHN EDWIN GEOFFREY (Geoff), *leader, trombone;* b. Leeds, Yorkshire, England, 6/30/24. Pl. w. Freddy Randall '48-9; Joe Daniels '50-1, own band from '52. Many broadcasts w. BBC Rhythm Club etc. Favs: Teagarden, L. McGarity, G. Chisholm.

Addr: c/o National Jazz Federation, 37 Soho Sq., London W.1, England.

SPANIER, HERBERT ANTHONY CHARLES (Herby), *trumpet;* also *piano, reeds, percussion;* b. Cupar, Sask., Canada, 12/25/28. Father and two uncles pl. instruments. First stud. trumpet for three months in high school; self-taught since then. Pl. w. local bands. To NYC, playing w. Claude Thornhill '55; Paul Bley at Carnegie Hall and Birdland '55. Worked in LA '58, w. Hal McIntyre in Reno, Nev., New Year's '59. Ret. to Canada and was feat. on Timex TV shows from Toronto, June & Oct. '59. Fav: Roy Eldridge.

Addr: 2166 St. Luke St., Montreal, Quebec, Canada.

SPANIER, FRANCIS JOSEPH (Muggsy), *cornet, leader;* b. Chicago, Ill., 11/9/06. Drums, cornet in school band and local cabarets. Studied cornet with Noah Tarintiono. Played with Elmer Schoebel 1921; Sig Meyers '22-4; Charlie Straight, Charles Pierce, Floyd Towne, 1925-6; Joe Kayser, Ray Miller 1928. During these years his associates included Mel Stitzel, Jess Stacy, Geo. Wettling; he was heard on records with the Bucktown Five and other jazz combos.

Touring with Ted Lewis' band from 1929-36, Muggsy visited England and France in 1930; he was seen with Lewis in the films *Is Everybody Happy?* and *Here Comes The Band.* From '36 until Jan. '38 he was with Ben Pollack's band, then suffered a physical collapse and spent three months in the Touro Infirmary in New Orleans. His miraculous recovery there, after many weeks at the point of death, was later celebrated in two of his blues records: *Relaxin' At The Touro; Oh Doctor Ochsner* (for Dr. Alton Ochsner, who saved his life).

Muggsy returned to music April 1939 in Chicago with the Ragtime Band combo, which made sixteen memorable sides for Bluebird, some of which have been reissued on Victor. He rejoined Ted Lewis for a few months in 1940, then joined Bob Crosby in Sept. 1940. In Feb. '41 he formed his own big band in NYC. This group, which stayed together until 1943 and recorded for Decca, was one of the best big bands ever to feature Dixieland style; sidemen included Mel Powell, Fazola, Vernon Brown; arrangements by Deane Kincaide. From 1944-8 Muggsy led various small groups, mostly at Nick's NYC. From '49 he toured for several years with his own sextet, incl. Darnell Howard, Floyd Bean, Ralph Hutchinson and Truck Parham. He later settled in San Francisco, working w. Earl Hines' combo at the Hangover '57-9.

Spanier is one of the true individualists of jazz, best identified through his exquisite use of the plunger mute. His open work shows the influence of King Oliver and Louis Armstrong, both idols of his youth. His recording career goes back to Feb. 1924, when he made his debut on Gennett with the Bucktown Five. Own LPs on Vict., Weathers, Merc.; w. Bucktown Five and Stomp Six in *Chicago Jazz* (River.), two tracks in *Dixieland At Jazz Ltd.* (Atl.); LPs w. Ted Lewis (Epic), one no. w. F. Teschemacher in *Introduction To Jazz* (Decca), *Jam Session* w. Sidney Bechet (Rondo.).

Addr: 303 South Street, Sausalito, Calif.

SPANN, LESLIE L., JR., *guitar, flute;* b. Pine Bluff, Ark., 5/23/32. Stud. guitar in high school in Jamaica, N.Y. 1949; majored in music ed. and flute at Tennessee State U. '50-7. Pl. with Tennessee State Collegians, others around Nashville; w. Phineas Newborn '57; Ronnell Bright briefly, then joined Dizzy Gillespie Aug. '58, remaining until Aug. '59. Toured w. Quincy Jones in *Free And Easy* '59-60. Favs: Wes Montgomery, Phineas Newborn, Dizzy Gillespie. LPs w. Gillespie, Ellington-Hodges, Ben Webster (Verve).

SPARGO, TONY (Anthony Sbarbaro), *drums;* b. New Orleans, La., 6/27/1897. Member of Original Dixieland

Jazz Band from 1914, leaving New Orleans 1916, and rec. with the band in New York, Feb. 1917. After the band broke up in 1925, he worked with society bands around NYC, then recorded and toured with the reorganized Original Dixieland group off and on from 1935-40. During the '40s and early '50s he free-lanced in New York with various Dixieland groups led by Miff Mole, Phil Napoleon, Big Chief Russell Moore and many others, most often at Nick's. Was with Pee Wee Erwin, '54-5, '57 and '59, Phil Napoleon, '55 & '59, Jimmy Lytell, '57-8; many sessions at Central Plaza, NYC and w. Tony Parenti at Ryan's. In 1957, recording with Connee Boswell for a Memphis Five LP on Victor, he found himself in the same studio in which he had recorded with the ODJB 40 years earlier. Spargo has often taken solos on the kazoo, a toy instrument. LPs w. ODJB (Comm.), Napoleon (Mercury), Erwin (Urania), C. Boswell (Victor), Eddie Condon, Max Kaminsky (Comm.).

Addr: 73-44 Austin St., Forest Hills 75, N.Y.

SPECKLED RED (Rufus Perryman), *piano;* b. Hampton, Ga., 10/23/91. Self-taught on organ; pl. for church at 13. Family moved to Atlanta and he began playing for house parties. Father objected to his playing blues, and he had to play for church; when he was grown he went back to playing blues. Pl. in both Detroit and Memphis before settling in St. Louis. Brother is Piano Red, who has own radio show in Atlanta. Predominantly a solo performer, he also played a few gigs around St. Louis with local bands. Visited England June 1960. Fav: Fats Waller. Art Tatum was early influence. Rec. for Brunswick, Victor, Delmar.

Addr: 1535 Franklin, St. Louis, Mo.

SPENCER, WILLIAM O'NEIL, *drums, singer;* b. Springfield, Ohio, 11/25/09; d. NYC, 7/24/44. Played with small bands around Buffalo 1926-30; Blue Rhythm Band (later known as Lucky Millinder Orch.) 1931-6; John Kirby 1937-41. A first-class swing drummer, he recorded in the late '30s with many combos including Red Allen, Sidney Bechet, Jimmie Noone, Johnny Dodds, Frankie Newton, Milt Herth, Lil Armstrong. LP w. Kirby (Epic).

SPERLING, JACK, *drums;* b. Trenton, N. J., 8/17/22. Parents musical; stud. drums w. Henry Adler in NYC 1942; w. Bunny Berigan '41-2; w. Tex Beneke Navy orch. '43-45 and again w. Tex '46-49; Les Brown '50-4; Bob Crosby TV show '54-7, also free-lancing w. Dave Pell Octet and various recording dates in Calif. Made many sides w. Miller Band on Victor. Favs: Dave Tough, Jo Jones, Don Lamond. LPs w. Les Brown (Col., Cor.), Hi-Lo's (Col.), Dave Pell (Trend, Cap.), Bob Crosby (Cor.).

Addr: 6649 Hesperia Ave., Reseda, Calif.

SPRECHER, ROBERT J. (Bob, Muggsy), *cornet;* b. Independence, Wisc., 9/15/21. Father played clarinet, mother piano, brother trumpet. Studied piano and cornet in public school. Became professional in 1942. Joined Sammy Gardner '55. Favs: Bunny Berigan, Wild Bill Davison. LPs w. Gardner (Roul., Evst., Mound City).

Addr: 251 Perthshire Road, St. Louis 37, Mo.

STABULAS, NICHOLAS (Nick), *drums;* b. Brooklyn, N.Y., 12/18/29. Stud. w. Henry Adler, 1946-8. Work was confined to commercial music for some time, but from '54 he gigged and/or recorded with Phil Woods, Jon Eardley, Jimmy Raney, later with Bob Brookmeyer, Urbie Green, Lennie Tristano, Chet Baker, Kenny Drew, Bill Evans, Al Cohn & Zoot Sims. Steady, driving percussionist. Favs: Clarke, Blakey, Roach. LPs w. Phil Woods (Epic, Pres.), Geo. Wallington (Atl.), Al Cohn (Coral), Zoot Sims (ABC-Par.).

Addr: 205-10 35th Avenue, Bayside 61, L.I., N.Y.

STACY, JESS ALEXANDRIA, *piano;* b. Cape Girardeau, Mo., 8/4/04. Chiefly self-taught. Prof. debut on riverboat 1920-2. Moved to Chicago; pl. w. M. Spanier, F. Teschemacher in Floyd Towne's orch. at Midway Gardens, also w. Art Kassel, Louis Panico. Rose to swing-era fame in Benny Goodman band June '35-July '39. After three years w. Bob Crosby band ret. to Goodman briefly '43; Horace Heidt, T. Dorsey '44; own big band '45. Back w. Goodman for occasional gigs in late '40s, then w. J. Teagarden et al on West Coast; Los Angeles cocktail bars as single during '50s. Clean, incisive, Hines-derived style made him one of top swing pianists. Won DB poll 1940-3; Met. award '40, '41, '44. Own LPs: Bruns., *Tribute to Goodman* (Atl.), one track each in *Great Jazz Pianists* (Cam.), *String of Swingin' Pearls* (Vict.), *History of Jazz, Vol. 3* (Cap.); LPs w. Goodman (Col., Vict., MGM), Harry James in *64,000 Jazz* (Col.), Gene Krupa (Cam.), *Chicago Jazz* (Decca), Bob Crosby (Coral), *Gene Krupa Story* (Verve).

Addr: 8700 Lookout Mountain Avenue, Los Angeles 46, Calif.

STANLEY, WILLIAM FREDERICK GATES (Bill), *tuba, bass;* b. Hull, Texas, 2/17/23. St. on tuba in high school, 1938. Has been mainly active in NBC-TV and ABC-TV commercial shows, and occasional concerts w. *Symphony of the Air*, but has also played on the following LPs: Red Onion Jazz Band (Riverside, Empirical), Bob Helm (River.), *Young Moderns* (Baton). Fav. own solo: *Song of the Islands* w. Red Onion Band (Empirical).

Addr: 839 West End Ave., New York 25, N.Y.

STARK, BOBBY, *trumpet;* b. New York City, 1/6/06; d. New York City, 12/29/45. Played w. Chick Webb, 1927 and '34-9; Fletcher Henderson '28-9; Ella Fitzgerald '39-40; Army 1942, then free-lanced in NYC. Stark's work showed apparent Armstrong influence, but was individual, and provided many impressively well-constructed solos. He was feat. on *Dee Blues, Got Another Sweetie Now* and *Bugle Call Rag* with the Chocolate Dandies, 1931; *New King Porter Stomp* w. Fletcher Henderson; *Liza, Clap Hands, Here Comes Charlie, Spinnin' The Webb* w. Chick Webb.

STARLING, RAYMOND LESLIE, *trumpet, mellophone, piano;* b. London, Eng., 1/4/33. Mother concert violinist; brother drummer; stud. piano in England, trumpet in NYC 1952-4. Worked w. Paul Bley '56; had own quintet '57-8, also worked w. Sal Salvador in clubs and for rec. dates. Names Stan Kenton, Anthony Ortega and Sal Salvador as musical influences. LPs w. Anthony Ortega (Beth.), Sal Salvador (Decca).

Addr: 1464 Ocean Ave., Brooklyn 30, N.Y.

STARR, KAY (Kathryn Starks), *singer;* b. Dougherty, Okla., 7/21/22. Raised in Dallas; debut on local radio while in high school. Subbed briefly for Marion Hutton in Glenn Miller band, July 1939. Early exp. w. Bob Crosby and Joe Venuti orchs. Left Venuti 1942 and was first well-known in jazz as vocalist w. Ch. Barnet, '43-5. Soon after leaving Barnet she was signed by Dave Dexter to record for Capitol and became nationally known as a solo artist. Steeped in the tradition of Bessie Smith and the big-voiced blues singers of the past, she retained some of their jazz qualities in her work despite its increasingly pop-aimed emphasis in later years. LPs: Capitol, Victor, Liberty.

STATON, DAKOTA (Aliyah Rabia), *singer;* b. Pittsburgh Pa., 6/3/32. Stud. voice at Filion School of Music, Pittsburgh. St. singing w. brother's orch. for local engagements, then pl. numerous club dates in U.S. and Canada. Won *Down Beat* award for most promising newcomer of the year, 1955. Rose rapidly to national popularity '58-9. Dynamic stylist recalling at times elements of Dinah Washington and Sarah Vaughan. Fav: Ella Fitzgerald. Own LPs: Capitol; also w. George Shearing (Cap.).

STEGMEYER, WILLIAM JOHN (Bill), *composer, clarinet;* b. Detroit, Mich., 10/8/16. To Lexington, Ky., 1934-6 on scholarship to Transylvania Coll., where Billy Butterfield was his roommate. Alto and clarinet w. Glenn Miller, 1938; Bob Crosby, 1939; before and after these jobs he did radio work in Detroit. In NYC from 1942, wrote for Paul Lavalle on Basin Street broadcasts, led own band at Kelly's Stable, arr. for B. Butterfield band, 1946-7, pl. and arr. for Yank Lawson, Will Bradley et al. In Detroit, 1948-50. In NYC from '50; arrangements for *Hit Parade* '50-58. Worked mainly in pop music during '50s but continued to play (and occasionally arrange) for jazz record dates. LPs w. Lawson-Haggart (Decca, Evst.), Jimmy McPartland (Bruns., Jazz.), Yank Lawson (Bruns., Han.), *Musical History of Jazz* (Gr. Award), *Porgy & Bess* w. Bob Crosby (Dot), Billy Maxted, Billy Butterfield, Cootie Williams, Ruby Braff (Vict.).

Addr: 4 Azalea Drive, Syosset, L.I., N.Y.

STEIN, HAROLD JEROME (Hal), *alto, tenor saxes;* also *clarinet;* b. Weehawken, N.J., 9/5/28. Clarinet at 11, tenor at 15; Town Hall concert w. Don Byas, Specs Powell at 15. Worked w. Rudy Williams, Roy Haynes 1946. Stud. at Juilliard '50-1; Army '51-4 during which time he pl. w. Toshiko in Japan for seven months. Switched from tenor to alto while in Korea; pl. w. Teddy Charles '55, Les Elgart '56, Larry Sonn '57; week ends w. Thornhill, Warren Covington, Sam Donahue '58-9. W. show band at Bal Tabarin, NYC latter part of '59. Bachelor of Mus. from Manhattan Sch. of Music on clar. '59, Masters in music education, Jan. '60; plans to teach. Favs: Parker, Coltrane, Rollins, Wayne Shorter. LPs w. Teddy Charles (Atl.), *Four Altos* (Pres.).

Addr: 4409 Palisade Ave., Union City, N.J.

STEIN, LOUIS (Lou), *piano;* b. Philadelphia, Pa., 4/22/22. Played alto sax first; started professionally on piano at 14. Early associate of Buddy De Franco, Ch. Ventura, Bill Harris in jam sessions at Billy Kretchmer's. Played w. Ray McKinley in 1941. In Army he played w. Glenn Miller in New Haven but did not go overseas with this band. After discharge in '46 went back with McKinley for a year, then joined Ch. Ventura, with whom he wrote and recorded *East of Suez.* Settled in NYC and studied extensively, played with symphonies at Westchester Coll. and took advantage of his versatility, playing effectively with both Dixieland and bop groups as well as many commercial outfits. In 1958-60 wrote jazz style jingles for TV and radio commercials. Own LPs: Merc., Jub., Epic, Bruns; LPs w. Lawson-Haggart (Dec.), K. Winding (Roost), N. Hefti (Epic), L. Bellson (Verve), Ch. Ventura (Reg.).

Addr: 13 Cedarwood Road, White Plains, N.Y.

STEVENS, LEITH, *composer, conductor;* b. Mt. Moriah, Mo., 9/13/09. Parents, both piano teachers, moved to Kansas City in 1911 and started piano school. Stud. from infancy; as child, pl. piano in local movie theater. Pl. w. Chicago Grand Opera Company Orch; was acc. for Madame Schumann-Heink. At height of swing era, made important contribution to jazz as leader on CBS radio series, *Saturday Night Swing Session.* Moved to Hollywood '39; writing for films since '41. Is President of Composers and Lyricists Guild of America. Pioneered by starting jazz background film score trend. Composed and conducted for *The Wild Ones, Private Hell 36* and *The Bob Mathias Story;* more recently *The Five Pennies, The Gene Krupa Story.* Has composed and conducted scores for more than 50 movies. Own LPs: Decca, Coral, Omega; *The Five Pennies* (Dot), *The Gene Krupa Story* (Verve).

Addr: 7411 Woodrow Wilson Dr., Los Angeles 46, Calif.

STEVENSON, GEORGE EDWARD, *trombone;* b. Baltimore, Md., 6/20/06. Father, brother Cyrus and son George all musicians. Stud. w. Albert Jack Thomas and made prof. debut in his city concert band. In NYC w. Irwin Hughes at Arcadia Ballroom, 1928; Ch. Johnson at Smalls', '32; Jimmie Smith's Night Hawks at Savoy; Jack Butler, Hot Chocolates show; Fletcher Henderson at Roseland '35; Claude Hopkins at Cotton Club '36; Ovie Alston at Ubangi '37; Jack Carter '38; Lucky Millinder '40-3; Cootie Williams, Roy Eldridge '44; Cat Anderson '47. From Dec. '55 to May '56 toured

Europe w. Sam Price and rec. in Paris w. Price and S. Bechet. Also has worked around NYC w. Don Redman, Sy Oliver, Chris Columbus, Henry Goodwin, Kaiser Marshall, Rex Stewart, Pops Foster, Danny Barker, Willie the Lion Smith, Hot Lips Page, Tony Parenti. In '59 worked w. own band at club in Wantagh, N.Y. Plays saxophones also, but mainly known as trombonist. LP w. Willie the Lion Smith (Urania).

Addr: 100 W. 139th St., New York, N.Y.

STEWARD, HERBERT (Herbie), *tenor, alto sax, flute;* b. Los Angeles, Cal., 5/7/26. Clarinet at 9; tenor at 13; quit school at 16 to join Bob Chester band, which then incl. Bill Harris, John La Porta, Johnny Bothwell. Jobbed in LA w. Barney Bigard, F. Slack; joined Artie Shaw late '44 and remained with him, except for short Army service, until band's breakup in '46. Spent a year w. Alvino Rey, then worked w. Butch Stone and Gene Roland. When Woody Herman organized the second Herd in fall of '47, Steward was featured on tenor as one of the original "Four Brothers" on the record by that name (with Stan Getz, Zoot Sims, Serge Chaloff) and others with a similar reed-section sound. After three months w. Herman he free-lanced in LA, working briefly w. Red Norvo in '48; rejoined Shaw, '49; worked w. T. Dorsey, Elliot Lawrence, '50-1; Harry James, '51-4. Though accorded less recognition, Steward ranks with other young Herman alumni among the top tenor men of the cool school. In Feb. '57 he was reunited w. Sims and Chaloff in *Four Brothers Together Again* on Vik (now unavailable). This was his only recent appearance in jazz. Pl. w. Al John's orch. in Las Vegas '59-60. Rec. for Roost in early '50s, never released on LP. LPs: w. George Handy, Ralph Burns in *The Jazz Scene* (Verve); Woody Herman, Harry James (Col.), Buddy Childers (Lib.), Artie Shaw (Rondo.—feat. on *The Hornet*); Louis Arcaraz (Vict.).

Addr: 10932 Huston St., North Hollywood, Calif.

STEWART, BUDDY, *singer;* b. Derry, N.H., 1922; d. New Mexico, 2/1/50. Went on the road at age eight doing comedy and songs in vaudeville act; formed vocal trio at fifteen. In NYC, 1940, worked w. Martha Wayne (known in movies, after her marriage to him, as Martha Stewart); after two months w. Glenn Miller in a quartet, they became part of the Snowflakes w. Claude Thornhill. After serving in the Army 1942-4, Buddy joined Gene Krupa's band, teamed w. Dave Lambert and, with him, made the Krupa record *What's This,* the first recorded bop vocal. On his own or with Lambert, he was featured in bop vocals during the next two years, touring w. Ch. Ventura in 1947 and w. Kai Winding in '48, Ch. Barnet 1949. Though best known for his wordless rhythmic vocals, he was a first-class ballad singer. Won DB poll as band vocalist 1947. LPs w. Ventura (Regent, Em.), George Wallington (Savoy).

STEWART, REX WILLIAM, *cornet;* b. Philadelphia, Pa., 2/22/07. Raised in Washington, D. C. from 1914. Stud. w. marine band instructor and grade school teacher. To Phila. w. Oliver Blackwell in Negro musical comedy 1921; to NYC with the Musical Spillers Oct. '21. After year and half with this band, worked at Leroy's, Smalls', Garden of Joy and other Harlem cabarets, then spent 1½ years w. Bobby Brown band and in '24-5 was w. Elmer Snowden.

Stewart spent a few months with Fletcher Henderson in 1926, then two years with Horace Henderson; back with Fletcher in '28 for 2½ years, then with McKinney's Cotton Pickers to '32 and again with Fletcher. He had his own band for 20 months w. Sid Catlett et al; a few months w. Luis Russell, then joined Duke Ellington Dec. '34, and except for brief absences stayed with him until 1944 and was one of the band's most distinctive personalities. His big hit with Duke was *Boy Meets Horn,* a novelty in which he used the "half-valve" tonal effect obtained by depressing a valve halfway.

Stewart formed his own combo after leaving Ellington. He was out of the US from 1947-51, touring Europe and Australia. In the fall of '51 he settled in Johnsonville, near Troy, N.Y., working as a disc jockey and program director on local radio stations WTRY and WROW, as well as gigging in the area. He returned to NYC Dec. '56 and played local gigs; helped organize and direct a reunion of Fletcher Henderson sidemen at the '57 and '58 Great South Bay jazz festivals. Many TV shows incl. *Sound of Jazz,* CBS; Art Ford's *Jazz Party.* Joined Eddie Condon at latter's club, Feb. '58, staying until July '59; later led own combos in NYC.

Though he was, and has remained an impressive stylist, Stewart is best represented by the records he made with Ellington, and by those dates for which he led combos of Duke's sidemen. He won *Met.* poll 1945. Own LPs: Fels., Uran., Gr. Award, *Porgy And Bess Revisited* (War. Bros.); as leader of Fletcher Henderson reunion band on UA, Uran.; w. Ellington groups: *The Duke's Men, Ellington Sidekicks* (Epic), one no. in *History of Jazz, Vol. 3* (Cap.); Ellington (Col., Vict.), Cozy Cole, Will Bradley (Gr. Award).

Addr: 255 West 108th Street, New York 25, N.Y.

STEWART, LEROY (Slam), *bass;* b. Englewood, N. J., 9/21/14. St. in Newark w. Sonny Marshall, then stud. Boston Cons. Worked w. Peanuts Holland in Buffalo, 1936. Met Slim Gaillard at Jock's Place in Harlem 1937; teamed as "Slim & Slam," 1938, they scored national hit w. *Flat Foot Floogee.* Team broke up 1942 when Slim entered Army. Seen in film *Stormy Weather* with Fats Waller, 1943. Toured and recorded with Art Tatum trio, 1943-4; Benny Goodman band, '44-5. Formed own trio, featuring Billy Taylor (later Beryl Booker) on piano, Johnny Collins on guitar. Rejoined Tatum several times in early 1950s. Often teamed w. Beryl Booker, '55-7; Rose Murphy, '57-60. Achieved unique reputation through his novel manner of humming an improvised jazz solo and simultaneously bowing it, in octave unison, on the bass. He was one of the most recorded jazz artists of the mid-'40s. In 1948 he took part in the Jazz Festival in Paris. Won Esq. Silver Award 1945-6; Met poll '46. Own LP on Savoy; LPs w. Erroll Garner (Savoy), Lionel Hampton in *Just Jazz* (Decca), Art Tatum (Cap., Bruns, Roost), Dizzy Gillespie (Rondo.), Benny Goodman (Col.).

Addr: c/o Rose Murphy, 114-28 180th St., St. Albans, L.I., N.Y.

STEWART, THOMAS (Tom), *tenor horn, trumpet;* b. Bridgeport, Conn., 12/26/31. Local groups in New England, 1946-9, and North Carolina, '49-51; Duke Ambassadors, '51-3; local groups around Conn. '53-5; Billy Butterfield and own combo in '56; Whitey Mitchell, fall '56; Bob Zieff group '58-9, incl. appearance at Randalls Island Festival in '59. Favs: B. Clayton, B. Hackett, D. Gillespie. Own LP: ABC-Paramount; LP w. W. Mitchell (ABC-Par.).

Addr: 63 Riverside Drive, New York 24, N.Y.

STITT, EDWARD (Sonny), *tenor, alto, baritone saxes;* b. Boston, Mass., 2/2/24. Father a college music prof., brother is concert pianist. Piano at seven, then clar. and alto. An early disciple of Ch. Parker, whom he heard on records of J. McShann band and in person from '43. Early jobs around Newark and Detroit, also on tour w. Tiny Bradshaw band. Prominent in NYC '45-6 w. D. Gillespie; then inactive until 1949, when he led a band for two years jointly with Gene Ammons. He then worked with his own combo, also toured with Norman Granz, visiting Britain with JATP in '58 and '59, playing tenor and alto. He rejoined Gillespie's combo for three months early in '58. One of the first and most successful bop alto men after Ch. Parker, who greatly admired him, Stitt has shown great individuality and tremendous lift and drive, especially on tenor. He won the *Esq.* New Star award on alto in '47. Film: *Jazz on a Summer's Day.* Own LPs: Roost, Verve, Prestige, Argo; LPs w. Gillespie (Verve, Rondo.), Roy Eldridge (Verve); Stitt-Ammons group (Pres.), *Battle of Birdland* w. Eddie Davis (Roost); *For Musicians Only, Modern Jazz Sextet, Peterson, Eldridge, Stitt, Jo Jones At Newport* (Verve); w. Bud Powell in *Opus De Bop* (Savoy).

Addr: 224 No. Fifth St., Saginaw, Mich.

STOLLER, ALVIN, *drums;* b. New York City, 10/7/25. St. w. Van Alexander, Raymond Scott, Teddy Powell; rec. debut w. Vaughn Monroe at 16. Stoller has rec. and/or toured with most of the top name bands incl. B. Goodman, '42; T. Dorsey, '45-7; Ch. Spivak, H. James, Flanagan, Thornhill, Sy Oliver, Bob Crosby, B. May, Ch. Barnet, also many rec. dates for Norman Granz w. JATP, Shavers, Webster, Flip Phillips etc. Movies: *Pin Up Girl* w. Spivak; *The Fabulous Dorseys.* Though absorbed into the commercial music world in recent years, he is a first-rate, swinging drummer. Prominently featured on Fred Astaire TV show late '59. LPs w. Art Tatum-Roy Eldridge, Fred Astaire, Oscar Peterson, Hawkins-Webster (Verve), Paul Smith (Savoy), T. Dorsey (Vict.), w. Georgie Auld in *Jumpin' Bands* (Savoy); two tracks in *Hi-Fi Drums* (Cap.).

Addr: 4108 Beck Avenue, Studio City, Calif.

STOVALL, DONALD (Don), *alto saxophone;* b. St. Louis, Mo., 12/12/13. Vln. first, then stud. sax under Jimmy Harris, bro. of Arville Harris of early Calloway band. Early jobs w. Dewey Jackson, Fate Marable on riverboats. Own band in Buffalo, '37-8; to NYC '39, worked w. Sam Price, Eddie Durham, '40; Cootie Williams '41, with latter's orig. big band. In 1942 he joined Red Allen's combo, remaining for eight years and impressing many listeners with his firm, hard-swinging style. In 1950 he retired permanently from music. Favs: J. Hodges, Tab Smith. LPs: *Kansas City Jazz* w. Hot Lips Page (Decca).

Addr: 114-39 172nd St., St. Albans, L.I., N.Y.

STRAND, LES (Leslie Roy Strandt), *electric organ, piano, pipe organ;* b. Chicago, Ill. 9/15/24. Father was theater organist and Strand began teaching self piano, then organ at 5. At 18, he was introduced to A. Tatum by a friend. Stud. formally beginning 1944, at Baldwin-Wallace Conservatory in Ohio and Augustana College in Rock Island, Ill. In late '47 was introduced to the work of D. Gillespie and Parker and began using modern style on organ. Jobs in Chicago area; first recordings w. C. Hawkins on Peacock. Fav. own solo: *If I Had You* (Fant.). Favs: Tatum, Gillespie, Parker, Tristano, Jimmy Smith. Own LPs: Fant.

Addr: 917 Diversey Pkwy., Chicago 14, Ill.

STRASEN, ROBERT M. (Bob), *singer;* b. Strasbourg, France, 4/1/28. Raised in Milwaukee. Sang in choirs for many years; led male chorus in Army in Japan. Got into pop music through Gene Puerling and was a member of the Hi-Lo's from Apr. '53 to summer of '59. Fav. singers: Jackie Cain, Roy Kral. LPs w. Hi-Lo's: Col.

STRATTON, DONALD PAUL (Don), *trumpet;* b. Woburn, Mass., 12/9/28. Stud. New England Conservatory and private tutors. Started in 1945 w. Ray Borden, out of whose group grew the Nat Pierce combo, '49-51; also worked w. Tommy Reynolds, '49, Victor Lombardo, '50, Dean Hudson, '51-2, Mal Hallett, '52, Tony Pastor, '52-3. Later worked w. Les Elgart, Elliot Lawrence, Tex Beneke, Boyd Raeburn, Buddy Morrow, Claude Thornhill and Jim Chapin. Originally influenced by Muggsy Spanier and Harry James. Own LP on ABC-Par.; *Blues for Night People* (Savoy); LP w. Jim Chapin (Classic Edit.).

Addr: 568 Grand St., New York 2, N.Y.

STRAYHORN, WILLIAM (Billy or Swee'Pea), *composer, piano;* b. Dayton, Ohio, 11/29/15. Raised partly in Hillsboro, N. Carolina; school in Pittsburgh, private teacher; played classics in school orchestra. In Dec. 1938 he met Duke Ellington, for whom he hoped to work as lyricist, and played him a song he had written called *Lush Life.* Three months later Ellington made his first record of a Strayhorn tune, *Something To Live*

For. After working briefly w. Mercer Ellington's orchestra in '39, Strayhorn became a permanent associate of Duke Ellington. At first he wrote and pl. for records by the Bigard, Hodges and other combos drawn from the band; later in '39 he became a regular arranger and occasional pianist w. Ellington's orch.

In his peak creative years, 1940-2, he composed and arranged some of the most significant music ever recorded by Ellington, including the Ravel-tinged *Chelsea Bridge,* the swinging riff tune *Take the A Train,* which became the band's theme; *After All, Day Dream, Raincheck, Johnny Come Lately, Passion Flower, Midriff.* He collaborated w. Ellington on the *Perfume Suite* and many of the other concert works. The musical vibrations between Strayhorn and Ellington were so sympathetic that sometimes neither they themselves nor members of the band could recollect at what point the work of one had left off and the other had begun.

In the late '40s and early '50s Strayhorn, living in NYC, was considerably less productive, scoring popular songs and occasional instruments such as *Smada* and *Boo'dah* but in the late '50s he became more active again, collaborating with Ellington on such works as *Such Sweet Thunder,* written especially for the Stratford, Ontario Shakespeare Festival, and *A Drum Is A Woman.* He also led his own trio w. Johnny Hodges and Jimmy Grissom called the Ellington Indigos in Florida, Spring '58. As a pianist, he possesses an excellent technique and airy, swinging style that has been heard on occasional duets with Ellington as well as on many records for which he has replaced Duke at the keyboard. Except for the band's European tour in 1950 he has rarely appeared in public with Ellington. He won the Esquire Silver Award as arranger, 1945 and '46, DB poll 1946 and '48. LPs: see Ellington; also Clark Terry (River. 12-246), *Ellingtonia '56* (Verve 8145), Al Hibbler (Bruns. BL 54036), one no. in *Town Hall Concert Plus* (Vict. LPM 1443), one track w. Mercer Ellington (Coral 57293).

Addr: 15 West 106th St., New York 25, N.Y.

SULIEMAN, IDREES DAWUD, *trumpet;* b. St. Petersburg, Fla., 8/27/23. Father plays piano and tuba. Stud. Boston Conservatory. Early experience w. Carolina Cotton Pickers Orch.; Fess Clark, in St. Petersburg. Featured during 1940s w. Tommy Reynolds, Gerry Mulligan, Cab Calloway, Mercer Ellington, Illinois Jacquet, Earl Hines, Count Basie, Lionel Hampton, Erskine Hawkins, Dizzy Gillespie. W. Friedrich Gulda at Birdland and NJF '56, Randy Weston '58-9. Then overseas, playing w. own group in Paris and Casablanca. Jazz record debut on Blue Note w. Thelonious Monk. Favs: Rafael Mendez, Clifford Brown, Dizzy Gillespie. Ambition: To record with strings. LPs: *Interplay, Three Trumpets,* Mal Waldron, Gene Ammons, Jerry Valentine (Pres.), *Top Brass,* Andre Hodeir (Savoy), Randy Weston (UA), Thelonious Monk (Blue Note), Coleman Hawkins (River.), Teddy Charles (Elektra), *Roots* (New Jazz), Friedrich Gulda (Vict.).

SULLIVAN, IRA BREVARD, JR., *trumpet, saxophones;* b. Washington, D.C., 5/1/31. From a musical family, he received his early training on trumpet from his father, on sax from his mother. Started jobs when still in high school. In 1952, for 2½ years, he was part of the house band at the Bee Hive in Chicago, and there worked w. B. Green, P. Quinichette, S. Stitt, H. McGhee, W. Gray, L. Young, R. Eldridge and C. Parker. Later worked w. Bill Russo's group. Was w. A. Blakey briefly in 1956; then ret. to Chi., pl. there to '60. Also gigged w. Trademarks in Louisville '59. Favs: Gillespie, Davis, Navarro, Edison, Terry; Parker, Hawkins, Young, Rollins. Own LP: ABC-Par.; LPs w. Red Rodney (Fant.), J. R. Monterose (Blue Note), Art Blakey (Col.).

SULLIVAN, JOE (Dennis Patrick Terence Joseph O'Sullivan), *piano, composer;* b. Chicago, Ill., 11/5/06. Studied at Chicago Cons. of Mus. An intimate of the Condon-Wettling-Krupa-Spanier-Freeman-Teschemacher-Russell clique in Chicago, he recorded with many jazz groups from 1927, also working with commercial bands in Chicago and NYC, among them Roger Wolfe Kahn, Russ Columbo, Louis Panico, Coon-Sanders, Ozzie Nelson; accompanied Bing Crosby in early '30s, recorded w. Red Nichols, Joe Venuti, Benny Goodman. Played w. Bob Crosby band 1937, then left music business for almost two years owing to illness. On recovering, he worked as studio accompanist for Bing for a year, rejoined Bob Crosby briefly, then opened at Cafe Society, late 1939, with his own sextet incl. Edmond Hall. Led his own band at Nick's 1940. Later worked as single in many night clubs throughout US incl. Eddie Condon's. Joined Louis Armstrong briefly in '52; spent most of the rest of the '50s as single in San Francisco, working at the Hangover in recent years.

Inspired by Fats Waller and Hines, Sullivan was one of the most popular jazz pianists of the late '30s and took part in many excellent record sessions. As a writer he contributed a few tunes that became well known, notably *Little Rock Getaway* and *Gin Mill Blues.* Own LPs: Riverside, Verve, also some tracks on *The Art of Jazz Piano* (Epic); LPs w. Louis Armstrong, Benny Goodman (Col.), Bob Crosby (Coral), Red Nichols (Bruns.), w. Jack Teagarden in *History of Jazz,* Vol. 2 (Cap.), w. Eddie Condon in *Chicago Jazz* (Decca), Bud Freeman (Em.), Max Kaminsky (Comm.).

SULLIVAN, MAXINE (Marietta Williams), *singer,* b. Homestead, Pa., 5/13/11. Mostly self-taught, she was discovered singing at the Benjamin Harrison Literary Club in Pittsburgh by Gladys Mosier, pianist in Ina Ray Hutton's band, who introduced her to Claude Thornhill. As Thornhill's protégée she made her record debut, accompanied by his band. She sang at the Onyx Club and began a partnership w. John Kirby, the bandleader there, to whom she was married from 1937-41.

Her first big hit was a swing version of the Scottish folk song *Loch Lomond;* as a result of it she was "typed" and depended on other similar performances for many subsequent records, despite her ability to adapt all kinds of pop and standard material to her cool, soft voice and subtle, intimate style.

She appeared in the movies *St. Louis Blues* and *Going Places;* on stage she was seen in *Swingin' The Dream* 1939; *Take A Giant Step* 1953. She toured Great Britain 1948 and again in 1954. In the late '50s she branched out surprisingly in two new areas, stud. to become a nurse and also stud. valve trombone, which she played in several jazz concerts and festivals from '58. She has continued to appear occasionally in night clubs. LPs: *The Complete Charlie Shavers and Maxine Sullivan* (Beth.); own on Period.

Addr: 818 Ritter Place, New York 59, N.Y.

SUMMERLIN, EDGAR E. (Ed), *tenor sax, composer;* also *clarinet;* b. Marrianna, Fla., 9/1/28. Stud. violin in Lexington, Mo. public schools. St. to play clar. w. local band. B.M.E. from Missouri St. Coll., M.M. from Eastman Sch. of Mus. Currently teaching and studying for Ph.D. at North Texas State Coll. Add. studies w. Hall Overton, Teddy Charles and George Russell in late '50s. Pl. w. Johnny Long Jan. '56-Mar. '57; Ted Weems '58. In '59 composed a jazz work to accompany a Methodist Sunday morning service, the most effective venture of its kind to date. After several performances in various churches, it was recorded and in Feb. '60, Summerlin brought a nine-piece band from the Texas college to play it at university chapels in the East and South. The jazz service was also seen and heard on *World Wide '60* (NBC-TV) in the same month. Favs: Rollins, Coltrane, Mobley; fav. arr: Gil Evans. LP: *Liturgical Jazz* (Ecclesia).

Addr: 932 S. Elm St., Denton, Texas.

SUNKEL, PHILLIP CHARLES, JR. (Phil), *cornet, trumpet, composer;* b. Zanesville, Ohio, 11/26/25. Started on cornet at 14, switched to trumpet during Army service. Attended Cincinnati Cons. of Music; graduated in 1950 and pl. w. local bands around Ohio. Later worked w. name bands incl. Tommy Tucker, Claude Thornhill, Ch. Barnet, Tony Pastor, Ray Anthony, Dan Terry, Sauter-Finegan, Les Elgart, Vincentico Valdez. First prominent in jazz w. Stan Getz combo '55. Sunkel's use of the cornet, and his admiration for Bix Beiderbecke, have produced in him a stylistic blend of the old and the new. As an arr., he admires the work of Al Cohn, John Lewis and Thelonious Monk. Own LPs on ABC-Par. incl. *Jazz Concerto Grosso* feat. Mulligan, Brookmeyer; LPs w. Al Cohn (Vict.), Junior Bradley (Epic), Don Stratton (ABC-Par.); arrs. for Tony Fruscella (Atl.).

Addr: 133-22 Blossom Ave., Flushing 55, L.I., N.Y.

SUNSHINE, MONTY, *clarinet, soprano sax;* b. London, England, 4/8/28. Father was amateur violinist. Learned clarinet in RAF band. Studied art and painting for eight years but left in 1950 to join semi-pro, co-op band and play jazz. Pl. w. Crane River Jazz Band '51-3, Ken Colyer '53-4. Joined Chris Barber '54, visited US w. him '59. Pl. for films w. Barber: *Look Back In Anger, Holiday, Mamma Don't Allow.* Solo on Barber's hit recording of *Petite Fleur.* Favs: Noone, Bigard, Bechet, George Lewis. LPs: see Barber.

Addr: 8 Danby House, Well St., London E. 9, England.

SUTTON, DICK (Richard Schwartz), *trumpet, composer, leader;* b. New York City, 12/7/28. Self-taught. Has worked mostly with jazz combos around NYC, and in Newfoundland Sept. to Nov. 1951. After starting in Dixieland and becoming interested in more modern approaches, led own sextet in '54-5 combining characteristics of both schools. Favs: B. Hackett, Chet Baker, Armstrong, Beiderbecke.

SUTTON, RALPH EARL, *piano;* b. Hamburg, Mo., 11/4/22. Played around St. Louis from 1936; discovered by Jack Teagarden at Kirksville State Teachers' College prom, he joined Teagarden's band and toured with it for three years before entering the Army. After his discharge in 1945 he joined the Joe Schirmer trio in St. Louis, then did staff work at local radio stations. In New York, '47, he rejoined Teagarden for a while, then in Aug. '48 went to work at Eddie Condon's and gained a large following during his years as intermission pianist there, recreating the works of early ragtimers. Pl. at jazz festival in London 1952; subbed for Earl Hines as leader of group at Hangover in SF during Hines' British tour, fall '57. Specialist in recreating works and style of Fats Waller, James P. Johnson; one of the best of the later stride pianists. Own LPs: Harmony, Verve, Riverside, Commodore; LPs w. Wild Bill Davison (River.), *Jazz-New Orleans* (Savoy), Bob Scobey (Vict.), *Ragtime!* (River.).

Addr: c/o Forest Farm, Arroyo Road, Forest Knolls, Calif.

SVENSSON, REINHOLD, *piano, organ;* b. Husum, Sweden, 12/20/19. Extensive studies in a school for the blind in Stockholm; started on organ and later played piano in dance bands. Since 1948 he has toured mostly w. clarinetist Putte Wickman's combo. He became well known in the US after making a series of records with a quintet patterned after Geo. Shearing's. LPs: *Swedes From Jazzville* (Epic), one half of *Mainstream Jazz Piano* (Omega).

SWEATMAN, WILBUR C., *composer, conductor, clarinet;* b. Brunswick, Mo., 2/7/82. Early musical educ. from sister, who was pianist. Largely self-taught on violin and clar. Traveled w. large circus band; pl. w. Mahara's Minstrels. Org. all-Negro orch. in Minneapolis 1902; musical dir. in various theaters. Became famous in Chicago 1910. Wrote *Old Folks Rag, Boogie Rag* etc. Sweatman's only relationship to jazz is that in 1922 he was instrumental in bringing Duke Ellington to New York for the first time when Sonny Greer, Toby Hardwicke and Ellington came up from Washington to work briefly in his elaborate, quasi-symphonic orchestra.

Addr: 371 West 120th Street, New York City, N.Y.

SWOPE, EARL BOWMAN, *trombone;* b. Hagerstown, Md., 8/4/22. Parents, sister, three brothers all musicians. Pl. w. Sonny Dunham 1942; Boyd Raeburn '43-4; Georgie Auld, Don Lamond '45; Buddy Rich '46-7; Woody Herman '47-9; Elliot Lawrence '50-1, then free-lanced in NYC and Wash., D.C. Joined Jimmy Dorsey March '57 and remained after Lee Castle took over band. After ret. to Wash. again where he pl. for legitimate shows, the Ice Follies and numerous jazz jobs in both D.C. and NYC, Swope joined Louis Bellson's band '59. One of the first trombonists to adapt a modern style in the mid-'40s. Favs: Jack Jenney, Frank Rosolino, Rob Swope, Carl Fontana. LPs w. Herman (Col., Cap.), Willis Conover (Bruns.), Sonny Berman (Eso.), *Jazz Soul of Porgy and Bess* (UA), *Jazz Under The Dome* (Vik), Bellson (Verve).

Addr: 916 10th St., N.E., Wash. 2, D.C.

SWOPE, GEORGE ROBERT (Rob), *trombone;* b. Washington, D.C., 12/2/26. Brother of Earl Swope, whom he replaced in Buddy Rich's band 1947. Also worked w. Chubby Jackson '48, Gene Krupa '49-50, Elliot Lawrence '50-1; then in Washington w. own trio, The Orchestra and other local gigs. W. Larry Sonn in NYC '57, a few club dates w. Boyd Raeburn, Claude Thornhill; at Statler w. Jimmy Dorsey. Subbed for Juan Tizol in Louis Bellson band for a few weeks '59. Currently leading own group in Wash. Rec. w. Chubby Jackson (Col.). Favs: Earl Swope, Johnny Mandel. LPs w. Willis Conover (Bruns.), Freddy Merkle (Vik).

Addr: 916 10th St., N.E., Washington 2, D.C.

SYMS, SYLVIA BLACK, *singer;* b. New York City, 12/3/19. Self-taught. Debut at Kelly's Stable 1939. Soon after, she was discovered and encouraged by Benny Carter. Sang in night clubs during '40s; stage roles in *Diamond Lil* w. Mae West '49-50; also *Dream Girl* and *Rain.* Became nationally popular in '56 after her hit record of *I Could Have Danced All Night* from *My Fair Lady.* Ebullient pop singer with jazz influences. Favs: Holiday, Fitzgerald, Lee Wiley, Mildred Bailey. Own LPs: Decca, Atlantic.

Addr: 135 East 63rd Street, New York City, N.Y.

SYRAN, GEORGE, *piano, composer;* also *clarinet, tenor sax;* b. Youngstown, Ohio, 7/21/28. Stud. at Youngstown College 1946. Cinn. Cons. of Mus. '49-'50. Graduated from Man. Sch. of Mus. '57. Started on clarinet and tenor, prof. debut at 15. Jobs on saxophone w. Bob Astor, Bobby Sherwood, Hal McIntyre '47-9; piano w. Cannonball Adderley '52; Phil Woods '53. With trio at Tony Pastor's NYC '58-9. Says, "I originally switched from saxophone to writing, and what better way to learn writing than by playing piano and analyzing all the great piano works and scores." Favs: Bud Powell, Randy Weston, Thelonious Monk. Fav. arrs: Jon Eardley, Phil Sunkel. LPs: *Phil and Quill, Down East* w. Jon Eardley (Pres.).

Addr: 112 West Houston Street, New York, N.Y.

SZABO, GABOR I., *guitar;* b. Budapest, Hungary, 3/8/36. Guitar at 15; stud. only 3 months. Learned jazz via Voice of America; developed own fingering technique. Rec. w. many local groups, backed singers, did radio, movie sound tracks; made tape for Voice of America that was broadcast the night he left Hungary, 11/22/56. A Freedom Fighter, he arrived in U.S. as a refugee and was at Camp Kilmer before settling in Boston. Stud. at Berklee School '57-9 and gigged locally w. Toshiko and others. He was feat. in July '58 w. the Newport International Band. Favs: J. Smith, T. Farlow, S. Salvador. LP: Newport International Band (Col.).

Addr: c/o Berklee School, 284 Newbury St., Boston, Mass.

T

TAKAS, WILLIAM J. (Bill), *bass;* also *trumpet;* b. Toledo, Ohio, 3/5/32. Began on piano, then trumpet, finally bass. With Billy May in 1955; came to NYC in '56. Worked w. Sal Salvador, Zoot Sims, Jutta Hipp, Nat Pierce, Tal Farlow and Eddie Costa '56-7; Marian McPartland '58-9; Pee Wee Russell at Metropole, Bob Brookmeyer at Basin St. East '59. Favs: Blanton, Ray Brown, Red Mitchell, Koussevitsky. LPs w. Farlow (Verve), Russell (Dot), Bob Dorough, Frank Socolow (Beth.).

Addr: 329 Bleecker St., New York, N.Y.

TALBERT, THOMAS ROBERT (Tommy), *composer;* b. Crystal Bay, Minn., 8/4/24. Primarily self-taught on piano; became interested in arr. at 15. Led and arr. for own band on West Coast 1946-9; arr. for Claude Thornhill, Tony Pastor, Kai Winding, Oscar Pettiford, Don Elliott et al in '50s. Though rarely active in jazz, is a skilled and unusual arranger. LPs: arr. for Patty McGovern (Atl.). Own LP, *Bix, Fats, Duke* (Atl.).

Addr: 1625 Pillsbury Bldg., Minneapolis 2, Minn.

TAMPA RED (Hudson Whittaker), *singer, guitar;* b. Atlanta, Ga., 12/25/00. Raised in Tampa, Fla. Popular in Chicago in the late 1920s, where he scored a tremendous success in '28 with a blues novelty, *It's Tight Like That;* recorded several versions. Tampa Red's partner on the original record was Georgia Tom, accompanist for Ma Rainey, with whom Whittaker also recorded. Some of his records featured him playing kazoo. He was also heard on a series of Bluebird recordings from '34. In recent years he has been living in obscurity in Chicago.

TARTO, JOE (V. Joseph Tortoriello), *bass, tuba;* b. Newark, N.J., 2/22/02. Stud. w. Emil Weber of N.Y. Phil. Symph., 1916. Pl. w. many pop dance bands during 1920s and '30s, incl. visits to London w. Paul Specht, '23 and Vincent Lopez, '25. Heard on many early jazz records: Cotton Pickers, '24; Charleston Chasers, Miff Mole, '27; Eddie Lang, Dorsey Bros., Joe Venuti, '28-9. Wrote arrs. for Fletcher Henderson, Chick Webb, Ch. Teagarden. For many years has been on NBC staff in NYC; pl. on *Lower Basin St.* radio series 1940. W. Lionel Hampton's augmented orch. at Carnegie Hall 1945.

Addr: Gregory Ave., Somerville, N.J.

TATE, GEORGE HOLMES (Buddy), *tenor sax;* b. Sherman, Tex., 2/22/15. Rec. debut w. Troy Floyd 1931 in San Antonio. Worked w. T. Holder 1930-3; Andy Kirk '33-4. With Count Basie's first band in KC, then joined Nat Towles. Replaced Herschel Evans in Count Basie band 1939; remained w. Basie ten years; after playing w. Lucky Millinder and Hot Lips Page, formed own band, playing Celebrity Club and Savoy Ballroom in NYC. Tate's best solos w. Basie in his own opinion were *Rock-a-bye Basie* and *Super Chief.* Favs: Cobb, Jacquet, Getz, Young, Auld. Own LP, *Swingin' Like Tate* (Fels.); LPs w. Eddie Davis, *Very Saxy* (Pres.), Jimmy Rushing (Col., Vang.), Buck Clayton, Mel Powell (Col.), *Lester Young Memorial* (Epic—solos on *Moten Swing* and *Jump For Me*), *Buck Meets Ruby* (Van.), Roy Eldridge (Verve). Count Basie (Cam., Col.), Dickenson-Thomas (Atl.).

Addr: 1732 Amsterdam Ave., New York 31, N.Y.

TATE, ERSKINE, *leader, violin;* b. Memphis, Tenn., 12/19/1895. Prominent for a decade after World War I as bandleader at the Vendome Theatre in Chicago. He employed such noted sidemen as Louis Armstrong, Punch Miller, Buster Bailey, Freddie Keppard. He continued to lead a band until the mid-30s, later becoming a music teacher.

TATRO, DUANE LYSLE, *composer, tenor sax, clarinet.,* b. Van Nuys, Calif., 5/18/27. Extensive studies incl. École Normale de Musique in Paris w. Arthur Honegger; Darius Milhaud 1948-51, Russ Garcia '51-5. Pl. tenor saxophone in dance bands, started comp. while in Navy. Worked w. a group led by Mel Tormé in '44, Stan Kenton '45, Joe Venuti '46, Dick Pierce '47. Overseas, worked in Paris off and on, '48-51 and in Knokke, Belgium '49; Heidelberg, Germany and Tunis '50. In May of '58 received Bachelor of Music at USC; three of his pieces were pl. at Senior Recital. One of the best equipped and most stimulating writers among those who have tried to take jazz into atonal fields while retaining its basic rhythmic qualities. Favs: Jack Montrose, Mulligan, Bill Holman, Ralph Burns. Own LP: *Jazz For Moderns* (Contemp.); comp. & arr. of his own *Rubricity* for Red Norvo (Contemp.).

Addr: 7807 White Oak Ave., Reseda, Calif.

TATUM, ARTHUR (Art), *piano;* b. Toledo, O., 10/13/10; d. Los Angeles, Cal., 11/4/56. Blind in one eye and with only slight vision in the other, he took up violin at thirteen but abandoned this study to concentrate on the piano. He made his professional bow at radio station WSPD in Toledo, where he stayed for three years, doubling in local night clubs. After work of a similar nature in Toledo, on WUJ and in clubs, he came to NYC in 1932 as pianist for Adelaide Hall and made his first records accompanying her in August '32, cutting his first piano solos the following March, by which time he had caused great excitement among musicians through his work at the Onyx Club on 52nd St. Settling in Chicago for a couple of years, he led his own band at the Three Deuces. By the mid-'30s his reputation had become international, enabling him to make a successful appearance in London in 1938.

After many years as a soloist, Tatum started working in 1943 with a trio (Slam Stewart, bass; Tiny Grimes and later Everett Barksdale, guitar). He maintained the trio format at most of his appearances from that time His health began to fail and, in 1955, Tatum died of uremia. Visually there are no mementoes except a brief appearance in a film called *The Fabulous Dorseys.* Fortunately during the last few years of his life he was abundantly recorded by Norman Granz in a variety of contexts.

Tatum's appearance on the scene in the early '30s upset all the standards for jazz pianists. His fantastic technique and original harmonic variations placed him incomparably far ahead of earlier artists, eliciting the praise of Leopold Godowsky and making him the favorite jazz pianist of most of his contemporaries. (In the *Encycl. Yrbook. of Jazz* "Musicians' Musicians" poll 68 out of 100 musicians voted for him.) His unequaled technique was never abused to the point of removing him from his firm jazz roots; his work often showed traces of Waller, Hines and Wilson. The delicacy and lightness of his touch were the envy of thousands of aspiring youngsters. As an improvising jazzman, Tatum achieved some of his highest points of inspiration in his interplay with Grimes during their trio performances, the records of which give only a slight idea of their achievements. Tatum won the *Esq.* Gold Award 1944, Silver '45, tied for Silver '47; *Met.* poll '45; *DB* critics' poll '54, '55, '56.

Own LPs: unaccompanied piano solos, *The Genius of Art Tatum,* Vols. 1-5 (Verve 8036-8040), Vol. 6-10 (Verve 8055-8059), Vol. 11 (Verve 8095); *Here's Art Tatum* (Bruns. 54004), *Giants of the Piano* (Roost 2213), *Art Tatum* (Cap. T216), *Art Tatum Concert* (Harm. 7006); three nos. in *Modern Jazz Piano* (Cam. 384), one no. each in *Great Jazz Pianists* (Cam. 328) & *History of Jazz, Vol. 3* (Cap. T795); one no. w. Joe Turner in *Encyclopedia of Jazz on Records, Vol. 3* (Decca 8385); four nos. in *Jazz at the Hollywood Bowl* (Verve 8231-2), three nos. in *Piano Interpretations* (Verve 8127); *Presenting the Art Tatum Trio* (Verve 8118), *The Three Giants* w. Benny Carter & Louis Bellson (Verve 8013), *Makin' Whoopee* w. same group (Verve 8227), *The Art Tatum-Roy Eldridge-*

Alvin Stoller-John Simmons Quartet (Verve 8064), *Art Tatum-Buddy De Franco Quartet* (Verve 8229), *Art Tatum-Ben Webster Quartet* (Verve 8220), *The Art of Tatum* (Decca 8715), w. L. Hampton (Verve 8093).

TAYLOR, ARTHUR S., JR., *drums;* b. New York City, 4/6/29. Studied w. Chick Morrison. Pl. in neighborhood band in Harlem w. Jackie McLean, Kenny Drew, etc. First prof. job w. Howard McGhee. W. Coleman Hawkins 1950-51; Buddy De Franco '52; Bud Powell 53; Geo. Wallington, Art Farmer '54. W. Powell and Wallington trios again in '55-6. Also w. Gigi Gryce's Jazz Lab. Own group, Taylor's Wailers, at Pad in Greenwich Village '56. W. Miles Davis fall '57. France, Belgium, w. Donald Byrd, Bobby Jaspar, July-Dec. '58. W. Thelonious Monk '59. A much-in-demand, swinging drummer whose crisp style shows the influence of his two favorites, Blakey and Roach. Own LPs on Pres., New Jazz; LPs w. Red Garland (Pres.), Miles Davis (Pres., Col.), Monk (River.), *Wilbur Harden, Bird's Night* (Savoy), Art Blakey, *Orgy In Rhythm* (Blue Note), Bud Powell (BN, Verve, Vict.), countless other dates on BN, Pres.

Addr: 672 St. Nicholas Ave., New York, N.Y.

TAYLOR, WILLIAM (Billy), *bass;* b. Washington, D.C., 4/3/06. Started on tuba, 1919; to NYC 1924. Pl. during '20s w. Elmer Snowden, Willie Gant, Charlie Johnson, and from 1929 to '31 w. McKinney's Cotton Pickers. Switching from tuba to string bass, he was feat. again w. Johnson, in 1934 w. Fats Waller and from 1935-9 w. Duke Ellington. During the 1940s worked mostly at Cafe Society w. Joe Sullivan, Red Allen, etc. Was in great demand for record sessions 1943-6 w. Johnny Guarnieri, Don Byas, Teddy Wilson, etc. A light, swinging bassist in a style similar to that of the late John Kirby. Billy Taylor, Jr., his son (not related to the pianist) also plays bass. LP w. Bessie Smith (Col.), Ed Hall (Comm.).

TAYLOR, WILLIAM, JR. (Billy), *piano, composer;* b. Greenville, N.C. 7/21/21. Stud. from 1938-42 at Va. State Coll. Graduated with B. Mus. degree. Joined Ben Webster's quartet at Three Deuces NYC; later worked w. Dizzy Gillespie, and in Chicago with the trios of Eddie South and Stuff Smith. Seen on stage in *Seven Lively Arts* w. Cozy Cole's quintet 1945. Two months w. Machito, then joined Slam Stewart 1946. To Europe w. Don Redman band Sept. '46; remained for several months in Paris, recording and free-lancing. Formed duo with organist Bob Wyatt in NYC, 1948.

Own quartet, 1949-50; Artie Shaw fronted it in late '50, calling it his Gramercy 5. In 1951 Taylor worked almost continuously at Birdland with combos led by Auld, Gillespie, Eldridge, Gaillard, Gibbs, McGhee, Konitz, Mulligan, Pettiford, Winding, etc. Since 1952 he has played night clubs with his own trio. Playing in a smooth, modified bop style that reflects his own urbane personality, Taylor won great respect among fellow musicians and fans as a consistent and adaptable artist. He has written several instruction books (see bibliography) and given numerous lectures at music schools. In the late '50s he wrote a number of keenly perceptive articles for *Down Beat, Saturday Review* and other publications. Taylor won DB Critics' poll as New Star 1953.

Own LPs: ABC-Par., Argo, Pres., Atl., Roost, Savoy, River.; one no. each in *Know Your Jazz, Vol. 1* (ABC-Par.), *Jazztime U.S.A.* (Bruns.), *Roost Fifth Anniversary Album* (Roost); LPs w. Johnny Ray (Col.), Mundell Lowe (River.), *Billy Taylor Introduces Ira Sullivan* (ABC-Par.), Ernie Royal (Uran.), Met. All Stars (Verve), Jackie Paris (Bruns.).

Addr: 2171 Madison Avenue, New York 37, N.Y.

TAYLOR, CECIL PERCIVAL, *piano, composer;* b. New York City, 3/15/33. Stud. privately, then at NY Coll. of Mus. and 4 yrs. at New England Conservatory. Later gigs w. Hot Lips Page, Lawrence Brown, J. Hodges et al. In the late '50s began to be heard around NYC with, first, a quart. consisting of Steve Lacy, sop. sax; Buell Neidlinger, bass; and Dennis Charles, drums; for a long stay at the Five Spot, and app. at NJF, July '57. Late '57 had revamped quart. featuring vibes in place of sop. sax and app. in concert at Cooper Union. He has since free-lanced around NYC. Taylor is considered by several leading critics to be among the advance guard of a new jazz era, though some musicians have dismissed his work as an unhappy attempt to blend Bartok and Stravinsky with jazz. Nevertheless, he is clearly aware of the techniques and folk heritage of jazz and shows some ties to the ideas of Ellington and Monk. His execution is most impressive and his ideas are strikingly original. Favs: Monk, Ellington, Silver; also Powell, Peterson, J. Lewis, and many older mus. incl. Bechet, Hawkins, Armstrong. Own LPs: Verve, Transition, Contemp., UA.

Addr: 210 Clinton Street, New York 2, N.Y.

TAYLOR, EDMUND (Eddie), *drums;* b. Oldham, Lancashire, England, 2/12/29. Self taught. St. with school band, the "Royal Kiltie Juniors"; played with Johnny Dankworth Seven 1951, Tommy Whittle Quintet; nine months in band on RMS *Queen Mary;* joined Humphrey Lyttelton 1956 and toured US with him in '59. Favs: B. Rich, Roy Haynes, Philly Joe Jones, Max Roach.

Addr: 8 Great Chapel Street, London W.1, England.

TAYLOR, CALVIN EUGENE (Gene), *bass;* b. Toledo, Ohio, 3/19/29. To Detroit 1936; st. on sousaphone. Moved to Chicago, pl. piano briefly, then took up bass. Repl. Teddy Kotick w. Horace Silver '58. Favs: Johnny Miller, Slam Stewart, Ray Brown, Oscar Pettiford. LPs w. Silver, Duke Pearson (Blue Note).

Addr: 991 De Kalb Ave., Brooklyn 21, N.Y.

TAYLOR, JASPER, *drums;* b. Texarkana, Ark., 1/1/1894. Started w. Dandy Dixie Minstrels, also house drummer at Booker T. Washington Theatre in St. Louis. Joined W. C. Handy's band in Memphis 1913 and was playing w. him in '14 when Handy wrote *St. Louis Blues.* Drums and xyl. w. Clarence Jones and Ch. Elgar in Chicago '17. Drummer in US Army, France '18; rejoined Handy '19. Toured Quebec w. Chicago Jazz Band '20; played w. Dave Peyton '23, Fess Williams '27 in Chicago. Taylor was also heard on many early records incl. Jelly Roll Morton '23, Freddy Keppard '26. Own group rec. on Paramount '26; various groups w. Jimmy Blythe '25-8, Frankie Jaxon '28-9, Ruben Reeves '33. Still active around Chicago, Taylor in '59 was playing w. Lil Armstrong's group at the Red Arrow in Stickney, Ill.

Addr: 5630 Prairie Ave., Chicago 37, Ill.

TAYLOR, SAMUEL L. (Sam the Man), *tenor sax;* also *bar. sax, clarinet;* b. Lexington, Tenn., 7/12/16. Mother and sister pianists, father guitarist, brothers choir director and drummer. Started on clar., played with brother Paul Taylor's band in Gary, Ind. Worked w. Scat Man Crothers, 1937-8, Sunset Royal Orch. '39-41, Cootie Williams '41-3 and '45-6, Lucky Millinder, '44-5. From '46-52 he worked more or less regularly w. Cab Calloway, touring South America with him in '51 and the Caribbean in '52. After this he began to find himself in great demand for rhythm and blues record sessions, and by '55-6 was frequently being featured on gigs with his own combo. Though often required to play exhibitionistically, he is a superior tenor man with a fine grounding in genuine jazz. Favs: Coleman Hawkins, Ch. Ventura, Ben Webster. Own LP as jazzman: *Jazz for Commuters* (Metrojazz). Own pop or r & b LPs: MGM. LPs w. Mal Fitch, Quincy Jones (Merc.), Lawrence Brown (Verve).

Addr: 1001 East 223rd Street, Bronx 66, N.Y.

TEAGARDEN, CHARLES (Charlie), *trumpet;* b. Vernon, Tex., 7/19/13; brother of Jack Teagarden, with whom he was associated for many years from 1929, in the bands of Ben Pollack, Red Nichols, Paul Whiteman and Jack Teagarden. Free-lanced in LA from early 1940s; with Harry James '46; toured w. Jimmy Dorsey '47-51; rejoined Jack Teagarden briefly in '51. Jerry Gray band '51; own trio w. Ray Bauduc, Jess Stacy '51-2. Many dates w. Bob Crosby's Bobcats '54-8, then settled in Las Vegas, doing extensive hotel and TV free-lancing. Admirable tone and style suggesting a Bix Beiderbecke influence. LPs w. Bob Crosby, Kay Starr, Jack Teagarden (Cap.), Bob Crosby (Cor., Col.), *Chicago Jazz* (Decca), Benny Goodman, Jimmy Dorsey (Col.), Joe Venuti in *Encyclopedia Of Jazz On Records,* Vol. 1 (Decca).

Addr: 2117 Alta Drive, Las Vegas, Nevada.

TEAGARDEN, CLOIS LEE (Cub), *drums;* b. Vernon, Tex., 12/16/15. Brother of Jack, Charlie, Norma. Stud. mainly w. mother. An uncle, Joe Teagarden in San Angelo, Tex., helped him get started. Joined Frank Williams' Oklahomans in Detroit, 1929, as drummer and singer. During 1930s barnstormed around Tex. oil fields, at Chicago fair w. Charles LaVere; joined Jack Teagarden's big band for a year, 1939-40, then played w. Okla. Symphony, had own band. After free-lancing in Calif. he quit music. Since 1948 he has been with the Gen. Telephone Co. in Long Beach, doing a little teaching occasionally. Rec. w. Jack Teagarden (Bruns., Col. '39).

Addr: P.O. Box 1146, Riverton, Wyo.

TEAGARDEN, WELDON JOHN (Jack), *trombone, singer; leader;* b. Vernon, Texas, 8/20/05. Started on trombone at seven; almost entirely self-taught. An early influence was Peck Kelley, the pianist in whose band he played, 1921-2. After leading his own band in Kansas City and working with Doc Ross, Willard Robison and others, he came to NYC in 1927, made record dates with Sam Lanin, Roger Wolfe Kahn and others and made his debut as a recording vocalist on *Makin' Friends* w. Eddie Condon in 1928. He played with the Ben Pollack orch. from 1928 until early 1933; after working with Mal Hallett and free-lancing in NYC, he played with Paul Whiteman from mid-1934 until late 1938, also appearing with "The Three Ts" contingent from the band (with Ch. Teagarden and Frankie Trumbauer) Dec. 1936.

From Jan. 1939 until 1947 Teagarden toured with his own big band. Though never financially successful, the band produced some great music, early sidemen incl. Ch. Spivak, Lee Castle, Ernie Caceres, Dave Tough. In 1947 Teagarden was forced to work with a small combo and later that year joined Louis Armstrong's group, with which he remained until late 1951. He then formed his own small band, with which he has toured successfully, including Europe in the fall of '57, and a State Dept.-subsidized tour of the Far East Sept. '58-Jan. '59.

The advent of Jack Teagarden on the jazz scene in the late 1920s brought a new style to the annals of both jazz singing and trombone: a style that defies classification and has moved musicians of every school to the expression of unqualified enthusiasm. He is noted among musicians for his ability to play at great length under the most trying conditions with unflagging technique and inspiration. Miff Mole has called him "the best trombone player around today"; Bill Russo hailed him as "a jazzman with the facility, range and flexibility of any trombonist of any idiom or any time; his influence was essentially responsible for a mature approach to trombone jazz."

Teagarden has appeared in a number of motion pictures, among them *Birth of the Blues* with Bing Crosby in 1941, *The Glass Wall,* and *Jazz on a Summer's Day.* He won the following awards: *Esq.* Gold Award 1944; *Met.* poll 1937-42, '45; Playboy All Star Band '57-60. Own LPs: *Accent on Trombone* (Uran. 1205), *Big T's Jazz* (Decca 8304), *Big T's Dixieland Band* (Cap. T1095), *This Is Teagarden* (Cap. T 721), *Shades of Night* (Cap. T 1143), *Swing Low Sweet Spiritual* (Cap. T 820), *Blues and Dixie* (Rondo. 18), *Jazz Great* (Beth. 32), *Red Allen, Kid Ory and Jack Teagarden At Newport* (Verve 8233). LPs w. Louis

Armstrong *Concert Plus* (Vict. LPM 1443), Decca 8037, 8038, 8041, 83330); Bunny Berigan (Epic 3109), Eddie Condon (Col. CL 632, Vict. LPM 1373, *A String of Swingin' Pearls*); also one no. each w. Condon in Decca 8244, *An Introduction To Jazz;* Decca 8400, (*Encyclopedia of Jazz on Records, Vol. 3*), Bud Freeman (Harm. 7046), *Chicago/Austin High School Jazz In Hi-Fi* (Vict. LPM 1508), Benny Goodman (Col. CL 821), Bobby Hackett (Cap. T 933, T692), one no. w. Ben Pollack (Savoy 12090), w. Joe Venuti in *Encyclopedia of Jazz on Records,* Vol. 1 (Decca 8383), *Met. All Stars* (Harm. 7044), *History of Jazz, Vol. 2* (Cap. T794), *Paul Whiteman 50th Anniversary* (Gr. Award 33-901).

Addr: 3253 Tareco Dr., Los Angeles 28, Calif.

TEAGARDEN, NORMA LOUISE (Norma Friedlander), *piano;* b. Vernon, Tex., 4/28/11. Sister of Jack. Piano and violin from age six; taught by mother. Territory bands in N. Mex. and taught piano in Roswell, 1933-7; own group in Oklahoma City and WKY studio work '38-41; to Calif. in '42; worked with Jack Teagarden's large band '43-6, then led own groups in Long Beach until 1949. Started teaching in Long Beach. Also worked with Ben Pollack, Ada Leonard. Pl. w. Jack Teagarden's combo 1953-4. A Tatum fan, but says, "I can play more Bob Zurke type piano." LP w. Jack Teagarden (Beth.).

Addr: 89 Heather Avenue, San Francisco 18, Cal.

TEDESCO, THOMAS J. (Tommy), *guitar;* b. Niagara Falls, N.Y., 7/3/30. While attending Niagara U., auditioned for Ralph Marterie when his band played Senior Prom there, and toured with him for a year through Oct. '53, when he settled in LA. Pl. w. Joe Burton trio; formed own trio, pl. at Lighthouse. From 1955 worked mainly w. Dave Pell, also w. Chico Hamilton, Buddy De Franco, Jack Montrose, Mat Mathews, Herb Geller. Favs: Kessel, H. Roberts, Raney, Farlow. LPs w. Pell (Vict., Kapp); Tommy Alexander (Lib.), *Salute to Cole Porter* w. Eddie Cano (incl. own fav. solo, *Love for Sale,* Vict.); *Three Roads to Jazz* w. Jerry Vaughn (American).

Addr: 2104 N. Dymond, Burbank, Cal.

TEMPERLEY, JOSEPH (Joe), *tenor* and *baritone saxophones;* b. Fife, Scotland, 9/20/29. Self-taught; st. on alto. Worked with Joe Loss, Jack Parnell, Harry Parry, Tommy Sampson, Tommy Whittle, Tony Crombie; played at Youth Festival in USSR Aug. '57. Toured US with Humphrey Lyttelton band fall '59. Favs: H. Carney, Ch. Parker. LPs w. Lyttelton (London).

Addr: 53 Livingstone House, Windham House, London S.E.5, England.

TERRY, CLARK, *trumpet, fluegelhorn;* b. St. Louis, Mo., 12/14/20. Joined local drum & bugle corps, 1935; majored on valve trombone w. band teacher at high school. With all-star Navy band at Great Lakes, Chicago, 1942-5; after discharge, following three weeks w. Lionel Hampton, he joined Geo. Hudson in St. Louis for 18 months; then to Calif. to join Ch. Barnet for 10 months. Briefly w. Eddie Vinson, Ch. Ventura and back w. Hudson, then joined Count Basie, 1948, remaining with him in small band 1950-1. W. Duke Ellington from Nov. '51 until Nov. '59, when he joined Quincy Jones. After touring Europe w. Jones in *Free and Easy* he ret. to NYC and joined NBC staff Mar. '60. Terry, who uses "half-valve" effects à la Rex Stewart and double-time passages akin to Gillespie's, combines the best qualities of both to present a unique style of his own; is one of the most original trumpet players in contemporary jazz. Own LPs on Argo, River., Merc.; LPs w. Ellington (Col., Cap., Beth.), Billy Taylor, Paul Gonsalves, Jimmy Woode (Argo), Count Basie (Col.), Wardell Gray (Pres.), Dinah Washington, Quincy Jones (Merc.), *Jam Session, The Jazz School* (Em.), *One World Jazz* (Col.).

Addr: 112-25 34th Ave., Corona 68, L.I., N.Y.

TERRY, DAN (Daniel Kostraba), *leader, trumpet, arranger;* b. Kingston, Pa., 12/22/24. Father a choirmaster. Stud. trumpet privately; played w. Muggsy Spanier's big band Feb. to May '43, then entered Marines. Discharged Sept. '44; took over leadership of Hollywood Teenagers Band '45 in Los Angeles. To NYC 1948; eight months w. Sonny Dunham, then stud. theory at Coll. of Pacific '48-9. Has led own big bands on and off since summer of 1950; recorded with all-star personnel for Columbia. Appeared in film short *Birth Of A Band.* Active mainly as music copyist in late '50s, occasionally gigging w. band and pl. w. Buddy Rich and others. LPs: *Teen Age Dance Party* (Harm.).

TERRY, SONNY (Saunders Teddell), *harmonica, singer;* b. Durham, N.C., 10/24/11. Blind since 1924, he teamed with Blind Boy Fuller, rec. with him 1937. To NYC '38 for *Spirituals to Swing* concert, Carnegie Hall. Soon afterward he joined forces with Brownie McGhee and they worked almost exclusively as a team. Settled in NYC 1941; appeared on Broadway in *Finian's Rainbow* '46-7, *Cat on a Hot Tin Roof* '55-7 and on the road '57-8; ten weeks touring Britain and Continent '58; to Europe again '59 and to India '59-60. All these tours with McGhee. A superb country blues artist whose work has been largely unspoiled by a comparatively sophisticated urban life, he is capable of intensely moving vocal blues work which he punctuates with ferociously effective comments on his harmonica. Own LPs: Riverside, Folkways, Savoy, Vanguard, Fantasy. LPs w. Garry Moore (Col.), Josh White (Decca); *Spirituals To Swing* (Vang.).

Addr: 110 West 126th Street, New York 27, N.Y.

TESCHEMACHER, FRANK, *clarinet, saxes;* b. Kansas City, Mo., 3/14/06; d. Chicago, 2/29/32. Attended Austin High School in Chicago w. Jimmy McPartland, Bud Freeman and others of the "Austin High Gang" who played gigs together in 1924-5. The group expanded to become Husk O'Hare's Wolverines in Des Moines; later a similar unit w. Teschemacher and Muggsy Spanier played at the Midway Gardens in Chicago. "Tesch" worked w. Sig. Meyers, Art Kassel, Floyd

Towne in Chicago and w. Red Nichols and others in NYC. He met his death in an auto accident while driving to a rehearsal w. Wild Bill Davison. Influenced by Johnny Dodds and Jimmy Noone, "Tesch" was a trail blazer in white Chicago style jazz and is considered by some critics to have been unsurpassed in his field. LPs: *Chicago Style Jazz* (Col. CL 632), two nos. in *Chicago Jazz* (River. 12-107); selections in *History of Classic Jazz* (River. SDP 11), *Introduction To Jazz* (Decca 8244), *Encyclopedia of Jazz on Records, Vol. 1* w. Elmer Schoebel (Decca 8398).

THARPE, (Sister) ROSETTA (Rosetta Nubin), *singer, guitar;* b. Cotton Plant, Ark., 3/20/21. Her mother sang in local church choir and gave her a religious musical education from childhood. She came to prominence in a Cotton Club Revue w. Cab Calloway in 1938 and during the next few years enjoyed a great vogue working w. Calloway and Lucky Millinder bands, and as a single at Cafe Society and other clubs. Since the early 1940s she has recorded regularly for Decca, sometimes teamed with Marie Knight. Most of her performances, both vocally and on guitar, have a magnificent passion and folk quality unspoiled by her appearances before sophisticated audiences. In 1949 she recorded a duet session with her mother, Katie Bell Nubin. App. in London and Paris in late '50s. Concert at Town Hall, Oct. '59. LPs on Merc., Decca.

Addr: 759 So. 19th St., Phila., Pa.

THESELIUS, GOESTA, *composer, piano, tenor sax;* b. Stockholm, Sweden, 6/9/22. After working with the bands of Sam Samson, Thore Ehrling and others, he was prominent from 1950 as arranger for many of the best Swedish jazz dates by Rolf Ericson, Arne Domnerus, Harry Arnold et al; has also written film scores and worked for radio and TV. Theselius is Sweden's outstanding jazz writer; his work combines colorful and skilful voicings with constant concern for a vital beat. LPs: tenor sax w. Jimmy Raney in *Swingin' In Sweden* (Em.).

THIELEMANS, JEAN (Toots), *guitar, harmonica;* b. Brussels, Belgium, 4/29/22. Harmonica at 17 while stud. math. at coll. During World War II his family fled to France and after they returned to Belgium in '41 he heard Django Reinhardt; later bought a guitar and taught himself to play. By 1944 he was gigging at American GI clubs. Visited US '47; pl. at Paris Jazz Festival '49; toured Europe w. Benny Goodman Sextet '50. Emigrated to US Nov. '51; toured with Geo. Shearing quintet from early '53 to fall '59, then formed own combo. A splendid musician who combines a beat with a sense of humor, Thielemans plays firm, swinging guitar and is the only jazzman to come to prominence as a harmonica soloist, bringing to this odd instrument enough taste and musicianship to compensate for its tonal limitations. Own LPs: Decca, Riverside, Columbia, Hanover-Signature. LPs w. Shearing (MGM, Cap.).

Addr: 279 North Broadway, Yonkers, N.Y.

THIGPEN, EDMUND LEONARD (Ed), *drums;* b. Chicago, Ill., 12/28/30. Father, Ben Thigpen, played drums for many years with Andy Kirk orch. Drums, piano in LA schools; pl. w. Cootie Williams band Sept. '51-Feb. '52; Army bands to '54, toured w. Dinah Washington to Nov. '54. Briefly w. L. Tristano, J. Hodges, Gil Melle; Bud Powell trio Sept. '55, Jutta Hipp trio Mar. '56; Billy Taylor trio summer '56. Oscar Peterson trio Jan. '59. A brilliant and learned young drummer who has made extensive studies of percussion history and puts his knowledge most effectively to work. Took up residence in Toronto fall '59. LPs w. Peterson (Verve), J. Hipp (BN), Taylor (ABC-Par., Argo), B. Peiffer (Merc.), Toshiko (Story.), P. Quinichette, *Earthy* (Pres.), D. Ashby (Reg.), Teddy Charles (Beth.).

THOMAS, ROBERT (Bob), *trombone;* b. New Orleans, La., 8/27/98. Bought trombone from pawn shop for $8.00; began stud. with Jim Humphrey 1914; joined Young Olympia Brass Band '15, which incl. Louis Armstrong, Kid Rena et al. Worked w. various bands around NO; at Childs Paramount NYC; pl. Newport Jazz Festival w. George Lewis summer '57. Fav: Tommy Dorsey. LPs w. Paul Barbarin (Atl.); George Lewis (Cav.).

Addr: 1146 E. 50th Street, Los Angeles 11, Calif.

THOMAS, WALTER PURL (Foots), *tenor, sax, flute, composer;* b. Muskogee, Okla., 2/10/07. To NYC 1927. Played w. Jelly Roll Morton, 1927-9; Joe Steele, '29; w. The Missourians, '29, remained with this band when it was taken over by Cab Calloway the following year and played all tenor and occasional flute solos on early Calloway records incl. *St. Louis Blues, Happy Feet, Some of These Days, Aw You Dawg, Avalon.* Left Calloway '43, played w. Don Redman, Zanzibar NYC, then had own band there for 6 months. Quit playing and has been active as manager since 1948; his clients incl. Vi Burnside, Dizzy Gillespie, Bill Doggett, Bill Davis. Joined Shaw Artists Agency as booker of one night stands Jan. 1954. Also runs music publishing company in partnership w. Cozy Cole.

Addr: c/o Shaw Artists, 565 Fifth Avenue, New York 22, N.Y.

THOMAS, JOSEPH, JR., (Joe), *composer, tenor sax;* b. Muskogee, Okla., 12/23/08. Brother of "Foots" Thomas (see above). To NYC w. Jelly Roll Morton 1929. Worked w. Blanche Calloway and many other name bands during 1930s; w. Dave Martin in early '40s; then gave up playing to become vocal coach. Later artists and repertoire executive for Decca, 1949-50, Victor, '51-2; free-lance since then. Has directed and written innumerable r&b record dates since late 1940s.

Addr: 117 West 48th St., New York 36, N.Y.

THOMAS, JOSEPH LEWIS (Joe), *trumpet;* b. Webster Groves, Mo., 7/24/09. Studied in school. Early experience w. Cecil Scott 1928, then w. Darrell Harris in Ft. Wayne, Ind.; Eli Rice in Minneapolis, 1930;

Shuffle Abernathy in Milwaukee. In NYC worked w. Fletcher Henderson, 1934 and '36-7; Benny Carter, '39-40; in recent years has free-lanced in NYC, mostly in Dixieland and Swing jam sessions. One of the most underrated trumpeters of the Swing era, his fine tone and relaxed style can be heard on many records w. Lil Armstrong, Barney Bigard, Pete Brown, Don Byas, Harry Carney, Cozy Cole, Alex Hill, Jimmy Jones, Joe Marsala, Ted Nash, Red Norvo, Art Tatum, Dave Tough, Fats Waller, George Wettling, Sandy Williams, and his own groups. Most of these sessions were made between '44 and '46. Own LP: *Mainstream* (Atl.); LPs w. Tony Scott (Coral), Buck Clayton (Col.), one no. w. Geo. Wettling in *Boning Up On Bones,* one no. w. own group in *Trumpet Interlude* (Em.).

Addr: 473 West 158th St., New York 32, N.Y.

THOMAS, JOSEPH VANKERT (Joe), *tenor sax;* b. Uniontown, Pa., 6/19/09. Played w. Horace Henderson, 1929 to '30; Stuff Smith in Buffalo '30-1; tenor sax, clarinet and vocals w. Jimmie Lunceford from 1932 until Lunceford's death in '47, then took over the band jointly with Ed Wilcox for a while and later led a small combo of his own. In recent years, since settling in Kansas City, he has been in business as an undertaker. A big-toned, melodious and inspired soloist, he was one of the great personalities in the Lunceford band in the halcyon days, best performances being *Baby Won't You Please Come Home,* on which he played and sang; *Wham, Bugs Parade, Posin'* and *What's Your Story Morning Glory?* LPs w. Lunceford (Decca, Col.), *Lunceford In Hi Fi* (Cap.), w. Jonah Jones in *Battle Of The Saxes* (Em.).

Addr: 2506 Benton Blvd., Kansas City, Mo.

THOMAS, RENE, *guitar;* b. Liège, Belgium, 2/25/27. Studied guitar 1937-8; mainly self-taught. After free-lancing with various combos in France and Belgium (incl. dates with Chet Baker in Paris, 1955, and with other visiting American jazzmen) he emigrated to Canada. During visits to New York in 1958 he did recording and night club work with Sonny Rollins, who described him as "better than any of the American guitarists on the scene today." Favs: Charlie Parker, Django Reinhardt, Jimmy Raney. LPs w. Rollins, Toshiko (Metro.).

Addr: 2100 Vauquelin, Montreal, Canada.

THOMPSON, CHARLES EDMUND (Chuck), *drums;* b. New York City, 6/4/26. Father was violin maker. Stud. piano in NYC, later 5 yrs, of drum study in Hollywood. While attending Jefferson High in LA, worked w. Charlie Echols band for 6 months, 1943, then played weekends w. Sachel McVea, father of Jack McVea. Worked w. Sammy Yates, 1945, Cee Pee Johnson, '46, Ch. Parker, Howard McGhee, Benny Carter, '47, then intermittently w. Dexter Gordon, Wardell Gray, and various combos around the West Coast. Worked w. Hamp Hawes Trio '55-6. Later w. various groups in SF; featured at the Cellar in the Cellar Quartet, SF '59. Favs: Art Blakey, Philly Joe Jones, Kenny Clarke, Max Roach. LPs w. Hawes (Contemp.), Wardell Gray (Pres.), Dexter Gordon (Dooto), Red Mitchell (Beth.), Barney Kessel (Contemp.).

THOMPSON, LLOYD, *bass;* b. Ontario, Canada, 1934. Brother, a tenor player, leads band in NYC. Went to Europe w. Pia Beck trio; worked in Paris w. Allen Eager, Don Byas, Kenny Clarke, Al Levitt, Art Simmons, Zoot Sims; w. Dizzy Reece in London. LP w. Reece (BN).

THOMPSON, ELI (Lucky), *tenor, soprano saxes;* b. Detroit, Mich., 6/16/24. Stud. w. Bobby Byrne's father and w. Francis Hellstein of Detroit Symph; harmony, theory w. John Phelps. Toured w. 'Bama State Collegians, led by Trenier Twins; in NYC, 1943, worked w. Lionel Hampton, Ray Parker, Sid Catlett, Don Redman and the original Billy Eckstine band (1944); gigged w. Lucky Millinder, Slam Stewart, Erroll Garner. With Count Basie 1944-5. Living in Los Angeles, 1946-7, he became that city's most prolific jazz recording soloist, on sessions w. Boyd Raeburn, Dizzy Gillespie, Ike Carpenter, Buddy Baker, Dinah Washington and dozens more. Back in NYC 1948, free-lancing; from 1951, had his own band which played more or less regularly at the Savoy Ballroom for two years. Became songwriter and started his own publishing company, Great Music. Visiting France early in '56, he subbed in Stan Kenton's band on baritone; after their return to the US he rec. w. Kenton pl. tenor, May '56. Since '57 Thompson has been in Europe, working chiefly in France. Has taken up soprano sax, which he has played on some recordings.

A greatly frustrated musician in the US, Thompson showed a highly individual style and the pure, full-bodied, distinctive tone that won him the Esq. New Star award in '47. His first important jazz solo was *Just One More Chance* on a 1947 session for Victor. Like Don Byas and many other musical expatriates, Thompson found in France increased esthetic recognition, and enough work to keep him going more steadily than at home. Favs: Hawkins, Webster, Byas. Own LPs: ABC-Paramount, Urania, Dawn. LPs w. Miles Davis (Pres.), J. Teagarden (Urania), *Cats vs. Chicks* (MGM), Basie (Col.), Milt Jackson (Atl., Savoy), Jo Jones (Vang.), Quincy Jones, O. Pettiford (ABC-Par.), *Modern Jazz Society* (Verve).

THOMPSON, CHARLES PHILLIP (Sir Charles), *piano, composer, organ;* b. Springfield, Ohio, 3/21/18. Father a Methodist minister. Left home at 15 to join Lloyd Hunter orch. in Omaha. Played w. many midwestern bands incl. Nat Towles, Floyd Ray; joined Lionel Hampton 1940. After working w. Lester Young at Cafe Society, '41, settled in NYC, played on 52nd St. w. Roy Eldridge, Don Byas, Hot Lips Page, etc. With Lucky Millinder several times during '40s. To Calif. w. Coleman Hawkins, 1944-5. A year w. Illinois Jacquet, 1947-8, again '52; while w. Jacquet in '47 he composed *Robbins' Nest,* which became Jacquet's biggest hit record and a jazz standard. Lived for two years in Cleveland in late '40s, later free-lanced in East w. Ch. Barnet and many other combos. Combines partial bop style with Basie influence. Except for a European tour as pianist in '59, he has worked mainly in recent years as a Hammond organist leading a combo in Harlem bars. Own LPs: Col., Vanguard; LPs w. Buck Clayton (Col.); V. Dickenson, U. Green, John Sellers (Vang.), P. Quinichette (Merc.); *Saxomaniac* (Apollo).

THORNE, FRANCIS BURRITT, JR. (Fran), *piano, composer;* b. Bay Shore, L.I., N.Y., 6/23/22. Piano '29; majored in theory and comp. at Yale (grad. in '43); stud. w. Hindemith for two years, four years w. Richard Donovan. D. Ellington heard and encouraged him in 1955 after he had spent several years in stockbroking. Worked as single at Hickory House in NYC, fall '55 to mid-'56. Was associated w. producing the Great South Bay Jazz Festivals in 1957-8. Took up residence in Italy '58. Favs: O. Peterson, H. Silver, T. Wilson, J. Lewis. Own LP: Trans., no longer available.

THORNHILL, CLAUDE, *leader, composer, piano;* b. Terre Haute, Ind., 8/10/09. Stud. at Cincinnati Cons. and Curtis Inst. Got his first job with Austin Wylie's orch. through Artie Shaw, who was then in the band, and remained a close friend and associate of Shaw for many years. Later arranged for Hal Kemp, Bing Crosby, Benny Goodman; pianist and arranger w. Ray Noble 1935-6.

Sponsored Maxine Sullivan's NY debut and conducted her record of *Loch Lomond.* Own band, 1940-2; in the Navy, 1942-5, played with Artie Shaw and with his own service band. Organizing a new band in 1946, he impressed audiences with the rich range of sounds and with the variety of classical, pop and jazz material on which he drew. The nucleus of his sidemen (including Lee Konitz, Bill Barber, Joe Shulman and arranger Gil Evans) formed the basis of the Miles Davis band on Capitol. Thornhill has continued to lead a band periodically, using his own arrangements as well as those of Gerry Mulligan and Ralph Aldridge. The tonal texture of his original band, notably the manner in which he used French horns, earned him great prestige among musicians. Own LPs: Kapp, Decca, Camden, Design, Harmony.

Addr: c/o Kastriner & Harris, 67 West 44th Street, New York 36, N.Y.

THORNTON, ARGONNE DENSE: See HAKIM, Sadik

TIMER, JOE (Joseph Michael Theimer), *drums, composer, leader;* b. Alexandria, Va., 3/21/23; d. Washington, D.C., 5/15/55. Stud. Navy Sch. of Mus. '43; Catholic U. '47-8. Played w. Johnny Scat Davis '47; briefly w. L. Tristano, '49; Elliot Lawrence May-July '51; TV shows and concerts with "The Orchestra," a cooperative group presented by Willis Conover from Dec. '51. Favs: Kahn, Lamond, Haynes, Blakey. Fav. comps: Kahn, Mandel, Mulligan. Own LP: *House of Sounds* (Brunswick).

TIMMENS, JAMES F. (Jim), *composer;* b. Wyoming, N. Y., 4/15/20. Father and brother played sax; stud. piano as child, later attended Eastman School of Music. St. arr. for dance bands; came to NYC, stud. with Stefan Wolpe and began work in radio, TV and rec. Wrote arrs. for *Porgy and Bess Revisited, Gilbert and Sullivan Revisited* (War. Bros.); *Off the Cuff* (Vik). Favs: Duke Ellington, Eddie Sauter, Bill Finegan, Gil Evans, George Russell.

Addr: 11 E. Winant Ave., Ridgefield Park, N.J.

TIMMONS, ROBERT HENRY (Bobby), *piano;* b. Philadelphia, Pa., 12/19/35. Studied w. uncle, a musician, at six; went to Phila. musical academy for a year. Gigged around Phila. until he joined Kenny Dorham's Jazz Prophets, Feb. 1956. W. Chet Baker, April '56-Jan. '57; Sonny Stitt Feb.-Aug. '57; Maynard Ferguson, Aug. '57-March '58; Art Blakey, July '58-Sept. '59. Joined Cannonball Adderley, Oct. '59. Timmons reflects the intelligent absorption of a variety of modern influences. Favs: Bud Powell, Art Tatum, Red Garland. Own LP: River.; one no. with trio in *Pianists Galore* (Wor. Pac.); LPs w. Hank Mobley, Kenny Dorham, Lee Morgan, Kenny Burrell, Art Blakey (Blue Note), Cannonball Adderley, Pepper Adams (River.), Chet Baker (Wor. Pac.), Maynard Ferguson (Merc.), Art Farmer (UA).

Addr: 314 East 6th St., New York 10, N.Y.

TIZOL, JUAN, *trombone, composer;* b. San Juan, Puerto Rico, 1/22/00. Stud. w. uncle, Manuel Tizol. Played in municipal concert work in San Juan. To US 1920; in pit band at Howard Theatre, Washington, D.C. and w. Bobby Lee's Cotton Pickers. Joined Duke Ellington Sept. '29, remaining with the band until 1944. Since then, except for a period in '51-3 when he was back with Ellington, Tizol has been with Harry James. His mellifluous, Latin-tinged valve trombone style was an important element of the Ellington band in the '30s; he also worked with Ellington on the extraction of scores and, alone or with Duke, wrote such works as *Caravan, Bakiff, Pyramid, Moonlight Fiesta, Conga Brava, Sphinx, Keb-lah, Perdido.* LPs: see Ellington, James; also w. L. Bellson (Verve), Nat Cole (Cap.).

Addr: 2150 South Hobart Blvd., Los Angeles 18, Calif.

TJADER, CALLEN RADCLIFFE, JR. (Cal), *vibes, drums, bongos;* b. St. Louis, Mo., 7/16/25. Mother played piano; father was in vaudeville. Graduated from San Francisco State, majored in music and education. Studied drums under Walter Larew. Played w. Dave Brubeck Trio and Octet 1949-51; George Shearing Quintet Jan. '53 to April '54. Specialized in Latin-American music with own combo in San Francisco from 1954, and by 1960 had earned great popularity regionally (and on records nationally). In late '59 he undertook an Eastern tour. Despite his increasing identification with Latin music, Tjader is still active in regular jazz and is a first-class performer with, as John S. Wilson has said, "a light touch and a propulsive approach." Fav: Milt Jackson. Own LPs: Fantasy; also an early set on Savoy; LPs w. Brubeck (Fant.), Shearing (MGM 3175 incl. own comp. *Mood For Milt*).

TOGAWA, PAUL, *drums;* b. Los Angeles, Calif., 9/3/32. Stud. drums in high school after taking a few trumpet lessons in a relocation center during World War II. Formed 10-piece orch. after grad. high school; majored in music at East LA Junior Coll., then joined Lionel Hampton for a while. Has had own quart. and quint. on West Coast, app. in movies and TV. W. Eddie Cano '59. Fav: Philly Joe Jones. Own LP (Mode).

Addr: 1721 Barnett Road, Los Angeles 32, Calif.

TORME, MELVIN HOWARD (Mel), *singer, comp., drums, piano;* b. Chicago, Ill., 9/13/25. Six months singing w. Coon-Sanders Orch. at Blackhawk, 1929; continued to sing during early school years w. Buddy Rogers and other name bands. Stud. drums at seven; acted in radio soap operas, 1934-40. First song, *Lament to Love,* rec. by Harry James 1941. Toured w. Chico Marx band '42-3 movie debut in *Higher & Higher,* '43; led vocal group, the Mel-Tones, in Calif.; Army, '45-6. Since 1947 has been major name as solo singer, also known for comps. incl. *Stranger in Town, The Christmas Song, Born to Be Blue, County Fair.*

Mel Tormé is an inventive and gifted artist, a writer of first-class music and lyrics. He is greatly admired by other singers, songwriters and musicians. His LPs in the late 1950s invariably featured excellent songs, his interpretations of them backed by an all-star jazz orchestra with Marty Paich as director and arranger. Although his contribution is at least as valuable as that of any other popular singer, and although he is closer to jazz than most, Tormé has been granted far less recognition than he deserves. He was perhaps most appreciated by the British public during vaudeville tours in England, 1956 and '57.

LPs: *California Suite; Tormé Sings Astaire; At The Crescendo; It's a Blue World* (Beth.); *Prelude To a Kiss* (Tops); *Mel Tormé, Back In Town* w. Mel-Tones (Verve).

Addr: 11351 Thurston Circle, West Los Angeles, Cal.

TOSHIKO: See AKIYOSHI, Toshiko

TOTAH, NABIL MARSHALL (Knobby), *bass;* b. Ramallah, Jordan, 4/5/30. Came to US 1944 to attend Moses Brown school in Providence, R. I.; later att. Haverford Coll. where he became interested in jazz; began pl. bass in '53 after he graduated. In Army '53-4 pl. w. Toshiko and Hampton Hawes while in Japan; also w. 289th Div. Army Band. After discharge, pl. w. Roger King Mozian, Charlie Parker, Bobby Scott, Gene Krupa, Johnny Smith, Eddie Costa, Woody Herman, Zoot Sims. With Slide Hampton '60. Favs: Ray Brown, Oscar Pettiford, Red Mitchell. LPs w. Bobby Scott (ABC-Par.); Johnny Smith (Roost); Zoot Sims (Argo, Dawn, ABC-Par.), Sims-Cohn (UA), Herbie Mann (Verve).

TOUFF, CYRIL JAMES (Cy), *bass trumpet;* b. Chicago, Ill., 3/4/27. St. on piano 1932, later C melody sax, tpt., xyl. Trombone in Army band '44-6. After discharge stud. w. L. Tristano. Worked with Jimmy Dale, Jay Burkhardt, Ch. Ventura, Shorty Sherock, Ray McKinley, Boyd Raeburn, also NYC Opera Company. Switched to bass tpt. after hearing Johnny Mandel play one. Joined Woody Herman '53 and toured US and Europe, leaving the band in Jan. '56 to free-lance in Chicago with Chubby Jackson and commercial groups. His sound resembles that of a valve trombone and his style swings exuberantly. Own LPs: Argo, World-Pacific; LPs w. Herman (Cap., Col., Verve), Chubby Jackson (Argo), Nat Pierce (Fant.).

TOUGH, DAVID, *drums;* b. Oak Park, Ill., 4/26/08; d. Newark, N. J., 12/6/48. One of the "Austin High School Gang" in Chicago, he was an associate of Bud Freeman, Frank Teschemacher, Eddie Condon from 1925-7; worked in Europe 1927-8; free-lanced in NYC with Red Nichols and others 1928-30; then sank into obscurity during a long illness and was rehabilitated in early 1936 when he joined Tommy Dorsey. After working w. Bunny Berigan and Benny Goodman in 1938; Jack Teagarden and Joe Marsala, 1939; Artie Shaw, 1941; Ch. Spivak, 1942, and several return dates, during the same years, w. Goodman and Dorsey, he entered the Navy in 1942 and toured the S. Pacific w. Artie Shaw's Navy Band.

For a long time highly regarded among musicians, Tough earned belated public acclaim in 1944-5 in the band of Woody Herman, with which he also had played briefly in 1942. His career after he left Herman was punctuated by a series of breakdowns, alternating with periods of highly successful activity in both modern and Dixieland bands, including Joe Marsala's at the Hickory House, 1945, the Charlie Ventura-Bill Harris combo, 1947, and periodic engagements at Eddie Condon's club. Tough's tragic life ended when, on leave from a New Jersey Veteran's Hospital, he suffered a fractured skull after a fall in a Newark street.

Dave Tough may well be rated the greatest artist ever to work as a jazz drummer. Originally inspired by Baby Dodds and other New Orleans pioneers, he evolved continually through the years; toward the end of his career he idolized Max Roach and was a passionate devotee of modern jazz. Endowed with a brilliant mind and frustrated by an unresolved desire to become a writer, he contributed an excellent series of articles to the pages of *Metronome.* He won the Esquire Armed Forces Award 1944; Silver Award 1945-7; Gold Award 1946; DB poll 1945-6; Met. poll 1946-7.

LPs w. Woody Herman (Harm. 7013, Col. CL 592), Benny Goodman (MGM 3E9, Col. CL 523), Bud Freeman (Em. 36013), Eddie Condon in *Chicago Jazz* (Decca 8029), Wild Bill Davison (Comm. 30009).

TRAPPIER, ARTHUR BENJAMIN (Traps), *drums;* b. Georgetown, S. C., 5/28/10. Raised in NYC. Played w. Carl Brown, Ch. Skeets, 1928; Tiny Bradshaw, Blanche Calloway, Buddy Johnson during '30s; three years w. Fats Waller until shortly before Waller's death. Was w. Teddy Wilson, Ed Hall combos at Cafe Society; on road w. Sy Oliver '47, also NYC clubs w. Ralph Sutton, Art Hodes, Tony Parenti, Joe Sullivan. In late '50s had own trio in Bronx, played w. Ch. Beal Quartet; to Canada w. Willie (The Lion) Smith, also seen on *Omnibus* and other TV shows. Favs: Sid Catlett, who was a close friend and major influence; Jimmy Crawford. LPs w. Ed Hall (Comm., Bruns.), Conrad Janis (Jub.), W. Smith (Urania), Rex Stewart (Felsted).

Addr: 1155 Dean Street, Brooklyn 16, N. Y.

TRAVIS, NICK (Nicholas Anthony Travascio), *trumpet;* b. Philadelphia, Pa., 11/16/25. Stud. Mastbaum Sch. Played w. Johnny McGhee, Vido Musso, Mitch Ayres '42; Woody Herman Dec. '42 off and on until drafted, '44. Jazz concerts in Paris while in service. With Ray McKinley off and on '46-9, six months w. B. Goodman, back with Herman etc. Other name band jobs in '40s w. Wald, Krupa, Bob Chester, Ina Ray Hutton, Les Elgart, T. Dorsey, T. Beneke. Pit band, also gigs w. E. Lawrence, then w. Sauter-Finegan '53-6. On staff at NBC since '57. Fine jazzman and versatile trumpeter. Favs: Clifford Brown, Miles Davis, Harry Glantz. Own LP: Victor (incl. fav. own solo *In The Nick of Time*); LPs w. Sauter-Finegan (Vict.), Bill Holman (Cap.), E. Lawrence (Fant.), T. Aless (Roost), B. Byers, Al Cohn (Vict.); Zoot Sims (River.), Manny Albam (Coral, Victor).

Addr: 15 Spruce Street, Tenafly, N. J.

TREADWELL, GEORGE McKINLEY, *songwriter, trumpet;* b. New Rochelle, N. Y., 12/21/19. Played at Monroe's Uptown House 1941-2; 18 months w. Benny Carter, '42-3, then w. Sunset Royals orch., Tiny Bradshaw, and from late '43 to early '46 w. Cootie Williams. While w. J. C. Heard at Cafe Society, '46, he met Sarah Vaughan, starring in the show there; they were married 9/18/47. After acting as mus. dir. and tpt. player on some of her Musicraft recs. he quit playing and worked as her manager; they were later divorced but he continued to manage her for a couple of years; has also managed Ruth Brown, the Drifters, the Four Guys, and in 1959 enjoyed some success in r & b field as songwriter. LP w. Vaughan (Rondo).

Addr: 1650 Broadway, New York 19, N. Y.

TRENIER, CLAUDE AND CLIFFORD, *singers, leaders;* b. Mobile, Ala., 7/14/19. The twins, who have six other brothers and two sisters, led their own band at Ala. State College in 1941. Claude joined Jimmie Lunceford's band in 1943; Clifford replaced him in '44; two years later, when Claude was released from the Army, they both sang with the band. From 1946 they worked night clubs as a twin act, singing in a rowdy, extroverted r & b style accompanied by their own quintet. They have enjoyed great success in TV, night clubs and movies. Milton, their youngest brother, has toured with the act. LPs: Epic.

Addr: c/o Heller, 1626 N. Vine, Hollywood 28, Cal.

TRENNER, DONALD R. (Donn), *piano;* b. New Haven, Conn., 3/10/27. During school years stud. classical piano, also pl. tbn. Piano w. Yale Collegians '43, Ted Fio Rito '43-5, led Air Corps band '46. In '47 he was in the Buddy Morrow orch. along with his wife, singer Helen Carr; the following year he and Miss Carr had their own trio in SF, and in 1950-1 they worked w. Ch. Barnet. After playing w. Jerry Gray, Stan Getz, Ch. Parker, Geo. Auld, Jerry Fielding and Skinnay Ennis in '52-3, Trenner joined Les Brown's band '53 and has been with him intermittently since then. During one absence (Feb.-Oct. '57) he went to NY, worked w. Oscar Pettiford, Anita O'Day, and was in Europe for a while. Stud. in Florence, Italy, summer '58. LPs w. Les Brown (Coral, Capitol, Kapp); Howard McGhee, Frances Faye, Betty Roche (Beth.).

Addr: 17612 Burbank Blvd., Encino, Calif.

TRENT, ALPHONSO E. (Al or Fonnie), *piano, leader;* b. Fort Smith, Ark., 8/24/05. Began music in high school where father was principal. Influenced by W. C. Handy and Fletcher Henderson. Stud. music at Shorter Coll., Little Rock, Ark; org. first band 1923, gaining wide territorial fame. First Negro band to play top white hotel, the Adolphus in Dallas, Tex., '25-6. Sidemen at various times were Peanuts Holland, Mouse Randolph, Snub Mosley, Stuff Smith, Sy Oliver, Harry Edison. Trent quit the band in 1932 to attend to family affairs, but band cont. under his name. Back in the business in mid-30s w. sextet pl. through the Northwest and South. This group incl. Charlie Christian, Alex Hill et al. In recent years has led local quintet while managing real estate. Rec. for Gennett '27-31.

Addr: 1301 N. 9th St., Fort Smith, Ark.

TRIGLIA, WILLIAM E. (Bill), *piano;* b. Bronx, N. Y., 2/22/24. Parents both pianists. Stud. with an uncle, 1936-42; one year at Juilliard, '45-6, and a year at Louisville, Ky., '46-7. Professional debut after his return from the service in '45, playing jazz dates at Club Paradise in Nyack, N. Y. Name band experience incl. Les Elgart, '46; Alvino Rey, Sam Donahue, Johnny Bothwell, Geo. Auld, Terry Gibbs, Buddy Rich. Has played frequent club dates around NYC w. Davey Schildkraut, who helped him get started in jazz, incl. Cafe Bohemia '59. He has also been active since '48 as piano teacher. Record debut '54 in Hank D'Amico album. Favs.: Tatum, Bud Powell. LPs w. Tony Fruscella (Atl.), Sam Most (Vang., Beth.), Hank D'Amico (Beth.).

Addr: 459 Kinderkamack Rd., Westwood, N. J.

TRISTANO, LEONARD JOSEPH (Lennie), *piano, composer;* b. Chicago, Ill., 3/19/19. Weak-sighted from birth, he was totally blind by about 1928. During his extensive studies, which included attendance at the American Conservatory of Music, he played piano locally in saloons from age 12; as clarinetist, led his own Dixieland group. Played tenor sax and clarinet in rhumba band in Chicago, piano in various clubs. In 1946, encouraged by Chubby Jackson, he came to NYC. During the next five years, while playing intermittently with his own combos, he worked successfully to expand the harmonic horizons of jazz improvisation. Tristano, whose original influence was Earl Hines, now found himself the leader of an informal cult, a school of progressive ideas in which his principal disciples were Lee Konitz, Warne Marsh, Billy Bauer. They were the key men in a series of remarkable recordings on Capitol (1949) in which some of Tristano's theories were carried into practice.

Tristano opened his own studio in June, 1951, and since that time, aside from occasional club and concert appearances, has been active mainly as a teacher. Even musicians associated with earlier jazz schools, among them Bud Freeman and Bob Wilber, have come to him for instruction. One of the most determinedly radical thinkers in modern jazz, Tristano, who was aided by the continuous and enthusiastic support of Barry Ulanov, has had a great influence on a large number of followers and was the author of some pungent articles on jazz in the pages of *Metronome.*

In '58-9, he app. regularly, at frequent intervals, at the Half Note, NYC, with his quintet feat. Konitz and Marsh. Won *Met.* poll '50. Fav: Bud Powell. Own LPs: Atlantic 1224; three tracks in *Cool And Quiet* (Cap. T371); four tracks in *The Jazz Keyboard* (Savoy 12043); two tracks in *Advance Guard of The Forties* (Em. 36016); one track in *Modern Jazz Piano: Four Views* (Cam. 384); LPs w. Lee Konitz (Pres. 7004), *Metronome All Stars* (Cam. 426, Harm. 7044).

Addr: 8667 Palo Alto St., Hollis, L. I., N. Y.

TROTMAN, LLOYD NELSON, *bass, composer;* b. Boston, Mass., 5/25/23. Stud. New England Cons. and his father's school, the Music Lovers' Sch. of Mus. Pl. w. Joe Nevils' Ala. Aces 1941, toured w. Blanche Calloway; to NYC 1945. Pl. w. Eddie Heywood, Hazel Scott. Spent two months w. Duke Ellington, '45 (before Pettiford) and attributes every subsequent job to the prestige of having worked w. Duke. Worked w. Pete Brown on 52nd st.; Geo. James and Edmond Hall at Cafe Society; Wilbur De Paris at Childs. Spent a year w. Boyd Raeburn, '48-9, and a year w. Johnny Hodges, '51-2, also gigged w. Sonny Dunham, Jerry Wald. Mainly active in record work in recent years, he has made hundreds of r & b sessions for Atlantic, Mercury, etc. Pl. w. Red Allen at NJF, '59. Signed w. Brunswick Rec. '59; comp. & arr. *Take Five* feat. bass supported by vocal group and rhythm section, and has expressed ambition to find new means and new settings for melodic expression on bass. Favs: Blanton, Pettiford, Slam Stewart, Richard Davis. LPs w. Cecil Lloyd (20th-Fox), J. Hodges, Lawrence Brown (Verve).

Addr: 27-27 Gillmore Street, East Elmhurst, L. I., N. Y.

TROUP, ROBERT WILLIAM (Bobby), *singer, piano, composer;* b. Harrisburg, Pa., 10/18/18. Family owned music stores; early exp. working for them. While dancing in Mask & Wig show at U. of Pa., wrote first song hit, *Daddy.* With T. Dorsey as staff songwriter 1941; U. S. Marines '42-6 (Captain). Moving to Los Angeles to resume composing career, he commemorated the trip with his next hit, *Route 66.* Worked in bars as pianist, then added bass, later guitar; since 1949, trio work in LA clubs; 1954-5 personnel included Howard Roberts, guitar and Bob Enevoldsen, bass. From July '56 until Dec. '58 he was moderator of a successful television series, *Stars of Jazz,* seen locally on KABC-TV in Hollywood and for a few months in '58 on the ABC network. In '59 he was seen briefly, playing the role of Arthur Schutt, in the film *The Five Pennies;* later he played T. Dorsey in the *Gene Krupa Story.* Songs incl. *Snooty Little Cutie, Baby Baby All the Time.* Rec. *Brand New Dolly* w. Count Basie (Vict.). Ultra-sophisticated, jazz-tinged vocal style. Own LPs on Lib., Interlude, Vict., Beth., Cap. Also produced many LPs for Julie London (Lib.), his wife since January 1, 1960.

Addr: 4440 Vantage, North Hollywood, Calif.

TRUJILLO, WILLIAM LEE (Bill), *tenor sax, clarinet;* b. Los Angeles, Calif., 7/7/30. Stud. clar. in grammar and junior high schools, sax in high school; harmony and arr. at Westlake Coll. of Music. Pl. with dance bands in high school; w. Alvino Rey 1950; Woody Herman '53-4; Charlie Barnet '56. Toured w. Stan Kenton 1959. Favs: Lester Young, Zoot Sims, Stan Getz. LPs w. Bill Russo (Atl.), Woody Herman (Verve).

Addr: 1917 Thomas Street, Los Angeles 31, Calif.

TRUMBAUER, FRANKIE (Tram), *C melody sax;* b. Carbondale, Ill., 1900; d. Kansas City, Mo., 6/11/56. Raised in St. Louis. Stud. violin, piano, trombone, flute but became famous as the only jazzman to work mainly with C melody sax (often mistaken for alto). Had own band at 17; served in Navy in World War I. Known during 1920s as inseparable associate of Bix Beiderbecke, who played in his band at the Arcadia Ballroom, St. Louis 1925-6; later worked with Bix in the bands of Jean Goldkette and Paul Whiteman. Trumbauer led various recording bands from '29-36, often using a contingent from Paul Whiteman's orchestra; on some numbers he sang and occasionally played clarinet, alto sax and cornet. His most important contributions to jazz, however, were made in '27-8, when, in partnership w. Bix, he produced a memorable series of sides, many of which were reissued on Col. CL 845.

Trumbauer remained w. Paul Whiteman from '27-36 and had his own band from '37-9; in '40 he retired from music to join the Civil Aeronautics Authority. He returned in '45 to do studio work at NBC in NYC

w. the Raymond Paige orch. but except for occasional special appearances was inactive musically during the last sixteen years of his life. Although his importance as a jazz soloist is disputed, he made an incontestable place for himself as the catalyst of some of the greatest recorded jazz of the '20s. As the original influence of Lester Young, he was also an important link in jazz history. LPs w. Beidebecke (Col. CL 845, CL 846) and in *On The Road Jazz* (River.); one no. in *A String of Swingin' Pearls* (Vict.).

TRUNK, PETER, *bass;* also *trumpet, 'cello;* b. Frankfurt am Main, Germany, 5/17/36. Broadcasts and concerts with Kenny Clarke, Zoot Sims, 1957; Stan Getz, Rita Reys, '58; member of Albert Mangelsdorff septet '58-9. Records with Hans Koller, Sims, Mangelsdorff. Very promising young bassist. Favs: Pettiford, Chambers, Brown, Mitchell.

Addr: Schwindstr. 16, Frankfurt am Main, Germany.

TUCKER, BENJAMIN MAYER (Ben), *bass;* b. Nashville, Tenn., 12/13/30. Stud. tuba in high school 1948-9; majored in music at Tennessee State U. and st. bass there. Pl. in Nashville clubs for two years in service four years. Joined Warne Marsh after discharge; w. Art Pepper briefly; w. Carl Perkins at Tiffany Club in LA. Came to NYC early 1959, gigged w. various groups, then joined Roland Hanna. Toured w. Chris Connor fall '59. Favs: Ray Brown, Pettiford. LPs w. Freddie Gambrell (Wor. Pac.), Roland Hanna (Atco), Dempsey Wright (Andex), Warne Marsh (Imp.).

Addr: 423 N. Michigan Ave., Pasadena, Calif.

TUCKER, ROBERT (Bobby), *piano;* b. Morristown, N.J., 1922. Began jobbing at 14, using pay to study under Cecily Knechtel of Juilliard. Worked with the Barons of Rhythm, 1932; entered service '43 for three years and was trombonist in military band; pianist-arranger-leader w. post dance band. Was Mildred Bailey's accompanist soon after discharge. In the next three years he worked off and on for Billie Holiday, played in 52nd st. combos led by Lucky Thompson and Stuff Smith. He joined Billy Eckstine, June 1949, and has toured US and Europe with him, impressing listeners everywhere with his discreet, sensitive work. In his rare solo appearances he is revealed as a first-class bop-influenced performer. LPs w. Eckstine (MGM, Merc., Roul.); Les Thompson (Vict.), *Chase & Steeplechase* (Decca).

Addr: 34 Cleveland Avenue, Morristown, N. J.

TUCKER, GEORGE ANDREW, *bass;* b. Palatka, Fla., 12/10/27. Moving to NYC in 1948, he began study at New York Conservatory of Modern Music. Had become interested in music (through a record by Ellington w. O. Pettiford) in the Army. Worked w. various groups and instrumentalists, incl. E. Bostic, S. Stitt, J. Coltrane, and became house bassist in Continental Lounge in Bklyn. Stud. privately w. Fred Zimmerman at Juilliard '57-8. House bassist at Minton's Play House, working there as leader, also sideman w. Jerome Richardson and others '58-9. Favs: M. Davis, C. Parker, O. Pettiford. LPs w. Freddie Redd (River.), Clifford Jordan (Blue Note), Bennie Green (Enrica, Blue Note), Jackie McLean (Jub.), John Handy (Roul.), Joe Zawinul (Strand), *Jazz It's Magic* (Reg.), Johnny Smith (New Jazz).

Addr: 1800 7th Ave., New York 26, N. Y.

TURNER, BRUCE, *clarinet, alto sax;* b. Saltburn, Yorkshire, Eng., 7/5/22. Father a Shakespeare prof. Childhood in India, then to Dulwich Sch. in England. Self-taught; clar. 1934; alto '43 in RAF. Joined bop group in '46 but quit music to work in civil service until 1948; then pl. w. Freddy Randall to '50; led quartet on *Queen Mary* w. Dill Jones, Peter Ind, '50; w. Ronnie Ball Quintet for three months in '51; then back w. Randall '51-3. Humphrey Lyttelton band, '53-7 (also Kenny Baker in '56 and concerts w. Condon, Bechet); own "Jump Band" from '57. Has pl. w. own groups all over Europe incl. Bucharest, Warsaw, Moscow, Vienna. Many recs. for Pye-Nixa, Polygon, Esquire (British labels). Fav. own solo: *Lightly and Politely* w. Lyttelton. Fav: J. Hodges.

TURNER, JOSEPH (Big Joe), *singer,* b. Kansas City, Mo., 5/18/11. Sang for many years around KC, often in partnership with pianist Pete Johnson. Came to NYC in 1938 and was featured in concert at Carnegie Hall, then worked at Cafe Society and during the next two years made records w. Joe Sullivan, Art Tatum, Pete Johnson and others. In the early 1950s, after some years of comparative obscurity, Turner enjoyed a new vogue as a top-selling r & b artist on Atlantic, his first big hit being *Chains of Love.* He is one of the most unspoiled of blues shouters in the great tradition in which sonority and conviction take precedence over clarity of diction. Won Esq. Silver Award 1945. Own LPs on Atl., LPs w. Pete Johnson (Merc.), *Kansas City Jazz, Encyclopedia of Jazz on Records, Vol. 3* (Decca), *Upright and Lowdown* (Col.), *Spirituals To Swing* (Vang.).

TURNER, JOE, *piano;* b. Baltimore, Md., 11/3/07. Not related to the blues singer of the same name. Early experience in Harlem bands w. Jimmy Harrison, June Clark *et al;* was also heard w. Louis Armstrong in the 1930s and accompanied Adelaide Hall, touring Europe with her. After World War II he returned to Europe and has remained there in recent years. A swinging pianist in the James P. Johnson-Fats Waller tradition.

TURRENTINE, STANLEY WILLIAM, *tenor saxophone;* b. Pittsburgh, Pa., 4/5/34. Studied tenor from 1947. Pl. w. Ray Charles '52, Earl Bostic '53, Max Roach '59-60. Favs: Don Byas, Coleman Hawkins, Sonny Rollins. Own LP: Time.

TURRENTINE, THOMAS WALTER, JR., *trumpet;* b. Pittsburgh, Pa., 4/22/28. Studied from 1940. Pl. w. Snookum Russell '45-6, Benny Carter '46, George Hudson '48-50, Earl Bostic '52-3, Charlie Mingus '56, Max Roach '59-60. Favs: Gillespie, Kenny Dorham, Art

Farmer. Own LP: Time. LPs w. Max Roach (Mercury), Bostic (King).

TWARDZIK, RICHARD (Dick), *piano;* b. Danvers, Mass., 1931; d. Paris, France, 10/21/55, during a tour with Chet Baker's quartet. Prof. debut in Boston, 1951 w. Serge Chaloff. Later worked in Boston w. Ch. Parker, Ch. Mariano, and toured for several months w. Lionel Hampton band. Twardzik's untimely death robbed jazz of a potentially great talent; he was developing into an outstandingly individual modern stylist. Own LP: trio on half an LP, shared w. Russ Freeman, also one no. in *Pianists Galore* (Wor. Pac.); LPs w. Chet Baker (Wor. Pac.).

U

UMILIANI, PIERO, *composer, piano;* also *vibes;* b. Florence, Italy, 7/17/26. Stud. piano from age 6, composition and harmony from 1952. Leads own groups but is mainly concerned with the writing of background scores for films. A recent soundtrack featured Chet Baker. Favs: Ellington, Mulligan.

Addr: V. Stresa, 66, Rome, Italy.

URSO, PHILIP (Phil), *tenor sax;* b. Jersey City, N.J., 10/2/25. Started on clarinet at thirteen; stud. in high school in Denver, Colo. To NYC 1947; Elliot Lawrence, '48-50; Woody Herman, '50-1; Jimmy Dorsey, '51; Terry Gibbs, Miles Davis, '52; Oscar Pettiford, '53; then free-lanced at Birdland, etc. around NYC. Joined Chet Baker, 1955. Later worked in Denver; with Ernie Ross Quartet in Las Vegas '59-60. Solos on *Elevation, Devil And The Deep Blue Sea* (Col.), with Lawrence: *Leo The Lion, By George* (MGM), with Herman. Favs: Getz, Sims, Cohn, Rollins. Own LPs on Savoy, Reg.; LPs w. Chet Baker (Wor. Pac.), *Rocky Mountain Jazz* w. Jomar Dagron (Golden Crest), Woody Herman (MGM).

URTREGER, RENE, *piano;* b. Paris, France, 7/16/34. St. on piano at five; lived in southern France and N. Africa 1939-45; after war, returned to Paris, resumed studies. Prof. debut at 19 worked w. Pierre Michelot and various modern combos in Paris. Toured w. Birdland show on Continent for 25 days in '56, accompanying Miles Davis, Lester Young. John Lewis, who heard him during several visits to Paris, supervised a recording session for him in April '57 (for Atlantic). Orig. infl. Basie, Garner, Tatum, Waller; later Bud Powell, Monk, Lewis. LPs: two w. Lionel Hampton (Merc.), own group (Atlantic), w. Miles Davis in *Jazz Track* (Col.).

USSELTON, WILLIAM HUGH (Billy), *tenor sax;* also *clarinet, bass clarinet, oboe;* b. Newcastle, Pa., 7/2/26. While at high school in Youngstown, Ohio, was heard jamming in a night club by Bubbles Becker, whose band he then joined. Pl. w. Sonny Dunham '47-8, Ray Anthony '48-9 and '51-2, Tommy Dorsey '49-50. Had own group w. Bill Harris in Fla. '52-3. W. Les Brown '54-'60 incl. trips to Europe, N. Africa and Far East '57-'58. Married Brown's vocalist Lauri Johnson '58. Feat. on *Opus 2* w. Tommy Dorsey (Vict.), all Les Brown Coral and Capitol LPs since '54; led own jazz combo on Kapp. Fav. own solo: *Twilight Time* in *The Les Brown Story* (Cap.). Fav: S. Getz.

Addr: 6500 Blucher Ave., Van Nuys, Calif.

V

VALDAMBRINI, OSCAR, *trumpet, composer;* b. Turin, Italy, 5/11/24. Son of noted violinist. Stud. music at Cons. of Turin. St. on violin but soon switched to trumpet. Just after World War II pl. in Switzerland, then in Turin, later settling in Milan where he has dominated the jazz scene since '55, the year his Sestetto Italiano made its debut at the National Jazz Festival. Later formed quintet w. tenor man Gianni Basso which has pl. for several seasons at Taverna Mexico in Milan. In '57-8 broadcast regularly w. big band of Armando Trovajoli in Rome. As composer, strongly infl. by Shorty Rogers. Rec. w. Chet Baker '59. LP: one track on *San Remo Festival* (Verve).

VALDEZ, CARLOS (Potato), *conga drum;* b. Havana, Cuba, 11/4/26. To US Oct. 1953. Played for four years w. Machito; then w. Tito Puente. Joined Herbie Mann's Afro-Cuban combo June '59 and toured Africa w him '60. LPs w. Herbie Mann (UA), Art Blakey, Kenny Dorham (Blue Note).

Addr: 246 East 112th St., New York 29, N. Y.

VALENTE, CATERINA, *singer, guitar;* b. Paris, France, 1/14/31. Fourth show-business generation of French-Italian family; parents, brothers, sister all musicians. Prof. debut at five in vaud. act w. mother. Took up guitar 1945; combo work in Toulouse w. Django Reinhardt's cousin, Chalin Ferret, '46; w. Erling Grönsted combo, Sweden, '47-8. Stage work w. brother Silvio. During '50s, popular throughout Continent as multilingual stage, night club singer; many movies from '54. To US '55 and '56 for hotel, TV work. Many rec. for Polydor, Decca, RCA; session playing and singing w. Chet Baker in Germany. Biggest hits: *Malaguena, The Breeze and I.* Though known mainly as variety and film figure rather than jazz artist, she is more a jazz singer than many artists so identified in US; her conception, phrasing and timbre are exceptional. LPs: Decca.

Addr: Postbox 270, Lugano, Switzerland.

VALENTINE, GERALD (Jerry), *composer, trombone;* b. Chicago, Ill., 9/14/14. Stud. piano as a child in Champaign, Ill., later composition and harmony in high school. Self-taught on trombone, which he began in 1937. Worked w. Jimmy Raschel and Richard Fox; joined Earl Hines on trom. 1940, and made several arrangements for the band, incl. *Second Balcony Jump.* Ret. to Chicago in '43; w. Dallas Bartley and King Kolax combos; arr. for shows at Club DeLisa and Joe's DeLuxe Club, before joining Billy Eckstine's band in '44 as trombonist-arr. Cont. his association w. Eckstine after the band broke up in '47, arr. the numbers that brought solo vocal fame to Eckstine. Had an a & r job at National Records '50-52; since then has written occasional arrangements, but has been in semi-retirement. Was very important in the development of the Eckstine orch. when it was one of the first big bands to feature bop. LP: *Outskirts of Town* w. Blues-Swingers (Pres.).

Addr: 56 W. 91st Street, New York City.

VANCE, RICHARD THOMAS (Dick), *composer, trumpet;* b. Mayfield, Ky., 11/28/15. Raised in Cleveland; private studies on violin, then trumpet. Toured w. Frank Terry band 1932-4; w. Lil Armstrong in Buffalo, '35; to NYC '36, worked w. Kaiser Marshall, Willie Bryant; Fletcher Henderson '36-8, then w. Chick Webb and Ella Fitzgerald to '41. During '40s, worked w. Eddie Heywood, Don Redman, Ch. Barnet, and in pit bands for shows incl. *Memphis Bound, St. Louis Woman, Pal Joey, Beggars' Holiday* and offstage band in *Streetcar Named Desire.* Studied comp. and trumpet at Juilliard, 1944-7. As arr. he wrote most of Ella's material while w. Webb; staff arr. for Cab Calloway, Don Redman; also for Glen Gray 1939-41; arr. for Sarah Vaughan while she was with Earl Hines, for B. Eckstine's big band, Lena Horne and many arrs. for Harry James. Arr. *How High The Moon, Stomping at Savoy, In The Mood, Flyin' Home* for D. Ellington. Since 1954 has been leading his own band, which played often at the Savoy Ballroom until its closing in 1958, and at the Celebrity Club. LP as arr: *Ellington '55* (Cap.); LP w. Eddie Heywood (Decca); *Like Who?* w. Paul Quinichette (UA).

Addr: 337 West 138th Street, New York 30, N. Y.

VAN DAMME, ART, *accordion;* b. Norway, Mich., 4/9/20. Raised in Chicago. Stud. piano, accordion w. P. Caviani in Iron Mountain, Mich.; accordion w. Andy Rizzo in Chicago. Played w. Ben Bernie band, 1941; local combos and bands in Chicago until 1944, when he became a staff musician at NBC. Has led own quintet, heard on records during past fifteen years, in many pleasant, neatly-arranged performances better classified as pop music than as jazz. Won DB poll '52-8. Own LPs: Cap., Col.

VANDERPOOL, SYLVIA, *guitar, singer;* b. New York City, 5/29/35. Stud. piano as a child. Was singing w. bands at 14 and recording as "Little Sylvia." Met Mickey Baker, took up guitar, and as "Mickey and Sylvia" they had wide popularity in '57-8 in the rhythm and blues field. Fav: Mickey Baker.

Addr: 461 Central Park West, New York, N. Y.

VAN EPS, GEORGE, *guitar;* b. Plainfield, N. J., 8/7/13. Noted musical family incl. father, Fred Van Eps, banjo; brothers, Bobby, piano & arr.; Fred, arr.; John, saxes. George was self-taught on banjo, 1924; pl. w. Smith Ballew, 1929-31; Freddy Martin, '31-3; Benny Goodman, '34-5; Ray Noble, '35-6 and '39-41; free-lance radio and records in Hollywood 1936-9 and 1945-55, incl. house band work w. Paul Weston since 1945. Worked for father in sound rec. research laboratory, Plainfield, '42-4. Fine musician, emphasizing chords rather than single-string modern style. Film: *Pete Kelly's Blues;* also same TV series. Won Met. poll 1937. (Also an engineer; after years of research, he completed, in 1954, what he believed to be the world's smallest fully operating live steam locomotive.) Own LPs: Col.; LPs w. Marvin Ash (Decca), Jerry Colonna (Lib.), Matty Matlock in *Pete Kelly At Home* (Vict.), *Pete Kelly Lets His Hair Down* (War. Bros.).

Addr: 436 So. Fairview St., Burbank, Calif.

VAN KRIEDT, DAVID (David N. Kriedt), *composer, tenor sax;* b. Berkeley, Calif., 6/19/22. Stud. flute, clar. in high school, composition w. Darius Milhaud at Mills Coll. and in Paris. Worked w. dance bands 1938-9; early associate of Dave Brubeck, '40. W. D. C. Band, Presidio, SF '42-6. Assoc. w. Jazz Workshop Ensemble early '47 (later became Brubeck Octet); worked w. Jacques Dieval in Paris early '48 w. Kenny Clarke and Dick Collins, and other groups in France and throughout Continent '47-8; Hal Mead, '49-52. Toured w. Stan Kenton summer '55. Van Kriedt has free-lanced extensively around SF and was also active for six months as French teacher in SF City College. Ambition: To invent new forms, incorporate jazz into standard symphonic repertoire. Favs: Stan Getz, Zoot Sims; fav. arrs. Bill Holman, Shorty Rogers, Alec Wilder. LPs w. Kenton (Cap.), Brubeck: *Reunion* (Fant.).

Addr: 1139 N. Ogden Drive, Los Angeles 46, Calif.

VAN LAKE, TURK (Vanig Hovsepian), *composer, guitar;* b. Boston, Mass., 6/15/18. Stud. harmony w. Otto Cesana. Played w. Ch. Spivak, Teddy Powell, Hudson-De Lange, 1941; G. Auld, 1942 & '44; Sam Donahue, '42; Ch. Barnet '43. Arr. for Basie, Hampton, Buddy Rich, B. Goodman, V. Lopez, '45-8. Stud. at Boston Cons. '47-50. Worked as teacher 1950-4. Own quartet June to Sept. '54, then joined Les Elgart. While with Elgart (Nov. '54-Sept. '58) took time out for USAFE trip to bases in France, Germany, N. Africa w. C. Thornhill band, Dec. '56. Concert tours w. B. Goodman Sept. '58 and Mar. '59. Comp. *Georgie-Porgie, In the Middle, Co-Pilot* for Auld. Pl. on *Cheerful Little Earful* w. Terry Gibbs etc. Favs: Chuck Wayne, Freddie Green. Fav. arr: Don Redman. LPs w. Gibbs (Merc.), Big Miller (UA), Eddie Vinson (Beth.), Les Elgart (Col.), Larry Elgart (Vict.), B. Goodman (Col., Chess).

Addr: 496 Arden Ave., Annadale, Staten Island, N. Y.

VAUGHAN, SARAH LOIS, *singer;* b. Newark, N.J., 3/27/24. Her father, now retired, was a carpenter, her mother a laundress. As a child Sarah sang at the Mt. Zion Baptist Church in Newark. She took piano lessons from 1931 to '39, also studied organ. After winning an amateur contest at the Apollo Theatre, NYC, she was recommended by Billy Eckstine, who was then Earl Hines' vocalist, for a job with the band, and made her debut as vocalist and second pianist with Hines at the Apollo, Apr. 1943. She joined the new band formed by Eckstine in 1944 and made her own first record session, organized by this writer, 12/31/44 for Continental (reissued on Remington LP).

Except for a couple of months in the winter of 1945-6, when she was vocalist with John Kirby's combo at the Copacabana, NYC, Sarah worked as a solo act after she left Eckstine in '45. Helped mainly by a Musicraft recording contract and by the enthusiasm of musicians such as Dizzy Gillespie and Charlie Parker, who had long been hailing her voice as a new development in jazz, she worked her way up very slowly into choicer club jobs and more general public acceptance. Working at Cafe Society, she met George Treadwell, trumpeter with the J. C. Heard sextet there, and after their marriage, 9/18/47, Treadwell devoted himself to building her career. (After they were divorced Treadwell continued to manage her for a couple of years.)

By 1949, when she signed with Columbia records, Sarah had benefited from the active support of Dave Garroway and other radio and TV stars. Within the following two years she at last gained international recognition, toured successfully in England and France, and became a major concert attraction in the US.

Sarah Vaughan's voice, completely different from that of Billie Holiday, Ella Fitzgerald or any of the other great jazz stylists before her, brought to jazz an unprecedented combination of attractive characteristics: a rich, beautifully controlled tone and vibrato; an ear for the chord structure of songs, enabling her to change or inflect the melody as an instrumentalist might; a coy, sometimes archly naive quality alternating with a sense of great sophistication. The emotional impact she can convey was memorably demonstrated in non-jazz, "straight" performances such as *The Lord's Prayer* and *Sometimes I Feel Like a Motherless Child,* which she recorded in the 1940s for the now long-defunct Musicraft label and which on the level of passionate communication are superior to almost any of her jazz solos.

Some of her recordings during the 1950s featured run-of-the-mill commercial tunes with lush string backgrounds and are devoid of jazz content. Her best jazz work on records has been done in performances with small groups, or with large swinging bands using Basie's sidemen etc. She has won the following awards: *Esquire* New Star 1947; DB poll '47-52; Met poll '48-52.

Own LPs: *After Hours* (Col. CL 660); *After Hours at London House* (Merc. 20383); *At Mister Kelly's* (Merc. 20326); *At the Blue Note* (Merc. 20094); *Best of Irving Berlin* with Billy Eckstine (Merc. 203161); *Favorites* (Harmony 7208); *Great* (Harmony 7158); *Great Songs from Hit Shows* (two LPs) (Merc. MGP 2-100); *with Her Trio* (EmArcy 36109); *In a Pensive Mood* (Rond. 102); *In a Romantic Mood* (Merc. 20223); *In Hi-Fi* (Col. CL 745); *In The Land of Hi Fi* (EmArcy 36058); *Linger Awhile* (Col. CL 914); *No 'Count Sarah* (Merc. 20441); *Sarah* (EmArcy 36004); *Sarah Vaughan* (Lion 70052); *Sassy* (EmArcy 36089); *Sings* (Rond. 853); *Sings Gershwin* (two LPs) (Merc. MGP 2-101); *Songs of Broadway* (Rond. 35); *Vaughan and Violins* (Merc. 20370); *Wonderful Sarah* (Merc. 20219); *Sarah Vaughan Sings* (first sessions) (Masterseal MS-55).

Addr: 394 Woodland Avenue, Englewood Cliffs, N. J.

VENTURA, CHARLIE (Charles Venturo), *saxophones, leader;* b. Philadelphia, Pa., 12/2/16. The fourth of 13 children. Started on C melody sax 1931. Early influence was Chu Berry. Worked in father's hat factory, and from 1940-2 at Navy Yard, jamming frequently with Bill Harris, Gillespie, Eldridge, De Franco. Played tenor w. G. Krupa '42-3 and '44-6; Teddy Powell, '43-4. Own big band '46-7. From '47-9 he led a series of small bop combos that earned him great popularity as a leader. He made frequent use of bop singing (first w. Buddy Stewart, then Jackie Cain and Roy Kral), often in unison with his own horn. He had his own big band again for a year, but gave it up in Feb. '51; ran his own night club, the Open House, outside Phila. from Dec. 1950 until summer '54. Featured in the "Big Four" with Buddy Rich, Chubby Jackson, Marty Napoleon from Aug. 1951; w. G. Krupa trio Jan. to June 1952, visited Japan w. Krupa; in the late '50s he led his own small groups, building a large popular following in Las Vegas night clubs.

Known mainly as a tenor saxophonist, Ventura has also performed occasionally on soprano, alto, baritone and bass sax. He won the following polls: *Esquire* New Star award 1946; *Down Beat* poll '45 on tenor sax and '48 for small combo; *Metronome* poll '49 for tenor sax and small combo. Own LPs: Reg., Merc., GNP, Decca, Bruns., Verve, Tops. LPs w. *Saturday Night Swing Session* (Ctpt.), Met. All Stars (Cam.), Gene Krupa (Col., Verve), JATP (Verve).

VENUTI, GIUSEPPE (Joe), *violin, leader;* b. aboard a ship that was bringing his family to US as immigrants from Italy, 9/1/04; raised in Philadelphia. From 1925 he was a frequent partner and recording associate of guitarist Eddie Lang; together they participated in hundreds of major jazz record dates during the following eight years (Lang died in 1933). Venuti, putting his classical training and expert craftsmanship to unprecedented use, became known as the first jazz violinist. One of his innovations was the playing of all four strings at once for chord passages by tying the bow around the instrument.

In addition to appearing and/or recording with Red Nichols, Frank Trumbauer, Paul Whiteman, Roger Wolfe Kahn, Jean Goldkette, Hoagy Carmichael, Phil Napoleon, Dorsey Bros., Adrian Rollini and Red McKenzie, Venuti began a series of records under his own name in Sept. 1926, the most famous of which were by "Venuti's Blue Four," members including Lang and, from time to time, Rollini, Trumbauer, Lennie Hayton, Jimmy Dorsey. They achieved a unique style, a tonal finesse and jazz-chamber-music quality hitherto unknown in jazz.

Venuti played with great success in England in 1934. In the next two decades he toured almost continuously, usually with his own band, but never accomplished anything equalling his early artistic achievements, though his musicianship remained peerless. In Dec. '56 he appeared on Jackie Gleason's CBS-TV memorial tribute to Tommy Dorsey; aside from this he has been in relative obscurity in recent years, leading small groups in LA clubs etc. In contrast with his smooth and serene musical personality, Venuti has always been known among his contemporaries as something of a screwball personality, many of whose wild escapades and practical jokes are recalled in Bing Crosby's autobiography *Call Me Lucky* (Simon & Schuster). Venuti was elected to the *Down Beat* All Time Swing band, 1936. Own LP: Grand Award; two tracks on Paul Whiteman 50th Anniv. album (Grand Award); one track in *Encyclopedia of Jazz on Records, Vol. I* (Decca).

VENUTO, JOSEPH (Joe), *vibes, drums, misc. percussion;* b. Bronx, N.Y., 6/20/29. Father a drummer. Studied w. Henry Adler, Phil Kraus, Alfred Fried. Master's degree from Manhattan Sch. of Mus. Prof. debut 1943 in Catskill Mts. and USO work. Society bands in NYC, jazz dates in Long Island clubs '46-9. Own quartet in NYC '50-2. Feat. on vibes, xylophone and misc. percussion w. Sauter-Finegan '54-6. W. Benny Goodman, summer '56, then house orch. at Radio City Music Hall under Raymond Paige '56-8, Johnny Richards '58-9; commercial TV work, etc. App. w. Don Butterfield at NJF '58. Own LP: *Sounds Different* (Evst.); LPs w. Sauter-Finegan, Billy Byers (Vict.), *Westchester Jazz Workshop* (Unique), Rex Stewart (Des.), Jim Timmens (War. Bros.), Johnny Richards (Cap., Roul.), Geo. Romanis (Coral).

Addr: 310 Kimball Ave., Yonkers, N.Y.

VER PLANCK, JOHN FENNO (Billy), *composer, trombone;* b. Norwalk, Conn., 4/30/30. First prof. job w. Jess Stacy band at 15. Has written music for many name bands, also played first trombone w. C. Thornhill 1952, Dorsey Bros. May-Dec. '56, and on the last record date (*So Rare*) under Jimmy Dorsey's name. First jazz original to be recorded was *Chicken Boogie* pl. by R. Marterie (Merc.) in '52. Rarely takes jazz solos but was heard on *Du-Udah-Udah* in *Jazz for Playgirls* (Savoy). Favs: Bill Harris, T. Dorsey. Fav. arrs: Marion Evans, N. Hefti, B. Strayhorn, Hall Overton, C. Basie, D. Ellington. Own LPs on Savoy, WW.

Addr: 42 W. 65th St., New York, N.Y.

VINNEGAR, LEROY, *bass;* b. Indianapolis, Ind., 7/13/28. Self-taught, first on piano, then bass. Started as pianist in local jam sessions; pl. w. Jimmy Coles' band. Moved to Chicago 1952, worked in house group at Beehive, and at Blue Note w. Bill Russo. To Los Angeles '54, worked w. Stan Getz, Herb Geller, Barney Kessel, Pete Candoli. Toured w. Shelly Manne for 18 months '55-6. Also w. Chico Hamilton Quintet and many local jobs with jazz combos. One of the most admired bassists on the West Coast, particularly among fellow-musicians such as Red Mitchell, who said: "I can't think of anyone who gasses me more than Leroy as a rhythm player." Favs: Ray Brown, Heath, Pettiford. Own LP: Contemporary; LPs w. Stan Getz, De Franco (Verve), Cy Touff (Wor. Pac.), Shorty Rogers (Atl.), Dexter Gordon (Dooto, Beth.), Stan Levey (Beth.), Serge Chaloff (Cap.), Herb Geller (Merc.), Frank Morgan (GNP), Shelly Manne, Buddy Collette (Contemp.), Chet Baker-Russ Freeman (Wor. Pac.).

Addr: 2521 Clyde Avenue, Los Angeles 16, Cal.

VINSON, EDDIE (Mr. Cleanhead), *singer, alto sax;* b. Houston, Tex., 12/18/17. Prof. debut with Milton Larkins band. Worked with Floyd Ray orch., then joined Cootie Williams' big band in '42 and during three years with Williams established himself as a powerful blues singer with a personal, broken-toned style. His big hits with Cootie were *Cherry Red* and *Somebody's Got To Go.* In 1945 he formed his own group and scored a big hit with *Kidney Stew Blues.* His 16-piece orchestra worked at the Zanzibar on Broadway in '47 and toured the country in '48-9. His popularity waned and he reduced to sextet format, then worked as a single. He rejoined Williams for four months in 1954, then worked around Chicago with his own and other small groups. Rec. w. all star band in NYC Sept. '57. Vinson plays alto in a coarse-toned, ruggedly swinging blues vein. His vocal style has tended to become mannered but is still capable of authenticity with a leavening of humor. Own LP: Bethlehem.

Addr: c/o Universal Attractions, 200 West 57th St., New York 19, N.Y.

VLADY (Wladimiro Bas Zabache), *alto sax;* b. Bilbao, Spain, 2/2/29. Stud. w. father, who plays viola in symphony, saxophone in dance bands. Extensive studies at Bilbao Cons., until economic difficulties forced him to start making living as jazzman and dance band musician. Moving to Madrid, pl. in leading hotels, clubs and in jam sessions w. drummer Jose Farreras and other top Spanish jazzmen. Many commercial rec. w. Rafael Cardona, Blue Stars of Madrid, Perez Prado *et al.;* Newport International band at NJF and Brussels Fair

'58; TV in Bilbao and Madrid. Zabache is known professionally by the single name Vlady. Fav. mus: J. S. Bach, Ellington, Basie, Kenton, Mulligan, Tristano, Konitz. LP w. Int. Band (Col.).

Addr: Virgen de Africa 6, Madrid, Spain.

W

WALD, JERRY, *clarinet, leader;* b. Newark, N.J., 1/15/19. Soprano sax at seven; alto, clarinet later w. private teachers. Own band at Childs' Spanish Garden, NYC 1941 (incl. Billy Bauer); Lincoln Hotel, '42. Had a fair swing-style band during most of the 1940s, playing in a pseudo-Artie Shaw style. Ran Studio Club in Hollywood, '49-51 and led combo there. Back in NYC, had own groups off and on from '52. Not related to the motion picture producer of the same name. Rec. for Decca, Col., MGM, Merc. Own LP: Kapp.

WALDRON, MALCOLM EARL (Mal), *piano, composer;* b. New York City, 8/16/26. Stud. composition under Karol Rathaus at Queens Coll, where he received his B.A. Originally an alto saxophonist; later switched to piano and worked around NYC with the groups of Big Nick Nicholas, Ike Quebec 1949-53. After being forced to work at times with rock-'n'-roll bands, he began a fruitful association w. Ch. Mingus, with whom he worked off and on 1954-March '57, including NJF '55 and '56. Also worked w. Lucky Millinder and Lucky Thompson summer '55; Gigi Gryce Nov.-Dec. '56. In Apr. '57 he started as accompanist to Billie Holiday and remained with her until her death, visiting France and Italy with her Nov. '58 and London Feb. '59. When Miss Holiday was not working he made numerous appearances with his own combo at the Five Spot in NYC.

A composer of exceptional talent with considerable academic scope, Waldron wrote modern ballet scores for the Henry Street dance group and others and has been emerging slowly in recent years, through his own albums, both as an exciting pianist and major writing talent. Some of the records featured vocals by his wife, Elaine. Favs: Powell, Monk, Herbie Nichols. Fav. arrs: John Lewis, Ellington. Own LPs on Pres., New Jazz; w. Teddy Charles (Atl.), Mingus (Atl., Deb.); P. Quinichette, J. Coltrane, T. Macero, Thad Jones, F. Wess (Pres.).

Addr: 187-17 Quencer Rd., St. Albans 12, N.Y.

WALKER, AARON (T-Bone), *singer, guitar;* b. Linden, Tex., 1913. Self-taught; as a youth, he accompanied a number of blues singers incl. Ida Cox, Ma Rainey, Blind Lemon Jefferson. Moved to Calif. in '34 and enjoyed great popularity while with the Les Hite orchestra which played on both West and East Coast in 1939-40. It was with Hite that he first recorded his celebrated *T-Bone Blues.* Throughout the 1940s and '50s he worked as a single all over the country, frequently making successful records for the r & b juke box market. He is a singer of convincing, earthy authority and a guitarist with compelling rhythmic intensity. Own LP: Atlantic.

Addr: 197 West 43rd Place, Los Angeles 37, Calif.

WALKER, JIM DADDY, *guitar;* b. Kansas City, Mo., 1914; d. Kansas City, Mo., 5/10/49. Pl. w. Jap Allen's KC band which incl. Ben Webster, Clyde Hart. Rec. w. Pete Brown, J. C. Higginbotham (Session). A very important though almost forgotten figure, he had a personal influence on Charlie Christian.

WALLER, THOMAS (Fats), *piano, organ, singer, songwriter;* b. New York City, 5/21/04; d. Kansas City 12/15/43, in a train on his way back from LA to NYC. Father, a clergyman, wanted Fats to follow a similar career, but after lengthy private studies he became a professional pianist at the age of 15 and was heard in many cabarets and theatres during the 1920s, accompanying Bessie Smith and other blues singers as well as playing organ and piano solos. He worked in Chicago with Erskine Tate in 1925. During the late 1920s he made a name for himself as a composer of popular songs for such shows as *Connie's Hot Chocolates,* in collaboration with lyricist Andy Razaf.

After a long series of broadcasts over WLW in Cincinnati, Waller made a brief trip to France in 1932. Soon after this he started working with a small band in New York. In May 1934 he began a famous series of Victor record sessions with six-piece groups, generally featuring his own satirical treatments of current pop songs that were a main identification for the rest of his life. In later years he toured (and occasionally recorded) with a bigger band, but the sides cut with the sextets, usually featuring Herman Autrey on trumpet, Gene Sedric on clarinet and tenor and Al Casey on guitar, best reflected Waller's unique style and personality. Waller, who had recorded on pipe organ on several occasions, recorded on Hammond organ from time to time in 1940-2. The best-known product of this innovation was his composition *Jitterbug Waltz,* rec. Mar. '42.

As a pianist, Waller added to the James P. Johnson style a symmetry and delicacy without precedent in jazz. At times light and airy, but occasionally forceful with a mighty "stride" left hand, Waller could make a gem out of the tritest pop song. His biggest record hit, *I'm Gonna Sit Right Down and Write Myself a Letter,* ironically was not one of his own compositions, though he scored other big hits with tunes that were his own, among them *Ain't Misbehavin', Honeysuckle Rose, Keepin' Out of Mischief Now, Blue Turning Gray Over You,* and many instrumental piano numbers. His earliest composition was *Squeeze Me,* written with Spencer Williams in 1918.

Waller was the first musician to play jazz successfully

and tastefully both on the pipe organ and the Hammond organ. As a singer, he was mainly regarded as a comedy personality, though the jazz qualities shone through even on his slapdash performances of third-rate Tin Pan Alley tunes which he frequently had to learn at the recording session. He was seen in several movies, the most successful of which was the last one, *Stormy Weather,* in 1943.

Fats left a legacy of great records recalling a gay, insouciant personality that contrasted oddly with his serious stature as a major jazz creator. Since his death many pianists, notably Johnny Guarnieri, Ralph Sutton and Joe Sullivan, have kept the Waller tradition alive. Modern pianists, among them Th. Monk and Bud Powell, have occasionally played brief passages in a Waller-like stride style, though sometimes for satirical effect to contrast with the more complex rhythmic left-hand punctuations of later idioms. Own LPs: *Young Fats Waller* (River. 12-103), *Handful of Keys* (Vict. LPM 1502), *Ain't Misbehavin'* (Vict. LPM 1246), *The Amazing Mr. Waller* (River. 12-109), *The Real Fats Waller* (Cam. 473), *One Never Knows, Do One?* (Vict. LPM 1503), *"Fats"* (Vict. LPT 6001). Other LPs: w. T. Dorsey, Berigan in *A String of Swingin' Pearls* (Vict. LPM 1373); nos. in *Great Jazz Pianists* (Cam. 383), w. Eddie Condon (Comm. 30010).

WALLIN, BENGT-ARNE, *trumpet, composer;* b. Linköping, Sweden, 7/13/26. Self-taught; entered profession through amateur contests. Played with Malte Johnson, 1949; Seymour Österwall '51; Arne Domnerus since '53. Records with Harry Arnold, Monica Zetterlund, Domnerus. Favs: Gillespie, Davis, Clifford Brown. One of Sweden's finest modern jazz trumpets. LP w. Herbie Mann (Pres.).

Addr: Essinge Brogata 7, Stockholm, Sweden.

WALLINGTON, GEORGE (Giorgio Figlia), *piano, songwriter;* b. Palermo, Sicily, 10/27/24. Father, an opera singer, immigrated to US, 1925. Stud. privately from 1933; quit high school at 15 to gig with local bands in Brooklyn and Greenwich Village. An early friend of Max Roach and charter member of the bop inner circle, he played in Dizzy Gillespie's first combo at the Onyx on 52nd St. in 1944. Later played a year w. Joe Marsala at the Hickory House. He worked w. innumerable combos in NYC incl. Georgie Auld, Allen Eager, Ch. Parker, Red Rodney. Well known as a writer, he enjoyed his biggest successes w. *Lemon Drop* and *Godchild;* he does not orchestrate, however, and has always had other composers score his tunes for him. Aside from two weeks in Europe w. Lionel Hampton in the summer of 1953, Wallington has worked exclusively with his own small groups. He is one of the most technically adroit performers in modern jazz. Own LPs on Pres., Verve, Savoy, Atl., East-West, *52nd St.,* (Inter.); one-half of *Swingin' In Sweden* (Merc.); LPs w. Metronome All Stars (Verve), Gerry Mulligan, *The Brothers* (Pres.), Tommy Talbert (Atl.), Bobby Jaspar (River.), Al Cohn (Savoy).

Addr: 601 West 113th St., New York, N.Y.

WALTON, CEDAR ANTHONY JR., *piano;* b. Dallas, Tex., 1/17/34. Studied w. mother, a piano teacher; stud. clarinet in high school. Started gigging around Dallas while in high school in rhythm and blues bands. Came to NYC in 1955; in Army '56-8; back to NYC, gigged w. Gigi Gryce, Lou Donaldson et al; joined Jay Jay Johnson Dec. '58. Favs: Bud Powell, Art Tatum, Thelonious Monk. LPs w. Johnson (Col.); two tracks w. Kenny Dorham in *New Blue Horns* (River.).

WARD, CLARA, *singer;* b. Philadelphia, 4/21/24. Sang sacred songs from age of 5 at Baptist Church under tutelage of her mother, a choir leader. Stud. piano at 8. By age 10, was appearing with sister and mother in local church events. Two new members, Henrietta and Marion Waddy, were added to the group, which by the time she had finished high school was well known locally. The Ward Singers first became nationally known in 1943 after appearing at a Baptist convention. Since then, they have been in constant demand, seen by audiences of up to 25,000 in stadiums, armories, etc. During the past decade, the gospel group has also been heard on records for the Duke, Savoy, Gotham and Peacock labels. They toured nationally in such shows as The Big Gospel Cavalcade of 1957, and in 1957 were heard at the Newport Jazz Festival. The group has a peripheral relationship to jazz; like many Negro gospel groups it has a strong emotional appeal melodically and rhythmically akin to that of earlier jazz forms. Its esthetic value has been questioned, critic Whitney Balliett calling it "lively but somewhat affected." LPs: Savoy.

WARD, HELEN, *singer;* b. New York City, 9/19/16. Self-taught both as singer and pianist. When just out of high school, joined Nye Mayhew band, then worked w. Eddy Duchin, Nat Brandwynne, Will Osborne, 1933; Rubinoff, Enric Madriguera, 1933-4; had her own show on WOR with Roxanne's Orch. Best known as vocalist with the Benny Goodman band during its first era of fame, she toured and recorded with him from Dec., 1934 to Dec., 1936. In retirement, 1937-41, except for occasional records w. Teddy Wilson, Joe Sullivan. Toured w. Hal McIntyre, 1942-3; joined Harry James, 1944. Produced and directed musical shows at WMGM, NYC, 1946-7. Has since been in retirement except for occasional appearances and records w. Benny Goodman. Married to Walter C. Newton, Jr. A very able performer, with a warm, honest ballad style. Like many pop singers, she earned a quasi-jazz reputation through her chance association with a band that played jazz. Own LP: Col. LPs w. Goodman (Col., Vict.); Peanuts Hucko (Vict.); *Wide Wide World of Jazz* (Vict.).

Addr: 873 Boston Post Road, Rye, N.Y.

WARE, LEONARD, *composer, guitar;* b. Richmond, Va., 12/28/09. Stud. at Tuskegee Inst., pl. oboe in band there. Began pl. guitar 1934; had own trio, popular in Greenwich Village in early 1940s. Retired from music, later was employed by the post office in NYC for a number of years. Songs incl. *Hold Tight, I Dreamt I Dwelt In Harlem.*

WARE, WILBUR BERNARD, *bass;* b. Chicago, Ill., 9/8/23. First became interested in music in church run by foster father who played drums, guitar, bass, trombone, sax. With his help, Ware taught himself first banjo, then bass, from childhood, and was soon playing in amateur string groups in Chicago, later prof. gigs locally and elsewhere in the Mid-west w. Stuff Smith, R. Eldridge, S. Stitt and others. In 1953 had own groups at the Bee Hive and Flame Lounge in Chicago playing w. Monk, J. Griffin and others; w. E. Vinson '54-5. Toured w. A. Blakey in '56, ending in NYC w. B. De Franco and Monk during 1957. Own trio at Bohemia, w. Monk, other local gigs '58. Worked w. J. R. Monterose in Albany summer '59; ret. to Chi. Oct. '59 for local concerts etc. Ware is one of the most adroit new bassists technically, capable of remarkable use of double-stops and imaginative solo work heard to advantage on the LPs listed. Own LP: Riverside; LPs w. Ernie Henry, Th. Monk, J. Griffin (River.), L. Morgan, H. Mobley, S. Rollins (BN).

WARREN, EARLE RONALD, *alto sax, composer;* b. Springfield, Ohio, 7/1/14. Own combo in Springfield, then pl. w. Marion Sears (brother of Al Sears) in Cleveland for 2½ years, 1933-5. Rejoined Sears '36; later had own 17-piece band in Cincinnati, where Count Basie heard him. Joined Basie as lead alto and ballad singer, April 1937. Excellent section leader and virtual director of the band for Basie; solos on *Out The Window, Sent for You Yesterday, Pound Cake.* Leaving the band in 1945, he led his own combo in Cincinnati and New York. He rejoined Basie twice: first in Dec. '48 for a few months, then from Sept. '49 until early '50. After working for some time as manager of Johnny Otis, he settled in the East, free-lancing as musical director at Apollo and Howard theatres in New York and Washington respectively, etc. Alto, mus. dir. and manager w. Eddie Heywood, 1954-5. In late '50s directed shows at Apollo, NYC and theatres in Washington, Baltimore, Chicago, also emceed and directed for Alan Freed stage shows in NYC. Toured Britain and Continent with Buck Clayton combo in NJF show fall '59. Warren composed (but did not orchestrate) several tunes for Basie incl. *Tom Thumb, Wiggle Woogie, Circus in Rhythm, Rockin' The Blues,* and with Buster Harding *9:20 Special.* LPs w. Basie (Dec., Vict., Col., Vang., Epic), Sir Ch. Thompson (Vang.), Buck Clayton (Col., Vang.), Milt Buckner (Cap.); *Session At Riverside* (Cap.), Lester Young (Savoy).

Addr: 50 West 106th Street, New York 25, N.Y.

WARREN, GUY, *drums;* b. Accra, Ghana, W. Africa, 5/4/23. Despite family opposition, he stud. jazz through records, and theory at Achimota Coll.; also by mail from US School of Music, Port Washington, N.Y. Until 1953, he worked in Accra off and on w. own groups, in addition working in England w. Kenny Graham's Afro-Cubists and other groups and free-lancing for a while in Paris. In 1954 he worked in Monrovia. On the Gold Coast (Ghana) he was disc jockey and newspaper editor. Came to the US (Chicago) in '55, working with and meeting such former idols as D. Gillespie, C. Parker and L. Young. Moved to NYC in July '57 and had own trio at the African Room. On a return visit to Accra Jan.-May '59, did educational radio series on jazz and worked as lecturer, drummer, journalist. Has a detailed authentic knowledge of African music, as is evident from his playing. Favs: J. Costanzo, K. Clarke. Fav. own solos: *My Story, Talking Drum Looks Ahead* in *Themes for African Drums.* Own LPs: *Themes for African Drums* (Vict.), *Africa Speaks, America Answers* (Decca).

Addr: P.O. Box 1246, Accra, Ghana, W. Africa.

WARWICK, WILLIAM CARL (Bama), *trumpet;* b. Brookside, Ala., 10/27/17. To N.J. at 13. Att. mus. sch. w. C. Shavers. Met D. Gillespie when they worked in Frank Fairfax band in Phila. Pl. w. Hardy Bros., NYC, '33, then w. Millinder, Bradshaw, T. Hill, R. Eldridge, B. Berigan; to Army '41 for 3½ years, in charge of 60-piece military band in Boston. Later worked w. many pop bands (Milt Britton, Abe Lyman, etc.); also w. Woody Herman, 1944-6, Buddy Rich '47 (feat. on rec. *Baby, Baby All The Time,* Merc.) and several Latin bands. Own combo w. Brew Moore in San Francisco, 1954-5; toured w. D. Gillespie '56-7. Though never considered a jazz soloist, Warwick at one time has worked in most of the name jazz bands and is a dependable all-round section man.

Addr: 167 Bleecker Street, New York 12, N.Y.

WASHBOARD SAM (Robert Brown), *singer, washboard;* b. Arkansas, 1910. Half brother of Big Bill Broonzy. Came to Chicago in 1932; recorded for Bluebird, also worked under the name of Shufflin' Sam in a series of Vocalion records w. Broonzy. One of his best-known blues was *I've Been Treated Wrong* on Bluebird. He continued to record until '47; since then, retired from music, he has been on the Chicago police force.

WASHINGTON, DINAH (Ruth Jones), *singer;* b. Tuscaloosa, Ala., 8/29/24; raised in Chicago, where she was immersed in religious music, playing piano for a church choir. At 15 she won an amateur contest at the Regal Theatre in Chicago; in 1942 she opened at the Garrick Bar, where Joe Glaser heard her and recommended her to Lionel Hampton, whose band she joined in 1943. She made her record debut 12/29/43 in a session organized by this writer, with a sextet from the Hampton band. After quitting Hampton she went to work as a single in 1946, having already established herself by this time as probably the most important new r&b recording star of the decade. Her gutty, forthright blues style, combining jazz qualities with more than a hint of her religious singing background, was later applied to pop and standard tunes, which extended her renown far beyond the r&b field. In June

1959 she appeared with the author's all star group on a BBC broadcast in London, then played with great success for a few weeks in Stockholm. Film: *Jazz on a Summer's Day.*

Own LPs: *After Hours with Miss D* (EmArcy 36028), *Best in Blues* (Merc. 20247), *Bessie Smith Blues* (Merc. 36130), *Dinah* (36065), *Dinah Jams* (36000), *For Those in Love* (36011), *In The Land of Hi Fi* (36073), *Music for a First Love* (20119), *Music for Late Hours* (20120), *The Queen* (20439), *Sings Fats Waller* (36119), *Swingin' Miss D* (36104), *What a Diff'rence a Day Makes* (20479). Also *Blues* (Grand Award 33-318); one track w. Lionel Hampton on Decca 8088.

Addr: 345 West 145th St., New York City, N.Y.

WASHINGTON, FORD LEE (Buck), *piano, singer, dancer, trumpet, comedian;* b. Louisville, Ky., 10/16/03; d. New York City, 1/31/55. Formed partnership w. John "Bubbles" Sublett when they were children, and toured in vaudeville from 1909, coming to NYC 1919. The team of "Buck & Bubbles" later earned world renown, while Buck earned a secondary reputation as a competent Hines-style pianist and fair trumpeter. He rec. on piano w. Louis Armstrong (*Dear Old Southland, My Sweet,* 1930) and Coleman Hawkins '34. Buck & Bubbles broke up in '53; during '54 Buck toured with Timmie Rogers' combo. The Buck & Bubbles team was seen in the films *Cabin In The Sky* and *A Song is Born.* LP w. L. Armstrong (Col.).

WASHINGTON, RONALD JACK, *baritone, alto saxophones;* b. Kansas City, Mo., 1912. Played w. Bennie Moten. From 1935-50, with the exception of time out for Army service, he was in Count Basie's band. Best known for his participation on earlier records incl. *Doggin' Around, Topsy, Somebody Stole My Gal.* Feat. on *Lopin'* w. rhythm section backing on *Count Basie* (Vict. LPM 1112). After leaving Basie he settled in Oklahoma City, taking a job at the airport and gigging occasionally. Came to New York for a few days to record w. Paul Quinichette in '59, Prestige label. LPs w. Basie (Decca, Vang., Col., Epic, Bruns., Vict.); w. Quinichette in *Basie Reunion* (Pres.).

WASSERMAN, EDWARD JOSEPH (Eddie), *tenor sax, clarinet, flute*: b. Smackover, Ark. 3/5/23. Studied sax w. private teacher in Texas; pl. in dance band there 1939. Army '43-6; grad. from Juilliard '48. Has been sideman in numerous bands incl. Benny Goodman, Artie Shaw, Ch. Barnet, Buddy De Franco, Charlie Spivak, Noro Morales, Stan Kenton, Chico O'Farrill, Louis Bellson. Joined Gene Krupa Oct. '57, playing record and club engagements as well as a JATP European tour in May '59. Joined Gerry Mulligan band March 1960. LPs w. Tony Scott, Geo. Williams (Victor), Krupa, Bellson (Verve), Elliot Lawrence (Fant.).

Addr: 17 West 70th St., New York 23, N.Y.

WASSERMAN, HERBERT (Herb), *drums;* b. New York City, 6/13/22. Stud. violin 1930. Pl. with local bands in the Bronx, later worked in NYC w. Cy Coleman, B. Butterfield, J. Carisi, H. Mann, and extensively w. the Barbara Carroll trio. To Paris w. Lena Horne combo May '54. On Broadway in *Me and Juliet* w. Barbara Carroll. LPs w. J. Carisi (Vict.), Barbara Carroll (Atl., Vict.).

Addr: 332 W. 49th St., New York 19, N.Y.

WATANABE, SADAO, *alto sax;* also *flute;* b. Utsunomiya, Japan, 2/1/33. Father taught Biwa, an old Japanese instrument. Took up clarinet in first grade of junior high school; entered music business because he "was fascinated by ad lib and spirit of freedom of jazz." Pl. for three years w. Toshiko's quartet before she went to US, then assumed leadership of the group. Pl. alto in the *Charlie Parker Story* on NHK (Radio Japan) in Tokyo. Ambition is to play w. Miles Davis or Sonny Rollins. Fav: Parker. Rec. on Japanese labels incl. session w. fellow winners of *Swing Journal* poll '58.

Addr: 2515 5-chome Kamimeguro, Meguro-ku, Tokyo, Japan.

WATERS, BENJAMIN (Benny), *clarinet, tenor sax;* b. Brighton, Md., 1/23/02. Pl. w. Ch. Miller in Phila., 1918-21; stud. in Boston, '22; w. Ch. Johnson, '26-31, also rec. with King Oliver, Clarence Williams. During 1930s spent three years each w. Claude Hopkins, Fletcher Henderson, Hot Lips Page. After a year w. J. Lunceford, 1941, had own band at Red Mill, NYC, for two years. To Calif., led own band for four years, then joined Roy Milton. Back in NYC, joined Jimmy Archey 1949 and went to Europe with him; later pl. on the continent with Bill Coleman. Favs: Goodman, Jacquet, Hawkins. LP w. King Oliver (River.).

Addr: c/o Clarence Waters, 59 Holland Avenue, Ardmore, Pa.

WATERS, ETHEL, *singer;* b. Chester, Pa., 10/31/00. Debut at five, billed as "Baby Star," singing in church. Tall and very thin as a youngster, she was billed as "Sweet Mama Stringbean" in early appearances in Philadelphia and Baltimore. Came to NYC 1917 to work at Lincoln Theatre in Harlem. During the 1920s she became a popular recording star in the Negro market, accompanied by Fletcher Henderson and other top jazzmen on many blues for Black Swan, Columbia, etc. Later she gained nation-wide acceptance as a star in night club revues and on stage, incl. *Blackbirds, Rhapsody In Black;* her biggest hits were *As Thousands Cheer,* 1934; *Mamba's Daughters,* in which she played a dramatic part and which she has frequently revived since its original presentation in 1939; and *Member of the Wedding,* 1952. She introduced and popularized such hit songs as *Dinah,* 1924; *Memories of You, You're Lucky To Me,* 1929-30; *Stormy Weather,* '33. Her best known motion pictures are *Cabin In The Sky, Tales of Manhattan, Pinky* and *The Sound And The Fury.* She appeared in a *One Night Stand,* WNTA-TV '59. Principally a great show business personality and only incidentally and indirectly a jazz performer, Ethel Waters has retained a full-bodied, wide-range voice in which vibrato and phrasing are distinctly jazz-tinged. An intimate study of her extraordinary life appeared as an autobiography, co-authored by Charles Samuels, published in 1951 by Doubleday & Co.: *His Eye Is On The Sparrow*. LP: Mercury.

WATERS, MUDDY (McKinley Morganfield), *guitar, singer;* b. Rolling Fork, Miss., 4/4/15. Learned to play harmonica and began singing at 10; father taught him guitar. Raised in Clarksdale, Miss. by his grandmother after his mother's death. Worked in cotton fields, where he was discovered by folklorist Alan Lomax, for whom he made some recordings for the Library of Congress. Came to Chicago in 1943, pl. in various south-side clubs. Rec. for Aristocrat label, later bought by Chess, for which company he has recorded since. Has been playing in Chicago ever since he moved there, making annual southern tours. Was a hit when he toured England in '58; featured in folk music concert at Carnegie Hall April '59. Names piano accompanist Otis Spann, who is his half-brother, as his most important influence. LP: selections in *Folk Song Festival* (UA).

Addr: 4339 Lake Park Ave., Chicago, Ill.

WATKINS, DOUGLAS (Doug), *bass;* b. Detroit, Mich., 3/2/34. Stud. Cass Tech High School, where schoolmates incl. bassist Paul Chambers, who is his cousin by marriage, and trumpeter Donald Byrd. Stud. in 1950 with Gaston Brohan. First left Detroit w. James Moody band Summer, '53. Worked mainly for next year w. Barry Harris trio, which backed visiting jazz stars incl. Stan Getz, Ch. Parker, Coleman Hawkins. Settled in New York, Aug., '54; first gigged w. Kenny Dorham, later at Minton's, etc. w. Horace Silver, Hank Mobley et al. One of the most able of the young Detroiters heard in NYC in the late '50s. Favs: P. Heath, R. Brown, Slam Stewart. LPs w. Art Blakey (Blue Note, Col.), Horace Silver (Blue Note), Art Farmer-Donald Byrd, Gene Ammons, Hank Mobley, Sonny Rollins, P. Quinichette, Kenny Burrell (Pres.), Jackie McLean (Pres., Jub.), Pepper Adams (Wor. Pac.), Wilbur Harden (Savoy).

WATKINS, EARL THOMAS, JR., *drums;* b. San Francisco, Calif., 1/29/20. Mostly self-taught originally, but stud. piano and drums briefly in '30s, resuming studies '46-7. Pl. in Navy band '42-5; led own bands around SF area '45-7. Sideman w. various combos after that, incl. Bob Scobey '54-5; Earl Hines at Club Hangover, SF '55-60. Has worked w. hundreds of name singers and soloists on their visits to SF. Member of Board of Dir. of Local 669, A. F. of M. since '45. Worked as real estate salesman '56. Innumerable records since '46, when he recorded w. Wilbert Baranco and w. own group. Fav. own solo: *Hindustan* w. Bob Scobey (Good Time Jazz). Main infls: Jo Jones, Rich, Krupa, Roach, Morello. LPs w. Flip Phillips, Kid Ory (Verve), Hines (Fant., Felsted).

Addr: 1816 San Benito St., Richmond, Calif.

WATKINS, JULIUS, *French horn, composer;* b. Detroit, Mich., 10/10/21. Took up French horn at age nine in grammar school. Worked w. Ernie Fields 1943-6. Lived in Colo. for a year, then ret. to Detroit, where he had his own band for a while. Cont. his studies w. Francis Hellstein of Detroit Symph., Robert Schultze of NY Phil.; three years at Manhattan Sch. of Mus. Worked w. Milt Buckner's big band, 1949; rec. w. Kenny Clarke, Babs Gonzales; night club and rec. dates w. Oscar Pettiford combo. Toured w. Pete Rugolo orch. '54. Early in '56 he and Charlie Rouse, tenor sax, formed a combo which they called Les Modes. The group worked together off and on until '59. Watkins also pl. in Johnny Richards' orch. and pl. summer symph. concerts w. the NY Municipal orch. In Aug. '59 he joined George Shearing's big band. LPs w. Les Modes (Dawn); w. Pete Rugolo (Col.); Art Farmer (UA); Mat Mathews: *Four French Horns* (Elek.), Thelonious Monk (Pres.), *Baritones and French Horns* (Prestige-16 rpm).

Addr: 195 St. Nicholas Ave., New York 26, N.Y.

WATSON, LEO, *singer;* b. Kansas City, Mo., 2/27/1898; d. Los Angeles, Cal., 5/2/50. Prominent during 1930s as the unique "scat" singer w. the Spirits of Rhythm, vocal-instrumental novelty group in which he played tiple (small instrument of guitar family). Toured for a few months w. G. Krupa band 1938-9 and had brief solos on three numbers w. Artie Shaw in '38. Lived in Calif. during 1940s; made two record sessions, not yet reissued, in which he demonstrated probably the most fantastic combination of rhythmic style and stream-of-consciousness sense of humor ever heard in jazz. Won Esq. Silver Award 1944.

WATTERS, LU, *trumpet, leader;* b. Santa Cruz, Cal., 12/19/11. Bugle at St. Joseph's Military Academy, trumpet in school's brass band. While at high school in SF formed own jazz band 1926 and worked during vacations as ship musician. While on scholarship at U. of SF, played in band at Palace Hotel. Toured the West for five years w. Carol Lofner, then went to China as ship musician. Back in SF worked with various jazz combos; led 11-piece band at Sweet's Blrm. in Oakland 1938-43; organized the Yerba Buena jazz band, 1940, retaining it until Dec. 1950 except for his years of Navy service, June 1942 to Sept. '45, when he led 20-piece Navy band based in Hawaii. The Yerba Buena band was perhaps the most vital factor in the reawakening of public interest in traditional jazz on the West Coast. In 1951 Watters retired temporarily from music, devoting his time to the study of geology. After returning briefly with a new band, he retired permanently from music and in '59 was working as a chef at a state institution in Cotati, Calif. Own LPs on Verve, GTJ, River.

WAYNE, CHUCK (Charles Jagelka), *guitar;* b. New York City, 2/27/23. Father a cabinetmaker. St. as mandolinist w. Russian balalaika band. When the mandolin began to warp he threw it into the furnace and bought a guitar. In 1941, after working as an elevator operator, he played w. the Clarence Profit and Nat Jaffe trios on 52nd St. Army Feb. '42-Mar. '44; Joe Marsala at Hickory House '44-6; Woody Herman, May-Dec. '46; Phil Moore Four '47; Barbara Carroll trio, Alvy West's Little Band '48; George Shearing quint. '49 to early '52. Free-lanced w. own combos in NYC '52-3; toured as accompanist to singer Tony Bennett '54-7. Also wrote and played music for Broadway show *Orpheus Descending* spring '57. Free-lanced and led various combos in NYC '57-9; CBS staff work '59-60. Wayne, who was one of the first and best guitarists of the bop era, made many combo records in the mid-'40s w. L. Young, Slam Stewart, B. Bigard et al. Favs: Segovia, C. Christian. Own LPs: *String Fever* (Vik), Savoy; LPs w. Shearing (MGM), Woody Herman (Col.), Gil Evans (Wor. Pac.), Dick Katz (Atl.); *Four Most Guitars* (ABC-Par.).

Addr: 589 Walton Ave., Bronx 51, N.Y.

WAYNE, FRANCES (née Chiarina Francesca Bertocci), *singer;* b. Boston, Mass., 8/26/24. To NYC with her brother Nick Jerret's combo, 1942. Joined Ch. Barnet, 1942, then worked for a year in Boston clubs. Joined Woody Herman late 1943 and achieved fame with *Happiness is a Thing Called Joe,* which she recorded with him Feb. '45 (arr. Ralph Burns). Married in 1945 to Neal Hefti, who was also with Herman, she moved to Calif. 1946 and worked as a single in night clubs, later going into semi-retirement. Returning to New York, she toured in a band organized by Hefti '52-3, then retired except for recordings. Sensitive, rich-toned ballad singer. Won Esq. New Star Award '46. Own LPs on Epic, Bruns., Atl.; LP w. Herman (Harmony).

Addr: 161 West 75th St., New York, N.Y.

WEATHERFORD, TEDDY, *piano;* b. Bluefield, W. Va., 10/11/03; d. Calcutta, India, 4/25/45. Moved to New Orleans when he was 12 and began on piano 2 years later. In Chi. in early '20s w. Erskine Tate and others, where he was considered one of the most advanced pianists of the time, sometimes compared w. Earl Hines. Beginning in 1926, he went to California and subsequently to China w. Jack Carter's band (which incl. Albert Nicholas). Then Japan, India and the East Indies. He remained in the Far East the rest of his life, except for a European tour in 1937 incl. several mos. in Paris.

WEBB, WILLIAM (Chick), *leader, drums;* b. Baltimore, Md., 2/10/02; d. Baltimore, Md., 6/16/39. Came to NYC 1924, joined Edward Dowell. Formed his own band '26, early members of which incl. Johnny Hodges and Bobby Stark, later Jimmy Harrison, Benny Carter. The band worked in many Harlem spots and made one session for Brunswick in '31 but did not achieve national prominence until '34, when it began to record regularly. Key members at that time were Edgar Sampson, alto sax and arranger; Taft Jordan, trumpet and vocals; John Kirby, bass. The band achieved its greatest fame after Webb discovered Ella Fitzgerald in '34 and used her on records, June '35. From this point on Webb's band, one of the great swing outfits of its day, played frequently at the Savoy Ballroom, was broadcast nationally, and produced a long series of extraordinary records for Decca.

After Webb died of tuberculosis in 1939 the band continued under Ella Fitzgerald's leadership for two years. Surmounting the handicaps of Jim Crow and of his own physical deformity, Webb rose to become one of the most dynamic figures in jazz, a powerful, pulsating drummer whose magnificent control of bass drum and cymbals lent the band much of its personality, both in ensemble work and in his occasional solos. A favorite drummer of G. Krupa and many other contemporaries, he was, according to Barry Ulanov in *A History of Jazz in America,* "perhaps the greatest of jazz drummers, a gallant little man who made his contribution to jazz within an extraordinary framework of pain and suffering." LPs: two selections in *Five Feet of Swing* (Decca 8045); one in *Encyclopedia of Jazz on Records, Vol. 2* (Decca 8384).

WEBB, S. LAWRENCE (Speed), *leader, singer;* also *drums;* b. Peru, Ind., 7/18/11. Stud. violin, peckhorn, drums; prof. debut at Forest Park, Toledo, O. Prominent as bandleader in late '20s and early '30s in Buffalo, Indianapolis, LA, ballrooms around the country, and w. Ethel Waters in early talking picture *On With the Show.* Wingy Manone pl. several dates with the band, which was known as Speed Webb's Hollywood Blue Devils; other sidemen were Teddy Wilson, Vic Dickenson, Roy and Joe Eldridge; Gus Wilson (Teddy's brother) on trombone, Eli Robinson, Reunald Jones. Rec. for Gennett, Vocalion and Okeh. Webb quit music in '40, became funeral director, inspector for Board of Health, public relations manager and political broadcaster in South Bend, Ind. In the opinion of many former members his was one of the best bands of its day.

Addr: 421 North College St., South Bend, Ind.

WEBSTER, BENJAMIN FRANCIS (Ben), *tenor sax;* b. Kansas City, Mo., 2/27/09. Stud. violin, piano; mainly self-taught on saxophone. Prof. debut as pianist in a band in Enid, Okla. Piano w. Dutch Campbell, alto and tenor w. Gene Coy, then worked w. Jap Allen, Blanche Calloway, Andy Kirk. Came to NYC 1932 w. Bennie Moten. Played w. Benny Carter and Fletcher Henderson, 1933-4; later w. Willie Bryant, Cab Calloway, Stuff Smith. Best known through a long intermittent association with Duke Ellington which began in 1935; he was w. Duke continuously from late 1939 until '43 and again for a few months in '48. In the mid-40s he worked mainly with local bands in Kansas City. After his last departure from Ellington he toured w. JATP and worked in the East, usually with his own combo.

Praised by Barry Ulanov as "one of the warmest and most sensitive of performers in the Coleman Hawkins tradition," Webster belongs, along with Hawkins and Chu Berry, among the earliest figures to bring full maturity to the tenor saxophone; he has also shown himself to be one of the most durable. He is of the old school in the sense that his tone is big and warm, his style vivid and forceful, yet the style he represents is timeless and his work has been respected and eulogized by critics, fans and musicians of every era from the 1930s up to the present.

Webster is best remembered for the records he made with the Ellington band of 1940-2: *Cotton Tail, Conga Brava, Just A-Settin' And A-Rockin', All Too Soon, C Jam Blues* etc. He was also heard on numerous records in the late '30s and early '40s with the following: Red Allen, Geo. Auld, B. Bigard, Sid Catlett, Cozy Cole, Al Hall, L. Hampton, W. Herman, B. Holiday, James P. Johnson, Pete Johnson, B. Morton, Hot Lips Page, Tony Scott, Rex Stewart, J. Teagarden and Teddy Wilson. App. on *Sound Of Jazz,* CBS-TV Dec. '57, *The Subject Is Jazz,* NBC-TV Apr. '58.

Own LPs on Verve: *The Kid And The Brute* (8065), *Sophisticated Lady* (2026), *Soulville* (8274), *King of the Tenors* (8020), *Coleman Hawkins Encounters Ben Webster* (8327), *Music With Feeling* (8130), *Ben Webster And Associates* (8318); half an LP in *The Big Sounds* (Bruns. 54016). LPs w. Harry Edison (Verve 8097, 8211), Bill Harris (Fant. 3263), Woody Herman (Verve 2069), Red Norvo (Vict. LPM 1729), Art Tatum-Ben Webster Quartet (Verve 8220), Georgie Auld (Gr. Award 316), JATP, Vol. 17 (Verve), Buddy Rich (Verve 2075), Duke Ellington (Vict. LPM 1364, LPM 1715, LPM 1092), *One World Jazz* (Col. WL 162).

Addr: 110-08 174th St., Jamaica 33, L.I., N.Y.

WEBSTER, FREDDIE, *trumpet;* b. Cleveland, Ohio, 1917; d. Chicago, Ill., 1947. Long associated w. Tadd Dameron, with whom he played in local bands, Webster was heard in NYC during the '40s w. Lucky Millinder, Earl Hines, Benny Carter, Jimmie Lunceford and on records w. Geo. Auld, Frankie Socolow, Sarah Vaughan. An early influence on Miles Davis, he was one of the most soulful performers among modern jazz trumpeters. LP: Solos on *My Kinda Love, If You Could See Me Now* w. Sarah Vaughan (Rondo.).

WEBSTER, PAUL FRANK, *trumpet;* b. Kansas City, Mo., 8/24/09. Stud. Fisk U. and William Inst. After working w. Geo. E. Lee, Andy Kirk, Bennie Moten, pl. lead tpt. w. J. Lunceford '35-42. With Cab Calloway off and on '44-52; Ch. Barnet '46-7, '52-3. Worked for immigration office '54-5, later had clerical day job, still gigging occasionally w. Sy Oliver and with show *Simply Heavenly.* Solos w. Lunceford incl. *Organ Grinder's Swing, For Dancers Only, Annie Laurie, Lunceford Special, Swinging On C, Blues In The Night.* LPs w. Lunceford (Decca, Col.), Sy Oliver (Decca).

Addr: 2394 Seventh Avenue, New York 30, N.Y.

WECHSLER, MORRIS LOUIS (Moe), *piano;* b. Jersey City, N.J., 10/15/20. St. playing w. high school band; stud. violin and bass at Juilliard. Played w. numerous bands in 1940s and '50s incl. Ray McKinley, Glenn Miller, Louis Prima, Benny Goodman, Bobby Hackett et al. Has free-lanced in NYC in recent years for rec. and TV. Favs: Bud Powell, Horace Silver, Art Tatum. LPs w. Billy Byers, Ralph Burns (Decca).

Addr: 73-04 193rd Street, Flushing 66, N.Y.

WEED, HAROLD (Buddy), *piano, composer, leader;* b. Ossining, N.Y., 1/9/18. Sister was first teacher. Played w. Ch. Spivak, 1940; Teddy Powell, '41; got big break when Geo. Simon introduced him to Paul Whiteman, on whose Capitol record of *I Found a New Baby* he was feat. in '42. On staff at ABC, NYC, since '45, also active in commercial jingle field for radio and TV, and soloist on concerts w. Whiteman. In '40s was heard on a few jazz rec. dates incl. one by S. Bechet. Own LP: Judson, Col.; LPs w. Joe Venuti (Grand Award); Paul Whiteman 50th Anniv. (Grand Award).

Addr: 15 West 55th St., New York 19, N.Y.

WEIN, GEORGE THEODORE, *piano, singer;* b. Boston, Mass., 10/3/25. Studied piano 1933-8 w. Margaret Chaloff, mother of Serge Chaloff; later w. Sam Saxe, Teddy Wilson. Through his years at Boston Univ. he was active as jazz pianist in local clubs. Played w. Max Kaminsky, '46; Edmond Hall '47; Bill Davison '49; Bobby Hackett, Pee Wee Russell, Jo Jones, Vic Dickenson, Jimmy McPartland and many other combos since '50, mostly at his own clubs, the best-known of which is Storyville in Boston. Starting in '54 he produced the annual Jazz Festivals in Newport, R.I., expanding in '59 to present festivals under Newport auspices in French Lick, Ind., Toronto, and Boston, also touring as producer and pianist with an all-star Newport Festival show in Europe. Own LP, *Wein, Women and Song* (Atl.); LP w. *Jazz At Storyville* (Savoy).

Addr: c/o Storyville, Copley Square Hotel, Boston, Mass.

WEINKOPF, GERRY, *flute;* b. Moravska Ostrava, Czechoslovakia, Dec. 1925. First stud. piano, later violin; while in early teens, he could play concertos by Beethoven, Mozart and Bach. Hurt hand in accident in 1945, ending his violin career, but he had already moved to Germany and had played alto sax in various GI clubs there. Switched from alto to tenor '47; began on flute after hearing Frank Wess w. Count Basie in '54. Won *Podium* jazz poll on flute in '56-7. Pl. with Erwin Lehn orch. in Stuttgart. John Lewis chose him to play featured role on his *European Windows* album for Vict. in '58.

WELLS, WILLIAM (Dickie), *trombone;* b. Centerville, Tenn., 6/10/09. Raised in Louisville, Ky. Originally inspired by Jimmy Harrison, he came to NYC in 1927, pl. with Ch. Johnson, Lloyd and Cecil Scott, Elmer Snowden and Luis Russell. Toured w. Benny Carter

1932; Fletcher Henderson '33-4; Teddy Hill '35-8, incl. European tour in '37; Count Basie '38-45 and '47-50; Buck Clayton, Sy Oliver off and on since '47; Jimmy Rushing '50-2. Worked in France '52; various small combos in NYC '53-4; Earl Hines '54. Toured Europe w. NJF show in Buck Clayton's group fall '59. Wells was one of the outstanding trombonists of the 1930s, gifted with a unique vibrato and a dashing, sometimes humorous style, full of imagination and rhythmic ingenuity. A great favorite in France, where he has won many jazz polls, he made some of his best records leading all-star combos there in 1937. An absorbing analysis of Wells' style, with musical illustrations, appeared in André Hodeir's *Jazz: Its Evolution and Essence* (Evergreen). Own LP: *Bones for the King* (Felsted); LPs w. Rex Stewart: *Chatter Jazz* (Vict.); Fletcher Henderson All-Stars (UA, Urania), P. Quinichette (Em.), Basie (Decca, Bruns., Vang.); Dickenson-Thomas (Atl.)

Addr: 153 W. 139th St., New York 30, N.Y.

WELLSTOOD, RICHARD MacQUEEN (Dick), *piano;* b. Greenwich, Conn., 11/25/27. Private teachers in Boston and New York, to 1946. Prof. debut at Jimmy Ryan's w. Bob Wilber, in whose combo he played from '46-50. Worked w. Jimmy Archey '50-2, incl. European tour '52. With Roy Eldridge '53; joined Conrad Janis '53 and remained with him off and on through 1960. Also worked as solo pianist at Eddie Condon's '56; matinees at Metropole w. Tony Parenti, also gigged w. S. Bechet, Rex Stewart, J. Windhurst, Red Allen. Favs: Wynton Kelly, Monk, James P. Johnson, Ray Charles. Own LP on River.; LPs w. R. Eldridge: *Swing Goes Dixie* (Verve), Bob Wilber (River., Music Minus One), Conrad Janis (Jub.); also rec. w. S. Bechet.

Addr: 129 E. 90th St., New York 28, N.Y.

WESS, FRANK WELLINGTON, *tenor sax, flute, composer;* b. Kansas City, Mo., 1/4/22. Started on alto in Oklahoma, then tenor in Washington, D.C., w. Bill Baldwin and house band at Howard Theatre; toured w. Blanche Calloway for year. Army '41-4. Played w. Billy Eckstine Orch. '44-5, then Eddie Heywood, Lucky Millinder, year w. Bull Moose Jackson, home to Washington, where he studied flute 1949. Joined Basie, June 1953, rapidly made name as exceptional tenor man and as first jazz star to record extensively and with complete success as flute soloist. Won DB critics' poll New Star Award '54. Arrs. for Basie incl. *Basie Goes Wess, Yesterdays.* LPs: *North, South, East-Wess, Flute Suite, Trombones & Flute, Opus De Jazz, Opus In Swing, No Count, Jazz For Playboys* (Savoy), *Olio, After Hours, Wheelin' And Dealin'* (Pres.); LPs w. Count Basie (Verve), Dorothy Ashby (Reg., Pres., New Jazz), Joe Newman (Coral), Tony Scott (Vict.), *West Coast vs. East Coast* (MGM), *The Saxophone Section* (WW), Billy Taylor (River.), Bennie Green (Vee-Jay).

Addr: 185-40 Ilion Ave., St. Albans 12, L.I.

WEST, HAROLD (Doc), *drums;* b. Woolford, N. Dak., 8/12/15; d. Cleveland, Ohio, 5/4/51. Pl. with many name bands during 1930s incl. Tiny Parham, Erskine Tate, Roy Eldridge; he subbed for Chick Webb for several months before Chick's death. Prominent during early '40s as frequent employee at Minton's and associate of many early boppers, he recorded with Tiny Grimes, Ch. Parker, 1944; Slam Stewart, '45-6; Erroll Garner '45 and '47. LPs w. Slam Stewart, Ch. Parker (Savoy).

WESTBROOK, CHAUNCEY LEON (Lord), *guitar;* b. Jacksonville, Fla., 10/21/21. Mother pianist and teacher. Stud. violin and piano w. private teacher NYC. Got start as a band boy and asst. road mgr., then began playing w. various groups incl. Buddy Johnson, Hot Lips Page, Mercer Ellington, Rose Murphy. Toured Europe w. Babs Gonzales 1951; had own groups of various sizes for a while. Appeared w. Fletcher Henderson alumni band under Rex Stewart's leadership at Great South Bay Jazz Festival summer '58. Fav: Charlie Christian. LP, *Henderson Homecoming* (UA).

Addr: 676 St. Nicholas Ave., New York, N.Y.

WESTON, RANDOLPH E. (Randy), *piano, composer;* b. Brooklyn, N.Y., 4/6/26. Private teacher. Overseas in Army 1945; owned restaurant '47-9 and did not enter music business until '49, when he worked w. Geo. Hall, Art Blakey. Worked w. Frank Culley 1950; Bull Moose Jackson '51; Eddie Vinson, Kenny Dorham '53; Cecil Payne '54; staff worker at Riverside records NYC 1954-5. Since then has had his own trio and quartet, pl. at New York clubs incl. the Bohemia, Vanguard, Composer and Five Spot. App. w. trio at NJF '58. As a pianist, although one of the first to show the direct influence of Thelonious Monk, Weston has his own individual style; as a composer he has shown an affinity for jazz pieces in the waltz idiom, writing such successful ones as *Little Niles, Pam's Waltz.* Other comps. incl. *Machine Blues, Hi Fly, Bantu Suite.* Favs: Tatum, Bud Powell, Monk. Own LPs: River., UA, Jub., Dawn; one half of *New Faces At Newport* (MGM).

Addr: 204 E. 13th St., New York 3, N.Y.

WETTLING, GEORGE GODFREY, *drums;* b. Topeka, Kans., 11/28/07. Raised in Chicago from 1921. Stud. w. Roy Knapp. Baby Dodds was early influence and fav. drummer. Prof. debut '24; worked w. Floyd Towne, Jack Chapman, the Seattle Harmony Kings, Art Jarrett. First trip to NYC w. US band of British bandleader Jack Hylton '35. Settling in NYC in '36 he pl. in Artie Shaw's first band, then worked w. Bunny Berigan '37; Red Norvo '37-8; Paul Whiteman '38-40; Muggsy Spanier '40; Joe Marsala '41, and the Ben Pollack band fronted by Chico Marx, '42. Staff mus. at ABC network, NYC, '43-52, also pl. at Condon's and other jazz spots. Own Dixieland combo at Jack Dempsey's etc. '53; Jimmy McPartland at Metropole '54; regularly w. Eddie Condon from '56, including

British tour Jan. '57. Left Condon Jan. '59, free-lanced in NYC w. Bud Freeman at Metropole, etc.

Described by John S. Wilson as a "firm but unobtrusive" drummer with "taste, imagination and sense of propriety," Wettling has been considered one of the best products of the Chicago jazz era ever since he made his record debut in 1927, with Spanier and Teschemacher in the Jungle Kings' *Friars Point Shuffle.* An old friend of painter Stuart Davis, he has been active as a painter himself since 1947; exhibitions of his works have been held several times. He is also a witty and trenchant writer whose contributions have appeared in *Down Beat* and *Playboy.*

Own LPs: Stere-o-craft, Harmony, Kapp, Weathers; four numbers w. own group in Chicago Jazz Album (Decca); LPs w. Condon (Comm., Col.), Bud Freeman (Merc., Beth.), Brother Matthew (ABC-Par.), *Ragtime* (River.), Muggsy Spanier (Weathers), Wild Bill Davison, Max Kaminsky (Comm.).

Addr: 43 Seventh Avenue, New York City, N.Y.

WETZEL, BONNIE (née Bonnie Jean Addleman), *bass;* b. Vancouver, Wash., 5/15/26. Spent many years studying violin; self-taught on bass. After graduation, toured for two years w. Ada Leonard; later played w. Marion Gange trio. Married Ray Wetzel, 1949; played with him in Tommy Dorsey band, '51, until Ray's death. Gigged in NYC w. Ch. Shavers, Roy Eldridge; worked w. Lou Carter, Herb Ellis, as "Soft Winds Trio"; toured w. Beryl Booker trio '53-4 incl. Europe, Jan.-Feb. '54. Free-lanced w. small groups in New York area since.

WETZEL, RAY, *trumpet;* b. Parkersburg, W. Va., 1924; d. Sedgwick, Colo., 8/17/51. Played w. Woody Herman 1943-5. Prominent w. Stan Kenton's band 1945-8 and 1951. While w. Ch. Barnet in 1949 he was feat. on *Over The Rainbow* (Cap.). Killed in an automobile accident while he was with Tommy Dorsey's band. He was feat. w. Kenton on *Dynaflow, Intermission Riff;* worked w. Henry Jerome as trumpeter and vocalist 1950 in NYC. LPs w. Kenton, Barnet (Cap.), Woody Herman (Bruns.).

WHETSOL, ARTHUR, *trumpet;* b. Punta Gorda, Fla., 1905; d. 5/1/40. Raised in Washington, D.C., he was an early friend of Duke Ellington and a member of his band from its inception until 1937, when he was forced by illness to leave. Mainly known as a fine section man, but was featured on many Ellington records of the late '20s, incl. *Dicty Glide, Stevedore Stomp, Black Beauty* (Vict.), *Big House Blues, Rocky Mountain Blues, Misty Morning* (Okeh). LP w. Ellington (Bruns.).

WHITE, ROBERT E. (Bobby), *drums;* b. Chicago, Ill., 6/28/26. Stud. in Los Angeles, 1942 with Ralph Collier. Has played with many groups around LA incl. Vido Musso, Gerry Mulligan, Alvino Rey, Harry James, Ch. Barnet, Art Pepper, Chet Baker. Toured Europe in Buddy De Franco quartet Jan.-Feb., '54, and was the hit of the show nightly with his two-bass-drum solo specialty. First-class technician and modern drummer. Favs: Roach, Blakey, Rich. LPs w. Art Pepper (Savoy), Buddy De Franco (Verve), Chet Baker (Wor. Pac.), Cal Tjader (Fant.).

Addr: 5140 Zakon Road, Torrance, Calif.

WHITE, HARRY ALEXANDER (Father), *trombone, composer;* b. Bethlehem, Pa., 6/1/1898. Worked as drummer on Keith Circuit from 1914. Started on trombone, 1923, in Washington, working w. Duke Ellington, Elmer Snowden; to NYC '25 w. Snowden. Several months w. Ellington at Cotton Club, 1929; Cab Calloway, 1930. Led Mills Blue Rhythm Band jointly w. Edgar Hayes, 1931-2; rejoined Calloway, '32-5. Comp. and arr. for Calloway *Evenin'* (later made famous by Jimmy Rushing w. Count Basie), *Zah Zuh Zah, Chinese Rhythm.* During this period w. Calloway, White coined the word "jitterbug," originally meaning a man suffering from alcoholic nerves. The word was used as the title of a number written by Cab's trumpeter Edwin Swayzee, recorded by Calloway Jan. 1934.

After playing for a year w. Louis Armstrong, 1935-6, White went into a physical decline. He made a remarkable recovery in 1947 and resumed playing occasionally. Since 1952 he has been working in a Manhattan bank and playing gigs from time to time.

Addr: 11 Sylvan Terrace, New York 32, N.Y.

WHITE, JOSHUA (Josh), *singer, guitar;* b. Greenville, S.C., 2/11/08. Started singing spirituals in childhood under guidance of father, a preacher; spent many years as a youth acting as guide and accompanist for blind singers, among them Blind Lemon Jefferson. About 1932 he came to NYC and began recording under the pseudonyms Pinewood Tom and The Singing Christian as well as under his own name; he also accompanied Leroy Carr and other blues singers on their records. During the late 1930s he began to acquire a reputation in Greenwich Village clubs; he recorded with a small jazz group for Blue Note in 1940 and went to Mexico on a good will tour for the US government in '41. During the 1940s he became a major night club attraction, especially in such NYC clubs as Cafe Society and the Blue Angel, singing folk songs, blues and songs of social significance. During the 1950s he made several highly successful visits to Europe and became especially popular in England.

White's performances, both instrumentally and vocally, acquired too much of a veneer of urban sophistication to be classified as genuine folk music, but compensated in personal charm and style for what they lacked in authenticity. Own LPs: Elek., Merc., Per., Decca, Lond., Stin., ABC-Par.

Addr: 539 West 150th St., New York 31, N.Y.

WHITE, KITTY, *singer;* b. Los Angeles, Calif., 7/7/24. Has been popular for a decade mainly in LA night clubs. Miss White has occasionally used jazz musicians in her record accompaniments, but is not a jazz artist. Own LPs: Merc., Pacifica, Roul.

WHITE, ELLERTON OSWALD (Sonny), *piano;* b. Panama City, Canal Zone, 11/11/17. Pl. w. Jesse Stone 1937; Willie Bryant, Teddy Hill '38; Frankie Newton at Cafe Society '39; Benny Carter, off and on, '39-47. Rec. w. Mezzrow '37; several sessions w. Billie Holiday '39-40; Artie Shaw '41. While in Army organized combo and pl. shows for Third Army units '44-5 in Europe. Later worked w. Hot Lips Page; from '47-54 was feat. at Cinderella Club in Greenwich Village, NYC. Started at Jimmy Ryan's on 52nd St., Dec. '54 w. Wilbur De Paris. Made African tour w. him '57. Favs: Teddy Wilson, Tatum. Fav. own rec: *Strange Fruit* w. Billie Holiday; *Back Bay Boogie, Cocktails For Two* w. Benny Carter. LPs w. De Paris (Atl.), Billie Holiday (Comm.).

Addr: 922 Boston Rd., Bronx, N.Y.

WHITEMAN, PAUL, *leader;* b. Denver, Colo., 3/28/1890. Originally a violinist, Whiteman was perhaps the biggest figure in the pop bandleading world of the 1920s. On 2/24/24 he premiered George Gershwin's *Rhapsody In Blue* at the Aeolian Hall, NYC. He was starred in a movie, *King Of Jazz,* in '30. Through the '20s and '30s many famous jazzmen passed through the ranks of his band, among them Bix Beiderbecke, Frankie Trumbauer, Red Norvo, the Dorsey brothers, Eddie Lang and Joe Venuti.

Despite this, most jazz critics and many musicians have challenged Whiteman's right to the title "King Of Jazz." According to Wilder Hobson in *American Jazz Music* (Norton), "Whiteman drew very little from the jazz language except some of its simpler rhythmic patterns . . . there was little more than a trace of the personal expression, improvisation, counterpoint, or rhythmic subtlety of natural jazz . . . Whiteman's band included fine jazz players, but their improvising talent (was) subordinated in the 'symphonic' orchestrations."

In recent years Whiteman has been active as mus. dir. at American Broadcasting Company in New York. LPs: one no. in *History of Jazz* (Cap.); 50th Anniversary album on Grand Award, recorded in 1956, features Tommy and Jimmy Dorsey, Johnny Mercer, Jack Teagarden, Bing Crosby, Hoagy Carmichael and Joe Venuti in addition to Whiteman and his orch.

Addr: Walking Horse Farm, Rosemont, N.J.

WHITLOCK, VON VARLYNN (Bob), *bass;* b. Roosevelt, Utah, 1/21/31. Studied piano as child; took up bass in high school, pl. for school dances. Worked with Steve White at Lighthouse, Hermosa Beach, Cal., 1949; numerous groups in Los Angeles area in '50s, incl. G. Mulligan, Art Pepper, Chet Baker, Z. Sims, B. De Franco, also had own quartet. Worked on Ph.D. at U. of Calif. and taught music theory there. Favs: Ch. Parker, Lester Young, G. Mulligan. LPs w. Mulligan, Chet Baker (Wor. Pac.), Art Pepper (Savoy), Stan Getz (Verve), Joe Albany (River.).

WICKMAN, PUTTE, *clarinet;* b. Falun, Sweden, 9/10/24. Played w. Hasse Kahn, then formed own group modeled on the lines of the Benny Goodman sextet in 1948, and has toured with his own unit ever since. In May 1949 he appeared at the International Jazz Festival in Paris. Wickman is Sweden's foremost clarinetist; his style is original rather than derivative and belongs strictly in the modern school. He has recorded with numerous all star groups for the American market, often featuring his pianist Reinhold Svensson. In recent years he has played dance music at the Grand Hotel in Stockholm in addition to touring on jazz dates with his own sextet. Visiting NYC May-June '59, he played a few gigs incl. S. Bechet Memorial concert at Carnegie Hall.

Addr: Mabärsstigen 22 Vällingby, Stockholm, Sweden.

WIGGINS, GERALD FOSTER, *piano;* b. New York City, 5/12/22. Stud. Martin Smith Mus. Sch. and High Sch. of Mus. & Art. After a year acc. Stepin Fetchit, toured for 1½ years w. Les Hite, a year w. Louis Armstrong, then in East w. Benny Carter until entered Army 1944. Pl. with Army band at Fort Lewis, Wash. Discharged in '46, jobbed in Seattle, then back w. Carter. Toured US and Europe acc. Lena Horne 1950-1. Had own trio in Los Angeles; TV series w. Jerry Fielding, many rec. dates w. Frances Faye, Ella Mae Morse, Les Baxter et al. Pianist w. Spike Jones & Helen Grayco '56-8; acc. Kay Starr '56-9. Acc. at MGM studios for *Les Girls;* at Goldwyn Studios for *Some Like It Hot* '59. Pl. with Harry James band '59. Too busy and too versatile to seek specific recognition from jazz fans, Wiggins remains, from any standpoint, one of the most dependable pianists on the West Coast. Fav: Tatum. Own LPs: Challenge, Motif, Tampa, Dig, Spec.; LPs w. Paul Horn, Rusty Bryant (Dot), Nat Cole: *Welcome to the Club* (Cap.), Kay Starr: *Rockin' with Kay* (Vict.), Joe Morello (Intro.).

Addr: 1404 S. Hobart Blvd., Los Angeles 6, Calif.

WIGGS, JOHNNY (John Wigginton Hyman), *cornet;* b. New Orleans, La., 7/28/1899. Daughter is classical pianist. Stud. mandolin 1907; pl. w. brass band in Ocean Springs, Miss. '11. Pl. violin w. amateur string band in New Orleans; pl. w. The Owls '25; repl. Emmet Hardy in Brownlee's Jazz Band, '25. W. Happy Schilling, Peck Kelley '26; Jimmy McGuire '27; Tony Parenti '28; Ellis Stratakos' Hotel Jung Roof Band '29-30; Earl Crumb's Suburban Gardens Band '31; then retired from jazz. Teaching mechanical drawing to Orleans Parish School Board '30-60; had WSMB radio house band '46-7 and has gigged and recorded occasionally since then. Favs: Beiderbecke, Armstrong. Recorded for Victor under the name of John Hyman's Bayou Stompers '27. Many sessions since '46 incl. duets w. guitarist Snoozer Quinn on own Wiggs Inc. label; other albums on New Orleans, Commodore, Tempo, Paramount, S/D, Southland, Oriole, Good Time Jazz, Golden Crest, Delmar.

Addr: 345 Betz Place, New Orleans 20, La.

WILBER, ROBERT SAGE, *clarinet, soprano sax;* b. New York City, 3/15/28. Moved to Scarsdale, N.Y., 1935. Took up clar. '41. Leader of jazz group in high school days which became nucleus of the Wildcats, one of the first young bands to reëxamine New Orleans jazz. Stud. at Juilliard, Eastman Sch. of Mus., '45-6; clar., sop. sax w. S. Bechet, '46-8. Pl. w. Mezzrow at jazz festival in Nice, '48. Led combo at Savoy, Boston, '48-50; opened Storyville Club, Boston, '51, with band feat. Sid Catlett, De Paris Bros. Wilber then began transition from trad. to modern jazz, stud. w. Lennie Tristano, '52. In Army '52-4 taught theory, led jazz group at Fort Dix. After discharge att. Manh. Sch. of Mus., stud. cl. w. Leon Russianoff. Member of coöperative group, "The Six", '54-6; with E. Condon, on tour of England, and at his club from May '56; doubled on reeds and vibes w. Bobby Hackett late '57; joined Max Kaminsky Mar. '58; saxes with Benny Goodman, '58-9. LP w. Condon, *The Roaring Twenties* (Col.); Wild Bill Davison with strings (Col.); *Dixieland Goes Progressive* (Gold. Cr.), R. Braff (Beth.), J. McPartland (Epic), *Young Men with Horns, Creole Reeds* (River.), *The Six* (Beth.), Jim Chapin (Classic Edit.), B. Goodman (Col.).

Addr: 245 Henry Street, Brooklyn 1, N.Y.

WILCOX, EDWIN FELIX (Eddie), *piano, arranger;* b. Method, N.C., 12/27/07. Played w. Jimmie Lunceford 1946-7. Led the band jointly w. Joe Thomas after Lunceford's death. From '49 had commercial band mostly in r & b field. Had trio at Brooklyn club '58-60, also partner of Teddy McRae in music publishing and record companies. Far more important as writer than as pianist, he contributed many valuable arrangements for Lunceford incl. *Miss Otis Regrets, Rhythm Is Our Business, Impromptu, Like A Ship at Sea, Knock Me a Kiss, Easy Street.* LPs: see Lunceford. Also arrs. for Ed Hall (Rae-Cox).

Addr: 611 W. 148th St., New York, N.Y.

WILDER, ALEXANDER LAFAYETTE CHEW (Alec), *composer;* b. Rochester, N.Y., 2/17/07. Studied at Eastman Sch. of Music. From the late 1930s he was responsible for a series of albums of original works that combined jazz influences with an instrumentation then considered highly unorthodox in jazz circles, feat. woodwinds and harpsichord; has also written a cello concerto, several string quartets and many others works in the classical field. As a pop writer he is best known for *I'll Be Around, While We're Young, It's So Peaceful In The Country* and *Who Can I Turn To?* A skilled and original musician, Wilder attracted the enthusiastic patronage of many important personalities in the music business during the '40s; among them was Frank Sinatra, who lent his name to Wilder's efforts by conducting an album of his compositions. LPs: Octets (MGM); Golden Crest, *Songs For Patricia* (River.).

Addr: Algonquin Hotel, 59 West 44th St., New York 36, N.Y.

WILDER, JOSEPH BENJAMIN (Joe), *trumpet;* b. Colwyn, Pa., 2/22/22. Raised in Phila., where his father now leads a band. Debut on local radio amateur show for talented Negro children. Attended Mastbaum School of Music along with Buddy De Franco, Red Rodney. Joined Les Hite (in same section w. Dizzy Gillespie), 1941-2. L. Hampton '42-April '43, when he joined Marines, became asst. bandmaster. Back w. Hampton '45-6; then to Lunceford (was with band when Lunceford died), Lucky Millinder, Sam Donahue, Herbie Fields, Noble Sissle; pit bands of Broadway musicals incl. three years w. *Guys & Dolls.* After working w. Count Basie's band Jan.-June '54 (incl. European tour), he returned to pit band, working until the fall of '57, when he became a staff musician at ABC-TV studios in NYC. He has continued to do occasional jazz work, also concert appearances w. symphony orchestras. A versatile artist and fluent soloist, Wilder has a unique tone and a highly personal manner of phrasing. He was featured on *Softly With Feeling* w. Basie (Verve) and on *Blitzen* in *The Swinging Seasons* (MGM). Own LPs: Col., Epic, Savoy. LPs w. Michel Le Grand (Col.), Hank Jones (Savoy), *Soul of Jazz* (WW).

Addr: 640 Riverside Drive, New York 31, N.Y.

WILEN, BERNARD JEAN (Barney), *tenor sax;* b. Nice, France, 3/4/37. Uncle sent him an old alto; self-taught musician. Pl. with American jazzmen visiting Paris; leader of own group in Club St. Germain there. Considered most promising of younger French tenor men. Flew to US to appear at Newport Jazz Festival 1959. Favs: Charlie Parker, Sonny Stitt, Sonny Rollins, John Coltrane. LPs: *Afternoon In Paris* w. John Lewis (Atl.); *Jazz Track* w. Miles Davis (Col.).

Addr: 69 Boulevard Victor Hugo, Nice, France.

WILEY, LEE, *singer, composer;* b. Port Gibson, Okla., 10/9/15. Ran away from home at 15, and within two years had become a top singer in Chicago and New York clubs, working w. Leo Reisman and doing dramatic work on radio. During the 1930s was one of the most successful singers in the pop field, enjoying a long association w. Victor Young, broadcasting w. Paul Whiteman and later w. Willard Robison on CBS, featuring orchestrations by William Grant Still. From '39 she became closely associated w. Eddie Condon and his Dixieland entourage, recording several albums of show tunes with accompaniments that included Max Kaminsky, Joe Bushkin, Fats Waller.

In the mid-'40s, during a five year marriage to pianist Jess Stacy, she toured with a big band led by him. In the late '40s she worked as a single in night clubs; one of her compositions of the '30s, *Any Time, Any Day, Anywhere,* became a big r & b hit via the Joe Morris-Laurie Tate recording. She has continued to make occasional appearances on TV, in concert and on records through the '50s.

Lee Wiley's is one of the few completely distinctive feminine voices in jazz. There is a husky, erotic warmth to her work, in which her wide vibrato is the most recognizable quality; combined with her ability to select superior tunes and interpret the lyrics sensitively, her unique characteristics have produced many memorable, timeless records. Own LPs on Storyville, Columbia, Victor.

Addr: 60 Sutton Place South, New York, N.Y.

WILKINS, ERNEST (Ernie), *composer, alto, tenor saxophone;* b. St. Louis, Mo., 7/20/22. Mother started him on piano; after studying at Wilberforce Univ., entered Navy for three years, playing at Great Lakes w. Clark Terry, Willie Smith, Gerald Wilson. With Geo. Hudson in St. Louis, Earl Hines' last big band '48, back to St. Louis; joined Basie May '51. Settling in NYC '55, he gave up playing almost entirely except for touring w. Dizzy Gillespie overseas '56. He wrote a number of arrangements for Tommy Dorsey during the year before Dorsey's death. In '58-60, he worked mainly for Harry James' band; also did scoring for numerous record dates and continued to write for Basie. Wilkins is an adaptable writer whose contribution to the Basie band during the 1950s was one of the most important factors in its success; he was also important in the modernization of the James band. Own LPs: *Trumpets All Out, Top Brass, Flutes and Reeds, Clarke-Wilkins Septet* (Savoy), *Drum Suite* (Vict.); also many arrangements on LPs by Nat Adderley (Merc.), Newport Youth Band (Coral), Basie (Verve, Roul.), James (Cap., MGM), Candido (ABC-Par.), J. Cleveland, *Dinah Washington Sings Fats Waller, Sarah Vaughan in the Land of Hi Fi* (Merc.).

Addr: 1804 Second Ave., New York, N.Y.

WILLIAMS, ALFRED (Al), *piano, organ, composer;* b. Memphis, Tenn., 12/17/19. Studied in Chicago (where he lived from 1922) w. several teachers from '28; att. school w. Nat Cole. Prof. debut '36 leading 12-piece dance band. Gigged w. many Chicago groups, '38-42, then had own act, the Three Dudes. Joined Red Allen at Down Beat Room '43; later worked in Chi. w. Jimmie Noone, Erskine Tate; formed act, Alfred & Audrey, '48; arr. for Dallas Bartley and many other Chi. bands, stud. at Lincoln Cons. In early '50s was in NYC working with many groups at Savoy Ballroom incl. Erskine Hawkins, Jimmy Rushing, Lucky Millinder, Dick Vance; also pl. w. Benny Carter, Hot Lips Page, Stuff Smith. Staff pianist for Atlantic Rec. rock 'n' roll dates, '53. To Bermuda w. King Curtis, '53. Gigs w. Sam Taylor in NYC '56-7. Feat. w. Sol Yaged and Dixieland groups at Metropole, NYC from Jan. '57. Toured Europe w. NJF concert unit fall '59 as member of Buck Clayton's band. Capable blues pianist in swing-era style. LP: *The Weary Blues* w. Langston Hughes (MGM), Buck Clayton (Col.), Vic Dickenson-Joe Thomas (Atl.), Sam "The Man" Taylor (MGM).

Addr: 242 Bradhurst Avenue, New York 39, N.Y.

WILLIAMS, CLARENCE, *composer, pianist, leader;* b. Plaquemine, La., 10/8/93. Pl. piano, guitar and organ; as youth, began working in Storyville clubs in New Orleans, touring w. minstrel shows and working w. Bunk Johnson, Sidney Bechet et al; various bands around Texas and Louisiana. As early as 1913 active as a song publisher and writer, some of his early hits included *Royal Garden Blues,* co-authored by Spencer Williams (no relation), *Sugar Blues, Gulf Coast Blues* and *I Ain't Gonna Give Nobody None of My Jelly Roll.* Williams' main importance to jazz was his direction, during the '20s, of a long series of record sessions, mostly for Okeh. Williams himself sometimes appeared as pianist and singer, sometimes only as director of these dates. Between '23 and '28 he was responsible for developing such names as Louis Armstrong, Buster Bailey, Sidney Bechet and a number of singers, among them Eva Taylor (his wife), Sara Martin and Sippie Wallace. During these years Williams was heard on records w. Bessie Smith, whom he accompanied off and on until '31 and who rec. many of his blues compositions.

During the '30s Williams was less active as a recording artist, spending much of his time running his own music publishing company on Broadway. In recent years he has been in wealthy semi-retirement from music, running a hobby shop in Harlem. His daughter, Irene Williams, born in 1931, was featured for a time w. the Herman Chittison trio and in '59-60 toured w. musical show *Free And Easy.* LPs: one no. w. own group in *History of Classic Jazz* (Riverside); LPs w. King Oliver (River.), Bessie Smith (Col.).

Addr: 717A Madison St., Brooklyn, N.Y.

WILLIAMS, CHARLES MELVIN (Cootie), *trumpet, leader;* b. Mobile, Ala., 7/24/08. Drums at 14; later played trumpet in school band. Prof. debut w. Eagle Eye Shields' Band in Florida 1925-6, then joined Alonzo Ross '26-8, coming to New York w. Ross. After three weeks w. Chick Webb he switched to Fletcher Henderson's band, leaving in the spring of '29 to join Duke Ellington, replacing Bubber Miley. His work with Duke, both in open solos and in plunger work and other muted performances, was one of the distinctive sounds of the Ellington band through the 1930s. His best known performances were *Echoes of Harlem,* 1936, and *Concerto For Cootie,* first recorded in 1940 and later turned into the pop song *Do Nothing Till You Hear From Me.* During the late '30s he was also featured on many record dates w. Teddy Wilson, L. Hampton and the Ellington contingents led by Barney Bigard and Johnny Hodges, as well as w. his own groups.

Cootie's departure from the Ellington band in Nov. 1940 to join B. Goodman was considered so significant that Raymond Scott wrote and recorded a number entitled *When Cootie Left the Duke.* After a year with Goodman, during which he was featured on such memorable sextet sides as *Wholly Cats* and *Royal*

Garden Blues, as well as with the full band on *Superman,* etc., Cootie left to form his own big band, which enjoyed moderate success until the late 1940s. He later cut down to combo size; by the early '50s he had buried his jazz value in r & b band that gave less prominence to his own work than to exhibitionistic tenor saxophonists. Played at Savoy Ballroom until it closed; toured Europe early 1959 for a few weeks; formed quartet and played at Embers and other clubs '59, returning to a style reflecting more closely his original personality. In his heyday, Cootie was a magnificent product of the best of Bubber Miley and Louis Armstrong and probably the best all-around trumpet player in jazz. He won the Esquire Gold Award 1945-46, Silver Award '44. Own LP on Vict.; LPs w. Duke Ellington (Vict.), Rex Stewart (Jazz.), Ronnie Gilbert (Vict.), *The Duke's Men, Ellington Sidekicks* (Epic).

Addr: 175-19 Linden Blvd., St. Albans 12, L.I., N.Y.

WILLIAMS, GEORGE DALE (The Fox), *leader, composer;* b. New Orleans, La., 11/5/17. Worked as arr. w. Sonny Dunham; nine months w. Glenn Miller (also occasionally subbing at piano) '41-2. Maritime Service '43-6. Arr. for G. Krupa '46-9, Ray Anthony '50-3, writing almost all Anthony's recorded arrs. Later w. Harry James, Vaughn Monroe, Ch. Ventura, and own rec. band. Own LPs: United Artists, Brunswick, Victor.

Addr: 21 Strawberry Hill Rd., Hillsdale, N.J.

WILLIAMS, JOE (Joseph Goreed), *singer;* b. Cordele, Ga., 12/12/18. Lived in Chicago from the age of three. Professional debut in 1937, when he worked with the late Jimmie Noone. During the 1940s he worked around Chicago with local groups, also singing w. Coleman Hawkins' big band at Cafe Society, Chicago, in '41, and then w. Lionel Hampton band. He made a road tour w. Andy Kirk, spent a couple of months with the boogie-woogie piano team of Albert Ammons and Pete Johnson, and worked in local night clubs w. Red Saunders. During '50, when Count Basie led a septet at the Brass Rail in Chicago, Williams worked with him for ten weeks. He rejoined Basie Christmas day, '54, scoring his first big record hit with Basie a few months later in *Every Day,* an old blues which he had heard sung many years ago by Memphis Slim. During '55, his success w. Basie was so phenomenal that he elevated the entire band to a new plateau of commercial success.

Joe Williams has aroused less than unanimously enthusiastic reactions among the critics: Whitney Balliett dismissed him as "a loud imitation of a blues singer," but British writer Raymond Horricks said that "though he may be inferior to Jimmy Rushing as a blues singer, he is one of the very few to emerge in the 1950s with a strongly individual character." According to Barry Ulanov he is "capable of endowing every sort of vocal line with a contagious lilt." Williams' work at its best combines an authentic earthy quality with a degree of musicianship and discreet, natural showmanship rare among contemporary singers. After concentrating on blues for some years he became increasingly active from 1958 as a pop ballad singer. Favs: Joe Turner, Nat Cole, Ray Charles. Own LPs and LPs w. Basie: Verve, Roulette, Regent.

Addr: c/o Willard Alexander Inc., 425 Park Avenue, New York 22, N.Y.

WILLIAMS, JOE, *singer, guitar;* b. Crawford, Miss., 10/16/03. Spent many years in work gangs along the Mississippi, later playing and singing at picnics and dances. To Chicago 1930; recorded for Paramount '31 under the name of King Solomon Hill. After working in levee gangs during the depression years, he began singing again about '38 and recorded for Bluebird. Some of his best-known numbers were *Please Don't Go* and *Highway 49.* During the late '40s Williams was in St. Louis teamed with another singer, Charlie Jordan; he recorded again for a St. Louis company in '59. He is not related to the Joe Williams heard with Count Basie.

WILLIAMS, JOHN, *alto sax, clarinet;* b. Memphis, Tenn., 4/13/05. High school in Kansas City; mostly self-taught, he launched his prof. career w. Paul Banks 1922. Had own band '24-8; w. Andy Kirk '28-39. Retired from music until '42 when he joined Cootie Williams. Rec. w. Cecil Scott (Vict.), Kirk (Decca).

WILLIAMS, JOHN, *piano;* b. Windsor, Vt., 1/28/29. Played w. Mal Hallett's last band in 1945 around Boston. To NYC 1949; Army, Jan. '51-3. Later was with Ch. Barnet, Stan Getz, Zoot Sims and other small groups around NYC. Not related to West Coast pianist John Towner Williams. Favs: Powell, Silver, Brookmeyer. Own LP: Mercury; LPs w. Nick Travis (Vict.), Brookmeyer (Storyville, Wor. Pac.), Getz (Verve), Cannonball Adderley (Merc.), Z. Sims (Argo, Dawn), Phil Woods (Pres.), J. Cleveland (Merc.).

WILLIAMS, JOHN TOWNER, *piano, composer;* b. Flushing, N.Y., 2/8/32. Father, Johnny Williams, was drummer w. Raymond Scott Quintet in late 1930s. Active since '55 as pianist-conductor for pop singers, film and TV studios, etc.; composer-conductor for *M-Squad, Wagon Train* TV series and pianist on *Staccato* TV show. Own LPs on Kapp, Beth., *Piano Jazz Quartet* (Vict.); other LPs *Bell, Book and Candoli* (Dot), *Music From Peter Gunn* (Vict.).

Addr: 4200 Hayvenhurst Drive, Encino, Calif.

WILLIAMS, MARY LOU (Mary Elfrieda Winn), *piano, composer;* b. Pittsburgh, Pa., 5/8/10. Prof. debut 1925 on tour w. Seymour & Jeanette, a vaudeville act. First band job with a group led by alto saxman John Williams, later her first husband. Best known through her long association with Andy Kirk's orch. from 1929 as arranger and '31-42 also as pianist. After several successful years in KC, she and the band came East and she wrote some arrs. for Benny Goodman incl. *Camel Hop, Roll 'Em,* '37. Her best known work for Kirk incl.

Froggy Bottom, Walkin' & Swingin', Little Joe From Chicago.

For a while in 1942 Mary Lou had her own small band with Shorty Baker, her second husband, on trumpet. Later she worked solo or with small groups at Cafe Society in NYC; wrote *Trumpets No End (Blue Skies)* and other arrs. for Duke Ellington, and completed *The Zodiac Suite,* which she introduced at a Town Hall concert in '45; it was played by the New York Phil. in '46. Her close association with Thelonious Monk and Bud Powell led to the gradual evolution of her piano style, which earlier had shown the influence of Earl Hines and of the boogie-woogie fad. Her popular song hits of the late '40s incl. *In The Land of Oo-Bla-Dee,* a "bop fairy tale," and *Pretty-Eyed Baby.* In '48 she wrote and played briefly for Benny Goodman. In Dec. '52 she left for England, spending a year there and most of '54 in Paris. Back in the US in '55, she devoted more and more of her time to religious activities and was completely out of music for two or three years. Occasional night club and concert dates in '58-60.

As Nat Shapiro has observed, Mary Lou Williams is "the best example of a musician who has refused to be imprisoned by either style or tradition." Barry Ulanov wrote that she "has steadily met the demanding art of jazz keyboard performance . . . (she has) a great skill in all the modern idioms; her sense of musical responsibility accounts for the consistency of her playing and writing, and for her steady growth from the early years." Own LPs: Atlantic, Folkways, Storyville, Contemporary. Other LPs: heard in *Jazztime USA* (Bruns.), *Kansas City Jazz* (Decca), *Modern Jazz Piano: Four Views* (Camden), w. *Dizzy Gillespie at Newport* (Verve).

Addr: 63 Hamilton Terrace, New York 31, N.Y.

WILLIAMS, NELSON (Cadillac), *trumpet;* b. Montgomery, Ala., 9/26/17. Prof. debut 1932 w. Cow-Cow Davenport. Pl. w. Tiny Bradshaw; three years in Pacific w. US military band, and briefly w. John Kirby. After touring w. Duke Ellington, '49-51, he settled in Europe, touring the continent w. various bands. LPs w. Ellington (Col.).

WILLIAMS, PINKY, *baritone sax;* b. Tuscaloosa, Ala., 10/6/14. Brother Skippy Williams plays tenor sax. Stud. violin as child at Cleveland, Ohio Cons.; harmony and theory in high school there; pl. lead alto w. Earl Hines before he had any lessons on sax; w. Claude Hopkins in NYC 1944-5; pl. in concerts w. Billy Eckstine and Sarah Vaughan '47; had own group '47-50; later w. Lucky Millinder, Earl Bostic. Joined brother's band '52; has made many rock and roll record dates. Favs: Harry Carney, Leo Parker, Gerry Mulligan. LP w. Rex Stewart, Cootie Williams et al; *Porgy and Bess Revisited* (War. Bros.).

WILLIAMS, SANDY, *trombone;* b. Somerville, S.C., 10/24/06. Father a minister. Started w. Miller Bros. in Washington, D.C., then worked w. Claude Hopkins, 1927-30; Horace and Fletcher Henderson until '33, when he joined Chick Webb. After Webb's death, remained w. band under Ella Fitzgerald's leadership until 1940. Worked w. Duke Ellington 1943; also during early '40s w. Coleman Hawkins, L. Millinder, F. Henderson. Toured Europe w. Rex Stewart '47-8. In '55 he was in the hospital for six months, lost his teeth, but from late '57 gigged intermittently in a determined effort to make a successful comeback, playing Dixieland dates at Central Plaza, Local 802-sponsored concerts in NYC parks. Williams, who made his record debut in 1930 w. Jelly Roll Morton, was one of the best trombonists of the '30s, in a style reminiscent of Jimmy Harrison. Rec. with Bunk Johnson, Art Hodes and Rex Stewart are no longer available. LPs: w. S. Bechet (Blue Note), one track w. Bechet in *Great Jazz Reeds* (Cam.).

Addr: 337 W. 138th St., New York, N.Y.

WILLIAMS, SKIPPY, *tenor sax;* also *clarinet;* b. Tuscaloosa, Ala., 7/27/16. Brother, Pinky Williams, plays baritone sax (see above). Stud. soprano sax at Cleveland's Central High in 1930. Pl. school dances, then organized own group for local dances; personnel incl. Tadd Dameron, Freddie Webster. Pl. w. Chester Clark '33-4, Frank Terry '34-5; Eddie Cole in Chicago '36-9, also copyist for Fletcher Henderson. Replaced Herschel Evans in Basie band '39, then w. Edgar Hayes; Earl Bostic June '39. USO shows for 18 months, Jimmy Mundy's band for a year, Duke Ellington, Bob Chester, Tommy Reynolds. Own band for a year; own small combo in Fla. in late '40s and early '50s; NYC and road since late '50s. Favs: Chu Berry, Lester Young. Recs. w. Bill Haley.

Addr: Alvin Hotel, 223 West 52nd St., New York, N.Y.

WILLIAMS, SPENCER, *songwriter;* b. New Orleans, La., 10/14/1889. Ed. St. Charles Univ. in New Orleans. Active from 1907 in Chicago as pianist and singer. Early associate (not relative) of Clarence Williams. A successful song writer since World War I, he wrote *Squeeze Me* w. Fats Waller in 1918. Went to Paris 1925 to write music for Josephine Baker at Folies Bergère. Williams' biggest hits have incl. *I Ain't Got Nobody, Basin St. Blues, Mahogany Hall Stomp, Royal Garden Blues, I Found a New Baby, Everybody Loves My Baby, Shim-Me-Sha-Wabble, I Ain't Gonna Give Nobody None of My Jelly Roll, Tishomingo Blues.* Williams made a few records, singing and playing piano, w. Lonnie Johnson for Okeh and w. Teddy Bunn, 1930. After vacationing in France w. Fats Waller, 1932, he moved to England and lived there until 1951, later making his home in Sweden.

WILLIAMSON, CLAUDE BERKELEY, *piano;* b. Brattleboro, Vt., 11/18/26. Brother of Stu Williamson. Started piano at 7. 10 years of classical study until grad. high school, then 3 years at New England Cons. in Boston.

Entered music bus. in Cal. w. Charlie Barnet '47; w. Red Norvo Sextet Nov. '48, then ret. to Barnet '49; acc. June Christy '50-1 and occasionally since. Own trio; also w. Bud Shank quartet in '50s incl. European-N. African tour, spring '58. Early infls: Wilson, Stacy. Favs: B. Powell, Silver, Lou Levy. Rec. debut, *Claude Reigns* w. Barnet '49. Own LPs: Criterion, Beth.; LPs w. Barnet (Cap.), Tal Farlow (Verve), Stu Williamson (Beth.), Bud Shank (Wor. Pac.), Art Pepper (Savoy), Bob Cooper (Cap.), Barney Kessel, Lighthouse All Stars (Contemp.).

Addr: 7715 Ethel Ave., North Hollywood, Calif.

WILLIAMSON, JOHN LEE (Sonny Boy), *singer, harmonica;* b. Jackson, Tennessee, 1914; d. Chicago, 1948. Heard on Bluebird country blues records such as *Elevator Woman,* Williamson punctuated his vocal phrases with ingenious harmonica interpolations. Among his performances were *Wartime Blues, Decoration Day Blues, Black Panther Blues, T.B. Blues.* While working at the Plantation Club in Chicago, he was stabbed to death with an icepick wielded by an unknown assailant.

WILLIAMSON, STUART LEE (Stu), *trumpet, valve trombone;* b. Brattleboro, Vt., 5/14/33. Brother of Claude Williamson. Stud. tpt. w. Del Staigers. Made second "Innovations" tour w. Stan Kenton, 1951; toured for a year w. Woody Herman, '52-3. Living in LA since 1949, has also jobbed w. Billy May, Ch. Barnet, Skinnay Ennis. Took up valve trombone '54. Worked w. Shelly Manne quintet '54-7; free-lanced since then, rejoining Manne at Monterey Festival '58. To Alaska w. Bob Hope '59. Solos w. Herman: *Buck Dance, Wooftie.* Fav: Gillespie. LPs w. Howard Lucraft (Decca), S. Manne (Contemp.), M. Paich (War. Bros.), Kenton, Bob Cooper (Cap.), Rugolo (Col.), Duane Tatro, Lennie Niehaus, Lighthouse All Stars (Contemp.).

Addr: 10925 Bluffside, North Hollywood, Calif.

WILSON, RICHARD (Dick), *tenor sax;* b. Mt. Vernon, Ill., 11/11/11; d. New York City, 11/24/41. Featured w. Andy Kirk band for six years before his death. An impressive soloist in a style recalling Herschel Evans and Chu Berry, he was described by Mary Lou Williams as "very advanced" and can be heard to advantage on such Kirk records (not currently available but likely to be reissued on Decca) as *Bearcat Shuffle, Steppin' Pretty, Christopher Columbus, Lotta Sax Appeal, A Mellow Bit of Rhythm, Wednesday Night Hop.* One track, *Walkin' & Swingin',* is in the *Jazz of the '30s* volume of Decca's *Encyclopedia of Jazz* series. He can also be heard w. Mary Lou Williams in *Kansas City Jazz* (Decca).

WILSON, GARLAND, *piano;* b. Martinsburg, W. Va., 6/13/09; d. Paris, France, 5/31/54. First came to NYC 1930; to Europe '32 acc. Nina Mae McKinney. Worked mostly on the Continent in night clubs until '39; played at Bon Soir and other NYC clubs in '40s, returning to Paris and spending the last few years of his life there. A fine, Hines-influenced pianist, at his best on the blues. He made very few recordings; none now available.

WILSON, GERALD STANLEY, *composer, leader, trumpet;* b. Shelby, Miss., 9/4/18. To Detroit '32; studied w. mother, a pianist, and Bobby Byrne's father at Cass Tech. High. Worked w. Plantation Club Orch., Detroit, 1936-7, then went on road w. Chic Carter; repl. Sy Oliver w. Jimmie Lunceford band 1939, remaining until Apr., 1942. Settled in L.A., 1942; worked w. Les Hite, Benny Carter, Phil Moore; Willie Smith's band at Gr. Lakes Naval Training Station, Chicago, 1943-4. Formed his own big band LA, Dec., 1944, and retained it for several years despite fluctuating success. Pl. and arr. w. Count Basie off and on 1948-9; also six months w. Dizzy Gillespie, 1948. Retired from music, spending a year in grocery business, 1951; returned as bandleader, San Francisco, 1952. Made a gradual return to full scale activity in LA and SF during the late '50s; debut as TV actor in *The Lineup,* Oct. '59.

Wilson is a writer, leader and soloist of outstanding talent who, for no good reason, had been, until recently, virtually ignored in books about jazz. His arrangements for Gillespie included *Katy* and *Dizzier & Dizzier* (Victor); for Lunceford *Hi Spook* (Decca); for Ellington *Smile* and *If I Give My Heart To You* (Cap.); many others for Basie and his own band. Fav. arrs: Oliver, Rugolo, Mulligan. Fav. tpts: Gillespie, Chet Baker, Clifford Brown, Clark Terry. LPs w. Leroy Vinnegar (Contemp.), Jimmy Witherspoon (Wor. Pac.).

Addr: 209 41st Street, Manhattan Beach, Cal.

WILSON, JOHN H., *trumpet;* b. Waynesburg, Pa., 7/9/26. Stud. w. staff trombonist of radio station KDKA in Pittsburgh; B.A. in Music from New York U. 1950; M.S. in '54. Pl. in '40s and '50s w. Al Donahue, Jimmy Palmer, Benny Goodman, Les Elgart, Pete Rugolo, Sauter-Finegan; in Army bands '44-6. Amb. to be teacher. Favs: Dizzy Gillespie, Clifford Brown, Billy Butterfield. LP w. Jimmy Raney (Pres.); w. Raney in *Fourmost Guitars* (ABC-Par.).

WILSON, NANCY, *singer;* b. Chillicothe, O., 2/20/37. School in Columbus. After singing with local groups, joined Rusty Bryant band May '56, touring the Midwest and Canada with him until '58, then worked as single. Came to NYC 1959, working as secretary while awaiting release of her first LP. Admired by George Shearing and other musicians who have predicted a bright future for her, she has shown a promising combination of sensitive phrasing, secure intonation and a strong jazz feeling. Own LP: Capitol.

Addr: c/o John Levy, 119 West 57th Street, New York 19, N.Y.

WILSON, ROBERT EDWARD (Juice), *violin, clarinet, alto sax;* b. St. Louis, Mo., 1/21/04. Went to Chicago at age three. Pl. drums in school; stud. violin beginning 1912 and pl. for dances. Pl. w. Eddie South; w. Freddie Keppard '18-9; pl. Great Lakes excursion boats after leaving Keppard; w. James P. Johnson, Luckey Roberts, various bands in East '19-28. Came to New York City and joined Lloyd Scott at the Savoy. Was on numerous records acc. blues artists. Went to Europe w. Noble Sissle 1929; remained there, joining Leon Abbey 1930. Soon gave up violin for alto, clarinet. Toured N. Africa; to Malta '37, remaining 17 years w. various bands. From 1954 worked in Lebanon, Italy, Gibraltar in various American bars, then settled in Tangier, where he was playing in 1960 at the Safari Club. Though never adequately recorded on violin, he is said to have been one of the few outstanding jazz artists on the instrument. Favs: Hodges, De Franco; other fav. mus. Gillespie, Armstrong, Ellington.

WILSON, ROSSIERE (Shadow), *drums;* b. Yonkers, N.Y., 9/25/19; d. New York City, 7/11/59. Pl. w. Frank Fairfax, Lucky Millinder, Jimmy Mundy, 1939; Benny Carter, Tiny Bradshaw, '40; Lionel Hampton, '40-1; Earl Hines '41-3; Geo. Auld, Louis Jordan, '44; Count Basie, Oct. '44-Jan. '46 and again in '48. With Illinois Jacquet, '46-7, '50, '53-4; Woody Herman, '49; Erroll Garner trio '51-2; Ella Fitzgerald acc. unit. unit '54-5; Thelonious Monk at Five Spot, NYC, '57-8; occasional odd jobs in NYC until shortly before his death. Wilson, who had the unenviable job of following Jo Jones in the Basie band, was one of the great drummers of the day; at his peak in the late '40s, he won the Esquire New Star Award in '47. Feat. w. Basie on *Queer Street* (Col.); also on *Jacquet Jumps* (Verve). LPs w. Sonny Stitt (Roost, Pres.), Joe Newman (Vict.), Monk (River., Blue Note), Woods-Quill, T. Scott (Vict.), Lee Konitz (Verve), Basie (Col.).

WILSON, STANLEY C. (Stan), *singer, guitar;* b. Oakland, Calif., 5/2/27. Self-taught, st. playing at parties. Club dates and TV work in Calif. and Hawaii; primarily a folk and calypso artist. Favs: Andres Segovia, Josh White, Charlie Christian. Own LPs on Cav. and Verve.

Addr: 1024 Montgomery St., San Francisco, Calif.

WILSON, THEODORE (Teddy), *piano, composer;* b. Austin, Tex., 11/24/12. Piano and four years of violin study at Tuskegee; music theory major at Talladega College. Moved to Detroit, 1929, played w. local bands; joined Milton Senior in Toledo, 1930, traveling with him to Chicago. From 1931 to '33 played in Chicago with Louis Armstrong, Erskine Tate, Jimmie Noone and François' Louisianians. Joined Benny Carter in New York, 1933, first attracting international jazz attention on record date supervised by John Hammond that year with Carter's Chocolate Dandies, for foreign market (*Once Upon a Time, Blue Interlude* etc.).

After playing with Willie Bryant's band, 1934-5, and accompanying the Charioteers vocal group, Wilson made national news when, after recording with Benny Goodman and Gene Krupa in July 1935, he went on tour as part of this Benny Goodman Trio, the swing era's first interracial group. Wilson remained with Goodman until spring 1939, when he left to form his own excellent but short-lived big band which broke up in June 1940. From 1940 to '44 Wilson worked mainly with a sextet at the two Cafes Society on Sheridan Square and East 58th St.

After rejoining Goodman for the *Seven Lively Arts* show on Broadway, 1945, he devoted all his time to teaching, broadcasting and recording in New York; except for occasional TV shows and club dates he rarely appeared in public. He was on staff at WNEW, NYC, from 1949 to 1952. In addition to giving annual summer courses at Juilliard 1945-52, he has done a great deal of private teaching. He made concert appearances in Scandinavia, 1952, and England, '53. He has frequently been reunited with Goodman for special concerts, records and benefits. In '54-5 he was on staff at CBS, NYC, on Peter Lind Hayes show, own program (radio) and on *Crime Photographer*. In '56 the renewed interest brought about by his acting and playing role in the film *The Benny Goodman Story* led to his touring extensively with a trio in night club work. He cont. to play regularly in clubs through '60, using Jo Jones or Bert Dahlander, drums; Gene Ramey or Arvell Shaw, bass. Appeared at Brussels Worlds Fair 1958.

Wilson's style, evolved from the influence of Hines, Tatum and Waller, achieved a neat, quietly swinging symmetry, mostly in single-note lines, that was revolutionary in piano jazz and influenced countless musicians during the decade after his rise. In the late 1930s he took part in a long series of great record dates with pick-up bands, for Brunswick under his own name (often with vocals by Billie Holiday), and for Vocalion under Billie Holiday's name. (Both series now belong to Columbia, and many have been reissued on this label.)

A little-known aspect of Wilson's career is his skill as an orchestrator. He composed or arranged many of the best numbers recorded by his big band in 1940. Later he became regrettably inactive as a writer. Wilson won the Esquire Gold Award '45, '47; Silver Award '46; DB poll '36-8; Met. poll '37, '39, '46. Own LPs: *For Quiet Lovers* (Verve 2029), *Gypsy* (Col. CL 1352), *I Got Rhythm* (Verve 2073), *Impeccable Mr. Wilson* (Verve 8272), *Intimate Listening* (Verve 2011), *Mr. Wilson & Mr. Gershwin* (Col. CL 1318). LPs with Benny Goodman on Columbia, MGM, Victor; with Billie Holiday (Col. CL 637); Krupa, Hampton (Verve 8066); Edmond Hall (Comm. 30012).

Addr: 415 Central Park West, New York 25, N.Y.

WINCHESTER, LEMUEL DAVIS (Lem), *vibes;* b. Philadelphia, Pa., 3/19/28. Grandfather pl. drums for Bert Williams and other comedians in 1920s. Stud. piccolo in high school in Wilmington, Del.; later tenor and baritone sax. Took up vibes '47 after experimenting with two-finger-style piano. During the 1950s, though regularly working as member of the Wilmington police force, he continued to play local jobs as a sideline. Played at Newport Jazz Festival 1958 as this writer's presentation for the "Critics' Choice" concert. A supple and inventive modern soloist clearly reflecting strong influence of his favorite, Milt Jackson. Own LPs: Argo, New Jazz; also *New Faces at Newport,* Metrojazz.

Addr: 526 S. Buttonwood St., Wilmington, Del.

WINDHURST, JOHN HENRY (Johnny), *trumpet;* b. Bronx, N.Y., 11/5/26. Self-taught, never learned to read music. Prof. debut 1944; to Boston w. Sidney Bechet early '45. Worked at Jazz Ltd. in Chicago, gigged w. Ed Hall; most of '47-'48 in Calif., where he played jam sessions w. Louis Armstrong, dates w. Nappy Lamare. Later had own band in series of engagements in Columbus, Ohio, and Boston; 14 months at Eddie Condon's '52-3; six months w. George Wettling '53. In jazz band on stage in Huntington Hartford's production *Joyride,* Hollywood and Chicago '56. In '57-9 he led his own group at various times in Columbus and Dayton, Ohio, made concert tours of eastern colleges, and played several gigs in Florida. At Eddie Condon's, NYC, Oct. '59. Favs: Armstrong, Hackett, Gillespie. LPs w. Barbara Lea (Pres.), Jack Teagarden (Decca).

Addr: 354 Mosholu Pkwy, New York 58, N.Y.

WINDING, KAI CHRESTEN, *trombone, composer;* b. Aarhus, Denmark, 5/18/22. To US 1934 with family. Took up trombone in '37 while attending Stuyvesant High School. Played a summer season in burlesque house, then worked in Shorty Allen band '40; Bobby Day, Sonny Dunham, Alvino Rey, '41. Joined Coast Guard '42, played in service band led by Bill Schallen; during this period, made record debut with Roy Stevens on Manor. Played w. Benny Goodman Oct. '45-Jan. '46, but no rec. solos. Toured w. Stan Kenton to April '47; featured on *Artistry in Percussion,* in *Bolero,* in *Boogie, Collaboration* etc. Worked with Ch. Ventura combo to Feb. '48; led small unit with singer Buddy Stewart to Dec. '48. In '49 headed combos at Royal Roost, Bop City, did TV, radio w. Patti Page, *Hit Parade* etc., doubling with pop and jazz jobs until Aug. '54, when he teamed with J. J. Johnson to form quintet, which displayed a tasteful blending of the strikingly similar styles developed in the mid-'40s by the two trombonists. After this group disbanded Winding formed a septet, featuring four trombones and rhythm, Oct. '56, and built a big commercial following for the group—especially at colleges, where he played most of his dates '58-60. He disbanded briefly to reunite with Johnson for a European tour in the fall of '58. His own group was heard at the *Playboy* festival '59 and at many other festivals.

Winding, who like Johnson has doubled occasionally on a new instrument called the trombonium, plays in a brittle yet volatile and emphatic style; praised by Nat Hentoff for "unusually expert and warmly imaginative trombone artistry."

Own LPs: *Trombone Panorama, The Trombone Sound, The Swingin' States, Dance To The City Beat* (Col.); selections w. own groups in *In The Beginning . . . Bebop, Loaded* (Savoy), *Trombone By Three* (Pres.). LPs w. J. J. Johnson: Col., Savoy, Beth., Pres. (see Johnson for nos.). Other LPs: w. Kenton (Cap.), Woody Herman (Col.), *Jazztime USA* (Bruns.), *The Brothers* (Pres.), *Hot vs. Cool* (MGM), Miles Davis (Cap.), *Trombone Rapport* (Debut).

Addr: 120 Bellair Drive, Dobbs Ferry, N.Y.

WINESTONE, BENJAMIN (Benny), *tenor, alto saxes;* also *clarinet, flute;* b. Glasgow, Scotland, 12/20/06. Brother, a professional pianist, was killed in London air raid 1941. Father was a cantor who taught him to read music when he was 7. Took violin lessons at 9 in Glasgow. Bought alto sax and became prof. at 20. To London where he worked w. Ted Heath in Sidney Lifton's band '37. Pl. w. Frank Bogart in Toronto '41-2, Jess Stacy in US '45, Maynard Ferguson in Montreal '47-8. Own group w. trumpeter Herby Spanier in Toronto '51. W. Steve Garrick at Chez Paree in Montreal '59. Film: *A Yank at Oxford* '38. Early infls: Carter, Trumbauer, J. Dorsey; later, Lester Young, Charlie Parker. LP: one track w. George Chisholm in *Scrapbook of British Jazz. 1926-1956* (Lond.).

Addr: 1465 Metcalfe St., Montreal, Quebec, Canada.

WISE, ROBERT RAYMOND (Buddy), *tenor sax;* b. Topeka, Kan., 2/20/28; d. Las Vegas, Nev., July 1955. Prof. debut 1943. Pl. w. Hal Wasson, Mal Hallett to '45, then five years w. G. Krupa, nine months w. Woody Herman, 18 months w. Ray Anthony. Fav. own solos on Fats Waller tunes rec. by Krupa. Favs: Al Cohn, Z. Sims. Feat. on *These Foolish Things* w. Krupa (Vict.). LPs w. Ray Anthony (Cap.), Gene Krupa (Camden).

WITHERSPOON, JAMES (Jimmy), *singer;* b. Gurdon, Ark., 8/8/23. No musical training, though he sang in Baptist church choir at seven. While with the Merchant Marine in the Pacific 1941-3, had his first experience as a blues performer during a stopover in Calcutta, where he sang with Teddy Weatherford's band. In 1944 he joined the Jay McShann orchestra, in Vallejo, Cal., replacing Walter Brown, and toured with McShann for four years. Working later as a solo artist, he had his first hit single record, *'Tain't Nobody's Business,* in '52; other hits followed, incl. *Big Fine Girl, The Wind Is Blowing, No Rollin' Blues.* Despite these successes in the r & b market, he was ignored by most jazz listeners and critics until he began to make LPs in '58. He had a great success at the Monterey, Cal. Jazz Festival in Oct. '59. A big-voiced, extroverted blues singer in an unspoiled traditional style. Own LPs: HiFiJazz (recorded at Monterey), Victor, World-Pacific, Atlantic.

WOOD, MITCHELL JR. (Bootie), *trombone;* b. Dayton, O., 12/27/19. Stud. w. Clarence Francois at Dunbar High. Got into music through Snookie Young, first in local band, then in Chick Carter orch. in which they both played 1938-9. Played w. Jimmy Raschel, '40-1;

Tiny Bradshaw, '42-3; Lionel Hampton '43-7 (with time out for service in Navy band under Willie Smith '44-5); Arnett Cobb '47-8; Erskine Hawkins '48-9; back w. Cobb for a year, Hawkins again to early '51, then six months w. Count Basie, after which he worked for Dayton Post Office as postman '51-9, also leading own local group from '54. Joined Duke Ellington 9/7/59, touring Europe with him shortly afterward. Favs: Fred Beckett, Trummy Young.

Addr: 2328 Greenway St., Dayton, Ohio.

WOODE, JAMES BRYANT (Jimmy), *bass, composer, piano;* b. Philadelphia, Pa., 9/23/28. Father, a music teacher, played baritone horn with Dixieland bands. Stud. piano at Phila. Acad. of Mus., Schillinger system under Clarence Cox, later at Boston U. Sch. of Mus., Boston Cons., and under bassist Paul Gregory in Calif. To Navy as radar operator, then Special Services '45 in Philippines; sang w. Navy band. Pl. piano and sang w. vocal group, the Velvetaires, then formed own trio, '46. Living in Boston, spent two years as house bassist at Storyville, then a year touring w. Flip Phillips, a year w. Sarah Vaughan and Ella Fitzgerald. Worked w. Nat Pierce off and on '51-2. Joined Duke Ellington Jan. '55. A serious, scholarly musician whose interests include the study of philosophy, religion and languages, he is well represented in his own LP as composer and soloist. Ambition: to give up traveling, study and teach music. Left Ellington Feb. '59. First infl: Mose Allen of old Lunceford band; then Blanton, Pettiford, Ray Brown; later favs. Duvivier, Chambers, Richard Davis. Own LP: Argo. Feat. w. Ellington *Sonnet in Search of a Moor* from *Such Sweet Thunder* (Col.), *Satin Doll in Bal Masque* (Col.), many others on Cap., Beth., Col.

Addr: 106-24 Ditmars Blvd., East Elmhurst, L.I., N.Y.

WOODMAN, BRITT, *trombone;* b. Los Angeles, Calif., 6/4/20. Worked with Phil Moore, 1938; Les Hite, '39-42; Army, '42-6. Boyd Raeburn, '46; three months w. Eddie Heywood, then w. Lionel Hampton '46-7. Stud. at Westlake Coll. in LA '48-50. Joined Duke Ellington '51. Featured on *One O'Clock Jump, Things Ain't What They Used to Be* (Cap.), *Sonnet to Hank Cinq* in *Such Sweet Thunder* (Col.), *Black Butterfly* w. Mercer Ellington (Cor.), etc. Highly inventive musician, often not heard extensively enough with Ellington to reveal his full capabilities. Fav: J. J. Johnson. LPs w. Ellington (Vict., Cap., Col., Beth.), Miles Davis (Debut), Mercer Ellington (Coral), J. Hodges (Verve), Billy Taylor (Argo).

Addr: 200 West 49th Street, Los Angeles 37, Cal.

WOODS, PHILIP WELLS, *alto sax, clarinet;* b. Springfield, Mass., 11/2/31. Heir to a deceased uncle's alto, he stud. locally until 1948, then moved to NYC, where he stud. w. Lennie Tristano and for one semester at Manhattan Sch. of Mus.; Juilliard for 4 years, majoring in clarinet. Briefly w. Richard Hayman, Ch. Barnet '54; concerts and rec. w. Jimmy Raney, '55; George Wallington '56; Friedrich Gulda at Birdland and NJF '56; toured US and abroad w. Dizzy Gillespie Mar.-Dec. '56; led combo with Gene Quill, '57; many freelance jobs around NYC, incl. return to Wallington, then mainly with Buddy Rich, '58-9; joined Quincy Jones Oct. '59.

Phil Woods, who happens to be the stepfather of the young son of Charlie Parker, has inherited the Parker style and modified it to his own ends more successfully than almost any other alto man except Julian Adderley. He plays with soul, fire, melodic ingenuity and complete command. Fav: Parker. Own LPs on Prestige, Epic; LPs w. Gene Quill (Pres., Vict.), *52nd Street* w. L. Feather (Interlude), G. Russell (Decca), *Bird Feathers* (New Jazz), N. Hefti (Epic), Joe Newman (Vict.), Jackie Cain-Roy Kral (ABC-Par.), Q. Jones (ABC-Par., Merc.), Manny Albam (Coral), Gillespie (Verve), G. Wallington (Pres., New Jazz, Savoy), *Bird's Night,* Sahib Shihab (Savoy), Jim Chapin (Classic Edit.), *Saxes, Inc.* (War. Bros.), Bill Potts, Zoot Sims-Al Cohn (UA).

Addr: Stover Park Road, Point Pleasant, Pa.

WOODYARD, SAMUEL (Sam), *drums;* b. Elizabeth, N.J., 1/7/25. Self-taught; no musicians in family. Early exp. sitting in locally around Newark and North Jersey. Joined Paul Gayten r & b band 1950-1. Pl. w. Joe Holiday combo '51; Roy Eldridge, '52; Milt Buckner, '53-5, then joined Duke Ellington, who hailed him as the best drummer in his band since Louis Bellson and featured him in the latter's old specialties such as *Skin Deep.* Some critics have disagreed with Ellington's appraisal: Whitney Balliett wrote that Woodyard "persists in a slogging, ticking after-beat that becomes hypnotic" at times, and that on other occasions he "handled every number as if he were breaking rocks." In the summer of 1959 Woodyard left the band, then returned to form a drum duo with Jimmy Johnson. While the band was in Europe, Oct. '59, he played with Mercer Ellington's orch. at Birdland. Favs: Roach, Blakey, Jo Jones, Krupa, Roy Haynes, Rich. LPs w. Ellington: Col.; feat. on *Hi Fi Fo Fum* (*Ellington at Newport '58.*

Addr: 730 Macon Street, Brooklyn 33, N.Y.

WOOTTEN, LAWRENCE B. (Red), *bass;* b. Social Circle, Ga., 11/5/22. Father pl. trombone, brother bassist in Las Vegas. Stud. at Chadek Cons., Chattanooga, Tenn. Guitar in 1944, then bass (private study). Prof. début with Gene Austin, 1940. Bass with Jan Savitt, '45, Randy Brooks, '46, Tony Pastor, '47, T. Dorsey, '49, W. Herman, '51, Ch. Barnet '56, Red Norvo '57; along w. Norvo joined Benny Goodman dectet on European tour Oct. '59. Film w. Norvo: *Screaming Mimi.* Favs: Blanton, Pettiford et al. Ambition: to study composition intensively. LPs w. Herman (MGM), *Lonely Street* w. Barnet (Verve), Goodman (MGM), Harry Babasin (Merc.).

Addr: 20632 Skouras Drive, Canoga Park, Cal.

WORMWORTH, JAMES EDWARD III (Jimmy), *drums;* b. Utica, N.Y., 8/14/37. Father pl. drums, piano; uncle, Dick Mariani, tenor sax. Stud. w. Geo. Claesgens in Utica from 1947. Worked with combos in Europe summer '56 and '57. Joined Nellie Lutcher Feb. '58; Jazz Modes June '58; Lou Donaldson, Phineas Newborn '58-9; Mal Waldron Feb.-June '59. Toured with Lambert, Hendricks & Ross from Oct. '59. One of the most promising young drummers on the New York scene. LPs w. Lambert, Hendricks & Ross (Col.), Hendricks (Wor. Pac.), Donaldson (Blue Note), Jazz Modes (Atl.).

Addr: 429 East Sixth Street, New York 9, N.Y.

WRIGHT, DEMPSEY, *guitar;* b. Calumet, Okla., 7/14/29. From 1941, played violin in string bands at local parties, riding to all jobs on horseback. After leaving Junior College in '48 to join Otho Swink's western-music band, started on guitar and took up jazz. Leaving for Calif. in '53, he worked with Frankie Carle; toured service bases in Japan, Korea, Okinawa '55-6; violin and guitar w. Harry Babasin's Jazzpickers '57-8; w. Freddie Slack trio in LA '59; toured w. Chico Hamilton Quintet '59. A vital and subtle guitarist in the tradition of his fellow-Oklahomans, Charlie Christian and Barney Kessel. Own LP: Andex; LPs w. Harry Babasin (Merc.).

WRIGHT, ELMON, *trumpet;* b. Kansas City, Mo., 10/27/29. Son of Lammar Wright, Sr. Joined Dizzy Gillespie 1946 and remained with him for the duration of his big band leadership (to '50). Worked with Roy Eldridge and other bands around NYC; toured w. Earl Bostic, '54-5; house bands at Apollo, rock 'n roll groups, etc. '56-60, also w. Buddy Rich and Earle Warren, '59.

WRIGHT, EUGENE JOSEPH (Gene), *bass;* b. Chicago, Ill., 5/29/23. Stud. cornet at school; self-taught on bass until recent studies w. Paul Gregory in Los Angeles. Had own 16-piece band, the Dukes of Swing, 1943-6. Worked w. Gene Ammons, '46-8 and '49-51; Count Basie, '48-9, Arnett Cobb, '51-2; Buddy De Franco quartet, '52-5, touring Europe with him Jan.-Feb., '54. Went to Australia w. Red Norvo trio, '55. Made movie short w. Ch. Barnet. Joined Dave Brubeck Feb. '58. A serious, dependable and capable musician. Fav: Milt Hinton. LPs w. Dave Brubeck (Col.), Gene Ammons, Sonny Stitt (Pres.), Cal Tjader (Fant.), B. De Franco (Verve).

Addr: 1189 W. 36th Pl., Los Angeles 7, Calif.

WRIGHT, LAMMAR, JR., *trumpet;* b. Kansas City, Mo., 9/28/27. Joined Lionel Hampton's band at 16 and remained with him for three years; feat. w. Ch. Barnet, 1947-8.

WRIGHT, LAMMAR, SR., *trumpet;* b. Texarkana, Tex., 6/20/12. Pl. w. Bennie Moten, 1923-8. Joined the Missourians, later taken over by Cab Calloway, and remained with the band under Calloway for 17 years, returning to him occasionally since 1945. Since leaving Calloway he has been first trumpet w. Don Redman, Claude Hopkins, Cootie Williams, Louis Armstrong, Lucky Millinder, Sy Oliver; also led several combos and became teacher in NYC. Played w. Perez Prado '56, Sauter-Finegan '57, George Shearing big band '59. Featured on *Lammar's Boogie* w. Sy Oliver (MGM). His two sons Elmon and Lammar Jr. both play trumpet. Fav: Louis Armstrong.

Addr: 275 West 150th St., New York 39, N.Y.

WRIGHT, LEO NASH, *alto sax, flute, clarinet, piccolo;* b. Wichita Falls, Tex., 12/14/33. Father pl. alto w. Boots and His Buddies band out of Houston, and still plays. Stud. alto with father during World War II while in Calif. Ret. to Texas to finish high school, where he learned more about the sax from John Hardee. Att. Huston-Tillitson Coll. and San Francisco State; pl. with Saunders King. Came to New York, joined Charles Mingus for a while; joined Dizzy Gillespie August 1959. Fav: Charlie Parker, but names Johnny Hodges, Benny Carter, Willie Smith, Jimmy Dorsey as earlier favorites. LP w. Virgil Gonsalves (Omega), Gillespie (Verve).

Addr: 429 E. 6th Street, New York 9, N.Y.

WRIGHT, CHARLES (Specs), *drums;* b. Philadelphia, Pa., 9/8/27. Uncle was music teacher. Played in band at South Philadelphia High, then Army band; discharged 1947. Pl. with Jimmy Heath's 17-piece band; six months w. Howard McGhee incl. trip to France 1948. Worked w. D. Gillespie's big band and combo '49-51, then free-lanced in Phila. until '55 except for a tour w. E. Bostic in '53. Worked for a year w. Cannonball Adderley '55-6, then joined Carmen McRae's accompanying trio. Later pl. with Benny Golson-Curtis Fuller, etc. LPs w. Art Blakey: *Orgy in Rhythm* (BN), *Drum Suite* (Col.); Carmen McRae (Decca), Ray Bryant, Red Garland (Pres.), Nat Adderley (Em.).

WRIGHTSMAN, STANLEY (Stan), *piano;* b. Oklahoma City, Okla., 6/15/10. Stud. privately in Springfield, Mo. At 14, joined band led by father who played piano, sax, guitar. Left Springfield 1927; pl. w. hotel band in Gulfport, Miss. Later worked w. Ray Miller, 1930, in New Orleans; Hank Halstead and many other bands in Texas, Louisiana and Okla. After a year in Chicago w. Ben Pollack, 1935-6, settled in Los Angeles. Has been feat. on many Dixieland records w. local jazz combos, mostly led by Bob Crosby or by various alumni of the Crosby band, as well as with Joe Yukl, Artie Shaw, Wingy Manone. Active free-lancing in TV and advertising jingles. Films: background for *Picnic,* duets in *Five Pennies;* TV: *M Squad, Bourbon Street Beat.* Original infl. was Earl Hines; other favs: Teddy Wilson, Tatum. LPs w. Matty Matlock (Col., War. Bros.), Pete Fountain (Coral), *Dixieland Jubilee* (GNP), Claire Austin (Contemp.); Nappy Lamare in *History of Jazz, Vol. 1* (Cap.).

Addr: 11826½ Riverside Drive, North Hollywood, Calif.

WROBLEWSKI, PTASZYN (Jan), *tenor sax;* b. Kalisz, Poland, 3/27/36. St. on piano, then clarinet, baritone, tenor. Had own student dance group, 1954; bari, clar. w. Sekstet Komedy '56-7, then tenor and arr. w. Jazz Believers. Former group pl. jazz festivals at Sopot, Poland, and at world youth festival, Aug. '57, in Moscow, where he rec. silver award. Has broadcast often on Warsaw radio since '56; TV in Lodz, Poznan, Warsaw, Katowice. He pl. w. Newport International Band at NJF and Brussels '58. As a result of his appearance with the band he became the most celebrated musician in Poland and has since been extremely busy as performer and writer. LP: Newport International Band (Col.).

Addr: Pukaskiego 1, Kalisz, Poland.

WYANDS, RICHARD, *piano;* b. Oakland, Calif., 7/2/28. St. professional career in 1944 working w. local groups. Pl. in house band at clubs and acc. many prominent instrumentalists. Was acc. for Ella Fitzgerald during part of '56; later w. Carmen McRae. Moved to NYC Jan. '58, worked w. Roy Haynes, Ch. Mingus; Kenny Burrell at Minton's, and several months w. J. Richardson '59. W. Gigi Gryce '60. LPs w. Cal Tjader (Savoy), Ch. Mingus (UA), Gryce (New Jazz).

Addr: 564 St. Mark's Ave., Brooklyn, N.Y.

WYBLE, JIMMY, *guitar;* b. Port Arthur, Tex., 1/25/22. Stud. with private teacher at 13; pl. around Houston w. Peck Kelley and other local musicians. Staff musician on Houston radio station 1941-2; in Army '42-6; moved to LA, working in several movie studios since then. W. Red Norvo '59-60, touring with him in Benny Goodman band. Stud. classical guitar with Laurindo Almeida. Favs: Charlie Christian, Tal Farlow, Jimmy Raney. LPs w. Red Norvo (Tampa, Vict.), Bob Harrington (Imp.), Goodman (MGM).

WYNN, ALBERT, *trombone;* b. New Orleans, La., 7/29/07. Was prom. in Chicago during the twenties w. various groups, incl. Earl Hines. Toured Europe w. Sam Wooding in 1928. Back in Chi. was active in the thirties w. Carroll Dickerson and at the Apex Club w. Jimmie Noone. With Fletcher Henderson during 1937-8. Played w. the groups of Baby Dodds, Lil Armstrong, Little Brother Montgomery; since '56 featured w. Franz Jackson Orch. at the Red Arrow in Stickney, Ill. Despite his origin, Wynn was influenced more by Jimmy Harrison and Jack Teagarden than by the early tailgate style. LP w. Franz Jackson (Replica, Merc.); also rec. w. Little Brother Montgomery, Lil Armstrong on Ebony.

Addr: 6125 Eberhart Ave., Chicago 37, Ill.

Y

YAGED, SOLOMON (Sol), *clarinet;* b. Brooklyn, N.Y., 12/8/22. Stud. w. Simeon Bellison of NY Phil. Played w. various symph. and chamber groups around NYC. A familiar figure for many years at jam sessions and jazz concerts in NYC, Yaged has free-lanced with virtually every Dixieland and swing combo ever heard on 52nd St. and in Greenwich Village since the late 1930s. Among the hundreds of leaders for whom he has worked are Phil Napoleon, Max Kaminsky, Fletcher Henderson, Eddie Condon, Claude Hopkins, Muggsy Spanier, Hot Lips Page, Red Allen, Pee Wee Erwin, Jimmy McPartland. He rec. with his own group for the Voice of America. Played in movie *Carnegie Hall.* Idolizes Benny Goodman, to whom he has a slight physical resemblance, and would like to have a swing band similar to Goodman's outfit of the late 1930s. He taught Steve Allen clarinet before Allen appeared in title role of *The Benny Goodman Story,* July '55. Own LP: Herald; LPs w. Jack Teagarden (Ur.), Chubby Jackson (Evst.).

Addr: 2844 West 28th St., Brooklyn, N.Y.

YANCEY, JAMES (Jimmy), *piano;* b. Chicago, Ill., 1894; d. Chicago, 9/17/51. Self-taught. Toured US and Europe for many years as singer and tap-dancer; later pl. blues piano at rent parties in Chicago but was largely inactive as musician after World War I. For more than thirty years he worked as groundskeeper for the Chicago White Sox at Comiskey Park. After his name had come to light through recordings of *Yancey Special* by Meade Lux Lewis, 1936, and Bob Crosby, 1938, he was brought to the recording studios and made a series of sessions off and on from 1939 until shortly before his death. On some of his records he accompanied vocals by his wife, blues singer Estella "Mama" Yancey. LPs: *Yancey's Getaway* (River.), *Pure Blues* w. Mama Yancey (Atl.).

YANKEE, PAT (Patricia Millicent Weigum), *singer;* b. Lodi, Calif., 7/2/29. At age of 14 was a prof. tap dancer; turned to singing in 1951. Made movies for Columbia Pictures while in her teens, later local TV in San Francisco for three years. While working as a single in a night club in Anchorage, Alaska, she met Turk Murphy, whose band she joined in 1958. Originally a pop singer, she turned to traditional jazz and has stud. the recordings of Ma Rainey, Bessie Smith et al, whom she names as influences. Fav: Ella Fitzgerald. LPs w. T. Murphy (Roul.).

Addr: 1011 Bush St., San Francisco, Calif.

YAW, RALPH PERCY, *composer, piano;* b. Enosburg Falls, Vt., 10/22/1898. Stud. with mother, a Boston Cons. graduate and piano teacher; also w. Julius Hartt, Ralph Baldwin. To LA 1919; toured with bands in Ariz. and Calif. Began arranging in 1927 w. Bob Stowell band. Managed and played at Coconut Grove dance hall, Bakersfield, Cal., 1927-34. Arr. for Eddie Barefield, 1934-5; Cab Calloway, 1935-9, also for Chick Webb, Isham Jones and a few for Basie, Les Brown. Back to LA, arr. 40 originals for Stan Kenton, whom he had first met in 1930. Yaw's work, perhaps the most important factor in the original Kenton band, included *Two Moods, Smoky, You Alone, Blues in*

Asia Minor, Night, Balboa Bash and *Down in Chihuahua.* Arr. for Duke Shaeffer, 1942, also for Red Nichols, Johnny Richards. Gave up arranging in 1947; since then, living in Bakersfield, teaching, playing w. western bands and writing western tunes incl. the big Hank Snow hit *No Longer a Prisoner.* Collaborated on songs w. poetess Georgie Starbuck Galbraith, 1954-5. Fav. arrs. Johnny Richards, Kenton. LP: *The Kenton Era* (Cap.).

Addr: Rt. 5, Box 529C, Bakersfield, Cal.

YOUNG, WILLIAM (Bill), *drums, flute, piano;* b. Salt Lake City, Utah, 2/11/28. Started playing drums in 1949 when he heard M. Roach on a C. Parker record. Played w. Salt Lake City Symphony. In 1950 was w. Gene Mayl's Dixieland Rhythm Kings; in '52 was w. D. Gordon in San Francisco, later w. Brew Moore. Formed trio w. wife Jean Hoffman (q.v.) in 1957. Favs: Roach, Parker, Bobby Donaldson. LP w. Jean Hoffman (Fant.).

Addr: 245 Bristol Blvd., San Leandro, Calif.

YOUNG, ELDEE, *bass;* also *cello;* b. Chicago, Ill., 1/7/36. Father pl. mandolin. Stud. guitar w. brother, later bass in high sch. and at Amer. Cons. of Music in Chicago. Pl. with King Kolax 1951. Traveled w. r&b singer Chuck Willis '54, and acc. various other r&b singers such as Joe Turner, T-Bone Walker, Joe Williams. Feat. w. Ramsey Lewis trio. Fav: Ray Brown. Fav. own solo: *I Had the Craziest Dream* w. Lewis (Argo).

Addr: 3263 W. Fulton Blvd., Chicago, Ill.

YOUNG, LEONIDAS RAYMOND (Lee), *drums;* b. New Orleans, La., 3/7/17. Brother of Lester Young; with Lester and their sister Irma, formed part of saxophone trio in school. Started on trombone, soprano and alto saxes, studying with father and touring vaudeville circuit in "Young Family" act. Went to school in Minneapolis. In Los Angeles, 1934, played w. Mutt Carey. Worked w. Buck Clayton band, 1935-6; eight months w. Eddie Barefield, briefly w. Eddie Mallory, then Fats Waller. Began to work for Geo. Stoll at Paramount studios, later MGM and other major movie studio assignments, also jobbing w. Les Hite. Toured w. Lionel Hampton, Sept. '40-Jan. '41; own sextet with Lester Young, 1942; staff work at Columbia Pictures 1944-8, then free-lance studio jobs. Joined Nat Cole combo June 1953. Young's studio jobs incl. dubbing drum parts for Mickey Rooney in *Strike Up The Band,* appearance w. Hazel Scott in *I Dood It,* writing of drum specialty for *Skirts Ahoy;* worked w. Marge & Gower Champion in *Everything I Have Is Yours.* LPs: w. Cole (Cap.); JATP (Verve).

Addr: 2331 Second Ave., Los Angeles 18, Calif.

YOUNG, LESTER WILLIS (Prez), *tenor sax,* also *composer, clarinet;* b. Woodville, Miss., 8/27/09; d. New York City, 3/15/59. His father, a trained musician who had studied at Tuskegee, instructed him on trumpet, violin, alto sax and drums. Family lived in New Orleans from Lester's infancy until 1919. At ten Lester played drums in the family band with his brother Lee and sister Irma; at the age of 13 he decided to concentrate on saxophone. By this time he was living in Minneapolis; during the carnival season the family traveled with the minstrel show in which his father played, touring through the Dakotas, Kansas and Nebraska.

Frankie Trumbauer was Young's original idol; he attributed his original sound on tenor sax in later years to an attempt to duplicate the quality of Trumbauer's C melody saxophone. Young's first major job with a touring band was as baritone saxophonist with the Bostonians around 1929-30. During the early 1930s he was heard around Kansas, Missouri, Oklahoma and Minnesota with such bands as King Oliver's and Walter Page's Blue Devils. While working at the Paseo Club in KC with the Benny Moten-George Lee band, he sat in one night with Fletcher Henderson, subbing for Coleman Hawkins. A few months later, when he was with a small combo led by Count Basie, he received an offer to replace Hawkins, who had left for Europe. He did not remain long in the Henderson band, as he was criticized for lacking Hawkins' big sound. He next worked with Andy Kirk for six months, then rejoined Basie, playing at the Reno Club in KC in the summer of '36; made his first recordings with a Basie quintet for Columbia in Chicago, 10/9/36. From then until 12/13/40, when he left Basie, Young had the most vital influence since Hawkins on the jazz approach to the tenor saxophone, ultimately becoming the founding factor in a new school of jazz thought and the original influence on virtually all new tenor men in the late '40s and the '50s.

After leading a short-lived combo of his own that played in 1941 at Kelly's Stable in NYC (recording only as background for a vocal date by Una Mae Carlisle on Victor-Bluebird), Lester teamed with his brother, Lee Young; their sextet played at Cafe Society in 1942 as well as in California. Lester toured for USO Camp Shows with Al Sears' band and was also back in Basie's band for a few months from Dec. '43. He entered the Army in Oct. '44 and during his 15 months in the service, according to Jo Jones and others who were close to him at that time, suffered traumatic experiences with racial prejudice that had a devastating effect on his life and his career.

From the time he reentered civilian life until his death Young alternated between leading his own small combo, one that usually was poorly integrated and sometimes included inferior musicians, and touring the US and overseas with Norman Granz' Jazz at the Philharmonic unit. The last three years of his life were marked by a series of catastrophes including a nervous breakdown, hospitalization for malnutrition and alcoholism; there were a few brief attempts to return to full-scale activity. He had just returned from a night club engagement in Paris when he died of a combination of ailments in his New York hotel.

Lester Young was, with Coleman Hawkins, one of

the two most vital influences in the course of the tenor sax in jazz; more, he was credited by many as the chief figure in the switch from hot to cool jazz, symbolized by the transition from big, full tone and dotted-eight-and-sixteenth-note phrasing to a moodier, more laconic sound and series of evenly placed eighth notes played legato.

As a composer Young was best known for some original works he wrote for the early Basie band such as *Tickle Toe;* also for a blues riff, *Jumpin' With Symphony Sid.* The most valuable of the few records he made playing clarinet were those with the Kansas City Six, on Commodore. He was seen in Norman Granz' film short *Jammin' The Blues* in 1944. He won the *Esquire* Silver Award in '45 and '47; the DB poll '44 and was elected to the DB Hall of Fame in '59. Fav. own recs: *Taxi War Dance* w. Basie (Epic), *Back in Your Own Backyard, Sailboat in the Moonlight* w. Billie Holiday (Col.). He was heard on many record dates in the late '30s with Teddy Wilson and Billie Holiday, and on one date each with Glenn Hardman (Col.) and Sam Price (Decca).

LPs on Verve: *Tenor Saxes* 8125, *Pres & Sweets* 8134, *with Oscar Peterson Trio* 8114, *Jazz Giants '56* 8146, *Lester's Here* 8161, *Pres* 8162, *Lester Young-Buddy Rich Trio* 8164, *Lester Swings Again* 8181, *It Don't Mean a Thing* 8187, *Verve Compendium of Jazz #1* 8194, *Pres and Teddy* 8205, *Anatomy of Improvisation* 8230, *The Lester Young Story* 8308, *Going for Myself* 8298, *Laughin' To Keep from Cryin'* with Eldridge 8316, *Jazz at the Phil.* Vols. 1, 2, 4, 5, 7, 8, 9, 11. Also *Blue Lester* (Savoy 12068), *The Greatest* (Intro 603), *Lester Leaps In* (Epic 3107), *Master's Touch* with Basie (Savoy 12071), *Memorial Album* with Basie (two LPs) (Epic SN-6031), *Swingin'* (Intro 602).

LPs with Basie (Bruns. 58019, Decca 8049), tracks in *Kansas City Jazz* (Decca 8044), *Basie at Newport* (Verve 8243), *The Jazz Scene* (Verve 8060), Billy Eckstine (MGM), *Benny Goodman Carnegie Hall Concert* (Col. OSL 160), *Spirituals to Swing* (Vang. 8523-4), Billie Holiday (Col.).

YOUNG, EUGENE EDWARD (Snookie), *trumpet;* b. Dayton, Ohio, 2/3/19. First instruction came from parents and private teacher. His first important engagement was w. Chick Carter in 1937. Subsequently he was w. J. Lunceford '39-42, C. Basie '42, L. Hampton '43-4, B. Carter '44, Gerald Wilson '45, Basie again '45-7. Returned to Dayton in '47 and had own group there until Oct. '57, when he rejoined Basie. Appeared in several films during '40s, incl. *Blues in the Night* as the off-screen trumpeter for Jack Carson in one sequence. Fav. own solos: *Uptown Blues* and *Time To Jump and Shout* w. Lunceford (Col.). Favs: The young Armstrong, M. Davis, R. Eldridge, C. Shavers, C. Spivak. LPs w. Basie (Roul.); *Like Who?* w. Paul Quinichette (UA), Lunceford (Col.).

Addr: 1502 Hockwalt St., Dayton, Ohio.

YOUNG, JAMES OSBORNE (Trummy), *trombone, singer;* b. Savannah, Ga., 1/12/12. Raised in Washington, D.C. Prof. debut in 1928 in Booker Coleman's Hot Chocolates. Later worked w. Hardy Bros. and Tommy Miles. Rose to prominence during his engagements w. Earl Hines, 1934-7 and Jimmie Lunceford, 1937-43. In 1943-4 worked w. Ch. Barnet and had his own band for a while on 52nd St. and in Chicago. After playing w. Boyd Raeburn and appearing w. JATP and in other combos, he moved to Hawaii, where he lived from 1947-52. Since the summer of '52 he has been on tour w. Louis Armstrong's group. Trummy's extroverted, technically brilliant trombone solos, his intimate, breathless style, and his humorous vocals were outstanding features of the Lunceford band in the late '30s. His biggest hit was *Margie,* which he first recorded w. Lunceford 1/6/38. Movie: *The Glenn Miller Story.* Other movies w. Louis Armstrong. Won Esq. New Star Award '47. LPs w. Lunceford (Decca 8050, Col. CL 634), Armstrong (Decca, Col.), Buck Clayton (Col. CL 567, CL 701).

Addr: 2947 Somerset Drive, Los Angeles 16, Calif.

YOUNG, WEBSTER, *trumpet;* b. Columbia, S.C., 12/3/32. Raised in Washington, D.C., played in Army band w. Hampton Hawes; later gigs in Washington w. local groups. Came to NYC, June '56. Recorded several albums for Prestige and gigged; returned to Washington 1959. Favs: M. Davis, Gillespie. LP w. R. Draper (Pres.). Own LP: Pres.

YUKL, JOSEPH (Joe), *trombone;* b. New York City, 3/5/09. Stud. violin w. father; trombone w. Ch. Randall, T. Dorsey's teacher. Started w. newsboys' band in Baltimore; toured w. Maryland Collegians. Settled in NYC at suggestion of Dorsey, 1927. Worked w. Red Nichols, Roger Wolfe Kahn, Dorsey bros., and Baltimore theatres; toured w. Joe Haymes, then Dorsey bros. again. To Calif. w. Jimmy Dorsey 1935; free lance studio work in LA ever since. Acting and playing role in film *Rhythm Inn;* sound-tracked solo for James Stewart in jam session scene of *The Glenn Miller Story.* App. on Red Rowe TV show '59-60. Favs: Dorsey, Teagarden, Mole. Recs. w. Eddie Skrivanek on MacGregor, Charlie La Vere on Jump are no longer available.

Addr: 13571 Rangoon St., Pacoima, Calif.

Z

ZARCHY, RUBIN (Zeke), *trumpet;* b. New York City, 6/12/15. Pl. w. Joe Haymes, 1935; Benny Goodman, '36; Artie Shaw, '36-7; Bob Crosby, '37-9; T. Dorsey, '39-40; Glenn Miller, '40; NBC staff, NYC, '40-2. Service, '42-5, overseas w. Glenn Miller AAF band 1944-5. Free-lance radio, TV, recording in Hollywood since then. Favs: Armstrong, Butterfield, Gillespie. LPs: No jazz solos on records.

Addr: 11034 Wrightwood Place, North Hollywood, Cal.

ZAWINUL, JOSEF (Joe), *piano;* also *bass trumpet, organ, vibes;* b. Vienna, Austria, 7/7/32. Stud. Vienna Cons. from age 7. Own trio for Special Service clubs in France & Germany, 1952; with Horst Winter, Austria's leading band, '53-4; Johannes Fehring, Friedrich Gulda, '54-6; piano, bass trumpet, vibes w. Fatty George combo, '57-8. To USA, toured for eight months w. Maynard Ferguson '59. Zawinul earned great popularity in Austria, leading his own radio quartet 1954-8 and recording on countless dates as house pianist for Polydor. After leaving Ferguson he gigged and rec. w. Slide Hampton; joined Dinah Washington as acc. Oct. '59. A facile and exciting soloist on piano, certainly one of the most valuable imports from Europe in recent years. Favs: Tatum, Powell. Own LP: Strand; LPs w. Slide Hampton (Strand), M. Ferguson (Roulette).

Addr: 245 Carlton Ave., Brooklyn, N.Y.

ZELNICK, MELVIN M. (Mel), *drums;* b. New York City, 9/28/24. Stud. at Christopher Columbus High School, 1939-42; joined union in '42. Early associate of Arnold Fishkin and Shorty Rogers. Played w. Les Elgart, Bob Chester and Scat Davis, '45, Herbie Fields and Jerry Wald, '46, Chubby Jackson, '47, then back w. Fields. Benny Goodman sextet (w. Stan Hasselgard, Wardell Gray), '48; Lennie Tristano, '49, Boyd Raeburn, '50; since then has worked around New York w. Pete Rugolo, Eddie Bert, Marian McPartland, Don Elliott et al, and on staff w. Jerry Jerome at WPIX-TV. Own trio gigs in recent years at Embers, etc., also many pop and rock 'n' roll rec. dates. Favs: Rich, Roach, Jo Jones. LPs w. Lenny Hambro (Col.), Don Elliott (Beth.), Johnny Plonsky (Crest).

Addr: 64-34 102nd Street, Forest Hills 74, L.I., N.Y.

ZENTNER, SIMON H. (Si), *trombone, leader;* b. Brooklyn, N.Y., 6/13/17. St. on vln. at 4. In 1933 won Philh. Scholarship from Guggenheim Foundation, on tbn. After summer jobs in Catskills, he worked w. Les Brown, 1940-2; Harry James to '43; J. Dorsey to '44, then free-lanced in LA to '49. On staff at MGM studios, '49-57, then started own dance band. Firm believer in future of big bands, strongly supported by *Down Beat.* Feat. on Sleepy Lagoon (Lib.). Fav: T. Dorsey. Own LPs: Bel Canto, Liberty.

Addr: 3456 Laurelvale Drive, Los Angeles, Cal.

ZETTERLUND, MONICA, *singer;* b. Hagfors, West Sweden, 9/20/37. Mother a bassist, father pl. tenor sax; sang with their band at 14. After working with Ib Glindemann band in Denmark she was heard by Arne Domnerus, returned to Sweden and sang with Domnerus' combo from Sept. '58. To England for TV shows and Bath Jazz Festival '59. First visit to U.S. Dec. '59-Mar. '60, for night clubs, Steve Allen TV show, recording. Acclaimed by US musicians (incl. Donald Byrd, who played on her first LP in Stockholm) as one of the most promising young singers ever developed in Europe, with a keen harmonic ear and excellent musicianship. Favs: B. Holiday, Peggy Lee, Sinatra, Ray Charles. Own LP: Hanover.

Addr: Forshagagatan 22, Farsta, Sweden.

ZIEFF, ROBERT LAWRENCE (Bob), *composer;* b. Lynn, Mass., 6/4/27. Stud. trumpet briefly; music at Boston U. Wrote series of originals for Chet Baker, rec. Dec. '57. First appearance as leader playing all originals, at Randall's Island festival Aug. '59, using unusual instrumentation with six woodwinds and brass. LPs: comp. for A. Ortega, D. Wetmore (Beth.), C. Baker (Wor. Pac.), J. Nimitz-Bill Harris (ABC-Par.).

Addr: 48 West 97th Street, New York 25, N.Y.

ZIMMERMAN, ROY EMILE, *piano;* b. New Orleans, 10/23/13. Stud. privately. The late Fate Marable helped him get started in music. Has worked with many local groups in New Orleans incl. Geo. Hartman, '39, Monk Hazel, '41, Sharkey Bonano, '45, Irving Fazola, '46, Leon and Louis Prima, '47, Basin Street Six, '50, Phil Zito and Tony Almerico. Favs: Earl Hines, Fats Waller, Bob Zurke. LPs w. Al Hirt, Jack Delaney, Raymond Burke, Santo Pecora (South.), *Basin Street Six* (Merc.).

ZOLLER, ATTILA CORNELIUS, *guitar;* also *bass, trumpet;* b. Visegrad, Hungary, 6/13/27. Father was conductor and music teacher; sister plays violin and piano. Father gave him lessons on violin at age four; took up trumpet at nine, and played for six years in high school symphony orchestra. After the second World War started to play guitar in various small clubs in Budapest. Pl. w. Tabanyi Pinoccio jazz ensemble 1946-8. To Vienna Oct. '48 playing there until '54 w. the Vera Auer combo. W. Jutta Hipp in Germany '54-5, Hans Koller, Apr. '56-Feb. '59. In this period also played on different tours w. Bud Shank, Bob Cooper, Tony Scott. Toured w. Oscar Pettiford, Kenny Clarke, and Koller end of '58. To US '59; stud. at School of Jazz, Lenox, Mass., summer '59. Favs: Reinhardt, Christian, Farlow, Raney, Hall, Burrell, Bauer. Ambition is to have own trio w. bass and drums. Rec. w. Koller, Pettiford in Germany.

Addr: 617 West 169th St., New York 32, N.Y.

ZURKE, ROBERT (Bob), *piano;* b. Detroit, Mich., 1910; d. Los Angeles, 2/16/44. Came to prominence when he repl. Joe Sullivan w. Bob Crosby band, late 1936. During the next three years he enjoyed great popularity with jazz fans and was considered one of the leading boogie-woogie performers, winning the DB poll on piano, 1939. After leaving Crosby in April, 1939, he led his own big band, but had no commercial success with it and spent the last three years of his life working as a single at the Hangover Club in Los Angeles. Own LP: Victor; LPs w. Bob Crosby: Coral, Decca.

The jazzman as critic: the blindfold test

Duke Ellington once remarked: "If it sounds good, it is good." Such a simple truth should be axiomatic in music. Certainly the average jazz enthusiast would agree, as would most musicians. The critics, however, subconsciously have evolved a variation. It runs: "Even if it seems to sound good, I must determine who is playing, how it compares with his other works, whether the style is original or imitative, what type of music it represents, and several other matters before I decide whether it really is good." Subconsciously, many critics, including the writer, have adopted this attitude. For this reason, and because most musicians are better qualified to be jazz reviewers than many who hold these jobs, I instituted the blindfold test as a feature in *Metronome* in September 1946. Since March 1951 it has been a regular feature of *Down Beat* and the excerpts that follow are some highlights that appeared during the 1951-60 period.

The objective of the blindfold test is honest subjective reaction. The blindfoldee is always reminded that commercial values are secondary, and that the guessing of the artist's identity is of less consequence than the listener's evaluation on a purely esthetic level.

The ratings are: FIVE STARS, outstanding; FOUR STARS, very good; THREE STARS, good; TWO STARS, fair; ONE STAR, poor.

The material quoted in this chapter from various Blindfold Tests is reprinted by special permission of *Down Beat* magazine, copyrighted by Maher Publications.

The name of the musician interviewed appears in italics at the beginning of the paragraph of comments.

REACTIONS TO DUKE ELLINGTON

Duke Ellington. *Lady in Red* (Columbia). Harry Carney, baritone.

Tony Scott: There's two sax sections in Duke's band—one is the sax section, and the other is Harry Carney. Having played with the band, I know what it feels like to play along with Harry . . . It's a fantastic thing.

Duke Ellington. *Lady Mac*, from *Such Sweet Thunder* (Columbia). Russell Procope, alto; Clark Terry, trumpet.

Sonny Rollins: This record is immediately recognizable as having a Duke Ellington sound. The soloists sound like Russell Procope, possibly, and Clark Terry on trumpet. It's very important to have a sound that you can recognize immediately, and, of course, Duke is an institution now in music. He's one of my particular favorites. Always has been a great inspiration to me. This was very well arranged. All the parts have a significance to the whole thing. I'd rate this four and a half stars.

Duke Ellington. *Satin Doll* (Capitol).

Leonard Bernstein: Well, that's about the quintessence of slick, professional, expert boring arrangement. I couldn't say offhand who it was. As I say, I haven't heard jazz for a year. I found it dull—methodical and extremely slick—the last word in polish and professionality—but dull.

Duke Ellington. *Stormy Weather* (Capitol). Harry Carney, baritone; Willie Cook, Ray Nance, Cat Anderson, trumpets; Billy Strayhorn, arranger.

Miles Davis: Oh, God! You can give that twenty-five stars! I *love* Duke. That sounded like Billy Strayhorn's arrangement; it's warmer than Duke usually writes . . . I think all the musicians should get together on one certain day and get down on their knees and thank Duke. Especially Mingus, who always idolized Duke and wanted to play with him; and why he didn't mention it in his Blindfold Test, I don't know. Yes, everybody should bow to Duke and Strayhorn—and Charlie Parker and Diz . . . Cat Anderson sounds good on that; Ray *always* sounds good.

The beginning soloist sounded real good, too. That's Harry Carney, too, in there; if he wasn't in Duke's band, the band wouldn't be Duke . . . They take in all schools of jazz . . . Give this all the stars you can.

Bay Big Band. *Things Ain't What They Used to Be* (Omega). Jean Evans, piano; Mercer Ellington, composer. Belgian orchestra recorded in Brussels; other soloists not credited.

Mercer Ellington: That must come from that new Ellington album . . . It's refreshing to hear Ellington play piano—if that is him. I think Johnny Hodges is in a position to be more greatly appreciated now than ever before. He sounds very good . . . I think that's Clark Terry on trumpet . . . Four stars.

Nat Cole: I liked the ending best; that little countermelody idea against *Me and My Shadow* . . . Piano sounded as though there was too much going on behind him—the drummer was noisy. Piano didn't play too much himself, at that. He seems to be from the Thelonious Monk class, I would say. I don't know who's on the saxophone; sounded to me like Lee Konitz and several other guys . . . I'll give it one.

Dave Brubeck. *St. Louis Blues* (Columbia). Paul Desmond, alto; Norman Bates, bass.

Willie The Lion Smith: I give them five, and if they were all put on the stage together, they would capture the prize anywhere—not only in a concert hall, but in a back room or any place. They upset me . . . The minute they start playing, that feeling and beat is there.

I like the piano because he plays like the guys I told you about at the brickyards in Haverstraw, New York, where the blues was born . . . He has heavy hands, but hits some beautiful chords . . . You could put this on at anybody's house, and they'd dance all night.

REACTIONS TO DAVE BRUBECK

Dave Brubeck Trio. *How High The Moon* (Fantasy).

Sy Oliver: This is the first Shearing record I've ever heard that I didn't like.

Dave Brubeck Quartet. *Take Five* (Columbia). Paul Desmond, comp. & alto sax.

Ray Bryant: That's one of those 5/4 things . . . those rhythms don't usually get me . . . I wouldn't say this swung, but it had a sort of lope to it. Three stars.

Dave Brubeck. *Rondo* (Fantasy). Brubeck, composer.

Benny Goodman: I should know this. I don't know who it is, but I'll take a guess. I know it's a jazz group playing it, and it sounds a little bit like Milhaud, I guess. Sounds a little bit like *Scaramouche* by Milhaud. I don't think it should be given a rating.

The performance isn't first class; not by any means. I don't think it's very good. I think that's the sort of thing that should be done by amateur groups . . . I don't think it should be put out on a commercial record. On the other hand, I won't criticize it because I think it's a good endeavour. If you're going to compete with the Boston Orchestra, with first-class classical musicians, "longhair musicians," playing this stuff, then that's bad.

Dave Brubeck Quartet. *Me and My Shadow* (Fantasy). Paul Desmond, alto; Herb Barman, drums.

REACTIONS TO TRADITIONAL JAZZ

Jelly Roll Morton. *Mamamita* (Riverside). Morton, piano, composer. Recorded 1924.

Phineas Newborn: That's very old. Ha! Ha! It sounded like it might have been as old as Jelly Roll Morton . . . It reminded me a lot of Jelly Roll—a march-like thing. It's obviously where Fats Waller came from. This is something I'd like to really get a closer listen to.

Jelly Roll Morton. *Shake It* (Commodore). Red Allen, trumpet. Recorded 1940.

Jimmy McPartland: Must be Rex Stewart on the trumpet there, or cornet.

Marian McPartland: Whoever it is, it doesn't kill me.

Jimmy: They never did get going, it was chopped up too much for them to get into the groove. Sluggish.

Marian: The piano did nothing to me. I'd give it one and a half.

Jimmy: The trumpet tried, but he couldn't get it going. Give it one.

Jelly Roll Morton. *Black Bottom Stomp* (Victor). Recorded 1926.

Louis Armstrong: Put four on them. They played it too fast for five stars; they couldn't keep up with it. The trumpet player attacked his notes like Joe Oliver and Mutt Carey. The piano, if that ain't Buster Wilson, it's that other boy that went to California in the early days—it's one of the old-timers. It could be Harvey Brooks. Or Freddie Washington? From New Orleans? This is worth a hell of a rating over that bop stuff, but not a five-star rating for a cat that would like to dance by it. Give it four.

Jelly Roll Morton. *The Pearls* (Victor). Recorded 1927.

Willie The Lion Smith: Those guys should be driving trucks! There's a lot of guys who think they can play instruments, but this must be some guys that *never* knew. The word square is a modern term, but that's what those guys are . . . They never could hear and never could play. Didn't know how to wear pants, talk, or nothing . . . There's some of them still around. The phrasing is bad—old-fashioned, and they've never learned the formula of music. I don't give this any stars.

Jelly Roll Morton. *Grandpa's Spells* (Label "X"). Morton, composer; recorded 1926. Morton, piano; John Lindsay, bass.

Coleman Hawkins: Well, I suppose those fellows did the best they could with that piece . . . That's strictly Dixieland fellers . . . I really don't want to rate that at all. You know, all that Dixieland sounds alike to me. They're pretty precise, usually; take that boy Pee Wee Erwin, he's correct, he's real precise in his playing . . . This is a lot of hodgepodge; I wouldn't even be particular about listening to that any more. (*Feather:* Do you hear any musical value in it?) Actually, no. The piano? I didn't notice—wasn't that like the rest of it? The bass sounded like Pops Foster—was that Pops Foster? He's the only one I can even come close to identifying—because of that popping sound. Well, Dixieland is a type of music, you can't get away from it; if it's good, it's good—but I've heard a lot better than this. Fair is two? Well, give it two.

Wilbur De Paris. *It's All Right With Me* (Atlantic).

André Previn: Take it off . . . you don't have to play this all the way through. That's a new high in incongruity. I think Cole Porter would go back to the Ambulance Corps, or whatever he was in during World War I, if he heard this. No stars at all . . .

Bunk Johnson. *When The Saints Go Marching In* (Victor). Recorded 1945. George Lewis, clarinet.

Jimmy McPartland: The trumpet is sharp . . . clarinet sounds like Omer Simeon; Johnny Dodds style . . . it sounds a little like the old King Oliver New Orleans style—which was good in its day, but nothing stands still in this world.

Marian McPartland: . . . I'll give it one and a half for their enthusiasm. At least they all played loud.

Turk Murphy-Wally Rose. *Tom Cat Blues* (Columbia). Murphy, trombone; Bob Short, tuba.

Jay Jay Johnson: . . . I can't give a fair judgment . . . let's say three stars for the tuba solo and no further comment!

Kai Winding: It's pretty corny, but it makes you tap your feet . . . possibly it's a burlesque or recreation of something . . . I'd rather not rate it.

Kid Ory. *Milneburg Joys* (Good Time Jazz). Don Ewell, piano.

Shorty Rogers: Yeah! Happy New Year! . . . I think this is wonderful Dixieland. It has a very good spirit, honest performance, and they're swinging in their own way. I really appreciate it. I haven't heard any Dixieland records lately, but it's kind of a kick to hear it. I don't know any of the individuals—the piano player kind of gassed me. Four stars.

Kid Ory. *Tiger Rag* (Verve).

Jay Jay Johnson: Well! It was certainly a lively performance. Dixieland players playing Dixieland, and it came off as such, with lots of spirit. On the strength of that, I'd give it two and a half. I didn't recognize any of the players or soloists. They weren't particularly outstanding individually, but as a unit they were quite on the ball . . . Somehow I got the feeling that the trombonist had more than he could handle with the tempo. Any guess I would make would be a stab in the dark—was it Wingy Manone?

Kid Ory. *Maryland, My Maryland* (Good Time Jazz). Ory, trombone; Mutt Carey, trumpet; Darnell Howard, clarinet.

Vic Dickenson: For being the age they are and playing that way, I'll give them three stars . . . If they weren't old-timers, they fooled me. If they were some *young*-timers, better give them one star!

REACTIONS TO LOUIS ARMSTRONG

Louis Armstrong. *Pennies from Heaven* (Victor). Recorded at Town Hall, New York City.

Dave Garroway: Well, this record is what's wrong with Norman Granz. This is the Boston Symphony Hall concert, I think. You notice quickly that they don't try to have a climax every thirty seconds.

Actually Norman's are the best of the concerts that try to have a climax every thirty seconds, but you can't do that! Louis' band has maybe one or two big moments a night, and they work up to that. As incandescent as the man is, I don't see how he's going to get along without Teagarden and Hines. But he's done it before; he's never depended much on the band. Another thing, Louis' music is less non-arranged than most of the music at these concerts. These boys fit together. Four stars.

Louis Armstrong. *Ain't Misbehavin'* (Victor).

Leonard Bernstein: Well, I love it, as long as Louis is around. It's so refreshing in the midst of all this contrived mental stuff—it's a breath of fresh air —warm and spontaneous, simple and meaningful, and besides he makes beautiful phrases on the trumpet.

Louis Armstrong. *Ain't Misbehavin'* (Victor). Bobby Hackett, Armstrong, trumpets; Jack Teagarden, trombone.

Miles Davis: I like Louis! Anything he does is all right. I don't know about his *statements,* though . . . I could do without them. That's Bobby Hackett, too; I always did like Bobby Hackett—anything by him. Jack Teagarden's on trombone. I'd give it five stars.

FOREIGN MUSICIANS

Hans Koller. *Beat* (Discovery). Koller, tenor.

Charlie Shavers: . . . I liked the tenor player very much. I figured possibly it might be Stan Getz or somebody Getzing Stan, which, of course, would be a derivative of Pres, but I still liked it. I'd give that at least four stars.

Roman New Orleans Jazz Band. *Muskrat Ramble* (Victor).

Charlie Shavers: If there's anything I hate worse than bad bop it's bad Dixieland! It sounded a little bit like Eddie Condon's group, and I'm a little surprised at him because usually he has some pretty good Dixieland musicians . . . Maybe it wasn't Eddie Condon, but if it was, I don't think he liked it either. It sounded like everybody was drunk—maybe everybody was. I'll give them credit for being drunk. Let's give them half a star.

Lars Gullin. *Holiday for Piano* (Prestige).

Sammy Davis, Jr.: I like that very, very much . . . I think it's Gerry Mulligan, isn't it? . . . I love the record. I'd give it four.

Bernard Peiffer. *Slow Burn* (Roost).

Dave Brubeck: It's Garner—for the first time today I'm really positive I know who it is. It's real relaxed, swings a lot. The effect is like you've got a guitar man playing the beat, only it's the pianist's left hand. If that isn't Erroll, somebody sure picked it up well. I'd rate it four.

Vic Lewis. *Everywhere* (English Esquire). John Keating, trombone; Bill Harris, composer.

Bill Harris: I haven't heard this in a long time . . . It doesn't even sound like me . . . Wait a minute. There's something wrong here. Who the hell made that thing? I noticed a couple of spots where the phrasing was different, and he goofed a little near the end . . . well, they say this is the sincerest form of flattery. It's a rather nice performance, but who would want to repeat everything so closely? . . . Is it foreign? . . . Two stars.

Humphrey Lyttelton. *Take the "A" Train* (London). Arr. Mo Miller.

Art Farmer: It sounds like a prison band, and they should be *kept* in prison as long as they play like that. The arranger should be taken out and given some lessons—from the warden.

George Romanis. *A Foggy Day* (Coral). Al Cohn, tenor sax.

Manny Albam: I think this is an English band . . . I would say Dankworth perhaps, but I didn't hear any alto solos. I think the tenor player listens to people like Al Cohn quite a bit.

DOUBLE TAKE

Don Elliott, Rusty Dedrick. *Gargantuan Chant* (Riverside). Dick Hyman, comp., arr., piano; Dedrick, first trumpet solo; Don Elliott, second trumpet solo; Mundell Lowe, guitar. (Blindfold test, September 21, 1955.)

Miles Davis: Sounds kind of fine. Sounds like Howard McGhee and Ray Nance but I don't know who it is. The arrangement was pretty nice, but not the interpretation. Piano, whoever he is, is crazy. That's about all I can say about it. Two stars. Guitar was nice. I preferred the last trumpet solo to the earlier one for that kind of thing.

Miles Davis: (Blindfold test, Aug. 7, 1958. Same record.) I don't know who that was, Leonard. Sounds good in spots, but I don't like that kind of trumpet playing. The guitar sounds good in spots, and the piano player sounds good. It's a good little number except for that interlude and that tired way of playing trumpet. I'll give that three stars. Who were those two trumpet players?

RIDDLE OF THE RACES

After a long stay in France, the land of Crow Jim (see the chapter "Jazz In American Society"), Roy Eldridge made a bet with me that he would be able to distinguish white musicians from Negroes. He did not even guess the 50% to which the law of averages entitled him. Following are racial guesses from Eldridge's and other interviews:

George Shearing. *To Be or Not to Bop* (London). Shearing, piano; accompanied by white English musicians, Jack Fallon, bass; Norman Burns, drums.

Roy Eldridge: This could be three or four people I know . . . On this kind of playing it's hard to tell white from colored. The piano player *might* be white; the bass player, I think—yes, I think he's colored. The drummer's colored, too. It's very well executed, doesn't kill me too much, but gets going nicely when he goes into the block-chords stuff. Two stars.

Miles Davis. *Venus de Milo* (Capitol). Gerry Mulligan, baritone and arranger.

Eldridge: Haven't the slightest idea who this is; it's a nice-sounding thing . . . I couldn't tell whether this is white or colored. Most of these guys play with hardly any vibrato, and a sound without vibrato is an easier thing to capture than one with a distinctive vibrato. One minute I thought it might be Miles Davis, but it's not quite like his sound. The baritone I didn't care for. Arrangement very nice. Three stars.

Billy Taylor quartet. *All Ears* (Coral). All colored musicians.

Eldridge: This is a fair side, combining bop influences with boogie-woogie. Sounded nice on the first chorus. I liked the pianist. Couldn't tell who was colored and who was white. They could be Eskimos for all I know. Two stars.

Billy Strayhorn-Duke Ellington. *Tonk* (Mercer).

Eldridge: This is nice little ditty. Let's see now, what two-piano teams are there? White or colored? It's impossible to tell. Two stars.

Afterthoughts by Roy Eldridge: I guess I'll have to go along with you, Leonard—you can't tell just from listening to records. But I still say that I could spot a white imitator of a colored musician immediately. A white musician trying to copy Hawkins, for instance. And, in the same way, I suppose I could recognize a colored cat trying to copy Bud Freeman. I can only talk about individual sounds that have made it, highly individual sounds. But you take a sound like Tommy Dorsey gets—any good musician could get that. Okay, you win the argument!

Buddy Collette. *Cycle* (Contemporary). Collette, tenor sax.

Miles Davis: I can't tell . . . All those white tenor players sound alike to me.

Fifty-Second Street. *Shaw Nuff* (Interlude). Thad Jones, trumpet.

Julian (Cannonball) Adderley: Funny thing—I never knew a white trumpet player who was influenced by Dizzy as strong as this guy is . . . you can just say it's a white trumpet player who is influenced by Dizzy. I like it.

THE INIMITABLES

Some of the sounds considered unique in jazz have gone unrecognized, or have been confused with the sounds of others. This has happened several times in the case of Benny Goodman, whom leading jazzmen have failed to identify in recent years, and Billie Holiday, for whom other singers have been mistaken. Henry Mancini's reference below to Reginald Kell alludes to Goodman's studies with Kell, during which he changed his embouchure and, according to some musicians, his style.

Benny Goodman. *Happy Session Blues* (Columbia).

Tony Scott: I don't know who the clarinet player is . . . It's not a definite enough style for me to grab onto.

Quincy Jones: I have no idea who the clarinet player could be.

Benny Goodman. *Obsession* (from *Benny in Brussels*) (Columbia).

Henry Mancini: The clarinet player stumped me a bit. I thought it might be Benny after Reginald Kell —it wasn't Benny *before* Reginald Kell.

Marilyn Moore: *Trav'lin' All Alone* (Bethlehem).

Jimmy Rushing: That's Billie Holiday. If it ain't Billie, it's somebody just like her . . . Whoever is playing those instruments is very good, but I do know it's Billie. I'll give it five.

DINAH WASHINGTON

Some of the least inhibited reactions ever heard in a blindfold test have been those of Miss Dinah Washington. Following are some of her more vehement comments, after which her own work is reviewed by one of the objects of her disaffection. (Note: Joni James is the singer selected by Louis Armstrong for his "New Star" vote in the *Encyclopedia of Jazz* poll.)

Chris Connor. *Something to Live For* (Atlantic).

Dinah Washington: Well! . . . When *I'm* hoarse, I sound bad enough . . . but this! ! !

Joni James. *Hey Good Lookin'* (MGM).

Dinah Washington: Has she got a cold? I want to know, who could sound that bad? It's a movie star . . . She's not a singer, because singers don't sound like that. When she says, "Say, what-cha got cookin'," it should have been *her* that was cookin'. She sings out of her nose. Well, I'd like to compliment her on nothing. No stars.

Eugenie Baird with Mercer Ellington Orch. *I Let A Song Go Out of My Heart* (Design).

She really fixed Duke's song there—she fixed it but good. When she comes to that line "to make amends," I was thinking, the only amends that can be made is to break the record.

Jane Russell, Connie Haines, Beryl Davis, Della Russell. *Do Lord* (Coral).

Dinah Washington: I don't care for that at all, because they seem to be playing with a sacred song. That *really* didn't kill me. It's in *very* bad taste. When I do a sacred song, I do it with sacredness. I think that's terrible. I don't give that *no* rating. And I don't know who it is! But they should all be punched in the face.

Dinah Washington. *The Lord's Prayer* (Mercury).

Jane Russell: Well, I didn't recognize the gal until the very end . . . the end was the part I liked. It's Dinah Washington. I like Dinah better singing things that are more her own typical style. Of course, I like the song very much, and possibly if I heard it in church, I'd think it was the greatest; but when I heard it just as a record, mixed in with a lot of other records, I'm not particularly impressed. Maybe it's just a mood you have to be in. It isn't because it's churchy, particularly; it's just a fair record. Two.

REACTIONS TO (AND BY) ORNETTE COLEMAN

Ornette Coleman. *The Sphinx* (Contemporary). Coleman, alto; Don Cherry, trumpet.

Zoot Sims: The alto player sounded like he was playing *slide* alto! Both he and the trumpet player sounded like the changes were too much for them, and the tempo . . . They never got off the ground.

Herbie Mann: There's two driving forces for every jazz player—the playing and the writing . . . Ornette's writing was a little bit ahead of his playing when this record was made. He has a wonderful sense of humor, and the compositions are very interesting. But I don't think he plays his compositions as well as he wrote them.

Ornette Coleman. *Mind and Time* (Contemporary). Coleman, alto.

Ruby Braff: Once I heard Charlie Parker sound a little bit like that when he was completely sick—as sick as he could possibly be . . . utter confusion and madness—terrible! What is that? . . . I have never heard anything as disjointed and mixed-up and crazy as that in my life. Good Heavens!

Ornette Coleman. *Eventually* (from *The Shape of Jazz To Come*) (Atlantic). Coleman, alto; Don Cherry, trumpet.

Jon Hendricks: For technical skill in getting around their horns, I'd have to give it five stars, but for singing, melodically, and for putting things together well so that they create a beautiful melody, ain't that much happening. I'll pass.

Ornette Coleman. *Endless* (Contemporary).

Art Farmer: . . . This style of playing is very extreme, but it does show that there is more freedom to be taken advantage of than is, as a rule . . . I like Ornette's approach to writing. I wish I could see more of a link between the writing and the solos. It's like a building without any foundation and something's got to keep it up in the air. Even an atom-powered submarine has to go back to home base sometimes . . . You've got to know where home is. You've got to acknowledge that somewhere. Three stars.

Yusef Lateef. *Sounds of Nature* (Savoy). Instrumentation includes earth board, fluegelhorn, Indian reed whistle, flute, and ocarina.

Ornette Coleman: I mostly like things that have causes more than effects, and this seemed to be a tune that is mostly effects. I don't get the cause clearly.

George Russell. *Livingston, I Presume* (Victor). Art Farmer, trumpet.

Ornette Coleman: When I hear a tune played I like to hear a difference between the tune and the improvising . . . like I believe that the execution of improvising should blend with the emotion . . . but in certain cases where the technical part of a tune hinders a musician from free improvising, it seems I don't get the message that they actually hear something to play in that style of tune . . . Art Farmer seems more experienced in playing, free-improvising, with that sort of writing, where the thing they're playing, the way they're playing it doesn't sound like it's notated that way, and Arthur's the only one I know who seems to be able to improvise in the form of playing. Four stars.

REACTIONS TO ROLLINS

Sonny Rollins. *I Found A New Baby* (Contemporary).

Herbie Mann: Sonny is not what I would call a real far-out modern player. When he's not doing what I call his sarcastic catcalls and things, he sounds like Georgie Auld. . . . I don't know if he's a sarcastic person but that's what I get from his playing. . . . I would like to hear Sonny just play without being—if he considers it is—humorous . . . I like to hear people just play. . . . Two stars.

Sonny Rollins. *Grand Street* (Metrojazz).

Zoot Sims: I love that—it's a great band, and the soloists were perfect! It sounded like Coltrane to me . . . He sounded great on that, whoever it was . . . five stars.

Sonny Rollins. *Rockabye Your Baby with a Dixie Melody* (Contemporary).

Jack Teagarden: I can almost see his cheeks puffed out a mile. His tonguing is draggy; he doesn't tongue the instrument in the right way . . . He doesn't have much imagination. He's got about three notes there, and it's about all in that range . . . there's no tone there . . . One star.

MONK

Sonny Rollins with Thelonious Monk. *The Way You Look Tonight* (Prestige).

Miles Davis: I don't see how a record company can record something like that. You know the way Monk plays—he never gives any support to a rhythm section. When I had him on my date, I had him lay out until the ensemble. I like to hear him play, but I can't stand him in a rhythm section unless it's one of his own songs . . . I can't understand a record like this.

Randy Weston. *I've Got You Under My Skin* (Riverside).

George Wallington: That I liked. That's Monk . . . I think Monk has developed a certain thing, where it's not the ordinary left hand like Teddy Wilson and a lot of piano players used to use; he's done something different. Artistically, I don't think this is that great. I'd give it about three. The piano on this needs an awful lot of fixing—the action, the tuning. They shouldn't have recorded at all on that piano.

Thelonious Monk. *Four in One* (Blue Note). Milt Jackson, vibes; Sahib Shihab, alto.

Count Basie: I know this from somewhere—it seems as though every time I turn on a radio this seems to slip in; and I've always liked it. It's cute, real cute; and although it's sort of not in my department and I don't know too much about that type of music, I like it an awful lot. Wonderful piano; vibes sound like what's-his-name, Gibbs, a little bit; and the alto, if it's not the Bird, he loves Bird. All the solos were wonderful. I've got to give it four stars.

BIRD

George Handy. *Crazy Lady* (Label X). Dave Schildkraut, alto.

Charles Mingus: That could be Bird on alto . . .

Charlie Parker. *Cosmic Rays* (Clef). Recorded 1953.

Charlie Mingus: . . . If that wasn't Bird, I quit . . . You know what's funny? Now I know that Bird was progressing still. The other cats were the ones that were standing still and making Bird sound old, you know? Bird isn't just playing riffs on here, the way his imitators do. You know how he used to be able to talk with his horn, the way he could tell you what chick he was thinking about? That's the way he's playing here. How many stars? FIFTY!

Charlie Parker. *Relaxin' with Lee* (Mercury). Dizzy Gillespie, trumpet; Thelonious Monk, piano.

Sy Oliver: I don't know who this one is, but it's one of those bop records in the sense that I detest it. I am not equipped to distinguish one group of this kind from another. I don't like it. I feel there is nothing derogatory about commercial values; I think in the final analysis the music that lives is the music that the greatest number of people buy, and this isn't it.

If this form of musical expression makes them happy, okay. No musical effort is entirely wasted. Sure, they have tremendous talent. Hitler was one of the greatest orators and spellbinders who ever lived; but greatness does not mean goodness. For my personal preference, no stars.

Charlie Parker, with Dave Lambert Singers. *Old Folks* (Verve).

Bob Morse (of the Hi-Lo's): . . . The saxophone seemed so inappropriate with that song. It seems to go along with that group; I mean it's on a par with them. Is the saxophone player a famous player?

Gene Puerling (of the Hi-Lo's): It sounded like a member of the Charlie Parker school. I've never liked that school—it's one of those out-of-tune, honking-type things . . .

Lennie Tristano, in a 1951 blindfold test, observed: I want to say something about Charlie Parker, his importance in the picture. As great as we all think Bud Powell is, where would he be if it hadn't been for Bird? He's the first one that should remember it—he told me himself that Bird showed him the way to a means of expression.

George Shearing shows a good deal of personality, but it's still a take-off on Parker. You take *Groovin' High,* or pick at random any five records by well-known boppers, and compare the ideas and phrases. You'll see that if Charlie Parker wanted to invoke plagiarism laws, he could sue almost everybody who's made a record in the last 10 years. If I were Bird, I'd have all the best boppers in the country thrown into jail!

International polls

Following are the results of a number of popularity polls published in recent years in the United States and overseas.

Though neither the readers' nor the critics' polls can be construed as a reflection of relative artistic merit, the former are of some value as a weather-vane of general opinion among jazz enthusiasts and the latter as a reflection of changing tastes among the experts.

The *Down Beat* Critics' Poll is based on a point system. The voters are asked to name three musicians in each category. Three points are awarded for a first-place vote, two points for a second-place vote, and one point is awarded for a third-place vote.

	Down Beat Critics' Poll 1960		Down Beat Readers' Poll 1959		Metronome Readers' Poll 1960	
MUSICIAN OF THE YEAR			Miles Davis	604		
			Duke Ellington	273		
			Lambert, Hendricks & Ross	261	Count Basie	507
ORCHESTRA	Duke Ellington	59	Count Basie	1276	Duke Ellington	486
	Count Basie	45	Maynard Ferguson	781	Stan Kenton	441
	Quincy Jones	10	Duke Ellington	678		
COMBO	MJQ	38	Dave Brubeck	735	MJQ	579
	Miles Davis	13	MJQ	712	Dave Brubeck	522
	Oscar Peterson	11	Miles Davis	708	Oscar Peterson	478
COMPOSER-ARRANGER	Duke Ellington	41	Gil Evans	901	John Lewis	530
	Gil Evans	37	Duke Ellington	406	Quincy Jones	491
	Benny Golson	14	John Lewis	346	Gil Evans	477
MALE SINGER	Jimmy Rushing	39	Frank Sinatra	1902	Frank Sinatra	791
	Louis Armstrong	28	Joe Williams	510	Ray Charles	501
	Joe Turner	14	Johnny Mathis	180	Jimmy Rushing	417
FEMALE SINGER	Ella Fitzgerald	48	Ella Fitzgerald	1326	Ella Fitzgerald	640
	Sarah Vaughan	19	Anita O'Day	304	Anita O'Day	553
	Ernestine Anderson	12	Annie Ross	303	June Christy	477
ALTO SAXOPHONE	Cannonball Adderley	39	Paul Desmond	1090	Paul Desmond	922
	Johnny Hodges	32	Cannonball Adderley	1084	Lee Konitz	389
	Sonny Stitt	22	Johnny Hodges	391	Johnny Hodges	225
TENOR SAXOPHONE	Coleman Hawkins	33	Stan Getz	1087	Stan Getz	811
	[John Coltrane / Ben Webster]	22	Sonny Rollins	589	Sonny Rollins	788
	Stan Getz	21	John Coltrane	558	John Coltrane	315
BARITONE SAXOPHONE	Gerry Mulligan	55	Gerry Mulligan	2740	Gerry Mulligan	1266
	Harry Carney	46	Pepper Adams	404	Harry Carney	323
	Pepper Adams	22	Harry Carney	391	Pepper Adams	282
CLARINET	Buddy De Franco	22	Tony Scott	1111	Tony Scott	666
	Edmond Hall	16	Jimmy Giuffre	805	Benny Goodman	574
	[Benny Goodman / Tony Scott]	15	Buddy De Franco	783	Jimmy Giuffre	509
TRUMPET	[Miles Davis / Dizzy Gillespie]	40	Miles Davis	1856	Miles Davis	701
	Art Farmer	15	Dizzy Gillespie	460	Dizzy Gillespie	468
	Louis Armstrong	13	Maynard Ferguson	293	Art Farmer	399

Playboy Readers' Poll 1960		Melody Maker Readers' Poll 1960	%	Jazz Hot Readers' Poll 1960		Jazz-Echo Readers' Poll 1959	%
		Duke Ellington	23.5			John Lewis	26.0
		Miles Davis	16.7			Miles Davis	25.5
Stan Kenton	5065	John Lewis	14.0			Sonny Rollins	11.6
Duke Ellington	3018	Count Basie	57.0	Count Basie	3560	Count Basie	30.6
Count Basie	2824	Duke Ellington	31.7	Duke Ellington	3038	Duke Ellington	29.0
		Stan Kenton	4.2	Miles Davis - Gil Evans	655	Stan Kenton	9.3
Dave Brubeck	3751	MJQ	44.4	MJQ	2444	MJQ	33.8
Ahmad Jamal	2348	Dave Brubeck	17.8	Art Blakey	2398	Gerry Mulligan	13.9
MJQ	1914	Miles Davis	6.7	Miles Davis	1225	Art Blakey	12.8
		Buck Clayton	6.7				
		Duke Ellington	47.0	Gil Evans	1944	John Lewis	23.7
		John Lewis	26.3	Duke Ellington	1408	Duke Ellington	10.2
		Benny Golson	3.7	Quincy Jones	1112	Gerry Mulligan	9.6
Frank Sinatra	10,851	Frank Sinatra	41.3	Louis Armstrong	2745	Louis Armstrong	29.4
Johnny Mathis	2247	Jimmy Rushing	18.2	Ray Charles	1836	Jimmy Rushing	24.5
Joe Williams	1150	Joe Williams	16.8	Jimmy Rushing	1380	Joe Turner	10.3
Ella Fitzgerald	6074	Ella Fitzgerald	70.7	Ella Fitzgerald	3783	Ella Fitzgerald	40.3
June Christy	1835	Sarah Vaughan	10.0	Sarah Vaughan	2615	Sarah Vaughan	18.9
Dakota Staton	1716	June Christy	3.0	Mahalia Jackson	1133	Billy Holiday	12.7
Paul Desmond	10,051	Paul Desmond	45.5	Johnny Hodges	2154	Lee Konitz	27.4
Earl Bostic	6378	Johnny Hodges	21.4	Sonny Stitt	1859	Bud Shank	17.8
Bud Shank	4609	Cannonball Adderley	7.5	Lee Konitz	1357	Sonny Stitt	13.1
Stan Getz	9501	Stan Getz	40.5	Sonny Rollins	2435	Stan Getz	23.4
Coleman Hawkins	4570	Sonny Rollins	20.3	Stan Getz	1654	Sonny Rollins	20.0
Sonny Rollins	3393	Coleman Hawkins	13.0	John Coltrane	1465	Bill Perkins	11.9
Gerry Mulligan	15,640	Gerry Mulligan	70.4	Gerry Mulligan	3750	Gerry Mulligan	47.4
Bud Shank	1286	Harry Carney	17.5	Harry Carney	2722	Pepper Adams	10.7
Jimmy Giuffre	897	Ronnie Ross	8.7	Pepper Adams	649	Harry Carney	8.2
Benny Goodman	6403	Jimmy Giuffre	26.0	Jimmy Giuffre	2371	Jimmy Giuffre	26.2
Jimmy Giuffre	2972	Edmond Hall	19.7	Benny Goodman	1707	Tony Scott	19.7
Buddy De Franco	2346	Benny Goodman	10.9	Tony Scott	1634	Benny Goodman	19.2
Miles Davis	11,190	Miles Davis	41.0	Miles Davis	3319	Miles Davis	39.3
Louis Armstrong	9533	Louis Armstrong	17.3	Dizzy Gillespie	2190	Louis Armstrong	12.9
Dizzy Gillespie	6935	Dizzy Gillespie	12.6	Louis Armstrong	1174	Dizzy Gillespie	11.3

	Down Beat Critics' Poll 1960		Down Beat Readers' Poll 1959		Metronome Readers' Poll 1960	
TROMBONE	J.J. Johnson	43	J.J. Johnson	1705	J.J. Johnson	714
	[Curtis Fuller Vic Dickenson]	19	Bob Brookmeyer	389	Bob Brookmeyer	587
			Kai Winding	259	Kai Winding	300
	Jack Teagarden	16				
VIBRAPHONE	Milt Jackson	62	Milt Jackson	2086	Milt Jackson	1241
	Red Norvo	21	Lionel Hampton	576	Red Norvo	440
	Lionel Hampton	20	Terry Gibbs	538	Terry Gibbs	421
PIANO	Thelonious Monk	32	Oscar Peterson	871	Erroll Garner	497
	Oscar Peterson	25	Thelonious Monk	511	Oscar Peterson	404
	Bill Evans	23	Dave Brubeck	390	Thelonious Monk	308
GUITAR	Kenny Burrell	23	Barney Kessel	1195	Barney Kessel	699
	Barney Kessel	21	Herb Ellis	372	Jim Hall	530
	Freddie Green	19	Charlie Byrd	358	Herb Ellis	296
BASS	Ray Brown	49	Ray Brown	994	Ray Brown	544
	Charlie Mingus	31	Paul Chambers	679	Red Mitchell	462
	Oscar Pettiford	12	Red Mitchell	351	Leroy Vinnegar	390
DRUMS	Max Roach	39	Shelly Manne	901	Shelly Manne	540
	Philly Joe Jones	27	Max Roach	552	Max Roach	511
	Art Blakey	14	Joe Morello	517	Chico Hamilton	472
ACCORDION			Art Van Damme	1711		
			Pete Jolly	418		
			Mat Mathews	324		
FLUTE	Frank Wess	45	Herbie Mann	1483		
	Herbie Mann	19	Frank Wess	648		
	Jerome Richardson	12	Bud Shank	616		
MISCELLANEOUS INSTRUMENTS	Julius Watkins (Fr. horn)	19	Don Elliott (mellophone)	685	Don Elliott (mellophone)	983
	Stuff Smith (violin)	16	Miles Davis (fluegelhorn)	232	Herbie Mann (flute)	590
	Miles Davis (fluegelhorn)	15			Fred Katz (cello)	253
VOCAL GROUP	Lambert, Hendricks & Ross	45	Lambert, Hendricks, & Ross	407	Lambert, Hendricks, & Ross	5111
	Hi-Lo's	8	Four Freshman	889	Four Freshman	382
	Jackie Cain&Roy Kral	5	Hi-Lo's	743	Hi-Lo's	334

Playboy Readers' Poll 1960		Melody Maker Readers' Poll 1960	%	Jazz Hot Readers' Poll 1960		Jazz-Echo Readers' Poll 1959	%
J.J. Johnson	15,688	J.J. Johnson	50.8	J.J. Johnson	3695	J.J. Johnson	32.5
Kai Winding	12,755	Kid Ory	7.6	Kai Winding	1064	Bob Brookmeyer	17.5
Bob Brookmeyer	8372	Dickie Wells	7.5	Bob Brookmeyer	1002	Kai Winding	16.9
		Milt Jackson	75.5	Milt Jackson	4189	Milt Jackson	49.0
		Lionel Hampton	18.3	Lionel Hampton	2840	Lionel Hampton	14.6
		Victor Feldman	3.6	Red Norvo	759	Red Norvo	14.3
Erroll Garner	3580	Erroll Garner	21.7	Thelonious Monk	2904	John Lewis	18.6
Dave Brubeck	3174	Dave Brubeck	19.3	Erroll Garner	1152	Erroll Garner	17.5
Ahmad Jamal	3112	Oscar Peterson	13.1	Bud Powell	854	Oscar Peterson	15.4
Barney Kessel	6992	Barney Kessel	44.2	Barney Kessel	2445	Barney Kessel	27.5
Eddie Condon	2406	Freddie Green	15.4	Tal Farlow	1938	Tal Farlow	15.8
Johnny Smith	1424	Herb Ellis	12.6	Jimmy Raney	1207	Jim Hall	15.1
Ray Brown	3616	Ray Brown	28.0	Oscar Pettiford	2335	Ray Brown	26.9
Oscar Pettiford	1927	Percy Heath	24.4	Percy Heath	1909	Percy Heath	19.3
Leroy Vinnegar	1486	Oscar Pettiford	9.7	Ray Brown	1730	Paul Chambers	14.2
Shelly Manne	8200	Shelly Manne	26.3	Art Blakey	2490	Max Roach	26.0
Gene Krupa	2516	Joe Morello	23.0	Max Roach	2349	Art Blakey	16.3
Cozy Cole	1477	Max Roach	11.9	Kenny Clarke	1595	Kenny Clarke	14.4
		Frank Wess	62.1			Bud Shank	36.5
		Bud Shank	14.5			Frank Wess	33.8
		Buddy Collette	8.9			Herbie Mann	9.1
Lionel Hampton	5713	Miles Davis (fluegelhorn)	17.8	Frank Wess (flute)	2304	Fred Katz (cello)	16.5
Milt Jackson	2746	Stuff Smith (violin)	11.6	Jimmy Smith (organ)	1305	Bob Cooper (oboe)	12.9
Cal Tjader	1707	Stephane Grappelly (violin)	8.8	Stuff Smith (violin)	916	Joe Venuti (violin)	11.5
Four Freshman	5111	Four Freshman	37.7				
Kingston Trio	4561	Hi-Lo's	35.1				
		Lambert, Hendricks, & Ross	21.5				

Jazz overseas

A 1958 cartoon in *The New Yorker* showed a group of diplomats seated around a conference table earnestly listening to their chairman, who was making a grave pronouncement. The caption read: "This is a diplomatic mission of the utmost delicacy. The question is, who's the best man for it—John Foster Dulles or Satchmo?"

There is something more than humor in the message of this cartoon. It is possible to infer correctly that jazz, unknown or ignored only a few years ago on most artistic and diplomatic levels in the United States, has become one of the few exports from this country that can be depended upon to be greeted with devotion and enthusiasm rather than with the uneasy resentment that has met many of our shipments in the recent past.

A glance at the biographical references in this volume under the names of many top American jazzmen tells its own story. Despite the tremendous advances made by American jazz on the domestic front, there have been few events at home to match the warmth of welcome accorded to Gerry Mulligan and the Modern Jazz Quartet and the Count Basie band in Europe, Benny Goodman in Asia, Louis Armstrong and Tony Scott and Wilbur de Paris in Africa, John Dizzy Gillespie in South America, Lionel Hampton in Australia. These names are drawn at random from the dozens who have been among America's unofficial ambassadors. In recent years there have even been penetrations of the Soviet Union and satellite countries, discussed later in this chapter. The stepping up of these tours has led to higher standards in the jazz played by local musicians in many countries; to point this up a specially assembled "Tower of Babel" orchestra was assembled for the 1958 Newport festival incorporating talent from 16 European countries.

Most experts have agreed that England, France, Sweden and Germany have produced the best jazz outside the United States; accordingly the first reports below are from these countries. In sharp contrast these reports are followed by reviews of conditions in areas that might seem least likely to have developed any jazz culture: three countries behind the Iron Curtain, where jazz for many years was officially forbidden.

GREAT BRITAIN

It is the proud boast of the British that in their country may be found the best jazz anywhere outside the United States. In the last few years, the claim has certainly had its application, though not quite in its intended sense. Since the British Musicians' Union lifted its unconditional ban on all foreign jazz artists publicly appearing in Britain, the élite of the jazz world has beaten a path to Britain's door. After Kenton had broken the ice in the spring of 1956, there followed at regular intervals Count Basie, the Mulligan Quartet, the Teagarden-Hines All-Stars, the Louis Armstrong All-Stars, the Lionel Hampton band, the Condon circus, the Modern Jazz Quartet, the Dave Brubeck Quartet, June Christy, Sarah Vaughan and, as an appropriate climax to the pilgrimage, Jazz at the Philharmonic, with Dizzy, Oscar, Ella; and Norman Granz trailing clouds of incandescent though vicarious glory.

British jazz audiences are invariably very generous, but as American jazzmen have lost their rarity value, there has been a noticeable stiffening of esthetic judgment. The Kenton concerts were conducted in an atmosphere of near-hysteria, no doubt because this was the first visit of an American band in twenty years. When I deputized for two concerts with the Kenton band on baritone saxophone, I found that people who knew of my feat held me in a new and unnatural regard. Illogical but understandable.

As the Harold Davison Office continued with its band-exchange policy, the critical faculty began to reassert itself, until by the time Hampton came here a year later there were many who carped about the low jazz content in his concerts.

Almost every one of these tours was commercially successful, with triumph reaching its giddy climax as JATP tickets were hustled around with an expertise reminiscent of *My Fair Lady*. An artist like Jack Teagarden, perhaps in partial eclipse at home, brought an unmistakable smile to the faces of the entrepreneurs. However much Teagarden's reputation may have fluctuated in the States, he was still a legend in Britain and support for him was widespread.

Fears that all this competition would harm the cause of British jazz have proved only partly well-founded, and there have been compensations. It is naturally harder now to induce audiences to attend all-British concerts, but the influence on the scene in general has been a beneficent one. However, the touring band business in Britain, only three or four years ago such a staple part of every musician's livelihood, has disintegrated completely, shattered by the tide of shamateurism which has appeared in the form of the rock-'n'-roll and skiffle phenomena. By the end of 1957 there were barely half a dozen bands worthy of the name left on the road. With the Ted Heath orchestra confining itself more and more to studio performances and foreign tours, the first place in the big band polls has passed to the Johnny Dankworth orchestra. The crown is Johnny's through sheer esthetic justice, for his is the only big band in Britain that plays a jazz program of any appreciable quality. Dankworth has become one of the leaders of the British jazz movement, particularly as a spokesman to the outside world. His appearances at the Oxford Union debates and his series of autobiographical pieces in the London *Star* (circulation 880,000) broke new ground in lay territory.

Another British jazz figurehead, Humphrey Lyttelton, has suffered in recent years something of a fall from grace with his once fanatically loyal fans. Lyttelton, for so long an adherent of the theory that musically, at least, time can be made to go backwards, suddenly stopped doing a Gatsby and began to remodel his band on more imaginative lines. The importation of a Hodges-style altoist to replace a Dodds-style clarinetist is a fairly accurate indication of the extent of his first advances. But the alto of Bruce Turner proved to be the thin end of the wedge of an entire saxophone section. Although the musical value of Lyttelton's band rose sharply as he imported more and more proficient musicians from the modern ranks, like ex-Dankworth drummer Eddie Taylor and modern-club star attraction Jimmie Skidmore, Humphrey's fan following took a drop in inverse proportion to the quality of the music, from which fact may be deduced a homily far too terrifying for this writer to acknowledge.

The developments in Lyttelton's band were some of the most interesting to take place in Britain recently, and Humphrey's comparative eclipse as the leader of British traditionalism, a position surely befitting one whose grandfather had once captained an English Test Match team, coincided with the phenomenal commercial success of rival traditionalist Chris Barber, an undistinguished trombonist surrounded by an undistingished collection of traditionalist musicians and a surprisingly good blues singer called Ottilie Patterson, known to advertising copy-writers as "Utterly" Patterson. Barber, braving the circuits once confined to the big commercial orchestras now defunct, broke house records previously held by Ted Heath in almost every hall in the Four Kingdoms. To date, Barber's ascendancy over all his rivals remains unchallenged, except perhaps for the even more primitive band of clarinetist Cy Laurie, snugly installed in his own club a stone's throw from the Eros Statue in Piccadilly Circus with a several-thousand-strong membership of pencil-trousered poseurs and dangly-haired demi-mondaines; and Acker Bilk, leader of an indifferent band that has become a box-office factor by virtue of high-pressure salesmanship; on sleeve covers the band dresses in a vaguely Edwardian manner and addresses the leader as "Mister."

For the moderns, as one door closed, so another has opened. The touring bands, once the last resort of unemployed modernists, have, like the dodo and the brontosaurus before them, proved unable to adapt themselves to changing conditions and have paid the price. Which raises the subject of the Little Jazz Clubs phenomenon, one that distinguishes Britain, and particularly London, from all other jazz cities.

In London have survived for some years now establishments that are jazz clubs in every sense of the phrase. Holding four or five hundred people at most, and changing premises as circumstances dictated or rents rose, these clubs catered primarily to the jazz fan. The sale of alcohol in these modern clubs is still an almost unknown phenomenon. There are no bars or drinking licenses. The programs consist of two groups and a *compère*, the amenities of tables and chairs and a small dance floor.

In the past few years, with interest stimulated by American visitors and the subsequent belated acknowledgment of the existence of jazz as something more than a source of delinquency and viciousness, the Little Clubs went from strength to strength until soon they were not so little. Crowds of a thousand were not unheard of during the brief but glorious life of Jazz City; nor are club programs of three nights a week of music at the Flamingo. It is calculated that on a normal Saturday night in London, about five thousand people pay for admission into the Little Clubs, with an equal division between traditional and modern.

Most of the modern groups these fans hear when they get inside the building are the same groups they have been hearing for the past five years, or sometimes new groups composed of permutations of old faces. Accepted as the best of these groups for two or three years were the Jazz Couriers, a five-piece unit co-led by tenorists Ronnie Scott and Tubby Hayes. Scott was for two years leader of the cooperative band that was the most successful modern group in Britain, and Hayes, doubling on vibes, broke up his own touring band to help form the Couriers, who appeared as the supporting attraction on the Sarah Vaughan touring show.

With the breakup of the Couriers, Hayes formed his own quartet and Scott in October 1959 opened the Ronnie Scott Club, which very soon became the hangout for jazz musicians in town, the place for visitors to "drop in" (Manny Albam, MJQ, Donna Hightower, Ray Nance) and a spawning ground for younger musicians who might never get work at the older-established clubs because of their lack of a reputation. Scott's most important find to date: Peter King, an eighteen-year-old alto player who appeared out of the hills of Surrey to astound the jazz world with a Parkeresque facility remarkable in a musician who had only been playing three years.

Other outstanding personalities include West Indian altoist Joe Harriott, currently leading his own quintet; baritonist Ronnie Ross, selected to appear at the 1958 Newport Festival; and the inseparable three, Jimmie Deuchar (trumpet), Derek Humble (alto) and Ken Wray (trombone), who for some time enjoyed self-imposed exile in Germany with the Kurt Edelhagen band.

Generally influential figures on the jazz scene, for instance commentators like Dankworth and Lyttelton, are able to wield a certain persuasive influence because of the existence of a genuine body of respectful fans. Musician-columnist Steve Race, for example, was largely responsible for the successful booking in Britain of the Brubeck Quartet, for whom, by his consistent championing of the group in his weekly columns, he cleared the way.

Johnny Dankworth's action in rejecting the offer of a lucrative return appearance in South Africa, because of the racial angle, was another action typical of the man, which earned unanimous approval and lent a moral force to the voice of jazz that can only strengthen its position in the social life of the land. In the meantime, South Africa seems to be the first outpost of the Empire being opened up by the jazz pioneers, for after the Dankworth appearance there in 1954, the first ever in the Union by an imported jazz star, American jazzmen began to include the Union as part of their world tour itineraries. Apart from a few traditional flutters from Australia from the Graeme Bell band, which toured Britain so successfully in the early '50s, the British Empire seems quiescent in the face of the advancing jazz muse. Perhaps that is because the sun never sets on the Empire and jazz is essentially the after-hours art.

—BENNY GREEN

FRANCE

France was without doubt the first country in the world to offer official acknowledgment to jazz as a genuine art form rather than a mere novelty. As early as 1928, Parisian intellectuals, headed by Jean Cocteau, proclaimed the right of jazz to recognition along with the motion picture and modern painting.

Only in recent years has jazz extended beyond the borders of a limited *succès d'estime* among a minority to reach into the great mass of the French people. Perhaps the most characteristic illustration of the trend can be found in the appearance in the "pops" programs at the Olympia, the great Parisian music hall, of a large number of American and French jazzmen. In the past few years the Olympia has offered its stage to such figures as Louis Armstrong, Lionel Hampton, Gerry Mulligan, Miles Davis, Count Basie, Erroll Garner, J. J. Johnson, Earl Hines, Jack Teagarden, in addition to annual visits of the Jazz at the Philharmonic tour.

Another popular music hall, the Alhambra, presented Harry James and his orchestra and the Stan Kenton band. The Modern Jazz Quartet enjoyed a triumphant success at the Théâtre des Champs-Elysées. An increasing number of night clubs have offered on a regular basis the music of numerous jazz combos, some of them featuring American musicians residing in Paris, others especially imported from the United States: among the latter were Miles Davis, Bud Powell and the Modern Jazz Quartet.

Another aspect of the French jazz scene that points up significantly the increased respect in which jazz is held is its frequent use for motion picture sound tracks. For the film *No Sun in Venice*, Roger Vadim commissioned John Lewis to write the musical score, which was interpreted by the Modern Jazz Quartet. For another picture, *Elevator to the Gallows*—which, incidentally, enjoyed a great success in France—Louis Malle, the director, used Miles Davis as instrumentalist and composer. According to experts, the music created by Miles was one of the major factors in the commercial success of the film. Other production companies are now frequently calling upon American and French jazzmen to provide the music for their movies. An outstanding example was *Les Liaisons Dangereuses,* with Thelonious Monk, the Jazz Messengers and Barney Wilen, which enjoyed a big success in Paris but ran into censorship problems elsewhere and could not be exported.

Television in France is represented by a sole outlet, controlled by the government. Clearly, this solitary network attempts to satisfy the most diversified popular tastes. Nevertheless, and this fact, too, may be considered symptomatic, a half-hour broadcast entitled *A La Recherche Du Jazz,* seen once every month, explains the characteristics of this music to the uninitiated. In addition the Modern Jazz Quartet, during one of its visits to Paris, was accorded the privilege of occupying the small screen at a peak viewing hour—9 p.m.—with no production of any kind, except for a simple series of panels announcing the titles of the tunes. A performance of this kind might not be accomplished even in the United States; it is even more astonishing when one takes into consideration the fact that the audiences had no alternate program selection available to them, so that everyone in France and Belgium who owned a television set and had it turned on at that time was bound to see the Modern Jazz Quartet's performance. Moreover, the directors of the network received many congratulations for their "happy initiative."

Radio, as might be expected, offers a much more important place to jazz; quite a large number of broadcasts can be heard. Since the early 1950s an American, Sim Copans, has been in charge of a very popular show heard on the official Government channel. A very successful station, Europe No. 1, from the very beginning dedicated a full hour every evening (two hours on Sunday) to jazz. These broadcasts bring in an extraordinarily large amount of mail, attesting to the quantity of the French fan following, as well as to the quality and intensity of their enthusiasm.

Jazz record sales similarly have enjoyed a remarkable upsurge since 1956. As many as 60 per cent of the jazz records published in the United States are released in France and are satisfactorily absorbed by the French market, an impressive fact considering the relative population (less than one-third that of the United States). Some companies, such as RCA Victor, prepare for release in France special LPs some of which are not even available in the US, such as reissues of old masters by Morton, Hampton, Waller and others.

The jazz magazines are faring especially well. *Jazz Hot,* the oldest, recently celebrated its 27th anniversary, while *Jazz Magazine,* after five years of existence, had a circulation of well over 25,000. In late 1959 the first issue appeared of *Les Cahiers du Jazz,* a scholarly quarterly; in addition, a number of larger daily newspapers, as well as several weekly publications, now have regular jazz departments.

The tastes of the French public have evolved considerably in the past few years in the direction of a broader acceptance of all styles. During the period immediately after World War II, only Dixieland jazz (or New Orleans style, as it is called in France) had any real commercial value. Today, modern jazz is consistently becoming more fashionable.

Given these favorable conditions, the quality of jazz produced by French musicians has developed commendably. The performers are not only more numerous than ever, but find more opportunities for work as jazzmen. The performance level of the soloists has shown a sharp improvement; several outstanding artists, in the opinion of visiting American musicians who have heard them, are comparable if not superior to many of their distinguished and celebrated confrères across the Atlantic.

In the night clubs of Paris, it is possible today to hear such veterans as Stéphane Grappelly (one of the original members of the Quintet of the Hot Club of France with Django Reinhardt in the middle '30s), as well as many promising young stars. Among the latter are Barney Wilen, a tenor saxophonist who has emulated the styles of Sonny Rollins and John Coltrane; René Urtreger and Martial Solal, the pianists; Pierre Michelot, an outstanding bassist; and at least a dozen other talented musicians. Among the adherents of a more classical style, Guy Lafitte and Michel de Villers represent the "middle-jazz" era, while the Dixielanders still have Maxime Saury and Claude Luter as the local kings of this venerable genre.

As for the American colony in Paris, for many years before his death Sidney Bechet was in a class by himself, a figure of national glory in France on the same level of acceptance as Maurice Chevalier or Edith Piaf. American jazzmen resident in France during the 1950s included Albert Nicholas, Bill Coleman, Nelson Williams, Don Byas, Mezz Mezzrow, Jimmy Gourley, Kenny Clarke and many others.

To sum up all the happy developments on the French scene, it might be apt to quote an American girl now living in Paris who remarked: "I had to come over here to live before I realized what an important part jazz could play in the artistic life of a country."

—DANIEL FILIPACCHI

GERMANY

"They take it so much as an art form—as what it really is; much more than we do in our country." John Lewis said this when he was touring Germany in the winter of 1957-58, expressing what he and the other members of his Modern Jazz Quartet thought about their overwhelming success and the appreciation they found in this country.

Many other famous American jazzemen have made similar comments. There seems to be, in this country, a kind of jazz appreciation which relates to the famous German tendency to take everything very seriously. Nowhere else in Europe are there so many discussions on jazz. And the market for books on jazz is nowhere better than here. On the other hand, the market for jazz records is, compared to other European countries, just average—maybe not even that.

Until a few years ago, Lee Konitz and the Lennie Tristano school were the most important influences on jazz in Germany. When this writer, some time ago, in a television show, asked each musician in a German all-star group about his favorite American jazzmen, everyone named Lee Konitz. The musicians were fascinated by Lee's long, flowing lines, his harmonic conceptions, and—most important of all—by an attitude of playing which more often than not is represented as being cerebral (although, in fact, it is as "intuitive" as any good jazz from Oliver to Rollins).

Of course, during these last years—as everywhere in the world—the picture changed gradually to a more basic conception—influenced especially by Sonny Rollins and Horace Silver.

Tenor man Hans Koller and trombonist Albert Mangelsdorff are the best known jazz solists in Germany. George Wein, of the Newport Festival, and Marshall Brown, of the Farmingdale High School Band, selected Albert as Germany's representative for their International Big Band to be presented at the Newport Festival in 1958. Albert plays a lyrical, sensitive, cool trombone. He says he formed his style by adopting the Lee Konitz way of playing to the trombone.

Hans Koller, also, derived from Konitz but, during the last few years, has changed completely. He now is a great improviser on the Al Cohn-Count Basie "classicistic" line with all the Cohn "moanings" in his phrasing and a "down home" jazz feeling. Hans was a member of the big band that the American arranger, Eddie Sauter, built for the Südwestfunk—the Southwestern German Radio Network in Baden-Baden. He now has his own combo to which, in 1959, Oscar Pettiford and the Westcoast drummer Jimmy Pratt belonged—the best combo ever in German Jazz.

Two other German radio networks have regularly employed big jazz bands: Radio Stuttgart has Erwin Lehn and Radio Cologne has Kurt Edelhagen. Lehn has a very musicianly and clean-playing, Basie-orientated orchestra with the remarkable pianist Horst Jankowski and a wonderful flutist, Gerry Weinkopf. Gerry was used when John Lewis recorded his album "European Windows" with the Stuttgart Symphony Orchestra. Kurt Edelhagen assembled what he calls "a U.N. in jazz" insofar as he has a kind of all-European big band with leading jazz improvisers from England, Belgium, France, Switzerland, Italy, Austria and, of course, Germany. That things of this kind are possible in jazz at a time when Europe still is full of borders and political jealousy is one of this music's most awesome aspects.

All these bands have regular programs on the networks. In addition the radio networks have—about four times a week—regular jazz shows with commentaries by jazz critics. Since there are eight radio networks in Germany there is a good deal of jazz on the air here.

There are many jazz combos in Germany; it is impossible to name all of them. The Helmut Brandt Quintet and the Michael Naura Quintet—both from Berlin, but mostly playing in Western Germany—are outstanding. Baritone saxophonist Brandt is a good arranger, fascinated by the Miles Davis Capitol band and astonishingly successsful in adapting its feeling to his own two-horn combo. Piano player Michael Naura acquired the most promising new jazz improviser in Germany for his Quintet: Wolfgang Schlüter, a vibes player with fluent ideas and very modern harmonic conceptions. There are two other excellent vibes players, Bill Grah from the Fatty George Band and Fritz Hartschuh from Heidelberg.

Emil Mangelsdorff, Albert's brother, is considered the leading alto saxophonist. He was playing jazz as early as the Nazi era. Pepsi Auer is an intelligently swinging pianist, who plays in Albert Mangelsdorff's Frankfurt Combo, for which he and Joki Freund write most of the arrangements. Joki is a swinging tenor saxophonist, who used to play in the Four Brothers idiom and changed to the Rollins style. He was among the many musicians who made the change from cool music to hard bop.

Most of the musicians live in Frankfurt, considered to be the German jazz capital. Some fled here from countries beyond the iron curtain because at home they had difficulties when playing jazz, among them the Hungarian-Austrian guitarist Attila Zoller (who in 1959 emigrated to the United States) and the Jugoslavian trumpeter Dusko Gojkovic, who plays with Edelhagen.

All the professional musicians are assembled, each year, at the German Jazz Festival in Düsseldorf. There is also an annual Amateur Jazz Festival in Düsseldorf. When the first amateur festival was held, in 1955, only 26 groups applied for participation. In 1956 we had about 60 groups, the year after it was 150 and in 1958 about 300 applications came in, representing more than 1,500 musicans. In the beginning of 1959, a German magazine estimated the number of amateur musicians playing jazz in Germany at 15,000.

To both festivals, jazz groups from the Eastern part of Germany are invited. Jazz, now, is tolerated in the East but not encouraged. Reginald Rudorf, the busiest jazz worker in the East, was condemned to two years of convict prison and forced labor, not officially because of his jazz work, but for "political conspiracy"; however, jazz, of course, had something to do with it. Many people in the East love jazz, and they love it so feverishly that you can feel how very much is in it, both of their love for the music and their love for the whole world of what jazz means for them. The musicians in the East are diligent and enthusiastic but they do not seem to get real jazz feeling—especially in their phrasing.

Coming back to the Western part of this country, jazz had its biggest breaks in 1957, when it was presented at the Donaueschingen Music Festival, and when both Protestant and Catholic Churches showed a keen interest in it. It took this writer many years to convince the Festival organizers that jazz is just as contemporary as any other "contemporary" music. But when, in late 1957, for the second time in its history the Festival had two jazz concerts on its program, they were a sensational success, overshadowing even Stravinsky conducting his brilliant *Agon* Ballet. The Modern Jazz Quartet, André Hodeir's experimental group from Paris with an all-star French and Belgian personnel, and the Eddie Sauter band were heard at the Festival.

Jazz meetings and conventions have been held in church seminars, Protestant academies and Catholic youth meetings, and attempts have been made to incorporate jazz elements into church music. Heinz Werner Zimmermann, Director of the Protestant Church Musical Institute at the Heidelberg University, wrote a *Church Concerto* for Jazz Combo, leaving room for improvised solos, and a *Psalm Concerto* for Jazz Band and Singers. These works have been played in churches.

German hit (popular) music has become so ordinary that, in comparison, American hit songs are works of art. With this in mind, a church official explained what the reason for the church's jazz interest might be: "In a period where no real folk music lives in Germany anymore, where classical music is appreciated only by a minority of highbrow people, and even these people very often do not appreciate modern symphonic music, jazz is the only thing to keep the youth away from the banality and sentimentality of the Schlager."

—JOACHIM E. BERENDT

CZECHOSLOVAKIA

The first impact of jazz in Czechoslovakia came with the importation of American records and, in 1925, the first visit by an American band, that of Sam Wooding, featuring Tommy Ladnier, Gene Sedric and Garvin Bushell. Wooding still remembers the excited response to his music during the band's two weeks in Prague.

This was authentic jazz, but we could not yet absorb it fully; it was too strange. Later came another American group, led by a violinist, Leon Abbey. One of the first Czech jazz units was Jaroslav Jezek's pit band in a comedy theater. In 1934 Jezek, a gifted pianist and composer, made his first recordings. He later became almost blind, left Czechoslovakia when the Germans came, and died in the U.S.A. in 1942.

1936 was an important year for jazz in Czechoslovakia. Joe Turner (the pianist, not the singer) visited the country, also a very fine Cootie Williams-style trumpeter from Brazil, Gabriel Dores. Turner was a center of attraction with all jazzmen; his influence was tremendous. He recorded two remarkable dates with the Czech Grammo Club combo. But there was still some indefinable non-American quality present in the work of Czech musicians.

Finally in 1938 we developed three who had the right accent on the right notes, and even Leonard Feather (blindfolded) could never have guessed that these were musicians from the heart of middle Europe. They were the wonderful pianists Lada Horcik and George Verberger, and a violinist, Alex Vizvary. Verberger combined Fats Waller with Teddy Wilson; Horcik already had his own distinctive style; Vizvary, who had a classical background, was a gypsy who played in the style of Grappelly but was, in my opinion, much better.

In 1939 another jazz musician appeared, Fritz Weiss, a fine clarinetist and arranger. Of course when the Germans came in March 1939 jazz was suddenly illegal and *verboten* as the product of degenerate races. However, jazz was not dead. We listened to American short wave stations, risking our lives in doing so. Weiss and many other Jewish jazzmen were deported to the concentration camp at Theresienstadt (Terezin) not far from Prague, where in a rare switch of fate jazz was not only permitted but ordered by the German SS. Thus the "Ghetto Swingers" were founded, and with the help of some Jewish jazz musicians from Germany, Holland and Denmark this band played terrific jazz. After the band was presented as a special attraction to an international Red Cross commission as proof that there is music in concentration camps, the members of the band were deported to Auschwitz, where most of them died in the gas chambers. Among them was Fritz (Bedrich) Weiss, Czechoslovakia's greatest jazzman of pre-war fame.

The golden age of the Czech jazz scene began after the war. There were plenty of combos and big bands. One of the best was Karel Vlach's big band, with a star alto player, Karel Krautgartner. The most important organization was Rhythmus 47, Czechoslovakia's first bop combo. A mediocre American military band was in Prague, and I will never forget the impression Rhythmus 47 made when the Americans visited the so-called "jazz center of middle Europe," Prague's Pygmalion, and heard this combo. They stopped eating and were speechless for minutes when Rhythmus began its program with *Lemon Drop*. The star of this quintet was a young trumpeter, Dunca Broz, in my opinion the best Europe ever had; in the U.S.A. he would figure among the best. John Hammond, who visited Prague in 1947, was very much impressed by him. Around this time there were some visitors from abroad, the British Negro group of the late Leslie (Jiver) Hutchinson and the Australian Dixieland combo of Graeme Bell. There was a jam session every night at the Pygmalion featuring musicians comparable with the best Americans. Jazzwise, Czechoslovakia was far in front of all other European nations, including Sweden.

But this period was of short duration. When in 1948 Czechoslovakia became suddenly a nation with a Communist government, jazz was again taboo, criticized as the product of American capitalism and alien to the inner feelings of the Czech musician. This pressure receded slowly, and today jazz is again a respected art form. Marshall Brown, visiting Prague with George Wein in 1958, picked Zdenek Pulec, whom he described as a fine trombonist, to play at Newport with his International Band. Pulec was unable to get permission to leave the country. Karel Vlach is still playing and has the leading big band, but among the many new organizations there is Gustav Brom's band, which shows a West Coast influence, as well as dozens of new combos and several jazz clubs.

—ERIC T. VOGEL

SWEDEN

Sweden in recent years has been considered second only to the United States in the extent of its interest in and support of jazz. However, in the late 1950s there were some significant changes. In the days when our records enjoyed their warm initial reception from American fans and critics, the interest here was concentrated mainly on local talent such as Bengt Hallberg and Lars Gullin. Currently there appears to be a trend among younger jazz lovers and critics to minimize the importance of Swedish jazz in general. The reason could possibly be that stars like Hallberg and Gullin have been comparatively inactive in jazz in recent years; the former devotes more and more of his time to commercial studio work and Gullin has had to fight several personal problems which have limited his musical capacities. One must also consider the enormously increased output of American jazz released here on records.

Stockholm, the only real jazz center in Sweden (Gothenburg is more or less a dead city these days), has a unique place where jazz reigns for more than eight months each years. Nalen, a huge dance hall with five steadily employed bands, is the scene for jam sessions twice a week and generally adds American solo talent to its impressive artist roster. Individual visitors in Stockholm during the past few years have included Tony Scott (a tremendous hit at Nalen both with musicians and fans), Don Byas, Lucky Thompson, Sonny Rollins, Mose Allison, Donna Hightower, Stan Getz, French pianist Martial Solal and an amazing new alto sax from Jamaica, Harold McNair.

There are no other clubs or dance halls in Stockholm concentrating entirely on jazz. Several attempts have been made to start informal after-hours spots, but the Swedish police always keeps an eye on them and generally closes them after a few weeks. All over Sweden, however, there is a network of local jazz clubs that are knitted together in a federation with about a thousand members.

Apart from records—most American LPs reach us rather fast and are often split up into EPs—there are two major factors that keep the jazz interest alive: radio, and concerts by visiting United States stars. Jazz on the radio—there are two networks, controlled by the Government—is scattered throughout the week's programming. On television, by the way, jazz is almost nonexistent, but then TV here is still in its infancy.

Lately there has been a catastrophic drop in public enthusiasm for jazz concerts, which nowadays are limited to Stockholm instead of being spread through half a dozen Swedish towns as formerly. Still, several American attractions, either packages or big bands and sometimes a single soloist, continue to visit here yearly. In 1959 the only artist to play all over Sweden to capacity houses was Louis Armstrong. Earlier, Count Basie and Gerry Mulligan enjoyed outstanding successes. Norman Granz has been a steady visitor with JATP and in 1960 brought three different shows here. Lionel Hampton's band returned to Sweden several times, with most unpleasant riots as a result. Dave Brubeck was among the more successful concert performers in 1958. Big bands have included Kenton, Goodman and McKinley. Benny played to sellout houses but was completely murdered by the critics. There are no jazz concerts during the summer. Two bands, however, have toured Sweden in the summer. The first, headed by Swedish trumpeter Rolf Ericson of Woody Herman fame, started traveling in June 1956, but Ericson had to change his personnel a couple of weeks later after some of the most scandalous behavior ever exhibited by musicians visiting this country. He sent his men back to the 'States and enlisted new sidemen with the help of jazz correspondent Claes Dahlgren in New York, joined forces with Lars Gullin and was able to finish out his contract with less disastrous results. Jay Jay Johnson presented his quintet in the summer of 1957 and gave splendid performances throughout. Jazz fans here found it hard to understand why this group was not brought back the next summer, as both the music and the box office reports were excellent.

There are two magazines, devoted exclusively to jazz, that have been operating in Sweden for more than twenty years, *Estrad* and *Orkester Journalen.* The former also owns a concert bureau. Jazz is given much space in the morning and afternoon dailies and also in most weeklies.

Jazz in Sweden is almost entirely modern. Traditional jazz is fast losing its grip on the audiences and the number of revival bands has decreased with astonishing speed. Concerning the modern influences, Swedish musicians have always been very alert to accept new trends, but it definitely seems that our jazzmen are turning back to reliable sources of inspiration like Ellington and Basie. Of course, modern giants like Bud Powell, Miles Davis, Sonny Rollins, John Lewis and Milt Jackson, to name a few, are extremely popular, especially among the younger set, but actually very few musicians here play that way. The best, steadily organized band is by far the Arne Domnerus Orchestra, which seems inspired by a wide variety of styles, from Duke, *via* Bird to West Coast jazz.

New talent is coming up in greater profusion than ever. One could mention at least fifty names, but this writer will limit himself to naming tenor saxophonist Bernt Rosengren. Bernt, who follows the Sonny Rollins trend, was chosen as the Swedish representative in the European band that appeared during the 1958 Newport Jazz Festival.

Mainly due to the number of American releases flooding this country, Swedish jazz records are almost as scarce these days as in the '30s and '40s. Furthermore, jazz records are almost never made here, except when ordered from a United States company, *e.g*, the Atlantic label. There have, however, been some impressive albums, of which Bengt Hallberg's trio LP was warmly received and chosen with a huge majority of votes as the best album made in Sweden in 1957. American critics were obviously not as enthusiastic as their Swedish colleagues when the record was released in the States on the Epic label.

A story on Swedish jazz would not be complete without mentioning Harry Arnold and his Swedish Radio Studio Orchestra, a band composed of our leading talents and organized only for broadcasts, recordings and an occasional concert. As many American critics and musicians will verify, this band is quite something and the first LP by Arnold, released in the United States with the "Mystery Band" gimmick, is the best jazz seller this country has ever seen. Quincy Jones contributed to the second LP, which won a Golden Disc award in 1958. Quincy had only superlatives for the Swedish musicians and named the Arnold band as one of the very best in the world.

In short: Swedish jazz is better off than ever, with more promising newcomers, more good bands and a broader audience. It is getting more publicity in one year's time than it did during the whole previous decade. The record sales have been amazing for such a small country. Some of us, however, mourn the fact that the easily identified, national brand of jazz is dying out. Our music is entirely Americanized these days and it is hard to put your finger on a specific record made here now and state that it definitely was made in the land of the Midnight Sun. This, however, should not deter jazz enthusiasts from visiting Sweden. As our American visitors will gladly tell you, it's a swinging country!

—CARL-ERIK LINDGREN

POLAND

Although jazz behind the Iron Curtain has long been politically discredited as a product of an allegedly bankrupt democratic system, the interest among young people has been so persistent, and the reception accorded to visiting musicians so tumultuous, that Poland by 1960 had as firm and fanatical a jazz cadre as any country in Eastern Europe.

Reporting in the quarterly American magazine *Jazz,* Roman Waschko, president of the Federation of Polish Jazz Clubs, stated that there were a dozen jazz clubs in Poland whose members organized live concerts featuring domestic groups. One of these units, The Jazz Believers, has been under the direction of Jan Wroblewski, who in 1958 played with the International Band at Newport and Brussels.

After the end of World War II there was immediate interest in jazz among a small but enthusiastic clique. Concerts were inaugurated within a couple of years, initiated by the Polish YMCA.

The Polish government, along with the other Communist regimes, took an officially dim view of jazz on ideological grounds, but Waschko says it was impossible to halt the movement. The youngsters who were forbidden to play jazz at concerts went underground and began to hold sessions behind closed doors in private apartments in Warsaw, Cracow, Poznan and Lodz.

It was not until 1955 that the official ban on jazz was lifted and concerts began to be held in the open. So great was the response among elated Polish fans that the first national Polish Jazz Festival was soon held at Sopot, a Baltic summer resort. Fans came from all over Poland, and from other Iron Curtain countries, to watch the celebration, which began with a New Orleans style street parade with eight bands, six domestic, one Czechoslovakian and one British.

Before long the jazz movement was thriving throughout Poland. In the spring of 1957 the revived Glenn Miller orchestra, under the direction of Ray McKinley, made a highly successful visit; a year later the Dave Brubeck quartet spent two memorable weeks in Poland and Kid Ory apeared there during the course of a European tour in 1959. The Louis Armstrong film *Satchmo The Great,* released to Polish audiences in 1959, enjoyed similar success.

Polish jazz groups soon began to make records: one of the most popular groups is a combo called Zygmunt Wichary and his Dixielanders, who have toured Eastern Germany, Rumania, Hungary, Bulgaria and the USSR. The Jan Kwasnicki quartet was invited to play at a jazz fesival in Belgium. In addition to the Americans, visitors arrived from several European countries; among them was the Birdland Group, a modern style combo from Holland.

Poland inevitably was one of the stops made by Willis Conover, Voice of America's disc jockey, during his international good will trip in 1959. Further good will was engendered by the organization known as Jazz Lift, which mailed many jazz records from the US to Poland free of charge. As soon as these records began to reach the hands of eager Polish fans the Federation of Polish Jazz Clubs was besieged with requests for Jazz Lift's address.

Held back for many years by the combined problems of a devastating war and an official government taboo, Poland has shown remarkable signs of catching up both in the extent of its jazz enthusiasm and in the quantity and quality of its domestic exponents.

USSR

From time to time during the 1950s there were reports that the Soviet Union, like Poland, had eased its anti-jazz propaganda and was even sanctioning the development of local talent.

Ulysses Kay, one of four American composers who went to Russia under State Department sponsorship, reported in 1959 on jazz activities in Moscow and Tiflis. Quoted by Ralph J. Gleason in the *San Francisco Chronicle,* Mr. Kay, who is a nephew of Joseph "King" Oliver, said: "Moscow is where we heard our first Soviet jazz, played by the house band of the Hotel Leningradsky. The tunes were largely unfamiliar but played with quite a clear melodic line, good harmony and a steady beat. At the Hotel Ukraine (also in Moscow) the house band—three reeds, three brass and three rhythm—had a less rhapsodic quality but more ensemble and power.

"I attended a jazz concert in Tiflis. It featured the Jazz Band of Eddie Rosner. This group consisted of eight brass, seven reeds, eight strings and four rhythm with Rosner fronting the band very suavely and featured on trumpet à la Harry James of the early 40s. The music was heavy, well voiced, a bit old fashioned . . . The house was jammed and they loved it. A Glenn Miller ballad and a pop song by a young Armenian composer, Arno Babajanian, brought mention of them as composers and great applause. Still, nothing swung.

"Jazz interest in the Soviet Union . . . is definitely increasing. At our first meeting at the Moscow House of Composers, a young legit composer eagerly approached me with many questions about new jazz trends in America. 'What is Ellington doing? What's with Kenton?' etc., etc. In the midst of answering, through an interpreter, the guy abruptly turned to the piano and began playing *Take the A Train* while proudly asking, 'Do you know this?' I asked him where he learned the tune. 'Oh, we hear a lot of good jazz—two hours a day on the Voice of America!' he said."

In September 1959, *Life Magazine* quoted a guide in the book exhibit at the American national exhibition in Moscow. "The most popular reference books," she stated, "are *The Encyclopedia of Jazz,* a one-volume edition of Salvador Dali, and the Sears, Roebuck mail-order catalog."

The Russians' interest in jazz, frustrated for many years by the government's failure to allow any official visits by American artists, led in 1959 to a unique situation that enabled two US musicians to bring authentic jazz to the country for the first time—not on an official level, but through the back door, by smuggling themselves in as members of a Yale vocal chorus. They were Dwike Mitchell and Willie Ruff, details about whom will be found in the biographical section. Carefully preparing for their objective by studying Russian for several months and by taking records and jazz magazines as gifts for Russian fans, they arrived in Moscow June 24th, 1959.

On the duo's second day in Moscow, Willie Ruff, looking around for a concert site, decided to visit the conservatory in search of official sanction for a performance. After meeting several of the professors and students he returned the next day with Mitchell and played for faculty members in a small recital hall, illustrating improvisation, harmonies, rhythms and forms. The interest was so great that arrangements were made for a formal concert a few days later in Tchaikovsky Hall. This time not only students and teachers but many musicians from Bolshoi Ballet Orchestra and the Moscow Philharmonic were present. After relaxing himself and the audience with an announcement in Russian, Ruff joined Mitchell for the opening number, *Walkin'*.

"We never played for a more responsive audience," he declared later in a special report for *Down Beat.* "No hand-clapping, foot-stomping or head-shaking, just a sea of Russian faces registering delight at things familiar, smiles at things humorous, and compassion at things soulful . . . after the intermission we opened with *Lullaby of Birdland,* the most popular jazz tune in Russia. Their reaction to this was their first open outburst; they went wild."

Mitchell and Ruff shrewdly gauged the audience reactions: "We played it very cool, favoring the intellectual rather than too much hard emotion. A riot was all the Ministry of Culture needed to prove that jazz was not compatible with Socialist realism." After playing what was planned as the finale, the Soviet Union's most popular song of the moment *Moscow Nights,* the duo was unable to conclude: "They insisted on dozens of encores, standing and cheering after each." After the show they were questioned for hours about jazz. The students and faculty of the conservatory, Ruff wrote, "did not know the government's stand on jazz. There was nothing in *Pravda* about the refusal to allow Armstrong to play." News of the Mitchell and Ruff triumph was picked up by the *New York Times* and by wire services who carried the story throughout the United States. A few days later their historic precedent was followed up in Leningrad, where they played a concert at the Conservatory and were guests of the Leningrad Jazz Club. The club has two groups of players, a modern unit and a Dixieland combo. The latter group included a cornet player who, said Ruff, "was 18 and didn't speak a word of English, but if you closed your eyes you'd swear it was Louis Armstrong . . . there was something about this 18-year-old 7,000 miles from New Orleans, playing Pops' solos on *Saints, Tin Roof Blues* and *Muskrat Ramble* that even Pops would dig. This kid got every inflection and its meaning." Musicians like these, he pointed out, do most of their playing at parties and sessions, since there are no organized professional jazz bands in Russia. There are, however, some student groups that are attracting considerable attention. One is a modern combo led by Nikolai Kapustin, which plays in a style apparently influenced by Gerry Mulligan and Shorty Rogers.

Though the Soviet Union may be farther behind than any other country in the world in terms of jazz, by 1960 it seemed inevitable that the next decade would produce the long-delayed importation of top American stars, probably leading in short order to major improvements in the standards of domestic jazz. As the incoming mail at Voice of America headquarters has long shown, the Soviet Union is perhaps more eager for a stepped-up jazz diet, after a longer period of deprivation, than any other country in the world.

The above reports give a general indication of a trend that began to take shape in 1945 and had reached world-wide proportions by 1960. There were similar developments in almost every other country. To cite an example at random, the Hong Kong Jazz Club, with 250 members, has been enjoying resounding successes with its concerts, all of them reported at great length in the local press. Japan, which during the 1950s saw the successful presentation of Jazz at the Philharmonic, Louis Armstrong and other American visitors, probably is more advanced in the level of jazz appreciation and performance than any other Asiatic country. A series of LPs by Japanese jazzmen representing Dixieland, swing and modern jazz, has been released on the Japanese King label. Music played (via hi fi sound systems) in the Tokyo coffee houses is perhaps hipper than that heard in their San Francisco counterparts.

In December 1959 the American clarinetist Tony Scott arrived in Japan on the first segment of a projected two-year world tour. A few days after his arrival a "Jazz Spectacular" entitled *Welcome Tony Scott* was produced by Radio Tokyo TV, featuring Scott joining forces with all the top Japanese jazz musicians plus a 65-piece orchestra. Also heard on the program were Japan's top male and female jazz singers, and a combo featuring the tenor saxophonist Sleepy Matsumoto, generally regarded as the country's foremost jazz soloist. Scott later assembled a group of his own to play for an audience of 2,000 jazz fans at another TV broadcast.

Scott's plans for 1960-62 included visits to the Philippines, Australia, New Zealand, Indonesia, Malaya, Cambodia, Thailand, Burma, India, Pakistan, Ceylon, Afghanistan, Nepal, Iran, Armenian USSR, Turkey, Syria, Lebanon, Egypt, Israel, Arabia, Ethiopia, East Africa and West Africa, North Africa, Spain and the whole of Europe and Russia. It seemed certain that his ambitious itinerary would prove to him at first hand what is gradually becoming clear to students of jazz everywhere: that the music once indigenous to the United States, a form that for so many years could be interpreted with authenticity only by Americans, had become unmistakably a music of the world.

Jazz and classical music: by Gunther Schuller

After a checkered history of some forty odd years, the dream of fusing jazz and "classical" music seems to be still very much alive. Despite the direst predictions and countless "authoritative" pronouncements that the two idioms will never amalgamate properly—the famous line about the incompatibility of oil and water is always quoted at this point—that the very idea of mixing the two idioms is invalid, the dream persists in one way or another. In fact, judging by an increase of activity in this area within the last two or three years, it is safe to assume that we are at the beginning of a new phase in this combinative trend.

Objections to these attempts at collaboration are, as might be expected, as persistent as the movement itself. It seems to me, however, that the main problem is one of definition, since no two people evidently agree exactly on what "jazz" or "classical music" is. When discussions turn to combining the two, the semantic confusion is accordingly compounded. There seem to be as many definitions of this fusion as there are definers. Actually diatribes to the effect that the two musics should not be merged remind me a little of Don Quixote fighting the windmills. Nobody of any consequence is interested in "merging" either music with the other at the expense of one or the other. I think *that* phase of the process is a thing of the past. But I think it should be understood once and for all, that most musicians, composers and players, look upon all phases of music as part of a total experience. The musicologists and critics may partition jazz off from the classics, and folk music from both. But to the active musician anything that is of quality, that holds his interest, is liable to become grist for his musical mill. If he is a great musician he will integrate these outside influences artistically as part of his personal style; in a lesser musician the various elements may never alloy properly. But the blame in that case should be placed on the musician, and not on the concept of fusion itself. Basically, it becomes a matter of using some or all of the materials available at a given time, limited only by the education of the ears and mind of the creator.

This is especially so in our time, which, if it can be characterized at all, can be called an age of synthesis. The many innovations in the early part of our century (those of Stravinsky, Schoenberg and Webern, as well as the evolution of jazz as an art form) are all moving rapidly into the sights of composers and players with open minds and ears. If a gifted creative musician is exposed to a particular kind of music, it will eventually find its way into his music. The qualifying factor, of course, is that these influences must be genuinely felt—not just adopted—and must become an inseparable part of the creator's style. Seen from this viewpoint I feel that in the hands of certain creative musicians, the fusing of jazz and classical elements can and will lead to genuine enduring works of art.

To the purists on either side of the musical fence, such talk, of course, is heresy. This, despite the fact that the whole history of music has been one long process of absorption, synthesis and cross-fertilization. Is the using of jazz elements in stricter, more complexly organized compositional frameworks less valid than the incorporation of the semi-improvised secular lyrics of the French troubadors into the sacred music of the Flemish polyphonists, or in our time, the blending into Bartok's personal idiom of the folk music of the Balkans? Furthermore, the "pure" jazz that some wish to preserve is itself the result of vigorous crossbreeding of several European and African musical traditions. On this specific point the semantic muddle becomes really exasperating. The protagonists of fusion call it "synthesis," while its detractors use the term "hybrid" in its derogatory sense.

But while the selfappointed critics *argue*, the musicians *create*, unmindful of musical pedigrees or the lack of same. It is clearly not a question of preserving the purity of each idiom and keeping them forever apart, but rather a question of retaining the *essence* of those elements to be combined. If this can be done—and the movement is still too young (in its new phase) to have yielded conclusive evidence pro or con—I for one feel that some very vital music may develop, and that in the process the two idioms may even fructify each other.

Seen from a vantage point of some forty years, the entire movement divides itself roughly into two distinct phases, separated by a more or less dormant period. The first phase encompassed the initial discovery of jazz by European and American composers in the 1920s. The names involved are illustrious enough—Stravinsky, Milhaud, Krenek, Ravel, Copland, Carpenter, Gruenberg, Gershwin and so on—but since improvisation, the lifeblood of jazz, could not figure in these experiments, and since the composers involved had in almost all cases a very peripheral, and sometimes even denigrating knowledge of jazz, very few of these works were of more than topical or historical interest. Their validity is in direct proportion to their authors' awareness of noncommercial improvised jazz. Milhaud's *La Creation du Monde* of 1923 comes closest to fulfilling this condition.

On the jazz side, there were similar dreams of uniting somehow with the revered classical world. An early example was the vogue of "symphonic jazz," as performed by the orchestras of Wilbur Sweatman and Noble Sissle. A few years later, the music of Duke Ellington (who, significantly, had played with Sweatman) began to show a slight, indirect (and possibly unconscious) awareness of classical music. Still later, Ellington's mentor, James P. Johnson, composed a number of extended form symphonic works, pieces which languish in obscurity to date. And then there was Bix Beiderbecke's dream of "the jazz symphony," vaguely inspired by a Stravinsky concert in Carnegie Hall and unfulfilled because of his untimely death.

The thirties and forties remained relatively uncommitted regarding a possible rapprochement between jazz and classical music. The assimilation of the many innovations of the first two decades of the century preoccupied musicians on both sides. Even more significant was the lack of instrumentalists who could perform authoritatively in both fields. The jazzmen couldn't read music, by and large, and the classical musicians couldn't improvise and hadn't the faintest notion of what "swinging" was.

The reactivation in recent years of this inclination to bring the two idioms together coincides precisely with the emergence of musicians who can perform authoritatively in both areas. The bringing together into a positive relationship of the spontaneity and sense of timing in jazz with the disciplines of classical music is recognized as desirable by most forward-looking musicians, although it is decried (as usual) by the cavilling jazz purists. Nonetheless, it is the emergence of such musicians that constitutes the greatest differentiating factor between the present second phase and the earlier period in the twenties. And it is this factor which opens up possibilities not realizable before, which therefore makes prediction, especially of the negative sort, so ill advised.

This has become a broad trend of international proportions. Even a limited survey of present efforts will give an indication of the range and fervor of activity in the field. The myriad gradations of emphasis and proportion in combining elements of the two idioms is in itself, it seems to me, an indication of the vigorous, youthful health of the movement.

Perhaps the most influential catalyst in the rapprochement between jazz and classical music has been the Modern Jazz Quartet. In its appearances at non-jazz festivals (like the important Donaueschingen festival of contemporary music, or the May Festival of Florence—both heretofore reserved only for "classical" music), and in the performances of works by the quartet's pianist and musical mentor, John Lewis, works which have successfully synthesized blues elements with earlier classically oriented contrapuntal techniques, the Modern Jazz Quartet has won the admiration and respect of musicians and music lovers on both sides of the apparent musical dividing-line.

Other jazzmen, whose primary allegiance has been to jazz, have incorporated one or several aspects of classical thinking in their work. Jimmy Giuffre, for instance, conducted somewhat inconclusive experiments with an implied rather than explicit beat, while Lennie Tristano, even earlier, made successful attempts to apply a more advanced harmonic-melodic language—largely inspired by Hindemith and Schoenberg—to his improvisations. Both Giuffre and Tristano became involved also with contemporary contrapuntal techniques. J. J. Johnson's extended works show a clear Hindemithian influence, while a recent composition by pianist Bill Evans entitled *Peace Piece* breathes the spirit of Chopin, without sacrificing the vitality of the improvisatory approach. Evans' awareness, incidentally, of classical music from Bach to Webern, and his ability to perform it authentically, combined with his strong sense of swing and structure in improvisation, make him one of the most important creative performers to watch in this development. A man of similar talents, although not as involved in jazz as a performer, is the composer and teacher Hall Overton. Three other pianists who seem to be equally versed in both fields are Friedrich Gulda, André Previn and Dr. Roland Kovac.

Other primarily jazz-oriented musicians who have worked in varying degrees of emphasis with "classical techniques" have been Bill Russo, Teo Macero, Bill Smith, John Graas, Teddy Charles and Bob Prince. Russo's ambivalent position, alternately embracing and denying jazz, has prevented him from producing, with one exception, any truly convincing works in this area. The exception is an experiment in combining a "legitimate" string quartet with the superimposed improvisations of Lee Konitz, which constitutes an important addition to the literature of the combinative approach.

In an entirely different way, Ornette Coleman, working strictly within the confines of jazz and evidently unencumbered by any "classical" notions, has miraculously produced a music whose basic precepts and listening requirements are very close to those of certain advanced "serial" composers in this country and abroad.

Many classically-oriented composers have sufficient empathy for jazz and the characteristics of its performance to have produced works of quality. This group of composers can be divided roughly into those who retain the more or less explicit beat of a rhythm section and those that do not. The German composer Werner Heider, the American Harold Shapero, Howard Brubeck and the German-born, Minneapolis-based musician Herb Pilhofer belong in the former category. Brubeck's *Dialogues* was performed by his brother's famous quartet and the New York Philharmonic under Bernstein, while Pilhofer's work, also in the quartet plus orchestra format, was performed by the composer's own group with the Minneapolis symphony—both during the 1960 season.

Composers working in the second category are the very gifted Edwin London, Meyer Kupferman, and Princeton professor Milton Babbitt, who although raised in a Tin Pan Alley milieu has a remarkable understanding of the nature of jazz. Significantly the composers in this group have (in the works known to me) excluded improvisation.

Many others, while basically adhering to one or the other rhythmic approach, have written pieces using both methods at times. They include the Parisian composer and critic, André Hodeir; the Canadian Norman Symonds, who has a number of large-scale works in this genre; the young theater composer David Amram; and this writer, who has composed works ranging from completely composed pieces to almost totally improvised works (one of the latter type written for the Modern Jazz Quartet and orchestra). The number of works, incidentally, composed for a solo group and orchestra is already sizable, and performances by the Modern Jazz, Brubeck and other quartets are becoming more and more frequent. A highly successful (in terms of audience reception and publicity value) though cliché-ridden forerunner of all these pieces was the *Concerto for Jazzband and Orchestra* (1954) by the Swiss-German composer Rolf Liebermann. A more recent addition (intended as a companion piece to the Liebermann work) is the combined effort of British bandleader Johnny Dankworth and the Hungarian born Matyas Seiber. (The latter, incidentally, was as far as is known the first composer to give a course on the nature of jazz—no, not in America, but in 1931 in Frankfurt, Germany!)

It is understood, I trust, that the works listed above do not necessarily qualify as "masterpieces" of a new genre. Understandably they achieve their goals in a variety of diverse ways and with varying degrees of success. While their artistic merits may be debatable in the opinion of this or that writer, they are all serious attempts to grapple with the issue at hand and are, for better or for worse, a part of the trend. Nor do I claim completeness for the list, as there must be many composers in the genre not yet known to me.

The greatest obstacle in bringing jazz groups together with symphony orchestras is the lack of real jazz feeling and the unyielding techniques of string players. But even here there are now signs that a break is about due, that something may be done about this deficiency, and that before too many years have passed, even Beiderbecke's vision of hearing an entire orchestra swing may become a reality.

The direction the whole movement takes from now on will be determined largely by the performers. And if, in the process, the jazz musician can instill some of the rhythmic vitality and effortless precision in classical musicians; and, by the same token, if the jazz musician can absorb some of the *re*creative disciplines of classical performers and the compositional skill of the best contemporary composers, the possibilities musically would seem to be enormously exciting. Whether the mating of these two musical concepts will produce a new third species, or whether at some future date, one or other idiom will gradually absorb its alternate, are questions only the future can answer.

Histories of jazz on records; recommended jazz records

HISTORIES OF JAZZ ON RECORDS

The Encyclopedia of Jazz on Records

Under the title *The Encyclopedia of Jazz on Records,* an album of four twelve-inch LPs was assembled by the author for release by Decca as a reference volume and musical parallel for *The Encyclopedia of Jazz.*

The first LP is entitled *Jazz of the Twenties.* Featured are King Oliver and his orchestra, Johnny Dodds' Black Bottom Stompers, featuring Louis Armstrong and Earl Hines, James P. Johnson, Pinetop Smith, Red Nichols and his Five Pennies, Jimmie Noone, Benny Goodman, Jelly Roll Morton, the New Orleans Rhythm Kings, the Eddie Lang-Joe Venuti All-Stars, with Jack Teagarden, Elmer Schoebel's Friars' Society Orchestra with Frank Teschemacher, and the early Ellington band.

The second volume, *Jazz of the Thirties,* features Count Basie and his original band, Bob Crosby's orchestra, the Dorsey Brothers, Sidney Bechet, the orchestras of Glen Gray, Fletcher Henderson, Jimmie Lunceford, Andy Kirk, Glenn Miller, John Kirby, Chick Webb's orchestra with Ella Fitzgerald, and Sister Rosetta Tharpe.

In the third volume, *Jazz of the Forties,* the artists are: Nat "King" Cole's trio, Eddie Condon's group, Roy Eldridge, Eddie Heywood with Don Byas and Ray Nance; Lionel Hampton, Woody Herman's Orchestra featuring Juan Tizol and Johnny Hodges, Stan Kenton's Orchestra, Billie Holiday, Coleman Hawkins, Jay McShann's orchestra featuring Charlie Parker, Artie Shaw's orchestra, and Art Tatum with Joe Turner.

In the final volume, *Jazz of the Fifties,* the artists are Louis Armstrong's All-Stars, Ralph Burns' orchestra, Les Brown's orchestra, Erroll Garner, Benny Green's combo, Terry Gibbs' group with Don Elliott, John Graas' group with Gerry Mulligan, Jimmy and Marian McPartland, Red Norvo Trio, Tony Scott's Quartet, a Shorty Rogers arrangement played by Elmer Bernstein; Charlie Ventura with Jackie Cain and Roy Kral.

The Encyclopedia Of Jazz On Records is available in a special album on Decca DX 140. Individual volumes are also obtainable separately as follows: Jazz of the Twenties: Decca DL 8398; Jazz of the Thirties: Decca DL 8399; Jazz of the Forties: Decca DL 8400; Jazz of the Fifties: Decca DL 8401.

Capitol History of Jazz

The History of Jazz is the title of a four-volume set produced by Dave Dexter Jr. and released on Capitol Records. Jazz styles that were current before the founding of Capitol Records (1942) are conveyed through recreations of early performances, or late recordings of artists representing these styles.

Volume one: *N'Orleans Origins,* with tracks by Sonny Terry, the Mt. Zion Church Choir, Leadbelly, Zutty Singleton Trio; Lizzie Miles, Eddie Miller Quartet, Bugle Sam DeKemel, Armand Hug's Louisianans, Blue Lu Barker, Sharkey's Band, Wingy Manone's Dixielanders and Nappy Lamare's Levee Loungers.

Volume two: *The Turbulent Twenties.* Paul Whiteman's orchestra, Sonny Greer and The Duke's Men, Julia Lee, Bus Moten, Marvin Ash's band, Red Nichols' 5 Pennies, Walter Brown, Jack Teagarden's Chicagoans, Tiny Brown, Bud Freeman.

Volume three: *Everybody Swings.* Glen Gray and Casa Loma orchestra, Benny Goodman band, Duke Ellington orchestra, Art Tatum, International Jazzmen, Red Norvo's Nine, Bob Crosby's Dixieland Band, Jess Stacy, Tommy Douglas' band, Rex Stewart's Big Eight, Bobby Hackett's band.

Volume four: *Enter The Cool.* Al Casey Sextet, Coleman Hawkins, Dizzy Gillespie's band, Lennie

Tristano, Woody Herman's Herd, Metronome All-Stars, Miles Davis, George Shearing, Stan Kenton's orchestra, Dave Pell Octet, Duke Ellington's orchestra.

These four volumes are available singly on Capitol T 793, 794, 795 and 796 respectively.

History of Classic Jazz

Riverside Records' *History of Classic Jazz* was produced by Bill Grauer Jr. and Orrin Keepnews. It includes a 20,000 word introductory essay by Charles Edward Smith, illustrated by photographs of early jazz figures. The album is composed of five twelve-inch LPs. The contents are as follows:

Side one: Backgrounds. African drums, Street cries of Charleston; Blind Lemon Jefferson, Rev. J. M. Gates and congregation; Sodero's Military Band; Fred Van Eps, ragtime banjo solo.

Side two: Ragtime. Scott Joplin, James Scott, Joseph Lamb, Jelly Roll Morton, Cow Cow Davenport.

Side three: The Blues. Ma Rainey, Bessie Smith, Ida Cox, Chippie Hill, Blind Lemon Jefferson, Big Bill Broonzy.

Side four: New Orleans. King Oliver, Jelly Roll Morton, New Orleans Rhythm Kings, Memphis Melody Boys, Red Onion Band.

Side five: Boogie-Woogie. Wesley Wallace, Jimmy Yancey, Cripple Clarence Lofton, Meade Lux Lewis, Art Hodes, Pete Johnson.

Side six: South Side Chicago. Johnny Dodds with Tiny Parham, Freddie Keppard, Barrelhouse Five, State Street Ramblers, Lovie Austin, Doc Cook's Dreamland Orchestra.

Side seven: Chicago Style. Muggsy Spanier, Bix Beiderbecke, Original Wolverines, Charles Pierce, Jungle Kings, Wingy Manone.

Side eight: Harlem. James P. Johnson, Fats Waller, Cliff Jackson, Clarence Williams, Duke Ellington, and Fletcher Henderson orchestras.

Side nine: New York Style. Original Memphis Five, California Ramblers, Red Nichols and Miff Mole, Wild Bill Davison, Yank Lawson, Muggsy Spanier.

Side ten: Revival. Kid Ory, Bunk Johnson, George Lewis, Lu Watters, Bob Helm, Dixieland Rhythm Kings.

History of Classic Jazz is available on Riverside SDP 11.

The Jazz Story

The Jazz Story, a three-volume anthology produced by the author and narrated by Steve Allen, contains a number of classic jazz recordings previously unavailable on LPs, most of them reproduced in their entirety, a few excerpted to present solo highlights.

The first side includes a specially recorded series of reminiscences of the ragtime era spoken and played by Willie (The Lion) Smith, as well as excerpts including King Oliver; the New Orleans Rhythm Kings, Trixie Smith, Jelly Roll Morton, Johnny Dodds with Louis Armstrong, Red Nichols and Art Hodes.

Side two is devoted to pianists, featuring: Duke Ellington, Meade Lux Lewis, Pete Johnson, Albert Ammons, Bob Crosby with Marvin Ash, Jimmie Noone with Earl Hines, Bob Howard with Teddy Wilson, Art Tatum.

Side three features bands and soloists of the 1930s: Fletcher Henderson, Don Redman, the Dorsey Brothers, Jimmie Lunceford, Roy Eldridge's Delta Four, Coleman Hawkins, Joe Venuti, John Kirby, Johnny Hodges with Eddie Heywood.

Side four features singers: Jimmy Rushing with Count Basie, Mildred Bailey, Ella Fitzgerald, Billie Holiday, Jack Teagarden with Paul Whiteman; Joe Turner.

Side five features Lionel Hampton's 1944 band, the original King Cole Trio, Count Basie's band, Charlie Parker with Jay McShann's band in 1941, Charlie Ventura, Erroll Garner.

Side six features music of the 1950s: Terry Gibbs and Don Elliot, Jimmy McPartland, Manny Albam's band featuring Gerry Mulligan; Bob Crosby, John Graas.

The Jazz Story is available in a three-record box, Coral CJE-100.

The Seven Ages of Jazz

Recorded in 1958 at a live concert presentation in Wallingford, Conn., with a narration by the author, this two-record album presents seven aspects of jazz history: folk, blues, ragtime, Dixieland, swing, bop and modern. The artists participating in the concert were Georgie Auld, Buck Clayton, Don Elliott, Tyree Glenn, Coleman Hawkins, Milt Hinton, Don Lamond, Willie (The Lion) Smith, Billie Holiday, Brownie McGhee and Maxine Sullivan, with Dick Hyman playing and serving as musical director.

Side one offers spiritual, work song and blues illustrations sung and played by Brownie McGhee; ragtime and "stride piano" by The Lion, Dixieland by the band, and a Bix impression by Don Elliott.

Side two includes, besides performances by the band, impressions of Meade Lux Lewis, Fats Waller, Earl Hines and Teddy Wilson by Dick Hyman; Billie Holiday accompanied by Mal Waldron.

Side three includes numbers by the band, Maxine Sullivan, Coleman Hawkins.

Side four has Dick Hyman's impression of Erroll Garner; a ballad medley featuring Buck Clayton, Georgie Auld and Coleman Hawkins; vibes impressions by Don Elliott; and an original Hyman composition played by the band.

The Seven Ages of Jazz is available in a two-record album on Metrojazz (MGM) 2-E 1009.

RECOMMENDED JAZZ RECORDS

The records listed below do not constitute a "basic jazz library", since the practice among record companies in recent years of deleting many important items while reissuing others makes any stable list impossible. I have tried to select LPs that are representative of some significant talent or trend and seem likely to remain available. Students concerned with records involving the pre-history of jazz, African origins etc. will find them in basic library suggestions among the various jazz history books listed in the bibliography.

Ragtime

Piano roll transcriptions, Riverside 12-110 and 12-126. James Scott, Scott Joplin, Tom Turpin. See also side two of *History of Classic Jazz* (above).

Early Jazz: Vocal

Big Bill Broonzy, Riverside 12-125.

Great Blues Singers, Riverside 12-121. Ma Rainey, Ida Cox, Sara Martin, Bessie Smith, Trixie Smith, Mary Johnson, Hociel Thomas, Chippie Hill.

Blind Lemon Jefferson, Riverside 12-125.

Bessie Smith, Vols. I, II, III, IV, Columbia CL 855, 856, 857, 858.

Spoken Documentary

Lil Armstrong. *Satchmo and Me,* Riverside 12-120. The pianist speaks of her early days in jazz before and during her marriage to Louis Armstrong.

Louis Armstrong. *Satchmo: A Musical Autobiography,* Decca DXM 155 (four records). Mainly music, but with long spoken introductions.

Coleman Hawkins. *A Documentary,* Riverside 12-117, 118. A two-record series of reminiscences.

Willie (The Lion) Smith. *The Lion Roars,* Dot 3094. Part music, part talk. Reminiscences in an interview with the author, and 13 piano solos.

Early Jazz: Instrumental

The Louis Armstrong Story Vols. I, II, III, IV. Columbia CL 851, 852, 853, 854. Covers the period 1925-31, with Earl Hines, Kid Ory, Johnny Dodds, Zutty Singleton and many others.

The Bix Beiderbecke Story, Vols. I, II, III. Columbia CL 844, 845, 846. With various small and large groups 1927-9, including Frank Trumbauer and members of the Paul Whiteman band.

Chicago Style Jazz. Columbia CL 632. White jazz groups 1927-35 led by Eddie Condon, Miff Mole, Bud Freeman, Paul Mares.

History of Classic Jazz. Riverside (see Histories of Jazz, above).

Jazz of the Twenties (see Encyclopedia of Jazz on Records, above).

Kings of Classic Jazz. Riverside 12-131. One track each by Ma Rainey (with Armstrong), Freddie Keppard, Johnny Dodds, King Oliver, New Orleans Rhythm Kings, Bix Beiderbecke, Jelly Roll Morton, James P. Johnson, Jimmy Yancey, Kid Ory, George Lewis, Sidney Bechet.

Jelly Roll Morton. Riverside 12-128. Small groups, 1923-6.

New Orleans Rhythm Kings. Riverside 12-102.

The Red Nichols Story. Brunswick 54047. "Five Pennies" groups, 1926-30, with Jack Teagarden, Benny Goodman, Jimmy Dorsey, Glenn Miller, Gene Krupa, Babe Russin, Joe Sullivan, Vic Berton, et al.

The Swing Era

Count Basie & His Orchestra, Brunswick 54012. Some of the band's definitive 1937-9 recordings, incl. *Jumpin' at the Woodside, Every Tub, Shorty George, Time Out, Blue and Sentimental, Cherokee, Topsy.*

Sidney Bechet Jazz Classics, Blue Note 1201. Various combo tracks, among them the famous 1939 *Summertime* solo.

Duke Ellington at his Very Best, Victor 1715. Excerpts from the original *Black, Brown and Beige* (far superior to the later Columbia version), and such 1940 masterpieces as *Jack The Bear, Concerto for Cootie, Ko-Ko, Warm Valley.*

Five Feet of Swing, Decca 8045. Covering 1934-7: the Bob Crosby band, the Dorsey Brothers, Chick Webb's

Orchestra with Ella Fitzgerald, Glen Gray's Casa Loma Orchestra.

Benny Goodman Carnegie Hall Jazz Concert, Columbia OSL 160 (two records). The Goodman Orchestra, Trio and Quartet with guest stars, Bobby Hackett and members of the Ellington and Basie bands.

Great Jazz Pianists, Camden 328. One track each by Oscar Peterson, Earl Hines, Meade Lux Lewis, Jelly Roll Morton, Albert Ammons, Pete Johnson, Fats Waller, Art Tatum, Jess Stacy, Erroll Garner, Duke Ellington, James P. Johnson, Mary Lou Williams.

Lionel Hampton. *Jivin' The Vibes,* Camden 402. Various small combos, 1937-9, including members of the Goodman, Ellington and Calloway bands as well as Benny Carter, Cozy Cole and four of the John Kirby sextet.

Billie Holiday. *Lady Day,* Columbia 637. Some of the best tracks of the 1935-8 period, featuring Teddy Wilson and various all-star combos. *Miss Brown to You, I Wished On The Moon, Summertime, Billie's Blues, Easy Living, I Cried for You* etc.

Jazz of the Thirties (see *Encyclopedia of Jazz on Records,* above).

Kansas City Jazz, Decca 8044. 1937-40. Includes the Basie band, Andy Kirk's band, and combo tracks led by Pete Johnson, Joe Turner, Mary Lou Williams, Hot Lips Page, Eddie Durham.

Jimmie Lunceford & His Orch., Decca 8050. Twelve tracks from 1934-41, including *Annie Laurie, Swanee River, Margie, Pigeon Walk, My Blue Heaven.*

Metronome All Stars, Harmony 7044. Top jazz poll winners of 1940, '41, '46 and '50. Includes Basie, Charlie Christian, Teagarden, James, Goodman, Benny Carter.

Spirituals to Swing, Vanguard 8523-4 (two records). An indispensable set, recorded at the Carnegie Hall concerts organized in 1938-9 by John Hammond. The Benny Goodman Sextet, Helen Humes, tracks by members of the Basie band, the band with Hot Lips Page, are heard on the first side.

Side two has the Kansas City Six, Charlie Christian, a Count Basie piano solo, members of the Basie band, James P. Johnson, Bechet's New Orleans Feetwarmers.

Side three: Goodman Sextet, Golden Gate Quartet, Ida Cox; Goodman, Basie, and boogie-woogie pianists Lewis, Ammons and Johnson in a jam session.

Side four has Sonny Terry, Joe Turner; Lewis, Ammons and Johnson with Big Bill Broonzy; Mitchell's Christian Singers, the Kansas City Six.

Lester Young Memorial Album, Epic 6031 (two records). By the Count Basie Quintet, 1936, and the Basie band 1939-40. Includes vocals by Jimmy Rushing; other soloists are Buck Clayton, Dickie Wells. Original versions of *Rock-a-Bye Basie, Taxi War Dance, Lester Leaps In, Tickle Toe, Let Me See,* etc.

Transitional, Bop, Cool

Charlie Christian. *The Harlem Jazz Scene 1941,* Counterpoint 548. Recorded at Monroe's Uptown House and Minton's Play House, with Gillespie, Monk et al.

Miles Davis. *Birth of the Cool,* Capitol 762. Incl. arrs. by Mulligan, Gil Evans, John Lewis. *Move, Jeru, Moon Dreams, Venus de Milo, Budo, Deception, Godchild, Boplicity, Rocker, Israel* and *Rouge.*

Ella Fitzgerald. *Lullabies of Birdland,* Decca 8149. Bop, blues and ballad vocals, incl. *How High The Moon, Basin Street, Angel Eyes.*

Dizzy Gillespie. *Groovin' High,* Savoy 12020. 1945-6 combo and band tracks incl. *Hot House, Salt Peanuts, Things to Come, Ray's Idea, Our Delight, Emanon.* Personnel includes Charlie Parker, Milt Jackson, Sonny Stitt.

Woody Herman. *Summer Sequence,* Harmony 7093. Best tracks of the mid-'40s.

Jazz at the Philharmonic. Volume 1, Verve MG 1. *How High the Moon, Bellboy Blues* with Buck Clayton, Flip Phillips, Trummy Young, Coleman Hawkins; *Lady be Good, After You've Gone* with Dizzy Gillespie, Lester Young, Charlie Parker.

Jazz of the Forties (see *Encyclopedia of Jazz on Records,* above).

Lee Konitz, Prestige 7004. With Lennie Tristano, Warne Marsh, Billy Bauer.

Metronome All Stars, Camden 426. Like the similarly titled LP on Harmony, this belongs partly to the swing era; however, four tracks include such soloists as Charlie Parker, Buddy De Franco, Flip Phillips, Tristano, Ventura, Winding, and a chase sequence featuring Dizzy Gillespie, Miles Davis and Fats Navarro.

Thelonious Monk. *Genius of Modern Music,* Blue Note 1510. Includes *'Round Midnight, Ruby My Dear, Well You Needn't, I Mean You, Epistrophy* in the original 1947-50 versions.

Charlie Parker Memorial, Vol. 1, Savoy 12000. Various takes on combo tracks of the mid-'40s including *Barbados, Constellation, Parker's Mood, Ah-Leu-Cha, Steeplechase, Buzzy.*

Bud Powell. *The Amazing Bud Powell,* Vol. 1. Blue Note 1503. Solo and combo tracks incl. *Un Poco Loco, Dance of the Infidels, Night in Tunisia, Wail, 52nd*

St. Theme, Parisian Thoroughfare, Ornithology. With Fats Navarro, Sonny Rollins.

Sarah Vaughan, Masterseal 55. 1944-5 tracks with Gillespie et al; the LP also includes two tracks by a Cozy Cole combo and one by Red Norvo's Quintet.

The Anatomy of Improvisation. Verve MGV 8230. Tracks featuring Gillespie, Eldridge, De Franco, Parker, Hodges, Hawkins, Young, Tatum, T. Wilson, B. Powell, corresponding with solos reproduced and analyzed in *The Book of Jazz.*

Contemporary Aspects

Cannonball Adderley Quintet in San Francisco, Riverside 12-311. Recorded at the Jazz Workshop.

Clifford Brown Memorial, Prestige 7055. Representative not only of Brown but of Swedish jazz, as one side shows Brown and Art Farmer with Arne Domnerus, Lars Gullin, Ake Persson, Bangt Hallberg et al. 1953.

Dave Brubeck Quartet. *Jazz at Oberlin,* Fantasy 3245. Recorded during a college concert, 1953.

Ray Charles, Atlantic 8006. Some of his first important titles, incl. *Hallelujah I Love Her So, I Got a Woman, Greenbacks, Come Back Baby, Mess Around, Mary Ann.*

Ornette Coleman. *The Shape of Jazz to Come,* Atlantic 1317. Six originals by Coleman's quartet, with Don Cherry on cornet.

Miles Davis. *Miles Ahead,* Columbia 1041. With Gil Evans Orchestra.

Stan Getz. West Coast Jazz, Verve 8028. With Conte Candoli, Lou Levy, Stan Levey, Leroy Vinnegar.

Jazz of the Fifties (see *Encyclopedia on Jazz on Records,* above).

Stan Kenton. *New Concepts of Artistry in Rhythm,* Capitol 383. Includes *Portrait of a Count, 23°N 82°W,* Mulligan's *Young Blood* and a semi-documentary *Prologue* in which Kenton introduces the members of the band (early 1950s).

Lambert, Hendricks & Ross. *The Swingers!,* World Pacific 1264. Vocal versions of Parker's *Now's The Time,* Miles Davis' *Four,* Rollins' *Airegin* etc.

Shelly Manne and his Friends, Vol. 2. *My Fair Lady,* Contemporary 3527. The catalytic LP that started the trend for jazz versions of show tunes. With André Previn, Leroy Vinnegar.

Charles Mingus. *Mingus Ah Um,* Columbia CS 8171. Includes *Goodbye Pork Pie Hat, Fables of Faubus, Better Git It In Your Soul* and six other Mingus originals.

Modern Jazz Concert, Columbia WL 127. Six works commissioned by the 1957 Brandeis U. Festival of the Arts. Conducted by Gunther Schuller, George Russell; other writers are Harold Shapero, Jimmy Giuffre, Charles Mingus, Milton Babbitt.

Modern Jazz Quartet. Django, Prestige 7057. Includes *One Bass Hit, Milano, The Queen's Fancy, Delaunay's Dilemma, La Ronde, Autumn in New York, But Not For Me.*

Modern Sounds, Capitol 691. Two West Coast groups, led by Shorty Rogers and Gerry Mulligan.

New York, N.Y. George Russell & Orchestra, Decca 79216. Narration by Jon Hendricks; solos are by Brookmeyer, Frank Rehak, Bill Evans, John Coltrane, Art Farmer, Benny Golson, Phil Woods, Max Roach and others.

One World Jazz. Columbia WS 314. International jam session in which leading jazzmen in London, Paris and Stockholm play (via overdubbing) with Clark Terry, Ben Webster, J. J. Johnson and a rhythm section in New York.

Oscar Peterson at Newport, Verve 8239. One side by the Peterson Trio, augmented on the other by Roy Eldridge, Sonny Stitt and Jo Jones.

Playboy All Stars, Volume 3, Playboy 1959 (three records). First disc includes tracks by Basie, Hawkins, Manne, Getz, Four Freshmen, Garner, Teagarden, J. J. Johnson, Chet Baker, Brookmeyer, Second has Fitzgerald, Kenton, Goodman, Ray Brown, Hi-Los, Giuffre, Armstrong, Kessel, Brubeck, Miles Davis. Third features Peterson, Gillespie, Winding, Earl Bostic, Mulligan, Hampton, Desmond, Milt Jackson, Sinatra, Rollins.

Max Roach. *Jazz in ¾ Time,* Mercury 36108. Representative of the recent interest in jazz waltzes. Quintet, with Sonny Rollins, Kenny Dorham.

Sonny Rollins & The Big Brass, Metrojazz SE 1002. Presents Rollins in three settings: with a large orchestra (brass and rhythm), a trio (himself, bass and drums) and, on one track *(Body and Soul),* completely unaccompanied. Band plays Ernie Wilkins arrangements.

Horace Silver & The Jazz Messengers, Blue Note 1518. Includes Silver's compositions *The Preacher, Doodlin'* etc., by a quintet with Hank Mobley and Art Blakey.

Jimmy Smith, Blue Note 1514. The Hammond organist, with guitar and drums, in *The Champ, Bayou, Deep Purple* etc.

Musicians' birthdays

JANUARY

1 Helmut Brandt; Papa Celestin; Milt Jackson; Al McKibbon; Jasper Taylor
2 Nick Fatool; Henry Goodwin
3 Al Belletto; John Jenkins; Musa Kaleem; Eddie Lang; Herbie Nichols
4 Al Dreares; Slim Gaillard; Noro Morales; Frank Newton; Ray Starling; Frank Wess
5 Jack Brokensha; Wild Bill Davidson; Chuck Flores; Bob Keene; Joe Marsala; Dizzy Reece
6 Lee Abrams; Vernon Brown; Keith Christie; Bobby Stark
7 Red Allen; Kenny Davern; Haywood Henry; Don Payne; Keg Purnell; Dave Schildkraut; Sam Woodyard
8 Wendell Culley; Elvis Presley; Bobby Tucker
9 Kenny Clarke; Ed Garland; Roger Guerin; Charlie Harris; Betty Roche; Carson Smith; Buddy Weed
10 Allen Eager; Buddy Johnson; Johnny Ray; Lyle Ritz; Max Roach
11 Wilbur De Paris; Bob Enevoldsen; Guy Lafitte; Osie Johnson; Jack Nimitz; Bud Scott
12 Jay McShann; Trummy Young
13 Danny Barker; Quentin Jackson; Melba Liston; Louis Mucci
14 Billy Butterfield; Jimmy Crawford; Maxwell Davis; Joe Muranyi; Caterina Valente
15 Ronnie Free; Steve Jordan; Gene Krupa; Dick Lammi; Alan Lomax; Jerry Wald
16 Ivie Anderson; Sandy Block; G. T. Hogan
17 Big Sid Catlett; George Handy; Vido Musso; Tommy Reynolds; Larry Sonn; Cedar Walton
18 John Costa; Christian Kellens; Irene Kral; Ray Sims
19 Israel Crosby; Bubber Miley; J. R. Monterose; Hod O'Brien; Horace Parlan
20 Ray Anthony; Jimmy Cobb; John Hawksworth; Jimmy Johnson; Bill Le Sage
21 Billy Maxted; Bob Whitlock; Juice Wilson
22 André Hodeir; Jay Jay Johnson; Teddy McRae; Juan Tizol
23 Ray Abrams; Fred Beckett; Dave Black; Scoops Carry; Curtis Counce; Richie Crabtree; Ken Errair; Bob Freedman; Erich Kleinschuster; Teddy Napoleon; Marty Paich; Django Reinhardt; Benny Waters
24 Jimmy Forrest; Lennie McBrowne; Avery Parrish; Bobby Scott
25 Wellman Braud; Barbara Carroll; Benny Golson; Truck Parham; Floyd Smith; Jimmy Wyble
26 Page Cavanaugh; Talib Dawud; Stephane Grappelly; Dick Nash; Stan Puls
27 Abe Aaron; Jimmy Bond; Will Marion Cook; Skitch Henderson; Charlie Holmes; Dick Meldonian; Hot Lips Page; Milt Raskin
28 Louis Nelson; Mert Oliver; Zilmer Randolph; Ronnie Scott; Johnny Williams
29 Frank Assunto; Sacha Distel; Beverly Kenney; Ulysses Livingston; Arnold Ross; Eddie Shaughnessy; Joan Shaw; Don Shirley; Earl Watkins
30 Ahmed Abdul-Malik; Ruth Brown; Roy Eldridge; Gene Gammage; Bob Harrington; Tubby Hayes; Horst Jankowski; Mitch Leigh, Bernie Leighton
31 John Anderson; Bobby Hackett; Jose Magalhaes; Benny Morton; Ottilie Patterson

FEBRUARY

1 Langston Hughes; James P. Johnson; Ruben McFall; Tricky Sam Nanton; Sadao Watanabe
2 Stan Getz; Tony Gottuso; Joe Mondragon; Sonny Stitt; Vlady
3 Chico Alvarez; John Handy; Paul Knopf; Snookie Young
4 Gil Bernal; Arthur Bernstein; Wally Cirillo; Tony Fruscella; Jutta Hipp; Manny Klein; Wade Legge

5 Rozelle Claxton; Don Goldie; Bull Ruther; Gene Schroeder; Will Shade
6 Nelson Boyd; George Brunis; Don Fagerquist; Bernie Glow; Conrad Gozzo; Howard McGhee; John Pisano
7 Eubie Blake; Marty Holmes; Wilbur Sweatman
8 Lonnie Johnson; Joe Maini; Buddy Morrow; Pony Poindexter; Jimmy Skidmore
9 Joe Dodge; Arthur Edwards; Peanuts Holland; Walter Page
10 Roland Hanna; Terry Lopez; Foots Thomas; Chick Webb
11 Ike Carpenter; Bob Carter; Matt Dennis; Conrad Janis; John Mills; George Roumanis; Josh White; Bill Young
12 Paul Bascomb; Tex Beneke; Buddy Childers; Hans Koller; Art Mardigan; Mel Powell; Bernie Privin; Eddie Taylor
13 Lennie Hayton; Les Hite; Ron Jefferson; Clyde Lombardi; Wingy Manone; Arthur Rollini
14 Perry Bradford; Elliott Lawrence; Jack Lesberg; Dwike Mitchell
15 Eddie Bonnemere; Will Bradley Jr.; Walter Fuller; Frank Horrox; Taft Jordan
16 Benny Barth; Bill Doggett; Charlie Fowlkes; Machito; Junior Raglin; Jerry Segal
17 Bill Blakkestad; Buddy De Franco; Will Davis; Harry Dial; Buddy Jones; Bill Stanley; Alec Wilder
18 George Baquet; Frank Butler
19 Stan Kenton; Kid Shots Madison
20 Frank Isola; Bobby Jaspar; Phil Moore; Fred Robinson; Nancy Wilson; Buddy Wise
21 Tadd Dameron; Eddie De Haas; Lil Green; Ed Higgins
22 Dave Bailey; James Reese Europe; Whitey Mitchell; Al Sears; Rex Stewart; Joe Tarto; Buddy Tate; Billy Triglia; Joe Wilder
23 John Benson Brooks; John Carisi; Les Condon; Philip Darois; Hall Overton
24 Eddie Chamblee; Clyde Hart; Michel LeGrand; Ralph Pena
25 Sandy Brown; Ralph Hutchinson; Fred Katz; Joe Saye; René Thomas
26 Fats Domino; Teddy Edwards; James Moody; Dave Pell; Flip Phillips; Red Press; Lou Singer
27 Mildred Bailey; Dexter Gordon; Abe Most; Jesse Powell; Maxim Saury; Leo Watson; Chuck Wayne; Ben Webster
28 Svend Asmussen; Lee Castle; Bill Douglass; Louis Metcalf
29 Jimmy Dorsey

MARCH

1 Kenny Baker; Barrett Deems; Bob Hardaway; Eddie Jones; Glenn Miller; Benny Powell
2 Lockjaw Davis; Ram Hall; Buell Neidlinger; Red Saunders; Doug Watkins
3 Barney Bigard; Clark Burroughs; Jimmy Garrison
4 Don Rendell; Cy Touff; Barney Wilen
5 Lou Levy; Bill Pemberton; George Probert; Bill Takas; Eddie Wasserman; Joe Yukl; Pee Wee Moore
6 Red Callender; Wes Montgomery; Billy Root
7 Mahlon Clark; Frank Morelli; Alcide Pavageau; Lee Young
8 Heinie Beau; George Coleman; Sam Donahue; Al Hall; Dick Hyman; George Mitchell; Gloria Smyth; Gabor Szabo
9 Vic Ash; Herschel Evans; Lloyd Price
10 Don Abney; Bix Beiderbecke; Don Trenner
11 Mercer Ellington; Allan Ganley; Jackie Mills; Miff Mole; Chauncey Morehouse; Calo Scott
12 Johnny Dunn; Willie Maiden
13 Bob Haggart; Roy Haynes; Ina Ray Hutton; Dick Katz; Blue Mitchell
14 Les Brown; Volly De Faut; Joe Dolney; Luther Henderson; Quincy Jones; Arif Mardin; Shirley Scott; Frank Teschemacher
15 Vinnie Burke; Jerry Fuller; Harry James; Jimmy McPartland; Bob Wilber
16 Ruby Braff; Tommy Flanagan; Leon Rappolo
17 Nat Cole; Paul Horn; Leroy Lovett
18 Jean Goldkette; Pat Halcox; Deane Kincaide
19 Harry Babasin; Ornette Coleman; Buster Harding; Bill Henderson; Steve Lewis; Doug Mettome; Curly Russell; Lennie Tristano; Lem Winchester
20 Burt Bales; John Davies; Larry Elgart; Marian McPartland; Sonny Russo
21 Hank D'Amico; Freddie Gambrell; Sir Charles Thompson; Joe Timer
22 Sonny Burke; Charlie Christian
23 Johnny Guarnieri; Dave Pike
24 June Clark; King Pleasure
25 Bunny Berigan; Percy Brice; Linton Garner; Paul Motian
26 Donald Bailey; Jimmy Blanton; Joe Loco; Maurice Simon
27 Burt Collins; Carl-Henrik North; Pee Wee Russell; Sarah Vaughan; Jan Wroblewski
28 Bill Anthony; Eric Dixon; Herb Hall; Ike Isaacs; Thad Jones; Cripple Clarence Lofton; Chummy MacGregor; Barry Miles; Skip Morr; Paul Whiteman
29 Sidney Arodin; Pearl Bailey; George Chisholm; Leslie Gilbert; Abe Lincoln; Remo Palmier; Gene Taylor
30 John Eaton; Ted Heath; Frankie Laine; Big Maceo
31 Freddie Green; Lizzie Miles; Red Norvo; Santo Pecora; Gene Puerling; Tommy Shepard

APRIL

1 Don Butterfield; Harry Carney; Alberta Hunter; Duke Jordan; Harry Sheppard; Bob Strasen
2 Booker Little; Marty Marsala; Herbert Mills; Boomie Richman; Hymie Shertzer
3 Bill Finegan; Stan Freeman; Art Harris; Ken Kersey; Scott La Faro; Pierre Michelot; Bill Potts; Billy Taylor (bass)
4 Elmer Bernstein; Buster Cooper; Gene Ramey; Stan Turrentine; Muddy Waters
5 Herb Flemming; Stan Levey; Knobby Totah
6 Dorothy Donegan; Bill Hardman; Eddie Hubble; Rosy McHargue; Gerry Mulligan; André Previn; Charlie Rouse; Snookum Russell; Arthur Taylor; Randy Weston
7 Victor Feldman; Ralph Flanagan; Al Hayse; Billie Holiday; Peanuts Hucko; Pete La Roca
8 Carmen McRae; Monty Sunshine
9 Sharkey Bonano; Julian Dash; Teddy Roy; Art Van Damme
10 Claude Bolling; Morty Corb; Fud Livingston; Chano Pozo
11 Ralph Blaze; Nick La Rocca; John Levy
12 Johnny Dodds; Russ Garcia; Lionel Hampton; Dick Marx
13 Teddy Charles; Bud Freeman; Slick Jones; John La Porta; John Williams
14 Gene Ammons; Gil Fuller; Bill Harris (guitar); Lucy Reed; Shorty Rogers
15 Bernard Addison; Richard Davis; Herb Pomeroy; Casper Reardon; Bessie Smith; Charlie Smith; Jim Timmens
16 Gerard Badini; Boyce Brown; Benny Green; Bobby Henderson; Hank Mancini; Herbie Mann; Tony Rizzi
17 Chris Barber; Warren Chiasson; Johnny St. Cyr; Sam Noto; Derek Smith; Paul Smith
18 Ken Colyer; Tony Mottola; James Rowser
19 Don Barbour; Tommy Benford; Joe Rushton
20 Emile Christian; Tito Puente; Henri Renaud
21 Sonny Berman; Joe Dixon; Slide Hampton; Tony Jackson; Mundell Lowe; Clara Ward
22 Candido; Paul Chambers; Charles Mingus; Lou Stein, Tom Turrentine
23 Benny Harris; Jimmie Noone
24 Aaron Bell; Jimmy De Brest; Fatty George; Johnny Griffin; Ray Leatherwood
25 Earl Bostic; Ella Fitzgerald; Sal Franzella; Rick Henderson
26 Fred Dutton; Herman Foster; Jimmy Giuffre; Ma Rainey; Dave Tough
27 Denzil Best; Larry Fotine; Connie Kay; Matty Matlock; Sal Mosca; Calvin Newborn
28 Everett Barksdale; Blossom Dearie; Norma Teagarden
29 Ray Barretto; Errol Buddle; Duke Ellington; Donald Mills; Paul Nero; Ward Pinkett; Andrew Simpkins; Jon Tilmans
30 Buddy Arnold; Percy Heath; Billy Ver Planck

MAY

1 Hayes Alvis; Billy Byers; Henderson Chambers; Ira Sullivan
2 Van Alexander; Bing Crosby; Jim Dahl; Torbjorn Hultcrantz
3 James Cleveland; Rudy Jacobs; Kinichi Kawabe; Yank Lawson; John Lewis
4 Ron Carter; Maynard Ferguson; Don Friedman; Lars Gullin; Mary Ann McCall; Sonny Payne; Maurice Purtill; Guy Warren
5 Paul Barbarin; Frankie Carlson; Pete Daily; Roy East
6 Charles Irvis; Fred Randall
7 Vic Berton; Ed Inge; Floyd O'Brien; Paul Quinichette; Herbert Steward
8 Jack Bland; Peter Littman; Red Nichols; Mary Lou Williams
9 Bob Zurke
10 Jim Europe; Al Hendrickson; Joe Holiday; Pee Wee Hunt; Mel Lewis; Dave Lindup; Bob Prince
11 John Coppola; Dick Garcia; Jay C. Higginbotham; Lennart Jansson; Moon Mullens; King Oliver; Oscar Valdambrini.
12 Barbara Dane; Jack Jenney; Gerry Wiggins
13 Buddy Catlett; Bert Dahlander; Gil Evans; Red Garland; Squire Gersh; Mitsuko Miyake; Bobby Plater; Maxine Sullivan
14 Sidney Bechet; Jim Buffington; Bobby Darin; Joe Knight; Skip Martin; Al Porcino; Zutty Singleton; Stu Williamson
15 Sonny Clay; Joe Gordon; Ed Hall; Ellis Larkins; Bonnie Wetzel
16 Dud Bascomb; Eddie Bert; Betty Carter; Friedrich Gulda; Woody Herman; Red Holt; Marlowe Morris
17 Dick Hixson; Lee Katzman; Jackie McLean; Little Brother Montgomery; Joe Roland; Larry Shields; Warren Smith; Peter Trunk
18 Dick McPartland; Duane Tatro; Big Joe Turner; Kai Winding
19 Georgie Auld; Pops Foster
20 Rod Cless; Dave Pochonet; Louis Smith
21 Bill Barber; Tommy Bryant; Bill Holman; Lawrence Marable; John Marabuto; Fats Waller
22 Jackie Cain; Eric Delaney; Eddie Edwards; Elaine Leighton; Roger Segure
23 Julian Euell; Fred Guy; Humphrey Lyttelton; Artie Shaw; Les Spann
24 Gianni Basso; Max Bennett; Herbie Fields; Charles Greenlee; Moondog; Frank Signorelli

25 Milt Bernhart; Miles Davis; Jimmy Hamilton; Edgar Hayes; Lloyd Trotman
26 Vernon Alley; Harold Baker; Gene Di Novi; Ziggy Elman; Calvin Jackson; Peggy Lee
27 Jock Carruthers; Albert Nicholas; Brother John Sellers; Bud Shank
28 Dave Barbour; Joe Burton; Reginald Foresythe; Russ Freeman; Andy Kirk; Tommy Ladnier; Arno Marsh; Traps Trappier
29 Dick Hafer; Sandy Mosse; Freddie Reed; Thornel Schwartz; Sylvia Vanderpool; Gene Wright
30 Sidney De Paris; Pee Wee Erwin; Benny Goodman; Dave McKenna; Armando Perrazza; Bobby Sherwood
31 Bill Castagnino; Gene Gifford; Louis Hayes; Toby Hardwicke; Al Heath; Jimmy Shirley

JUNE

1 Herbie Lovelle; Hal McKusick; Nelson Riddle; Harry White
2 Gildo Mahones; Jeff Morton; Marty Napoleon; Burnie Peacock; Ernie Royal; Milt Sealey
3 Lillian Briggs; Carl Pruitt; Dakota Staton
4 Sammy Gardner; Morgana King; Teddy Kotick; Oliver Nelson; Chuck Thompson; Britt Woodman; Bob Zieff
5 Kurt Edelhagen; Pete Jolly; Specs Powell
6 Raymond Burke; Lennie Bush; Eddie Cano; Gilberto Cuppini; Al Grey; Ted Lewis; Jimmie Lunceford; Dave Matthews; John Mehegan
7 Beryl Booker; Tal Farlow; Glen Gray; Anthony Ortega; Prince Robinson
8 Horst Fischer; Toni Harper; Kurt Jaernberg; Dante Martucci; Freddie Webster
9 Sanford Gold; Jimmy Gourley; Les Paul; Goesta Theselius
10 Bertell Knox; Carl Halen; Wes Hensel; Dickie Wells
11 John Glasel; Bob Gordon; Nils Lindberg; Shelly Manne; Kaiser Marshall; Lennie Niehaus; Hazel Scott; Pinetop Smith
12 Al Fairweather; Gene Hall; Zeke Zarchy
13 Eddie Beal; Phil Bodner; Doc Cheatham; Clarence Hutchenrider; Richard M. Jones; Si Zentner; Attila Zoller
14 Joe Cinderella; Cy Coleman; Nappy Lamare
15 Jaki Byard; Erroll Garner; George Kawaguchi; Allan Reuss; Turk Van Lake; Stan Wrightsman
16 Jimmy Ford; Marilyn Moore; Ted Sommer; Lucky Thompson
17 Chris Columbus; Jerry Fielding; Tony Scott; Gene Sedric
18 Ray Bauduc; Mat Mathews; Ray McKinley; Babe Russin
19 Jerry Jerome; Dave Lambert; Lloyd Morales; Joe Thomas (tenor sax); Dave Van Kriedt
20 Dennis Budimir; Doc Evans; Thomas Jefferson; George Stevenson; Joe Venuto; Lammar Wright, Sr.
21 Dewey Jackson; Jamil Nasser (George Joyner); Helen Merrill
22 Lem Davis; Ella Johnson; Ben Pollack; Mouse Randolph
23 Milt Hinton; Stanley Mendelson; Eddie Miller; Eli Robinson; George Russell; Hank Shaw; Sahib Shihab; Fran Thorne
24 Manny Albam; Bill Grah; George Gruntz; Memphis Minnie
25 Bill Russo; Johnny Smith
26 Big Bill Broonzy; Jimmy Deuchar; Clarence Profit; Maurice Rocco
27 Shad Collins; Ben Homer; Elmo Hope; Tony Spargo
28 Pete Candoli; Jimmy Mundy; Adrian Rollini; Joe Smith; Robert White
29 Mousie Alexander; Ralph Burns; Julian Priester
30 Eric Dolphy; Mort Herbert; Lena Horne; Andy Marsala; Roger King Mozian; Dean Reilly; Buddy Rich; Harry Shields; John Sowden

JULY

1 Ruth Olay; Earl Warren
2 Herbie Harper; Charlie Kennedy; Jabbo Smith; Billy Usselton; Richard Wyands; Pat Yankee
3 Ronnell Bright; Lawrence Brown; John Coles; Pete Fountain; Jerry Gray; Corky Hale; Tommy Tedesco
4 Louis Armstrong; Jack Dupree; Timmie Rogers; Aaron Sachs
5 Vern Friley; Richard Healey; Bruce Turner
6 Dick Kenny; Karl Kiffe; Della Reese; Frank Rehak
7 Nick Brignola; Otto Cesana; Mary Ford; Tiny Grimes; Hank Mobley; Doc Severinsen; Bill Trujillo; Kitty White; Joe Zawinul
8 Billy Eckstine; Ken Hanna; Louis Jordan; Johnny Mince; Andy Russo
9 Buddy Bregman; Joe Darensbourg; Hal Gaylor; Irv Kluger; John Wilson
10 Milt Buckner; Dick Cary; Buddy Clark; Major Holley; Lee Morgan; Noble Sissle
11 Andres Ingolfsson; Blind Lemon Jefferson
12 Will Bradley; Conte Candoli; Christian Chevallier; Rusty Dedrick; Paul Gonsalves; Sam the Man Taylor
13 Michel De Villers; George Lewis; Adolph Sandole; Leroy Vinnegar; Bengt-Arne Wallin; Herb Wasserman
14 Stan Dawson; Billy Kyle; Stan Rubin; Claude and Clifford Trenier; Dempsey Wright
15 Ralph Gari; Sadik Hakim; Joe Harriott; Philly Joe Jones
16 John "Teddy" Buckner; Nat Pierce; Cal Tjader

17 Danny Bank; George Barnes; Ray Copeland; Vince Guaraldi; Jerry Lloyd; Wilfred Middlebrooks; Joe Morello; Mary Osborne; Piero Umiliani

18 Don Bagley; Lou Busch; Joe Comfort; Carl Fontana; Bob Helm; Speed Webb

19 David Allen; Buster Bailey; Dick Collins; Kenny Graham; Cliff Jackson; Charlie Teagarden

20 Arnold Fishkin; Peter Ind; Ernie Wilkins

21 Sonny Clark; Arthur Edgehill; Plas Johnson; Omer Simeon; Kay Starr; George Syran; Billy Taylor (piano)

22 Keter Betts; Junior Cook; Lou McGarity; Paul Moer; Bill Perkins; Hal Schaefer

23 Danny Barcelona; Emmett Berry; Jim Chapin; Richie Kamuca; Steve Lacy; Claude Luter

24 Rudy Collins; Herbie Haymer; Ronny Lang; Joe Thomas (trumpet); Cootie Williams

25 Happy Caldwell; Don Ellis; Johnny Hodges; Johnny Wiggs

26 Louis Bellson; Patti Bown; Bob Davis; Erskine Hawkins; Kitty Noble; Charlie Persip

27 Bob Morse; Charlie Queener; Skippy Williams

28 Corky Corcoran; Leon Prima; A. K. Salim

29 Nick Jerret; Vic Lewis; Don Redman; Al Wynn

30 Jimmy Blanton; Vernel Fournier; Hilton Jefferson

31 Kenny Burrell; Bill Clark; Hank Jones; George Kelly; Bjarne Nerem

AUGUST

2 Roy Crimmins; Natty Dominique; Big Nick Nicholas

3 Ray Draper; Les Elgart; Claude Hopkins; Eddie Jefferson; Charlie Shavers

4 Bill Coleman; Herb Ellis; Mel Henke; Howie Mann; Don Prell; Jess Stacy; Earl Swope; Tom Talbert

5 Luis Russell; Jeri Southern

6 Dorothy Ashby; Buddy Collette; Vic Dickenson; Norman Granz; Abbey Lincoln; Reese Markewich; Eddie McFadden; Tony Parenti; Jack Parnell

7 Warren Covington; Don Michaels; Luckey Roberts; Freddie Slack; George Van Eps

8 Harry Arnold; Benny Carter; Vinnie Dean; Charles Gaines; Urbie Green; Lucky Millinder; Jimmy Witherspoon

9 Nat Jaffe; Bill Napier

10 Arnett Cobb; Lea Mathews; Al Morgan; Salvatore Pace; Claude Thornhill

11 Russell Procope; Johnny Rae; Johannes Rediske

12 Earl Coleman; Roy Gaines; Doc West

13 Benny Bailey; Dale Jones; Charles Lee; Big Chief Russell Moore; Joe Puma; George Shearing

14 Ray Beckenstein; Eddie Costa; Frank Devito; Buddy Greco; Stuff Smith

15 Joe Castro; Bill Dowdy; Morey Feld; Joe Garland; Monk Hazel; Tommy Pederson; Oscar Peterson; Terry Pollard

16 Tony Almerico; Bill Evans; Al Hibbler; Howard Lucraft; Carl Perkins; Dick Shreve; Mal Waldron

17 Larry Clinton; George Duvivier; Duke Pearson; Ike Quebec; Jack Sperling

18 Don Lamond; Knocky Parker; Eddie Shu

19 Eddie Durham; Manzie Johnson; Harry Mills; Spud Murphy; Michael Naura; Jimmy Rowles; Lee Roy

20 Frank Capp; Freddie Moore; Jimmy Raney; Frank Rosolino; Joya Sherrill; Jack Teagarden

21 Count Basie; Savannah Churchill; Addison Farmer; Art Farmer

22 Tony Aless; Rolf Billberg; Bob Flanigan; Brick Fleagle; Lex Humphries; Bumps Myers

23 Gil Coggins; Bob Crosby; John Lindsay; Martial Solal

24 George Devens; Phil Gomez; Eddie Phyfe; Alphonso Trent; Paul Webster

25 Leonard Bernstein; Leonard Gaskin; Rune Gustafsson; Billy Moore; Wayne Shorter

26 Peter Appleyard; Norman Bates; Jimmy Rushing; Mickey Simonetta; Buster Smith; Frances Wayne

27 Tony Crombie; Jack Delaney; Med Flory; Idrees Sulieman; Bob Thomas; Lester Young

28 Mutt Carey; Kenny Drew; Don Shelton

29 Jerry Dodgion; Rolf Ericson; Red Kelly; Charlie Parker; Dinah Washington

30 Floyd Bean; Willie Bryant; Kenny Dorham

31 Todd Rhodes; Edgar Sampson

SEPTEMBER

1 Bob Bates; Alex Kallao; Velma Middleton; Art Pepper; Willie Ruff; Mike Simpson; Joe Venuti

2 Laurindo Almeida; Walter Davis Jr.; Clifford Jordan; Phil Napoleon; Emil Richards; Horace Silver

3 Trigger Alpert; Ernie Henry; Clyde Hurley; Memphis Slim; Paul Togawa

4 Al Norris; Gerald Wilson

5 Joki Freund; Virgil Gonsalves; Albert Mangelsdorff; Richie Powell; Hal Stein

6 Eddie Duran; Chippie Hill; Johnny Letman; Angelo De Pippo; Sol Schlinger; Bill Slapin

7 Alvin Alcorn; Max Kaminsky; Joe Newman; Sonny Rollins; Harry South

8 Arthur Anton; Dave Bowman; James Clay; Billy Graham; Elmer Schoebel; Wilbur Ware; Specs Wright

9 Walter Benton; Honore Dutry; Elvin Jones

10 John Keating; Cliff Leeman; Raymond Scott; Hans Solomon; Putte Wickman

11 Bert Courtley; Lorraine Geller; Peck Morrison

12 Cat Anderson; Charles Bateman; Gus Cannon; Ella Mae Morse; Bryce Rohde; Joe Shulman

13 Chu Berry; Bengt Hallberg; Leith Stevens; Mel Torme

14 Jay Cameron; Kid Rena; Jerry Valentine

15 Cannonball Adderley; Al Casey; Bobby Nichols; Bob Petersen; Gene Roland; Arvell Shaw; Bobby Short; Bob Sprecher; Les Strand

16 Charlie Byrd; Jon Hendricks; Jan Johansson; Mamie Smith; Garland Wilson

17 Sil Austin; Sam Butera; Earl May; Leon Merian; Ralph Sharon

18 Pia Beck; Teddi King; Frankie Socolow

19 Lovie Austin; Helen Ward

20 John Collins; Johnny Dankworth; Bill De Arango; Joe Guy; Red Mitchell; Jelly Roll Morton; Jackie Paris; Joe Temperley; Monica Zetterlund

21 Chico Hamilton; Gene Harris; Shafi Hadi; Papa Laine; Frank Orchard; Tommy Potter; Slam Stewart

22 Jean Hoffman; Ray Wetzel

23 Albert Ammons; Ray Charles; John Coltrane; Frank Foster; George Matthews; Jimmy Woode

24 Jack Costanzo; Fats Navarro

25 Garvin Bushell; Anton Lada; Albert Mangelsdorff; Shadow Wilson

26 George Gershwin; Julie London; Romano Mussolini; Nelson Williams

27 Sammy Benskin; Teddy Brannon; Bill Dolney; Bud Powell; Red Rodney

28 Morris Nanton; Lammar Wright, Jr., Mel Zelnick

29 Freddie Keppard; Rolf Kuhn

30 Jon Eardley; Carmen Leggio; Oscar Pettiford

OCTOBER

1 Harry Lookofsky; Sherwood Mangiapane; Ann Richards

2 Bob Corwin; Howard Roberts; Wally Rose; Ronnie Ross; Phil Urso

3 Gene Estes; George Wein

4 Marvin Ash; Walter Bishop; Buddy Featherstonhaugh; Stan Hasselgard; Chino Pozo

5 Bob Astor; Fred Norman

6 Jack Buck; Carmen Mastren; Sammy Price; Pinky Williams

7 Marty Flax; Jo Jones; Alvin Stoller

8 Pepper Adams; Flavio Ambrosetti; J. C. Heard; Sonny Igoe; Hal Singer; Bill Stegmeyer; Clarence Williams

9 Pops Snowden; Lee Wiley

10 Lee Blair; Harry Edison; Fats Heard; Harold Holmes; Freddie Jenkins; Roy Kral; Milton Larkins; Junior Mance; Thelonious Monk; Monk Montgomery; Howard Reay; Julius Watkins

11 John Acea; Papa Jac Assunto; Art Blakey; Bob Dukoff; Billy Higgins; Tony Kinsey; Teddy Weatherford

12 Jimmy Archey; Tubby Hall; Sleepy Matsumoto

13 Edward Baker; Ray Brown; Scoville Brown; Terry Gibbs; Lee Konitz; Art Tatum

14 Dusko Gojkovic; John Graas; Red McKenzie; Spencer Williams

15 Mickey Baker; Al Killian; Nellie Lutcher; John Plonsky; Moe Wechsler

16 Lenny Hambro; Buck Washington; Joe Williams (guitar-singer)

17 Cozy Cole; Lee Collins; George Girard; Jimmy Harrison; Barney Kessel

18 Bobby Troup

19 Ronnie Greb; Roger Wolfe Kahn; Jack Noren; Alphonse Picou; Red Richards; Leon Sash; Howard Smith

20 John Best; Willie Jones; Carl Kress; Ray Linn

21 Don Byas; Don Elliott; Dizzy Gillespie; Chauncey Westbrook

22 Jesse Drakes; John Neves; Bernard Peiffer; Ralph Yaw

23 Betty Bennett; Sonny Criss; Speckled Red; Fats Sadi; Roy Zimmerman

24 Stella Brooks; Lawrence Marrero; Wendell Marshall; Jimmy Powell; Sonny Terry; Sandy Williams

25 Sascha Burland; Jimmy Heath; Chubby Jackson; Kas Malone; Edmond Souchon

26 Charlie Barnet; Hank Duncan; Mahalia Jackson; Warne Marsh; Kenny O'Brien

27 Sonny Dallas; Babs Gonzales; Boyd Raeburn; George Wallington; Carl Warwick; Elmon Wright

28 Bill Harris (trombone); Dink Johnson; Chico O'Farrill; Rudy Powell

29 Rollie Culver; Neal Hefti; Pim Jacobs; Zoot Sims

30 Clifford Brown; Teo Macero; John Murtaugh

31 Booker Ervin; Bob Graettinger; Illinois Jacquet; Julia Lee; Ted Nash; Ethel Waters

NOVEMBER

1 Lou Donaldson; Alonzo Levister; Sam Margolis; John Markham; Johnny Scott

2 Herb Geller; Johnny Richards; Bill Rubenstein; Phil Woods

3 Henry Grimes; Joe Howard; Billy Mitchell; Joe Turner (piano)

4 Joe Benjamin; Larry Bunker; Peter Schilperoort; Ralph Sutton; Potato Valdes

5 Jack McVea; Terry Shannon; Joe Sullivan; Johnny Windhurst; George Williams; Red Wootten

6 Ozzie Bailey; Dick Cathcart; Ray Conniff; Andy Gibson; Jimmy Lyon

7 Joe Bushkin; Roland Kovac; Howard Rumsey

8 Pete Beilmann; Chris Connor; Georg Riedel; Dizzy Sal

9 Pete Brown; Tommy Douglas; Mezz Mezzrow; Muggsy Spanier

10 Paul Bley; Vince Cattolica; Arnold Johansson; Billy May

11 Mose Allison; Ernestine Anderson; Hoagy Carmichael; Willie Cook

12 Buck Clayton; Sam Jones; Merle Koch; Charlie Mariano; Audrey Morris; Wolfgang Schlüter

13 Ernie Farrow; Bennie Moten (leader); Singleton Palmer; Dick Sherman

14 Billy Bauer; Don Ewell; Clancy Hayes; Art Hodes; Carlos Valdez

15 Eddie Harvey; Gus Johnson; Seldon Powell

16 Jim Bates; Eddie Condon; W. C. Handy; Al Lucas; Nick Travis

17 Dave Amram; Wayne Andre; Chuck Andrus; Max Miller; Shorty Sherock

18 Don Cherry; Claes-Göran Fagerstedt; Allyn Ferguson; Lil Greenwood; Johnny Mercer; Boots Mussulli; Claude Williamson

19 Tommy Dorsey; Keg Johnson; Andre Persiany

20 Skeeter Best; June Christy

21 Claire Austin; Jimmy De Preist; Coleman Hawkins; Charlie Johnson; Jack Millman; Sal Salvador; Arthur Schutt

22 Ernie Caceres; Billy Exiner; Jimmy Knepper; Cecil Scott; Gunther Schuller

23 Robert Alexander; Tyree Glenn; Gloria Lynne; Johnny Mandel; Jack Marshall; Bob McCracken; Vito Price; Willie The Lion Smith

24 Serge Chaloff, Al Cohn; Wild Bill Davis; Scott Joplin; Teddy Wilson

25 Nat Adderley; Gus Bivona; Palle Bolvig; Joe Carroll; Charles Crosby; Paul Desmond; Matthew Gee; Willie Smith; O'Neil Spencer; Dick Wellstood

26 Bernie McKinney; Frank Melrose; Jack Perciful; Phil Sunkel

27 Tom Montgomery; Loumell Morgan; Frank Ortega; Eddie South

28 Al Beldiny; Jerry Coker; Ethel Ennis; Gigi Gryce; Ralph Martin; Dick Vance; George Wettling

29 Danny Alvin; Ed Bickert; Harry Blons; Otto Bredl; Tony Coe; Bobby Donaldson; Nat Gershman; Hal McIntyre; Dennis Sandole; Billy Strayhorn

30 Roy Burnes; Brownie McGhee; Benny Moten (bass); Jack Sheldon

DECEMBER

1 Ted Brown; John Bunch; Lurlean Hunter; Dick Johnson; Jimmy Lytell

2 Sidney Desvignes; Wynton Kelly; Fate Marable; Eddie Sauter; Rob Swope; Charlie Ventura

3 Fred Assunto; Tommy Goodman; Brad Gowans; Russell Jacquet; Paul Lingle; Pat Riccio; Sylvia Syms; Webster Young

4 Herman Autrey; Dennis Charles; Frank Flynn; Jim Hall; Eddie Heywood

5 Gene Allen; Arthur Davis; Kay Davis; Kansas Fields; Marshall Royal

6 Dave Brubeck; Bob Cooper; Frankie Dunlop; Azira Miyazawa; Annie Ross

7 Teddy Hill; Louis Prima; Dick Sutton

8 Jimmy Smith; Sol Yaged

9 Donald Byrd; Benny Green; Gil Rodin; Bob Scobey; Elsie Smith; Don Stratton

10 Irving Fazola; Matty Malneck; Stuart McKay; Pat Moran; Ray Nance; Don Sebesky; Guitar Slim; George Tucker

11 Marky Markowitz

12 Toshiko Akiyoshi; Eddie Barefield; Bob Dorough; Dodo Marmarosa; Frank Sinatra; Don Stovall; Joe Williams

13 Jackie Davis; Sonny Greer; Tiger Haynes; Mickey Sheen; Ben Tucker

14 Ted Buckner; Wallace Eckhardt; Chuck Gentry; Budd Johnson; Phineas Newborn; Cecil Payne; Clark Terry; Leo Wright

15 Ed Allen; Buddy Cole; Curtis Fuller; Barry Harris; Curtis Lowe; Jimmy Nottingham; Gene Quill; Dannie Richmond

16 Bobby Gutesha; Sam Most; Turk Murphy; Andy Razaf; Johnny Smith (organ); Cub Teagarden

17 Walter Bolden; Bob Drasnin; Sonny Red Kyner; Sy Oliver; John Ore; Al Williams

18 Barry Galbraith; Fletcher Henderson; Harold Land; Larry Lucie; Big Miller; Anita O'Day; Nick Stabulas; Eddie Vinson

19 Bob Brookmeyer; Santos Miranda; Erskine Tate; Bob Timmons; Lu Watters

20 Arne Domnerus; Reinhold Svensson; Benny Winestone

21 Dave Baker; Marshall Brown; Panama Francis; Pleasant Joseph; Rita Reys; George Treadwell

22 Ronnie Ball; Bill Hitz; Reunald Jones; Dan Terry

23 Chet Baker; Henry Cuesta; John Drew; Joe Harris; Herman Schoonderwalt; Joe Thomas Jr.

24 Ray Bryant; Cab Calloway; Jimmy Campbell; Henry Coker; Baby Dodds; Ralph Marterie; Punch Miller; Fumio Nanri; Rune Ofwerman; Bernt Rosengren; Moe Schneider

25 Wayman Carver; Eddie Gibbs; Pat Jenkins; Harry Klein; Oscar Moore; Kid Ory; Tiny Parham; Tampa Red; Jerome Richardson; Little Richard; Jim Robinson; Pete Rugolo; Eddie Safranski; Herby Spanier

26 Steve Allen; Butch Ballard; Billy Bean; Monty Budwig; Una Mae Carlisle; Tom Stewart

27 Bill Crow; John Frigo; Bunk Johnson; Walter Norris; Eddie Wilcox; Bootie Wood

28 Earl Hines; Al Klink; Bill Mackel; Ed Thigpen; Leonard Ware

29 Irving Ashby; Cutty Cutshall; Snub Mosley; Dave Pearson

30 Bo Diddley; Charlie Creath; Jimmy Jones; Jack Montrose

31 Ross Barbour; Simon Brehm; Jonah Jones; John Kirby; Harvey Leonard; Gil Melle; Odetta

Musicians' birthplaces

ALABAMA—*Anniston:* Cow Cow Davenport, Lucky Millinder; *Birmingham:* John Anderson, Dud Bascomb, Paul Bascomb, Hillard Brown, Harry Dial, Joe Guy, Wilbur Harden, Erskine Hawkins, Haywood Henry, Teddy Hill, Al Killian, Odetta, Avery Parrish, Carl Pruitt, Johnny Smith; *Brookside:* Bama Warwick; *Evergreen:* Herman Autrey; *Florence:* W. C. Handy; *Mobile:* James Reese Europe, Urbie Green, Lil Greenwood, Harold Holmes, Claude Trenier, Cliff Trenier, Cootie Williams; *Montgomery:* Nat Cole, John Collins, Joe Morris, Nelson Williams; *Troy:* Pinetop Smith; *Tuscaloosa:* Dinah Washington, Pinky Williams, Skippy Williams.

ARIZONA—*Komatke:* Big Chief Russell Moore; *Miami:* Joe Castro; *Nogales:* Charlie Mingus; *Phoenix:* Sonny Clay, Howard Roberts.

ARKANSAS—Washboard Sam; *Brinkley:* Louis Jordan; *Cherry Hill:* Bob Dorough; *Cotton Plant:* Sister Rosetta Tharpe; *Dermott:* Zilmer Randolph; *Fort Smith:* Alphonso Trent; *Gurdon:* Jimmy Witherspoon; *Hope:* Buddy Jones; *Jonesboro:* Bill Clark; *Little Rock:* Scoops Carry, Volly De Faut, Al Hibbler, Alex Hill, Snub Mosley, Walter Norris; *Pine Bluff:* Les Spann; *Smackover:* Eddie Wasserman; *Texarkana:* Jasper Taylor.

CALIFORNIA—*Antonito:* Joe Mondragon; *Berkeley:* David van Kreidt; *Brawley:* Howard Rumsey; *Concord:* Dave Brubeck, Howard Brubeck; *Fairmead:* Bob Helm; *Gardena:* Art Pepper; *Gilroy:* Ivie Anderson; *Inglewood:* Zoot Sims; *Lodi:* Pat Yankee; *Long Beach:* Larry Bunker, Buddy Catlett.

Los Angeles: Dennis Budimir, Walter Benton, Gil Bernal, Clark Burroughs, Billy Byers, Buddy Collette, Joe Comfort, Eddie Cano, Eric Dolphy, Don Ellis, Gil Fuller, Herb Geller, Dexter Gordon, Norman Granz, Chico Hamilton, Toni Harper, Hampton Hawes, Billy Higgins, Karl Kiffe, Jimmy Knepper, Larry Marable, Warne Marsh, Ruben McFall, Jack McVea, Anthony Ortega, Frankie Ortega, George Probert, Tony Rizzi, Ernie Royal, Herbie Steward, Paul Togawa, Bill Trujillo, Kitty White, Britt Woodman, Bill Douglass.

Manhattan Beach: Bob Keene; *Monterey:* Virgil Gonsalves; *Oakland:* Russ Garcia, Fred Higuera, John Marabuto, Johnny Markham, Marty Paich, Jerome Richardson, Wally Rose, Stan Wilson; *Olive:* Bill Holman; *Ontario:* Bob Graettinger; *Orange:* Chuck Flores; *Palermo:* Turk Murphy; *Pasadena:* Mary Ford, Bob Morse; *Puente:* Herb Flemming; *Redlands:* Eddie Beal; *Richmond:* Jerry Dodgion; *Riverside:* Gil Melle; *San Diego:* Ann Richards, Paul Smith; *San Francisco:* Bill Castagnino, Vince Cattolica, Paul Desmond, Eddie Duran, Don Friedman, Squire Gersh, Vince Guaraldi, Ruth Olay, Bill Perkins, Carson Smith, Earl Watkins; *San Jose:* Fred Dutton; *Santa Barbara:* Eddie Hubble; *Santa Cruz:* Lu Watters; *Santa Monica:* Don Prell; *Santa Rosa:* Julie London; *Vallejo:* Johnny Otis; *Van Nuys:* Duane Tatro.

COLORADO—*Denver:* Paul Lingle, Paul Quinichette, Paul Whiteman; *Lamar:* Marvin Ash.

CONNECTICUT—*Bridgeport:* Tom Stewart; *Cromwell:* Hal McIntyre; *Danbury:* Hilton Jefferson, Al Klink; *Greenwich:* Alonzo Levister, Dick Wellstood; *Hartford:* David Allen, Walter Lee Bolden, Dick Cary, Johnny Mehegan, Emil Richards; *Manchester:* Wayne Andre; *Meriden:* Ben Homer; *Middletown:* Tony Pastor; *New Britain:* Conrad Gozzo; *New Haven:* Sonny Berman, Bob Carter, Les Elgart, Eddie Gibbs, Pete Jolly, Buddy Morrow, Donn Trenner; *New London:* Gus Bivona, Larry Elgart; *Norwalk:* Horace Silver, Billy Ver Planck; *Putnam:* Manzie Johnson; *Waterbury:* Phil Bodner, Stan Freeman; *West Haven:* Bernie Leighton; *Westport:* Buell Neidlinger.

DELAWARE—*Wilmington:* Clifford Brown, Betty Roche.

DISTRICT OF COLUMBIA—*Washington:* Jimmy Cobb, Will Marion Cook, Duke Ellington, Mercer Ellington, Freddie Gambrell, Henry Goodwin, Otto Hardwicke, Rick Henderson, Buck Hill, Claude Hopkins, Cliff Jackson, Osie Johnson, Marky Markowitz, Jack Nimitz, Leo Parker, Andy Razaf, Charlie Rouse, Ira Sullivan, Rob Swope, Billy Taylor (bass).

FLORIDA—*Dunnellon:* Sil Austin; *Jacksonville:* Blind Blake, Jackie Davis, Al Hall, Sam Jones, Dwike Mitchell, Lord Westbrook; *Key West:* Al Dreares, Fats Navarro; *Leesburg:* Fred Norman; *Miami:* Panama Francis, Jimmy Garrison, George Kelly, Blue Mitchell; *Palatka:* George Tucker; *Pensacola:* Junior Cook, Gigi Gryce; *Punta Gorda:* Arthur Whetsol; *St. Petersburg:* Buster Cooper, Idrees Sulieman; *Tampa:* Julian Adderley, Nat Adderley, Lem Davis, Machito.

GEORGIA—*Albany:* Ray Charles, Harry James; *Americus:* Gene Gifford; *Athens:* Lou McGarity; *Atlanta:* Perry Bradford, Eddie Chamblee, Gene Gammage, Eddie Heywood, Jay C. Higginbotham, Duke Pearson, Tampa Red; *Burkeville:* Freddie Guy; *Claxton:* Jabbo Smith; *Cordele:* Joe Williams; *Cuthbert:* Fletcher Henderson, Horace Henderson; *Eastman:* Hank Mobley; *Greensville:* Eli Robinson; *Hampton:* Speckled Red; *Macon:* Emmett Berry, Little Richard; *Moultrie:* Teddy Brannon; *Savannah:* Lee Blair, Kaiser Marshall, Johnny Mercer, James Moody, Sahib Shihab, Trummy Young; *Social Circle:* Red Wootten.

HAWAII—*Honolulu:* Danny Barcelona.

IDAHO—*Boise:* Jim Bates, Norm Bates; *Moscow:* Jack Perciful; *Pocatello:* Bob Bates.

ILLINOIS—*Alton:* Miles Davis; *Beardstown:* Red Norvo; *Carbondale:* Frankie Trumbauer.

Chicago: Hayes Alvis, Albert Ammons, Gene Ammons, Eddie Baker, Lavern Baker, Vic Berton, Josh Billings, Buddy Bregman, Ronnell Bright, Boyce Brown, Scoville Brown, Joe Burton, Happy Caldwell, Jack Costanzo, Israel Crosby, Richard Davis, Will Davis, Dorothy Donegan, Bud Freeman, Russ Freeman, John Frigo, Benny Goodman, Bennie Green, Lil Green, Johnny Griffin, Bill Henderson, Mel Henke, Darnell Howard, Ina Ray Hutton, Tom Jefferson, John Jenkins, Jimmy Jones, Jo Jones, Quincy Jones, Richard M. Jones, Clifford Jordan, Lee Katzman, Lee Konitz, Irene Kral, Roy Kral, Gene Krupa, Anton Lada, Frankie Laine, Ronny Lang, Lou Levy, Meade Lux Lewis, Abbey Lincoln, Ray Linn, Curtis Lowe, Junior Mance, Joe Marsala, Marty Marsala, Dick Marx, Al McKibbon, Dick McPartland, Jimmy McPartland, Mezz Mezzrow, Skip Morr, Audrey Morris, Ray Nance, Jack Noren, Floyd O'Brien, Hod O'Brien, Anita O'Day, Frank Orchard, Truck Parham, Gil Rodin, Ben Pollack, A. K. Salim, Tommy Shepard, Mickey Simonetta, Bill Russo, Leon Sash, Muggsy Spanier, Les Strand, Joe Sullivan, Ed Thigpen, Mel Tormé, Cy Touff, Lennie Tristano, Jerry Valentine, Wilbur Ware, Bobby White, Gene Wright, Jimmy Yancey, Eldee Young, Julian Priester.

Chicago Heights: George Barnes, Johnny Mince, Johnny Pate; *Danville:* Rosy McHargue, Jack Pettis, Bobby Short; *Du Quoin:* Les Hite, Teddy Roy; *East St. Louis:* Elmer Schoebel; *Evanston:* Kay Davis, Tom Montgomery, Joe Rushton; *Freeport:* Corky Hale; *Highland Park:* Pepper Adams; *Irving:* Buddy Cole; *La Grange:* John Lewis; *Macomb:* Al Sears; *Mount Vernon:* Dick Wilson; *Oak Park:* Dave Tough; *Roanoke:* Glen Gray; *Robinson:* Skip Martin; *Rock Falls:* Louis Bellson; *Rock Island:* Franz Jackson; *Springfield:* June Christy, Barrett Deems; *Sumner:* Frank Melrose; *Venice:* Vernon Brown.

INDIANA—*Batesville:* Joe Howard; *Bloomington:* Hoagy Carmichael; *Clinton:* Danny Polo; *Crawfordsville:* Sidney de Paris, Wilbur de Paris; *East Chicago:* Gene Allen, Willie Cook; *Evansville:* Sid Catlett; *Fort Wayne:* Rudy Jackson; *Gary:* Mousie Alexander, Johnny Bothwell; *Goodland:* Eddie Condon; *Greenfield:* Richard Curry; *Indianapolis:* Trigger Alpert, Dave Baker, Benny Barth, J. J. Johnson, Reunald Jones, Wes Montgomery, Monk Montgomery, Carl Perkins, Bobby Sherwood, Noble Sissle, Leroy Vinnegar; *Logansport:* Med Flory; *Michigan City:* Dick Cathcart; *Mishawaka:* Conte Candoli, Pete Candoli; *Peru:* Speed Webb; *Portland:* Pete Daily; *Richmond:* Andrew Simpkins; *South Bend:* Jerry Coker; *Terre Haute:* Claude Thornhill; *Tipton:* John Bunch; *Valparaiso:* Milt Bernhardt.

IOWA—*Clarinda:* Glenn Miller; *Council Bluffs:* Addison Farmer, Art Farmer; *Davenport:* Bix Beiderbecke, Bob Petersen; *Des Moines:* Max Bennett; *Dubuque:* John Graas; *Keokuk:* Jack Buck; *Ladora:* Floyd Bean; *Lenox:* Rod Cless; *Mason City:* Jack Jenney; *Scandia:* Eddie Barefield; *Sioux City:* Big Miller.

KANSAS—*Caney:* Clancy Hayes; *Chapman:* Kansas Fields; *Cherokee:* Page Cavanaugh; *El Dorado:* Jack Marshall; *Emporia:* Roy Burnes; *Eskridge:* Tommy Douglas; *Independence:* Maxwell Davis; *Kansas City:* Bob Brookmeyer, Charlie Parker; *Lawrence:* Lawrence Brown; *Marysville:* Moondog; *Parsons:* Buck Clayton; *Salina:* Herbie Harper; *Topeka:* George Wettling, Buddy Wise; *Wichita:* Stan Kenton, Ray Sims.

KENTUCKY—*Bowling Green:* Hank Duncan; *Flemingsburg:* Herman Chittison; *Lexington:* Dan Burley, Edgar Hayes; *Louisville:* Mickey Baker, Lou Bush, Al Casey, Lionel Hampton, Jimmy Harrison, Helen Humes, Jonah Jones, George Mitchell, Jimmy Raney, Johnny Smith (organ), Buck Washington; *Mayfield:* Dick Vance; *Newport:* Andy Kirk; *Paducah:* Harry Lookofsky, Kas Malone, Fate Marable, Matty Matlock; *Paris:* Bill Coleman; *Pineville:* Charlie Queener.

LOUISIANA—*Abend:* King Oliver; *Alexandria:* Henderson Chambers; *Algiers:* Red Allen, John Lindsay, Memphis Minnie; *Baton Rouge:* Joe Darensbourg; *Broussard:* Illinois Jacquet, Russell Jacquet; *Bunkie:*

Zutty Singleton; *Deeringe:* Jim Robinson; *Gulfport:* Jelly Roll Morton; *Harvey:* Monk Hazel; *Kentwood:* Little Brother Montgomery; *Lafourche:* Papa Celestin; *Lake Charles:* Papa Jac Assunto, Nellie Lutcher; *La Place:* Kid Ory; *Lutheran:* Leon Rappolo; *Mandeville:* Tommy Ladnier; *McCall:* Pops Foster; *Milneburg:* Sharkey Bonano; *Monroe:* Carl Fontana; *Mooringsport:* Leadbelly; *New Iberia:* Elsie Smith.

New Orleans: Alvin Alcorn, Tony Almerico, Louis Armstrong, Sidney Arodin, Frank Assunto, Fred Assunto, Bob Astor, George Baquet, Paul Barbarin, Danny Barker, Al Belletto, Ray Bauduc, Sidney Bechet, Barney Bigard, Buddy Bolden, Sterling Bose, Connee Boswell, Rabbit Brown, Steve Brown, Tom Brown, George Brunis, Willie Bryant, Raymond Burke, Sam Butera, Papa Mutt Carey, Savannah Churchill, Emile Christian, Lee Collins, Jack Delaney, Sidney Desvignes, Baby Dodds, Johnny Dodds, Natty Dominique, Fats Domino, Champion Jack Dupree, Honore Dutrey, Eddie Edwards, Irving Fazola, Pete Fountain, Vernel Fournier, Sal Franzella, Ed Garland, George Girard, Armand Hug, Tony Jackson, Mahalia Jackson, Preston Jackson, Bunk Johnson, Dink Johnson, Lonnie Johnson, Plas Johnson, Snags Jones, Freddie Keppard, Papa Laine, Julian Laine, Nappy Lamare, Nick La Rocca, John Levy, George Lewis, Steve Lewis, Kid Shots Madison, Sherwood Mangiapane, Wingy Manone, Paul Mares, Lawrence Marrero, Stanley Mendelson, Lizzie Miles, Eddie Miller, Punch Miller, Al Morgan, Big Eye Nelson, Joe Newman, Albert Nicholas, Wooden Joe Nicholas, Jimmie Noone, Tony Parenti, Alcide Pavageau, Buddy Petit, Santo Pecora, Fats Pichon, Alphonse Picou, Pony Poindexter, Benny Powell, Lloyd Price, Leon Prima, Louis Prima, Henry (Kid) Rena, Bud Scott, Harry Shields, Larry Shields, Omer Simeon, Edmond Souchon, Tony Spargo, Johnny St. Cyr, Bob Thomas, Johnny Wiggs, George (Fox) Williams, Spencer Williams, Albert Wynn, Lee Young, Roy Zimmerman.

Plaquemine: Clarence Williams; *Reserve:* Edmund Hall, Herb Hall; *Sellers:* Ram Hall, Tubby Hall; *St. James:* Wellman Braud; *Wallace:* Pleasant Joseph.

MAINE—*Donaldsonville:* Dave Nelson; *Houlton:* John Benson Brooks; *Portland:* Cliff Leeman.

MARYLAND—*Annapolis:* Bernard Addison; *Baltimore:* Don Abney, Eubie Blake, Pete Brown, Ethel Ennis, Don Ewell, Ken Hanna, Clyde Hart, Billie Holiday, Dick Katz, John Kirby, Ellis Larkins, Bill Mackel, Eddie McFadden, Elmer Snowden, George Stevenson, Joe Turner (piano), Chick Webb; *Brighton:* Benny Waters; *Hagerstown:* Earl Swope.

MASSACHUSETTS—*Attleboro:* Ray Conniff; *Billerica:* Brad Gowans.

Boston: Ruby Braff, Harry Carney, Serge Chaloff, Bobby Donaldson, Paul Gonsalves, Joe Gordon, Jerry Gray, Charlie Holmes, Teddi King, Dave Lambert, Jack Lesberg, Charlie Mariano, Toots Mondello, Phil Napoleon, Bobby Nichols, Milt Raskin, Arnold Ross, Sonny Stitt, Lloyd Trotman, Turk Van Lake, Frances Wayne, George Wein.

Brockton: Sonny Dunham, Dick Johnson, Max Kaminsky, Boomie Richman; *Cambridge:* Ed Higgins, Johnny Hodges; *Chicopee Falls:* Teddy Charles; *Danvers:* Dick Twardzik; *Dorchester:* Sam Margolis; *Framingham:* Marshall Brown; *Gloucester:* Herb Pomeroy; *Great Barrington:* Shorty Rogers; *Haverhill:* Teddy Kotick; *Holyoke:* Chuck Andrus; *Lawrence:* Leonard Bernstein; *Lynn:* Phil Darois, Joe Dixon, Bob Zieff; *Mansfield:* John Neves; *Medford:* Peter Littman, Hal McKusick; *Milbury:* Nick Fatool; *Milford:* Boots Mussulli; *Monson:* Sal Salvador; *Newton:* Ralph Burns; *Norwell:* Lloyd Morales; *Roxbury:* Bob Alexander, Roy Haynes; *Saugus:* Johnny Rae; *Somerville:* Irving Ashby, Nick Jerret, Dick Nash, Ted Nash, Nat Pierce; *South Braintree:* Leon Merian; *Springfield:* Joe Morello, Phil Woods; *Woburn:* Don Stratton; *Worcester:* Jaki Byard, Frank Capp, Barbara Carroll, Wendell Culley, Bob Dukoff, Don Fagerquist, Harry Sheppard.

MICHIGAN—*Bangor:* Hall Overton; *Battle Creek:* Sy Oliver; *Benton Harbor:* Bill Dowdy, Gene Harris.

Detroit: Dorothy Ashby, Everett Barksdale, Kenny Burrell, Donald Byrd, Barbara Dane, Sam Donahue, Ken Errair, Tommy, Flanagan, Curtis Fuller, Slim Gaillard, Charles Greenlee, Roland Hanna, Barry Harris, Louis Hayes, Al Hayse, Major Holley, Frank Isola, Milt Jackson, Oliver Jackson, Herb Jeffries, Sonny Red Kyner, Hugh Lawson, Willie Maiden, Art Mardigan, Jack Millman, J. R. Monterose, Jack Montrose, Frank Morelli, Sandy Mosse, Dave Pike, Terry Pollard, Della Reese, Timmie Rogers, Frank Rosolino, Bill Stegmeyer, Lucky Thompson, Doug Watkins, Julius Watkins, Bob Zurke, Bernie McKinney.

Ferndale: Ron Carter; *Flint:* Betty Carter; *Grand Rapids:* Arno Marsh; *Lansing:* Big Nick Nicholas; *Norway:* Art Van Damme; *Pontiac:* Elvin Jones, Hank Jones, Thad Jones; *Port Huron:* Earl Coleman; *Saginaw:* Chummy MacGregor.

MINNESOTA—*Crystal Bay:* Tommy Talbert; *Duluth:* Sadik Hakim; *Halstead:* Skitch Henderson; *Mahnomen:* Jim Dahl; *Minneapolis:* Bill Blakkestad, Bob Davis, John Murtaugh, Shorty Sherock; *Spring Valley:* Doc Evans; *St. Paul:* Harry Blons, Johnny Plonsky; *Watkins:* Tommy Pederson.

MISSISSIPPI—*Byhalia:* Mike Bryan; *Clarksdale:* John Lee Hooker, Lurlean Hunter, Robert Johnson, Brother John Sellers; *Crawford:* Joe Williams (guitar-singer); *Greenwood:* Guitar Slim; *Indianola:* Brew Moore; *Jackson:* Teddy Edwards, Kokomo Arnold; *Laurel:* Mundell Lowe; *Mayhew:* Moon Mullens; *McCombs:* Bo Diddley; *Meridian:* Cleo Brown; *Red Banks:* Gus Cannon; *Rolling Fork:* Muddy Waters; *Rosedale:* Red

Holt; *Scott:* Big Bill Broonzy; *Shelby:* Gerald Wilson; *Tippo:* Mose Allison; *Tupelo:* Fred Beckett, Elvis Presley; *Vicksburg:* Milt Hinton; *West Point:* Jock Carruthers; *Woodville:* Lester Young; *Yazoo City:* Tommy McClennan.

MISSOURI—*Brunswick:* Wilbur Sweatman; *Cape Girardeau:* Jess Stacy; *Fulton:* Jimmie Lunceford; *Gallatin:* Walter Page; *Glasgow:* Wild Bill Davis; *Hamburg:* Ralph Sutton; *Ironton:* Charlie Creath; *Joplin:* Langston Hughes; *Louisiana:* Eddie South.

Kansas City: Frank Butler, Chris Connor, Curtis Counce, Billy Graham, Luther Henderson, Ed Inge, Pete Johnson, Julia Lee, Harlan Leonard, Melba Liston, Billy Mitchell, Bennie Moten (bandleader), Tiny Parham, Dick Shreve, Frank Teschemacher, Joe Turner (singer), Jim Daddy Walker, Jack Washington, Leo Watson, Ben Webster, Paul Webster, Frank Wess, Elmon Wright, Lamar Wright Jr.

Marshall: Vern Friley; *Mt. Moriah:* Leith Stevens.

St. Louis: Shorty Baker, Chuck Berry, Jimmy Blanton, Milt Buckner, Ted Buckner, Buddy Childers, Wallace Eckhardt, Jimmy Forrest, Sammy Gardner, Bob Gordon, Jimmy Gourley, Dewey Jackson, Wendell Marshall, Red McKenzie, Louis Metcalf, Velma Middleton, Oliver Nelson, Lennie Niehaus, Singleton Palmer, Mouse Randolph, Pee Wee Russell, Gene Sedric, Arvell Shaw, Floyd Smith, Don Stovall, Clark Terry, Cal Tjader, Ernie Wilkins, Juice Wilson.

St. Joseph: Coleman Hawkins; *Sedalia:* Jack Bland; *Trenton:* Yank Lawson; *Webster Groves:* Joe Thomas (trumpet).

MONTANA—*Billings:* Bob Enevoldsen; *Red Lodge:* Dick Lammi; *Shelby:* Red Kelly; *Sidney:* Richie Crabtree; *Stevensville:* Burt Bales.

NEBRASKA—*Belgrade:* Chuck Gentry; *Cedar County:* Dale Jones; *Falls City:* Pee Wee Erwin; *Hastings:* Neal Hefti; *Lexington:* Merle Koch; *Lincoln:* Betty Bennett; *Omaha:* Junior Raglin; *Pender:* Monty Budwig; *Royal:* Jeri Southern.

NEVADA—*Jarbidge:* Ralph Pena; *Winnemucca:* Vernon Alley.

NEW HAMPSHIRE—*Derry:* Buddy Stewart.

NEW JERSEY—*Atlantic City:* Joe Albany, Joe Benjamin, Chris Columbus, Sam Most, Gene Quill; *Bayonne:* Arnold Fishkin, Joya Sherrill; *Camden:* Butch Ballard, Nelson Boyd, Buddy De Franco, Larry Fotine, Jimmy Lyon; *East Orange:* Cozy Cole, Walter Davis Jr.; *Elizabeth:* Shad Collins, Herbie Fields, Sam Woodyard; *Englewood:* Slam Stewart; *Garfield:* Tony Aless; *Hackensack:* Whitey Mitchell; *Hasbrouck Heights:* John Carisi; *Hoboken:* Frank Sinatra; *Jersey City:* Herbie Haymer, Sonny Igoe, Ed Shaughnessy, Phil Urso, Moe Wechsler; *Kearney:* Tony Mottola; *Long Branch:* June Clark, Sonny Greer; *Montclair:* Faye Adams; *Morristown:* Roger Wolfe Kahn, Charlie Persip, Tony Scott, Bobby Tucker.

Newark: Vinnie Burke, Mike Cuozzo, Bill Finegan, Don Goldie, Babs Gonzales, Al Haig, Carl Kress, Scott La Faro, Matty Malneck, Barry Miles, Bobby Plater, Ike Quebec, Wayne Shorter, Joe Tarto, Sarah Vaughan, Jerry Wald.

New Brunswick: Ralph Blaze, James P. Johnson; *Newton:* Will Bradley; *Nutley:* Jackie Paris; *Oradell:* Nelson Riddle; *Orangeburg:* Tony Fruscella; *Paterson:* Ralph Martin; *Perth Amboy:* Morris Nanton, Don Sebesky; *Plainfield:* Bill Evans, George van Eps; *Red Bank:* Count Basie; *Somerville:* Don Elliott, Mort Herbert; *Trenton:* John Coles, George Romanis, Jack Sperling; *Weehawken:* Hal Stein.

NEW MEXICO—*Tucumcari:* Bob Scobey.

NEW YORK—*Albany:* Dick Kenney; *Bay Shore, L.I.:* Fran Thorne; *Bronx:* Burt Collins, Bobby Darin, George Devens, Bill Dolney, Clyde Lombardi, Marlowe Morris, Aaron Sachs, Bobby Scott, Bill Triglia, Joe Venuto, Johnny Windhurst.

Brooklyn: Ahmed Abdul-Malik, Danny Bank, Ray Beckenstein, Al Beldiny, Artie Bernstein, Larry Clinton, Al Cohn, Gene Di Novi, Arthur Edgehill, Billy Exiner, Charlie Fowlkes, Leonard Gaskin, George Gershwin, Terry Gibbs, Tommy Goodman, Walter Gross, George Handy, Ernie Henry, Marty Holmes, Lena Horne, Jerry Jerome, Willie Jones, Duke Jordan, Fred Katz, Irv Kluger, Joe Knight, Mitch Leigh, Herbie Lovelle, Gloria Lynne, Herbie Mann, Reese Markewich, Andy Marsala, Lennie McBrowne, Jackie Mills, Jeff Morton, Marty Napoleon, Teddy Napoleon, Jimmy Nottingham, Cecil Payne, Dave Pell, Flip Phillips, Bernie Privin, Frank Rehak, Buddy Rich, Andy Russo, Sonny Russo, Red Richards, Max Roach, Eddie Sauter, Mickey Sheen, Randy Weston, Sol Yaged, Si Zentner.

Buffalo: Dave Bowman, Frankie Dunlop, Jim Hall, Mel Lewis, Sam Noto; *Cohoes:* Carmen Mastren; *Delevan:* Rusty Dedrick; *East Durham:* Blossom Dearie; *Freeport, L.I.:* Teddy Bunn; *Geneva:* John Coppola; *Glens Falls:* Teo Macero; *Goshen:* Willie The Lion Smith; *Harrison:* Beverly Kenney; *Hollis, L.I.:* Bob Corwin; *Hornell:* Bill Barber; *Huntington, L.I.:* Wally Cirillo, Kenny Davern, Maurice Purtill; *Jamaica, L.I.:* Don Michaels; *Jackson Heights:* Gunther Schuller; *Little Falls:* Casper Reardon; *Long Island City:* Vito Price; *Mount Vernon:* Vinnie Dean, Bob Freedman, Sal Mosca; *New Rochelle:* Stan Rubin, George Treadwell.

New York City: Lee Abrams, Ray Abrams, Van Alexander, Steve Allen, Danny Alvin, Bill Anthony, Arthur Anton, Buddy Arnold, Ozzie Bailey, Dave Barbour, Charlie Barnet, Ray Barretto, Billy Bauer, Sam Benskin, Elmer Bernstein, Denzil Best, Walter Bishop, Eddie Bonnemere, Bill Bradley, Percy Brice, Sascha Burland, Joe Bushkin, Jay Cameron, Frank Carlson,

Benny Carter, Lee Castle, Jim Chapin, Gil Coggins, Cy Coleman, Rudy Collins, Eddie (Lockjaw) Davis, Sammy Davis, Jr., Jesse Drakes, Ray Draper, Kenny Drew, George Duvivier, Allen Eager, Julian Euell, Marty Flax, Frank Flynn, Jerry Fuller, Dick Garcia, John Glasel, Bernie Glow, Tony Gottuso, Johnny Guarnieri, Bob Haggart, Adelaide Hall, Lenny Hambro, Benny Harris, Lennie Hayton, Bobby Henderson, Paul Horn, Elmo Hope, Margie Hyams, Dick Hyman, Chuck Israels, Chubby Jackson, Nat Jaffe, Conrad Janis, Ron Jefferson, Freddy Jenkins, Walter Johnson, Eddie Jones, Steve Jordan, Tiny Kahn, Manny Klein, Paul Knopf, Bertell Knox, Steve Lacy, Pete La Roca, Freeman Lee, Elaine Leighton, Harvey Leonard, Al Levitt, Jerry Lloyd, Joe Loco, Jimmy Lytell, Gildo Mahones, Johnny Mandel, Howie Mann, Shelly Manne, Dante Martucci, Earl May, Jackie McLean, Carmen McRae, Helen Merrill, Red Mitchell, Benny Morton, Abe Most, Benny Moten (bass), Roger King Mozian, Gerry Mulligan, Tricky Sam Nanton, Herbie Nichols, Remo Palmier, Sonny Payne, Bill Pemberton, John Pisano, Jimmy Powell, Al Porcino, Red Press, Clarence Profit, Bob Prince, Bud Powell, Mel Powell, Richie Powell, Rudy Powell, Specs Powell, Russell Procope, Tito Puente, Joe Puma, Freddie Redd, Allan Reuss, Dannie Richmond, Joe Roland, Adrian Rollini, Arthur Rollini, Sonny Rollins, Curly Russell, Edgar Sampson, Hal Schaefer, Dave Schildkraut, Sol Schlinger, Charlie Shavers, Artie Shaw, Dick Sherman, Hymie Shertzer, Joe Shulman, Frank Signorelli, Lou Singer, Charlie Smith, Teddy Sommer, Bobby Stark, Alvin Stoller, Dick Sutton, Sylvia Syms, Arthur Taylor, Cecil Taylor, Chuck Thompson, Sylvia Vanderpool, Mal Waldron, Fats Waller, Helen Ward, Herb Wasserman, Chuck Wayne, Gerald Wiggins, Bob Wilber, Joe Yukl, Zeke Zarchy, Mel Zelnick.

Niagara Falls: Tommy Tedesco, Chauncey Morehouse; *Ossining:* Buddy Weed; *Pleasantville:* Morgana King; *Port Chester:* Keter Betts; *Rochester:* Ted Brown, Cab Calloway, Hank D'Amico, Bill Rubenstein, Alec Wilder; *Rockaway:* Lex Humphries; *Roosevelt, L.I.:* Miff Mole; *Schenectady:* Johnny Richards; *Staten Island:* Eric Dixon, Charlie Kennedy; *Syracuse:* Peanuts Hucko, Louis Mucci; *Tarrytown:* Carmen Leggio; *Tuckahoe:* Connie Kaye; *Utica:* Frank Divito; *White Plains:* Sal Pace; *Wyoming:* Jim Timmens; *Yonkers:* Eddie Bert, Elmer James, Shadow Wilson.

NORTH CAROLINA—*Asheville:* Bill Napier; *Badin:* Lou Donaldson; *Durham:* Ike Carpenter, Sonny Terry; *Greensboro:* Tal Farlow; *Greensville:* Billy Taylor (piano); *Hamlet:* John Coltrane; *Kinston:* Skeeter Best, Tab Smith; *Method:* Eddie Wilcox; *Nashville:* Bill Harris (guitar); *Raleigh:* Loumell Morgan, Pee Wee Moore; *Rockingham:* Blind Boy Fuller; *Rocky Mount:* Thelonious Monk; *Shelby:* John Best; *Thomasville:* Linton Garner; *Washington:* Freddie Moore; *Wilmington:* Percy Heath.

NORTH DAKOTA—*Jamestown:* Peggy Lee; *Minot:* Mary Osborne; *Woolford:* Doc West.

OHIO—*Akron:* Ike Isaacs, Tommy Reynolds; *Chillicothe:* Nancy Wilson; *Cincinnati:* Frank Foster, Jimmy Mundy, Dave Pearson, George Russell, Bill Slapin, Mamie Smith; *Circleville:* Ted Lewis.

Cleveland: Benny Bailey, Sandy Block, Tadd Dameron, Bill De Arango, Joe Dolney, Morey Feld, Mal Fitch, Sanford Gold, Buster Harding, Bill Hardman, Screamin' Jay Hawkins, Fats Heard, Wes Hensel, Bull Moose Jackson, Hank Mancini, Lyle Ritz, Freddie Webster.

Columbus: Bobby Byrne, Harry Edison; *Dayton:* J. C. Heard, Bud Shank, Billy Strayhorn, Bootie Wood, Snooky Young; *Defiance:* Wild Bill Davison; *Dover:* Lee Roy (Leo Anthony); *Hamilton:* Carl Halen; *Lorain:* Ralph Flanagan; *Martins Ferry:* Joe Muranyi; *Middletown:* Billy Butterfield; *Mt. Healthy:* Pee Wee Hunt; *Newark:* Jon Hendricks; *New Philadelphia:* Max Miller; *Oxford:* Maurice Rocco; *Piqua:* Donald Mills, Harry Mills, Herbert Mills; *Portsmouth:* Stuff Smith; *Ripley:* Joe Smith; *Steubenville:* Paul Howard; *Springfield:* Garvin Bushell, Don Frye, Quentin Jackson, Cecil Scott, O'Neil Spencer, Sir Charles Thompson, Earl Warren; *Toledo:* Bill Takas, Art Tatum, Gene Taylor; *Xenia:* Una Mae Carlisle, Vic Dickenson; *Youngstown:* Charles Bateman, Dick Healey, Kitty Noble, George Syran; *Zanesville:* Andy Gibson, Phil Sunkel.

OKLAHOMA—*Ardmore:* Howard Smith; *Bessie:* Moe Schneider; *Boley:* Claude Jones; *Calumet:* Dempsey Wright; *Dougherty:* Kay Starr; *Eagle City:* Ed Lewis; *Enid:* Pat Moran; *Fort Gibson:* Lee Wiley; *Guthrie:* Joe Liggins; *Haskell:* John Simmons; *McAlester:* Lea Mathews, Dave Matthews; *Muskogee:* Aaron Bell, Don Byas, Barney Kessel, Jay McShann, Joe Thomas (tenor sax), Foots Thomas; *Oklahoma City:* Don Cherry, Wardell Gray, Don Lamond, Marilyn Moore, Jimmy Rushing, Stan Wrightsman; *Okmulgee:* Oscar Pettiford; *Sapulpa:* Marshall Royal; *Tulsa:* Earl Bostic, Howard McGhee, Hal Singer; *Yale:* Chet Baker.

OREGON—*Arlington:* Doc Severinsen; *Dallas:* Johnnie Ray; *Portland:* Norma Carson, Lorraine Geller, Jean Hoffman, Phil Moore.

PENNSYLVANIA—*Allentown:* Lillian Briggs; *Altoona:* Jon Eardley; *Arnold:* John Costa; *Atlas:* Eddie Costa; *Bellefonte:* John Mills; *Bentleyville:* Ray Anthony; *Bethlehem:* Harry (Father) White; *Chester:* Ethel Waters; *Colwyn:* Joe Wilder; *Duquesne:* Earl Hines; *Duryea:* Ronnie Greb; *Germantown:* Leroy Lovett; *Hanover:* Brick Fleagle; *Harrisburg:* Art Davis, Bobby Troup; *Herminie:* Sonny Clark; *Homestead:* Maxine Sullivan; *Jeannette:* Slide Hampton; *Jersey Shore:* Jim Buffington; *Kane:* Al Norris; *Kingston:* Dan Terry; *Lancaster:* Pete Bielmann, Abe Lincoln, Peck Morrison; *Marietta:*

Alan Dawson; *Meadville:* Paul Moer; *Newcastle:* Ralph Gari, Billy Usselton; *Norristown:* Jimmy Smith.

Philadelphia: John Acea, Dave Amram, Ernie Andrews, Donald Bailey, Billy Bean, Dave Black, James Bond, Beryl Booker, Ray Bryant, Tommy Bryant, Joe "Bebop" Carroll, Warren Covington, Jimmy De Brest, Willie Dennis, Jimmy De Preist, Bill Doggett, Johnny Eaton, Ziggy Elman, Herman Foster, Charles Gaines, Nat Gershman, Stan Getz, Benny Golson, Buddy Greco, Henry Grimes, Shafi Hadi, Art Harris, Bill Harris, Al Heath, Jimmy Heath, Bill Hitz, Calvin Jackson, Eddie Jefferson, Charlie Johnson, Jimmie Johnson (drums), Philly Joe Jones, Richie Kamuca, Billy Kyle, Eddie Lang, John La Porta, Elliot Lawrence, Stan Levey, Perry Lopez, Mary Ann McCall, Teddy McRae, Jimmy Merritt, Louis Mitchell, Lee Morgan, John Ore, Luckey Roberts, Tommy Potter, Jimmy Rowser, Adolph Sandole, Dennis Sandole, Thornel Schwartz, Shirley Scott, Jerry Segal, Red Rodney, Billy Root, Lou Stein, Rex Stewart, Bobby Timmons, Nick Travis, Charlie Ventura, Clara Ward, Lem Winchester, Jimmy Woode, Specs Wright.

Pittsburgh: Art Blakey, Ray Brown, Paul Chambers, Kenny Clarke, Bob Cooper, Sonny Dallas, Billy Eckstine, Roy Eldridge, Jerry Fielding, Barry Galbraith, Erroll Garner, Joe Harris, Ahmad Jamal, Alex Kallao, Dodo Marmarosa, Billy May, Horace Parlan, Babe Russin, Bull Ruther, Eddie Safranski, Dakota Staton, Stan Turrentine, Tom Turrentine, Mary Lou Williams.

Reading: Arthur Schutt; *Reinerton:* Les Brown; *Scranton:* Sonny Burke; *Shenandoah:* Jimmy Dorsey, Tommy Dorsey; *Uniontown:* Joe Thomas (tenor sax); *Waynesburg:* John Wilson (trumpet); *Wilkes-Barre:* Jimmy Campbell; *Wyomissing:* Dick Hafer.

RHODE ISLAND—*Providence:* Angelo Di Pippo, Bobby Hackett, Joe Maini, Dick Meldonian, Paul Motian; *Woonsocket:* Dave McKenna.

SOUTH CAROLINA—*Aiken:* Bubber Miley; *Charleston:* Julian Dash, Ronnie Free, Freddie Green, Chippie Hill, Fud Livingston, Willie Smith (alto sax); *Cheraw:* Dizzy Gillespie; *Columbia:* Snookum Russell, Webster Young; *Dillon:* Jimmy Hamilton; *Darlington:* Buddy Johnson, Ella Johnson; *Florence:* Taft Jordan; *Georgetown:* Traps Trappier; *Greenville:* Cat Anderson, Josh White; *McCormick:* Johnny Letman; *Somerville:* Sandy Williams; *Union:* Jimmy Shirley.

SOUTH DAKOTA—*Faith:* Boyd Raeburn.

TENNESSEE—*Bessie:* Bob Shoffner; *Bristol:* Ulysses Livingston; *Centerville:* Dickie Wells; *Chattanooga:* Lovie Austin, Yusef Lateef, Wilfred Middlebrooks, Bill Oldham, Bessie Smith; *Columbia:* Burnie Peacock; *Dyersburg:* Walter Fuller; *Jackson:* Big Maybelle, Sonny Boy Williamson; *Kingsport:* Cripple Clarence Lofton; *Knoxville:* Ida Cox, Brownie McGhee; *Lexington:* Sam The Man Taylor.

Memphis: Johnny Ace, Lil Armstrong, Buster Bailey, Evans Bradshaw, Rozelle Claxton, George Coleman, Jimmy Crawford, Sonny Criss, Charles Crosby, Johnny Dunn, Alberta Hunter, George Joiner, Booker Little, Memphis Slim, Calvin Newborn, Fred Robinson, Fred Saunders, Will Shade, Louis Smith, Erskine Tate, Washboard Sam, Al Williams, John Williams (alto sax).

Nashville: Ed Allen, Leroy Carr, Doc Cheatham; *Oakdale:* King Pleasure; *Wartrace:* Jimmy Cleveland; *Whiteville:* Phineas Newborn.

TEXAS—*Amarillo:* Gene Estes, Don Payne; *Austin:* Alan Lomax, Oscar Moore, Gene Ramey, Teddy Wilson; *Centerville:* Lightning Hopkins; *Corsicana:* Tyree Glenn.

Dallas: Harry Babasin, Charlie Christian, James Clay, Henry Coker, Red Garland, Jimmy Giuffre, Budd Johnson, Keg Johnson, Bob McCracken, Hot Lips Page, Gene Roland, Cedar Walton; *Denison:* Booker Ervin; *Denton:* Herschel Evans; *Eastland:* Al Hendrickson; *Ellis County:* Buster Smith; *Fairfield:* Kenny Dorham.

Fort Worth: Tex Beneke, Ornette Coleman, Arthur Edwards, Clyde Hurley, Ray McKinley, Jesse Powell; *Galveston:* G. T. Hogan, Blind Lemon Jefferson; *Honey Grove:* Sam Price; *Houston:* Ernestine Anderson, Arnett Cobb, Jimmie Ford, Roy Gaines, Matthew Gee, Cedric Haywood, Deane Kincaide, Harold Land, Milton Larkins, Maurice Simon, Eddie Vinson; *Hull:* Bill Stanley; *Itasca:* Ray Leatherwood; *Linden:* T-Bone Walker; *Mansfield:* Ella Mae Morse; *Marlin:* Blind Willie Johnson; *McAllen:* Henry Cuesta; *McKinley:* Herb Ellis; *Palmer:* Knocky Parker; *Paris:* Jesse Crump; *Port Arthur:* Jimmy Wyble; *Rockport:* Ernie Caceres; *San Antonio:* Morty Corb; *San Marcos:* Eddie Durham; *Sherman:* Teddy Buckner, Buddy Tate; *Texarkana:* Scott Joplin, Lammar Wright Sr.; *Texas City:* Charles Brown; *Tyler:* Gus Johnson, Don Shelton; *Vernon:* Charlie Teagarden, Cub Teagarden, Jack Teagarden, Norma Teagarden; *Waco:* Clarence Hutchenrider; *Whitewright:* Gene Hall; *Wichita Falls:* Leo Wright; *Winters:* Mike Simpson.

UTAH—*Ogden:* Red Nichols; *Roosevelt:* Bob Whitlock; *Salt Lake City:* Don Bagley, Doug Mettome, Spud Murphy, Bill Young.

VERMONT—*Brattleboro:* Claude Williamson, Stu Williamson; *Enosburg Falls:* Ralph Yaw; *Windsor:* John Williams (piano).

VIRGINIA—*Aldie:* Al Grey; *Alexandria:* Charlie Harris, Joe Timer; *Arlington:* Bill Potts; *Emory:* Frankie Newton; *Emporia:* Lawrence Lucie; *Herndon:* Mert Oliver; *Lawrenceville:* Seldon Powell; *Newport News:* Pearl Bailey, Ella Fitzgerald, Tiny Grimes, Joan Shaw, Ward Pinkett; *Norfolk:* Jimmy Archey, Ray Copeland, Joe Garland, Peanuts Holland, Pat Jenkins, Prince Robinson, Keely Smith; *Portsmouth:* Dave Bailey, Ruth Brown, Wayman Carver, Mahlon Clark, Skip Hall; *Richmond:* Red Callender, Leonard Ware; *Roanoke:* Slick Jones; *Suffolk:* Charlie Byrd.

WASHINGTON—*Auburn:* Dean Reilly; *Centralia:* Don Butterfield; *Othello:* Bill Crow; *Seattle:* Patti Bown, Stella Brooks, Dick Collins, Matt Dennis; *Spokane:* Bob Crosby, Jimmy Rowles; *Tacoma:* Corky Corcoran, Bing Crosby; *Tekoa:* Mildred Bailey; *Vancouver:* Bonnie Wetzel; *Yakima:* Claire Austin.

WEST VIRGINIA—*Bluefield:* Teddy Weatherford; *Charleston:* Tommy Benford, Bob Drasnin, Keg Purnell; *Clarksburg:* Bumps Myers; *Huntington:* Ernie Farrow, Wade Legge; *Martinsburg:* Garland Wilson; *Middlebourne:* Warren Smith; *Parkersburg:* Billy Moore Jr., Ray Wetzel; *Piedmont:* Don Redman; *Wheeling:* Chu Berry, Musa Kaleem.

WISCONSIN—*Appleton:* Stan Puls; *Calvary:* Heinie Beau; *Fond du Lac:* Rollie Culver; *Fox Lake:* Bunny Berigan; *Independence:* Muggsy Sprecher; *Kenosha:* Buddy Clark; *LaCrosse:* Eddie Phyfe, Freddie Slack; *Madison:* Gene Schroeder; *Marshfield:* Bob Harrington, Lucy Reed; *Milwaukee:* Jackie Cain, Bob Hardaway, Woody Herman, Gene Puerling, Bob Strasen; *Monroe:* Joe Dodge; *Racine:* Billy Maxted; *Waukesha:* Les Paul.

WYOMING—*Cheyenne:* Buster Johnson.

CANAL ZONE—*Careening Cay:* Luis Russell; *Panama City:* Sonny White.

PUERTO RICO—*Ponce:* Santos Miranda; *San Juan:* Noro Morales, Juan Tizol.

VIRGIN ISLANDS—*St. Croix:* Dennis Charles, Tiger Haynes.

FOREIGN

ALGERIA—*Algiers:* Martial Solal.

AUSTRALIA—Graeme Bell; *Adelaide:* Erroll Buddle; *Nailsworth, Adelaide:* Jack Brokensha.

AUSTRIA—*Graz:* Erich Kleinschuster; *Vienna:* Fatty George, Friedrich Gulda, Hans Koller, Roland Kovac, Hans Salomon, Joe Zawinul.

BELGIUM—*Andenne:* Christian Kellens, Fats Sadi; *Brussels:* Toots Thielemans; *Liège:* Bobby Jaspar, René Thomas; *Liverchies:* Django Reinhardt.

BRAZIL—*São Paulo:* Laurindo Almeida.

BRITISH WEST INDIES—*Antigua:* Talib Dawud; *Jamaica:* Joe Harriott, Wynton Kelly, Dizzy Reece, Don Shirley; *Trinidad, Port of Spain:* Hazel Scott.

BURMA—*Rangoon:* Dizzy Sal.

CANADA—BRITISH COLUMBIA—*Kamloops:* Phil Nimmons; MANITOBA—*Hochfeld:* Ed Bickert; NOVA SCOTIA —*Sydney:* Warren Chiasson; ONTARIO — Lloyd Thompson; *Harrow:* Ken Kersey; *Port Arthur:* Pat Riccio; *Toronto:* Abe Aaron, Georgie Auld, Gil Evans, Moe Koffman, Murray McEachern; *Windsor:* Al Lucas; QUEBEC—*Montreal:* Chico Alvarez, Paul Bley, Hal Gaylor, Stew MacKay, Oscar Peterson, Milt Sealey; *Verdun:* Maynard Ferguson; SASKATCHEWAN —*Cupar:* Herby Spanier.

CUBA—*Camaguey:* Calo Scott; *Havana:* Candido, Chico O'Farrill, Armando Peraza, Carlos Valdez; *Matanzas:* Chano Pozo, Chino Pozo, Perez Prado.

CZECHOSLOVAKIA—*Karlsbad:* Georg Riedel; *Moravska-Ostrava:* Gerry Weinkopf.

DENMARK—*Aarhus:* Kai Winding; *Copenhagen:* Svend Asmussen, Palle Bolvig.

DOMINICAN REPUBLIC—Manny Albam, George Matthews.

ENGLAND—*Birmingham:* Ronnie Ball, Tony Kinsey; *Blackpool:* Keith Christie, Eddie Harvey; *Brighton:* Ray Noble; *Bristol:* Johnny Scott; *Bolton:* Frank Horrox; *Canterbury:* Tony Coe; *Cleethorpes:* Peter Appleyard; *Great Lever:* Jack Hylton; *Great Yarmouth:* Ken Colyer; *Leeds:* Benny Green, John Sowden.

London: Bert Ambrose, Vic Ash, Chris Barber, Lennie Bush, Les Condon, Roy Crimmins, Tony Crombie, Johnny Dankworth, Eric Delaney, Leonard Feather, Victor Feldman, Reginald Foresythe, Kenny Graham, Pat Halcox, Johnny Hawksworth, Tubby Hayes, Ted Heath, Spike Hughes, Harry Klein, Bill LeSage, Vic Lewis, Howard Lucraft, Jack Parnell, Freddy Randall, Terry Shannon, Ronnie Scott, Ralph Sharon, Hank Shaw, George Shearing, Jimmy Skidmore, Harry South, Ray Starling, Monty Sunshine.

Manchester: Bert Courtley; *Newcastle:* Ralph Hutchinson; *Northampton:* Roy East; *Oldham:* Eddie Taylor; *Oxbridge:* Peter Ind; *Saltburn:* Bruce Turner; *Seamham Harbour:* Howard Reay; *Sheffield:* Leslie Gilbert; *Stratford:* Derek Smith; *Surrey:* Annie Ross; *Tolworth:* Allan Ganley; *Windsor:* Humphrey Lyttelton, Marian McPartland; *Withersnea:* Kenny Baker; *Wivelsfield:* John Davies; *Worthing:* Dave Lindup.

FRANCE—*Angers:* Christian Chevallier; *Cannes:* Claude Bolling; *Enghien:* Maxim Saury; *Epinal:* Bernard Peiffer; *Nice:* Barney Wilen.

Paris: Gerard Badini, Sacha Distel, Buddy Featherstonhaugh, Stephane Grappelly, André Hodeir, Michel Le Grand, Claude Luter, André Persiany, Dave Pochonet, Caterina Valente; *Saarebruck:* Roger Guérin; *St. Denis:* Pierre Michelot; *St. Gaudens:* Guy

Lafitte; *Valenciennes:* Jean Goldkette; *Villedieu:* Henry Renaud; *Villeneuve sur Lot:* Michel De Villers.

GERMANY—*Berlin:* Helmut Brandt, Horst Jankowski, André Previn, Johannes Rediske, Wolfgang Schlüter; *Chemnitz:* Horst Fischer; *Cologne:* Bill Grah, Rolf Kuhn; *Frankfurt am Main:* Joki Freund, Albert Mangelsdorff, Peter Trunk; *Hamburg:* Paul Nero; *Herne:* Kurt Edelhagen; *Leipzig:* Jutta Hipp.

GHANA—*Accra:* Guy Warren.

HOLLAND—*Eindhoven:* Herman Schoonderwalt; *Hilversum:* Pim Jacobs, Rudolph Jacobs; *The Hague:* Pia Beck, Mat Mathews, Peter Schilperoort; *Rotterdam:* Rita Reys.

HUNGARY—*Budapest:* Gabor Szabo; *Visegrad:* Attila Zoller.

ICELAND—Andres Ingolfsson.

INDIA—*Calcutta:* Ronnie Ross; *Izatnagar:* Sandy Brown.

INDONESIA—*Bandoeng, Java:* Eddie De Haas.

IRELAND—*Comber:* Ottilie Patterson.

ITALY—*Asti:* Gianni Basso; *Brescia:* Otto Cesana; *Carpena:* Romano Mussolini; *Milan:* Gilberto Cuppini; *Naples:* Ralph Marterie; *Palestrina:* Nunzio Rotondo; *Turin:* Oscar Valdambrini; *Florence:* Piero Umiliani.

JAPAN—Kinichi Kawabe, George Kawaguchi, Sleepy Matsumoto, Akira Miyazawa, Fumio Nanri, Sadao Watanabe.

JORDAN—*Ramallah:* Knobby Totah.

MANCHURIA—Toshiko Akiyoshi, Mitsuko Miyake.

MEXICO—*Mazatlan:* Phil Gomez.

NORWAY—*Oslo:* Bjarne Nerem.

PHILIPPINES—*Manila:* Fred Elizalde.

POLAND—*Kalisz:* Jan Wroblewski.

PORTUGAL—*Lisbon:* Jose Magalhaes.

SCOTLAND—*Dundee:* Jimmy Deuchar; *Edinburgh:* Al Fairweather, John Keating; *Fife:* Joe Temperley; *Glasgow:* George Chisholm, Joe Saye, Benny Winestone.

SICILY—*Agira:* Joe Holiday; *Carrini:* Vido Musso; *Palermo:* George Wallington; *San Piero:* Pete Rugolo.

SPAIN—*Bilbao:* Vlady.

SWEDEN—*Bandhagen:* Rune Gustafsson; *Bollnas:* Stan Hasselgard; *Boxholm:* Arnold Johansson; *Falun:* Putte Wickman; *Gaule:* Kurt Jaernberg; *Gothenburg:* Bert Dahlander, Bengt Hallberg; *Hagfors:* Monica Zetterlund; *Hälsingborg:* Harry Arnold; *Hässleholm:* Aake Persson; *Husum:* Reinhold Svensson; *Karlskrona:* Lennart Jansson; *Linköping:* Bengt-Arne Wallin; *Lund:* Rolf Billberg.

Stockholm: Simon Brehm, Arne Domnerus, Rolf Ericson, Claes-Goran Fagerstedt, Bob Laine, Bernt Rosengren, Gösta Theselius, Torbjorn Hultcrantz, Rune Ofwerman; *Soderhamn:* Jan Johansson; *Uppsala:* Nils Lindberg; *Västeras:* Carl-Henrik Norin.

SWITZERLAND—*Basle:* George Gruntz; *Lugano:* Flavio Ambrosetti.

TASMANIA—*Hobart:* Bryce Rohde.

TURKEY—*Istanbul:* Arif Mardin.

U.S.S.R.—Buzzy Drootin; *Memel, Lithuania:* Michael Naura; *Nikolaev:* Art Hodes.

YUGOSLAVIA—*Jajce:* Dusko Gojkovic; *Sarajevo:* Bobby Gutesha.

Jazz organizations, schools and booking agencies

JAZZ ORGANIZATIONS AND SCHOOLS

BERKLEE SCHOOL OF MUSIC, Lawrence Berk, 284 Newbury Street, Boston 15, Massachusetts.

DUKE ELLINGTON JAZZ SOCIETY, Bill Ross, Box 2486, Hollywood 28, California.

INSTITUTE OF JAZZ STUDIES, Marshall W. Stearns, Exec. Dir., 108 Waverly Place, New York 11, N.Y.

JAZZ INTERNATIONAL, Howard Lucraft, P.O. Box 91, Hollywood 28, California.

MONTEREY JAZZ FESTIVAL, James Lyons, Big Sur, California.

NATIONAL BAND CAMP, Dr. Eugene Hall, Dean, Box 221, South Bend, Indiana.

NEW ORLEANS JAZZ CLUB, Jo Schmidt, 2417 Octavia Street, New Orleans 15, Louisiana.

NEWPORT JAZZ FESTIVAL INC., Louis L. Lorillard, Newport, Rhode Island.

SCHOOL OF JAZZ, MUSIC INN (Lenox, Mass.), Jule Foster, Dean, Room 1510, 270 Madison Avenue, New York 17, N.Y.

WESTLAKE COLLEGE OF MUSIC, 7190 Sunset Boulevard, Hollywood 46, California.

BOOKING AGENCIES AND PERSONAL MANAGEMENT OFFICES

WILLARD ALEXANDER INC., 425 Park Ave., New York 22, N.Y. PLaza 1-7070. 333 North Michigan, Chicago 1, Ill. CEntral 6-2460.

ASSOCIATED BOOKING CORP. (Joe Glaser), 745 Fifth Avenue, New York 22, N.Y. PLaza 9-4600. 203 North Wabash Ave., Chicago, Ill. CEntral 6-9451. 8619 Sunset Blvd., Hollywood 46, Calif. OLympia 2-9940.

GENERAL ARTISTS CORP., 640 Fifth Avenue, New York 19, N.Y. CIrcle 7-7543. 8 South Michigan, Chicago, Ill. STate 2-6288. 9650 Santa Monica Blvd., Beverly Hills, Calif. CRestview 1-8101.

INTERNATIONAL TALENT ASSOCIATES (Bert Block, Larry Bennett), 527 Madison Avenue, New York 22, N.Y. PLaza 1-3344. 916 Kearny St., San Francisco, Calif. EXbrook 2-2576.

JOHN LEVY ASSOCIATES, 119 West 57th St., New York 19, N.Y. CIrcle 5-2488.

WILLIAM MORRIS AGENCY INC., 1740 Broadway, New York 19, N.Y. JUdson 6-5100. 919 North Michigan, Chicago, Ill. WHitehall 3-1744. 151 El Camino Drive, Beverly Hills, Calif. CRestview 4-7451.

MUSIC CORP. OF AMERICA, 598 Madison Avenue, New York 22, N.Y. PLaza 9-7500. 430 North Michigan, Chicago, Ill. DElaware 7-1100. 9370 Santa Monica Blvd., Beverly Hills, Calif. CRestview 6-2001.

PRODUCTION AND MANAGEMENT ASSOCIATES (George Wein, Ed Sarkesian), 50 Central Park West, New York 23, N.Y. TRafalgar 3-0733.

SHAW ARTISTS CORP., 565 Fifth Avenue, New York 17, N.Y. OXford 7-7744. 203 North Wabash, Chicago, Ill. RAndolph 6-0131. 9033 Wilshire Blvd., Beverly Hills, Calif. CRestview 1-7294.

UNIVERSAL ATTRACTIONS (Ben Bart), 200 West 57th Street, New York 19, N.Y. JUdson 2-7575. 3849 S. Western Ave., Los Angeles 62, Calif. AXminster 2-0517.

Record companies

Aamco, c/o Alison Enterprises Inc., 1604 Broadway, New York, N.Y.
ABC-Paramount, 1501 Broadway, New York, N.Y.
Abner, 1449 So. Michigan Ave., Chicago 5, Ill.
Ad-Lib, 20-43 19th St., Long Island City, N.Y.
Aladdin, 451 N. Canon Drive, Beverly Hills, Calif.
Allegro, 510 22nd St., Union City, N.J.
American Music, 600 Chartres St., New Orleans, La.
American Recording Society, 100 6th Ave., New York, N.Y.
Andex, c/o Rex Productions, 8715 W. 3rd St., Los Angeles 48, Calif.
Angel, 38 W. 48th St., New York 36, N.Y.
Apollo, 457 W. 45th St., New York 36, N.Y.
Argo, 2120 S. Michigan, Chicago, Ill.
Atlantic, 157 W. 57th St., New York 19, N.Y.
Atco, see Atlantic
Audiophile, Saukville, Wisc.
Audio Fidelity, 770 11th Ave., New York 19, N.Y.
Audio Lab, 1540 Brewster Ave., Cincinnati 7, Ohio

Baton, 108 W. 44th St., New York, N.Y.
Bel Canto, 2919 S. LaCienega Blvd., Culver City, Calif.
Bethlehem, see King
Blue Note, 43 W. 61st St., New York 23, N.Y.
Brunswick, 445 Park Ave., New York, N.Y.

Cadence, 119 W. 57th St., New York, N.Y.
Camden, see RCA Victor
Capitol, Sunset and Vine, Hollywood 28, Calif.
Carlton, 345 W. 58th St., New York, N.Y.
Carnival, 706 Bourbon St., New Orleans, La.
Cavalier, 298 9th St., San Francisco, Calif.
Challenge, 6920 Sunset Blvd., Hollywood, Calif.
Chess, see Argo
Checker, see Argo
Colpix, 711 5th Ave., New York, N.Y.
Columbia, 799 7th Ave., New York 19, N.Y.
Commodore, 252 D Lake Ave., Yonkers, N.Y.
Contemporary, 8481 Melrose Pl., Los Angeles 46, Calif.
Cook, 101 2nd St., Stamford, Conn.
Coral, 445 Park Ave., New York, N.Y.
Counterpoint, 333 6th Ave., New York 14, N.Y.
Criterion, 1491 Vine St., Hollywood, Calif.
Crown, see Modern

Dawn, 39 W. 60th St., New York 14, N.Y.
Decca, 445 Park Ave., New York, N.Y.
Delmar, 439 So. Wabash, Chicago 5, Ill.
Design, 33 34th St., Brooklyn 32, N.Y.
Dig, 2180 W. Washington Blvd., Los Angeles, Calif.
Dixieland Jubilee, see GNP
Dooto, 9512 S. Central Ave., Los Angeles 2, Calif.
Dot, 157 W. 57th St., New York, N.Y.

East-West, see Atlantic
Ecclesia, Box 8022, Dallas, Texas.
Elektra, 361 Bleecker St., New York, N.Y.
EmArcy, 745 5th Ave., New York 22, N.Y.
Epic, see Columbia
Esoteric, see Counterpoint
Euterpean, 506 S. Coast Blvd., Laguna Beach, Calif.
Everest, 112-03 14th Ave., College Point, N.Y.

Fantasy, 654 Natoma St., San Francisco, Calif.
Felsted, see London
Folkways, 117 W. 46th St., New York, N.Y.
Fraternity, 413 Race St., Cincinnati, Ohio

GNP (Gene Norman Presents), 8600 Lookout Mt. Ave., Hollywood 6, Calif.
Golden Crest, 220 Broadway, Huntington Station, N.Y.
Good Time Jazz, see Contemporary
Grand Award, 8 Kingsland Ave., Harrison, N.J.

Harmony, see Columbia
Herald, 1697 Broadway, New York, N.Y.
HiFiRecord, 7803 Sunset Blvd., Hollywood 38, Calif.
Hip, Box 2337, Van Nuys, Calif.

Imperial, 6425 Hollywood Blvd., Los Angeles 28, Calif.
Intro, see Aladdin

Jazzland, see Riverside
Jazzman, 6420 Santa Monica Blvd., Hollywood 38, Calif.
Jazzology, 3918 Bergenline Ave., Union City, N.J.

Jazztone, see American Recording Society
Jazz: West, see Aladdin
Josie, see Jubilee
Jubilee, 1721 Broadway, New York 19, N.Y.
Judson, see Riverside

Kapp, 119 West 57th St., New York, N.Y.
King, 1540 Brewster Ave., Cincinnati, Ohio

Liberty, 1556 N. LaBrea, Hollywood 28, Calif.
London, 539 W. 25th St., New York 1, N.Y.

Mayfair, 1755 Broadway, New York, N.Y.
Mercury, 35 E. Wacker Dr., Chicago, Ill.
Metrojazz, see MGM
MGM, 1540 Broadway, New York 36, N.Y.
Modern, 9317 W. Washington Blvd., Culver City, Calif.
Mode, 8295 Sunset Blvd., Hollywood, Calif.
Motif, 6269 Selma Ave., Hollywood 28, Calif.
Music Minus One, 719 10th Ave., New York, N.Y.
Musidisc International, 666 Fifth Ave., New York 19, N.Y.

New Jazz, see Prestige

Offbeat, see Washington
Omega Records, P.O. Box 558, North Hollywood, Calif.
Opus, P.O. Box 106, Forest Hills 75, N.Y.

Period, 304 E. 74th St., New York, N.Y.
Playback, 1501 Broadway, New York, N.Y.
Prestige, 203 S. Washington, Bergenfield, N.J.

Rama, see Roulette
Rainbow, 767 10th Ave., New York 19, N.Y.
RCA Victor, 155 E. 24th St., New York 10, N.Y.
Regent, see Savoy
Replica, 7210 Westview Dr., Desplaines, Ill.
Request, 443 W. 49th St., New York 19, N.Y.
Richmond, see London
Riverside, 235 W. 46th St., New York 36, N.Y.
RKO-Unique, 1440 Broadway, Rm. 1972, New York 36, N.Y.
Rondo, 220 W. Locust, Chicago, Ill.
Roost, 625 10th Ave., New York 36, N.Y.
Roulette, 659 10th Ave., New York 36, N.Y.

San Francisco Jazz, 217 Kearny St., San Francisco, Calif.
Savoy, 56 Ferry St., Newark, N.J.
Score, 5352 W. Pico Blvd., Los Angeles, Calif.
S-D, 1637 N. Ashland Ave., Chicago, Ill.
Seeco, see Dawn
Soma, 29 Glenwood Ave., Minneapolis, Minn.
Somerset, Media, Pa.
Southland, 58 St. Louis St., New Orleans 16, La.
Specialty, 8508 Sunset Blvd., Hollywood 46, Calif.
Starlite, 6671 Sunset Blvd., Hollywood 28, Calif.
Stepheny, 1080 Asbury Ave., Evanston, Ill.
Stere-O-Craft, 1650 Broadway, New York, N.Y.
Stereo Spectrum, Pickwick Sales Corp., Dept. E., Brooklyn, N.Y.
Stinson, 27 Union Sq. W., New York, N.Y.
Storyville, 75 State St., Boston, Mass.
Strand, 680 5th Ave., New York, N.Y.
Sunset, 6671 Sunset Blvd., Hollywood 28, Calif.

Tampa, 117 N. El Centro Ave., Hollywood, Calif.
Tempo, 8540 Sunset Blvd., Hollywood 46, Calif.
Time, 2 West 45th St., New York, N.Y.
Top Rank, 24 W. 57th St., New York, N.Y.
Tops, 83 Crosby St., New York, N.Y.
Trans-Disc, 615 Albany St., Boston, Mass.
Twentieth Century Fox, 157 W. 57th St., New York, N.Y.

United Artists, 729 7th Ave., New York, N.Y.
United Telefilm, 701 7th Ave., New York 36, N.Y.
Urania, 625 8th Ave., New York 18, N.Y.

Vanguard, 154 W. 14th St., New York, N.Y.
Vee-Jay, 1449 So. Michigan Ave., Chicago 5, Ill.
Verve, 451 N. Canon Dr., Beverly Hills, Calif.

Warner Bros., 666 5th Ave., New York, N.Y.
Washington, 1340 Connecticut Ave., N.W., Washington, D.C.
Westminster, 275 7th Ave., New York 1, N.Y.
World-Pacific, 8255 Sunset Blvd., Hollywood 46, Calif.
World-Wide, 324 Plane St., Newark, N.J.

Bibliography: books and periodicals

The bibliography of jazz has expanded in recent years as astonishingly as its discography. Far more books on the subject were published during the period 1955-60 than in the entire 50-year preceding period. The change from famine to glut has been so rapid that by 1960 many bookstores were complaining of the surfeit of material and it seemed that the supply at last had outstripped the demand. Nevertheless, the quality and quantity of available books did not abate.

The sole exception to the rule remained in the realm of fiction. In 1960 there was still not a single novel with a jazz theme that could qualify both as first-class literature and as an accurate reflection of the mentality, personality and social environment of the jazz musician. The books listed are merely typical examples of what has appeared to date, ranging from the well-written and readable (but not completely authentic) to the mediocre and utterly spurious. The only items in the former group, in the author's opinion, are *Young Man with a Horn, The Horn* and *Blow Up a Storm.*

A revised and comprehensive listing of books, periodicals and magazine articles entitled *The Literature of Jazz: A Selective Bibliography* was published in 1959 by the New York Public Library. Compiled by Robert George Reisner, with an introduction by Prof. Marshall W. Stearns, it may be obtained for $1 from the New York Public Library, Fifth Avenue and 42nd Street, New York 17, N. Y. No attempt has been made below to duplicate the information in the Reisner work, since the latter is indispensable to anyone concerned with a comprehensive examination of the bibliography of jazz.

An amazingly comprehensive international bibliography, which attempts to list every significant book, newspaper and magazine article on jazz published up to the end of 1950, was published in 1954 under the title *A Bibliography of Jazz.* Compiled by Alan P. Merriam with the assistance of Robert J. Benford and containing some 3,300 separate entries, all elaborately indexed, the book may be obtained from the American Folklore Society, Box 5, Bennett Hall, University of Pennsylvania, Philadelphia 4, Pa.

The books listed below are currently obtainable in the U.S. or, if out of print, still likely to be found in public libraries.

HISTORIES, BIOGRAPHIES, AUTOBIOGRAPHIES

ARMSTRONG, LOUIS. *Satchmo: My Life In New Orleans.* Prentice-Hall, 1954. Autobiography.

BALLIETT, WHITNEY. *The Sound of Surprise.* E. P. Dutton, 1959. 46 pieces from *The New Yorker.*

BLESH, RUDI. *Shining Trumpets.* Knopf, 1946; revised 1958.

BLESH, RUDI and HARRIET JANIS. *They All Played Ragtime.* Knopf, 1950; revised 1959.

BRUNN, H. O. *The Story of the Original Dixieland Jazz Band.* Louisiana State University Press.

BRUYNOGHE, YANNICK. *Big Bill Blues.* Biography of the late Bill Broonzy.

CARMICHAEL, HOAGY. *The Stardust Road.* Rinehart, 1946. Autobiography.

CHARTERS, SAMUEL B. *Jazz: New Orleans 1885-1957.* Walter C. Allen, 1958. An index to the older Negro jazzmen of New Orleans.

The Country Blues. Rinehart, 1959. Stories of blues singers from Blind Lemon Jefferson to Lightnin' Hopkins.

CONDON, EDDIE and THOMAS SUGRUE. *We Called It Music.* Henry Holt, 1947.

CONNOR, DONALD. *B. G. Off The Record.* Gaildonna, 1958. A bio-discography of Benny Goodman. Autobiography.

DEXTER, DAVE. *Jazz Cavalcade.* Criterion, 1946.

EATON, JEANETTE. *Trumpeter's Tale.* William Morrow, 1955.

FEATHER, LEONARD. *Inside Jazz* (originally *Inside Bebop*). Consolidated Mus. Pub. Inc., 1949. History, technical analysis and biographies of jazz and jazzmen 1940-49.

The Book of Jazz. Horizon, 1957. Chapter-by-chapter history of each instrument; technical analysis of improvisation, etc.

Jazz. Trend Books, 1959. History of jazz from 1942-59.

FINKELSTEIN, SIDNEY. *Jazz: A People's Music.* Citadel, 1948.

FRANCIS, ANDRÉ. *Jazz.* Grove Press Inc.

GOFFIN, ROBERT. *Horn of Plenty.* Allen, Towne and Heath, 1947. Biography of Louis Armstrong.

Jazz: From the Congo to the Metropolitan. Doubleday, 1944.

GOODMAN, BENNY and IRVING KOLODIN. *The Kingdom of Swing.* Stackpole, 1939. Autobiography.

GROSSMAN, WILLIAM L. and JACK W. FARRELL. *The Heart of Jazz.* New York University Press, 1956.

HANDY, W. C. *Father of the Blues.* Macmillan, 1941. Autobiography.

HARRIS, REX. *The Story of Jazz.* Grosset & Dunlap, 1955.

HOBSON, WILDER. *American Jazz Music.* W. W. Norton, 1939.

HODEIR, ANDRÉ. *Jazz: Evolution and Essence.* Grove Press, 1956. Series of essays including technical analyses.

HOLIDAY, BILLIE with WILLIAM DUFTY. *Lady Sings The Blues.* Doubleday, 1956. Autobiography.

HORRICKS, RAYMOND. *Count Basie and his Orchestra.* Citadel, 1957. Series of biographies of Basie and sidemen; with discography.

HUGHES, LANGSTON. *Famous Negro Music Makers.* Dodd, Mead, 1955.

The First Book of Jazz. Franklin Watts, 1955. For children.

JOHNSON, GRADY. *The Five Pennies.* Dell, 1959. Story of Red Nichols.

LOMAX, ALAN. *Mister Jelly Roll.* Duell, Sloan & Pearce, 1950; paperback, Grove Press, 1956. Story of Jelly Roll Morton.

MANONE, WINGY and PAUL VANDERVOORT II. *Trumpet on the Wing.* Doubleday, 1948. Autobiography.

MEZZROW, MEZZ and BERNARD WOLFE. *Really The Blues.* Random House, 1946; paperback, Dell. Autobiography.

RAMSEY, FREDERIC and CHARLES EDWARD SMITH. *Jazzmen.* Harcourt, Brace, 1939; paperback, Harvest, 1959.

REISNER, ROBERT GEORGE. *The Jazz Titans.* Doubleday, 1960. 33 profiles.

SARGEANT, WINTHROP. *Jazz: Hot and Hybrid.* E. P. Dutton, 1946. A reissue of the first book ever to deal with the technical aspects of jazz.

SHAW, ARTIE. *The Trouble With Cinderella.* Farrar, Straus & Young, 1952. Autobiography.

SPAETH, SIGMUND. *A History of Popular Music In America.* Random House, 1948.

STEARNS, MARSHALL. *The Story of Jazz.* Oxford, 1956. Extensive documentation of African origins and prehistory of jazz.

TERKEL, STUDS. *Giants of Jazz.* Thomas Y. Crowell, 1957. For teenagers.

ULANOV, BARRY. *Duke Ellington.* Creative Age, 1946. Biography and story of Ellington and his orchestra.

A History of Jazz In America, Viking, 1952.

A Handbook of Jazz. Viking, 1957.

WATERS, ETHEL and CHARLES SAMUELS. *His Eye Is on the Sparrow.* Doubleday, 1951. Autobiography.

WOODWARD, WOODY. *Jazz Americana.* Trend Books, 1956.

ANTHOLOGIES AND REFERENCE BOOKS

Art of Jazz, The. Edited by Martin T. Williams. Oxford, 1959.

ASCAP Biographical Dictionary of Composers, Authors and Publishers, The. Edited by Daniel I. MacNamara. Thomas Y. Crowell, 1952.

Collector's Jazz: Traditional and Swing. John S. Wilson. Lippincott, 1958.

Collector's Jazz: Modern. John S. Wilson. Lippincott, 1959.

Down Beat Record Reviews. Annually from 1956. Maher Publications.

Down Beat Yearbook. Annually from 1956. Maher Publications.

Duke Ellington: His Life and Music. Roy, 1960.

Hear Me Talkin' To Ya. Edited by Nat Shapiro and Nat Hentoff. Rinehart, 1955. Story of jazz told in the musicians' own words.

Jam Session. Edited by Ralph J. Gleason. Putnam's, 1958. Background stories, personality pieces, general essays and fiction.

Jazz. Edited by Nat Hentoff and Albert J. McCarthy. Rinehart, 1959. Essays by twelve writers.

Jazzmakers, The. Edited by Nat Shapiro and Nat Hentoff. Rinehart, 1957. Paperback Grove Press 1959. Studies of 21 jazzmen by nine writers.

Jazz Scene, The. By Francis Newton. Monthly Review Press, 1960.

Jazz Word, The. Edited by Dom Cerulli, Burt Korall and Mort Nasatir. Ballantine (paperback), 1960. Essays, poetry, humor, fiction etc.

Metronome Yearbook. Annually from 1950.

Pictorial History of Jazz, A. Edited by Orrin Keepnews and Bill Grauer. Crown, 1955.

Treasury of Jazz, A. Edited by Eddie Condon and Richard Gehman. Dial, 1956. Essays, personality stories, humor and fiction.

MUSICAL INSTRUCTION OR METHOD

ELLINGTON, DUKE. *Piano Method For Blues.* Robbins Music Corp., 1943. A history and analysis of the blues form.

HANDY, W. C. and ABBE NILES. *A Treasury of the Blues.* C. Boni, 1949. Complete words and music of 67 songs by Handy and others, with an historical and critical text by Niles.

MEHEGAN, JOHN. *Jazz Improvisation.* Watson-Guptill, 1959. Mainly an analysis of harmonic and melodic principles.

MILLER, GLENN. *Method For Orchestral Arranging.* Mutual Music Society, Inc., 1943. Excellent technical book including two scores.

PAPARELLI, FRANK. *The Blues and How to Play 'Em.* Leeds Music Corp., 1942. *Eight to the Bar.* Leeds, 1941. *Two to the Bar.* Leeds, 1946. Technical guides to blues, boogie-woogie and Dixieland, respectively.

TAYLOR, BILLY. *Basic Be-Bop Instruction; Dixieland Piano Solos; Mambo Piano Solos; Ragtime Piano Solos.* Charles H. Hansen Music Co., 1949-50. Four brief (16-page) low-priced books containing original music for piano, with admirably succinct explanations of the styles and how to play them.

FICTION

BAKER, DOROTHY. *Young Man With A Horn.* Houghton, Mifflin, 1938.

BORNEMAN, ERNEST. *Tremolo.* Harper, 1948.

CURRAN, DALE. *Dupree Blues.* Knopf, 1948; Berkeley (paperback).

DUKE, OSBORN. *Sideman.* Criterion, 1956.

EWING, ANNEMARIE. *Little Gate.* Rinehart, 1947.

FLENDER, HAROLD. *Paris Blues.* Ballantine, 1957.

GILBERT, EDWIN. *The Hot and the Cool.* Doubleday, 1953; paperback, Popular Library, 1954.

HOLMES, CLELLON. *The Horn.* Random House, 1958.

HUNTER, EVAN. *Second Ending.* Simon & Schuster, 1956; paperback version, *Quartet In H.*

KANIN, GARSON. *Blow Up a Storm.* Random House, 1959.

LEA, GEORGE. *Somewhere There's Music.* Lippincott, 1958.

STEIG, HENRY. *Send Me Down.* Knopf, 1941; paperback, Avon.

UPDYKE, JAMES. *It's Always Four O'Clock.* Random House, 1956.

WALLOP, DOUGLASS. *Night Light.* W. W. Norton, 1953; paperback, Cardinal.

WHITMORE, STANFORD. *Solo.* Harcourt, Brace, 1955.

PERIODICALS

Australian Jazz Quarterly, Box 2440 V, G.P.O., Melbourne, Australia.

Billboard, 1564 Broadway, New York 36, N.Y.

Bulletin Du Hot Club De Genève, 7 Pl. Longmalle, Geneva, Switzerland.

Coda, P.O. Box 87, Station "J", Toronto 6, Ontario, Canada.

Down Beat, 205 West Monroe St., Chicago 6, Ill.

Estrad, Tunnelgatan 12, Stockholm C, Sweden.

Jazz: A Quarterly of American Music, 1483 Solano Avenue, Albany 6, California.

Jazz, Gdansk, Waly Jagiellonskie 1, Poland.

Jazzbladid, Ranargotu 34, Reykjavik, Iceland.

Jazz-Echo, included as supplement in *Gondel Magazine,* 9 Adolphsbrucke, Hamburg 11, Germany.

Jazz Hot, 14 Rue Chaptal, Paris 9, France.

Jazz Journal, The Cottage, 27 Willow Vale, London W. 12, England.

Jazz Magazine, 3, Rue de l'Echelle, Paris 1, France.

Jazzmania, Gascón 252 "A", Buenos Aires, Argentina.

Jazz Monthly, The Old Bakehouse, Back Road East, St. Ives, Cornwall, England.

Jazz News, Aldeman House, 37 Soho Square, London W. 1, England.

Jazz Podium, Vogelsangstr. 32, Stuttgart W., Germany.

Jazz Review, 124 White St., New York 13, N.Y.

Melody Maker, 4 Arne Street, London, W.C. 1, England.

Metronome, 114 East 32nd Street, New York 16, N.Y.

Musica Jazz, Galleria Del Corso 4, Milan, Italy.

New Musical Express, 5 Denmark Street, London, W.C. 2, England.

Orkester Journalen, Regeringsgatan 22, Stockholm, Sweden.

Record Mirror, 20 Rupert Street, Piccadilly, London, W. 1, England.

Rhythme, Gagelstraat 83b, Eindhoven, Holland.

Rytmi, Fredrikenkatu 68 A. 2., Helsinki, Finland.

Schlagzeug, 136 Kurfürstendamm, Berlin-Halensee, Germany.

Second Line, 1227 Webster Street, New Orleans, La.

Swing Journal, 55 1-chome, Minamisakumacho, Siba, Minato-ku, Tokyo, Japan.

Variety, 154 West 46th Street, New York 36, N.Y.

OVER NIGHT BOOK

This book must be returned before the first class on the following school day.

DEMCO NO. 28-500

The new edition of the encyclopedia of jazz

DATE			
Peterson			